# TH[...]
# AND CRUCIFIXION
# OF JESUS

## Texts and Commentary

David W. Chapman & Eckhard J. Schnabel

HENDRICKSON
PUBLISHERS

**The Trial and Crucifixion of Jesus:**
**Texts and Commentary**

Revised Edition © 2019 by Hendrickson Publishers Marketing, LLC
P.O. Box 3473
Peabody, Massachusetts 01961-3473
www.hendrickson.com

ISBN 978-1-68307-266-9

Originally published in 2015 in Tübingen, Germany, by Mohr Siebeck, as *The Trial and Crucifixion of Jesus: Texts and Commentary*, Wissenschaftliche Untersuchungen zum Neuen Testament 344.

*Printed in the United States of America*

Typesetting: E. J. Schnabel, NotaBene Lingua Workstation Version 12

**Library of Congress Cataloging-in-Publication Data**

Chapman, David W., Schnabel, Eckhard J.
    The trial and crucifixion of Jesus : texts and commentary / David W. Chapman, Eckhard J. Schnabel.
        pages cm
    Includes bibliographical references and index.
    ISBN 978-1-68307-266-9
    1. Bible. Gospels—Antiquities. 2. Jesus Christ—Trial, Crucifixion, Death.

# Preface

The significance of Jesus' death is apparent from the space that Matthew, Mark, Luke, and John devote to the passion narrative, from the emphasis of many speeches in the Book of Acts, and from the missionary preaching and the theology of the Apostle Paul, who asserts that when he preaches the gospel, he proclaims nothing "except Jesus Christ and him crucified" (1 Cor 2:2). The significance of Jesus' death is recognized by historians, who view Jesus' trial as one of the most famous criminal cases of antiquity (see CORNELIUS HARTZ, Tatort Antike. Berühmte Kriminalfälle des Altertums. Mainz: Zabern, 2012). And the significance of Jesus' death on the cross is apparent from the history of Christian theology, piety, and art (see JOHANN ANSELM STEIGER / ULRICH HEINEN, eds., Golgatha in den Konfessionen und Medien der Frühen Neuzeit. Arbeiten zur Kirchengeschichte 113. Berlin: De Gruyter 2010), not least on account of the Lord's Supper or Eucharist, which regularly focuses the attention of Christians on Jesus' death. The significance of Jesus' death is connected, certainly in the texts of the New Testament, with the historical details of Jesus' trial and crucifixion. Exegetical discussions of Jesus' trial and death have employed biblical (Old Testament) and extra-biblical texts in order to understand the events during the Passover of A.D. 30 that led to Jesus' execution by crucifixion. The purpose of our book is to publish the primary texts that have been cited in the scholarly literature as relevant for understanding Jesus' trial and crucifixion. The texts in Part 1 deal with Jesus' trial / interrogation before the Sanhedrin, the texts in Part 2 with Jesus' trial before Pontius Pilatus, and the texts in Part 3 with crucifixion as a method of execution in antiquity. The sequence of texts follows a chronological order where possible.

Each Part and sub-section will have brief introductions. For each document, we provide the original text and a translation. The translations are our own, unless otherwise indicated (Old and New Testament texts are taken from the NRSV). In an age in which the study of Greek, Hebrew, and Latin are regarded by some as gratuitous, we unapologetically present Greek, Hebrew, and Latin texts, convinced that any truly serious study of antiquity requires analyzing documents in their original languages. Globalization should not be confused with linguistic imperialism where everything is reduced to English but should be taken as an opportunity to learn, master, and use the languages of other cultures with as much ease as is possible in a lifetime. The major editions and translations of the primary sources are listed in the bibliography. The commentary will describe the literary context and the purpose of each document in context before clarifying details and commenting on its contribution to Jesus' trial and crucifixion. The commentary will refer only to the most relevant and more recent discussions in the secondary literature; completeness is neither possible nor desirable in a collection of texts. The careful reader may notice slightly different criteria for source selection between the sections on the trial of Jesus and the section on crucifixion. This is because our selection of source material has been influenced by the various kinds of questions that have engaged contemporary scholarship. Scholarly treatments of crucifixion frequently present a general depiction of crucifixion in the Roman world, with secondary application to the specifics of Jesus' death. Thus the goal in Part 3 will be to include a vast array of sources from throughout the ancient world that report or discuss crucifixion and penal suspension. Meanwhile, academic study on the trial of Jesus has typically focused on specific questions concerning the degree to which the Gospels' trial narratives cohere with first-century Jewish and Roman legal practices and other historical data. This necessitates a selection of sources that is more driven by specific questions arising from the legal procedures reportedly employed in Jesus' trial.

We thank Prof. Heinrich von Siebenthal for help with the translation of some of the Greek texts, Prof. Jörg Frey, the editor of the Wissenschaftliche Untersuchungen zum Neuen Testament, and Dr. Henning Ziebrizki of Mohr Siebeck, for the support of this project, Nadine Schwemmreiter-Vetter and Jana Trispel for editorial help, Steve Siebert of NotaBene for a truly superb word-processing software which allowed the production of camera-ready copy of the manuscript, and for help with specific questions, Steven White and Cheryl Eaton for help with proofreading, Karis Chapman for meticulously producing the drawings in Part 3, Benjamin Schnabel for producing the graphics files, Justin Allison for help with the indexes, and the institutions at which we teach for their support for research and writing: Covenant Theological Seminary and Gordon-Conwell Theological Seminary.


David W. Chapman
Eckhard J. Schnabel

# Preface to the American Edition

We thank Hendrickson Publishers, in particular Paul Hendrickson, for their interest and initiative in accepting our manuscript for an American Edition. We thank Dr. Henning Ziebrizki for granting copyright. We have corrected orthographical mistakes and other infelicities but otherwise preserved the original edition. Reviews of our work were uniformly positive, although some reviewers begged to differ on details; see Bulletin of Biblical Research 25 (2015) 407–409 (S. Gathercole); Revista Estudios Bíblicos (2015) 485–487 (J. M. Garcia); Themelios 40 (2015) 506–508 (B. R. Wilson); Actualidad Bibliográphica 2016, 17–24 (V. Fabrega); Comparative Legal History 4 (2016) 249–251 (W. Decock); Journal of the Evangelical Theological Society 56 (2016) 620–622 (A. W. White); Journal for the Study of the New Testament 38 (2016) 24 (M. Y. Marshall); Religious Studies Review 42 (2016) 41 (B. Wright); Studia Biblica Athanasiana 17 (2016) 162–163 (X. Géza); Studien zum Neuen Testament und seiner Umwelt 41 (2016), 205–208 (A. Heindl); Theologische Literaturzeitung 141 (2016) 270–271 (A. Puig i Tàrrech); Archivio Teologico Torinese 23 (2017) 214–219 (G. Ghiberti); Journal of Theological Studies 68 (2017) 290–293 (J. G. Cook); European Journal of Theology 27 (2018) 92–93 (C. Stenschke). We thank Cheryl Eaton and Alexander M. Schurman, our assistants, for help with fresh proof-reading.

We want to take this opportunity to list new and relevant publications. ECKHARD SCHNABEL has used his material on Jesus' trial before the Sanhedrin and before Pontius Pilatus in: Mark, Tyndale New Testament Commentary 2, London/Downers Grove: Inter-Varsity Press/IVP Academic, 2017, and in Jesus in Jerusalem: The Final Days, Grand Rapids: Eerdmans, 2018. BERNARDO SANTALUCIA, 'Lo portarono via e lo consegnarono al governatore Ponzio Pilato' (Matth. 27,2): la giurisdizione del prefetto di Giudea, pages 85–104 in Il processo contro Gesù, edited by F. Amarelli and F. Lucrezi, Quaestiones 2. Napopi: Jovene, 1999, investigates the juridicial authority of Pontius Pilatus, which is also discussed by MASSIMO MIGLIETTA, I.N.R.I. Studie riflessioni intorno al processo a Gesù, Napoli: Saturna, 2011 and ANTONELLO CINCOTTA, L'Affaire Gesù. Il processo, sincronie, diacronie giuridiche e futuribili scientifici. Suggestioni e ipotesi a proposito di alcuni recenti contributi, Historia et ius 11 (2017): 1–23. SOFÍA TORALLAS TOVAR and KLAAS A. WORP, Greek Papyri from Montserrat (P. Monts. Roca IV), Scripta orientalia 1, Barcelona: Publicacions de l'Abadia de Montserrat, 2014, No. 70 (pp. 99–204), is a bilingual, Latin and Greek (fragmentary) text of trial proceedings (see below, Nos. 100, 101); the document mentions three persons by name: the lawyer Soterichus, a *nauclerus* with the name Theodorus, and the judge presiding over the lawsuit, the *praefectus annonae Alexandeae* Flauius Cratinus who held office in A.D. 378/379. CRAIG A. EVANS, Jesus and the Remains of His Day: Studies in Jesus and the Evidence of Material Culture, Peabody: Hendrickson, 2015, surveys the literary and archaeological evidence for Caiaphas, Pilatus, and Simon of Cyrene, as well as the trial of Jesus, the offer of a Passover pardon, and crucifixion (pp. 49–66, 155–65). STEVE MASON, A History of the Jewish War: AD 66–74, Cambridge: Cambridge University Press, 2016, discusses the use of Josephus' works for gleaning historical information (see below, pp. 5–6) and evaluates the two Pontius Pilatus episodes in Josephus, *B. J.* 2. 169–177, concluding that these incidents indicate the prefect's determination to work closely with the priestly elite in Jerusalem (pp. 60–137, 215–16, 265–66). DAVID A. BRONDOS, Jesus' Death in New Testament Thought, 2 vols, Mexico City: Theological Community of Mexico/Instituto Internacional de Estudios Superiores, 2018, attempts a theological and exegetical exploration of the understanding of Jesus' death in the New Testament and the early Patristic tradition.

SHUA AMORAI-STARK et al., An Inscribed Copper-Aloy Finger Ring from Herodium Depicting a Krater, *IEJ* 68 (2018): 208–220, describe the sealing ring discovered in excavations at Herodion which depicts a krater circled by a Greek inscription reading Πιλάτο(υ), "of Pilatus"; the authors of the study conclude that it is unlikely that the ring belonged to Pontius Pilatus himself, allowing for the possibility that it belonged to a person in his administration. The ossuary of Mariam daughter of Yeshu'a son of Qayafa, discovered in the Elah Valley (J. PRICE, in WALTER AMELING et al., eds. Corpus Inscriptionum Iudaeae/Palaestinae IV: Iudaea/Idumaea, Berlin: De Gruyter, 2018, No. 3295, pp. 717–718; *editio princeps* in IEJ 61, 2011, 74–95), is most plausibly associated with the first-century tomb outside of Jerusalem with two ossuaries bearing the name *Qy/wp'* (CIIP I 461, 463; see below p. 13), identified with Joseph Caiaphas, the high priest; this ossuary answers the objection that the person named *Qyp'* of the Jerusalem tomb lacks any indication of a priestly background: Qayafa/Caiaphas is identified as "priest of (the course) Ma'aziya from Beit 'Imri" (Ma'aziya is the last of the 24 priestly courses listed in 1 Chron 24:7–18; Beit 'Imri can perhaps be identified with the Arab village Beit 'Ummar in the northern Hebron hills). ANNA DOLGANOV, Reichsrecht and Volksrecht in Theory and Practice: Roman Justice in the Province of Egypt (P. Oxy. II 237, P. Oxy. IV 706, SB XII 10929), in Administration, Law and Administrative Law: Comparative Studies in Imperial Bureaucracy and Officialdom, edited by M. Jursa and H. Täuber, Papyrologica Vindobonensia, Wien: Verlag der Österreichischen Akademie der Wissenschaften, 2019, revisits the use of the Roman legal order in the provinces and the status of local laws, including the "laws of the Egyptians" (see below, No. 74).

A regularly-updated annotated bibliography of works about crucifixion can be found in JOHN GRANGER COOK and DAVID W. CHAPMAN, "Crucifixion," in Oxford Bibliographies in Biblical Studies, edited by Christopher Matthews, New York: Oxford University Press, 2018. JOHN GRANGER COOK continues to publish sage and important studies on the cross, including his expanded Crucifixion in the Mediterranean World, second edition, WUNT 327, Tübingen: Mohr Siebeck, 2019. Also see his Maxentius's Crosses: CIL VIII, 18261, Vigiliae Christianae 68 (2014): 192–205 (a Latin inscription from Numidia implies that Maxentius's regular use of crucifixion was reversed by Constantine); also see COOK's related articles Crucifixion in the West: From Constantine to Recceswinth, Zeitschrift für antikes Christentum 16 (2012): 226–246 (Constantine desired to end the practice of crucifixion, though scattered later crucifixions occurred); A Note on SEG 53, 633: Crucifixion in Imperial Thessalonica, Early Christianity 2 (2011): 387–390 (a third-century A.D. epitaph from Thessalonica prescribes the cross for any who defile its tomb); R. Gest. Div. Aug. 25,1: Triginta fere millia capta dominis ad supplicium sumendum tradidi, Zeitschrift für Papyrologie und Epigraphik 201 (2017): 68–71 (the *Res Gestae* implies that many thousands of captured fugitive slaves from the army of Sextus Pompeius would have been crucified, both by Octavian and by those slaves' former masters). The debate over ancient crucifixion terminology and the definition of crucifixion continues with GUNNAR SAMUELSSON's cautious summary article "Crucifixion" in The Oxford Encyclopedia of the Bible and Law, edited by Brent A. Strawn, Oxford: Oxford University Press, 2015, 1:138–142; and with his review of COOK's first edition of Crucifixion in the Mediterranean World in Theologische Literaturzeitung 141 (2016): 329–331; COOK's rejoinder can be found in the preface to his second edition. Earlier mention should have been made of GIOVANNI LENZI, Talah in PreMishnaic Halakhah, Review of Rabbinic Judaism 11 (2008): 33–48; he contends that the Hebrew term *talah* never refers to crucifixion in any ancient text; however, LENZI relies heavily on later rabbinic writings, and his claim appears difficult to sustain among the earlier Jewish sources (see below pp. 499–500, 503–505; and esp. CHAPMAN, Crucifixion, 14–26). An important new contribution on impalement in Assyrian inscriptions and reliefs summarizes the evidence and argues that the legal penalty against local criminals preceded later usage in siege warfare; see KAREN RADNER, High Visibility Punishment and Deterrent: Impalement in Assyrian Warfare and Legal Practice, Zeitschrift für Altorientalische und Biblische Rechtsgeschichte 21 (2015): 103–128. For crucifixion understood within the range of Roman and Greek capital penalties, see also EVA CANTARELLA, I supplizi capitali: Origine e funzioni delle pene di morte in Grecia e a Roma, Nuova edizione rivista, Milan: Feltrinelli, 2005; paperback reprint Milan: Feltrinelli, 2011 (esp. pp. 77–82, 203–215). On the Palatino graffito (No. 462), see now also HERMANN LICHTENBERGER, Das Spottkruzifix vom Palatin und die Inattraktivität des Christentums in der hellenistisch-römischen Welt, Pages 173–88 in "Make Disciples of All Nations": The Appeal and Authority of Christian Faith in Hellenistic-Roman Times, edited by L. T. Stuckenbruck, B. Langstaff, and M. Tilly, WUNT 2.482, Tübingen: Mohr Siebeck, 2019.

A possible second archaeological discovery of crucified remains, from Roman-era strata in Gavello in the Po Valley of northern Italy, has been published; the find consists of a poorly preserved male skeleton with a circular hole in the right heel/calcaneum evidencing a *peri-mortem* blow inflicted from medial to lateral (from the inside of the foot to the outside); the left heel is not preserved, the tibiae show no evidence of *crucifragium* (fracturing during crucifixion), no nails were discovered with the skeleton, and the arms show no clear evidence of fixation (esp. nailing). Due to the poor preservation of the remains, some will likely continue to debate the osteologists' case for this as a crucifixion (with the leg pinned by a circular nail from the inside of the heel). See EMANUELA GUALDI-RUSSO, URSULA THUN HOHENSTEIN, NICOLETTA ONISTO, ELENA PILLI, and DAVID CARAMELLI, A Multidisciplinary Study of Calcaneal Trauma in Roman Italy: A Possible Case of Crucifixion? Archaeological and Anthropological Sciences, April 2018, accessed online at https://doi.org/10.1007/s12520-018-0631-9 (no print publication as of yet).

Recent discussion and debate has focused on portrayals of crucifixion in early Christian art, a topic that connects with our discussion on p. 676. B. W. LONGENECKER has renewed and expanded arguments for Christian crosses from imagery at Pompeii and Herculaneum in BRUCE W. LONGENECKER, The Cross Before Constantine: The Early Life of a Christian Symbol, Minneapolis: Fortress, 2015; idem, The Crosses of Pompeii: Jesus-Devotion in a Vesuvian Town, Minneapolis: Fortress, 2016. Contrast JOHN GRANGER COOK, Alleged Christian Crosses in Herculaneum and Pompeii, Vigiliae Christianae 72 (2018): 1–20; he responds that an inscription and two key artifacts employed by LONGENECKER are incorrectly identified as Christian crosses. Those wishing to pursue early Christian representations of the cross will greatly benefit from FELICITY HARLEY, Images of the Crucifixion in Late Antiquity: The Testimony of Engraved Gems, Ph.D. Thesis, Adelaide University, 2001; also see her published works (more recently as FELICITY HARLEY-MCGOWAN) in Picturing the Bible: The Earliest Christian Art, edited by JEFFREY SPIER, New Haven: Yale University Press, 2007; esp. pp. 227–232; "Gems of Heaven": Recent Research on Gemstones in Late Antiquity, AD 200–600, edited by CHRIS ENTWISTLE and NOËL ADAMS, London: British Museum, 2011; esp. pp. 214–220; Envisioning Christ on the Cross: Ireland and the Early Medieval West, edited by JULIET MULLINS, JENIFER NÍÍ GHRAÌDAIGH, and RICHARD HAWTREE, Dublin: Four Courts, 2013; esp. pp. 13–33; The Art of Empire: Christian Art in its Imperial Context, edited by

LEE M. JEFFERSON and ROBIN M. JENSEN, Minneapolis: Fortress Press, 2015; esp. pp. 115–158; and The Routledge Handbook of Early Christian Art, edited by ROBIN M. JENSEN and MARK D. ELLISON, New York: Routledge, 2018; esp. pp. 290–307. Further see The Eerdmans Encyclopedia of Early Christian Art and Archaeology, edited by PAUL CORBY FINNEY, 3 vols., Grand Rapids: Eerdmans, 2017, with articles on Cross (KARL SANDIN), Crucifixion (FELICITY HARLEY-MCGOWAN), and Gemstone: Cross (JEFFREY SPIER). Also note ALLYSON EVERINGHAM SHECKLER and MARY JOAN WINN LEITH, The Crucifixion Conundrum and the Santa Sabina Doors, Harvard Theological Review 103 (2010): 67–88; ROY D. KOTANSKY, The Magic "Crucifixion Gem" in the British Museum, Greek, Roman, and Byzantine Studies 57 (2017): 631–659. Finally, note the learned and wide-ranging summary by ROBIN M. JENSEN, The Cross: History, Art, and Controversy, Cambridge: Harvard University Press, 2017; also JENSEN's articles The Suffering and Dead Christ in Early Christian Art, ARTS 8 (1995): 22–28; The Passion in Early Christian Art, in Perspectives on the Passion: Encountering the Bible through the Arts, edited by CHRISTINE JOYNES, London: T & T Clark, 2007, pp. 53–84.


David W. Chapman
Eckhard J. Schnabel

# Table of Contents

(1) Josephus, *Antiquitates judaicae* 18.26 (2) Josephus, *A. J.* 18.34
(3) Josephus, *A. J.* 18.95 (4) Josephus, *A. J.* 20.198 (5) Josephus,
*Bellum judaicum* 5.506 (6) *t. Menahot* 13:21 (7) Josephus, *A. J.* 18.35
(8) Josephus, *A. J.* 18.95

(9) CIIP I/2 2 (10) Philo, *De legatione ad Gaium* 306–308 (11) Josephus,
*A. J.* 18.2 (12) Josephus, *A. J.* 20.199–203 (13) Josephus, *B. J.* 2.117
(14) Josephus, *B. J.* 6.126 (15) *Megillat Taanit* 6 (16) *y. Sanhedrin* 18a,42–43
(17) *b. Sanhedrin* 41a (18) *b. ʿAbodah Zarah* 8b

(19) 11QTemple LIV, 8 – LV, 10 (20) 11QTemple LVI, 8–11
(21) 11QTemple LXI, 7–12 (22) 11QTemple LXIV, 6–13 (23) CD IX, 1
(24) 4Q266 Frag. 6 II, 5–10 (25) Philo, *De specialibus legibus* 1.54–55
(26) Philo, *Spec.* 1.315–316 (27) Philo, *Spec.* 2.27–28 (28) Philo, *Spec.*
2.242–243 (29) Philo, *Spec.* 2.252– 254 (30) Josephus, *B. J.* 1.96–97
(31) Josephus, *A. J.* 14.177 (32) *m. Sanhedrin* 4:1 (33) *m. Sanh.* 4:5
(34) *m. Sanh.* 6:1–2 (35) *m. Sanh.* 6:4–6 (36) *m. Sanh.* 7:4 (37) *m. Sanh.*
7:6–7 (38) *m. Sanh.* 7:10 (39) *m. Sanh.* 7:11 (40) *m. Sanh.* 11:5
(41) *t. Sanh.* 10:11 (42) *t. Sanh.* 11:7 (43) *y. Sanh.* 25c,74–25d,10
(44) *b. Sanh.* 46a (45) *b. Sanh.* 89a (46) Origen, *Commentarii in
epistulam ad Romanos* 6.7.11

(47) Susanna 44–62 (48) CD IX, 2–8 (49) CD IX, 16 – X, 2
(50) 1QS VI, 1 (51) Josephus, *A. J.* 4.219 (52) *m. Sanh.* 5:1–5
(53) *t. Sanh.* 6:3

(281) Cicero, *Verr.* 2.5.165–166 (282) Cicero, *Verr.* 2.5.163
(283) Cicero, *Verr.* 2.5.168 (284) Cicero, *Verr.* 2.5.169 (285) Cicero,
*Verr.* 2.5.170–171 (286) Cicero, *Verr.* 2.1.6–7 (287) Cicero, *Verr.* 2.1.9
(288) Cicero, *Verr.* 2.1.12–13 (289) Cicero, *Verr.* (290) Cicero, *Verr.* 2.3.58–59
(291) Cicero, *Verr.* 2.3.70 (292) Cicero, *Verr.* 2.3.112 (293) Cicero, *Verr.*
2.4.24 (294) Cicero, *Verr.* 2.4.26 (295) Cicero, *Pro Rabirio* 3.10
(296) Cicero, *Rab. Perd.* 4.11 (297) Cicero, *Rab. Perd.* 4.13
(298) Cicero, *Rab. Perd.* 5.16–17 (299) Cicero, *Rab. Perd.* 10.28
(300) Appian, *Bella Civilia* 3.1.3 (301) Suetonius, *Galba* 9.1

(302) Plautus, *Mostellaria* 348–361 (303) Plautus, *Mostellaria* 55–57
(304) Plautus, *Mostellaria* 69–71 (305) Plautus, *Mostellaria* 741–744/745
(306) Plautus, *Mostellaria* 1128–1134 (307) Plautus, *Aulularia* 56–59
(308) Plautus, *Bacchides* 358–365 (309) Plautus, *Miles Gloriosus* 368–374
(310) Plautus, *Miles Gloriosus* 182–184 (311) Plautus, *Miles Gloriosus* 305–312
(312) Plautus, *Asinaria* 545–557 (313) Terence, *Andria* 616–625
(314) Appian, *Bell. civ.* 4.4.29 (315) Appian, *Bell. civ.* 4.5.35
(316) Appian, *Bell. civ.* 4.10.81 (317) Appian, *Bell. civ.* 5.8.70
(318) Tacitus, *Historiae* 4.3 (319) Tacitus, *Hist.* 4.11 (320) Tacitus, *Hist.* 2.72
(321) Juvenal, *Saturae* 6.219–224 (322) *Historia Augusta* 8 [Pertinax] 9.10
(323) *Historia Augusta* 18 [Severus Alexander] 23.7–8

(324) Dionysius of Halicarnassus, *Ant. rom.* 5.51.3
(325) Dionysius of Halicarnassus, *Ant. rom.* 12.6.4–6 (326) Appian, *Bell. civ.*
1.14.119 (327) Appian, *Bell. civ.* 1.14.120 (328) Cicero, *Verr.* 2.5.7
(329) Cicero, *Verr.* 2.5.10–11 (330) Cicero, *Verr.* 2.5.12
(331) Cicero, *Verr.* 2.5.14

(332) *Leges XII Tabularum* 8.5 (333) Epitaph from Amyzon
(334) *Lex Libitinaria* from Puteoli 2.8–14 (335) Seneca, *De Clementia* 1.23
(336) *Pauli Sententiae* 5.17.2 (337) *Pauli Sententiae* 5.21.4
(338) *Pauli Sententiae* 5.21a.1–2 (339) *Pauli Sententiae* 5.22.1
(340) *Digesta* 48.19.38.2 (341) *Pauli Sententiae* 5.23.1
(342) *Pauli Sententiae* 5.23.14–17 (343) *Pauli Sententiae* 5.25.1
(344) *Pauli Sententiae* 5.30b.1 (345) *Historia Augusta* 18 [Severus
Alexander] 28.4–5

(346) *Digesta* 48.19.28.15 (347) Apuleius, *Metamorphoses* 3.9.1–3
(348) Firmicus Maternus, *Mathesis* 8.22.3

(349) Appian, *Mithridatica* 5.29 [113–114] (350) Appian, *Bell. civ.*
2.13.90 [377] (351) [Pseudo-] Caesar, *De Bello Hispaniensi* 20.5

(384) Petronius, *Satyricon* 112 (385) *Semaḥot* 2.11 [44b]
(386) Josephus, *Vita* 420–421

(387) Cicero, *De Finibus* 5.30.92 (388) Philo, *De Providentia* 2.24
(389) Dio Chrysostom, *Orationes* 17.15 (390) Lucian, *Contemplantes* 14
(391) Valerius Maximus, *Facta et Dicta Memorabilia* 6.9 ext. 5

(392) Arrian, *Indica* 5.10–11 (393) Lucian, *De Sacrificiis* 6

(394) Greek Text of Esther (395) Philo, *De Josepho* 96, 98 (396) Philo, *De Josepho* 156 (397) Philo, *De Somniis* 2.213 (398) Josephus, *A. J.* 2.72–73 (399) Josephus, *A. J.* 6.374 (400) Josephus, *A. J.* 11.103 (401) Josephus, *A. J.* 11.267 (402) Targumim on Genesis 40:19

(403) Seneca, *De Ira 3 (Dialogue 5)* 3.6 (404) Philo, *De Posteritate Caini* 25–27

(405) *Anthologia Graeca* 11.192 (from Lucillius) (406) Chariton, *De Chaerea et Callirhoe* 3.4.18 (407) Apuleius, *Metamorphoses* 1.15.4 (408) *Anthologia Graeca* 9.378 (from Palladas)

(409) Josephus, *Antiquities* 19.94–95 (410) Suetonius, *Gaius Caligula* 57.3–4 (411) Juvenal, *Saturae* 8.183–188

(412) Martial, *Epigrammaton – Liber de spectaculis* 7.1–12

(413) Artemidorus, *Oneirocritica* 2.53

## List of Illustrations

# Abbreviations

| | |
|---|---|
| AB | Anchor Bible |
| ABD | Anchor Bible Dictionary. Edited by D. N. Freedman. New York, 1972 |
| AE | Année épigraphique |
| AGAJU | Arbeiten zur Geschichte des antiken Judentums und des Urchristentums |
| AGR | Akten der Gesellschaft für griechische und hellenistische Rechtsgeschichte |
| AHAW.PH | Abhandlungen der Heidelberger Akademie der Wissenschaften. Philosophisch-historische Klasse |
| AHw | Akkadisches Handwörterbuch. Edited by W. von Soden. Wiesbaden 1965–1981 |
| AJAH | American Journal of Ancient History |
| AJT | American Journal of Theology |
| AJP | American Journal of Philology |
| ANE | Ancient Near East |
| ANEP | Ancient Near Eastern Pictures Relating to the Old Testament. Edited by J. B. Pritchard. Princeton 1969 |
| ANET | Ancient Near Eastern Texts Relating to the Old Testament. Edited by J. B. Pritchard. Princeton 1969 (1955) |
| ANRW | Aufstieg und Niedergang der römischen Welt. Edited by W. Haase, H. Temporini. Berlin, 1972– |
| AOS | American Oriental Series |
| APVG | Archiv für Papyrusforschung und verwandte Gebiete |
| AREA | Arbeiten zur römischen Epigraphik und Altertumskunde |
| ASP | American Studies in Papyrology |
| ASV | American Standard Version |
| AYB | Anchor Yale Bible |
| BAR | Biblical Archaeology Review |
| BBR | Bulletin for Biblical Research |
| BDAG | Bauer, W., F. W. Danker, W. F. Arndt, F. W. Gingrich. A Greek-English Lexicon of the New Testment and Other Early Christian Literature. Third Edition. Chicago, 2000 |
| BDB | Brown, W., S. R. Driver, C. A. Briggs, Hebrew and English Lexicon of the Old Testament. Oxford 1968 |
| BDF | Blass, F., A. Debrunner, and R. W. Funk. A Grammar of the New Testament and Other Early Christian Literature. Chicago, 1961 [Reprint 1982] |
| BECNT | Baker Exegetical Commentary on the New Testament |
| BEThL | Bibliotheca Ephemeridum Theologicarum Lovaniensium |
| BHS | Biblia Hebraica Stuttgartensia |
| Bib | Biblica |
| BJS | Brown Judaic Studies |
| BNot | Biblische Notizen |
| BNP | Brill's New Pauly. Edited by H. Cancik, H. Schneider. Leiden, 2002–2012 |
| BRev | Bible Review |
| BSac | Bibliotheca Sacra |

| | |
|---|---|
| BSGRT | Bibliotheca Scriptorum Graecorum et Romanorum Teubneriana |
| BSJJGW | Berichte aus den Sitzungen der Joachim Jungius-Gesellschaft der Wissenschaften |
| BSJS | Brill's Series in Jewish Studies |
| BWANT | Beiträge zur Wissenschaft vom Alten und Neuen Testament |
| BZ | Biblische Zeitschrift |
| BZNW | Beihefte zur Zeitschrift für die neutestamentliche Wissenschaft |
| CAD | The Assyrian Dictionary of the Oriental Institute of the University of Chicago. Edited by I. J. Gelb et al. Chicago, 1956–2010 |
| CBET | Contributions to Biblical Exegesis and Theology |
| CBQ | Catholic Biblical Quarterly |
| CEFR | Collection de l'École Française de Rome |
| CHANE | Culture and History of the Ancient Near East |
| CHL | Commentationes humanarum litterarum |
| CIIP | Corpus Inscriptionum Iudaeae/Palestinae. Edited by H. M. Cotton, L. Di Segni, W. Eck, B. Isaac, A. Kushnir-Stein, H. Misgav, J. Price, I. Roll, A. Yardeni, W. Ameling. Berlin 2010–2014 |
| CIJ | Corpus Inscriptionum Judaicarum. Edited by J. B. Frey. New York, 1975 |
| CNT | Commentaire du Nouveau Testament |
| CPJ | Corpus Papyrorum Judaicarum. Edited by V. Tcherikover, A. Fuks. Cambridge, 1957–1964 |
| CSCT | Columbia Studies in the Classical Tradition |
| DJD | Discoveries in the Judaean Desert [of Jordan]. Oxford, 1955–2002 |
| DJG | Dictionary of Jesus and the Gospels. Edited by J. B. Green, S. McKnight, I. H. Marshall. Downers Grove, 1992 |
| DLNTD | Dictionary of the Later New Testament and Its Developments. Edited by P. H. Davids, R. P. Martin. 1997 |
| DNTB | Dictionary of New Testament Background. Edited by C. A. Evans, S. E. Porter. Downers Grove, 2000 |
| DSSSE | The Dead Sea Scrolls Study Edition. Edited by F. García Martínez, J. C. E. Tigchelaar. Leiden, 1997–1998 |
| EBC | Expositor's Bible Commentary |
| EBR | Encyclopedia of the Bible and its Reception. Edited by Dale C. Allison et al. Berlin / Boston 2009– |
| EDNT | Exegetical Dictionary of the New Testament. Edited by H. Balz, G. Schneider. Grand Rapids, 1990–1993 |
| EDSS | Encyclopedia of the Dead Sea Scrolls. Edited by L. H. Schiffman, J. C. VanderKam. Oxford, 2000 |
| EHS | Europäische Hochschulschriften |
| EKK | Evangelisch-Katholischer Kommentar |
| EBib | Études Bibliques |
| EHS | Europäische Hochschulschriften |
| EstEcl | Estudios eclesiásticos |
| ET | English Translation |
| ETL | Ephemerides theologicae lovanienses |
| FGH | Fragmente der griechischen Historiker. Edited by F. Jacoby. Berlin 1923–1958 |
| FilNT | Filología Neotestamentaria |
| FIRA | Fontes iuris romani anteiustiniani. 3 vols. Edited by S. Riccobono, V. Arangio Ruiz. Florence 1940–1941; Second Edition 1968 |
| FO | Folia Orientalia |
| FRLANT | Forschungen zur Religion und Literatur des Alten und Neuen Testaments |

| | |
|---|---|
| FS | Festschrift |
| fzb | Forschungen zur Bibel |
| GELS | T. Muraoka, A Greek-English Lexicon of the Septuagint. Leuven, 2009 |
| Georges | Ausführliches lateinisch-deutsches Handwörterbuch. K. E. Georges. Darmstadt 1992 (1912/1918) |
| GLA | Greek and Latin Authors on Jews and Judaism. 3 vols. Edited by M. Stern. Jerusalem, 1974–1984 |
| GNB | Gute Nachricht Bibel |
| HALOT | The Hebrew and Aramaic Lexicon of the Old Testament in English. Edited by L. Koehler, W. Baumgartner, J. J. Stamm. Leiden, 1994–2000 |
| HCS | Hellenistic Culture and Society |
| HdA | Handbuch der Altertumswissenschaft. Begründet von Iwan von Müller |
| HNT | Handkommentar zum Neuen Testament |
| HThK | Herders Theologischer Kommentar zum Neuen Testament |
| HTR | Harvard Theological Review |
| ICC | International Critical Commentary |
| IEJ | Israel Exploration Journal |
| IG | Inscriptiones Graecae |
| IGLS | Inscriptions grecques et latines de la Syrie. Edited by L. Jalabert, R. Mouterde, J.-P. Rey-Coquais, M. Sartre, P.-L. Gatier. 21 vols. Paris 1911–1993 |
| IGR | Inscriptiones Graecae ad res Romanas pertinentes. Edited by E. Leroux. Paris, 1906–1927; reprint Chicago, 1975 |
| IJudO | Inscriptiones Judaicae Orientis. Edited by D. Noy, A. Panayotov, H. Bloedhorn, W. Ameling. Tübingen, 2004 |
| ILS | Inscriptiones latinae selectae. Edited by H. Dessau, Berlin 1892–1916 [1954–1962] |
| IMC | Inscriptions Reveal: Documents from the Time of the Bible, the Mishna and the Talmud. Edited by Ruth Hestrin. Israel Museum Catalogue 100. Jerusalem 1973 |
| Int | Interpretation |
| ISBE | The International Standard Bible Encyclopedia. Edited by G. W. Bromiley. Grand Rapids, 1979–1988 |
| JAC | Jahrbuch für Antike und Christentum |
| JECS | Journal of Early Christian Studies |
| JBL | Journal of Biblical Literature |
| JETS | Journal of the Evangelical Theological Society |
| JGRChJ | Journal of Greco-Roman Christianity and Judaism |
| JHS | Journal of Hellenic Studies |
| JJS | Journal of Jewish Studies |
| JPT | Journal of Pentecostal Theology |
| JSJ | Journal the Study of Judaism in the Persian, Hellenistic, and Roman Periods |
| JSJSup | Journal the Study of Judaism Supplement Series |
| JSNT | Journal for the Study of the New Testament |
| JSNTSup | Journal for the Study of the New Testament Supplement Series |
| JSP | Journal for the Study of the Pseudepigrapha |
| JSPSup | Journal for the Study of the Pseudepigrapha Supplement Series |
| JTS | Journal of Theological Studies |
| JRA | Journal of Roman Archaeology |
| JRASup | Journal of Roman Archaeology Supplementary Series |
| KEK | Kritisch-exegetischer Kommentar über das Neue Testament |
| KJV | King James Version |
| LASBF | Liber annus Studii biblici franciscani |

| | |
|---|---|
| LCL | Loeb Classical Library |
| LD | Lectio Divina |
| LEH | Lust, J. E. Eynikel, K. Hauspie. A Greek-English Lexicon of the Septuagint. Stuttgart, 1992–1996 |
| Levy | Wörterbuch über die Talmudim und Midrashim. Second Edition by H. L. Fleischer, L. Goldschmidt, Darmstadt 1963 (orig. 1924) |
| LGPN | A Lexicon of Greek Personal Names. Vols. I–VA. Edited by P. M. Fraser, E. Matthews. Oxford, 1987–2009 |
| LN | Louw, J. P., E. A. Nida. Greek-English Lexicon of the New Testament Based on Semantic Domains. New York, 1988 |
| LNTS | Library of New Testament Studies |
| LSJ | H. G. Liddell, R. Scott, H. S. Jones. A Greek-English Lexicon. Ninth Edition, with revised supplement edited by Peter G. W. Glare. Oxford, 1996. |
| Luther | Luther-Bibel (1984) |
| LXX | Septuagint; the LXX texts are taken from the Göttingen Septuaginta |
| Maj | Majority Text |
| MAMA | Monumenta Asiae Minoris Antiqua |
| MBPAR | Münchener Beiträge zur Papyrusforschung und antiken Rechtsgeschichte |
| MJS | Münsteraner Judaistische Studien |
| MM | J. H. Moulton, G. Milligan. The Vocabulary of the Greek Testament Illustrated from the Papyri and Other Non-Literary Sources. Grand Rapids, 1982 [1930] |
| MT | Masoretic Text |
| Muraoka | T. Muraoka, A Greek-English Lexicon of the Septuagint, Leuven 2009 |
| NA$^{28}$ | Nestle-Aland. Novum Testamentum Graece. 28th Revised Edition. Edited by B. Aland, K. Aland, J. Karavidopoulos, C. M. Martini, B. M. Metzger, H. Strutwolf. Stuttgart, 2012 |
| NAC | New American Commentary |
| NCBC | New Century Bible Commentary |
| NEAEHL | The New Encyclopedia of Archaeological Excavations in the Holy Land. Edited by E. Stern. Jerusalem and New York, 1993 |
| NET | New English Translation |
| NICNT | New International Commentary on the New Testament |
| NIDB | New Interpreter's Dictionary of the Bible. Edited by K. D. Sakenfeld. Nashville, 2006–2009 |
| NIDNTT | The New International Dictionary of New Testament Theology. Edited by C. Brown. Grand Rapids, 1975–1978 |
| NIDOTTE | New International Dictionary of Old Testament Theology and Exegesis. Edited by W. A. VanGemeren. Grand Rapids, 1997 |
| NIGTC | New International Greek Testament Commentary |
| NIV | New International Version |
| NJB | New Jerusalem Bible |
| NLT | New Living Translation |
| NovT | Novum Testamentum |
| NovTSup | Novum Testamentum Supplements series |
| NRSV | New Revised Standard Version |
| NTA | Neutestamentliche Abhandlungen |
| NTD | Neues Testament Deutsch |
| NTOA | Novum Testamentum et Orbis Antiquus |
| NTS | New Testament Studies |
| OCD | Oxford Classical Dictionary. Edited by S. Hornblower, A. Spawforth. Fourth Edition. Oxford, 2012 |

| | |
|---|---|
| OCT | Oxford Classical Texts |
| OGIS | Orientis Graeci Inscriptiones Selectae. Edited by W. Dittenberger. 2 vols. Leipzig 1903–1905 |
| OLA | Orientalia Lovaniensia Analecta |
| ÖTK | Ökumenischer Taschenbuchkommentar |
| P. Coll. Youtie | Collectanea Papyrologica: Texts published in Honor of H. C. Youtie. Edited by A. E. Hanson, et al. |
| P. Oxy. | Oxyrhynchus Papyri. Edited by B. P. Grenfell, A. S. Hunt, et al. |
| P. Yale | Yale Papyri in the Beinecke Rare Book and Manuscript Library. Edited by J. F. Oates, et al. |
| PEFQS | Palestine Exploration Fund Quarterly Statement |
| PEQ | Palestine Exploration Quarterly |
| PKNT | Papyrologische Kommentare zum Neuen Testament |
| PNTC | Pillar New Testament Commentary |
| PSI | Papiri greci e latini. Edited by G. Vitelli, M. Norsa, V. Bartoletti, et al. Florence 1912–2008 |
| QD | Questiones disputatae |
| RAr | Revue archéologique |
| RB | Revue Biblique |
| RdQ | Revue de Qumran |
| RE | Real-Encyclopädie der classischen Altertumswissenschaft. Edited by A. F. Pauly, G. Wissowa, W. Kroll, K. Mittelhaus, K. Ziegler, H. Gärtner. Stuttgart, 1894–1980 |
| REA | Revue des études anciennces |
| REB | Revised English Bible |
| RHDFE | Revue historique de droit français et étranger |
| RNT | Regensburger Neues Testament |
| RPP | Religion Past and Present: Encyclopedia of Theology and Religion. Edited by H. D. Betz, D. S. Browning, B . Janowski, E. Jüngel. Leiden, 2007–2013 |
| RRJ | Review of Rabbinic Judaism |
| RSV | Revised Standard Version |
| RV | Revised Version |
| SAG | Studien zur Alten Geschichte |
| SB | Sammelbuch griechischer Urkunden aus Aegypten. Edited by F. Preisigke, et al. |
| SBLDS | Society of Biblical Literature Dissertation Series |
| SCI | Scripta Classica Israelica |
| SDHI | Studia et Documenta Historiae et Iuris |
| SEG | Supplementum Epigraphicum Graecum. 55 vols. Edited by J. J. E. Hondius, H. W. Pleket, R. S. Stroud, J. H. M. Strubbe. Leiden, 1923–2010 |
| SFSHJ | South Florida Studies in the History of Judaism |
| SHAR | Studies in the History and Anthropology of Religion |
| SJ | Studia Judaica |
| SJLA | Studies in Judaism in Late Antiquity |
| SJOT | Scandinavian Journal of the Old Testament |
| SNTSMS | Society of New Testament Studies Monograph Series |
| SP | Sacra Pagina |
| SRG | Schriften zur Rechtsgeschichte |
| ST | Studia theologica |
| STDJ | Studies on the Texts of the Desert of Judah |
| TAM | Tituli Asiae Minoris |
| TANZ | Texte und Arbeiten zum neutestamentlichen Zeitalter |

| | |
|---|---|
| TDNT | Theological Dictionary of the New Testament. Edited by G. Kittel, G. Friedrich. Grand Rapids, 1964–1976 |
| TDOT | Theological Dictionary of the Old Testament. Edited by G. J. Botterweck, H. Ringgren, H.- J. Fabry. Grand Rapids, 1974–2006 |
| TFPL | Travaux de la Faculté de Philosophie et Lettres, l'Université Libre de Bruxelles |
| ThHK | Theologischer Handkommentar zum Neuen Testament |
| TLNT | Theological Lexicon of the New Testament. Edited by C. Spicq. Peabody, 1995 |
| TLOT | Theological Lexicon of the Old Testament. Edited by E. Jenni, C. Westermann. Peabody, 1997 |
| TNIV | Today's New International Version |
| TNTC | Tyndale New Testament Commentary |
| TRE | Theologische Realenzyklopädie. Edited by G. Krause, G. Müller. Berlin, 1977–2007 |
| TrJ | Trinity Journal |
| TynBul | Tyndale Bulletin |
| VC | Vigiliae Christianae |
| WBC | Word Biblical Commentary |
| WMANT | Wissenschaftliche Monographien zum Alten und Neuen Testament |
| WUNT | Wissenschaftliche Untersuchungen zum Neuen Testament |
| ZB | Züricher Bibel |
| ZDPV | Zeitschrift des Deutschen Palästina-Vereins |
| ZNW | Zeitschrift für die neutestamentliche Wissenschaft |
| ZPE | Zeitschrift für Papyrologie und Epigraphik |
| ZSSR. RA | Zeitschrift der Savigny-Stiftung für Rechtsgeschichte. Romanistische Abteilung |
| ZTK | Zeitschrift für Theologie und Kirche |

The abbreviations of ancient sources follow PATRICK H. ALEXANDER ET AL. The SBL Handbook of Style: For Ancient Near Eastern, Biblical, and Early Christian Studies. Peabody: Hendrickson, 1999, and HUBERT CANCIK, HELMUTH SCHNEIDER, and MANFRED LAND-FESTER, eds. Brill's New Pauly: Encyclopedia of the Ancient World. Leiden: Brill, 2002–2010. For abbreviations of papyri see JOHN F. OATES, ROGER S. BAGNALL, ET AL., Checklist of Greek, Latin, Demotic and Coptic Papyri, Ostraca and Tablets. http://scriptorium. lib.duke.edu/papyrus/texts/clist.html (last updated June 2011); for inscriptions see the abbreviations in L'Année Philologique.

Part 1

# The Jewish Trial before the Sanhedrin

The most important discussion of Jesus' trial in the 20th century by a Jewish author was the study of JEAN JUSTER on the Jews in the Roman Empire. He argued that the Sanhedrin in Jerusalem, the highest Jewish court before A.D. 70, had the right to indict Jews who were accused of capital charges and to execute capital punishment.[1] HANS LIETZMANN, in his *Akademieabhandlung* of 1931 on Jesus' trial, used Juster's conclusions to argue that Mark's depiction of Jesus' trial before the Sanhedrin (Mark 14:55–65) cannot be accepted as historical.[2] Lietzmann believed that if Jesus had indeed been tried by the Sanhedrin and indicted on capital charges, he would have been stoned. Since Jesus was crucified according to Roman law, he was neither tried nor condemned by the Sanhedrin. While skepticism concerning the historicity of a Sanhedrin trial continues to find support, JOSEF BLINZLER,[3] AUGUST STROBEL,[4] RUDOLF PESCH,[5] RAYMOND BROWN,[6] ERIKA HEUSLER,[7] MONIKA

---

[1] JEAN JUSTER, Les Juifs dans l'empire romain. Leur condition juridique, économique et sociale (2 vols.; Paris: Geuthner, 1914), 2:132–45. EMIL SCHÜRER, The History of the Jewish People in the Age of Christ (175 B.C. – A.D. 135) (revised by G. Vermes, F. Millar, M. Black, and M. Goodman; Edinburgh: T & T Clark, 1973–1987), 2:261, argues the same point.

[2] HANS LIETZMANN, Der Prozess Jesu, in Sitzungsberichte der preussischen Akademie der Wissenschaften Nr. XIV (Berlin: Verlag der Akademie der Wissenschaften in Kommission bei Walter de Gruyter, 1931) = HANS LIETZMANN, Der Prozess Jesu, in Kleine Schriften II (Texte und Untersuchungen 68; Berlin: Akademie-Verlag, 1958), 251–263.

[3] JOSEF BLINZLER, Der Prozeß Jesu (Vierte, erneut revidierte Auflage; orig. 1951; repr., Regensburg: Pustet, 1969); the translation by Isabel and Florence McHugh is based on the shorter 2nd German edition 1951: JOSEF BLINZLER, The Trial of Jesus (Cork: Mercier, 1959).

[4] AUGUST STROBEL, Die Stunde der Wahrheit. Untersuchungen zum Strafverfahren gegen Jesus (WUNT 21; Tübingen: Mohr Siebeck, 1980).

[5] RUDOLF PESCH, Das Markusevangelium (2 vols.; orig. 1976–1977; repr., HThK 2; Freiburg: Herder, 1980), 2:442–43.

[6] RAYMOND E. BROWN, The Death of the Messiah: From Gethsemane to the Grave. A Commentary on the Passion Narratives in the Four Gospels (2 vols.; Anchor Bible Reference Library; London: Chapman, 1994), 1:553–60.

[7] ERIKA HEUSLER, Kapitalprozesse im lukanischen Doppelwerk. Die Verfahren gegen Jesus und Paulus in exegetischer und rechtshistorischer Analyse (NTA 38; Münster: Aschendorff, 2000), 8–46, 239–43, who argues that Luke 22:66–23:25 corresponds to the *accusatio* in the *ordo* of Roman criminal trials (discussed in ibid. 218–38).

SCHUOL[8] and others[9] argue that there was a trial or examination of Jesus by the high priest and the Sanhedrin and that the Jewish authorities share the legal responsibility for Jesus' conviction with Rome. Recent investigations of the legal situation in Roman provinces, in particular in Judea, have suggested that an interrogation of Jesus by the Sanhedrin, convened *ad hoc* by the high priest, is historically plausible when we understand the episode not as a formal trial but as an investigation in which the members of the Sanhedrin had a consultative function.[10] F. WIENACKER suggests that due to the messianic implications of the *seditio* charge, the Roman prefect temporarily yielded the preliminary investigation to the Sanhedrin under Caiaphas, a procedure that neither robbed the sentence and execution of the character of a Roman trial nor called into question the monopoly of Roman capital punishment.[11]

The documents presented in Part 1 have been cited by various scholars as relevant for understanding the Gospel narratives of Jesus' trial / interrogation before the Sanhedrin. The texts are grouped into seven areas: (1) Annas and Caiaphas, the two high priests who were present during Jesus' interrogation by the Sanhedrin; (2) the jurisdiction of the Sanhedrin in the early first century A.D.; (3) capital cases in Jewish law, including stipulations concerning the interrogation of witnesses; (4) interrogation of witnesses; (5) blasphemy in Jewish law; (6) seducers of the people (*mesit, maddiah*) in Jewish law; (7) the charge of sorcery; (8) the abuse of prisoners in Jewish sources; and (9) the transfer of court cases.

## 1.1 Annas and Caiaphas

The Gospel accounts of Jesus' interrogation before the transfer to Pilate mention two Jewish leaders: Annas and Caiaphas. Annas is mentioned for the first time in Luke's dating of the ministry of John the Baptist: "In the fifteenth year of the reign of Emperor Tiberius, when Pontius Pilate was governor of Judea,

---

[8] MONIKA SCHUOL, Augustus und die Juden. Rechtsstellung und Interessenpolitik der kleinasiatischen Diaspora (SAG 6; Frankfurt: Antike, 2007), 188–89, 198–99.

[9] Cf. DIETER KRIMPHOVE, "Wir haben ein Gesetz ...!" Rechtliche Anmerkungen zum Strafverfahren gegen Jesus (2. völlig bearbeitete Auflage; orig. 1997; repr., Ius Vivens B: Rechtsgeschichtliche Abhandlungen 5; Münster / Berlin: LIT, 2006), 37–188.

[10] Cf. GUIDO O. KIRNER, Strafgewalt und Provinzialherrschaft. Eine Untersuchung zur Strafgewaltspraxis der römischen Statthalter in Judäa (6–66 n.Chr.) (SRG 109; Berlin: Duncker & Humblot, 2004), 167–68, 259.

[11] FRANZ WIEACKER, Römische Rechtsgeschichte. Zweiter Abschnitt: Die Jurisprudenz vom frühen Prinzipat bis zum Ausgang der Antike im weströmischen Reich und die oströmische Rechtswissenschaft bis zur justinianischen Gesetzgebung. Ein Fragment (ed. J. G. Wolff; HdA X/3.2; München: Beck, 2006), 366 n. 60. Commenting on the killing of Stephen and on Paul's trial in Acts, WIEACKER concludes that these accounts fit reliably into the outlines of what we know about the criminal jurisdiction in the Roman provinces (ibid. 367).

and Herod was ruler of Galilee, and his brother Philip ruler of the region of Ituraea and Trachonitis, and Lysanias ruler of Abilene, during the high priesthood of Annas and Caiaphas, the word of God came to John son of Zechariah in the wilderness" (Luke 3:1–2). John relates that immediately after his arrest, Jesus was taken to Annas: "First they took him to Annas, who was the father-in-law of Caiaphas, the high priest that year" (John 18:13). After the interrogation, during which Jesus refers the high priest to his public teaching, Annas sends Jesus to Caiaphas: "Then Annas sent him bound to Caiaphas the high priest" (John 18:24). Annas is mentioned again by Luke when he describes the interrogation of Peter and John after their arrest in the Temple: "The next day their rulers, elders, and scribes assembled in Jerusalem, with Annas the high priest, Caiaphas, John, and Alexander, and all who were of the high-priestly family" (Acts 4:5–6).

*Annas (Ananus, son of Seth)*

**(1)** Josephus, *Antiquitates judaicae* 18.26

Κυρίνιος δὲ τὰ Ἀρχελάου χρήματα ἀποδόμενος ἤδη καὶ τῶν ἀποτιμήσεων πέρας ἐχουσῶν αἳ ἐγένοντο τριακοστῷ καὶ ἑβδόμῳ ἔτει μετὰ τὴν Ἀντωνίου ἐν Ἀκτίῳ ἧτταν ὑπὸ Καίσαρος, Ἰωάζαρον τὸν ἀρχιερέα καταστασιασθέντα ὑπὸ τῆς πληθύος ἀφελόμενος τὸ ἀξίωμα τῆς τιμῆς Ἄνανον τὸν Σεθὶ καθίσταται ἀρχιερέα.

*Translation.* After Quirinius had sold the property of Archelaos and when the census, which took place in the thirty-seventh year after Caesar's victory over Anthony at Actium, had been concluded and Joazar was overpowered by a majority of the people, he (Quirinius) stripped him of the dignity of his office and appointed Ananus, the son of Seth, as high priest.

*Commentary.*[12] Josephus begins Book 18 of *Antiquitates* with the arrival of

[12] The Greek text of Josephus's works used throughout is that of BENEDIKT NIESE, Flavii Josephi Opera (7 vols.; Berlin: Weidmann, 1885–1895). For other editions of the Greek text and translations cf. SAMUEL ADRIANUS NABER, Flavii Iosephi Opera Omnia (6 vols.; BSGRT; Leipzig: Teubner, 1888–1896); H. ST. JOHN THACKERAY / RALPH MARCUS / LOUIS H. FELDMAN, Josephus (10 vols.; LCL; Cambridge: Harvard University Press, 1926–1965); OTTO MICHEL and OTTO BAUERNFEIND, Flavius Josephus, De Bello Judaico. Der jüdische Krieg (Griechisch und Deutsch. 3 vols.; Darmstadt: Wissenschaftliche Buchgesellschaft, 1959–1969); ÉTIENNE NODET, Flavius Josèphe. Les Antiquités juives (4 vols.; Paris: Cerf, 1990–2005); STEVE MASON, Judean War 2 (Flavius Josephus: Translation and Commentary 1B; Leiden: Brill, 2008); see also HEINRICH CLEMENTZ, Des Flavius Josephus Jüdische Altertümer (orig. 1899–1923; repr., Wiesbaden: Fourier, 1994); HEINRICH CLEMENTZ, Flavius Josephus, Geschichte des jüdischen Krieges. (orig. 1900; repr., Wiesbaden: Fourier, 1984); WILLIAM WHISTON, The Works of Flavius Josephus (Complete and Unabridged. Updated ed.;

Quirinius, the new Roman legate of the province of Syria, and his assessment of property in Judea (18.1–3), followed by an account of the revolt instigated by Judas from Gamala and Zaddok the Pharisee (18.4–10). He then provides a description of the three "philosophies" of the Pharisees, Sadducees, and Essenes and of the "fourth philosophy" established by Judas the Galilean and his followers (18.11–25). Josephus resumes his account of the history of Judea and of Quirinius' activities in 18.26, noting the liquidation of the estate of Archelaos, the completion of the registration of property in Judea, the deposition of the high priest Joazar who had faced serious opposition by a popular faction, and the appointment of Ananus as high priest. The Annas ("Αννας) mentioned in the New Testament is identical with Ananus ("Ανανος),[13] the high priest mentioned by Josephus, the son of Seth, an unknown member of a leading priestly family. Publius Sulpicius Quirinius was probably proconsul of Creta-Cyrenae in c. 15 B.C., appointed consul in 12 B.C., legate of Galatia-Pamphylia perhaps between 5–3 B.C., then perhaps proconsul of the province of Asia. He accompanied C. Iulius Caesar, Augustus' adopted son, as tutor on his mission to the East in A.D. 2–3. Shortly thereafter he was appointed governor of Syria. It is unclear how long he remained in Syria. The reference to "the thirty-seventh year" reckons with the Actian era (the battle of Actium took place in September of 31 B.C.), i.e., the census took place in A.D. 6. Quirinius' funerary inscription has been found in 1764 near Tibur (*titulus Tiburtinus*).[14]

---

orig. 1737; repr., Peabody: Hendrickson, 1987), which is based on the inferior text of SIWART HAVERKAMP, Flavii Josephi quae reperiri potuerunt, opera omnia graece et latine cum notis et nova versione Joannis Hudsoni (2 vols.; Amsterdam: Wetstenios, 1726). The Greek version of *B. J.* appeared between A.D. 79–81, *A. J.* was published A.D. 93–94.

[13] Annas is the abbreviated form of Ananias ('Ανανίας), in Hebrew Hananiah (חֲנַנְיָה), meaning "Yah[weh] has shown favor"); cf. TAL ILAN, Lexicon of Jewish Names in Late Antiquity (TSAJ 91.126.141.148; Tübingen: Mohr Siebeck, 2002–2011), 1:99–102, who lists 39 occurrences of the name. Other Greek transcriptions of the name are "Ανανος, "Ανανος, 'Αναν. On Annas cf. JAMES C. VANDERKAM, From Joshua to Caiaphas: High Priests After the Exile (Minneapolis: Fortress, 2004), 420–24; RAINER METZNER, Die Prominenten im Neuen Testament. Ein prosopographischer Kommentar (NTOA 66; Göttingen: Vandenhoeck & Ruprecht, 2008), 234–37, 342–43; MARTIN HENGEL / ANNA MARIA SCHWEMER, Jesus und das Judentum (Geschichte des frühen Christentums Band I; Tübingen: Mohr Siebeck, 2007), 79–80; RAINER METZNER, Kaiphas: der Hohepriester jenes Jahres: Geschichte und Deutung (Ancient Judaism and early Christianity 75; Leiden: Brill, 2010), 21–26, 61–67, 256–66.

[14] ILS 918 = CIL XIV 3613; cf. VICTOR EHRENBERG and ARNOLD H. M. JONES, Documents Illustrating the Reigns of Augustus and Tiberius (Second ed.; orig. 1955; repr., Oxford: Clarendon, 1976), No. 199. P. Sulpicius Quirinus is not mentioned in the text; for the most recent arguments that the inscription ILS 918 refers to Quirinius cf. GEZA ALFÖLDY, Un celebre frammento epigraphico tiburtino anonimo (P. Sulpicius Quirinius?), in Le iscrizione dei Cristiani in Vaticano (ed. I. Di Stefano Manzella; Inscriptiones Sanctae Sedis 2; Città del Vaticano Roma: Monumenti, Musei e gallerie pontificie Distribuzione esclusiva, Edizioni Quasar, 1997), 199–208; cf. ALEXANDER DEMANDT, 'Hände in Unschuld'. Pontius Pilatus in der Geschichte (Köln: Böhlau, 1999), 75–76.

Quirinius died in A.D. 21.[15] The next governor of Syria that we have information about is Caecilius Metellus Creticus Silanus (A.D. 12–17).

Josephus connects Ananus' appointment to the events of the year A.D. 6, the thirty-seventh year after 31 B.C., the year when Augustus defeated Mark Anthony in the battle of Actium. Caesar, i.e., the emperor Augustus, deposed Archelaos, son of Herod I, as ethnarch of Judea and sent him into exile in Vienne in Gaul. He ordered Quirinius to assess people's property in a census and to dispose of the property of Archelaos, and he appointed Coponius as prefect of Judea (Josephus, *A. J.* 18.1–2; see No. 11). Ananus succeeded Joazar, son of Boethus, whom Quirinius deposed in response to the activities of a "majority of the people" or "a popular faction" which might have been connected with the nationalist Judas the Galilean (*A. J* 18.23–25).[16] Annas was thus the first high priest appointed by a Roman governor after the imposition of direct Roman rule in Judea.

EMIL SCHÜRER regarded Josephus as a "preserver of facts."[17] Much has changed in Josephus scholarship since the early 20th century. HORST MOEHRING argued in his 1957 dissertation, on the basis of composition-critical analyses, that Josephus is the author of the works ascribed to him in the true sense of the term: the material in Josephus' works is more or less freely created, with no necessary connection to historical events.[18] PER BILDE's study of Josephus similarly uses composition criticism, with little interest in history, to portray Josephus as a competent author.[19] STEVE MASON believes that composition- and narrative-critical analyses of Josephus have shown that "we have no place to stand that affords traction for getting behind Josephus" because "where we have only one relevant narrative and no other evidence, we cannot hope to produce probable solutions to our historical questions."[20] He argues that "one can

---

[15] Cf. WERNER ECK, Sulpicius [II 13] P. S. Quirinius, BNP 13 (2008): 939–940; SCHÜRER, History, 1:259.

[16] RICHARD A. HORSLEY, High Priests and the Politics of Roman Palestine: A Contextual Analysis of the Evidence in Josephus, JSJ 17 (1986): 23–55, 21.

[17] EMIL SCHÜRER, Geschichte des jüdischen Volkes im Zeitalter Christi (3 vols. 4. Auflage; Leipzig: Hinrichs, 1901–1911); SCHÜRER, History. The phrase "preserver of facts" is from STEVE MASON, Josephus as Authority for First-Century Judea, in Josephus, Judea, and Christian Origins: Methods and Categories (Peabody: Hendrickson, 2009), 7–43, 16, who is unnecessarily polemical when he refers to SCHÜRER and "his many followers in the NT-*Umwelt* industry" (ibid. 24); cf. STEVE MASON, Josephus and the New Testament, the New Testament and Josephus: An Overview, in Josephus und das Neue Testament. Wechselseitige Wahrnehmungen (ed. C. Böttrich and J. Herzer; WUNT 209; Tübingen: Mohr Siebeck, 2007), 15–48, 33. For the following survey cf. STEVE MASON, Contradiction or Counterpoint? Josephus and Historical Method [2003], in Josephus, Judea, and Christian Origins: Methods and Categories (Peabody: Hendrickson, 2009), 103–137.

[18] HORST R. MOEHRING, Novelistic Elements in the Writings of Flavius Josephus (Chicago: University of Chicago, 1957), 64, 87, 144.

[19] PER BILDE, Flavius Josephus between Jerusalem and Rome: His Life, his Works and their Importance (JSPSup 2; Sheffield: JSOT, 1988).

[20] MASON, Contradiction, 136, 134; cf. STEVE MASON, Flavius Josephus on the Pharisees: A Composition-Critical Study (SPB 39; Leiden: Brill, 1991); STEVE MASON, Josephus and the New Testament (Second ed.; Peabody: Hendrickson, 2003), 27–31; MASON, Authority.

no longer use Josephus as a fact-book for NT study."[21] Undeterred, SHAYE COHEN argues that an event narrated by Josephus is doubtful or spurious (only) when an apologetic interest can be identified.[22] TESSA RAJAK, responding to the skepticism of MOEHRING and COHEN, argues that "from the narrative provided by the historian, which, if nothing else, is full and circumstantial, and from his analysis, treated itself as a pertinent fact, a full and realistic picture emerges.[23] In deliberate contrast to compositional-critical studies, DANIEL SCHWARTZ challenges the notion that narrative criticism precludes historical reconstruction and uses Josephus to reconstruct the life of Agrippa I, and more recently defended reading Josephus with a view to "reconstruct not only stories but also history."[24] MARTIN GOODMAN and JONATHAN PRICE reconstruct the Jewish War on the basis of Josephus' works, relying on his "detailed narrative, attaching special significance to every snippet of information which appears to contradict the main thrust of his apologetic."[25] MARTIN HENGEL and ANNA MARIA SCHWEMER insist, against S. MASON and other skeptics, that Josephus remains "der wichtigste 'Augenzeuge' für die neutestamentliche Zeit."[26] MONIKA SCHUOL, a classical scholar, argues that it is justified and methodologically acceptable to use Josephus as source for the history of the Jews in the Greco-Roman period, particularly if the relevant texts are analyzed source-critically.[27] Several recent volumes investigate Josephus' reliability and significance as a historian.[28]

## (2) Josephus, *Antiquitates judaicae* 18.34

ὃς παύσας ἱερᾶσθαι Ἄνανον Ἰσμάηλον ἀρχιερέα ἀποφαίνει τὸν τοῦ Φαβί καὶ τοῦτον δὲ μετ' οὐ πολὺ μεταστήσας Ἐλεάζαρον τὸν Ἀνάνου τοῦ ἀρχιερέως υἱὸν ἀποδείκνυσιν ἀρχιερέα.

*Translation.* He (Valerius Gratus) deposed Ananus from his priestly office and appointed Ishmael, the son of Phabi, as high priest. Not long afterwards he removed him also and appointed Eleazar, the son of the high priest Ananus.

---

[21] MASON, Overview, 36.

[22] SHAYE J. D. COHEN, Josephus in Galilee and Rome: His Vita and Development as a Historian (orig. 1979; repr., CSCT 8; Leiden: Brill, 2002), 144.

[23] TESSA RAJAK, Josephus: The Historian and His Society (Philadelphia: Fortress, 1983), 106–7. She explains Josephus' portrayal of Pontius not with the author's literary aims, but with the fragmentary information available to him (ibid. 67).

[24] DANIEL R. SCHWARTZ, Agrippa I: The Last King of Judaea (TSAJ 23; Tübingen: Mohr Siebeck, 1990), and DANIEL R. SCHWARTZ, Reading the First Century: On Reading Josephus and Studying Jewish History of the First Century (WUNT 300; Tübingen: Mohr Siebeck, 2013), quotation 25. See also cf. DANIEL R. SCHWARTZ, Composition and Sources in *Antiquities* 18: The Case of Pontius Pilate, in Making History: Josephus and Historical Method (ed. Z. Rodgers; JSJSup 110; Leiden: Brill, 2007), 125–146, contra STEVE MASON, Contradiction or Counterpoint? Josephus and Historical Method, RRJ 6 (2003): 145–188.

[25] MARTIN GOODMAN, The Ruling Class of Judaea: The Origins of the Jewish Revolt Against Rome A.D. 66–70 (Cambridge: Cambridge University Press, 1987), 20–21; similarly JONATHAN J. PRICE, Jerusalem Under Siege: The Collapse of the Jewish State 66–70 C.E. (BSJS 3; Leiden: Brill, 1992), 186.

[26] HENGEL / SCHWEMER, Jesus, 130.

[27] SCHUOL, Augustus, 67–75.

[28] JOSEPH SIEVERS and GAIA LEMBI, eds., Josephus and Jewish History in Flavian Rome and Beyond (JSJSup 104; Leiden: Brill, 2005); JACK PASTOR, PNINA STERN, and MENAHEM MOR, eds., Flavius Josephus: Interpretation and History (JSJSup 146; Leiden: Brill, 2011).

*Commentary.* Ananus was removed as high priest by Valerius Gratus, the new prefect of the province of Judea (A.D. 15–26), who had just been appointed by the emperor Tiberius to replace Annius Rufus (*A. J.* 18.33).[29] Ananus' replacement was not prompted by Roman dissatisfaction with his tenure: within a year he appointed Eleazar, one of Ananus' sons, to the high priestly office.[30] Perhaps Gratus wanted to demonstrate his authority in the province by appointing a new high priest,[31] after his predecessors Coponius (A.D. 6–9), Marcus Ambibulus (A.D. 9–12), and Annius Rufus (A.D. 12–15) had worked with Ananus, who thus officiated as high priest for nine years from A.D. 6–15.

**(3)** Josephus, *Antiquitates judaicae* 20.197

Πέμπει δὲ Καῖσαρ Ἀλβῖνον εἰς τὴν Ἰουδαίαν ἔπαρχον Φήστου τὴν τελευτὴν πυθόμενος ὁ δὲ βασιλεὺς ἀφείλετο μὲν τὸν Ἰώσηπον τὴν ἱερωσύνην τῷ δὲ Ἀνάνου παιδὶ καὶ αὐτῷ Ἀνάνῳ λεγομένῳ τὴν διαδοχὴν τῆς ἀρχῆς ἔδωκεν.

*Translation.* When the emperor heard of Festus' death, he sent Albinus to Judea as procurator. The king removed Joseph from the high priesthood and gave the succession to this office to Ananus' son who was also called Ananus.

*Commentary.* The fact that Josephus mentions Ananus in his report of the accession of Ananus the younger to the high priestly office in A.D. 62 hints at the influence of the father in Judean politics. The following comment in *A. J.* 20.198 (No. 4) underlines the significance of Ananus in first-century Judea. Porcius Festus was governor of Judea in A.D. 59–62, either as *praefectus* or as presidial *procurator* of an independent province.[32] Lucceius Albinus was officeholder of Judea in A.D. 62–64.[33]

---

[29] Cf. JOSEF RIST, Gratus [2] Valerius G., BNP 5 (2004): 996.

[30] Cf. E. MARY SMALLWOOD, The Jews under Roman Rule: From Pompey to Diocletian. A Study in Political Relations (Orig. 1976; repr., SJLA 20; Leiden: Brill, 2001), 159.

[31] VANDERKAM, High Priests, 423.

[32] WERNER ECK, Porcius [II 2] P. Festus, BNP 11 (2007): 636; SCHÜRER, History, 1:467–68; SMALLWOOD, Jews, 271; KLAUS-STEFAN KRIEGER, Geschichtsschreibung als Apologetik bei Flavius Josephus (TANZ 9; Tübingen/Basel: Francke, 1994), 173–77; METZNER, Die Prominenten, 514–26.

[33] WERNER ECK, Lucceius [II 1] L. Albinus, BNP 7 (2005): 835. Albinus plundered public and private funds, took bribes, and mismanaged the province to such an extent that "the audacity of the revolutionaries was stimulated" (*B. J.* 2.274). Cf. SCHÜRER, History, 1:468–70; SMALLWOOD, Jews, 271–72, 279–82; WERNER ECK, Die römischen Repräsentanten in Judaea: Provokateure oder Vertreter der römischen Macht? [2011], in Judäa – Syria Palästina. Die Auseinandersetzung einer Provinz mit römischer Politik und Kultur (TSAJ 157; Tübingen: Mohr Siebeck, 2014), 166–185, 179; DANIEL R. SCHWARTZ, Josephus on Albinus: The Eve of Catastrophe in Changing Retrospect, in The Jewish Revolt Against Rome: Interdisciplinary Perspectives (ed. M. Popović; JSJSup 154; Leiden: Brill, 2011), 291–309.

**(4)** Josephus, *Antiquitates judaicae* 20.198

τοῦτον δέ φασι τὸν πρεσβύτατον Ἄνανον εὐτυχέστατον γενέσθαι· πέντε γὰρ ἔσχε παῖδας καὶ τούτους πάντας συνέβη ἀρχιερατεῦσαι τῷ θεῷ αὐτὸς πρότερος τῆς τιμῆς ἐπὶ πλεῖστον ἀπολαύσας ὅπερ οὐδενὶ συνέβη τῶν παρ' ἡμῖν ἀρχιερέων.

*Translation.* It is said that the elder Ananus was most fortunate because he had five sons, all of whom were high priests of God after he himself had enjoyed the office for a very long time, which had never happened to any other of our high priests.

*Commentary.* Josephus describes Ananus/Annas as the patriarch of the most influential high priestly family in the first century. Five sons of Annas were high priests: Eleazar (A.D. 16–17), Jonathan (A.D. 36–37), Theophilus (A.D. 37–41), Matthias (A.D. 42–43?), and Ananus (A.D. 62).[34] Caiaphas, whose appointment as high priest is the occasion of Josephus' comment in *A. J.* 20.198, was Annas' son-in-law (high priest from A.D. 18–36). Caiaphas' eighteen-year tenure as high priest has been explained with the continued influence of Annas in Judean politics as an *éminence grise*, which also explains why Luke mentions Annas and Caiaphas together as high priests (Luke 3:1; Acts 4:6) and why John's trial account relates an interrogation of Jesus by Annas (John 18:13–24).[35] The family of Annas has to be regarded as the leading group of the Sadducees and as the main opponents of the Christians. Their opposition began with Jesus' trial in A.D. 30 in which both Annas and Caiaphas played the decisive role, and included the killing of Stephen in A.D. 30 in which Caiaphas was involved (Acts 7:1), as well as the execution of James, the brother of Jesus, in A.D. 62 in which Annas the Younger was involved.[36]

**(5)** Josephus, *Bellum judaicum* 5.506

μεθ' ἣν ἀναβαίνων κατὰ τὸ Ἀνάνου τοῦ ἀρχιερέως μνημεῖον καὶ διαλαβὼν τὸ ὄρος, ἔνθα Πομπήιος ἐστρατοπεδεύσατο, πρὸς κλίμα βόρειον ἐπέστρεφε

*Translation.* beyond which [i.e., the Valley of the Fountain] the wall ascended toward the tomb of Ananus the high priest and, encompassing the mountain where Pompey had built his camp, turned in a northerly direction.

---

[34] VANDERKAM, High Priests, 424, 436–43, 448–53, 476–82.

[35] MARTIN HENGEL, Das Johannesevangelium als Quelle des antiken Judentums, in Judaica, Hellenistica et Christiana. Kleine Schriften II (WUNT 109; Tübingen: Mohr Siebeck, 1999), 293–334, 328, 329.

[36] Josephus, *A. J.* 20.200. HENGEL, Johannesevangelium, 325; DAVID FLUSSER, Caiaphas in the New Testament, ʾAtiqot 21 (1992): 63–71; GOODMAN, The Ruling Class, 44, 141–44.

*Commentary.*[37] This text belongs to Josephus' description of the wall that Titus constructed around Jerusalem during the siege of A.D. 70. The area of Ananus' tomb (μνημεῖον) is south of the city, the site of the Akeldama tombs. An elaborate tomb with a triple entrance that has been discovered at the site is identified by some as Ananus' family tomb.[38]

## (6) *t. Menaḥot* 13:21

על אלו ועל כיוצא בהן ועל דומה להן ועל עושין כמעשיהן היה אבא שאול בן בטנית ואבא יוסי
בן יוחנן איש ירושלים אומר אוי לי מבית ביתוס אוי לי מאלתן אוי לי מבית קדרוס אוי לי
מקולמסן אוי לי מבית אלחנן אוי לי מבית לחישתן אוי לי מבית אלישע אוי לי מאגרופן אוי לי
מבית ישמעאל בן פיאבי שהם כהנים גדולים ובניהם גזברין וחתניהן אמרכלין ועבדיהן באין
וחובטין עלינו במקלות.

*Translation.* Regarding these people, and people like them, and people similar to them, and people who do things as they do, did Abba Saul, the son of Bitnit, and Abba Yose, the son of Yohanan of Jerusalem, say "Woe is me because of the House of Boethus; woe is me because of their rods. Woe is me because of the House of Qadros; woe is me because of their pen. Woe is me because of the House of Elhanan; woe is me because of their whispering mouth. Woe is me because of the House of Elisha; woe is me because of their fist. Woe is me because of the House of Yishmael, son of Phiabi; for they are high priests, and their sons are treasurers, and their sons-in-law are supervisors, and their slaves come and beat us with rods."

*Commentary.*[39] This passage, which has a parallel in *b. Pesaḥ* 57a, pronounces judgment on priests who took by force things that did not belong to them (*t. Menaḥ.* 13:18–20). The "House of Elhanan" or "Hanin" (*b. Pesaḥ* 57a) could be a reference to the family of Ananus (Hebr. Hananiah). If this identification is correct, Ananus and his sons and son-in-law, who were also high priests, are accused of resorting to violent actions in taking material possessions that did not belong to them.[40] This is a critique found in the Rabbinic

---

[37] For text, text editions, and translations see No. 1.

[38] LEEN RITMEYER and KATHLEEN RITMEYER, Akeldama: Potter's Field or High Priest's Tomb, BAR 20 (1994): 22–35,76–78; VANDERKAM, High Priests, 424.

[39] Text: MOSES SAMUEL ZUCKERMANDEL, ed., Tosephta (Based on the Erfurt and Vienna Codices with Parallels and Variants. With Supplement by Saul Lieberman. New Edition with Additional Notes and Corrections; Jerusalem: Wahrmann, 1970). For translations cf. BØRGE SALOMONSEN, Die Tosefta. Seder IV: Nezikin, 3: Sanhedrin–Makkot. Übersetzt und erklärt (Rabbinische Texte. Erste Reihe: Die Tosefta; Stuttgart: Kohlhammer, 1976); JACOB NEUSNER, The Tosefta. Translated from the Hebrew, with a New Introduction (Orig. 1977–1986; repr., Peabody: Hendrickson, 2002).

[40] Cf. VANDERKAM, High Priests, 423.

sources with regard to other Sadducean high priests, although a special animosity toward the family of Ananus as greedy and repressive can be observed.[41]

*Annas and Jesus' trial*. The fact that Annas interrogates Jesus immediately after his arrest and before he was sent to Caiaphas, the incumbent high priest (John 18:12–24), underscores Annas' continued influence in A.D. 30, fourteen years after his deposition. The fact that he is called "high priest" (ὁ ἀρχιερεύς) in John 18:15, 16, 19, 22 is most plausibly explained by the suggestion that former high priests retained the title "high priest".[42] The use of this title, and the identification as the father-in-law (πενθερός) of Caiaphas in John 18:13, together with the fact that he was the father of a former high priest Eleazar and the father of four future high priests (Jonathan, Theophilus, Matthias, and Ananus the Younger; see No. 4), underscore his preeminence in the priestly hierarchy in Jerusalem. It is quite plausible that Jesus was interrogated by Annas (John 18:13) *and* by Caiaphas (Matt 26:57).[43]

*Caiaphas (Joseph Caiaphas)*

**(7)** Josephus, *Antiquitates judaicae* 18.35

οὐ πλείων δὲ καὶ τῷδε ἐνιαυτοῦ τὴν τιμὴν ἔχοντι διεγένετο χρόνος, καὶ Ἰώσηπος ὁ καὶ Καϊάφας διάδοχος ἦν αὐτῷ. καὶ Γρᾶτος μὲν ταῦτα πράξας εἰς Ῥώμην ἐπανεχώρει ἕνδεκα ἔτη διατρίψας ἐν Ἰουδαίᾳ, Πόντιος δὲ Πιλᾶτος διάδοχος αὐτῷ ἧκεν.

*Translation*. When he (Simon, the son of Camit) had occupied this office for not more than a year, Joseph who is also called Caiaphas became his successor. After having done these things, Gratus returned to Rome, having stayed in Judea for eleven years. Pontius Pilatus became his successor.

*Commentary*. Caiaphas[44] was the third member of the family of Annas, whose

---

[41] BROWN, Death, 1:409.

[42] RAYMOND E. BROWN, The Gospel According to John (2 vols.; Anchor Bible; New York: Doubleday, 1966–1970), 1:820–21; VANDERKAM, High Priests, 420.

[43] STROBEL, Stunde, 9; BROWN, Death, 1:407–9. Cf. HENGEL / SCHWEMER, Jesus, 593–95, who think Annas interrogated Jesus while the members of the Sanhedrin gathered for a night session convened and presided over by Caiaphas.

[44] For the name Caiaphas cf. ILAN, Lexicon, 1:408. Greek Καϊάφας renders the Aramaic determinate form קיפא (Qayafa), in Hebrew הקיף (Ha-Qayaf); the lack of a second *yod* in the ossuary inscription renders the identification with Caiaphas the high priest uncertain, although it should be noted that some NT manuscripts read the variant Καίφα; the Latin has *Caiphas* and the Syriac reads ܩܝܦܐ. *A. J.* 18.95 (Ἰώσηπον τὸν Καϊάφαν ἐπικαλούμενον) suggests that Καϊάφας was a nickname or family name of the high priest Joseph. Cf. JONATHAN J. PRICE and HAGGAI MISGAV in Hannah M. Cotton, et al., Corpus Inscriptionum Iudaeae / Palestinae

son-in-law he was, to serve as high priest. Josephus mentions Caiaphas only in connection with his appointment by Valerius Gratus, prefect of the province of Judea from A.D. 15–26, and in connection with his removal as high priest (No. 8), despite the fact that he had held the high priestly office for eighteen years. Rabbinic sources mention the family of Qifai (or Neqifai, Qifa) from Bet Meqoshesh (location uncertain), commenting that some members of this priestly family became high priests (*t. Yebam.* 1:10; *y. Yebam.* 6a,3; *y. Maʿaś.* 52a). C. A. EVANS holds that the identification of this family with that of Caiaphas is probable.[45]

**(8)** Josephus, *Antiquitates judaicae* 18.95

Οὐιτέλλιος δὲ ἐπὶ τῷ ἡμετέρῳ πατρίῳ ποιεῖται τὴν στολήν ᾗ τε κείσοιτο μὴ πολυπραγμονεῖν ἐπισκήψας τῷ φρουράρχῳ καὶ ὁπότε δέοι χρῆσθαι. καὶ ταῦτα πράξας ἐπὶ εὐεργεσίᾳ τοῦ ἔθνους καὶ τὸν ἀρχιερέα Ἰώσηπον τὸν Καϊάφαν ἐπικαλούμενον ἀπαλλάξας τῆς ἱερωσύνης Ἰωνάθην καθίστησιν Ἀνάνου τοῦ ἀρχιερέως υἱόν.

*Translation.* Vitellius placed the vestments under our ancestral power and instructed the commander of the garrison not to inquire into the question of where they were stored or when they were to be used. After he had provided these things for the benefit of the nation, he removed the high priest Joseph, called Caiaphas, from his priestly office and appointed Jonathan, son of Ananus the high priest.

*Commentary.* Joseph Caiaphas' long tenure as high priest ended in A.D. 36 when Lucius Vitellius, governor of Syria, forced a change in the office in connection with his deposition of Pontius Pilatus, whom he ordered to return to Rome after Pilatus' clashes with the Samaritans (see No. 83). Caiaphas was high priest for eighteen years, during two Roman prefects in Judea, viz. Valerius Gratus (A.D. 15–26, or 15–19) and Pontius Pilatus (A.D. 26–36, or 19–36; see introduction to 2.1). Caiaphas' exceptionally long tenure attests to his shrewd political talent and to the continued influence of his father-in-law, Annas.[46] Rabbinic sources mention the family name Caiaphas; the Mishnah refers to "Elyoʿenai the son of ha-Qayaf [הקיף]" (*m. Parah* 3:5).[47] The Tosefta

_____

(Vols. I-II; Berlin: De Gruyter, 2010–2012), 482–485 (No. 461); VANDERKAM, High Priests, 426–36; HELEN K. BOND, Caiaphas: Friend of Rome and Judge of Jesus (Louisville: Westminster John Knox Press, 2004); OLIVER GUSSMANN, Das Priesterverständnis des Flavius Josephus (TSAJ 124; Tübingen: Mohr Siebeck, 2008), 419–20; METZNER, Die Prominenten, 76–84, 343; METZNER, Kaiphas, 35–176; REINHARTZ, Caiaphas the High Priest (Studies on Personalities of the New Testament; Minneapolis: Fortress, 2013 [2011]).

[45] CRAIG A. EVANS, Jesus and the Ossuaries (Waco: Baylor University Press, 2003), 105.

[46] Cf. HENGEL, Johannesevangelium, 328, who describes Annas as *éminence grise*.

[47] Some Mishnah manuscripts read הקיף, which renders the identification uncertain.

refers to the high priestly "family of the house of Qayapha [קיפא] of Bet Me-qoshesh" (*t. Yebam.* 1.10).[48] Vitellius' visit to Jerusalem and his actions there are conceivable if Pilatus is absent and Tiberius had not yet appointed Marcellus as the next prefect.[49]

H. J. SCHONFIELD believes that Caiaphas was removed from office because Vitellius wanted to conciliate the Jews who hated the high priest for his involvement of Jesus' indictment.[50] This is hardly plausible, since Caiaphas' was evidently not criticized for his role in Jesus' trial by the early Christians and since there is no evidence that Vitellius had to placate any Jews regarding Caiaphas' role in Jesus' trial.[51] A. VICENT CERNUDA suggests that Caiaphas was removed from office because he became a followers of Jesus, after Paul's return to Jerusalem three years after his conversion (Gal 1:18–23).[52] The (rarely defended) position that Caiaphas became a Christian is presupposed by the Arabic Infancy Gospel which refers in ch. 1 to a "book of Joseph the high priest ... who some say is Caiaphas."[53] The assumed conversion of Caiaphas is not likely to be historical: the early Christian tradition would hardly have been silent about the conversion of such a prominent member of the high priestly families.[54] H. BOND suggests that when Vitellius returned to Jerusalem in A.D. 37 and granted tax relief on agricultural products and handed over the high priestly garments (Josephus, *A. J.* 18.90–95), he must have been pressured by

---

[48] This tradition is also mentioned in *b. Yebam.* 15b, with a reference to "the house of Ben Quphai [קופאי] of Bet Meqoshesh." Bet Meqoshesh is a village in the vicinity of Jerusalem. Another tradition refers to "Menahem, son of Maxima, the brother of Jonathan Caiapha [יונתן קיפא]" (*p. Maʿaserot* 52a). Cf. CRAIG A. EVANS, Excavating Caiaphas, Pilate, and Simon of Cyrene: Assessing the Literary and Archaeological Evidence, in Jesus and Archaeology (ed. J.H. Charlesworth; Grand Rapids: Eerdmans, 2006), 323–340, 326.

[49] ÉTIENNE NODET, Josephus and Discrepant Sources, in Flavius Josephus: Interpretation and history (ed. J. Pastor, P. Stern, and M. Mor; JSJSup 146; Leiden: Brill, 2011), 259–277, 273.

[50] HUGH J. SCHONFIELD, The Passover Plot: New Light on the History of Jesus (New York: Random, 1965), 143, 149.

[51] METZNER, Kaiphas, 169.

[52] ANTONIO VICENT CERNUDA, Jésus ante Anás, in Cum vobis et pro vobis (FS M.R. Cabanellas; ed. R. Arnau-García and R. Ortuño Soriano; Valentina 27; Valencia: Facultad de Teologia San Vicente Ferrer, 1991), 53–71, 60–65; ANTONIO VICENT CERNUDA, La Conversión de Caifás y el Hallazgo de sus Huesos, Estudios Bíblicos 54 (1996): 35–78; cf. ANTONIO VICENT CERNUDA, Jesús perseguido a muerte. Estudios exegéticos sobre las personas y los hechos (Monografías 82; Madrid: Fundación Universitaria Española, 2002).

[53] JAMES K. ELLIOTT, The Apocryphal New Testament.(Oxford: Oxford University Press, 1993), 102; Elliot points to the tradition of the Syrian Jacobites who believed that Caiaphas had become a Christian (ibid. 100). MARIA JOSUA and FRIEDMANN EISLER, Das arabische Kindheitsevangelium, in Antike christliche Apokryphen in deutscher Übersetzung. I. Band: Evangelien und Verwandtes (ed. C. Markschies and J. Schröter; Tübingen: Mohr Siebeck, 2012), 963–982, 964, date origins the Arabic Infancy Gospel earlier than the 5th century; they do not mention the potential connection with the Syrian Jacobites.

[54] BROWN, Death, 410 n. 18.

Caiaphas to do so, who used the power vacuum after Pilatus' removal to gain concessions for the Jewish people; Vitellius agreed in order to keep the peace, but removed Caiaphas as he feared that the incumbent high priest was becoming too powerful.[55] There is no evidence, however, that Vitellius was susceptible to pressure after Pilatus' removal from office, nor that Caiaphas put pressure on him. C. A. EVANS surmises that Caiaphas' removal from office may be linked with Pilatus' removal from office as prefect, as the two had worked well together.[56] R. METZNER suggests that Caiaphas was old and too weak for the office of high priest and was thus removed.[57]

A burial cave discovered just south of Mt. Zion in Jerusalem in 1990 has been identified as the burial site of Caiaphas.[58] Two of the undisturbed ossuaries had the name Qapha (קפא) inscribed. An ornate ossuary (ossuary No. 6) contained the bones of a sixty-year-old man as well as the bones of two infants, a toddler, a young boy, and a woman.[59] The ossuary bears two inscriptions: an inscription on the long rear side that reads, יהוסף בר קפא (*Yhwsp br Qp*'; "Yehosef son of Qafa"), and an inscription on the narrow side that reads, יהוסף בר קיפא (*Yhwsp br Qyp*'; "Yehosef son of Qaifa [or Qofa]").[60] Some suggest that the name inscribed on the ossuary is a two-syllable name, probably Qôphaʿ, Qûphaʿ, or Qēphaʿ.[61] Some scholars have doubts about the identification.[62] For J. J. PRICE and H. MISGAV, the most serious objection is that "the inscriptions indicate no connection to the high priesthood,"[63] compared with "the neat and competent inscription of the granddaughter of the high priest Theophilus, duly noting his title."[64] They acknowledge that the title of high

---

[55] BOND, Caiaphas, 86–87. For the following critique cf. METZNER, Kaiphas, 170–71.

[56] EVANS, Excavating Caiaphas, 333; for a critique cf. METZNER, Kaiphas, 168, who misunderstands EVANS.

[57] METZNER, Kaiphas, 171: if Caiaphas became high priest when he was 43 years old, he would have been ca. 60 years old when he was removed from office (ibid. n. 577).

[58] ZVI GREENHUT, Discovery of the Caiaphas Family Tomb, Jerusalem Perspectives 4 (1991): 6–11; ZVI GREENHUT, The Caiaphas Tomb in North Talpiot, Jerusalem, in Ancient Jerusalem Revealed (Reprinted and Expanded Edition; ed. H. Geva; Jerusalem: Israel Exploration Society, 2000), 219–222.

[59] Cf. JOSEPH ZIAS, Human Skeletal Remains from the 'Caiaphas' Tomb, ʾAtiqot 21 (1992): 78–80.

[60] Editio princeps: RONNY REICH, Ossuary Inscriptions from the 'Caiaphas' Tomb, ʾAtiqot 21 (1992): 72–77, No. 5; WILLIAM HORBURY, The 'Caiaphas' Ossuaries and Joseph Caiaphas, PEQ 126 (1994): 32–48; DAVID FLUSSER, Jesus (Jerusalem: Magnes, 1997), 195–206; EVANS, Jesus and the Ossuaries, 104–12; RONNY REICH, Ossuary Inscriptions of the Caiaphas Family from Jerusalem, in Ancient Jerusalem Revealed (Reprinted and Expanded Edition.; ed. H. Geva; Jerusalem: Israel Exploration Society, 2000), 223–225; CIIP I/1 461 (J. J. Price, H. Misgav); cf. CIIP I/1 463.

[61] BOND, Caiaphas, 1–8; Evans, "Excavating Caiaphas", 328–29.

[62] Cf. HORBURY, The 'Caiaphas' Ossuaries; ÉMILE PUECH, A-t-on redécouvert le tombeau du grand-prêtre Caïphe? Le Monde de la Bible 80 (1993): 42–47.

[63] J. J. PRICE / H. MISGAV, in CIIP I/1, 484.

[64] CIIP I/1 534 = IEJ 36 (1986) 39–44.

priest is absent in two inscriptions that probably refer to high priests or their families.[65] The identification with the high priest Joseph Caiaphas is based on (1) the agreement in spelling with the rabbinic traditions; (2) the agreement with Josephus who relates the fact that the full name of the high priest Caiaphas was "Joseph Caiaphas;" (3) the ornate decoration of the ossuary,[66] one of the most impressive ever discovered.

*Caiaphas and Jesus' trial.* John mentions twice that Caiaphas was the high priest in the year of Jesus' crucifixion (John 11:49; 18:13). He is mentioned twice in conjunction with Annas, his father-in-law (John 18:13, 24). Luke mentions Caiaphas together with Annas twice, albeit in different contexts (Luke 3:2; Acts 4:6). Since Caiaphas was high priest during the entire tenure of Pontius Pilatus, he must have maintained an excellent relationship with the prefect of the province of Judea. M. HENGEL surmises that Caiaphas must have been "a genius of balance, diplomatically flexible in his dealings with the prefects and the Herodian rulers, conscious of his power and yet not hated by the people to a degree which would have prompted strong protests."[67] Having control over what happened in the Temple, including supervision of the trade with sacrificial animals and the exchange of foreign currencies, Caiaphas, together with Annas' entire aristocratic family, must have been able to build up a considerable fortune, which would have been used to consolidate and expand dominance in the affairs of Judea. While some interpreters such as H. BOND and A. REINHARTZ regard the Gospels as virtually useless for a historical assessment of Caiaphas' role in Jesus' trial,[68] others are much less

---

[65] CIIP I/1 674 = IEJ 20 (1970) 7. EVANS, Jesus and the Ossuaries, 107–8, thinks that the poor quality of the inscriptions on the ossuaries is a problem; MAGNESS, JODI. Stone and Dung, Oil and Spit: Jewish Daily Life in the Time of Jesus. Grand Rapids: Eerdmans, 2011, 248 n. 33, argues that there is "no correlation between the deceased and the quality of the inscriptions on ossuaries."

[66] The decoration consists of five floral designs arranged around a central, spiraling flower. BRUCE CHILTON AND DARRELL L. BOCK, A Comparative Handbook to the Gospel of Mark: Comparisons with Pseudepigrapha, the Qumran Schrolls, and Rabbinic Literature (The New Testament Gospels in their Judaic Contexts 1; Leiden: Brill, 2010), 340, point out that "the palm design that surrounds the circles on Caiaphas' ossuary picks up a motif in the Temple's decoration. Placed in the tunnel to the south of the cave, his ossuary was in fact oriented to face that Temple. His status, and his connections to the Temple, the preeminent sacred place in Judaism, are attested by this find."

[67] HENGEL, Johannesevangelium, 327. For the following point cf. HENGEL / SCHWEMER, Jesus, 591–92.

[68] BOND, Caiaphas, 143, thinks that none of the evangelists had any real interest in Caiaphas as an individual and that the discussions of Jesus' death in the Gospels "have moved a long way from historical accuracy ... Caiaphas and his colleagues ... appear in the Gospels as caricatures." REINHARTZ, Caiaphas, 24, 50, claims that imaginative construction played a major role as the evangelists "reenacted a past that no longer existed, and which they did not themselves experience," and that they "did not know exactly what role, if any, Caiaphas played in the events leading to Jesus' death."

skeptical, using the material in the Gospels and Josephus as well as the available knowledge about the leading priestly families, the Temple, and the Sanhedrin for a reconstruction of Caiaphas' life and actions. E. P. SANDERS suggests that Caiaphas was forced to eliminate Jesus to keep order in Judea.[69] M. HENGEL, M. SCHWEMER, and J. P. MEIER argue that Caiaphas and his father-in-law regarded Jesus' proclamation of the dawn of the kingdom of God, the implied messianic claim, and the ensuing critique of the Temple cult as a threat to their authority over the Jewish people which the Roman government protected.[70] R. METZNER argues that Caiaphas was not involved in the attempt to eliminate Jesus at first: leading priests and the Sadducean priestly aristocracy decided to move against Jesus (Mark 14:1–2); Caiaphas interrogated Jesus in a fair examination, during which he became convinced that Jesus was dangerous; when Jesus blasphemously claimed quasi-divine authority to condemn his opponents as the coming judge, Jewish law forced him to impose the death sentence; since only the Roman prefect could execute convicted criminals, Jesus' messianic claims were more relevant for a Roman trial than his blasphemous utterance before the Sanhedrin, which is why Jesus was accused before Pontius Pilatus as a political insurrectionist.[71]

## 1.2 The Jurisdiction of the Sanhedrin

The question of whether the Sanhedrin in Jerusalem had jurisdiction over capital cases has been vigorously discussed.[72] According to John 18:31, the Jewish leaders who took Jesus' case to Pontius Pilatus, responded to the latter's suggestion to judge Jesus according to Jewish law ("Take him yourselves and judge him according to your law") with the statement, "We are not permitted to put anyone to death." Since LUSTER and LIETZMANN,[73] many accepted the thesis that the Sanhedrin in Jerusalem in fact did have full jurisdiction, including capital cases, before A.D. 70.[74] Newer studies since BLINZLER, have dem-

---

[69] E. P. SANDERS, The Historical Figure of Jesus (London: Penguin, 1993), 268: "When Caiaphas ordered Jesus to be arrested, he was carrying out his duties, one of the chief of which was to prevent uprisings."

[70] HENGEL / SCHWEMER, Jesus, 575–580.592; JOHN P. MEIER, A Marginal Jew: Rethinking the Historical Jesus (New York: Doubleday, 1991–2009), 3:624–625.

[71] METZNER, Kaiphas, 134–35.

[72] For summaries of the debate cf. BLINZLER, Prozeß, 229–44; DAVID R. CATCHPOLE, The Trial of Jesus: A Study in the Gospels and Jewish Historiography from 1770 to the Present Day (Studia Post-Biblica 18; Leiden: Brill, 1971), 221–60; STROBEL, Stunde, 18–45; BROWN, Death, 1:363–73; HEIKE OMERZU, Der Prozeß des Paulus. Eine exegetische und rechtshistorische Untersuchung der Apostelgeschichte (BZNW 115; Berlin: De Gruyter, 2002), 346–49.

[73] JUSTER, Juifs, 2:132–45; LIETZMANN, Prozess, 318–19.

[74] Cf. ROBERT H. LIGHTFOOT, History and Interpretation in the Gospels (The Bampton

onstrated that a Roman governor could not delegate jurisdiction in capital cases (*ius gladii*), given to him personally by the emperor, to other provincial officials.[75] It appears that the Roman administration in Judea allowed jurisdiction in cases in which the sanctity of the Jerusalem Temple had been violated, evidently permitting executions in such cases. The conclusion of BROWN summarizes the view of most scholars: "The Romans permitted the Jews to execute for certain clear religious offenses, e.g., for violating the prohibitions against circulating in certain quarters of the Temple, and perhaps for adultery. Beyond this specified religious sphere the Jewish authorities were supposed to hand over cases to the Romans, who would decide whether or not to pass and execute a death sentence."[76] Recent studies argue that the Sanhedrin in Jerusalem was, at this time, not a permanent administrative institution but a consultative body convened ad hoc by the incumbent or a former high priest for the purpose of deliberating political questions as well as investigating religious offenses.[77] The following texts present Jewish sources regarding jurisdiction in capital cases in Judea; in section 2.2 non-Jewish sources will be discussed.

**(9)** CIIP I/1 2

Copy One:
μηθένα ἀλλογενὴ εἰσπο-
ρεύεσθαι ἐντὸς τοῦ πε-
ρὶ τὸ ἱερὸν τρυφάκτου καὶ
περιβόλου· ὃς δ᾽ἂν λη-
φθῇ ἑαυτῶι αἴτιος ἔσ-
ται διὰ τὸ ἐξακολου-
θεῖν θάνατον

Copy Two:
[μη]θένα ἀλλο[γενῆ εἰσπορεύεσθαι]
[ἐν]τὸς τοῦ π[ερὶ τὸ ἱερὸν τρυφ-]
[ακ]του καὶ [περιβόλου· ὃς δ᾽ἂν]
[λ]ηφθῇ αὐ[τῷ αἴτιος ἔσται]
[δ]ιὰ τὸ ἐξ[ακολουθεῖν]
θάνατ[ον]

---

Lectures; London: Hodder & Stoughton, 1935), 147–48; HANS JÜRGEN EBELING, Zur Frage nach der Kompetenz des Synhedrion, ZNW 35 (1936): 290–295; T. ALEC BURKILL, The Trial of Jesus, VC 12 (1958): 1–18; PAUL WINTER, On the Trial of Jesus (ed. T. A. Burkill and G. Vermes; orig. 1961; repr., Studia Judaica 1; Berlin: De Gruyter, 1974), 90–130.

[75] Cf. KARLHEINZ MÜLLER, Möglichkeit und Vollzug jüdischer Kapitalgerichtsbarkeit im Prozeß gegen Jesus von Nazareth, in Der Prozeß gegen Jesus (ed. K. Kertelge; QD 112; Freiburg: Herder, 1988), 41–83, 52–58; OMERZU, Prozeß, 348–49.

[76] BROWN, Death, 1:371.

[77] JAMES S. MCLAREN, Power and Politics in Palestine: The Jews and the Governing of their Land, 100 BC – AD 70 (JSNTSup 63; Sheffield: JSOT Press, 1991), who builds on GOODMAN, The Ruling Class, 27–134. Cf. ECKHARD J. SCHNABEL, Sanhedrin, NIDB 5 (2009): 102–106. For the rabbinic evidence cf. GÜNTHER STEMBERGER, Die Umformung des palästinischen Judentums nach 70 – der Aufstieg der Rabbinen [1999], in Judaica Minora II (TSAJ 138; Tübingen: Mohr Siebeck, 2010), 179–83, who points out that *m. Mak.* 1:10 and *m. Soṭa.* 9:11 state explicitly that there has been no Sanhedrin since the destruction of the Temple (at least with regard to capital jurisdiction). On the other hand, *t. Sanh.* 8:1 seems to imply the existence of a rabbinic Sanhedrin.

*Translation.* No foreigner is to enter within the balustrade and forecourt around the sacred precinct. Whoever is caught will himself be responsible for (his) consequent death.

*Commentary.*[78] Two exemplars of stone slabs with the warning sign inscription were discovered in 1871 and 1935 in Jerusalem.[79] Josephus twice refers to the content of these warning signs.[80] The stone slabs were set in the balustrade (δρύφακτος; *soreg* in *m. Mid.* 2:3), which separated the large outer court of the Temple Mount, where foreigners (non-Jews) were allowed, from the inner courts and the sanctuary. In the inscription, the term περίβολος (translated by PRICE as "forecourt," by EVANS as "barrier") refers to the area between the balustrade (δρύφακτος) and the wall surrounding the inner courts, an area that was fourteen steps wide (Josephus, *B. J.* 5.195). It should be pointed out that it would have been very difficult to identify a Gentile who was determined to enter the Temple as being a Gentile.[81] The legal origins of the warning inscriptions are generally located by scholars in the Jerusalem priesthood.[82] S. R. LLEWELYN and D. VAN BEEK argue that the death penalty stipulated by the warning inscriptions – instead of the more usual fine[83] – was

---

[78] Editio princeps – Copy One: Charles Clermont-Ganneau, "Discovery of a Tablet from Herod's Temple," *PEFQS* 3 (1871): 132–33; CHARLES CLERMONT-GANNEAU, Une stèle due temple de Jérusalem, RAr 23 (1872): 214–234, 290–296 = CIJ II 1400 = OGIS II 598; Copy Two: JOHN H. ILLIFFE, The ΘΑΝΑΤΟΣ Inscription from Herod's Temple: The Fragment of a Second Copy, QDAP 6 (1938): 1–3 = SEG VIII 169. Cf. CIJ II 329; SEG XX 477; XXXIV 1626; IMC No. 169. The text and translation follows JONATHAN J. PRICE in CIIP I 2.

[79] The first stone (60 x 90 x 39 cm), found in secondary use in a courtyard north of the Temple Mount, is in the Istanbul Archaeological Museum; the second stone (49 x 27 x 31 cm), found in secondary use outside the Lion's Gate, is in the Israel Museum in Jerusalem (inv. no. 1936-989). The Greek text is also published in *OGIS* II 598; SEG VIII 169; XX 477; XXXIX 1626; CIJ II 1400; II 329; IMC No. 169; CIIP I; PERETZ SEGAL, The Penalty of the Warning Inscription from the Temple of Jerusalem, IEJ 39 (1989): 79–84; EVANS, Jesus and the Ossuaries, 31–35; S. R. LLEWELYN / D. VAN BEEK, in GREG H. R. HORSLEY and STEPHEN R. LLEWELYN, eds., New Documents Illustrating Early Christianity (Macquarie University: North Ryde, New South Wales, Australia, 1981–2012), 10:136–139; PRICE in CIIP, 42–45.

[80] Josephus, *B. J.* 5.194: "in this [i.e. the stone balustrade separating the outer court from the inner courts] stood stone slabs (στῆλαι) at regular intervals, some in Greek and some in Latin characters, which gave warning with regard to the law of purification, namely that no foreigner (ἀλλόφυλον) was permitted to enter the holy place;" *A. J.* 15.417: "Within [the first court] and not very far away was a second court, accessible by a few steps and surrounded by a stone balustrade with an inscription (γραφῇ) which prohibited the entrance of a foreigner (ἀλλοεθνῆ) under threat of the penalty of death (θανατικῆς ἀπειλουμένης τῆς ζημίας)."

[81] SHAYE J. D. COHEN, The Beginnings of Jewishness: Boundaries, Varieties, Uncertainties (HCS 31; Berkeley: University of California Press, 1999), 65–66.

[82] SCHWARTZ, Agrippa I, 124–30; STEFAN KRAUTER, Bürgerrecht und Kultteilnahme. Politische und kultische Rechte und Pflichten in griechischen Poleis, Rom und antikem Judentum (BZNW 127; Berlin: De Gruyter, 2004), 144–92; SEGAL, Penalty.

[83] See, e.g., the *programma* of Antiochus III, as reported by Josephus, *A. J.* 12.145–146: "It is unlawful for any foreigner to enter the enclosure of the temple which is forbidden to the

instituted by Herod I.[84] The warning inscriptions have been taken to support the view that the Sanhedrin was allowed limited jurisdiction over capital cases by the Roman governor.[85] Suggestions vary concerning the judicial authority which would have carried out the death sentence against Gentiles who entered the area inside the balustrade, including the inner courts (Court of the Women, Court of the Israelites). They range from lynch killing,[86] spontaneous communal administration of justice,[87] and violent vigilante action,[88] to the execution of the perpetrator following a legal trial and sentencing.[89] The latter suggestion seems the most plausible in view of Josephus' comment in *B. J.* 6.126 (see No. 11). The Romans seemed to have respected the autonomy of the Jerusalem Temple by accepting a limited curtailment of Roman jurisdiction in capital cases as a concession to the jurisdiction of the Jews. It seems unlikely, however, that they would have allowed a lynch killing or a spontaneous honor killing, for example, by the priests. The Roman governor would have insisted on regular legal proceedings before the Sanhedrin and on the confirmation of the death sentence by the Roman governor before the Jewish authorities could execute the perpetrator. The plausibility of this assumption is supported by the episode in Acts 21:26–30 in which Paul is accused of violating the prohibition and the subsequent actions of the commander of the Roman troops (Acts 21:31–40; 22:22–30; 23:23–30).

---

Jews, except to those of them who are accustomed to enter after purifying themselves in accordance with the laws of the country ... the person who violates any of these statutes shall pay to the priests a fine of three thousand drachmas of silver."

[84] STEPHEN R. LLEWELYN / DIONYSIA VAN BEEK, Reading the Temple Warning as a Greek Visitor, JSJ 42 (2011) 1–22; cf. HORSLEY and LLEWELYN, New Documents, 10:136–139.

[85] CATCHPOLE, Trial, 240; STROBEL, Stunde, 22–24.

[86] MARTIN HENGEL, Die Zeloten. Untersuchungen zur jüdischen Freiheitsbewegung in der Zeit von Herodes I. bis 70 n. Chr. (3., durchgesehene und ergänzte Auflage; ed. R. Deines and C. J. Thornton; WUNT 283; Tübingen: Mohr Siebeck, 2011), 216–17; cf. MARTIN HENGEl, The Zealots: Investigations into the Jewish Freedom Movement in the Period from Herod I until 70 A.D. (Edinburgh: T & T Clark, 1989), 214, with reference to *m. Sanh.* 9:6; cf. SACHA STERN, Jewish Identity in Early Rabbinic Writings (AGAJU 23; Leiden: Brill, 1994), 169.

[87] ELIAS J. BICKERMAN, The Warning Inscription of Herod's Temple [1947], in Studies in Jewish and Christian History. A New Edition in English (2 vols.; AGAJU 68; Leiden: Brill, 2007), 1:483–496: "the trespasser will be executed by the outraged community he had polluted by his act" (491). Also HELMUT SCHWIER, Tempel und Tempelzerstörung. Untersuchungen zu den theologischen und ideologischen Faktoren im ersten jüdisch-römischen Krieg (66–74 n.Chr.) (NTOA 11; Fribourg / Göttingen: Universitätsverlag / Vandenhoeck & Ruprecht, 1989), 59–61.

[88] TORREY SELAND, Establishment Violence in Philo and Luke: A Study of Non-Conformity to the Torah and Jewish Vigilante Reactions (Biblical Interpretation 15; Leiden: Brill, 1995), 284–85.

[89] MÜLLER, Kapitalgerichtsbarkeit, 68–69.

**(10)** Philo, *De legatione ad Gaium* 306–308

τότε μὲν οὖν ἀσπίδες ἦσαν, αἷς οὐδὲν ἀνεζωγράφητο μίμημα· νυνὶ δὲ κολοσσιαῖος ἀνδριάς. καὶ τότε μὲν ἡ ἀνάθεσις ἐν οἰκίᾳ τῶν ἐπιτρόπων ἦν· τὴν δὲ μέλλουσάν φασιν ἐσωτάτω τοῦ ἱεροῦ κατ' αὐτὰ τὰ ἄδυτα γίνεσθαι, εἰς ἃ ἅπαξ τοῦ ἐνιαυτοῦ ὁ μέγας ἱερεὺς εἰσέρχεται τῇ νηστείᾳ λεγομένῃ μόνον ἐπιθυμιάσων καὶ κατὰ τὰ πάτρια εὐξόμενος φορὰν ἀγαθῶν εὐετηρίαν τε καὶ εἰρήνην ἅπασιν ἀνθρώποις. [307] κἂν ἄρα τίς που, οὐ λέγω τῶν ἄλλων Ἰουδαίων, ἀλλὰ καὶ τῶν ἱερέων, οὐχὶ τῶν ὑστάτων, ἀλλὰ τῶν τὴν εὐθὺς μετὰ τὸν πρῶτον τάξιν εἰληχότων, ἢ καθ' αὑτὸν ἢ καὶ μετ' ἐκείνου συνεισέλθῃ, μᾶλλον δὲ κἂν αὐτὸς ὁ ἀρχιερεὺς δυσὶν ἡμέραις τοῦ ἔτους ἢ καὶ τῇ αὐτῇ τρὶς ἢ καὶ τετράκις εἰσφοιτήσῃ, θάνατον ἀπαραίτητον ὑπομένει. [308] τοσαύτη τίς ἐστιν ἡ περὶ τὰ ἄδυτα φυλακὴ τοῦ νομοθέτου μόνα ἐκ πάντων ἄβατα καὶ ἄψαυστα βουληθέντος αὐτὰ διατηρεῖσθαι.

*Translation.* Now at that time it was shields on which no representation of any living creature had been painted; this time it is a colossal statue. Then the dedication took place in the residence of the governors; now they say the dedication shall take place right inside the Temple, in the innermost sanctuary itself, into which the high priest enters only once a year, on the so-called Fast Day, to burn incense and to pray according to ancestral practice for blessings in abundance and prosperity and peace for all mankind. (307) If anyone else – I am not speaking of any Jewish person, but even any one of the priests, and not merely one of the junior priests but one of the priests who are ranked directly below the high priest – enters it alone, or even with the high priest, or indeed if the high priest himself goes in on two days of the year, or three or four times on the same Fast Day,[90] he faces a death against which there can be no appeal. (308) This is the elaborate protection for the sanctuary laid down by our lawgiver, who wanted this one part of the Temple alone to be inaccessible and untouched.

*Commentary.*[91] Philo's *Legatio ad Gaium* is set in the context of the attack of

---

[90] According to Lev 16:12-15 (and *m. Yoma* 5:1-4; 7:4), the High Priest entered the Holy of Holies four times during the ritual of the Day of Atonement: "first to place a censer of incense of the Ark (or, after the loss of the Ark, on a stone marking its site); then to sprinkle the blood of a sacrificed bullock round the chamber; then to repeat the action with the blood of a he-goat; and finally to remove the censer" (E. MARY SMALLWOOD, Philonis Alexandrini Legatio ad Gaium. With an Introduction, Translation, and Commentary [Second ed.; Leiden: Brill, 1970], 308).

[91] Text: SIEGFRIED REITER, in LEOPOLD COHN, PAUL WENDLAND, and SIEGFRIED REITER, Philonis Alexandrini opera quae supersunt (Editio Maior. 7 vols.; orig. 1896–1930; repr., Berlin: De Gruyter, 1962), 6:155–223; for other text editions and translations cf. FRANCIS H. COLSON, GEORGE H. WHITAKER, and RALPH MARCUS, Philo. Works. Greek Text and English Translation (LCL; London: Heinemann, 1929–1962), 10:1–187; PEDER BORGEN, KÅRE FUGLSETH, and ROALD SKARSTEN, Philo Judaeus. The Works of Philo: Greek Text with Mor-

the citizens of Alexandria against the Jews in A.D. 38, which prompted the Alexandrian Jews to send a delegation to Gaius Caligula in A.D. 39/40 with the goal of having their claim to citizenship recognized. As the delegation, led by Philo, was waiting to see the emperor, they received news that Gaius intended to set up a statue of himself in the Temple in Jerusalem. In his description of Agrippa's intervention, Philo cites a long letter (*Legat.* 276– 329) in which Agrippa appeals to Gaius to show consideration for the Jewish nation, the city of Jerusalem and the Temple.[92] A grandson of Herod I, Agrippa had been brought up in Rome and was a friend of Gaius, who had made him king over Judea (A.D. 41–44). In his letter, Agrippa reminds Gaius of the honor earlier emperors had shown the Temple. And he emphasizes the sanctity of the Jerusalem Temple, pointing out that its innermost room (τὰ ἄδυτα, the Holy of Holies) can be accessed only once a year during the Fast Day[93] (i.e., the Day of Atonement in September/October on which the Jews are fasting) and only by a single person (the high priest). Philo asserts that this long-established tradition had been recognized and honored by the Roman authorities, who allowed automatic death penalties in the case of Temple violations: Anyone who intends to violate the sanctity of the Temple must know that "death without appeal" (θάνατον ἀπαραίτητον; 307) awaits him.

A. STROBEL interprets this text as evidence for the *Sonderdelikt* (special offense) that corresponds to the crossing of the barrier surrounding the Temple and its inner courts, which was subject to its own particular jurisdiction. This special offense, with its stipulated penalty, cannot be taken as evidence that the Sanhedrin had the right to issue death penalties and execute convicted criminals.[94]

---

phology (Bellingham, WA: Logos Reserach Systems, 2005); LEOPOLD COHN, ISAAK HEINEMANN, MAXIMILIAN ADLER, and WILLY THEILER, Philo von Alexandrien. Die Werke in deutscher Übersetzung (7 vols.; Berlin: De Gruyter, 1962–1964), 7:166–266; SMALLWOOD, Legatio ad Gaium, 53–147.

[92] Cf. Josephus, *A. J.* 18.143–160, 224–239. Josephus describes Agrippa's intervention in the Temple affair in *A. J.* 18.289–309, Philo in *Legat.* 261–338.

[93] Josephus, *A. J.* 14.66, 487, also uses ἡ νηστεία for the Day of Atonement; cf. Lev 16 and the tractate *Yoma* in the Mishnah. The fear that something might happen to the High Priest while officiating in the Holy of Holies was so great that at the end of the Day of Atonement, the High Priest "made a feast for his friends for that he was come forth safely from the Sanctuary" (*m. Yoma* 7:4); SMALLWOOD, Legatio ad Gaium, 307.

[94] STROBEL, Stunde, 38, who argues against EBELING, Kompetenz, 294.

**(11)** Josephus, *Antiquitates judaicae* 18.2

Κωπώνιός τε αὐτῷ συγκαταπέμπεται τάγματος τῶν ἱππέων, ἡγησόμενος Ἰουδαίων τῇ ἐπὶ πᾶσιν ἐξουσίᾳ. παρῆν δὲ καὶ Κυρίνιος εἰς τὴν Ἰουδαίαν προσθήκην τῆς Συρίας γενομένην ἀποτιμησόμενός τε αὐτῶν τὰς οὐσίας καὶ ἀποδωσόμενος τὰ Ἀρχελάου χρήματα.

*Translation.* Coponius, who was of equestrian rank, was sent along with him [i.e., Quirinius] to rule over the Jews with full authority. Quirinius visited Judea, which had been annexed to Syria, in order to value the property of the Jews and to dispose of the estate of Archelaos.

*Commentary.* Josephus' description of the origins of the "fourth philosophy" in the activities of Judas from Gamala and Zaddok the Pharisee who organized the Jewish opposition against the census of Quirinius, the governor of Syria (18.1–10), includes a comment on the administrative authority of Coponius, the prefect of Judea, which had just come under Roman rule (see No. 11). According to Josephus, the mandate of the distinguished ex-consul Publius Sulpicius Quirinius (see No. 1), included conducting a property census in both Syria and Judea (*A. J.* 18.2). He was accompanied and supported (συγκαταπέμπεται) by Coponius, who had full authority over Judea. The situation "thus precisely fulfills the hope of the Judean elders who went to Rome following Herod's death in 4 BCE: they asked to be delivered from kingship, to become instead a part of Syria ... and subject to the Roman commanders there."[95] While the text underlines the superior authority of the governor of the province of Syria over the Roman official in charge of Judea, Josephus' comment that Coponius had "full authority" (τῇ ἐπὶ πᾶσιν ἐξουσίᾳ) leaves no doubt that the Roman prefects of Judea had full legal and administrative jurisdiction.[96] While the prefects of Judea did not have *imperium* as did the procurators of Syria, they were granted the *ius gladii* as its equivalent, which included jurisdiction in capital cases, guaranteeing that they could administer Judea effectively.[97] See the parallel in *B. J.* 2.117 (No. 13).

**(12)** Josephus, *Antiquitates judaicae* 20.199–203

ὁ δὲ νεώτερος Ἄνανος, ὃν τὴν ἀρχιερωσύνην ἔφαμεν εἰληφέναι, θρασὺς ἦν τὸν τρόπον καὶ τολμητὴς διαφερόντως, αἵρεσιν δὲ μετήει τὴν Σαδδουκαίων, οἵπερ εἰσὶ περὶ τὰς κρίσεις ὠμοὶ παρὰ πάντας τοὺς Ἰουδαίους, καθὼς ἤδη

---

[95] MASON, Judean War 2, 78 n. 718, commenting on *A. J.* 18.2; cf. *A. J.* 17.314; *B. J.* 2.91.

[96] WERNER ECK, Rom und Judaea. Fünf Vorträge zur römischen Herrschaft in Palaestina (Tübingen: Mohr Siebeck, 2007), 27–28, translates ἡγησόμενος Ἰουδαίων τῇ ἐπὶ πᾶσιν ἐξουσίᾳ as "zur Wahrnehmung der höchsten Gewalt in Judaea."

[97] KIRNER, Strafgewalt, 142.

δεδηλώκαμεν. ²⁰⁰ ἄτε δὴ οὖν τοιοῦτος ὢν ὁ Ἄνανος, νομίσας ἔχειν καιρὸν ἐπιτήδειον διὰ τὸ τεθνάναι μὲν Φῆστον, Ἀλβῖνον δ᾽ ἔτι κατὰ τὴν ὁδὸν ὑπάρχειν, καθίζει συνέδριον κριτῶν καὶ παραγαγὼν εἰς αὐτὸ τὸν ἀδελφὸν Ἰησοῦ τοῦ λεγομένου Χριστοῦ, Ἰάκωβος ὄνομα αὐτῷ, καί τινας ἑτέρους, ὡς παρανομησάντων κατηγορίαν ποιησάμενος παρέδωκε λευσθησομένους. ²⁰¹ ὅσοι δὲ ἐδόκουν ἐπιεικέστατοι τῶν κατὰ τὴν πόλιν εἶναι καὶ περὶ τοὺς νόμους ἀκριβεῖς βαρέως ἤνεγκαν ἐπὶ τούτῳ καὶ πέμπουσιν πρὸς τὸν βασιλέα κρύφα παρακαλοῦντες αὐτὸν ἐπιστεῖλαι τῷ Ἀνάνῳ μηκέτι τοιαῦτα πράσσειν· μηδὲ γὰρ τὸ πρῶτον ὀρθῶς αὐτὸν πεποιηκέναι. ²⁰² τινὲς δ᾽ αὐτῶν καὶ τὸν Ἀλβῖνον ὑπαντιάζουσιν ἀπὸ τῆς Ἀλεξανδρείας ὁδοιποροῦντα καὶ διδάσκουσιν, ὡς οὐκ ἐξὸν ἦν Ἀνάνῳ χωρὶς τῆς ἐκείνου γνώμης καθίσαι συνέδριον. ²⁰³ Ἀλβῖνος δὲ πεισθεὶς τοῖς λεγομένοις γράφει μετ᾽ ὀργῆς τῷ Ἀνάνῳ λήψεσθαι παρ᾽ αὐτοῦ δίκας ἀπειλῶν. καὶ ὁ βασιλεὺς Ἀγρίππας διὰ τοῦτο τὴν Ἀρχιερωσύνην ἀφελόμενος αὐτὸν ἄρξαντα μῆνας τρεῖς Ἰησοῦν τὸν τοῦ Δαμναίου κατέστησεν.

*Translation.* The younger Ananus, who had been appointed to the high priesthood as we have said earlier, had a rash temper and was unusually audacious. He belonged to the school of the Sadducees, who are more heartless than any of the other Jews when they judge cases, as I have already explained. (200) Inasmuch as Ananus had such a character, he thought that he had an opportunity because Festus was dead and Albinus was still on the way. So he convened the judges of the Sanhedrin and brought before them a man called James, the brother of Jesus who was called the Messiah, and certain others. After he had accused them of having broken the law, he handed them over to be stoned. (201) But those inhabitants of the city who were considered the most fairminded and precise in observance of the laws took offense at this. They secretly sent to King Agrippa, urging him to order Ananus not to do such things, for this was not the first time[98] that he had not acted justly. (202) Some of them even went to Albinus, who was on his way from Alexandria, and informed him that Ananus was not authorized to convene the Sanhedrin without his approval. (203) Convinced by these words, Albinus wrote in anger to Ananus, threatening that he would punish him. And so King Agrippa removed Ananus from the high priesthood, which he had held for three months, because of this action, and appointed Jesus, the son of Damnaeus, as high priest.

*Commentary.* Josephus' report of the execution in A.D. 62 of James, the brother of Jesus and leader of the church in Jerusalem since A.D. 41/42,[99] confirms that the Sanhedrin in Jerusalem did not have jurisdiction in capital cases

---

[98] FELDMAN translates "Ananus had not even been correct in his first step," with our translation mentioned as a possibility in note (c).

[99] Some suggest that the phrase τὸν ἀδελφὸν Ἰησοῦ τοῦ λεγομένου Χριστοῦ is a Christian interpolation (MÜLLER, Kapitalgerichtsbarkeit, 56 n. 29); others accept it as plausibly authentic (VANDERKAM, High Priests, 477 n. 213). Cf. SCHÜRER, History, 1:430 n. 1.

and could not execute people convicted as criminals without the consent of the Roman governor (on Festus and Albinus see No. 3). The opponents of Ananus, the high priest, who had been appointed in A.D. 62,[100] bring two complaints before King Agrippa (who resided in southern Lebanon and who had supervision rights over the Temple in Jerusalem) and before Albinus, who is the new governor of Judea: Ananus' convening of the Sanhedrin was illegal, and the death sentences against James and others were illegal as well.[101] The passage clearly implies that the Sanhedrin in Jerusalem did not have jurisdiction over capital cases when Roman governors ruled Judea (i.e., in A.D. 6–41 and 44–66). And the passage seems to indicate that during this period the high priests needed the approval of the Roman governor to convene a meeting of the Sanhedrin. Ananus' belief that he could claim jurisdiction in capital cases when the Roman governor was physically absent from Judea – for example, during the transition period from one governor to the next – was erroneous. When the Roman governor was absent, capital cases could not be tried in a Roman province.[102] When Albinus arrived in Judea, he deposed Ananus from the high priestly office. In addition, Josephus states that the Sadducees were much stricter in the interpretation and application of the law than any of the other Jews, i.e., the Pharisees (cf. *A. J.* 13.294).

**(13)** Josephus, *Bellum judaicum* 2.117

Τῆς δὲ Ἀρχελάου χώρας εἰς ἐπαρχίαν περιγραφείσης ἐπίτροπος τῆς ἱππικῆς παρὰ Ῥωμαίοις τάξεως Κωπώνιος πέμπεται μέχρι τοῦ κτείνειν λαβὼν παρὰ Καίσαρος ἐξουσίαν.

*Translation.* The territory of Archelaos was now marked off for a province, and Coponius, who belonged to the equestrian order among the Romans, was sent as the procurator, having received from the emperor full powers, including the infliction of the death penalty.

*Commentary.* When he died in 4 B.C., Herod I appointed Archelaos as king (βασιλεύς) in charge of Judea (*B. J.* 1.668). Augustus eventually confirmed Archelaos as ruler of Judea, albeit with the lesser title ethnarch (ἐθνάρχης; *B. J.* 2.93). Josephus relates that when Archelaos returned from Rome to Jerusalem to take possession of his ethnarchy, he "did not forget old feuds" and

---

[100] On the influential family of Ananus/Annas see No. 4.

[101] EBELING, Kompetenz, 290–95. Cf. CATCHPOLE, Trial, 244, who concludes after a discussion of πρῶτον: "The situation was accordingly that complaints were made to Agrippa in view of the injustice of the proceedings, and to Albinus in view of the infringement of the laws of the occupying power."

[102] CATCHPOLE, Trial, 241–44; MÜLLER, Kapitalgerichtsbarkeit, 55–57; STROBEL, Stunde, 31–36.

treated the people with excessive brutality (*B. J.* 2.111). Archelaos was denounced by delegations that the Jews and the Samaritans sent to Rome, resulting in his removal. In A.D. 6, after Archelaos had ruled Judea nine years, Augustus exiled him to Vienne in the province of Gallia Narbonensis, and confiscated his property (*B. J.* 2.111). In *B. J.* 117, Josephus relates that when Judea was "marked off for a province"[103] after Archelaos' removal from office, Coponius was appointed as procurator (ἐπίτροπος; Lat. *procurator*). This title is anachronistic; it must have been ἔπαρχος (*praefectus*).[104] (See below the introduction to section 2.1.) Judea did not become an autonomous province in A.D. 6: it was part of the province of Syria, with auxiliary units rather than Roman legions, governed by a *praefectus* of equestrian rank rather than by a senator.[105] The governor of the province of Syria could order the prefect of Judea to travel to Rome and defend himself before the emperor against complaints lodged by the Samaritans.[106] Josephus emphasizes specifically that Coponius had the authority (ἐξουσία) to indict on capital charges and impose the death penalty. In order to maintain peace, the emperor granted the prefect military, administrative, and legal powers (ἐξουσία), including capital jurisdiction (*ius gladii*), which was denied the local authorities. This corresponds to the practice in the other Roman provinces.[107] Only the governor of the province, in this case both the procurator of the province of Syria and the prefect of Judea, had the authority to try and decide capital cases and order the execution of a person who had been sentenced to death.

---

[103] Following the translation of MASON.

[104] Thus the title of Annius Rufus (*A. J.* 18.32) and Valerius Gratus (*A. J.* 18.33), successors of Coponius. The Pilate inscription from Caesarea gives the title *praefectus Iudaeae* (see No. 76). MASON, Judean War 2, 80 n. 720, thinks it possible that "perhaps Judea's early governors had both prefectural and procuratorial functions, and Claudius merely began to insist on the procuratorial title only – whether because he wanted to advertise the non-militarized state of the provinces or he wished to emphasize the governors' direct responsibility to him, rather than to neighboring senatorial governors;" cf. BARBARA LEVICK, Claudius (New Haven: Yale University Press, 1990), 48–49.

[105] FERGUS MILLAR, The Roman Near East, 31 BC – AD 337 (Cambridge: Harvard University Press, 1993), 44–45, calls Judea "a second-rank province," and HENGEL / SCHWEMER, Jesus, 76, speak of "a Roman province 'third class'." See ECK, Rom und Judaea, 24–43.

[106] Thus in the case of Pontius Pilate who was ordered by L. Vitellius, the governor in Syria, to defend himself in Rome against complaints of the Samaritans, an affair which led to his removal from office in A.D. 36 (Josephus, *A. J.* 18.85–89).

[107] Cf. WERNER ECK, Die Leitung und Verwaltung einer prokuratorischen Provinz [1988], in Die Verwaltung des römischen Reiches in der Hohen Kaiserzeit. Ausgewählte und erweiterte Beiträge. Band 1 (AREA 1; Basel / Berlin: Reinhardt, 1995), 327–340, 334, 336–37; ECK, Rom und Judaea, 40; KIRNER, Strafgewalt, 140–42.

**(14)** Josephus, *Bellum judaicum* 6.126

οὐχ ἡμεῖς δὲ τοὺς ὑπερβάντας ὑμῖν ἀναιρεῖν ἐπετρέψαμεν, κἂν Ῥωμαῖός τις ᾖ;

*Translation.* Did we not permit you to execute anyone who passed (the balustrade before the Temple), even if he were a Roman citizen?

*Commentary.* Josephus describes how, during the siege of Jerusalem in A.D. 70, the Roman general Titus rebuked the Jewish rebels who had barricaded themselves inside the Temple and had killed a large number of Jewish deserters so that "the surrounding court of the Temple resembled a burial ground" (*B. J.* 6.121). At the beginning of his speech, Titus points to the balustrade that the Jews had built around the Temple (124) to remind the rebels of the Temple's sanctity, which they had now violated. He argues that if he is now forced to pollute the Temple, this is their responsibility alone (127). In *B. J.* 6.126, Titus reminds the rebels that the Roman authorities had granted the Jews the right to execute people who desecrated the Temple. The reference to Roman permission (ἐπετρέψαμεν) implies restrictions imposed by the Roman governor on Jewish jurisdiction in death penalty cases.[108] At the same time, the statement clearly indicates that in cases of the violation of the Temple, the Jewish authorities had jurisdiction and could impose the death penalty. This is evidently the scenario envisioned by Luke in Acts 21:27–31, where Jews who accuse Paul of having defiled the Temple, seized Paul and wanted to kill him.[109] It has been argued that the fact that the Roman governors of Judea allowed an exception with regard to capital jurisdiction, even in the case of a Roman citizen who profaned the Jerusalem Temple, makes it highly unlikely that the Jewish authorities could pronounce a death sentence without the involvement of the Roman governor and a Roman court deciding capital cases.[110]

**(15)** *Megillat Taʿanit* 6 [13–15]

[13] באַרבעה באליל חנכת שור ירושלם די לא למספד

[14] בשבעת עשר ביה נפקו רומאי מן ירושלם

[15] בעשרין ותרין ביה תבנא לקטל[א] רשיעיא.

*Translation.* On the 4th of Elul is the day of the dedication of the wall of Jerusalem, on which it is also not permitted to mourn. 14 On the 17th of the same

---

[108] BROWN, Death, 1:367.

[109] On the legal aspects of this episode cf. OMERZU, Prozeß, 310–84.

[110] MÜLLER, Kapitalgerichtsbarkeit, 67–68. As regards the concession that Jews can execute Roman citizens if they entered the Temple, note Diodorus Siculus 1.83.8: a Roman envoy in Egypt was killed because he had put to death a cat, regarded as a holy animal by the local population. *B. J.* 6.126 may indeed reflect historical reality; OMERZU, Prozeß, 350–51.

month the Romans withdrew from Jerusalem. 15 On the 22nd of the same month we started again to kill the evildoers.[111]

*Commentary.*[112] The document *Megillat Ta'anit* or *Scroll of Fasts*[113] provides a list of thirty-five days on which mourning was forbidden. This is the earliest complete enumeration of the Jewish names of the months of the year, listing them in the correct sequence. Since *Megillat Ta'anit* is mentioned in the Mishnah (*m. Ta'anit* 2:8), the document originated in the mid-second century at the latest. K. BEYER interprets the text as a Pharisaic festival calendar. Since the individual days refer to events during the Maccabean period[114] until the beginning of the First Jewish Revolt, some scholars suggest that the document may have been compiled about A.D. 67–70.[115] Line 13 refers to the dedication of the wall that secured the eastern expansion of Jerusalem. This is the third wall that king Agrippa I (A.D. 41–44) had started and which was finished in the month of Elul (August/September) in A.D. 67. The withdrawal of the Roman troops mentioned in line 14 took place in A.D. 66. Josephus dates the evacuation of Herod's Palace by the Roman forces under their commander Metilius to the 6th of the month Gorpiaeus, i.e., the month of Elul (Josephus, *B. J.* 2.439–440). The withdrawal of the Roman troops and the killing of stragglers by the Jewish insurrectionists marked the beginning of a new era of Jewish freedom – and the beginning of the war.

The 22nd of Elul commemorated the day when the Jews became fully independent from the Romans, demonstrated by the fact that Jews could indict perpetrators on capital charges and execute convicted criminals (line 15). It seems that five days after the withdrawal of the Roman troops, a Jewish court tried an accused person on criminal charges, issued a death sentence, and ordered the execution. This reference implies that Jewish courts could not indict on capital charges and execute the convicted criminal while Roman

---

[111] BEYER translates line 15: "Am zweiundzwanzigsten desselben kehrten wir zur Hinrichtung der Verbrecher zurück" (on the 22nd we returned to the execution of criminals).

[112] Text: KLAUS BEYER, Die aramäischen Texte vom Toten Meer (3 vols.; Göttingen: Vandenhoeck & Ruprecht, 1984–2004), 1:354–58; cf. also PAUL RIESSLER, Die Fastenrolle, in Altjüdisches Schrifttum außerhalb der Bibel (Orig. 1928; repr., Heidelberg: Kerle, 1982), 346–347; HANS LICHTENSTEIN, Die Fastenrolle. Eine Untersuchung zur jüdisch-hellenistischen Geschichte, HUCA 8–9 (1931–32): 257–351.

[113] Besides RIESSLER und LICHTENSTEIN, cf. WILLIAM R. FARMER, Maccabees, Zealots, and Josephus: An Inquiry into Jewish Nationalism in the Greco-Roman Period (New York: Columbia University Press, 1956), 151–58; HUGO D. MANTEL, Fastenrolle, TRE 11 (1983): 59–61.

[114] Fifteen days celebrate victories of the Hasmoneans over Israel's enemies.

[115] None of the festival days dates after A.D. 67, with the exception of the day of Trajan (line 29) which, however, is missing from the best manuscripts. Some manuscripts state at the end of the document that *Megillat Ta'anit* was written by Elieser ben Hanania ben Hezekiah from the House of Guron; this Elieser has been identified by some with Eleasar ben Hanania, the leader of the Zealots. Cf. LICHTENSTEIN, Fastenrolle 257–58.

troops were in the city. The 22nd of Elul was memorable also because it was the day of the Feast of Oil in the Essene calendar and the day on which Jews were massacred in Caesarea, signalling the beginning of the rebellion against the Romans (Josephus, *B. J.* 2.457–458).[116] The commemoration of Jewish jurisdiction in capital cases on the 22nd of Elul, possibly due to the withdrawal of Roman troops from Jerusalem (they later returned in A.D. 70, when Jerusalem was besieged and destroyed), implies the lack of Jewish jurisdiction in capital cases before A.D. 66.

As regards the jurisdiction of the Roman governors in the province of Judea and the relevance of this question for Jesus' trial, A. STROBEL argues that *Megillat Ta'anit* 6 "fügt sich glatt in die Überlieferung des Josephus über den ersten Prokurator von Judäa ein. Als nämlich Coponius im Jahre 6 n.Chr. die Herrschaft des Archelaus ablöste, empfing er, was ausdrücklich vermerkt wird (Jos., Bell. Iud. II,8,1 § 117), vom Kaiser die Vollmacht (ἐξουσία) μεχρὶ τοῦ κτείνειν ... d.i. das Recht über Leben und Tod in letzter Instand (*ius gladii* oder *potestas gladii*). Es wurde vom Kaiser als Spezialmandat dem einzelnen Statthalter erteilt (Ulpian 1,21,1,1 *imperium merum*) und war nicht auf andere Personen übertragbar."[117]

## (16) *y. Sanhedrin* 18a,42–43

תַּנֵּי קוֹדֶם לְאַרְבָּעִים שָׁנָה עַד שֶׁלֹּא חָרַב הַבַּיִת נִיטְלוּ דִינֵי נְפָשׁוֹת מִיִּשְׂרָאֵל

*Translation.* It has been taught: forty years before the house (i.e., the Temple) was destroyed, they took away capital jurisdiction from Israel.

*Commentary.*[118] This rabbinic tradition, preserved in a baraita, i.e., presented as an early tradition, states that jurisdiction for capital cases (דיני נפשות)[119] was taken away from the Jews forty years before the destruction of the Temple. This implies the year A.D. 30 as the time when this change happened.[120] There is no evidence and no historically plausible reason why such a change in jurisdiction regarding capital cases would have occurred in the middle of Pontius

---

[116] JOACHIM JEREMIAS, Zur Geschichtlichkeit des Verhörs Jesu vor dem Hohen Rat, ZNW 43 (1950–51): 145–150, 150; CATCHPOLE, Trial, 245; STROBEL, Stunde, 26–27.

[117] STROBEL, Stunde, 27 mit Verweis auf THEODOR MOMMSEN, Römisches Strafrecht (orig. 1899; repr., Darmstadt: Wissenschaftliche Buchgesellschaft, 1961), 243–44.

[118] Cf. GERD A. WEWERS, Sanhedrin. Gerichtshof (Übersetzung des Talmud Yerushalmi IV/4; Tübingen: Mohr Siebeck, 1981), 3. A virtually identical text is *y. Sanh.* 24b,48–50.

[119] NEUSNER renders דיני נפשות as "capital cases;" GUGGENHEIMER "criminal jurisdiction," WEWERS "Lebensrechtsfälle."

[120] HEINRICH W. GUGGENHEIMER, The Jerusalem Talmud. Fourth Order: Neziqin. Tractates Sanhedrin, Makkot, and Horaiot. Edition, Translation, and Commentary (SJ 51; Berlin/New York: De Gruyter, 2010), 13, n. 32, comments "when Judea came under direct Roman rule" but does not discuss the specific date that the *baraita* implies.

Pilatus' tenure as prefect of Judea (A.D. 26–36). Some scholars suggest that "forty" is a round number,[121] or that here it is tantamount to saying "over one generation before the Temple was destroyed."[122] If we accept the possibility of "forty years" representing a round number, the baraita may refer to the assignment of *procuratores* as provincial governors by Claudius (A.D. 41–54).[123] The most plausible date for the transfer of jurisdiction in capital cases to the Roman governor is A.D. 6, when Archelaos, one of Herod's sons, was removed as ethnarch and when Judea became a Roman province governed by a prefect. On capital cases in Roman law, cf. 2.3.

## (17)  *b. Sanhedrin* 41a

ותניא ארבעים שנה קודם חורבן הבית גלתה סנהדרי וישבה לה בחנות ואמר ר' יצחק בר
אבודימי לומר שלא דנו דיני קנסות דיני קנסות ס"ד אלא שלא דנו דיני נפשות

*Translation.* And it has also been taught: Forty years before the destruction of the Temple, the Sanhedrin was exiled and took up residence in Ḥanuth. And Rabbi Isaac son of Abudimi said: "This is to teach that they did not try cases of fines." Do you think it was cases of fines? Rather, the Sanhedrin did not try capital cases.

*Commentary.* This rabbinic tradition, which is an anonymous comment not attributed to a rabbinic authority and thus cannot be dated, also states that forty years before the destruction of the Temple, the Sanhedrin did not have jurisdiction over capital charges. The rhetorical question "Do you think it was cases of fines?" implies that cases involving penalties could be tried anywhere in Palestine and were not restricted to the main Sanhedrin in Jerusalem.[124] The reference to the "exile" of the Sanhedrin refers to the transfer of the sessions of the Sanhedrin in Jerusalem from the Chamber of Hewn Stone on the Temple Mount to a hall in the city. According to the Mishnah, the Great Sanhedrin met in the Chamber of Hewn Stone (לִשְׁכַּת הַגָּזִית, *Lishkat hagazit*), probably located in the southeast corner of the inner enclosure (*Azarah*), giving access to the Court of the Priests and the Court of Israel.[125] This Chamber measured 12 by 11 meters and was large enough for the assembly of the mem-

---

[121] JEREMIAS, Geschichtlichkeit, 148.

[122] STROBEL, Stunde, 28, who points out that the fortieth year is often given as the year in which bad things took place. STROBEL argues for the basic historicity of the rabbinic tradition, as does CATCHPOLE, Trial, 238–39.

[123] We thank David Instone-Brewer for pointing out this possibility.

[124] JACOB SCHACHTER and AARON M. FREEDMAN, Sanhedrin (Hebrew-English Edition of the Babylonian Talmud. New ed.; ed. I. Epstein; London: Soncino, 1969), note d(6).

[125] Cf. *m. Sanh.* 11:2; *m. Mid.* 5:4. The later text *b. Yoma* 25a calls this structure "like a great basilica" (כמין בסלקי גדולה). Cf. EHUD NETZER, The Architecture of Herod, the Great Builder (Grand Rapids: Baker, 2008), 156.

bers of the Sanhedrin. On the other hand, since the term "hewn stone" (גָּזִית) is translated in the LXX as ξυστός (1 Chron 22:2; Amos 5:11),[126] the Hebrew expression could be understood as "the Hall beside the Xystos." According to Josephus, the council (βουλή), or council hall (βουλευτήριον), was located in the Upper City on the west side of the Temple Mount between the latter and the so-called Xystos, which was connected with the Temple Mount by a bridge.[127] This rabbinic tradition asserts that forty years before the destruction of the city (i.e., c. A.D. 30), the Sanhedrin moved from its previous location in the Chamber of Hewn Stone to the Ḥanut (חָנוּת; or חניות, "shops"). This tradi-tion is also found in *b. Roš Haš.* 31b.[128] The remains of a large hall dating to the Second Temple period have been discovered near Wilson's Arch, which is part of the bridge over the Tyropoean Valley leading to the Kipunus Gate. This structure, called Hasmonean Hall, has been described as follows: "The walls are built of ashlars. Pilasters at the corners and along the walls originally bore Corinthian capitals, one of which is preserved in the northeastern corner. In the eastern wall was a double door with a lintel."[129] The text connects the change of venue of Sanhedrin meetings with the fact that the Sanhedrin did not have jurisdiction over capital cases (דיני נפשות).[130]

## (18) *b. 'Abodah Zarah* 8b

אמר להו מאה ושמנים שנה קודם שנחרב הבית פשטה מלכות הרשעה על ישראל פ' שנה עד לא
חרב הבית גזרו טומאה על ארץ העמים ועל כלי זכוכית מ' שנה עד לא חרב הבית גלתה סנהדרין

---

[126] Cf. LSJ s.v. ξυστός 1, "walking place" in the grounds of a private residence or in a gymnasium; meaning 2, "*covered colonnade* in a gymnasium."

[127] Josephus, *B. J.* 5.144; 6.354; cf. 2.344. Cf. SCHÜRER, History, 2:223–24. The Xystos was the covered colonnade of the gymnasium built during the Maccabean period (1 Macc 1:14–15; 2 Macc 4:11–15), which was now used as a public plaza.

[128] See *b. Roš Haš.* 31b: "The Sanhedrin was exiled from the Chamber of Hewn Stone to the market, and from the market into Jerusalem, and from Jerusalem to Yabneh, and from Yabneh to Usha, and from Usha to Yabneh, and from Yabneh to Usha, and from Usha to Shefar, and from Shefar to Beth , and from Beth Shearim to Sepphoris, and from Sepphoris to Tiberias." The first two of the ten places of "exile" (or banishment) of the Sanhedrin date to the period before the destruction of Jerusalem and of the Temple in A.D. 70. For the context of this text cf. CHILTON / BOCK, Mark, 484–86. Scholars who assume that there was a "city coun-cil" (βουλή) beside the Sanhedrin as "supreme court" locate this civic body in the area of the Huldah Gates south of the Temple Mount (cf. *t. Ḥag.* 2:9; *t. Sanh.* 7:1).

[129] HILLEL GEVA, Jerusalem: The Temple Mount and its Environs, NEAEHL 2 (1993): 736–744, 742, who continues, "The original hall was presumably part of a large Herodian public building that some scholars have identified with the Chamber of Hewn Stones (the Xystos) or with the Council Building, both referred to by Josephus as being in this area." Cf. Josephus, *B. J.* 5.144.

[130] CHILTON / BOCK, Mark, 489, connect this text (as well as *b. 'Abodah Zarah* 8b; cf. No. 18) with "the arrangements in the Temple which Caiaphas innovated."

וישבה לה בחנות למאי הלכתא א"ר יצחק בר אבדימי לומר שלא דנו דיני קנסות דיני קנסות
סלקא דעתך ... אמר רב נחמן בר יצחק לא תימא דיני קנסות אלא שלא דנו דיני נפשות

*Translation*. (Rabbi Yishmael, son of Rabbi Yose) said to them, "One hundred and eighty years before the house of the Temple was destroyed, the evil kingdom began to dominate Israel. Eighty years before the destruction of the Temple, the decree was issued that the lands of the neighboring nations around Israel and all glass vessels were to be regarded as unclean. Forty years before the destruction of the Temple the Sanhedrin went out into exile from the Temple and held its sessions in Hanuth.[131] Has this any legal relevance? Rabbi Isaac, son of Abdimi, said, "It indicates that [from that time onward] they did not deal with cases of fines."[132] You say cases of fines? ... Rabbi Nahman, son of Isaac, said, "Say not that cases of fines ceased, but that capital cases ceased."

*Commentary*. The statement that forty years before the destruction of the Temple the Jewish Sanhedrin lost jurisdiction over capital cases (and moved from the Temple Mount to a hall in the city) is attributed to Rabbi Nahman, son of Isaac, who lived c. A.D. 325. The three dates given by Rabbi Yishmael, son of Rabbi Yose (c. A.D. 200), are most plausibly interpreted as round dates.[133]

*The jurisdiction of the Sanhedrin and Jesus' trial*. The primary sources demonstrate the historical accuracy of the Jewish leaders' assertion before Pilatus that they do not have jurisdiction in capital cases (John 18:31). Exceptions to the rule – capital cases in Roman provinces were the exclusive responsibility of the Roman governor – were allowed, in Judea, in cases where the Temple had been defiled. The fact that the Sanhedrin first sought to indict Jesus on the charge of plotting the destruction of the Temple (Matt 26:61; cf. Matt 27:40 / Mark 14:58; 15:29) fits the evidence. If the Jewish leaders' trial strategy had been successful, they might have been able to execute Jesus, granted that the destruction of the Temple implies the ultimate defilement of the Temple. Lack of jurisdiction to execute convicted persons in cases not involving the specific charge of defilement of the Temple did not preclude the Sanhedrin from interrogating persons on the relevant charges with the goal of taking the case to the Roman governor.[134]

---

[131] NEUSNER translates "in a stall [on the Temple mount]." For the relocation of the Sanhedrin cf. No. 17.

[132] NEUSNER translates "extrajudicial penalties."

[133] BLINZLER, Prozeß, 169–70; STROBEL, Stunde, 28. JOSEF LENGLE, Zum Prozess Jesu, Hermes 790 (1935): 312–321, suggests that the forty years refers to capital punishment *de facto*, not *de jure*, from the time of Pontius Pilatus onwards, with very few exceptions allowed; the Jewish authorities had to obtain the approval of the Roman governor for executions; cf. BROWN, Death, 1:366 n. 86.

It seems a moot point whether such an event can be called an official judicial trial (whose irregularities are then variously explained),[135] or whether it should be treated as an interrogation.[136] Sadducean champions of the Law, who had concluded that it was their responsibility to eliminate Jesus, might have been eager to see the proceedings as an official act of the highest Jewish authorities, while Pilatus would have regarded any legal proceedings of the Sanhedrin as part of the concessions granted to local authorities in a Roman province. As a result of these ambiguities, the location of Jesus' trial (or interrogation) by the Sanhedrin – evidently held in the house of Caiaphas, rather than in the Chamber of Hewn Stone or in the Hasmonean Hall – can hardly be regarded as a problem for the historicity of the Synoptics' portrayal.[137]

## 1.3 Capital Cases in Jewish Law

The following texts document how capital cases were handled according to Jewish law. It should be noted that there are no extant primary sources from the first century that document the proceedings of the Sanhedrin in Jerusalem in capital cases. While there continues to be debate about the relevance of the rabbinic evidence for trial proceedings in the first half of the first century, some scholars are more confident than others that the Qumran evidence suggests a continuity in the Jewish legal tradition regarding capital cases from Second Temple Judaism to the rabbinic period.

**(19)** 11QTemple LIV, 8 – LV, 10

8    אִם יָקוּם בְּקִרְבְּכָה נָבִיא אוֹ חוֹלֵם חֲלוֹם וְנָתַן אֵלֶיכָה אוֹת אוֹ

9    מוֹפֵת וּבָא אֵלֶיכָה הָאוֹת אוֹ הַמּוֹפֵת אֲשֶׁר דִּבֶּר אֵלֶיכָה לֵאמוֹר

10    נֵלְכָה וְנַעֲבוֹדָה אֱלוֹהִים אֲחֵרִים אֲשֶׁר לוֹא יְדַעְתֶּמָה לוֹא

11    תִשְׁמַע אֶל דִּבְרֵי הַנָּבִיא הַהוּא אוֹ לְחוֹלֵם הַחֲלוֹם הַהוּאָה כִּי

12    מְנַסֶּה אָנוֹכִי אֶתְכֶמָה לָדַעַת הֲיִשְׁכֶם אוֹהֲבִים אֶת יהוה

13    אֱלוֹהֵי אֲבוֹתֵיכֶמָה בְּכוֹל לְבַבְכֶם וּבְכוֹל נַפְשְׁכֶמָה אַחֲרֵי יהוה

14    אֱלוֹהֵיכֶמָה תֵלְכוּן וְאוֹתוֹ תַעֲבוֹדוּן וְאוֹתוֹ תִירָאוּ וּבְקוֹלוֹ תִשְׁמָעוּן

15    וּבוֹ תִדְבָּקוּן וְהַנָּבִיא הַהוּא אוֹ חוֹלֵם הַחֲלוֹם יוּמַת כִּי דִבֶּר סָרָה

16    עַל יהוה אֱלוֹהֵיכָה אֲשֶׁר הוֹצִיאָכָה מֵאֶרֶץ מִצְרַיִם וּפְדִיתִיכָה

17    מִבֵּית עֲבָדִים לְהַדִּיחֲכָה מִן הַדֶּרֶךְ אֲשֶׁר צִוִּיתְכָה לָלֶכֶת בָּה וּבְעַרְתָּ

---

[134] See Josephus, *B. J.* 6.300–309, discussed in No. 65.

[135] E.g., STROBEL, Stunde, 5–95.

[136] Cf. recently CHILTON / BOCK, Mark, 487.

[137] Differently EDUARD LOHSE, Der Prozeß Jesu Christi [1961], in Die Einheit des Neuen Testaments. Exegetische Studien zur Theologie des Neuen Testaments (Göttingen: Vandenhoeck & Ruprecht, 1973), 88–103, 96–97.

הָרָע מִקִּרְבְּכָה 18

וְאִם יְשִׁיתְכָה אָחִיכָה בֶן אָבִיכָה אוֹ בֶן אִמְּכָה אוֹ בִנְכָה אוֹ בִתְּכָה 19

אוֹ אֵשֶׁת חֵיקְכָה אוֹ רֵיעֲיכָה אֲשֶׁר כְּנַפְשְׁכָה בַּסֵּתֶר לֵאמוֹר 20

נֵלְכָה וְנַעֲבוֹדָה אֱלוֹהִים אֲחֵרִים אֲשֶׁר לוֹא יְדַעְתַּמָה אַתָּה 21

[וְאַב]וֹתֵיכה מֵאֱלוֹהִי ה[עמים אשר סביבותיכמה הקרובים אליכה] 01[^138]

[אוֹ הרחוקים ממ]כה מקצי הארץ ועד קצ[י הארץ לוא תואבה] 02

[לו ולוא תשמע אליו ולוא תחוס עינ]כה עליו ולוא תחמל ע[ליו] 03

[ולוא תכסה עליו כי הרוג תהרגנו ידכה תהיה בו ברא]ישונה 04

[להמיתו ויד] כול העם באחרונה וסקלתו באבנים וימות כי 05

[בקש לה]דיחכה [מעל יהוה אלוהיכה המוציאכה מארץ מצרים] 06

[מבית עבדים וכול ישראל ישמעו ויראון ולוא יוסיפו לעשות] 07

[כַּדָּבָר הָרָע הַזֶּה] בְּקִרְבְּכָה] 1

אִם תִּשְׁמַע בְּאַחַ[ת עָרֶיכָה אֲשֶׁר א]נוכִי נוֹתֵן לְכָה לָשֶׁ[בֶת שָׁם] 2

לֵאמוֹר יָצְאוּ אֲנָשִׁ[י]ם בְּנֵי [בְלִיַ]עַל מִקִּרְבְּכָה וַיַּדִּיחוּ אֶת כּוֹל [י]וֹשְׁבֵי 3

עִירָמָה לֵאמוֹר נֵלְכָה וְנַעֲבוֹדָה אֱלוֹהִים אֲשֶׁר לוֹא יְדַעְתָּמָה 4

וְשָׁאַלְתָּה וְדָרַשְׁתָּה וְחָקַרְתָּה הֵיטֵב וְהִנֵּה אֱמֶת נָכוֹן הַדָּבָר 5

נֶעֶשְׂתָה הַתּוֹעֵבָה הַזֹּאת בְּיִשְׂרָאֵל הַכֵּה תַכֶּה אֶת כּוֹל יוֹשְׁבֵי 6

הָעִיר הַהִיא לְפִי חֶרֶב הַחֲרֵם אוֹתָהּ וְאֶת כּוֹל אֲשֶׁר בָּהּ וְאֶת 7

כּוֹל בְּהֶמְתָּהּ תַּכֶּה לְפִי חֶרֶב וְאֶת כּוֹל שְׁלָלָהּ תִּקְבּוֹץ אֶל תּוֹךְ 8

רְחוֹבָהּ וְשָׂרַפְתָּה בָאֵשׁ אֶת הָעִיר וְאֶת כּוֹל שְׁלָלָהּ כָּלִיל לַיהוה 9

אֱלוֹהֶיכָה וְהָיְתָה לְתֵל עוֹלָם לוֹא תִבָּנֶה עוֹד 10

*Translation.* LIV, 8 If a prophet rises up among you, or a dreamer of dreams, and gives to you a sign or 9 or a miracle, and it actually occurs for you, the sign or miracle which he declared to you saying, 10 "Let us go and serve other gods whom you have not known," you shall not 11 listen to the word of that prophet or that dreamer of dreams, for 12 I am testing you to know whether you continue loving YHWH, 13 the God of your fathers, with all your heart and all your soul. After YHWH, 14 your God, you shall go, and him you shall serve, and him you shall revere, and to his voice you shall listen, 15 and to him you shall cling. And that prophet or dreamer of dreams shall be put to death, for he spoke a falsehood 16 against YHWH, your God, who brought you out of the land of Egypt and ransomed you 17 from the house of slavery, to mislead you from the way which I am ordering you to go. And you shall remove 18 the evil from among you. *Blank.* 19 And if anyone urges you,[139] your brother, the son

---

[^138] The restoration of the zero lines follows Deut 13:7–12; LAWRENCE H. SCHIFFMAN, ANDREW D. GROSS, and MICHAEL C. RAND, Composite Text of the Temple Scroll: Hebrew Text, in Temple Scroll and Related Documents (ed. J. H. Charlesworth; The Dead Sea Scrolls 7; Tübingen: Mohr Siebeck, 2011), 266–405, 370.

[^139] FLORENTINO GARCÍA MARTÍNEZ and EIBERT J. C. TIGCHELAAR, The Dead Sea Scrolls Study Edition (2 vols. Leiden: Brill, 1997–1998), 1275, translate the verb יְשִׁיתְכָה as "provoke;" JOHANN MAIER, Die Tempelrolle vom Toten Meer und das "Neue Jerusalem" (3., völlig neu bearbeitete und erweiterte Auflage; UTB 829; München: Reinhardt, 1997), 230, translates "verführt;" ANNETTE STEUDEL, Die Texte aus Qumran II. Hebräisch/Aramäisch und

of your father or the son of your mother, or your son, or your daughter, [20] or the wife of your bosom, or your friends who are as your own soul, secretly saying, "Let us go and serve other gods whom you have not known," you [LV, 01] and your fathers, from the gods of the [peoples who are around you, those near you] [02] [or distant from] you, from the ends of the land and to the end[s of the land, you shall not yield] [03] [to him, and you shall not listen] to him, and you shall not have pity in your eyes on him, and you shall not have mercy upon him, [04] [and you shall not forgive him. For you shall surely kill him, your hand shall be on him fir]st [05] to put him to death and the hand of [all the people afterward, and you shall pelt him with stones, and he shall die for] [06] [he sought to d]rive you away [from YHWH, your God, who brought you out of the land of Egypt], [07] [from the house of slavery. And all Israel shall hear and see, and they shall not continue to act] [1] [in accordance with this evil thing][140] among you. [...] [2] If you hear (a report) in on[e of your cities, which I] am giving to you to dwe[ll ...] [3] that says, "Men, sons of [Beli]al have emerged from among you and have led astray all the inhabitants [4] of their town, saying, 'Let us go and serve gods whom you have not known,'" [5] then you shall ask, investigate, and inquire carefully, and, indeed, if it is established as true, [6] that this abomination has been done in Israel, you shall surely kill all the inhabitants of [7] that town by the sword; it is under the ban and all that is in it. [8] All its domesticated animals you shall kill by the edge of the sword and you shall collect all its booty in the midst of [9] its square and shall burn with fire the town and its booty as a whole-offering for YHWH [10] your God. And it shall be a rubble forever; it shall never be rebuilt.

*Commentary.*[141] This text is part of the *Temple Scroll*, which dates, as a

Deutsch. Mit masoretischer Punktation, Übersetzung, Einführung und Anmerkungen (Darmstadt: Wissenschaftliche Buchgesellschaft, 2001), 117, has "verleitet."

[140] Restoration LAWRENCE H. SCHIFFMAN, ANDREW D. GROSS, and MICHAEL C. RAND, Temple Scroll Defining Edition 11Q19 (11QTempleᵃ): Hebrew Text, in Temple Scroll, and Related Documents (ed. J. H. Charlesworth; The Dead Sea Scrolls 7; Tübingen: Mohr Siebeck, 2011), 1–173, 139 n. 459.

[141] Text: SCHIFFMAN / GROSS / RAND, Temple Scroll Defining Edition. The translations have been adapted. For the punctuation of the Hebrew text cf. STEUDEL, Texte aus Qumran II. The other major editions have been consulted; cf. YIGAEL YADIN, The Temple Scroll (3 vols. with Supplementary Plates; Jerusalem: Israel Exploration Society, 1977–1983); ELISHA QIMRON, The Temple Scroll: A Critical Edition with Extensive Reconstructions (Judean Desert Studies; Beer Scheva/Jerusalem: Ben-Gurion University of the Negev Press/Israel Exploration Society, 1996); FLORENTINO GARCÍA MARTÍNEZ, EIBERT J. C. TIGCHELAAR, and ADAM S. VAN DER WOUDE, Qumran Cave 11.II (11Q2–18, 11Q20–30) (DJD 23; Oxford: Clarendon, 1998), 357–414; ÉMILE PUECH, Qumrân Grotte 4.XVIII: Textes hébreux (4Q521–4Q528, 4Q576–4Q579) (DJD 25; Oxford: Clarendon, 1998), 85–114; ELISHA QIMRON, The Dead Sea Scrolls: The Hebrew Writings (3 vols.; Jerusalem: Yad Ben-Zvi, 2010), 1:193–94. For all Qumran texts, in addition to DJD, we also consulted the following editions: GARCÍA MARTÍNEZ and TIGCHELAAR, Dead Sea Scrolls Study Edition; MARTIN G. ABEGG, Qumran Sectarian Manuscripts (With Morphological and Lexical Tags; Bellingham: Logos Research

whole, to the second half of the reign of John Hyrcanus (135–104 B.C.), i.e., after 120 B.C. It was written by an author or redactor who belonged to the Sadducean (Zadokite) heritage of those who founded the Qumran group, and who "called for a thoroughgoing revision of the existing Hasmonean order, advocating its replacement with a Temple, sacrificial system, and government representing his own understanding of the law of the Torah."[142] The Law of the King (preserved in 4Q524, the oldest extant manuscript of the scroll)[143] is a polemic against the Hasmonean rulers in Jerusalem. The text belongs to the last major section of the *Temple Scroll*, which presents general laws (cols. XLVIII – LXVI)[144] that paraphrase large parts of Deuteronomy 12–23.[145] After laws regarding purity, the courts, the death penalty for bribery and corruption,[146] and the cultus, the author addresses idolatry (LIV, 8 – LVI, 04). The laws of Deuteronomy concerning idolatry are treated in five passages.[147] (1) Prohibition of various idolatrous practices, such as erecting pillars or figure stones for the worship of Ashera (LI, 19 – LII, 3; cf. Deut 16:21–22). (2) A prophet or interpreter of dreams who incites to idolatrous worship (LIV, 8–18, cf. Deut 13:2–6). (3) An individual who seduces others to idolatrous worship (LIV, 19 – LV, 1; cf. Deut 13:7–12).[148] (4) A town that had been seduced to idolatrous worship (LV, 2–14; cf. Deut 13:13–19). (5) An individual who seduces to idolatrous worship (LV, 15 – LVI, 04; cf. Deut 17:2–7).

The text follows Deuteronomy closely, with only minor textual variations apart from the laws concerning the town that was enticed to idolatrous worship. Here the author/redactor introduced specific halakhic rulings, indicating that all inhabitants must worship idols for this law to apply, that all the inhabitants are to be executed, and that all animals must be destroyed.[149] The crimi-

---

Systems, 2003); EMANUEL TOV, The Dead Sea Scrolls Electronic Library (rev. ed.; Leiden: Brill, 2006).

[142] LAWRENCE H. SCHIFFMAN, The Courtyards of the House of the Lord: Studies on the Temple Scroll (ed. F. García Martínez; STDJ 75; Leiden: Brill, 2008), xviii; for the relationship between 11QTemple and the Qumran group cf. ibid. xviii–xx; SCHIFFMAN / GROSS / RAND, Temple Scroll Defining Edition, 4–5.

[143] PUECH, Qumrân Grotte 4.XVIII, 87–88, dates 4Q524 to the early Hasmonean period, c. 150–125 B.C.

[144] MAIER, Tempelrolle, 8–20; JOHANN MAIER, Die Qumran-Essener: Die Texte vom Toten Meer (3 vols.; UTB; Reinhardt: München/Basel, 1995–1996), 1:406–28.

[145] Cf. LAWRENCE H. SCHIFFMAN, The Deuteronomic Paraphrase of the *Temple Scroll* [1992], in The Courtyards of the House of the Lord: Studies on the Temple Scroll (ed. F. García Martínez; STDJ 75; Leiden: Brill, 2008), 443–469.

[146] On the law of judges in 11QTemple LI, 11–18 see below the commentary on 11QTemple LXI, 7–12 (No. 21).

[147] LAWRENCE H. SCHIFFMAN, Laws concerning Idolatry in the *Temple Scroll* [1994], in The Courtyards of the House of the Lord: Studies on the Temple Scroll (ed. F. García Martínez; STDJ 75; Leiden: Brill, 2008), 471–486, here 472.

[148] This is the rabbinic *mesit* or *maddiakh*; SCHIFFMAN, Laws concerning Idolatry, 472.

[149] This modification agrees with the LXX. Cf. SCHIFFMAN, Deuteronomic Paraphrase,

nal offense of idolatry is described as "serve other gods" (נַעַבְדָה אֱלֹהִים אֲחֵרִים). The cause of idolatry by Israelites is connected with the activity of a prophet (נָבִיא) or dreamer of a dream (חוֹלֵם חֲלוֹם), i.e., with people who claim to have received a revelation from God, either through direct verbal revelation or through dreams and visions.[150] The content of the alleged revelation is the "permission" to worship the gods of the non-Israelite nations. The prophet and dreamer claims his message is divinely authenticated by the performance of a sign (אוֹת) or miracle (מוֹפֵת),[151] which he announces and which actually occurs. At the same time, he operates in secret (בַּסֵּתֶר). The alleged divine message of such prophets or dreamers is evaluated: (1) as constituting a test (מְנַסֶּה) of Israel's faithfulness to her covenant God in response to a falsehood (סָרָה) against YHWH (because it is falsely claimed that the message came from God), (2) as evil (הָרַע), and (3) as an abomination (תּוֹעֵבָה). The activity of these prophets and dreamers is described with the verbs שׁוּת (for סות) and נדח denoting "entice, seduce, lead astray." They "emerge from among you" (מִקִּרְבְּךָ): they can be a brother, indeed a most closely related brother ("the son of your father or the son of your mother"), a son, a daughter, a beloved wife, or beloved friends. Yet they are "sons of Belial" (אֲנָשִׁים בְּנֵי בְלִיַּעַל): they are inspired by the "Angel of Darkness," the leader of the demonic forces who rules the world and seeks to ensnare the faithful with the three nets of unchasteness, wealth, and defiling the sanctuary.[152] In Old Testament texts, "Belial" denotes a concrete-personal entity as well as the abstract-conceptual reality of wickedness, uselessness, and destruction. People who entice Israelites to worship foreign gods, which is "the cardinal cultic sin," are "men who are sons of Belial" (Deut 13:14 [13]).[153] No miracle can ever prove that YHWH allows his people to worship other gods besides the God of their fathers. They must always love (אוֹהֲבִים) YHWH with all their heart and soul; they must always go (תֵּלְכוּן) after him, serve (תַעֲבֹדוּן) him, revere (תִּירָאוּ) him, listen (תִּשְׁמָעוּן) to his voice alone, and cling (תִדְבָּקוּן) to him.

The charge that a Jew has attempted to seduce a town to worship foreign gods must be thoroughly investigated: one shall ask (שָׁאַלְתָּ), investigate (דָרַשְׁתָּ), inquire carefully (חָקַרְתָּ הֵיטֵב), and establish as true (אֱמֶת נָכוֹן הַדָּבָר) the alleged crime of seducing to idolatry (LV, 5). This line uses the same

---

456–58; SCHIFFMAN, Laws concerning Idolatry, 480–83, pointing out that the author may have been influenced here by Gen 18:24–25 and Ezek 18:1–20.

[150] According to Job 7:14, God sends dreams. Cf. Num 12:6–8; Job 33:16; 1 Sam 28:6. For Deut 13:1–6, compare Jer 23:25–32; 27:9–10; 29:8; Zech 10:2.

[151] The text of 11QT clarifies with regard to MT that the Torah intends either a sign or a miracle, not both together; SCHIFFMAN, Laws concerning Idolatry, 476.

[152] Michael Mach, Demons, EDSS (2000): 199–192. For Belial's three nets cf. CD IV, 12–18; for the Angel of Darkness see the "Treatise on the Two Spirits" 1QS III, 13 – IV, 26.

[153] BENEDIKT OTZEN, "בְּלִיַּעַל, TDOT 2 (1975): 131–136, 135. The English versions of Deut 13:14[13] have "scoundrel" (NRSV), "wicked men" (NIV1984), "troublemakers" (NIV2011).

verbs as Deut 13:15[14] (with a different sequence of the verbs: "you shall in-quire [דרש] and you shall make search [חקר] and you shall investigate [שאל]"). The verb שאל denotes, in legal and sacral-legal settings, the asking of ques-tions in a careful examination of accusations. The verb דרש, again in legal set-tings, is used for the process of investigating accusations on the basis of exist-ing legal regulations. The verb חקר stands for cognitive, analytical examina-tion and testing; the hiphil infinitive absolute הֵיטֵב indicates the exactness of the investigation.[154] In the phrase אֱמֶת נָכוֹן הַדָּבָר, the verb כּוּן stands for assert-ing the truth of statements,[155] specifically the statements of the witnesses who heard the prophet or dreamer of dreams suggest that one can and indeed should worship a foreign deity. The parallelism of the verbs makes clear dis-tinctions impossible. The text indicates, however, that a careful investigation is made into the charges that a particular person wanted to seduce others to idolatry. While the mandate of a careful investigation is only mentioned with regard to cases involving general reports of attempted seductions of towns, it can be assumed that the same careful investigation must be conducted in cases when specific witnesses, perhaps family members, have reported the activity of a prophet who attempted to seduce to worship foreign gods.

If the investigation leads to a confirmation of the charges, the court must pronounce the death penalty. The prophet or dreamer of dreams who has been convicted in a legal investigation of inciting Israelites to worship foreign gods "shall be put to death" (יוּמַת)[156] and thus "remove" (בִעַרְתָּ) the evil from Israel. If an entire town has committed the crime of idolatrous worship, all the inhab-itants of that town shall be executed (הַכֵּה תַכֶּה) and the town shall be burnt to the ground, never to be rebuilt. The verb נכה, used mostly in the hiphil, denotes here, as in many Old Testament passages (Deut 16:16 [15]; 19:6; Num 25:14–15), the punishment of a serious transgression, here of idolatry, by executing the offender. The verb focuses on the act causing the violent death and on the fact that the offender "is removed definitively by the quickest possible means."[157] The town and its inhabitants are all "put under the ban" (הַחֲרֵם), i.e., destroyed, for abandoning YHWH by violating the first command-ment of the Decalogue.[158] A false prophet who claims to speak for Israel's God but who in fact abandons Israel's uniqueness by adapting the beliefs of God's people to the religious worldview of the idolatrous pagans shall be

---

[154] HANS F. FUHS, שאל, TDOT 14 (2004): 249–264, 254; SIEGFRIED WAGNER, דרש, TDOT 3 (1978): 293–307, 296; MATITYAHU TSEVAT, חקר, TDOT 5 (1986):148–150, 149.

[155] KLAUS KOCH, כּוּן, TDOT 7:89–101, 95.

[156] The hophal forms of מות, used both "in threats and in legal stipulations concerning the death penalty" formulates here an act-consequence prescription; KARL-JOHAN ILLMAN, HELMER RINGGREN, and HEINZ-JOSEF FABRY, מות, TDOT 8 (1997): 185–209, 201 (Illman).

[157] JOACHIM CONRAD, נכה, TDOT 9 (1998): 415–23, 418.

[158] Cf. NORBERT LOHFINK, חרם, TDOT 5 (1986): 180–199, 185, with regard to Deut 13.

carefully investigated, condemned, and executed, together with his followers, even if he performs miracles.

The author of the *Temple Scroll* closely follows the text of Deuteronomy, seeing little need to add to the legislation of the Torah regarding idolatry, with the exception of the law concerning the idolatrous city, where his halakhic modifications minimize the possibility of enforcing the law that required the destruction of an entire town. This prompts L. H. SCHIFFMAN to conclude that the author wrote in a historical context in which idolatrous practices by Jews were not a substantial problem.[159] The Zadokite provenance of the scroll and the close adherence to the laws of Deuteronomy suggests in a first-century A.D. context of a Sanhedrin trial over which the high priest presided a thorough investigation of witnesses in a death-sentence case. See the comments on 11QTemple LXI, 7–12 (No. 21). A. STROBEL refers to this text for the argument that the later rabbinic law regarding the death penalty for seducers of the people (*mesit*, *maddiakh*) was in force in the first century A.D.[160]

**(20)** 11QTemple LVI, 8–11

8 ... וְהָאִישׁ אֲשֶׁר לוֹא יִשְׁמַע וְיַעַשׂ בְּזָדוֹן לְבִלְתִּי

9 שְׁמוֹעַ אֶל הַכּוֹהֵן הָעוֹמֵד שָׁמָּה לְשָׁרֵת לְפָנַי אוֹ אֶל

10 הַשּׁוֹפֵט יוּמַת הָאִישׁ הַהוּא וּבְעַרְתָּה הָרַע מִיִשְׂרָאֵל וְכוֹל

11 הָעָם יִשְׁמְעוּ וְיִרָאוּ וְלוֹא יָזִידוּ עוֹד בְּיִשְׂרָאֵל

*Translation.* And the man who does not listen and who acts with presumption, who does not [9] listen to the priest who stands there to serve before me or to [10] the judge, that man shall be put to death. Thus you will remove the evil from Israel, and all [11] the people shall listen and fear,[161] and no one will behave presumptuously again in Israel.

*Commentary.* This text reproduces Deut 17:12–13, which is part of the law of the central tribunal (Deut 17:8–13), "the high court of referral at the central sanctuary" that decided cases too difficult for the local courts in the towns.[162]

---

[159] SCHIFFMAN, Laws concerning Idolatry, 486: "Such an analysis fits the Hasmonean period better than that of Yadin's, as the Hasmoneans had extirpated idolatry, both Jewish and non-Jewish, from the Land of Israel." YADIN, Temple Scroll, 2:230, argues that the scroll's treatment of idolatry constituted "a rebuke of Hellenizers in the Hasmonean period."

[160] STROBEL, Stunde, 83. CHILTON / BOCK, Mark, 421, cite 11QTemple LIV, 8–16 with regard to Jesus' warning concerning false prophets in Mark 13:21–22, but not in the context of Jesus' trial.

[161] JAMES H. CHARLESWORTH and JACOB MILGROM, Temple Scroll Defining Edition 11Q19 (11QTemple^a): Translation, in Temple Scroll, and Related Documents (ed. J. H. Charlesworth; The Dead Sea Scrolls 7; Tübingen: Mohr Siebeck, 2011), 1–173, 145, translate וְיִרָאוּ as "revere" (SCHIFFMAN / GROSS / RAND, Temple Scroll Defining Edition, 145), GARCÍA MARTÍNEZ / TIGCHELAAR as "fear," MAIER as "sehen."

[162] DUANE L. CHRISTENSEN, Deuteronomy (WBC 6; Dallas: Word, 2001–2002), 373.

The priests and the judge at the sanctuary investigate the matter (LVI, 2) and base their judgment on the book of Torah (LVI, 4) which they interpret with authority (LVI, 5–7). The decision reached by this court was final. Lines 8–11 address the case of a person who refuses to obey the decision of the priests and the judge of the central court at the sanctuary: he is to be executed so that "the evil" would be purged from Israel. This ruling regarding the presumptuous man (who either thinks he has superior insight into the meaning of the Torah, or who does not care about the high court's interpretation) applies whether or not the case in question is a capital offense in the first place. This text documents the death penalty for persons who disregard the considered judgment of Israel's highest court. The verb translated as "act with presumption" (זִיד) denotes arrogant behavior that disregards the decision of the priests and the judge of the highest court, who speak in the name of YHWH.[163] And the text indicates that the specific reason for the death penalty was made public: "all the people" shall hear why the presumptuous man who does not accept the ruling of the central court is condemned to death. Such a public announcement was necessary not only in the case of a presumptuous man, but in other cases as well. According to *b. Sanh.* 89a, "public announcement must be made for four (malefactors): a *mesit* (seducer), a stubborn and rebellious son, a rebellious elder, and witnesses who were proved false witnesses" (cf. No. 45). If Jesus was investigated as *mesit* and condemned as someone who disobeyed the highest court by arrogantly disregarding the priests and the judge, the death sentence becomes inevitable, and a public proclamation of both the charges and the sentence is plausible.[164]

**(21)**  11QTemple LXI, 7–12

7     ...          אִם יָקוּם עֵד חָמָס בְּאִישׁ לַעֲנוֹת

8     בּוֹ סָרָה וְעָמְדוּ שְׁנֵי הָאֲנָשִׁים אֲשֶׁר לָהֵמָּה הָרִיב לְפָנַי וְלִפְנֵי הַכּוֹהֲנִים וְהַלְוִיִּים וְלִפְנֵי

9     הַשּׁוֹפְטִים אֲשֶׁר יִהְיוּ בַיָּמִים הָהֵמָּה וְדָרְשׁוּ הַשּׁוֹפְטִים וְהִנֵּה עֵד שֶׁקֶר הֵעִיד שֶׁקֶר

10    עָנָה בְאָחִיהוּ וַעֲשִׂיתָה לּוֹ כַּאֲשֶׁר זָמַם לַעֲשׂוֹת לְאָחִיהוּ וּבִעַרְתָּה הָרַע מִקִּרְבְּכָה

11    וְהַנִּשְׁאָרִים יִשְׁמְעוּ וְיִרָאוּ וְלוֹא יוֹסִיפוּ עוֹד לַעֲשׂוֹת כַּדָּבָרהָרָע הַזֶּה בְּקִרְבְּכָה לוֹא

12    תָחוֹס עֵינְכָה עָלָיו נֶפֶשׁ בְּנֶפֶשׁ עַיִן בְּעַיִן שֵׁן בְּשֵׁן יָד בְּיָד רֶגֶל בְּרֶגֶל

---

[163] JOSEPH SCHARBERT, זִיד, זוּד, TDOT 4 (1980): 46–51. In 1QH VI, 35 the "presumptuous" are the enemies of the community who oppose the will of God with premeditated defiance (ibid. 49). LXX translates יַעֲשֶׂה בְזָדוֹן in Deut 17:12 with ποιήσῃ ἐν ὑπερηφανίᾳ; BDAG defines ὑπερηφανία as "a state of undue sense of one's importance bordering on insolence, *arrogance, haughtiness, pride.*"

[164] On the last point cf. STROBEL, Stunde, 6 n. 3, arguing against LIETZMANN, Prozess, 313-22, who asserted that any report about a trial of Jesus before the Sanhedrin is suspect since there would not have been people who witnessed the legal proceedings.

*Translation.* If a malicious witness should stand up against a man to accuse him [8] of wrongdoing, the two men between whom there is the legal dispute shall stand before me, the priests, the Levites, and [9] the judges who will be there in those days; and the judges shall investigate. And if it happens that the witness has given false testimony, falsely [10] accusing his brother, then you shall do to him so as he intended to do to his brother. Thus you shall remove the evil from among you. [11] The rest shall hear it and fear so that they will not do such an evil thing among you again. Not [12] shall your eye have pity on him: a life for a life, eye for eye, tooth for tooth, hand for hand, foot for foot.

*Commentary.* This text, which reproduces the law of testimony in Deut 19:15–21, addresses the case of a malicious witness (עֵד חָמָס),[165] who deliberately makes a false declaration against the accused (לַעֲנוֹת בּוֹ סָרָה)[166] before the high court at the sanctuary (לְפָנַי, "before me"). When the lie is uncovered during the investigation of the court, the false witness is to receive the punishment that his testimony was intended to bring upon the accused. The formula וּבִעַרְתָּה הָרָע מִקִּרְבְּכָה ("thus you shall remove the evil from among you") shows that the false witness is to be put to death.[167] Note that in the law of judges (LI, 11–18), the *Temple Scroll* stipulates that judges who take bribes shall be subject to the death penalty (LI, 16–18). This is an original section that adds material to Deut 16:18–21. The author concludes by linking Deut 1:17 (לֹא תָגוּרוּ מִפְּנֵי־אִישׁ, "you shall not be afraid of any man"), which speaks of the avoidance of favoritism in judgment, with Deut 18:22 (לֹא תָגוּר מִמֶּנּוּ, "do not be afraid of him"), which speaks of the obligation to execute the false prophet. The author concluded that "just as the death penalty was required for the false prophet, so it was for judges who accepted bribes."[168] This ruling fits the view of the author that judicial corruption defiles the Temple (LI, 13–15).

---

[165] HERBERT HAAG, חָמָס, TDOT 4 (1980): 476–87, 484, thinks that in Deut 19:16, the עֵד חָמָס is "the plaintiff, who with his false accusation, makes an attempt on the defendant's life," with reference to ISAC LEO SEELIGMANN, Zur Terminologie für das Gerichtsverfahren im Wortschatz des biblischen Hebräisch, in Hebräische Wortforschung (FS W. Baumgartner; VTSup 16; Leiden: Brill, 1967), 251–278, 263.

[166] Cf. HALOT s.v. II סָרָה 2 "falsehood", with דִּבֶּר "to speak falsely," with I ענה "to make a false declaration (in court)" (Deut 19:16).

[167] HAAG, חָמָס 484, regarding Deut 19:18–19. Cf. SAMUEL BELKIN, Philo and the Oral Law: The Philonic Interpretation of Biblical law in Relation to the Palestinian Halakah (HSS 9; Cambridge: Harvard University Press, 1940), 147–49.

[168] SCHIFFMAN, Deuteronomic Paraphrase, 463–468; LAWRENCE H. SCHIFFMAN, The Prohibition of Judicial Corruption in the Dead Sea Scrolls, Philo, Josephus, and Talmudic Law [1998], in The Courtyards of the House of the Lord: Studies on the Temple Scroll (ed. F. García Martínez; STDJ 75; Leiden: Brill, 2008), 189–212, 197. For the following point cf. ibid. 195–96. Philo, Josephus, and the rabbinic sources do not specify a particular punishment for taking bribes by judges to pervert justice, "seeing these simply as negative commandments (לֹאוִיל) which normally incur the penalty of flogging" (ibid. 210).

During Jesus' trial, false witnesses came forward (Mark 14:56: πολλοὶ γὰρ ἐψευδομαρτύρουν κατ' αὐτοῦ; 14:57: τινες ἀναστάντες ἐψευδομαρτύρουν κατ' αὐτοῦ; Matt 26:60: προσελθόντων ψευδομαρτύρων), some of which accused Jesus of conspiring to destroy the Temple. According to Mark 14:55, "the chief priests and the whole council" looked for testimony they could use to convict Jesus of a crime punishable by death. The witnesses who had been summoned did not agree, and their testimony was not used to convict Jesus (Mark 14:56, 59). Neither Mark nor Matthew states that the members of the Sanhedrin were summoning false witnesses; had they done so, they would have coordinated the testimony, resulting in accusations by two or three witnesses that would have thus been confirmed as accurate and would have led to a conviction. Neither Mark nor Matthew comments on what happened to these witnesses: if the law of Deut 19:15–21 had been applied, they would have had to have been punished by death since some of them evidently accused Jesus of serious crimes. Had Jesus threatened to destroy the Temple, he would have been subject to severe punishment, probably execution. See Josephus, *B. J.* 6.300–309 (No. 65).

## (22) 11QTemple LXIV, 6–13

כִּי ...  6

7 יִהְיֶה אִישׁ רָכִיל בְּעַמִּי[169] וּמַשְׁלִים אֶת עַמִּי לְגוֹי נֵכָר וְעוֹשֶׂה רָעָה בְעַמִּי

8 וּתְלִיתֶמָה אוֹתוֹ עַל הָעֵץ וְיָמֵת עַל פִּי שְׁנַיִם עֵדִים וְעַל פִּי שְׁלוֹשָׁה עֵדִים

9 יוּמַת וְהֵמָּה יִתְלוּ אוֹתוֹ הָעֵץ VACAT? כִּי יִהְיֶה בְאִישׁ חֵטְא מִשְׁפַּט מָוֶת וְיִבְרַח אֶל

10 תּוֹךְ הַגּוֹאִים וִיקַלֵּל אֶת עַמּוֹ [א]ֶת בְּנֵי יִשְׂרָאֵל וּתְלִיתֶמָה גַם אוֹתוֹ עַל הָעֵץ

11 וְיָמוּת וְלוֹא תָלִין נִבְלָתֶמָה עַל הָעֵץ כִּי קָבוֹר תִּקוֹבְרֶמָ(ה)[170] בַּיּוֹם הַהוּא כִּי

12 מְקוּלְלֵי אֱלוֹהִים וַאֲנָשִׁים תָּלוּי עַל הָעֵץ וְלוֹא תְטַמֵּא אֶת הָאֲדָמָה אֲשֶׁר אָנוֹכִי

13 נוֹתֵן לְכָה נַחֲלָה ...

*Translation.* If ⁷ a man passes on information against[171] my people, and betrays my people to a foreign nation, and does evil against my people, ⁸ you shall hang him on a tree, and he shall die. On the testimony[172] of two wit-

---

[169] Following QIMRON, MAIER, SCHIFFMAN; cf. QIMRON, The Dead Sea Scrolls, 1:203, who now reads עמי. Differently YADIN, PUECH, GARCÍA MARTÍNEZ / TIGCHELAAR, and STEUDEL who read עמו.

[170] The copyist erased ה after מ. QIMRON adds ה in brackets; SCHIFFMAN / GROSS / RAND, Temple Scroll Defining Edition, 396, and STEUDEL omit ה, with an explanatory note.

[171] GARCÍA MARTÍNEZ; cf. HALOT s.v. בְּ 12b "hostile *against*." CHARLESWORTH / MILGROM, Temple Scroll Defining Edition, 167, assume a locative sense: "an informer among my people." MAIER switched from an adversarial understanding ("wenn ein Mann Nachrichten über mein Volk weitergibt;" MAIER, Texte vom Toten Meer, 1:425) to a locative meaning ("wenn ein verräterischer Mann in meinem Volk vorhanden sein sollte;" MAIER, Tempelrolle, 280).

[172] In the phrase עַל פִּי, the term פֶּה ("mouth") means "declaration," in a legal context "evi-

nesses or on the testimony of three witnesses, [9] he shall be put to death, and they shall hang him on the tree. *Blank.* If a person is guilty of a sin requiring a judgment of death, and he escapes [10] among the nations and curses my people, the sons of Israel, you shall also hang him on the tree, [11] and he shall die. And you shall not leave their corpses on the tree; you shall bury them on that day because [12] those hanged on a tree are cursed by God and the people. And you shall not defile the land which I [13] give to you as an inheritance.

*Commentary.* This text begins the author's discussion of measures that serve to protect the community. This section treats crimes against the people of Israel, explaining what kinds of people merit the penalties of Deut 21:22–23.[173] Two types of crime are mentioned that are punishable by death. (1) The death penalty is stipulated for cases of treason involving slander or deception (רָכִיל)[174] against Israel,[175] abandoning (מַשְׁלִים)[176] the people to a foreign nation, and committing evil acts (עוֹשֶׂה רָעָה) against Israel (lines 6–9). (2) The death penalty is stipulated for cases in which a Jewish person who has committed a crime and refuses to be tried by a Jewish court escapes (יִבְרַח) to a pagan city, where he curses (יקַלֵּל) God's people (lines 9–11). After such a criminal has been executed by suspension, the corpse must be taken down before nightfall in order not to pollute the land. The stipulation of a speedy burial, formulated with plural forms (lines 11–12), applies to both these cases. Execution is to be preceded by a trial in which at least two witnesses (שְׁנַיִם עֵדִים) – preferably three witnesses (שְׁלוֹשָׁה עֵדִים) – give evidence. In view of the fact that CD IX, 16–23 requires three witnesses for capital matters (see No. 49), the stipulation that (apparently) two witnesses might suffice in testifying in a capital case can be explained either by the non-sectarian origin of the *Temple Scroll* – the two texts representing different legal traditions – or by the fact that the *Temple Scroll* envisions special treatment of informers, being less rigorous in the case

---

dence" (HALOT s.v. פֶּה 8). Cf. GARCÍA MARTÍNEZ; CHARLESWORTH / MILGROM translate "on the testimony of [lit. mouth of]," STEUDEL "Aussage," MAIER "auf Grund von."

[173] Differently MOSHE J. BERNSTEIN, *Midrash Halakhah* at Qumran? 11QTemple 64:6–13 and Deuteronomy 21:22–23, Gesher 7 (1979): 145–166, who argues that the legal material of this text came not from an interpretation of Deut 21 but from a different source. For the discussion cf. MICHAEL O. WISE, A Critical Study of the Temple Scroll from Qumran Cave 11 (SAOC 49; Chicago: Oriental Institute of the University of Chicago, 1990), 121–27; DAVID W. CHAPMAN, Ancient Jewish and Christian Perceptions of Crucifixion (WUNT 2.244; Tübingen: Mohr Siebeck, 2008), 129–30.

[174] The term רְכִיל describes dishonorable activities, with the connotation of a person engaging in "swindle" and "deception;" cf. EDOUARD LIPIŃSKI, רָכִיל, TDOT 13:498–99. PUECH, Qumrân Grotte 4.XVIII, 101, interprets the expression איש רכיל as "traitor against his people," i.e. as spy, with reference to Ezek 22:9; 1QS VII, 15–16; 1QHᵃ XIII, 27.

[175] Or among Israel; cf. CHARLESWORTH / MILGROM: "informer among my people."

[176] KARL-JOHAN ILLMAN, שָׁלֵם, TDOT 15:97–105, here 102–2, has "abandon" for the hiphil of the verb in Isa 38:12–13; cf. HALOT s.v. שלם hif. 2 "to deliver up."

of such criminals.[177] For a discussion of the mode of execution – suspension, perhaps crucifixion – see below (No. 274). Jesus' prophecy of the destruction of the Jerusalem Temple (Mark 13:2, 14–23 / Matt 24:2, 15–28 / Luke 21:6, 20–24 referring to "armies," "nations," and "Gentiles") could be construed as constituting the first of these crimes. Announcing the destruction of the Temple by foreign armies without expecting God's intervention before, during, or after their invasion is tantamount to abandoning Israel to a Gentile nation, thus committing – or at least condoning – an evil act.

## (23) CD IX, 1

כָּל אָדָם אֲשֶׁר יַחֲרִים אָדָם מֵאָדָם בְּחוּקֵּי הַגּוֹיִם[178] לְהָמִית הוּא

*Translation.* Any man who destroys[179] a man among men according to the statutes of the Gentiles shall be put to death.

*Commentary.* Column IX of CD has been recognized as the continuation of column XVI.[180] The column begins with a law about a "ban" of destruction. This law stipulates the death sentence for any Jew who seeks recourse before a Gentile court. The requirement that all cases must be tried before Jewish courts implies the exclusive validity of Jewish law for the members of the Jewish people.[181] The law is based on a legal exegesis of Lev 20:23 ("You

---

[177] LAWRENCE H. SCHIFFMAN, Sectarian Law in the Dead Sea Scrolls: Courts, Testimony and Penal Code (BJS 33; Chico: Scholars Press, 1983), 77–78.

[178] QIMRON, The Dead Sea Scrolls, 1:41, reads הגואים (line 192).

[179] GARCÍA MARTÍNEZ / TIGCHELAAR translate יחרים "vows to destruction," LOHSE: "einen Bannspruch verhängt;" MAIER has "weiht," thus also BEN ZION WACHOLDER, The New Damascus Document. The Midrash on the Eschatological Torah: Reconstruction, Translation, and Commentary (STDJ 56; Leiden: Brill, 2004), 82–83, who reads (instead of כל אדם) כל אדם חרם: "any devotion in which a person proscribes another person." See 4Q266 Frag. 6 II, 8 and JOSEPH M. BAUMGARTEN, Qumran Cave 4.XIII: The Damascus Document (4Q266–4Q273) (DJD 18; Oxford: Clarendon Press, 1996), 66: the quotation formula at the beginning of the line should be followed by the text of Lev 27:29; see also 4Q270 Frag. 6 III, 16; cf. JOSEPH M. BAUMGARTEN, Damascus Document 4Q266–273 (4QD^a–h), in Damascus Document II: Some Works on the Torah, and Related Documents (ed. J. H. Charlesworth; The Dead Sea Scrolls 3; Tübingen: Mohr Siebeck, 2006), 1–185, 144 with n. 146. Cf. HALOT s.v. חרם I, hifil: "1. to put under a ban, to devote to destruction; 2. to dedicate something to YHWH by the ban and rule out redemption."

[180] Cf. JOSEPH M. BAUMGARTEN / DANIEL R. SCHWARTZ, Damascus Document (CD), in Damascus Document, War Scroll, and Related Documents (ed. J. H. Charlesworth; The Dead Sea Scrolls 2; Tübingen: Mohr Siebeck, 1995), 4–57, 5; AHARON SHEMESH, Scriptural Interpretations in the Damascus Document and their Parallels in Rabbinic Midrash, in The Damascus Document: A Centennial of Discovery (ed. J. M. Baumgarten, E. G. Chazon, and A. Pinnick; STDJ 34; Leiden: Brill, 2002), 168–69.

[181] Cf. SCHIFFMAN, Sectarian Law, 10; for the next point cf. ibid. 20 n. 16. SHEMESH, Scriptural Interpretations, 169–73, argues that the law in CD IX, 1 is based on the laws of dedication in Lev 27:28–29.

shall not follow the practices of the nation that I am driving out before you. Because they did all these things, I abhorred them"); Lev 27:28–29 ("Nothing that a person owns that has been devoted to destruction for the LORD, be it human or animal, or inherited landholding, may be sold or redeemed; every devoted thing is most holy to the LORD"); Gen 9:6 ("Whoever sheds the blood of a human, by a human shall that person's blood be shed; for in his own image God made humankind"). The use of חרם for people who deliver others to their death by hostile authorities is also found Micah 7:2 ("The faithful have disappeared from the land, and there is no one left who is upright; they all lie in wait for blood, and they hunt each other with nets [יָצוּדוּ חֵרֶם]"); *Targum Jonathan* renders the last line as גְּבַר יַת אֲחוּהִי מָסְרִין לְגַמֵּירָא ("each man delivers his brother to destruction").[182] The text may deal with idolatrous vows.[183]

Besides the delivery of a man to his death by Gentile law (CD IX, 1), other offenses listed as capital crimes in Qumran legal texts but not in biblical law are seditious talk against the community (CD XII, 3), entry into the Temple by a woman who has recently given birth and is in a state of uncleanness (4Q266 Frag. 6 II, 9–10), and disclosure of national secrets to the Gentiles (4Q270 Frag. 2 II, 13). Offenses for which biblical law stipulated the death penalty and which are mentioned in Qumran legal texts are necromancy (CD XII, 3), the deliberate violation of the Sabbath (CD XII, 3–4), and premarital promiscuity by a betrothed virgin (4Q159 Frag. 2–4, 8–9). J. M. BAUMGARTEN argues that the Qumran community accepted, in principle, the biblical death penalties but had moral scruples about taking a human life, with the result that the most severe penalty imposed for serious infractions of the law seems to have been expulsion, which was conceptually tantamount to death: the person who was expelled may die due to starvation.[184]

---

[182] BAUMGARTEN, Qumran Cave 4.XIII, 66; comment on 4Q266 Fag. 8 II, 8.

[183] WACHOLDER, New Damascus Document, 316. DONALD W. PARRY, Notes on Divine Name Avoidance in Scriptural Units of the Legal Texts of Qumran, in Legal Texts and Legal Issues (Proceedings of the Second Meeting of the International Organization for Qumran Studies, Cambridge, 1995. FS Joseph M. Baumgarten; ed. M. J. Bernstein, F. García Martínez, and J. Kampen; STDJ 23; Leiden: Brill, 1997), 437–449, 448 n. 22, suggests that the author of CD IX, 1–15, citing Amos 5:26–27, deliberately avoids "revelatory formulas."

[184] JOSEPH M. BAUMGARTEN, The Avoidance of the Death Penalty in Qumran Law, in Reworking the Bible: Apocryphal and Related Texts at Qumran (Proceedings of a Joint Symposium by the Orion Center for the Study of the Dead Sea Scrolls and Associated Literature and the Hebrew University Institute for Advanced Studies Research Group on Qumran, 15–17 January, 2002; ed. E. G. Chazon, D. Dimant, and R. A. Clements; STDJ 58; Leiden: Brill, 2005), 31–38. In addition to a close reading of the texts, BAUMGARTEN points to 1QS X, 17–18; 4Q275 Frag. 2: the members of the general assembly shall not lean to excessive harshness in punishment, they were made to "solemnly promise not to put any man to death," and Josephus, *B. J.* 2.144: when an Essene who had been expelled was "on the verge of death" due to starvation, this "was deemed to be a sufficient fulfillment of the sentence" (ibid. 38).

**(24)** 4Q266 Frag. 6 II, 5–10

5 ואשה אשר [תזרי]ע וילדה זכר [וטמאה א]ת שבעת [הימים]185
6 [כ]י[מי] נדת [דאותה וביום השמיני ימול בשר] ערלת[ו]
7 [ושלושת ושלושים יום תשב בדם טוהרה ואם נקבה תלד]
8 [וטמאה שבועים כנדת ד]אותה ו[ששה וששים יום תשב בדם]
9 [טוהרה והיאה] לא תוכל [קודש ולא תבו אל המקדש]
10 [כי מ]שפט מות הו[א]ה

*Translation.* And a woman who conceives and bears a male child shall be unclean for seven days ⁶ as in the days of her menstrual impurity. And on the eighth day the flesh of his foreskin shall be circumcised. For ⁷ thirty-three days she shall remain in her blood purification. If she bears a female child ⁸ she shall be unclean two weeks as in her menstrual impurity. And sixty-six days she shall remain in her blood ⁹ purification. And she shall not eat any holy thing, nor come into the sanctuary ¹⁰ for it is a capital precept.

*Commentary.* Following stipulations concerning menstruation, the author of 4Q266 turns to laws concerning childbearing, paraphrasing Lev 12:2–4. Lines 9–10 state that entering the Temple during the mother's period of defilement is a capital offense. This law has been called extreme In view of the statement in CD XII, 3–5 absolving from capital punishment all who have performed prohibited labor on the Sabbath (a capital offense according to rabbinic law) and stipulating incarceration instead.[186] J. M. BAUMGARTEN refers to Num 19:20 as an explanation:[187] "But if a person who is unclean does not purify himself, he must be cut off from the community, because he has defiled the sanctuary of the Lord: the water of cleansing has not been sprinkled on him, and he is unclean." If the author developed his ruling from this passage, he interpreted כרת ("to cut off") as implying a capital offense: biblical texts which prescribe כרת similarly refer to death penalty cases.

**(25)** Philo, *De specialibus legibus* 1.54–55

Τῶν δ' ἀπὸ τοῦ ἔθνους εἴ τινες καθυφίενται τὴν τοῦ ἑνὸς τιμήν, ὡς λιπόντες τὴν ἀναγκαιοτάτην τάξιν εὐσεβείας καὶ ὁσιότητος ταῖς ἀνωτάτω τιμωρίαις ὀφείλουσι κολάζεσθαι, σκότος αἱρούμενοι πρὸ αὐγοειδεστάτου φωτὸς καὶ τυφλὴν ἀπεργαζόμενοι διάνοιαν ὀξὺ καθορᾶν δυναμένην ⁵⁵ καὶ ἐπιτετράφθαι

---

¹⁸⁵ Restorations according to BAUMGARTEN / SCHWARTZ, Damascus Document, 40–43; ABEGG, Qumran Sectarian Manuscripts.

¹⁸⁶ WACHOLDER, New Damascus Document, 273.

¹⁸⁷ BAUMGARTEN / SCHWARTZ, Damascus Document, 42 n. 320. On bodily discharges in CD and related manuscripts cf. IAN C. WERRETT, Ritual Purity and the Dead Sea Scrolls (STDJ 72; Leiden: Brill, 2007), 46–60.

δὲ καλὸν ἅπασι τοῖς ζῆλον ἔχουσιν ἀρετῆς ἐκ χειρὸς ἀναπράττειν ἀνυπερθέτως τὰς τιμωρίας, μήτ᾽ εἰς δικαστήριον μήτ᾽ εἰς βουλευτήριον μήτε
συνόλως ἐπ᾽ ἀρχὴν ἄγοντας, ἀλλὰ τῷ παραστάντι μισοπονήρῳ πάθει καὶ
φιλοθέῳ καταχρῆσθαι πρὸς τὰς τῶν ἀσεβῶν ἀπαραιτήτους κολάσεις,
νομίσαντας αὐτοὺς ὑπὸ τοῦ καιροῦ τὰ πάντα γεγενῆσθαι, βουλευτάς,
δικαστάς, στρατηγούς, ἐκκλησιαστάς, κατηγόρους, μάρτυρας, νόμους, δῆμον,
ἵνα μηδενὸς ὄντος ἐμποδὼν ἄφοβοι σὺν ἀδείᾳ πολλῇ προαγωνίζωνται
ὁσιότητος

*Translation.* But if some people of the nation compromise the honor due to
the One, they shall suffer the utmost penalties, because they have abandoned
the most important ordinance of piety and holiness, because they have chosen
darkness in preference to the brightest light and blinded the mind which had
the power of keen vision. [55] And it is well that all who are zealous for virtue
should be permitted to inflict the penalties without delay, without bringing the
offender before a jury or council or any magistrate, as they give vent to the
feelings which consume them, hating evil and loving God which urges them
to inflict punishment without mercy on the impious. They should think that
the occasion has made them councillors, judges, governors, members of the
peoples' assembly, accusers, witnesses, laws, the people, everything in fact, so
that they may fight for holiness without fear or hindrance with full indemnity.

*Commentary.* Philo's treatise *On the Special Laws* is an exposition of the
Decalogue (*Spec.* 1.1). Book 1 treats the first and second commandments: the
existence and worship of the one true God,and the prohibition of worshiping
idols; Book 2 discusses laws that can be assigned to the third, fourth, and fifth
commandments: not taking God's name in vain, keeping the sabbath, and
honoring parents. Having just warned the proselytes not to blaspheme the
gods worshiped in the cities (*Spec.* 1.53), he turns to a discussion of cases in
which Jews betray the honor due to God, which constitutes the crime of apostasy, falling away from the One true God. He describes apostasy as refusing to
give to God the honor due to him, as preferring darkness to the brightest light,
and as separating oneself from the people who have the power of clear vision,
i.e., who know God.[188] The punishment described as "the utmost penalties"
(ταῖς ἀνωτάτω τιμωρίαις) is capital punishment, as is indicated by the example of the Pinehas episode in the subsequent comments (*Spec.* 1.56–57; cf.
Num 25:1–13), and by his summary of the punishment to be exacted on those
who break the first five commandments (*Spec.* 2.242–243; No. 28). Jews who
have abandoned religious observance shall be punished with "the supreme
penalty of extermination."[189] Philo asserts that Jews who are (emotionally)

---

[188] For a fuller discussion of this passage cf. SELAND, Establishment Violence, 103–36.

[189] LOUIS H. FELDMAN, Philo's Portrayal of Moses in the Context of Ancient Judaism
(Notre Dame: University of Notre Dame Press, 2007), 107.

zealous[190] for virtue shall put the offender to death – without courts, judges, or due process, without witnesses and without any regard for the laws. The offenders should be executed "without delay" (ἀνυπερθέτως) and "without mercy" (ἀπαραιτήτους).[191] Philo's willingness to consider, even welcome and recommend, the circumvention of the traditional legal process in dealing with Jews who sell out God's honor is all the more remarkable when we consider the fact that he was not the leader of a rebel movement but a Torah scholar.

**(26)** Philo, *De specialibus legibus* 1.315–316

Κἂν μέντοι τις ὄνομα καὶ σχῆμα προφητείας ὑποδύς, ἐνθουσιᾶν καὶ κατέχεσθαι δοκῶν, ἄγῃ πρὸς τὴν τῶν νενομισμένων κατὰ πόλεις θρησκείαν θεῶν, οὐκ ἄξιον προσέχειν ἀπατωμένους ὀνόματι προφήτου· γόης γὰρ ἀλλ' οὐ προφήτης ἐστὶν ὁ τοιοῦτος, ἐπειδὴ ψευδόμενος λόγια καὶ χρησμοὺς ἐπλάσατο ³¹⁶ κἂν ἀδελφὸς ἢ υἱὸς ἢ θυγάτηρ ἢ γυνὴ ἡ οἰκουρὸς ἢ γνήσιος φίλος ἤ τις ἕτερος εὔνους εἶναι δοκῶν εἰς τὰ ὅμοια ἐνάγῃ προτρέπων συνασμενίζειν τοῖς πολλοῖς καὶ ἐπὶ τὰ αὐτὰ ἱερὰ καὶ τὰς αὐτὰς σπονδάς τε καὶ θυσίας ἀφικνεῖσθαι, κολαστέον ὡς δήμιον καὶ κοινὸν ἐχθρὸν ὄντα ὀλίγα φροντίσαντας οἰκειότητος καὶ τὰς παραινέσεις αὐτοῦ διαγγελτέον πᾶσι τοῖς εὐσεβείας ἐρασταῖς, οἳ ἀνυπερθέτῳ τάχει ταῖς κατ' ἀνδρὸς ἀνοσίου τιμωρίαις ἐπιδραμοῦνται κρίνοντες εὐαγὲς τὸ κατ' αὐτοῦ φονᾶν

*Translation.* And if anyone assumes the name and guise of a prophet and, claiming to be inspired, seeks to lead us to the worship of the gods that are recognized in the different cities, we ought not to listen to him and be deceived by the name of a prophet. For such a person is not a prophet but an impostor, since his oracles and his pronouncements are falsehoods that he has invented. ³¹⁶ And if a brother or son or daughter or wife or housekeeper or friend, however legitimate, or anyone else who seems to be friendly, seeks to lead us in a similar course, exhorting us to take pleasure in the same things as the crowds, visit their temples and join them in their libations and sacrifices, we must punish him as a public and general enemy, having no regard for the relationship that binds us to him. And we should report his proposals to all the lovers of piety, who will rush to inflict punishment on the impious man with speed and without delay, and regard it as a religious duty to seek his death.

*Commentary.* In the context of describing what God wants of his people in *Spec.* 1.299–311, drawing on Deut 10:12–21, and emphasizing the importance of clinging to God in *Spec.* 1.312–314, using Deut 12:29–31, Philo turns

---

[190] On "zeal" (ζῆλος) in Philo cf. SELAND, Establishment Violence, 126–31.
[191] With regard to punishments, the term ἀπαραίτητος means "not to be averted by prayers, inevitable, unmerciful" (LSJ).

to false prophets, who are treated in Deut 13:2–11.[192] Philo omits the description of the seducer as a person who has dreams and performs signs and wonders. He focuses on the seducer as a false prophet who promulgates invented oracles. Claiming to have prophetic inspiration (ἐνθουσιᾶν), he seeks to entice Jewish people to worship other gods beside the One true God. Such activity constitutes deception (ἀπατωμένους).[193] Such a person is not a prophet but an "impostor" (γόης), a charlatan who leads the people astray.[194] The reference to brothers, sons, and other relatives clarifies that the false prophet who seeks to seduce the people is a Jewish person. Philo advises that when the community deals with a seducer of the people who falsely claims divine inspiration, vigilante actions are permitted, even necessary. Those who witness the activities of such an impostor shall inform "all lovers of piety" (πᾶσι τοῖς εὐσεβείας ἐρασταῖς) and arrange for his punishment as "a public and general enemy" (δήμιον καὶ κοινὸν ἐχθρόν). When the pious rush to the place where the seducer is being held, he ought to be put to death "with speed and without delay" (ἀνυπερθέτῳ τάχει). The crime of false prophet and deception of the people was so serious that the transgressor was to be killed on the spot.

**(27)** Philo, *De specialibus legibus* 2.27–28

δίκαι δὲ κατ᾽ ἐπιόρκων αἱ μὲν ἀνάκεινται τῷ θεῷ, αἱ δὲ ἀνθρώποις, θεῷ μὲν αἱ ἀνωτάτω καὶ μέγισται ἵλεως γὰρ οὐ γίνεται τοῖς οὕτως ἀσεβοῦσιν, ἀλλὰ μένειν εἰς ἀεὶ δυσκαθάρτους ἐᾷ, δικαίως, οἶμαι, καὶ προσηκόντως· ὁ γὰρ ἀμελήσας τί δεινὸν εἰ ἀνταμεληθήσετ οἷς δίδωσι τὰ ἴσα καρπούμενος; [28] αἱ δ᾽ ἀπ᾽ ἀνθρώπων διάφοροι, θάνατος ἢ πληγαί, τῶν μὲν ἀμεινόνων καὶ περιττῶν εἰς εὐσέβειαν θανάτου δίκας βεβαιούντων, τῶν δὲ μαλακώτερον χρωμένων ὀργαῖς δημοσίᾳ μάστιγι τυπτόντων ἀναφανδὸν ἐν κοινῷ· εἰσὶ δὲ καὶ πληγαὶ τοῖς μὴ δουλοπρεπέσιν οὐκ ἔλαττον δίκης θανάτου

*Translation.* As regards the penalties for perjury, some depend on God, some on human beings. The highest and the greatest are from God, who is not gracious to people who commit such impiety, but allows them to remain forever in their all but hopeless uncleanness, a just and fitting penalty, I hold. For the person who is careless in such dangerous matters,[195] how can he complain if he is ignored in his turn, being repaid in kind? [28] The penalties which are given by men are different, being death or the lash. The better people whose piety is extraordinary affirm the death penalty, while those who have a more gentle disposition have the offenders scourged by order of the state in a public

---

[192] For Philo, *Spec.* 1.315–318 cf. SELAND, Establishment Violence, 136–60.

[193] The LXX of Deut 13 uses πλανάω instead of ἀπατάω.

[194] The term γόης also designates a sorcerer, wizzard, or cheat (LSJ).

[195] COLSON translates "for he who has ignored God."

place and before the eyes of all people. Except to people who have the disposition of a slave, a flogging is not inferior to the penalty of death.

*Commentary.* Philo treats the third commandment in *Spec.* 2.1–38, confining it to perjury. The Torah has no specific punishment for perjury, in contrast to the punishment for bearing false witness, which was punishable by death (Exod 20:7; Lev 24:16). Philo knows of two punishments: execution and flogging. He prefers the stricter penalty, viz. death, as *Spec.* 2.252 (No. 29) confirms. Philo is not a "liberal" Jew with a more gentle disposition: he sees himself as belonging to the "better people," whose piety is superior to that of the others.[196] Philo suggests that oaths are best avoided since an oath may turn out, accidentally, to be false, with the consequence that the divine name was profaned as a result (*Spec.* 2.2–3). Instead of taking an oath in the name of God, an oath that cannot be avoided could be taken "by -----" with no reference to anybody after it, or in the name of "earth, sun, stars, heaven, the whole universe" appealing to the certainty of the existence of the earth (or the sun) as the basis for the truthfulness of the statement that is being made (*Spec.* 2.4–5).[197] L. H. SCHIFFMAN sees a parallel development from 1QS VI, 27 – VII, 2 to CD XV, 1–5 and in other sources of the Second Temple period, as in early Tannaitic traditions, which have reservations about the use of swearing oaths but also know of the use of the name of God – the Tetragrammaton as well as other names – in oaths, requiring that "judicial oaths be taken by the Tetragrammaton."[198] In sum, according to Philo, the person who swears false oaths deserves the death penalty.

**(28)**  Philo, *De specialibus legibus* 2.242–243

Τὰ μὲν δὴ κατὰ τὴν προτέραν δέλτον πέντε κεφάλαια νόμων καὶ ὅσα τῶν κατὰ μέρος εἰς ἕκαστον ἐλάμβανε τὴν ἀναφορὰν διεξῆλθον χρὴ δὲ καὶ τὰς ὁρισθείσας ἐπὶ τῇ τούτων παραβάσει τιμωρίας δηλῶσαι. [243] κοινὸς μὲν οὖν ἐστι κατὰ πάντων θάνατος δι' ἣν ἔχει τἀδικήματα πρὸς ἄλληλα συγγένειαν

*Translation.* I have now discussed the five heads of the laws belonging to the first table, and all the particular enactments which may be classed under each of the five.[199] But I must now also state the penalties stipulated for transgressions of these laws. [243] They have one common punishment, namely death, the result of the close relationship which the offenses have to each other.

---

[196] Cf. SELAND, Establishment Violence, 169–70.

[197] Cf. SCHIFFMAN, Sectarian Law, 139.

[198] SCHIFFMAN, Sectarian Law, 140, with reference to *m. Šebuʿot* 4.13, for the latter point *Sifre* Num 14 (ed. Horovitz p. 19); *Mekhilta᾿ de-Rabbi Ishmael* Mishpaṭim 16 (ed. Horovitz-Rabin p. 303); *b. Šebuʿot* 35 baraita.

[199] The translation follows here COLSON; cf. YONGE, who has "all the particular points which had any reference to any individual."

*Commentary.* At the end of his treatment of the first five commandments (κεφάλαια, "heads"), Philo asserts that the penalty for violating these five commandments is death. He then goes on to comment on the punishments and the reason for the death penalty: first on the punishment for breaking the fifth commandment, i.e., honoring the parents (2.243b–248), then for breaking the fourth, i.e., profaning the Sabbath (2.249–251), the third, i.e., the prohibition of giving false witness (2.252–254), the first, i.e., denying the existence of the true God (2.255a), and the second, i.e., the prohibition of worshiping idols (2.255b–256).

**(29)** Philo, *De specialibus legibus* 2.252–254

τοῖς μάρτυρα καλοῦσιν ἐπὶ μὴ ἀληθεῖ θεὸν ὥρισται δίκη θανάτου· προσηκόν-
τως· οὐδὲ γὰρ ἄνθρωπος τῶν μετρίων ἀνέξεταί ποτε παρακληθεὶς συνεπιγρά-
ψασθαι ψεύδεσιν, ἀλλ᾽ ἐχθρὸν ἄπιστον ὑπολαβεῖν ἄν μοι δοκεῖ τὸν εἰς ταῦτα
προτρέποντα. ²⁵³ ὅθεν ῥητέον· τὸν ὀμνύντα μάτην ἐπ᾽ ἀδίκῳ θεὸς ὁ τὴν φύσιν
ἵλεως οὔποτε τῆς αἰτίας ἀπαλλάξει δυσκάθαρτον καὶ μιαρὸν ὄντα κἂν
διαφύγῃ τὰς ἀπ᾽ ἀνθρώπων τιμωρίας. διαδράσεται δ᾽ οὐδέποτε· μυρίοι γὰρ
ἔφοροι, ζηλωταὶ νόμων, φύλακες τῶν πατρίων ἀκριβέστατοι, ἐπὶ καταλεύσει
τι δρῶσιν ἀμειλίκτως ἔχοντες· εἰ μὴ ἄρα ἐπὶ μὲν ἀτιμίᾳ πατρὸς ἢ μητρὸς
φονᾶν ἄξιον, ἐπὶ δ᾽ ὀνόματι τῷ καὶ αὐτῆς εὐκλεεστέρῳ σεμνότητος ὑπ᾽ ἀσεβῶν ἀτιμουμένῳ μετριώτερον οἰστέον ²⁵⁴ ἀλλ᾽ οὐχ οὕτως ἐστί τις ἀνόητος, ὡς
ἕνεκα τῶν ἐλαττόνων κτείνων τοὺς αἰτίους ἐπὶ τοῖς μείζοσιν ἐᾶν· μεῖζον δ᾽
ἀσέβημα τοῦ πρὸς, γονεῖς, κακηγορουμένους, καί, ὑβριζομένους τὸ περὶ τὴν
ἱερὰν πρόσρησιν θεοῦ γενόμενον ἐκ ψευδορκίας

*Translation.* For people who call God as a witness to assertions which are not true, death is the stipulated punishment, and rightly so, for a person, if he is reasonable, will not tolerate a summon to be named jointly as a witness to an untruth, but would, it seems to me, regard anyone who proposed such a thing as an enemy not to be trusted. ²⁵³ Therefore we must say that God, even though gracious by nature, will never set free from guilt the person who swears falsely to an injustice as he is repulsive and hard to purify²⁰⁰ even if he escapes human punishment. Such a person will never escape, for there are thousands who have their eyes upon him,²⁰¹ zealous admirers of the laws, strictest guardians of the ancestral customs, pitiless to those who do anything to subvert them. Otherwise we are prepared to say that while it is right to seek the death

---

²⁰⁰ COLSON translates δυσκάθαρτον as "almost beyond possibility of purification," which weakens the sense. HEINEMANN has "den wird der gnadenreiche Gott von seiner Schuld nimmer lossprechen, weil er befleckt und nicht reinzuwaschen ist." Cf. LSJ s.v. δυσκάθαρτος: "hard to purify, hard to satisfy by purification or atonement."

²⁰¹ Thus COLSON; the term ἔφοροι designates overseers, guardians, rulers, in Sparta the ephors, in many cities the magistrates (LSJ).

of a person who dishonors a father or a mother, more moderation should be extended when sacrilegious people dishonor the name which is more glorious than dignity itself. [254] But nobody is so senseless as to punish with death people who are guilty of the lesser offenses and spare the people who are guilty of the greater; the sacrilege involved in slandering and insulting parents is not so great as that committed by perjury against address to God.

*Commentary.* The comments on the penalty for breaking the third commandment, i.e., for committing perjury, are parallel to *Spec.* 2.27– 28 (No. 27). This text, while not commenting on a specific Old Testament text, alludes to Exod 20:7 (Deut 5:11) and Lev 19:12; 24:16.[202] Philo understands these texts to prohibit uttering the Tetragrammaton, which explains his reluctance to swearing oaths in general in which God's name may be carelessly uttered. He regards perjury as a very serious crime: it represents a subversion of the laws (νόμων) and of the ancestral customs (τῶν πατρίων [ἐθῶν]),[203] i.e., it threatens Israel's constitution of the people of God. The death penalty is to be carried out by the witnesses to this crime; if the offender is spared, he (she) cannot escape God, who will treat perjurers forever as impure and thus unworthy of his presence and blessing. Philo asserts that there will be countless Jews willing and ready to take decisive action against perjurers: Jews eager to detect and remove violators of the law of God, zealous in their commitment to the law, and consistent in guarding the ancestral customs and thus the constitution of the Jewish commonwealth. Such pious Jews are pitiless (ἀμειλίκτως) against all who violate this basic law. While Philo may have exaggerated the possibility of lynch justice exacted by Jews on Jewish violators of the commandments of Torah whose violation warranted death, his statement suggests that he regarded the scenario that Jews zealous for the law would take action against transgressors as a real (or at least desirable) possibility in Roman Alexandria.[204]

## (30) Josephus, *Bellum judaicum* 1.96–97

Οὐ μὴν τό γε λοιπὸν πλῆθος ὑποχωρησάντων τῶν συμμάχων κατέθεντο τὰς διαφοράς, συνεχῆσ δὲ πρὸς Ἀλέξανδρον ἦν αὐτοῖς ὁ πόλεμος, μέχρι πλείστους ἀποκτείνας τοὺς λοιποὺς ἀπήλασεν εἰς Βεμέσελιν πόλιν καὶ ταύτην καταστρεψάμενος αἰχμαλώτους ἀνήγαγεν εἰς Ἱεροσόλυμα. [97] προύκοψεν δ᾽ αὐτῷ δ᾽ ὑπερβολὴν ὀργῆς εἰς ἀσέβειαν τὸ τῆς ὠμότητος· τῶν γὰρ ληφθέντων ὀκτακοσίους ἀνασταυρώσας ἐν μέσαὐτῶν ἀπέσφαξεν ταῖς ὄψεσι, καὶ ταῦτα πίνων καὶ συγκατακείμενος ταῖς παλλακίσιν ἀφεώρα.

---

[202] SELAND, Establishment Violence, 161–63.

[203] Cf. Philo, *Mos.* 2.193; *Spec.* 2.148; *Praem.* 106; *Flacc.* 43, 52, 53; *Legat.* 170, 300; *Hypoth.* 7.11. On Philo's understanding of ἔθος cf. SELAND, Establishment Violence, 173–74.

[204] Cf. SELAND, Establishment Violence, 171–72, 175.

*Translation.* The rest of the people, however, did not abandon their disagreements when their allies withdrew, but engaged in continuous war against Alexander. After he killed a very large number of them, he drove the rest into Bemeselis and, having subdued this town, he took them to Jerusalem as prisoners. [97] His fury became so extreme that his savagery progressed to impiety. He had eight hundred of the prisoners crucified in the center of the city, and cut the throats of their wives and children before their eyes while he watched, drinking, with his concubines reclining beside him.

*Commentary.* The massacre of 800 opponents in Jerusalem by Alexander Jannaeus c. 90 B.C. is regarded by some as evidence for crucifixion as mode of execution during the Second Temple period (see No. 277). Josephus' account is taken to presuppose the crime of treason, as stipulated in 11QTemple LXIV, 6–13 (see No. 22).[205] The fact that Alexander Jannaeus did not kill the prisoners in Bemeselis but took them to Jerusalem may suggest the execution followed a trial and conviction.

**(31)** Josephus, *Antiquitates judaicae* 14.177

Ὑρκανὸς δὲ ὁρῶν ὡρμημένους πρὸς τὴν ἀναίρεσιν τὴν Ἡρώδου τοὺς ἐν τῷ συνεδρίῳ τὴν δίκην εἰς ἄλλην ἡμέραν ἀνεβάλετο καὶ πέμψας κρύφα πρὸς Ἡρώδην συνεβούλευσεν αὐτῷ φυγεῖν ἐκ τῆς πόλεως· οὕτω γὰρ τὸν κίνδυνον διαφεύξεσθαι.

*Translation.* When Hyrcanus saw that the members of the Sanhedrin were eager to putting Herod to death, he adjourned the trial for another day and secretly sent word to Herod, advising him to flee from the city and thus escape the danger.

*Commentary.* Hyrcanus II[206] was the son of Alexander Jannaeus (103–76 B.C.) and Salome Alexandra (who ruled as Queen from 76–67 B.C.). He had been appointed high priest by Salome Alexandra in 76 B.C. and was evidently deposed by his brother Aristobulus II in 67 B.C. Hyrcanus was supported by Antipater, an Idumean by birth (*A. J.* 14.8; *B. J.* 1.123), who administered Idumea. Hyrcanus was reinstated by Pompey in 63 B.C. after the Roman army defeated Aristobulus and his allies who had barricaded themselves on the Temple Mount. In 57 B.C., Gabinius confirmed Hyrcanus as high priest, while

---

[205] MAIER, Tempelrolle, 278–79; MARTIN HENGEL, Mors Turpissima Crucis. Die Kreuzigung in der antiken Welt und die 'Torheit' des 'Wortes vom Kreuz' [1976], in Studien zum Urchristentum. Kleine Schriften VI (ed. C.-J. Thornton; Tübingen: Mohr Siebeck, 2008), 594–652, 644; MARTIN HENGEL, Crucifixion in the Ancient World and the Folly of the Message of the Cross (Translated by John Bowden; Philadelphia: Fortress, 1978), 84–85; HENGEL / SCHWEMER, Jesus, 611–12. Cf. WISE, Temple Scroll, 123–25.

[206] For Hyrcanus II see VANDERKAM, High Priests, 337–39, 345–85.

making the leading Jewish families responsible for the administration and the dispensation of justice.[207] After Julius Caesar's victory in Egypt, Hyrcanus was appointed ethnarch of the Jews and confirmed as high priest in 47 B.C., while Antipater, appointed procurator of Judaea, was given "power to rule in whatever form he preferred" (*A. J.* 14.143). Josephus relates that when Antipater saw that Hyrcanus was "dull and sluggish," he appointed his eldest son, Phasael, as governor of Jerusalem and Judea and his second son, Herod, as governor in Galilee (*A. J.* 14.158). According to *A. J.* 14.163, "the leading Jews" (οἱ ἐν τέλει τῶν Ἰουδαίων) resented the increasing power of Antipater and his sons. The "chief Jews" (οἱ πρῶτοι τῶν Ἰουδαίων) became convinced that Herod was both powerful and reckless and desired to rule as a tyrant (τυραννίς; *A. J.* 14.165). These Jewish aristocrats, presumably members of the Sanhedrin and lower councils[208] and representatives of the priestly and lay aristocracy,[209] demanded that Hyrcanus put Herod on trial (*A. J.* 14.165–166). They accused Herod specifically of having killed Ezekias and many of his men in violation of the Jewish Law that forbids Jews "to slay a man, even an evildoer, unless he has first been condemned by the Sanhedrin to suffer this fate" (*A. J.* 14.167). The mothers of the men killed by Herod implored the king (i.e., Hyrcanus) and the people (i.e., the Jewish leaders) to have Herod "brought to judgment in the Sanhedrin for what he had done" (*A. J.* 14.168). The events connected with Herod's trial are described in *A. J.* 14.169–184 and *B. J.* 1.210–215.[210] According to *A. J.* 14.177, Hyrcanus postponed the trial. The reason Josephus gives is the eagerness of the members of the Sanhedrin to execute Herod. This has been taken to confirm the Mishnaic law that a condemned criminal shall not be executed on the same day the trial began.[211] Others argue that the postponement of the trial was the only course of action that allowed Hyrcanus to save Herod.[212] In view of *A. J.* 14.170 (*B. J.* 1.211), this seems correct: Sextus Caesar, the governor of Syria, intervened and ordered Herod cleared of the charge of manslaughter, a request Hyrcanus gladly obliged because "he loved Herod." Josephus is not clear regarding the relationship between Hyrcanus' acquittal of Herod and any decision the Sanhedrin

---

[207] HENGEL / SCHWEMER, Jesus, 46.

[208] VANDERKAM, High Priests, 358 n. 313.

[209] HENGEL / SCHWEMER, Jesus, 49.

[210] For differences between the two accounts cf. PETER RICHARDSON, Herod: King of the Jews and Friend of the Romans (orig. 1996; repr., Fortress: Minneapolis, 1999), 108–13, who argues that the value of the Samaias story in *A. J.* 14.171–176 for a reconstruction of Herod's trial is "almost negligible." HENGEL / SCHWEMER, Jesus, 49, are less skeptical, assuming that Josephus' source for his account of Herod's appearance before the Sanhedrin and for Samaias' speech is Nicolaus of Damascus.

[211] SOLOMON ZEITLIN, Who Crucified Jesus? (orig. 1942; repr., New York: Harper, 1947), 73. Cf. STROBEL, Stunde, 52–53, interprets Hyrcanus' action as being based on a legal argument. However, *A. J.* 14.177 is not as "eindeutig" as STROBEL claims.

[212] BLINZLER, Prozeß, 223.

might have taken.[213] He describes Hyrcanus, the high priest, as exercising the right to summon people accused of capital crimes, even a governor of Galilee, to face the Sanhedrin, and his account implies that the Sanhedrin could go against the wishes of the high priest.

Since there is no evidence that the rights and responsibilities of either the Sanhedrin or the incumbent high priest were clearly defined, and since those rights had changed under the impact of Roman rule, this text cannot be given too much weight when assessing the legal maneuvers of either side during Jesus' trial.

**(32)** *m. Sanhedrin* 4:1

אֶחָד דִּינֵי־מָמוֹנוֹת וְאֶחָד דִּינֵי־נְפָשׁוֹת בִּדְרִישָׁה וּבַחֲקִירָה שֶׁנֶּאֱמַר מִשְׁפָּט אֶחָד יִהְיֶה לָכֶם: מַה־בֵּין דִּינֵי מָמוֹנוֹת לְדִינֵי־נְפָשׁוֹת? דִּינֵי־מָמוֹנוֹת בִּשְׁלֹשָׁה וְדִינֵי־נְפָשׁוֹת בְּעֶשְׂרִים וּשְׁלֹשָׁה וו דִּינֵי־מָמוֹנוֹת פּוֹתְחִין לוֹ בֵּין לִזְכוּת בֵּין לְחוֹבָה וְדִינֵי־נְפָשׁוֹת פּוֹתְחִין בִּזְכוּת וְאֵין פּוֹתְחִין בְּחוֹבָה וו דִּינֵי־מָמוֹנוֹת מַטִּין עַל־פִּי־עֵד אֶחָד בֵּין לִזְכוּת בֵּין לְחוֹבָה וְדִינֵי־נְפָשׁוֹת מַטִּין עַל־פִּי־אֶחָד לִזְכוּת וְעַל־פִּי־שְׁנַיִם לְחוֹבָה וו דִּינֵי־מָמוֹנוֹת מַחֲזִירִין בֵּין לִזְכוּת בֵּין לְחוֹבָה וְדִינֵי־נְפָשׁוֹת מַחֲזִירִין לִזְכוּת וְאֵין מַחֲזִירִין לְחוֹבָה וו דִּינֵי מָמוֹנוֹת הַכֹּל מְלַמְּדִין זְכוּת וְחוֹבָה וְדִינֵי־נְפָשׁוֹת הַכֹּל מְלַמְּדִין זְכוּת וְאֵין הַכֹּל מְלַמְּדִין חוֹבָה וו דִּינֵי־מָמוֹנוֹת הַמְלַמֵּד חוֹבָה מְלַמֵּד זְכוּת וְהַמְלַמֵּד זְכוּת מְלַמֵּד חוֹבָה וְדִינֵי־נְפָשׁוֹת הַמְלַמֵּד חוֹבָה מְלַמֵּד זְכוּת אֲבָל הַמְלַמֵּד זְכוּת אֵינוֹ יָכוֹל לַחֲזוֹר וּלְלַמֵּד חוֹבָה: דִּינֵי־מָמוֹנוֹת גּוֹמְרִין בּוֹ בַּיּוֹם בֵּין לִזְכוּת בֵּין לְחוֹבָה וְדִינֵי־נְפָשׁוֹת גּוֹמְרִין בּוֹ בַיּוֹם לִזְכוּת וּבְיוֹם שֶׁלְּאַחֲרָיו לְחוֹבה וו לְפִיכָךְ אֵין דָּנִין לֹא בְּעֶרֶב־שַׁבָּת וְלֹא בְּעֶרֶב־יוֹם טוֹב:

*Translation.* Both cases of money (property cases) and cases of life (capital cases) have examination and interrogation (of witnesses), as it is said (Lev. 24:22), *You shall have one law.* What is the difference between property cases and capital cases? Property cases (are tried) by three (judges), and capital cases by twenty-three (judges). Property cases begin either (with arguments) to acquit or to convict, and capital cases begin (with arguments) to acquit and not (with arguments) to convict. Property cases are decided by (a majority of) one either to acquit or to convict, and capital cases are decided by (a majority of) one to acquit or by (a majority of) two to convict. In property cases (the verdict) can change from acquittal to conviction, and capital cases can change (the verdict) to acquittal but not to conviction.[214] In property cases all (judges) can rule to acquit or to convict, and in capital cases all (judges) can argue to acquit but all (judges) do not argue for conviction. In property cases, one who argues for conviction can argue for acquittal and one who argues for acquittal can also argue for conviction; in capital cases, one who argues for conviction

---

[213] VANDERKAM, High Priests, 361; for the following point see ibid.

[214] NEUSNER translates this stipulation, "In property cases they reverse the decision whether in favor of acquittal or in favor of conviction, while in capital cases they reverse the decision in favor of acquittal, but they do not reverse the decision in favor of conviction."

can argue for acquittal, but one who argues for acquittal cannot turn around and argue for conviction. Property cases can be tried during the day and finish during the night, and capital cases are tried during the day and must finish during the (following) day. Property cases come to a conclusion on the same day, whether for acquittal or conviction, and capital cases come to a conclusion on the same day for acquittal and the next day for conviction; therefore they do not try (capital cases) on the evening of the Sabbath or on the evening before a holiday.

*Commentary.*[215] These stipulations, which are presented as interpretation of Lev 24:22[216] and may date to the Usha period (A.D. 125–170),[217] specify the following proceedings for trials in which the death penalty is being sought: (1) A capital case must be tried by twenty-three judges. (2) Capital trials must begin with arguments for the acquittal of the accused.[218] (3) A majority of one judge is sufficient for acquittal, whereas a majority of two judges is needed for conviction. (4) Once a decision is made in favor of acquittal, the decision cannot be reversed in favor of conviction, whereas a decision in favor of conviction can be reversed if new evidence surfaces that suggests the innocence of the accused. (5) All may argue for acquittal, but not all – i.e., not the rabbinic disciples present in court but not yet independent law experts[219] – may argue for conviction. (6) A judge who argues for conviction can change his mind and argue for acquittal, whereas a judge who has been arguing for acquittal cannot retract his arguments and decide for conviction.[220] (7) The trial must be held during the day, it cannot be held during the night; if one day is not sufficient to finish the trial during daylight hours, it must be finished on the next day. (8) A decision of acquittal can be reached on the same day the trial began, while a guilty verdict can be reached no earlier than the following day

---

[215] Text: SAMUEL KRAUSS, Sanhedrin–Makkot (Die Mischna IV/4–5; Gießen: Töpelmann, 1933), 140–46.

[216] Lev 24:22 stipulates, "You shall have one law for the alien and for the citizen: for I am the Lord your God."

[217] JACOB NEUSNER, A History of the Mishnaic Law of Damages (5 vols.; SJLA 35; Leiden: Brill, 1982–85), 5:101–103, 169–73.

[218] The phrase לוֹ פּוֹתְחִין refers not to the opening of the trial but to the sequence of the arguments; in trials regarding property cases, the arguments for acquittal or for conviction can be given in any order. KRAUSS, Sanhedrin–Makkot, 142–43.

[219] KRAUSS, Sanhedrin–Makkot, 145.

[220] SAMUEL KRAUSS, The Mishnah Treatise Sanhedrin. Edited with an Introduction, Notes and Glossary (Semitic Study Series 11; Leiden: Brill, 1909), 40; KRAUSS, Sanhedrin–Makkot, 145, points out with reference to the explanation of (4) in *b. Sanh.* 33b, that revoking a vote happens when a judge has made an error of law, not if there is an error of judgment. The statement in (6) is modified in the gemara in *b. Sanh.* 34a: Rab said that a judge who argued for acquittal cannot change his mind during the trial proceedings (וּמַתָּן מַשָּׂא); however, after the verdict has been rendered, a judge who had argued for acquittal but now thinks that he has been wrong can petition for conviction; cf. KRAUSS, ibid., 145.

after the start of the trial. This means trials in capital cases are not held on the evening of the Sabbath day (Friday evenings) or on the evening before a Festival; there can be no convictions on the Sabbath or during a Festival. These stipulations demonstrate the seriousness of capital charges in comparison with cases involving personal property. And they demonstrate the rabbis' concern that a person accused of a capital crime receive special protections to avoid a miscarriage of justice. It is more difficult to convict a person accused of a capital crime than it is to decide on acquittal.

These legal stipulations for capital cases are cited as establishing irregularities in the Evangelists' description of Jesus' trial before the Sanhedrin:[221] Jesus was tried during the night (Matt 26:34, 57; John 13:30; 18:2, 13, 24); he was tried on the day before Passover (John 18:28); he was convicted of a capital crime on the same day his trial had begun, i.e., there was no interval of at least a night between the judges' arguments and Jesus' conviction. J. BLINZLER argues that the legal stipulations of tractate Sanhedrin in the Mishnah, which reflect the more humane Pharisaic viewpoint, were not in force in the first century A.D.[222] C. A. EVANS argues that if the gathering of priests and elders at the home of Caiaphas during the night is regarded as "an informal hearing designed to gain a consensus among Jewish authorities that Jesus should be handed over to the Romans with a capital recommendation," there would be no violations of the rules of capital trials.[223] D. A. HAGNER suggests that by the standard of the Mishnaic stipulations, the "trial of sorts" was a sham, "but under the very special circumstances, it could not have been otherwise."[224] A. STROBEL argues: (1) there is no basic difference between Sadducean law in central legal questions (which the Jerusalem Sanhedrin would have followed before A.D. 70); (2) the legal stipulations of Mishnah (and Tosefta), particu-

---

[221] Cf. LOHSE, Prozeß, 96–97; DONALD JUEL, Messiah and Temple: The Trial of Jesus in the Gospel of Mark (SBLDS 31; Missoula: Scholars Press, 1977), 59–60; STROBEL, Stunde, 46–48; BROWN, Death, 1:358–59; WOLFGANG REINBOLD, Der älteste Bericht über den Tod Jesu. Literarische Analyse und historische Kritik der Passionsdarstellungen der Evangelien (BZNW 69; Berlin: De Gruyter, 1994), 252.

[222] JOSEF BLINZLER, Das Synedrium von Jerusalem und die Strafprozeßordnung der Mischna, ZNW 52 (1961): 54–65; BLINZLER, Prozeß, 216–29; also BROWN, Death, 1:357–63, and HENGEL / SCHWEMER, Jesus, 592, who conclude that since we do not know the more severe Sadducean criminal law of the first century A.D., we are not in a position to confirm or gainsay the possibility or impossibility and the legality of a Sanhedrin session during the second half of the night of Passover.

[223] CRAIG A. EVANS, Mark 8:27–16:20 (WBC 34B; Nashville: Nelson, 2001), 444, who refers to C. E. B. CRANFIELD, The Gospel according to Saint Mark (Cambridge Greek Testament Commentary; Cambridge: Cambridge University Press, 1963), 440; also JOEL MARCUS, Mark (AYB 27; New York: Doubleday / Yale University Press, 2000–2009), 2:1127; CHILTON / BOCK, Mark, 487.

[224] DONALD A. HAGNER, Matthew (WBC 33; Dallas: Word, 1993–95), 2:797; the "special circumstances" are Judas' unexpected actions and the eagerness of the authorities to act quickly before the climax of Passover (ibid.).

larly regarding capital cases, reflect the legal situation during the first century; (3) capital cases involving a seducer of the people (*mesit*) followed different rules from that of ordinary criminal cases (cf. No. 38, 41, 42, 43, 45). He concludes that in Jesus' trial before the Sanhedrin, no legal rules were broken as Jesus was tried as a seducer of the people.[225]

**(33)** *m. Sanhedrin* 4:5

כֵּיצַד מְאַיְּמִין עַל עֵדֵי־נְפָשׁוֹת הָיוּ מַכְנִיסִין אוֹתָן וּמְאַיְּמִין עֲלֵיהֶן שֶׁמָּא תֹאמְרוּ מֵאֹמֶד מִשְּׁמוּעָה עֵד מִפִּי־עֵד מִפִּי־אָדָם נֶאֱמָן שָׁמַעְנוּ אוֹ שֶׁמָּא אֵין אַתֶּם יוֹדְעִין שֶׁסּוֹפֵנוּ לִבְדֹּק אֶתְכֶם בִּדְרִישָׁה וּבַחֲקִירָה. הֱיוּ יוֹדְעִין שֶׁלֹּא כְדִינֵי־מָמוֹנוֹת דִּינֵי־נְפָשׁוֹת. דִּינֵי־מָמוֹנוֹת אָדָם נוֹתֵן מָמוֹן וּמִתְכַּפֵּר לוֹ וְדִינֵי־נְפָשׁוֹת דָּמוֹ וְדַם־זַרְעִיּוֹתָיו תְּלוּיִן בּוֹ עַד סוֹף־הָעוֹלָם. שֶׁכֵּן מָצִינוּ בְקַיִן שֶׁהָרַג אֶת־אָחִיו שֶׁנֶּאֱמַר קוֹל דְּמֵי־אָחִיךָ אֵינוֹ אוֹמֵר דַּם־אָחִיךָ אֶלָּא דְמֵי־אָחִיךָ דָּמוֹ וְדַם־זַרְעִיּוֹתָיו. דָּבָר אַחֵר דְּמֵי־אָחִיךָ שֶׁהָיָה דָמוֹ מֻשְׁלָךְ עַל־הָעֵצִים וְעַל־הָאֲבָנִים. לְפִיכָךְ נִבְרָא הָאָדָם יְחִידִי בָעוֹלָם לְלַמֶּדְךָ שֶׁכָּל־הַמְאַבֵּד נֶפֶשׁ אַחַת מַעֲלִין עָלָיו כְּאִלּוּ אִבַּד עוֹלָם מָלֵא וְכָל־הַמְקַיֵּם נֶפֶשׁ אַחַת מַעֲלִין עָלָיו כְּאִלּוּ קִיֵּם עוֹלָם מָלֵא. וּמִפְּנֵי־שְׁלוֹם־הַבְּרִיּוֹת שֶׁלֹּא יֹאמַר אָדָם לַחֲבֵרוֹ אַבָּא גָדוֹל מֵאָבִיךָ. וְשֶׁלֹּא יְהִיּוּ הַמִּינִין אוֹמְרִים רְשֻׁיּוֹת הַרְבֵּה בַּשָּׁמַיִם. וּלְהַגִּיד שִׁבְחוֹ שֶׁל־מֶלֶךְ מַלְכֵי־הַמְּלָכִים הַקָּדוֹשׁ בָּרוּךְ הוּא שֶׁאָדָם טוֹבֵעַ מֵאָה מַטְבְּעוֹת בְּחוֹתָם אֶחָד וְכֻלָּן דּוֹמִין זֶה לָזֶה וּמֶלֶךְ מַלְכֵי־הַמְּלָכִים הַקָּדוֹשׁ בָּרוּךְ הוּא טוֹבֵעַ אֶת־כָּל־הָאָדָם בְּחוֹתָמוֹ שֶׁל־אָדָם הָרִאשׁוֹן וְאֵין אֶחָד דּוֹמֶה לַחֲבֵרוֹ. לְפִיכָךְ כָּל־אֶחָד וְאֶחָד חַיָּב לוֹמַר בִּשְׁבִילִי נִבְרָא הָעוֹלָם. שֶׁמָּא תֹאמְרוּ מַה־לָּנוּ לְצָרָה הַזֹּאת וַהֲלֹא כְבָר נֶאֱמַר וְהוּא עֵד אוֹ רָאָה אוֹ יָדַע וְשֶׁמָּא תֹאמְרוּ מַה־לָּנוּ לָחוּב בְּדָמוֹ שֶׁל־זֶה וַהֲלֹא כְבָר נֶאֱמַר וּבַאֲבוֹד רְשָׁעִים רִנָּה:

*Translation.* How do they admonish witnesses in capital cases? They bring them in and admonish them [as follows]: "Perhaps you will say what is but supposition or hearsay or as witness from the testimony of [another] witness, or (you may be thinking) 'we heard it from a reliable person.' Or perhaps you do not know that we will test you with interrogation and examination. You should know that capital cases are not the same as property cases. In property cases a person pays money and thus achieves atonement. In capital cases the blood [of the accused] and the blood of all who were [potentially] born from him [who was wrongfully convicted] are held against him [who gives false testimony] to the end of the world. For so we find in the case of Cain who slew his brother, as it is written, 'The bloods of your brother cry.' It does not say 'The blood of your brother" but 'The bloods of your brother' – his blood and the blood of all his [potential] descendants. Another word: 'The bloods of your brother' – because his blood was spattered on trees and stones. Therefore man was created alone, to teach you that if any man destroys a single soul,[226] Scripture regards him as if he had destroyed a whole world. And if any man

---

[225] STROBEL, Stunde, 46–92.

[226] Several manuscript witnesses (followed by DANBY and NEUSNER) add the restriction מִיִּשְׂרָאֵל ("from Israel") thus also in the next sentence. The addition does not make sense, since the first human being was not an Israelite. The word may have been added since the persons to whom this admonition is addressed were Jews (KRAUSS).

saves a single soul, Scripture regards him as if he had saved a whole world. And [a single man was created] for the sake of peace among mankind, so that nobody should say to his fellow, 'My father is greater than your father.' And [a single man was created] so that the *minim* should not say, 'There are many powers in heaven.' And [a single man was created] to proclaim the praise of the King of all kings, the Holy One, blessed is He. For a man mints a hundred coins with a single seal, and they are all like one another. But the King of kings, the Holy One, blessed is He, minted all human beings with the seal of the first human being, yet not one of them is like anyone else. Therefore everyone is obligated to say, 'The world was created for my sake'. And if you [the witnesses] perhaps would like to say, 'Why should we be involved in this trouble?' – it has once been written, 'And he is a witness, or he has seen it or he knows.' And perhaps you [the witnesses] would like to say, 'Why should we be guilty of the blood of this person? – it has once been written, 'When the wicked perish there is rejoicing.'"

*Commentary.* In capital cases, the court admonishes witnesses before they give testify that they cannot base their testimony on supposition, on hearsay, on what they have heard second-hand from another witness or on what they have heard from a person they deem reliable. A witness' testimony must be based on what that witness has personally seen or heard. The judges inform witnesses that they will establish the truth of their testimony through interrogation and cross-examination. The admonition to give truthful, first-hand testimony is based on two arguments: (1) A person who murders a human being kills not only that human being but all his potential descendants as well. This is why the damage resulting from false testimony in a capital case that leads to the conviction and execution of the accused cannot be remedied, in contrast to the monetary damages resulting from false testimony give in a property case, which can be remedied by the payment of money. This is confirmed by the citation of Gen 4:10: Abel's blood and the blood of his descendents (thus the plural דמים) cried out against Cain. (2) God created a single person (Adam), which means that every human being is unique. The fact that God created a single person has a four-fold purpose: it teaches us that to destroy a single human being is tantamount to destroying the entire world; it establishes the equality of every human being; it rules that the existence of other heavenly powers who might be credited to have created other worlds (as assumed in Gnostic systems); and it proclaims the greatness of God who made human beings who are distinct and unique and yet who are all his creation. The potential objection of the witnesses why they should get involved in the business of testifying before the court if their testimony might turn out to be wrong is answered with a quotation of the first part of Lev 5:1 ("And he is a witness, or he has seen it or he knows"), the continuation of which is decisive: "if he does not speak it, then he shall bear his iniquity." A person who has witnessed a crime and does not testify before participates in the guilt of the perpetrator. This is the reason why the penalty for giving false witness was the death penalty (*m. Sanh.* 11:6). The objection that it might be preferable not to get involved as a witness in a capital case in order not to be responsible for the death of another person is answered with a quotation of Prov 11:10: the death of a wicked person as a result of a conviction in a court of law is not a minor matter but a reason for rejoicing. As regards Jesus' trial, Mark does not report that the witnesses were admonished.[227] R. H. GUNDRY argues, "Mark has no reason to mention such a warning. His silence does not imply that there was none."[228]

### (34) *m. Sanhedrin* 6:1–2

נִגְמַר הַדִּין מוֹצִיאִין אוֹתוֹ לְסָקְלוֹ וּבֵית־הַסְּקִילָה הָיָה חוּץ לְבֵית־דִּין שֶׁנֶּאֱמַר הוֹצֵא אֶת־הַמְקַלֵּל
אֶל־מְחוּץ לַמַּחֲנֶה וְאֶחָד עוֹמֵד עַל פֶּתַח־בֵּית־דִּין וְהַסּוּדָרִין בְּיָדוֹ וְאָדָם אֶחָד רוֹכֵב עַל־הַסּוּס רָחוֹק
מִמֶּנּוּ כְּדֵי שֶׁיְּהֵא רוֹאֵהוּ אוֹמֵר אֶחָד יֵשׁ־לִי לְלַמֵּד עָלָיו זְכוּת וְהוּא מֵנִיף בַּסּוּדָר וְהַסּוּס רָץ וּמַעֲמִידוֹ
אֲפִלּוּ הוּא עַצְמוֹ אִם אָמַר יֶשׁ־לִי לְלַמֵּד עַל עַצְמִי זְכוּת מַחֲזִירִין אוֹתוֹ אֲפִלּוּ אַרְבָּעָה וַחֲמִשָּׁה פְּעָמִים
וּבִלְבַד שֶׁיְּהֵא מַמָּשׁ בִּדְבָרָיו אִם מָצְאוּ לוֹ זְכוּת פְּטָרוּהוּ וְאִם לָאו יוֹצֵא לִסָּקֵל וְהַכָּרוֹז יוֹצֵא לְפָנָיו
אִישׁ פְּלוֹנִי בֶּן־פְּלוֹנִי פְּלוֹנִי יוֹצֵא לִסָּקֵל עַל־שֶׁעָבַר עֲבֵירָה פְּלוֹנִית וּפְלוֹנִי וּפְלוֹנִי עֵדָיו כָּל־מִי שֶׁיּוֹדֵעַ
לוֹ זְכוּת יָבֹא וִילַמֵּד עָלָיו:
הָיָה רָחוֹק מִבֵּית־הַסְּקִילָה עֶשֶׂר אַמּוֹת אוֹמְרִים לוֹ הִתְוַדֵּה שֶׁכֵּן דֶּרֶךְ כָּל־הַמּוּמָתִין מִתְוַדִּין
שֶׁכָּל־הַמִּתְוַדֶּה יֶשׁ־לוֹ חֵלֶק לָעוֹלָם הַבָּא שֶׁכֵּן מָצִינוּ בְּעָכָן שֶׁאָמַר לוֹ יְהוֹשֻׁעַ בְּנִי שִׂים־נָא כָבוֹד לַה'
אֱלֹהֵי־יִשְׂרָאֵל וְתֶן־לוֹ תוֹדָה וגו' וַיַּעַן עָכָן אֶת־יְהוֹשֻׁעַ וַיֹּאמַר אָמְנָה אָנֹכִי חָטָאתִי לַה' אֱלֹהֵי־יִשְׂרָאֵל
וּמִנַּיִן שֶׁנִּתְכַּפֵּר לוֹ בְוִדּוּיוֹ שֶׁנֶּאֱמַר וַיֹּאמֶר יְהוֹשֻׁעַ מֶה עֲכַרְתָּנוּ יַעְכָּרְךָ ה' בַּיּוֹם הַזֶּה הַיּוֹם הַזֶּה אַתָּה
עָכוּר וְאִי אַתָּה עָכוּר לֶעָתִיד לָבֹא וְאִם אֵינוֹ יוֹדֵעַ לְהִתְוַדּוֹת אוֹמְרִים לוֹ אֱמוֹר תְּהֵא מִיתָתִי כַפָּרָה
לְכָל־עֲוֹנוֹתַי רַבִּי יְהוּדָה אוֹמֵר אִם הָיָה יוֹדֵעַ שֶׁהוּא מוּזָּם אוֹמֵר תְּהֵא מִיתָתִי כַפָּרָה לְכָל־עֲוֹנוֹתַי
חוּץ מִן הֶעָוֹן הַזֶּה אָמְרוּ לוֹ אִם כֵּן יְהֵא כָּל־אָדָם אוֹמְרִים כָּךְ כְּדֵי לְנַקּוֹת אֶת־עַצְמָן:

*Translation.* (1) When sentence [of the death penalty] has been passed, they take him out to stone him. The place of stoning is well outside the court, as it is written, *Bring forth him who cursed to a place outside the camp* (Lev 24:14). One person stands at the door of the court with a piece of cloth[229] in his hand, and another person on a horse stands some distance from him so that he can see him. If [in the court] one of the judges said, "I have something to

---

[227] Thus HERBERT DANBY, The Bearing of the Rabbinical Criminal Code on the Jewish Trial Narratives in the Gospels [1920], in The Historical Jesus: Critical Concepts in Religious Studies (ed. C. A. Evans; London: Routledge, 2004), 51–76, 202, in a recital of the critique of the account of Jesus' trial in the Gospels by writers "eager to discover irregularities."

[228] ROBERT H. GUNDRY, Mark: A Commentary on His Apology for the Cross (Grand Rapids: Eerdmans, 1993), 893.

[229] The term סוּדָרִין (Greek σουδάριον; Latin *sudarium*), while plural, is meant as a singular, cf. the next sentence where סוּדָר is used.

say in favor of his acquittal," the person at the door waves the cloth,[230] and [the person on] the horse runs and stops [the execution]. And even if he [the convicted person] says, "I have something to say in favor of my own acquittal," they must bring him back, be it four or five times, provided that there is substance in what he says. If they then found him innocent, they release him. If not, he goes out to be stoned. A herald[231] goes out before him, calling, "So-and-so, the son of so-and-so, is going out to be stoned because he committed such-and-such a transgression. So-and-so and so-and-so are witnesses against him. If anyone knows something [that is grounds] for acquittal, let him come and speak on his behalf."

(2) When he was ten cubits[232] from the place of stoning, they say to him, "Confess!," for it is common for those who have been condemned to death to confess, because whoever confesses has a share in the world to come. For so we found concerning Achan; Joshua said to him, *My son, I ask you, give glory to the Lord, the God of Israel, and confess to him [and tell me now what you have done; do not hide it from me.] And Achan answered Joshua and said, Truly have I sinned against the Lord, the God of Israel, and thus and thus I have done* (Josh 7:19–20). How do we know that his confession made atonement for him? Because it is written, *And Joshua said, Why have you troubled us? The Lord shall trouble you this day* (Josh 7:25) – *this day* the Lord shall trouble you, but you shall not be troubled in the world to come. If he does not know how to confess,[233] they say to him, "Say, 'Let my death be an atonement for all my transgressions.'" Rabbi Yehudah says, "If he knew that he was condemned because of false testimony, he says, 'Let my death be atonement for all my sins, except for this particular sin [of which I have been convicted by perjury].'" They said to him, "If so, then everyone will say that to show his innocence."

*Commentary.* This text discusses the situation of a condemned person just before execution when there is still time for exculpatory evidence to be brought before the court and when the condemned person is given time to confess his transgressions.[234] The person condemned to death is led to a place (בַּיָת) outside (מוֹצִיאִין), i.e., outside the city.[235] The stipulations of 6:1 reflect the

---

[230] Reference is made to cloths or flags for signalling, attested for the great synagogue at Alexandria; cf. *t. Sukkah* 4:6; *y. Sukkah* 5a,51. KRAUSS, Mishnah Treatise Sanhedrin, 42.

[231] The term כָּרוֹז probably comes from Greek κῆρυξ; cf. SAMUEL KRAUSS, Griechische und lateinische Lehnwörter im Talmud, Midrasch und Targum (Berlin: Calvary, 1898–99), 1:129 (§246); GUSTAV H. DALMAN, Aramäisch-Neuhebräisches Handwörterbuch zu Targum, Talmud und Midrasch (orig. 1938; repr., Hildesheim: Olms, 1967), 207; MARCUS JASTROW, A Dictionary of the Targumim, the Talmud Babli, and Yerushalmi, and the Midrashic Literature (orig. 1903; repr., Peabody: Hendrickson, 2005), 664, s.v. כָּרוֹז translates "public crier."

[232] A cubit is the distance between the tip of the middle finger and the point of the elbow (ca. 45 cm). Ten cubits would have been 4.5 m (15 feet).

[233] The accused cannot remember his other sins; KRAUSS, Sanhedrin–Makkot, 187.

caution with which accused persons convicted of capital crimes were treated. The stipulation in 6:2 that the person about to be executed should confess his sins so his death could be an atonement demonstrates that in Jewish legal reasoning, the death of an executed person who confesses his sins before his execution achieved atonement for his sins that could not be forgiven by other means (including sacrifices), allowing him to have a share in the world to come.[236]

The use of Lev 24:14 in confirming the stipulation that executions must take place outside the city and reference to Josh 7:19–20 regarding confession of sins by the condemned to be executed has been taken as evidence that Mishnaic law was derived from the legal stipulations of the Pentateuch and agreed with Sadducean law regarding criminal cases.[237] The stipulation of *m. Sanh.* 6:2 seems to have been standard practice before A.D. 70, as suggested by *t. Sanh.* 9:5 which relates the execution of an innocent man who confessed his sins before his death.[238]

## (35) *m. Sanhedrin* 6:4–6

בֵּית־הַסְּקִילָה הָיָה גָבוֹהַּ שְׁתֵּי־קוֹמוֹת וְאֶחָד מִן הָעֵדִים דּוֹחֲפוֹ עַל מָתְנָיו נֶהְפַּךְ עַל לִבּוֹ הוֹפְכוֹ עַל מָתְנָיו אִם מֵת בָּהּ יָצָא וְאִם לֹא נוֹטֵל אֶת־הָאֶבֶן וְנוֹתְנָהּ עַל לִבּוֹ אִם מֵת בָּהּ יָצָא וְאִם לָאו רְגִימָתוֹ בְּכָל־יִשְׂרָאֵל שֶׁנֶּאֱמַר יַד־הָעֵדִים תִּהְיֶה־בּוֹ בָרִאשׁוֹנָה לַהֲמִיתוֹ וְיַד כָּל־הָעָם בָּאַחֲרוֹנָה: כָּל־הַנִּסְקָלִין נִתְלִין דִּבְרֵי־רַבִּי־אֱלִיעֶזֶר וַחֲכָמִים אוֹמְרִים אֵינוֹ נִתְלֶה אֶלָּא הַמְגַדֵּף וְהָעוֹבֵד עֲבוֹדָה

---

[234] Note the possible link with the call to confession "Give glory to God. We know that this man is a sinner" in John 9:24.

[235] The baraita *b. Sanh.* 42b asserts that the place of stoning was outside of three "camps," interpreted by Rashi as the sanctuary, the Temple Mount, and the city of Jerusalem. The gemara *b. Sanh.* 42b finds, besides the proof from Scripture, two further reasons: the court thus avoids being regarded as a company of murderers, and the distance of the place of stoning from the courthouse guarantees the possibility of rescue for the condemned. There are two exceptions as regards the stipulation concerning the place of stoning: a betrothed virgin committing adultery in her father's house is stoned at the door of her father's house or where she committed adultery (*t. Sanh.* 10:10), and a man or woman convicted of idolatry are stoned at the door of the courthouse (*b. Ketub.* 45b). Cf. KRAUSS, Sanhedrin–Makkot, 182.

[236] Cf. EDUARD LOHSE, Märtyrer und Gottesknecht. Untersuchungen zur urchristlichen Verkündigung vom Sühntod Jesu Christi (2., durchgesehene und erweiterte Auflage; orig. 1955; repr., FRLANT 64; Göttingen: Vandenhoeck & Ruprecht, 1963), 38–50. See also *t. Sanh.* 9:5; *b. Sanh.* 44b; *y. Sanh.* 23b,46. KRAUSS, Sanhedrin–Makkot, 187, compares with the exhortation given to judges in civil trials in *m. 'Abot* 1:8: "While the litigants stand before you, regard them as wicked men, and when leave you, regard them as innocent as soon as they have accepted the judgment."

[237] STROBEL, Stunde, 57–58.

[238] LOHSE, Märtyrer, 40, arguing that this must have happened at a time when the Jews had the ius gladii. BLINZLER, Prozeß, 223–24, remains unconvinced that *m. Sanh.* 6:2 and *t. Sanh.* 9:5 prove that the Mishnaic criminal law obtained at the time of Jesus; against BLINZLER cf. STROBEL, Stunde, 53.

זָרָה הָאִישׁ תּוֹלִין אוֹתוֹ פָּנָיו כְּלַפֵּי־הָעָם וְהָאִשָּׁה פָּנֶיהָ כְּלַפֵּי־הָעֵץ דִּבְרֵי־רַבִּי־אֱלִיעֶזֶר וַחֲכָמִים
אוֹמְרִים הָאִישׁ נִתְלֶה וְאֵין הָאִשָּׁה נִתְלֵית אָמַר לָהֶם רַבִּי אֱלִיעֶזֶר וַהֲלֹא מַעֲשֶׂה בְּשִׁמְעוֹן בֶּן־שָׁטַח
שֶׁתָּלָה שְׁמֹנִים נָשִׁים בְּאַשְׁקְלוֹן אָמְרוּ לוֹ שְׁמוֹנִים נָשִׁים תָּלָה וְאֵין דָּנִין שְׁנַיִם בְּיוֹם אֶחָד:
כֵּיצַד תּוֹלִין אוֹתוֹ מְשַׁקְּעִין אֶת־הַקּוֹרָה בָּאָרֶץ וְהָעֵץ יוֹצֵא מִמֶּנָּה וּמַקִּיף שְׁתֵּי יָדָיו זוֹ עַל גַּב זוֹ וְתוֹלֶה
אוֹתוֹ רַבִּי יוֹסֵי אוֹמֵר הַקּוֹרָה מַטָּה עַל הַכֹּתֶל וְתוֹלֶה בָּהּ כְּדֶרֶךְ שֶׁהַטַּבָּחִים תּוֹלִין וּמַתִּירִין אוֹתוֹ מִיָּד
וְאִם לָאו עוֹבְרִין עָלָיו בְּלֹא תַעֲשֶׂה שֶׁנֶּאֱמַר לֹא תָלִין נִבְלָתוֹ עַל־הָעֵץ וְגו' כְּלוֹמַר מִפְּנֵי־מָה זֶה תָּלוּי
מִפְּנֵי שֶׁבֵּרַךְ אֶת־הַשֵּׁם וְנִמְצָא שֵׁם־שָׁמַיִם מִתְחַלֵּל:

*Translation.*[239] The place of stoning was twice the height of a man. One of the witnesses knocks him on his hips so that he (comes to lie) turned on his heart; then he turns him over on his hips again; if he dies, it sufficed;[240] if not, he[241] takes the stone and puts it on his heart; if he dies, it sufficed; if not, the second witness takes the stone and puts it on his heart; if he dies, it sufficed; if not, the throwing of stones[242] (takes places) by all Israel, as it is written, *The hand of the witnesses shall be first upon him to put him to death*, and then it says, *and afterward the hand of all the people* (Deut 17:7).

(5) All those who are stoned are hanged.[243] These are the words of Rabbi Eliezer. But the Sages say, "Only the blasphemer and the one who worships an idol are hanged." A man is hanged with the face towards the people, and a woman is hanged with the face towards the wood.[244] These are the words of Rabbi Eliezer. But the sages say, "The man is hanged, but the woman is not hanged." Rabbi Eliezer said to them, "Did not Simeon ben Shetach hang eighty women in Ashkelon?" The sages answered, "He hanged eighty women, and they ought not to judge not even two (persons) on a single day!"

(6) How do they hang him? They drive a beam into the ground and a piece of wood (a crossbeam) juts out from it; they tie together[245] his two hands and thus they hang him. Rabbi Yose says, "The beam was made to lean against a wall, and one hanged him on it as the butchers do." And they untie him immediately; if not, one transgresses a negative command (a prohibition), because it is written, *You shall not leave his body over night on the tree* etc. (*but you shall surely bury him on the same day, for he who is hanged is a curse against God*) (Deut. 21:23). As if to say, why was this (person) hanged? Because he cursed the Name. And the Name of Heaven was found profaned.

---

[239] The numbering of paragraphs follows KRAUSS' edition in which *m. Sanh.* 6 has eight paragraphs; NEUSNER's edition has six paragraphs.

[240] KRAUSS: "hat er [der Pflicht] genügt."

[241] According to the Mishnah manuscript followed by KRAUSS, this is still the first witness.

[242] KRAUSS translates רְגִימָה as "Steinbewerfung," to distinguish the term from סְקִילָה which is the standard word for "stoning;" cf. JASTROW s.v. רכימא. NEUSNER translates with "stoning."

[243] NEUSNER translates נִתְלִין "are hanged on a tree;" the location is not specified in the text.

[244] The term עֵץ denotes the gallows; cf. KRAUSS, DANBY; NEUSNER has "toward the tree."

[245] KRAUSS translates וּמַקִּיף שְׁתֵּי יָדָיו זוֹ "worauf er seine beiden Hände eine über die andere bog": in order to make the hanging possible, they interlocked the hands and tied them backwards to the cross-beam.

*Commentary.* Mishnaic law stipulates that a person condemned to death is executed by stoning. The person to be stoned is pushed face forward from an elevated place. The specification "twice the height of a man" or four cubits corresponds to 3,52 meters; the height of a man is usually reckoned to be three cubits to the shoulders and four cubits if the head is included. In *t. Sanh.* 9:6 the height of the man is added to the twofold height indicated in the Mishnah, thus assuming twelve cubits or 5,28 meters. If the convicted person survives the fall, which is ascertained by turning the perpetrator on the back, he or she is killed by the throwing of stones. J. BLINZLER argues that the method of execution described in *m. Sanh.* 6:4 – the perpetrator is killed by stoning only if he survives a fall from an elevated place – is a later development; it differs from the original method of execution, followed in the first century, in which stones were thrown only.[246] A. STROBEL argues against a later development, emphasizing that the procedure of stoning is established in this mishnah on the basis of a Scriptural passage (Deut 17:7, which, however, does not mention that the convicted person is first pushed from an elevated place before being stoned).[247]

People who were executed by stoning were subsequently hanged (post-mortem exposure).[248] According to R. Eliezer (c. A.D. 120), this was true for all people condemned to suffer the death penalty. The more generally held opinion asserted that only people who were convicted of blasphemy and idolatry were to be hanged. The latter opinion is found in Josephus' summary of the Mosaic Law: ὁ δὲ βλασφημήσας θεὸν καταλευσθεὶς κρεμάσθω δι᾽ ἡμέρας καὶ ἀτίμως καὶ ἀφανῶς θαπτέσθω ("Let him who blasphemes God be stoned, then hung for a day, and buried ignominiously and in obscurity;" *A. J.* 4.202).[249] The stipulation that a blasphemer is to be hanged after the stoning is

---

[246] BLINZLER, Prozeß, 217–18, with reference to John 8:7; Josephus, *A. J.* 4.202; 16.394; Philo, *Mos.* 2.202. Cf. DORIS LAMBERS-PETRY, How to Become a Christian Martyr: Reflections on the Death of James as Described by Josephus and in Early Christian Literature, in Internationales Josephus-Kolloquium Paris 2001: Studies on the Antiquities of Josephus (ed. F. Siegert and J. U. Kalm; MJS 12; Münster: Lit, 2002), 104 n. 10, who states that "the procedure described in mSanh. VI 1–6 seems not to have been in use yet (if it ever was)."

[247] STROBEL, Stunde, 58.

[248] The baraita on this passage in *b. Sanh.* 45a wants to prove from Exod 19:13 that דְּחִיָּה (hurling down) is equivalent to סְקִילָה (stoning), that both methods of execution can be in view, and that hurling down sometimes suffices: "One of the witnesses pushed him: Our Rabbis taught: Whence do we know that it [the execution] was accomplished by hurling down? Scripture states, *And he shall be cast down* (Exod 19:13). And Whence the necessity of stoning? Scripture states, *He shall be stoned* (Exod 19:13). And whence do we know that both stoning and hurling down [were employed]? From the verse, *He shall surely be stoned or thrown down* (Exod 19:13). And whence do we know that if he died through being hurled down, it is enough? Scripture states, *or cast down*." Differently *y. Sanh.* 23c,6–26 where the rabbis insist that both hurling down and stoning is described as required by Scripture. Cf. KRAUSS, Sanhedrin–Makkot, 193.

[249] DAVID M. GOLDENBERG, The Halakhah in Josephus and in Tannaitic Literature: A

established on the basis of Deut 21:(22–)23: וְכִי־יִהְיֶה בְאִישׁ חֵטְא מִשְׁפַּט־מָוֶת וְהוּמָת
וְתָלִיתָ אֹתוֹ עַל־עֵץ: לֹא־תָלִין נִבְלָתוֹ עַל־הָעֵץ כִּי־קָבוֹר תִּקְבְּרֶנּוּ בַּיּוֹם הַהוּא כִּי־קִלְלַת אֱלֹהִים תָּלוּי
וְלֹא תְטַמֵּא אֶת־אַדְמָתְךָ אֲשֶׁר יְהוָה אֱלֹהֶיךָ נֹתֵן לְךָ נַחֲלָה: ("When someone is convicted of
a crime punishable by death and is executed, and you hang him on a tree, his
corpse must not remain all night upon the tree; you shall bury him that same
day, for anyone hung on a tree is under God's curse. You must not defile the
land that the Lord your God is giving you for possession"). The LXX interprets the *status constructus* קִלְלַת אֱלֹהִים as a subjective genitive (κεκατηραμένος ὑπὸ θεοῦ):[250] the person who blasphemed, i.e., cursed God, is himself
*cursed by God*, indicated by the fact that the blasphemer is displayed on a tree
(or piece of wood) after he has been stoned.

## (36) *m. Sanhedrin 7:4*

אֵלּוּ הֵן הַנִּסְקָלִין הַבָּא עַל־הָאֵם וְעַל־אֵשֶׁת־אָב וְעַל־הַכַּלָּה הַבָּא עַל־הַזָּכוּר וְעַל־הַבְּהֵמָה וְהָאִשָּׁה
הַמְּבִיאָה אֶת־הַבְּהֵמָה וְהַמְגַדֵּף וְהָעוֹבֵד עֲבוֹדָה זָרָה וְהַנּוֹתֵן מִזַּרְעוֹ לַמֹּלֶךְ וּבַעַל אוֹב וְיִדְּעוֹנִי וְהַמְחַלֵּל
אֶת־הַשַּׁבָּת וְהַמְקַלֵּל אָבִיו וְאִמּוֹ וְהַבָּא עַל־נַעֲרָה מְאוֹרָסָה וְהַמֵּסִית וְהַמַּדִּיחַ הַמְכַשֵּׁף וּבֶן סוֹרֵר
וּמוֹרֶה:

*Translation.* These are they [the felons] who are stoned: he who has sexual
relations with his mother, the wife of his father, his daughter-in-law, a male, a
beast, a woman who lets a beast come on top of her, the blasphemer, he who
performs foreign worship (the idolater), he who gives of his seed to Molech,
he who has a familiar spirit (the necromancer), he who is a soothsayer, he who
profanes the Sabbath, he who curses his father or his mother, he who has sexual relations with a betrothed girl, he who seduces [to idolatry] and he who
leads astray [an entire town to idolatry], the sorcerer, the stubborn and incorrigible son.

*Commentary.* For some of the offenses in this list, the Mosaic Law explicitly
stipulates execution by stoning as punishment. In the case of the other
offenses mentioned here, the death sentence of stoning is inferred from the
phrase דָּמָיו בּוֹ or דְּמֵיהֶם בָּם (his blood is upon himself, or their blood is upon
them), which is mentioned in Lev 20:27 together with stoning with reference
to a medium and a wizard. In those cases in which this phrase is missing, the

---

Comparative Study, Ph.D. Dissertation (Philadelphia: Dropsie University, 1978), 66–68, 204–
11, argues that Josephus is in agreement with the earlier tannaitic halakhah (attributed in *m.
Sanh.* 6:4 to R. Eliezer), drawing on a proto-rabbinic work that existed in written form; cited
by LOUIS H. FELDMAN, Judean Antiquities 1–4. Translation and Commentary (Flavius
Josephus: Translation and Commentary 3; Leiden: Brill, 2000), 400–401 nn. 593, 596.

[250] Deut 21:22–23 LXX: Ἐὰν δὲ γένηται ἔν τινι ἁμαρτία κρίμα θανάτου καὶ ἀποθάνῃ καὶ
κρεμάσητε αὐτὸν ἐπὶ ξύλου, οὐκ ἐπικοιμηθήσεται τὸ σῶμα αὐτοῦ ἐπὶ τοῦ ξύλου, ἀλλὰ ταφῇ
θάψετε αὐτὸν ἐν τῇ ἡμέρᾳ ἐκείνῃ, ὅτι κεκατηραμένος ὑπὸ θεοῦ πᾶς κρεμάμενος ἐπὶ ξύλου·
καὶ οὐ μιανεῖτε τὴν γῆν, ἣν κύριος ὁ θεός σου δίδωσίν σοι ἐν κλήρῳ.

penalty of stoning is inferred with one of Hillel's hermeneutical rules.[251] The list of crimes to be punished by stoning begins with six sexual crimes and five religious transgressions; the following six transgressions (beginning with the profanation of the Sabbath) do not seem to form a deliberate group.[252] The following section of 7:4, not reproduced here, provides an exposition of the sexual sins of the list. J. NEUSNER dates these stipulations to the Usha period (A.D. 125–170).[253]

This mishnah is often quoted for the possible charges against Jesus. J. BLINZLER specifies blasphemy (Mark 2:7; John 5:18; 8:59; cf. Lev 24:16; Exod 22:27), profanation of the Sabbath (Mark 2:24; 3:2–6; John 5:16; 9:16 etc.; cf. Num 15:35; Exod 31:14–15; 35:2), necromancy and sorcery (Mark 3:22; John 8:48; 10:20; cf. Exod 22:17; Lev 19:26, 31; 20:27; Deut 18:10–11), false prophecy (Mark 6:15; Matt 21:11, 46; Luke 7:16, 39; 13:33; John 6:14; 7:40, 52; 9:17; cf. Deut 13:6; 18:20).[254] A. STROBEL argues that the charge of false prophecy combined with the even more serious charge of seducing the people – the person who seduces (מֵסִית, *mesit*) to idolatry and the person who leads astray (מַדִּיחַ, *maddiakh*) an entire town (see No. 38) – was the charge on which Jesus was convicted.[255]

## (37) *m. Sanhedrin* 7:6–7

הָעוֹבֵד עֲבוֹדָה זָרָה אֶחָד הָעוֹבֵד וְאֶחָד הַזּוֹבֵחַ וְאֶחָד הַמְקַטֵּר וְאֶחָד הַמְנַסֵּךְ וְאֶחָד הַמִּשְׁתַּחֲוֶה וְהַמְקַבְּלוֹ עָלָיו לֶאֱלוֹהַּ וְהָאוֹמֵר לוֹ אֵלִי אָתָּה. אֲבָל הַמְגַפֵּף וְהַמְנַשֵּׁק וְהַמְכַבֵּד וְהַמְרַבֵּץ הַמַּרְחִיץ הַסָּךְ הַמַּלְבִּישׁ וְהַמַּנְעִיל עוֹבֵר בְּלֹא תַעֲשֶׂה. הַנּוֹדֵר בִּשְׁמוֹ וְהַמְקַיֵּם בִּשְׁמוֹ עוֹבֵר בְּלֹא תַעֲשֶׂה: הַפּוֹעֵר עַצְמוֹ בְּבַעַל־פְּעוֹר זוֹ הִיא עֲבוֹדָתוֹ: וְהַזּוֹרֵק אֶבֶן לְמַרְקוּלִיס זוֹ הִיא עֲבוֹדָתוֹ: הַנּוֹתֵן מִזַּרְעוֹ לַמֹּלֶךְ אֵינוֹ חַיָּב עַד שֶׁיִּמְסוֹר לַמֹּלֶךְ וְיַעֲבִיר בָּאֵשׁ. מָסַר לַמֹּלֶךְ וְלֹא הֶעֱבִיר בָּאֵשׁ הֶעֱבִיר בָּאֵשׁ וְלֹא מָסַר לַמֹּלֶךְ אֵינוֹ חַיָּב עַד שֶׁיִּמְסוֹר לַמֹּלֶךְ וְיַעֲבִיר בָּאֵשׁ. וּבַעַל אוֹב זֶה הַפִּיתוֹם וְהַמְדַבֵּר מִשֶּׁחְיוֹ. וְיִדְעוֹנִי זֶה הַמְדַבֵּר בְּפִיו. הֲרֵי אֵלּוּ בִסְקִילָה וְהַנִּשְׁאָל בָּהֶם בְּאַזְהָרָה:

*Translation.* The person who performs foreign worship (the idolator) – it is the same whether he worships, or sacrifices, or burns incense, or pours out a libation, or bows down, or accepts it as his god, or says to him, 'You are my god.' But the person who hugs it, kisses it, polishes it, cleans it, washes it, anoints it, clothes it, or puts shoes on it, [merely] transgresses a negative commandment. He who makes a vow in its name or carries out a vow in its name transgresses a negative commandment. The person who excretes to Baal Peor

---

[251] KRAUSS, Sanhedrin–Makkot, 215.

[252] NEUSNER, A History of the Mishnaic Law of Damages, 3:193.

[253] NEUSNER, A History of the Mishnaic Law of Damages, 5:104–5, 107; ibid. 169–73.

[254] BLINZLER, Prozeß, 86, who cites the passages listed above; he allows that Jesus, after his arrest, was ridiculed as a false prophet but disputes that Jesus' conviction was based on the charge of false prophecy; blasphemy was the decisive charge (ibid. 187).

[255] STROBEL, Stunde, 81–86.

– [he is to be stoned, because] this is how one performs an acts of worship to it. The person who throws a stone at Merkolis – [he is to be stoned, because] this is how one performs an act of worship to it.

(7) The person who gives of his seed to Molech is not liable unless he gives it (i.e., the child) to Molech and passes him through the fire; if he gave it (i.e., the child) to Molech but did not pass it through fire, if he passed it through fire but did not give it to Molech, he is not culpable, until he has both given it to Molech and passed it through fire. The necromancer – this is a person who has a Python which speaks from his armpits; and he who is a soothsayer – this is a person who speaks through his mouth: these are [to be put to death] by stoning, and the person who inquires of them is subject to a warning.

*Comment*ary. This text continues the explanation of the crimes deserving capital punishment in 7:4 (for 7:5 see No. 57). The negative commandments to which 7:6 refers are, respectively, Exod 20:5 ("You shall not bow down to them or worship them; for I the Lord your God am a jealous God ...") and Exod 23:13 ("Be attentive to all that I have said to you. Do not invoke the names of other gods; do not let them be heard on your lips"). The term Merkolis (מַרְקוּלִיס) refers to the stone pillar with the head of Mercurius / Hermes (herms) that marked the entrance of houses, private property boundaries, and city limits. Travelers threw stones at the herms, a custom that "had the pragmatic function clearing stones from the road" besides the cultic act of "controlled aggression aimed against the challenge of the apotropaic sign; "as a cultic marker on the border between gardens and uncultivated land, herms were resting-places" where the owners of the gardens left fruit and the shepherds, milk as sacrificial offerings to Hermes, which were available as provisions to travelers who rested there.[256] The opening line of 7:7 comes from Lev 20:2 / 18:21 (cf. Deut 18:10). Molech worship is punishable by death. Parents would hand over their child to the priests of Molech, who either sacrifice the child[257] or carry the child between two fires. The child is not burned, as this would be murder, a capital crime that would render the discussion of the details of Molech worship unnecessary.[258] Passing between fires may have been thought to replace human sacrifice or as an initiation rite.[259] The high point of Molech worship in Judah occured in the 8th to the 6th centuries. At the time of the rabbis, the Molech cult no longer existed. The necromancer

---

[256] GERHARD BAUDY, Hermes I. Cult and Mythology, BNP 6 (2005): 214–19, 215.

[257] JOHN DAY, Molech: A God of Human Sacrifice in the Old Testament (Cambridge: Cambridge University Press, 1989). Since O. EISSFELDT, scholars dispute the existence of a Molech; cf. ED NOORT, Child Sacrifice in Ancient Israel: The Status Quaestionis, in The Strange World of Human Sacrifice (ed. J. N. Bremmer; SHAR 1; Leuven: Peeters, 2006), 103–125.

[258] Cf. GUGGENHEIMER, Tractates Sanhedrin, Makkot, and Horaiot, 267; cf. *b. Sanh.* 64b.

[259] SALOMONSEN, Sanhedrin–Makkot, 165 n. 38, on *t. Sanh.* 10:4.

(בַּעַל אוֹב) is a person who raises the spirits of the dead; the term "Python" (פִּיתוֹם; from Greek πύθων)[260] designates a "spirit of divination" and was used of ventriloquists, who were believed to have such a spirit dwelling in their bellies.[261] The soothsayer (יִדְּעוֹנִי) is a person who predicts the future, speaking with his mouth. According to Deut 18:20, a false prophet must be executed: "But any prophet who speaks in the name of other gods, or who presumes to speak in my name a word that I have not commanded the prophet to speak – that prophet shall die." While Lev 19:31 and Deut 18:10–11 forbid turning to necromancers and fortune-tellers, the biblical text does not stipulate a punishment, while this mishnah prescribes the death sentence. People who consult necromancers and mediums receive a warning.

After Jesus' conviction, he was mocked as a false prophet: "Some began to spit on him, to blindfold him, and to strike him, saying to him, 'Prophesy!'" (Mark 14:65; cf. Matt 26:67–68). Some scholars infer that Jesus was charged and convicted as a false prophet.[262] It is unclear how Jesus' prophecy concerning the destruction of the Temple (Matt 24:2 / Mark 13:2 / Luke 21:6), which is mentioned prominently in the interrogation of the witnesses (Matt 26:60–61 / Mark 14:57–58), could have been the basis for a conviction on the charge of being a false prophet. It has been suggested that Jesus was charged with being a deceiver who leads people astray through magic and false prophecy, as he was not upholding Israel's inalienable symbols (Sabbath, food, nation, land, Temple) but claiming through his actions and words that God was reconstituting Israel through his (Jesus') ministry.[263]

---

[260] The meaning of the term πύθων is derived from πύθεσθαι ("to decay"), referring to the corpse of the snake, or from πυνθάνεσθαι ("to inquire [from the gods]," or from πυθμήν ("bottom") referring to the "chasm of the earth" which allowed for the inquiry of the oracle. The Python myth speaks of an enormous female dragon (or snake) called Python, which Apollo killed near Delphi; the town and the god were given the nickname Pytho. Apollo is said to have brought Cretans as priests to the sanctuary he established at the foot of the mountain at Delphi, and where Pythia, a prophetic seer of the oracles of Apollo Pythios, was sought out by the Greek cities. Cf. *Hymni Homerici* 3.300–374; Euripides, *Iph. taur.* 1245–52. Cf. TIM JUNK, Python I, BNP 12 (2008): 298; WOLFGANG DECKER, Pythia, BNP 12 (2008): 291–94.

[261] Cf. Plutarch, *Mor.* 414e, who describes Apollo as inspiring πύθωνες or ἐγγαστρίμυθοι ("belly-talkers"), i.e. ventriloquists, identified as "people who prophesy from the belly" (ἐγγαστρίμαντις) by Pollianus 2.168. Cf. LSJ s.v. ἐγγαστρίμυθος; BDAG s.v. πύθων.

[262] JOACHIM JEREMIAS, Die Abendmahlsworte Jesu (4. Auflage; Göttingen: Vandenhoeck & Ruprecht, 1967 [1935]), 72–73; JOACHIM JEREMIAS, Neutestamentliche Theologie. Erster Teil: Die Verkündigung Jesu (4. Auflage; Gütersloh: Mohn, 1988), 82–83. See the critique of BLINZLER, Prozeß, 187–88; OTTO BETZ, Probleme des Prozesses Jesu, ANRW II/25.1 (1982): 565–647, 638, argues that Jesus was mocked as a false messiah, not a false prophet.

[263] N. T. WRIGHT, Jesus and the Victory of God (Christian Origins and the Question of God Vol. 2; Minneapolis: Fortress, 1996), 438–42, 549–51.

**(38)** *m. Sanhedrin* 7:10

הַמֵּסִית זֶה הֶדְיוֹט הַמֵּסִית אֶת־הַהֶדְיוֹט אָמַר לוֹ יֵשׁ יִרְאָה בְמָקוֹם כָּךְ אוֹכֶלֶת כָּךְ שׁוֹתָה כָּךְ
מֵטִיבָה כָּךְ מְרֵעָה. כָּל־חַיָּבֵי־מִיתוֹת שֶׁבַּתּוֹרָה אֵין מַכְמִינִין עֲלֵיהֶן חוּץ מִזּוֹ:
אָמַר לִשְׁנַיִם וְהֵן עֵדָיו מְבִיאִין אוֹתוֹ לְבֵית־דִּין וְסוֹקְלִין אוֹתוֹ אָמַר לְאֶחָד וְהוּא אוֹמֵר לוֹ יֵשׁ־לִי
חֲבֵרִים רוֹצִים בְּכָךְ אִם הָיָה עָרוּם אֵינוֹ יָכוֹל לְדַבֵּר בִּפְנֵיהֶן אֶלָּא מַכְמִינִין לַאֲחוֹרֵי־הַגָּדֵר וְהוּא אוֹמֵר
לוֹ אֱמוֹר מַה־שֶּׁאָמַרְתָּ לִי בְּיִחוּד וְהוּא אוֹמֵר וַהֲלָה אוֹמֵר הֵיאַךְ נַנִּיחַ אֶת־אֱלֹהֵינוּ שֶׁבַּשָּׁמַיִם וְנֵלֵךְ
וְנַעֲבוֹד עֵצִים וַאֲבָנִים אִם חָזַר בּוֹ מוּטָב וְאִם אָמַר כָּךְ הוּא חוֹבָתֵנוּ וְכָךְ יָפֶה לָנוּ הָעוֹמְדִים
מֵאֲחוֹרֵי־הַגָּדֵר מְבִיאִין אוֹתוֹ לְבֵית־דִּין וְסוֹקְלִין אוֹתוֹ:
הָאוֹמֵר אֶעֱבוֹד אֵלֵךְ וְאֶעֱבוֹד נֵלֵךְ וְנַעֲבוֹד אֲזַבֵּחַ אֵלֵךְ וַאֲזַבֵּחַ נֵלֵךְ וּנְזַבֵּחַ אֲקַטֵּר אֵלֵךְ וַאֲקַטֵּר נֵלֵךְ
וּנְקַטֵּר אֲנַסֵּךְ אֵלֵךְ וַאֲנַסֵּךְ נֵלֵךְ וּנְנַסֵּךְ אֶשְׁתַּחֲוֶה אֵלֵךְ וְאֶשְׁתַּחֲוֶה נֵלֵךְ וְנִשְׁתַּחֲוֶה.
הַמַּדִּיחַ זֶה הָאוֹמֵר נֵלֵךְ וְנַעֲבוֹד עֲבוֹדָה זָרָה:

*Translation.* The seducer[264] – he is a layperson[265] who seduces a layperson; he says to him, "There is a god in a certain place who eats this, who drinks that, who does good in this way, who does harm in that way." They may not lie in wait[266] against anyone who is liable to the death penalties stipulated in the Law except in this case alone. If he spoke to two people, and they can act as witnesses against him, they bring him to the court and stone him. If he spoke to one person, he shall say to him, "I have companions who desire this." If he was crafty, he would not speak in their presence; but they lie in wait behind the wall,[267] and he says to him, "Tell me what you told me privately." And he tells. The person says, "How can we leave our God who is in Heaven and go and worship wood and stone?" If he retracts, it is good; but if he said, "It is our duty and it is auspicious for us," then those who are behind the wall shall bring him to the court and stone him. The person who says, "I will worship [another god], or "I will go and worship," or "Let us go and worship," or "I will sacrifice," or "I will go and sacrifice," or "Let us go and sacrifice," or "I will burn incense," or "I will go and burn incense," or "Let us go and burn incense," or "I will make a libation," or "I will go and make a libation," or "Let us go and make a libation," or "I will bow down," or "I will go and bow down," or "Let us go and bow down," [he is culpable]. The person who leads astray[268] [an entire town] is he who says, "Let us go and worship idols."

---

[264] The term מֵסִית is the hiphil participle of יסת "to cause to do, stir up, instigate;" cf. JASTROW, who renders מֵסִית as "he who stirs people up to worship idols" (s.v. יסת). Cf. HALOT s.v. סות hif. "to mislead, incite; to entice away; to incite against."

[265] The term הֶדְיוֹט derives from Greek ἰδιώτης. DANBY translates with "common man," NEUSNER with "ordinary fellow, " KRAUSS with "Privatmann."

[266] NEUSNER translates "place witnesses in hiding."

[267] The term translated as "wall" (גָּדֵר) refers to a dry-stone wall made without mortar from loose stones from a field (HALOT; cf. Num 22:24), e.g. in a vineyard or a sheep pen; here it could refer to the wall of the meeting house; cf. KRAUSS, Sanhedrin–Makkot, 235–36.

[268] The term מַדִּיחַ is the hiphil participle of נדח "to slip, move away," hiphil "to lead astray." DANBY and NEUSNER translate מַדִּיחַ as "he who leads astray" (a whole town); KRAUSS

*Commentary.* This text explains the statement concerning death penalty cases against the seducer of the people (*mesit*) and the person who leads astray (*maddiakh*) in *m. Sanh.* 7:4 (No. 36). The difference between a *mesit* and a *maddiakh* is the scope of the seduction: a *mesit* seduces an individual or several individuals, whereas a *maddiakh* incites an entire town to idolatry.[269] A. STROBEL understands the *mesit* as the educated ideologue who is openly active as heretic in a small circle of people, while the *maddiakh* is the uneducated demagogue who wants to influence through his secret teachings the masses.[270] Text No. 38 highlights the danger the *mesit* poses by describing him as a הֶדְיוֹט: he is not a sage or a rabbi but a common man who is not automatically recognized and who is therefore able to propagate his teachings under the radar. The mishnah explains what is legally allowed in proceedings against the *mesit*. The *mesit* is described as a layperson who seduces another layperson to serve other gods. The term הֶדְיוֹט excludes the false prophet who leads people astray, whose punishment is strangulation rather than stoning. The statement, "There is a god in a certain place who eats this, who drinks that, who does good in this way, who does harm in that way," reviews what a *mesit* might say. The provision "if he spoke (in this fashion) to two people, and they can act as witnesses against him" refers to two people who can act as witnesses against the *mesit* (because they are not related to him). The assertion of a single person whom the *mesit* has contacted, stating that he has "companions who desire this" is a ruse to get the *mesit* to speak to a larger group of people so that a larger number of witnesses hear his words. The person who says, "Tell me what you told me privately" is the person who was contacted by the *mesit* alone, i.e., without witnesses.[271] The section beginning with the statement, "The person who says, 'I will worship [another god],'" specifies the utterances of the *mesit* as well as the words spoken by the people who have been seduced. The mishnah emphasizes the importance of multiple (at least two) witnesses whom the *mesit* has seduced into being willing to engage in unsanctioned worship. And the mishnah asserts that a person who has heard the seductive talk of the *mesit* by himself has the right, indeed the duty, to entrap the *mesit* by secretly positioning his friends behind a wall where they

---

has "der Verstoßer," which is meant to refer to "the disowned city" ("soll auf die 'verstoßene' Stadt verweisen") (KRAUSS, Sanhedrin–Makkot, 217 n. 13). WEWERS, Sanhedrin, 207: "der Abtrünnigmachende" (on 7:18 [25d]).

[269] Cf. KRAUSS, Sanhedrin–Makkot, 216–17, n. 13, 236 n. 1. The term "city led astray" (עִיר הַנִּדַּחַת) is used in *m. Sanh.* 1:5; 9:1, and the legal procedures against the "city led astray" are described in *m. Sanh.* 10:4–6.

[270] STROBEL, Stunde, 82–83. On the *mesit* of the rabbis cf. JOSHUA J. SCHWARTZ, Peter and Ben Stada in Lydda, in The Book of Acts in its Palestinian Setting (ed. R. Bauckham; The Book of Acts in Its First-Century Setting, Volume 4; Exeter: Paternoster, 1995), 391–414, 400–3: the legal rules were stacked against the *mesit* because he threatened the very fabric of the Jewish commonwealth.

[271] KRAUSS, Sanhedrin–Makkot, 234–35.

can hear the *mesit* repeat his suggestive invitations to idolatry (the ancient version of the hidden wire worn by an undercover officer or informer to collect incriminating evidence). The mishnah explicitly states that while the *mesit* can be caught by people lying in wait for the purpose of entrapment, which is not allowed for all other persons who are guilty of offenses (כָּל־חַיָּבֵי־מִיתוֹת) for which the Law stipulates the death penalty (שֶׁבַּתּוֹרָה): the *mesit* is the only exception (חוּץ מִזּוֹ) to the rule that potential witnesses shall not lie in wait[272] against offenders (אֵין מַכְמִינִין עֲלֵיהֶן). The exception that mishnaic law allows for the *mesit* underlines the danger the *mesit* poses: measures otherwise illegal are permitted so he can be condemned by a sufficient number of witnesses in the subsequent trial.

J. NEUSNER dates the stipulations of this mishnah to the Usha period (A.D. 125–170).[273] A. STROBEL argues that these mishnaic stipulations were part of Jewish law by the first century as follows.[274] First, the terms *mesit* and *maddiakh* are technical terms of Jewish law that derive from Deuteronomy:

Deut 13:5 (ET 13:6): But those prophets or those who divine by dreams shall be put to death for having spoken treason against the LORD your God – who brought you out of the land of Egypt and redeemed you from the house of slavery – to turn you (לְהַדִּיחֲךָ) from the way in which the LORD your God commanded you to walk. So you shall purge the evil from your midst (NRSV).

Deut 13:7–12 (ET 13:6–11): If anyone secretly entices (יְסִיתְךָ) you – even if it is your brother, your father's son or your mother's son, or your own son or daughter, or the wife you embrace, or your most intimate friend – saying, "Let us go worship other gods," whom neither you nor your ancestors have known, ⁷ any of the gods of the peoples that are around you, whether near you or far away from you, from one end of the earth to the other, ⁸ you must not yield to or heed any such persons. Show them no pity or compassion and do not shield them. ⁹ But you shall surely kill them; your own hand shall be first against them to execute them, and afterwards the hand of all the people. ¹⁰ Stone them to death for trying to turn you away from the LORD your God, who brought you out of the land of Egypt, out of the house of slavery. ¹¹ Then all Israel shall hear and be afraid, and never again do any such wickedness (NRSV).

Deut 13:13–18 (ET 13:12–17): If you hear it said about one of the towns that the LORD your God is giving you to live in, ¹³ that scoundrels from among you have gone out and led the inhabitants of the town astray (וַיַּדִּיחוּ), saying, "Let us go and worship other gods," whom you have not known, ¹⁴ then you shall inquire and make a thorough investigation. If the charge is established that such an abhorrent thing has been done among you, ¹⁵ you shall put the inhabitants of that town to the sword, utterly destroying it and everything in it – even putting its livestock to the sword. ¹⁶ All of its spoil you shall gather into its public square; then burn the town and all its spoil with fire, as a whole burnt offering to the LORD your God. It shall remain a perpetual ruin, never to be rebuilt (NRSV).

Second, the Temple Scroll confirms that the mishnaic stipulations against seducers were integral elements of Jewish law before the first century

---

[272] The verb כמן means "to be hidden, lie in wait" (JASTROW); LEVY s.v. כמן hiphil, "jemdn. verbergen, im Versteck, auf der Lauer halten" (2:344, with citation of this mishnah).

[273] NEUSNER, A History of the Mishnaic Law of Damages, 5:106–10, cf. ibid. 169–73.

[274] STROBEL, Stunde, 81–84.

(11QTemple LIV, 8 – LV, 10; cf. No. 19). The subject of being led astray (נדח) is often mentioned in the Dead Sea Scrolls.[275] Note, however, that the usual term for the concept of enticing or seduction in the Scrolls is פתה,[276] and that the nominalized participles מֵסִית and מַדִּיחַ do not occur in the Scrolls. The assertion of A. STROBEL that the concept of the seducer was "without doubt" legally defined for a long time[277] goes beyond the evidence, at least linguistically. There is little doubt, however, that the stipulations of *m. Sanh.* 7:10 regarding the seducer (*mesit*) are in keeping with the stipulations of Deut 13 and 11QTemple LIV–LV. These texts underline the seriousness of the offense committed by a person who seduces others.

The permission to entrap the seducer in order to obtain the required number of witnesses can be linked with Mark 14:1 as an explanation for the irregularities in Jesus' trial:

Mark 14:1: It was two days before the Passover and the festival of Unleavened Bread. The chief priests and the scribes were looking for a way to arrest Jesus by stealth (ἐν δόλῳ)[278] and kill him (NRSV).

**(39)** *m. Sanhedrin* 7:11

הַמְכַשֵּׁף זֶה הָעוֹשֶׂה מַעֲשֶׂה לֹא הָאוֹחֵז אֶת־הָעֵנַיִם. רַבִּי עֲקִיבָה אוֹמֵר מִשּׁוּם רַבִּי יְהוֹשֻׁעַ שְׁנַיִם לוֹקְטִין קִשּׁוּאִין אֶחָד לוֹקֵט פָּטוּר וְאֶחָד לוֹקֵט חַיָּב הָעוֹשֶׂה מַעֲשֶׂה חַיָּב וְהָאוֹחֵז אֶת־הָעֵנַיִם פָּטוּר:

*Translation.* The sorcerer – he who performs a deed, and not the person who (merely) deceives the eyes.[279] Rabbi Aqiba says in the name of Rabbi Jehoshua, "If two (people) were gathering cucumbers (by sorcery), one gatherer may be exempt (from punishment), and one gatherer may be liable: the person who performs a deed is liable, but the person who only deceives the eyes is exempt.

---

[275] Cf. 1QM XIV, 9; 1QHᵃ XII, 8, 9; 4Q200 Frag. 6, 8; 4Q504 Frags. 1–2 V, 12; 4Q509 Frags. 12 I – 13, 1; 11Q5 XVIII, 6. In 4Q491 Frags. 8–10 I, 7 the author praises God for now allowing the people belonging to the empire of Belial to "separate" the members of the community from his covenant.

[276] Cf. CD XV, 11; 1QHᵃ XII, 16; XIV, 19; Frag. 4, 8; 4Q184 1,17; 4Q266 Frag. 8 I, 2; 4Q270 Frag. 6 II, 8; 4Q417 Frag. 1 II, 12, 13; 4Q430 4; 11QTemple LXVI, 8. The term that STROBEL, Stunde, 84, translates as "Verführung" in CD XII, 2–3 is סָרָה which means, rather, "Abtrünnigkeit" ("rebellion, falsehood"); for סָרָה see also CD V, 21; 4Q177 Frags. 1–4, 14; 4Q267 Frag. 2, 5; Frag. 4, 13; 4Q270 Frag. 2 II, 14; 4Q271 Frag. 5 I, 18; 4Q408 Frag. 11, 5; 11QTemple LIV, 15; LXI, 8.

[277] STROBEL, Stunde, 84; the following point ibid. 85.

[278] TNIV "looking for some sly way" is too negative; BDAG offers "deceit, cunning, treachery," for the dative δόλῳ "by cunning or stealth."

[279] NEUSNER dissolves the metaphor of the phrase הָאוֹחֵז אֶת־הָעֵנַיִם and translates as "creates an illusion."

*Commentary*. This text, which comments on the death penalty for the sorcerer (מְכַשֵּׁף) mentioned in *m. Sanh*. 7:4, distinguishes between a concrete act (מַעֲשֶׂה) performed by magic and tricks which deceive the eyes but cause nothing to happen by occult powers. The example of two people gathering cucumbers was presumably a well-known conjuring trick.[280] A person who gathers cucumbers by means of a concrete magic act is liable to be punished with death by stoning, as the Law in Exod 22:17 states (which is quoted twice in the parallel passage *y. Sanh*. 25d,12–21). If a person collects cucumbers with the help of a conjuring trick, he is not liable to the death penalty (which could either mean that this is still prohibited but not punished with the death penalty or that conjuring tricks are allowed).[281] The explanations in Talmud Yerushalmi (*y. Sanh*. 25d,55–61) and in the Babylonian Talmud (*m. Sanh*. 67a-b) provide several examples for this distinction.

*y. Sanh*. 25d,55–61: Rabbi Yannai said, "I (once) walked on a road from Sepphoris and saw a heretic (מיני) who took a stone, threw it in the air, and it came down and it had become a calf." But Rabbi Le'azar said in the name of Rabbi Yose bar Zimra, "If all who have come into the world were to gather together, they could not create a fly and put life in it. Shall we say that the heretic did not take a stone, threw it in the air, and it came down and it had become a calf? Rather, he called a crook[282] who stole for him a calf from a farmyard and brought it to him." Rabbi Hinena be Rabbi Hananya said, "I (once) walked in Gufta near Sepphoris and saw a heretic (מיני) who took a skull, threw it into the air, and it came down and it had become a calf. I came and told this to my father. He said to me, 'If you ate from it, it was an act [i.e., a real act of magic], if not, it was (merely) a deception of the eyes [i.e., a conjuring trick].'"

## (40) *m. Sanhedrin* 11:5

נְבִיא־הַשֶּׁקֶר וְהַמִּתְנַבֵּא מַה־שֶּׁלֹּא שָׁמַע וּמַה־שֶּׁלֹּא נֶאֱמַר לוֹ אֲבָל הַכּוֹבֵשׁ אֶת־נְבוּאָתוֹ וְהַמּוֹתֵר עַל־
דִּבְרֵי־הַנָּבִיא וְנָבִיא שֶׁעָבַר עַל־דִּבְרֵי־עַצְמוֹ מִיתָתוֹ בִּידֵי־שָׁמַיִם שֶׁנֶּאֱמַר אָנֹכִי אֶדְרֹשׁ מֵעִמּוֹ

*Translation*. "The false prophet" – one who prophesies something which he has not heard or something which was not said to him (is put to death by man). But he who holds back his prophecy, and he who adds to the words of a prophet, and the prophet who transgresses his own words – he is put to death by the hand of Heaven, because it is said, "I will require it of him" (Deut 18:19).

*Commentary*. This mishnah explains the term "false prophet" (נְבִיא־הַשֶּׁקֶר, "prophet of falsehood") in the list *m. Sanh*. 11:1, which itemizes the offenders who are to be executed by strangulation. The phrase "one who prophesies something which he has not heard" (הַמִּתְנַבֵּא מַה־שֶּׁלֹּא שָׁמַע) explains the phrase

---

[280] WEWERS, Sanhedrin, 208 n. 293.
[281] KRAUSS, Sanhedrin–Makkot, 239.
[282] JASTROW (s.v. סריא) and WEWERS read סריה (with MS Leiden 460).

"he who prophesies in the name of foreign worship (i.e., idolatry)" (הַמִּתְנַבֵּא לְשֵׁם־עֲבוֹדָה זָרָה) from 11:1. The false prophet whose teaching leads to apostasy is to be executed. Prophets who are not prosecuted and executed but left to God's judgment are: the prophet who does not speak even though he has received a message from God, the prophet who adds to the words spoken by another prophet (KRAUSS; NEUSNER: "he who disregards the words of another prophet"), and the prophet who acts in opposition to his own words (as the prophet in 1 Kings 13:26). This discussion follows after a mishnah, which explains why, according to Rabbi Aqiba, certain criminals shall be executed not in the local towns but in Jerusalem at the time of the next pilgrimage festival (*m. Sanh.* 11:3). Reference is made to this mishnah as evidence for Jesus' execution during the Passover Festival[283] and as possible explanation for Jesus' arrest.[284] In their explanation of the mishnah in 11:5, the later rabbis distinguished six categories of false prophets: three are executed in human courts – a person who prophecies what he has not heard, presuming to speak in the name of God; a person who prophesies what was not told him, prophesying words which God did not command him to speak; a person who prophesies in the name of an idol – and three are dealt with by God: a prophet who suppresses his prophecy (e.g., Jonah, the son of Amittai), a prophet who disregards the words of a prophet (e.g., the colleague of Micah, the son of Imlah), and a prophet who transgresses his own words (e.g., Iddo, the prophet); *b. Sanh.* 89a–b.

## (41)  *t. Sanhedrin* 10:11

כל חייבי מיתות שבתורה אין ממיתין עליהן חוץ מן המסית כיצד מוסרין לו שני תלמידי חכמים
בבית הפנימי והוא יושב בבית החיצון ומדליקין לו את הנר כדי שיהו רואין אותו ושומעים את
קולו וכן עשו לבן סטדא בלוד נימנו עליו שני תלמידי חכמים וסקלוהו פותחין את דינו ביום
וגומרין אף בלילה פותחין וגומרין בו ביום בין לזכות בין לחובה מטין על פי אחד בין לזכות בין
לחובה הכל מלמדין זכות וחובה המלמד זכות יכול לחזור וללמד חובה הסריס ומי שלא ראה לו
בנים יושבין בדין ור' יהודה מוסיף אף האכזרי

*Translation.* For all those who are guilty of the death penalties [mentioned] in the Torah, one may not keep witnesses hidden[285] except for the Mesit.[286] How [do they proceed]? [The court] gives him [the person who has been exposed to

---

[283] JEREMIAS, Abendmahlsworte, 72–73; cf. BLINZLER, Prozeß, 45.

[284] BLINZLER, Prozeß, 86, 187.

[285] מכן means "to be hidden, to lie in wait;" the Hifil is translated as "to keep witnesses hidden" (while eliciting a confession); cf. JASTROW, 646. Manuscript E reads אין ממיין ("one does not kill"), which implies that only the death sentences are carried out that have been pronounced against people convicted of being a *mesit*. The translation of the text is adapted from SALOMONSEN and NEUSNER.

[286] Cf. *m. Sanh.* 7:10 (No. 38); cf. ibid. for the *mesit*. See *b. Sanh.* 67a Baraita.

seduction] two[287] disciples of the sages [who are put] in an inside room of the house, while he [the suspect] sits outside; and they light a candle for him, so that they can see him and hear his voice. This is what they did in the case against Ben Stada in Lud [Lydda]. The two disciples of the sages were appointed [as witnesses] against him, and they stoned him. [The judges] can begin the trial by day and complete it even during the night; they can begin and complete the trial on the same day, whether [the trial] leads to acquittal or to conviction; they can decide the trial with the majority of a single vote, whether for acquittal or conviction. All can argue for acquittal or for conviction; he who argues for acquittal can change his position and argue for conviction. A eunuch and a person who has never had children can serve on the court. And Rabbi Yehudah says, "also the cruel person [may sit on the court in the trial of this type]."

*Commentary.* This text suggests that the usual precautions stipulated for capital cases (cf. *m. Sanh.* 4:1; No. 32) were suspended for legal proceedings involving a *mesit* who seduces other lay persons to idolatry.[288] The first part of the text (until "and they stoned him") corresponds to *m. Sanh.* 7:10, while the following stipulations complement the stipulation of the same mishnah: "They may not lie in wait against anyone who is liable to the death penalties stipulated in the Law except in this case alone," permitting procedures that are normally applicable only in property cases (*m. Sanh.* 4:1). The accusers are permitted to set a trap for the person accused of being a *mesit*. The fact that it was generally prohibited to set a trap for a transgressor of the law or for the opposing party in a court case is confirmed by *y. Sanh.* 21c,5: המכמין עידיו אחרי גדר לא עשה כלום ("he who hides his witnesses behind a fence [so that they hear the confession of a debtor] has done nothing," i.e., their testimony is unusable. The use of a trap is prohibited in capital cases in particular because it makes the obligatory warning impossible.[289]

The case against Ben Stada is cited as an example for setting a trap in order to gather evidence against a *mesit*. As regards the name Ben Stada, the standard printed editions of the Tosefta have איש אחד ("a certain man"), while MS Vienna reads "the house of Stada;" other rabbinic traditions speak of "Ben Stada" (בן סטדא). Ben Stada is only mentioned in rabbinic literature.[290] In some traditions, Ben Stada was an Egyptian sorcerer,[291] in others a seducer

---

[287] According to Deut 17:6, two witnesses are required in a capital case.

[288] Cf. SALOMONSEN, Sanhedrin–Makkot, 172 n. 81.

[289] Cf. SALOMONSEN, Sanhedrin–Makkot, 170 n. 74.

[290] JASTROW, 972 explains סָטְדָא as probably of Greek origin, comparable to the proper noun ὁ σταδιεύς, "one who runs in a stadium." R. TRAVERS HERFORD, Christianity in Talmud and Midrash (1903; repr., Jersey City, NJ: Ktav, 2006), 344 links סָטְדָא with ὁ ἀνάστατος, "the one who rises up, the insurgent." See the commentary below.

[291] *m. Šabb.* 11:15; *y. Šabb.* 13d,27; *b. Šabb.* 104b Bar.

who was stoned and hanged on the eve of Passover in Lydda.[292] It has been suggested that Ben Stada is Jesus,[293] James the brother of Jesus,[294] or Peter.[295]

The text allows, in trials involving a *mesit*, that the judges of the court complete the trial at night, i.e., that a verdict is reached after sundown. Such trials are permitted to be started and completed on the same day, with a majority of one sufficient for conviction (the Mishnah required a majority of two for conviction and stipulated a conviction could not be reached until the following day; acquittals could be reached the same day as the trial started). All sages on the court can argue for both acquittal and conviction (according to the Mishnah, only the judges, not all sages present, can argue for conviction). Judges who argue for acquittal can change their mind and argue for conviction (according to the Mishnah, sages who argued for conviction can change the mind and later argue for acquittal, but sages who argued in favor of acquittal cannot change and argue in favor of conviction). A eunuch and a person who has never had children can serve as judges, according to R. Yehudah even a mean (or cruel) person can serve on a court which decides a capital case. The corresponding mishnah in *m. Sanh.* 7:10 dates to the Usha period (A.D. 125–170).[296] A. STROBEL regards *t. Sanh.* 10:11 as evidence that Jesus' trial before the Sanhedrin adhered to the legal requirements of a trial against a *mesit* or *maddiakh* during which the usual precautionary measures which insisted on fair and humane proceedings were suspended.[297]

---

[292] *m. Sanh.* 10.11; *y. Sanh.* 25d,2–3; *y. Yebam.* 15d,64; *b. Sanh.* 67a.

[293] LEVY, 3:499, interprets בן סטדא as a derogatory name consisting of the elements סטדיא = דא סוטה דא, a phrase which describes Jesus as "son of a *sotah*," i.e. a woman suspected of adultery (with reference to Mark 6:1–6 par and Matt 1:16 where Jesus is named after his mother (rather than his father). Cf. JOSEPH KLAUSNER, Jesus of Nazareth: His Life, Times, and Teaching (London: Allen & Unwin, 1925), 21–22; MORRIS GOLDSTEIN, Jesus in the Jewish Tradition (New York: Macmillan, 1950), 57–62; DAVID ROKEAH, Ben Stara is Ben Pantera – Toward the Clarification of a Philological-Historical Problem, Tarbiz 39 (1970): 9–18; PETER SCHÄFER, Jesus im Talmud (2, durchgesehene Auflage; Tübingen: Mohr Siebeck, 2010), 31–36, 277 (= PETER SCHÄFER, Jesus in the Talmud [Princeton: Princeton University Press, 2007], 16–18, 141); DAVID INSTONE-BREWER, Jesus of Nazareth's Trial in the Uncensored Talmud, TynBul 62 (2011): 269–294, 272. See also SALOMONSEN, Sanhedrin–Makkot, 170–71. For arguments against the identification of Ben Stada with Jesus cf. JOSEPH DERENBOURG, Essai sur l'histoire et la géographie de la Palestine (Paris: Imprimerie impériale, 1867), 468–71. LOUIS GINZBERG, Some Observations on the Attitude of the Synagogue Towards the Apocalyptic-Eschatological Writings, JBL 41 (1922): 115–136. HERFORD, Christianity in Talmud and Midrash, 345, argues that Ben Stada was both an Egyptian sorcerer and the seducer who was executed in Lydda, later confused with Jesus.

[294] J. LOEWY, Die drei Jacobus, Das Juedische Literaturblatt 7/4 (1878): 15; HANS-JOACHIM SCHOEPS, Simon Magus in der Haggada? *HUCA* 2 (1948): 257–274.

[295] B. KÖNIGSBERGER, Miscellen aus der juedischen Alterthumskunde, Das Juedische Literaturblatt 20 (1891): 40; SCHWARTZ, Peter and Ben Stada, 391–414.

[296] NEUSNER, A History of the Mishnaic Law of Damages, 5:106–10, cf. ibid. 169–73.

[297] STROBEL, Stunde, 84–85 (where "TSanh VII,11" refers to *t. Sanh.* 10:11 (correct ibid. 87 n. 232). The evidence of the Tosefta for explaining the differences between the Gospel

**(42)** *t. Sanhedrin* 11:7

בן סורר ומורה וזקן ממרא על פי בית דין והמסית והמדיח ונביא השקר ועדים זממין אין ממיתין
אותן מיד אלא מעלין אותן לבית דין הגדול שבירושלים ומשמרין אותן עד הרגל וממיתין אותן
ברגל שנאמר וכל העם ישמעו ויראו ולא יזידון עוד דברי ר' עקיבה אמר לו ר' יהודה וכי נאמר
וכל העם יראו ויראו אלא לא נאמר אלא כל העם ישמעו ויראו ולמה מעניין את דינו של זה אלא
ממיתין אותו מיד וכותבין ושולחין בכל המקומות איש פלוני נגמר דינו בבית דינו של פלוני
ופלוני ופלוני עדיו וכך וכך עשה וכן עשו לו.

*Translation.* A rebellious and incorrigible son, a person who defies the court,[298] a *mesit*, a *maddiakh*, a false prophet, and witnesses proved perjurers: they are not executed immediately, but they are taken to the Supreme Court in Jerusalem and kept imprisoned until the (next) festival, and they are executed on the festival, as it is said, "And all the people shall hear and fear, and no more sin presumptuously" (Deut 17:13). [These are] the words of Rabbi Aqiba. Rabbi Yehudah said to him, "Is it said, 'And all the people shall see and fear'? It is not thus stated, however, but rather: 'And all the people shall hear and fear.' Why should they postpone the [execution of the] sentence of this person at all? But they execute him immediately, and they send the following written messages everywhere: 'So-and-so – his sentence was pronounced by the court in such-and-such, his witnesses are such-and-such and such-and-such, he did this and that, and this is what they did to him.'"

*Commentary.* This text supplements *m. Sanh.* 8:5–7[299] and parallels *m. Sanh.* 11:5 (No. 40) and *b. Sanh.* 89a baraita (No. 45). The six categories of criminals[300] are linked with different death sentences. What unites them is the practice that they are not executed immediately after conviction.[301] Among them is the *mesit* (המסית), i.e., the layperson who seduces another layperson to idolatry, and the *maddiakh* (המדיח), i.e., the person who leads a town into apostasy, as well as the false prophet (נביא השקר). Rabbi Aqiba and Rabbi Yehudah agree that the trial and the conviction of these six types of criminals can take place outside of Jerusalem. They disagree concerning the place of execution. Aqiba

---

accounts of Jesus' trial before the Sanhedrin and later rabbinic law is ignored by most scholars before Strobel's study; cf. BROWN, *Death*, 1:362, whose (only) reference to *t. Sanh.* 11.7 cites JOACHIM JEREMIAS, *The Eucharistic Words of Jesus* (orig. 1966; repr., London: SCM, 1976), 79 with n. 1.

[298] SALOMONSEN, *Sanhedrin–Makkot*: "einen gegen das Gericht ungehorsamen"; NEUSNER, *Tosefta*: "defiant elder."

[299] Cf. NEUSNER, *A History of the Mishnaic Law of Damages*, 3:206.

[300] The obstinate and intractable son (Deut 21:18–21), the scribe who rebels against the court (Deut 17:8–13), the seducer to idolatry (Deut 13:7–12), the seducer of an entire community to idolatry (Deut 13:13–19), a false prophet (Deut 18:20), and a false witness (Deut 19:18–21).

[301] This is the usual practice, out of consideration for the transgressor; cf. *m. Sanh.* 6:1. Cf. SALOMONSEN, *Sanhedrin–Makkot*, 180 n. 48.

insists that they can be executed only in Jerusalem during the next pilgrimage festival (Passover, Weeks, or Tabernacles), a ruling which necessitates a postponement of the execution, while Rabbi Yehudah argues that they can be executed immediately. According to Aqiba, these six categories of criminals are not executed immediately upon conviction but taken to Jerusalem and executed during one of the main Jewish festivals. The phrase עד הרגל means that the convicted criminal is kept imprisoned until the next of the three pilgrimage festivals. He is executed ברגל, i.e., during the next festival. This procedure is defended with Deut 17:13. Two authorities disagree about the interpretation of ישמעו in the biblical text.[302] Aqiba takes the verb to mean that the people shall participate in the execution and thus have fear (as a deterrent). Rabbi Yehuah interprets the verb literally and argues that the people are not present: they hear of the execution after it has taken place. The question, "Why should they postpone the [execution of the] sentence of this person at all?," refers to deterrence as the reason for the postponement of the execution, which is rejected by Rabbi Yehudah.[303] He goes on to assert that there is no need to take the convicted criminal to Jerusalem (and thus postpone the execution): as a provincial court has ruled on the death sentence of these culprits, so the provincial court can proceed to execute the criminals in that town, immediately. The ruling of Aqiba (c. A.D. 40–135) may derive from his interpretation of Deut 17:13, or it may be an attempt to confirm a local tradition, while Rabbi Yehuah's ruling seems more likely to be historical in the context of the second century A.D.[304]

J. JEREMIAS refers to *t. Sanh.* 11:7 as evidence that executions of people convicted of the most serious offenses should be carried out during one of the pilgrimage feasts when "all the people" were assembled in Jerusalem, in fulfillment of Deut 17:13, and that the Gospel narratives of Jesus' crucifixion thus "portray no incident which could not have taken place on Nisan 15."[305]

## (43) *y. Sanhedrin* 25c,74–25d,10

הַמֵּסִית זֶה הֶדְיוֹט כּוּל'. הָא חָכָם לֹא. מִכֵּיוָן שֶׁהוּא מֵסִית אֵין זֶה חָכָם. מִכֵּיוָן שֶׁהוּא נִיסִּית אֵין זֶה חָכָם. כֵּיצַד עוֹשִׂין לְהַעֲרִים עָלָיו. מַכְמִינִין עָלָיו שְׁנֵי עֵדִים בַּבַּיִת הַפְּנִימִית וּמוֹשִׁיבִין אוֹתוֹ בַבַּיִת הַחִיצוֹן וּמַדְלִיקִין אֶת הַנֵּר עַל גַּבָּיו כְּדֵי שֶׁיְּהוּ רוֹאִין אוֹתוֹ וְשׁוֹמְעִין אֶת קוֹלוֹ. שֶׁכֵּךְ עָשׂוּ לְבֶן סוֹטָדָא בְּלוֹד וְהִכְמִינוּ עָלָיו שְׁנֵי תַלְמִידֵי חֲכָמִים וְהֱבִיאוּהוּ לָבֵית דִּין וּסְקָלוּהוּ. וָכָה אַתְּ אָמַר הָכֵן. שַׁנְיָיא הִיא דְּאָמַר. אֲנִי. וְאָמַר אוֹף הָכָא. אֲנִי. שֶׁלֹּא יַעֲרִים. וְיַעֲרִים. שֶׁלֹּא יֵלֵךְ וְיַסִּית עַצְמוֹ וְיַסִּית אֲחֵרִים

---

[302] For the following interpretation cf. SALOMONSEN, Sanhedrin–Makkot, 180–81.

[303] According to *b. Sanh.* 43a Bar, the reason for the postponement is the possibility that a witness who might speak for acquittal may need time to travel to Jerusalem.

[304] SALOMONSEN, Sanhedrin–Makkot, 181 n. 55.

[305] JEREMIAS, Eucharistic Words, 78–79, quotation 79 (highlighted by Jeremias with italics). Cf. STROBEL, Stunde, 84 with n. 222. Also BROWN, Death, 1:362, who asserts, however, that "overall the evidence is really not clear."

מֵסִית אוֹמֵר בְּלָשׁוֹן גָּבוֹהַּ וְהַמַּדִּיחַ אוֹמֵר בְּלָשׁוֹן נָמוּךְ. מֵסִית שֶׁאָמַר בְּלָשׁוֹן נָמוּךְ נַעֲשָׂה מַדִּיחַ. וּמַדִּיחַ שֶׁאָמַר בְּלָשׁוֹן גָּבוֹהַּ נַעֲשָׂה מֵסִית. מֵסִית אוֹמֵר בְּלָשׁוֹן הַקּוֹדֶשׁ וּמַדִּיחַ אוֹמֵר בְּלָשׁוֹן הֶדְיוֹט. מֵסִית שֶׁאָמַר בְּלָשׁוֹן הֶדְיוֹט נַעֲשָׂה מַדִּיחַ. וּמַדִּיחַ שֶׁאָמַר בְּלָשׁוֹן הַקּוֹדֶשׁ נַעֲשָׂה מֵסִית:[306]

*Translation.* "The seducer (*mesit*) is an ordinary person," etc. Therefore not a Sage? Insofar as he seduces (to idolatry), he is not a Sage. Insofar as he is seduced, he is not a Sage. How do they proceed to outsmart (the seducer to idolatry)? One hides two witnesses inside the house, (25d) and puts him into an outer room, lights a candle near him so that they can see him and hear his voice. This is what they did to Ben Sotada in Lydda, where they hid two disciples of Sages, and (in consequence of what they saw and heard) they brought him to the courthouse, and stoned him. Do you say this here?[307] This is a different case because he (the man in *m. Yebam.* 16:6) said, "I am" (because the man is heard to speak of himself, the witnesses do not need to identify him further). But here he also said "I am"? (Nevertheless, here he is outsmarted) so that the does not outsmart (the others) and flees, so that he does not go and seduce himself and others with him. The seducer (*mesit*) speaks in an elevated voice, and the beguiler (*maddiakh*) speaks in a low voice. The seducer who speaks in a low voice is treated as (or becomes) a beguiler, and the beguiler who speaks in an elevated voice is treated as a seducer. The seducer speaks in the holy language (i.e., Hebrew), and the beguiler speaks in an ordinary language. The seducer who speaks in an ordinary language is treated as a beguiler, and the beguiler who speaks in the holy language is treated as seducer.

*Commentary.* This text[308] discusses the mishnah in *m. Sanh.* 7:10. The rabbis clarify that a *mesit* who seduces another person to engage in idolatry, a crime punishable by death, is a layperson (הדיוט), not a Sage (חכם), i.e., a trained rabbi. A long section is devoted to a discussion of the means by which evidence against a *mesit* can be gathered. A *mesit* presents a problem for law enforcement. If he seeks to seduce a single person, this person cannot appear in court as a witness, given that two witnesses are required.[309] Thus, in contrast to the standard precautions stipulated for capital cases, which prohibited setting a trap for people suspected of a crime,[310] the rabbis argue that a *mesit* can be exposed by two hidden witnesses who overhear the man trying to seduce others to worship other gods. Witnesses who testify against a *mesit* in court are not required to have personally confronted (and warned) the seducer.

---

[306] Punctuation adopted from GUGGENHEIMER, Tractates Sanhedrin, Makkot, and Horaiot.

[307] In view of the different ruling concerning the death of a husband in *m. Yebam.* 16:6, in which the rabbis stipulate that "they may give evidence by the light of a lamp or by the light of the moon, and they may suffer a woman to marry again [solely on evidence afforded] by an echo" – in the latter case, one does *not* see the person. WEWERS, Sanhedrin, 207 n. 290.

[308] The first three paragraphs are paralleled in *y. Yebam.* 15d,61–68.

[309] Cf. GUGGENHEIMER, Tractates Sanhedrin, Makkot, and Horaiot, 277 n. 351.

[310] Cf. *m. Sanh.* 4:1 (No. 32); *y. Sanh.* 21c,5.

It is sufficient that they saw him (and thus can identify him) and that they heard his voice. The case against Ben Sotada (Ben Stada) is cited as an example for testifying against a *mesit*. The fact that these procedures, and the case of Ben Stada, parallel *t. Sanh.* 10:11 (No. 41), suggests an early date for this legal tradition. The discussion in *y. Sanh.* 25d,5–10 adds that the *mesit* speaks with an elevated or loud voice using the "holy language" (בלשון הקודש), i.e., Hebrew, while the *maddiakh* (who entices an entire town to idolatry) speaks in a low or soft voice and speaks "in an ordinary language" (בלשון הדיוט), i.e., a language of the Gentiles. The latter distinction may be explained with respect to location: A town that can be seduced to idolatry is conceivable only outside of Jewish territory; it is thus a town where the *maddiakh* would have to use a common or non-Jewish language.[311] This text formulates the possible exceptions from the rule of what distinguishes a *mesit* and a *maddiakh*.[312] The *mesit* is an educated person who can speak with a soft voice in the context of his family and acquaintances, conveying his seductive message in a face-to-face conversation. Similarly, the *maddiakh*, who generally seeks to incite an entire town into idolatry through his public demagoguery, may on occasion agitate with a "low voice," i.e., in secret. The key factor is not the specific behavior but the intention (to seduce to idolatry) and the effects of their message (idolatrous actions).

## (44) *b. Sanhedrin* 46a

תניא ר"א בן יעקב אומר שמעתי שבית דין מכין ועונשין שלא מן התורה ולא לעבור על דברי
תורה אלא כדי לעשות סייג לתורה ומעשה באחד שרכב על סוס בשבת בימי יונים והביאוהו
לבית דין וסקלוהו לא מפני שראוי לכך אלא שהשעה צריכה לכך שוב מעשה באדם אחד שהטיח
את אשתו תחת התאנה והביאוהו לבית דין והלקוהו לא מפני שראוי לכך אלא שהשעה צריכה
לכך

*Translation.* It has been taught: Rabbi Eliezer b. Jacob says, "I heard that the court may impose floggings and pronounce (capital) sentences even if they are not in accord with the Torah. Yet (this is not so) with the intention of disregarding the words of the Torah but (on the contrary) in order to establish a fence around the Torah. And there is the precedent of the man who rode a horse on the Sabbath in the time of the Greeks, and they brought him before the court and stoned him, not because he was liable (to be stoned), but because the times required it. And there is the other precedent of a man who had intercourse with his wife under a fig tree, and they brought him before the court and flogged him, not because he deserved it but because the times required it."

---

[311] KRAUSS, Sanhedrin–Makkot, 237.
[312] For the following explanation cf. STROBEL, Stunde, 82–83.

*Commentary.* This text belongs to the larger context of the rabbis' discussion of the Scriptural basis of the death penalty as described in *m. Sanh.* 6:4, more specifically the extra-legal penalties stipulated by Simeon b. Shetah. Rabbi Eliezer b. Jacob insists, on the basis of the authority of his teachers (שמעתי), that harsh sentences could be imposed even in cases for which the Torah did not stipulate a particular sentence. The reason for going beyond the Torah is not the intention to disregard the teaching of the Torah (לא לעבור על דברי תורה), but in order to erect a "fence around the Torah" (סייג לתורה), i.e., with the intention of safeguarding against its violation. Extraordinary measures have became necessary "because the times required it" (השעה צריכה לכך).[313] One precedent (מעשה) is cited from the time of the Greeks (יונים), i.e., the pre-Maccabean period. A man who rode a horse on the Sabbath was stoned, even though the prohibition against riding on the Sabbath is not stipulated in the Torah.[314] The second precedent, which is not dated, relates to a man who had intercourse with his wife under a fig tree, i.e., in public, and was subsequently flogged, a punishment not stipulated in the Torah for such an action. This and similar passages relate trial procedures in which rabbis appeal to the principle of "a decision under an emergency" (הוֹרָאת שָׁעָה).[315] E. STAUFFER cites this principle as explanation for the irregularities of Jesus' trial before the San-hedrin.[316] The legal problems of Jesus' trial would be immediately solved if it could be assumed that his conviction by the high priest was based on the prin-ciple of "a decision under an emergency." It is unclear, however, whether this legal principle existed in the early first century A.D. Rabbi Eliezer b. Yacob is either a Tanna who lived c. A.D. 70–90, or, due to more frequent references, much more likely a Tanna who lived c. A.D. 150. It is doubtful הוֹרָאת שָׁעָה was ever accepted as a legal principle. It can hardly have been a principle used by Pharisees since they tended to protect the accused against arbitrary procedures and rulings, nor would a Sadducean court resort to an "emergency decision"

---

[313] Cf. JASTROW, 1301 s.v. צָרִיךְ: "the condition of the time required such a measure" (with reference to *y. Ḥag.* 78a and *b. Sanh.* 46a).

[314] SHAYE J. D. COHEN, Pagan and Christian Evidence on the Ancient Synagogue [1987], in The Significance of Yavneh and Other Essays in Jewish Hellenism (TSAJ 136; Tübingen: Mohr Siebeck, 2010), 244–265, here 256, cites *b. Sanh.* 46a as well as *y. Ḥag.* 77b (2:1); *Ber. Rab.* 65:22, as texts which mention apostates riding horses on the Sabbath.

[315] Cf. JASTROW, 341 s.v. הוֹרָיָה, הוֹרָאָה, describing the phrase הוֹרָאת שָׁעָה as "a decision under an emergency, a special dispensation (not to be taken as a precedent); cf. ibid. 1609 s.v. שָׁעָה, where he describes the same phrase as "temporary, special legislation," in both cases referring to *b. Yoma* 69b. Note that *b. Sanh.* 46a uses a different phrase, a fact that seems to have been missed by STROBEL, Stunde, 85 n. 227. Note below *Sifre Devarim* §221 on Deut 21:22 (No. 62), discussed in this context by BLINZLER, Prozeß, 204–6 n. 68.

[316] ETHELBERT STAUFFER, Neue Wege der Jesusforschung, Wissenschaftliche Zeitschrift der Martin-Luther-Universität Halle-Wittenberg 7/2 (1958): 451–476. Cf. BØRGE SALOMONSEN, Einige kritische Bemerkungen zu Stauffers Darstellung der spätjüdischen Ketzergesetzgebung, ST 18 (1964): 91–118, for a critique.

that went beyond the Torah since they tended to uphold the letter of the Law.[317]

## (45) *b. Sanhedrin* 89a

תנו רבנן אין ממיתין אותו לא בבית דין שבעירו ולא בבית דין שביבנה אלא מעלין אותו לב"ד
הגדול שבירושלים ומשמרין אותו עד הרגל וממיתין אותו ברגל שנאמר וכל העם ישמעו ויראו
דברי רבי עקיבא אמר לו ר' יהודה וכי נאמר יראו ויראו והלא לא נאמר אלא ישמעו ויראו למה
מענין דינו של זה אלא ממיתין אותו מיד וכותבין ושולחין בכל מקום איש פלוני נתחייב מיתה
בבית דין  ת"ר ארבעה צריכין הכרזה המסית ובן סורר ומורה וזקן ממרא ועדים זוממין בכולהו
כתיב בהו וכל העם וכל ישראל בעדים זוממין כתיב והנשארי' דלא כולי עלמא חזו לסהדותא

*Translation.* Our rabbis taught: He [i.e., the rebellious elder] was executed neither by the court of his own town nor by the court at Yabneh; rather, he was taken to the Supreme Court in Jerusalem, and they kept him there until the [next] festival, and they execute him during the festival, as it is written, "And all the people shall hear and fear" (Deut 17:13); these are the words of Rabbi Aqiba. But Rabbi Yehudah said to him, "Is it stated, ' They shall see and fear'? What is stated is only, 'They shall hear and fear.' Why delay the sentence of this person? Rather, he is executed immediately, and a message is written and sent to all places, "So-and-So has been sentenced to death by the court." Our rabbis taught: Public announces are required for four (classes of criminals): a seducer (*mesit*), a stubborn and rebellious son, a rebellious elder, and witnesses who have been proved to have committed perjury. In the case of all of them [except the fourth], it is written, "And all the people," or "and all Israel;" but in the case of witnesses proved perjurers, it is written, "And those that remain shall hear and fear" (Deut 19:20), since not all are eligible to be witnesses.

*Commentary.* This baraita parallels the material in *t. Sanh.* 11:7 (No. 42; see there for a discussion of the date of the tradition). Based on the authority of Rabbi Aqiba, the rabbis taught that the execution of a rebellious elder is to be delayed until the next pilgrimage festival, i.e., Passover, Weeks, or Tabernacles. The reason, again, is deterrence: when a criminal is executed in Jerusalem during one of the main festivals when all Israel is gathered together, all the people will take notice of the crime and its punishment. The dissenting Rabbi Yehudah argues that the wording of Deut 17:13 requires only that the people of Israel hear about the crime and its punishment, not that all Israelites personally see the criminal executed. A. STROBEL cites this baraita to counter

---

[317] Thus the critique of BLINZLER, Prozeß, 204–6, who suggests that the theory of הוֹרָאַת
שָׁעָה was a legal fiction used by later rabbis to justify decisions in past legal cases that ignored the standard legal norms based on the Torah. STROBEL, Stunde, 85 n. 227, asserts that the question of the validity of this principle for Jesus' trial must remain open.

H. LIETZMANN who had argued that any report of a trial of Jesus by the Sanhedrin is spurious since there would have been no outside witnesses present during the proceedings.[318]

**(46)** Origen, *Commentarii in epistulam ad Romanos* 6.7.11 (Rom 7:2–6)

Ubi uero uerbum caro factum est et habitauit in nobis et praesentia eius Ierusalem terrena cum templo et altari atque omnibus quae inibi gerebantur euersa est, tunc mortuus est uir eius, id est secundum litteram lex. An non iure dicetur in hac parte mortuus sermo legis cui nulla sacrificia nullum sacerdotium nulla leuitici ordinis ministeria deferuntur? Homicidam punire non potest nec adulteram lapidare; haec enim sibi uindicat Romanorum potestas; et dubitas adhuc si mortua sit secundum litteram lex? Ter in anno apparere Domino omnis masculus non ascendit: ouis in festiuitate paschae in ciuitate quam elegisse putatur Dominus Deus nulla iugulatur; manipuli primitiarum nulla celebratur oblatio; nulla lepra nulla peccati purgatur immunditia. Et dubitari potest in his omnibus mortuam esse litteram legis?

*Translation.* But when the Word became flesh and lived among us, his earthly presence in Jerusalem with its temple and altar and everything that was borne there, was torn down at that time her husband died, that is the law according to the letter. Or will it not rightly be said in this passage that the message of the law is dead, since no sacrifices, no priesthood, and no ministries associated with the Levitical order are being offered? It cannot punish the murderer or stone the adulteress, because the power of the Romans reserves this for itself. Do you still doubt whether the law according to the letter is dead? No male goes up to appear before the Lord three times a year, no sheep is being slaughtered at the Passover festival in the city that is believed to have been chosen by the Lord God, no offering of the piles of first-fruits are being celebrated, no leprous diseases and no defilement of sin are being cleansed. Is it possible to doubt in all these things that the letter of the law is dead?

*Commentary.*[319] Origen illustrates Paul's argument in Rom 7:4 that believers in Jesus as Savior "have died to the law through the body of Christ" with two

---

[318] LIETZMANN, Prozess, 315; STROBEL, Stunde, 6 n. 3.

[319] The Latin text of Rufinus' translation of Origen's commentary is taken from CAROLINE P. HAMMOND BAMMEL, ed., Der Römerbriefkommentar des Origenes. Kritische Ausgabe der Übersetzung Rufins (3 vols.; Vetus Latina: Aus der Geschiche der Lateinischen Bibel 16.33.34; Freiburg: Herder, 1990–98), 2:490–91 (lines 139–153). For other text editions and translations cf. ORIGENES, Commentarii in epistulam ad Romanos/Römerbriefkommentar (Lateinisch-Deutsch. 5 vols.; ed. Theresia Heither; Fontes Christianae 2/1–5; Freiburg: Herder, 1990–1996); ORIGEN, Commentary on the Epistle to the Romans (ed. Thomas P. Scheck; The Fathers of the Church 103–104; Washington, DC: Catholic University of America Press, 2001–2002), 2:25.

specific examples: the destruction of the Temple in Jerusalem after ministry of Jesus who is the incarnated Word, and the abolishment of the cultic service in the Temple together with the officiating priesthood. He goes on to make the point that the law cannot punish a murderer or an adulteress because "the power (*potestas*) of the Romans reserves this for itself." Origen's point is the theological argument that the law has been abolished: People no longer visit the Temple on pilgrimages, nor do they slaughter lambs for the Passover festival, nor offer the first-fruits. While the law stipulated the execution of a murderer and the stoning of an adulteress (Lev 20:10; Deut 22:22), Origen argues that the punishment of criminals is the prerogative of the Roman provincial authorities. It has been argued that since Origen alludes to the pericope about the woman caught in adultery (John 7:53–8:11),[320] he reflects not simply on the political situation in the third century A.D. but, more specifically, on the Jewish authorities' lack of jurisdiction in capital cases.[321]

## 1.4  Interrogation of Witnesses

The Jewish legal tradition insisted on trials in which the accused were treated fairly. Legal texts thus describe and discuss the composition of courts, the qualifications for judges and witnesses, and the rights and privileges of plaintiffs and defendants. The importance of safeguards against injustice was particularly important in capital cases. A major factor in securing judicial fairness was the stipulation in the Mosaic law that a minimum of two witnesses is required for conviction:

(Deut 17:6) עַל־פִּי שְׁנַיִם עֵדִים אוֹ שְׁלֹשָׁה עֵדִים יוּמַת הַמֵּת לֹא יוּמַת עַל־פִּי עֵד אֶחָד
ἐπὶ δυσὶν μάρτυσιν ἢ ἐπὶ τρισὶν μάρτυσιν ἀποθανεῖται ὁ ἀποθνῄσκων· οὐκ ἀποθανεῖται ἐφ᾽ ἑνὶ μάρτυρι[322]
A person is to be executed on the testimony of two witnesses or three witnesses; a person must not be executed on the testimony of only one witness

לֹא־יָקוּם עֵד אֶחָד בְּאִישׁ לְכָל־עָוֹן וּלְכָל־חַטָּאת בְּכָל־חֵטְא אֲשֶׁר יֶחֱטָא עַל־פִּי שְׁנֵי עֵדִים אוֹ עַל־פִּי שְׁלֹשָׁה־עֵדִים יָקוּם דָּבָר (Deut 19:15)
Οὐκ ἐμμενεῖ μάρτυς εἷς κατὰ ἀνθρώπου κατὰ πᾶσαν ἀδικίαν καὶ κατὰ πᾶν ἁμάρτημα καὶ κατὰ πᾶσαν ἁμαρτίαν, ἣν ἂν ἁμάρτῃ· ἐπὶ στόματος δύο μαρτύρων καὶ ἐπὶ στόματος τριῶν μαρτύρων σταθήσεται πᾶν ῥῆμα.
A single witness shall not suffice to convict a person of any crime or offense

---

[320] ULRICH BECKER, Jesus und die Ehebrecherin. Untersuchungen zur Text- und Überlieferungsgeschichte von Joh. 7,53–8,11 (BZNW 28; Berlin: Töpelmann, 1963), 120–21.

[321] BLINZLER, Prozeß, 235–36; STROBEL, Stunde, 38–41; cf. MOMMSEN, Strafrecht, 120.

[322] The Greek text is taken from JOHN W. WEVERS, Deuteronomium (2. Auflage; Septuaginta III.2; Göttingen: Vandenhoeck & Ruprecht, 2006), 213.

regarding any offense that may be committed. A case shall be established on the testimony of two witnessees or three witnesses.

Witnesses not only played a role in the trial itself but even before the trial. The legal experts of the Qumran community required that an offender be warned of the consequences of an offense before he was accused in court. SCHIFFMAN explains that Jewish law "was concerned to guarantee that the accused had been fully cognizant that his actions violated the law and that he knew of the punishment for his crime before committing the forbidden action. Otherwise, he could not be considered a purposeful violator and could not be punished."[323]

**(47)** Susanna 44–62

Καὶ ἰδοὺ ἄγγελος κυρίου ἐκείνης ἐξαγομένης ἀπολέσθαι, καὶ ἔδωκεν ὁ ἄγγελος, καθὼς συνετάγη, πνεῦμα συνέσεως νεωτέρῳ ὀνόματι Δανιηλ [48] διαστείλας δὲ Δανιηλ τὸν ὄχλον καὶ στὰς μέσος αὐτῶν εἶπεν Οὕτως μωροὶ οἱ υἱοὶ Ισραηλ; οὐκ ἀνακρίναντες οὐδὲ τὸ σαφὲς ἐπιγνόντες ἀπεκτείνατε θυγατέρα Ισραηλ; [51] καὶ νῦν διαχωρίσατέ μοι αὐτοὺς ἀπ᾽ ἀλλήλων μακράν, ἵνα ἐτάσω αὐτοὺς [51a] ὡς δὲ διεχωρίσθησαν, εἶπε Δανιηλ τῇ συναγωγῇ Νῦν μὴ βλέψητε ὅτι οὗτοί εἰσι πρεσβύτεροι, λέγοντες Οὐ μὴ ψεύσωνται· ἀλλὰ ἀνακρινῶ αὐτοὺς κατὰ τὰ ὑποπίπτοντά μοι. [52] καὶ ἐκάλεσε τὸν ἕνα αὐτῶν, καὶ προσήγαγον τὸν πρεσβύτερον τῷ νεωτέρῳ, καὶ εἶπεν αὐτῷ Δανιηλ Ἄκουε ἄκουε, πεπαλαιωμένε ἡμερῶν κακῶν· νῦν ἥκασί σου αἱ ἁμαρτίαι, ἃς ἐποίεις τὸ πρότερον [53] πιστευθεὶς ἀκούειν καὶ κρίνειν κρίσεις θάνατον ἐπιφερούσας καὶ τὸν μὲν ἀθῷον κατέκρινας, τοὺς δὲ ἐνόχους ἠφίεις, τοῦ κυρίου λέγοντος Ἀθῷον καὶ δικαιον οὐκ ἀποκτενεῖς· [54] νῦν οὖν ὑπὸ τί δένδρον καὶ ποταπῷ τοῦ παραδείσου τόπῳ ἑόρακας αὐτοὺς ὄντας σὺν ἑαυτοῖς; καὶ εἶπεν ὁ ἀσεβὴς Ὑπὸ σχῖνον [55] εἶπε δὲ ὁ νεώτερος Ὀρθῶς ἔψευσαι εἰς τὴν σεαυτοῦ ψυχήν· σήμερον γὰρ ὁ ἄγγελος κυρίου σχίσει σου τὴν ψυχήν. [56] καὶ τοῦτον μεταστήσας εἶπε προσαγαγεῖν αὐτῷ τὸν ἕτερον· καὶ τούτῳ δὲ εἶπε Διὰ τί διεστραμμένον τὸ σπέρμα σου, ὡς Σιδῶνος καὶ οὐχ ὡς Ιουδα; τὸ κάλλος σε ἠπάτησεν [ἢ μικρὰ ἐπιθυμία]· [57] καὶ οὕτως ἐποιεῖτε θυγατράσιν Ισραηλ, καὶ ἐκεῖναι φοβούμεναι ὡμιλοῦσαν ὑμῖν, ἀλλ᾽ οὐ θυγάτηρ Ιουδα ὑπέμεινε τὸ νόσημα ὑμῶν ἐν ἀνομίᾳ ὑπενεγκεῖν· [58] νῦν οὖν λέγε μοι Ὑπὸ τί δένδρον καὶ ἐν ποίῳ τοῦ κήπου τόπῳ κατέλαβες αὐτοὺς ὁμιλοῦντας ἀλλήλοις; ὁ δὲ εἶπεν Ὑπὸ πρῖνον. [59] καὶ εἶπε Δανιηλ Ἁμαρτωλέ, νῦν ὁ ἄγγελος κυρίου τὴν ῥομφαίαν ἕστηκεν ἔχων, ἕως ὁ λαὸς ἐξολεθρεύσει ὑμᾶς, ἵνα καταπρίσῃ σε. [60–62] καὶ πᾶσα ἡ συναγωγὴ ἀνεβόησεν ἐπὶ τῷ νεωτέρῳ, ὡς ἐκ τοῦ ἰδίου στόματος ὁμολόγους αὐτοὺς

---

[323] LAWRENCE H. SCHIFFMAN, Qumran and Jerusalem: Studies in the Dead Sea Scrolls and the History of Judaism (Studies in the Dead Sea Scrolls and Related Literature; Grand Rapids: Eerdmans, 2010), 105.

κατέστησεν ἀμφοτέρους ψευδομάρτυρας· καὶ ὡς ὁ νόμος διαγορεύει, ἐποίησαν αὐτοῖς, καθὼς ἐπονηρεύσαντο κατὰ τῆς ἀδελφῆς. καὶ ἐφίμωσαν αὐτοὺς καὶ ἐξαγαγόντες ἔρριψαν εἰς φάραγγα· τότε ὁ ἄγγελος κυρίου ἔρριψε πῦρ διὰ μέσου αὐτῶν. καὶ ἐσώθη αἷμα ἀναίτιον ἐν τῇ ἡμέρᾳ ἐκείνῃ.

*Translation.* And behold, there was an angel of the Lord as she was led out (of the city assembly) to be executed. And the angel, as he was ordered, gave the spirit of insight to a young man with the name Daniel. [48] Daniel separated the crowd, stood among them, and said, "Are you such fools, sons of Israel? Do you kill a daughter of Israel without examination and without knowing the plain truth? [51] And now, separate them far from one another so that I can test them." [51a] When they had been separated, Daniel said to the assembly, "Now, do not pay attention to the fact that they are elders, saying, 'Surely they would not lie!' Instead, I will examine them according to my impressions."[324] [52] And he called one of them, and they brought the elder to the youth, and Daniel saids to him, "Hear, hear, you who has grown old in wicked days! Your sins have now come, which you have formerly committed, [53] when people trusted you to hear and (only then) to judge cases carrying a death sentence; you condemned the innocent while acquitting the guilty, even though the Lord says, 'You shall not kill an innocent and righteous person.' [54] Now, therefore, under what tree and in which location of the orchard did you see them together?" And the impious one said, "Under a mastic tree." [55] But the youth said, "You have truly lied against your own life; because this very day the angel of the Lord will split your soul." [56] And after he had this (witness) removed, he told them to bring the other to him. And he said to him, "Why is your offspring perverted, like that of Sidon, and not like that of Judah? Beauty has deceived you [or trivial[325] lust]. [57] And you have treated the daughters of Israel in this manner, and they had intercourse with you because they were afraid; but a daughter of Judah did not tolerate bearing your (moral) disease in lawlessness. [58] Now, therefore, tell me: Under what tree and in which location of the orchard[326] did you catch them having intercourse with each other?" And he said, "Under a holm-oak."[327] [59] And Daniel said, "Sinner! Now, the angel of the Lord stands with the sword until the people utterly destroy you so that he may saw you in pieces. [60-62] And the whole assembly shouted at the youth, how he had established them both as false witnesses by their own mouth, even though they had agreed (in their testimony). And as the law explicitly prescribes, they did to them just as they had wickedly intended against the sister.

---

[324] Thus the translation of τὰ ὑποπίπτοντα in MURAOKA, s.v. ὑποπίπτω 3.

[325] RAHLFS and ZIEGLER's first edition suggested μιαρά ("abominable, repulsive") instead of μικρά. ZIEGLER / MUNNICH print the phrase ἢ μικρὰ ἐπιθυμία in square brackets and thus treat it as an explanatory gloss.

[326] The term here is κῆπος, parallel to παράδεισος in v. 54; MURAOKA suggests "orchard" for both terms.

[327] MCLAY and NRSV translate "evergreen oak;" MURAOKA suggests "holm-oak."

And they muzzled them and led them out and threw them into a ravine. Then the angle of the Lord threw fire in their midst. And guiltless blood was saved on that day.

*Commentary.*[328] Set during the Babylonian exile, the story relates the vindication of Susanna, the beautiful wife of a certain Joakim (v. 7). Susanna is falsely accused by two infatuated men of having committed adultery (vv. 36–39). The assembly (συναγωγή) believes the two men, who were elders (πρεσβύτροι) and judges (κρίται; v. 41). When Susanna is about to be executed (v. 44), Daniel intervenes. He accuses the assembly of having convicted the woman without examining the case (οὐκ ἀνακρίναντες ) in order to establish the truth (ὁ σαφές) of what happened (v. 48). He asks that the two witnesses be cross-examined separately (διαχωρίσατέ ... αὐτούς), an inquiry that he will conduct himself (ἐτάσω;[329] v. 51). The cross-examination focuses in each case on two questions: (1) The precise location of the alleged crime, and (2) the more general location of the alleged crime. The close questioning of the witnesses, who are intimidated by Daniel, yields two different answers. The Greek terms for the two different trees constitute puns for the fate that will befall two men unmasked as false witnesses: σχῖνος ("mastic tree") and πρῖνος ("holm-oak") is punned as σχίσε ("split, cleave apart") and καταπρίσῃ ("cut down with a saw"). The false witnesses are punished with the same punishment they wanted to inflict on the woman: they are executed. The reference to the fire from the Lord serves to confirm the vindication of the woman. This text shows the importance – and the legal practice – of the cross-examination of witnesses. The truth of the testimony of witnesses must be established through separate interrogation concerning details relevant for the alleged crime. If the cross-examination of witnesses reveals discrepancies, it cannot be used for a conviction.

J. MARCUS points to the crowd in the Susanna story, depicted as "'fickle, malleable, and readily manipulated' by the corrupt elders of the nation" in his explanation of Mark's depiction of the chief priests stirring up the crowds to

---

[328] The text of the Old Greek (OG) version is taken from JOSEPH ZIEGLER and OLIVIER MUNNICH, Susanna, Daniel, Bel et Draco (Zweite Auflage; Septuaginta XVI.2; Göttingen: Vandenhoeck & Ruprecht, 1999), 226–30. For translations cf. R. TIMOTHY MCLAY, in ALBERT PIETERSMA and BENJAMIN G. WRIGHT, eds., A New English Translation of the Septuagint and the Other Greek Translations Traditionally Included unter that Title (Oxford: Oxford University Press, 2007), 986–990; Helmut Engel, in WOLFGANG KRAUS and MARTIN KARRER, eds., Septuaginta Deutsch. Das griechische Alte Testament in deutscher Übersetzung (Stuttgart: Deutsche Bibelgesellschaft, 2009), 1418–23. The translation in NRSV follows the later and longer Theodotion version (TH), which includes vv. 46–47, 49–50.

[329] MURAOKA s.v. ἐτάζω 3, "to make enquiries into" (human subjects).

seek Jesus' crucifixion.[330] R. E. BROWN refers to the "both false and inconsistent testimony" of the witnesses who testified against Susanna in his discussion of the false witness testimony during Jesus' trial concerning statements
about the Temple.[331] C. A. EVANS cites this text in his explanation of Mark
14:59 asserting that the witnesses against Jesus were not in agreement: "Under
separate cross-examination, the testimonies of these individuals did not agree
and so were not admissible against Jesus."[332]

**(48)** CD IX, 2–8

וַאֲשֶׁר אָמַר לֹא תִקּוֹם וְלֹא תִטּוֹר אֶת בְּנֵי עַמֶּךָ וְכָל אִישׁ מַבִּיאוֹ 2

הַבְּרִית אֲשֶׁר יָבִיא עַל רֵעֵהוּ דָּבָר אֲשֶׁר לֹא בְהוֹכֵחַ לִפְנֵי עֵדִים 3

וֶהֱבִיאוֹ בַחֲרוֹן אַפּוֹ אוֹ סִפֵּר לִזְקֵנָיו לְהַבְזוֹתוֹ נוֹקֵם הוּא וְנוֹטֵר 4

וְאֵין כָּתוּב כִּי אִם נוֹקֵם הוּא לְצָרָיו וְנוֹטֵר הוּא לְאוֹיְבָיו 5

אִם הֶחֱרִישׁ לוֹ מִיּוֹם לְיוֹם וּבַחֲרוֹן אַפּוֹ בוֹ דִּבֶּר בּוֹ בִדְבַר מָקֹות 6

עָנָה בוֹ יַעַן אֲשֶׁר לֹא הֵקִים אֶת מִצְוַת אֵל אֲשֶׁר אָמַר לוֹ הוֹכֵחַ 7

תּוֹכִיחַ אֶת רֵעֶיךָ וְלֹא תִשָּׂא עָלָיו חֵטְא 8

*Translation.* And as to that which he said, 'You shall not take vengeance nor
bear resentment against the sons of your people' (Lev 19:18), anyone of those
who enter ³ the covenant who brings an accusation against his neighbor without reproof before witnesses, ⁴ but brings it in his burning wrath or tells it to
his elders to bring shame on him, he is the one who takes vengeance and bears
resentment. ⁵ It is written only, 'He takes vengeance against his adversaries
and bears resentment against his enemies' (Nah 1:2). ⁶ If he kept silent from
day to day and in his burning wrath accused him of a capital offense, ⁷ his
iniquity is upon him,[333] for he did not fulfill the commandment of God which
says to him, 'You shall surely ⁸ reprove your neighbor so that you do not incur
sin because of him' (Lev 19:17).

*Commentary.* The Qumran community required that an offender be reproved
for a previous commission of the same offense before he could be officially
accused and subsequently punished for the offense. The requirement of
reproof is derived from Lev 19:18: if someone sees an offense, he must
immediately warn the offender; if he does not and later accuses him of the
offense, he violates the commandment of Lev 19:18 by "bearing resentment"
and "taking revenge." The author quotes Nah 1:2 arguing that God alone can

---

[330] MARCUS, Mark, 2:1030, citing ERICH S. GRUEN, Heritage and Hellenism: The Reinvention of Jewish Tradition (HCS 30; Berkeley: University of California Press, 1998), 176.

[331] BROWN, Death, 1:445.

[332] EVANS, Mark, 447.

[333] Cf. BAUMGARTEN / SCHWARTZ, Damascus Document, 43. GARCÍA MARTÍNEZ and
TIGCHELAAR, Dead Sea Scrolls Study Edition, 565: "he has testified against himself."

take vengeance or bear resentment.[334] Reproof had to be given on the very day the offense was witnessed. The subsequent stipulations in CD IX, 10–23 indicate that reproof was a regular part of legal procedure in Qumran, that it had to take place in the presence of the Examiner and the offender, and that records of the case be kept by the Examiner. According to 1QS IX, 16–18, the legal requirement of reproof before an accusation can be brought before an offender was limited to members of the community; it was not followed with regard to non-members, which indicates that "this process of reproof was not part of the legal system in the rest of Palestine."[335] The legal requirement of the rabbinic הַתְרָעָה ("warning") is similar, but not identical. In the early Tannaitic period, the rabbis required a warning only for offenses incurring death penalties: the witnesses had "to explain formally to the transgressor the exact penalty for the offense he was about to commit. Only if he then answered in the affirmative, demonstrating his acceptance of the warning, could he be convicted of violating the law."[336] The Qumran community required reproof after a first offense, and it appears that at least two occurrences of an offense were required for conviction. In rabbinic law, a warning had to take place before the very same offense for which an offender could be tried, which means that only one offense was required for conviction. But both procedures served the same purpose: "Neither legal system was willing to convict a person until it was certain that he fully understood the nature of his offense and the required penalty. Only then could he be considered a purposeful offender. Further, both systems required that the witnesses to the crime play the main role in ensuring the understanding of the offender."[337]

The discussion in X, 16–23 resolves the requirement in Deut 17:6; 19:15 of "two witnesses or three witnesses": capital cases require three witnesses (or occurrences), while monetary cases require only two witnesses. The testimony before court may combine the testimony of witnesses who saw discrete violations of the law (i.e., each violation may have been witnessed by only one witness); this legal procedure is not allowed in later rabbinic halakhah.[338]

---

[334] For the law of reproof cf. SCHIFFMAN, Sectarian Law, 89–109; LAWRENCE H. SCHIFFMAN, Reproof as a Requisite for Punishment in the Law of the Dead Sea Scrolls, in Jewish Law Association Studies II (The Jerusalem Conference Volume; ed. B. S. Jackson; Atlanta: Scholars Press, 1986), 59–74. Other relevant passages are CD VII, 2–3; 1QS V, 24 – VI, 1; 4Q286–290. On the latter text cf. BILHAH NITZAN, The Laws of Reproof in 4QBerakhot (4Q286–290) in Light of their Parallels in the Damascus Document and Other Texts from Qumran, in Legal Texts and Legal Issues (Proceedings of the Second Meeting of the International Organization for Qumran Studies, Cambridge, 1995. FS Joseph M. Baumgarten; ed. M. J. Bernstein, F. García Martínez, and J. Kampen; STDJ 23; Leiden: Brill, 1997), 149–165. See also Sir 19:13–17; *T. Gad* 6:3–7; in the New Testament: Matt 18:15–17; Gal 6:1; 2 Thess 3:15; 2 Tim 3:23–25.

[335] SCHIFFMAN, Sectarian Law, 96.

[336] SCHIFFMAN, Sectarian Law, 97; cf. *t. Sanh.* 11:1; *b. Sanh.* 8b; 80b; *b. Sanh.* 40b–41a.

[337] SCHIFFMAN, Sectarian Law, 97.

**(49)** CD IX, 16 – X, 2

16 ...          כָּל דָּבָר אֲשֶׁר יִמְעַל
17 אִישׁ בַּתּוֹרָה וְרָאָה רֵעֵיהוּ וְהוּא אֶחָד אִם דְּבַר מָוֶת הוּא וִידִיעֵהוּ
18 לְעֵינָיו בְּהוֹכִיחַ לַמְּבַקֵּר וְהַמְּבַקֵּר יִכְתְּבֵהוּ בְיָדוֹ עַד עֲשׂוֹתוֹ
19 עוֹד לִפְנֵי אֶחָד וְשָׁב וְהוֹדִיעַ לַמְּבַקֵּר אִם יָשׁוּב וְנִתְפַּשׂ לִפְנֵי
20 אֶחָד שָׁלֵם מִשְׁפָּטוֹ וְאִם שְׁנַיִם הֵם וְהֵם מְעִידִים עַל
21 דָּבָר אַחֵר (אֶחָד) וְהוּבְדַּל הָאִישׁ מִן הַטָּהֳרָה לְבַד אִם נֶאֱמָנִים
22 הֵם וּבְיוֹם רְאוֹת הָאִישׁ יוֹדִיעָה לַמְּבַקֵּר וְעַל הַהוֹן יְקַבְּלוּ שְׁנֵי
23 עֵדִים נֶאֱמָנִים וְעַל אֶחָד לְהַבְדִּיל הַטָּהֳרָה וְאַל יְקוּבַּל
1 עוֹד לַשׁוֹפְטִים לְהָמִית עַל פִּיהוּ אֲשֶׁר לֹא מָלְאוּ יָמָיו לַעֲבוֹר
2 עַל הַפְּקוּדִים יְרֵא אֶת אֵל ...

*Translation.*[339] Any matter in which a man violates the Torah, and his neighbor sees him and he is but one, if it is a capital matter, he shall report it [18] in
his presence with reproof to the Examiner. And the Examiner shall write it
down with his hand, until he does it [19] again in the presence of someone who
again reports it to the Examiner; if he is caught again in the presence of [20]
someone, his judgment is complete. And if there are two and they testify
about [21] a different matter, the man shall only be separated from the purity, on
the condition that [22] they are reliable. And on the day when a man sees it, he
shall make it known to the Examiner. And concerning property, they shall
receive two [23] reliable witnesses, while one is sufficient to separate (him
from) the purity. No witness shall be [X, 1] received by the judges to put someone to death upon the basis of his testimony unless he has reached the age to
pass [2] among those who are enrolled (and) is God fearing.

*Commentary.* The law of testimony, as presented in this text, understood the
stipulations of Deut 17:6–7 and 19:15 regarding "two or three witnesses" in
terms of property law and capital case law. Two witnesses are required for a
conviction in financial matters, irrespective of whether they witnessed the violation of the Torah simultaneously or sequentially. In capital cases, three witnesses are required.[340] The interpretation of Deut 17:6 allows the combination of eyewitness testimony of three men who individually (sequentially) testify to a discrete violation of a capital law. J. M. BAUMGARTEN asserts, "One
may assume, however, from Deut 17:6 (cf. 11QTemple 64.8) that two wit-

---

[338] JOSEPH M. BAUMGARTEN, Judicial Procedures, EDNT 2:455–460, 456.

[339] Text and (modified) translation follow BAUMGARTEN / SCHWARTZ, Damascus Document, 42–45; cf. QIMRON, The Dead Sea Scrolls, 1:43, lines 206–215.

[340] SCHIFFMAN, Sectarian Law, 73–81; see ibid. 76–78 and LAWRENCE H. SCHIFFMAN,
The Relationship of the *Zadokite Fragments* to the *Temple Scroll* [2000], in The Courtyards
of the House of the Lord: Studies on the Temple Scroll (ed. F. García Martínez; STDJ 75;
Leiden: Brill, 2008), 149–162, 156, on the different law in 11QTemple LXIV, 8–9 whose
author seems to assume only two witnesses testify in a criminal case.

nesses testifying about a single capital offense would be valid for imposing the maximum penalty."[341] L. H. SCHIFFMAN argues that CD derives the laws pertaining to the judiciary from biblical law but extends it considerably, while the *Temple Scroll* basically "recapitulates the biblical laws on this matter with only small changes."[342]

The fragmentary text 4Q477, known under the title "Rebukes Reported by the Overseer,"[343] records the excommunication from the community of several members who had sinned. The name of each offender is followed by a list of three offenses; the latter use the term וגאף ("and also") which underscores the compounding of offenses. S. PFANN lays out the text 4Q477 Frag. 2 II, 3–8 as follows:[344]

| | |
|---|---|
| Johnathan ben Mat [ ... was rebuked [ | |
| because] he is short tempered [ | {OFFENSE NO. 1} |
| and also he gives the evil eye | {OFFENSE NO. 2} |
| and also he has a boastful spirit is with him [ ] | {OFFENSE NO. 3} |
| he [apostacized so let him be commit]ted to the darkness/the pit. | |
| Hanania Notos was rebuked | |
| because he [ | {OFFENSE NO. 1} |
| ] to hire/shut up the spirit of the Yahad | {OFFENSE NO. 2} |
| and] also created mixture in Israel [ | {OFFENSE NO. 3} |
| And ... ben Yo]sef was rebuked | |
| because he gives the evil eye [ ] | {OFFENSE NO. 1} |
| and also doesn't [ ] his [ ] | {OFFENSE NO. 2} |
| and also he loves his kin | {OFFENSE NO. 3} |

This text highlights the fact that the Community excommunicated members with grave faults only after the third infraction, while implying at the same time that a record of faults was kept. As the Sanhedrin dismissed the "false witnesses" who testified in the examination of Jesus (Mark 14:56, 57; Matt 26:60) in the context of a death penalty case, they seemed to have taken seriously the necessity of having three witnesses testifying to the offense punishable by death.

---

[341] BAUMGARTEN / SCHWARTZ, Damascus Document, 45, n. 146.

[342] LAWRENCE H. SCHIFFMAN, The Zadokite Fragments and the Temple Scroll, in The Damascus Document: A Centennial of Discovery (ed. J. M. Baumgarten, E. G. Chazon, and A. Pinnick; STDJ 34; Leiden: Brill, 2002), 133–145, 140.

[343] HANAN ESHEL, 477. 4QRebukes Reported by the Overseer (Pl. XXXII), in Qumran Cave 4.XXVI: Cryptic Texts and Miscellanea, Part 1 (ed. S. Pfann; DJD 36; Oxford: Clarendon, 2000), 474–485.

[344] Cf. STEPHEN PFANN, The Essene Yearly Renewal Ceremony and the Baptism of Repentance, in The Provo International Conference on the Dead Sea Scrolls. Technological Innovations, New Texts, and Reformulated Issues (ed. D. W. Parry and E. Ulrich; STDJ 30; Leiden: Brill, 1999), 337–352, 343 n. 7.

**(50)** 1QS VI, 1

וְגַם אַל יָבִיא אִישׁ עַל רֵעֵהוּ דָּבָר לִפְנֵי הָרַבִּים אֲשֶׁר לוֹא בְתוֹכַחַת לִפְנֵי עֵדִים ...

*Translation.* And also, let no man accuse his companion before the Many without reproof in the presence of witnesses.

*Commentary.* This passage stipulates the same legal requirement as CD IX, 2–8 (No. 48). The legal procedure of reproof requires that an offender be warned of the consequences of an offense before he is accused in court. The Many (הָרַבִּים), the assembly of the community, act here as its highest court. This stipulation clarifies that witnesses be present when the offender is reproved – other witnesses than those who saw the offense.[345] The term תוֹכַחַת, translated here as "reproof,"[346] could be interpreted as referring to evidence in a legal sense. In this case, the stipulation forbids accusing a person without adequate testimony: such an accusation would amount to slander, which is forbidden by biblical law. This interpretation is less likely than seeing here a reference to the procedure of reproof.[347]

**(51)** Josephus, *Antiquitates judaicae* 4.219

Εἷς δὲ μὴ πιστευέσθω μάρτυς, ἀλλὰ τρεῖς ἢ τὸ τελευταῖον δύο, ὧν τὴν μαρτυρίαν ἀληθῆ ποιήσει τὰ προβεβιωμένα. γυναικῶν δὲ μὴ ἔστω μαρτυρία διὰ κουφότητα καὶ θράσος τοῦ γένους αὐτῶν· μαρτυρείτωσαν δὲ μηδὲ δοῦλοι διὰ τὴν τῆς ψυχῆς ἀγένειαν, οὓς ἢ διὰ κέρδος εἰκὸς ἢ διὰ φόβον μὴ τἀληθῆ μαρτυρῆσαι. ἂν δέ τις ψευδομαρτυρήσας πιστευθῇ, πασχέτω ταῦτ᾽ ἐλεγχθεὶς ὅσα ὁ καταμαρτυρηθεὶς πάσχειν ἔμελλεν

*Translation.* Do not trust a single witness, but let there be three or, at the least, two, whose credibility[348] is attested by their previous life. Testimony of women shall not be accepted because of the levity and rashness[349] of their

---

[345] SCHIFFMAN, Sectarian Law, 94–95.

[346] Following GARCIA MARTINEZ. JAMES H. CHARLESWORTH, ed., Rule of the Community and Related Documents (The Dead Sea Scrolls 1; Tübingen: Mohr Siebeck, 1994), 27 n. 134 explains the verb *ykḥ* in terms of "a reasoning together (in a legal matter), reprove, and an argument with someone."

[347] SCHIFFMAN, Sectarian Law, 95.

[348] Thus FELDMAN, Judean Antiquities 1–4, 411. THACKERAY translates μαρτυρία here as "evidence" (cf. LSJ); WHISTON with "testimony."

[349] FELDMAN translates θράσος as "boldness," THACKERAY as "temerity." LSJ offers "courage, confidence," in a bad sense: "over-boldness, rashness, insolence." BDAG writes, "in a good sense 'courage', but when a pers[on] is undisciplined an impulse for bold action can deteriorate into 'recklessness' or 'rashness' and one projects the impression of lacking regard for the feelings, concerns, or thoughts of others."

gender. Neither shall slaves give testimony because of the ignobility of their soul, since it is likely that they do not bear witness to the truth, whether because of their desire of gain or because of fear. And if a person gives false testimony and is believed, he shall, when he is convicted, suffer the penalty that the one against whom he gave false testimony was going to incur.

*Commentary.* Beginning in *A. J.* 4.196, Josephus describes the "constitution" (πολιτεία) that Moses had given to the Jewish people.[350] In 4.197 he defends his decision not to follow the chronological order of the laws as recorded in the Pentateuch, but to arrange the laws topically, which he regards as an innovation.[351] In 4.198 he emphasizes that he presents the laws relevant for the constitution of the Jewish people. He promises to present the laws regarding communal matters in a later work. As regards his projected work "Customs and Causes," THACKERAY comments (on *A. J.* 1.25) that this was evidently never completed, although the reference to its "four books" (*A. J.* 20.268) and allusions to the work through *A. J.* suggest that "it had taken shape in the author's mind and was actually begun."[352] The stipulation concerning witnesses in 4.219 paraphrases Deut 19:15 (see above); see also Deut 17:6: ἐπὶ δυσὶν μάρτυσιν ἢ ἐπὶ τρισὶν μάρτυσιν ἀποθανεῖται ὁ ἀποθνήσκων· οὐκ ἀποθανεῖται ἐφ᾽ ἑνὶ μάρτυρι ("On two witnesses or upon three witnesses, the one who is to die shall die; he shall not die on the basis of one witness") and Num 35:30: Πᾶς πατάξας ψυχήν, διὰ μαρτύρων φονεύσεις τὸν φονεύσαντα, καὶ μάρτυς εἷς οὐ μαρτυρήσει ἐπὶ ψυχὴν ἀποθανεῖν ("Every one, when he strikes a soul, through witnesses you shall kill the murderer, and one witness shall not bear witness against a soul that he should die"). Josephus cites, and agrees with, the biblical law stipulating that convictions must be based on the testimony of at least two witnesses.[353] He asserts that the past life of a witness affects the credibility of his testimony,[354] and that neither women nor slaves

---

[350] The significance of the constitution of the Law is a major theme in the *Antiquities*. Cf. FELDMAN, Judean Antiquities 1–4, 396 n. 568.

[351] Josephus was actually anticipated by Philo's *De Specialibus Legibus*; cf. FELDMAN, Judean Antiquities 1–4, 397, n. 574, with reference to MENACHEM ELON, Jewish Law: History, Sources, Principles (4 vols.; Philadelphia: Jewish Publication Society, 1994), 3:1055 n. 72.

[352] THACKERAY / MARCUS / FELDMAN, Josephus, 4:13 note b.

[353] Philo, *Spec.* 4.53–54 gives two reasons why conviction must not be based on the evidence of a single witness: possible misunderstanding in the testimony of a witness, and the need for a preponderance of evidence. FELDMAN, Judean Antiquities 1–4, 411 n. 671.

[354] The previous life of a witness does not come into view in Deut 17:6. According to *m. Sanh.* 3:3, a person who plays dice, who lends money on interest, who races pigeons, and who does business in produce in a sabbatical year, may not serve as judge or as witness.

can give testimony in a court of law.[355] The statement "if a person gives false testimony" implies the cross-examination of witnesses. The statement paraphrases Deut 19:18–19: καὶ ἐξετάσωσιν οἱ κριταὶ ἀκριβῶς, καὶ ἰδοὺ μάρτυς ἄδικος ἐμαρτύρησεν ἄδικα, ἀντέστη κατὰ τοῦ ἀδελφοῦ αὐτοῦ· καὶ ποιήσετε αὐτῷ ὃν τρόπον ἐπονηρεύσατο ποιῆσαι τῷ ἀδελφῷ αὐτοῦ, καὶ ἐξαρεῖς τὸν πονηρὸν ἐξ ὑμῶν αὐτῶν ("and if the judges make a thorough inquiry and, look, an unjust witness has testified unjustly, he has stood up against his brother, then you shall do to him just as he connived to do to his brother. And you shall remove the evil one from yourselves"). According to *m. Mak.* 1:6, the Sadducees interpreted the phrase "then you shall do to him as he had meant to do to his brother" in the sense that the false witnesses were executed only when the accused had actually been put to death; the Pharisees argued that the false witnesses could be executed even if it had been established that their false testimony had been false before the execution of the accused. Josephus sides with the Pharisees: perjured witnesses in a capital case shall be executed, irrespective of what happened, or will happen, with the accused. He does not address the question how it is established that the witnesses had given false testimony.[356] Mark 14:56–59 seems to suggest that members of the Sanhedrin cross-examined the witnesses who testified against Jesus and established that their testimony did not agree.[357] The text does not indicate whether the Pharisees in the court demanded the execution of the false witnesses.[358]

## (52) *m. Sanhedrin* 5:1–5

הָיוּ בוֹדְקִין אוֹתָן בְּשֶׁבַע חֲקִירוֹת[359] בְּאֵיזוֹ שָׁבוּעַ בְּאֵי זוֹ שָׁנָה בְּאֵי זוֹ חֹדֶשׁ וּבְכַמָּה בַחֹדֶשׁ בְּאֵיזֶה יוֹם וּבְאֵיזוֹ שָׁעָה וּבְאֵיזֶה מָקוֹם רַבִּי יוֹסִי אוֹמֵר בְּאֵיזֶה יוֹם בְּאֵיזוֹ שָׁעָה בְּאֵיזֶה מָקוֹם מַכִּירִין אַתֶּם אוֹתוֹ הִתְרֵיתֶם בּוֹ הָעוֹבֵד עֲבוֹדָה זָרָה אֶת־מָה עָבַד וּבַמֶּה עָבָד.
כָּל־הַמַּרְבֶּה בִּבְדִיקוֹת הֲרֵי־זֶה מְשֻׁבָּח. מַעֲשֶׂה שֶׁבָּדַק בֶּן־זַכַּאי בְּעָקְצֵי־תְאֵנִים. וּמַה־בֵּין חֲקִירוֹת לִבְדִיקוֹת חֲקִירוֹת אֶחָד אָמַר אֵינִי יוֹדֵעַ עֵדוּתוֹ בְּטֵלָה בְּדִיקוֹת אֶחָד אָמַר אֵינִי יוֹדֵעַ אֲפִלּוּ שְׁנַיִם

---

[355] Deut 17:6 mentions neither the disqualification of women nor the disqualification of slaves. But see *m. Šebu.* 4:1; *Sifre Dev.* §190 and *m. Roš Haš.* 1:8; *m. B. Qam.* 1:3; *b. B. Qam.* 88a. Other rabbinic traditions imply that women can testify in certain cases, cf. *t. Ketub.* 1:6; *b. B. Qam.* 114b.

[356] Cf. FELDMAN, Judean Antiquities 1–4, 412 n. 677.

[357] EVANS, Mark, 447.

[358] BLINZLER, Prozeß, 198. PESCH, Markusevangelium, 2:432 wonders whether the statement "for many gave false testimony against him" (Mark 14:56) indirectly incriminates the Sanhedrin as well as those who summoned these witnesses. PESCH emphasizes that Mark has not interfered in the text he uses: he faithfully reproduces the tradition (ibid. 429).

[359] The editio princeps (Napels 1492) reads between חקירות and באיזו the following: אם אמר אחד מהם איני יודע עדותן בטלה בדיקות ("If one of them said, 'I do not know,' their witness is invalid. Cross-examinations." KRAUSS, Sanhedrin–Makkot, 168, prints the text of the editio princeps while suggesting that this is probably incorrect (see nn. 2–3). We omit the line.

אוֹמְרִים אֵין אָנוּ יוֹדְעִין עֵדוּתָן קַיֶּמֶת. אֶחָד חֲקִירוֹת וְאֶחָד בְּדִיקוֹת בִּזְמַן שֶׁהֵן מַכְחִישִׁין זֶה אֶת־זֶה עֵדוּתָן בְּטֵלָה:

אֶחָד אוֹמֵר בִּשְׁנַיִם בַּחֹדֶשׁ וְאֶחָד אוֹמֵר בִּשְׁלֹשָׁה עֵדוּתָן קַיֶּמֶת שֶׁזֶּה יָדַע בְּעִבּוּרוֹ שֶׁל־חֹדֶשׁ וְזֶה לֹא יָדַע בְּעִבּוּרוֹ שֶׁל־חֹדֶשׁ. אֶחָד אוֹמֵר בִּשְׁלֹשָׁה וְאֶחָד אוֹמֵר בַּחֲמִשָּׁה עֵדוּתָן בְּטֵלָה. אֶחָד אוֹמֵר בִּשְׁתֵּי־שָׁעוֹת וְאֶחָד אוֹמֵר בְּשָׁלֹשׁ עֵדוּתָן קַיֶּמֶת. אֶחָד אוֹמֵר בְּשָׁלֹשׁ וְאֶחָד אוֹמֵר בְּחָמֵשׁ עֵדוּתָן בְּטֵלָה. רַבִּי יְהוּדָה אוֹמֵר עֵדוּתָן קַיֶּמֶת. אֶחָד אוֹמֵר בְּחָמֵשׁ וְאֶחָד אוֹמֵר בְּשֶׁבַע עֵדוּתָן בְּטֵילָה שֶׁבְּחָמֵשׁ חַמָּה בַּמִּזְרָח וּבְשֶׁבַע חַמָּה בַּמַּעֲרָב:

הָיוּ מַכְנִיסִין אֶת־הַשֵּׁנִי וּבוֹדְקִין אוֹתוֹ אִם נִמְצְאוּ דִבְרֵיהֶם מְכֻוָּנִין פּוֹתְחִין בִּזְכוּת. אָמַר אֶחָד מִן הָעֵדִים יֶשׁ־לִי לְלַמֵּד עָלָיו זְכוּת אוֹ אֶחָד מִן הַתַּלְמִידִים יֶשׁ־לִי לְלַמֵּד עָלָיו חוֹבָה מְשַׁתְּקִין אוֹתוֹ. אָמַר אֶחָד מִן הַתַּלְמִידִים יֶשׁ־לִי לְלַמֵּד עָלָיו זְכוּת מַעֲלִין וּמוֹשִׁיבִין אוֹתוֹ עִימָּהֶם וְלֹא הָיָה יוֹרֵד מִשָּׁם כָּל־הַיּוֹם. אִם יֵשׁ־מַמָּשׁ בִּדְבָרָיו שׁוֹמְעִין לוֹ. אֲפִילּוּ אָמַר הוּא יֶשׁ־לִי לְלַמֵּד עַל עַצְמִי זְכוּת שׁוֹמְעִין לוֹ וּבִלְבַד שֶׁיְּהֵא מַמָּשׁ בִּדְבָרָיו:

אִם מָצְאוּ לוֹ זְכוּת פְּטָרוּהוּ וְאִם לָאו מַעֲבִירִין אוֹתוֹ עַד לְמָחָר. וּמִזְדַּוְּגִין זוּגוֹת זוּגוֹת וּמְמַעֲטִין בְּמַאֲכָל וְלֹא הָיוּ שׁוֹתִים יַיִן כָּל־הַיּוֹם וְנוֹשְׂאִין וְנוֹתְנִין בַּדָּבָר כָּל־הַלַּיְלָה. וּלְמָחֳרַת מַשְׁכִּימִים וּבָאִים לְבֵית־דִּין הַמְזַכֶּה אוֹמֵר אֲנִי הוּא הַמְזַכֶּה וּמְזַכֶּה אֲנִי בִּמְקוֹמִי וְהַמְחַיֵּב אוֹמֵר אֲנִי הוּא הַמְחַיֵּב וּמְחַיֵּב אֲנִי בִּמְקוֹמִי. הַמְלַמֵּד חוֹבָה מְלַמֵּד זְכוּת אֲבָל הַמְלַמֵּד זְכוּת אֵינוֹ יָכוֹל לַחֲזוֹר וּלְלַמֵּד חוֹבָה. אִם טָעוּ בַדָּבָר סוֹפְרֵי־הַדַּיָּנִין מַזְכִּירִין אוֹתוֹ. אִם מָצְאוּ לוֹ זְכוּת פְּטָרוּהוּ וְאִם לָאו עוֹמְדִין עַל הַמִּנְיָן. שְׁנַיִם עָשָׂר מְזַכִּין וְאַחַד־עָשָׂר מְחַיְּבִין זַכַּי. שְׁנֵים עָשָׂר מְחַיְּבִין וְאֶחָד־עָשָׂר מְזַכִּין (חַיָּב). אַחַד עָשָׂר מְזַכִּין וְאַחַד־עָשָׂר מְחַיְּבִין אֲפִלּוּ עֶשְׂרִים וּשְׁנַיִם מְזַכִּין אוֹ מְחַיְּבִין וְאֶחָד אוֹמֵר אֵינִי יוֹדֵעַ יוֹסִיפוּ הַדַּיָּנִים. עַד כַּמָּה מוֹסִיפִין שְׁנַיִם שְׁנַיִם עַד שִׁבְעִים וּשְׁנַיִם וְאֶחָד. שְׁלֹשִׁים וְשִׁשָּׁה מְזַכִּין וּשְׁלֹשִׁים וַחֲמִשָּׁה מְחַיְּבִין זַכַּי. שְׁלֹשִׁים וְשִׁשָּׁה מְחַיְּבִין וּשְׁלֹשִׁים וַחֲמִשָּׁה מְזַכִּין (חַיָּב). שְׁלֹשִׁים וְשִׁשָּׁה מְזַכִּין וּשְׁלֹשִׁים וְשִׁשָּׁה מְחַיְּבִין דָּנִין אֵלּוּ כְּנֶגֶד אֵלּוּ עַד שֶׁיִּרְאֶה אֶחָד מִן הַמְחַיְּבִין אֶת־דִּבְרֵי־הַמְזַכִּין:

*Translation.* (1) They examined them [the witnesses] with seven points of interrogation: In what week of years? In what year? In what month? On what day of the month? On what day [of the week]? In what hour? In what place? Rabbi Yose says, "On what day? In what hour? In what place?" Do you know him? Did you warn him?" [In the case of] one who worships an idol: What did he worship? And how did he worship it?

(2) The more they expand the interrogation, the more he deserves to be praised. Ben Zakkai once examined the evidence inquiring [the witness] about the stems of figs. And what is the difference between interrogation and examination? In the case of interrogation, [if] one [of the two witnesses] said, "I do now know," his testimony is invalid. In the case of examination, [if] one [of the two witnesses] said, "I do now know," or if they both answered, "We do not know," their testimony remains valid. Yet whether during interrogation or examination: if they contradict one another, they testimony is invalid

(3) [If] one [of the witnesses] said, "on the second day of the month," and the other said, "on the third," their testimony remains valid, since one may have known about the intercalation of the month, and the other did not know about the intercalation of the month. [If] one said, "on the third," and the other said, "on the fifth," their testimony is invalid. [If] one said, "at the second hour," and the other said, "at the third," their testimony remains valid. [If] one

said, "at the third hour," and the other said, "at the fifth," their testimony is invalid. Rabbi Judah says, "It remains valid." [If] one said, "at the fifth hour," and the other said, "at the seventh," their testimony is invalid, since at the fifth hour the sun is in the east and at the seventh it is in the west.

(4) And afterward they brought in the second [witness] and examined him. If their words were found to agree, they begin [the argument] in favor of acquittal. [If] one of the witnesses says, "I have something to say in favor of acquittal," or [if] one of the disciples said, "I have something to say in favor of conviction," they silence him. [If] one of the disciples said, "I have something to say in favor of acquittal," they bring him up and seat him among them (the judges), and he does not come down from there the entire day. If there is substance in what he says, they listen to him. And even if the accused said, "I have something to say in favor of my acquittal," they listen to him, provided that there is substance in his words.

(5) If they found him innocent, they set him free; if not, they postpone judging him[360] until the next day. They went together in pairs, they did not each much or drink wine the entire day, and they discussed the matter all night. And the next day they came to the courthouse. The one who favors acquittal says, "I declared him innocent [yesterday], and I still declare him innocent today." And the one who favored conviction says, "I declared him guilty [yesterday], and I still declare him guilty." The one who argued in favor of conviction may [now] argue in favor of acquittal, but the one who argued in favor of acquittal may not now retract and argue in favor of conviction. [If] they made an error in some matter, the scribes[361] of the judges remind them [of what had been said]. If they find him innocent, they set him free; if not, they decide by vote. [If] twelve favor acquittal and eleven favor conviction, he is acquitted. [If] twelve vote for conviction and eleven vote for acquittal, or even if eleven favor acquittal and eleven favor conviction and one says, "I have no opinion," they must add to the number of the judges. Up to what number may they add to them? Two by two, until there are seventy-one. [If] thirty-six vote for acquittal and thirty-five vote for conviction, he is acquitted. [If] thirty-six vote for conviction and thirty-five vote for acquittal, they debate the matter until one of those who favored conviction accepts the arguments of those who favor acquittal.

*Commentary.* The interrogation (חֲקִירָה) of witnesses has to cover seven questions in order to precisely establish the date, time, and place of the crime (5:1). The discussion in *b. Sanh.* 40a provides the Scriptural basis for all seven questions. The term שָׁבוּעַ refers to the "year-week" or septennate, i.e., the particular seven-year period of the fifty-year jubilee. The term שָׁנָה refers to the year of

---

[360] The editio princeps reads אוֹתוֹ, which would refer to the accused; the majority of editions reads דִּינוֹ referring to the lawsuit or judgment (KRAUSS).

[361] NEUSNER follows editions which speak of two (שְׁנֵי) scribes.

the septennate. The inquiry regarding the day of the week (יוֹם) was rendered superfluous due to the indication of the day of the month (וּבְכַמָּה בַחֹדֶשׁ ); it seems to have provided a further point of agreement of the witnesses in case they disagreed on one of the other questions (KRAUSS) According to R. Yose, only three questions were asked in the cross-examination (date, hour, place). The query about whether a witness knew the accused[362] may relate to the question whether the accused was a Jew or Gentile. The question whether the accused has been warned of the consequences of the deed renders convictions on the basis of witness testimony difficult and in the case of murder, virtually impossible (KRAUSS). The last two questions belong to the specific case of a person accused of idolatry (עֲבוֹדָה זָרָה): What particular foreign deity did the accused worship, and did he worship the foreign deity with sacrifices, incense, libations, and/or expressions of adoration?

While the interrogation of witnesses is subject to specific regulations, the examination of witnesses about minor matters is not regulated. This is why it is praiseworthy if they ask many questions during the examination of the witnesses (5:2). In a case involving witnesses who testified that the murder took place under a fig tree, Yohanan ben Zakkai asked questions about the character of the stems of the figs (according to *b. Sanh.* 41a, he asked whether the stems were thin or thick). Interrogation (חֲקִירוֹת) differs from examination (בְּדִיקוֹת) as regards the consequences of not knowing the answer to a judge's question. For the testimony of witnesses to be valid as the basis for conviction, both witnesses must be able to answer all (seven) questions; when they are examined about minor matters and cannot answer a judge's question, their testimony on the major questions is not affected. However, if the witnesses contradict each other during examination about minor matters, their testimony becomes invalid, as is the case regarding contradictory testimony during interrogation. The discussion about the testimony of witnesses concerning the date and time of the crime in 5:3 accepts discrepancies based on the intercalation of the month as well as on the difficulty of giving the precise time of the day. A witness may not be aware that the month in question was intercalated; a discrepancy of nearly two hours is regarded as acceptable, a discrepancy of nearly three hours is generally not accepted, although Rabbi Judah accepts even a discrepancy of three hours.

The discussion in 5:4 resumes 5:1 with a treatment of the second witness. The arguments for acquittal are heard first. They can be advanced by a witness, by a rabbi's disciple (student), or by the accused. A disciple was not permitted to speak against the accused (in capital cases; cf. 4:1). According to

---

[362] This and the following question are included by NEUSNER in 5:1 C, the section on R. Yose's statement, who is thus understood to have asked five questions. KRAUSS seems to treat this and the following question as additional questions besides the seven queries mentioned at the beginning of the section.

5:5, an accused person acquitted by a majority of the judges is released on the same day, while the case of an accused person who is not acquitted is decided on the following day. During the deliberations, whether by day or through the night, the judges were not allowed to eat much nor drink wine. As had already been stipulated in 4:1 (No. 32), a judge who first argued for conviction can change his mind as a result of the deliberations and vote for acquittal, while a judge who first argued for acquittal cannot now vote for conviction. A simple majority was sufficient for acquittal. Conviction required a majority of at least two judges (cf. 4:1). If twelve judges voted for conviction and eleven for acquittal, the number of judges had to be increased by two additional judges, a process that continued until the court voted for acquittal or reached a verdict of condemnation with the necessary majority of two votes. The maximum number of judges that could be reached through this process was seventy-one.

It appears that during Jesus' trial, only witnesses who spoke for conviction appeared before the Sanhedrin. Mark and Matthew relate that there were "many" (πολλοί) witnesses who testified for conviction but whose testimony did not agree (Mark 15:56 / Matt 26:60). In particular, two witnesses testified that Jesus claimed to be able to destroy the Temple to rebuild it in three days (Matt 26:61). Mark speaks of "some" witnesses who testify to such a statement, (Mark 15:57–58). The fact that the testimony of these witnesses did not agree (Mark 15:59; implied in Matt 26:62, in which the high priest seeks to elicit a statement from Jesus that would prove the validity of these witnesses) implies that the witnesses were cross-examined, as stipulated by *m. Sanh.* 5:1.[363] The Gospels do not indicate whether Sanhedrin members who sympathized with Jesus, such as Joseph of Arimathea (Mark 15:43; Luke 23:50) and Nicodemus (John 3:1; 7:50; 19:39), or members who were cautious in capital cases, such as Gamaliel (Acts 5:33–39), spoke in favor of acquittal. It is not clear whether they were present during Jesus' examination. Jesus' silence during the examination suggests that he did not himself advance arguments for his acquittal, which *m. Sanh.* 5:4 allows. This is true irrespective of whether Jesus was present during the cross-examination of the witnesses.[364] His response to the direct question of Caiaphas is hardly information that would provide grounds for acquittal. On the contrary, it helped the high priest secure a conviction.

---

[363] GUNDRY, Mark, 893: "the Sanhedrin's finding of disagreement in the testimony which they heard against Jesus and consequently throwing out that testimony implies careful examination." CHILTON / BOCK, Mark, 487, refer to this Mishnah text for the assertion that the session described in Mark 14:53–72 "does not correspond to a formal meeting of the Sanhedrin, but a gathering of evidence." It cannot be ruled out that the session was a formal trial, particularly if the witnesses who testified against Jesus were members of the Sanhedrin who heard Jesus speak and saw him act during the previous week.

[364] Cf. PESCH, Markusevangelium, 2:435. STROBEL, Stunde, 67, assumes that Jesus was not present, with reference to *t. Sanh.* 6:3 (No. 53).

**(53)** *t. Sanhedrin* 6:3

כיזה צד הן דנין הדייינין יושבים ובעלי דינין עומדין לפניהם וכל התובע את חבירו הוא פותח
ראשון ואם יש עדים מכניסין אותו ומאיימין עליהן ומוציאין אותן לחוץ ומשייירין את הגדול
שבהם ושומעין את דבריו ומוציאין אותן לחוץ ואחר כך מכניסין את שניהם כאחד ואומ' זה בפני
זה ושומעין את דבריו ומוציאין אותו לחוץ ואח"כ מכניסין את שניהן כאחד ואומרים דבריהם זה
בפני זה אם אמ' זכאי זכאי אם אמ' חייב חייב אחד דיני ממונות ואחד דיני נפשות דיני ממונות
בשלשה שנים מזכין ומחייבין ואחד או' איני יודע יוסיפו הדייינין יפה כח האומר חייב מכח האו'
איני יודע עד כמה מוסיפין עד פחות משנים יוסיפו הדייינין אם אמ' זכאי זכאי אם אמ' חייב
אחד אומ' זכאי ואחד או' איני יודע יוסיפו הדייינין שעד עכשיו בית דין שקול אחד א' חייב ואחד
א' זכאי ואחד א' איני יודע יוסיפו הדייינין שעד עכשיו לא הוסיפו אלא אחד:

*Translation.* How do they judge? The judges sit and the litigants remain
standing before them. The one who brings a claim against his neighbor is the
one who opens the proceedings. If there are witnesses, they bring them in and
they admonish them; then they take them out and they keep back the most
important witness; they hear his testimony and bring him out. Then they bring
in both parties together and one speaks in the presence of the other. If [all the
judges] rule that he is innocent, he is innocent. If they rule [unanimously] that
he is guilty, he is guilty. The rule is the same for civil and capital cases. Civil
cases are tried by three [judges]. If two [judges] acquit or declare guilty, while
one of them says, "I do not know," they add to the judges. The power of the
one who says, "Guilty," is greater than the power of the one who says, "I do
now know." How many [judges] do they add? Not less than two judges [at
once]. If [both judges that were last added] say, "He is innocent," he is innocent. If they say, "He is guilty," he is guilty. If one says, "He is innocent," and
one says, "I do not know," they add to the judges, because in this case the
court is evenly balanced. If one says, "He is guilty," and one says, "I do not
know," they add to the judges, for up to now they have added only one judge
at a time.

*Commentary.* The first section of this text clarifies the procedure by which a
court of law arrives at a verdict. The following matters are addressed: (1) The
judges sit during the court session. (2) The litigants and witnesses stand
before the judges. (3) The plaintiff speaks first; he is given the opportunity to
formulate his complaint. (4) Before the witnesses are crossexamined, they are
brought before the court and admonished to speak the truth.[365] The wording of
the admonition is provided neither here nor in *m. Sanh.* 3:6. According to
*b. Sanh.* 29a, Rabbi Judah said that witnesses (in civil cases) were warned that
if they provided false evidence, they might cause a drought (reference to Prov
25:14); Rabba said that witnesses were warned that false testimony might

---

[365] The conditional formulation עדים יש אם ("If there are witnesses") implies cases that can
be decided without witnesses on the basis of documentary evidence.

cause a plague to come upon the world (reference to Prov 25:18); and Nathan ben Mar Zutra said that witnesses were warned that if they gave false testimony, their employer would despise them (reference to 1 Kings 21:10). The admonition in capital cases is provided in *m. Sanh.* 4:5 (No. 33). After the admonition, the witnesses are led out of the courtroom. (6) The examination of the witnesses begins with the main witness. The plaintiff and the accused are both present when the witnesses are cross-examined.[366] (7) Both the plaintiff and accused argue their cases in the presence of the other party. (8) The judges vote based on the arguments of the plaintiff and the accused and the testimony of the witnesses. If they agree on a verdict, whether acquittal or conviction, the case is decided. (9) In civil (monetary) cases, the court consists of three judges who must agree on a verdict. If only two agree, and the third has no opinion, the legal case cannot be decided since the judge who has no opinion is no longer regarded as a member of the court (which must have at least three judges).[367] Two judges are added, and the legal case is heard again by the court; the previously undecided judge continues to be a member of the court, which has now five judges. If two judges vote to convict, two acquit and the fifth remains undecided, the court is evenly divided (בית דין שקול).[368]

## 1.5  The Charge of Blasphemy

According to Mark 14:64 / Matt 26:65, the high priest Caiaphas asserts that Jesus has committed the offense of blasphemy, which is taken to be the grounds for the guilty verdict:

ἠκούσατε τῆς βλασφημίας τί ὑμῖν φαίνεται; οἱ δὲ πάντες κατέκριναν αὐτὸν ἔνοχον εἶναι θανάτου (Mark 14:64)
"You have heard the blasphemy! What do you think?" They all condemned him as deserving the death penalty.

τότε ὁ ἀρχιερεὺς διέρρηξεν τὰ ἱμάτια αὐτοῦ λέγων· ἐβλασφήμησεν· τί ἔτι χρείαν ἔχομεν μαρτύρων; ἴδε νῦν ἠκούσατε τὴν βλασφημίαν (Matt 26:65)[369]

---

[366] SALOMONSEN, Sanhedrin–Makkot, 96 n. 19, suggests that this procedure allowed both the plaintiff and the accused to comment on statements the witnesses made during cross-examination. Differently STROBEL, Stunde, 67, who thinks that the cross-examination of the witnesses took place without either the plaintiff or the accused being present.

[367] Differently *m. Sanh.* 4:1, which stipulates that civil cases can be decided by a majority of one vote

[368] Cf. SALOMONSEN, Sanhedrin–Makkot, 97–98 nn. 25, 26 for a discussion of the respect shown for the undecided judge, who is not put under pressure to arrive at a verdict. The text is not entirely clear.

[369] Note the blasphemy charge according to John 10:36: ὃν ὁ πατὴρ ἡγίασεν καὶ ἀπέστειλεν εἰς τὸν κόσμον ὑμεῖς λέγετε ὅτι βλασφημεῖς, ὅτι εἶπον· υἱὸς τοῦ θεοῦ εἰμι;

Then the high priest tore his clothes and said, "He has blasphemed! Why do we need any more witnesses? Look, you have now heard the blasphemy."

Caiaphas' assertion follows his question, "Are you the Messiah, the Son of the Blessed One?" (Mark 14:61), to which Jesus responded: "I am. And you will see the Son of Man sitting at the right hand of the Power and coming on the clouds of heaven." H. LIETZMANN and others argue that the charge of blasphemy required, according to contemporary legal understanding (cf. *m. Sanh.* 7:5), the pronunciation of the divine name, taking the discrepancy as evidence that Mark created the scene.[370] Since J. BLINZLER, most scholars assume a wider understanding of blasphemy.[371] The following texts have been cited for understanding blasphemy as pronouncing the divine name, claiming divine prerogatives, profaning holy things, threatening the Temple, and attacking the divinely appointed leadership.

*Pronouncing the divine name.* The Torah stipulates in Lev 24:16: "One who blasphemes[372] the name of YHWH shall be put to death. The whole assembly must stone him. The alien as well as the native citizen, when they blaspheme the Name, shall be put to death" (וְנֹקֵב שֵׁם־יְהוָה מוֹת יוּמָת רָגוֹם יִרְגְּמוּ־בוֹ כָּל־הָעֵדָה כַּגֵּר כָּאֶזְרָח בְּנָקְבוֹ־שֵׁם יוּמָת). The LXX interprets the verb נקב ("blaspheme") in terms of speaking the Tetragrammaton: ὀνομάζων δὲ τὸ ὄνομα κυρίου θανάτῳ θανατούσθω· λίθοις λιθοβολείτω αὐτὸν πᾶσα συναγωγὴ Ἰσραήλ· ἐάν τε προσήλυτος ἐάν τε αὐτόχθων, ἐν τῷ ὀνόμασαι αὐτὸν τὸ ὄνομα κυρίου τελευτάτω ("Whoever names the name of the Lord – by death let him be put to death; let the whole congregation of Israel stone him with stones. Whether a guest or a native, when he names the name, let him die;" Lev 24:16 LXX).[373] The following texts from Philo, Josephus, and the Mishnah are most relevant for the discussion of the charge of blasphemy understood as pronouncing the name YHWH.

---

[370] LIETZMANN, Prozess, 6; cf. LOHSE, Prozeß, 121–22. For a recent defense of the historicity of the scene cf. DARRELL L. BOCK, Blasphemy and the Jewish Examination of Jesus, in Key Events in the Life of the Historical Jesus: A Collaborative Exploration of Context and Coherence (ed. D. L. Bock and R. L. Webb; WUNT 247; Tübingen: Mohr Siebeck, 2009), 589–667.

[371] Cf. BLINZLER, Prozeß, 152–56, 188–97. For the various interpretations cf. DAVID R. CATCHPOLE, You Have Heard His Blasphemy, TynB 16 (1965): 10–18; BROWN, Death, 1:534–44; DARRELL L. BOCK, Blasphemy and Exaltation in Judaism: The Charge against Jesus in Mark 14:53–56 (Orig. 1998; repr., Grand Rapids: Baker, 2000), 6–26. Cf. ADELA YARBRO COLLINS, The Charge of Blasphemy in Mark 14:6 [2004], in The Trial and Death of Jesus: Essays on the Passion Narrative in Mark (ed. G. Van Oyen and T. Shepherd; CBET 45; Leuven: Peters, 2006), 149–170; BOCK, Blasphemy and the Jewish Examination of Jesus.

[372] The Hebrew verb נקב means, here, "to denote unfavourably: to curse, slander" (HALOT s.v. נקב 3b. Most English versions render the verb with "blaspheme."

[373] JOHN W. WEVERS, Leviticus (Septuaginta II.2; Göttingen: Vandenhoeck & Ruprecht, 1986), 260. Translation of Dirk L. Büchner in PIETERSMA / WRIGHT, Septuagint, 103.

**(54)** Philo, *De vita Mosis* 2.203–208

μετὰ δὲ τὴν τοῦ ἀνοσίου καὶ παλαμναίου τίσιν ἐγράφη διάταγμα καινόν, οὐκ ἄν ποτε προηγουμένης ἀξιωθὲν γραφῆς, ἀλλ᾽ αἱ ἀπροσδόκητοι νεωτεροποιίαι καινοὺς νόμους εἰς ἀνακοπὴν ἁμαρτημάτων ἐπιζητοῦσιν αὐτίκα γοῦν νομοθετεῖται τάδε· ὃς ἂν καταράσηται θεόν, ἁμαρτίας ἔνοχος ἔστω, ὃς δ᾽ ἂν ὀνομάσῃ τὸ ὄνομα κυρίου, θνησκέτω. ²⁰⁴ εὖ γ᾽, ὦ πάνσοφε, μόνος ἀμιγοῦς ἠκρατίσω σοφίας· τοῦ καταρᾶσθαι χεῖρον τὸ ὀνομάζειν ὑπείληφας; οὐ γὰρ ἂν τὸν μὲν βαρύτατον ἀσέβημα εἰργασμένον ἐπεκούφιζες διημαρτηκόσιν ἐπιεικέστερον συντάττων, κατὰ δὲ τοῦ βραχύτερον ἠδικηκέναι δόξαντος τὴν ἀνωτάτω τιμωρίαν, θάνατον, ὥριζες ²⁰⁵ ἀλλ᾽ ὡς ἔοικε " θεοῦ" τὰ νῦν οὐχὶ τοῦ πρώτου καὶ γεννητοῦ τῶν ὅλων ἀλλὰ τῶν ἐν ταῖς πόλεσι μέμνηται· ψευδώνυμοι δ᾽ εἰσὶ γραφέων καὶ πλαστῶν τέχναις δημιουργούμενοι ξοάνων γὰρ καὶ ἀγαλμάτων καὶ τοιουτοτρόπων ἀφιδρυμάτων ἡ οἰκουμένη μεστὴ γέγονεν, ὧν τῆς βλασφημίας ἀνέχειν ἀναγκαῖον, ἵνα μηδεὶς ἐθίζηται τῶν Μωυσέως γνωρίμων συνόλως θεοῦ προσρήσεως ἀλογεῖν· ἀξιονικοτάτη γὰρ καὶ ἀξιέραστος ἡ κλῆσις. ²⁰⁶ εἰ δέ τις οὐ λέγω βλασφημήσειεν εἰς τὸν ἀνθρώπων καὶ θεῶν κύριον, ἀλλὰ καὶ τολμήσειεν ἀκαίρως αὐτοῦ φθέγξασθαι τοὔνομα, θάνατον ὑπομεινάτω τὴν δίκην. ²⁰⁷ οὐδὲ γὰρ τῶν φυτευσάντων καίτοι θνητῶν ὑπαρχόντων οἷς μέλει γονέων τιμῆς τὰ ὀνόματα προφέρουσιν, ἀλλὰ τὰ κύρια διὰ τὸν ἐπ᾽ αὐτοῖς σεβασμὸν ἡσυχάζοντες τοῖς τῆς φύσεως ἀνακαλοῦσι πατέρα καὶ μητέρα προσαγορεύοντες δι᾽ ὧν εὐθὺς αἰνίττονται τὰς ἐξ ἐκείνων ἀνυπερβλήτους εὐεργεσίας καὶ τὴν αὐτῶν εὐχάριστον διάθεσιν ²⁰⁸ ἔτι νῦν συγγνώμης ἀξιούσθωσαν οἱ κατ᾽ ἐπισυρμὸν γλώττης ἀκαιρευόμενοι καὶ λόγων ἀναπλήρωμα ποιούμενοι τὸ ἁγιώτατον καὶ θεῖον ὄνομα;

*Translation.* After this impious murderer had been punished, a new ordinance was enacted which had not seem to be required before this event. But unexpected disorders demand new laws as a check to sinful actions. And so on this occasion the following law was enacted: Anybody who curses god shall be guilty of sin, and anybody who names the name of the Lord shall die. ²⁰⁴ Well done, you most wise man! You alone have drunk of the pure wine of wisdom. You have determined that the naming is a greater sacrilege than the cursing, for you could never treat lightly a person guilty of the gravest impiety and rank him with the milder offenders, while you decreed the extreme penalty of death for a person who appeared to have committed the lesser iniquity. ²⁰⁵ But as it seems, here he does not use the word 'god' for the Most High,[374] the Begetter of the Universe, but for those who are regarded as gods in the different cities. They are falsely called gods, being fashioned by the skill of painters and sculptors. For the world is full of images carved of wood and statues and such images set up in honor of a god. We must refrain from speaking in an

---

[374] Thus BADT ("den Höchsten") for τοῦ πρώτου; COHEN translates "the Primal God", YONGE as "the first being who had any existence."

insulting manner of these, in order that no one of Moses' disciples ever gets into the habit of treating the appellation 'god' lightly; for the title is worthy of the highest respect and love. [206] But if anyone, I will not say defames the Lord of human beings and of gods, but is even bold enough to utter his name in an inopportune moment, he shall face the penalty of death. [207] For even those who have proper regard for the honor of their parents, even though they are mere mortals, abstain from using their personal names and, leaving them unsaid, rather call them by the terms indicating their natural relationship, that is 'father' and 'mother' – terms which are at once seen as an acknowledgement of the unsurpassed benefits which they have received from them and as an expression of their own grateful disposition. [208] After this, can we still deem worthy of pardon those who, with a reckless tongue, use the most holy name divine name in inopportune moments and as expletive?

*Commentary.*[375] In the second volume of his Moses biography, Philo follows Suetonius in giving a topical treatment of Moses.[376] He describes and explains Moses' roles as Lawgiver (*Mos.* 2.8–65), high priest (*Mos.* 2.66–186), and prophet (*Mos.* 2.187–291). Philo begins with a discussion of the second and third kind of divine utterances in the Pentateuch, i.e., revelation that comes through question and answer and utterances which are spoken by Moses "when possessed by God and carried away out of himself" (*Mos.* 2.188). In legal cases with no precedent, Moses communicated directly with God, asking about matters on which he has been seeking knowledge and receiving God's instruction. The first case Philo recounts as an example for Moses' revelatory role concerns the case of the blasphemer in Lev 24:10–16. A man whose father was an Egyptian and whose mother was a Jewess (*Mos.* 2.193) became so angry at one point that he lost control of himself, and, since he was beholden to "Egyptian atheism," he cursed God (*Mos.* 2.196). For Philo, the sin of blaspheming God is particularly egregious because it implies the refusal to honor parents and country and benefactors (*Mos.* 2.198).[377] Moses was prepared to kill the offender on the spot but feared this would be too light a penalty, realizing that "to devise an adequate punishment for such an impiety was beyond human powers" (*Mos.* 2.197). Moses ordered the man imprisoned and then implored God to reveal what punishment would be appropriate for such a monstrous and unheard-of crime (*Mos.* 2.201). God commanded that he be stoned (ὁ δὲ προστάττει καταλευσθῆναι), for apparently (οἶμαι) two reasons:

---

[375] Text: Borgen / FUGLSETH / SKARSTEN; for translations cf. C. D. YONGE, B. BADT (in COHN / HEINEMANN / ADLER / THEILER), F. H. COLSON.

[376] FELDMAN, Philo's Portrayal of Moses, 22–23; on Moses as Lawgiver ibid. 258–79, as priest and theologian ibid. 291–97, as prophet ibid. 297–308.

[377] FELDMAN, Philo's Portrayal of Moses, 158, suggests that Philo expanded the story of the blasphemer and emphasized that he was an Egyptian because of "the attraction that the Egyptian way of life had for some of the Jews of his own day."

stoning is the fitting punishment for a man who has a stony and hard soul (λιθίνην καὶ ἀπόκροτον ψυχὴν ἔχοντος), and it is a mode of execution in which all the people can participate by hurling missiles against the offender (*Mos.* 2.202). As a result of this incident, a new law was drawn up. Philo proceeds to quote Lev 24:15–16 (*Mos.* 2. 203–204). He interprets Lev 24:15b as referring to the gods of the different cities, of which Jews may not speak in an insulting manner because the title "god" deserves respect and love (*Mos.* 2.205).[378] The punishment stipulated in Lev 24:15b ("let him bear the guilt of his sin") is not explained by Philo.[379] He focuses on Lev 24:16: a person who defames (blasphemes) "the Most High, the Begetter of the Universe" (*Mos.* 2.205) and utters his name, shall be executed. The qualification "in inopportune moments" (ἀκαίρως) exempts the high priest from this new law when he pronounces the name of God in the Temple. This text stipulates the death penalty for blasphemy that involves pronouncing the name of Israel's God.[380]

**(55)** Josephus, *Antiquitates judaicae* 4.198, 202

ἔχει δὲ οὕτως ἡ διάταξις ἡμῶν τῶν νόμων τῶν ἀνηκόντων εἰς τὴν πολιτείαν. οὓς δὲ κοινοὺς ἡμῖν καὶ πρὸς ἀλλήλους κατέλιπε τούτους ὑπερεθέμην εἰς τὴν περὶ ἐθῶν καὶ αἰτιῶν ἀπόδοσιν, ἣν συλλαμβανομένου τοῦ θεοῦ μετὰ ταύτην ἡμῖν τὴν πραγματείαν συντάξασθαι πρόκειται ... Ὁ δὲ βλασφημήσας θεὸν καταλευσθεὶς κρεμάσθω δι' ἡμέρας καὶ ἀτίμως καὶ ἀφανῶς θαπτέσθω.

*Translation.* This is the arrangement of our laws that are relevant to the constitution. Those [laws] that he left relating to communal affairs and our relations with one another, I have put off for the account concerning customs and causes which, with God's help, I intend to compose after this undertaking[381] ... "Let a person who blasphemes God be stoned and hanged for a day; he shall be buried without honor and in obscurity."

*Commentary.* Josephus begins his presentation of the laws of the constitution of the Jews in *A. J.* 4.199–201 with the laws concerning Jerusalem as the one holy city God selects for himself, and concerning the one Temple of the Jews

---

[378] Cf. Philo, *QE* 2.5, where he gives three additional reasons why Jews should not revile the religion of the Gentiles: praise is better than disparagement, contempt of the piety of others leads to war, and refraining from contempt of the pagan gods may lead Gentiles to speak well of God. Cf. FELDMAN, Philo's Portrayal of Moses, 160; on the case of the blasphemer in *Mos.* 2.192–208, cf. ibid. 156–60.

[379] For a recent discussion of Lev 24:15–16 cf. BERNON P. LEE, Leviticus 24:15b–16: A Crux Revisited, BBR 16 (2006): 345–349, who argues that both laws of Lev 24:15b and Lev 24:16 have the same case in view, with the second law providing a more explicit expression of the crime of blasphemy and the punishment of the death penalty.

[380] Cf. SCHIFFMAN, Sectarian Law, 151 n. 88. On this passage see also COLLINS, Charge of Blasphemy, 159–60.

[381] THACKERAY translates "after the present work."

built in Jerusalem (Deut 12:5; Exod 20:25, 26, 23; Deut 27:5–6; 12:11). L. H. FELDMAN explains that the central issue in the *Antiquities* is the constitution and ideal state of the Jews, and that Josephus, proud of his priestly status, "naturally began by emphasizing the importance of Jerusalem and the Temple."[382] The second law is the law about blasphemy (*A. J.* 4.202): the person who blasphemes God is executed by stoning, hanged for a day, and buried without the traditional honors accorded the dead. Josephus follows Lev 14:16; the hanging of the corpse on a tree is mentioned in Deut 21:22–21. Neither of these biblical texts specify how or where the body is to be buried. The rabbinic halakhah does not mention a disgraceful burial of the blasphemer. According to *m. Sanh.* 6:5–6, the executed criminal is not buried in the burial grounds of his ancestors but in a separate graveyard, and his relatives mourn privately, but not publicly. Josephus goes on to present the laws concerning the annual pilgrimage festivals, the tithe of fruit, blasphemy of alien gods and robbing of foreign temples, etc. By substituting ὀνομάζων δὲ τὸ ὄνομα κυρίου (Lev 14:16 LXX) with the phrase βλασφημήσας θεόν, Josephus signals that "blasphemy" means uttering or pronouncing the divine name.[383] D. L. BOCK interprets "blaspheme" in *A. J.* 4.202 in the light of 4.207, in which Jews are directed not to blaspheme the gods other peoples revere or rob foreign temples out of respect for the very word "God":[384] "The issue of respect, whether in words or in things associated with the presence of the deity, is the central concern. Blasphemy is seen as the verbal element, but the underlying concern is offense against things closely associated with the god in question."[385]

**(56)** *m. Sanhedrin* 6:4

כָּל־הַנִּסְקָלִין נִתְלִין דִּבְרֵי־רַבִּי־אֱלִיעֶזֶר. וַחֲכָמִים אוֹמְרִים אֵינוֹ נִתְלֶה אֶלָּא הַמְגַדֵּף וְהָעוֹבֵד עֲבוֹדָה
זָרָה ... מִפְּנֵי־מָה זֶה תָּלוּי מִפְּנֵי שֶׁבֵּרַךְ אֶת־הַשֵּׁם וְנִמְצָא שֵׁם־שָׁמַיִם מִתְחַלֵּל:

*Translation.*[386] All who have been stoned are hanged. These are the words of Rabbi Eliezer. But the Sages say: "nobody is hanged except the blasphemer and the idolator" ... Why was he hanged? Because he cursed[387] the Name, and the Name of Heaven was found profaned.

*Commentary.* In an extended discussion about stoning a convicted criminal in

---

[382] FELDMAN, Judean Antiquities 1–4, 396–97 n. 569, responding to NODET, Flavius Josèphe. Les Antiquités juives, ad loc.

[383] Cf. COLLINS, Charge of Blasphemy, 162.

[384] Cf. FELDMAN, Judean Antiquities 1–4, 401 n. 594, with further reference to Josephus, *C. Ap.* 2.237; Philo, *Mos.* 2.38, 205.

[385] BOCK, Blasphemy, 54–55.

[386] KRAUSS includes these two texts in *m. Sanh.* 6:5, 6. We follow DANBY and NEUSNER.

[387] The term בֵּרַךְ ("blessed") is used euphemistically for "cursed;" some manuscripts read קִלֵּל ("cursed").

*m. Sanh.* 6, Rabbi Eliezer b. Hyrcanus (c. A.D. 90) is quoted as stating that every person who has been stoned to death is subsequently hanged on a pole, in contrast to the tradition of the Sages, who assert that only the person who blasphemed God (הַמְגַדֵּף) and who worshiped foreign gods (הָעוֹבֵד עֲבוֹדָה זָרָה) is hanged subsequent to stoning. After discussing whether a woman who has been stoned to death should be hanged and how the hanging is to be carried out, the section ends with a statement that highlights the fact that blaspheming God and worshiping foreign gods are heinous crimes. As terrible as murder is, attacking the honor of God is worse, thus requiring the disgrace of the executed felon whose corpse is publicly displayed on a pole. Blaspheming God (גדף), which is tantamount to worshiping foreign gods, is described as profaning (חלל hitp.). The text does not specify what "blaspheming" entails.[388]

## (57) *m. Sanhedrin* 7:5

הַמְגַדֵּף אֵינוֹ חַיָּב עַד שֶׁיְּפָרֵשׁ אֶת־הַשֵּׁם. אָמַר רַבִּי יְהוֹשֻׁעַ בֶּן־קָרְחָה בְּכָל־יוֹם דָּנִין אֶת־הָעֵדִים בְּכִנּוּי
יַכֶּה יוֹסֵי אֶת־יוֹסֵי נִגְמַר הַדִּין לֹא הָיוּ הוֹרְגִין בְּכִנּוּי אֶלָּא מוֹצִיאִין אֶת־כָּל־הָאָדָם לַחוּץ וּמְשַׁיְּרִין
אֶת־הַגָּדוֹל שֶׁבָּהֶן וְאוֹמְרִים לוֹ אֱמֹר מַה שֶּׁשָּׁמַעְתָּ בְּפֵירוּשׁ וְהוּא אוֹמֵר וְהַדַּיָּנִין עוֹמְדִין עַל־רַגְלֵיהֶן
וְקוֹרְעִין וְלֹא מְאַחִין וְהַשֵּׁנִי אוֹמֵר אַף אֲנִי כָּמוֹהוּ וְהַשְּׁלִישִׁי אוֹמֵר אַף אֲנִי כָּמוֹהוּ:

*Translation.* The blasphemer is not culpable (to be executed by stoning) unless he clearly pronounces[389] the Name. Rabbi Joshua b. Qorha says: "On every day of a trial they examined the witnesses with a substituted name,[390] [such as] 'May Yose smite Yose.' When the trial is over, they would not execute him [on the basis of evidence given] with the substituted name, but they sent out all the people and ask the most important of the witnesses, saying to him, 'Say, what exactly[391] did you hear?' And he says what he heard. And the judges stand up on their feet and tear their clothing and never mend them again. And the second witness says, 'I also [heard] what he heard.' And the third witness says, 'I also [heard] what he heard.'"

*Commentary.* This mishnah states that a blasphemer (הַמְגַדֵּף) is liable to death by stoning if he explicitly pronounces the divine Name (עַד שֶׁיְּפָרֵשׁ אֶת־הַשֵּׁם).

---

[388] Differently BOCK, Blasphemy, 67, 234; BOCK, Blasphemy and the Jewish Examination of Jesus, 657, who cites the text in support of the statement that blasphemy included the use of the divine name in an inappropriate way. Note that הַשֵּׁם ("the Name") is a circumlocution for יהוה and does not suggest here that the accused had pronounced the tetragrammaton. Cf. JACOB NEUSNER, Eliezer ben Hyrcanus: The Traditions and the Man (2 vols.; Leiden: Brill, 1973), 1:218–19; 2:118, who does not discuss the pronunciation of the tetragrammaton.

[389] JASTROW s.v. פָּרַשׁ pi 4, "to specify, express clearly," with reference to *m. Sanh.* 7:5 ("until he mentions the Name expressly [uses the Tetragrammaton]."

[390] JASTROW s.v. כִּנּוּי "by-name, surname; attribute, substituted word."

[391] JASTROW s.v. פֵּירוּשׁ "distinct expression, directness," בפירוש "distinctly, explicitly, directly;" with reference to *m. Sanh.* 7:5 ("tell plainly now what thou hast heard [the blasphemer say, i.e. repeat without euphemistic disguise").

This stipulation is derived from Lev 24:14 where הַמְקַלֵּל is used: הוֹצֵא אֶת־הַמְקַלֵּל אֶל־מִחוּץ לַמַּחֲנֶה וְסָמְכוּ כָל־הַשֹּׁמְעִים אֶת־יְדֵיהֶם עַל־רֹאשׁוֹ וְרָגְמוּ אֹתוֹ כָּל־הָעֵדָה: ("Take the one who has cursed[392] outside the camp; and let all who heard him lay their hands on his head, and let the whole congregation stone him;" cf. LXX: Ἐξάγαγε τὸν καταρασάμενον ἔξω τῆς παρεμβολῆς, καὶ ἐπιθήσουσιν πάντες οἱ ἀκούσαντες τὰς χεῖρας αὐτῶν ἐπὶ τὴν κεφαλὴν αὐτοῦ, καὶ λιθοβο-λήσουσιν αὐτὸν πᾶσα ἡ συναγωγή). However, note Num 15:30, in which the person who acts defiantly "blasphemes" (מְגַדֵּף; LXX παροξύνει) YHWH. Rabbi Joshua b. Qorha (c. A.D. 150) explained the process by which a person who pronounced the divine name is convicted in court. The witnesses first give testimony using a substitute for the divine name. After the public has been excused from the courtroom, the most important witnesses repeat exactly (בְּפֵירוּשׁ) what the accused has said. Once the judges hear the divine name pronounced, they stand up and rend their clothing. The accused is convicted when three witnesses repeat explicitly what he has said.

R. H. GUNDRY argues that Jesus did pronounce the divine name when he alluded to Psalm 110:1, which was suppressed in the public reports of the scene and in Mark's account in order that the blasphemy not be repeated.[393] J. BLINZLER asserts that the narrow understanding of blasphemy reflected in this text was not applied in the courts during Jesus' time.[394] D. JUEL argues, "If this second-century conception of blasphemy is an appropriate reflection of early first-century legal standards, it is impossible that Jesus could have been legally condemned for this offence. In fact, his response to the question of the high priest contains clear indications of respectful avoidance of the name of God ('The right hand of power')."[395] D. L. BOCK suggests that the text "re-

---

[392] Cf. KJV, NASB, RSV; NIV, NLT NRSV translate "the blasphemer."

[393] GUNDRY, Mark, 915–18; ROBERT H. GUNDRY, The Old is Better: New Testament Essays in Support of Traditional Interpretations (WUNT 178; Tübingen: Mohr Siebeck, 2005), 98–110. See the discussion in BOCK, Blasphemy and the Jewish Examination of Jesus, 610–613, who argues with *m. Soṭah* 7:6; *m. Yoma* 62, and the evidence of 1QIsaᵃ that "it is not certain that even if Jesus cited Ps 110:1 he would have read the divine name as written."

[394] BLINZLER, Prozeß, 153; he argues ibid. 216–29 that the Mishnah reflects the more humanitarian interpretation of the Law by the Pharisees, which had no legal relevance before A.D. 70 when the Sanhedrin followed Sadducean law; for a critical discussion cf. STROBEL, Stunde, 48–61, who argues for the unity of the Pharisees' and the Sadducees' legal thinking in special religious offenses. BLINZLER refers to JOSEPH KLAUSNER, Jesus von Nazareth. Seine Zeit, sein Leben und seine Lehre (3., erweiterte Auflage; orig. 1907, 1922; repr., Jerusalem: Jewish Publishing House, 1952), 463; ELIAS BICKERMAN, Utilitas crucis. Observations sur les récits du procès de Jésus dans les Évangiles canoniques [1935], in Studies in Jewish and Christian History (AGJU 9; Leiden: Brill, 1976), 1:82–138, 87–88; EDUARD MEYER, Ursprung und Anfänge des Christentums (3 vols.; orig. 1921–1923; repr., Darmstadt: Wissenschaftliche Buchgesellschaft, 1962), 2:452.

[395] JUEL, Messiah and Temple, 97. He asserts that scholars who assume a broader legal definition of blasphemy in the first century still cannot explain "what in the question of the high priest or Jesus' response would constitute a blasphemous statement or claim" (ibid. 98).

presents the narrowest interpretation of this law, a restricting of capital punishment during a period when capital punishment was a largely theoretical discussion anyway."[396]

*Claiming divine prerogatives.* Most scholars link the blasphemy charge with the content of Jesus' answer to Caiaphas' question in Mark 14:62, in particular with his allusion to the enthroned authority of the regal figure in Psalm 110:1 and to the authoritative figure of one like a Son of Man in Dan 7:13. MORNA D. HOOKER writes, "To claim for oneself a seat at the right hand of power, however, is to claim a share in the authority of God; to appropriate to oneself such authority and to bestow on oneself this unique status in the sight of God and man would almost certainly have been regarded as blasphemy."[397] DARRELL L. BOCK, who wrote the most extensive study of the blasphemy charge, concurs: "Jesus' bold affirmation of his presence at the side of God and coming authority (whether as judge, ruler, or merely as a vindicated person) is what they found offensive ... not only will God vindicate Jesus, but he will exalt him to a place of honor that is shared with God. This position is what the saying indicates the leadership heard as blasphemous ... It is the juxtaposition of seating and coming on the clouds that makes clear the transcendent function that Jesus gives himself here, with the reference to clouds making it apparent that more than a pure human and earthly messianic claim is present."[398] The following texts are relevant.

**(58)** Philo, *De somniis* 2.129–132

καὶ μὴν οὗτος αὐτὸς ἐγὼ τὰ λεχθέντα, ἔφη, πάντα εἰμί, τυφώς, πόλεμος, κατακλυσμός, κεραυνός, λιμηρὰ καὶ λοιμώδης νόσος, ὁ τινάττων καὶ κυκῶν τὰ παγίως ἑστῶτα σεισμός, εἱμαρμένης ἀνάγκης οὐκ ὄνομα, ἀλλ᾽ ἐμφανὴς ἐγγὺς ἑστῶσα δύναμις. [130] τί οὖν τὸν ταῦτα λέγοντα ἢ διανοούμενον αὐτὸ μόνον εἶναι φῶμεν; ἆρ᾽ οὐκ ἐκτόπιον; ὑπερωκεάνιον μὲν οὖν ἢ μετακόσμιόν τι καινὸν κακόν, εἴ γε τῷ πάντα μακαρίῳ ὁ πάντα βαρυδαίμων ἑαυτὸν ἐξομοιοῦν ἐτόλμησεν [131] ὑπερθεῖτ᾽ ἂν οὗτος ἥλιον καὶ σελήνην καὶ τοὺς ἄλλους ἀστέρας βλασφημεῖν, ὁπότε τι τῶν ἐλπισθέντων κατὰ τὰς ἐτησίους ὥρας ἢ μὴ συνόλως ἢ μὴ ῥᾳδίως ἀποβαίνοι, φλογμὸν μὲν θέρους, κρυμὸν δὲ καὶ χειμῶνος βαρὺν κατασκήπτοντος ἔαρος δὲ καὶ μετοπώρου, τοῦ μὲν πρὸς εὐκαρπίαν ἐστειρωμένου, τοῦ δὲ πρὸς νοσημάτων γενέσεις εὐτοκίᾳ χρωμένου; [132] πάντα μὲν οὖν ἀνασείων κάλων ἀχαλίνου στόματος καὶ κακηγόρου γλώττης, ὥσπερ τὸν εἰωθότα δασμὸν οὐκ ἐνεγκόντας τοὺς ἀστέρας αἰτιάσεται, τιμᾶσθαι

---

[396] BOCK, Blasphemy, 68.

[397] MORNA D. HOOKER, The Son of Man in Mark: A Study of the Background of the Term "Son of Man" and Its Use in St. Mark's Gospel (London: SPCK, 1967), 173.

[398] BOCK, Blasphemy and the Jewish Examination of Jesus, 616.

μονονοὺ καὶ προσκυνεῖσθαι δικαιῶν ὑπὸ τῶν οὐρανίων τὰπίγεια καὶ περι-
ττότερον ἑαυτόν, ὅσῳ καὶ τῶν ἄλλων ἄνθρωπος ὢν διενηνοχέναι ζῴων δοκεῖ

*Translation.* And he said, "And indeed I myself am all the evils which I have
mentioned: a whirlwind, war, deluge, thunderbolt, famine and plague, an
earthquake which shakes and stirs up what stood firm; I am the necessity of
fate, not its name, but its manifest power standing close."[399] [130] What shall we
say of a person who says or who merely thinks these things? Shall we not call
him a new evil, outlandish, monstrous, abysmal, miserable in every respect,
who dared to compare himself to the All-blessed? [131] Would he delay to utter
blasphemies against the sun and the moon and the other stars, if what he
hoped for at each season of the year did not happen at all or only with difficulty, if the summer falls upon him with scorching heat or the winter with icy
cold, if the spring did not yield fruit or the autumn produced diseases? [132]
Indeed, he will shake out every reef of his unbridled mouth and abusive
tongue and accuse the stars of not paying their customary tribute, all but
claiming that the things of heaven revere and pay homage to the things of the
earth, and to himself above them all, inasmuch as he, being a man, deems
himself to have been made superior to the other living creatures.

*Commentary.* Philo discusses in this text an unnamed governor of the Roman
province of Egypt who wanted to abolish the observance of the sabbath by the
Jews so that they would be able to serve him on that day as well. He argues
that they would surely abandon the observance of the sabbath if an enemy
would suddenly attack, if there was a flood, a fire, a thunderbolt, famine,
plague, earthquake or any other trouble caused by human beings or the gods
(*Somn.* 2.125). He then claims that he is all these things and that he has the
power to influence destiny. Philo states that a man who dares to claim the prerogatives of God for himself and to compare himself with God is a man who
would not hesitate to utter blasphemies (βλασφημεῖν, 2.131) against creation
when the sun, moon or seasons do not behave according to his wishes. The
term βλασφημεῖν is used "for a human being who claims a greater degree of
authority and power than he has a right to do."[400] D. L. BOCK suggests that
Jesus' statement in Mark 14:62 "would have been read as blasphemous" along
these lines.[401]

---

[399] COLLINS, Charge of Blasphemy, 157, translates the last clause as "I am constraining
destiny, not its name but its power, visible to your eyes and standing at your side."

[400] COLLINS, Charge of Blasphemy, 158.

[401] BOCK, Blasphemy and the Jewish Examination of Jesus, 618.

**(59)** Philo, *De decalogo* 61–63

καθάπερ οὖν τοῦ μεγάλου βασιλέως τὰς τιμὰς εἴ τις τοῖς ὑπάρχοις σατράπαις ἀπένειμεν, ἔδοξεν ἂν οὐκ ἀγνωμονέστατος μόνον ἀλλὰ καὶ ῥιψοκινδυνότατος εἶναι χαριζόμενος τὰ δεσπότου δούλοις, τὸν αὐτὸν τρόπον ἂν τοῖς αὐτοῖς εἴ τις γεραίρει τὸν πεποιηκότα τοῖς γεγονόσιν, ἴστω πάντων ἀβουλότατος ὢν καὶ ἀδικώτατος, ἴσα διδοὺς ἀνίσοις οὐκ ἐπὶ τιμῇ τῶν ταπεινοτέρων ἀλλ᾽ ἐπὶ καθαιρέσει τοῦ κρείττονος ⁶² εἰσὶ δ᾽ οἳ καὶ προσυπερβάλλουσιν ἀσεβείᾳ μηδὲ τὸ ἴσον ἀποδιδόντες, ἀλλὰ τοῖς μὲν τὰ πάντα τῶν ἐπὶ τιμῇ χαριζόμενοι, τῷ δ᾽ οὐδὲν νέμοντες ἀλλ᾽ οὐδὲ μνήμην, τὸ κοινότατον· ἐπιλήθονται γὰρ οὗ μόνου μεμνῆσθαι προσῆκον ἦν, ἐπιτηδεύοντες οἱ βαρυδαίμονες ἑκούσιον λήθην. ⁶³ ἔνιοι δὲ καὶ στομάργῳ κατεχόμενοι λύττῃ τὰ δείγματα τῆς ἐνιδρυμένης ἀσεβείας εἰς μέσον προφέροντες βλασφημεῖν ἐπιχειροῦσι τὸ θεῖον, ἀκονησάμενοι κακήγορον γλῶτταν, ἅμα καὶ λυπεῖν ἐθέλοντες τοὺς εὐσεβοῦντας, οἷς ἄλεκτον καὶ ἀπαρηγόρητον εὐθὺς εἰσδύεται πένθος τὴν ὅλην πυρπολοῦν ψυχὴν δι᾽ ὤτων· ἡ γὰρ τῶν ἀνοσίων ἑλέπολις τοῦτ᾽ ἐστίν, ᾧ μόνῳ τοὺς φιλοθέους ἐπιστομίζουσι νομίζοντας ὑπὲρ τοῦ μὴ παροξύνειν ἐν τῷ παρόντι κάλλιστον ἡσυχίαν

*Translation.* So just as anyone who rendered the honors of the Great King to the subordinate satraps would appear to be not only most ignorant and most foolhardy, giving to slaves what belonged to their master, in the same way anyone who honors the Creator with the same honor as that which he bestows on the creature may be assured that he is the most foolish and the most unjust of all people, because he gives equal measure to those who are not equal, although he does not honor the inferior but reduces the superior. ⁶² And there are some who exceed in impiety and do not even give this equal tribute but bestow on those others (the creatures) all honor, while to Him nothing at all, refusing to remember Him, the most common of tributes. They forget Him, who alone should be remembered, as miserable people willingly practicing forgetfulness. ⁶³ And again some people, seized with a loud-mouthed frenzy, present examples of their established impiety and attempt to blaspheme the Deity; and when they whet their evil-speaking tongue, they wish to grieve the pious who immediately feel indescribable and inconsolable grief which enters at their ears and burns the whole soul. For this is the siege engine of the unholy by which they silence those who love God who think that it is best at the moment to be silent in order not to give further provocation.

*Commentary.* This text belongs to Philo's description of worship in terms of a hierarchy in *Decal.* 52–81. He begins with the sublime worship of the One God, who is the transcendent source of all that exists, and then describes the ridiculous worship of the stars, pantheism, deification of certain elements, worship of idols, worship of domesticated animals, and worship of savage animals.[402] The "subordinate satraps" may be the four elements or the sun, moon and stars.[403] A person who regards anything in creation to share God's unique honor blasphemes (βλασφημεῖν) the Creator (63). D. L. BOCK argues that in view of Philo's strong, emotional reaction to the arrogance of pagans who think they can breach the gulf that exists between the one true God and created beings, the Sanhedrin, hearing Jesus' claim to sit at the right hand of God, "would have been offended by Jesus' remarks, made as they were by a Jew."[404]

**(60)** *y. Taʿanit* 65b,61–70

תני בשם רבי מאיר כי הנה ה' יצא ממקומו יוצא לו ממדה למדה יוצא לו ממדת הדין למדת רחמים על ישראל. כתיב לא איש אל ויכזב ר' שמואל בר נחמן ורבנן. רבי שמואל בר נחמן אמר הקדוש ברוך הוא אומר לעשות טובה לא איש אל ויכזב. אומר לעשות רעה ההוא אמר ולא יעשה ודבר ולא יקימנה ורבנן אמרי לא איש הוא שעשה דבריו של אל כאילו אינן למה ה' יחרה אפך בעמך. ובן אדם ויתנחם לא בן עמרם הוא שעשה לאל שיתנחם וינחם ה' על הרעה אשר דבר לעשות לעמו אמר רבי אבהו אם יאמר לך אדם אל אני מכזב הוא בן אדם אני סופו לתהות בו שאני עולה לשמים ההוא אמר ולא יקימנה

*Translation.* It has been taught in the name of Rabbi Meir, "'For behold, the Lord comes forth from his place (to punish the inhabitants of the earth for their iniquity, and the earth will disclose her blood and will no more cover her slain' [Isa 26:21]." He deduced from one attribute (of God) to another. He excluded the attribute of righteousness (in favor of) of the attribute of grace for the benefit of Israel. It is written, "God is not a man that he should lie (or the son of a man that he should change his mind)" (Num 23:19). Rabbi Samual bar Nahman and the Rabbis: Rabbi Samuel bar Nahman said, "The Holy One, blessed be He, says that he plans to do good, (thus): 'God is not a man that he should lie' (Num 23:19). (If) He said, 'to do evil,' would He not do it? And has He (ever) spoken and not fulfilled it? But the Rabbis said, "'He is not a man' (Num 23:19) (means), He could treat the words of God as if they were not. (Because it is written): 'O Lord, why does your wrath burn hot against your people?' (Exod 32:11) 'Or the son of a man that he should change his mind' (Num 23:19). Did not the son of Amram make God repent and become merciful? 'And the Lord relented over the evil that he had said he would do to his people' (Exod 32:14)." Rabbi Abbahu said, "If a man tells

---

[402] ALAN MENDELSON, Philo's Jewish Identity (BJS 161; Atlanta: Scholars Press, 1988), 34–38; FELDMAN, Philo's Portrayal of Moses, 146.

[403] COLLINS, Charge of Blasphemy, 158 n. 31.

[404] BOCK, Blasphemy and the Jewish Examination of Jesus, 619. Cf. MARCUS, Mark, 1008, who points to *Somn.* 2.129–131 and *Decal.* 61–69 as explanation for the blasphemy charge against Jesus: according to Philo, blasphemers are those who claim to be like God or who give the Creator and the creature equal honor.

you, 'I am God,' he is a liar; if he says, 'I am (the) son of man,' he will regret it in the end; 'I go up to the heavens,' he has said, but he shall not do it."

*Commentary.*[405] This text belongs to a discussion of the importance of repentance for Israel.[406] Repentance prevents punishment, since God is patient, as the example of the Ninivites demonstrates. God has stationed his angels who bring his punishment in a distant place, which means that it takes time for them to arrive, as Isa 13:5 demonstrates, which means that Israel has time to repent and reconcile. God is ready to replace his severe judgment by his merciful grace. This conviction is substantiated with reference to Num 23:19, which asserts that God's promises are certain. However, the three assertions of Num 23:19 – (a) God is not a man (לֹא אִישׁ אֵל) that he should lie, (b) nor a son of man (וּבֶן־אָדָם) that he should repent; (c) has he said, and will he not do it (הַהוּא אָמַר וְלֹא יַעֲשֶׂה)? or has he spoken, and will He not carry it out? – are ambiguous, a fact of which Rabbi Samuel b. Nachman (3rd century) took advantage in his interpretation. He interpreted assertion (a) in terms of God's promises and linked assertion (c) with God's threats, which God withdraws in the case of Israel's repentance. The Rabbis argued for a different interpretation based on Exod 32. They interpreted assertion (b) as reference to Moses, the בֶּן־אָדָם who achieved what is stated in Exod 32:14: "And the Lord relented over the evil that he had said he would do to his people." Rabbi Abbahu is quoted as asserting that any man who says that he is God is a liar; any man who claims to be (the) son of man will regret this claim (as God will punish him for uttering such a lie); and any man who asserts that he will go up to heaven is not able to do what he promised. Both Jewish and Christian scholars have interpreted the statement of R. Abbahu as a reference to Jesus and to Jewish anti-Christian polemic.[407] E. STAUFFER argues that the rabbinic polemic refers to Mark 14:62 rather than John 8:28: challenged by the high priest, Jesus uses "the highest form of divine self-revelation" in the sense of "I am who I am" in Exod 3:14.[408] W. G. KÜMMEL rejects the interpretation of the statement "I am God" in the rabbinic text with the phrase "I am who I am";

---

[405] The text follows the Krotoshin edition. The translation follows ANDREAS LEHNARDT, Ta'aniyot. Fasten (Übersetzung des Talmud Yerushalmi II/9; Tübingen: Mohr Siebeck, 2008), 49–50; JACOB NEUSNER, The Talmud of the Land of Israel. Volume 18: Besah and Taanit (Chicago: University of Chicago Press, 1987), 183.

[406] Cf. JOHANN MAIER, Jesus von Nazareth in der talmudischen Überlieferung (EdF 82; Darmstadt: Wissenschaftliche Buchgesellschaft, 1978), 76–77.

[407] HEINRICH GRAETZ, Geschichte der Juden von den ältesten Zeiten bis auf die Gegenwart (11 vols.; Leipzig: Leiner, 1853–76), 4:283–84; HERFORD, Christianity in Talmud and Midrash, 62– 63; HERMANN L. STRACK / GÜNTHER STEMBERGER, Einleitung in Talmud und Midrasch (7., völlig neu bearbeitete Auflage; München: Beck, 1982), 1:486; 2:542; JACOB Z. LAUTERBACH, Jesus in the Talmud, in Rabbinic Essays (New York: Ktav, 1973) 473–570, 551; cf. further MAIER, Jesus von Nazareth in der talmudischen Überlieferung, 287 n. 169.

[408] ETHELBERT STAUFFER, Jesus: Gestalt und Geschichte (Bern / München: Francke, 1957), 130–146; STAUFFER, Jesusforschung, 464.

while the rabbinic text is a polemic against the Christian's view of Jesus, it does not allude to Mark 14:62.[409] JOHANN MAIER interprets R. Abbahu's affirmation of God's promises in the context of the crisis of the third century, which increased the Jewish aversion against Rome, and noted that Num 23 is part of the Balak/Balaam narrative. He reads the statement of Rabbi Abbahu (c. A.D. 300) in the context of biblical and rabbinic parallels in which stereotypical characterizations of arrogant rulers play an important role. He argues that R. Abbahu speaks of the kings of the nations who elevated themselves to gods and were punished for their arrogance. A prominent example is Hiram, the king of Tyre, who in Ezek 28:2 claims to be a God (כֹּה־אָמַר אֲדֹנָי יְהוִֹה) and who was subsequently rebuked by God: "You are a man and not God" (אַתָּה אָדָם וְלֹא־אֵל). MAIER argues that R. Abbahu's statement should be understood as critical of Rome and the imperial cult but hardly as critique of Jesus' claims.[410] PETER SCHÄFER disagrees: in Ezek 28:2 it is the prophet, not Hiram, who is called "son of man" (בֶּן־אָדָם). The Hiram interpretation belongs to the first part of the midrash (God is not a man who lies: a man who tells you that he is God is a liar), not to the second part, which refers to בֶּן־אָדָם (God is not a Son of man who repents: a man who tells you that he is the Son of Man will regret it). In the sophisticated structure of the midrash, "Son of Man" corresponds directly to "God" and thus very likely understands "Son of Man" as a title referring to Jesus, who described himself as "Son of Man". The third part of the midrash (God does what he says: a man who tells you that he goes up to heaven will not perform what he has promised) may reject the arrogance of Nebuchadnezzar in Isa 14:13–14, but in the context of the sequence God – Son of Man – ascent to heaven, "it makes much more sense to conclude that R. Abbahu uses a complex midrash tradition in order to apply it to Jesus and his movement: Jesus is a common human being, not God, not the Son of Man, and he certainly did not ascend to heaven to return to his divine father."[411] If this interpretation is correct, the text is evidence of a Jewish tradition that accuses Jesus of having claimed to be God and the heavenly Son of Man. While R. Abbahu does not refer to Jesus' trial and death, the phrase "he will regret it in the end" (סופו לתהות) may imply a reference to Jesus' death as punishment for his claim. Note that the context of the discus-

---

[409] WERNER GEORG KÜMMEL, Verheißung und Erfüllung. Untersuchungen zur eschatologischen Verkündigung Jesu (2., völlig neu bearbeitete Aufl.; 1946; repr., AThANT 6; Zürich: Zwingli, 1953), 44–45. For a critique of STAUFFER's Ani Hu theory which understands ἐγώ εἰμι as the divine name, cf. CATCHPOLE, Trial, 133–34. BLINZLER, Prozeß, 45–46, follows KÜMMEL.

[410] MAIER, Jesus von Nazareth in der talmudischen Überlieferung, 77–82.

[411] SCHÄFER, Jesus in the Talmud, 107–9, quotation 109 (SCHÄFER, Jesus im Talmud, 217–21). SCHÄFER adds that this interpretation goes well with the fact that Rabbi Abbahu lived in Caesarea, the center of Palestinian Christianity in the third and fourth centuries; it is possible that he knew Origen (A.D. 184–253). Cf. LEHNARDT, Ta'aniyot , 50 n. 92, who allows that the passage is "möglicherweise nicht nur ... 'anti-christlich'".

sion speaks of God's punishment of people for their iniquity if they do not repent.

## (61) *b. Sanh.* 38b

הנך למה לי כדרבי יוחנן דא"ר יוחנן אין הקב"ה עושה דבר אא"כ נמלך בפמליא של מעלה שנאמר (דניאל ד) בגזירת עירין פתגמא ובמאמר קדישין שאילתא התינח כולהי עד די כרסוון רמיו מאי איכא למימר אחד לו ואחד דתניא אחד לו ואחד לדוד דברי ר"ע א"ל ר' יוסי עקיבא עד מתי אתה עושה שכינה חול אלא אחד לדין ואחד לצדקה קבלה מיניה או לא קבלה מיניה ת"ש דתניא אחד לדין ואחד לצדקה דברי ר"ע א"ל ר' אלעזר בן עזריא עקיבא מה לך אצל הגדה כלך אצל נגעים ואהלות אלא אחד לכסא ואחד לשרפרף כסא לישב עליו שרפרף להדום רגלי

*Translation.* Why were these (passages)[412] necessary? The answer accords with what Rabbi Yohanan said: "The Holy One, blessed be He, does nothing without consulting with his heavenly household, for it is written, 'The matter is by the decree of the watchers and the sentence by the word of the Holy Ones' (Dan 4:14)." Now this is satisfactory for all (the other passages), but how shall we explain (the phrase) "till thrones were placed' (Dan 7:9)? One (throne) is for himself and one for David. As it has been taught: "one is for himself and one for David," the words of Rabbi Aqiba. Rabbi Yose said to him, "Aqiba, how long will you profane the Shekinah?[413] Rather, one (throne) is for bestowing judgment and one for bestowing righteousness." Did he accept (this answer) from him or not? Come and hear, for it has been taught, "One is for bestowing judgment and one is for bestowing righteousness," the words of Rabbi Aqiba. Rabbi Eleazar ben Azariah said to him, "Aqiba, what have you to do with Haggadah? Confine yourself to the study of Negaim and Ohalot.[414] Rather, one is a throne, the other a footstool: a throne for a seat and a footstool in support of his feet."

*Commentary.* The larger context of the discussion is *m. Sanh.* 4:5, "that the Minim should not say, 'There are many ruling powers in heaven' – again to proclaim the greatness of the Holy One." In the context of a discussion of the dictum of Rabbi Yohanan (c. A.D. 80) that God does nothing without consulting his heavenly court,[415] Rabbi Aqiba (A.D. 110–135) asserts that the second throne in God's presence belongs to David, i.e., to the "son of man" who

---

[412] Referring to passages in which the Minim have found evidence for their heresy, in particular Gen 1:26; 1:27; 11:7; 11:5; 35:7; 35:3; Deut 4:7; 2 Sam 7:23; Dan 7:9.

[413] NEUSNER translates שכינה as "the Presence of God."

[414] NEUSNER translates, "Go over to rules governing the skin disease [of Lev. 13] and uncleanness imparted through overshadowing of the corpse [in Ohalot = Num. 19:1ff.]."

[415] JASTROW translates the loanword פְּמִילְיָיא (*familia*) as "the slaves in a household, family servants," frequently "divine agencies, ministers," and the construction פמליא של מעלה as "heavenly household."

is identified with the Davidic messiah,[416] implying that he shares divine authority and status. Rabbi Yose rebukes Aqiba, who immediately changes his mind, with Rabbi Eleazar ben Azariah suggesting that Aqiba should abandon his messianic speculations and concentrate on legal interpretation for which he was famous. C. A. EVANS suggests that this scene is a combination of fact and fiction: "Aqiba probably did interpret Daniel the way the tradition remembers, and he may very well have eventually changed his mind after ben Kosiba's defeat. But it is possible that Aqiba's interpretation paralleled too closely Christian interpretation in which Jesus was conceptualized as the enthroned and deified Son of man of Daniel 7."[417] This text is quoted to explain the high priest's charge of blasphemy. By relating Dan 7:13 and Ps 110:1 to himself, claiming to be the "son of God" in the sense of sitting on God's throne, Jesus asserted heavenly identity.[418] J. BLINZLER argues that while Aqiba placed the messiah next to God, sharing the role as judge on the Day of Judgment, he did not accord him divine status.[419] The accusation that Aqiba risks profaning the Shekinah, i.e., blaspheming, by suggesting that a human being sits beside God, shows, according to D. L. BOCK, how God's honor was protected as unique and "that offense could emerge from a remark not using the Name of God and that the offense could be accompanied by a warning."[420]

**(62)** *Sifre Devarim* §221 on Deuteronomy 21:22

(כב) **וכי יהיה באיש חטא משפט מות והומת** האיש נתלה ואין האשה נתלית רבי אליעזר אומר
אף האשה נתלית אמר להם רבי אליעזר והלא שמעון בן שטח תלה נשים באשקלון אמרו לו
שמונים נשים תלה ואין דנים דנים שנים ביום אחד אלא שהשעה צריכה ללמד בה את אחתים.
**ותלית אותו** יכול יהו כל הנסקלים נתלים תלמוד לומר כי **קללת אלהים תלוי** אחר שריבה
הכתוב מיעט הרי אנו למדים איתו מן המגדף מה מגדף מיוחד שפשט ידו בעיקר והרי הוא נתלה
כך כל הפושט ידו בעיקר הרי הוא נתלה רבי אליעזר אומר מה מגדף מיוחד שהוא נסקל והרי
הוא נתלה כך כל הנסקלים נתלים יכול יהו תולים אותו חי כדרך שהמלכות עושה תלמוד לומר
**והומת ותלית אותו על עץ**.
**אותו** ולא את כליו **אותו** ולא את עדיו **אותו** ולא את זממיו **אותו** ולא שנים ביום אחד.

---

[416] Cf. ALAN F. SEGAL, Two Powers in Heaven: Early Rabbinic Reports about Christianity and Gnosticism (SJLA 25; Leiden: Brill, 1977), 47–48.

[417] Cf. CRAIG A. EVANS, Jesus and His Contemporaries: Comparative Studies (AGAJU 25; Leiden: Brill, 1995), 208.

[418] Cf. CATCHPOLE, Blasphemy, 17–18; CATCHPOLE, Trial, 140–41; CATCHPOLE, Trial EVANS, Mark, 456; MARCUS, Mark, 1008–9. Cf. the references to *b. Sanh.* 38b in BROWN, Death, 537; ULRICH LUZ, Das Evangelium nach Matthäus (EKK I/1–4; Zürich / Neukirchen-Vluyn: Benziger / Neukirchener, 1985–2001), 4:182.

[419] BLINZLER, Prozeß, 194.

[420] BOCK, Blasphemy, 99.

**על עץ** יכול בעץ התלוש או בעץ המחובר תלמוד לומר כי **קבור תקברנו בעץ** שנקבר עמו אמור
מעתה בעץ התלוש ולא בעץ המחובר.

(כג) מנין למלין את מתו שהוא עובר בלא תעשה תלמוד לומר **לא תלין נבלתו על העץ** הלינו
לכבודו להביא לו ארון ותכריכים יכול יהא עובר עליו תלמוד לומר **על העץ** מה עץ מיוחד
שהוא ניוול לו אף כל שהוא ניוול לו יצא המלין לכבודו שאין ניוול לו. **לא תלין נבלתו על העץ**
מצות לא תעשה. **כי קבור תקברנו** מצות עשה כיצד עושים לו ממתינים לו עד חשיכה ותולים לו
ומתירים אותו ואם לן עוברים עליו בלא תעשה שנאמר **לא תלין נבלתו על העץ.**

**כי קללת אלהים תלוי** כלומר מפני מה זה תלוי מפני שקלל את השם ונמצא שם שמים מתחלל.
האיש נסקל ערום ואין האשה נסקלת ערומה רבי יהודה אומר אחד האיש ואחד האשה אלא
שהאיש תולים אותו ופניו כלפי העם ואחוריו כלפי העץ והאשה פניה כלפי העץ ואחוריה כלפי
העם האיש סרט אחד מלפניו והאשה שני סרטים אחד מלפניה ואחד מלאחריה מפני שכולה
ערוה. **ולא תטמא את אדמתך אשר ה' אלהיך נתן לך נחלה** להזהיר בית דין על כך סליק
פיסקא.

*Translation. And when a man has committed a sin worthy of death, and he is
executed (and you hang him on a tree)* (Deut 21:22). A man may be hanged,
but a woman may not. Rabbi Eliezer said to the Sages, "Did Simeon ben
Sheṭaḥ not hang women in Ashkelon?" They replied, "He hanged eighty
women (in one day); although no two persons may be sentenced to death on
the same day, this was an emergency intended as a lesson to others."

*And you hang him.* Are all those who are stoned (to death) hanged? Scripture says, *A curse of God is the one who has been hanged* (Deut 21:23). After
including, Scripture excludes. We learn this from (the case of) the blasphemer: just as the blasphemer is someone who extends his hand to the fundamental principle (of faith),[421] and is hanged as such, so all are hanged who
extend their hand to the fundamental principle (of faith). Rabbi Eliezer says,
"Just as the blasphemer is one who is stoned and hanged as such, so all who
are stoned are hanged." Perhaps he is hanged alive, as is the practice of the
state. Scripture says, "And he be put to death and you hang him on a tree."

*Him*, but not his clothes. *Him*, but not his witnesses. *Him*, but not those
who gave false testimony against him. *Him*, but not two persons on the same
day.

*On a tree.* Either on a tree that has been cut off or on a tree rooted in the
ground. Scripture says, *But you shall surely bury him* (Deut 21:23). (Thus
hang him) on a tree that is buried with him. From this we deduce that it is a
tree that has been cut off, and not one that is still rooted in the ground.

Whence (can it be proven that he) who permits a body to hang overnight
transgresses a prohibition? Scripture says, *His body shall not remain overnight on the tree* (Deut 21:23). Do they let him hang overnight on account of
his honor, to that they bring a coffin and shrouds, is it perhaps permitted to

---

[421] Thus HAMMER's translation of עיקר; BIETENHARD interprets the Hebrew term in a metaphorical sense and translates with "God." Cf. JASTROW s.v. עיקר 1. root, origin; 2. essence,
reality, main object, chief; in later Hebrew literature עִיקָרִים means "principles of faith."

transgress (a commandment)? Scripture says, *On the tree*. Just as the tree inflicts disgrace upon the body, so is anything that inflicts grace (included). Excluded is (the case when) they leave him overnight on account of his honor, because it does not inflict disgrace (on him). *His body shall not remain overnight on the tree*. This is a negative commandment. *But you shall surely bury him*. This is a positive commandment. What is to be done with him? One waits until dusk, then hangs him, and then releases the body. If it remains overnight, one transgresses a negative commandment (a prohibition), as it is said, *His body shall not remain overnight on the tree*.

*For the person who is hanged is a curse unto God* (Deut 21:23). That is to say, why was he hanged? Because he cursed the Name, and the Name of Heaven was found to be profaned.

[A man must be stoned naked, but not a woman. Rabbi Judah says, "Both men and women are (to be stoned naked), but when the man is hanged, his face is turned towards the people and his back towards the tree; but the face of the woman is turned towards the tree and the back towards the people. The man is covered with a strip of cloth in front, and the woman with two strips, one in front and one in the back, because all her nakedness is illicit.][422] *And you shall not defile your land that the LORD, your God, gives you for an inheritance* (Deut 21:23). In order to warn the court of law in this matter.

*Commentary*.[423] This text interprets Deut 21:22–23, focusing on the penalty of hanging for blasphemy. Rabbi Eliezer ben Hyrcanus (c. A.D. 90) argues that not only men but also women are hanged for blasphemy, citing the precedent of the eighty women who were hanged in Ashkelon on account of a ruling by Simeon ben Sheṭaḥ.[424] The action of Simeon ben Sheṭaḥ is regarded as violat-

---

[422] Cf. *m. Sanh.* 6:3; *t. Sanh.* 9:6. This section is not found in Vatican MS 32 and other manuscripts; cf. REUVEN HAMMER, Sifre: A Tannaitic Commentary on the Book of Deuteronomy (Yale Judaica 24; New Haven / London: Yale University Press, 1986), 467 n. 8; HANS BIETENHARD, Der tannaitische Midrasch Sifre Deuteronomium. Übersetzt und erklärt (Mit einem Beitrag von Henrik Ljungman; Judaica et christiana 8; New York: Lang, 1984), 526 n. 55.

[423] Text: LOUIS FINKELSTEIN, Sifre ad Deuteronomium (H. S. Horovitzii schedis usus cum variis lectionibus et adnotationibus. Editio nova; orig. 1939; repr., Corpus Tannaiticum III/3; New York: Jewish Theological Seminary of America, 1969), 253–55; this text supersedes the older edition of MEIR FRIEDMANN, Sifrè debê Rab, der älteste halachische und hagadische Midrasch zu Numeri und Deuteronomium (Wien: Selbstverlag, 1864). Quotations of the main Scriptural text are printed in bold. For translations cf. BIETENHARD, Sifre Deuteronomium, 523–26; HAMMER, Sifre, 231–33; JACOB NEUSNER, Sifre to Deuteronomy: An Analytical Translation (2 vols.; BJS 98.101; Atlanta: Scholars Press, 1987), 2:127–29.

[424] This incident is also discussed in *m. Sanh.* 6:4–5; *y. Sanh.* 23c,55–69. See MARTIN HENGEL, Rabbinische Legende und frühpharisäische Geschichte: Schimeon b. Schetach und die achtzig Hexen von Askalon (AHAW.PH 1984,2; Heidelberg: Winter, 1984), who interprets the story of the execution of witches for blasphemous acts as a symbolic reference to Sadducean friends of Alexander Jannaeus who were executed by the Pharisees, who had come back to power after the death of Jannaeus and proceeded to exact political revenge for sedi-

ing halakhah: if judges sentence two persons to death on a single day, they run the risk of not conducting the trials with due diligence.[425] However, due to the extraordinary nature of the situation, extraordinary measures were necessary: Simeon ben Sheṭaḥ wanted to establish a precedent for identical or similar cases. The hanging of convicted criminals who have been stoned is explained with the statement, "After including, Scripture excludes."[426] BIETENHARD explains: Scripture mentions a general case – a person who is executed is hanged; and, Scripture mentions a special case, referring in Deut 21:23 to someone who has blasphemed God (המגדף).[427] The blasphemer is described as a person who "extends his hand to the fundamental principle (of faith)" (מגדף מיוחד שפשט ידו בעיקר). Blasphemers are like idolators and are therefore hanged after execution (by stoning). Rabbi Eliezer disagrees: the blasphemer is mentioned as a special case as regards the penalty of stoning; the blasphemer is not hanged because he has blasphemed but because he has been executed by stoning. The practice of the "state" (המלכות), i.e., of the Roman empire, to hang a convicted criminal on a tree (or pole) while he is alive – a reference to execution by crucifixion – is rejected on account of what Scripture says: a convicted criminal is first executed, then his corpse is hanged on a tree. The phrase "not this clothes" implies that the criminal is hanged naked; the phrase "not his witnesses" refers to witnesses whose testimony were the basis of the conviction and execution and who subsequently turn out to be false witnesses; the phrase "not those who gave false testimony against him" refers to witnesses who testified that the testimony of the first witnesses was erroneous, and who subsequently were proved to be false witnesses by yet other witnesses.[428] The next section argues that convicted criminals who are hanged should be hanged not on a live tree but on a pole which is then buried with him. The following section argues that a criminal who has been executed and then hanged on a pole shall be buried on the same day. Hanging on a pole is then explained with reference to Deut 21:23): the blasphemer is a curse unto God (קללת אלהים תלוי), i.e., he has cursed God ("the Name") and thus profaned the "Name" of Heaven (שקלל את השם ונמצא שם שמים מתחלל).

J. BLINZLER refers to *Sifre Devarim* §221 on Deut 21:22 to illustrate his observation that even in later rabbinic periods blasphemy was defined more broadly than pronouncing the Tetragrammaton: "extending the hand to

---

tion. DARRREL L. BOCK, Crucifixion, Qumran, and the Jewish Interrogation of Jesus, in Literary Studies in Luke-Acts (FS Joseph B. Tyson; ed. R. P. Thompson and T. E. Phillips; Macon: Mercer University Press, 1998), 3–10, 9, argues that if this interpretation is correct, "this would mean that Essene, Sadducean, and Pharisaical sects all provide evidence for the use of crucifixion in cases of sedition."

[425] Cf. KRAUSS, Sanhedrin–Makkot, 197; BIETENHARD, Sifre Deuteronomium, 523 n. 13.

[426] HAMMER translates: "after extending the rule, Scripture limits it."

[427] BIETENHARD, Sifre Deuteronomium, 524 nn. 19–20; see nn. 26–29 for the following.

[428] BIETENHARD, Sifre Deuteronomium, 524 nn. 36–38.

(threaten) God" classifies as blasphemy as well.[429] D. L. BOCK comments, "Blasphemy is seen as among the worst of sins, which is why it is worthy of death. To see a violation of a fundamental of the faith is very similar to pointing out that blasphemy violates the first commandment."[430]

Even though it has been argued the halakhic sections of *Sifre Devarim* (§§55–303) can be traced back to Eliezer ben Hyrcanus, whose students begun the redaction of *Sifre Devarim* at the time of Yohanan ben Zakkai,[431] we can only affirm with some certainty the date of the final redaction in the late third century.[432] It remains uncertain, therefore, whether this text is relevant for a discussion of the blasphemy charge against Jesus.

*Despising the Torah and Profaning Holy Things.* One rabbinic text of the third century A.D. provides a broad understanding of blasphemy punishable by death that includes despising the Torah by speaking with impudence about its commandments and profaning holy things, including the festivals.

**(63)** *Sifre Bamidbar* §112 on Numbers 15:30–31

**והנפש אשר תעשה ביד רמה**, זה המגלה פנים בתורה כמנשה בן חזקיה **את ה' הוא מגדף** שהיה יושב ודורש בהגדה של דופי לפני המקום אמר לא היה לו לכתוב בתורה אלא וילך ראובן בימי קציר חטים (בראשית ל יד) ולא היה לו לכתיב בתורה אלא ואחות לוטן תמנע (שם לו כב) עליו מפורש בקבלה תשב באחיך תדבר בבן אמך תתן דופי אלה עשית והחרשתי דמית היות אהיה כמוך (תהלים נ כא) כסבור אתה שמא כדרכי בשר ודם דרכי המקום אוכיחך ואערכה לעיניך (שם). בא ישעיה ופירש בקבלה הוי מושכי העון בחבלי השוא וכעבותות העגלה חטאה (ישעיה ה יח). תחילתו של חטא הוא דומה לחוט של כויא אבל סופו היות כעבות העגלה חטאה. רבי אימר העושה מצוה אחת לשמה אל ישמח לאותה מצוד לסוף שגוררת מצות הרבה והעובר עבירה אחת אל ידאג לאותה עבירה לסוף שגוררת עבירות הרבה שמצוה גוררת מצוה ועבירה גוררת עבירה: **את ה' הוא מגדף,** ר' אלעזר בן עזריה אומר כאדם שאומר לחבירו גדפת את הקערה וחיסרתה. איסי בן עקביא אומר כאדם שאומר לחבירו גדפת את כל הקערה כולה ולא שיירתה ממנה כלום: **ונכרתה,** אין הכרתה אלא הפסקה: **הנפש ההיא,** מזידי דברי ר' עקיבא: **מעמיה,** ועמה שלום.

**כי דבר ה' בזה זה** צדוקי **ואת מצותו הפר** זה אפיקורוס. ד"א כי בזה זה המגלה פנים בתורה ואת מצותו הפר זה המפר ברית בשר. מיכן אמר רבי אלעזר המודעי המחלל את הקדשים והמבזה את המועדות והמפר בריתו של אברהם אבינו אע"פ שיש בידו מצות הרבה כדיי הוא

---

[429] BLINZLER, Prozeß, 153 with n. 53.

[430] BOCK, Blasphemy, 80.

[431] LOUIS FINKELSTEIN, Hashpaʿat Bêt Shammai al Sifrê Debarim, in Sefer Assaf (FS Simcha Assaf; ed. M. D. Cassuto, J. Klausner, and J. Guttmann; Jerusalem: Mossad Harav Kook, 1953), 415–426.

[432] Cf. HERMANN L. STRACK, GÜNTER STEMBERGER, and MARKUS BOCKMUEHL, Introduction to the Talmud and Midrash (Second ed.; Minneapolis: Fortress, 1996), 272–73; cf. ibid. 272 for a critique of J. NEUSNER's attempt to establish *Sifre Devarim* as an integral work.

לדחותה מן העולם אמר כל התורה כולה אני מקבל עלי חוץ מדבר זה זהו כי דבר ה' בזה אמר כל
התורה אמר מפי הקודש ודבר זה משה מפי עצמו אמרו <זהו כי דבר ה' בזה>. ד"א כי דבר ה'
בזה ר' מאיר אומר זה הלמד ואינו שונה לאחרים ר' נתן אומר זה היכול ללמוד ואינו לומד ר'
נהוראי אמר זה שלא השגיח על ד"ת כל עיקר. ר' ישמעאל אומר בע"ז הכתוב מדבר שנאמר כי
דבר ה' בזה שביזה על דבור הראשון שגאמר למשה מפי הגבורה אנכי ה' אלהיך לא יהיה לך
אלהים אחרים על פגי (שמות כ ב–ג): **הכרת תכרת הנפש ההיא**, הכרת בעוה"ו תכרת לעוה"ב
דברי ר' עקיבא אמר לו ר' ישמעאל לפי שהוא אומר <ונכרתה הנפש ההיא שומע אגי שלש
כריתות בשלשה עולמות מה ת"ל> הכרת תכרת הנפש ההיא דברה תורה כלשון בני אדם: **עונה**
**בה**, כל המתים במיתה מתכפרים אבל זו עונה בה כענין שנאמר שנאמר ותהי עונותם על עצמותם
(יחזקאל לב כו) או אפילו עשה תשובה ת"ל עונה בה ולא כל זמן שעשה תשובה וכן הוא אומר
שחת לו לא בניו מומם (דברים לב ה) כשמומם בם אינם בניו וכשאין מומם בם בניו הם.

*Translation. But the person who does anything with a high hand* (Num
15:30). This refers to the person who treats the Torah with impudence, like
Manasseh, the son of Hezekiah. *Who blasphemes the Lord.* [As Manasseh, the
son of Hezekiah,] who sat and lectured on defective haggadah before God.[433]
He said, "Could he not have written in the Torah something (different) than:
*And Reuben went out at the time of the wheat harvest [and found mandrakes
in the field and brought them to his mother Leah]* (Gen 30:14)? Could he not
have written in the Torah something (different) than: *And Lotan's sister was
Timna* (Gen 36:22)? In the tradition it is said explicitly about such a person:
*You sit and speak against your brother, you slander the son of your mother.
These things you have done and I (God) have been silent. You thought that I
was like yourself* (Ps 50:20–21). You think perhaps that the ways of flesh and
blood are the same as the ways of God. *I will rebuke you and lay the charge
before your eyes* (Ps 50:21). Isaiah came and explicitly says in the tradition:
*Woe to those who draw iniquity with ropes of nothing and who draw sin with
cart ropes* (Isa 5:18). In the beginning sin is like the threat of a spider, but in
the end it is (as strong as) the ropes of a cart. Rabbi says, "He who fulfills a
(single) commandment for its own sake, should not rejoice on account of (the
fulfillment of) this one commandment, for it results in (the fulfillment of )
many commandments. And he who engages in a single transgression should
not worry about that transgression alone, for it results in many transgressions.
The (fulfillment of a) commandment entails (further) (fulfillment of more)
commandments, and a transgression entails further transgressions. *He who
blasphemes the Lord.* Rabbi Eleazar ben Azariah says, "As when somebody
says to his fellow man: You have scraped out the dish and deprived it (of its
content)."[434] Issi ben Aqabia says, "As when somebody says to his fellow
man: You have scraped out the entire dish and left nothing at all in it." *He*

---

[433] NEUSNER translates המקום with "the Omnipresent."

[434] Cf. KUHN, who translates והיסרתה as "und zu wenig darin gelassen;" BÖRNER-KLEIN
translates "und sie beschädigt," NEUSNER "and so diminished [its contents]." Cf. JASTROW s.v.
חסר pi. "to lessen, omit; deprive."

*shall be cut off.* Cutting off means separation.[435] *That person.* Those who have sinned deliberately; words of Rabbi Aqiba. *From their people.* But the people will have peace.

*Because he has despised the word of the Lord* (Num 15:31). This refers to a Sadducee. *And he has broken his commandment.* This refers to an Epicurean. Another interpretation: *Because he has despised the word of the Lord*: this is the person who treats the Torah with impudence; *and he has broken his commandment*: this is the person who removes the covenant of the flesh. On this basis Rabbi Eleazar from Modiim says, "The person who desecrates the holy things and despises the festival seasons and breaks the covenant of Abraham, our father, even if he fulfills many commandments, deserves to be removed from the world." When a person says, "I have taken upon myself the entire Torah, except this (one) word," (this is a case of)[436] *because he has despised the word of the Lord.* When a person says, "The Holy One said the entire Torah with his own mouth, but this (one) word Moses said with his own mouth,"[437] (this is a case of) *because he has despised the word of the Lord.* Another interpretation: *Because he has despised the word of the Lord.* Rabbi Meir says, "This is the person who learns (Torah) but does not teach others." Rabbi Natan says, "This is the person who has the capacity to learn, but does not learn (Torah)." Rabbi Nehorai (says), "This is the person who never pays any attention whatsoever to the words of the Torah." Rabbi Yishmael says, "Scripture speaks of idolatry, for it is said, *because he has despised the word of the Lord.* For he has despised the first word [the first of the Ten Commandments] that was said to Moses from the mouth of the All-Powerful: *I am the Lord your God ... you shall have no other gods before me* (Exod 20:2–3). *This person shall surely be cut off* (Num 15:31). *Cut off* in this world. *Cut off* in the world to come, words of Rabbi Aqiba. Rabbi Yishmael said to him, "Since it is said, *And that person shall be cut off,* shall I infer that there is a threefold cutting off, in three worlds? What does Scripture say, *that person shall surely be cut off*? The wording of the Torah corresponds to human speech. *Their guilt remains on them* (Num 15:31). All those who die attain atonement through their death, but (not) this person, because it says, *and their guilt remains on them.* According to what it says, *Their guilt remained on their bones* (Ezek 32:27). Or: is this the case even if one has repented? Scripture says, *his guilt (remains) on him.* But not so long as he has repented. And so (Scripture) says, *They have dealt corruptly with him, they are no longer his children because of their blemish* (Deut 32:5). When they

---

[435] The term פסקה is translated (and explained) by NEUSNER as "interrupting [in that the man's life is interrupted and cut off from its normal span of years." Cf. JASTROW s.v. פסקא "cut; interruption; detached part."

[436] Following NEUSNER's interpretative gloss.

[437] NEUSNER translates, "The entirety of the Torah did Moses state on the instruction of the Holy One, but this one matter did Moses say on his own initiative;" cf. KUHN.

are blemished, they are not his children; when they are no (longer) blemished (because they have removed the blemish through repentance), they are his children.

*Commentary.*[438] The interpretation of Num 15:27–31 in *Sifre Bamidbar* §112 deals with sins committed either unwittingly or deliberately. The discussion about sins committed deliberately is quoted above. The preceding discussion deals with sins committed unwittingly and with the question of whether women fall under the rule that a person who sins unwittingly shall offer a sin offering. The subsequent context discusses the matter of repentance. The Torah stipulates in Num 15:30 that Israelites who deliberately break the Law shall be executed. The phrase "acting with a high hand" (תעשה ביד רמה) refers to the deliberate transgression of a commandment. The expression is interpreted in terms of a person acting with impudence (המגלה פנים) against the Torah. Manasseh, the son of Hezekiah, is cited as a prototype of a person who serves other gods and acts with impudence against God and the Torah (cf. 2 Kings 21; 2 Chron 33:1–9). He is described as someone who does what Num 30:31 condemns: he blasphemed (מגדף) God.

The term "blaspheme" is explained in terms of scoffing at the Torah; the reference to Gen 36:22 suggests a person who makes fun of the genealogies contained in the Torah. The author uses the technique of notarikon: the verb גדף ("to blaspheme") of the biblical text is explained as with the phrase בהגדה של דֻופִי ("defective haggadah").[439] The explanation that cites Isa 5:18 is connected in *Ber. Rab.* 22.6 with Aqiba, who warns of the seriousness of a first sin, which leads to ever more serious transgressions.[440] Rabbi is cited in support of this explanation which emphasizes the serious consequences of an initial sin. Aqiba and Rabbi interpret Num 15:30 in terms of the blasphemer (מגדף). Rabbi Eleazar ben Azariah and Rabbi Issi interpret the text in terms of the idolator: he is like a person who "scrapes out" (גדפת) a dish, i.e., who removes what God is due by worshipping other gods.[441] The term ונכרתה ("he

---

[438] Text: HAIM SAUL HOROVITZ, ed., Siphre ad Numeros adjecto Siphre zutta (Cum variis lectionibus et adnotationibus; orig. 1917; repr., Corpus Tannaiticum III/3: Siphre d'be Rab 1; Jerusalem: Wahrmann, 1966), 120–21. Quotations of the main Scriptural text are printed in bold. For translations cf. KARL GEORG KUHN, Sifre zu Numeri (Rabbinische Texte II/3; Stuttgart: Kohlhammer, 1959), 324–32; JACOB NEUSNER, Sifré to Numbers: An American Translation and Expansion (2 vols.; BJS 118/119; Atlanta: Scholars Press, 1986), 2:168–70; DAGMAR BÖRNER-KLEIN, Der Midrasch Sifre zu Numeri. Übersetzung und Erklärung (Rabbinische Texte II/3; Stuttgart: Kohlhammer, 1997), 205–7.

[439] Thus KUHN, Sifre zu Numeri, 324 n. 37.

[440] Cf. KUHN, Sifre zu Numeri, 325 n. 45.

[441] Cf. KUHN, Sifre zu Numeri, 326–27 nn. 50, 53, who asserts that the rabbis who interpret Num 15:30 in terms of idolatry read מגרף instead of מגדף; see ibid. for a discussion of *y. Sanh.* 25b,12–13 and *b. Ker.* 7b which also mention the statements of Rabbi Eleazar ben Azariah and Rabbi Issi. Cf. the discussion of the parallel traditions *y. Sanh.* 25b,12–13, *b. Sanh. 99b*, and *b. Ker.* 7b in BÖRNER-KLEIN, Sifre zu Numeri, 684–86. Cf. JASTROW s.v.

shall be cut off") is explained in terms of a violent end of life, i.e., the death sentence. The next section explains what "despising" (בזי, בזה) the word of God means. Prime examples of people who despise the word of God and who should thus be treated as blasphemers are the Sadducees (צדוקי), who are often accused in rabbinic literature of diverging in their teaching and in their prac-tice from the Torah,[442] and the Epicureans (אפיקורוס),[443] i.e., secular Jews who ignore the Torah. The following six examples further explain what it means to "despise" the word of God and thus to blaspheme Yahweh:[444] (1) to act with impudence against the commandments of the Torah; (2) to reverse circumci-sion;[445] (3) to profane holy things, including the festivals of God's covenant people; (4) to refuse to be obedient to a particular commandment of the Torah; (5) to declare a particular instruction in the Torah to come not from God but from the human author, e.g., Moses; (6) to learn Torah but not to teach Torah to others, i.e., to regard it as not relevant for others; (7) to refuse to learn Torah when the opportunity presents itself; (8) to ignore the commandments of the Torah entirely. Rabbi Yishmael explains that despising the word of God revealed in the Torah is tantamount to breaking the first commandment of the Decalogue and thus committing idolatry, a sin for which the Torah stipulates the death sentence. According to Rabbi Aqiba, a person who despises God by breaking the first commandment will have no part in the world to come: He is excluded from eternal life.

J. BLINZLER mentions *Sifre Bamidbar* §112 on Numbers 15:30–31 as a text that demonstrates that the definition of blasphemy is not restricted to pro-nouncing the divine name: A person who speaks with impudence against the Torah can also be regarded as a blasphemer.[446] D. L. BOCK discusses this text since it "relates and compares blasphemy to a series of sins that deal more with actions than with words ... It indicates a kind of fluidity in the approach

---

גדף pi 1. to hollow out, scrape, chisel; 2. to scrape, to empty to the dregs; transferred: to blas-pheme (God), to revile, reproach; s.v. גרף to scrape, sweep.

[442] KUHN, Sifre zu Numeri, 328 n. 59, refers to the text cited by HERMANN L. STRACK / PAUL BILLERBECK, Kommentar zum Neuen Testament aus Talmud und Midrasch (6 vols.; Ninth ed.; München: Beck, 1986), 4:344–52.

[443] JASTROW s.v. אפיקורוס, one irreverent of authority or religion, sceptic, heretic; note the comment, "The peculiar form and also the meaning assigned to our w[ord] found a ready sup-port in the phonetic coincidence with *Epicurus*, the philosopher." KUHN and BÖRNER-KLEIN translate as "Epikuräer," NEUSNER has "unbeliever [Epicurean]."

[444] KUHN, Sifre zu Numeri, 328–29, nn. 61, 64, discusses the redaction of this section.

[445] Some Jews reversed circumcision through a medical procedure; cf. Aulus Cornelius Celsus, *De Medicina* 7.25; Martial 7.82; 1 Macc 1:15; 1 Cor 7:18; Josephus, *A. J.* 12.241; *Ass. Mos.* 8:3; cf. BDAG s.v. ἐπισπάω 3; cf. ROBERT G. HALL, Epispasm and the Dating of Ancient Jewish Writings, JSP 2 (1988): 71–86; ANDREAS BLASCHKE, Beschneidung. Zeugnisse der Bibel und verwandter Texte (TANZ 28; Tübingen: Francke, 1998), 139–41, 350–53.

[446] BLINZLER, Prozeß, 153 with n. 53.

taken to blasphemy. Technically it requires the pronunciation of the Name, but practically it can involve actions that reflect total unfaithfulness."[447]

Since the final redaction of *Sifre Bamidbar* took place c. A.D. 250–300,[448] it is uncertain whether this text should be regarded as relevant for the blasphemy charge in Jesus' trial.

*Threatening the Temple*. During the trial, two witnesses testified that Jesus claimed to be involved in destroying the Temple (Matt 26:61; Mark 15:57–58). While some scholars doubt the historicity of the scene concerning the interrogation of witnesses and the statement about the Temple,[449] others accept the historicity of the scene.[450] If this accusation had been proven, the charge of blasphemy could have been based on this claim.

**(64)** Josephus, *Antiquitates judaicae* 12.406

Ἔτι δ᾽ αὐτῷ κατιόντι ἀπὸ τῆς ἄκρας εἰς τὸ ἱερὸν ἀπαντήσαντες τῶν ἱερέων τινὲς καὶ πρεσβυτέρων ἠσπάζοντο καὶ τὰς θυσίας ἐπεδείκνυον ἃς ὑπὲρ τοῦ βασιλέως ἔλεγον ἐπιφέρειν τῷ θεῷ. ὁ δὲ βλασφημήσας αὐτοὺς ἠπείλησεν εἰ μὴ παραδοίη τὸν Ἰούδαν ὁ λαὸς αὐτῷ καθαιρήσειν ὅταν ἐπανέλθῃ τὸν ναόν.

*Translation.* And again, when Nicanor came down from the Akra to the Temple and when some of the priests and elders met him, they greeted him and showed him the sacrifices which they said they were offering to God on behalf of the king. He, however, cursed them and threatened that, unless the people gave Judas up to him, he would destroy the Temple when he returned.

*Commentary.* Demetrios I, the king of Syria since 162 B.C., had sent his general Nicanor with a large army against Judea in support of Alcimus, the high priest, in a new attempt to quell the rebellion led by Judas (Maccabaeus). After a failed plot to arrest Judas and having suffered losses at a battle near Kapharsalama, Nicanor went to Jerusalem where he threatened to destroy the Temple unless the priests and elders handed over Judas and his army.[451] If

---

[447] BOCK, Blasphemy, 79; BOCK, Blasphemy and the Jewish Examination of Jesus, 635, 636.

[448] Cf. STRACK / STEMBERGER / BOCKMUEHL, Introduction, 267.

[449] Cf. REINBOLD, Bericht, 241–56. KURT PAESLER, Das Tempelwort Jesu. Die Tradition von Tempelzerstörung und Tempelerneuerung im Neuen Testament (FRLANT 184; Göttingen: Vandenhoeck & Ruprecht, 1999), 11–22, 203–28, concludes that the statement about the Temple was derived from Hellenistic circles of the early church (ibid. 121–22).

[450] Cf. BLINZLER, Prozeß, 174–83; JOEL B. GREEN, The Death of Jesus: Tradition and Interpretation in the Passion Narrative (WUNT 2.33; Tübingen: Mohr-Siebeck, 1988), 275–83; PESCH, Markusevangelium, 2:416–18, 442–43; HENGEL / SCHWEMER, Jesus, 147.

[451] On Nicanor's portrayal in 2 Macc 14–15 cf. TOBIAS NICKLAS, Die 'Fratze' des Feindes: Zur Zeichnung des 'Nikanor' in 2 Makk 14–15, SJOT 17 (2003): 141–155.

αὐτούς is taken as the direct object of the verb ἠπείλησεν, the threat to destroy the Temple (καθαιρήσειν ... τὸν ναόν) is described as an act of blasphemy ( ὁ δὲ βλασφημήσας); if αὐτούς is taken as the direct object of the participle βλασφημήσας, Nicanor's threat to destroy the Temple can still be regarded as blasphemous if read in the context of 1 Macc 7:37–38 ("You have selected this house for your name to be invoked in it, to be a house of prayer and supplication for your people. Execute vengeance on this man and on his army, and let them fall by the sword. Remember their blasphemies [μνήσθητι τῶν δυσφημιῶν αὐτῶν], and do not allow them to endure").[452] The priests react with tears and supplication, asking God to deliver them from their enemies (*A. J.* 12.407). Nicanor and his army were defeated by Judas on 13 Adar 161 B.C. in a decisive battle at Adasa near Beth-horon (*A. J.* 12.408–412). D. L. BOCK discusses this text as it shows a connection between blasphemy and attacking the Temple as the locale of God's presence, and between blasphemy and attacking God's people.[453]

**(65)** Josephus, *Bellum judaicum* 6.300–309

τὸ δὲ τούτων φοβερώτερον, Ἰησοῦς γάρ τις υἱὸς Ἀνανίου τῶν ἰδιωτῶν ἄγροικος πρὸ τεσσάρων ἐτῶν τοῦ πολέμου τὰ μάλιστα τῆς πόλεως εἰρηνευομένης καὶ εὐθηνούσης, ἐλθὼν εἰς τὴν ἑορτήν, ἐν ᾗ σκηνοποιεῖσθαι πάντας ἔθος τῷ θεῷ, κατὰ τὸ ἱερὸν ἐξαπίνης ἀναβοᾶν ἤρξατο "φωνὴ ἀπὸ ἀνατολῆς, [301] φωνὴ ἀπὸ δύσεως, φωνὴ ἀπὸ τῶν τεσσάρων ἀνέμων, φωνὴ ἐπὶ Ἱεροσόλυμα καὶ τὸν ναόν, φωνὴ ἐπὶ νυμφίους καὶ νύμφας, φωνὴ ἐπὶ τὸν λαὸν πάντα." τοῦτο μεθ' ἡμέραν καὶ νύκτωρ κατὰ πάντας τοὺς στενωποὺς περιῄει κεκραγώς. [302] τῶν δὲ ἐπισήμων τινὲς δημοτῶν ἀγανακτήσαντες πρὸς τὸ κακόφημον συλλαμβάνουσι τὸν ἄνθρωπον καὶ πολλαῖς αἰκίζονται πληγαῖς. ὁ δὲ οὔθ' ὑπὲρ αὐτοῦ φθεγξάμενος οὔτε ἰδίᾳ πρὸς τοὺς παίοντας, ἃς καὶ πρότερον φωνὰς βοῶν διετέλει. [303] νομίσαντες δὲ οἱ ἄρχοντες, ὅπερ ἦν, δαιμονιώτερον τὸ κίνημα τἀνδρὸς ἀνάγουσιν αὐτὸν ἐπὶ τὸν παρὰ Ῥωμαίοις ἔπαρχον. [304] ἔνθα μάστιξι μέχρι ὀστέων ξαινόμενος οὔθ' ἱκέτευσεν οὔτ' ἐδάκρυσεν, ἀλλ' ὡς ἐνῆν μάλιστα τὴν φωνὴν ὀλοφυρτικῶς παρεγκλίνων πρὸς ἑκάστην [305] ἀπεκρίνατο πληγήν "αἰαὶ Ἱεροσολύμοις." τοῦ δ' Ἀλβίνου διερωτῶντος, οὗτος γὰρ ἔπαρχος ἦν, τίς εἴη καὶ πόθεν, καὶ διὰ τί ταῦτα φθέγγοιτο, πρὸς ταῦτα μὲν οὐδ' ὁτιοῦν ἀπεκρίνατο, τὸν δὲ ἐπὶ τῇ πόλει θρῆνον εἴρων οὐ διέλειπεν, μέχρι καταγνοὺς μανίαν ὁ Ἀλβῖνος ἀπέλυσεν αὐτόν. [306] ὁ δὲ τὸν μέχρι τοῦ πολέμου χρόνον οὔτε προσῄει τινὶ τῶν πολιτῶν οὔτε ὤφθη λαλῶν, ἀλλὰ καθ' ἡμέραν ὥσπερ εὐχὴν μεμελετηκώς "αἰαὶ Ἱεροσολύμοις" ἐθρήνει. [307] οὔτε δέ τινι τῶν τυπτόντων αὐτὸν ὁσημέραι κατηρᾶτο οὔτε τοὺς τροφῆς μεταδιδόντας εὐλόγει,

---

[452] Translation of GEORGE T. ZERVOS in PIETERSMA / WRIGHT, Septuagint, 490.
[453] BOCK, Blasphemy, 56–57, 111, 205; BOCK, Blasphemy and the Jewish Examination of Jesus, 621.

μία δὲ πρὸς πάντας ἦν ἡ σκυθρωπὴ κληδὼν ἀπόκρισις. ³⁰⁸ μάλιστα δ᾽ ἐν ταῖς ἑορταῖς ἐκεκράγει· καὶ τοῦτ᾽ ἐφ᾽ ἑπτὰ ἔτη καὶ μῆνας πέντε εἴρων οὔτ᾽ ἤμβλυνεν τὴν φωνὴν οὔτ᾽ ἔκαμεν, μέχρις οὗ κατὰ τὴν πολιορκίαν ἔργα τῆς κληδόνος ἰδὼν ἀνεπαύσατο. ³⁰⁹ περιιὼν γὰρ ἀπὸ τοῦ τείχους "αἰαὶ πάλιν τῇ πόλει καὶ τῷ λαῷ καὶ τῷ ναῷ" διαπρύσιον ἐβόα, ὡς δὲ τελευταῖον προσέθηκεν "αἰαὶ δὲ κἀμοί", λίθος ἐκ τοῦ πετροβόλου σχασθεὶς καὶ πλήξας αὐτὸν παραχρῆμα κτείνει, φθεγγομένην δ᾽ ἔτι τὰς κληδόνας ἐκείνας τὴν ψυχὴν ἀφῆκε.

*Translation.* But what was even more troubling than these matters was the following: four years before the war, when the city enjoyed peace and prosperity in the highest degree, a certain Jesus ben Ananias, an uneducated man from the countryside, came to the festival at which it is the custom of all to erect a booth to God, stood in the Temple, ³⁰¹ and suddenly began to cry out, "A voice from the east, a voice from the west, a voice from the four winds, a voice against Jerusalem and the Temple, a voice against the bridegroom and the bride, a voice against all the people!" He went about all the alleyways shouting day and night. ³⁰² Some of the distinguished citizens who were angry at these evil words⁴⁵⁴ arrested him and maltreated him with many blows. But he did not utter a sound, neither on his own behalf nor specifically⁴⁵⁵ against those who were striking him, only continuing to yell the same shouts as before. ³⁰³ Thus the authorities believed, as was indeed the case, that the man was engaged in a divine commotion,⁴⁵⁶ and they brought him before the prefect appointed by the Romans. ³⁰⁴ There he was flogged to the bone with whips, but he did not beg for mercy nor did he shed tears; rather, he responded to each blow with the most mournful modulation that he could give to his voice, "Woe to Jerusalem!" ³⁰⁵ When Albinus (he was the prefect) asked him, who he was, where he was from, and why he uttered these cries, he did not

---

⁴⁵⁴ LSJ suggests "evil" or "ominous words" for the passage; MICHEL / BAUERNFEIND translate κακόφημον "Unglücksgeschrei."

⁴⁵⁵ Following CLEMENTZ and MICHEL / BAUERNFEIND who interpret ἰδίᾳ in terms of a specific word of judgment (which Jesus ben Ananias did not utter while being tortured); differently THACKERAY who links ἰδίᾳ with πρὸς τοὺς παίοντας ("for the private ear of those who smote him"). Cf. MICHEL / BAUERNFEIND, De Bello Judaico, II/2, 189 n. 145.

⁴⁵⁶ Most translators and commentators interpret the phrase δαιμονιώτερον τὸ κίνημα in a theological-psychological sense; cf. WHISTON: "that this was a sort of divine fury in the man;" THACKERAY: "that the man was under some supernatural impulse;" MICHEL / BAUERNFEIND: "daß den Mann eine übermenschliche Macht treibe." PETER EGGER, "Crucifixus sub Pontio Pilato". Das "crimen" Jesu von Nazareth im Spannungsfeld römischer und jüdischer Verwaltungs- und Rechtsstrukturen (NTA 32; Münster: Aschendorff, 1997), 143–44, argues that κίνημα is used by Josephus, with one exception, for "insurgency," "commotion" or "rebellion" and should be given a political meaning here as well, and suggests that δαιμόνιος, which means "caused by God" ("gottgefügt") in Josephus, is not part of the evaluation of the Jewish leaders but, rather, Josephus' interpretation of the prophecies of Jesus. Cf. CHRISTOPH RIEDO-EMMENEGGER, Prophetisch-messianische Provokateure der Pax Romana. Jesus von Nazaret und andere Störenfriede im Konflikt mit dem Römischen Reich (NTOA 56; Fribourg / Göttingen: Academic Press / Vandenhoeck & Ruprecht, 2005), 241–42.

answer him, but continued his lament over the city until Albinus pronounced him mad and let him go. [306] During the period until the outbreak of the war he did not approach any of the citizens, nor was he seen talking to anyone, but he shouted every day his lament, as if he had rehearsed a prayer, "Woe to Jerusalem!" [307] He did not curse any of those who beat him day by day, nor did he bless those who gave him food. This gloomy utterance was the one answer he had for all. [308] He cried loudest at the festivals. And he did this continuously for seven years and five months. His voice never became dull nor did he grow tired, until he rested at the time of the siege, when he saw his omen become reality. [309] For while he was going around and shouted with a piercing voice from the wall, "Woe again to the city and to the people and to the Temple," he added at the end, "and woe to me also," a stone released from the catapult struck him so that he died immediately, giving up his life while uttering these shouts.

*Commentary.* The case of Jesus ben Ananias appears in discussions of the question of what constituted Jesus' offense in his trial, and, more frequently, in discussions of the jurisdiction of the Sanhedrin and of the Roman prefect in death penalty cases.[457] Josephus dates the appearance of the prophet Jesus ben Ananias to the governorship of Lucceius Albinus (62–64 A.D.).[458] The context of the passage is a series of omens and prophecies concerning the fall of Jerusalem and the destruction of the Temple (*B. J.* 6.288–315). Jesus ben Ananias is described as an uneducated peasant from the countryside whose activity in Jerusalem began on the Feast of Tabernacles (Sukkoth) of the year A.D. 62, four years before the beginning of the Jewish revolt, and continued daily for seven years and five months.[459] He predicts that a disaster would fall on Jerusalem, the Temple, and the people. Josephus emphasizes that Jesus ben Ananias prophesied during festivals, when the city would be filled with pilgrims (6.308). His prophecy consists of two strophes with three lines each, formulated in synonymous parallelism, with the third line summarizing and developing the first two lines (*B. J.* 6.301).[460] As regards form, his pronouncements of woe correspond to the kind of lamentation found in settings of real or anticipated grief, loss, or calamity (Psalm 120:5; Isa 6:5; Micah 7:1). Unlike woe oracles in the biblical and Jewish tradition, Jesus' oracle does not specify the nature of the calamity, although Josephus was obviously con-

---

[457] As regards the latter, *B. J.* 6.303–305 will be discussed in No. 75.

[458] For sustained discussion of *B. J.* 300–309 cf. EGGER, Crucifixus, 136–47; REBECCA GRAY, Prophetic Figures in Late Second Temple Jewish Palestine: The Evidence from Josephus (New York: Oxford University Press, 1993), 28–30, 158–63; RIEDO-EMMENEGGER, Provokateure, 240–43. For Albinus see No. 3.

[459] On these dates cf. MICHEL / BAUERNFEIND, De Bello Judaico, 189–90.

[460] Cf. DAVID E. AUNE, Prophecy in Early Christianity and the Ancient Mediterranean World (Grand Rapids: Eerdmans, 1983), 136; for the following comments on the form and content of the oracle see ibid. 136–37.

vinced that it was fulfilled in the events of A.D. 70. The location of Jesus ben Ananias' activity in the Temple is paralleled only by Jeremiah's prophecy of the Temple's destruction in the Temple precincts (Jer 7:1–15; 26:4–9) and by Jesus of Nazareth's symbolic announcement of the fall of the Temple (Mark 11:15–17 par.). The voice (φονή), mentioned six times as coming from all directions and announcing calamity for Jerusalem, the Temple, and the people, is the voice of God.[461]

Jesus ben Ananias is harmless since he has no followers. But his activities represent a provocation for the Sadducean leadership, who are responsible for law and order, and thus, at least potentially, for the Roman administration.[462] Even though Jerusalem is described as a city enjoying peace and prosperity at the time of Jesus' appearance (6.300), the Jewish magistrates do not want to risk a repeat of the riot that broke out in the Temple during the Feast of Passover under Cumanus (A.D. 48–52), when a Roman soldier had made an obscene gesture at the crowd, forcing the governor to call in his troops and resulting in a stampede that killed 20,000 people (*B. J.* 2.224–227; *A. J.* 20.105–111). Jesus ben Ananias' pronouncements of divine judgment during the Feast of Tabernacles left the Jewish magistrates with little choice since "no one could predict the effect that a prophet of doom might have on the huge crowds that flooded the city ... it was better to move quickly to eliminate the source of the problem than to risk the outbreak of a serious disturbance."[463] Josephus describes the action of the Jewish aristocracy (τῶν δὲ ἐπισήμων τινὲς δημοτῶν; *B. J.* 6.302), identified with the political authorities (οἱ ἄρχοντες; 6.303), as follows: (1) they arrest Jesus ben Ananias (συλλαμβάνουσι); (2) they torture him (πολλαῖς αἰκίζονται πληγαῖς); (3) they interrogate him,[464] without success since he stayed silent (ὁ δὲ οὔθ᾽ ὑπὲρ αὐτοῦ φθεγξάμενος; 6.302); (4) they conclude that he wants to create a commotion or rebellion (κίνημα); (5) they transfer him to the Roman governor (ἀνάγουσιν αὐτὸν ἐπὶ τὸν παρὰ Ῥωμαίοις ἔπαρχον). The transfer of the court case and the trial of

---

[461] The reference to the bridegroom and the bride allude to Jeremiah's prophecies; cf. Jer 7:34; 16:9; 25:10; 33:11. They are singled out to underline that even the happiest people will suffer in the looming catastrophe.

[462] MÜLLER, Kapitalgerichtsbarkeit, 83; RIEDO-EMMENEGGER, Provokateure, 242. BENT NOACK, Jesus Ananiassøn og Jesus fra Nasaret. En drøftelse af Josefus, Bellum Judaicum VI,5,3 (Tekst og Tolkning 6; Copenhagen: Gyldendal, 1975), 54, suggests that Jesus' prophecy implied the destruction of Jerusalem by the Romans, which should have prompted the Jewish leadership to take anti-Roman actions. RIEDO-EMMENEGGER, ibid. 242 n. 1925, remains unconvinced. RICHARD A. HORSLEY and JOHN S. HANSON, Bandits, Prophets, and Messiahs: Popular Movements in the Time of Jesus (orig. 1985; repr., Harrisburg: Trinity Press International, 1999), 173–75, 186, argue that Jesus was a proponent of the common people and opposed the aristocracy. RIEDO-EMMENEGGER, ibid. 242–43 n. 1931, counters by pointing to the religious and economic importance of the Temple for all social classes in Judea.

[463] GRAY, Prophetic Figures, 162.

[464] RIEDO-EMMENEGGER, Provokateure, 241 n. 1919.

Jesus ben Ananias before the Roman governor is discussed below (No. 75). After being released by the governor, who concludes that the man is insane, Jesus ben Ananias continues to proclaim his woe oracle against Jerusalem and the Temple. Despite these warnings, the Jews continued to plan a rebellion against the Romans, which eventually led to the destruction of Jerusalem. In the context of the other omens and prophecies concerning the fall of Jerusalem, the episode underlines the point that since the Jewish leaders and the people are unwilling to recognize the will of God, shouted out by Jesus ben Ananias, the catastrophe of the war and the destruction of Jerusalem and of the Temple are inevitable.[465] In the context of Josephus' larger project, he seeks to encourage the Jewish people to accept Roman rule and renounce all further plans to rebellion.[466]

Several authors interpret Jesus ben Ananias' threats against Jerusalem and the Temple against the background of Jer 26:8–11 as blasphemy and thus as a capital crime that requires the death penalty.[467] The transfer to the Roman governor, who seems to begin a trial on capital charges (note the flogging of Jesus),[468] can be interpreted as implying that the Jewish leaders had tried Jesus ben Ananias on a death penalty charge.

*Attacking the Divinely Appointed Leadership.* Josephus' report about John Hyrcanus' fury at the Pharisees and his turning to the Sadducees indicates that reviling Israel's leadership could be regarded as blasphemy. The earlier text 11QTemple LXIV, 6–12 has already been discussed (see No. 22).

**(66)** Josephus, *Antiquitates judaicae* 13.293–296

Τῶν δ' ἐκ τῶν Σαδδουκαίων τῆς αἱρέσεως οἳ τὴν ἐναντίαν τοῖς Φαρισαίοις προαίρεσιν ἔχουσιν Ἰωνάθης τις ἐν τοῖς μάλιστα φίλος ὢν Ὑρκανῷ τῇ κοινῇ πάντων Φαρισαίων γνώμῃ ποιήσασθαι τὰς βλασφημίας τὸν Ἐλεάζαρον ἔλεγεν· καὶ τοῦτ' ἔσεσθαι φανερὸν αὐτῷ πυθομένῳ παρ' ἐκείνων τίνος ἄξιός ἐστιν ἐπὶ τοῖς εἰρημένοις κολάσεως. ²⁹⁴ τοῦ δὲ Ὑρκανοῦ τοὺς Φαρισαίους ἐρομένου τίνος αὐτὸν ἄξιον ἡγοῦνται τιμωρίας· πειραθήσεσθαι[469] γὰρ οὐ μετὰ τῆς ἐκείνων γνώμης γεγονέναι τὰς βλασφημίας τιμησαμένων αὐτὸν τῷ

---

[465] Cf. EGGER, Crucifixus, 140–41.

[466] BILDE, Flavius Josephus between Jerusalem and Rome, 77; RIEDO-EMMENEGGER, Provokateure, 240.

[467] URBANUS HOLZMEISTER, Zur Frage der Blutgerichtsbarkeit des Synedriums, Bib 19 (1938): 43–59, 151–174, 161–65; BLINZLER, Prozeß, 243; cf. CATCHPOLE, Trial, 126–132; STROBEL, Stunde, 25. BOCK, Blasphemy, does not use this text.

[468] Cf. GERD THEISSEN / ANNETTE MERZ, Der historische Jesus. Ein Lehrbuch (Göttingen: Vandenhoeck & Ruprecht, 1996), 520; GERD THEISSEN and ANNETTE MERZ, The Historical Jesus: A Comprehensive Guide (London/Minneapolis: SCM/Fortress, 1998), 603.

[469] The text follows NIESE (P F L); MARCUS reads πεισθήσεσθαι (A M V W).

μέτρῳ τῆς δίκης πληγῶν ἔφασαν καὶ δεσμῶν· οὐ γὰρ ἐδόκει λοιδορίας ἕνεκα θανάτῳ ζημιοῦν ἄλλως τε καὶ φύσει πρὸς τὰς κολάσεις ἐπιεικῶς ἔχουσιν οἱ Φαρισαῖοι. ²⁹⁵ πρὸς τοῦτο λίαν ἐχαλέπηνεν καὶ δοκοῦν ἐκείνοις ποιήσασθαι τὰς βλασφημίας τὸν ἄνθρωπον ἐνόμισεν. μάλιστα δ'ʼ αὐτὸν ἐπιπαρώξυνεν Ἰωνάθης καὶ διέθηκεν οὕτως, ²⁹⁶ ὥστε τῇ Σαδδουκαίων ἐποίησεν προσθέσθαι μοίρᾳ τῶν Φαρισαίων ἀποστάντα καὶ τά τε ὑπ᾽ αὐτῶν κατασταθέντα νόμιμα τῷ δήμῳ καταλῦσαι καὶ τοὺς φυλάττοντας αὐτὰ κολάσαι μῖσος οὖν ἐντεῦθεν αὐτῷ τε καὶ τοῖς υἱοῖς παρὰ τοῦ πλήθους ἐγένετο.

*Translation.* There was a certain Jonathan, a close friend of Hyrcanus who belonged to the school of the Sadducees whose convictions are opposed to those of the Pharisees, who said that Eleazar had made his slanderous (blasphemous) statement with the general approval of all the Pharisees; and this would become clear to him if he inquired of them what punishment he (Eleazar) deserved for what he had said.²⁹⁴ When Hyrcanus asked the Pharisees what penalty they thought he deserved, and that he would be testing whether the slanderous (blasphemous) statement had not been made with their approval if they awarded the penalty proportional to the crime, they replied that he deserved to be flogged and bound; it did not seem right to them to sentence a man to death for insulting speech, and besides, the Pharisees are by nature reasonable in the matter of punishments. ²⁹⁵ Hyrcanus became very angry at this and believed that this man had slandered (blasphemed) him with their approval. Jonathan inflamed his anger above all, and arranged it ²⁹⁶ so that he made him join the party of the Sadducees and desert the Pharisees, and to abolish the regulations which they had established for the people, and punish those who observed them. This was the reason for the hatred of the masses for him and his sons.

*Commentary.* In Book 13, Josephus describes the zenith of the Hasmonean dynasty which was reached in the reign of John Hyrcanus I (134–104 B.C.).⁴⁷⁰ Hyrcanus achieved a compromise with the Seleucid rulers at the beginning of his reign. He agreed to pay tribute and provide military support for the eastern campaign of Antiochus VII Sidetes while the latter agreed not to maintain a military garrison in Jerusalem.⁴⁷¹ During his last years, Hyrcanus conquered Idumea and Samaria, and he was forced to deal with internal opposition. Josephus relates that Hyrcanus was a "disciple" (μαθητής) of the Pharisees. On the occasion of a feast to which he had invited the Pharisees, Hyrcanus asked them to correct him and lead him back to the right path if they happened to observe him doing anything wrong (*A. J.* 13.289–290).⁴⁷² One of the guests,

---

⁴⁷⁰ On John Hyrcanus I see JOSEPH SIEVERS, The Hasmoneans and Their Supporters: From Mattathias to the Death of John Hyrcanus I (SFSHJ 6; Atlanta: Scholars Press, 1990), 135–56, on his dealings with the Pharisees ibid. 147–50.

⁴⁷¹ Josephus, *A. J.* 13.236–253; *B. J.* 1.61; also Diodorus Siculus 34–35.1.1–5.

⁴⁷² For a comparison of the banquet story in Josephus' account and in the close parallel

a certain Eleazar, immediately takes Hyrcanus at his word and suggests that if Hyrcanus really wanted to be righteous (δίκαιος), he would give up the high-priesthood and be content with governing the people (*A. J.* 13.291). When asked for the reason, Eleazar asserts that since Hyrcanus' mother was a captive during the reign of Antiochus IV Epiphanes, he does not have the genealogical qualifications for the high-priesthood.[473] Josephus asserts that this information was false, that Hyrcanus was furious, and that "all the Pharisees" were indignant with Eleazar (*A. J.* 13.292). In *A. J.* 13.293–296 Josephus relates how a certain Sadducee named Jonathan takes the opportunity presented by Eleazar's request to persuade Hyrcanus to re-evaluate his loyalty to the Pharisees and switch his allegiance to the Sadducees. Jonathan tells Hyrcanus that all the Pharisees approved of Eleazar's request, a fact that Hyrcanus could easily ascertain if he asked them what punishment they deem appropriate for Eleazar's statement (*A. J.* 13.293). According to Josephus, Jonathan calls the assertion that Hyrcanus is not qualified to be high priest a "slanderous" or "blasphemous" statement (τὰς βλασφημίας; 13.293), an assessment with which Hyrcanus agrees (13.294, 295). In their response, the Pharisees call Eleazar's statement "insulting speech" (λοιδορία) that should be punished with flogging and imprisonment (πληγῶν ... καὶ δεσμῶν) rather than the death penalty (θανάτῳ). Hyrcanus, impressed by the counsel of Jonathan the Sadducean, is incensed at their reply, expecting the Pharisees to agree with his assessment that Eleazar's statement constitutes βλασφημία, a crime (δίκη) that deserves the death sentence. Hyrcanus abandons the Pharisees, abolishes the regulations that had been enacted as a result of their legal work, and joins the Sadducean party (13.296).[474] According to this episode, the Sadducees interpret the vilification, or verbal abuse, of the high priest as "blasphemy" punishable by death, and demand Eleazar's execution. The key passage is Exod 22:27(28), which prohibits both "reviling God" (אֱלֹהִים לֹא תְקַלֵּל; LXX Θεοὺς οὐ κακολογήσεις) and "cursing a leader of your people" (וְנָשִׂיא בְעַמְּךָ לֹא תָאֹר; LXX καὶ ἄρχοντας τοῦ λαοῦ σου οὐ κακῶς ἐρεῖς).[475] In *C. Ap.* 2.194, Josephus alludes to this passage and asserts: ὁ τούτῳ μὴ πειθόμενος ὑφέξει δίκην ὡς εἰς θεὸν αὐτὸν ἀσεβῶν ("The person who disobeys him [the high

---

b. *Qidd.* 66a cf. JACOB NEUSNER, *The Rabbinic Traditions about the Pharisees before 70* (3 vols.; Leiden: Brill, 1971), 1:173–76; JOSHUA EFRON, *Studies on the Hasmonean Period* (SJLA 39; Leiden: Brill, 1987), 161–89; SCHWARTZ, *Reading,* 127–28.

[473] Lev 21:14 stipulates concerning the high priest: "A widow, or a divorced woman, or a woman who has been defiled, a prostitute, these he shall not marry."

[474] MARTIN HENGEL, E. P. Sanders' 'Common Judaism', Jesus, and the Pharisees [1995], in *Judaica et Hellenistica. Kleine Schriften I* (WUNT 90; Tübingen: Mohr Siebeck, 1996), 392–479, 463–62, describes the Sadducees, in this historical context, as the military and feudal aristocracy consisting of priests and non-priestly elite Jews.

[475] Exod 22:27(28) uses the verb קלל which occurs in Lev 24:10–23, which discusses blasphemy and its punishment.

priest] will pay a penalty as if he were sacrilegious towards God himself").[476]

A. M. SCHWEMER refers to this text as evidence explaining the blasphemy charge in Jesus' trial. By claiming to have the authority to be seated at the right hand of God (Mark 14:62), Jesus usurps a place on the divine throne that only Enoch, the eschatological Son of Man, or Moses could claim, thus blaspheming God. And by claiming to come with the clouds of heaven, Jesus is claiming to be the judge of the high priest and his colleagues,which constitutes a form of blasphemy, and thus has to be sentenced to death.[477]

*Jesus as a blasphemer*. The charge of blasphemy against Jesus is most plausibly connected with Jesus' allusions to the enthroned authority of a royal figure from Psalm 110:1 and the authoritative figure of the one like a Son of Man from Daniel 7:13, claiming the prerogative of being instrumental in the final judgement sitting next to God in heaven, and attacking Israel's leadership, thereby putting the nation at risk of possible intervention by Roman authorities. The charge of blasphemy could also have been linked with Jesus' statements concerning the Temple, which evidently were interpreted as a threat, and with his statements that could be interpreted as despising the Torah and profaning Holy Things.

## 1.6  The Charge of being a Seducer

Some scholars emphasize that Jesus was tried as a seducer of the people. On the *mesit* and *maddiakh* in rabbinic law see Texts No. 36, 38, 41, 42, 43, 45. The following New Testament texts suggest that Jesus was indicted on the charge of being a seducer of the people.

---

[476] Translation of JOHN M. G. BARCLAY, Against Apion (Flavius Josephus: Translation and Commentary 10; Leiden: Brill, 2006).

[477] ANNA MARIA SCHWEMER, Die Passion des Messias nach Markus und der Vorwurf des Antijudaismus, in Der messianische Anspruch Jesu und die Anfänge der Christologie (M. Hengel and A. M. Schwemer; WUNT 138; Tübingen: Mohr Siebeck, 2001), 133–163, 149–50; cf. RICHARD J. BAUCKHAM, For What Offence Was James Put to Death? in James the Just and Christian Origins (ed. B. D. Chilton and C. A. Evans; NTSup 98; Leiden: Brill, 1999), 199–232, 224; COLLINS, Charge of Blasphemy, 163. Cf. BOCK, Blasphemy and the Jewish Examination of Jesus, 624. JEFFREY B. GIBSON, The Function of the Charge of Blasphemy in Mark 14:64, in The Trial and Death of Jesus: Essays on the Passion Narrative in Mark (ed. G. Van Oyen and T. Shepherd; Leuven: Peeters, 2006), 171–187, argues that what lies at the heart of the blasphemy charge "is not *what* Jesus claims about himself. Rather, it is the fact that it is *Jesus* who is making messianic claims ... the path that Jesus advocates as divinely mandated for Israel is not only one that God does not endorse, it is one that, if followed, will bring his elect to ruin and make God's name a mockery among the Gentiles" (173, 184).

Matt 27:62–63: The next day, the day after Preparation Day, the chief priests and the Pharisees went to Pilatus. [63] "Sir," they said, "we remember that while he was still alive that deceiver (ἐκεῖνος ὁ πλάνος) said, 'After three days I will rise again.'"

Luke 23:1–2, 5: Then the whole assembly rose and led him away to Pilatus. [2] And they began to accuse him, saying, "We have found this man perverting our nation (διαστρέφοντα τὸ ἔθνος ἡμῶν). He opposes paying taxes to the emperor and he claims to be the Messiah, a king" ... They insisted and said, "He incites the people (ἀνασείει τὸν λαὸν) as he teaches throughout all Judea, beginning in Galilee (and now he has come) this far."

John 7:12: There was much secret discussion about him among the crowds. Some said, "He is a good man." Others said, "No, he deceives the people (πλανᾷ τὸν ὄχλον)."

John 7:45–49: The temple police went back to the chief priests and Pharisees, who asked them, "Why did you not arrest him?" [46] The police answered, "Never has anyone spoken like this!" [47] Then the Pharisees replied, "Surely you have not been deceived too, have you? (μὴ καὶ ὑμεῖς πεπλάνησθε;) [48] Has any one of the authorities or of the Pharisees believed in him? [49] But this crowd, which does not know the law – they are accursed."

Two later texts (Josephus, *A. J.* 18.63; Justin Martyr, *Dialogue* 69.7) confirm this tradition. See also *b. Sanh.* 43a (No. 71).

### (67) Josephus, *Antiquitates judaicae* 18.63

Γίνεται δὲ κατὰ τοῦτον τὸν χρόνον Ἰησοῦς σοφὸς ἀνήρ, εἴγε ἄνδρα αὐτὸν λέγειν χρή· ἦν γὰρ παραδόξων ἔργων ποιητής, διδάσκαλος ἀνθρώπων τῶν ἡδονῇ τἀληθῆ δεχομένων, καὶ πολλοὺς μὲν Ἰουδαίους, πολλοὺς δὲ καὶ τοῦ Ἑλληνικοῦ ἐπηγάγετο.

*Translation.* At this time there lived Jesus, a wise man, if indeed one ought to call him a man. For he was one who performed incredible actions and he was a teacher of people who accept the truth with pleasure. He won over many Jews and many Greeks.

*Commentary.* The verb ἐπηγάγετο which is usually translated "he won over"[478] means "bring over to oneself, win over" (LSJ s.v. ἐπάγω II.7), but it can also mean "lead on by persuasion, influence" (ibid. I.3). G. N. STANTON suggests the meaning "bring trouble to" and even "seduce, lead astray."[479] While the noun ἐπαγωγή means "calamity, trouble" (LSJ, MURAOKA), BDAG dropped the information that the figurative sense of ἐπάγω is "bring something bad upon someone" (BAGD; in BDAG we find the following: "to cause a state or condition to be or occur, bring on, bring some-thing upon someone, mostly something bad"). The authenticity of Josephus' statement about Jesus in *A. J.*

---

[478] FELDMAN, in THACKERAY / MARCUS / FELDMAN, Josephus, 9:51.

[479] GRAHAM N. STANTON, Jesus of Nazareth: A Magician and a False Prophet Who Deceived God's People? in Jesus of Nazareth: Lord and Christ (FS I. H. Marshall; ed. J. B. Green and M. Turner; Grand Rapids/Carlisle: Eerdmans/Paternoster, 1994), 164–180, 170.

18.63–64 is debated.[480] Many scholars hold that Josephus included a description of Jesus and his ministry and that a Christian editor made some alterations in the originally "neutral" Josephus text. The statement that Jesus "won over" many people – perhaps in the negative sense of "deceive" or "seduce" – probably derives from Josephus. See for a fuller discussion No. 82.

**(68)** Justin Martyr, *Dialogus cum Tryphone* 69.6–7

Πηγὴ ὕδατος ζῶντος παρὰ θεοῦ ἐν τῇ ἐρήμῳ γνώσεως θεοῦ, τῇ τῶν ἐθνῶν γῇ, ἀνέβλυσεν οὗτος ὁ Χριστός, ὃς καὶ ἐν τῷ γένει ὑμῶν πέφανται, καὶ τοὺς ἐκ γενετῆς καὶ κατὰ τὴν σάρκα πηροὺς καὶ κωφοὺς καὶ χωλοὺς ἰάσατο, τὸν μὲν ἅλλεσθαι, τὸν δὲ καὶ ἀκούειν, τὸν δὲ καὶ ὁρᾶν τῷ λόγῳ αὐτοῦ ποιήσας· καὶ νεκροὺς δὲ ἀναστήσας καὶ ζῆν ποιήσας, [καὶ] διὰ τῶν ἔργων ἐδυσώπει τοὺς τότε ὄντας ἀνθρώπους ἐπιγνῶναι αὐτόν. [7] Οἱ δὲ καὶ ταῦτα ὁρῶντες γινόμενα φαντασίαν μαγικὴν γίνεσθαι ἔλεγον· καὶ γὰρ μάγον εἶναι αὐτὸν ἐτόλμων λέγειν καὶ λαοπλάνον.

*Translation.* The spring of living water which gushed forth from God in the land destitute of the knowledge of God, namely the land of the Gentiles, was this Christ, who also appeared in your nation, and healed those who were maimed, and deaf, and lame in body from their birth, causing them to leap, to hear, and to see, by his word. And having raised the dead, and causing them to live, by his deeds he compelled the men who lived at that time to recognize him. [7] But though they saw such works, they asserted it was magical art. For they dared to call him a magician and a deceiver of the people.

*Commentary.*[481] According to Justin Martyr, who wrote *Dialogue with Trypho* c. A.D. 160,[482] Jesus' contemporaries regarded his works (ἔργα), specified as

---

[480] PAUL WINTER in SCHÜRER, History, 1:428–41; ERNST BAMMEL, Zum Testimonium Flavianum (Jos Ant 18,63–64) [1974], in Judaica: Kleine Schriften I (WUNT 37; Tübingen: Mohr Siebeck, 1986), 177–189; GEZA VERMES, The Jesus Notice of Josephus Re-Examined, JJS 38 (1987): 1–10; JOHN P. MEIER, Jesus in Josephus: A Modest Proposal, CBQ 52 (1990): 76–103; MEIER, Marginal Jew, 1:56–88; THEISSEN / MERZ, Der historische Jesus, 74–82 (= THEISSEN / MERZ, Historical Jesus, 64–74); PIER ANGELO GRAMAGLIA, Il Testimonium Flavianum: Analisi linguistica, Henoch 20 (1998): 153–177; ALICE WHEALEY, Josephus on Jesus: The Testimonium Flavianum Controversy from Late Antiquity to Modern Times (Studies in Biblical Literature 36; New York: Lang, 2003).

[481] Text: MIROSLAV MARCOVICH, Iustini Martyris Dialogus cum Tryphone (Patristische Texte und Studien 47; Berlin: De Gruyter, 1997). Justin's works are preserved in a single manuscript: Parisinus graecus 450, dated 11 September 1363, evidently copied in Mistra near Sparta. Cf. EDGAR J. GOODSPEED, Dialogus com Tryphone, in Die ältesten Apologeten. Texte mir kurzen Einleitungen (orig. 1914; repr., Göttingen: Vandenhoeck & Ruprecht, 1984).

[482] Cf. SARA PARVIS and PAUL FOSTER, eds., Justin Martyr and His Worlds (Minneapolis: Fortress, 2007), xiii. WOLFRAM KINZIG, Justin Martyr, RPP 7 (2010): 127–128, dates *Dialogue* to A.D. 155–160.

his healing the maimed, the deaf, and the lame and raising people from the dead, as constituting magical art (φαντασίαν μαγικήν). They asserted that he was a magician (μάγον εἶναι) and a deceiver of the people (λαοπλάνος). This corresponds to the charge against Jesus in Matt 27:63 and John 7:12, 47. The only reference for λαοπλάνος listed in LSJ, and the earliest attested occurrence, is to Josephus, *A. J.* 8.232, where the term is used by the prophet Jadon (evidently Iddo of 2 Chron 9:29) against king Jeroboam, who has made himself high priest, and against his priests, who are about to offer sacrifices at the altar in Bethel. Both the king and his priests are accused of misleading the people and of being impostors and ungodly (λαοπλάνων τούτων καὶ ἀπατεώνων καὶ ἀσεβῶν). Josephus uses the term as equivalent of the Hebrew term מַדִּיחַ (*maddiakh*), the "deceiver" or "enticer" who leads a large number of people into idolatry.[483] Justin relates that Jesus' opponents brought two charges against him: he was a sorcerer and he was a deceiver of the people.

*Jesus as a seducer of the people.* A. STROBEL has argued that Jesus was tried and condemned by the Jewish leaders as a seducer of the people.[484] The main criticism of this explanation concerns the focus of the seduction in Deut 13 and in the various Jewish texts: the death penalty is stipulated for individuals who seduce others to idolatry, a charge not leveled against Jesus.[485] J. D. G. DUNN points out that other testimony besides the charge of having threatened to destroy the Temple was brought against Jesus (Mark 14:55–56 par Matt 26:59–60); the charge that Jesus leads people astray (Matt 27:63; John 7:12, 47) is unknown to Mark and "not a part of the accusation at the trial."[486] Other scholars find STROBEL's position generally convincing.[487] D. NEALE argues that Jesus' announcement that his activities divide families,[488] as well as his rejection in the towns of Galilee,[489] fit the profile of a *mesit*.[490] G. N. STAN-

---

[483] Cf. INSTONE-BREWER, Trial, 281.

[484] STROBEL, Stunde, 81–92. Early studies who argued for this position include ROBERT VON MAYR, Der Prozeß Jesu, Archiv für Kriminal-Anthropologie und Kriminalistik 20 (1905): 269–305, 296–97; FRIEDRICH DOERR, Der Prozeß Jesu in rechtsgeschichtlicher Beleuchtung. Ein Beitrag zur Kenntnis des jüdisch-römischen Provinzialstrafrechts (orig. 1908; repr., Berlin: Kohlhammer, 1920), 39–42.

[485] BLINZLER, Prozeß, 187; MÜLLER, Kapitalgerichtsbarkeit, 70 n. 51; REINBOLD, Bericht, 255; EGGER, Crucifixus, 170–71. Cf. BROWN, Death, 1:543–44, 2:1290, who thinks that this tradition is post-70, following GERHARD SCHNEIDER, Das Verfahren gegen Jesus in der Sicht des dritten Evangeliums (Lk 22,54 - 23,25). Redaktionskritik und historische Rückfrage, in Der Prozeß gegen Jesus (ed. K. Kertelge; QD 112; Freiburg: Herder, 1988), 111–130, 121–25.

[486] JAMES D. G. DUNN, Jesus Remembered (Christianity in the Making I; Grand Rapids: Eerdmans, 2003), 632 n. 95.

[487] Cf. THEISSEN / MERZ, Der historische Jesus, 405 (= THEISSEN / MERZ, Historical Jesus, 463); WRIGHT, Jesus, 439–42, 548–51; BOCK, Blasphemy and the Jewish Examination of Jesus, 627–28; KRIMPHOVE, Strafverfahren, 79–90, 170–90.

[488] Luke 12:52–53; cf. Matt 10:21, 35–36; compare Deut 13:6, 9.

[489] Matt 10:14–15, 17, 23; 11:20–24; 23:34; Luke 4:28–29; 9:58; 10:13–15; cf. Deut

TON demonstrates that later Jewish accusations against Jesus being a magician and a false prophet who deceived God's people date to Jesus' own lifetime.[491] P. STUHLMACHER argues that "seduction" has a broader meaning in the relevant texts than merely seduction to worship foreign gods and that Deut 13:2–12; 17:12; 18:20 allows for a wider range of accusations against a seducer (*mesit*).[492] M. HENGEL and A. M. SCHWEMER argue that since Jesus was tried and sentenced as messianic pretender, he was regarded as a false prophet, a seducer of the people and someone who had blasphemed God.[493]

## 1.7  The Charge of Sorcery

Jesus was regarded by some Jerusalem scribes as a magician. Relevant to this are the New Testament texts that follow.

Mark 3:22: And the scribes who came down from Jerusalem said, "He has Beelzebul (Βεελ-ζεβοὺλ ἔχει), and by the ruler of the demons he casts out demons."

Matt 12:22–24 (par Luke 11:14–15): Then they brought to him a demoniac who was blind and mute; and he cured him, so that the one who had been mute could speak and see. [23] All the crowds were amazed and said, "Can this be the Son of David?" [24] But when the Pharisees heard it, they said, "It is only by Beelzebul, the ruler of the demons (ἐν τῷ Βεελζεβοὺλ ἄρχοντι τῶν δαιμονίων), that this fellow casts out the demons." Cf. Matt 9:34; 10:25.

While the standard Greek term for magician (μάγος) is not used in the accusation against Jesus, the fact that Jesus is associated with Beelzebul, the prince of demons, by whose power he performs acts of exorcism is tantamount to the charge that he is a sorcerer who performs acts of magic. Some suggest that Jesus was tried and condemned as a magician.[494] The following texts are cited (for Justin Martyr, *Dialogus cum Tryphone* 69.6–7, see No. 68).

---

13:13–17 on the protection of the cities.

[490] DAVID A. NEALE, Was Jesus a *Mesith*? Public Response to Jesus and his Ministry, TynBul 44 (1993): 89–101.

[491] STANTON, Magician, 164–180.

[492] PETER STUHLMACHER, Biblische Theologie des Neuen Testaments. Band 1: Grundlegung. Von Jesus zu Paulus (3., neubearbeitete und ergänzte Auflage; Göttingen: Vandenhoeck & Ruprecht, 2005), 146–47, who argues contra JOACHIM GNILKA, Jesus von Nazareth. Botschaft und Geschichte (HThK Sup 3; Freiburg: Herder, 1990), 308 n. 69.

[493] HENGEL / SCHWEMER, Jesus, 599.

[494] STAUFFER, Jesus, 19, 73, 81; BLINZLER, Prozeß, 188 n. 14, also points to DUNCAN FISHWICK, The Talpioth Ossuaries Again, NTS 10 (1963): 49–61. See also the interpretation of Jesus' activity as that of a magician by MORTON SMITH, Jesus the Magician (San Francisco: Harper & Row, 1978); recently SHIMON GIBSON, The Final Days of Jesus: The Archaeological Evidence (New York: HarperOne, 2009), 173.

**(69)** Origen, *Contra Celsum* 1.6,38,68

Κατηγορεῖ δ᾽ ἐν τοῖς ἑξῆς καὶ τοῦ σωτῆρος ὡς **γοητείᾳ δυνηθέντος ἃ ἔδοξε παράδοξα πεποιηκέναι καὶ προϊδόντος ὅτι μέλλουσι καὶ ἄλλοι τὰ αὐτὰ μαθήματα** ἐγνωκότες ποιεῖν **τὸ αὐτό, σεμνυνόμενοι τῷ θεοῦ δυνάμει ποιεῖν· οὕστινας ἀπελαύνει τῆς ἑαυτοῦ πολιτείας ὁ Ἰησους.**
³⁸ ἀνέπλασε δέ τι ἕτερον, συγκατατιθέμενος μέν πως ταῖς παραδόξοις δυνάμε-
σιν, ἃς Ἰησοῦς ἐποίησεν, ἐν αἷς τοὺς πολλοὺς ἔπεισεν ἀκολουθεῖν αὐτῷ ὡς
Χριστῷ, διαβάλλειν δ᾽ αὐτὰς βουλόμενος ὡς ἀπὸ μαγείας καὶ οὐ θείᾳ δυνάμει
γεγενημένας ... ⁶⁸ πλὴν ὡς χρήσιμον αὐτῷ εἰς τὰ προκείμενα τοῖς ἀπὸ μαγείας
ὁμοιοῖ τὰ περὶ Ἰησοῦ ἱστορούμενα. Καὶ ἦν ἂν ὅμοια, εἰ μέχρι ἀποδείξεως
ὁμοίως τοῖς μαγγανεύουσιν ἔφθανεν δείξας· νυνὶ δὲ οὐδεὶς μὲν τῶν γοήτων δι᾽
ὧν ποιεῖ ἐπὶ τὴν τῶν ἠθῶν ἐπανόρθωσιν καλεῖ τοὺς θεασαμένους οὐδὲ φόβῳ
θεοῦ παιδαγωγεῖ τοὺς καταπλαγέντας τὰ θεάματα, οὐδὲ πειρᾶται πείθειν οὕτω
ζῆν τοὺς ἰδόντας, ὡς δικαιωθησομένους ὑπὸ θεοῦ.

*Translation.* He (Celsus) next proceeds to bring a charge against the Savior
himself, alleging that "it was by magic that he was able to do the miracles
which he appeared to have performed; and because he foresaw that others
would know the same formulas as well and do the same thing, and boast that
they did so by the power of God, Jesus expelled them from his society."
³⁸ He (Celsus) invents something altogether different, admitting somehow the
miraculous works done by Jesus, by means of which he persuaded the multitude to follow him as the Messiah, yet he wants to discredit them as being
done by magic and not by divine power ... ⁶⁸ As it helps his purpose, he
(Celsus) compares the miracles related of Jesus to the results produced by
magic. There would indeed be a resemblance between them if Jesus, like
those who engage in magical tricks, had performed his works only for show.
But now there is not a single magician who uses his tricks to call his spectators to reform their manners, nor does he educate by the fear of God those
who are amazed at what they see, nor does he attempt to persuade the spectators to live as men who will be judged by God.

*Commentary.*⁴⁹⁵ In these and similar texts,⁴⁹⁶ Origen responds to Celsus'

---

⁴⁹⁵ Text: MIROSLAV MARCOVICH, Origenes. Contra Celsum libri VIII (VCSup 54; Leiden:
Brill, 2001). The direct tradition of *Contra Celsum* consists of the single manuscript
Vaticanus graecus 386, written in the 13th century; the indirect tradition is represented by an
anthology of passages from Origen's work in the *Philocalia*, composed in the 4th century by
Basil and Gregory Nazianzen, and by excerpts from Books I and II in the Cairo papyrus
88747, dated to the 7th century. The *Philocalia* does not contain *Cels.* 1.6, 38, 68. The most
authoritative edition of *Contra Celsum* was CHARLES DELARUE, Origenis opera omnia (4
vols.; Paris: Vincent, 1733–1759), 1:315–799, reproduced in JACQUES-PAUL MIGNE,
Patrologia Graeca (161 vols.; Paris: Imprimerie Catholique, 1857–1866), 11:637–1632. The
first critical edition was published by PAUL KOETSCHAU, Contra Celsum (Die griechischen
christlichen Schriftsteller der ersten drei Jahrhunderte. Origenes Werke I-II; Leipzig: Hinrichs,

assertion that Jesus was a sorcerer just like other men who went to Egypt to learn the tricks of the magical arts, yet none of whom claims to be the son of God (1.68). Celsus allows that Jesus performed incredible feats (παράδοξα) but argues that he did so by means of sorcery (γοητεία; 1.6), i.e., by magic (ἀπὸ μαγείας; 1.38, 68), and that he can be compared to others who engage in magical tricks (ὁμοίως τοῖς μαγγανεύουσιν; 1.68).[497] Celsus suggests that the claim that Jesus and his followers performed real miracles by the power of God is only an affectation (σεμνυνόμενοι; 1.6). Origen counters by arguing that Jesus did not perform miracles for show (μέχρι ἀποδείξεως, 1.68); rather than aiming at effects that can be merely seen with the eyes, Jesus' works are sincere and authentic since they cause people to change the way they live towards a commitment to divine righteousness. Origen wrote *Contra Celsum* c. A.D. 248.[498]

**(70)** *b. Sanh.* 43a

והתניא בערב הפסח תלאוהו לישו הנוצרי והכרוז יוצא לפניו ארבעים יום ישו הנוצרי יוצא
ליסקל על שכישף והסית והדיח את ישראל כל מי שיודע לו זכות יבא וילמד עליו ולא מצאו לו
זכות ותלאוהו בערב פסח אמר עולא ותסברא הנוצרי בר הפוכי זכות הוא מסית הוא ורחמנא
אמר לא תחמול ולא תכסה עליו שאני ישו הנוצרי דקרוב למלכות הוה:

*Translation.* It was taught: On the Eve of Passover they hanged Yeshu the Notzri. And the herald went out before him for forty days (before the execution took place) [saying], "Yeshu the Notzri will go out to be stoned for sorcery and misleading and enticing Israel [to idolatry]. Anyone who can say anything in his favor, let him come forward and plead on his behalf." But no one came forward in his favor, so they hung him on the Eve of the Passover! Ulla said, "Do you suppose that the Notzri was one for whom a defense could be made? He was a deceiver," and the Merciful says, You shall not spare and you shall not shield him (Deut 13:9). With Yeshu the Notzri, however, it was different, for he was close to the government."

1899). A new critical edition with a French translation was published by MARCEL BORRET, Origène, Contre Celse (5 vols.; Sources chrétiennes 132, 136, 147, 150, 227; Paris: Cerf, 1967–1969). The classic English translation is that of HENRY CHADWICK, Origen: Contra Celsum (orig; 1953; repr., Cambridge: Cambridge University Press, 1980). The direct quotations from Celsus' work are printed in bold and in the translation with quotation marks.

[496] See also Origen, *Contra Celsum* 1.71; 2.9, 14, 16; 3.1; 5.51; 6.42.

[497] The verb μαγγανεύω means "use charms, play tricks;" note the nouns ὁ μαγγανάριος "conjurer," ἡ μαγγανεία "trickery, esp. of magical arts," τὸ μαγγάνευμα "trickery," τὸ μάγγανον "means for charming or bewitching others," ὁ μαγγανευτής "impostor, quack."

[498] MARCOVICH, Origenes. Contra Celsum, ix; cf. Eusebius, *Hist. eccl.* 6.36.2.

*Commentary.*[499] In many Talmud editions this passage has been censored, as were other texts mentioning Jesus (almost all late anti-Christian polemics).[500] The discussion at this point relates to *m. Sanh.* 6:1 (No. 34), which described how a trial should end and how a herald walks before the condemned person on the way to execution, calling for last-minute evidence that may support the case of the defense. The discussion is opened by Rabbi Abaye (c. A.D. 320–350), whose comment is followed by a comment from an anonymous rabbi (והתניא, "it was taught") introducing the older tradition about Jesus' trial; he is probably a rabbi in Palestine c. A.D. 220–250. This tradition is commented by Rabbi Ulla bar Ishmael (c. A.D. 300), who had moved from Palestine to Babylonia. This is followed by a list of five disciples of Jesus who were also executed, and by two comments from Rabbi Joshua b. Levi (c. A.D. 220–250). The traditions of the trials of Jesus and of the disciples date to about A.D. 200. The references to the herald in the Mishnah and in the comment of the anonymous rabbi differ. According to the Mishnah, the herald's call for last-minute evidence follows the trial and occurs during the condemned man's walk to the place of execution. In the tradition about Jesus' trial, the herald's call occurs forty days before the trial (or on the fortieth day before the execution is carried out).[501] P. SCHÄFER explains that the tension is "solved" by Ulla: "Since Jesus had friends in high places, the Jews took extra precautions before executing him: they went beyond the letter of the law so none of his powerful friends could accuse them of executing an innocent man. Accordingly, this exchange seems to conclude, his case was not a halakhically valid precedent but rather a

---

[499] This is the text of the Munich Talmud (München Codex Hebraicus 95), the earliest full manuscript of the Talmud, produced in Paris in 1343 (STRACK / STEMBERGER / BOCKMUEHL, Introduction, 209); cf. HERMANN L. STRACK, Der Babylonische Talmud nach der einzigen vollständigen Handschrift München Codex Hebraicus 95, mittelst Facsimile-Lichtdruck vervielfältigt (2 vols.; Leiden: Sijthoff, 1912), 1:679. The translation is adapted from SCHACHTER and INSTONE-BREWER; cf. also GÜNTER MARK, Jesus 'Was Close to the Authorities': The Historical Background of a Talmudic Pericope, JTS 60 (2009): 437–466, 437–38. The reference *b. Sanh.* 43a is artificial: it refers to the folio page of Bomberg's edition (and subsequent editions) which, however, omits this passage.

[500] Cf. INSTONE-BREWER, Trial, 269–76, who provides the Hebrew text and a translation. The church began to censor the text of the Talmud after the Christian-Jewish disputation of Barcelona in 1263 (SCHÄFER, Jesus im Talmud, 263 = SCHÄFER, Jesus in the Talmud, 132). The Soncino edition (between 1484–1519) erased Jesus' name, while the edition of Bomberg (the Vilna edition, printed 1880–1886) omits the whole passage. Cf. INSTONE-BREWER, Trial, 275–80, for the following discussion of the context of the passage and of the dating of the edited tradition. Cf. MAIER, Jesus von Nazareth in der talmudischen Überlieferung, 219–35; BROWN, Death, 1:372–81; RAYMOND E. BROWN, The Babylonian Talmud on the Death of Jesus, NTS 43 (1997): 158–159; THEISSEN / MERZ, Der historische Jesus, 82–84 (= THEISSEN / MERZ, Historical Jesus, 74–76); SCHÄFER, Jesus im Talmud, 131–52 (= SCHÄFER, Jesus in the Talmud, 64–75); INSTONE-BREWER, Trial, 274–94.

[501] SCHÄFER, Jesus im Talmud, 133 (= SCHÄFER, Jesus in the Talmud, 65), who thinks the latter is more likely.

real exception; in other words, the Baraita dos [sic] not contradict the Mishnah."[502] D. INSTONE-BREWER argues that since no rabbi proposed a correction to either tradition, both traditions were being treated "as having comparable standing in terms of age and authority."[503]

The anonymous rabbi cites a tradition that gives three reasons for Jesus' execution, said to be stoning followed by hanging (in agreement with Deut 21:22–23): (1) Jesus practiced sorcery (שכישף);[504] (2) Jesus misled the people (והסית); (3) Jesus enticed Israel to idolatry (והדיח את ישראל). Ulla later confirms that the Notzri was a "deceiver" (הוא מסית). This agrees with the Mishnah, which includes the *mesit*, the *maddiakh*, and the *mekhashef* (sorcerer) in a longer list of crimes punishable by death. On the charge that Jesus was a *mesit* see No. 36, 38, 41, 42, 43, 45. According to the rabbis of the early third century, Jesus was not only a *mesit* who seduced an individual to idolatry,[505] and a *maddiakh* who publicly seduced the entire people of Israel to idolatry, but worse yet, he was a sorcerer who employed magical practices. This implies that "Jesus had real power, because rabbinic law did not prescribe death for magic tricks carried out by illusionists."[506]

Since the Mishnah connects idolatry with blasphemy, we can assume that the rabbis of the Bavli also ascribed to Jesus the offense of blasphemy.[507] The rabbis would have interpreted Jesus' assertion that he was the Messiah as claim that he was the Son of God and thus as blasphemy, and they could have interpreted the witnesses' statement that Jesus claimed to be able to destroy the Temple and rebuild it in three days as constituting sorcery. Jesus' practice of driving out demons, explicitly linked with messianic claims,[508] could be similarly interpreted.

The emphasis that the herald of the court announced Jesus' execution forty days before it took place underlines the notion that there were no witnesses in Jesus' defense coming forward, despite the fact that there was time to do so. Perhaps implied is the further thought that Jesus' repeated predictions of his

---

[502] SCHÄFER, Jesus in the Talmud, 65 (= SCHÄFER, Jesus im Talmud, 133); cf. MAIER, Jesus von Nazareth in der talmudischen Überlieferung, 223.

[503] INSTONE-BREWER, Trial, 279.

[504] JASTROW s.v. כשׁף (piel "to charm, practice sorcery") refers to the passage about Jesus "suppressed in later eds." in *b. Sanh.* 43a about ישׁו.

[505] MARK, Close to the Authorities, 466, argues that after the Council of Chalcedon, when the church became dominant, Ulla equates a *mesit* with a person who is "close to the authorities" and thus introduces a new meaning for the term: the *mesit* now "conveys the notion that *for Jews* (the Talmud has no quarrel with Gentiles who turn their back on paganism and join the church) Christianity is a form of idolatry, and all the rules that pertain to idolaters in the biblical and mishnaic sense also apply to Jewish converts to Christianity" (465).

[506] INSTONE-BREWER, Trial, 286.

[507] SCHÄFER, Jesus im Talmud, 138–39 (= SCHÄFER, Jesus in the Talmud, 68); for the following interpretation of the text see ibid. 139–45 (= ibid. 69–71).

[508] Matt 12:23-24; Mark 3:22; Luke 11:15.

death[509] serve to unmask him as a charlatan and false prophet, who claimed to prophesy an event that had already been announced by the Sanhedrin.

The description of Jesus' execution as stoning (ליסקל) followed by hanging (תלאוהו)[510] ignores the fact that Jesus was condemned by the Roman authorities to death by crucifixion (which the rabbis were aware of)[511] and underlines the Jewish perspective of Jesus' execution as that of a blasphemer and idolater who had seduced Israel. With this reading, the rabbis brought Jesus "home" into the Jewish people, only to decisively repudiate his claims and the claims of his followers: Jesus was indeed able to win over many people, but this was the result of the deception perpetrated by a Jewish heretic who has been tried, convicted, and executed according to Jewish initiative and to Jewish Law.

The Baraita mentions the precise day of Jesus' execution: He was hanged on the eve of Passover, which agrees with John 19:14. The Firenze manuscript of this Talmud passage states that Jesus' was executed on the eve of the Sabbath (i.e., Friday), which agrees with the evidence in all four Gospels.[512]

Ulla's comment that Jesus was close to the government agrees with the narrative in the Gospels that Pontius Pilatus wanted to save Jesus and have Barabbas crucified instead.[513] Ulla thus "exonerates the Roman government from the blame of Jesus' condemnation and consequently, adopting the Gospels' message, puts the thrust of the accusation on the Jews ... the later Babylonian discourse may not want to accept the Gospels' *blame* for Jesus' death; rather, like the Baraita but with different reasoning, it may want to convey the message: yes, the Roman governor wanted to set him free, but we did not give in. He was a blasphemer and idolater, and although the Romans probably could not care less, we insisted that he get what he deserved. We even convinced the Roman governor (or more precisely: forced him to accept) that this heretic and impostor needed to be executed – and we are proud of it."[514]

D. INSTONE-BREWER argues that the earliest core tradition – "on the Eve of Passover they hung Yeshu the Nozri for sorcery and enticing Israel [to idolatry]" – "originates from the actual charge sheet for the trial of Jesus. This would explain how it carried enough authority to ensure that all the sources

---

[509] Mark 8:31 par; Mark 9:30–31 par; Mark 10:32–34 par.

[510] The verb סקל denotes "to stone, put to death by stoning," and תלי/תלה means "to swing, raise;to suspend, hang" (JASTROW s.v. סקל, תלי, 1020, 1670).

[511] Cf. *Sifre Devarim* §221 on Deut 21:22 (No. 62). Cf. INSTONE-BREWER, Trial, 285, who suggests that "without any reference to another form of execution, the assumption in the First or Second Centurywould be that 'hang' refers to crucifixion."

[512] SCHÄFER, Jesus im Talmud, 147 n. 56 (= SCHÄFER, Jesus in the Talmud, 170 n. 55).

[513] Matt 27:17–23; Mark 15:9–15; Luke 23:13–25; John 18:38–19:16.

[514] SCHÄFER, Jesus in the Talmud, 73, 74 (= SCHÄFER, Jesus im Talmud, 150, 151), who continues: "What we then have here in the Bavli is a powerful confirmation of the New Testament Passion narrative, a creative rereading, however, that not only knows some of its distinct details but proudly proclaims Jewish responsibility for Jesus' execution" (ibid. 74).

maintain the reversed order of the charges, the unscriptural mode of execution and the impious trial date."[515]

## (71) *b. Sanhedrin* 107b

יומא חד הוה קא קרי קריאת שמע אתא לקמיה סבר לקבולי אחוי לי' בידיה הוא סבר מידחא דחי
לי' אזל זקף לבינתא והשתחוה לה אמר ליה הדר בך אמר ליה כך מקובלני ממך כל החוטא
ומחטיא את הרבים אין מספיקין בידו לעשות תשובה ואמר מר יש"ו כישף והסית והדיח את
ישראל.

*Translation.* One day he (Rabbi Yehoshua) was reciting the Shema, when Jesus came before him. He intended to receive him and made a sign to him. He (Jesus) thinking that it was to repel him, went, put up a brick, and worshipped it. "Repent," he (Rabbi Yehoshua) said to him. He replied, "I have thus learned from you: he who sins and causes others to sin is not afforded the means of repentance." And a Master has said, "Jesus the Nazarene practiced magic, he seduced and he deceived Israel."[516]

*Commentary.* This text confirms that the rabbis of the Bavli know and repeat a tradition according to which Jesus committed blasphemy (he worshipped[517] a brick) practiced sorcery (כישף) and seduced (הסית) and deceived (הדיח) Israel.[518] This tradition is linked here with Rabbi Yehoshua ben Perachia,[519] presented as Jesus' teacher, and with an unnamed authority.

---

[515] INSTONE-BREWER, Trial, 294; cf. the discussion ibid. 291–94. INSTONE-BREWER argues that the additions concerning the herald and the reference to stoning and to Jesus being charged as a misleader (*mesit*) were introduced later "as explanatory glosses to help the reader with problems which became particularly acute" in the latter half of the 2nd century. The traditions about the trials of Jesus and his disciples were brought into the Talmudic discussions early in the 3rd century and removed in the 15th and 16th centuries.

[516] SCHACHTER / FREEDMAN, Sanhedrin, 107b (c) n. 1, citing the uncensored edition.

[517] The term והשתחוה denotes prostration for prayer; cf. JASTROW s.v. השתחואה.

[518] INSTONE-BREWER, Trial, 280, thinks that *b. Sanh.* 107b originally had only two charges "because a scribe would be more inclined to add a missing charge in b.San.107b to harmonise with b.San.43a than to delete a charge."

[519] Yehoshua ben Perachia is one of the earliest Pharisaic authorities, belonging to the second pair of sages in *m. Abot* 1; STRACK / STEMBERGER, Einleitung, 72–73 (STRACK / STEMBERGER / BOCKMUEHL, Introduction, 64). Cf. LOUIS FINKELSTEIN, The Pharisaic Leadership after the Great Synagogue (170 B.C.E.- 135 C.E.), in The Cambridge History of Judaism. Vol. 2: The Hellenistic Age (ed. W. D. Davies and L. Finkelstein; Cambridge: Cambridge University Press, 1989), 229–244, who thinks that Yehoshua ben Perachia presided over the Pharisaic associations c. 142 B.C.; STRACK / BILLERBECK, Kommentar, 6:172, give 104–78 B.C. as date. NEUSNER, Rabbinic Traditions about the Pharisees, 1:84–86, argues that the story in *b. Sanh.* 107a cannot date before A.D. 100; he surmises that the last statement ("A Master has said ...") is probably the earliest element.

*Jesus as a sorcerer*. Since Jesus was accused during his ministry of being in league with the devil, it is not impossible that he was accused during the trial as a sorcerer or magician.[520] G. N. STANTON concludes his examination of the charge that Jesus was a magician by stating, "The allegations of the contemporary opponents of Jesus confirm that he was seen by many to be a disruptive threat to social and religious order. His claims to act and speak on the basis of a special relationship to God were rightly perceived to be radical. For some they were so radical that they had to be undermined by an alternative explanation of their source."[521] The trial accounts do not suggest that such a charge was level against Jesus.[522]

## 1.8  Abuse of Prisoners

All four Gospels state that Jesus was mistreated both during the interrogation and after the guilty verdict in the Sanhedrin: He was spat on in the face (Mark 14:65 / Matt 26:67), blindfolded (Mark 14:65 / Luke 22:64), and struck (Mark 14:65 / Matt 26:67 / Luke 22:63; cf. John 18:22: struck in the face). The following text confirms the practice, if not legality, of abusing prisoners who stand before a Jewish court of law.

**(72)**  Josephus, *Bellum judaicum* 6.302

τῶν δὲ ἐπισήμων τινὲς δημοτῶν ἀγανακτήσαντες πρὸς τὸ κακόφημον συλλαμβάνουσι τὸν ἄνθρωπον καὶ πολλαῖς αἰκίζονται πληγαῖς. ὁ δὲ οὔθ᾽ ὑπὲρ αὐτοῦ φθεγξάμενος οὔτε ἰδίᾳ πρὸς τοὺς παίοντας, ἃς καὶ πρότερον φωνὰς βοῶν διετέλει.

*Translation*. Some of the distinguished citizens who were angry at these evil words arrested him and maltreated him with many blows. But he did not utter a sound, neither on his own behalf nor specifically against those who were striking him, only continuing to yell the same shouts as before.

*Commentary*. For the arrest and interrogation of Jesus ben Ananias who uttered prophecies of doom against Jerusalem and the Temple, see No. 65. After the Jewish leaders arrested (συλλαμβάνουσι) the peasant who prophesied doom for Jerusalem and the Temple, they maltreat him (αἰκίζονται) by

---

[520] Most recently JOHN W. WELCH, Miracles, Maleficium, and Maiestas in the Trial of Jesus, in Jesus and Archaeology (ed. J. H. Charlesworth; Grand Rapids: Eerdmans, 2006), 349–383, who argues that Jesus was thus not convicted of the crime of *maiestas* but of *maleficium* (and *seditio*).

[521] STANTON, Magician, 175–80, quotation 180.

[522] See the critique of BLINZLER, Prozeß, 188.

striking (παίοντας) him with "many blows" (πολλαῖς πληγαῖς), i.e., repeatedly, evidently during the interrogation.

## 1.9  Transfer of Court Cases

Literary and documentary sources illustrate the complex relationship between the Roman provincial administration and the local courts. Text No. 73 illustrates the transfer of court cases from a local Egyptian court to the Greek courts of the Ptolemaic administration. Text No. 74 demonstrates the existence of a traditional "national" law in the Roman provinces, in this case "the law of the Egyptians," which could be read before Roman judges. The case of Jesus ben Ananias (No. 75) demonstrates the cooperation between the local Jewish authorities in Jerusalem and the Roman governor.

**(73)** P. Helsinki I 1

[βασιλεῖ Πτ]ολεμαίωι καὶ β[α]σι[λ]ίσ[σηι Κλεοπάτραι τῆι ἀδελφῆι]
[Θεοῖς Ἐπι]φανές[ι] καὶ Εὐ[χ]αρ[ίς]τοις [χαίρειν    vacat } ]
[π]αρ᾽ Ἀσκληπι[ά]δου. ἀδ[ικοῦμαι ὑπὸ Πεταῦτος    ca. 8    ἐκ-]
[λα]βόντος γὰρ μοῦ μετ᾽ ἄλλων τὴν ἕκ[την τῶν παραδείσων ? τῆς]
5 [Δι]καίου τοῦ Ἀρσινοίτου νομοῦ τῶι ἔτει ι[· καὶ Πεταῦτος τοῦ]
[πρ]ογεγραμμένου μετέχοντός μοι τῆ[σ αὐτῆς ὠνῆς πρὸς τὸ τέ-]
[τ]αρτον μέρος, περὶ ὧν καὶ ὅρκον ἐγραψάμεθ[α καὶ ὑπεκεχειρο-]
[γ]ράφει ἕκαστος ἡμῶν τοῖς ἰδίοις γράμμασι, κ[αὶ τούτου μὲν]
[ο]ὐχ ὑπομένοντος διεγγυῆσαι τοῦ ἐπιβ[άλλοντος αὐτῶι]
10 μέρους τετάρτου, ἀλλὰ κελεύοντος πα[ρ᾽ αὐτοῦ δανείζεσθαι ?]
οὗ ἂν ἐγγυήσηται καὶ πραχθῆ ὑπὲρ ἡμ[ῶν Αὖγχις ἡ γυνή μου,]
περὶ ὧν καὶ ἐγραψά[μ]ην αὐτῶι συγγραφὴ[ν δανείου χαλκοῦ]
(ταλάντων) ζ, καὶ τούτο[υ τετε]λεσμένου τὸ διε[γγύημα αὐτοῦ κατ-]
εστήσαμε[ν . . . . . .]ν καὶ ἄλλων ἀντ[ὶ        ca. 14        ]
15 ἐ . . . . . [ . . . . ] . . . . σὺν τῆι αὐτοῦ ἀπομ[ο]ί[ραι . . . . ]
[ . . . . .] . . . . [ . . . . . . ] χαλκοῦ (τάλαντα) ε Γωκη, ὥστε ἀπέχε[ιν]
[τοῦτο]. νυνὶ δὲ ἡ[μᾶς δια]σειόμενος [δια]σευομενος καὶ συκοφαντῶν πεποί-
ηται καταβόησιν ἐπὶ τῶν λαοκριτῶν κατ᾽ Αὔγχιος τῆς
γυναικός μου φάμενος ταύτην ἔγγυον γεγενῆσθαι, διὰ τῆς
20 τοῦ δανείου συγγραφῆς ἧς ἐγραψάμην αὐτῶι μετὰ τῶν μετόχων,
τοῦ ἐπιβάλλοντός μοι μέρους τρίτου. ἐπεὶ οὖν τὸ δάνειον
ὃ ἀπαιτεῖ τὴν ἄνθρωπόν μου ἀντὶ τῆς ἐγγύης ἧς ἐνεγύησα κ[α-]
θ᾽ ἡμᾶς (?) ἐστιν {εισιν} ἣν καὶ κεκόμισται, ἐπισυκοφαντῶν δὲ
καθέστακεν ταύτην ἐπὶ τοὺς λαοκρίτας, ἀξιῶ ὧν συν-

25 ἐπείγων καὶ καθήκο<ν>τός μοι ἐπὶ τῶν τὰ προσοδικὰ κρινόντ[ων]
χρηματιστῶν τὸ δίκαιον λαμβάνειν καὶ διδόναι, καὶ ἔστιν
τὰ προγεγραμμένα ἀπὸ τῆς προσόδου τῆς Φιλαδέλφου,
ἀποστεῖλαι μοῦ τὸ ὑπ[ό]μνημα ἐπ᾽ αὐτούς, ὡς ἂν χρηματί-
σαντες αὐτὸ εἰς κρίς[ι]ν ἀνακαλέσωνται τὸν Πεταῦν,
30 καὶ ἐὰν ἀποδείξωμεν μετεσχηκότα ἡμῖν τὴν ἕκτην
καὶ ἀπέχοντος αὐτοῦ τὸ διεγγύημα ὑπὲρ οὗ καὶ ἐγραψά-
μεθα αὐτῶι τὴν προγεγραμμένην δανείου συγγραφὴν
συνκρίνωσιν οἱ χρηματισταὶ ἀποτεῖσαι αὐ[τὸν . . . . ]
[. . . . . τὸ ἐπι]βάλλον αὐτῶι μέρος τέταρτον [ ca. 8]
35 [                    ]ν προσδέχουσι δ[
[                 τὴν τοῦ] δανείου συγγραφὴ[ν      ]

]  . . [ . . . ] . . [

*Translation.*

[To king Pt]olemaeus and queen [Cleopatra, his sister,]
[to the gods man]ifest and blessed, [greetings]
from Asclepiades. [I am wronged by Petaus ... ]
since I with others contracted the six[th-part (tax) on gardens for]
5  Dikaiou (Nesus) in the Arsinoite nome in the 10th year [and Petaus, the]
aforementioned, shared with me the [same sale to a fo]urth
part, concerning which we wrote an oath [and]
each of us signed (it) with his own letters, and [this (Petaus), however,]
did not submit to give security for the fourth
10 part [which fell to him,] but he told (us) [to borrow from himself,] for
whom [my wife Aynchis] should give security and be made actionable for
us,
concerning which I wrote for him a contract [for a loan of]
7 [bronze] talents and, this done, we established [his surety]
... and other instead of ...
15 ... with his portion ...
... of 5 bronze (talents), 3828 (drachmae) so that he repay
[this.] But now intimidating and falsely accusing [us]
he has laid a charge before the *laokritai* against Aynchis,
my wife, saying that she had become the one giving surety, by the
20 contract of loan which I wrote for him with my partners,
for the third part which falls to me. Since, therefore, the loan, which
he demands from my woman against the surety which I guaranteed,
is against us, which also he has received, and falsely accusing
has stood her before the *laokritai*, I request, since I
25 am eager and it is appropriate for me before the *chrematistai* who judge
matters of revenue to receive and give justice – and the

aforewritten is from the revenue (of the village) of Philadelphia –
to send my petition to them, that deliberating
on this they might summons Petaus to judgment,
30 and if we demonstrate that he shared with us the sixth-part (tax)
and received the surety for which we wrote
for him the aforementioned contract of loan
the *chrematistai* might conclude that he repay ...
... the fourth part which falls to him ...
35 ... they accept ...
... [the] contract of loan ...
......

*Commentary.*[523] The papyrus, taken from mummy cartonage, dates to 194–
180 B.C. The text concerns a dispute between Asklepiades, the petitioner, and
Petaus regarding a partnership that had been formed to collect taxes for the
village of Dikaiou Nesus. The agreement (μετοχή) included the subscription
of each partner (Aynchis, the wife of Asklepiades, was the guarantor of the
portion of her spouse's loan) and an oath, formalized in a handwritten agreement (συγγραφή). "It was usual for the collection of taxes to be sold for discrete areas, village by village. An individual won the contract from the government to collect the tax (ἀρχώνης), but he then drew in others as partners
(μέτοχοι). The contract from the government's point of view devolved on the
ἀρχώνης, but the partners could participate in the business by widening the
property base and security of the sale. However, they were not active participants in the actual collection of taxes."[524] Petaus, rather than providing a guarantor for his portion of the loan, seems to have made a loan of seven talents to
Asklepiades and the two other partners. Petaus then sued Aynchis before the
*luokritai* for the sum she had guaranteed. S. R. LLEWELYN comments, "Why
he should want to do this is unclear. Perhaps he thought that he might be able
by this procedure to limit his liability to the state for any shortfall in collection
... If so, Asclepiades was justified in his fear, for in *ll.* 16–17 we learn that
only 5 talents 3828 drachmae were repaid ... In other words, there was a shortfall of 1 talent 2172 drachmae between the value of the guarantee (seven talents) which secured a fourth portion of the purchase price and the amount collected ... Petaus pressed his case and sought distraint against Asclepiades'
guarantor for his portion of the loan, an amount (a third part of the value of
the loan, i.e., 2 talents 2,000 drachmae, *l.* 21) which would more than cover

---

[523] Editio princeps by HENRIK ZILLIACUS in JAAKKO FRÖSÉN, ed., Papyri Helsingienses I.
Ptolemäische Urkunden (P. Hels. I) (CHL 80; Helsinki: Societas Scientiarum Fennica, 1986),
18–22 (No. 1), with German translation and notes; cf. STEPHEN R. LLEWELYN, in HORSLEY
and LLEWELYN, New Documents, 9:45–47 (No. 18), who also provides a translation, which is
used here; discussion of the text ibid. 47–53.
[524] LLEWELYN, in HORSLEY and LLEWELYN, New Documents, 9:48.

his loss."[525] The legal situation is not entirely clear, partly due to the fragmentary preservation of lines 13–17. D. KALTSAS suggests on the basis of lines 10–11 that Petaus suggested to his fellow contractors that he be a guarantor of the loan rather than a leaseholder, a change of status perhaps triggered by the desire to minimize the financial risk of the contract to collect taxes. As guarantor, he could only loose the seven talents for which he stood surety (or real estate or houses, if such had been put down as bond). As lease-holder, he could loose much more; he could be made responsible for the entire deficit of the year. It is unclear why Asklepiades and the two other partners agreed to Petaus' offer. The loan seems to have been the surety for Petaus as the guarantor.[526]

The editor, HENDRIK ZILLIACUS, regards the text as a petition (ἔντευξις, Enteuxis) addressed to Ptolemy V Epiphanes and Queen Cleopatra, which accounts for the reconstruction of the damaged first two lines of the papyrus. S. R. LLEWELYN comments, "It was usual Ptolemaic practice to address petitions to the king. The personal jurisdiction of the king for the most part was concerned with matters of fiscal governance and state security, but it also took a direct part in legal matters from the private domain ... But from the second half of the third century the addressing of petitions to the king became a mere formality as they were submitted to the office of the *strategos* and were directly dealt with there."[527] In view of the language of the petition in line 28, this has been disputed.[528] Rather than submitting his Enteuxis, nominally addressed to the king, directly to the *chrematistai*, the petitioner chose to take his petition to a higher official and ask him to forward the petition to the *chrematistai*, who should summon Petaus to "judgment" or "trial" (κρίσις).[529] The reason for the unusual procedure may have been Asklepiades' hope for a speedy resolution: He wanted to terminate the legal proceedings before the *laokritai*, hoping that the intervention of a higher official was more likely than the cooperation of the Eisagogeus of the *chrematistai*.

The case involves the issue of competing jurisdictions of the indigenous

---

[525] LLEWELYN, in HORSLEY and LLEWELYN, New Documents, 9:48, 49.

[526] DEMOKRITOSS KALTSAS, Ein Streit zwischen Epergoi in P. Hels 1, ZPE 142 (2003): 214–220, 217–18.

[527] LLEWELYN, in HORSLEY and LLEWELYN, New Documents, 9:47, with reference to HANS JULIUS WOLFF, Das Justizwesen der Ptolemäer (Zweite, durchgesehene Auflage; orig. 1962; repr., MBPAR 44; München: Beck, 1970), 8, 10.

[528] GREGG W. SCHWENDNER, Literary and Non-literary Papyri from the University of Michigan Collection, Ph.D. Dissertation (University of Michigan, 1988), 106; KALTSAS, Streit, 214; the following point ibid. The name of the official is mentioned in line 1, which, according to SCHWENDNER and KALTSAS, was wrongly restored by ZILLIACUS.

[529] CHRISTINA M. KREINECKER, 2. Thessaloniker (PKNT 3; Göttingen: Vandenhoeck & Ruprecht, 2010), 125, refers to P. Hels. I 1, line 28–29, to illustrate the meaning of κρίσις as "Prozess" (trial").

Egyptian court and the Greek (Ptolemaic) court.[530] Petaus initiated his legal action before the (Egyptian) court of the *laokritai*. Asklepiades attempts to have the case transferred to the (Greek) court of the *chrematistai*. The *laokritai* were boards of Egyptian judges; the proceedings before these courts were conducted in the vernacular. The judgment conformed to the enchoric law. The *chrematistai* were travelling groups of judges appointed by the king to provide direct royal relief to the population living in the *chora* (i.e., country districts, the territory of Egypt outside of the three Greek cities of Ptolemaic Egypt). By about 200 B.C. a local board of *chrematistai* served in each administrative district (nome) as a permanent authority, representing the king, whose διαγράμματα, προστάγματα and πολιτιλοὶ νόμοι were to be obeyed. "The court of the *laokritai* continued to function until the early first century but increasingly under the encroachment of the *chrematistai* ... the individual was not assigned to a legal system on the basis of his or her racial origin as such, but rather each system was attached to a particular court by the will of the king. Individuals, however, tended to litigate in accord with their ethnic laws and thus before the court which respected them. But this was not always possible for the mixed population of Egypt where persons of different ethnicity became parties to all forms of legal relationship. Also, at the same time as the growing encroachment of the court of the *chrematistai*, the documentary evidence shows the distinctions between the legal system being blurred. One finds contracting parties at will availing themselves of legal documents and practices of either Greek or Egyptian provenance ... In the event of a dispute and trial, it further appears that a party was not constrained to argue the case within one particular legal system but might actually draw on rules from various legal systems."[531] It appears that Petaus lodged his complaint before the (Egyptian) court of the *laokritai* because both he and Aynchis, the guarantor, were Egyptian (as suggested by their names). Asklepiades wants to transfer the case to the court of the *chrematistai*, not because of his ethnicity but, at least according to the reasons stated in lines 25–27, because the court of the *chrematistai* dealt with matters related to state revenue.[532] If we read instead of ἀξιῶ ὧν συν|επείγων, with D. KALTSAS, ἀξιῶ ὧν των | ἐπέργων ("I request, since I am one of the Epergoi"), Asklepiades describes himself as a financial official: Papyrus texts use the term *epergos* for (lower) finance official and also leaseholders of the collection of taxes.[533]

S. R. LLEWELYN compares "the complexity of multiple legal systems" in Roman Egypt with "the overlapping jurisdictions of Roman governors and the indigenous Jewish court, the Sanhedrin," evident in the legal procedures

---

[530] Cf. LLEWELYN, in HORSLEY and LLEWELYN, New Documents, 9:50–52.

[531] LLEWELYN, in HORSLEY and LLEWELYN, New Documents, 9:51, who relies on WOLFF, Justizwesen der Ptolemäer.

[532] LLEWELYN, in HORSLEY and LLEWELYN, New Documents, 9:52.

[533] KALTSAS, Streit, 215–16.

against Jesus and Paul. The legal competence of the Jewish court in capital cases must be seen in this context. "If the court was not competent to sentence a prisoner to death, one can well understand why Jesus might be handed over to the Roman governor to decide his fate once he had been found guilty by the Sanhedrin."[534]

**(74)** P. Oxy. II 237 Col. VII, 29–38

Τιτιανός· διαφέρει παρὰ τίνι βούλεται εἶναι ἡ γεγαμημένη. ἀνέγνων.
σεσημ(είωμαι). ἐξ ὑπομ(νηματισ)μῶν
Πακωνίου Φήλικος ἐπιστρατήγου. (ἔτους) ιη θεοῦ Ἀδριανοῦ, Φαῶφι ιζ, ἐν τῇ
    παρὰ ἄνω Σεβεννύτου, ἐπὶ τῶν κατὰ Φλαυήσιος
Ἀμμούνιος ἐπὶ παρούσῃ Ταειχήκει θυγατρὶ αὐτοῦ πρὸς Ἥρωνα Πεταήσιος.
    Ἰσίδωρος ῥήτωρ ὑπὲρ Φλαυήσιος εἶπεν, τὸν οὖν αἰτιώμενον
ἀποσπάσαι βουλόμενον τ[ὴ]ν θυγατέρα αὐτοῦ συνοικοῦσαν τῷ ἀντιδίκῳ
    δεδικάσθαι ὑπογύως πρὸς αὐτὸν ἐπὶ τοῦ ἐ[πι]στρατήγου
καὶ ὑπερτεθεῖσθαι τὴν δίκην ὑμεῖν ἵνα ἀναγνωσθῇ ὁ τῶν Αἰγυπτίω[ν νό]μος.
    Σεούρου καὶ Ἡλιοδώρου ῥητόρων ἀποκρειναμένων
Τειτιανὸν τὸν ἡγεμονεύσαντα ὁμοίας ὑποθέσεως ἀκούσαντα [ἐξ] Αἰγυπτια-
    κῶν προσώπων μὴ ἠκολουθηκέναι τῇ τοῦ νό-
μου ἀπανθρωπίᾳ ἀλλὰ τ[ῇ] ἐπι[νοί]ᾳ τῆς παιδός, εἰ βούλεται παρὰ τ[ῷ ἀνδρὶ]
    μένειν, Πακώνιος Φῆλιξ· ἀναγνωσθήτω ὁ ν[ό]μ[ος. ἀ]να-
γνωσθέντος Πακώνιος [Φῆ]λιξ· ἀνάγνωται καὶ τὸν Τειτιανοῦ ὑπομ[ν]ημα-
    τισμόν. Σεούρου ῥήτορος ἀναγν[όντος], ἐπὶ τοῦ ιβ (ἔτους) Ἁ[δρια]νοῦ
Καίσαρος τοῦ κυρίου, Παῦν[ι] η, Πακώνιος Φῆλιξ· καθὼς ὁ κράτιστος
    Τ[ειτ]ιανὸς ἔκρεινεν, πεύσονται τῆς γυναικός· καὶ ἐκέλευ[σε]ν δι' [ἑρ]μη-
νέως αὐτὴν ἐνεχθῆν[α]ι, τί βούλεται. εἰπούσης, παρὰ τῷ ἀνδρὶ μένειν,
    Π[α]κώνιος Φῆλιξ ἐκέλευσεν ὑπομνηματι[σ]θῆναι.

*Translation.* Extract from the minutes of Flavius Titianus, epistrategos. The 18th year of the deified Hadrian, Phaophi 17, at the court in the upper division of the Sebennyte nome, in the case of Phlauesis, son of Ammounis, in the presence of his daughter Taeichekis, against Heron, son of Petaësis. Isidorus, advocate for Phlauesis, said that the plaintiff therefore, wishing to take away his daughter who was living with the defendant, had recently brought an action against him before the epistrategos and the case had been deferred in order that the law of the Egyptians might be read. Severus and Heliodorus, advocates (for Heron), replied that the late governor Titianus heard a similar plea advanced by Egyptian witnesses, and that his judgement was in accordance not with the inhumanity of the law but with the choice of the daughter, whether she wished to remain with her husband. Paconius Felix said, "Let the

---

[534] LLEWELYN, in HORSLEY and LLEWELYN, *New Documents,* 9:53.

law be read." When it had been read, Paconius Felix said, "Read also the minute of Titianus." Severus the advocate having read "The 12th year of Hadrianus Caesar the lord, Payni 8 (etc.)," Paconius Felix said, "In accordance with the decision of the esteemed Titianus, they shall find out from the woman," and he ordered that she should be asked through an interpreter what was her choice. On her replying "To remain with my husband," Paconius Felix ordered that the judgement should be entered on the minutes.

*Commentary.*[535] The long papyrus P. Oxy. II 237, dated A.D. 186, is a petition of Dionysia to Pomponius Faustianus, the governor of Egypt, against her father Chaeremon, a former gymnasiarch of Oxyrhynchus, who had dissolved her marriage and taken her dowry against her will. In support of her case, Dionysia, who argues that the wife alone should decide the course of her marriage, provides four precedents, three of which are extracts from the minutes of court proceedings in which a Roman judge had ruled against a father who wanted to dissolve a marriage.[536] The second case quoted in Dionysia's petition is the case before the epistrategos Paconius Felix (in A.D. 133), who provides an interpreter when needed (δι' [ἑρ]μηνέως) and allows the content of "the law of the Egyptians" (ὁ τῶν Αἰγυπτίων νόμος) to be read, which the governor T. Flavius Titianus (in the first case quoted) had ignored due to its alleged inhumanity. The fact that "the law of the Egyptians" could be *read* indicates that it was a written collection "of precepts of different origin – both Greek and Egyptian – that was adhered to in early Roman Egypt," created in order "to make provincial practices accessible to Roman judges whenever they heard cases involving non-Roman litigants. The details of Dionysia's petition indicate that this law "was an object of ongoing study, interpretation, and development by a group of local experts who acted as consultants in provincial courts of law."[537]

---

[535] Editio princeps of Cols. IV–VIII in BERNARD P. GRENFELL / ARTHUR S. HUNT, eds., The Oxyrhynchus Papyri (London: Egypt Exploration Fund, 1898–), 2:152–64; translation adapted from ibid. 170–71.

[536] For a description and analysis of the case cf. GRENFELL / HUNT, The Oxyrhynchus Papyri, 2:141–51. The phrase ἐξ ὑπομ(νηματισ)μῶν ("extract from the minutes") is taken by RAPHAEL TAUBENSCHLAG, The Law of Greco-Roman Egypt in the Light of the Papyri 332 B.C. – 640 A.D. (Second Edition, Revised and Enlarged. Ristampa Anastatica; orig. 1955, 1944; repr., Milan: Cisalpino Goliardica, 1972), 520 with n. 10, to indicate that the sentence "was dictated and communicated to the parties."

[537] Cf. URI YIFTACH-FIRANKO, Law in Greco-Roman Egypt: Hellenization, Fusion, Romanization, in The Oxford Handbook of Papyrology (ed. R. S. Bagnall; Oxford: Oxford University Press, 2009), 541–560, here 551, 552. For the "law of the Egyptians" cf. JOSEPH MODRZEJEWSKI, Droit impérial et traditions locales dans l'Égypte romaine (Aldershot: Brookfield, 1990); HANS JULIUS WOLFF, Das Recht der griechischen Papyri Ägyptens in der Zeit der Ptolemäer und des Prinzipats. Band 1: Bedingungen und Triebkräfte der Rechtsentwicklung (HdA X/5.1; München: Beck, 2002), 74–75, 117–21. WOLFF, ibid. 76 n. 22 and 119, points to line 35 for his point that the Romans rejected the application of the Egyptian

When Pontius Pilatus counters the Jewish leaders' demand that he should crucify Jesus with the statement, "I find no basis for a charge against him" (John 19:6, NIV), the Jewish leaders in Jerusalem affirm, "We have a law (ἡμεῖς νόμον ἔχομεν) and according to that law, he ought to die because he has claimed to be the Son of God" (John 19:7). The reference to their own νόμος is likely more than a means to exert moral pressure on the Roman governor.[538] It may well be a reference not simply to the Mosaic Torah[539] but to the non-Roman legal precepts, practices, and interpretations of the law of the Jews that were normative for the local courts of law. While Pontius Pilatus would not have been obligated to follow the law of the Jews, it was certainly appropriate for Jewish participants in a legal case before Roman authorities to cite the tradition of the law of the Jews and relevant precedents.

**(75)** Josephus, *Bellum judaicum* 6.303–305

νομίσαντες δὲ οἱ ἄρχοντες, ὅπερ ἦν, δαιμονιώτερον τὸ κίνημα τἀνδρὸς ἀνάγουσιν αὐτὸν ἐπὶ τὸν παρὰ Ῥωμαίοις ἔπαρχον. ³⁰⁴ ἔνθα μάστιξι μέχρι ὀστέων ξαινόμενος οὔθ' ἱκέτευσεν οὔτ' ἐδάκρυσεν, ἀλλ' ὡς ἐνῆν μάλιστα τὴν φωνὴν ὀλοφυρτικῶς παρεγκλίνων πρὸς ἑκάστην ³⁰⁵ ἀπεκρίνατο πληγήν "αἰαὶ Ἱεροσολύμοις." τοῦ δ' Ἀλβίνου διερωτῶντος, οὗτος γὰρ ἔπαρχος ἦν, τίς εἴη καὶ πόθεν, καὶ διὰ τί ταῦτα φθέγγοιτο, πρὸς ταῦτα μὲν οὐδ' ὁτιοῦν ἀπεκρίνατο, τὸν δὲ ἐπὶ τῇ πόλει θρῆνον εἴρων οὐ διέλειπεν, μέχρι καταγνοὺς μανίαν ὁ Ἀλβῖνος ἀπέλυσεν αὐτόν.

*Translation.* Thus the magistrates believed, as was indeed the case, that the man was impelled by a supernatural impulse, and they brought him before the prefect appointed by the Romans. ³⁰⁴ There he was flogged to the bone with whips, but he did not beg for mercy nor did he shed tears; rather, he responded to each blow with the most mournful modulation that he could give to his voice, "Woe to Jerusalem!" ³⁰⁵ When Albinus (he was the prefect) asked him, who he was, where he was from, and why he uttered these cries, he did not

law as "inhumane" since the early 2nd century; for the Romans, the guiding legal principle was *aequitas*. RANON GEDALIA KATZOFF, Sources of Law in Roman Egypt: The Role of the Prefect, ANRW II.13 (1980): 807–844, 843, argues that the epistrategos relied not on the binding force of precedent but on the key argument of the inhumanity of the law of the Egyptians, even though he allowed it to be read in court.

[538] BLINZLER, Prozeß, 249; see ibid. 331 n. 31 for the comment that the law in question is the Jewish law, not the Roman law, as ZEITLIN, Who Crucified Jesus?, 168, asserts.

[539] ULRICH WILCKENS, Das Evangelium nach Johannes (NTD 4; Göttingen: Vandenhoeck & Ruprecht, 1998), 285. C. K. BARRETT, The Gospel According to St. John (Second Edition; London/Philadelphia: SPCK/Westminster, 1978), 541, interprets in terms of "the law of blasphemy" (with reference to Lev 24:16; *m. Sanh.* 7:5; *m. Ker.* 1:1-2); cf. BROWN, John, 877; ANDREAS KÖSTENBERGER, John (BECNT; Grand Rapids: Baker, 2004), 533 with n. 62, who refers to Lev 24:16 for the "local law" that a Roman prefect was responsible for maintaining.

answer him, but continued his lament over the city until Albinus pronounced him mad and let him go.

*Commentary.* The context of this passage has been discussed in No. 65. The measures of the Jewish leadership to silence Jesus ben Ananias are unsuccessful. Since the man continues to predict calamity for Jerusalem and the Temple, they take him (ἀνάγουσιν αὐτὸν) to Albinus, the Roman governor of Judea (A.D. 62–64; see No. 3). C. RIEDO-EMMENEGGER explains this transfer with the principle of subsidiarity:[540] "die Mitverantwortung der lokalen Behörden für die öffentliche Ruhe [ist] als *Eigenverantwortung* konzipiert. Erst dort, wo die Mittel der lokalen Behörden nicht ausreichen, greift die römische Besatzungsmacht gemäss dem Subsidiaritätsprinzip mit härteren Mitteln bis hin zum militärischen Einsatz ein."[541] The local authorities are duty-bound to prevent riots and re-establish law and order in case of disturbances; they assist the Roman prefect in matters of criminal justice as the authority responsible for arresting and imprisoning criminals and transferring them to the Roman authorities. Josephus relates four elements of the trial before Albinus. (1) Jesus ben Ananias is brutally flogged (μάστιξι μέχρι ὀστέων ξαινόμενος), which may suggest that his proclamation of doom for Jerusalem and the Temple was regarded as a capital offense.[542] (2) Albinus interrogates Jesus with the purpose of establishing his identity (τίς εἴη), origin (πόθεν), and motivation for his activity (διὰ τί ταῦτα φθέγγοιτο). (3) Albinus pronounces him to be mad (καταγνοὺς μανίαν) because he continues to shout oracles of doom. (4) Albinus releases him (ὁ Ἀλβῖνος ἀπέλυσεν αὐτόν). P. EGGER believes that the scene reports *coercitio* measures rather than a formal trial.[543] Roman magistrates had the authority to impose penal *coercitio* measures on non-Roman provincials at their discretion.[544] This is not convincing, given the interrogation and the meaning of the verb καταγινώσκειν which describes legal verdicts in *B. J.* 2.245; 7.154. The verdict of the prefect is binding for the local authorities: Despite the fact that Jesus continues to proclaim oracles of doom for Jerusalem and the Temple (6.306–309), he is not rearrested. The beatings (6.307) are evidently the actions of individuals who want to silence Jesus.[545]

---

[540] RIEDO-EMMENEGGER, Provokateure, 242. Cf. MÜLLER, Kapitalgerichtsbarkeit, 70, who speaks of an "etablierter Instanzenzug ... der keine Zufälligkeiten und Improvisationen zu erkennen gibt." CATCHPOLE, Trial, 245, who interprets Jesus ben Ananias' offense as solely religious, has been criticized for missing the political implications of prophecies of doom; cf. RIEDO-EMMENEGGER, ibid. 242 n. 1927; also EGGER, Crucifixus, 145 n. 590; THEISSEN / MERZ, Der historische Jesus, 520.

[541] RIEDO-EMMENEGGER, Provokateure, 108; the following comment ibid.

[542] Cf. BLINZLER, Prozeß, 243; STROBEL, Stunde, 24–25; THEISSEN / MERZ, Der historische Jesus, 520.

[543] EGGER, Crucifixus, 146.

[544] Cf. CHRISTIAN G. GIZEWSKI, Coercitio, BNP 3 (2003): 508–509.

[545] Cf. EGGER, Crucifixus, 146 n. 595; RIEDO-EMMENEGGER, Provokateure, 242.

The cooperation of the Jewish authorities in Jerusalem with the Roman governor in the case of a prophet who announced a calamity befalling Jerusalem and the Temple during an already tense festival period helps us, as S. MASON asserts, "to imagine some cooperation between the Jewish leadership and the Roman governor in the trial of Jesus."[546] K. MÜLLER explains that Jesus' prophecy, which announced the destruction of the Temple,[547] had to trigger the cooperation between the Jewish and Roman authorities that Josephus reports in the case of Jesus ben Ananus. In both cases, the arrest by the Jewish authorities and the examination by the Sanhedrin was followed by a formal decision to transfer the prisoner to court of the Roman prefect who carried out his own investigation and issued a decisive verdict.[548] P. BILDE argues that the Jewish authorities, in their desire to bring the proclamation of this eschatological prophet to an end, sought the help of the Roman authorities to resolve a conflict that was an internal Jewish conflict; they were unsuccessful, however, unlike the Jewish authorities in the case of Jesus of Nazareth.[549]

---

[546] MASON, Josephus and the New Testament, 188.

[547] Cf. Mark 14:56–61 / Matt 26:60-62; see Mark 13:2, 14–20 / Matt 24:2, 15–21; Luke 21:6, 20–24; Mark 15:29 / Matt 27:40; Acts 6:14; John 2:19.

[548] MÜLLER, Kapitalgerichtsbarkeit, 83.

[549] PER BILDE, Der Konflikt zwischen Gaius Caligula und den Juden über die Aufstellung einer Kaiserstatue im Tempel von Jerusalem, in Kult und Macht. Religion und Herrschaft im syro-palästinensischen Raum. Studien zu ihrer Wechselbeziehung in hellenistisch-römischer Zeit (ed. A. Lykke and F. T. Schipper; WUNT 2/319; Tübingen: Mohr Siebeck, 2011), 9–48, 41–42.

Part 2

# The Roman Trial before Pontius Pilatus

Judea was placed under direct Roman rule in A.D. 6, when Augustus removed Archelaos, who had ruled the southern part of the client kingdom of Herod I, his father, since 4 B.C. Roman Judea was not an independent province, however. The highest Roman official, based in Caesarea Maritima, was a prefect from the equestrian order (*ordo equester*) who was subordinate to the consular governor of the province of Syria.[1] The imperial *legati Augusti pro praetore* who governed the Roman province of Syria had senatorial rank. P. KEHNE explains, "During the Empire, a *legatus Augusti pro praetore* of consular or praetorial rank, standing in for the emperor equipped with *imperium proconsulare*, administered the latter's provinces or conducted war ... In senatorial provinces, the proconsul with praetorial rank was assisted by a *legatus*."[2] As members of the Roman senate, the imperial legates came mostly from established senatorial families. They had all been consuls and thus belonged to the leadership of the senate. They were the most loyal senators, responsible, as governors of Syria, for the protection of the Roman empire in the East against attacks from the outside and against internal unrest in the province. Attaining the governorship of Syria would have been the climax of their senatorial careers. The prefects (*praefecti*), on the other hand, were far removed from the socio-political status and influence of the imperial legates: they had only equestrian rank; they did not belong to the established Roman families; they were novices in the administration of the empire; they did not belong to a permanent political institution and they evidently had not had an administrative position before becoming prefects in Judea.[3] Josephus never dares to criticize

---

[1] Cf. ECK, Rom und Judaea, 1–51. See the introduction to section 2.1.

[2] PETER KEHNE, Legatus, BNP 7 (2005): 354–355, 355. The governors of the senatorial provinces were called *proconsules*. The Roman province of Syria was an imperial province. For the following description see WERNER ECK, Beförderungskriterien innerhalb der senatorischen Laufbahn, dargestellt an der Zeit von 69 bis 138 n. Chr, ANRW II.1 (1974): 158–228; ECK, Repräsentanten, 168-170; cf. EDWARD DĄBROWA, The Governors of Roman Syria from Augustus to Septimius Severus (Antiquitas Reihe 1, Abhandlungen zur alten Geschichte 45; Bonn: Habelt, 1998). For Roman Syria see KEVIN BUTCHER, Roman Syria and the Near East (Los Angeles: Paul Getty Museum, 2003).

[3] Cf. ECK, Repräsentanten, 170-171; WERNER ECK, Praefectus, BNP 11 (2007): 751–756. Among the extant monuments there is no single example of a monument erected for an equestrian procurator; ECK, Leitung, 340 n. 63.

the imperial legates of Syria, even when they brutally suppressed Jewish dissent, unlike the prefects of Judea, who are repeatedly censured.[4]

The equestrian order (*ordo equites*) described the second rank after that of the senators. By the early principate, the *ordo equites* had become an honorary civic status whose political significance had increased. The right to wear the golden ring and to occupy the first 14 rows at the theater was accorded to those "who could demonstrate free descent for three generations and wealth of 400,000 HS."[5] There was no fixed norm for an equestrian career, but as a rule, they served first in the military and in modest civil posts and then progressed to higher positions. They would have been shaped through their military service by the hierarchical command structure and dependency upon the emperor, developing a "professionalism" that focused their lives on the tasks and duties of the state.[6] While they were sent to serve as administrators in various and diverse regions and functions, there is little evidence of specialization. Most served in a particular province for 2–4 years, but Josephus knows of prefects who stayed for 10 or more years (Valerius Gratus and Pontius Pilatus). For all practical purposes, there was little difference between the military and administrative competency of the equestrian prefects administering provinces and the *imperium* of the *legati Augusti pro praetore*. The *imperium* of the *praefectus Aegypti* probably served as a model for the authority of other *praefecti* administering provinces and subordinate regions. The very first equestrian prefect of Judea (Coponius, A.D. 6–9; Josephus, *B. J.* 2.117) had the right of capital punishment. The prefects commanded all troops stationed in their province, which (with the exception of Egypt) were composed of auxiliary troops.[7] They were responsible for adjudicating civil and criminal cases as well as for the general administration of their territory, e.g. the building of city walls, the repair of aqueducts, and the dedication of temples. The administration of finances was a special case. While the *legati Augusti pro praetore* were not involved in collecting taxes or paying the troops (these were tasks for which a procurator was responsible), the procurators of the equestrian provinces had full responsibility for the financial administration. As regards the prefects who ruled Roman Judea, it should be noted that from the standpoint

---

[4] ECK, Repräsentanten, 173.

[5] ANDREW W. LINTOTT, Equites Romani, BNP 5 (2004): 1–4, 4, with reference to Pliny, *Nat.* 33.32; cf. ibid. for the following comment.

[6] For the following description cf. ECK, Leitung, 329–40.

[7] On the Roman army and its administration cf. DAVID KENNED, ed., The Roman Army in the East (JRASup 18; Ann Arbor: Journal of Roman Archaeology, 1996); ARMIN EICH, ed., Die Verwaltung der kaiserzeitlichen römischen Armee (FS Hartmut Wolff; Historia. Einzelschriften 211; Stuttgart: Steiner, 2010); for Judea in the later part of the first century cf. HANNAH M. COTTON, The Impact of the Roman Army in the Province of Judaea/Syria Palaestina, in The Impact of the Roman Army (200 BC-AD 476): Economic, Social, Political, Religious and Cultural Aspects (ed. L. de Bois and E. Lo Cascio; Impact of Empire 6; Leiden/Boston: Brill, 2007), 393–408.

of the population, an equestrian prefect was just as much the all-powerful representative of the Roman empire and of the emperor as the imperial legate in Syria.[8] This means the prefect of Roman Judea, while not having the *imperium* of an imperial or senatorial legate, possessed full legal authority, including the (sole) authority to decide capital cases (*ius gladii*).

Our knowledge of the Roman administration in first-century Judea is rudimentary due to the paucity of relevant primary sources. Criminal jurisdiction of Roman Judea is so far not attested in the papyri.[9] As a result of the rich finds of documentary papyri in Egypt, we are much better informed about the legal situation in Ptolemaic and Roman Egypt.[10] J. G. MANNING describes the system of law and order in Ptolemaic Egypt as "a complex system that joined royal decree, i.e., royal *authority*, with norms and practices that developed at the local level."[11] H. J. WOLFF speaks of a symbiosis of Greek and Egyptian law that continued to exist side by side.[12] The two different sources of law were integrated only in the sense that they were subsumed under the sovereignty of the king.[13] The Roman conquest did not substantially alter the region's legal practices. U. YIFTACH-FIRANKO summarizes the evidence as follows: "In Egypt, the language of the courts was not particularly Roman, nor did Roman judges apply Roman legal concepts or institutions more than non-Roman ones in formulating their rulings. The Latin language and formulae were also not very common in legal documents. In general, Romans and non-Romans in Egypt issued the same Greek legal documents, applied local institutions and mechanisms, and usually administered justice according to the

---

[8] ECK, Leitung, 340; KIRNER, Strafgewalt, 141; cf. ibid. for the following point; also ECK, Rom und Judaea, 39–41.

[9] HANNAH M. COTTON and WERNER ECK, Roman Officials in Judea and Arabia and Civil Jurisdiction, in Law in the Documents of the Judaean Desert (ed. R. Katzoff and D. Schaps; JSJSup 96; Leiden/Boston: Brill, 2005), 23–44, 23 n. 1.

[10] Publication of political and administrative edicts, letters, rescripts or orders, served legal and practical purposes. Due to the material used for the publication – wood tablets (*tabulae dealbatae*) and papyrus – the vast majority of such texts are lost. Publication of political and administrative texts must be distinguished from the public presentation of edicts, letters, or rescripts on bronze tablets or in marble inscriptions. Cf. WERNER ECK, Administrative Dokumente: Publikation und Mittel der Selbstdarstellung [1998], in Judäa – Syria Palästina. Die Auseinandersetzung einer Provinz mit römischer Politik und Kultur (TSAJ 157; Tübingen: Mohr Siebeck, 2014), 3–24.

[11] JOSEPH G. MANNING, The Last Pharaohs: Egypt Under the Ptolemies, 305–30 BC (Princeton: Princeton University Press, 2010), 167, emphasis by Manning.

[12] WOLFF, Das Recht der griechischen Papyri Ägyptens I, 71–86; he speaks of "Zweispurigkeit des Rechts" and "Rechtspluralismus."

[13] HANS JULIUS WOLFF, Plurality of Laws in Ptolemaic Egypt, Revue internationale des Droits de L'antiquité 3 (1960): 191–223, 212; cf. MANNING, Egypt Under the Ptolemies, 168–69. On the law of the king in Ptolemaic Egypt cf. WOLFF, Das Recht der griechischen Papyri Ägyptens I, 49–54. See the collection of the extant prostagmata published by MARIE-THÉRÈSE LENGER, Corpus des Ordonnances des Ptolémées (Second ed.; orig. 1964; repr., Mémoires 64.2; Bruxelles: Palais des Académies, 1980).

same non-Roman guidelines."[14] At the same time, the Roman prefect had, for all practical purposes, unlimited executive and legal authority, including the *ius gladii*. Of at least equal importance was that he also exercised the *ius edicendi*, the authority to set legal norms and issue edicts (διάταγμα, Lat. *edictum*).[15] While the vast majority of documentary papyri concerns civil cases, the fact that there was no clear boundary between civil and criminal cases[16] means that a wider range of papyri beyond those specifically describing criminal cases are relevant for a description of the legal realities in Roman Egypt. It remains true, however, as R. S. BAGNALL has stated, that "criminal sentencing is effectively nonexistent in the papyri."[17] Also, it should be noted that Roman Egypt was a special case in that the legal decisions and the edicts of the Roman prefects in Egypt were accepted as binding for decades after the prefect had been succeeded by other prefects.[18] Significant is the principle expressed by Cicero: the local communities in the provinces can craft and employ their own laws only to the extent that larger Roman interests did not require Roman involvement in legal or administrative matters (Cicero, *Pro Balbo* 22; see No. 82). The edict of Gaius Petronius Mamertinus, prefect of Egypt in A.D. 133–137, illustrates the prerogative of a provincial governor to have criminal cases transferred to his jurisdiction (P. Yale II 162; No. 87).

The texts in this section will be discussed under ten headings: (1) Pontius Pilatus, (2) the jurisdiction of Roman governors, (3) capital cases in Roman law, (4) reports of trial proceedings, (5) languages used in provincial court proceedings, (6) amnesty and *acclamatio populi*, (7) mocking and beating of the convicted criminal, (8) requisitioning of provincials, (9) carrying the crossbeam, (10) the *titulus*.[19]

---

[14] YIFTACH-FIRANKO, Law in Greco-Roman Egypt, 557; cf. ERWIN SEIDL, Rechtsgeschichte Ägyptens als römischer Provinz: Die Behauptung des ägyptischen Rechts neben dem römischen (Sankt Augustin: Richarz, 1973), 13–49.

[15] WOLFF, Das Recht der griechischen Papyri Ägyptens I, 105–6. For a list of the edicts of the Roman prefects in Egypt cf. KATZOFF, Sources of Law in Roman Egypt, 810–19.

[16] BENJAMIN KELLY, Petitions, Litigation, and Social Control in Roman Egypt (Oxford: Oxford University Press, 2011), 81–82.

[17] ROGER S. BAGNALL, Official and Private Violence in Roman Egypt [1989], in Later Roman Egypt: Society, Religion, Economy and Administration (Variorum Collected Studies; Aldershot: Ashgate, 2003), 201–216, 211 n. 38. He cites the largely negative findings of the study of BARBARA ANAGNOSTOU-CANAS, Juge et sentence dans l'Égypte romaine (Études de philosophie et d'histoire du droit 6; Paris: L'Harmattan, 1991).

[18] KATZOFF, Sources of Law in Roman Egypt, 823–25; WOLFF, Das Recht der griechischen Papyri Ägyptens I, 106–7.

[19] The numerous texts on Herod Antipas, before whom Jesus appeared in the course of the Roman trial (Luke 23:6–12), will not be separately discussed. On Antipas cf. MORTEN HØRNING JENSEN, Herod Antipas in Galilee: The Literary and Archaeological Sources on the Reign of Herod Antipas and its Socio-Economic Impact on Galilee (Second ed.; orig. 2006; repr., WUNT 2/215; Tübingen: Mohr Siebeck, 2010), where the relevant texts are discussed.

# 2.1 Pontius Pilatus

This section collects all non-Christian texts on Pontius Pilatus, the prefect of Judea who condemned Jesus to be executed by crucifixion.[20] The *praenomen* Pontius is Oscan and an Oscan/Latin gentilic.[21] It is possible but cannot be proved that Pontius Pilatus belonged to the old Samnite family of the Pontii, several of whom are known: Gavius Pontius was a Samnite general who defeated the Romans at Caudium in 321 B.C.; Pontius Telesinus was a general of the Samnites in the Social War in 90 B.C. who was defeated in 82 B.C.; Pontius Aquila was tribune in 45 B.C. who was possibly dispossessed as a result for remaining seated when Caesar, the dictator, passed him in the triumphal march and who was involved in Caesar's murder in 44 B.C. First- and second-century Roman officials with the name Pontius whose descent from the Samnite Pontii is unclear include: C. Pontius Paelignus, a knight who was accepted into the senate and served as military tribune, quaestor, aedil, and praetor before being appointed by both the senate and the emperor Tiberius as special legate in the province of Asia; C. Petronius Pontius Nigrinus who was adopted by one of the senatorial Petronii of the Augustan-Tiberian period and served as consul during Tiberius' principate in A.D. 37; M. P. Laelinanus who was consul in A.D. 163 and legate of Moesia; and M. Pontius Laelianus Larcius Sabinus who was a senator under Hadrian, governor in Pannonia, a consular legate in Syria probably in A.D. 150–164 who was honored by the senate with a statue in Trajan's Forum.[22] The *cognomen* Pilatus means "hairy,

---

[20] We will consistently use the Latin name of the prefect of Judea. Introductory studies on Pontius Pilatus in the New Testament include JEAN-PIERRE LÉMONON, Pilate et le gouvernement de la Judée. Textes et monuments (EBib; Paris: Gabalda, 1981); HELEN K. BOND, Pontius Pilate in History and Interpretation (orig. 1998; repr., SNTSMS 100; Cambridge: Cambridge University Press, 2004); WARREN CARTER, Pontius Pilate: Portraits of a Roman Governor (Interfaces; Collegeville, MN: Liturgical Press, 2003); JEAN-PIERRE LÉMONON, Ponce Pilate (Ivry-sur-Seine: Atelier, 2007). A commentary on the relevant New Testament texts provides METZNER, Die Prominenten, 96–123, 175–88, 281–96, 318–34.

[21] KARL-LUDWIG ELVERS, Pontius, BNP 11 (2007): 596.

[22] Cf. CHRISTIAN MÜLLER, Pontius [I 1] Pontius, Gavius, BNP 11 (2007): 596; KARL-LUDWIG ELVERS, Pontius [I 4] P.Telesinus, BNP 11 (2007): 597; JÖRG FÜNDLING, Pontius [I 3] P. Aquila, BNP 11 (2007): 596–597, with reference to Cicero, *Att.* 14.21.3; Cassius Dio 46.38.3; WERNER ECK, Pontius [II 6] C. P. Paelignus, BNP 11 (2007): 597; WERNER ECK, Prosopographica II. 1. Zur Laufbahn des C. Pontius Paelignus. 2. Lucilius Capito oder Cn. Vergilius Capito auf Cos? ZPE 106 (1995): 249–254; WERNER ECK, Pontuis [II 3] M. P. Laelianus, BNP 11 (2007): 597; WERNER ECK, Pontius [II 4] M. P. Laelianus Larcius Sabinus, BNP 11 (2007): 597. On the possible connection between these officials and Pontius Pilatus cf. BLINZLER, Prozeß, 264; JEAN-PIERRE LÉMONON, Ponce Pilate: documents profanes, Nouveau Testament et traditions ecclésiales, ANRW II.26/1 (1992): 741–778, 744–45. Unproven connections between Pontius Pilatus and these men with the name Pontius are often assumed by novelistic-fictional treatments or popular reconstructions of the life of the Roman prefect of Judea; cf. PAUL L. MAIER, Pontius Pilate: A Novel (Grand Rapids: Kregel, 1968), 313; ANN WROE, Pontius Pilate: The Biography of an Invented Man (orig. 1999.; repr., New

shaggy" or "armed with javelins (*pila*)", depending on whether the "i" is long or short.[23] Josephus identifies him as Pontius Pilatus in *A. J.* 18.35, as does Luke in Luke 3:1; Acts 4:27 (cf. 1 Tim 2:11) and Ignatius in *Magn.* 11:1, *Trall.* 9:1, and *Smyrn.* 1:2. The fuller name is also attested in the fragmentary inscription from Caesarea (see No. 76). Pontius Pilatus was a Roman knight (*eques*) who was appointed *praefectus Iudaeae* by Tiberius (A.D. 14–37), perhaps as early as A.D. 19 (the traditional date is A.D. 26). He administered Judea until A.D. 36.

The dates of Pilatus' rule are usually derived from Josephus, *A. J.* 18.35, which mentions his predecessor, Valerius Gratus, in Judea for 11 years, and *A. J.* 18.89, which relates that Pilatus stayed for 10 years in office. This calculation accords with Eusebius' claim that Pilatus began to govern in the 12th year of Tiberius, i.e., in A.D. 26 (*Hist. eccl.* 1.9). Challenging this consensus, D. R. SCHWARTZ argues that Pontius Pilatus took office as early as A.D. 19.[24] The following arguments are relevant.[25] (1) According to Josephus, Valerius Gratus left Judea after having deposed four high priests in quick succession, each having served about a year from A.D. 15, and after having appointed Caiaphas (see Texts No. 2, 7). (2) Josephus' account of Gratus' tenure is very brief (*A. J.* 18.34–35), while Pilatus' tenure is reported extensively (*A. J.* 18.35–89). (3) The long tenure of Caiaphas as high priest (A.D. 18–36) is best explained in terms of a change of prefects and their policies regarding the tenure of high priests. (4) The events connected with the beginning of Caiaphas' tenure – the founding of Tiberias in A.D. 19, the rule of Orodes as king of Armenia (A.D. 16–18), the death of Germanicus in A.D. 19, and the expulsion of Judeans and Egyptians from Rome in A.D. 19 (*A. J.* 18.36–38, 52, 53–54, 65–84; on the latter cf. Tacitus, *Ann.* 2.85) – suggest that Pilatus arrived in Judea at roughly the same time. As regards the numbers 11 and 10 for Gratus' and Pilatus' years in Judea, SCHWARTZ suggests that they are based on textual corruption or reflect deliberate Christian rewriting to disprove the false *Acts of Pilate*.[26] Independently, K. A. LÖNNQVIST argues, based on the metallurgy of the coins issued between A.D. 17–30,[27] that Pontius Pilatus may have replaced

---

York: Random / Modern Library, 2001). Commenting on WROE in the London Review of Books 21/8 (1999) 17–18, F. KERMODE states, "The present book is a modern 'Acts of Pilate', with copious allusion to these and other traditions, much spontaneous invention, and some speculation of a more modern sort about the kind of person Pilate may have been."

[23] IIRO KAJANTO, The Latin Cognomina (orig. 1965; repr., Commentationes humanarum litterarum 2; Rome: Bretschneider, 1982), 354.

[24] DANIEL R. SCHWARTZ, Pontius Pilate's Appointment to Office and the Chronology of Josephus' *Antiquities*, Books 18–20 [1982/1983], in Studies in the Jewish Background of Christianity (WUNT 60; Tübingen: Mohr Siebeck, 1992), 182–201; DANIEL R. SCHWARTZ, Pontius Pilate, ABD 5 (1992): 395–401; SCHWARTZ, Reading, 139–45. He revives the suggestion of ROBERT EISLER, Ἰησοῦς βασιλεύς οὐ βασιλεύσας. Die messianische Unabhängigkeitsbewegung vom Auftreten Johannes des Täufers bis zum Untergang Jakobs des Gerechten. Nach der neuerschlossenen Eroberung von Jerusalem des Flavius Josephus und den christlichen Quellen (2 vols.; Religionswissenschaftliche Bibliothek 9; Heidelberg: Winter, 1929–1930), 1:125–30.

[25] Cf. the summary in MASON, Judean War 2, 139 n. 1054.

[26] SCHWARTZ, Pontius Pilate's Appointment, 184, asserting that "it is curious, or suspicious, that, of all seventeen Roman governors of Judaea mentioned by Josephus, only for Gratus and Pilate are we given data regarding the length of their tenures" (ibid.).

[27] The lead content of coins minted between A.D. 17/18–31/32 dropped from ca. 11% to virtually nil; it was replaced by a bronze alloy of tin and copper, and returned to its previous

Gratus in A.D. 17/18.[28] While some scholars do not find these proposals convincing,[29] Josephus experts find the case for an early date of Pilatus' appointment compelling.[30] If the early date is correct, Josephus' readers would find it easier to understand his quick movement from Tiberius' accession in A.D. 14 to Pilatus' appointment in A.D. 18/19. Josephus' brief treatment of Gratus' tenure corresponds to his treatment of the brief 2- and 3- year terms of Coponius, Ambibulus, and Rufus, and it is easy to understand why he would focus on the Roman official who spent 18 or 19 years in Judea. Pilatus' long tenure fits Tiberius' policy of leaving provincial governors in office as long as possible.[31] If Pontius Pilatus was prefect of Judea from A.D. 18 or 19 onwards, this would mean that "Pilate and Caiaphas served in their respective offices for a lengthy and almost identical period of time, some eighteen years for Caiaphas (from 18 to early 37) and seventeen for Pilate (from 19 to early 37)."[32] É. NODET suggests that Pilatus' removal should be dated at A.D. 35, shortly after Vitellius' arrival in Antioch.[33] B. MAHIEU argues that Pilatus was deposed after Vitellius' visit at Passover A.D. 36 in the winter of A.D. 36–37.[34]

W. ECK has repeatedly objected to the label "governor" for Pontius Pilatus: he was not an independent provincial governor but a *praefectus* (Greek ἔπαρχος) and should thus be called "prefect."[35] Philo, Josephus, and Tacitus use the term ἐπίτροπος / *procucator* ("governor,"

---

levels under Claudius and Nero. Cf. KENNETH A. LÖNNQVIST, Pontius Pilate – Aqueduct Builder? Recent Findings and New Suggestions, Klio 82 (2000): 459–475, 465. LÖNNQVIST argues that Pilatus removed lead from his coins to be used for the building of the Jerusalem aqueduct; lead has been discovered in the contemporary aqueduct system at Panias.

[28] Cf. LÖNNQVIST, Pontius Pilate, 467–68.

[29] BOND, Pontius Pilate, 1 n. 2; JULIA WILKER, Für Rom und Jerusalem. Die herodianische Dynastie im 1. Jahrhundert n. Chr. (SAG 5; Frankfurt: Verlag Antike, 2007), 93 n. 107; MONIKA BERNETT, Der Kaiserkult in Judäa unter den Herodiern und Römern. Untersuchungen zur politischen und religiösen Geschichte Judäas von 30 v. bis 66 n. Chr. (WUNT 1.203; Tübingen: Mohr Siebeck, 2007), 199 n. 111.

[30] MASON, Authority, 24; MASON, Judean War 2, 139 n. 1054; the following point ibid. Cf. JENS HERZER, Zwischen Loyalität und Machtstreben: sozialgeschichtliche Aspekte des Pilatusbildes bei Josephus und im Neuen Testament, in Josephus und das Neue Testament. Wechselseitige Wahrnehmungen (ed. C. Böttrich and J. Herzer; WUNT 209; Tübingen: Mohr Siebeck, 2007), 429–449, 432.

[31] Cf. Josephus, *A. J.* 18.170; Tacitus, *Ann.* 1.80; Suetonius, *Tib.* 41.

[32] EVANS, Excavating Caiaphas, 337.

[33] NODET, Sources, 274, arguing that "the usual dating of 36 CE takes at face value Vitellius' two visits in Jerusalem at Passover, but the data can hardly be reconciled."

[34] BIEKE MAHIEU, Between Rome and Jerusalem: Herod the Great and His Sons in Their Struggle for Recognition. A Chronological Investigation of the Period 40 BC – 39 AD With a Time Setting of New Testament Events (OLA 208; Leuven: Peeters, 2012), 406 with n. 66.

[35] Cf. ECK, Leitung, 340; WERNER ECK, Pontius [II 7] P. Pilatus, BNP 11 (2007): 597–598; WERNER ECK, Die Benennung von römischen Amtsträgern und politisch-militärisch-administrativen Funktionen bei Flavius Iosephus: Probleme der korrekten Identifizierung, ZPE 166 (2008): 218–226; ECK, Rom und Judaea, 35–39; ECK, Repräsentanten, 169-170. Cf. MAURIZIO GHIRETTI, Lo 'status' della Guidea dall' età Augustea all' età Claudia, Latomus 44 (1985): 751–766; HANNAH M. COTTON, Some Aspects of the Roman Administration of Judaea/Syria-Palaestina, in Lokale Autonomie und römische Ordnungsmacht in den kaiserzeitlichen Provinzen vom 1. bis 3. Jahrhundert (ed. W. Eck and E. Müller-Luckner; Schriften des Historischen Kollegs 42; München: Oldenbourg, 1999), 75–91, 76–79; ECKHARD MEYER-ZWIFFELHOFFER, Πολιτικωῶς ἄρχειν. Zum Regierungsstil der senatorischen Statthalter in den kaiserzeitlichen griechischen Provinzen (Historia Einzelschriften 165; Stuttgart: Steiner, 2002), 44–45; BERNETT, Kaiserkult, 310–13.

"Statthalter") for the Roman official governing in Roman Judea. For Philo, see *Legat*. 299 (Pontius Pilatus); for Josephus, see *B. J.* 2.169 (Pontius Pilatus), 2.117 (Coponius); *B. J.* 2.220, *A. J.* 15.406; 20.2, 97 (C. Cuspius Fadus); *B. J.* 2.220, 223 (Ti. Iulius Alexander); *B. J.* 2.223, *A. J.* 20.107, 132 (Ventidius Cumanus); *B. J.* 2.247, 252, 271, *A. J.* 20.142, 162 (M. Antonius Felix; *B. J.* 2.271 (Porcius Festus); *B. J.* 6.303, *A. J.* 20.197 (Lucceius Albinus); *A. J.* 20.257 (Gessius Florus); for Tacitus see *Ann.* 15.44.3 (Pontius Pilatus); *Hist.* 5.10.1 (Gessius Florus). This designation is anachronistic. Under Augustus and his immediate successors, the designation ἐπίτροπος / *procurator* is used only for officials responsible for the finances of the emperor in a single province (sometimes in several provinces concurrently). No *procurator* was provincial governor before the time of Claudius (A.D. 41–54).[36] Josephus uses the correct term ἔπαρχος (Lat. *praefectus*) in *B. J.* 6.303 (Lucceius Albinus); *A. J.* 18.33 (Annius Rufus, Valerius Gratus), 19.363 (C. Cuspius Fadus), 20.197 (Lucceius Albinus), and 20.197 (Porcius Festus).[37] Both Josephus and Titus knew that Roman officials of equestrian rank were responsible for Judea during this period, but Josephus also knew that Judea became an independent province under the Flavian emperors, a situation that continued into the first decades of the 2nd century, when Tacitus wrote. Both Josephus and Tacitus often (but not consistently) use later terminology in describing the chief Roman officials in Judea appointed by the emperors before the time of Vespasian. Also, both knew of equestrian procurators who acted as *praesides*, i.e., as representatives of the emperor ("governors," "Statthalter"), which resembled the function of the *equites* who were in charge of Judea in the early 1st century A.D., granted one did not look too closely into the respective responsibilities.[38]

As regards the historical reliability of Josephus, see the discussion at the end of No. 1. Despite the perspectival nature of Josephus' historical narratives – indeed of all narratives – the agnostic skepticism of S. MASON is unwarranted.[39]

---

[36] ECK, Rom und Judaea, 32; WERNER ECK, Procurator, BNP 11 (2007): 928–930, 928. LEVICK, Claudius, 48–49, surmises that "the use of the title 'procurator' emphasizes Claudius' personal control of the province; prefects might have been taken to be the appointees of the preceding senatorial commander, and that was not to be tolerated." MASON, Judean War 2, 80 n. 721, wonders whether "perhaps Judea's early governors had both prefectural and procuratorial functions, and Claudius merely began to insist on the procuratorial title only."

[37] Cf. MASON, Judean War 2, 80 n. 720, who notes the following pattern: "at their first mention in *War*, Josephus *invariably* uses 'procurator,' whereas he never uses this term in *Antiquities*. Thus, when he mentions the governor a second time, whether this is later in *War* or (mainly) in *Antiquities*, he varies his language ... In *War*, again, Josephus seems concerned to stress the low character and status of Judea's equestrian governors, in order to help explain the origins of the conflict" (ibid.).

[38] ECK, Rom und Judaea, 27–39. Pace ROBERT L. WEBB, The Roman Examination and Crucifixion of Jesus, in Key Events in the Life of the Historical Jesus: A Collaborative Exploration of Context and Coherence (ed. D. L. Bock and R. L. Webb; WUNT 247; Tübingen: Mohr Siebeck, 2009), 669–773, 725. KIRNER, Strafgewalt, 140–61, follows W. ECK in distinguishing the status of the imperial legates in the province of Syria and the equestrian prefects in Judea but still describes the latter as "Statthalter."

[39] MASON, Authority, 24, asserts, "*what Pilate did* during his long stay in Judea, and *why he did it* ... seem impossible to recover, even where we have several lines of independent evidence. For the vast majority of cases, where Josephus provides the sole evidence, we simply have no means of recreating the past that he knew from his surviving works of art" (italics Mason); cf. MASON, Overview, 34.

Pontius Pilatus served as prefect of Judea under three governors of Roman Syria: L. Aelius Lamia (A.D. 23[?]–32), Lucius Pomponius Flaccus, and Lucius Vitellius.[40] As highest Roman official in Judea, the *praefectus* Pontius Pilatus represented the power of the Roman empire in the region he administered. The *praefecti* of Roman Judea resided not in Jerusalem but in Caesarea Maritima, using the palace built by Herod I as *praetorium* (cf. Acts 23:35).[41] The competencies Pontius Pilatus had been given as prefect of Judea included the responsibility to maintain law and order, especially as far as Roman citizens were concerned.[42] He monitored the Jewish authorities, i.e., the high priest and the Sanhedrin. He alone had the authority to try capital cases (*ius gladii*) in the province. He had auxiliary troops at his disposal. The use of Roman legions was the prerogative of the imperial legate who governed the province of Syria and evidently also retained the right to collect taxes and other dues (and control over the high-priestly garments, unless these were under the jurisdiction of a client king of Herodian descent).

Most information on Pontius Pilatus comes from Josephus. He devotes much more attention to this governor (*B. J.* 2.169–177; *A. J.* 18.55–64, 85–89) than to his predecessors, a fact that cannot be explained by any special interest in the history of Christianity; his account "must reflect the relative richness of material available to him."[43] At the same time, it should be noted that both Josephus and Philo relate only "negative" events for Pilatus.

A further source of information on Pontius Pilatus are the coins he minted in A.D. 29 (16th year of Tiberius), 30 (17th year of Tiberius), and 31 (18th year of Tiberius).[44] The series of small bronze perutahs, evidently minted in

---

[40] Cf. DĄBROWA, The Governors of Roman Syria , 35–41; WERNER ECK, Aelius [II 16] Ae. Lamia, L., BNP 1 (2002): 205; WERNER ECK, Pomponius [II 10] L. P. Flaccus, BNP 11 (2007): 579–580; WERNER ECK, Vitellius [II 3] L. V., BNP 15 (2010): 476–477; KRIEGER, Geschichtsschreibung, 48–59.

[41] Cf. BARBARA BURRELL, Palace to Praetorium: The Romanization of Caesarea, in Caesarea Maritima: A Retrospective after Two Millenia (ed. A. Raban and K. G. Holum; Documenta et monumenta Orientis antiqui 21; Leiden: Brill, 1996), 228–247; KENNETH G. HOLUM, AVNER RABAN, and JOSEPH PATRICH, eds., Caesarea Papers 2: Herod's Temple, the Provincial Governor's Praetorium and Granaries, the Later Harbor, a Gold Coin Hoard, and Other Studies (JRASup 35; Portsmouth, R.I.: Journal of Roman Archaeology, 1999).

[42] For the authority of the *praefectus* in Roman Judea cf. ECK, Rom und Judaea, 39–43; KIRNER, Strafgewalt, 140–245.

[43] DANIEL R. SCHWARTZ, Pontius Pilate's Suspension from Office: Chronology and Sources [1981/1982], in Studies in the Jewish Background of Christianity (WUNT 60; Tübingen: Mohr Siebeck, 1990), 202–217, 202. He regards it as possible "that the richness of sources stemmed from Christians' attempts to collect and preserve as much as possible about this period; perhaps Josephus had access to such a collection. Note, in this connection, that the only other ancient writer to refer to Pilate, apart from Philo (*Leg.* 299–305), Josephus, and the New Testament writers, does so in a Christian context (Tacitus, *Ann.* 15.44 – GLA II, pp. 88–93)" (ibid. n. 1).

[44] Cf. YA'AKOV MESHORER, A Treasury of Jewish Coins: From the Persian Period to Bar

Jerusalem, do not include the name of the issuer, but by the combination of the names of the emperor (Tiberius) and the date of issue, the coins can be securely attributed to the prefect. There are two types of coins; type 1 coins give the date after the legend on the obverse; type 2 coins have the date inside the wreath. The dates are given in the form of the Latin letter "L" (for Greek λύκαβας, "year"), followed by Latin-Greek letter-numbers: LIS, LIZ, LIH (year 16, 17, and 18 of Tiberius' reign). The obverse of the type 1 coins has the legend ΙΟΥΛΙΑ ΚΑΙCΑΡΟC ("Iulia, of Caesar"). Livia was given the title "Iulia Augusta" after Augustus' death in A.D. 14. The legend surrounds three ears of barley. The reverse bears the Greek legend ΤΙΒΕΡΙΟΥ ΚΑΙCΑΡΟC ("of Tiberius Caesar"), surrounding a *simpulum*. The obverse of the type 2 coins has the legend ΤΙΒΕΡΙΟΥ ΚΑΙCΑΡΟC ("of Tiberius Caesar"), surrounding a *lituus*. The reverse gives the date within a wreath. Pilatus' coins broke with the tradition of the coins issued by his predecessors, depicting symbols of Roman cult practices which was unprecedented on coins minted in Judea. The three ears of barley on the obverse of the type 1 coins could symbolize the agricultural produce of Judea.[45] In view of the legend honoring Iulia, Tiberius' mother, who is frequently associated with Ceres, and in view of the distinctive depiction of two of the three ears of barley drooping (suggesting cut wheat or barley used in a cereal festival) and positioned in a display frame or tripod, as if they are used in a ritual, it is more likely that the coin commemorates Livia (Iulia Augusta), who was "cut down by death in the year of the coin's issue, 29 CE."[46] The *simpulum* on the reverse represents a small ladle-shaped utensil used in Roman cults by a priest for tasting the wine before it was poured on the head of the sacrificial animal; it was often used as a symbol for the *pontifex*. Since the *simpulum* is surrounded by the text "of Tiberius Caesar," it serves to honor the emperor Tiberius in his role as *pontifex maximus* and is thus a reference to the imperial cult.[47] The *lituus* on the reverse of the type 2 coins (issued in A.D. 30 and 31) is a wooden or metal staff ending in a crook or spiral and used as a cultic instrument by the augurs

---

Kokhba (Jerusalem/Nyack: Yad ben-Zvi Press/Amphora, 2001), 170–73; DAVID HENDIN, Guide to Biblical Coins (Fifth ed.; New York: Amphora, 2010), 316–18, 327–28 (No. 1341–1346). Cf. HELEN K. BOND, The Coins of Pontius Pilate: Part of an Attempt to Provoke the People or to Integrate Them into the Empire? JSJ 27 (1996): 241–262; JEAN-PHILIPPE FONTANILLE and SHELDON LEE GOSLINE, The Coins of Pontius Pilate (Warren Center, Pa.: Shangri-La Publications, 2001); JOAN E. TAYLOR, Pontius Pilate and the Imperial Cult in Roman Judaea, NTS 52 (2006): 555–582, 556–64; JENSEN, Herod Antipas, 203; BERNETT, Kaiserkult, 202–5; WEBB, Roman Examination, 707–14.

[45] BOND, Coins, 250; cf. YAA'KOV MESHORER, Ancient Jewish Coinage (2 vols.; New York: Amphora, 1982), 2:179, who interprets the three ears of grain as indication that Pilatus' intentions were not as negative as Philo suggests; it may have been "his ignorance rather than his unsympathetic nature which was the major cause of his difficulties."

[46] TAYLOR, Pontius Pilate, 561, followed by WEBB, Roman Examination, 710.

[47] WEBB, Roman Examination, 711.

for quartering the heavens (*templum*) into regions.[48] Since the *lituus* is surrounded by the legend "of Tiberius Caesar," it most likely refers to the emperor's role as augur in the imperial cult.[49] The wreath on the reverse of the type 2 coins, which also appears on Jewish coins, is a symbol of power and victory; in connection with the legend of the observe, it honors the emperor Tiberius as "the person who has ultimate political power over the region."[50] The coins minted by Pontius Pilatus are neither a deliberate provocation of the Jewish population in Judea[51] – he did not depict the image of the emperor on his coins – nor do they represent "an attempt to continue the attempt of Herod I and his successors to integrate Judaea into the empire."[52] R. L. WEBB concludes that Pilatus pursued three interrelated aims with the coins he minted: (1) to honor the Roman emperor and his family, as the prefect of a Roman province that had a largely non-Roman population; (2) to honor Tiberius and his religious roles in the imperial cult;[53] and (3) to emphasize that Rome and specifically the emperor Tiberius, had political power in Judea.[54]

Pontius Pilatus is mentioned 57 times in the New Testament: Matt 27:2, 13, 17, 22, 24, 58 (bis), 62, 65; Mark 15:1, 2, 4, 5, 8, 12, 14, 15, 43, 44; Luke 3:1; 13:1; 23:1, 3, 4, 6, 11, 12, 13, 20, 24, 52; John 18:28, 29, 31, 33, 35, 37, 38; 19:1, 4, 5, 6, 8, 10, 12, 13, 15, 19, 21, 22, 31, 38 (bis); Acts 3:13; 4:27; 13:28; 1 Tim 6:13. Both nomen and cognomen – Pontius Pilatus – are mentioned in Luke 3:1; Acts 4:27; 1 Tim 6:13 (varia lectio in Matt 27:2 in A C W Θ 0250 f$^{1.13}$ Maj latt sy$^h$). He is described as ἡγεμῶν ("head imperial provincial administrator," BDAG s.v. ἡγεμῶν 2) in Matt 27:2, 11, 14, 15, 21, 27; 28:14; cf. Luke 3:1 where the verb ἡγεμονεύειν ("to exercise an administrative position," BDAG s.v. ἡγεμονεύω, correctly translating "while P.P. was prefect of Judaea") is used. Luke 3:1 mentions Pontius Pilatus in connection

---

[48] V. ANNE SIEBERT, Lituus, BNP 7 (2005): 737.

[49] Cf. BOND, Coins, 252; TAYLOR, Pontius Pilate, 559; WEBB, Roman Examination, 711.

[50] WEBB, Roman Examination, 712, going further than TAYLOR, Pontius Pilate, 561–62, in the interpretation of the wreath.

[51] Thus ETHELBERT STAUFFER, Christus und die Cäsaren. Historische Skizzen (orig.1948; repr., Hamburg: Wittig, 1966), 114–15 (= ETHELBERT STAUFFER, Christ and the Caesars: Historical Sketches [London: SCM, 1955], 119); also SMALLWOOD, Jews, 167.

[52] BOND, Coins, 260, who interprets the ears of barley and the wreath as a purely "Jewish design" that Pilatus placed on one side, while engraving the other side with a symbol of the Roman imperial cult (cf. ibid. 250, 251).

[53] Cf. TAYLOR, Pontius Pilate, 582, who concludes: "Pontius Pilate in his coinage honours the emperor Tiberius by celebrating his membership of two Roman priestly colleges in depicting Roman emblems symbolic of these colleges, but he also does more. It was the *pontifices* and *augures* who were the representatives of Roman religion in the two imperial cult temples of Caesarea Maritima and in Sebaste, located in the province he governed ... Pilate was promoting Roman religion, manifested largely in the imperial cult, in an environment in which there were strong sensibilities."

[54] WEBB, Roman Examination, 731. DEMANDT, Pontius Pilatus, 72, insists that Pilatus' coins do not represent a deliberate affront to Jewish sensibilities.

with the beginning of the public ministry of John the Baptist, which is also linked with the 15th regnal year of emperor Tiberius and the rule of the tetrarch Herod (Antipas) in Galilee, the rule of tetrarch (Herod) Philip in Ituraea and Trachonitis, the rule of the tetrarch Lysanias in Abilene, and the high priesthood of Annas and Caiaphas; cf. also Luke 20:20.

The apocryphal *Acts of Pilate*, which constitute the first part of the apocryphal *Gospel of Nicodemus*, date to c. A.D. 360–370 (*Acts Pil.* 1–11) and to c. A.D. 415 (*Acts Pil.* Prologue, chap. 12–16).[55] This text purports to contain the records of Jesus' trial; the consistent theological conception that intrudes into the *accusatio* before Pilatus attests to the fact that the text is fictional. Neither this text nor later Pontius Pilatus literature – Letter of Pilatus to Claudius; Letter of Pilatus to Tiberius; Letter of Tiberius to Pilatus; Letter of Pilatus to Herod; Letter of Herod to Pilatus; Report of Pilatus (*Anaphora Pilati*); Handing over of Pilatus (*Paradosis Pilati*); *Cura sanitatis Tiberii*; *Vindicta Salvatoris*; *Mors Pilati*; Narrative of Joseph of Arimathaea (*Narratio Josephi*)[56] – contains relevant information that helps illuminate Jesus' trial.

A funerary inscription, discovered in Kazan in North Galatia, dating to the Byzantine period, erected for an unknown man, mentions Pontius Pilatus.[57] The author invokes Jesus Christ who bore witness before Pontius Pilatus:

| | |
|---|---|
| ✠ τοῦ εὐδοκιμωτά- | This is the grave of a most distinguished |
| του ὂν βοηθήσῃ ὁ Κ[ύ]- | man, whom the Lord |
| ριος  IC XC[58] ὁ μαρτυρ[ῶν] | Jesus Christ, bearing witness |
| ἐπὶ Ποντίου Πιλά[του] | before Pontius Pilatus |
| 5  τὴν καλὴν ὁμολ[ογί]- | to a fair confession, |

---

[55] MONIKA SCHÄRTLI, Das Nikodemusevangelium, die Pilatusakten und die 'Höllenfahrt Christi', in Antike christliche Apokryphen in deutscher Übersetzung. I. Band: Evangelien und Verwandtes (ed. C. Markschies and J. Schröter; Tübingen: Mohr Siebeck, 2012), 231–261, 238 (German translation ibid. 240–61). JAMES K. ELLIOTT, The Apocryphal New Testament. A Collection of Apocryphal Christian Literature in an English Translation based on M. R. James (Oxford: Oxford University Press, 1993), 165, dates the *Acts of Pilate* proper to the 5th/6th century (English translation ibid. 169–85). For the Greek and Latin texts cf. CONSTANTIN VON TISCHENDORF, Evangelia apocrypha (orig. 1852, 1876; repr., Hildesheim: Olms, 1987), 1:210–486.

[56] Cf. MONIKA SCHÄRTLI, Die sonstige Pilatusliteratur, in Antike christliche Apokryphen in deutscher Übersetzung. I. Band: Evangelien und Verwandtes (ed. C. Markschies and J. Schröter; Tübingen: Mohr Siebeck, 2012), 262–279; ELLIOTT, Apocryphal New Testament, 205–25. Pilate was eventually regarded as a Christian martyr; his feast day in the Coptic Church is June 19.

[57] MITCHELL, STEPHEN, DAVID FRENCH, and JEAN GREENHAIGH. Regional Epigraphic Catalogues of Asia Minor II: The Ankara District. The Inscriptions of North Galatia. British Archaeological Reports International Series 135. Oxford: British Institute of Archaeology, 1982, 157 (No. 186), with translation (used here in slightly modified form). The stone (48 x 35 cm), now used as stairs inside a house, is a red-streaked marble altar; in a circle above the inscription is a part of a Maltese cross, incised by a small cross.

[58] IC XC abbreviates Ἰησοῦς Χριστός.

αν τὴν ἡμετέρ[αν σω]-        and salvation, shall help.
τηρίαν· ἀμήν              Amen
[Κ]ύριον σε ὁ ἀνα[γινώς]-      He who reads this,
ϙων εὖξε ὑπὲρ [τελευ]-       let him pray to you, Lord, on behalf
10 [τήσ]αντος (?)          of the dead man

Outside of these Christian texts, Pilatus is mentioned in an inscription from Caesarea, in one text by Philo, in three texts by Josephus, and once by Tacitus.

**(76)** AE 1971 477

[NAVTI]S TIBERIEVM       [Nauti]s Tiberieum
[PO]NTIVS PILATVS        [Po]ntius Pilatus
[PRAEF]ECTVS IVDAE[A]E     [praef]ectus Iudae[a]e
[    REF]E[CIT      ]     [    ref]e[cit]

*Translation.* [Sailor']s Tiberieum / [Pon]tius Pilatus / [Pref]ect of Jude[a] / [ restor]e[d ...]
Pontius Pilatus, prefect of Judea, restored the (lighthouse) Tiberieum for the sailors.

*Commentary.*[59] The stone, discovered during the Italian excavations in the theater of Caesarea, is inscribed with an architectural dedication dating to A.D. 31–36.[60] The fragmentary inscription has four lines. The block was reused in the fourth century as a step at the level of the orchestra at the northern end in the remodeled theater of Caesarea. Other suggestions include an administra-

---

[59] Editio princeps: ANTONIO FROVA, L'iscrizione di Pontio Pilato a Cesarea, in Rendiconti dell'Istituto Lombardo, Accademia di Scienze e Lettere (Classe di Lettere e Scienze Morali e Storoiche 95; Milan: Istituto Lombardo, 1961), 419–434 = AE 1971 477 = CIIP II 1277. Cf. CLAYTON M. LEHMANN and KENNETH G. HOLUM, The Greek and Latin Inscriptions of Casearea Maritima (Joint Expedition to Caesarea Maritima: Excavation Reports 5; Boston: American Schools of Oriental Research, 2000), 67–70 (No. 43). We follow the reconstruction of the inscription by GEZA ALFÖLDY, Pontius Pilatus und das Tiberieum von Caesarea Maritima, SCI 18 (1999): 85–108; GEZA ALFÖLDY, Nochmals: Pontius Pilatus und das Tiberieum von Caesarea Maritima, SCI 21 (2002):133–148; cf. AE 1999 1681 = AE 2002 1556. Cf. LÉMONON, Pilate, 23–32; LÉMONON, Ponce Pilate: documents profanes, 749–52; LAURA BOFFO, Iscrizioni greche e latine per lo studio della Bibbia (Biblioteca di storia e storiografia dei tempi biblici 9; Brescia: Paideia, 1994), 217–33 (No. 25); LÉMONON, Ponce Pilate, 23–33; DEMANDT, Pontius Pilatus, 72–74; BERNETT, Kaiserkult, 205–14.

[60] LEHMANN / HOLUM, Inscriptions, 67–68. The letters of the inscription "are constricted, square, and have serifs. They measure 58–61 mm high in line 1 (the T is 68 mm), 55 in line 2 (the tall I and Ts are 65 mm), 48 in line 3 (the T is 69), and ca. 45 in line 4. The lettering is a monumental alphabet of the first two centuries" (ibid. 68). For the older literature cf. BLINZLER, Prozeß, 266 n. 199; the most recent bibliography is given by W. ECK in CIIP II, 229–30. The stone is in the Israel Museum, Jerusalem (inv. no. 1961-529).

tive building,[61] perhaps a library,[62] a building for the cult of Tiberius,[63] the theater itself,[64] games in honor of Tiberius,[65] a *porticus* connected with the theater or with the stadium,[66] or a sacred grove.[67] W. ECK argues that such speculations fail to take seriously the size of the stone and the type of the inscription: it is hardly doubtful that the building was called *Tiberieum*.[68] According to G. ALFÖLDY's reconstruction, the inscription commemorates the restoration (or rebuilding) of a lighthouse called Tiberieum, a project that benefitted the seamen who approached the harbor. The entrance had two monumental lighthouses, one of which was named Drusion (Δρούσιον), after Drusus, the younger stepson of Augustus (Josephus, *B. J.* 1.412; *A. J.* 15.336). Josephus does not give a name for the second lighthouse, but it seems plausible that he named it after Tiberius, the brother of Drusus.[69] The inscription at the lighthouse in Patara, put up by Nero, also mentions sailors as the people for whom the tower was erected.[70] ALFÖLDY's reconstruction has been widely accepted,[71] although M. BERNETT remains skeptical.[72]

---

[61] LÉMONON, Pilate, 31; LÉMONON, Ponce Pilate, 31. LÉMONON has consistently remained skeptical about the possibility of determining the nature of the building; he believes that the small size of the block suggests a brief inscription recording the name of a secular building – "ce pourrait être un temple, mais beaucoup plus vraisemblablement une place, une colonnade, voire an bâtiment administratif. Ce bâtiment pouvait être un élément d'un espace sacré ... il est difficile de préciser davantage sa nature" (ibid.).

[62] GILBERT LABBÉ, Ponce Pilate et la munificence de Tibère: l'inscription de Césarée, REA 93 (1991): 277–297.

[63] ATTILIO DEGRASSI, Sull'iscrizione di Ponzio Pilato, in Rendiconti dell'Accademia Nazionale dei Lincei Ser. 8 (Classe di Scienze morali, storiche ee filologiche 19; Rome: Accademia dei Lincei, 1964), 59–65; BERNETT, Kaiserkult, 205–14.

[64] IVAN DI STEFANO MANZELLA, Pontius Pilatus nell'iscrizione di Cesarea di Palestina, in Le iscrizioni dei cristiani in Vaticano. Materiali e contributi scientifici per una mostra epigrafica (Inscriptiones Sanctae Sedis 2; Città del Vaticano Roma: Monumenti, Musei e gallerie pontificie Distribuzione esclusiva, Edizioni Quasar, 1997), 209–215.

[65] TIBOR GRÜLL, Pilate's 'Tiberieum': A New Approach, Acta antiqua Academiae Scientiarum Hungaricae 41 (2001): 267–278.

[66] LEHMANN / HOLUM, Inscriptions, 31.

[67] WOLFGANG BURR, Epigraphischer Beitrag zur neueren Pontius-Pilatus-Forschung, in Vergangenheit, Gegenwart, Zukunft (ed. W. Burr; Unitas Schriftenreihe 1; Würzburg: Verlag des Wissenschaftlichen Katholischen Studentenvereins Unitas, 1972), 37–41.

[68] ECK, Rom und Judaea, 16–17; idem, CIIP II, 229.

[69] Cf. ALFÖLDY, Pontius Pilatus, 94–101, for a reconstruction of the historical context.

[70] HAVVA İŞKAN-IŞIK, WERNER ECK, and HELMUT ENGELMANN, Der Leuchtturm von Patara und Sex. Marcius Priscus als Statthalter der Provinz Lycia von Nero bis Vespasian, ZPE 164 (2008): 91–121. The relevant line 8–9 reads: τὸν φάρον κατεσκεύασεν πρό[ς ἀς]φά / λ[ει]αν [τῶ]ν πλοϊ[ζομένω]ν; Nero Claudius Caesar Augustus Germanicus "hat diesen Leuchtturm zum Schutz der Seefahrenden errichten lassen."

[71] Cf. ALFÖLDY, Nochmals: Pontius Pilatus, 134–35 n. 10; BERNETT, Kaiserkult, 212; ECK, Rom und Judaea 16–17 n. 3; EVANS, Excavating Caiaphas, 334–36; DEMANDT, Pontius Pilatus, 74; W. ECK, in CIIP II, 229.

[72] BERNETT, Kaiserkult, 211–14.

The inscription confirms that his title was *praefectus Iudaeae*,[73] which proves, according to W. Eck, "that he was not a governor in charge of an independent province Iudaea, but subordinate to the legate of Syria."[74] On the *praefecti* of the provincial administration in the Roman Empire see the Introduction to Part 2. And the inscription attests to building activity initiated by Pontius Pilatus, at least for Caesarea Maritima, the political capital of Roman Judea.

**(77)** Philo, *De legatione ad Gaium* 299–305

ἔχω δέ τι καὶ φιλοτίμημα αὐτοῦ προσδιηγήσασθαι καίτοι μυρίων ἀπολελαυκὼς ὅτε ἔζη κακῶν· ἀλλὰ τἀληθὲς φίλον καὶ σοὶ τίμιον. Πιλᾶτος ἦν τῶν ὑπάρχων ἐπίτροπος ἀποδεδειγμένος τῆς Ἰουδαίας· οὗτος οὐκ ἐπὶ τιμῇ Τιβερίου μᾶλλον ἢ ἕνεκα τοῦ λυπῆσαι τὸ πλῆθος ἀνατίθησιν ἐν τοῖς κατὰ τὴν ἱερόπολιν Ἡρῴδου βασιλείοις ἐπιχρύσους ἀσπίδας μήτε μορφὴν ἐχούσας μήτε ἄλλο τι τῶν ἀπηγορευμένων, ἔξω τινὸς ἐπιγραφῆς ἀναγκαίας, ἢ δύο ταῦτα ἐμήνυε, τόν τε ἀναθέντα καὶ ὑπὲρ οὗ ἡ ἀνάθεσις. [300] ἐπεὶ δὲ ᾔσθοντο οἱ πολλοί – καὶ περιβόητον ἦν ἤδη τὸ πρᾶγμα –, προστησάμενοι τούς τε βασιλέως υἱεῖς τέτταρας οὐκ ἀποδέοντας τό τε ἀξίωμα καὶ τὰς τύχας βασιλέων καὶ τοὺς ἄλλους ἀπογόνους καὶ τῶν παρ' αὐτοῖς τοὺς ἐν τέλει παρεκάλουν τὸ νεωτερισθὲν περὶ τὰς ἀσπίδας εἰς ἐπανόρθωσιν ἀγαγεῖν καὶ μὴ κινεῖν ἔθη πάτρια τὸν πρὸ τοῦ πάντα αἰῶνα διαφυλαχθέντα καὶ πρὸς βασιλέων καὶ πρὸς αὐτοκρατόρων ἀκίνητα. [301] στερρῶς δὲ ἀντιλέγοντος – ἦν γὰρ τὴν φύσιν ἀκαμπὴς καὶ μετὰ τοῦ αὐθάδους ἀμείλικτος –, ἀνεβόησαν· 'μὴ στασίαζε, μὴ πολεμοποίει, μὴ κατάλυε τὴν εἰρήνην· οὐκ ἔστιν ἀτιμία νόμων ἀρχαίων αὐτοκράτορος τιμή. μὴ πρόφασις τῆς εἰς τὸ ἔθνος ἐπηρείας ἔστω σοι Τιβέριος· οὐδὲν ἐθέλει τῶν ἡμετέρων καταλύεσθαι. εἰ δὲ φῄς, αὐτὸς ἐπίδειξον ἢ διάταγμα ἢ ἐπιστολὴν ἤ τι ὁμοιότροπον, ἵνα παυσάμενοι τοῦ σοὶ διενοχλεῖν πρέσβεις ἑλόμενοι δεώμεθα τοῦ δεσπότου.' [302] τὸ τελευταῖον τοῦτο μάλιστα αὐτὸν ἐξετράχυνε καταδείσαντα, μὴ τῷ ὄντι πρεσβευσάμενοι καὶ τῆς ἄλλης αὐτὸν ἐπιτροπῆς ἐξελέγξωσι τὰς δωροδοκίας, τὰς ὕβρεις, τὰς ἁρπαγάς, τὰς αἰκίας, τὰς ἐπηρείας, τοὺς ἀκρίτους καὶ ἐπαλλήλους φόνους, τὴν ἀνήνυτον καὶ ἀργαλεωτάτην ὠμότητα διεξελθόντες. [303] οἷα οὖν ἐγκότως ἔχων καὶ βαρύμηνις <ὢν> ἄνθρωπος ἐν ἀμηχάνοις ἦν, μήτε καθελεῖν τὰ ἅπαξ ἀνατεθέντα θαρρῶν μήτε βουλόμενός τι τῶν πρὸς ἡδονὴν τοῖς ὑπηκόοις ἐργάσασθαι, ἅμα δὲ καὶ

---

[73] Eck, Rom und Judaea, 35, emphasizes, that Pontius Pilate is not called *praefectus provinciae Iudaeae*, prefect of the province of Judea, and certainly not *procurator Iudaeae*. The inscription demonstrates that despite the designation ἐπίτροπος / *procurator* for the chief Roman official in Judea by Josephus and Tacitus, the title was ἔπαρχος / *praefectus*, at least until A.D. 41 when emperor Claudius introduced the title *praeses* for equestrian procurators in some provinces.

[74] W. Eck, in CIIP II, 229.

τὴν ἐν τούτοις σταθερότητα Τιβερίου μὴ ἀγνοῶν· ἅπερ ὁρῶντες οἱ ἐν τέλει καὶ συνιέντες, ὅτι μετανοεῖ μὲν ἐπὶ τοῖς πεπραγμένοις δοκεῖν δὲ οὐ βούλεται γράφουσι Τιβερίῳ δεητικωτάτας ἐπιστολάς. ³⁰⁴ ὁ δὲ διαναγνοὺς οἷα μὲν εἶπε Πιλᾶτον, οἷα δὲ ἠπείλησεν· ὡς δὲ ὠργίσθη, καίτοι οὐκ εὔληπτος ὢν ὀργῇ, περιττόν ἐστι διηγεῖσθαι τοῦ πράγματος ἐξ αὐτοῦ φωνὴν ἀφιέντος. ³⁰⁵ εὐθέως γὰρ οὐδὲ εἰς τὴν ὑστεραίαν ὑπερθέμενος ἐπιστέλλει, μυρία μὲν τοῦ καινουργηθέντος τολμήματος ὀνειδίζων καὶ ἐπιπλήττων, κελεύων δὲ αὐτίκα καθελεῖν τὰς ἀσπίδας καὶ μετακομισθῆναι ἐκ τῆς μητροπόλεως εἰς τὴν ἐπὶ θαλάττῃ Καισάρειαν, ἐπώνυμον τοῦ προπάππου Σεβαστήν, ἵνα ἀνατεθεῖεν ἐν τῷ Σεβαστείῳ· καὶ ἀνετέθησαν. οὕτως ἀμφότερα ἐφυλάχθη, καὶ ἡ τιμὴ τοῦ αὐτοκράτορος, καὶ ἡ περὶ τὴν πόλιν ἀρχαία συνήθεια.

*Translation.* I can also tell you of an act on which he (i.e., the emperor Tiberius) prided himself, even though I suffered countless ills when he was alive. But you love and honor the truth. Pilatus was an official who had been appointed governor of Judea. He set up shields plated with gold in Herod's palace in the Holy City, not so much to honor Tiberius, but with the intention of annoying the Jews. They bore no figure nor anything else that was forbidden (by the law), but only the briefest possible inscription, which stated two things: the name of the person who made the dedication, and the name of the person in whose honor the dedication was made. ³⁰⁰ But when the people learnt (of Pilatus' action), which was already much talked about,[75] they chose as their spokesmen[76] the king's four sons, who in prestige and position[77] were not inferior to a king, his other descendants, and their own officials, and appealed to Pilatus to correct his innovation with respect to the shields and not to violate their native customs which had been invariably safeguarded in the past by kings and emperors. ³⁰¹ When he (Pilatus) stubbornly refused – a man inflexible by nature, arrogant, and cruel – they shouted, "Do not cause a revolt! Do not cause a war! Do not break the peace! Disgracing our ancient laws does not honor the emperor. Do not use Tiberius as an excuse for insulting our nation: he does not wish any of our customs to be abolished. If you say that he does, show us some decree or letter or something of the sort so that we may cease troubling you and appeal to our lord by means of an embassy." ³⁰² This last point particularly exasperated him, because he was afraid that if they really sent an embassy, they would expose[78] his administration as well by specifying in detail his taking of bribes, his violence, his robberies, his assaults, his hostile attitude, his executions without trial in quick succession,

---

[75] The adjective περιβόητον is also used with the negative sense of "notorious, scandalous" (LSJ s.v. περιβόητος 2); thus YONGE: "when the circumstance became notorious."

[76] Following SMALLWOOD for describing the king's four sons as "spokesmen."

[77] Cf. LSJ s.v. τύχη IV.3: position, station in life, rank.

[78] BDAG s.v. ἐξελέγχω; cf. LSJ s.v. ἐξελέγχω 1. convict, confute, refute; 2. put to the proof, bring to the test. SMALLWOOD translates "bring accusations," YONGE "impeach."

and his endless and supremely grievous savagery. [303] So, as he was a spiteful man with a furious temper, he was in a serious dilemma. He did not have the courage to remove what he had once set up, nor did he have the will to do anything which would please his subjects. At the same time he knew full well Tiberius' firmness regarding these matters. When the (Jewish) officials[79] saw this and realized that he regretted his actions, but did not wish to show it, they wrote a letter with the most earnest supplication[80] to Tiberius. [304] When he read it, what words, what threats Tiberius uttered against Pilatus! There is no need to describe his anger, although he was not easily provoked to anger, since his reaction speaks for itself. [305] For he wrote to him (Pilatus) immediately, without even waiting for the next day, reproaching and rebuking him a thousand times for his unprecedented audacity, and telling him to remove the shields at once and have them taken from the capital to Caesarea on the coast (the city named Sebaste after your great-grandfather), to be dedicated in the temple of Augustus. This was duly done. In this way both the honor of the emperor and the traditional policy regarding Jerusalem were safeguarded.

*Commentary.* This text belongs to the memorandum that King Agrippa I (A.D. 37–44), the grandson of Herod I, a friend of Gaius Caligula, wrote to Gaius in a renewed attempt to convince the emperor to abandon his plans regarding the Temple (*Legat.* 276–329). Gaius had commanded Publius Petronius, the legate of the province of Syria in A.D. 39–42, to make a colossal statue of himself and erect it in the Temple in Jerusalem.[81] Agrippa was in Rome in the summer of A.D. 39.[82] In his memorandum to the emperor, Agrippa describes (1) the significance of Jerusalem and the attitude of the Jews concerning the city (*Legat.* 278—289); (2) the respect shown by M. Vipsanius Agrippa and others for the Temple (290–298); (3) the prohibition of the emperor Tiberius regarding Pontius Pilatus' introduction of votive shields into Jerusalem (299–305); (4) the sanctity of the Holy of Holies in the Temple (306–308); (5) the protection of the religious liberty of the Jews by Augustus (309–318); (6) the gifts of Livia to the Temple (319–320); (7) an appeal to precedent (321–322); (8) the former kindness of Gaius to Agrippa (323–329).[83]

Philo's report about the decision of Pilatus to set up gold-plated shields in Herod's palace (Ἡρῴδου βασιλείοις) in Jerusalem in honor of Tiberius is regarded by some scholars as another version of Josephus' report about the Roman standards brought by the troops to Jerusalem (*B. J.* 2.169–177; see No.

---

[79] Thus SMALLWOOD translating οἱ ἐν τέλει; COLSON translates "the magnates."

[80] SMALLWOOD translates δεητικωτάτας ἐπιστολάς with "a letter ... pleading their case as forcibly as they could."

[81] Philo, *Legat.* 188, 207–208; Josephus, *A. J.* 18.261–262; *B. J.* 2.185–187; cf. Tacitus, *Hist.* 5.9.

[82] SANDRA GAMBETTI, The Alexandrian Riots of 38 C.E. and the Persecution of the Jews: A Historical Reconstruction (JSJSup 135; Leiden: Brill, 2009), 266.

[83] Cf. SMALLWOOD, Legatio ad Gaium, 51–52.

78).[84] It seems more likely that these were two different incidents.[85] (1) The objects of dispute are different. In Philo's report they were shields with an inscription but no pictorial representation. In Josephus' account they were military standards with displayed an image of the emperor. (2) The location of the conflict differs. The affair of the gilded shields takes places in Jerusalem: Pilatus is present in Jerusalem and confronted there by the Jewish protest. The affair of the military standards takes place in both Jerusalem and Caesarea: the standards are brought from Caesarea to Jerusalem, but Pilatus stays in Caesarea, which is where the Jewish protests take place. (3) The form and organization of the protest differ. In Josephus' report, Jewish crowds protest spontaneously against the presence of the military standards in Jerusalem; no leaders of the protest are mentioned; Pilatus makes the decision to give in to the protesters. In Philo's report, it is members of the Herodian dynasty, chosen as spokesmen by the Jewish population, who articulate the Jewish protest before Pilatus, who refuses to compromise, and then before the emperor who forces Pilatus to respect the Jewish customs.

The incident related by Philo most likely took place after the incident described by Josephus.[86] In view of the inscription inscribed on the shields honoring the emperor Tiberius (see below), it can be assumed that the incident happened shortly after the fall of Sejanus (October 18, A.D. 31), when Pilatus would have wanted to demonstrate his loyalty to Tiberius.[87] Herod's palace stood in the western part of the upper city; it served both as a luxurious residence and a fortress.[88] The shields were probably set up in one of the two reception and banqueting halls, which were the most impressive parts of the palace "with which the Temple itself bore no comparison; these he named after his friends, the one Caesareum, the other Agrippeum" (Josephus, *B. J.* 1.402; cf. 5.179; *A. J.* 15.318). The fact that four Herodian princes and Pilatus were in Jerusalem at the same time suggests that the event of *Legat.* 299–305

---

[84] Already Eusebius in *Dem. ev.* 8.2.122–123, in contrast to *Hist. eccl.* 2.5.7; 6.4. More recently DANIEL R. SCHWARTZ, Josephus and Philo on Pontius Pilate, in The Jerusalem Cathedra: Studies in the History, Archaeology, Geography and Ethnography of the Land of Israel (ed. L. I. Levine; Jerusalem: Yad Izhak Ben-Zvi Institute, 1983), 3:26–45; DEMANDT, Pontius Pilatus, 87–89; MANUEL VOGEL, Herodes: König der Juden, Freund der Römer (Leipzig: Evangelische Verlagsanstalt, 2002), 299; HERZER, Loyalität, 433.

[85] Cf. SMALLWOOD, Legatio ad Gaium, 302; LÉMONON, Ponce Pilate: documents profanes, 758; LÉMONON, Ponce Pilate, 133-34, 189–90; BOND, Pontius Pilate, 37–38; WILKER, Dynastie, 101–3; W. ECK, in CIIP I/1, 61. For the following points see especially WILKER, ibid. 102–3. Differently SCHWARTZ, Reading, 115–21.

[86] On the date of the two incidents cf. BOND, Pontius Pilate, 45–46.

[87] PAUL L. MAIER, The Episode of the Golden Shields at Jerusalem, HTR 27 (1969): 109–121, 113–14; GIDEON FUKS, Again on the Episode of the Gilded Roman Shields at Jerusalem, HTR 75 (1982): 503–507; BOND, Pontius Pilate, 45–46; WILKER, Dynastie, 101 n. 137.

[88] Cf. EHUD NETZER, The Architecture of Herod, the Great Builder (Grand Rapids: Baker, 2008), 129–32. See the description by Josephus in *B. J.* 5.176–181.

occurred during a festival. The four Herodian princes whose prestige and status is compared to that of kings are the tetrarchs Antipas and Philip, and either Herod (son of Mariamne), Herod (son of Cleopatra), or Phasael (son of Pallas). Herod's "other descendants" might have included the brothers Agrippa I, Herod II, and Aristobulos.[89]

Philo relates that these members of the Herodian dynasty, together with other Jewish officials in Jerusalem, prompted by the population, articulated the protest both before Pontius Pilatus (300) as well as before the emperor to whom they sent a protest letter (δεητικωτάτας ἐπιστολάς; 303). This letter may have been the cause of the enmity that existed between Antipas and Pilatus at the time of Jesus' trial (Luke 23:12).[90]

Philo describes Pilatus as ὕπαρχος, i.e., an "official" (*Legat.* 299). The Greek term is used for a "subordinate commander" or "lieutenants," but also for a "subordinate governor"[91] as well as for proconsuls for the *praefectus Aegypti*,[92] or the *praefectus praetorio*.[93] The translation "official"[94] is helpfully vague about Pilatus' status at the time of his appointment as *praefectus Iudaeae*. When Philo uses the term ἐπίτροπος, i.e., *procurator*,[95] for Pilatus (299, 302), this is anachronistic (see the introduction to Part 2).

The shields were round shields (ἄσπις, Lat. *clupeus* or *clipeus*), presumably made of bronze and plated with gold. They were sometimes used to honor a person, often decorated with an image of the honoree or displaying inscriptions. The senate in Rome honored Augustus in 27 B.C. in the Curia Julia with a golden *clipeus virtutis*.[96] The inscription on the gold-plated shields (ἐπίχρυσοι ἀσπίδες) that Pilatus set up in Jerusalem would have been in Latin. The first part was, most likely, the text *Ti(berio) Caesari Augusto*, the second part *Pontius Pilatus praefectus Iudaeae*.[97] Philo asserts that the shields "bore no figure nor anything else that was forbidden (by the law)" (μήτε μορφὴν ἐχούσας μήτε ἄλλο τι τῶν ἀπηγορευμένων). E. M. SMALLWOOD surmises, "The episode of the iconic military standards may have awakened the Jews to

---

[89] Cf. SMALLWOOD, Legatio ad Gaium, 303; KLAUS-STEFAN KRIEGER, Pontius Pilatus - ein Judenfeind? Zur Problematik einer Pilatusbiographie, BNot 78 (1995): 63–83, 65 n. 10; BERNETT, Kaiserkult, 201 n. 121; WILKER, Dynastie, 96–97.

[90] SMALLWOOD, Legatio ad Gaium, 306, with reference to A. D. DOYLE, Pilate's Career and the Date of the Crucifixion, JTS 42 (1941): 190–193; cf. NIKOS KOKKINOS, The Herodian Dynasty: Origins, Role in Society and Eclipse (JSPSup 26; Sheffield: Sheffield Academic Press, 1997), 195–96; HERZER, Loyalität, 447.

[91] The term is used of a Persian satrap by Herodotus, 3.70; 4.166.

[92] Arrianus, *An.* 3.5.7.

[93] IGRom III 435. Cf. LSJ s.v. ὕπαρχος.

[94] SMALLWOOD. YONGE and COLSON translate as "lieutenant."

[95] Cf. LSJ s.v. ἐπιτροπή II.2 "office of a Roman procurator."

[96] Monumentum Ancyranum 34; cf. DEMANDT, Pontius Pilatus, 85.

[97] WERNER ECK, in CIIP 1/1, 61 (No. 14); the title *praefectus Iudaeae* is taken from the Pilatus inscription from Caesarea, following G. Alföldy's reconstruction (see No. 76).

the fact that aniconic objects also could have religious significance for the Romans, and made them anxious to keep even those out of Jerusalem ... as Pilate had met stiff opposition when he had openly flouted Jewish religious feeling, he might now be initiating another attack by a seemingly innocent action which was to be the forerunner of some definite contravention of the Law."[98] The anger of the Jews seems to have been provoked by the fact that the reference to Tiberius contained the filiation *divi Aug(usti) f(ilio) divi Iuli nep(oti)* ("for Tiberius, the son of the divine Augustus, grandson of the divine Iulius [Caesar]."[99] W. ECK comments that if this is correct, "Pilate did not deliberately try to provoke the Jews, but insisted on using the standard formula for the name of Tiberius as attested in many other epigraphical documents."[100] Philo's report is obscure and somewhat self-contradictory: he allows that the shields Pilatus set up in Jerusalem contained nothing that should have offensive to the Jews, while on the other hand he relates that their presence in Jerusalem triggered riots. W. ECK surmises that there must have been people in Jerusalem who described Pilatus' action to other Jews in such a manner that the actual event as described by Philo was massively distorted. However, Philo does not intimate which people would benefit from a violent reaction of a large part of the Jewish population. Since Philo has a massive interest in portraying the emperor Tiberius as a protector of Jewish interests, we can hardly expect an objective description of the incident which would do justice to Pontius Pilatus.[101]

Philo's characterization of Pilatus is consistently negative. He describes him as a man who was "inflexible by nature" (τὴν φύσιν ἀκαμπὴς; 301), "arrogant" (αὐθάδης), "cruel" (ἀμείλικτος); as an official who engages in "taking of bribes" (δωροδοκία, 302), "violence" (ὕβρις),[102] "robberies"

---

[98] SMALLWOOD, Legatio ad Gaium, 304.

[99] Cf. ILS 114. 6080; in ILS 113. 152. 153 etc. the title *pontifex maximus* is added. Cf. FUKS, Episode, 507; BOND, Pontius Pilate, 38–39; MORTEN HØRNING JENSEN, Herod Antipas in Galilee: The Literary and Archaeological Sources on the Reign of Herod Antipas and its Socio-Economic Impact on Galilee (WUNT 2/215; Tübingen: Mohr Siebeck, 2006), 108; WILKER, Dynastie, 96; W. ECK, CIIP I/1, 61. DEMANDT, Pontius Pilatus, 86, wonders why, if this is correct, Philo did not mention this fact.

[100] W. Eck, in CIIP I/1, 61, citing ILS 155, 156, 159; cf. ECK, Rom und Judaea, 59 n. 8. Differently GOTTFRIED SCHIMANOWSKI, Juden und Nichtjuden in Alexandrien: Koexistenz und Konflikte bis zum Pogrom unter Trajan (117 n. Chr.) (Berlin: Lit, 2006), 140, who interprets Pilatus' action as evidence for the deterioration of the legal situation of the Jews. On the religious duties of Roman officials in the provinces cf. WERNER ECK, Die religiösen und kultischen Aufgaben der römischen Statthalter in der Hohen Kaiserzeit [1992], in Die Verwaltung des römischen Reiches in der Hohen Kaiserzeit. Ausgewählte und erweiterte Beiträge. Band 2 (AREA 3; Basel / Berlin: Reinhardt, 1997), 203–217.

[101] ECK, Repräsentanten, 183.

[102] LSJ s.v. ὕβρις I. wanton violence, arising from the pride of strength or from passion; insolence; II. outrage.

(ἁρπαγη),[103] "assaults (αἰκία),[104] "hostile attitude" (ἐπήρεια), "executions without trial in quick succession" (οἱ ἄκρίτοι καὶ ἐπαλλήλοι φόνοι),[105] "endless and supremely grievous savagery" (ἡ ἀνήνυτος καὶ ἀργαλεωτάτης ὠμότης),[106] and as a man who is "spiteful" (ἐγκότως, 303) and who has "a furious temper" (βαρύμηνις ὢν ἄνθρωπος). Philo evaluates Pilatus' actions in equally negative terms: when he sets up the controversial shields in Jerusalem, he does so "with the intention of annoying the Jews" (ἕνεκα τοῦ λυπῆσαι τὸ πλῆθος, 299). He is "stubborn" (στερρῶς) in his refusal to respect precedent (301). He has neither the courage (μήτε ... θαρρῶν) to acknowledge his mistake and remove the shields, nor does he have the will (μήτε βουλόμενός) to do something that would please the Jews (303). In contrast to Pilatus, the emperor Tiberius is characterized by "firmness" (σταθερότης, 303): he arrives at the correct decision in the matter without delay, commanding Pilatus to remove the shields at once and to set them up in the temple of Augustus in Caesarea, thus demonstrating the honor of the emperor and safeguarding the traditional policy regarding Jewish sensibilities (305).

Some scholars accept Philo's negative portrayal of Pontius Pilatus as reflecting historical reality.[107] M. PLAULT attributes Pilatus' plan to bring the shields of the Roman cohort, stationed in Caesarea, to Jerusalem to his euphoria over his promotion to governor.[108] Others are more skeptical. J. BLINZLER thinks that Philo's portrayal does not do Pontius Pilatus full justice, but nevertheless accepts that the prefect was antisemitic.[109] E. M. SMALLWOOD explains Pilatus' obstinacy in the context of the earlier conflicts with the Jewish population: in the episode of the standards (Josephus, *B. J.* 2.169–174; *A. J.* 18.55–59), he had ultimately given way and had them removed; by the time of the incident of the aqueduct (*B. J.* 2.175–177; *A. J.* 18.60–62), "his attitude had hardened, and he had many Jews massacred for their opposition."[110] A. STROBEL argues that Pilatus could hardly have remained in his post for a

---

[103] LSJ s.v. ἁρπαγή 1. seizure robbery, forcible abduction; 2. booty, prey; 3. greediness.

[104] LSJ s.v. αἰκία 1. insulting treatment, outrage; 3. in Prose usu[ally] law-term, *assault*.

[105] Cf. LSJ s.v. ἄκρῑτος II.1. undecided, doubtful; 2. unjudged, untried, of persons and things; without trial; subject to no judge; s.v. ἐπαλληλος I. one close after another, in close order, in quick succession. The noun φόνος is used for "murder, slaughter, killing."

[106] Cf. LSJ s.v. ὠμότης I. rawness, crudeness; II. savagery, fierceness, cruelty. This phrase may allude to the massacre which ended the aqueduct episode (Josephus, *B. J.* 2.176–177) and to the massacre of Galileans (Luke 13:1); cf. SMALLWOOD, Legatio ad Gaium, 305.

[107] Cf. MARTIN HENGEL, Gewalt und Gewaltlosigkeit. Zur 'politischen Theologie' in neutestamentlicher Zeit [1971], in Jesus und die Evangelien: Kleine Schriften V (ed. C.-J. Thornton; Tübingen: Mohr Siebeck, 2007), 245–288, 268, with reference to Luke 13:1.

[108] MICHEL PLAULT, Affaire Jésus. Rapports de Ponce Pilate, préfet de Judée, à la Chancellerie romaine (Paris: Calmann-Lévy, 1965), 12. He thinks that despite the fact that Pilate had been in Judea for four years by A.D. 30, he would have hardly been a specialist in Jewish questions; at the same time he was not an anti-Semite (ibid. 17, 19).

[109] BLINZLER, Prozeß, 260, 264.

[110] SMALLWOOD, Legatio ad Gaium, 304.

decade had he been as corrupt and cruel as Philo (and Josephus) suggest: Philo's story attests to a certain stubborn defiance on the part of Pilatus, but also to an unmistakable respect regarding the stubbornness of the Jews, as well as to his timidity, if not cowardice regarding the emperor.[111] J. P. LÉMONON concludes that while Agrippa's (and thus Philo's) account needs to be read critically, the episode of the gilded shields reveals several faces of Pilatus: he does not want to hurt the Jews systematically, but he is insensitive to the protests of the Jewish population, whose sensibilities he refuses to comprehend; he is fearful of the emperor who has the ultimate power over him; he is not insulting nor cantakerous, but embarrassed by the situation into which he got himself.[112] H. K. BOND argues that Philo's characterization of Pontius Pilatus stems largely from his political rhetoric "in which he tries to persuade Claudius not to adopt Gaius' attitude to the Jews, and from his theology, in which the enemies of Judaism are the enemies of God and are thus portrayed extremely negatively;" she concludes that Philo's description of the facts seems trustworthy: the setting up of the shields was not an aggressive act, as the lack of imperial portraits and the location inside the headquarters of the Roman administration show, but aimed at demonstrating his loyalty to the emperor; when protest arose, he was afraid that the removal of the shields would negate the project of honoring the emperor.[113] W. ECK doubts whether we should expect an objective account of the incident from Philo, considering his massive interest in portraying Tiberius as protector of Jewish interests; it is not possible, however, to establish at what places Philo sugarcoated or sharpened his account.[114] M. BERNETT concludes that most scholars today view the episode of the shields as a marginal event that Philo elevated to a conflict between the Roman governor and the Jews in order to highlight the enormity of Gaius Caligulas' claim to have the authority to be worshiped in Jerusalem as God; Pilatus respected the aniconic tradition of the Jews; nevertheless, the shields were offensive because their inscription was connected with the cult of Tiberius.[115] R. L. WEBB explains Pilatus' alleged character qualities (301, 303) as part of Philo's polemical rhetoric, but regards the more specific charges – venality, robbery, executions without trial (302) – are more likely to be historical: the episode related by Philo "reveals Pilate as a governor intent on maintaining the power and honor of the Roman empire he served and represented."[116]

---

[111] STROBEL, Stunde, 100, 104.

[112] LÉMONON, Pilate, 226; LÉMONON, Ponce Pilate, 203–4.

[113] BOND, Pontius Pilate, 47.

[114] ECK, Repräsentanten, 183.

[115] BERNETT, Kaiserkult, 202, wtih reference to KRIEGER, Pontius Pilatus, 75–76.

[116] WEBB, Roman Examination, 720.

**(78)** Josephus, *Bellum judaicum* 2.169–174

Πεμφθεὶς δὲ εἰς Ἰουδαίαν ἐπίτροπος ὑπὸ Τιβερίου Πιλᾶτος νύκτωρ κεκαλυμμένας εἰς Ἱεροσόλυμα εἰσκομίζει[117] τὰς Καίσαρος εἰκόνας, αἳ σημαῖαι καλοῦνται. [170] τοῦτο μεθ' ἡμέραν μεγίστην ταραχὴν ἤγειρεν Ἰουδαίοις· οἵ τε γὰρ ἐγγὺς πρὸς τὴν ὄψιν ἐξεπλάγησαν ὡς πεπατημένων αὐτοῖς τῶν νόμων, οὐδὲν γὰρ ἀξιοῦσιν ἐν τῇ πόλει δείκηλον τίθεσθαι, καὶ πρὸς τὴν ἀγανάκτησιν τῶν κατὰ τὴν πόλιν ἄθρους ὁ ἐκ τῆς χώρας λαὸς συνέρρευσεν. [171] ὁρμήσαντες δὲ πρὸς Πιλᾶτον εἰς Καισάρειαν ἱκέτευον ἐξενεγκεῖν ἐξ Ἱεροσολύμων τὰς σημαίας καὶ τηρεῖν αὐτοῖς τὰ πάτρια. Πιλάτου δὲ ἀρνουμένου περὶ τὴν οἰκίαν πρηνεῖς καταπεσόντες ἐπὶ πέντε ἡμέρας καὶ νύκτας ἴσας ἀκίνητοι διεκαρτέρουν. [172] Τῇ δ' ἑξῆς ὁ Πιλᾶτος καθίσας ἐπὶ βήματος ἐν τῷ μεγάλῳ σταδίῳ καὶ προσκαλεσάμενος τὸ πλῆθος ὡς ἀποκρίνασθαι δῆθεν αὐτοῖς θέλων, δίδωσιν τοῖς στρατιώταις σημεῖον ἐκ συντάγματος κυκλώσασθαι τοὺς Ἰουδαίους ἐν τοῖς ὅπλοις. [173] περιστάσης δὲ τριστιχεὶ τῆς φάλαγγος Ἰουδαῖοι μὲν ἀχανεῖς ἦσαν πρὸς τὸ ἀδόκητον τῆς ὄψεως, Πιλᾶτος δὲ κατακόψειν εἰπὼν αὐτούς, εἰ μὴ προσδέξαιντο τὰς Καίσαρος εἰκόνας, γυμνοῦν τὰ ξίφη τοῖς στρατιώταις ἔνευσεν. [174] οἱ δὲ Ἰουδαῖοι καθάπερ ἐκ συνθήματος ἀθρόοι καταπεσόντες καὶ τοὺς αὐχένας παρακλίναντες ἑτοίμους ἀναιρεῖν σφᾶς[118] ἐβόων μᾶλλον ἢ τὸν νόμον παραβῆναι. ὑπερθαυμάσας δὲ ὁ Πιλᾶτος τὸ τῆς δεισιδαιμονίας ἄκρατον ἐκκομίσαι μὲν αὐτίκα τὰς σημαίας Ἱεροσολύμων κελεύει.

*Translation.* Pilatus, who had been sent by Tiberius to Judea as procurator, introduced to Jerusalem at night and under cover the images[119] of Caesar which are called standards. [170] This stirred up an immense upheaval among the Jews on the following day. Those who were close to the spectacle were shocked at their appearance, thinking that their laws had been trampled, because they do not permit any representation to be set up in the city. Stirred by the indignation of the people in the city, the people from the countryside flowed into the city all at once. [171] They rushed headlong to Pilatus in Caesarea and implored him to remove the standards from Jerusalem and to preserve their ancestral customs. When Pilatus refused, they fell down prostrate around his residence, and for five days and as many nights they remained motionless in that position. [172] On the following day Pilatus sat on the tribunal-platform[120] in the great stadium, and, summoning the crowd with the apparent intention of answering them, he gave a signal to his soldiers, accord-

---

[117] THACKERAY reads παρεισκομίζει, attested in Eusebius' quotation of this passage (*Hist. eccl.* 2.6.4).

[118] The active infinitive is read in manuscripts PA; the easier reading εἰς ἀναίρεσιν ("[declared themselves ready] for elimination" seems "an accommodation to a more expected passive formulation," as in the parallel *A. J.* 18.59 (MASON, Judean War 2, 145 n. 1093).

[119] THACKERAY translates "effigies," MICHEL / BAUERNFEIND "Kaiserbilder."

[120] Following the translation of MASON; WHISTON and THACKERAY translate "tribunal," MICHEL / BAUERNFEIND have "Richterstuhl."

ing to a scheme, to surround the Jews with weapons. [173] Being surrounded by the infantry column three-deep, the Jews were stunned at this unexpected sight. Pilatus threatened to cut them to pieces if they refused to accept the images of Caesar, and signaled to the soldiers to draw their swords. [174] The Jews fell to the ground all at once, as if an agreed signal; they exposed their necks and shouted that they were ready to be killed rather than transgress the law. Greatly surprised by the purity of their religious zeal,[121] Pilatus ordered the immediate removal of the standards from Jerusalem.

*Commentary.* Josephus' description of the history of Judea after Herod's death begins with a description of the rule of his son Archelaos, ethnarch of Judea, which ends in anarchy and in Archelaos' banishment to Vienne in Gaul (2.1– 116). Augustus placed Judea under direct Roman rule in A.D. 6. Josephus reports relatively little for the next thirty-one years, until the reign of Agrippa I from A.D. 41–44 (2.178–220). He mentions only two Roman prefects of Judea for the period from A.D. 6–41: Coponius, a Roman of the equestrian order, "who belonged to the equestrian order among the Romans, was sent as the procurator, having received from the emperor full powers, including the infliction of the death penalty" (2.117; No. 13), and Pilatus (2.169–177).

Between Coponius and Pilatus, Josephus provides a description of the Essenes (2.119–161) and the Pharisees and Sadducees (2.162–166). And he briefly reports on the rule of Philip and Antipas, the other sons of Herod I who had been given territories by Augustus, who continued to rule as tetrarchs after Judea had become a Roman province (2.167) and after Augustus' death when Tiberius became emperor in A.D. 14 (2.168). Josephus relates in *Bellum* two incidents involving Pilatus: the affair of the standards (2.169–174) and the affair of the aqueduct (2.175–177; see No. 79).

Pilatus' residence (οἰκία; 2.171) was most likely the palace of Herod I in Caesarea (see No. 77). The tribunal-platform (βῆμα; Lat. *rostrum*; 2.172) was an elevated podium, shaped in a variety of forms, and stood in a central location (forum, theater); it was "the central place for the representation of the power of the ruler, a place for speeches and addresses."[122] Here, the *bema* was probably the VIP box in the center of the stadium.[123] Herod's amphitheater (stadium), built on the seashore next to his palace, used by the prefects of Judea as praetorium, was ca. 316 x 64 m and seated 7,000–13,000 people on

---

[121] MASON, Judean War 2, 145, translates "superstition" and comments that, given the usually negative connotation of the term δεισιδαιμονία (e.g. *B. J.* 1.113; and in Plutarch, *Mor.* 164C–171) and given the positive meaning in *B. J.* 2.230, "it remains unclear – perhaps artfully so – whether the word should reflect Pilate's negative judgment on his foreign 'superstition' or whether the word itself should take a less pejorative sense here" (145 n. 1096).

[122] CHRISTOPH HÖCKER, Rostrum, BNP 12 (2008): 741–742, 741.

[123] DEMANDT, Pontius Pilatus, 86; according to Josephus, *A. J.* 18.57, the platform was "specially constructed for this hearing" (MASON, Judean War 2, 143 n. 1076).

twelve rows of seats.[124] The affair of the standards[125] was triggered by the decision of Pilatus to bring military "standards" (σημαῖαι; Lat. *signa*) into Jerusalem, perhaps at the beginning of his tenure as prefect of Judea,[126] each of which bore the "image" (εἰκῶν; Lat. *imago*; 2.169) of Caesar (Tiberius), understood by the Jewish population as a "representation" (δείκηλον)[127] that the Law prohibits (2.170). This is a reference to the second commandment which forbids the production of a cut or hewn image (פֶּסֶל) representing anything in the sky, the earth, or the water (Exod 20:4: "You shall not make for yourself an idol, whether in the form of anything that is in heaven above, or that is on the earth beneath, or that is in the water under the earth").[128] The problem for the Jews may have been not such much the military cult of the *signa* but the imperial cult which was connected with the *signa* since the time of Augustus.[129] D. R. SCHWARTZ writes, "what motivated the Jews was a notion of there being such a thing as a Jewish capital city and (accordingly) a Jewish land and the concomitant notion that Jewish law – the law of the Jewish sovereign – should govern what happened in that land."[130]

The *signum* "represented a more or less richly orna-mented long lance: tassel and crescent moon on the lower end, discs in the middle, crown, hand,[131]

---

[124] Herod's amphitheater was uncovered between 1992–1998; cf. YOSEF PORATH, Herod's 'Amphitheater' at Caesarea: A Multipurpose Entertainment Building, in The Roman and Byzantine Near East: Some Recent Archaeological Research (JRASup 14; Ann Arbor, MI: Journal of Roman Archaeology, 1995), 15–27; JOSEPH PATRICH, The *Carceres* of the Herodian Hippodrome/Stadium at Caesarea Maritima and Connections with the Circus Maximus, *JRA* 14 (2001): 269–283. The hippodrome to the east dates to the 2nd century A.D.

[125] For the account in *A. J.* 18.55–59 see No. 80; cf. the comparative analysis in KRIEGER, Geschichtsschreibung, 32–34, 36–42; SCHWARTZ, Reading, 152–54, 164–66. Cf. MASON, Judean War 2, 138–43. For the suggestion that this is the same affair as the incident related by Philo, *Legat.* 299–305, cf. No. 77.

[126] Cf. SMALLWOOD, Jews, 161; BOND, Pontius Pilate, 79. Since Josephus relates relatively few incidents of Pilatus' tenure, the fact that the transfer of the military standards to Jerusalem is reported first does not prove that this happened at the beginning of his administration.

[127] Cf. LSJ s.v. δείκηλον I. representation; II.1 reflection, image; 2. sculptured figure. WHISTON and THACKERAY translate with "image."

[128] HALOT s.v. פֶּסֶל, "a divine image carved from wood or sculpted from stone, but later cast in metal." Cf. Deut 4:16, 23, 25; 27:15; also Isa 44:9–20; 48:5; Jer 10:14; Nah 1:14. MASON, Judean War 2, 141 n. 1061, points out, in light of the golden eagle that Herod I had placed above the Jerusalem Temple, the presence of animal motifs in Antipas' palace in Tiberias, and the figurative representations in the mosaics of later synagogues, "it seems that the precise import of the biblical prohibition was not self-evident."

[129] BERNETT, Kaiserkult, 201, with reference to KAY EHLING, Zu Th. Mommsens Auswertung der Münzzeugnisse im Judäa-Kapitel des 5. Bandes seiner Römischen Geschiche, Jahrbuch für Numismatik und Geldgeschichte 53–54 (2003–2004): 1–14, 8.

[130] SCHWARTZ, Composition and Sources, 134.

[131] The hand signified the soldiers' oath of loyalty.

and a short transverse pole with ribbons on the tip."[132] While the eagle (*aquila*) was the common standard of an entire legion, attached to the tip of a long lance, born by the first cohort,[133] the *signum* was the standard of the maniple, often a bull, ibex, or lion. The praetorian cohorts and perhaps also the *centuriae* received standards (*signa*) that were equipped with the image (*imago*) or bust of the emperor.[134] The cohorts of the auxiliary troops were identified by their *signum*. Evidence is slim, but does suggest that auxiliary troops, such as Pilatus commanded, had at least simple spearhead-capped standards with a rectangle of fabric that was hung down from a horizontal pole (*vexilla*), or standards adorned with medallions which enclosed an imperial portrait or a bull's head.[135] The standards of the auxiliary cohorts did not normally include imperial images. The soldier who carried the *signum* was called *signifer*; if he carried the *imago* of the emperor he was called *imaginifer*. In peace times, all standards were kept in a small sanctuary (*aedes signorum*), located in the center of the military camp.

The military standards of the infantry cohort[136] that Pilatus transferred to Jerusalem arrived "by night and under cover" (νύκτωρ κεκαλυμμένας; 2.169): either under cover of darkness or concealed by covers.[137] H. K. BOND thinks that "Pilate *knew* his actions would cause offence;" she adds that "the overriding impression, however, is one of insensitivity; Pilate's conduct was not blatant but combined a certain amount of stealth with secrecy and involved a disregard for the religious feelings of those under his rule."[138] M. BERNETT believes that Pilatus wanted to force the imperial cult on the Judeans.[139] S. MASON concludes that "it remains unclear whether his motive was to preclude confrontation (in hopes that the public would not see them) or to prepare the ground for it (by creating a *fait accompli*)."[140] Pilatus would have

---

[132] Cf. YANN LE BOHEC, Ensigns, BNP 4 (2004): 992–996, 995; for the following description cf. ibid. 992, 995. Cf. also GRAHAM WEBSTER, The Roman Imperial Army of the First and Second Centuries A.D. (Totowa, N.J.: Barnes, 1985), 133–50 and Plates IX–X.

[133] Pilatus did not have a legion at his disposal, only auxiliary troops.

[134] Cf. OLIVER STOLL, Der Adler im 'Käfig'. Zu einer Aquilifer-Grabstele aus Apamea in Syrien [1991], in Römisches Heer und Gesellschaft. Gesammelte Beiträge 1991–1999 (Mavors Roman Army Researches 13; Stuttgart: Steiner, 2001), 13–46, 38: Postamentrelief 7: "2 Signa mit Imago des Kaisers, darüber Adler auf 'Corona' (?), Flügel seitlich ausgebreitet" (early imperial period, perhaps Augustus and Livia).

[135] WEBSTER, Roman Imperial Army, Plate XIVb; cf. MASON, Judean War 2, 140 n. 1058.

[136] Cf. CARL HERMANN KRAELING, The Episode of the Roman Shields at Jerusalem, HTR 35 (1942): 263–289, 269–73.

[137] MASON, Judean War 2, 140 n. 1056, refers, for the latter possibility, to some reliefs which show images on military standards concealed by covers; cf. WEBSTER, Roman Imperial Army, Plate IXa.

[138] BOND, Pontius Pilate, 57; for the following point cf. ibid. 80. Following BOND, cf. WEBB, Roman Examination, 715.

[139] BERNETT, Kaiserkult, 199–201.

[140] MASON, Judean War 2, 140 n. 1056.

hardly understood why standards that one of his infantry cohorts used in Caesarea could not be brought to Jerusalem; as prefect responsible for law and order in Judea, he would have naturally insisted on the free deployment of his troops. BOND believes that the crowd's appeal to the Law was, to some extent, "a cover for a more political demand regarding the removal of the troops."[141]

As regards the scene in Caesarea (2.171–74), Josephus focuses on the Jews rather than on Pilatus' psychology: when he lets the Jewish protesters wait outside his residence for five days and nights, he shows "either patience or stubbornness," expecting the people to give up, accept the standards, and go home.[142] When the Jews hold out longer than he evidently thought they would, he does not simply give in, exhibiting the same lack of transparency as when he had the military standards taken to Jerusalem at night. He takes his seat on the *bema*, seemingly prepared to either hear the case of the protesters or announce an administrative decision. Instead, he gives a prearranged signal to his soldiers to surround the protesters, and threatens them to kill them unless they accept the imperial images. Having attempted to dispel the protesting crowds first by ignoring them, then by intimidating them and finally by threatening them, Pilatus gives in when the Jewish protesters express their willingness to die for their faith and for their law, which he finds utterly amazing (ὑπερθαυμάσας) (2.174). He did his duty as prefect of Judea and maintain law and order as long as he was able, "but he drew the line at the massacre of large numbers of passive unarmed protesters. In this case the symbols of Rome and personal pride were sacrificed in favour of peace in the province."[143] Pilatus orders (κελεύει) the removal of the standards, retaining some control of the situation. He may have wanted to test public opinion, willing to back down in the face of persistent, non-violent opposition of Jews who are willing to die for their religious convictions. W. ECK argues that if Pilatus wanted to provoke the Jews, he would have marched his troops with the military standards into Jerusalem by day, visibly bearing the image of the emperor: he wanted to do justice both to the traditions of the Roman army and to the sensibilities of the Jews.[144] The removal of the military standards is perhaps the event referred to in *Megillat Taʿanit* 9 [20],[145] which K. BEYER renders as follows: "Am dritten Kislew (26 n.Chr.) wurden die (römischen, mit Kaiserbilder geschmückten) Feldzeichen (die Pontius Pilatus gleich zu Beginn seiner Prokuratur [26–36 n.Chr.] nach Jerusalem hatte hineinbringen lassen, nach sechs

---

[141] BOND, Pontius Pilate, 83, suggesting that "writing an apology for Judaism to subjects of the Empire, Josephus has naturally covered up the political aspect of the affair." This may be correct, but evidence is lacking.

[142] BOND, Pontius Pilate, 58; for the next comment cf. ibid.

[143] BOND, Pontius Pilate, 59; the following point ibid. 79.

[144] ECK, Repräsentanten, 174-175.

[145] Thus MICHEL / BAUERNFEIND, De Bello Judaico, 1:441 n. 99.

Tagen wieder) aus dem äußeren Tempelhof beseitigt."[146] Josephus locates the
military standards in Pilatus' residence, not in the outer court of the Temple.[147]
R. L. WEBB comments, "Pilate appears to have been a prefect who wanted to
start his governorship with a clear statement of Rome's presence and authority
... he was being more blatantly pro-Roman than his predecessors."[148]

**(79)** Josephus, *Bellum judaicum* 2.175–177

Μετὰ δὲ ταῦτα ταραχὴν ἑτέραν ἐκίνει τὸν ἱερὸν θησαυρόν, καλεῖται δὲ κορβωνᾶς, εἰς καταγωγὴν ὑδάτων ἐξαναλίσκων· κατῆγεν δὲ ἀπὸ τετρακοσίων
σταδίων. πρὸς τοῦτο τοῦ πλήθους ἀγανάκτησις ἦν, καὶ τοῦ Πιλάτου παρόντος
εἰς Ἱεροσόλυμα περιστάντες τὸ βῆμα κατεβόων. [176] ὁ δέ, προῄδει γὰρ αὐτῶν
τὴν ταραχήν, τῷ πλήθει τοὺς στρατιώτας ἐνόπλους ἐσθῆσιν ἰδιωτικαῖς κεκα-
λυμμένους ἐγκαταμίξας καὶ ξίφει μὲν χρήσασθαι κωλύσας, ξύλοις δὲ παίειν
τοὺς κεκραγότας ἐγκελευσάμενος σύνθημα δίδωσιν ἀπὸ τοῦ βήματος. [177] τυ-
πτόμενοι δὲ οἱ Ἰουδαῖοι πολλοὶ μὲν ὑπὸ τῶν πληγῶν, πολλοὶ δὲ ὑπὸ σφῶν
αὐτῶν ἐν τῇ φυγῇ καταπατηθέντες ἀπώλοντο. πρὸς δὲ τὴν συμφορὰν τῶν
ἀνηρημένων καταπλαγὲν τὸ πλῆθος ἐσιώπησεν.

*Translation.* After these events he provoked a different kind of upheaval by
exhausting the sacred treasure, known as the *korbonas*, for the construction of
an aqueduct which brought water from a distance of 400 stadia. Expressing
indignation at this action, the crowd surrounded the tribunal-platform of
Pilatus when he was in Jerusalem, and kept yelling at him. [176] Having anticipated the disturbance, he had mixed his armed soldiers among the crowd, disguised in civilian clothes, with orders not to attack with their swords but to
beat the rioters with clubs. Then he gave the prearranged signal from the
tribunal-platform. [177] Many Jews who were beaten perished from the blows
which they received, but many others from being trampled by their own (people) in the ensuing flight. Terror-stricken on account of the calamity of those
who were killed, the crowd became silent.

*Commentary.* The second incident in *Bellum* that Josephus reports for Pilatus'
term as prefect in Judea concerns an aqueduct (cf. *A. J.* 18.60–62; see No. 81).
It has been suggested that the aqueduct (καταγωγὴ ὑδάτων, "water conduit")
that Pilatus built was the so-called low-level aqueduct that began at the lowest

---

[146] BEYER, Die aramäischen Texte, 1:357, with reference to SCHÜRER, History, 1:163 n.
63, 384; cf. SOLOMON ZEITLIN, Megillat Taanit as a Source for Jewish Chronology and History in the Hellenistic and Roman Periods (Philadelphia: Dropsie College for Hebrew and
Cognate Learning, 1922), 87–88.

[147] Eusebius, *Dem. ev.* 8.2.123 locates the standards also in the Temple courts, referring to
Philo's (lost) work on the persecution of the Jews under Tiberius and Caligula.

[148] WEBB, Roman Examination, 715.

of the three Solomon's Pools, about 10 km southwest of Jerusalem, following a winding course that was over 24 km long, delivering water to the system of cisterns in the southern part of the Temple Mount.[149] Pilatus may have repaired the aqueduct that was built by Herod or earlier. Others think that Pilatus extended the existing aqueduct by adding a 39 km long conduit from Solomon's Pools farther south through Wadi ʿArrub to ʿEin Kuweiziba, creating a 63 km long aqueduct.[150] The 400 stadia correspond to ca. 80 km; *A. J.* 18.60 specifies 200 stadia, corresponding to ca. 40 km, which fits the length of the ʿArrub aqueduct.[151] Since the cost of an aqueduct was enormous – about 2 million HS (sesterces) per linear km – financing required a combination of imperial grants, local funds, and private donations.[152] Pilatus financed the (re)construction of the aqueduct from the "sacred treasure" (τὸν ἱερὸν θησαυρόν), i.e., from the Temple treasury. The dues of the people for the support of the priests, the priestly vestments, the large quantity of gold and silver vessels used in sacrificial worship, supplies of flour, oil, wine, and fragrant substances, and funds deposited by private individuals, were kept in various chambers and guarded by treasurers (גזברים, γαζοφύλακες).[153]

It is not clear what provoked the residents of Jerusalem when Pilatus appropriated Temple funds for the construction, nor when the protest took place (building the aqueduct required at least two years).[154] According to the Mishnah, Temple funds could be used for constructing an aqueduct (*m. Šeqal.* 4:2). This may reflect a more liberal view. The Sadducees might have objected to the use of Temple funds for such "secular" projects. Assuming that such a use was permissible, the objection might have concerned the identity of the

---

[149] Cf. HILLEL GEVA, Jerusalem: The Second Temple Period. Water Supply, NEAEHL 2 (1993): 746–747; AMIHAI MAZAR, Die Untersuchungen über die Wasserleitungen nach Jerusalem, in Wasser im Heiligen Land. Biblische Zeugnisse und archäologische Forschungen (ed. W. Dierx and G. Garbrecht; Mainz: Zabern, 2001), 165–194, 167–69; KENNETH LÖNNQVIST, Pontius Pilatus – An Aqueduct Builder? Recent Findings and New Suggestions, Klio 82 (2000): 459–474. Cf. LÉMONON, Pilate, 168–70; LÉMONON, Ponce Pilate, 155–57.

[150] AMIHAI MAZAR, A Survey of the Aqueducts to Jerusalem, in The Aqueducts of Israel (ed. D. Amit, J. Patrich, and Y. Hirschfeld; JRASup 46; Portsmouth, RI: Journal of Roman Archaeology, 2002), 211–244, 211, 236–38; on the ʿArrub aqueduct ibid. 213–17; cf. JOSEPH PATRICH and DAVID AMIT, The Aqueducts of Israel: An Introduction, in The Aqueducts of Israel (ed. D. Amit, J. Patrich, and Y. Hirschfeld; JRASup 46; Portsmouth, RI: Journal of Roman Archaeology, 2002), 9–20, 18; LEE I. LEVINE, Jerusalem: Portrait of the City in the Second Temple Period (538 B.C.E. – 70 C.E.) (Philadelphia: The Jewish Publication Society, 2002), 216.

[151] Cf. MICHEL / BAUERNFEIND, De Bello Judaico, 1:441 n. 101; MASON, Judean War 2, 147–48 n. 1103.

[152] Cf. PHILIPPE LEVEAU, Aqueduct Building: Financing and Costs, in Frontinus' Legacy: Essays on Frontinus' De Aquis Urbis Romae (ed. D. R. Blackman and A. T. Hodge; Ann Arabor: University of Michigan Press, 2001), 85–101.

[153] For details and documentation cf. SCHÜRER, History, 2:279–84.

[154] Cf. LÖNNQVIST, Pontius Pilate, 473; MASON, Judean War 2, 147 n. 1103.

authority using Temple funds for the construction of an aqueduct: the problem was the use of the sacred monies by pagan authorities. It is also possible that the monies had been earmarked for the purchase of sacrificial offerings and were thus misused by Pilatus.[155] J. P. LÉMONON surmises that Pilatus may soon have taken his use of Temple funds for the aqueduct project for granted, treating them as is own *fiscus*.[156] H. K. BOND suggests that while the use of the verb ἐξαναλίσκω ("spend entirely, exhaust") may be exaggerated, "problems seem to have arisen when Pilate began to demand more than the surplus for his venture."[157] The use of Temple funds for the aqueduct project must have involved the cooperation of the Jewish leaders, at least of the high priest and the treasurer of the Temple.[158] Josephus does not mention leaders or representatives of the Jews; the upheaval was provoked by Jewish crowds.[159]

According to K. S. KRIEGER and H. K. BOND, the first incident related by Josephus shows that when the Judeans peacefully resist an action of Pilatus, they achieve a positive outcome, while the second incident demonstrates that militant resistance against Rome's representative has fatal consequences.[160] S. MASON remains unconvinced: neither reaction of the Jews to Pilatus' action is violent; the two narratives cannot be taken as models of two different kinds of behavior.[161] He thinks that Josephus tried to assimilate one story to the other, wanting to present two similar disturbances provoked by this unworthy Roman prefect: the parallel structure of the two episodes seems deliberate, and key vocabulary is repeated. The reference to many Jews being killed in the stampede takes away any credit for Pilatus' seemingly cautious military action.[162] D. R. SCHWARTZ compares the two episodes in *Bellum* with the corresponding narratives in *Antiquitates* and argues that "this text began as one friendly to Pilate, one bespeaking Pilate's point of view; perhaps it was a report composed by the governor, or by someone on his staff."[163]

The use of monies from temples for projects that served the community

---

[155] LEVINE, Jerusalem, 290 with n. 22. The term κορβωνᾶς denotes the treasury of the Jerusalem Temple; it is connected with κορβᾶν, a transliteration of the Hebrew term קָרְבָּן ("offering, gift"), "the commonest and vaguest expression for sacrifice" (HALOT); cf. BDAG s.v. κορβᾶν: "something consecrated as a gift for God and closed to ordinary human use." The term is used in Mark 7:11. SCHÜRER, History, 2:284, suggests that the Roman prefects had political supervision of the Temple treasury. The extant sources do not state this, however.

[156] LÉMONON, Pilate, 168; LÉMONON, Ponce Pilate, 155.

[157] BOND, Pontius Pilate, 86; cf. MASON, Judean War 2, 148 n. 1105. BOND places the story in *Bellum* into the context of Josephus' apologetic aims, suggesting that he wanted to illustrate "the disastrous effects when large numbers of people turn to rioting" (ibid. 88).

[158] Cf. BOND, Pontius Pilate, 86; DEMANDT, Pontius Pilatus, 91; WILKER, Dynastie, 104.

[159] Cf. WILKER, Dynastie, 103–4.

[160] KRIEGER, Geschichtsschreibung, 39–42; BOND, Pontius Pilate, 49–62.

[161] MASON, Overview, 33 n. 51; MASON, Authority, 23 n. 50.

[162] MASON, Judean War 2, 150 n. 1123.

[163] SCHWARTZ, Composition and Sources, 139–43, quotation 141.

was known in the Greco-Roman world.[164] In some cities, the main deity took responsibility for important public works of the city, whose costs were covered by funds from the temple. Under Augustus, Sextus Appuleius, the proconsul of the province of Asia, arranged for a street to be paved from the funds of the temple of Artemis Ephesia.[165]

Seen against this background, Pilatus acted responsibly. Josephus calls him a man of "foresight" (προήδει) who was not looking for trouble (2.176). Some Jewish authorities must have agreed to the use of Temple funds for the construction or repair of the aqueduct: Josephus does not say that Pilatus took the funds by force.[166] Pilatus wanted to avoid an escalation: he ordered the soldiers not to attack the protesters with their swords (ξίφει μὲν χρήσασθαι κωλύσας), i.e., not to kill them, but to beat them with wooden clubs (ξύλοις δὲ παίειν τοὺς κεκραγότας). Josephus emphasizes that it was the soldiers who escalated the situation and killed many Jews in the mêlée that ensued.[167]

(80) Josephus, *Antiquitates judaicae* 18.55–59

Πιλᾶτος δὲ ὁ τῆς Ἰουδαίας ἡγεμὼν στρατιὰν ἐκ Καισαρείας. ἀγαγὼν καὶ μεθιδρύσας χειμαδιοῦσαν ἐν Ἱεροσολύμοις ἐπὶ καταλύσει τῶν νομίμων τῶν Ἰουδαϊκῶν ἐφρόνησε, προτομὰς Καίσαρος, αἳ ταῖς σημαίαις προσῆσαν, εἰσαγόμενος εἰς τὴν πόλιν, εἰκόνων ποίησιν ἀπαγορεύοντος ἡμῖν τοῦ νόμου. ⁵⁶ καὶ διὰ τοῦτο οἱ πρότερον ἡγεμόνες ταῖς μὴ μετὰ τοιῶνδε κόσμων σημαίαις ἐποιοῦντο εἴσοδον τῇ πόλει. πρῶτος δὲ Πιλᾶτος ἀγνοίᾳ τῶν ἀνθρώπων διὰ τὸ νύκτωρ γενέσθαι τὴν εἴσοδον ἱδρύεται τὰς εἰκόνας φέρων εἰς τὰ Ἱεροσόλυμα. ⁵⁷ οἱ δ' ἐπεὶ ἔγνωσαν κατὰ πληθὺν παρῆσαν εἰς Καισάρειαν ἱκετείαν ποιούμενοι ἐπὶ πολλὰς ἡμέρας ἐπὶ μεταθέσει τῶν εἰκόνων. καὶ μὴ συγχωροῦντος διὰ τὸ εἰς ὕβριν Καίσαρι φέρειν, ἐπείπερ οὐκ ἐξανεχώρουν λιπαρεῖν κατὰ ἕκτην ἡμέραν ἐν ὅπλοις ἀφανῶς ἐπικαθίσας τὸ στρατιωτικὸν αὐτὸς ἐπὶ τὸ βῆμα ἧκεν. τὸ δ' ἐν τῷ σταδίῳ κατεσκεύαστο, ὅπερ ἀπέκρυπτε τὸν ἐφεδρεύοντα στρατόν. ⁵⁸ πάλιν δὲ τῶν Ἰουδαίων ἱκετείᾳ χρωμένων ἀπὸ συνθήματος περιστήσας τοὺς στρατιώτας ἠπείλει θάνατον ἐπιθήσειν ζημίαν ἐκ τοῦ ὀξέος, εἰ μὴ παυσάμε-

---

[164] For the following cf. ECK, Repräsentanten, 175-176, with reference to MAURICE SARTRE, L'orient romain. Provinces et sociétés provinciales en Méditerranée orientale d'Auguste aux Sévères (31 avant J.-C – 235 après J.-C.) (L'Univers historique; Paris: Seuil, 1991), 141; BEATE DIGNAS, Economy of the Sacred in Hellenistic and Roman Asia Minor (Oxford Classical Monographs; Oxford New York: Oxford University Press, 2002), 173.

[165] I. Eph II 459; SEG XL 971; AE 1991 1502; IK LIX 148: [Benef]icio Ca[esaris] Augusti ex rediti[bus] agrorum sacrorum quos is dianae de[dit] via strata Sex(to) Appul[eio] pro co(n)s(ule).

[166] Cf. ECK, Repräsentanten, 176.

[167] BOND, Pontius Pilate, 59–60, agrees that Pilatus appears to have acted appropriately, but finds his orders to his men "inconsistent with the final slaughter." This difficulty is resolved if we assume, with ECK, that it was the soldiers who escalated the situation.

νοι θορυβεῖν ἐπὶ τὰ οἰκεῖα ἀπίοιεν. [59] οἱ δὲ πρηνεῖς ῥίψαντες ἑαυτοὺς καὶ γυμνοῦντες τὰς σφαγὰς ἡδονῇ δέξασθαι τὸν θάνατον ἔλεγον ἢ τολμήσειν τὴν σοφίαν παραβήσεσθαι τῶν νόμων. καὶ Πιλᾶτος θαυμάσας τὸ ἐχυρὸν αὐτῶν ἐπὶ φυλακῇ τῶν νόμων παραχρῆμα τὰς εἰκόνας ἐκ τῶν Ἱεροσολύμων ἐπανεκόμισεν εἰς Καισάρειαν.

*Translation.* When Pilatus, the governor of Judea, brought the army from Caesarea and transferred it to winter quarters in Jerusalem, decided to subvert the customs of the Jews by introducing into the city the images of the emperor that attached to the military standards – our law prohibits the making of images. [56] This is the reason why previous governors used standards that did not have such decorations when they entered the city. Pilatus, out of ignorance of the people, was the first to bring the images into Jerusalem, which happened at night, and set them up. [57] When the people learnt about it, they went to Caesarea in great numbers and implored him for many days to take down the images. He refused to concede since this would be an outrage against the emperor. Since they did not cease to implore him, he secretly armed his troops on the sixth day and placed them in position, while he personally came to the tribunal which had been set up in the stadium, providing cover for the troops laying in wait. [58] When the Jews implored him again, he surrounded them with his soldiers at a prearranged signal and threatened to punish them at once with death if they did not end the tumult and went home. [59] But they threw themselves on the ground, exposed their necks and declared that they would rather accept death than dare break the wisdom of their laws. Pilatus was amazed by their commitment to keep their laws and immediately removed the images from Jerusalem, bringing them back to Caesarea.

*Commentary.* The parallel account in *B. J.* 2.169–174 has been discussed above (No. 78). The report of the affair of the military standards exhibits the following additions and reductions.[168] (1) Josephus gives more detail: the troops that were transferred from Caesarea to Jerusalem to set up winter quarters (χειμαδιοῦσαν ἐν Ἱεροσολύμοις; 18.55). In contrast to *B. J.* 2.169, where no reason for Pilatus' bringing his troops to Jerusalem is given, *A. J.* 18.55 portrays him as carrying out his normal responsibilities.[169] The military standards of Pilatus' troops entering Jerusalem exhibited "the images of the emperor" (προτομὰς Καίσαρος; 18.55). Previous prefects used military standards without the image of the emperor when they entered the city (18.56). (2) The strong sequence of cause and effect that characterized the account in *B. J.* is minimized. BOND believes that this suggests that "the actions and reactions of the central characters are no longer of primary significance."[170] The initial

---

[168] See generally MASON, Authority, 21–22; cf. SCHWARTZ, Composition and Sources, 132–43, interacting with MASON, Contradiction.

[169] Cf. SCHWARTZ, Composition and Sources, 137.

reaction is shortened, and the behavior of the Jewish crowd in Caesarea is portrayed in a less passive manner: the persistent entreaties to remove the standards is called a "tumult" (θορυβεῖν; 18.58). The Jews are still willing to die (18.59), but Pilatus has become more important: he "decided to subvert the customs of the Jews" (ἐπὶ καταλύσει τῶν νομίμων τῶν Ἰουδαϊκῶν ἐφρόνησε; 18.55).[171] He is the first (πρῶτος; 18.56) governor to bring military standards with the image of the emperor attached into Jerusalem. He acts "out of ignorance of the people" (ἀγνοίᾳ τῶν ἀνθρώπων; 18.56). His initial refusal to concede and remove and standards is explained with the conviction of Pilatus that "this would be an outrage against the emperor" (διὰ τὸ εἰς ὕβριν Καίσαρι φέρειν; 18.57). Rather than being more generally surpri-sed at the Jews' religious zeal, he is "amazed by their commitment to keep their laws" (θαυμάσας τὸ ἐχυρὸν αὐτῶν ἐπὶ φυλακῇ τῶν νόμων; 18.59). In sum, while Pilatus is compared unfavorably with preceding prefects, Josephus portrays him as a Roman official who is concerned about honor being shown to the emperor and who is willing to give in and remove the military standards from Jerusalem which offend Jewish sensibilities. His willingness to use force is not an indication of cruelty as a major personality trait of Pilatus: Roman officials in the provinces responsible for maintaining law and order have to demonstrate their willingness to use military force in order to avoid upheavals of the population.

**(81)** Josephus, *Antiquitates judaicae* 18.60–62

Ὑδάτων δὲ ἐπαγωγὴν εἰς τὰ Ἱεροσόλυμα ἔπραξεν δαπάνῃ τῶν ἱερῶν χρημάτων ἐκλαβὼν τὴν ἀρχὴν τοῦ ῥεύματος ὅσον ἀπὸ σταδίων διακοσίων, οἱ δ' οὐκ ἠγάπων τοῖς ἀμφὶ τὸ ὕδωρ δρωμένοις πολλαί τε μυριάδες ἀνθρώπων συνελθόντες κατεβόων αὐτοῦ. παύσασθαι τοῦ ἐπὶ τοιούτοις προθυμουμένου, τινὲς δὲ καὶ λοιδορίᾳ χρώμενοι ὕβριζον εἰς τὸν ἄνδρα, οἷα δὴ φιλεῖ πράσσειν ὅμιλος. [61] ὁ δὲ στολῇ τῇ ἐκείνων πολὺ πλῆθος στρατιωτῶν ἀμπεχόμενον, οἳ ἐφέροντο σκυτάλας ὑπὸ ταῖς στολαῖς, διαπέμψας εἰς ὃ περιέλθοιεν αὐτούς, αὐτὸς ἐκέλευσεν ἀναχωρεῖν. τῶν δὲ ὡρμηκότων εἰς τὸ λοιδορεῖν ἀποδίδωσι τοῖς στρατιώταις ὃ προσυνέκειτο σημεῖον. [62] οἱ δὲ καὶ πολὺ μειζόνως ἤπερ ἐπέταξεν Πιλᾶτος ἐχρῶντο πληγαῖς τούς τε θορυβοῦντας ἐν ἴσῳ καὶ μὴ κολάζοντες οἱ δ' εἰσεφέροντο μαλακὸν οὐδέν, ὥστε ἄοπλοι ληφθέντες ὑπ' ἀνδρῶν ἐκ παρασκευῆς ἐπιφερομένων πολλοὶ μὲν αὐτῶν ταύτῃ καὶ ἀπέθνησκον, οἱ δὲ καὶ τραυματίαι ἀνεχώρησαν. καὶ οὕτω παύεται ἡ στάσις.

---

[170] BOND, Pontius Pilate, 69; for the following observation cf. ibid. 70.

[171] KRIEGER, Geschichtsschreibung, 39–41; KLAUS-STEFAN KRIEGER, A Synoptic Approach to B 2:117–283 and A 18–20, in Internationales Josephus-Kolloquium Paris 2001: Studies on the Antiquities of Josephus (ed. J. Kalms and F. Siegert; Münster: Lit, 2002), 90–100, 92–93, argues that in contrast to the account in *Bellum*, here Josephus, in his effort to write an apologetic for the Jews, portrays Pilatus as malicious and ruthless enemy of the Jews.

*Translation.* He spent money from the Temple treasury for bringing water to Jerusalem,[172] taking the source of the stream at a distance of 200 stadia. The Jews were not pleased with what was being done with the water. Tens of thousands of people assembled and implored him to stop such designs. Some hurled insults and abuse at the man, as crowds will commonly do. [61] He then ordered a large number of soldiers to wear Jewish robes under which they carried clubs and sent them off in different directions so that they would surround the Jews whom he ordered to go away. When they continued to hurl abuse at him, he gave the soldiers the prearranged signal. [62] They, however, attacked (the Jews) with much harder blows than Pilatus had ordered, punishing in equal measure both those who were rioting and those who were not. But they showed no cowardice,[173] and since they were unarmed, caught by men prepared for an attack, many of them were killed on the spot, while the wounded withdrew. Thus the uprising ended.

*Commentary.* The parallel account *B. J.* 2.175–177 has been discussed above (No. 79). Pilatus is portrayed in a positive manner: he spends (ἔπραξεν) funds from the Temple treasury; the verb ἐξαναλίσκων used in *B. J.* 2.175 suggests a more hard-nosed attitude. The Jewish reaction is portrayed in stronger terms, albeit not in terms of militant violence: while in the case of the military standards the crowd argues "respectably for a legitimate cause," in the affair of the Temple funds the crowd argues "in an unrespectable manner and for an unjustified cause."[174] The angry mob prompts Pilatus to bring in his troops; in *Bellum* the troops are already in position, suggesting that Pilatus expected trouble.[175] Unlike *Bellum*, here Pilatus gives the Judeans a chance to withdraw after having stationed his troops, who are disguised among the crowd. It is the troops who are ruthlessly brutal, not Pilatus: they attack the Judeans "with much harder blows than Pilatus had ordered" (πολὺ μειζόνως ἤπερ ἐπέταξεν Πιλᾶτος ἐχρῶντο πληγαῖς; 18.62). H. K. Bond thinks that the account in *Antiquitates* is "a more accurate reflection of the historical situation" – the Jewish community was divided whether Pilatus' actions constituted an infringement of the Law or their customs, which seems plausible; Pilatus' policing action makes sense if there was a larger crowd in which a few more extreme Judeans rioted who could be dealt with by plain-clothes soldiers.[176]

---

[172] Feldman translates ὑδάτων ἐπαγωγὴν εἰς τὰ Ἱεροσόλυμα with "in the construction of an aqueduct to bring water into Jerusalem."

[173] Following Feldmann ("But the Jews showed no faint-heartedness"). Whiston translation ("nor did they spare them in the least") follows the conjecture of Niese (οἱ δ'] aut omittendum aut οὐδ' scribendum); cf. Feldman, in Thackeray / Marcus / Feldman, Josephus, 9:47, note d.

[174] Schwartz, Composition and Sources, 132.

[175] Cf. Bond, Pontius Pilate, 75. Krieger, Geschichtsschreibung, 40, thinks that Pilatus is portrayed as malicious and ruthless person.

[176] Bond, Pontius Pilate, 88.

**(82)** Josephus, *Antiquitates judaicae* 18.63–64

Γίνεται δὲ κατὰ τοῦτον τὸν χρόνον Ἰησοῦς σοφὸς ἀνήρ, εἴγε ἄνδρα αὐτὸν λέγειν χρή· ἦν γὰρ παραδόξων ἔργων ποιητής, διδάσκαλος ἀνθρώπων τῶν ἡδονῇ τἀληθῆ δεχομένων, καὶ πολλοὺς μὲν Ἰουδαίους, πολλοὺς δὲ καὶ τοῦ Ἑλληνικοῦ ἐπηγάγετο· ὁ χριστὸς οὗτος ἦν. ⁶⁴ καὶ αὐτὸν ἐνδείξει τῶν πρώτων ἀνδρῶν παρ' ἡμῖν σταυρῷ ἐπιτετιμηκότος Πιλάτου οὐκ ἐπαύσαντο οἱ τὸ πρῶτον ἀγαπήσαντες· ἐφάνη γὰρ αὐτοῖς τρίτην ἔχων ἡμέραν πάλιν ζῶν τῶν θείων προφητῶν ταῦτά τε καὶ ἄλλα μυρία περὶ αὐτοῦ θαυμάσια εἰρηκότων. εἰς ἔτι τε νῦν τῶν Χριστιανῶν ἀπὸ τοῦδε ὠνομασμένον οὐκ ἐπέλιπε τὸ φῦλον.

*Translation.* About this time there lived Jesus, a wise man, if indeed one ought to call him a man. He was the author of incredible deeds and a teacher of people who gladly accept the truth. He attracted many Jews and also many of the Greeks. He was the Messiah. ⁶⁴ When Pilatus had condemned him to the cross, having been indicted by the most prominent men among us, those who had loved him first did not leave him. He appeared to them on the third day, again alive, for the divine prophets had prophesied these and countless other wonderful things about him. And the tribe of the Christians, who are named after him, have still not disappeared to this day.

*Commentary.* Pilatus appears in this text as having condemned Jesus to the cross (σταυρῷ ἐπιτετιμηκότος Πιλάτου), after Jesus had been indicted (ἐνδείξει)[177] by the Jewish leaders (τῶν πρώτων ἀνδρῶν παρ' ἡμῖν). Some scholars hold that this text, the so-called *Testimonium Flavianum*, is authentic,[178] while some think that it is in its entirety a Christian interpolation,[179] perhaps inserted by Eusebius.[180] Most scholars think that the text derives essentially

---

[177] LSJ s.v. ἔνδειξις I.2, "as law-term, *laying of information against* one who discharged public functions for which he was legally disqualified, *writ of indictment* in such a case."

[178] FRANCIS C. BURKITT, Josephus and Christ, Theologische Tijdschrift 47 (1913): 135–144; ADOLF HARNACK, Geschichte der altchristlichen Literatur bis Eusebius (Vier Bände, 2. erweiterte Auflage; orig. 1893–1904; repr., Leipzig: Hinrichs, 1958), 1:858–60; 2:581; FRANZ DORNSEIFF, Zum Testimonium Flavium, ZNW 46 (1955): 245–250; ÉTIENNE NODET, Jésus et Jean-Baptiste selon Josèphe, RB 92 (1985): 321–348, 497–524; ÉTIENNE NODET, Pharisees, Sadducees Essenes, Herodians, in Handbook for the Study of the Historical Jesus. Vol. 2: The Study of Jesus (ed. T. Holmén and S. E. Porter; Leiden: Brill, 2011), 1495–1543, 1540–43; ULRICH VICTOR, Das Testimonium Flavianum. Ein authentischer Text des Josephus, NovT 52 (2012): 72–82.

[179] SOLOMON ZEITLIN, The Christ Passage in Josephus, JQR 18 (1927–28): 231–255; SOLOMON ZEITLIN, Josephus on Jesus (Philadelphia: Dropsie College, 1931); J. NEVILLE BIRDSALL, The Continuing Enigma of Josephus's Testimony about Jesus, BJRL 67 (1985): 609–622; ELLIS RIVKIN, What Crucified Jesus? (Nashville: Nelson, 1984), 64–67; BILDE, Flavius Josephus between Jerusalem and Rome, 223; DEMANDT, Pontius Pilatus, 68–69. MASON, Josephus and the New Testament, 234–36, is largely skeptical.

[180] KEN A. OLSON, Eusebius and the Testimonium Flavianum, CBQ 61 (1999): 305–322; LOUIS H. FELDMAN, On the Authenticity of the *Testimonium Flavianum* Attributed to

from Josephus, with some Christian interpolations.[181] JOHN P. MEIER reconstructs the original text as follows: "Around this time lived Jesus, a wise man. For he was a worker of amazing deeds and was a teacher of people who gladly accept the truth. He won over both many Jews and many Greeks. Pilate, when he heard him accused by the leading men among us, condemned him to the cross, [but] those who had first loved him did not cease [doing so]. To this time the tribe of Christians named after him has not disappeared."[182] This reconstruction is accepted by many scholars as a neutral reconstructon.[183] The phrase ὁ χριστὸς οὗτος ἦν ("He was the Messiah") is either eliminated as a Christian interpolation, or changed into a neutral statement: ὁ λεγόμενος Χριστός ("He was called Messiah"), in analogy to *A. J.* 20.200. Assuming that the neutral reconstruction is correct and the passage authentic, Josephus corroborates the Gospels' report that both the Jewish leaders and Pilatus were involved in Jesus' death, the former indicting him, the latter condemning him to death by crucifixion.

---

Josephus, in New Perspectives on Jewish-Christian Relations (ed. E. Carlebach and J. J. Schacter; Leiden: Brill, 2012), 13–30.

[181] KLAUSNER, Jesus of Nazareth, 55–56; H. ST. JOHN THACKERAY, Josephus, the Man and the Historian (orig. 1929; repr., New York: Ktav, 1967), 136–49; BAMMEL, Zum Testimonium Flavianum; LOUIS H. FELDMAN, The *Testimonium Flavium*: The State of the Question, in Cbristological Perspectives (FS H. K. McArthur; ed. R. F. Berkey and S. A. Edwards; New York: Pilgrim, 1982), 288–293; MEIER, Marginal Jew, 1:56–69; CRAIG A. EVANS, Jesus in Non-Christian Sources, in Studying the Historical Jesus: Evaluations of the State of Current Research (ed. B. Chilton and C. A. Evans; NTTS 19; Leiden: Brill, 1994), 443–478; GRAMAGLIA, Testimonium Flavianum; J. CARLETON PAGET, Some Observations on Josephus and Christianity [2001], in Jews, Christians and Jewish Christians in Antiquity (WUNT 251; Tübingen: Mohr Siebeck, 2010), 185–265; GIORGIO JOSSA, Jews, Romans, and Christians: From the Bellum Judaicum to the Antiquitates, in Josephus and Jewish History in Flavian Rome and Beyond (ed. J. Sievers and G. Lembi; Supplements to the Journal for the study of Judaism 104; Leiden / Boston: Brill, 2005), 331–342; FRIEDRICH-WILHELM HORN, Das Testimonium Flavianum aus neutestamentlicher Perspektive, in Josephus und das Neue Testament. Wechselseitige Wahrnehmungen (ed. C. Böttrich and J. Herzer; WUNT 209; Tübingen: Mohr Siebeck, 2007), 117–136; ALICE WHEALEY, Josephus, Eusebius of Caesarea, and the Testimonium Flavianum, in Josephus und das Neue Testament. Wechselseitige Wahrnehmungen (ed. C. Böttrich and J. Herzer; WUNT 209; Tübingen: Mohr Siebeck, 2007), 73–116; ROBERT E. VAN VOORST, Jesus Tradition in Classical and Jewish Writings, in Handbook for the Study of the Historical Jesus. Vol. 3: The Historical Jesus (ed. T. Holmén and S. E. Porter; Leiden: Brill, 2011), 2149–2180, 2168–71. Cf. SERGE BARDET, Le Testimonium Flavianum. Examen historique, considérations historiographiques (Paris: Cerf, 2002); WHEALEY, Josephus on Jesus.

[182] MEIER, Marginal Jew, 1:61.

[183] BROWN, Death, 1:373–74; THEISSEN / MERZ, Der historische Jesus, 74–82 (= THEISSEN / MERZ, Historical Jesus, 71–74); VAN VOORST, Jesus Tradition.

**(83)** Josephus, *Antiquitates judaicae* 18.85–89

Οὐκ ἀπήλλακτο δὲ θορύβου καὶ τὸ Σαμαρέων ἔθνος· συστρέφει γὰρ αὐτοὺς ἀνὴρ ἐν ὀλίγῳ τὸ ψεῦδος τιθέμενος κἀφ' ἡδονῇ τῆς πληθύος τεχνάζων τὰ πάντα, κελεύων ἐπὶ τὸ Γαριζεὶν ὄρος αὐτῷ συνελθεῖν, ὃ ἁγνότατον αὐτοῖς ὀρῶν ὑπείληπται, ἰσχυρίζετό τε παραγενομένοις δείξειν τὰ ἱερὰ σκεύη τῇδε κατορωρυγμένα Μωυσέως τῇδε αὐτῶν ποιησαμένου κατάθεσιν. ⁸⁶ οἱ δὲ ἐν ὅπλοις τε ἦσαν πιθανὸν ἡγούμενοι τὸν λόγον, καὶ καθίσαντες ἔν τινι κώμῃ, Τιραθανὰ λέγεται, παρελάμβανον τοὺς ἐπισυλλεγομένους ὡς μεγάλῳ πλήθει τὴν ἀνάβασιν εἰς τὸ ὄρος ποιησόμενοι. ⁸⁷ φθάνει δὲ Πιλᾶτος τὴν ἄνοδον αὐτῶν προκαταλαβόμενος ἱππέων τε πομπῇ καὶ ὁπλιτῶν, οἳ συμβαλόντες τοῖς ἐν τῇ κώμῃ προσυνηθροισμένοις παρατάξεως γενομένης τοὺς μὲν ἔκτειναν, τοὺς δ' εἰς φυγὴν τρέπονται ζωγρίᾳ τε πολλοὺς ἦγον, ὧν τοὺς κορυφαιοτά-τους καὶ τοὺς ἐν τοῖς φυγοῦσι δυνατωτάτους ἔκτεινε Πιλᾶτος. ⁸⁸ Καταστάν-τος δὲ τοῦ θορύβου Σαμαρέων ἡ βουλὴ παρὰ Οὐιτέλλιον ὑπατικὸν ἴασιν ἄνδρα Συρίας τὴν ἡγεμονίαν ἔχοντα καὶ Πιλάτου κατηγόρουν ἐπὶ τῇ σφαγῇ τῶν ἀπολωλότων· οὐ γὰρ ἐπὶ ἀποστάσει τῶν Ῥωμαίων, ἀλλ' ἐπὶ διαφυγῇ τῆς Πιλάτου ὕβρεως εἰς τὴν Τιραθανὰ παραγενέσθαι. ⁸⁹ καὶ Οὐιτέλλιος Μάρκελ-λον τῶν αὐτοῦ φίλων ἐκπέμψας ἐπιμελητὴν τοῖς Ἰουδαίοις γενησόμενον Πιλᾶτον ἐκέλευσεν ἐπὶ Ῥώμης ἀπιέναι πρὸς ἃ κατηγοροῖεν οἱ Σαμαρεῖται διδάξοντα τὸν αὐτοκράτορα. καὶ Πιλᾶτος δέκα ἔτεσιν διατρίψας ἐπὶ Ἰουδαίας εἰς Ῥώμην ἠπείγετο ταῖς Οὐιτελλίου πειθόμενος ἐντολαῖς οὐκ ὂν ἀντειπεῖν. πρὶν δ' ἐν τῇ Ῥώμῃ ἴσχειν αὐτὸν φθάνει Τιβέριος μεταστάς.

*Translation.* The nation of the Samaritans did not escape without disturbance. A man who thought that lying was nothing and who contrived everything with cunning so as to satisfy the mob rallied them, urging them to go to Mount Ge-rizim with him, which they hold to be the most sacred mountain. He insisted that once they had come, he would show them the sacred vessels which were buried there, deposited by Moses. ⁸⁶ They came in arms, believing his message to be plausible. They set themselves up in a certain village called Tirathana¹⁸⁴ and welcomed those who kept coming, planning to go up the mountain in large numbers. ⁸⁷ However, Pilatus blocked their way up by occupying in advance the route with a detachment of cavalry and heavily armed infantry. They fought those in the village who had arrived first; they killed some in a pitched battle, put some to flight, and took many prisoners. Pilatus executed the leaders and the most influential among the fugitives. ⁸⁸ When the uprising had been settled, the council of the Samaritans went to Vitellius, a man of consular rank who was governor of Syria, and charged Pilatus with the murder of the people who had been killed. For (they said) they went to Tirathana not to cause a revolt against the Romans but as a refuge from Pilatus' violence.

---

¹⁸⁴ Codex W reads τιραθαβᾶ (followed by Whiston, "Tirathaba").

[89] So Vitellius sent Marcellus, one of his friends to take charge of the administration of Judea and ordered Pilatus to return to Rome and to explain to the emperor the matters the Samaritans accused him of. And so Pilatus, who had spent ten years in Judea, hurried to Rome in obedience to Vitellius' orders which he could not refuse. Tiberius died before Pilatus reached Rome.

*Commentary.* Josephus describes Pilatus as energetic governor who uses his military to squash an armed uprising by Samaritans. According to Josephus, the uprising was provoked by a Samaritan man, whom he calls a liar, who may have presented himself as Taheb, the expected revealer of truth fulfilling the prophecy of Deut 18:18 concerning a coming prophet like Moses.[185] The reference to the "sacred vessels" (τὰ ἱερὰ σκεύη) that Moses buried may be connected with the assertion in the Samaritan Chronicles that God hid the ark of the covenant and sacred vessels in a cave on Mount Gerizim (*Kitab al-Tarikh*, written by Abu ᵓl'Fath in the 14th century, and the *Asatir*, written in Aramaic in the 10th century).[186] An older version of the story of the hiding of "sacred vessels" is found in 2 Macc 2:4–8: the tent, the ark of the covenant, and the altar of incense were taken to a cave on Mount Nebo by the prophet Jeremiah; the location of the cave will be revealed when God will again gather his people and when the glory of the Lord and the cloud will appear.[187] Since the Samaritans climbed Mount Gerizim three times every year to celebrate Tabernacles, Passover, and the Festival of Weeks, the Samaritan impostor probably chose one of these festivals for his action. The "sacred vessels" should probably be seen as *pars pro toto* for the tabernacle which, according to Samaritan tradition, was hidden and would be restored in the end-times.[188] Why the Samaritans came "in arms" (ἐν ὅπλοις; 18.86) is unclear. If the messianic interpretation of the event is correct, they would have prepared for the eschatological battle.[189] They claim, later, that they went to Tirathana so seek

---

[185] Cf. MARILYN F. COLLINS, The Hidden Vessels in Samaritan Tradition, JSJ 3 (1972): 97–116; REINHARDT PUMMER, The Mosaic Tabernacle as the Only Legitimate Sanctuary: The Biblical Tabernacle in Samaritanism, in The Temple of Jerusalem: From Moses to the Messiah (FS L. H. Feldman; ed. S. Fine; Leiden: Brill, 2011), 125–150, 137; JÜRGEN ZANGENBERG, ΣΑΜΑΡΕΙΑ. Antike Quellen zur Geschichte und Kultur der Samaritaner in deutscher Übersetzung (TANZ 15; Tübingen/Basel: Francke, 1994), 83. HANS GERHARD KIPPENBERG, Garizim und Synagoge. Traditionsgeschichtiche Untersuchungen zur samaritanischen Religion der aramäischen Periode (RVV 30; Berlin: De Gruyter, 1971), 250, suggests that the man saw himself as *Moses redivivus*, not as prophet like Moses or the Taheb.

[186] Cf. REINHARD PUMMER, The Samaritans in Flavius Josephus (TSAJ 129; Tübingen: Mohr Siebeck, 2009), 133–37. On the *Kitab al-Tarikh* and *Asatir* cf. ZANGENBERG, ΣΑΜΑΡΕΙΑ, 188–94, 229–31.

[187] The letter in which this passage is found claims to have been written in 163–160 B.C. Others date the letter to the time before Pompey's conquest of Jerusalem in 63 B.C. Cf. PUMMER, Samaritans, 236–37.

[188] PUMMER, Tabernacle, 137.

[189] DEMANDT, Pontius Pilatus, 193.

"refuge from Pilatus' violence" (ἐπὶ διαφυγῇ τῆς Πιλάτου ὕβρεως; 18.88). The planned ascent to Mount Gerizim suggests a religious motivation.

Pilatus seems to have believed that the actions of the Samaritan man and the movement that he initiated corresponded to similar messianic expectations and movements of the Jews, and thus used military means to put an end to this new development.[190] Pilatus did not overstep his authority as prefect:[191] he blocks the ascent of the Samaritans to Mount Garizim; when a battle ensues, his cavalry and infantry kill some people, scatter the rest, and take prisoners; after the battle, Pilatus executed the leaders of the uprising and those Samaritans who had the most influence among those who had been taken in by the impostor. A similar event in A.D. 67 forces Cerealis, Vespasian' general, to engage Samaritans at Mount Gerizim in battle, killing thousands (*B. J.* 3.32).

The "council" (ἡ βουλή) of the Samaritans comprised the political representatives of the Samaritan community.[192] Lucius Vitellius was the governor of the province of Syria.[193] It is unclear why Vitellius sent Pilatus to the emperor:[194] (1) Due to contradictory reports, Vitellius was not certain what happened, and since he had not authority to decide the matter, he sent Pilatus to Rome. (2) Vitellius regarded Pilatus' actions as too brutal and thus recalled him as prefect of Judea. (3) Since the Samaritans were on good terms with the emperor during this period, Vitellius wanted to do them a favor. (4) Since Vitellius respected the sensibilities of the Jews (cf. *A. J.* 18.90–95, 120–122), he might have respected the wishes of the Samaritans as well. (5) Vitellius might have been waiting for an opportunity to remove Pilatus, either because he found his administration ineffective (unlikely, considering Pilatus' long tenure), or because he had political reasons, perhaps wanting to promote one of his own protégés, using the Samaritans' complaint as a pretext.[195]

Since this event is linked with the removal of Pilatus, is should be dated to A.D. 35/36. Replacing Pilatus, Marcellus was sent to Judea as the "manager" or "curator" (ἐπιμελητής) of Judea. It is unclear whether he should be regarded as *praefectus* in the legal sense, although he certainly fulfilled the function of prefect until the arrival of Marullus in A.D. 37.[196] Tiberius died on

---

[190] FERDINAND DEXINGER, Josephus Ant 18, 85–87 und der samaritanische Taheb, in Proceeding of the First International Congress of the Société d'Études Samaritaines (ed. A. Tal and M. Florentin; Tel Aviv: Chaim Rosenberg School for Jewish Studies, University of Tel Aviv, 1991), 49–60, 55; MARTINA BÖHM, Samarien und die Samaritai bei Lukas (WUNT 2/111; Tübingen: Mohr Siebeck, 1999), 81, 162.

[191] Thus PUMMER, Samaritans, 241. Since a prefect depended on the cooperation of the local leaders, the execution of members of the Samaritan may be regarded as problematic.

[192] Cf. BÖHM, Samarien, 163; cf. RITA EGGER, Josephus Flavius und die Samaritaner: Eine terminologische Untersuchung zur Identitätsklärung der Samaritaner (NTOA 4; Fribourg / Göttingen: Editions Universitaires / Vandenhoeck & Ruprecht, 1986), 133–36.

[193] On Lucius Vitellius, cf. No. 8 and the introduction to 2.1.

[194] LÉMONON, Pilate, 237–38; LÉMONON, Ponce Pilate, 219; PUMMER, Samaritans, 241.

[195] Thus KRIEGER, Pontius Pilatus, 82–83.

March 15th or 16th, A.D. 37. Pontius Pilatus probably left Judea between mid-December A.D. 36 and the end of February A.D. 37.

**(84)** Tacitus, *Annales* 15.44

Et haec quidem humanis consiliis providebantur. mox petita [a] dis piacula aditique Sibyllae libri, ex quibus supplicatum Volcano et Cereri Proserpinae-que ac propitiata Iuno per matronas, primum in Capitolio, deinde apud proximum mare, unde hausta aqua templum et simulacrum deae perspersum est; et sellisternia ac pervigilia celebravere feminae, quibus mariti erant. Sed non ope humana, non largitionibus principis aut deum placamentis decedebat infamia, quin iussum incendium crederetur. ergo abolendo rumori Nero subdidit reos et quaesitissimis poenis adfecit, quos per flagitia invisos vulgus Christianos appellabat. auctor nominis eius Christus Tiberio imperitante per procuratorem Pontium Pilatum supplicio adfectus erat; repressaque in praesens exitiabilis superstitio rursum erumpebat, non modo per Iudaeam, originem eius mali, sed per urbem etiam, quo cuncta undique atrocia aut pudenda confluunt celebran-turque. igitur primum correpti qui fatebantur, deinde indicio eorum multitudo ingens haud proinde in crimine incendii quam odio humani generis convicti sunt. et pereuntibus addita ludibria, ut ferarum tergis contecti laniatu canum interirent, aut crucibus adfixi [aut flammandi atque], ubi defecisset dies in usu(m) nocturni luminis urerentur. hortos suos ei spectaculo Nero obtulerat et circense ludicrum edebat, habitu aurigae permixtus plebi vel curriculo insis-tens. unde quamquam adversus sontes et novissima exempla meritos miseratio oriebatur, tamquam non utilitate publica sed in saevitiam unius absumerentur.

*Translation.* These were the precautions taken as a result of human prudence. Then steps were taken to appease the gods. The Sibylline Books were consulted, at the suggestion of which prayers were offered to Vulcan, Ceres, and Proserpina, and propitiatory ceremonies were performed for Juno by married women, first on the Capitol, and then on the nearest part of the shore, where water was drawn for the sprinkling of the temple and the statue of the goddess. Married women also held ritual banquets and all-night festivals. But neither human help, nor the emperor's largesse, nor the appeasement of the gods could dispel the belief in the ugly rumor that the fire had been set by an order. In order to dispel the rumor, Nero placed the guilt on others on whom he inflicted the most extraordinary punishments. These were people hated for their shameful vices whom the common people called Christians. The man from whom this name is derived is Christus, who had been executed during the rule of Tiberius by the procurator Pontius Pilatus. The pernicious supersti-

---

[196] WERNER ECK, Marcellus [II 2] M., BNP 8 (2006): 299. KIRNER, Strafgewalt, 217, calls Marcellus "eine Art Interimsverwalter."

tion had been suppressed for a time, but it was starting to break out again, not merely in Judea, where the disease originated, but in the city (of Rome) as well, where all that is abominable and shameful in the world flows together and becomes popular. And so, at first, the people who confessed were arrested. Subsequently, vast numbers were convicted as a result of their disclosures, not so much on account of arson as for their hatred of mankind. Insult accompanied their end: they were wrapped in the skins of wild animals and perished by being torn to pieces by dogs; or they were nailed to crosses and, when daylight had gone, burned to provide lighting at night. Nero had offered his gardens as a venue for the spectacle, and he also organized circus entertainments during which he mixed with the crowd in his charioteer's outfit or standing in his chariot. As a result, even though they were guilty and deserved the most exemplary punishment, pity for them arose on account of the impression that they were destroyed not for the public good but to gratify one man's cruelty.

*Commentary.*[197] Cornelius Tacitus, who came from Gaul and had a successful senatorial career under the Flavian emperor (A.D. 70–96), was consul in A.D. 97 and proconsul in the province of Asia in A.D. 112.[198] The *Annales* treat in

---

[197] Text: HEINZ HEUBNER, P. Cornelii Taciti Libri qui supersunt. Tom. I. Ab excessu divi Augusti (Zweite Auflage; orig. 1983; repr., BSGRT; Stuttgart / Leipzig: Teubner, 1994); for other text editions and translations cf. KARL HALM, C. Cornelii Taciti libri qui supersunt. Tomus prior qui libros ab excessu divi Augusti continet. (Editionem quintam curavit Georgius Andresen; orig. 1855; repr., BSGRT; Leipzig: Teubner, 1913); HENRY FURNEAUX, Tacitus, Cornelius. Annalium ab excessu divi Augusti libri. The Annals of Tacitus (Second Edition Revised by H. F. Pelham and C. D. Fisher. 2 vols.; orig. 1896; repr., Oxford: Clarendon, 1907); WELLESLEY KENNETH, Cornelii Taciti Libri qui supersunt. Tomus I pars secunda: Ab excessu divi Augusti Libri XI–XVI (Stuttgart / Leipzig: Teubner, 1986); CLIFFORD H. MOORE and JOHN JACKSON, Tacitus. The Histories. The Annals (4 vols.; LCL; Cambridge: Harvard University Press, 1931–1937); MICHAEL GRANT, The Annals of Imperial Rome (Sixth Revised ed.; orig. 1956; repr., Penguin Classics; Harmondsworth: Penguin, 1989); WALTHER SONTHEIMER, Tacitus. Annalen (Stuttgart: Reclam, 1964–1967); FRANCIS R. D. GOODYEAR, The Annals of Tacitus (2 vols.; Cambridge Classical Texts and Commentaries; Cambridge: Cambridge University Press, 1972); NORMA P. MILLER, Tacitus. Annals Book 1 (Methuen's Classical Texts; London: Methuen, 1959); ERICH HELLER, Tacitus. Annalen (Lateinisch und deutsch; orig. 1992; repr., Sammlung Tusculum; München / Zürich: Artemis & Winkler, 1997); ANTHONY JOHN WOODMAN, Tacitus: The Annals (Indianapolis: Hackett, 2006); JOHN C. YARDLEY, Tacitus. The Annals: The Reigns of Tiberius, Claudius, and Nero (With Introduction and Notes by A. A. Barrett; Oxford World's Classics; Oxford: Oxford University Press, 2008).

[198] Cf. EGON FLAIG, Tacitus [1] (P.?) Cornelius T., BNP 14 (2009): 105–111; MARTIN SCHANZ and CARL HOSIUS, Geschichte der römischen Literatur. Zweiter Teil: Die römische Literatur in der Zeit der Monarchie bis auf Hadrian (Unveränderter Nachdruck der 4., neu bearbeiteten Auflage von Carl Hosius; orig. 1935; repr., HdA VIII.2; München: Beck, 1980), 603–643, on the *Annales* ibid. 626–32; also RONALD H. MARTIN, Structure and Interprtation in the 'Annals' of Tacitus, ANRW II.33.2 (1990): 1550–1581.

16 books, not all of which are preserved, the history of Rome, beginning with Augustus' death in A.D. 14 and presenting the reigns of the emperors Tiberius, Caligula, Claudius, and Nero. *Ann.* 15.44 ends Tacitus' account of the episode of the Great Fire of A.D. 64 (15.38–41; 15.42–43 treats Nero's building projects). The fire broke out in the early hours of 19 July and lasted for six days, a second outbreak lasted for another three days. The fire effectively levelling three of the fourteen regions of the city, leaving only four untouched.[199] Rumors suggested that Nero was the arsonist.[200] Tacitus remains skeptical, and rightly so: the fire did not start in the area which Nero later claimed for the Domus Aurea, it damaged his own newly built apartments on the Palatine and Oppian Hills, and a fire on such a grand scale would have incurred immense expenses for the emperor.[201] The precautions taken on account of *humanis consiliis* ("human prudence") refer to Nero's initiatives designed to improve the supply of water for fighting fires and to a new building code prohibiting houses from having party walls (15.43). The *petita dis piacula* ("steps to appease the gods") refers to the prayers and offerings performed for Vulcan, Ceres, and Proserpina, and Juno, later described as *deum placamentis*. The term *piaculum* denotes on the one hand the action which violated the *pax deorum*, requiring expiation of the offense, and on the other hand the ritual act of expiation, or the sacrificial used in the ritual act.[202] The cult places of Vulcan, the god of fire, were on the Campus Martius and near the Comitium; the temple of Ceres and Proserpina (Libera) was at the Circus Maximus; the temple of Iuno Moneta was on the Capitoline Hill.[203] Nero became apparently afraid of rumors that he was involved in starting the fire, and accused the Christians of arson, inflicting a punishment that fitted the crime. The notice on *Christus* is made "with documentary precision."[204] Those "who confessed"

---

[199] MIRIAM T. GRIFFIN, Nero: The End of a Dynasty (orig. 1984; repr., New York: Routledge, 2000), 129.

[200] One of the Praetorian officers involved in the Pisonian conspiracy accused Nero of having burnt Rome, cf. Tacitus, *Ann.* 15.67. See the later authors Dio Cassius 62.16; Suetonius, *Nero* 38; Pliny, *Nat.* 17.5, who suggest that Nero indulged in an act of malicious destruction; Suetonius thinks that the pretext for Nero's dislike of the city's ugliness.

[201] GRIFFIN, Nero, 132, the following point ibid.

[202] ANNE VIOLA SIEBERT, Piaculum, BNP 11 (2007): 227–229; cf. ERICH KOESTERMANN, Cornelius Tacitus. Annalen. Erläutert und mit einer Einleitung versehen (4 vols.; Wissenschaftliche Kommentare zu griechischen und lateinischen Schriftstellern; Heidelberg: Winter, 1963–1968), 4:252; KURT LATTE, Römische Religionsgeschichte (orig. 1967; repr., HdQA V.4; München: Beck, 1992), 47–50.

[203] KOESTERMANN, Tacitus. Annalen, 4:252.

[204] RONALD SYME, Tacitus (Oxford: Clarendon, 1958), 2:469. ERICH KOESTERMANN, Ein folgenschwerer Irrtum des Tacitus (Ann. 15,44, 2ff)? Historia 16 (1967): 456–469; KOESTERMANN, Tacitus. Annalen, 4:10–11, 253–54, argues that in Tacitus' source, followers of a Jewish agitator with the name Chrestus (cf. Suetonius, *Claud.* 25.4) were meant, causing him to make the most serious error of his historical work when he identified these Jewish followers of Chrestus with the Christians. PETER LAMPE, From Paul to Valentinus: Christians at

(*qui fatebantur*) probably confessed that they were Christians. Some commentators suggested that while the fire may have been accidental, "some Christians might have thought it was the destruction by fire that was expected to
mark the second coming ... and might consequently have helped it along."[205]
The punishment was death by fire was imposed on arsonists. However, in his
account Tacitus drops the charge of arson, and among later authors it is only
Sulpicius Severus, who relies on Tacitus, who mentions the fire as the cause
of the persecution of the Christians.[206]

This text, usually cited in the context of the history of the Christian community in the city of Rome, demonstrates the following points.[207] (1) The
Christians constituted "vast numbers" (*multitudo ingens*), which is confirmed
by Clement (1 Clem 6:1). (2) The torments that the Christians were subjected
to indicates that at least the Christians who were crucified did not possess
Roman citizenship. The torments that Tacitus mentions – wrapped in the skins
of wild animals (*ferarum tergis contecti*), torn to pieces by dogs (*laniatus
canum*), nailed to crosses (*crucibus affixit*), burned (*flammandi*) – are not so
much the result of Nero's cruelty as common Roman penal praxis.[208] Since
many Jews in Rome were Roman citizens, it follows that most Christians in
the city of Rome at this time were Gentile Christians. (3) Christians were
publicly known, and they had made a bad impression upon the people: the
"common people" (*vulgus*) "hated" them "for their shameful vices" (*per flagitia invisos*), accusing them of hating humankind (*odium humani generis*),[209]
which was the reason why they could be used as scapegoats. Tacitus charac-
terizes the Christians as "pernicious superstition" (*exitiabilis superstitio*). (4)
One could distinguish Christians and Jews at around A.D. 60. (5) At least
Roman historians knew several facts about the origins of the Christian movement in Judea: (a) the sect of the Christians was started by a man called
"Christus" (*auctor nominis eius Christus*); (b) this Christus had been executed

---

Rome in the First Two Centuries (Minneapolis: Fortress, 2003), 13 n. 4, calls this hypothesis
"a superfluous complication."

[205] YARDLEY, Tacitus: Annals, 495 with n. 360. KOESTERMANN, Irrtum, 464–65; cf.
KOESTERMANN, Tacitus. Annalen, 4:256, who relates *fastebantur* to "jüdische Krämer, die
durch Fahrlässigkeit den Ausbruch des Feuers in den Zirkusbuden verursacht haben."

[206] Cf. Eusebius, *Hist. eccl.* 4.29.9; Tertullian, *Apol.* 5.3; 21.25. Cf. STEPHEN BENKO,
Pagan Criticism of Christianity During the First Two Centuries A.D, ANRW II.23.2
(1980): 1055–1118, 1065.

[207] Cf. RAYMOND E. BROWN and JOHN P. MEIER, Antioch and Rome: New Testament Cradles of Catholic Christianity (New York: Paulist, 1983), 99; JAMES D. G. DUNN, Beginning
from Jerusalem (Christianity in the Making II; Grand Rapids: Eerdmans, 2009), 56–57;
LAMPE, Christians at Rome, 82–84.

[208] LAMPE, Christians at Rome, 82, refers to the Twelve Tablets (Gaius, *Dig.* 47.9.9);
Seneca, *Clem.* 1.23; Suetonius, *Claud.* 34; Modestinus, *Dig.* 48.9.9. For the following point
cf. LAMPE, ibid. 83–84.

[209] Tacitus similarly accuses the Jews of hating the human race (*odium humani generis*;
*Hist.* 5.5.1). In the second century Christians were accused of cannibalism and infanticide.

during the principate of Tiberius (*Tiberio imperitante*); (c) he was sentenced by Pontius Pilatus (*per procuratorem Pontium Pilatum supplicio adfectus erat*); (d) it spread from Judea to other cities, including Rome: it breaks out like a disease, but Tacitus does not know how it speads.[210]

Tacitus mentions Pontius Pilatus only because he wants to provide the historical context for the execution of Jesus, the instigator of the *superstitio* of the Christians, which he presents as the result of a legally correct trial. He has no interest in the person of Pontius Pilatus as such.[211]

*Pontius Pilatus*. As Roman prefect of Judea, Pontius Pilatus' effectiveness as Rome's representative depended on the cooperation with the aristocratic elite. His long tenure indicates that he was successful in maintaining a balance between his loyalty to Rome and his authority In Judea. Josephus and Philo report disturbances under Pilatus. The Roman authorities seem to have treated these and similar incidents as insignificant:[212] Tacitus, who reports a complaint in A.D. 17 in the provinces of Syria and Judea against the burden of Roman taxation,[213] asserts, with stark simplicity, *sub Tiberio quies* ("under Tiberius all was quiet;" *Hist.* 5.9.2). At the same time, Pilatus' long tenure as well as his abrupt departure from Judea suggest that he had either no ambitions or no options for more advanced appointments.[214]

Both Philo's and Josephus' narratives serve distinct purposes in the context of their literary aims. Philo's polemical description of Pilatus fits his rhetorical aims: as Tiberius did not tolerate the behavior of Pontius Pilatus, prefect of Judea, which triggered disturbances in Judea, so Gaius Caligula should not tolerate the actions of Flaccus, prefect in Egypt. Josephus, who writes *Bellum* both for a Jewish and (mostly) for a Roman audience (*B. J.* 1.3) and addresses *Antiquitates* to primarily Roman readers (*A. J.* 1.5), and who belongs himself to the Jewish aristocracy of Judea, wants to present a picture of Judaism which appears acceptable for his audience and which does not hurt Jewish sensibilities. He seems eager to keep the high priest out of the disturbances in Judea that he reports. This literary position can be compared with the political position of Pilatus.[215] He seeks to preserve his authority as Roman prefect in his dealings with the Judeans, willing to compromise when Jewish interests

---

[210] For the last point cf. EDWIN A. JUDGE, The First Christians in the Roman World: Augustan and New Testament Essays (ed. J. R. Harrison; WUNT 229; Tübingen: Mohr Siebeck, 2008), 434.

[211] HERZER, Loyalität, 433. For the anachronistic title *procurator* see the introduction to Section 2.1.

[212] MARTIN GOODMAN, Judaea, in Cambridge Ancient History. Volume X: The Augustan Empire, 43 B.C.–A.D. 69 (Second ed.; ed. A. K. Bowman, E. Champlin, and A. Lintott; orig. 1996; repr., Cambridge: Cambridge University Press, 2006), 737–781, 752.

[213] Tacitus, *Ann.* 2.42.5.

[214] Cf. HERZER, Loyalität, 435.

[215] HERZER, Loyalität, 444–45, 449.

are at stake. Josephus portrays Pilatus as Rome's representative in Judea whose authority is not challenged by the Jewish leadership – the high priest is never mentioned. Pilatus is a loyal Roman official who strives to maintain law and order in his territory and who is able to do justice to the various interests of both Rome, the Jewish leadership, and the Jewish population.[216] Josephus essentially exonerates Pilatus from the violence that breaks out at different times in Judea, which can be explained with the promotion of the imperial cult and of imperial "presence" in Judea. It is the Samaritans who, at the end of his tenure, report him to the Roman governor of Syria who removes him from office and sends him to Rome, probably for personal political interests.

In contrast to (largely older) scholarship that assumed a hatred of the Jews by Pilatus on account of his close relationship with Lucius Aelius Sejanus who was an enemy of the Jews,[217] and scholarship that regards Pilatus as being at least contemptuous of the Jews,[218] many scholars today no longer describe Pilatus in terms of being hostile to the Jews.[219] A. STROBEL emphasizes the difficulty of Pilatus' task as prefect of Judea, and explains both his clashes with the Jewish people and his behavior during Jesus' trial with a mixture of obstinacy and weakness of character.[220] J. P. LÉMONON explains the clashes between Pilatus and the Jewish population with Pilatus' character on the one hand and his understanding of the role of a prefect in a Roman province on the other hand: he expected the population of the province to accept his role as Roman prefect, and he sought to honor the emperor by bringing Judea in line with the other Roman provinces, despite Jewish sensibilities.[221] H. K. BOND

---

[216] HERZER, Loyalität, 449.

[217] Cf. STAUFFER, Jesus, 99–101 (= ETHELBERT STAUFFER, Jesus and His Story [London: SCM Press, 1960], 108–10); ERNST BAMMEL, Pilate and Syrian Coinage [1951], in Judaica: Kleine Schriften I (WUNT 37; Tübingen: Mohr, 1986), 47–50; ERNST BAMMEL, Philos tou Kaisaros, TLZ 77 (1952): 205–210; MAIER, Episode; WINTER, Trial, 70–89; MENAHEM STERN, The Province of Judea, in The Jewish People in the First Century. Historical Geography, Political History, Social, Cultural and Religious Life and Institutions (ed. S. Safrai and M. Stern; CRINT I; Assen: Van Gorcum, 1974), 308–376, 349–53; KIRNER, Strafgewalt, 157–58; MAHIEU, Herod, 480. For a critique of the Sejanus hypothesis and Sejanus' assumed hatred for the Jews cf. DIETER HENNIG, L. Aelius Seianus. Untersuchungen zur Regierung des Tiberius (Vestigia 21; München: Beck, 1975), 160–79; DEMANDT, Pontius Pilatus, 91–92; WEBB, Roman Examination, 722–23. STAUFFER challenged the standard view of Pilatus as a reasonably able governor; the standard treatment was GUSTAV ADOLF MÜLLER, Pontius Pilatus, der fünfte Prokurator von Judäa und Richter Jesu von Nazareth (Stuttgart: Metzler, 1888). The picture of Pilatus as contemptuous and intolerant toward the Jews was drawn already by SCHÜRER, Geschichte.

[218] Cf. BLINZLER, Prozeß, 260–71; SCHÜRER, History, 2:383–87; SMALLWOOD, Jews, 160–70; HENGEL / SCHWEMER, Jesus, 80–81.

[219] Cf. KRIEGER, Pontius Pilatus; HERZER, Loyalität, 435.

[220] STROBEL, Stunde, 99–131.

[221] LÉMONON, Pilate, 221–77; LÉMONON, Ponce Pilate, 200–61. Cf. BRIAN C. MCGING, Pontius Pilate and the Sources, CBQ 53 (1991): 416–438; BROWN, Death, 1:695–705.

portrays Pilatus as an essentially capable and prudent governor who is unwilling to take any nonsense from the people but who is also able to show flexibility and the willingness to stand down in the interest of preserving the peace; he was willing and able to work closely with the Jewish hierarchy, and he avoided undue aggression when his eagerness to bring Judea into line with other Roman provinces provoked unrest and clashes.[222] M. BERNETT argues that Pilatus may have deliberately used the symbolic language of the imperial cult in his coins in order to force the Jewish population to publicly acknowledge Roman rule. Seen in a more benign light, his initiatives can be interpreted as representing the normal actions or a Roman official in the context of the developments connected with the imperial cult. In the latter case, Pilatus would have either not understood or underestimated the problematic nature of the imperial cult for the Jewish population, and, once conflicts emerged, he refused to acknowledge the problem, a fact that led to repeated clashes.[223]

It comes as no surprise that the New Testament references to Pilatus are connected with Jesus' execution. The earliest reference comes from the Apostle Paul who refers to Pontius Pilatus, without mentioning his name, probably in the context of his collaboration with the Jewish aristocracy, when he writes: ἣν οὐδεὶς τῶν ἀρχόντων τοῦ αἰῶνος τούτου ἔγνωκεν· εἰ γὰρ ἔγνωσαν, οὐκ ἂν τὸν κύριον τῆς δόξης ἐσταύρωσαν ("None of the rulers of this age understood this; for if they had, they would not have crucified the Lord of glory;" 1 Cor 2:8). According to Acts 26:26–27, the church in Jerusalem linked Jesus' death with "kings" (οἱ βασιλεῖς) and "rulers" (οἱ ἄρχοντες), specifically with "Herod and Pontius Pilatus" (Ἡρῴδης τε καὶ Πόντιος Πιλᾶτος). Luke knows of the conflict between Pilatus and the Herodian princes such as Antipas (Luke 23:7). Luke's presentation of Pilatus (Luke 23:1–25) and of Herod Antipas (Luke 23:7) distances both from the accusation of the high priest and the leaders of the people: he sees the primary responsibility for Jesus' death with the priestly aristocracy of Jerusalem, who use the Jewish crowds to maneuver Pilatus into granting their request to execute Jesus.[224]

## 2.2  The Jurisdiction of Roman Prefects

Apart from the Pilatus texts, there is very little evidence for the jurisdiction of the Roman prefects in Judea in the first century. Cicero's statement in *Pro Balbo* 22 is indicative of Rome's fundamental attitude concerning her own

---

[222] BOND, Pontius Pilate, 203–4 (conclusions).

[223] BERNETT, Kaiserkult, 200. HENNIG, Seianus, 176–78, leaves open the question whether Pilatus deliberately provoked the Jews or whether his actions aimed at adapting the situation in Roman Judea to the standard of other Roman provinces.

[224] HERZER, Loyalität, 448.

interests and that of the cities, regions, and provinces Rome governed. The Cyrene edicts of Augustus are rarely mentioned in discussions of Jesus' trial before Pontius Pilatus, despite the fact that they demonstrate the power of the emperor to intervene in the affairs of the Roman provinces and the legal and administrative authority of the provincial governors who had full jurisdiction over capital cases, even when they worked in conjunction with local courts. The papyrus SB XII 10920 (P. Yale II 162) illustrates the legal arrangements in Roman Egypt. A province which Augustus placed under a *praefectus* of equestrian rank, Egypt served as a model for other provinces: the *imperium* that the emperor granted to the *praefectus Aegypti* even before 27 B.C. corresponded to the authority of the proconsuls,[225] and the same comprehensive authority over military, legal, financial, and general administrative matters was granted to the equestrian *praefecti* of the other imperial provinces.[226] In imperial provinces, the governors, appointed as *legati Augusti*, participated in the *imperium* of the emperor and thus could not delegate the jurisdiction in legal matters to others.[227] For texts that relate specifically to the province of Judea see section 1.2.

**(85)** Cicero, *Pro Balbo* 22

Cum aliquid populus Romanus iussit, id si est eius modi ut quibusdam populis sive foederatis sive liberis permittendum esse videatur, ut statuant ipsi non de nostris, sed de suis rebus, quo iure uti velint, tum, utrum fundi facti sint an non, quaerendum esse videtur; de nostra vero re publica, de nostro imperio, de nostris bellis, de victoria, de salute fundos populos fieri noluerunt.

*Translation.* When the Roman people enacted a law, if the law was of such a kind that it seemed it might be permitted to certain peoples, whether bound to us by treaty or free, to decide themselves – by consulting not our interests but their own – which law they wished to adopt: it is only in this case that the question arises whether or not they have given consent; that these states

---

[225] *Digesta* 1.17.1: *imperium, quod at similitudinem proconsulis lege sub Augusto ei datum est.*

[226] ECK, Leitung, 327–40. At the time of Claudius, thirteen provinces were governed by an equestrian *praefectus*: Mauretania Caesariensis, Mauretania Tingitana, Sardinia, Corsica (?), Alpes Maritimae, Alpes Cottiae, Alpes Graiae, Raetia, Noricum, Thracia, Cappadocia, Iudaea, and Aegyptus. ECK bases his conclusions on texts such as *Digesta* 1.18.4 (*praeses provinciae maius imperium in ea provincia habet omnibus post principem*) and Josephus, *B. J.* 2.117 (cf. No. 13) and Josephus, *A. J.* 18.1–2 (cf. No. 11).

[227] HARTMUT GALSTERER, The Administration of Justice, in Cambridge Ancient History. Volume X: The Augustan Empire, 43 B.C.–A.D. 69 (Second ed.; ed. A. K. Bowman, E. Champlin, and A. Lintott; orig. 1996; repr., Cambridge: Cambridge University Press, 2006), 397–413, 411. The *proconsules* of the senatorial provinces had an *imperium* of their own and thus could appoint *legati* to assist them in jurisdiction.

approve of our affairs of state, our rule, our wars, our victory, or our safety, was never desired.

*Commentary.*[228] Lucius Cornelius Balbus from Gades, a *civitas foederata*,[229] had been granted Roman citizenship by Cn. Pompeius for his services in the battle against Sertorius in 72 B.C., an act that the *lex Gellia et Cornelia de civitate* of 72 B.C. allowed. Balbus became an *eques* and served under Caesar as *praefectus fabrum* in 61 B.C. A year later he promoted the First Triumvirate, and had himself adopted by Theophanes of Mytilene. In 56 B.C. he was accused by radical Optimates of obtaining his citizenship illicitly. Crassus, Pompey, and Cicero defended him successfully. He was consul in 40 B.C., the first non-citizen by birth to achieve the consulship. Cicero's speech in support of Balbus, given in the second half of 56 B.C., is important for the theory of Roman citizenship.[230] The relevant law for the case was the *lex Papia* of 65 B.C.[231] The notion that the Roman *patria* is greater than the local region reflects the idea of the *maiestas populi romani* which figured in the treaties concluded by Rome since the end of the third century B.C.[232] Cicero emphasizes in his speech in defense of Balbus that the idea of *maiestas*, as defined by Rome, was confined to diplomatic and external relations, without interfering in matters of private law, customs, or institutions. Rome conceded the right to accept or refuse specific Roman laws both to new allies as well as to new citizens. C. NICOLET comments: "This 'guarantee' or 'endorsement' (*fundifactio*) recognized the sphere of individual relations, the family, customs and religion as an essential though subordinate aspect of public life: these constituted the 'natural *patria*' of which Cicero speaks. Embracing them, but at a higher level, was the national or imperial *patria* embodied in Rome and

---

[228] Text: TADEUSZ MASLOWSI, M. Tullius Cicero Scripta quae manserunt omnia. Fasc. 24: Oratio de provinciis consularibus. Oratio pro L. Cornelio Balbo (BSGRT; Berlin: De Gruyter, 2007); for other text editions and translations cf. CARL F. W. MÜLLER, M. Tullii Ciceronis scripta quae manserunt omnia (10 vols.; BSGRT; Leipzig: Teubner, 1885–1891), II/3; ROBERT GARDNER, Cicero. Pro Caelio. De provinciis consularibus. Pro Balbo (orig. 1958; repr., LCL; Cambridge: Harvard University Press, 2005), 611–717; MANFRED FUHRMANN, Marcus Tullius Cicero. Sämtliche Reden (7 vols.; Bibliothek der Alten Welt. Römische Reihe; Zürich / Stuttgart, 1970–1982), 6:93–136; MANFRED FUHRMANN, Marcus Tullius Cicero. Die Prozeßreden (Lateinisch-deutsch. 2 vols.; Sammlung Tusculum; Zürich / Düsseldorf: Artemis & Winkler, 1997), 1:230–309; JEAN COUSIN, Cicéron. Discours. Tome XV: Pour Caelius, Sur les provinces consulaires, Pour Balbus (Collection des universités de France 166; Paris: Belles Lettres, 1962).

[229] Cf. KARL-LUDWIG ELVERS, Cornelius [I 6] C. Balbus, L., BNP 3 (2003): 809.

[230] Cf. CARL HOSIUS, Geschichte der römischen Literatur. Erster Teil: Die römische Literatur in der Zeit der Republik (HdA VIII.1; München: Beck, 1927), 433; on Cicero ibid. 400–550. Balbus' Roman name suggests that he probably owed his promotion to L. Cornelius Lentulus Crus, the consul of 49 B.C.; cf. FUHRMANN, Cicero. Prozeßreden, 793.

[231] FUHRMANN, Cicero. Prozeßreden, 792.

[232] Cf. CLAUDE NICOLET, The World of the Citizen in Republican Rome (Berkeley / Los Angeles: University of California Press, 1988), 45.

the right of a Roman citizen."[233] According to Cicero, Rome has the right to interfere when Rome's interests are concerned, which includes Rome's *salus* ("safety," GARDNER translates "welfare"). During the imperial period, the autonomy of cities and regions was increasingly pulled back.[234] This means for Roman Judea that if the *praefectus* saw Rome's interests threatened, he could, indeed would be compelled to, interfere in Jewish affairs.

**(86)** Cyrene Edicts of Augustus (SEG IX 8)

I

αὐτοκράτωρ Καῖσαρ Σεβαστὸς ἀρχιερεὺς δημαρχικῆς ἐξουσίας
ἑπτακαιδέκατον αὐτοκράτωρ τεσσερασκαιδέκατον | λέγει·[235] | ἐπειδὴ τοὺς
5 πάντας εὑρίσκω Ῥωμαίους ἐν τῆι περὶ Κυρήνην ‖ ἐπαρχήαι πέντε καὶ δέκα
καὶ διακοσίους ἐκ πάσης ἡλικίας | δισχειλίων καὶ πεντακοσίων διναρίων ἢ
μείζω τίμησιν ἔχοντας, | ἐξ ὧν εἰσιν οἱ κριταί, καὶ ἐν αὐτοῖς τούτοις εἶναί
τινας συνωμοσίας | αἱ πρεσβῆαι τῶν ἐκ τῆς ἐπαρχήας πόλεων ἀπωδύραντο
τὰς ἐπιβαρού| σας τοῖς Ἕλληνας ἐν ταῖς θανατηφόροις δίκαις, τῶν αὐτῶν
10 ἐμ μέρει κα‖ τηγορούντων καὶ μαρτυρούντων ἀλλήλοις, κἀγὼ δὲ αὐτός
ἔγνωκα ἀ|ναιτίους τινὰς τῶι τρόπῳ τούτῳ καταβεβαρημένους καὶ ἐς τὴν
ἐσχά|την ἠγμένους τιμωρίαν, ἄχρι ἂν ἡ σύνκλητος βουλεύσηται περὶ
τούτου | ἢ ἐγὼ αὐτὸς ἄμεινον εὕρω τι δοκοῦσί μοι καλῶς καὶ προσηκόντως
ποιήσειν | οἱ τὴν Κρητικὴν καὶ Κυρηναικὴν ἐπαρχήαν καθέξοντες
15 προτιθέντες ἐν τῆι κατὰ ‖ Κυρήνην ἐπαρχήαι τὸν ἴσον ἀριθμὸν Ἑλλήνων
κριτῶν ἐκ τῶν μεγίστων τιμημά|των ὅσον καὶ Ῥωμαίων, μηδένα νεώτερον
πέντε καὶ εἴκοσι ἐτῶν, μήτε Ῥωμαῖον μή|τε Ἕλληνα, μηδὲ ἔλασ<σ>ον
ἔχοντα τίμημα καὶ οὐσίαν, ἄν γε εὐπορία τοιούτων ἀν|θρώπων ἦι,
δειναρίων ἑπτακισχειλίων καὶ πεντακοσίων, ἢ ἂν τούτωι τῶι | μη δύνηται
συμπληροῦσθαι ὁ ἀριθμός τῶν ὀφειλόντων προτίθεσθαι κριτῶν, τοὺς ‖
20 τὸ ἥμισυ καὶ μὴ ἔλασ<σ>ον τούτου τοῦ τιμ<ήμ>ατος ἔχοντας
προτιθέτωσαν κριτὰς ἐν | τοῖς θανατηφόροις τῶν Ἑλλήνων κριτηρίοις. ἐὰν
δὲ Ἕλλην κρινόμε|νος, πρὸ μιᾶς ἡμέρας ἢ τὸν κατήγορον ἄρξασθαι λέγειν,
δοθείσης ἐξου|σίας αὐτῷ πότερον ἅπαντας βούλεται κριτὰς αὐτῶι
Ῥωμαίους εἶναι ἢ τοὺς | ἡμίσους Ἕλληνας, ἕληται τοὺς ἡμίσεις Ἕλληνας,
25 τότε σηκωθεισῶν τῶν ‖ σφαιρῶν καὶ ἐπιγραφέντων αὐταῖς τῶν ὀνομάτων,

---

[233] NICOLET, Citizen, 46. KIMBERLY A. BARBER, Rhetoric in Cicero's *Pro Balbo:* An Interpretation (orig. 2004; repr., Studies in Classics 6; London: Routledge / Taylor & Francis, 2012), 51, comments that "given the differences between Balbus' situation and that of cities adopting the *leges* mentioned above [i.e. the *lex Furia, lex Voconia, lex Iulia*], and given the argument about Rome's sovereignty, it is most likely that Gades did not have to 'give consent' for Balbus' citizenship grant to be legitimate."

[234] THEODOR MOMMSEN, Römisches Staatsrecht (3 vols. Dritte Auflage; orig. 1871–1888; repr., HdA III.1; Leipzig: Hirzel, 1887–1888), 696–97.

[235] Written in extra large letters on the stone.

ἐγ μὲν τοῦ ἑτέρου κλη|ρωτηρίου τὰ τῶν Ῥωμαίων ὀνόματα, ἐγ δὲ τοῦ
ἑτέρου τὰ τῶν Ἑλλήνων κληρο[ύ]|σθω, ἕως ἂν {αν} ἐφ' ἑκατέροιυ γένους
ἀνὰ εἴκοσι πέντε ἐκπληρωθῶσιν, ὧν ἀνὰ ἕ|να ἐξ ἑκατέρου γένους ὁ
διῶκων, ἂν βούληται, ἀπολεγέτω, τρῖς δὲ ἐξ ἁπάντων | [ὁ] φεύγων, ἐφ' ὧι
οὔτε [Ῥ]ωμαίους πάντας οὔτε Ἑλληνας πάντας ἀπολέξει εἶτα οἱ ‖
30 ἄλλοι πάντες ἐπὶ τὴν ψηφοφορίαν ἀπολυέσθωσαν καὶ φερέτωσαν ἰδίαι μὲν
εἰς ἑτέ|ραν κίστην οἱ Ῥωμαῖοι τὴν ψῆφον, ἰδίαι δὲ οἱ Ἑλληνες εἰς
ἑτέραν· εἶτα γενομένης ἰδί|αι τῆς διαριθμήσεως τῶν ἑκατέρωθεν ψήφων, ὅ
τι ἃ οἱ πλείους ἐξ ἁπάντων δικάσω|σιν, τοῦτο ἐμφανῶς ὁ στρατηγὸς
ἀποφαινέσθω. καὶ ἐπεὶ τοὺς ἀδίκους θανάτους ὠ|ς τὸ πολὺ οἱ προσήκοντες
35 τοῖς ἀπολωλόσιν οὐκ ἀτειμωρήτους περιορῶσιν, εἰκός τέ ἐστιν ‖ τοῖς
ἐνόχοις μὴ ἐνλύφειν Ἑλληνας κατηγόρους τοὺς δίκην ὑπὲρ τῶν
ἀπολωλότων οἰκήων ἢ πολειτῶν πραξομένους, ὀρθῶς καὶ προσηκόντως
μοι δοκοῦσιν ποιή|σειν ὅσοι Κρήτης καὶ Κυρήνης στρατηγήσουσιν, εἰ ἐν
τῆ κατὰ Κυρήνην ἐπαρχήαι ὑπὲρ | Ἑλληνος ἀνδρὸς ἢ γυναικὸς
ἀναιρέσεως μὴ προσίοιντο κατήγορον Ῥωμαῖον Ἑλλη|νος, πλὴν τις
40 Ῥωμαιότητι τετειμημένος ὑπὲρ τινος τῶν οἰκήων ἢ πο‖λειτῶν θανάτου
δικάζοιτο

## II

αὐτοκράτωρ Καῖσαρ Σεβαστὸς ἀρχιε|ρεὺς δημαρχικῆς ἐξουσίας τὸ
ἑπτακαιδέκατον λέγει· φθόνος φόγος | τε εἶναι Ποπλίωι Σεξστίωι Σκεύαι
οὐκ ὀφείλει, ὅτι Αὖλον Στλάκκιον Λευ|κίου υἱὸν Μάξιμον καὶ Λεύκιον
Στλάκκιον Λευκίου υἱὸν Μακεδόνα καὶ Πόπλι|ον Λακουτάνιον Ποπλίου
45 ἀπελεύθερον Φιλέρωτα, ἐπειδὴ ἑατοὺς οὖτοι, ‖ ὅ πρὸς τὴν ἐμὴν σωτηρίαν
τά τε δημόσια πράγματα ἀνῆκεν, ἐπίστασθαι καὶ | βούλεσθαι εἰπεῖν
ἔφησαν, δεσμίους πρός με ἐκ τῆς Κυρηναικῆς ἐπαρχήασ{α}|
ἀναπεμφθῆναι ἐφρόντισεν· τοῦτο γὰρ ἐποίησεν Σέξστιος καθηκόντως καὶ
ἐ|πιμελῶς. λοιπὸν ἐπειδὴ τῶν πρὸς ἐμὲ καί τὰ δημόσια πράγματα ἀνηκόν|
των οὐδὲν γεινώσκουσι, τοῦτο δὲ ἐν τῆι ἐπαρχήαι εἶπαν ἑατοὺς πε‖
50 πλάσθαι καὶ ἐφεύσθαι φανερόν <τε> ἐποίησάν μοι, ἐλευθερωθέντας |
αὐτοὺς ἐκ τῆς παραφυλακῆς ἀφείημι. Αὖλον δὲ Στλάκκιον | Μάξιμον, ὃν
Κυρηναίων οἱ πρέσβεις αἰτιῶνται ἀνδριάντας ἐκ τῶν | δημοσίων τόπων
ἠρκέναι, ἐν οἷς καὶ τὸν ὧι ἡ πόλεις τὸ ἐμὸν ὄνομα ὑπέγραψεν, ἕως |
{ς} ἂν περὶ τούτου τοῦ πράγματος διαγνῶ, ἀπελθεῖν ἄνευ τῆς ἐμῆς
55 ἐπιταγῆς κω‖λύω

## III

αὐτοκράτωρ Καῖσαρ Σεβαστὸς ἀρχιερεὺς δημαρχικῆς ἐξουσίας | τὸ
ἑπτακαιδέκατον{ι} λέγει· εἴ τινες ἐκ τῆς Κυρηναικῆς ἐπαρχή|ας πολειτίαι
τετείμηνται, τούτους λειτουργεῖν οὐδὲν ἔλασ<σ>ον ἐμ μέρει τῶ τῶν |
Ἑλλήνων σώματι κελεύω, ἐκτὸς τ[ο]ύτ{ι}ων οἷς κατὰ νόμον ἢ δόγμα

συνκλή<του ἤ> | τῶι τοῦ πατρός μου ἐπικρίματι ἤ τῶι ἐμῶι ἀνεισφορία
60 ὁμοῦ σὺν τῆι πολειτήαι ‖ δέδοται· καὶ τούτους αὐτούς, οἷς ἡ ἀνεισφορία
δέδοται, τούτων τῶν πρα|γμάτων εἶναι ἀτελεῖς ὧν τότε εἶχον ἀρέσκει μοι,
ὑπὲρ δὲ τῶν ἐπικτήτων | πάντων τελεῖν τὰ γεινόμενα

IV

αὐτοκράτωρ Καῖσαρ Σεβαστὸς ἀρχιε|ρεὺς δημαρχικῆς ἐξουσίας τὸ
ἑπτακαιδέκατον λέγει· αἵτινες | ἀμφισβητήσ<ε>ις ἀνὰ μέσον Ἑλλήνων
65 ἔσονται κατὰ τὴν Κυρηναικὴν ἐπαρχήαν, ‖ ὑπεξειρημένων τῶν ὑποδίκων
κεφαλῆς, ὑπὲρ ὧν ὅς ἂν τὴν ἐπαρχήαν διακατέχῃ | αὐτὸς διαγεινώσκειν
κ[αὶ] ἱστάναι ἢ συμβούλιον κριτῶν παρέχειν ὀφείλει, | ὑπὲρ δὲ τῶν λοιπῶν
πραγμάτων πάν Ἕλληνας κριτὰς δίδοσθαι ἀρέσκει εἰ μή τις | ἀπαιτούμενος
ἢ ὁ εὐθυνόμενος πολείτας Ῥωμαίων κριτὰς ἔχειν βούληται· ὧν δ᾽ ἀνὰ |
{να} μέσον ἐκ τοῦδε τοῦ ἐμοῦ ἐπικρίματος Ἕλληνες κριταὶ δοθήσονται,
70 κριτὴν δίδοσθαι ‖ οὐκ ἀρέσκει ἐξ ἐκείνης τῆς πόλεως οὐδὲ ἕνα ἐξ ἧς ἂν ὁ
διώκων ἢ ὁ εὐθύνων ἔσται ἢ ἐκεῖ|νος ὁ {π} ἀπαιτούμενος ἢ ὁ εὐθυνόμενος

*Translation.*

I

Imperator Caesar Augustus, pontifex maximus holding the tribunician |
power for the seventeenth time,[236] imperator for the fourteenth time,
declares: Since I find that all the Romans in the province of Cyrene ‖
5  are two hundred and fifteen of every age | who have a census valuation of
twenty-five hundred denarii or more, | from whom the judges are (chosen),
and that there are conspiracies among these (Romans) | – so the embassies
of the cities from the province have complained – which have oppre|ssed
10 the Greeks in capital cases, the same people taking turns as ac‖cusers and
as witnesses for each other, and (since) I myself have found that some
in|nocent people in this way have been oppressed and brought to the
ulti|mate penalty, until the senate may decide about this | or I myself may
find something better, the fair and appropriate course of action, it seems to
me, | would be for those who govern the province of Crete and Cyrene to
15 set up (a list) in the ‖ province of Cyrene of Greek judges of the highest
census valuati|on, equal in number to the Roman (judges), none of them
younger than twenty-five years, Roman | or Greek, with a census valuation
and property, if there is a sufficient number of such m|en, of no less than
seventy-five hundred denarii,or, if in this way | the number of judges which
20 ought to be listed cannot be filled, ‖ they shall list those judges who have
half and no less than half of this census valuation to be judges in | capital
cases of the Greeks. If a Greek is on tri|al, one day before the accuser
begins to speak he shall be given the pow|er (to decide) whether he wishes

---

[236] I.e. 7/6 B.C.

his judges to be Romans or | half of them Greeks. If he chooses half
25 Greeks, then, after the balls have been weighed || and the names inscribed
on them, from the one ur|n the names of the Romans, and from the other
the names of the Greeks shall be drawn by lot, | until in each group twenty-
five have been selected. Of these names | the accuser, if he wishes, shall
reject one from each group, but the defendant (may reject) three of all the
names, | on the condition that he reject neither all Romans, nor all Greeks.
30 Then || all the others shall be sent to cast their votes and they shall cast their
votes, | the Romans separately into one basket, the Greeks separately into
another. Then, when the counting has been finished sep|arately for the
votes in each group, whatever the majority of all shall have | decided the
praetor (i.e., governor) shall declare publicly (as the verdict). And since
unjust deaths, for | the most part, the relatives of victims do not allow to go
35 unavenged, and it is likely that Greek accusers will not be lacking in
procuring justice for the guilty on behalf of their murdered | relatives or
(fellow) citizens, the correct and appropriate course of action, it seems to
me, wou|ld be if the future governors of Crete and Cyrene, | in the province
of Cyrene, would not permit a Roman to be the accuser of a Greek in a case
of the murder of a Greek man or woman, | except that someone who has
been honored with Roman citizenship may go to court on behalf of the
40 death of one of his relatives or (fellow) citizens. ||

## II

Imperator Caesar Augustus, pon|tifex maximus, holding the tribunician
power for the seventeenth time, declares: Ill-will and blame | ought not be
(directed) to(ward) Publius Sextius Scaeva because he saw to it that Aulus
Stlaccius Maximus son of Lu|cius, Lucius Stlaccius Macedo son of Lucius,
45 and Publi|us Lacutanius Phileros, freedman of Publius, when they || said
that they knew and wished to tell something that pertained to my safety and
to the Republic, | were sent in chains to me from the Cyrenaica, | for in this
Sextius acted properly and with vi|gilance. Moreover, since they know
nothing of matters that pertain to me and the Republic | and stated and
made it clear to me that this, which they said in the province, had been a
50 fa||brication and a falsehood, I have set them free | and released them from
custody. But (as for) Aulus Stlaccius | Maximus, whom envoys of the
Cyreneans accuse of removing statues from | public places, among them
being the one beneath which the city has inscribed my name, until | I have
formed an opinion about this matter, I forbid him to leave (Rome) without
my order. ||

## III

Imperator Caesar Augustus, pontifex maximus, holding the tribunician
power | for the seventeenth time, declares: If people from the provin|ce of
Cyrene have been honored with (Roman) citizenship, I order them to

perform the personal[237] liturgies, nevertheless, in their role | as Greeks. Excepted are those to whom in accordance with a law or decree of the senate | (or) decree of my father or of myself, immunity from taxation has
60 been granted along with the citizenship. || And it pleases me that these men to whom immunity has been given shall have exemption only for that pro|perty which they had at the time (of the grant). For all newly acquired property | they shall pay the taxes.

IV

Imperator Caesar Augustus, ponti|fex maximus, holding the tribunician power for the seventeenth time, declares: Whatever | disputes shall arise
65 between Greeks in the province of Cyrene, || except for those who are liable for capital offenses, in whose case the governor of the province | has the duty of conducting the investigation and rendering judgments himself or establishing a list of judges, | – for all other matters it pleases me that Greek judges be granted to them, unless some | defendant or accused wishes to have Roman citizens for judges. For the parties | to whom Greek judges will be given in consequence of this decree of mine, it pleases me
70 that no judge should be given || from that city from which the plaintiff or accuser comes, or th|e defendant or accused.

*Commentary.*[238] Four edicts of Augustus dated 7/6 B.C. were discovered in 1926 in the agora of Cyrene; a fifth edict, dated 5/4 B.C., inscribed on the same stone, communicates a *senatus consultum* of 4 B.C. which streamlined procedures for extortion cases (*repetundae*). The edicts[239] demonstrate that

---

[237] Cf. the discussion in ROBERT K. SHERK, Rome and the Greek East to the Death of Augustus (Translated Documents of Greece and Rome 4; Cambridge: Cambridge University Press, 1984), 102 n. 6; also ADRIAN NICOLAS SHERWIN-WHITE, The Roman Citizenship (Second ed.; Oxford: Clarendon, 1973), 334–36.

[238] SEG IX 8 = FIRA I² 68; editio princeps: GASPARE OLIVERIO, La stele di Augusto rinvenuta nell Agorà di Cirene, Notiziario Archeologico del Ministero delle Colonie 4 (1927): 15–67 (text, Latin and Italian translation, commentary, Tables II–V); cf. LUDWIG RADERMACHER, Fünf Erlässe des Augustus aus der Cyrenaica, Anzeiger der Wiener Akademie der Wissenschaften (Phil.-Hist. Klasse) 10 (1928): 69–82; JOHANNES STROUX and LEOPOLD WENGER, Die Augustus-Inschrift auf dem Marktplatz von Kyrene (Abhandlungen der Bayrischen Akademie der Wissenschaften, Philosophisch-philologische und historische Klasse 34.2; München: Verlag der Bayerischen Akademie der Wissenschaften, 1928), 8–17 (discussion ibid. 18–136); cf. FERNAND DE VISSCHER, Les édits d'Auguste découverts à Cyrène (Recueil de Travaux d'Histoire et de Philologie III.1; Louvain / Paris: Bibliothèque de l'Université / Les Belles Lettres, 1940), 16–26 (with photograph), 31–210 (commentary); EHRENBERG / JONES, Documents, 139–43 (No. 311); ROBERT K. SHERK, Roman Documents from the Greek East: Senatus Consulta and Epistulae to the Age of Augustus (Baltimore: Johns Hopkins University Press, 1969), 174–82 (No. 61); the translation is taken from SHERK, Rome and the Greek East, 127–32 (No. 102), with some modifications.

[239] The term λέγει ("declares, proclaims") in line 3 is the technical verb which always appears in imperial edicts, following the imperial titles.

Augustus could intervene in a senatorial province on the basis of his *imperium proconsulare*, which was superior to the *potestas* of the senatorial pro-consuls.[240] Edict I regulates the appointment of judges in the Roman province *Creta et Cyrene*. The minimum age of the judges (jurors) is lowered from 30 years (*lex Acilia*) to 25 years. As regards capital cases (ἐν ταῖς θανατηφόροις δίκαις, line 9), the list of judges should have as many Greeks as Romans, which would allow a Greek defendant to secure for himself a panel of judges with a majority of Greeks.[241] This stipulation represents Augustus' reaction to complaints of provincials that Romans control the courts and oppress the Greek population. Another measure which was meant to rectify abuses and grievances was the exclusion of Romans (unless they had both Greek and Roman citizenship) from the right of accusation if the accused was a Greek. The census valuation for admission to the *album iudicium selectorum* was lowered in order to procure the necessary number of people sitting as judges. Edict II deals with the transfer of three men who allegedly had knowledge about a planned conspiracy to the imperial court in Rome. It is not clear on what legal basis the three Roman citizens were sent to Augustus. The refer-ence to the "safety" (σωτηρία) of the emperor might be said to fall under the ban on consulting astrologers and soothsayers;[242] however, the earliest legisla-tion against the consultation of astrologers is a *senatus consultum* of A.D. 17, and there is no suggestion in the edict that the men had consulted astrologers. If we accept STROUX / WENGER and add the negation μή at the end of line 45, it follows that when the accused men were confronted by the governor with the demand that they disclose the information they possessed, they refused to do so, which would have allowed the governor to treat them as possible accomplices in a suspected conspiracy, warranting a transfer to Augustus.[243]

---

[240] The reason why Augustus does not refer to his *imperium proconsulare* in these edicts is the fact that they were promulgated not while Augustus was *extra pomerium* but while he was present in the city of Rome; cf. GÉZA ALFÖLDY, Das neue Edikt des Augustus aus El Bierzo in Hispanien, ZPE 131 (2000): 177–205, 194. Cf. JEAN-LOUIS FERRARY, The Powers of Augustus, in Augustus (ed. J. Edmondson; Edinburgh: Edinburgh University Press, 2009), 90–136, 117–8, points out that the broader interpretation of Augustus' *imperium* as greater than that of the governors of proconsular provinces, granted for the first time in 23 B.C., was for-mulated, as far as we know, for the first time in the law of A.D. 17. For the older discussion cf. STROUX / WENGER, Augustus-Inschrift, 71–73, 84–93; VISSCHER, Édics, 45–48, 119–34. The following summary of the Cyrene edicts follows SCHUOL, Augustus, 159–62.

[241] The balls on which the names of the judges are inscribed must all weigh the same (line 24) so that a particular name cannot be singled out in the selection process.

[242] De salute principis vel summa rei publicae; Paulus, *Sent.* 5.21.3; Ulpian, *Coll.* 1.15.2.

[243] RICHARD A. BAUMAN, The Crimen Maiestatis in the Roman Republic and Augustan Principate (Johannesburg: Witwatersrand University Press, 1967), 292. Differently VISSCHER, Édics, 82, who regards the addition of μή unnecessary: "Être détenteur d'un secret d'Etat, s'est déjà prêter au soupçon, s'est tout au moins se trouver indûment mêlé à des affaires qui ne regardent que le prince. Aussi le proconsul refuse-t-il d'en entendre davantage. Prudemment, il tient nos hommes au secret et les envoie d'urgence et sous bonne escorte à Rome pour être

The investigation in Rome did not establish that the men had relevant information; the men made it clear that what they had said in the province was false;[244] thus two of the men were set free. Publius Sextius Scaeva, the governor of the province, was publicly exonerated regarding the accusation of having been unduly harsh. Aulus Stlaccius Maximus remained in custody since he faced the additional charge of having removed statues of from public plazas, including one which the city had inscribed with Augustus' name. This was one of the crimes listed in the *lex Iulia de maiestate*,[245] prosecuted by the *quaestio maiestatis* or, in particularly serious cases when members of the imperial family or senators were involved, by the senate. In this case it was not the *quaestio maiestatis* that tried the case: Augustus dealt with the matter in his imperial court, probably on the basis of the principle of "violated majesty."[246] Edict III addresses the refusal of Greeks who also held Roman citizenship to perform the personal compulsory public services, with the argument that they are Roman citizens. Augustus limits the privilege of exemption to those who were explicitly granted *immunitas* when they became Roman citizens and to the property they possessed at the time when they were granted Roman citizenship. Edict IV, supplementing Edict I, stipulates that in civil disputes between Greeks, Greek judges (jurors) shall be assigned unless a defendant or accused wants to have Roman citizens as judges; no judge shall be assigned from the city from which either the plaintiff or the accused comes. In capital cases (ὑποδίκων κεφαλῆς, line 65), the governor of the province has two options: (a) he either conducts the investigation (αὐτὸς διαγεινώσκειν) and renders judgment himself (ἱστάναι), or (b) he sets up a panel of jurors (συμβούλιον κριτῶν παρέχειν). The edict implies that the governor of a province could intervene in nearly all legal or administrative matters arising in the cities of his province. Even though Edicts I and IV represent a far-reaching accommodation of the citizens of the Greek cities of the Cyrenaica and their legal views in a compromise between Greek jury courts and Roman trial law,[247] the juridical freedom of the provincials was limited: capital cases are reserved for the governor, who will judge them personally or appoint a jury.[248]

---

entendus par le prince ... La crainte des conspirations continuait de hanter l'esprit d'Auguste, et toute affaire de cet ordre demandait à être traitée avec la plus grande circonspection."

[244] Thus J. G. C. ANDERSON, Augustan Edicts from Cyrene, JRS 17 (1927): 33–48, 39; SHERK, Rome and the Greek East, 129. STROUX / WENGER, Augustus-Inschrift, 11, 36, who read the text as making the point that the statement which they were alleged to have made in the province had been falsely attributed to them.

[245] Cf. *Dig.* 48.4.6.

[246] BAUMAN, Crimen Maiestatis, 291.

[247] Cf. ARTHUR STEINWENTER, in RE Suppl. V, 353–356; DIETMAR KIENAST, Augustus. Prinzeps und Monarch (4. Auflage; orig. 1982; repr., Darmstadt: Wissenschaftliche Buchgesellschaft, 2009), 467.

[248] Emphasized by MIRIAM PUCCI BEN ZEEV, Jewish Rights in the Roman World: The Greek and Roman Documents Quoted by Josephus Flavius (TSAJ 74; Tübingen: Mohr

E. BAMMEL points to the Cyrene edicts as evidence for the jurisdiction of provincial governors in capital cases[249] and for the simultaneous existence of local courts who might try capital cases and the court of the provincial governor who has the right to try capital cases, with the latter increasingly becoming the exclusive prerogative of the governors.[250] The simultaneous existence of local and provincial courts is repeatedly emphasized by classical scholars who comment on the Cyrene edicts.[251] K. MÜLLER discusses Edicts I and II as evidence for the virtually unlimited jurisdiction of the Roman governors in the provinces: he alone determines what happens in capital cases – he can try and judge capital cases himself, or he can appoint a jury whose composition he controls.[252] He suggests that since the jury trials were as privilege of the Greeks in Cyrene, they cannot be simply assumed for Judea. Roman governors had exclusive jurisdiction in capital cases, without any limitations of their *coercitio*, especially when law and order needed to be maintained against troublemakers.

**(87)** SB XII 10929 (P. Yale II 162)

I

1a  Μά[ρκ]ος Π[ετρ]ῴγιος Μαμερ[τ]ε[ῖ]νος
.  ἔπαρχο[σ] Α[ἰγύ]πτου [λέ]γε[ι].
α . . . . ε.[. . διε]στείλατο [δ]ιὰ β[ι]βλει-
δ[ι . . . . ]εν[. . . . . ]ων γρα[. . . . ] ἀναφε-
5a  ρομεν . . [. . . . . ] . πι . . . . κόντων α-
. . . [. . ]εν[. . ] . κ[α]θάπερ [. . . . ]σ ἐν ἀρχῇ

---

Siebeck, 1998), 432. Cf. WOLFGANG KUNKEL, Quaestio [1963], in Kleine Schriften zum römischen Strafverfahren und zur römischen Verfassungsgeschichte (Weimar: Hermann Böhlaus Nachfolger, 1974), 33–110, 107. JOCHEN BLEICKEN, Augustus. Eine Biographie (orig. 1998; repr., Reinbek / Hamburg: Rohwolt, 2010), 395–96, emphasizes Augustus' power to introduce a new order for the courts by edict.

[249] ERNST BAMMEL, Zum Kapitalrecht in Kyrene [1954], in Judaica: Kleine Schriften I (WUNT 37; Tübingen: Mohr, 1986), 73–75. EDWIN A. JUDGE, What Kind of Ruler Did the Greeks Think Augustus Was? [1992], in The First Christians in the Roman World: Augustan and New Testament Essays (ed. J. R. Harrison; WUNT 229; Tübingen: Mohr Siebeck, 2010), 385–394, 387–88, quotes Edicts II and III for the point that "problems in other people's provinces tend now to be referred to him [i.e. Augustus]."

[250] ERNST BAMMEL, Die Blutgerichtsbarkeit in der römischen Provinz Judäa vor dem ersten jüdischen Aufstand [1974], in Judaica: Kleine Schriften I (WUNT 37; Tübingen: Mohr, 1986), 59–72, 59–62.

[251] Cf. MERET STROTHMANN, Augustus – Vater der res publica. Zur Funktion der drei Begriffe restitutio – saeculum – pater patriae im augusteischen Principat (Stuttgart: Steiner, 2000), 208–9; VERONIKA WANKERL, Appello ad principem. Urteilsstil und Urteilstechnik in kaiserlichen Berufungsentscheidungen (Augustus bis Caracalla) (MBPAR 101; München: Beck, 2009), 12 n. 62.

[252] MÜLLER, Kapitalgerichtsbarkeit, 59–62, the following points ibid. 61–62.

δ..[..]αμη.[... ἐ]πειδὰν λ[υ]σιτελὲς ἦ
].[.....]ησ[.].[.] ποιούμενοι
]..[..].ουσιν[

10a    ]..[.....].[

11        ὁ ἡγεμὼν διαγνώσεται

| II | | III |
|---|---|---|
| περὶ φόνου | | π(ερὶ) ὕβρεως ἀνηκέστου |
| περὶ ληστειῶν | | π(ερὶ) ὧγ ἐὰν μέμφωνται ο[ἱ] |
| περὶ φαρμακείας | 15 | ἐλευθερώσαντες ἀπε- |
| 5  περὶ πλαγιαρίας | | λευθέρους ἢ γονεῖς παῖδ(ας) |
| περὶ ἀπελατῶν | | οἱ λοιποὶ οὐκ ἄλλως |
| περὶ βίας σὺν ὅ- | | ὑπ' ἐμοῦ ἀκουσθήσονται |
| πλοις γεγενημένης | | εἰ μὴ ἐπικαλεσάμενοι |
| π(ερὶ) πλαστογραφίας | 20 | καὶ παραβόλιον θέντες |
| 10 καὶ ῥᾳδιουργίας | | τὸ τέ[ταρτον] μέρος ἐκ τιμή- |
| [π(ερὶ) ἀ]γῃρημένων | | μα[τος περὶ(?)] οὗ ἐδικάσθη |
| [δι]αθηκῶν | | |

*Translation.* (Col. 1) Marcus Petronius Mamertinus, prefect of Egypt, says ...
(Col. 2) The prefect will render judgement concerning homicide, robbery, poisoning, kidnapping, cattle-rustling, armed violence, forgery and fraud, the
annulment of wills, (Col. 3) aggravated assault, complaints in which patrons
bring a charge against (15) their own freedmen or parents against their children. the rest will not otherwise be heard by me unless they make an appeal
(20) and lodge as deposit a quarter of the fine applied concerning the case
which was adjudicated (in previous trials).

*Commentary.*[253] This edict of the Roman prefect in Egypt, Marcus Petronius
Mamertinus (A.D. 133–137), lists categories of crimes and offenses that the
prefect himself adjudicates.[254] Most of the offenses concern criminal cases; in

---

[253] Editio princeps: NAPHTALI LEWIS, Un nouveau texte sur la juridiction du préfet
d'Égypte (P. Yale inv. 1606 = SB XII 10929), RHDFE 50 (1972): 5–12; 51 (1973) 5–7;
republished with consecutive line numbering in NAPHTALI LEWIS, Emperor or Prefect? in Le
monde grec. Pensée littérature histoire documents, vol. Brussels (FS C. Préaux; ed. J. Bingen,
G. Cambier, and G. Nachtergael; TFPL 62; Éditions de l'Université de Bruxelles, 1975), 760–
765. Cf. NAPHTALI LEWIS, On Government and Law in Roman Egypt: Collected Papers (ASP
33; Atlanta: Scholars Press, 1995), 157–64, 165–67, 168–73. The papyrus is be republished
as P. Yale II 162. For translations and commentary cf. ERWIN SEIDL, Eine neue kaiserliche
Konstitution über die Apellation, SDHI 38 (1972): 319–320; JAMES H. OLIVER, Greek Applications for Roman Trials, AJP 100 (1979): 543–558; HORSLEY and LLEWELYN, New
Documents, 1:49–51; ANDREA JÖRDEN, Eine kaiserliche Konstitution zu den
Rechtsprechungskompetenzen der Statthalter, Chiron 41 (2011): 327–356.
[254] RANON GEDALIA KATZOFF, Law as *Katholikos,* in Studies in Roman Law in Memory

lines 14–16 civil cases are in view. The procedures set out in the edict will have applied only to Roman citizens.[255] Since the criminal charges all have Latin equivalents,[256] it is assumed that the text is a Greek translation of a Latin original. N. LEWIS thinks that the ἡγεμών of line 11, written across Columns II and III, is the Roman prefect who announces the criminal charges that he will hear personally. E. SEIDL suggests that ἡγεμών is the emperor: Columns II and III are a single imperial constitution; the emperor's *mandata* reflect the trend to limit appeals to the emperor in criminal cases, allowing a more effective local control of crime.[257] J. H. OLIVER suggests that the heading ὁ ἡγεμών διαγνώσεται in line 11 does not imply "that even the prefect is bound to hold a trial. He too can delegate, appoint a judge, postpone or refuse a trial which at his diagnosis he finds unnecessary".[258] Whatever the merits of this discussion,[259] the papyrus illustrates the legal arrangements in Egypt.

## 2.3 The *crimen maiestatis* in Roman Law

The following texts illustrate aspects of Roman law that are relevant for Jesus' trial before Pontius Pilatus, including the scope of the legal and administrative authority of governors and prefects responsible for the provinces, and in particular the *crimen maiestatis*. While the texts of Cicero, Suetonius, Seneca, Tacitus, the *Digesta* and the *Institutiones* do not establish the precise legal

---

of A. Arthur Schiller (ed. R. S. Bagnall and W. V. Harris; CSCT 13; Leiden: Brill, 1986), 119–126, 120. On the *proconsulare imperium* in the provinces cf. WIEACKER, Rechtsgeschichte II, 24–27.

[255] LEWIS, Un nouveau texte sur la juridiction du préfet d'Égypte, 12; followed by JOHN GRANGER COOK, Roman Attitudes Toward the Christians: From Claudius to Hadrian (WUNT 261; Tübingen: Mohr Siebeck, 2010), 145.

[256] Lines 2–13: de homocidio, de latrociniis, de veneneficio, de plagiaria, de abigeis, de vi armata, de falsariis et falso, de testamentis rescissis, de iniuria atroci.

[257] SEIDL, Eine neue kaiserliche Konstitution, 319–29; SEIDL, Rechtsgeschichte Ägyptens als römischer Provinz, 241 n. 124. It should be noted that SEIDL argued for his views before the publication of Col. I which clearly is the edict of a prefect. OLIVER, Applications, 550, thinks that the edict of the prefect (Col. I) cites a document in Columns II–III which he identifies as "a special order of Hadrian" while the last six lines (lines 17–22) are again part of the prefect's edict. KATZOFF, Law as *Katholikos*, 121, agrees that the quoted document was an imperial order. LEWIS, Emperor or Prefect, 764–65, leaves the question open whether the quoted document was a prefectural edict or an imperial constitution.

[258] OLIVER, Applications, 551. BARBARA ANAGNOSTOU-CANAS, La réparation du préjudice dans les papyrus grecs d'Egypte, in Symposion 2005. Vorträge zur griechischen und hellenistischen Rechtsgeschichte (Salerno, 14.–18.September 2005; ed. E. Cantarella; AGR 19; Wien: Österreichische Akademie der Wissenschaften, 2007), 307–326, agrees with OLIVER that the prefect heard the other cases unless there was an appeal to the emperor who (implicitly) refused to accept appeals with regard to crimes that are listed in the edict.

[259] WOLFF, Das Recht der griechischen Papyri Ägyptens I, 111, 175 n. 115, leaves the question open.

authority under which Pontius Pilatus operated in A.D. 30, they describe the legal context of Jesus' trial before the *praefectus Iudaeae*.

**(88)** Cicero, *De inventione* 2.17.52–55

Cum est nominis controversia, quia vis vocabuli definienda verbis est, constitutio definitiva dicitur. Eius generis exemplo nobis posita sit haec causa: C. Flaminius is, qui consul rem male gessit bello Punico secundo, cum tribunus plebis esset, invito senatu et omnino contra voluntatem omnium optimatium per seditionem ad populum legem agrariam ferebat. Hunc pater suus concilium plebis habentem de templo deduxit; arcessitur maiestatis. Intentio est: 'maiestatem minuisti, quod tribunum plebis de templo deduxisti.' Depulsio est: 'Non minui maiestatem.' quaestio est: maiestatemne minuerit. Ratio: 'in filium enim quam habebam potestatem, ea sum usus.' Rationis infirmatio: 'at enim, qui patria potestate [hoc est privata quadam] tribuniciam potestatem [hoc est populi potestatem] infirmat, minuit is maiestatem.' Iudicatio est: minuatne is maiestatem, qui in tribuniciam potestatem patria potestate utatur? ad hanc iudicationem argumentationes omnes adferre oportebit. [53] Ac ne qui forte arbitretur nos non intellegere aliam quoque incidere constitutionem in hanc causam, eam nos partem solam sumimus, in quam praecepta nobis danda sunt. Omnibus autem partibus hoc in libro explicatis quivis omni in causa, si diligenter adtendet, omnes videbit constitutiones et earum partes et controversias, si quae forte in eas incident; nam de omnibus praescribemus. Primus ergo accusatoris locus est eius nominis, cuius de vi quaeritur, brevis et aperta et ex opinione hominum definitio, hoc modo: maiestatem minuere est de dignitate aut amplitudine aut potestate populi aut eorum, quibus populus potestatem dedit, aliquid derogare. Hoc sic breviter expositum pluribus verbis est et rationibus confirmandum et ita esse, ut descripseris, ostendendum. Postea ad id, quod definieris, factum eius, qui accusabitur, adiungere oportebit et ex eo, quod ostenderis esse, verbi causa maiestatem minuere, docere adversarium maiestatem minuisse et hunc totum locum communi loco confirmare, per quem ipsius facti atrocitas aut indignitas aut omnino culpa cum indignatione augeatur. [54] Post erit infirmanda adversariorum descriptio. Ea autem infirmabitur, si falsa demonstrabitur. Hoc ex opinione hominum sumetur, cum, quemadmodum et quibus in rebus homines in consuetudine scribendi aut sermocinandi eo verbo uti soleant, considerabitur. Item infirmabitur, si turpis aut inutilis esse ostenditur eius descriptionis adprobatio et, quae incommoda consecutura sint eo concesso, ostendetur – id autem ex honestatis et ex utilitatis partibus sumetur, de quibus in deliberationis praeceptis exponemus – et si cum definitione nostra adversariorum definitionem conferemus et nostram veram, honestam, utilem esse demonstrabimus, illorum contra. [55] Quaeremus autem res aut maiore aut minore aut pari in negotio similes, ex quibus affirmetur nostra descriptio. Iam si res plures erunt definiendae: ut, si quaeratur, fur sit an sacrilegus, qui vasa ex privato sacra subripuerit, erit utendum pluribus definitionibus; deinde simili ratione causa tractanda. Locus autem communis in eius malitiam, qui non modo rerum, verum etiam verborum potestatem sibi arrogare conatus et faciat, quod velit, et id, quod fecerit, quo velit nomine appellet. Deinde defensoris primus locus est item nominis brevis et aperta et ex opinione hominum descriptio, hoc modo: Maiestatem minuere est aliquid de re publica, cum potestatem non habeas, administrare. Deinde huius confirmatio similibus et exemplis et rationibus; postea sui facti ab illa definitione separatio. Deinde locus communis, per quem facti utilitas aut honestas adaugetur.

*Translation.* When there is a dispute about the designation, the issue is known as the issue of definition, because the meaning of the concept must be defined. I propose the following case as an example of this class. When Gaius Flaminius, the man who fulfilled his task as consul in the Second Punic War but poorly, was tribune of the people, he seditiously proposed an agrarian law to the people against the will of the senate and generally against the consent of the Optimates. When he convened an assembly of the plebs, his own father dragged him from the rostrum; he is charged with *maiestas*.[260] The charge is, "You committed *maiestas* because you dragged a tribune of the people from the rostrum." The refutation is, "I did not commit *maiestas*." The matter of dispute is, "Did he commit *maiestas*?" The substantiation is, "I used the authority which I had over my son." The invalidation of the argument is, "On the contrary, one who uses the authority belonging to him as a father (that is, private authority) to lessen the authority of a tribune (that is, the authority of the people) is guilty of *maiestas*." The disputed point for the judge's decision is, "Is a person guilty of *maiestas* who used his authority as a father against the authority of a tribune?" All arguments must be directed to this disputed point. [53] But unless someone thinks that I am not aware of the fact that another matter arises in this case, I shall say that I am taking up only the part for I must at this time provide rules. When all types have been discussed in this book, anyone will, without discrepancy, recognize in all case all forms of substantiation as well as their types and oppositions, if he carefully pays attention, for I will give directions about all of them. The first topic in the prosecutor's argument is a brief, clear, and conventional definition of the word whose meaning is sought, as follows: *maiestas* is a lessening of the dignity, greatness, or power of the people or of those to whom the people have given power. This brief exposition must be supported by further words and substantiations, and shown to be as you have outlined it. Then it will be necessary to connect the act of the accused with your definition, and on the basis of what you have shown to

---

[260] NÜSSLEIN translates: "wegen der Verletzung der Hoheit des Volkes."

be, for example, the meaning of *maiestas*, to demonstrate that your opponent committed *maiestas*, and then to support the whole argument by a common topic in which you magnify and inveigh against the enormity of the deed itself or its heinousness or generally its guilt. Then the definition of the opposing counsel must be invalidated. This can be done if it is shown to be false. [54] Such an argument will be based on common belief when one considers how and in what connection people are accustomed to use such a word in ordinary writing or speech. It is also shown to be false if we show that to approve this definition is dishonorable or inexpedient, and if we point out the disadvantages that will follow if their definition is accepted – this is based on the concepts of honor and advantage, which I shall expound in giving the rules for speeches before deliberative bodies – and if we compare our definition with that of our opponents and prove that ours is true, honorable, and expedient, and theirs the opposite. [55] Further, we shall investigate similar cases of greater or lesser or equal seriousness to support our definition. In a case in which several words have to be defined – for example, when the question is whether it is theft or sacrilege if someone steals sacred vessels from a private house – one has to use of several definitions and then proceed to treat the case in the manner already laid down. Another common topic attacks the villainy of a man who, attempting to arrogate to himself the control not only of the actions but also of the words, who does what he pleases and then calls his deed by whatever name he pleases. The first topic for the defense is, likewise, a brief, clear, and conventional definition of the world, as follows: "*maiestas* consists in doing some public business without authority." Then follows the confirmation of this definition by similar examples and arguments, then the differentiation of one's action from the definition. Then follows a common topic which further emphasizes the advantage and the honor of the act.

*Commentary.*[261] Written early in Cicero's career (c. 80 B.C.),[262] the rhetorical handbook *De inventione* was meant to cover all parts of rhetoric: invention, arrangement, expression, memory, and delivery (*Inv.* 1.9); Cicero ended up treating only invention.[263] Cicero points out that every rhetorical discourse is

---

[261] Text: EDUARD STRÖBEL, M. Tulli Ciceronis scripta, quae manserunt omnia. Fasc. 2: Rhetorici libri duo, qui vocantur De inventione (orig. 1915; repr., Bibliotheca Scriptorum Graecorum et Romanorum Teubneriana; Stuttgart / Leipzig: Teubner, 1965); cf. MÜLLER, M. Tullii Ciceronis scripta quae manserunt omnia, I/1; HARRY M. HUBBELL, Cicero. De inventione. De optimo genere oratorum. Topica (LCL; London: Heinemann, 1949); THEODOR NÜSSLEIN, M. Tullius Cicero. De inventione. Über die Auffindung des Stoffes. De optimo genere oratorum. Über die beste Gattung von Rednern (Lateinisch und deutsch; Sammlung Tusculum; Düsseldorf / Zürich: Artemis & Winkler, 1998); GUY ACHARD, Cicéron. De l'invention (Collection des universités de France 320; Paris: Belles Lettres, 1994).

[262] JÜRGEN LEONHARDT, Cicero II. Cicero as Orator and Writer, BNP 3 (2003): 321–327.

[263] Cf. ROBERT N. GAINES, Roman Rhetorical Handbooks, in A Companion to Roman Rhetoric (ed. W. Dominik and J. Hall; Chicester: Wiley-Blackwell, 2010), 163–181, 169–70.

driven by an issue (2.12–13). His treatment of particular arguments is an exposition of forensic topics, in particular controversy about fact (2.14–51), definition of an act (2.52–56), correctness of procedure (2.57–61), and quality of an act (2.62–115). In his discussion of the issue of definition (*constitutio definitiva*), Cicero uses a case study that involves the crime of lèse-majesté (*maiestas*), which he defines as "a lessening of the dignity or greatness or authority of the people or of those to whom the people have given authority" (*maiestatem minuere est de dignitate aut amplitudine aut potestate populi aut eorum, quibus populus potestatem dedit, aliquid derogare*; 2.17.53). A subsequent definition, suggested for the defense, says, "lèse-majesté consists in doing some public business without authority" (*maiestatem minuere est aliquid de re publica, cum potestatem non habeas, administrare*; 2.17.55). The focus on the "dignity, greatness, and authority of the people" (*dignitas aut amplitudo aut potestas populi*) in the first definition reflects the notion in the Republican period that the state was the sum of its citizens.[264] *Maiestas* means, in general terms, "an unusual, unquestionably superior power and dignity to be respected," notably the sacredness of a god, the authority of the *pater familias* towards his relatives and slaves, and especially the majesty of the Roman people (*populus Romanus*), the state (*res publica*) and its highest offices and institutions, and later of the emperor.[265] The person who has *maiestas* is owed by all people, or by a specific class of people, or by individuals, respect (*reverentia*), deference (*honor*), and obedience (*obsequium*).

The first general law of *maiestas* was the *lex Appuleia*, passed probably in 103 B.C. by the tribune Lucius Appuleius Saturninus. This law seems to have provided a catalogue of specific offenses[266] but was otherwise vague regarding the meaning of *maiestas*.[267] The next general law was the *lex Cornelia de maiestate* of Lucius Cornelius Sulla, passed in 81 B.C.,[268] which also listed

---

[264] Cf. CLIFFORD ANDO, Imperial Ideology and Provincial Loyalty in the Roman Empire (Classics and Contemporary Thought 6; Berkeley: University of California Press, 2000), 65, who also refers to the definition of *maiestas* in *Rhet. ad Her.* 2.12.17; 4.25.35.

[265] CHRISTIAN GIZEWSKI, Maiestas, BNP 8 (2006): 185–187, 184; BERNHARD KÜBLER, Maiestas, RE XIV/1 (1928): 542–559, 542; for the following point cf. ibid. KÜBLER translates the Latin terms with "Ehrfurcht," "Ehrerbietung," "Gehorsam."

[266] Cf. Cicero, *Pis.* 50; *Dig.* 48.4.4.pr.; see below No. 90, 96.

[267] Cf. ROBIN SEAGER, *Maiestas* in the Late Republic: Some Observations, in Critical Studies in Ancient Law, Comparative Law and Legal History (FS A. Watson; ed. J. W. Cairns and O. F. Robinson; Oxford / Portland: Hart, 2001), 143–153, 144–48; for the prehistory of *maiestas* cf. BAUMAN, Crimen Maiestatis, 22–33. Cf. GOTTFRIED SCHIEMANN, Crimen, BNP 3 (2003): 940–942, 942; GOTTFRIED SCHIEMANN, Lex, leges, BNP 7 (2005): 460–466; GIZEWSKI, Maiestas, 184; KÜBLER, Maiestas; MOMMSEN, Strafrecht, 537–94; RICHARD A. BAUMAN, Impietas in Principem: A Study of Treason against the Roman Emperor with Special Reference to the First Century A.D. (MBPRG 67; München: Beck, 1974).

[268] Cf. KÜBLER, Maiestas, 547–58; SEAGER, Maiestas, 148–53; also BAUMAN, Crimen Maiestatis, 70–83.

specific offenses besides containing a general clause.[269] The punishment that was stipulated for a *crimen maiestatis* was enforced exile, which was a capital penalty in the first century B.C. Cicero does not tell us the outcome of the confrontation between Gaius Flaminius and his father: the former had *maiestas* because he held the position of *tribunus plebis*, the latter had *maiestas* in terms of the *patria potestas* of the *pater familias*. The father might have argued his case "under the *constitutio generalis* by pleading that he was carrying out the order of the Senate in restraining a seditious person (*remotio criminis*), or that the act was committed for the sake of a greater good (*comparatio*)."[270] Later, both Caesar and Augustus issued a *lex Iulia de maiestate*, which also did not provide a definition of the *crimen maiestatis* but listed specific offenses. For the discussion of the *lex maiestatis* in Jesus' Roman trial by New Testament scholars see the *Jesus' Roman trial and Roman law* at the end of section 2.3.

(89) Cicero, *Pro Cluentio* 97

At enim etiam Bulbus est condemnatus. Adde "maiestatis," ut intellegas hoc iudicium cum illo non esse coniunctum. At est hoc illi crimen obiectum. Fateor, sed etiam legionem esse ab eo sollicitatam in Illyrico C. Cosconi litteris et multorum testimoniis planum factum est, quod crimen erat proprium illius quaestionis, et quae res lege maiestatis tenebatur. At hoc obfuit ei maxime. Iam ista divinatio est; qua si uti licet, vide ne mea coniectura multo sit verior. Ego enim sic arbitror, Bulbum, quod homo nequam, turpis, improbus, multis flagitiis contaminatus in iudicium sit adductus, idcirco facilius esse damnatum. Tu mihi ex tota causa Bulbi, quod tibi commodum est, eligis, ut id esse secutos iudices dicas.

*Translation*. But Bulbus was also convicted. Yes, and you should add, "For *maiestas*,"[271] then you understand that my client's trial has no connection with his. "But they brought this charge against him." I admit it, but it was also made evident by the correspondence of Gaius Cosconius and the evidence of many witnesses that Bulbus had incited a legion in Illyricum; this charge belonged before that court, and the facts were covered by the *lex maiestatis*. "But it was this matter which told most heavily against him." Now this is only an assumption; if one can rely on something like this, then my own inference is certainly much more plausible. For I assume the following: with Bulbus they brought a ne'er-do-well, a scoundrel, and a miscreant before the court

---

[269] Cf. Cicero, *Fam.* 3.11.2–3; see No. 91. Cicero's speeches against C. Verres, especially the fifth, are "the closest approximations we possess to a prosecution speech for *maiestas*" under the *lex Cornelia*, thus SEAGER, Maiestas, 150; cf. BAUMAN, Crimen Maiestatis, 79–80.

[270] HUBBELL, Cicero. De inventione, 214–15 NOTE B.

[271] HODGE translates *maiestas* with "treason," FUHRMANN with "Staatsverbrechen."

who had dishonored himself by numerous outrageous actions, and thus he was convicted with no compunction. You select from the entire case against Bulbus the one point that suits your case, and then you say that it was that point which guided the judges.

*Commentary.*[272] Cicero's longest single speech, given in defense of Aulus Cluentius Habitus in a public criminal case (*causa publica*) when he was praetor, dates to 66 B.C. Aulus Cluentius Habitus, a Roman *eques* from Larinum, had suspected Statius Albius Oppianicus, his stepfather, of attempting to murder him with the help of Gaius Fabricius and his freedman Scamander, and secured the conviction of the three men in 74 B.C. (*Clu.* 43–61).[273] This trial had cased a political scandal in Rome because both sides had bribed senators who had served as jurors, resulting in the prosecution of 70 prominent people who were involved (*Verr.* 1.38–40). Cluentius was reprimanded by the censors (*Clu.* 117). When Oppianicus died in mysterious circumstances in 72 B.C., Cluentius' mother Sassia held her son responsible. In 66 B.C. Cluentius was charged by Statius Albius Oppianicus, his younger stepbrother, of patricide. In that year, there were three courts in Rome dealing with murder cases: two *questiones* for violent murders (*inter sicarios*), and one *questio* for murder by poisoning (*de veneficiis*). The case against Cluentius was handled by the latter court, which had 32 jurors, according to the *lex aurelia* of 70 B.C.; the accusations of murder by poisoning and bribery of judges (for which only members of the senate were liable) were punished in according to Sulla's law on murders of 81 B.C. (*lex Cornelia de sicariis et veneficis*).[274] Cicero defended Cluentius successfully, challenging in particular the accusation of juror bribery (*Clu.* 88–160) since, according to Cicero, the charge of poisoning was completely baseless and thus needed to be addressed only briefly (*Clu.* 160–194). The speech given in Cluentius' defense was regarded by Cicero himself as a masterpiece (*Or. Brut.* 107–108), and by Pliny as Cicero's finest speech (Pliny, *Ep.* 1.20.4).[275] Cluentius was charged under the *lex Cornelia de veneficiis et sicariis*, passed by Sulla to deal with cases of assassination and

---

[272] Text: MÜLLER, M. Tullii Ciceronis scripta quae manserunt omnia, II/2 (LUDWIG FRÜCHTEL); for other text editions and translations cf. HUMFREY G. HODGE, Cicero. Pro lege Manilia. Pro Caecina. Pro Cluentio (LCL; Cambridge: Harvard University Press, 1927); PIERRE BOYANCÉ, Cicéron. Discours. Tome VIII: Pour Cluentius (Collection des universités de France; Paris: Belles Lettres, 1953); FUHRMANN, Cicero: Sämtliche Reden, 2:7–115; FUHRMANN, Cicero. Prozeßreden, 1:362–581.

[273] Cf. KARL-LUDWIG ELVERS, Cluentius [2] C. Habitus, A., BNP 3 (2003): 483, for the description of the circumstances of the trial.

[274] Cf. FUHRMANN, Cicero. Prozeßreden, 1:861–62.

[275] For an analysis cf. CARL JOACHIM CLASSEN, Recht–Rhetorik–Politik. Untersuchungen zu Ciceros rhetorischer Strategie (Darmstadt: Wissenschaftliche Buchgesellschaft, 1985), 15–119; JOHN KIRBY, The Rhetoric of Cicero's Pro Cluentio (Amsterdam: Gieben, 1990), 98, on *Clu.* 97. Cf. GEORGE A. KENNEDY, A New History of Classical Rhetoric (Princeton: Princeton University Press, 1994), 132.

poisoning. Other statutes mentioned in the speech are the *lex Cornelia de repetundis*, designed by Sulla to check administrative malpractice, the *lex Calpurnia de Ambitu* which punished anyone guilty of corrupt practices in connection with an election, and the *lex Cornelia* concerning the *crimen maiestatis*. In *Clu.* 88–142, Cicero discusses previous verdicts which are quoted against Cluentius. After evaluating the case of Gaius Iunius (*Clu.* 89–96), who was convicted as the result of the violence of the mob incited by the tribune Quinctius, Cicero discusses the case of a certain Bulbus who had been convicted of treason, arguing that Bulbus' case has no connection with the case against Cluentius. Bulbus was convicted for treason (*maiestatis*). The prosecution had presumably used Bulbus' conviction for *maiestas* to argue that Cluentius' alleged murder of Statius Albius Oppianicus, his stepfather, was a crime against the *patria potestas* of the *pater familias* and thus fell under the *crimen maiestatis*. Cicero argues that Bulbus' crime was entirely different: in his trial, many witnesses provided evidence that Bulbus "had incited a legion in Illyricum" (*legionem esse ab eo sollicitatam in Illyrico*),[276] which is a charge (*crimen*) that was investigated by the court; the facts of the case were covered by the law of lèse-majesté (*res lege maiestatis tenebatur*). This is a reference to Sulla's *lex Cornelia de maiestate*, which contained a clause against soliciting the troops or inciting them to mutiny or riot *adversus rem publicam* (*Dig.* 48.4.1.1; cf. No. 96).[277] Cicero argues that since Cluentius' alleged crime is unconnected to inciting troops, he should not be accused of committing a *crimen maiestatis*.

**(90)** Cicero, *In Pisonem* 50

Hic si mentis esset suae, nisi poenas patriae disque immortalibus eas quae gravissimae sunt, furore atque insania penderet, ausus esset – mitto exire de provincia, educere exercitum, bellum sua sponte gerere, in regnum iniussu populi [Romani] aut senatus accedere, quae cum plurimae leges veteres, tum lex Cornelia maiestatis Iulia de pecuniis repetundis planissime vetat? Sed haec omitto; ille si non acerrime fureret, auderet, quam provinciam P. Lentulus, amicissimus huic ordini, cum et auctoritate senatus et sorte haberet, interposita religione sine ulla dubitatione deposuisset, eam sibi adsciscere, cum, etiam si religio non impediret, mos maiorum tamen et exempla et gravissimae legum poenae vetarent?

*Translation.* If he had been in his right mind, if he had not already been forced to paying the severest of all penalties to his country and to the immortal gods

---

[276] Gaius Cosconius was proconsul in the province of Illyria in 78–76 B.C.; KARL-LUDWIG ELVERS, Cosconius [I 1] C., C., BNP 3 (2003): 859.

[277] Cf. SEAGER, Maiestas, 148–49.

due to his fury and madness, would he have dared – I do not say: to leave his province, lead his army out of it, wage war on his own account, enter a king's territory without the orders of the Roman people or the senate (conduct expressly forbidden by numerous ancient statutes, and in particular by the law of Cornelius against *maiestas* and the law of Julius against malpractices) – but I say nothing of all this; would he have dared, I say, had he not been a raving madman, to appropriate to himself a province which Publius Lentulus, the faithful friend of the politics of this house, had renounced without any hesitation when a divine sign appeared in an impeding manner, though he held that province by the authority of the senate and by due allotment, would he have dared to do so, when – if he does not care even about divine warnings – even though it was prohibited by ancient usage, precedent, and the severest penalties of the law?

*Commentary.*[278] When Julius Caesar left Rome in 58 B.C. for Gaul, he used Publius Clodius, one of Cicero's personal enemies, and the two consuls of that year – Lucius Calpurnius Piso Caesoninus, his father-in-law, and Aulus Gabinius – to remove Cicero. Clodius introduced a law that any one who had a Roman citizen killed without a court sentence was to be shunned; the law was aimed at Cicero who had the immediate suspects of the Catiline conspiracy executed in 63 B.C. Cicero left Rome in March 58 B.C. and spent 15 months in exile in Thessalonica, before traveling to Dyrrhachium. As a reward, Piso received the province of Macedonia (57–55 B.C.), while Gabinius received Syria. After his return to Rome, Cicero, to the surprise of the Optimates, gave a speech in support of the triumvirate that united Pompey, Crassus, and Caesar (*De provinciis consularibus*; 56 B.C.); he argued for the necessity of giving Caesar more time in Gaul, and at the same time alleged that Piso and Gabinius had mismanaged their provinces, demanding that they should be replaced by praetorian governors. When Piso returned in disgrace in 55 B.C., he vented his anger and frustration against Cicero before the senate. Cicero's speech *In L. Calpurnium Pisonem* returned the favor.[279] In *Pis.* 50 he attacks Piso's colleague Aulus Gabinius, whom he charges with the *crimen maiestatis* while governor of the province of Syria. The list of charges listed in the *lex Cornelia*

---

[278] Text: MÜLLER, M. Tullii Ciceronis scripta quae manserunt omnia, III/2; for other text editions and translations cf. NEVILLE H. WATTS, Cicero. Pro Milone. In Pisonem. Pro Scauro. Pro Fonteio. Pro Rabirio Postumo. Pro Marcello. Pro Ligario. Pro rege Deiotaro (orig. 1931; repr., LCL; Cambridge: Harvard University Press, 1953), 138–259; ROBERT G. M. NISBET, M. Tullii Ciceronis in L. Calpurnium Pisonem Oratio. With Text, Introduction, and Commentary (Oxford: Clarendon, 1961); PIERRE GRIMAL, Cicéron. Discours. Tome XVI: Contre L. Pison, Pour Cn. Plancius, Pour M. Aemilius Scaurus (Collection des universités de France 16; Paris: Belles Lettres, 1966); FUHRMANN, Cicero. Prozeßreden, 2:310–433.

[279] On the date cf. NISBET, In L. Calpurnium Pisonem Oratio, 199–202: the speech was delivered between July and September 55, and rewritten for publication at the end of 55 or beginning of 54 B.C.

*maiestatis* and in the *lex Iulia de pecuniis repetundis* included the following:
1. leaving one's province (*exire de provincia*); 2. leading the army out of one'
province (*educere exercitum*); 3. waging war on one's own account (*bellum
sua sponte gerere*); 4. entering a king's realm without the orders of the Roman
people or senate (*in regnum iniussu populi Romani aut senatus accedere*).
With his appeal to the *lex Cornelia maiestatis*, Cicero put all governors of
Roman provinces on notice that they were subject to proceedings of *maiestas*
in case they exceeded their powers.

**(91)** Cicero, *Epistulae ad familiares* 3.11.1–3

Cum essem in castris ad fluvium Pyramum, redditae mihi sunt uno tempore a
te epistulae duae, quas ad me Q. Servilius Tarso miserat. earum in altera dies
erat ascripta Nonarum Aprilium, in altera, quae mihi recentior videbatur, dies
non erat. respondebo igitur superiori prius, in qua scribis ad me de absolutione
maiestatis. de qua etsi permulto a<n>te certior factus eram litteris, nuntiis,
fama denique ipsa (nihil enim fuit clarius, non quo quisquam aliter putasset,
sed nihil de insignibus ad laudem viris obscure nuntiari solet), tamen eadem
illa laetiora fecerunt mihi tuae litterae, non solum quia planius loquebantur et
uberius quam vulgi sermo sed etiam quia magis videbar tibi gratulari cum de
te ex te ipso audiebam. ² complexus igitur sum cogitatione te absentem,
epistulam vero osculatus etiam ipse mihi gratulatus sum. quae enim <a>
cuncto populo, a senatu, a iudicibus ingenio, industriae, virtuti tribuuntur, quia
mihi ipse adsentor fortasse, cum ea esse in me fingo, mihi quoque ipsi tribui
puto. Nec tam gloriosum exitum tui iudici exstitisse,sed tam pravam inimi-
corum tuorum mentem fuisse mirabar. 'de ambitu vero quid interest' inquies,
'an de maiestate?' ad rem, nihil; alterum enim non attigisti, alteram auxisti.
verum tamen est maiestas, etsi Sulla voluit ne in quemvis impune declamari
liceret, <ambigua>; ambitus vero ita apertam vim habet ut aut accusetur
improbe aut defendatur. quid enim? facta necne facta largitio, ignorari potest?
tuorum autem honorum cursus cui suspectus umquam fuit? me miserum, qui
non, adfuerim! quos ego risus excitassem! ³ sed de maiestatis iudicio duo mihi
illa ex tuis litteris iucundissima fuerunt: unum, quod te ab ipsa re publica
defensum scribis, quae quidem etiam in summa bonorum et fortium civium
copia tueri talis viros deberet, nunc vero eo magis quod tanta penuria est in
omni vel honoris vel aetatis gradu ut tam orba civitas talis tutores complecti
debeat; alterum, quod Pompei et Bruti fidem benevolentiamque mirifice
laudas. laetor virtute et officio quom tuorum necessariorum, meorum amicis-
simorum, tum alterius omnium saeculorum et gentium principis, alterius iam
pridem iuventutis, celeriter, ut spero, civitatis. de mercennariis testibus a suis
civitatibus notandis nisi iam factum aliquid est per Flaccum, fiet a me cum per
Asiam decedam.

*Translation.* While in camp on the river Pyramus, I received two letters from you at the same time, sent to me from Tarsus by Q. Servilius. One of them was dated the Nones of April (i.e., April 5); the other, which had no date, seemed to me more recent. I shall therefore reply first to the earlier letter in which you write of your acquittal on the charge of *maiestas*. It is true that I had been informed about it long before by letters, oral messages, and a general report; it was in all mouths – not that anyone expected a different result, but news concerning men of distinguished reputations seldom lack advertisement. Your letter added to the pleasure which these news had given me, not only because it spoke more distinctly and fully than the common talk, but also because I thought my congratulations were better justified as I heard the news from yourself. [2] Thus, in my mind I embraced you from afar and kissed the letter, congratulating myself as well as you. For any tribute paid by the whole people, the senate, and the jury to talent, energy, and virtue as paid also to me, flattering myself perhaps in imagining that I possess these qualities as well. What surprises me is not that your trial should have ended so gloriously, but that your enemies should have shown such perverseness. You may ask what differences it makes – corruption or *maiestas*. None that really matters. You never touched the former, and the latter you have enhanced. However, as a matter of fact, *maiestas* is an imprecise term, despite Sulla's ordinance which penalizes random declamation against individuals, whereas corruption is clearly defined that either the prosecution or the defense must be scandalously false.[280] Because obviously the fact cannot be unknown whether improper disbursements have or have not taken place. But who has ever suspected your successive public promotions? How I regret that I was not there! How I should have made them laugh! [3] However, in your letter about your trial on the charge of *maiestas* there are two points which have given me much pleasure. One is your remark that your defense was undertaken by the Republic herself. To be sure, the country ought to protect men like yourself, no matter how abundant the supply of honorable and honest citizens. But as matters stand now, when at every grade of rank and age there is so sore a scarcity, the State in her destitution should make the most of such guardians as yourself. The second point is your glowing praise for the loyalty and good will shown by Pompey and Brutus. I am delighted that they have been fair and courteous to you, not only because they are connections of yours relatives and very good friends of mine, but because one of them is the greatest man that any century or people has produced, while the other has long been a main figure among his contemporaries and will soon, I hope, become so in the state. As to the public censures to be passed upon the venal witnesses by the communities to

---

[280] Following SHACKLETON-BAILEY. WILLIAMS, following PURSER, reads *Sulla noluit* and translates, "although Sulla never meant it to be so, lest the public denunciation of any man should be allowed to pass unpunished."

which they belong, unless something has already been done through the agency of Flaccus, I shall take action myself on my way home through Asia.

*Commentary.*[281] Cicero's letter to Appius Pulcher was written June 16 in 50 B.C. Appius Claudius Pulcher was praetor in 57 B.C., consul in 54 B.C., proconsul in Cilicia in 53–51 B.C., censor in 50 B.C.[282] He plundered Cilicia to an extent otherwise only known of Verres; when Cicero, his successor, arrived in Cilicia, he described a "forever ruined and completely devastated province" (Cicero, *Att.* 5.16.2). Pulcher had just been acquitted of *maiestas*, a fact on which Cicero congratulates him. Cicero distinguishes *maiestas* from *ambitus*, a term that, in the political realm, describes the "circulation and supplication" for the purpose of campaigning for office, usually used in a negative sense, with unauthorized methods penalized in a series of laws.[283] Various laws[284] changed or confirmed prohibitions and limitations regarding campaigns for office, e.g. public games and banquets for campaign purposes, the buying of votes and donations, systematic propaganda with the help of clients and friends, the union of politicians for gathering votes. The penalties were fines, exile, prohibition against running for office, expulsion from the senate. Cicero argues that while the charge of *ambitus* is lucid and can easily be proven or disproven, the charge of *maiestas* (lèse-majesté), despite Sulla's law, is imprecise (*ambigua*) and thus gives rise to malicious prosecution and sophistic defense.[285] On the *lex Cornelia de maiestate* of Sulla see No. 88, 90.

---

[281] Text: DAVID R. SHACKLETON BAILEY, M. Tulli Cicero. Epistulae ad familiares libri I-XVI (Bibliotheca Scriptorum Graecorum et Romanorum Teubneriana; Stuttgart: Teubner, 1988); For other text editions and translations cf. LOUS C. PURSER, Cicero. Epistulae ad familiares (orig. 1901; repr., Oxford Classical Texts; Oxford: Oxford University Press, 1952); WILLLIAM S. WATT, M. Tulli Ciceronis Epistulae. Tomus I: Epistulae ad familiares (Oxford Classical Texts; Oxford: Oxford University Press, 1982); GLYNN W. WILLIAMS, Cicero. Letters to his Friends. Epistulae ad familiares (3 vols.; Cambridge: Harvard University Press, 1927–1929); HELMUT KASTEN, M. Tulli Ciceronis epistularum ad familiares Libri XVI / Marcus Tullius Cicero an seine Freunde (Lateinisch / Deutsch; orig. 1964; repr., München: Heimeran, 1989); DAVID R. SHACKLETON BAILEY, Cicero. Epistulae ad familiares (3 vols.; LCL; Cambridge: Cambridge University Press, 2001); DAVID R. SHACKLETON BAILEY, Cicero. Epistulae ad Familiares (2 vols.; orig. 1977; repr., Cambridge Classical Texts and Commentaries 16; Cambridge: Cambridge University Press, 2004).

[282] WOLFGANG WILL, Claudius [I 24] C. Pulcher, Ap., BNP 3 (2003): 394–395; the following description ibid.

[283] CHRISTIAN GIZEWSKI, Ambitus, BNP 1 (2002): 568–569; cf. ibid. for the following.

[284] Relevant are the *lex Cornelia Baebia de ambitu* of 181 B.C., the *lex Cornelia* of 81 B.C., and nine further *leges* in the years 70, 67–63, 61, 55, 52, and later in the *lex Iulia* of 18 B.C.

[285] SEAGER, Maiestas, 150.

## (92) Seneca, *De beneficiis* 3.26

Nostri saeculi exempla non praeteribo. Sub Tib. Caesare fuit accusandi frequens et paene publica rabies, quae omni ciuili bello grauius togatam ciuitatem confecit; excipiebatur ebriorum sermo, simplicitas iocantium; nihil erat tutum; omnis saeuiendi placebat occasio, nec iam reorum expectabantur euentus, cum esset unus. Cenabat Paulus praetorius in conuiuio quodam imaginem Tib. Caesaris habens ectypa et eminente gemma. Rem ineptissimam fecero, si nunc uerba quaesiero, quemadmodum dicam illum matellam sumpsisse; quod factum simul et Maro ex notis illius temporis uestigatoribus notauit et seruus eius, quoi nectebantur insidiae, ei ebrio anulum extraxit. Et cum Maro conuiuas testaretur admotam esse imaginem obscenis et iam sub-scriptionem conponeret, ostendit in manu sua seruus anulum. Si quis hunc seruum uocat, et illum conuiuam uocabit.

*Translation.* I will not omit examples from our own age. Under Tiberius Caesar there was a frequent and almost universal frenzy for bringing charges (of *maiestas*) which ruined[286] the state more than the entire civil war. It captured the talk of drunkards, the frank words of jesters. Nothing was safe. Anything served as an excuse to shed blood, and there was no need to wait in order to find out the fate of the accused, because there was only one outcome. Paulus, a praetorian, while dining on a particular festive occasion, was wearing a ring with a conspicuous stone on which the portrait of Tiberius Caesar was engraved in relief. It would be silly if I tried, at this point, to find a polite way of saying that he took in his hands a chamber-pot; the action was noticed simultaneously by Maro, one of the notorious informers of that time, and by a slave of the victim for whom the trap was being set, who pulled the ring from the finger of his drunken master. When Maro called the table companions to witness that the emperor's portrait had been brought into contact with some-thing indecent, and drew up the indictment, the slave showed that the ring was on his own hand. Whoever calls such a man a slave, will also call Maro a table companion!

*Commentary.*[287] Lucius Annaeus Seneca, called the Younger, was born

---

[286] Cf. GEORGES, s.v. conficio II.3.b: "politisch erschöpfen, in seiner Eristenz gefährden, aufreiben, zugrunde richten."

[287] Text: FRANÇOIS PRÉCHAC, Sénèque: Des bienfaits. De Beneficiis (2 vols.; orig. 1926–1927; repr., Budé; Paris: Belles Lettres, 1972); for other text editions and translations cf. MARTIN C. GERTZ, L. Annaei Senecae Libri De beneficiis et De clementia. Ad Codicem Nazarianum (Berlin: Weidmann, 1876); KARL HOSIUS, L. Annaei Senecae Opera quae supersunt. I/2: De beneficiis libri VII. De clementia libri II (BSGRT; Leipzig: Teubner, 1914); MANFRED ROSENBACH, L. Annaeus Seneca. Philosophische Schriften (Lateinisch und deutsch. 5 vols.; orig. 1999, 1969–84; repr., Darmstadt: Wissenschaftliche Buchgesellschaft, 2011), 5:95–593 (Budé); JOHN W. BASORE, Seneca. Moral Essays (3 vols.; orig. 1928–1935; repr., LCL; Cambridge: Harvard University Press, 1979), vol. 3.

around A.D. 1 in Corduba in a wealthy equestrian family of the province of
Baetica; he died A.D. 65 in Rome, forced to commit suicide by Nero.[288] The
seven books of the treatise *De beneficiis*, dedicated to Aeubutius Liberalis,
who is virtually unknown, were written between A.D. 56–62. Book III discusses the question whether ingratitude can be legally prosecuted (Seneca
does not think so), whether a slave can give his master a benefaction (Seneca
thinks the answer is yes), and whether children can give benefits to their parents which are greater than the benefits which they received from them.
Seneca's description of prosecutions during the time of Tiberius in *Ben.* 3.26
demonstrates the transition of *maiestas* being a crime against the state to a
crime against the person of the emperor and his family.[289] The protection of
the state by prosecutions on the basis of the *crimen laesae maiestatis* was
extended by Tiberius to the person of the emperor and even to the image of
the emperor on rings, coins, or statues; even gestures that could be interpreted
as showing disrespect towards the emperor could be punished.[290] The person
of the emperor was already protected by the *lex maiestate*: he exercised both
the *imperium* and the *potestas tribunicia*. However, the protection was
increased on account of the deification of his person and on account of the
emperor's identification with the state. Public actions that could be interpreted
as being critical of the emperor – such as replacing an emperor's head on a
statue with someone else's head or allowing a city to be honored on a day on
which the emperor is honored, or public gestures that could be interpreted as
disrespectful of the emperor – such as beating a slave near a statue of
Augustus, or changing clothes near an imperial statue, or taking a ring or coin
stamped with the image of the emperor into a latrine or a brothel – could be
prosecuted as *crimen laesae maiestatis*. It is not surprising that the *crimen
laesae maiestatis* was also seen as a religious crime (*sacrilegium*; Dig.
48.4.1.pr.). Dio Cassius describes the crime of *maiestas* as ἀσέβεια (*impietas*;
Dio 57.9.2; 78.12.1).

---

[288] On Seneca cf. KARLHANS ABEL, Seneca. Leben und Leistung, ANRW II.32.2
(1984): 653–775; JOACHIM DINGEl, Seneca [2] L. Annaeus S., DNP 13 (2008): 271–278;
SCHANZ / HOSIUS, Geschichte der römischen Literatur II, 679–722, on *De beneficiis* cf. ibid.
696–98; also FRANÇOIS-RÉGIS CHAUMARTIN, Les désillusions de Sénèque devant l'évolution
de la politique néronienne et l'aspiration à la retraite: le 'De vita beata' et le 'De beneficiis',
ANRW II.36.3 (1989): 1686–1723.

[289] Cf. KÜBLER, Maiestas, 550; for the following point ibid. 550–51.

[290] Cf. KÜBLER, Maiestas, 552; GIZEWSKI, Maiestas, 187; cf. ibid. for the following point.
See also BARBARA LEVICK, Tiberius the Politician (Second ed.; orig. 1976; repr., New York:
Routledge, 1999), 180–200 ("Tiberius and the Law: The Development of *maiestas*"). Cf.
ANDO, Imperial Ideology, 237, who comments that "the ability of portraits to demand venera-
tion, as it were, made them active forces within local affairs."

**(93)** Tacitus, *Annales* 1.72–73

Decreta eo anno triumphalia insignia A. Caecinae, L. Apronio, C. Silio ob res cum Germanico gestas. nomen patris patriae Tiberius, a populo saepius ingestum, repudiavit; neque in acta sua iurari, quamquam censente senatu, permisit, cuncta mortalium incerta, quantoque plus adeptus foret, tanto se magis in lubrico dict<it>ans. non tamen ideo faciebat fidem civilis animi; nam legem maiestatis reduxerat. cui nomen apud veteres idem, sed alia in iudicium veniebant: si quis proditione exercitum <a>ut plebem seditionibus, denique male gesta re publica maiestatem populi Romani minuisset: facta arguebantur, dicta inpune erant. primus Augustus cognitionem de famosis libellis specie legis eius tractavit, commotus Cassii Severi libidine, qua viros feminasque inlustris procacibus scriptis diffamaverat; mox Tiberius, consultante Pompeio Macro praetore, an iudicia maiestatis redderentur, exercendas leges esse respondit. hunc quoque asperavere carmina incertis auctoribus vulgata in saevitiam superbiamque eius et discordem cum matre animum. <sup>73</sup> Haud pigebit referre in Falanio et Rubrio, modicis equitibus Romanis, praetemptata crimina, ut quibus initiis quanta Tiberii arte gravissimum exitium inrepserit, dein repressum sit, postremo arserit cunctaque corripuerit, noscatur. Falanio obiciebat accusator, quod inter cultores Augusti, qui per omnis domos in modum collegiorum habebantur, Cassium quendam mimum corpore infamem adscivisset, quodque venditis hortis statuam Augusti simul mancipasset. Rubrio crimini dabatur violatum periurio numen Augusti. quae ubi Tiberio notuere, scripsit consulibus non ideo decretum patri suo caelum, ut in perniciem civium is honor verteretur. Cassium histrionem solitum inter alios eiusdem artis interesse ludis, quos mater sua in memoriam Augusti sacrasset; nec contra religiones fieri, quod effigies eius, ut alia numinum simulacra, venditionibus hortorum et domuum accedant. ius iurandum perinde aestimandum quam si Iovem fefellisset: deorum iniurias dis curae.

*Translation.* In this year, triumphal insignia were granted to Aulus Caecina, Lucius Apronius, and Gaius Silius for their services with Germanicus. Tiberius refused the title "Father of the Nation" which had been pressed on him on numerous occasions by the people, and he refused to allow an oath of obedience to his enactments despite a vote of the senate. He explained that all human affairs were uncertain, and the more he achieved, the more slippery the ground on which he stood. Yet he failed to inspire faith in his citizen spirit.[291] For he brought back the *lex maiestatis*, which had the same name in earlier times, but covered a different type of offense: betrayal of an army, seditious incitement of the people, any act of wrongdoing on an official level which

---

[291] Lat. *civilis*; YARDLEY translates "liberal sympathies," SONTHEIMER "Bürgersinn." JACKSON provides a loose paraphrase: "belief that his sentiments were not monarchical."

diminishes the majesty of the Roman nation. Actions were prosecuted, words remained unpunished. Augustus was the first who, provoked by Cassius Severus' immoderate slander of distinguished men and women with his scandalous compositions, initiated legal proceedings against defamatory writings under this statute. Afterwards, Tiberius, who was consulted by the praetor Pompeius Macer on the question whether cases of *maiestas* should go to trial, replied that "the laws should be applied." He, too, had been incensed by poems of unknown authorship about his ruthlessness, his arrogance, and his strained relations with his mother. [73] It will not be inapposite to recall the charges brought as prelude in the case of Falanius and Rubrius, two Roman equestrians of little importance, in order to show how the severe disaster began, how Tiberius' deftness[292] allowed it to creep in, how it was subsequently suppressed, and how it finally flared up to engulf everything. The person who accused Falanius alleged that he had admitted a certain Cassius, a mime-actor notorious on account of fornication,[293] among the votaries of Augustus who were maintained in all the great houses resembling collegia, and that he had disposed of a statue of Augustus when he sold his gardens. Rubrius was charged with having violated the divinity of Augustus by perjury. When Tiberius heard of this, he wrote to the consuls that his father had not been decreed divine status so that the honor could be turned to the destruction of his fellow citizens. Cassius, the actor, along with others in the same profession, he said, regularly attended the games that his mother had consecrated to the memory of Augustus; nor was it an act of sacrilege if the image (of Augustus), like other statues of deities, went with the property whenever a house or garden was sold; a perjury should be regarded as if the man had sworn falsely by Jupiter: offenses against the gods were the god's concern!

*Commentary.* Tacitus dates the beginning of the increased use of the *crimen maiestatis* by Tiberius (A.D. 14–37) to A.D. 15 when Aulus Caecina, Lucius Apronius, and Gaius Silius, who had served in Germania under Germanicus, were granted the triumphal insignia. Aulus Caecina Severus was commander of the Lower German army, at least from A.D. 14–16. Lucius Apronius was a legate in Germania in A.D. 15, responsible for the protection of the banks of the Rhine during the campaign against the Chatti. Gaius Silius Aulus Caecina Largus was commander under Germanicus of the Upper German army since A.D. 13 and took part in campaigns against the Germanic tribes in A.D. 15–16.[294] Tacitus has been criticized for stating that it was Tiberius' "deftness"

---

[292] Lat. *ars*, translated as "art" (JACKSON) or "cunning" (YARDLEY).

[293] JACKSON, YARDLEY translate "catamite," a term used for pederastic friendship, a term not used by Tacitus, who has *corpore infamem*; SONTHEIMER translates with "Unzucht."

[294] Cf. WERNER ECK, Caecina [II 8] C. Severus, A., BNP 2 (2003): 888–889; WERNER ECK, Apronius [II 1] L., BNP 1 (2002): 911; WERNER ECK, Silius [II 3] C., S. A. Caecina Largus, BNP 13 (2013): 459–460.

(*ars*) which was responsible for "bringing back" (*reduxerat*) the *crimen maiestatis* in A.D. 15: the last known trial for treason under Augustus took place in A.D. 12.[295] If Tacitus implies that the praetor Pompeius Macer asked Tiberius whether charges of *maiestas* were to be entertained at all, he is mistaken: it was the consuls of the princeps who presided over the senatorial court where *maiestas* cases were tried, not the praetor.[296] As president of the appropriate jury court, Macer asked if any cases were to be taken in that court (as well as in the senate). Tacitus asserts that Tiberius, like Augustus, was provoked to increase prosecutions for *maiestas* due to libel. When the first charges of *crimen maiestatis* were brought in A.D. 15, the new concept of the *maiestas* of the emperor was introduced.[297] The *crimen maiestatis* that was prosecuted consisted no longer of "actions" (*facta*), such as the betrayal of an army, incitement of the people to sedition, or acts of wrongdoing on an official, but also "words" (*dicta*). The *crimen maiestatis* against the deified Augustus could take two forms: defamation, and disrespect towards his image. The knight Falanius was accused of keeping a male prostitute in his domestic college of worshipers of Augustus and of selling a statue of Augustus, the knight Rubrius was accused of using the name of the emperor in a perjury. In these particular cases, the charges were dismissed or the accused were acquitted. Tiberius wrote in an opinion for the consuls that Augustus had not been deified so that his divine honor would lead to the destruction of Roman citizens; the actor Cassius had taken part in ceremonies held by Livia in memory of Augustus, her husband; there was nothing wrong about selling a statue along with gardens; and as far as perjury in which the name of a god is invoked, the maxim holds that gods can take care of themselves. It appears that Tiberius disapproved of the attempt to broaden the charge of *maiestas* in the direction that these cases suggested, which is surprising: "Even if religious offences had not been catered for in the *leges maiestatis* the deification of Augustus was an act of patent political significance for Tiberius. A light to the new deity could easily be construed as a slight to the *maiestas* of Tiberius himself."[298] B. LEVICK agrees that the number of prosecutions and convictions of the charge of *crimen maiestatis* increased during Tiberius' principate, but thinks that the increase in numbers "is exaggerated for us because we have the conscientious and hostile testimony of Tacitus and Dio and the sensational generalizations of Suetonius."[299]

---

[295] Dio 56.72.1; cf. LEVICK, Tiberius, 191; for the following cf. ibid. 191–95.

[296] ERICH KOESTERMANN, Die Majestätsprozesse unter Tiberius, Historia 4 (1955): 72–106, argues that Tiberius was invited at the beginning of his rule to abolish charges of *maiestas* and thus strike a new tone. Given the evidence, this is not plausible; cf. BAUMANN, Impietas in Principem, 221–22.

[297] Pliny, *Pan.* 11.1, claims that Tiberius deified Augustus, his predecessor, to that he might "usher in" (*induceret*) the law of *maiestas*.

[298] LEVICK, Tiberius, 193.

**(94)** Tacitus, *Annales* 2.50

Adolescebat interea lex maiestatis. et Appuleiam Varillam, sororis Augusti neptem, quia probrosis sermonibus divum Augustum ac Tiberium et matrem eius inlusisset Caesarique conexa adulterio teneretur, maiestatis delator arcessebat. de adulterio satis caveri lege Iulia visum; maiestatis crimen distingui Caesar postulavit damnarique, si qua de Augusto inreligiose dixisset; in se iacta nolle ad cognitionem vocari. interrogatus a consule, quid de iis censeret, quae de matre eius locuta secus argueretur, reticuit; dein proximo senatus die illius quoque nomine oravit, ne cui verba in eam quoquo modo habita crimini forent. liberavitque Appuleiam lege maiestatis: adulterii graviorem poenam deprecatus, ut exemplo maiorum propinquis suis ultra ducentesimum lapidem removeretur suasit. adultero Manlio Italia atque Africa interdictum est.

*Translation.* Meanwhile, the law of *maiestas* gained in strength. Appuleia Varilla, the granddaughter of Augustus' sister, was summoned by an informer to answer a charge under the statute. The basis for the charge was that she had ridiculed the deified Augustus as well as Tiberius and his mother, by scandalous conversations, and that she, a relative of the emperor, had committed adultery. As regards the charge of adultery, it was decided that the *lex Iulia* had made sufficient provisions. As regards the *crimen maiestas*, the emperor demanded that a distinction should be made: she should be convicted if she had made any impious comment about Augustus; remarks levelled against himself he did not wish to be made the subject of an inquiry. When the consul asked what he thought about the offensive remarks that Appuleia was said to have made about his mother, he gave no answer; but in the meeting of the senate on the following day he asked, also in the name of his mother, that no one should be charged for having uttered any kind of words against her. So he did not apply the *lex maiestatis* to Appuleia. In the matter of adultery, he made a plea against the heavier penalty, urging that precedent should be followed and she be removed by her relatives to a point beyond the two-hundredth milestone. Her lover, Manlius, was banned from residence in Italy and Africa.

*Commentary.* Appuleia Varilla was the daughter of Sextus Appuleius and granddaughter of Octavia, Augustus' sister.[300] In A.D. 17, an informer (*delator*) charged her with *crimen maiestatis*, trying to bring three doctrines under the umbrella of the *lex maiestatis*: verbal injury to the deified Augustus, verbal injury to the emperor and his mother, and adultery by a connection of the emperor.[301] Tiberius decided that the adultery should be dealt with according to the provisions of the *lex Iulia de adulteriis*. As regards the alleged

---

[299] LEVICK, Tiberius, 189.
[300] WERNER ECK, Appuleia, BNP 1 (2002): 903.
[301] Cf. BAUMANN, Impietas in Principem, 77–79, for the case of Appuleia Varilla.

insulting comments, a distinction should be made whether the alleged impious words (*inreligiose dicta*) ridiculed the deified Augustus – in which case the *lex maiestatis* applies – or whether they were directed to the incumbent emperor and his mother, in which case no action was to be taken. This leniency contrasts with the cases of Aelius Saturninus and Sextius Paconianus who were executed in *maiestas* trials in A.D. 23 and A.D. 35, respectively.[302] It may find its explanation in the eminence of Appuleia's family: she was spared the penalty prescribed by the *lex Iulia de adulteriis* (relegation to an island, confiscation of one-third of her property, loss of half of her dowry) and handed over to her family for punishment. The case demonstrates the emperor's power to intervene at any stage of a trial. R. A. BAUMAN argues that the decision of the senate (*senatus consultum*) to accept the charge of impious comments (*inreligiose dicta*) about the deified emperor is "the most important single ruling in the entire history of *impietas in principem*. Not only did it establish Divus Augustus' right to the protection of the *lex maiestatis* but it also laid the foundation for the ambivalent position of the living emperor, for the encroachment of *principalis maiestatis veneratio* on the perfectly logical preserve of *in notam aliquorum* ... Events moved to rapidly in the direction of equating the position of the emperor with that of the Divus that when Dio looked back to the case of Appuleia Varilla, all that he was able to discern was a series of charges of *asebeia* being driven home in respect of insults to Augustus, Livia and Tiberius alike."[303]

## (95) Suetonius, *Tiberius* 58

Sub idem tempus consulente praetore an iudicia maiestatis cogi iuberet, exercendas esse leges respondit et atrocissime exercuit. Statuae quidam Augusti caput dempserat, ut alterius imponeret; acta res in senatu et, quia ambigebatur, per tormenta quaesita est. Damnato reo paulatim genus calumniae eo processit, ut haec quoque capitalia essent: circa Augusti simulacrum servum cecidisse, vestimenta mutasse, nummo vel anulo effigiem impressam latrinae aut lupanari intulisse, dictum ullum factumve eius existimatione aliqua laesisse. Perit denique et is, qui honorem in colonia sua eodem die decerni sibi passus est, quo decreti et Augusto olim erant.

*Translation.* It was at about this time that a praetor asked him whether he should have the courts convened to consider cases of *maiestas*, to which he replied that the laws must be enforced, and he enforced them with the greatest cruelty. A certain man had removed the head from a statue of Augustus and substituted it with someone else's head. The case was tried in the senate, and

---

[302] Dio 57.22.5; Tacitus, *Ann.* 6.39; LEVICK, Tiberius, 192; the following point ibid. 197.
[303] BAUMANN, Impietas in Principem, 78–79; cf. Dio 57.19.1.

since the evidence was conflicting, the witnesses were examined under torture. After the defendant had been convicted, in time the following types of accusations resulted in capital trials: beating a slave near a statue of Augustus, changing one's clothes there, carrying a coin or a ring bearing his image into a latrine or a brothel, criticizing any of his words or deeds. Indeed, a man was executed merely for allowing honors to be offered him in his colony on the same day that honors had previously been offered to Augustus.

*Commentary*.[304] Gaius Suetonius Tranquillus was born in A.D. 70, perhaps in Hippo; he became an official at the court of emperor Hadrian, who ended his career in A.D. 122; many years of scholarly production followed. His *De vita Caesarum* seeks to "interpret the Principate in the sense of individualized embodiments of imperial history in the persons of the emperor: how Caesar's conception of the principate was calculated to preserve republican institutions; how Augustus tentatively realized that conception, Tiberius usurped it for his own ends, Gaius (Caligula) cynically abused it, Claudius administered it as a good bureaucrat, Nero used it as an instrument to realize his private artistic ambitions; and how, after the abortive initiatives of the year of four emperors, the pattern was repeated on a lesser scale under the Flavians."[305] Rather than being a chronique scandaleuse, his biography of the emperors must be accorded equal status with the annals and histories, exhibiting an astonishing historical reliability. As regards the *crimen laesae maiestatis*, Suetonius confirms what Seneca writes in *Ben.* 3.26.1 (cf. No. 92): public actions that could be interpreted as being critical of the emperor – such as replacing an emperor's head on a statue with someone else's head or allowing a city to be honored on a day on which the emperor is honored – or public gestures that could be interpreted as disrespectful of the emperor – such as beating a slave near a statue of Augustus, or changing clothes near an imperial statue, or taking a ring or coin stamped with the image of the emperor into a latrine or a brothel – could be understood as *crimen laesae maiestatis* and be punished severely.[306] For Suetonius, the trials prosecuting people for this crime during

---

[304] Text: MAXIMILIAN IHM, C. Suetonius Tranquillus Opera. De vita Caesarum Libri III (orig. 1907; repr., Bibliotheca Scriptorum Graecorum et Romanorum Teubneriana; Stuttgart / Leipzig: Teubner, 2003); for other text editions and translations cf. JOHN C. ROLFE, Suetonius. Lives of the Caesars (orig. 1913–1914; repr., LCL; Cambridge: Harvard University Press, 1998); ANDRÉ LAMBERT, Sueton: Caesarenleben (7. Auflage im Rahmenteil bearbeitet von R. Häußler; orig. 1955; repr., Stuttgart: Kröner, 1986); CATHERINE EDWARDS, Suetonius. Lives of the Caesars. A New Translation (orig. 2000; repr., Oxford World's Classics; Oxford: Oxford University Press, 2008); DONNA W. HURLEY, Suetonius. The Caesars. Translated, with Introductions and Notes (Indianapolis: Hackett, 2011).

[305] KLAUS SALLMANN, Suetonius [2] S. Tranquillus C, BNP 13 (2008): 918–922, 919; cf. KLAUS SALLMANN, Von der römischen zur christlichen Literatur, 117 bis 284 n. Chr. (HdA VIII.4; München: Beck, 1997), 47; the following ibid.

[306] Cf. KÜBLER, Maiestas, 552; GIZEWSKI, Maiestas, 187.

Tiberius' principate belong to the "many other cruel and savage deeds under the guise of strictness and improvement of the public morals" which in reality merely gratify his natural cruel instincts (*Tib.* 59).

## (96)  *Digesta* 48.4.1–11

Ad legem Iuliam maiestatis. [1] *Ulpianus libro septimo de officio proconsulis.* Proximum sacrilegio crimen est, quod maiestatis dicitur. (1) Maiestatis autem crimen illud est, quod adversus populum Romanum vel adversus securitatem eius committitur. Quo tenetur is, cuius opera dolo malo consilium initum erit, quo obsides iniussu principis interciderent: quo armati homines cum telis lapidibusve in urbe sint conveniantve adversus rem publicam, locave occupentur vel templa, quove coetus conventusve fiat hominesve ad seditionem convocentur: cuiusve opera consilio malo consilium initum erit, quo quis magistratus populi Romani quive imperium potestatemve habet occidatur: quove quis contra rem publicam arma ferat: quive hostibus populi Romani nuntium litterasve miserit signumve dederit feceritve dolo malo, quo hostes populi Romani consilio iuventur adversus rem publicam: quive milites sollicitaverit concitaveritve, quo seditio tumultusve adversus rem publicam fiat: [2] *Idem libro octavo disputationum* quive de provincia, cum ei successum esset, non discessit: aut qui exercitum deseruit vel privatus ad hostes perfugit: quive sciens falsum conscripsit vel recitaverit in tabulis publicis: nam et hoc capite primo lege maiestatis enumeratur. [3] *Marcianus libro quarto decimo institutionum.* Lex duodecim tabularum iubet eum, qui hostem concitaverit quive civem hosti tradiderit, capite puniri. Lex autem Iulia maiestatis praecipit eum, qui maiestatem publicam laeserit, teneri: qualis est ille, qui in bellis cesserit aut arcem tenuerit aut castra concesserit. Eadem lege tenetur et qui iniussu principis bellum gesserit dilectumve habuerit exercitum comparaverit: quive, cum ei in provincia successum esset, exercitum successori non tradidit: quive imperium exercitumve populi Romani deseruerit: quive privatus pro potestate magistratuve quid sciens dolo malo gesserit: quive quid eorum, quae supra scripta sunt, facere curaverit: [4] *Scaevola libro quarto regularum* cuiusque dolo malo iureiurando quis adactus est, quo adversus rem publicam faciat: cuiusve dolo malo exercitus populi Romani in insidias deductus hostibusve proditus erit: factumve dolo malo cuius dicitur, quo minus hostes in potestatem populi Romani veniant: cuiusve opera dolo malo hostes populi Romani commeatu armis telis equis pecunia aliave qua re adiuti erunt: utve ex amicis hostes populi Romani fiant: cuiusve dolo malo factum erit, quo rex exterae nationis populo Romano minus obtemperet: cuiusve opera dolo malo factum erit, quo magis obsides pecunia iumenta hostibus populi Romani dentur adversus rem publicam. Item qui confessum in iudicio reum et propter hoc in vincula coniectum emiserit. (1) Hoc crimine liberatus est a senatu, qui statuas imperatoris reprobatas conflaverit. [5] *Marcianus libro quinto regularum.* Non contrahit crimen maiestatis, qui statuas Caesaris vetustate corruptas reficit. (1) Nec qui lapide iactato incerto fortuito statuam attigerit, crimen maiestatis commisit: et ita Severus et Antoninus Iulio Cassiano rescripserunt. (2) Idem Pontio rescripsit non videri contra maiestatem fieri ob imagines Caesaris nondum consecratas venditas. [6] *Venuleius Saturninus libro secundo de iudiciis publicis.* Qui statuas aut imagines imperatoris iam consecratas conflaverint aliudve quid simile admiserint, lege Iulia maiestatis tenentur. [7] *Modestinus libro duodecimo pandectarum.* Famosi, qui ius accusandi non habent, sine ulla dubitatione admittuntur ad hanc accusationem. (1) Sed et milites, qui causas alias defendere non possunt: nam qui pro pace excubant, magis magisque ad hanc accusationem admittendi sunt. (2) Servi quoque deferentes audiuntur et quidem dominos suos: et liberti patronos. (3) Hoc tamen crimen iudicibus non in occasione ob principalis maiestatis venerationem habendum est, sed in veritate: nam et personam spectandam esse, an potuerit facere, et an ante quid fecerit et an cogitaverit et an sanae mentis fuerit. Nec lubricum linguae ad poenam facile trahendum est: quamquam enim temerarii digni poena sint, tamen ut insanis illis parcendum est, si non tale sit delictum, quod vel ex scriptura legis descendit vel ad exemplum legis vindicandum est. (4) Crimen maiestatis facto vel violatis statuis vel imaginibus maxime exacerbatur in milites. [8] *Papinianus libro tertio decimo responsorum.* In quaestionibus laesae maiestatis etiam mulieres audiuntur. Coniurationem denique Sergii Catilinae Iulia mulier detexit et Marcum Tullium consulem indicium eius instruxit. [9] *Hermogenianus libro quinto iuris epitomarum.* Eorum, qui maiestatis crimine damnati sunt, libertorum bona liberis damnatorum conservari divus Severus decrevit et tunc demum fisco vindicari, si nemo damnati liberorum existat. [10] *Idem libro sexto iuris epitomarum.* Maiestatis crimine accusari potest, cuius ope consilio dolo malo provincia vel civitas hostibus prodita est. [11] *Ulpianus libro octavo disputationum.* Is, qui in reatu decedit, integri status decedit: extinguitur enim crimen mortalitate. Nisi forte quis maiestatis reus fuit: nam hoc crimine nisi a successoribus purgetur, hereditas fisco vindicatur. Plane non quisque legis Iuliae maiestatis reus est, in eadem condicione est, sed qui perduellionis reus est, hostili animo adversus rem publicam vel principem animatus: ceterum si quis ex alia causa legis Iuliae maiestatis reus sit, morte crimine liberatur.

*Translation.* Lex Iulia on Treason. [1] ULPIAN, *Duties of Proconsul, Book 7*: Closest to sacrilege is that crime which is called treason. 1. The crime of treason is that which is committed against the Roman people or against their safety. He is liable, by whose agency a plan is formed with malicious intent to kill hostages without the command of the emperor; or that men armed with weapons or stones should be, or should assemble, within the city against the interests of the state, or should occupy places or temples; or that there should be an assembly or gathering or that men should be called together for seditious purposes; or by whose agency a plan is formed with malicious intent to kill any magistrate of the Roman people, or anyone holding *imperium* of power; or that anyone should bear arms against the state; or who sends a messenger or letters to the enemies of the Roman people, or gives them a password, or does anything with malicious intent, whereby the enemies of the Roman people may be helped with his counsel against the state; or who persuades or incites troops to make a sedition or tumult against the state. [2] ULPIAN, *Disputations, Book 8*: or who has failed to relinquish his province although his successor has arrived; or who has deserted the army, or, as a private citizen, has fled to the enemy; or has knowingly written or dictated a falsehood onto the public records; for this also is set out in the first chapter of the statute on treason. [3] MARCIAN, *Institutes, Book 14*: The *Law of the Twelve Tables* commands capital punishment for the man who stirs up the enemy or hands a Roman citizen over to them. But the *lex Iulia* on treason makes him liable who injures the public *maiestas*, such as he who surrenders in war or recklessly yields a citadel or camp. Under the same law, without the command of the emperor, wages or raises a levy or prepares an army; or who, though he has been superseded in his province, has not handed his military command over to his successor; or who has abandoned his *imperium* or an army of the Roman people; or who, being a private citizen, knowingly and with malicious intent acts as though holding office or magistracy; or who brings about the doing of any of the above. [4] SCAEVOLA, *Rules, Book 4*:[307] or he by whose malicious intent a person is induced to take an oath to act against the state; or by whose malicious intent an army of the Roman people is led into an ambush or betrayed to the enemy; or whose malicious action is alleged to have prevented enemies falling into the power of the Roman people; or by whose agency with malicious intent the enemies of the Roman people have been assisted with provisions, arms, weapons, horses, money, or any other thing; or who so acts that allies of the Roman people become their enemies; or by whose malicious intent it is brought about that the king of a foreign nation fails to make submission to the Roman people; or by whose agency with malicious intent it is brought about that hostages, money, or cattle are handed over to the enemies of the Roman people against the interests of the state; also the man who lets go someone charged and found guilty in a [treason] trial and for this reason cast into prison. 1. The senate cleared of this charge a man who had melted down rejected statues of the emperor. [5] MARCIAN, *Rules, Book 5*: He who has restored imperial statues which have fallen into disrepair with age does not incur a charge of treason. 1. Nor has someone committed the offense of treason if he happened to hit a statue [of an emperor] with a chance-thrown

---

[307] WIEACKER, Rechtsgeschichte II, 106, calls the quotation of a *lex Iulia de maiestate* from Scaevola's *Regulae* in 48.4.4 "ziemlich unerwartet."

stone, as Severus and Antoninus wrote in a rescript to Julius Cassianus. 2. The same [emperors] wrote in a rescript to Pontius that there did not seem to be lèse-majesté in selling likenesses of Caesar which had not yet been consecrated. [6] VENULEIUS SATURNINUS, *Criminal Proceedings, Book 2*: Persons are liable under the *lex Iulia* on treason who melt down statues or likenesses of the emperor which are already consecrated, or who commit anything of the same kind. [7] MODESTINUS, *Encyclopaedia, Book 12*: The infamous, who do not have the right of accusation, are nevertheless undoubtedly permitted this accusation. 1. Soldiers also, who cannot bring other kinds of actions; for those who are on guard to keep the peace should more and more be permitted this accusation. 2. Slaves also who bring [this] accusation are given a hearing, even against their masters, as are freedmen against their patrons. 3. But this charge should not be treated by judges as an opportunity for showing their reverence for the imperial majesty, but as a matter of fact; for the nature of the person must be considered; could he have done it, had he done or devised anything beforehand, and was he in his right mind? Nor should a slip of the tongue readily bring a man to punishment; for although thoughtless persons may deserve punishment, nevertheless, they should be pardoned as not of sound mind if their crime was not of such a kind that it derives from the actual wording of the statute or merits exemplary punishment. 4. The offense of treason in an action such as the violation of statues or images is very much aggravated in the case of a soldier. [8] PAPINIAN, *Replies, Book 13*: Women also are given a hearing in questions [of offenses] against the *maiestas* [of the Roman people]. It was indeed the woman Fulvia who revealed the conspiracy of Sergius Catiline and gave information to the consul M. Tullius [Cicero]. [9] HERMOGENIAN, *Epitome of Law, Book 5*: The deified Severus decreed that the property of freedmen of those condemned on a charge of treason should be saved for the children of the condemned, and should be claimed for the imperial treasury only if there were no surviving children of the condemned man. [10] HERMOGENIAN, *Epitome of Law, Book 6*: He by whose help and counsel, given with malicious intent, a province or a *civitas* has been betrayed to the enemy can be accused of the offense of treason. [11] ULPIAN, *Disputations, Book 8*: He who dies while under accusation dies with his status unimpaired; for the charge is extinguished by death. Unless perchance he has been charged with treason; for with this offense his inheritance is claimed by the imperial treasury, unless he is cleared by his successors. Clearly, not everyone charged with treason under the *lex Iulia* is on the same footing, but he who is charged with *perduellio*, animated by a hostile spirit against the state or the emperor [is liable even after death]; he who is charged under the *lex Julia* on treason on other grounds is cleared of the charge on his death.

*Commentary.*[308] The *Digesta* was produced as a result of the desire of emperor Justinian (A.D. 527–563) to codify the law of the empire with the goal of unifying the legal order and its application: the *Corpus iuris civilis*, published November 16, A.D. 534, included the *Digesta seu pandecta*, the *codex Iustinianus repetitae praelectionis*, and the *Institutiones.*[309] The *Digesta* is an anthology of excerpts from 1,528 books written by Roman lawyers from the first century B.C. to the fourth century A.D., divided into fifty books which represents a condensed (*digesta*) and comprehensive (*pandectae*) version of Roman law under 432 titles.[310] Over 40 percent of the *Digesta* texts are expressly attributed to Domitius Ulpian (c. A.D. 170–223), which means that the reader of the *Digesta* "is primarily reading a selected and revised version of Ulpian's writing, incorporating alternative versions of the law when appropriate."[311] The jurist Ulpian,[312] who hailed from Tyre and composed his writings during the principate of emperor Caracalla (A.D. 211–217), wrote *De officio proconsulis* in ten books with the goal of ordering, explaining, and publishing the general decrees and the individual decisions of the emperors for individual or for several senatorial provinces; the imperial decisions were

---

[308] Text: THEODOR MOMMSEN, Iustiniani Digesta (Corpus Iuris Civilis. Editio stereotypa quinta. Volumen Primum: Institutiones, Recognovit P. Krueger. Digesta, Recognovit T. Mommsen; Berlin: Weidmann, 1889), 1:793–94 (editio maior); reprinted in ALAN WATSON, ed., The Digest of Justinian (Latin Text Edited by Theodor Mommsen, With the Aid of Paul Krueger. English Translation edited by Alan Watson; Philadelphia: University of Pennsylvania Press, 1985), 4:802–3. Cf. JOP SPRUIT, et al., Corpus Iuris Civilis. Tekst en vertaling (12 vols.; Amsterdam: Royal Dutch Academy of Sciences / Amsterdam University Press, 1993–2011); eventually there will be a new bilingual Latin/German edition in OKKO BEHRENDS, et al., Corpus Iuris Civilis. Text und Übersetzung (5 vols.; Heidelberg: Müller, 1990–2005). The English translation of OLIVIA ROBINSON, in ALAN WATSON, ed., The Digest of Justinian: Revised English Language Edition (4 vols.; orig. 1985; repr., Philadelphia: University of Pennsylvania Press, 1998), is reprinted with permission of the University of Pennsylvania Press. For an older, only partially reliable translation cf. SAMUEL P. SCOTT, The Civil Law, including the Twelve Tables, the Institutes of Gaius, the Rules of Ulpian, the Opinions of Paulus, the Enactments of Justinian, and the Constitutions of Leo. Translated from the original Latin, edited, and compared with all accessible systems of jurisprudence ancient and modern (17 vols.; Cincinnati: Central Trust Company, 1932), 11: 25–33; for other translations cf. C. F. E. SINTENIS in CARL EDUARD OTTO / BRUNO SCHILLING / CARL FRIEDRICH FERDINAND SINTENIS, Das Corpus juris civilis in's Deutsche übersetzt von einem Vereine Rechtsgelehrter (7 vols.; Leipzig: Focke, 1830–1833), 4:934–37; GOTTFRIED HÄRTEL, Aus den Digesten, in Römisches Recht in einem Band (ed. L. Huchthausen; orig. 1975; repr., Berlin: Aufbau, 1989), 253–55. The most important manuscript is the Florentina, dating to the 6th (?) century.

[309] WIEACKER, Rechtsgeschichte II, 294–324; ON THE COMPILATION OF THE *DIGESTA* CF. IBID. 294–314; WULF ECKART VOSS, Digesta, BNP 4 (2004): 407–410.

[310] Cf. TONY HONORÉ, Justinian's Digest: Character and Compilation (Oxford: Oxford University Press, 2010), 2, 29.

[311] HONORÉ, Justinian's Digest, 6.

[312] On Ulpian cf. TONY HONORÉ, Ulpian (Oxford: Clarendon, 1982); WIEACKER, Rechtsgeschichte II, 130–38; SALLMANN, Literatur des Umbruchs, 175–87; on *De officio proconsulis*, cf. ibid. 181–82.

available in the archives. Criminal law is treated in Book 6 i.f.–10. The *Digesta* preserves only twenty-four lines of excerpts from Book 6. Ulpian did much more than record the status quo of legal matters in the provinces: he harmonized and disciplined the laws of the provincial administrations, and emphasized the moral responsibility of the provincial governors. T. HONORÉ suggests that when Ulpian cites the text of an imperial constitution, and often when he does not, "he has consulted the original text, a copy in the *liber libellorum rescriptorum*, or a collection which reproduced the text of the constitution."[313] P. BIRKS and G. MCLEOD represent the recent consensus which takes issue with earlier claims that Justinian's commissioners introduced doctrinal alterations; rather, they did not add legal material "except to tidy up or abbreviate the excerpt, or occasionally to adjust it."[314]

Under the heading *Ad legem Iuliam maiestatis*, the text in 48.4 cites eleven excerpts from the works of seven classical jurists: Ulpian, Marcian, Scaevola, Venuleius Saturninus, Modestinus, Papinian, and Hermogenian. A *lex iulia maiestatis* is also attested by *Inst.* 4.18.3 (cf. No. 97).[315] Since the laws of both Caesar and Augustus are known as *leges Iuliae*, a particular *lex Iuliae* can be linked with either Caesar or Augustus only if further evidence exists to sup-port an identification. The best argument for the existence of a *lex Iulia maiestatis* issued by Augustus has long been *Dig.* 48.4.3:[316] according to Marcian, a *lex Iulia maiestatis* prohibited levies and warfare *iniussu principis* ("without the command of the emperor"), and according to Ulpian, the same criterion applied to the execution of hostages (*Dig.* 48.4.1.1). In all other instances, the subject, where specified, is the people of Rome (*populus Romanus*) or the state (*res publica*). R. A. BAUMAN argues that *iniussu principis* in Ulpian and Marcian is probably an authentic citation from a *lex maiestatis* by Augustus, the full expression being *iniussu principis aut senatus* ("without the command of the emperor or the senate"), with the *aut* ("or") discarded by the compilers of the *Digesta* or their predecessors.[317] The stipulation is linked with the arbitration of war and peace. According to Strabo, when Augustus was granted "the foremost place of authority" (τὴν προστασίαν τῆς ἡγεμονίας), i.e., at the beginning of his principate, he was established as "lord for life of war and peace" (πολέμου καὶ εἰρήνης κατέστη κύριος διὰ βίου; Strabo, 17.3.25). This is corroborated by Dio Cassius who says that in 27 B.C.

---

[313] Honoré, Ulpian, 237–38.

[314] PETER BIRKS / GRANT MCLEOD, Justinian's Institutes (With the Latin Text of Paul Krueger; orig. 1987; repr., Ithaca: Cornell University Press, 1996), 10; cf. HONORÉ, Justinian's Digest, 107–8.

[315] Cf. BAUMAN, Crimen Maiestatis, 266–92, for the following discussion.

[316] Cf. VINCENZO ARANGIO-RUIZ, La Legislazione, in Augustus. Studi in occasione del bimillenario Augusteo (ed. P. de Francisci and S. Riccobono; Rome: Accademia Nazionale dei Lincei, 1938), 101–146, 136–37.

[317] BAUMAN, Crimen Maiestatis, 274, for the following point ibid. 274–75.

Augustus received the right to wage war and make peace (53.15.5). The rules that Dio assigns to 27 B.C. in 53.15.6 parallel *Dig.* 48.4.3 (Marcian) and 48.4.2 (Ulpian): Augustus' *lex Iulia de maiestate* reserved matters of war and peace for the decision of the emperor, and made it an offense for a provincial governor not to hand his province over to his successor. These rules were established both by a *senatus consultum* and by *lex* (Dio 53.12.1).[318] It appears that Augustus *lex Iulia de maiestate* went beyond the adjustments occasioned by the constitutional settlement of 27 B.C., necessitated by the transfer of provinces to Augustus. In addition to unauthorized levies and warfare, and wrongful retention of a province, Marcian cites actions that fell under the concept of *proditio* (in the general sense of treacherously handing over the person or interests of another to a hostile third party, including the defection of an ally and the more serious military crimes),[319] various forms of which were brought under the *crimen maiestatis*: surrender of positions to the enemy and desertion according to Marcian (*Dig.* 48.4.3), aiding the enemy and desertion according to Ulpian (*Dig.* 48.4.1.1; 48.4.2); Scaevola provides a full list (*Dig.* 48.4.4), including provisions against people whose actions cause allies of the Roman people to become their enemies, and through whose malicious intent it is brought about that the king of a foreign nation fails to make submission to the Roman people – two provisions that would have been relevant in Jesus' trial before Pilatus. The *crimen maiestatis* directed "against the Roman people and its safety" (*adversus populum Romanum vel adversus securitatem*; *Dig.* 48.4.1.1) could be committed by Roman citizens or by provincials who planned the killing of a magistrate or an armed revolt, who was bearing arms against the state, who liberated prisoners, who occupied public or sacred buildings, or who cooperated for an enemy power. The term *maiestas* "was applied to a number of criminal offenses including treason, sedition, and desertion. In the empire it covered any action which endangered the emperor or his family. The earlier crime of betrayal to an enemy, *perduellio*, was eventually held to be merely a way of committing this offense."[320] The *crimen maiestatis* was regarded as *crimen extraordinaria* and thus prosecuted in a proceeding *extra ordinem*; the "freedom" of this procedure meant that "a formal accusation was no longer required but mere notification (or rather denun-

---

[318] BAUMAN, Crimen Maiestatis, 275; cf. PETER SATTLER, Augustus und der Senat: Untersuchungen zur römischen Innenpolitik zwischen 30 und 17 v. Christus (Göttingen: Vandenhoeck & Ruprecht, 1960), 37, 45–46. For the following point BAUMAN, ibid. 277–28. For the history of the *crimen maiestatis* cf. No. 13.

[319] Cf. CHRISTOPH H. BRECHT, Perduellio. Eine Studie zu ihrer begrifflichen Abgrenzung im römischen Strafrecht bis zum Ausgang der Republik (MBPAR 29; München: Beck, 1938), 26–27.

[320] WATSON, Digest, 1:xxxiv; OLIVIA ROBINSON, the translator of *Dig.* 48, writes in a note on the heading of 48.4, "*Majestas* [sic] is translated regularly as treason, except where it is being contrasted with *perduellio* or means majesty or lèse-majesté." SINTENIS translates "Majestätsverbrechen."

ciation), by anyone – including slaves – was sufficient for criminal prosecution. The decision regarding the punishment was increasingly left to the decision-maker in each individual case."[321] During the investigation of the crime, "established trial norms could be disregarded, such as those which forbade the charging and questioning as witnesses, e.g. slaves of *infami*, or exclu-ded torture for accused persons of free status."[322] Depending on the status of the person convicted of treason, punishments ranged from deportation to death by wild animals in the arena or crucifixion (*Dig.* 48.19.38).[323]

**(97)** *Institutiones* 4.18

*De publicis iudiciis.* Publica iudicia neque per actiones ordinantur nec omnino quidquam simile habent ceteris iudiciis de quibus locuti sumus, magnaque diversitas est eorum et in instituendis et in exercendis. 1. Publica autem dicta sunt quod cuivis ex populo exsecutio eorum plerumque datur. 2. Publicorum iudiciorum quaedam capitalia sunt, quaedam non capitalia. capitalia dicimus quae ultimo supplicio adficiunt vel aquae et ignis interdictione vel deportatione vel metallo: cetera si qua infamiam irrogant cum damno pecuniario, haec publica quidem sunt, non tamen capitalia. 3. Publica autem iudicia sunt haec. lex Iulia maiestatis, quae in eos qui contra imperatorem vel rem publicam aliquid moliti sunt suum vigorem extendit. cuius poena animae amissionem sustinet et memoria rei et post mortem damnatur. 4. Item lex Iulia de adulteriis coercendis, quae non solum temeratores alienarum nuptiarum gladio punit, sed etiam eos, qui cum masculis infandam libidinem exercere audent. sed eadem lege Iulia etiam stupri flagitium punitur, cum quis sine vi vel virginem vel viduam honeste viventem stupraverit. poenam autem eadem lex irrogat peccatoribus, si honesti sunt, publicationem partis dimídiae, bonorum, si humiles, corporis coercitionem cum relegatione. 5. Item lex Cornelia de sicariis, quae homicidas ultore ferro persequitur vel eos, qui hominis occidendi causa cum telo ambulant. telum autem, ut Gaius noster in interpretatione legis duodecim tabularum scriptum reliquit, vulgo quidem id appellatur quod ab arcu mittitur: sed et omne significatur quod manu cuiusdam mittitur: sequitur ergo, ut et lapis et lignum et ferrum hoc nomine contineatur. dictumque ab eo quod in longinquum mittitur, a Graeca voce figuratum, ἀπὸ τοῦ τηλοῦ: et hanc significationem invenire possumus et in Graeco nomine: nam quod nos telum appellamus, illi βέλος appellant ἀπὸ τοῦ βάλλεσθαι. admonet nos Xenophon. nam ita scripsit: καὶ τὰ βέλη ὁμοῦ ἐφέρετο, λόγχαι, τοξεύματα,

---

[321] SCHIEMANN, Crimen, 942.

[322] GIZEWSKI, Maiestas, 187; see *Cod. Theod.* 9.6.2; *Dig.* 48.4.7; 48.4.8; *Cod. Iust.* 5.17.8.6; 9.1.20.

[323] Cf. RICHARD A. BAUMAN, Crime and Punishment in Ancient Rome (London: Routledge, 1996), 124–60.

σφενδόναι, πλεῖστοι δὲ καὶ λίθοι. sicarii autem appellantur a sica, quod significat ferreum cultrum. eadem lege et venefici capite damnantur, qui artibus odiosis, tam venenis vel susurris magicis homines occiderunt vel mala medicamenta publice vendiderunt. 6. Alia deinde lex asperrimum crimen nova poena persequitur, quae Pompeia de parricidiis vocatur. qua cavetur, ut, si quis parentis aut filii aut omino adfectionis eius, quae nuncupatione parricidii continetur, fata properaverit, sive clam sive palam id ausus fuerit, nec non is, cuius dolo malo id factum est, vel conscius criminis existit, licet extraneus sit, poena parricidii punietur et neque gladio neque ignibus neque ulla alia sollemni poenae subicietur, sed insutus culleo cum cane et gallo gallinaceo et vipera et simia et inter eius ferales angustias comprehensus, secundum quod regionis qualitas tulerit, vel in vicinum mare vel in amnem proiciatur, ut omni elementorum usu vivus carere incipiat et ei caelum superstiti, terra mortuo auferatur. si quis autem alias cognatione vel adfinitate coniunctas personas necaverit, poenam legis Corneliae de sicariis sustinebit. 7. Item lex Cornelia de falsis, quae etiam testamentaria vocatur, poenam irrogat ei qui testamentum vel aliud instrumentum falsum scripserit signaverit recitaverit subiecerit quive signum adulterinum fecerit sculpserit expresserit sciens dolo malo. eiusque legis poena in servos ultimum supplicium est, quod et in lege de sicariis et veneficis servatur, in liberos vero deportatio. 8. Item lex Iulia de vi publica seu privata adversus eos exoritur, qui vim vel armatam vel sine armis commiserint. sed si quidem armata vis arguatur, deportatio ei ex lege Iulia de vi publica irrogatur: si vero sine armis, in tertiam partem bonorum publicatio imponitur. sin autem per vim raptus virginis vel viduae vel sanctimonialis vel aliae fuerit perpetratus, tunc et peccatores et ei, qui opem flagitio dederunt, capite puniuntur secundam nostrae constitutionis definitionem, ex qua haec apertius possibile est scire. 9. Lex Iulia peculatus eos punit, qui pecuniam vel rem publicam vel sacram vel religiosam furati fuerint. sed si quidem ipsi iudices tempore administrationis publicas pecunias subtraxerunt, capitali animadversione puniuntur, et non solum hi, sed etiam qui ministerium eis ad hoc adhibuerunt vel qui subtracta ab his scientes susceperunt: alii vero, qui in hanc legem inciderint, poenae deportationis subiugentur. 10. Est inter publica iudicia lex Fabia de plagiariis, quae interdum capitis poenam ex sacris constitutionibus irrogat, interdum leviorem. 11. Sunt praeterea publica iudicia lex Iulia ambitus et lex Iulia repetundarum et lex Iulia de annona et lex Iulia de residuis, quae de certis capitulis loquuntur et animae quidem amissionem non irrogant, aliis autem poenis eos subiciunt, qui praecepta earum neglexerint. 12. Sed de publicis iudiciis haec euimus, ut vobis possibile sit summo digito et quasi per indicem ea tetigisse. alioquin diligentior eorum scientia vobis ex latioribus digestorum sive pandectarum libris deo propitio adventura est.

*Translation. Public trials.* Public trials are not ordered by forms of action, nor are they similar to the forms of action we have been dealing with so far. This is particularly true regarding the manner in which they are initiated and conducted. 1. They are called public because nearly every member of the public can set them in motion. 2. Some public trials are capital, and some are noncapital. We call capital trials those which involve the ultimate penalty or end in banishment from hearth and home or deportation or condemnation to the mines. The rest, which lead to disgrace and monetary fines, are still public, but not capital trials. 3. Public trials are instituted as follows. The *lex Iulia maiestatis* (Julian Act on Treason), which subjects to severe punishments all who conspire against the emperor or the state. The penalty it stipulates is the loss of life, and the memory of the guilty is condemned even after death. 4. Next, the *lex Iulia de adulteriis coercendis* (Julian Act on the Suppression of Adultery), which puts to the sword not only those who treat with contempt (through adultery) the marriages of others but also those who give themselves up to their unspeakable lust with males. The same law also punishes the crime of sexual intercourse where a man seduces, without violence, a virgin or a respectable widow. The penalty that the Act stipulates for such offenders is, for the highly placed (honesti), confiscation of half of their wealth, for common people (humiles) corporal punishment and banishment. 5. Next, the *lex Cornelia de sicariis* (Cornelian Acts on Assassins), which puts to the sword of vengeance murderers and those who go armed with a *telum* for the purpose of killing a man. According to the interpretation of our Gaius in his commentaries on the Twelve Tables, the word *telum* ordinarily refers to anything that is shot from a bow, but it also denotes anything flung from the hand. So the meaning of the term includes a stone, a piece of wood or of iron. For the term implies something propelled from a distance, derived from the Greek phrase ἀπὸ τοῦ τεηλοῦ. The equivalent Greek word has the same meaning, for what we call *telum* they call βέλος (missile), ἀπὸ τοῦ βάλλεσθαι (from throwing), as we learn from Xenophon, who says, "they carried the weapons (βέλη), spears, arrows, slings, and many stones." Assassins are called *sicarii* which comes from the word *sica* which is a metal knife. The Act also stipulates the death penalty for poisoners who use their detestable knowledge to kill men by poison or by magic spells or sell lethal drugs to the public. 6. Another law inflicts a rare punishment on the most horrible of crimes, called the *lex Pompeia de parricidiis* (the Pompeian Act on Parricide). It provides that anyone who openly or secretly dares to hasten the death of a parent or child or any other relative within the term *parricidium* (parricide, murder of a close relative), and anyone who instigates such a death, and anyone who is an accomplice in the commission of the crime even if he is not a member of the family, shall suffer the penalty for parricide: he is not put to the sword, nor to the fire, nor to any other customary penalty, but he is to be sewed up into a sack with a dog, a cock, a snake, and a monkey, and, locked up in this bestial tight spot, he shall be thrown into a nearby sea or river, as the nature of the place allows.

In this way he is deprived of the use of every element even while he still lives, and the sky is taken from him before he dies, and the earth is denied him when he is dead. If anyone kills a relation by blood or marriage outside the parricide degrees, he shall suffer the penalty of the *lex Cornelia de sicariis*. 7. Next, the *lex Cornelia de falsis* (Cornelian Act of Forgery), also called *testamentaria* (Cornelian Act on Wills), punishes anyone who has written a forged will or other document, seals one, reads one for witnessing, or substitutes a false one for a true one, also anyone who knowingly and with malicious intent makes or engraves or casts a duplicate seal. The penalty is, for slaves, the ultimate punishment, as stipulated by the *lex Cornelia* for assassins and poisoners; for free persons, the penalty is deportation. 8. Next, the *lex Iulia de vi publica seu privata* (Julian Act on Public or Private Force) punishes those who are guilty of using force, whether with arms or without. For violence with armed force, the penalty stipulated by the *lex Iulia de vi publica* is deportation; for violence without armed force, he suffers the confiscation of one third of his wealth. If force is used to rape a virgin or widow, whether religious or lay, the culprits and anyone who aided in the commission of the crime shall suffer the death penalty, according to the provisions of our constitution which provides fuller details. 9. Next, the *lex Iulia peculatus* (Julian Act on Embezzlement) punishes those who seal money or property which is public, sacred, or religious. If judges, of all people, take public money during their time of office, they shall suffer the death penalty, as also all those who have helped or knowingly received what they have plundered. Others who offend this Act are subject to the penalty of deportation. 10. To this list of crimes also belongs the *lex Fabia de plagiariis* (Fabian Act on Kidnapping) which stipulates, in certain cases, the death penalty according to the imperial constitutions; some have a lesser penalty. 11. The following laws also pertain to public prosecutions: the *lex Iulia ambitus* (Julian Act on Bribery), the *lex Iulia repetundarum* (Julian Act on Extortion), the *lex Iulia de annona* (the Julian Act on Interference with the Corn Supply), and the *lex Iulia de residuis* (Julian Act on Improper Application of Public Funds). These Acts all have their own specific provisions. They do not stipulate the death penalty but subject those who ignore their terms to lesser punishments. 12. This is what we say about public prosecutions so that you can touch them as with your finger and become acquainted with them at least by name. You can obtain a fuller understanding of these matters, with God's help, from the great books of the Digest or Pandects.

*Commentary*.[324] The *Institutiones* ("Introduction") provide the first principles

---

[324] Text: PAUL KRÜGER / THEODOR MOMMSEN, Digesta Iustiniani Augusti (2 vols.; Berlin: Weidmann, 1870), 55–56. For translations cf. BIRKS / McLEOD, Justinian's Institutes, 145, 147; THOMAS COLLETT SANDARS, The Institutes of Justinian, with English Introduction, Translation, and Notes (Eighth Edition, Revised and Corrected; London / New York: Longmans, Green, 1888), 503–8; OTTO / SCHILLING / SINTENIS, Corpus juris civilis, 1:197–

of Roman law, giving a bird's eye view of the material in the *Digesta* which is twenty times as comprehensive. The work was promulgated on November 21, 533, although it had been commissioned by Justinian only when the collection of the *Digesta* was completed.[325] Section 3 on public trials (*publica iudicia*) cites the *lex Iulia maiestatis* according to which people are to be severely punished "conspire against the emperor or the state" (*qui contra imperatorem vel rem publicam aliquid moliti sunt*). This means that plans to conspire against the emperor or the Roman state were sufficient for the charge of treason, without any overt act having been committed.

*Jesus' Roman trial and Roman law*. The Jewish leaders accuse Jesus before Pontius Pilatus, the prefect of the province of Judea, that he claimed to be the king of the Jews. This accusation, which is the background of Pilatus' question σὺ εἶ ὁ βασιλεὺς τῶν Ἰουδαίων; ("Are you the King of the Jews?"), is reported in all four Gospels (Mark 15:2; Matt 27:11; Luke 23:3; John 18:33).[326] A majority of New Testament scholars[327] and many classical historians[328] explain Jesus' conviction by Pontius Pilatus in terms of the *crimen maiestatis*, or more specifically the *crimen laesae maiestatis* towards the emperor. JUSTIN TAYLOR suggests the claim that Jesus is (another) king could be construed as falling within Cicero's definition of the crime of *maiestas* (Cicero, *Inv.* 2.53).[329] JOHN G. COOK regards a conviction for *maiestas* difficult since Jesus was a *peregrinus*,[330] following J. J. AUBERT who thinks the view that the Romans found Jesus guilty of *crimen maiestatis populi Romani imminutae* (i.e. „*perduellio*) is "debatable" since "the reported criminal procedure and Jesus' punishment, legal status (noncitizen), and social standing

---

200 (C. F. E. SINTENIS); OKKO BEHRENDS, et al., Corpus Iuris Civilis. Text und Übersetzung. Band I: Institutionen (3. überarbeitete Auflage; orig. 1990; repr., Heidelberg: Müller, 2007).

[325] BIRKS / MCLEOD, Justinian's Institutes, 12.

[326] Cf. BLINZLER, Prozeß, 278–79; STROBEL, Stunde, 73, 95; BROWN, Death, 1:732.

[327] Cf. ALEXANDER T. INNES, The Trial of Jesus Christ: A Legal Monograph (Edinburgh: Clark, 1899), 85; BLINZLER, Prozeß, 311–12, 339; STROBEL, Stunde, 92, 119, 135; BETZ, Probleme, 642–43; BROWN, Death, 717–19, 968; EGGER, Crucifixus, 199; GIORGIO JOSSA, Jews or Christians? The Followers of Jesus in Search of their Own Identity (WUNT 202; Tübingen: Mohr Siebeck, 2006), 57; WELCH, Miracles (*maiestas* and *maleficium*, i.e. magic); WEBB, Roman Examination, 754–55. See also the commentators, e.g. JOACHIM GNILKA, Das Evangelium nach Markus (EKK II/1–2; Zürich / Neukirchen-Vluyn: Benziger / Neukirchener, 1978–79), 2:304; MARCUS, Mark, 2:1034.

[328] Cf. DEMANDT, Pontius Pilatus, 153; SCHUOL, Augustus, 195–96, who points out that the first phase of Jesus' trial before Pilate in the *praetorium*, evidently held in closed session, was a *cognitio de plano*, corresponding to the fact that in Rome, *crimina laesae maiestatis* were not investigated not in public but in a trial before the emperor or the senate. The second phase was a *cognitio pro tribunali*, held in front of the people (ibid. 199–200).

[329] JUSTIN TAYLOR, The Roman Empire in the Acts of the Apostles, ANRW II.26.3 (1996): 2436–2500, 2462.

[330] JOHN GRANGER COOK, Crucifixion and Burial, NTS 57 (2011): 193–213, 199–203.

(lower-class) ... all speak against it."[331] COOK argues that he has not found any records of Roman trials in which a *peregrinus* was explicitly accused of *maiestas* by a magistrate, and suggests that Jesus was convicted by Pilatus on a charge of sedition (*seditio*) or troublemaking.[332] It should be noted that the various *leges* that addressed *maiestas* did not explicitly limit the crime to Roman citizens, that we have hardly any records for criminal offenses in the provinces, and that *seditio* could be classified as *maiestas*. COOK is certainly correct when he states that once Pilatus identified Jesus as a political criminal, "it is doubtful that he felt the need to consult juristic texts to justify execution."[333] E. HEUSLER, who investigates the trial account in the Gospel of Luke, argues that the crime Jesus was accused of by the Jewish authorities was *seditio*, which could be understood as *crimen (laesae) maiestatis* in the imperial period, that Jesus received a fair trial and that Pilatus deemed Jesus innocent but eventually gave in to the will of the Jewish people.[334] GUIDO KIRNER cautions that it is not clear that a provincial governor examining the alleged crime of a "foreigner" (*peregrinus*) needed to identify a specific criminal law for conviction.[335] A *peregrinus* "did not belong to the community of rights of the Roman citizens."[336] KIRNER argues that Jesus' waiver of a defense – by asserting that he indeed thinks that he is the king of the Jews, or by giving an ambiguous answer to Pilatus' question, or by silence – would have to be taken by Pilatus as a confession, in terms of a guilty plea; he would not have found it necessary to consult a *consilium* or imperative to formally announce his verdict: he sentenced Jesus to crucifixion as a *confessus* according to the principle *confessus pro iudicato est*.[337] M. SCHUOL hesitates, due to Pilatus' efforts to release Jesus: on the basis of the statement *confessus pro iudicato est*, Pilatus would have had no other option but accept the demand of Jesus' accusers who want a death sentence, had Jesus confessed that he claims to be king.[338] She allows that Jesus' refusal to make a statement in the *interrogatio* could be interpreted as recalcitrance or contumacy (*contumacia*) not only against the prefect but also against the emperor, whom the prefect

---

[331] JEAN-JACQUES AUBERT, A Double Standard in Roman Criminal Law? The Death Penalty and Social Structure in Late Republican and Early Imperial Rome, in Speculum Iuris: Roman Law as a Reflection of Social and Economic Life in Antiquity (ed. J. J. Aubert and B. Sirks; Ann Arbor: University of Michigan Press, 2002), 94–133, 122 n. 118.

[332] COOK, Crucifixion and Burial, 199, 202.

[333] COOK, Crucifixion and Burial, 202.

[334] Cf. HEUSLER, Kapitalprozesse, 202–3, 239–266 passim.

[335] KIRNER, Strafgewalt, 285 n. 133.

[336] GOTTFRIED SCHIEMANN, Peregrinus, BNP 10 (2007): 750–751.

[337] KIRNER, Strafgewalt, 269, 284–85. For Jesus' sentencing as *confessus* cf. WOLFGANG KUNKEL, Prinzipien des römischen Strafverfahrens [1968], in Kleine Schriften zum römischen Strafverfahren und zur römischen Verfassungsgeschichte (Weimar: Hermann Böhlaus Nachfolger, 1974), 1–31, 17–21.

[338] SCHUOL, Augustus, 193; the following point ibid.

represented. Cf. *Dig.* 11.1.11.4 (Ulpianus): *Qui tacuit quoque apud praeto-rem, in ea causa est, ut instituta actione in solidum conveniatur, quasi negaverit se heredem esse. nam qui omnino non respondit, contumax est: con-tumaciae autem poenam hanc ferre debet, ut in solidum conveniatur, quemad-modum si negasset, quia praetorem contemnere videtur* ("Also, if someone refuses to answer before the praetor, the position is that should an action be brought against him, he can be sued for the full amount, as though he had denied that he was heir; for he is held to display contempt for the praetor"); *Dig.* 42.1.53 (Hermogenianus): *Contumax est, qui tribus edictis propositis vel uno pro tribus, quod vulgo peremptorium appelatur, litteris evocatus praesentiam sui facere contemnet* ("A person is contumacious who, when three edicts are issued or one in lieu of three, which is called peremptory, and he has been summoned in writing, does not deign to enter an appearance"); *Dig.* 48.1.5 (Ulpianus): *Is qui reus factus est purgare se debet nec ante potest accuare, quam fuerit excusatus* ("Someone who has been charged must clear himself and cannot bring an accusation until he has been discharged").[339]

## 2.4 Reports of Trial Proceedings

The succinct account of Jesus' Roman trial in Mark 15:2–5 has been ex-plained with the help of Cicero, *Verr.* 18.55, a text where Cicero describes his prodecure in the trial proceedings against Gaius Verres, who ended up prema-turely ceding the case: Mark describes the official filing of the charges against Jesus by the high priest and the Jewish leaders (*accusatio, delatio nominis*), the registration of the name of the accused and of all relevant matters of the case (*inscriptio*), and the formal admission of the charges (*receptio nominis*) whereby the *delator* acquires the status of an accuser (*accusatio*).

Numerous papyri document trial proceedings. Since the evidence comes from Egypt, it is not always clear whether identical, similar, or very different practices and procedures were followed in Judea. In the papyri which contain copied reports of legal proceedings, the protocol is divided into four main sec-tions: the introductory formulae, the body of the trial, the judgment, and con-cluding matter. The majority of reports of legal proceedings in the papyri are private copies that have been made from the official court records; it should be noted that "these reports are not complete, since very likely only the por-tions directly interesting the person having the copy made would have been put down, but that they might be verbatim in so far as the utterances they con-tain could have been extracted as they stand without remodelling. This would presuppose the existence of much longer verbatim original records."[340] In

---

[339] SCHUOL, *Augustus*, 193, with n. 68.
[340] REVEL A. COLES, Reports of Proceedings in Papyri (Papyrologica Bruxellensia 4;

Egypt, the transition from recording trial proceedings in *oratio obliqua* to *oratio recta* seems to have been related to the political transition from Ptolemaic to Roman rule: the available evidence suggests that in Rome reports of trial proceedings adopted *oratio recta* subsequent to the development of a Latin shorthand system by the middle of the first century A.D. at the latest. The earliest indications of the use of shorthand in Rome date to the Catalinarian trial in 63 B.C. when Cicero was consul and evidently introduced ad hoc a rudimentary system, and to 50 B.C. by which time the Senate proceedings were recorded in *oratio recta*.[341] Seneca provides the first clear evidence that true shorthand was used to record the individual statements made in Senate meetings, which were subsequently drafted in *oratio recta* and thus reported verbatim: *quod in foro uiu(eb)at, dixit, quae notarius persequi non potuit et ideo non refero, ne aliis uerbis ponam quae ab illo dicta sunt* ("He [Janus] was living in the Forum and so spoke a lot glibly, which the shorthand secretary could not keep up with and which therefore I do not report, so as not to put in other words the things that were said by him;" Seneca, *Apocol.* 9.2).[342]

## (98) Cicero, *In Verrem* 1.18.55

Faciam hoc non novum, sed ab iis, qui nunc principes nostrae civitatis sunt, ante factum, ut testibus utar statim; illud a me novum, iudices, cognoscetis, quod ita testis constituam, ut crimen totum explicem; ut, ubi id [interrogando,] argumentis atque oratione firmavero, tum testes ad crimen accommodem, ut nihil inter illam usitatam accusationem atque hanc novam intersit, nisi quod in illa tum, cum omnia dicta sunt, testes dantur, hic in singulas res dabuntur, ut illis quoque eadem interrogandi facultas, argumentandi dicendique sit. Si quis erit, qui perpetuam orationem accusationemque desideret, altera actione audiet; nunc id, quod facimus, si ea ratione facimus, ut malitiae illorum consilio nostro occurramus, necessario fieri intellegat.

---

Bruxelles: Fondation égyptologique Reine Élisabeth, 1966), 16, quotation ibid. 16–17, with a discussion of P. Fam. Teb. 24 (A.D. 124).

[341] Cf. Plutarch, *Cat. Min.* 23; Cicero, *Sull.* 14.41–42; *Fam.* 8.11.4.

[342] Cf. PETER T. EDEN, Seneca. Apocolocyntosis (orig. 1984; repr., Cambridge Greek and Latin Classics; Cambridge: Cambridge University Press, 2002), 5. Seneca's *Apocolocyntosis* dates to A.D. 54. The text and translation follows EDEN, ibid. 44–45, who comments on the word *notarius*: "a word first occurring here, = 'stenographer', using a system of shorthand developed from the *notae Tironianae* of Cicero's secretary Tiro" (ibid. 109). The earliest text in Greek shorthand is *P. Brem.* 82 which dates to the time of Trajan or Hadrian; the earliest dated documentary reference to shorthand appears in *P. Oxy.* IV 724, a contract of apprenticeship to a shorthand writer dated A.D. 155; cf. HERBERT J. M. MILNE, Greek Shorthand Manuals: Syllabary and Commentary (London: Egypt Exploration Society, 1934), 1–2; COLES, Reports of Proceedings, 15. For a discussion of the use of shorthand in connection with Paul's letter writing cf. E. RANDOLPH RICHARDS, The Secretary in the Letters of Paul (WUNT 2/42; Tübingen: Mohr Siebeck, 1991), 26–43.

*Translation.* I will not use a new procedure, but I will do what those have done earlier who are now the leading men in our state: I will immediately call the witnesses. Judges, you will notice *one* novelty in my procedure: I shall call the witnesses in such a manner that I can present the prosecution point by point. When I have described a charge with arguments and comments, I shall call the witnesses relevant for that particular charge. Thus there is only one difference between the usual method of prosecution and this new one: in the former the witnesses are not called until the entire material has been presented in speeches, whereas in the latter they will be called as each new charge is introduced, with the proviso that the other side will have the same opportunity to ask questions, draw conclusions, and make comments. If somebody misses an uninterrupted speech of the prosecution: he will get it in the second hearing; he shall understand that our present procedure, which aims at preventing the perfidy of the opponents (of delaying the trial), comes from pure necessity.

*Commentary.*[343] While governor of Sicily between 73–71 B.C., Gaius Verres embezzled public funds, appropriated Greek works of art, and forced landowners to pay large sums in default of the grain levy. Cicero, who had been elected aedil in 70 B.C. and who was the Sicilians' patron, prosecuted Verres for extortion, charging that he had engaged in malicious and greedy policies and legal proceedings directed against Sicilian dignitaries, that he had corruptly raised taxes, that he extorted works of art, and that he had killed Roman citizens.[344] In late July, members of the senate were chosen by lot to sit as judges in the trial, of which Verres rejected six and Cicero one. Verres was represented by Q. Hortensius Hortalus, P. Cornelius Scipio Nasica, and L. Cornelius Sisenna. Cicero prosecuted the case by himself, perhaps aided by his nephew Lucius. The president of the court, which may have consisted of twenty members, was M. Acilius Glabrio, the praetor responsible for extortion

---

[343] Text: MÜLLER, M. Tullii Ciceronis scripta quae manserunt omnia, II.1 (ALFRED KLOTZ); for other editions and translations cf. WILLIAM PETERSON, M. Tulli Ciceronis Orationes III. Divinatio in Q. Caecilium. In Verrem (Editio altera recognita et emendata; orig. 1917; repr., Oxford Classical Texts; Oxford: Oxford University Press, 1993); LEONARD H. G. GREENWOOD, Marcus Tullus Cicero. The Verrine Orations (LCL. 2 vols.; orig. 1928; repr., London: Heinemann, 1988); HENRI DE LA VILLE DE MIRMONT, Cicéron. Discours. Tome II: Pour M. Tullius, Discours contre Q. Caecilius, dit 'la divination', Première action contre C. Verrès, Seconde action contre C. Verrès. Livre premier, La préture urbaine (Collection des universités de France; Paris: Belles Lettres, 1922); FUHRMANN, Cicero: Sämtliche Reden, 3:77–100; MANFRED FUHRMANN, Marcus Tullius Cicero. Die Reden gegen Verres. In C. Verrem (Lateinisch – deutsch. Sammlung Tusculum; Zürich: Artemis & Winkler, 1995).

[344] On the provincial governors in republican Rome, cf. RAIMUND SCHULZ, Herrschaft und Regierung. Roms Regiment in den Provinzen in der Zeit der Republik (Paderborn: Schöningh, 1997). On Cicero, Sicily, and Verres, cf. JULIEN DUBOULOZ and SYLVIE PITTIa, eds., La Sicilie de Cicéron. Lectures des Verrines (Presses universitaires de Franche-Comté: Besançon, 2007).

cases.[345] In view of the fact that some members of the jury had been newly elected to various offices and would have to be replaced in the new year, Hortenius wanted to delay the trial. Cicero's first speech, which opened the trial proceedings against Verres, was delivered in the afternoon of August 5, 70 B.C. In view of the abundance of witnesses and evidence, Verres prematurely ceded the case and went into exile – the five speeches of the *actio secunda* (*Verr.* 2.1–5) were never delivered.[346] At the end of the *prima actio*, Cicero explains that he wants to follow a novel procedure: rather than beginning with a long continuous speech presenting his case (first *actio*), he will immediately present his evidence and his witnesses.[347]

A. STROBEL refers to *Verr.* 1.18.55 in his discussion of the extremely succinct account of the Roman trial in Mark 15:2–5: the text describes the official filing of the charges against Jesus by the high priest and the Jewish leaders, i.e., the *accusatio* and the *delatio nominis*.[348] The name of the accused, together with all relevant matters concerning the accused and the alleged crime, was registered with the authorities (*inscriptio*), which seems in view in Mark 15:1. In the judicial criminal proceeding of the *cognitio extra ordinem* in which a government official dealt with the entire trial, the *accusatio* was "the sum total of the private share in the course of procedure [sic]."[349] The Jewish leaders, acting as representatives of the Sanhedrin of Jerusalem, i.e. the highest Jewish court, accused Jesus before the Roman prefect of claiming to be the "King of the Jews" (cf. Mark 15:2). The *delatio nominis* constituted an official procedure: accusers formally report a criminal act to a Roman official (*inscriptio*) by indicating the name of the suspect; the official has to formally admit the charges (*receptio nominis*) before a trial can take place, whereby the *delator* acquires the status of an accuser (*accusatio*).[350]

---

[345] Cf. FUHRMANN, Cicero. Die Reden gegen Verres,1:462–73.

[346] JENS BARTELS, Verres, C., BNP 15 (2010): 321–323. Cf. SHANE BUTLER, Hand of Cicero (London: Routledge, 2002). For a rhetorical analysis of the *actio secunda* cf. THOMAS D. FRAZEL, The Rhetoric of Cicero's "In Verrem" (Hypomnemata 179; Göttingen: Vandenhoeck & Ruprecht, 2009).

[347] Cf. ULRIKE STECK, Der Zeugenbeweis in den Gerichtsreden Ciceros (EHS 2/4839; Frankfurt: Lang, 2009), on witness evidence in Cicero's juridical speeches.

[348] STROBEL, Stunde, 96–97, with reference to MOMMSEN, Strafrecht, 381ff; DOERR, Prozeß, 52, who comments: "Ein zusammenhängender Vortrag konnte unterbleiben und die Beweis-führung auf die einzelnen Klagepunkte gestellt werden" (Cicero, *Verr.* 1.18.55; Tacitus, *Ann.* 2.30; Suetonius, *Nero* 15). For the following point STROBEL, ibid. 97.

[349] GOTTFRIED SCHIEMANN, Accusatio, BNP 1 (2002): 65; cf. KUNKEL, Quaestio, 74–78. On *cognitio extra ordinem* cf. MAX KASER, Das römische Zivilprozeßrecht (Zweite Auflage, neu bearbeitet von K. Hackl; orig. 1966; repr., HdA X/3,4; München: Beck, 1996), 435–514.

[350] Cf. GOTTFRIED SCHIEMANN, Delatio nominis, BNP 4 (2004): 199.

**(99)** P. Oxy. I 37

I

ἐξ ὑπομ[ν]ηματισμῶν Τι[βερίο]υ Κλαυδ[ίο]υ Πασίωνος στρατη(γοῦ).
(ἔτους) ἐνάτ[ο]υ Τιβερίου Κλαυδίου Καίσαρος Σεβαστοῦ Γερμανικοῦ
Αὐτοκ[ρά]τορος, Φαρμοῦθι γ, ἐπὶ τοῦ βήματος,
[Π]εσοῦρι[ς] πρὸς Σαραεῦν. Ἀριστοκλῆς ῥήτωρ
5 ὑπὲρ Πεσούριος· Πεσοῦρις, ὑπὲρ οὗ λέγω, ζ (ἔτους)
Τιβερίου Κλαυδίου Καίσαρος τοῦ κυρίου ἀνεῖλεν
ἀπὸ κοπρίας ἀρρενικὸν σωμάτιον ὄνομα Ἡρα-
κ[λᾶν]. τοῦτο ἐνεχείρισεν τῆι ἀντιδίκωι· ἐγένετο ἐνθάδε ἡ τροφῖτις εἰς υἱὸν τοῦ Πεσούριος.
10 τοῦ πρώτου ἐνιαυτοῦ ἀπέλαβεν τὰ τροφεῖα.
ἐνέστη ἡ προθεσμία τοῦ δευτέρου ἐνιαυτοῦ,
κα[ὶ] πάλιν ἀπέλαβεν. ὅτι δὲ ταῦτα ἀληθῆ λέγω,
ἔστιν γράμματα αὐτῆς δι’ ὧν ὁμολογεῖ εἰληφέναι. λιμαγχουμένου τοῦ σωματ[ί]ου ἀπέ-
15 σπασεν ὁ Πεσοῦρις. μετ[ὰ] ταῦτα καιρὸν εὑροῦσ[α]
εἰσεπήδησεν εἰς τὴν τοῦ ἡμετέρου [ο]ἰκίαν
καὶ τὸ σωμάτιον ἀφήρπασεν, καὶ βούλεται ὀν[ό]-
ματι ἐλευθέρου τὸ σωμάτιον ἀπενέγκασ-
θαι. ἔχω πρῶτον γράμμα τῆς τροφίτιδος,
20 ἔχω δεύτερο[ν] τῶν τροφείων τὴν [ἀ]ποχή[ν.]
ἀξιῶ ταῦ[τα] φυλαχθῆ[ν]αι. Σα[ρα]εῦς·
ἀπεγαλάκ[τισά] μου τὸ [π]αιδίον, κα[ὶ] τούτων
σωμάτιόν μοι ἐνεχειρίσθη. ἔλαβ[ον] παρ’ αὐτῶν τοὺ[ς] πάντας ὀκτὼ στατῆρας. μετὰ
25 ταῦτα [ἐτελεύ]τησεν τ[ὸ σ]ωμάτιο[ν ca.? στα]-
τήρων [μοι περ]ιόντων. νῦν βούλον[ται τὸ]

II

ἴ[δι]όν μου τέκνον ἀποσπάσαι. Θέων·
γράμματα τοῦ σωματίου ἔχομεν.
ὁ στρατηγός· ἐπεὶ ἐκ τῆς ὄψεως φαίνεται τῆς
30 Σαραεῦτος εἶναι τὸ παιδίον, ἐὰν χειρογραφήσῃ
αὐτή τε καὶ ὁ ἀνὴρ αὐτῆς ἐκεῖνο τὸ ἐνχει-
ρισθὲν αὐτῆι σωμάτιον ὑπὸ τοῦ Πεσούριος
τετελευτηκέναι, φαίνεταί μοι κατὰ τὰ ὑπὸ
τοῦ κυρίου ἡγεμόνος κριθέντα ἀποδοῦσαν
35 αὐτὴν ὃ εἴληφεν ἀργύριον ἔχειν τὸ [ἴδιο]ν
τέκνον.

*Translation.* From the records of the strategos Tiberius Claudius Pasion. The 9th year of the emperor Tiberius Claudius Caesar Augustus Germanicus Imperator, Pharmouthi 3, before the court. Pesouris against Saraeus. Aristokles, the advocate for Pesouris, said, "Pesouris, for whom I am speaking, picked up from the dung-heap a male infant named Heraklas in the 7th year of our sovereign Tiberius Claudius Caesar. He turned the infant over to the defendant. In this court a contract-arrangement was made for the nursing of the son of Pesouris. She received her wages for the first year when they became due. She also received them for the second year. To prove my assertions, there are the receipts in which she acknowledges that she received them. As the infant was being starved, Pesouris took him away. Afterwards, finding an opportunity, Saraeus burst into our house and carried off the infant and now wants to take him on the ground that he was free-born. I have here, first, the document of the contract with the nurse. I have here, second, the receipt of the nurse's wages. I demand their recognition.[351] Saraeus: "I weaned my own child, and the infant belonging to these people was placed in my charge. I received from them (my full wages of) eight staters. Later the infant died and I was left with the staters. Now they want to take away my own child." Theon: "We have the documents relating to the infant." The strategos: "Since in appearance the child appears to be that of Saraeus, if she and her husband will make a written declaration that the infant entrusted to her by Perouris died, I give judgment in accordance with the decision of our lord the prefect that she receive her own child when she pays back the money she has received."

*Commentary.*[352] This text, which dates to 29 March A.D. 49, is an abridged copy of the transcript of a trial, with the strategos Tiberius Claudius Pasion as the presiding judge. A woman named Pesouris initiated a lawsuit against a nurse Saraeus whom she accuses of baby-snatching. Pesouris had found a male infant on a dung-heap. Pesouris claims that after she had entrusted the boy to the nurse Saraeus and arranged for payment, she discovered that the nurse had let the boy starve, and so she took the boy back, who was then snatched by Saraeus from her house. The defense claims that the foundling

---

[351] TIM G. PARKIN / ARTHUR J. POMEROY, eds., Roman Social History: A Sourcebook (Routledge Sourcebooks for the Ancient World; London: Routledge, 2007), 305, translates ἀξιῶ ταῦτα φυλαχθῆναι as "I ask that the terms of the contract be enforced;" cf. JANE ROWLANDSON, ed., Women and Society in Greek and Roman Egypt: A Sourcebook (Cambridge: Cambridge University Press, 1998), 117: "I ask that these contractual agreements be safeguarded;" differently ALEXANDRA TRACHSEL in PAUL SCHUBERT, Vivre en Égypte gréco-romaine. Une sélection de papyrus (Chant du monde; Vevey: Aire, 2000), 55: "Je réclame que l'on conserve ces documents."

[352] P. Oxy. I 37; cf. ULRICH WILCKEN / LUDWIG MITTEIS, Grundzüge und Chrestomathie der Papyruskunde (Berlin: Teubner, 1912), No. 79; ORSOLINA MONTEVECCHI / MARIADELE MANCA MASCIADRI, Corpus Papyrorum Graecarum I: I Contratti di baliatico (Milan: Tibiletti, 1984), No. 19.

had died and that the infant away by Pesouris was Saraeus' own child. The strategos decides for the defense, arguing that the boy looks like his mother: Saraeus shall receive the boy back upon refunding the wages that she received as a nurse.

This papyrus is the earliest dated example of trial proceedings in *oratio recta*.[353] The introductory formula has five parts: (1) the "extract" phrase (ἐξ ὑπομ[ν]ηματισμῶν + gen.); (2) the names and title of the presiding official (formula ἐπὶ τοῦ βήματος; line three) from whose minutes the protocol was copied; (3) the date; (4) the location; (5) the names of the parties in the case (formula "A πρός B"). In the body of the trial report, the parties are given one name each (here without descriptive details, as in later protocols). The rhetor who speaks for the plaintiff and who opens the proceedings is specified (ῥήτωρ ὑπέρ + name). The presiding official is not called by name but introduced, as speaker, simply as ὁ στρατηγός (line 29). The judgment (κρίσις) is expressed in *oratio recta* after the introduction of ὁ στρατηγός as speaker.

Since Jesus stood before Pontius Pilatus as a *peregrinus*, in a case requiring urgent treatment, held on the spot out of the regular order (*extra ordinem*), with no possibility of appeal against the Roman prefect whose *imperium* to inflict punishment on non-Roman citizens was unfettered, the prefect may not have insisted on keeping trial records. On the other hand, given Jesus' significance which the high priest's and the Jerusalem Sanhedrin's initiative underline, Pilatus might have insisted on records.

## 2.5 Languages Used in Provincial Court Proceedings

New Testament scholars seem to assume that the Roman trial of Jesus was conducted in Greek. The assumption that the Sadducean leaders of the Sanhedrin, in particular the leading families who supplied the high priests during this period, spoke Greek, is plausible. Whether a Roman official composed official documents in Greek or in Latin was "a personal decision, conditioned by such factors as his origins, his upbringing, his attitude toward Hellenic culture and the degree of his competence in its language."[354] It can be assumed

---

[353] COLES, Reports of Proceedings, 9; for the following ibid. 29–31, 38–40, 50.

[354] NAPHTALI LEWIS, The Process of Promulgation in Rome's Eastern Provinces, in Studies in Roman Law in Memory of A. Arthur Schiller (ed. R. S. Bagnall and W. V. Harris; CSCT 13; Leiden: Brill, 1986), 127–139, 128 (= LEWIS, On Government and Law, 315–127, 316). He discusses P. Yale II 175 (= P. Coll. Youtie I 30 = SB XIV 12144), a letter addressed by the prefect of Egypt in A.D. 198/199, Q. Aemilius Saturninus, to the strategoi of some of the nomes in Egypt, and argues that "the original version of this letter issued from Saturninus' lips or pen in Latin" – the Greek of the letter "reeks of Latin terminology and idiom" (ibid. 136). Cf. A. ARTHUR SCHILLER, Legal Commentary, in Apokrimata: Decisions of Septimius Severus on Legal Matters (New York: Columbia University Press, 1954), 35–101, 39–42, 47,

that most Romans who wanted to be active in the administration of the empire learnt Greek and were able to speak it satisfactorily, if not always fluently.[355] When L. Aemilius Paullus, after the battle at Pydna in 168 B.C., proclaims to the Macedonians his political decisions, he did this in Latin and asked the praetor Cn. Octavius to repeat the explanations in Greek (Livius 45.29). Cicero was utterly conversant in Greek and would have spoken Greek as governor of the province of Cilicia (51 B.C.).[356] Arrianus of Nicomedia, proconsul of Baetica in the 2nd century A.D., wrote a poem honoring Artemis in Greek and had it published on a stone set up in Cordoba.[357] The texts in this section illustrate the switch between Greek and Latin in court proceedings before Roman officials in the provinces, and the use of translators for local people who understood neither Greek nor Latin. While the available evidence from the papyri comes from Egypt, it seems plausible to assume that the situation in Roman Judea was not much different.

**(100)** P. Oxy. LI 3619 Frag. 2, 23–26

] . ζ ...... αι ὑμεῖς οἱ βουλευταὶ πῶς ἐπράθη ὁ σῖτος. *Apollonius ex* [
] . *um.* (vac.) *quo uexato*          (vac.)
] . κων ἐξετάζω. ἐγχωρεῖ γὰρ το[ὺς] β[ο]υλευτὰς ψεύδεσθαι. *r(espondit).*
    τριάκοντα [
        ] ... *r(espondit).* ναί. (vac.) [          ] (vac.)

*Translation.* You councillors (must?) be investigated[358] on the manner of the sale of the grain ... Apollonius ... When he had been beaten ... I am enquiring (from the country folk?), for it is possible that the councillors are lying. He responded. Thirty ... He responded, Yes ...

*Commentary.* This fragmentary record of a transcript of the legal proceedings before the *praeses* of the (short-lived) province of Aegyptus Iouia, dated c. A.D. 314–325, illustrates the fact that when representatives of Roman power met provincials, multiple languages were sometimes used. In this case, the hearing was conducted in Greek. At several points the official switched to Latin. In Frag. 1, the beginnings of the extant seventeen lines introduce

---

who argues that P. Col. VI 123 confirms the view that "subscripts posted in Egypt and promulgated in the Greek language were actually translations from Latin."

[355] W. ECK, in a personal communication.

[356] For Cicero's use of Greek cf. SIMON SWAIN, Bilingualism in Cicero? The Evidence of Code-Switching, in Bilingualism in Ancient Society: Language Contact and the Written Text (ed. J. N. Adams, M. Janse, and S. Swain; Oxford: Oxford University Press, 2002), 128–167.

[357] SEG XXVI 1215; cf. SEG LVII 990.

[358] JOHN R. REA, The Oxyrhynchus Papyri. Volume LI (Graeco-Roman Memoirs No. 71; London: Egypt Exploration Society, 1985), 51, restores ἐπι]ζητεῖσθαι; the translation follows REA.

speeches of the *praeses* who is always mentioned with his name and Latin title: *Isidorus u(ir) p(erfectissimus) praes(es) Aeg(ypti) Ioui[a]e*. The probably mostly short questions of the *praeses* are introduced by *d(ixit)*, the short answers from other parties are introduced by *r(espondit)*; the papyrus fragment preserves only the left side of the column introducing the *praeses*, whose questions are not preserved; the answers of the other parties which were originally recorded on the same (long) lines are lost as well.

One of the most common situations in which Roman officials gave instructions to court personnel in Latin involved orders to beat one of the participants in order to elicit information.[359] In this particular case, "the *praeses* spoke here to his staff in Latin, saying something like *uexa] eum*," i.e., "beat him," which is followed by the confirmation "when he had been beaten" (*quo uexato*).[360] The code-switching into Latin can be understood as emphasizing the power of the judge; if the participants did not understand Latin, it would probably have been perceived as threatening.[361]

**(101)** P. Lips. I 40, Col. III, 20–25

*Fl. Leontius Beronician(us) v. c. pr. Tebaei(dis) d(ixit)*: τίνος ἕνεκεν ἐπῆλθες τῷ βουλευτῇ; *Et ad officium d(ixit)*: τυπτέσθω. *Et cumque buneuris caesus fuisset,*

*Fl. Leontius Beronicianus v. c. pr. Tebaei(dis) d(ixit)*: ἐλευθέρους μὴ τύπτητε. *Et ad officium d(ixit): parce. Cumque pepertum ei fuisset,*

*Fl. Leontius Beronician(us) v. c. pr. Tebaei(dis) d(ixit)*: εἰπὲ ποῦ ἐστιν τὸ χρυσίον ὕπερ ἥρπασας. *Acholius d(ixit):* τὸ ἱμάτιον αὐτοῦ ἀπεδύσατο καὶ δέδωκεν [τῇ] γυναικὶ τῇ ἀκολουθούσῃ αὐτῷ. οὐκ εἶ[δον].

*Fl. Leontius Beronician(us) v. c. pr. Tebaei(dis) d(ixit)* διέλεγξον αὐτὸν ὅτι χρυσίον σου ἄφείλατο. *Filammon d(ixit):* ἀπὸ τῆς μάχης ἔλυσεν ἀπὸ [τ]ῆς χειρίδος τοῦ υἱοῦ μ[ου] καὶ ἥρπασεν, εἷς ἐκράτησεν αὐτὸν κα[ὶ] ὁμολογεῖ ὅτι Γορ[γ]όνιος ἔδησεν αὐτοῦ τὰς χεῖρας. *Herminu(s) ad(vocatus) d(ixit):* ἀξιοῦμεν ἄλλους τοὺς συνεργήσαντας αὐτῷ οἰκέτας παρεῖναι. *Filammon d(ixit)*: Στεργόρ(γ)ιος τὴν κεφαλὴν αὐτοῦ ἐκροτάφισεν.

*Senecion d(ixit):* καταθῆται εἰ αὐτὸς μόνος ἦν ἢ ἄλλοι μετ᾽ αὐτοῦ, ἵνα ἀσφαλὲς ἡμῖν γένηται, ἵνα ὁ σκρίβας ἔλθῃ καὶ εἴπῃ.

---

[359] COLES, Reports of Proceedings, 48.

[360] REA, Oxyrhynchus Papyri LI, 51-52 on line 24; cf. JAMES N. ADAMS, Bilingualism and the Latin Language (Cambridge: Cambridge University Press, 2003), 384-85.

[361] ADAMS, Bilingualism, 384–85, followed by CHRISTINA M. KREINECKER, How Power and Province Communicate: Some Remarks on the Language of the (Non-)Conversation between Pilate and Jesus, in Light from the East: Papyrologische Kommentare zum Neuen Testament (ed. P. Arzt-Grabner and C. M. Kreinecker; Philippika 39; Wiesbaden: Harrassowitz, 2010), 169–185, 179–80.

*Translation.* Flavius Leontius Beronicianus, *vir clarissimus, praeses* of the Thebais, said, 'Why did you attack the counselor?' And he said to the staff, 'He shall be beaten.' And after he had been beaten with straps, Flavius Leontius Beronicianus, *vir clarissimus, praeses* of the Thebais, said, 'You shall not beat freemen.' And he said to the staff, 'Spare him!' And after he had been spared, Flavius Leontius Beronicianus, *vir clarissimus, praeses* of the Thebais, said, 'Say where is the money that you have stolen!' Acholios said, 'He stripped off his garment and gave it to the woman who followed him; I did not see it.' Flavius Leontius Beronicianus, *vir clarissimus, praeses* of the Thebais, said, 'Proof to him hat he took you money.' Philammon said, 'He took it out of the bag of my son during the fight and stole it; one held him, and he admits that Gorgonios bound his hands.' The lawyer Herminus said, 'We request that the other slaves who were involved are summoned. Philamon said, 'Stergorius hit his head.' Senecios said, 'He shall make a deposition whether he was alone or whether others were with him, so that we may have certainty, so that the secretary may come and make a statement.'

*Commentary.*[362] The legal proceedings recorded in this papyrus concern a certain Asynkritios, son of Philammon, who was attacked at night, beaten, and robbed. The main suspect is the slave Acholios; the other persons who were involved were able to get away. A certain Hermaion witnesses the attack; there was evidently also a break-in nearby. The speeches during the trial, which are largely in Greek, are introduced in Latin. Flavius Leontius Beronicianus, the presiding judge, addresses his staff in both Greek and Latin; his order to administer the beating is in Greek (τυπτέσθω) and the order to stop the beating is in Latin (*parce*). The switch into the language of the imperial power expressed the solidarity of the imperial power in the non-Latin speaking society of Roman Egypt; it created an element of uncertainty, it rendered the Roman official aloof from the participants who are allowed to use Greek, and "would have effectively symbolized the Romanness of that power, and it have left no doubt that this was a Roman hearing, whatever linguistic accommodation had been made to the Greek-speaking participants."[363]

*Language in court proceedings before Roman courts in Judea.* As Judea had been under direct Roman control since A.D. 6, that is twenty-four years by A.D. 30, it is plausible to assume that some members of the Jewish élite, in particular those who maintained regular contact with the Roman authorities, had learned enough Latin to be able to communicate in the language of the domi-

---

[362] For text, German translation, and discussion cf. ULRICH WILCKEN / LUDWIG MITTEIS, eds., Griechische Urkunden der Papyrussammlung zu Leipzig. Erster Band (APVG 10; Leipzig: Teubner, 1906); WILCKEN / MITTEIS, Griechische Urkunden, 127–37. The papyrus is dated before A.D. 381.

[363] ADAMS, Bilingualism, 386; cf. KREINECKER, Power, 180.

nant political power – at least on "level two bilingualism" which involves people (immigrants, natives) learning the language of the élite well enough in order to fit into the relevant social and economic contexts.[364] It can be assumed that when Jewish leaders presented documents before the Roman governor in a legal case, the relevant documents had to be written in Greek, perhaps in Latin. In Ptolemaic Egypt, when Egyptians appeared before a Greek court, "the royal judges or *chrematistai* or local officials, Demotic no longer suffices. They have to write a petition in Greek, their title deeds have to be translated into Greek, and they have to show in Greek that the taxes have been duly paid."[365] In Roman Egypt, the use of Latin documentation was "at best marginal" in most areas of private law, with the exception of the wills of Roman citizens which had to be written in Latin.[366] In court trials in Graeco-Roman Egypt, declarations of members of the local population often needed translation by official interpreters (P. Oxy. II 237; cf. No. 74).[367]

---

[364] CHARLOTTE HOFFMANN, An Introduction to Bilingualism (Longman Linguistics Library; London: Longman, 1991), 16–17. Cf. HORSLEY and LLEWELYN, New Documents, 5:6–26, with a discussion of the situation in Palestine. On the evidence for Latin in first century Palestine cf. ALAN R. MILLARD, Latin in First-Century Palestine, in Solving Riddles and Untying Knots: Biblical, Epigraphic and Semitic Studies (FS J. C. Greenfield; ed. Z. Zevit, S. Gitin, and M. Sokoloff; Winona Lake: Eisenbrauns, 1995), 451–458; ECK, Rom und Judaea, 157–200; WERNER ECK, Presence, Role, and Significance of Latin in the Epigraphy and Culture of the Roman Near East, in From Hellenism to Islam: Cultural and Linguistic Change in the Roman Near East (ed. H. M. Cotton, et al.; Cambridge: Cambridge University Press, 2009), 15–42. On the knowledge of Latin by non-native Latin speakers in the ancient world see BRUNO ROCHETTE, Le latin dans le monde grec. Recherches sur la diffusion de la langue et des lettres latines dans les provinces hellenophones de l'Empire romain (Collection Latomus 233; Bruxelles: Latomus, 1997).

[365] WILLY CLARYSSE, "Bilingual Papyrological Archives," in The Multilingual Experience in Egypt, from the Ptolemies to the Abbasids (ed. A. Papaconstantinou; Farnham: Ashgate, 2010), 47–72, here 71.

[366] YIFTACH-FIRANKO, Law in Greco-Roman Egypt, 553. For the use of Latin in Egypt see ADAMS, Bilingualism, 527–641. For the importance of archives cf. CLAUDE NICOLET, ed., La mémoire perdue. A la recherche des archives oubliées, publiques et privées, de la Rome antique (Paris: Sorbonne, 1994); for Egypt in the context of food distribution cf. JEAN-MICHEL CARRIÉ, "Archives municipales et distributions alimentaires dans l'Égypte romaine," in La mémoire perdue. Recherches sur l'administration Romaine (ed. C. Moatti; CEFR 243; Rome: École française de Rome, Palais Farnèse, 1998), 271–302.

[367] SOFÍA TORALLAS TOVAR, Linguistic Identity in Graeco-Roman Egypt, in The Multilingual Experience in Egypt, from the Ptolemies to the Abbasids (ed. A. Papaconstantinou; Farnham: Ashgate, 2010), 17–43, 30. For bilingual record-keeping and archives cf. CLARYSSE, "Bilingual Papyrological Archives,". For interpreters mentioned in papyri and literary sources cf. JACQUES SCHWARTZ, Traductions en Égypte gréco-romaine, in Mélanges Pierre Lévêque. Vol. 2, Anthropologie et Société (ed. M. M. Mactoux and E. Geny; Annales littéraires de l'Université de Besançon 82; Paris: Belles lettres, 1989), 379–386; BRUNO ROCHETTE, Traducteurs et traductions dans l'Egypte greco-romaine, Chronique d'Égypte 69 (1994): 313–322; PETER ROBERT FRANKE, Dolmetschen in hellenistischer Zeit, in Zum Umgang mit Fremdsprachlichkeit in der griechisch-römischen Antike (ed. Carl Werner Müller, Kurt Sier, and Jürgen Werner; Palingenesia 36; Stuttgart: Steiner, 1992), 85–96.

Professional translators (ἑρμηνεύς, lat. *interpres*) were used in particular in political and administrative contexts, both in oral and written communication. The use of an interpreter "did not necessarily indicate a deficiency in one's own bilingual ability or the inability to speak for oneself. It could also signal an attitude or an obligation, as was the case with Roman magistrates in the exercise of their official function."[368] Rome did not impose its language on its provinces, with the exception of the cities, colonies, and municipia organized by the Romans.[369]

Roman governors and prefects were not necessarily bilingual. The code-switching from Latin to Greek, e.g. by Cicero, does not constitute evidence "to prove that any educated Roman did regularly hold conversations in Greek with or write letters in Greek to his fellow Romans."[370] Depending on how well Romans spoke Greek, they were called *Graeci, semigraeci* (half-Greeks), or *Graeculi* (pseudo-Greeks).[371] Greek was the second language of the Roman administration in Judea.[372] In a papyrus from A.D. 152, written in Caesarea but discovered in Egypt, Aelius Amphigetes, an imperial freedman who had responsibilities in the financial administration of the province as *procurator*, uses Greek in the announcement of a legal decision.[373]

If Pontius Pilatus in fact spoke Greek, the interaction between the Jewish leaders and the Roman prefect would have been conducted in Greek, since by the first century the Jewish élite spoke Greek. This is the more likely scenario preferable to the assumption that the Jewish leaders were more or less fluent Latin. The bilingual transcripts of legal hearings from Egypt demonstrate that while the Roman administration allowed the use of the Greek language in hearings "as a form of pragmatically determined accommodation," occasional

---

[368] FRÉDÉRIQUE BIVILLE, Graeco-Romans and Graeco-Latin: A Terminological Framework for Cases of Bilingualism, in Bilingualism in Ancient Society: Language Contact and the Written Text (ed. J. N. Adams, M. Janse, and S. Swain; Oxford: Oxford University Press, 2002), 77–102, 85.

[369] WERNER ECK, Latein als Sprache politischer Kommunikation in den Städten der östlichen Provinzen, Chiron 30 (2000): 641–660, 641. Cf. WERNER ECK, Ein Spiegel der Macht: Lateinische Inschriften römischer Zeit in Iudaea/Syria Palaestina, ZDPV 117 (2000): 47–63; WERNER ECK, The Language of Power: Latin in the Inscriptions of Iudaea / Syria Palaestina, in Semitic Papyrology in Context: A Climate of Creativity (ed. L. A. Schiffman; CHANE 14; Brill: Leiden, 2003), 123–144

[370] Cf. SWAIN, Bilingualism in Cicero, 147. Cicero's use of Greek in his letters is evidence for his strategy of code-switching *in his Latin*, but "it is not possible to estimate Romans' fluency in Greek from this, for a high degree of bilingualism is not necessary to access the identity set which code-switched language advertises" (ibid. 167).

[371] BIVILLE, Graeco-Romans and Graeco-Latin, 90–91.

[372] ECK, Rom und Judaea, 161.

[373] P. Berol. 21652 (SB XII 11043); JOHN REA, Two Legates and a Procurator of Syria Palaestina, ZPE 26 (1977): 217–222; WERNER ECK, Ein Prokuratorenpaar von Syria Palaestina in P. Berol. 21652 [1998], in Judäa – Syria Palästina. Die Auseinandersetzung einer Provinz mit römischer Politik und Kultur (TSAJ 157; Tübingen: Mohr Siebeck, 2014), 266–274.

code-switching into Latin reminded participants "that there were an outside power."[374]

## 2.6 Amnesty and Acclamatio Populi

According to John 18:39, Pilatus referred to an amnesty of prisoners granted on the occasion of the Passover Festival, referred to as *privilegium paschale*: ἔστιν δὲ συνήθεια ὑμῖν ἵνα ἕνα ἀπολύσω ὑμῖν ἐν τῷ πάσχα· βούλεσθε οὖν ἀπολύσω ὑμῖν τὸν βασιλέα τῶν Ἰουδαίων; ("But you have a custom that I release someone for you at the Passover; do you want me to release for you the King of the Jews?" (cf. Mark 15:6: "Now he used to release a prisoner for them at the festival whom they requested").[375] The existence of a Passover amnesty has been disputed since J. MERKEL.[376] While some scholars question the historicity of the *privilegium paschale*,[377] others accept the possibility that Pilatus offered pardons on the occasion of the Passover Festival.[378] The texts in this section are relevant for the discussion.

---

[374] ADAMS, Bilingualism, 561; for examples see ibid. 383–90.

[375] Also Matt 27:15, and Luke 23:17 in ℵ D W θ Ψ Maj.

[376] JOHANNES MERKEL, Die Begnadigung am Passahfeste, ZNW 6 (1905): 293–316. Cf. BLINZLER, Prozeß, 301–20; STROBEL, Stunde, 118–24; ROBERT L. MERRITT, Jesus Barabbas and the Paschal Pardon, JBL 104 (1985): 57–68; BROWN, Death, 1:814–20. LUDWIG MITTEIS, Reichsrecht und Volksrecht in den östlichen Provinzen des Römischen Kaiserreichs (orig. 1891; repr., Leipzig: Teubner, 1935), 90, accepted it as historical evidence for the "Schonung der Stammeseigenthümlichkeiten" by the Romans in the provinces.

[377] In addition to R. E. BROWN, cf. ROGER DAVID AUS, The Release of Barabbas (Mark 15.6–15 par; John 18.39–40) and Judaic Traditions on the Book of Esther, in Barabbas and Esther and Other Studies in the Judaic Illumination of Earliest Christianity (SFSHJ 54; Atlanta: Scholars Press, 1992), 1–27; WINTER, Trial, 134; SIMON LÉGASSE, Le Procès de Jésus. I L'histoire. II La passion dans les quatre évangiles (LD 156; Paris: Cerf, 1994/1995), 109–10; GNILKA, Markus, 2:304; CHRISTOF NIEMAND, Jesus und sein Weg zum Kreuz. Ein historisch-rekonstruktives und theologisches Modellbild (Stuttgart: Kohlhammer, 2007), 423.

[378] In addition to J. BLINZLER, R. L. MERRITT, and A. STROBEL, cf. PESCH, Markusevangelium, 2:462; GUNDRY, Mark, 935; WILLIAM D. DAVIES / DALE C. ALLISON, The Gospel According to Saint Matthew (ICC; Edinburgh: T & T Clark, 1988–1997), 3:583; CRAIG S. KEENER, A Commentary on the Gospel of Matthew (Grand Rapids: Eerdmans, 1999), 668–69; LUZ, Matthäus, 4:273 n. 46; EVANS, Mark, 480; also WOLFGANG WALDSTEIN, Untersuchungen zum römischen Begnadigungsrecht. Abolitio–Indulgentia–Venia (Commentationes Aenipontanae 18; Innsbruck: Universitätsverlag Wagner, 1964), 41–44. MARCUS, Mark, 2:1028, thinks deems the institution of a paschal amnesty as a regular practice unlikely; he suggests that the Jews may have regularly asked the Roman governor to release prisoners at Passover and that the Romans would occasionally have granted such a request.

**(102)** Titus Livius, *Ab urbe condita* 8.35.4–7

tum dictator silentio facto 'bene habet' inquit, 'Quirites: vicit disciplina militaris, vicit imperii maiestas, quae in discrimine fuerunt an ulla post hanc diem
essent. ⁵ non noxae eximitur Q. Fabius, qui contra edictum imperatoris
pugnavit, sed noxae damnatus donatur populo Romano, donatur tribuniciae
potestati, precarium non iustum auxilium ferenti. ⁶ vive, Q. Fabi, felicior hoc
consensu civitatis ad tuendum te quam qua paulo ante exsultabas victoria.
vive, id facinus ausus, cuius tibi ne parens quidem, si eodem loco fuisset, quo
fuit L. Papirius, veniam dedisset. ⁷ mecum ut voles reverteris in gratiam:
populo Romano, cui vitam debes, nihil maius praestiteris quam si hic tibi dies
satis documenti dederit, ut bello ac pace pati legitima imperia possis'.

*Translation.* When silence was obtained, the dictator said: "It is well, Quirites.
The discipline of war, the majesty of government, received the victory, despite
the danger that this day would see the end of them. ⁵ Quintus Fabius is not
found guiltless, even though he fought against the orders of his general; but,
convicted of that guilt, he is granted as a boon to the people of Rome, he is
granted to the authority of the tribunes, who plead for him but can bring him
no legal relief. ⁶ Live, Quintus Fabius, more blest in this consent of your fellow citizens to save you, than in the victory over which, a little while ago, you
were exulting! Live, though you dared a deed which not even your sire would
have pardoned, had he been in the place of Lucius Papirius! ⁷ With me you
shall again be on good terms when you will. For the Roman People, to whom
you owe your life, you can do nothing greater than to show that you have
learned what this day clearly teaches: to submit in war and in peace to lawful
authority."

*Commentary.*³⁷⁹ Lucius Papirius Cursor, dictator in 325 and 310 B.C., was the
most important figure in the Second Samnite War (326–304 B.C.). ³⁸⁰ Quintus
Fabius Maximus Rullianus had a long and illustrious career. He was aedile in
331 B.C. and in 325 B.C. *magister equitum* of the dictator L. Papirius Cursor;
he was five times consul and in 315 and 313 B.C. he was himself dictator. His

---

³⁷⁹ Text: WILHELM WEISSENBORN, Titi Livi Ab urbe condita libri (Editio altera quam
curavit Moritz Müller; BSGRT; Teubner, 1887); for other text editions and translations cf.
CHARLES F. WALTERS and ROBERT S. CONWAY, Titi Livi Ab urbe condita. Tomus II. Libri
VI–X (orig. 1919; repr., Scriptorum Classicorum Bibliotheca Oxoniensis; Oxford: Clarendon,
1961); BENJAMIN O. FOSTER, Livy. Ab urbe condita. Books VIII–X (LCL; Cambridge: Harvard University Press, 1926); HANS JÜRGEN HILLEN, T. Livius, Römische Geschichte. Buch
VII–X. Fragmente der zweiten Dekade (Sammlung Tusculum; Zürich: Artemis & Winkler,
1994).

³⁸⁰ CHRISTIAN MÜLLER, Papirius [I 15] P. Cursor, L., BNP 10 (2007): 487–488; STEPHEN
P. OAKLEY, A Commentary on Livy, Books VI-X (3 vols.; Oxford: Clarendon, 1997–2005),
2:518-19. Papirius Cursor was consul in 326, 320, 319, 315, 313 B.C.

victory at Sentinum in 295 B.C. secured Rome's hegemony in Italy.[381] As *magister equitum* (Master of the Cavalry) he had been appointed by the dictator as deputy. The battle in question took place in 325 B.C. According to Livy's account, Q. Fabius engaged the Samnites in battle despite the command of L. Papirius who was absent (8.30.1–9).[382] Despite the fact that Q. Fabius had been victorious, L. Papirius was enraged and initiated legal proceedings, ready to execute the *magister equitum*. Since no pleas were able to sway the dictator, not even the imminent mutiny of the army, Q. Fabius fled the camp in order to have the case decided in Rome, where, at the instigation of his father M. Ambustus, the senate was summoned; when L. Papirius arrives during the senate session and orders Q. Fabius to be seized, his father exercises the right of *provocatio* (8.33.3–8). However, neither the senate, the tribunes of the plebs, or the *provocatio ad populum* were successful in finding a legal remedy: L. Papirius insists that he cannot abandon the just punishment for Q. Fabius' behavior (8.34.4). At this point Q. Fabius, his father, the tribunes, and the people "turn from argument to entreaty, thereby admitting the guilt of the *magister equitum* and the right of the dictator to punish him."[383] They adjure the dictator "to remit for their sake the punishment" of the *magister equitum* (ut sibi poenam magistri equitum dictator remitteret; 8.35.1). The tribunes supported this plea.

The quoted text relates the dictator's response: since he made his point, L. Papirius relents: he "gives" him to the Roman people (donatur populo Romano; line 5).[384] The joy of the senate and the people shows the rightness of his decision. The act of pardon is described with the verb *donare*, which corresponds to χαρίζομαι in P. Flor. I 61 line 61 (No. 103).[385] The act of pardon is described as *venia* (line 6), a term that was used since Cicero to refer to the pardon of people who had been convicted of a crime, either in the sense of clemency in view of extenuating circumstances, or in the sense of an act of grace irrespective of the question of guilt, usually before the verdict was pro-

---

[381] Cf. KARL-LUDWIG ELVERS, Fabius [I 28] F. Maximus Rullianus, Q., BNP 5 (2004): 293; OAKLEY, Commentary, 2:598–600; on the dispute between Fabius Rullianus and Papirius Cursor cf. ibid. 704–7.

[382] Cf. JAMES LIPOSVKY, A Historiographical Study of Livy Books VI–X (Monographs in Classical Studies; Salem: Ayer, 1984), 115–30, for an analysis of the quarrel of Papirius Cursor and Quintus Fabius Maximus Rullianus related in Titus Livius 8.30.1–37.2.

[383] OAKLEY, Commentary, 2:705.

[384] OAKLEY, Commentary, 2:743, points out that the phrase *non iustum auxilium ferenti* reflects the fact that "a tribune could not impede a dictator". Without commenting on the phrase *donatur populo Romano*, he continues, "The moral of the tale is that military discipline can be upheld without resort to needless brutality." The following comment ibid. 707.

[385] WALDSTEIN, Begnadigungsrecht, 74.

nounced. In the case of Q. Fabius, a guilty verdict had been rendered which, however, was being challenged. The historicity of these events is disputed.[386]

W. WALDSTEIN compares Pontius Pilatus' pardon on the occasion of the Passover Festival with the *venia* mentioned in Roman sources, which was practiced in various contexts and in different forms, and he argues that there is no good reason to doubt that a particular tradition could have been established under particular local circumstances, such as granting one prisoner *venia* on the Passover Festival.[387]

**(103)** *Papyrus Florentinus* I 61

I

ἀντίγραφ[ον ἐξ ὑπομνημα]τισμῶν
ἔτους δ [Αὐτοκράτο]ρος Καίσαρος Δομιτιανοῦ
Σεβαστ[οῦ Γερμανικοῦ Μ]εχεὶρ ιδ.
Ἰ[σί]δωρ[ος ὁ καὶ Φιβίων π]ρὸς Ἀχιλλεὺς .. ρα . . .
5   . χ . . . . [ . . . . . ] . . . . νψ . . .
[ὑ]πόθεσις [ . . . . . . ] . ἀπέχειν [ . . . . ]
. . . ρα . . . . [ . . . . . . ]
Σεπτίμιος Οὐέ[γετος . . . . ] . . . . [τ(?)]ὸν Φιβίωνα.
[π]αραστα[- ca.13 -]αμενος [ὀφε]ίλειν σοι
10   δι' ἃς αὐτ . [ . ] . . . [ . . . . ] . . . . . . εὐθέως
μαστιγω . . . . [ . . . Φι]β[ί]ων· τὸ πρᾶ[γ]μα χαρίζομαι
αὐτῶι, ἵν' ἀμελῶ[ς ἔχω (?)]
Σεπτίμιος Οὐέγετος· . [ . . .] ἐγκαλεῖς αὐτῶι;
Κεφάλων ῥήτωρ· τῆς σῆς εὐεργεσίας δεόμενος ἐντυγ-
15   χάνει σοι τὸ πρῶτον κ[α]ὶ ἀναγκαιότατον συ[γ]γνώμην
αἰτούμενος, ἐπεὶ ἐπλανήθη περὶ τὴν ἔντευξιν· ἔ-
δει γὰρ ἀναφόριόν σο[ι] δοῦναι, ὡς καὶ σὺ ἠθέλησας. δ[εό-]

---

[386] EDWARD J. PHILLIPS, Roman Politics during the Second Samnite War, Athenaeum 50 (1972): 337–356, here 341–42.

[387] WALDSTEIN, Begnadigungsrecht, 44; cf. BLINZLER, Prozeß, 304. WALDSTEIN rejects both *indulgentia* and *abolitio privata* as the legal background for Pilate's paschal amnesty (ibid. 43–44). The pardons granted on the occasion of festivals, adduced by MERRITT, Jesus Barabbas, 62–66, are not relevant for a discussion of Pilate's paschal amnesty since they are not evidence for legal traditions; cf. WALDSTEIN, ibid. On the occasion of the introduction of the *lectisternia* in Rome in 339 B.C., described by Livius 5.13.5–8, prisoners were released on the condition that they would return to prison at the end of the festival. Similarly, Ulpian states that the release of prisoners at a Greek festival was merely a parole for the duration of the festival; the bond that the prisoner had to provide was meant to ensure that he would return to prison; the release of prisoners during the Greater Dionysia and the Panathenaea guaranteed that the divine might be preserved as the paroled prisoners attend the festivals; cf. Ulpian, *Scholia* on Demosthenes 22.68 (KARL MÜLLER, ed., Oratores Attici: Fragmenta Oratorum Atticorum [Paris: Didot, 1888], 2:706); cf. MERRITT, ibid. 63.

μεθα οὖν μὴ μαστιγωθῆναι αὐτόν. τὸ δὲ ζήτημα [νῦν(?)]
ἐστι τοιοῦτο. ὁ πατὴρ τοῦ ἀντιδίκου ἐδανείσατο [παρὰ]
20 τοῦ πατρὸς τοῦ ἡμετέρου ἑκατὸν ἀρτάβας πυροῦ. κ[λη-]
ρονομικὸν δὲ τὸ δίκ[α]ιον. δοκῶ δὲ ὅτι οὐ τῶν χαρα[κτή-]
ρων μόνων κληρο[ν]όμους δεῖ εἶναι, ἀλλὰ καὶ τὰ ὀφ[ειλό-]
μενα ὑπὸ τῶν κληρονομηθέντων ἀποδ[ιδ]όναι.
[Ἀρ]ιστόνικος ῥήτωρ· ἀναγνώτω πῶς ὀφείλετα[ι ταῦτα.]
25 [Κε]φάλωνος ἀναγνόντος ἐπίσταλμα Ἀρχίου τοῦ [καὶ Πολυ-]
δεύκους ἐπὶ τοῦ ια (ἔτους) θεοῦ Κλαυδίου
Ἀριστόνικος· τὸν μὲν δ[ανειο]κόπον τοῦτο[ν . . . . .]
ἐνθάδε καλοῦνται ο[ἱ [δεδ]αν<εικότ>ες ἐκ πολλ[ῶν ἤδη χρο-]
νω[ν] ἄνθρωπον στα[τέον] εἰς τὰ θέατρ-
30 [α] . [ . ] . τα· ὁ δὲ ἡμ[έτερός ἐστι]ν εὐσχήμω[ν]
[ . . . .] . εν εννε[ . . . . . ]ν τοῦ μελ[ . . . . .]
[ . . . . . ] πότε δ[ . . . . . . ]γραφο . . [ . . . ]
[ . . . . . ]ε γραπ[ . . . . . . ]ωι . . [ . . . . . ]
[ . . . . ]νουτ[ . . . . . . . . . . ]

II

35 Φιβίων· ο[ὐ]κ οἶδα. Σεπτίμιος Οὐέγετος· ὅ γε σὺ οὐ-
κ οἶδας οὐδὲ ἡμει[ . . . ] . ωμεν.
Κεφάλων· τὸ μὲν ἐπίσταλμα τοῦ π[ατρ]ὸς τούτου
ἐστίν· προστάτης δὲ ὢν ὁ δοῦλος ὑπέγραψεν ὅτι
μετρήσει, οὐδὲν δὲ μεμέτρηκεν ἅπαξ ἀπὸ τοῦ ἐπι-
40 στάλματος. Σεπτίμιος Οὐέγετος· πρῶτον μὲν
ζητεῖται, εἰ τοῦ πατρὸς τούτου γράμματά ἐστιν, δεύ-
τερον διὰ τί ἕως σήμερον οὐκ ἀπήτησας· δύναται
γὰρ καὶ γεγραφέναι ὁ [ . . . . .]ιος καὶ μεμετρηκέναι.
Ἀριστόνικος· σὺ μὲν ζητ[εῖ]σ ὀρθῶς ταῦτα, ἐγὼ δέ σοι τὸ
45 καθολικὸν λέγω· ἡγημόνες πεν[τ]αετίον ὥρισαν
περὶ τῶν πολυχρονίων· ἀλλ' οἳ δεκαετίαν, οὐχ ὅπου
διαλογισμοὶ καὶ ἡγεμόνες παραγενόμενοι. πυθ[οῦ]
αὐτοῦ. πόσα ἔτη ὁ πατὴρ αὐτοῦ ἐπέζησεν.
Φιβίων· ἠρνήσατο οὗτος [τὴ]ν κλη[ρ]ονομίαν τοῦ πατρὸς
50 καὶ ἐγὼ τὴν καὶ ἐγὼ τὴν τοῦ ἰδίου πατρός, ἐπεὶ σιτο-
λόγοι ἦσαν καὶ ἀπητο[ῦ]ντο εἰς τὸν Κ[α]ίσαρος λόγον.
Ἀριστόνικος· εἰ οὖν καὶ ὠφείλετο εἰς τὸν Κ[α]ίσαρος λόγον,
διὰ τί οὐκ ἀπήτει τότε; Σεπτίμιος Οὐέγετος·
λειμοῦ γεν[ομ]ένου πε[ι]νῶν οὐκ ἀπή[τ]εις [τὸ]ν πυρόν,
55 εἰ ὠφείλετό σοι; Φιβίων· παρεκάλει με τέσσαρας
μνᾶς λαβεῖν. Ἀριστόνικος· ἐὰν τούτῳ προχωρή-
σῃ, ἐποίσουσιν μυρίοι χειρόγραφα τοῦ πατρὸς τούτου·

ἐν ὀρφανείᾳ γὰρ κατε[λί]πη οὗτος.
Σεπτίμιος Οὐέγετος τῶι Φιβίωνι· ἄξιος μ[ὲ]ν ἧς μαστι-
60   γωθῆναι, διὰ σεαυτοῦ [κ]ατασχὼν ἄνθρωπον
εὐσχήμονα καὶ γυν[αῖ]καν· χαρίζομαι δέ σε τοῖς ὄ-
χλοις καὶ φιλανθρωπ[ότ]ερ[ό]σ σοι ἔσομαι. διὰ τες[σ]ε-
ράκοντα ἐτῶν ἐπιφέ[ρε]ις ἐπίσταλ[μ]α· τὸ ἥμις[ύ] σοι
τοῦ χρόνου χαρίζομαι· [μ]ετὰ εἴκοσι ἔτη ἐπανε-
65   λεύσῃ πρὸς ἐμέ. καὶ ἐκ[έ]λευσε τὸ χειρ[ό]γραφον χια-
σθῆναι.

*Translation.* Transcript of the minutes, the fourth year of the Emperor Caesar Domitian Augustus Germanicus, the fourteenth day of the month Mechir. Isidoros, who is also called Phibion, against Achilleus ... [8] *Septimius Vegetus* ... Step forward ... [11] I will flog ... *Phibion*: I give him the matter so that (I?) (can live?) without worries. *Septimius Vegetus*: Of what do you accuse him? What is the basis of your complaint? *The lawyer Kephalon*: Begging your kindness and appealing [15] to you, they ask first and with utmost necessity for a lenient judgment, since he ought to have been in error about the petition; we had to give the petition to you, as you wished. Thus we beg you not to flog him. This is what we seek. The father of the defendant borrowed from [20] our father one hundred artaba of wheat. This liability is connected with the inheritance. It seems that they should not be heirs of the letters only, but they should also pay the debt incurred by those whose heirs they are. *The lawyer Aristonikos*: I certainly read how this is owed. [25] As Kephalon has read the promissory note of Archias, who is called Polydeukes, from the eleventh year of the divine Claudius. *Aristonikos*: The lenders are called in this case usurers already for a long time, they must appoint someone for the assembly ... [30] Our case is honorable ... [35] *Phibion*: I do not know. *Septimius Vegetus*: If you do not know ... *Kephalon*: The promissory note is from the father of this one here (i.e., of the accused, Achilleus). As his legal representative his slave signed that he would pay, but he has not once paid anything on account of the [40] promissory note. *Septimius Vegetus*: First I want to know whether this is the document of the father of this person, second, why the suit was not brought until today. For it is possible that the promissory note is correct but (that the debt is) already paid. *Aristonikos*: You are right in raising these questions, and [45] I will state the matter generally. The prefects set a five year limitation of actions, but those who stipulated ten years did not do so where circuit courts were available and prefects who travel. Inquire from him how long his father lived (lived after the certificate of debt had been signed). *Phibion*: He renounces the inheritance of his father, [50] and I (renounce) the inheritance of his father, since there were collectors of wheat and they demanded it back according to Caesar's ruling. *Aristonikos*: If he had to pay according to Caesar's ruling, why did he not make his demand when his father was alive? *Septimius*

*Vegetus*: Even when famines caused hunger, you did not demand back the wheat, [55] if he had to pay you? *Phibion*: He demanded that I take four mina. *Aristonikos*: If this one is successful, countless numbers will produce a written note of their father; for he has been left an orphan. *Septimius Vegetus to Phibion*: You deserve to be [60] flogged for keeping in your custody a decent man and his wife. But I give you to the people, and I will treat you with utmost kindness. You bring the promissory note after forty years: I give you half of this period; you will come to me after twenty years. [65] And he ordered that the written note be canceled.

*Commentary*.[388] This papyrus, which dates to February 8, A.D. 85,[389] contains the minutes of a trial before C. Septimius Vegetus, the prefect of Egypt. The accuser is a certain Phibion, represented by the lawyer Kephalon, the accused is Achilleus represented by the lawyer Aristonikos. Phibion insists on the validity of a promissory note (or certificate of debt; ἐπίσταλμα) of over 100 artaba of wheat, signed by Archias, the father of the Achilleus, in dealings with Phibion's father some decades earlier; the slave mentioned in line 35 was Archias' business manager. The accuser bases his claim on the fact that Achilleus took over his father's inheritance, which included the unpaid debt; as a result, Phibion had Achilleus and his wife arrested. The first speech by the prefect begins in line 8; what he says is not entirely clear as the papyrus is damaged; the prefect threatens to flog Phibion on account of his unilateral action of putting Achilleus and his wife in prison. The prefect raises two questions against the plaintiff (lines 40–43): was the document which has been produced in court authentic? why had a suit not been brought earlier? The accuser avoids answering the question and maintains a postponement of the statute of limitations by the *deliberatio heredis*. The phrase τὸ καθολικόν (line 45) means that "the statement of the law as it applies to all persons in such circumstances."[390] It seems that in Egypt the prefects stipulated five years for old debts, but those who stipulated ten did not do so where conventus and prefect

---

[388] Text: GIROLAMO VITELLI, Papiri Greco-Egizii. Volume Primo (No. 1–105). Papiri Fiorentini: Documenti pubblici e privati dell'età romana e bizantina (Supplementi filologico-storici ai Monumenti antichi; Pubblicati per cura della Reale Accademia dei Lincei; Milan: Hoepli, 1906), 113–15 (No. 61); LUDWIG MITTEIS, Ägyptischer Schuldprozeß v. J. 84/86 p. Chr., ZSSR.RA 27 (1906): 220–227; MITTEIS / WILCKEN, Chrestomathie, 2:88–89 (No. 80). As far as we know, what follows is the first complete translation of the papyrus. Cf. BENEDICT FRESE, Aus dem gräko-ägyptischen Rechtsleben (Halle: Niemeyer, 1909), 12–13; ULRICH WILCKEN, Zu den Florentiner und den Leipziger Papyri, Archiv für Papyrusforschung 4 (1907): 423–486, 444–48.

[389] GUIDO BASTIANINI, Lista dei prefetti d'Egitto dal 30ᵃ al 299ᴾ, ZPE 17 (1975): 263–328, 277 n. 1.

[390] KATZOFF, Law as *Katholikos*, 123; the phrase does not refer to an empire-wide edict since limitation of actions became a rule in the Roman empire only several centuries later under Theodosius II.

were available (lines 46–47).[391] In his decision (lines 59–65), Septimius Vegetus rescinds the flogging of Phibion which he had threatened earlier, asserting that he will treat him with more kindness than Phibion showed to Achilleus and his wife: he "gives (χαρίζομαι) him to the people" (line 61), i.e., he lets him go free.[392] In his kindness he cuts in half the forty years which had elapsed since the debt acknowledged in the promissory note had become due: but even reckoning with only twenty years, the statute of limitations has elapsed. The prefect then proceeds to declare null and void Phibion's claims based on the old promissory note, acknowledging that the statue of limitations for claims had expired. Details of the discussion about the statute of limitations in Attic, Doric, and Roman need not concern us here. L. MITTEIS points out that this papyrus provides a rare picture of the authority of Roman prefects: Septimius Vetegus threatens to whip the debtor, he "donates" him to the people, and then he destroys the promissory note that recorded his debt.[393]

Scholars cite P. Flor. I 61 lines 61–62 as evidence for isolated amnesties granted by Roman governors, illustrating John 18:39 and Mark 15:6, and especially Mark 15:15 ("Thus Pilatus, who wished to satisfy the crowd, released Barabbas for them; and after flogging Jesus, he handed him over to be crucified").[394] O. HIRSCHFELD doubted that Roman governors had the authority the pronounce amnesties.[395] This skepticism has been proven to be unjustified on account of P. Flor. I 61.[396]

---

[391] This is probably a reference to edicts issued by previous prefects; cf. TAUBENSCHLAG, Law, 427; WOLFF, Das Recht der griechischen Papyri Ägyptens I, 177 n. 122.

[392] On the language of amnesty cf. WALDSTEIN, Begnadigungsrecht, 16–17, who asserts that the terminology in the primary sources is diverse and confusing: in Roman sources we find *abolitio* (*abolere*), *amnestia, beneficium, fides, gratia, indulgentia* (*indulgere*), *impunitas, remissio, restitutio* (*restituere*), *venia,* in Greek sources we find ἀμνηστία, ἄδεια, φιλανθρωπία, συγχώρησις and related verbs, as well as loanwords from Latin and verbs such as χαρίζομαι (as in P. Flor. I 61, lines 61–62) and ἀπολύειν (as in Matt 27:15–16; Mark 15:6, 11; Luke 23:17; John 18:39); cf. ibid. 44 n. 21, 73–74, where he compares the phrase *donatur populo Romano* in Livius 8.35.5, which here clearly refers to a pardon of Q. Fabius by the dictator L. Papirius (*veniam dedisset*; 8.35.6).

[393] LUDWIG MITTEIS, Miszellen: Neue Urkunden I, ZSSR.RA 26 (1905): 484–487, 485, commenting that "in ganzen Bänden kann man das Imperium nicht so deutlich schildern."

[394] Thus already VITELLI, Papiri Fiorentini I, 116 note 61: "Involontariamente si pensa a Pilato e Barabba (p. es. Marc. 15,15 etc.)". Cf. ADOLF DEISSMANN, Licht vom Osten. Das Neue Testament und die neuentdeckten Texte der hellenistisch-römischen Welt (4., völlig neu bearbeitete Auflage; Tübingen: Mohr-Siebeck, 1923), 229; WALDSTEIN, Begnadigungsrecht, 42–43; STROBEL, Stunde, 124; BOND, Pontius Pilate, 199; PESCH, Markusevangelium, 2:462; LUZ, Matthäus, 4:273 n. 46; EVANS, Mark, 480.

[395] OTTO HIRSCHFELD, Die kaiserlichen Verwaltungsbeamten bis auf Diokletian (2. Auflage; orig. 1878; repr., Berlin: Weidmann, 1905), 406: "Das Recht der Begnadigung hat dem Prokurator sicherlich ebensowenig wie den übrigen Statthaltern zugestanden."

[396] WALDSTEIN, Begnadigungsrecht, 31 n. 56; he further refers to P. Oxy. XIV 1668, dated to the 3rd century A.D., a private letter in which a certain Charmus asks Sopatrus to return since the amnesty of the governor (ὁ ἡγεμὼν ἀμνησίαν ἔπεμψεν ἐνθάδε; lines 17–19) has

**(104)** Josephus, *Antiquitates judaicae* 20.215

Ὡς δ' ἤκουσεν Ἀλβῖνος διάδοχον αὐτῷ Γέσσιον Φλῶρον ἀφικνεῖσθαι, βουλόμενος δοκεῖν τι τοῖς Ἱεροσολυμίταις παρεσχῆσθαι προαγαγὼν τοὺς δεσμώτας, ὅσοι ἦσαν αὐτῶν προδήλως θανεῖν ἄξιοι, τούτους προσέταξεν ἀναιρεθῆναι, τοὺς δ' ἐκ μικρᾶς καὶ τῆς τυχούσης αἰτίας εἰς τὴν εἱρκτὴν κατατεθέντας χρήματα λαμβάνων αὐτὸς ἀπέλυεν. καὶ οὕτως ἡ μὲν φυλακὴ τῶν δεσμωτῶν ἐκαθάρθη, ἡ χώρα δὲ λῃστῶν ἐπληρώθη.

*Translation.* When Albinus heard that Gessius Florus was coming as his successor, he wanted to appear as somebody who had provided something for the Jerusalemites; he brought out those prisoners who clearly deserved to be put to death and ordered their execution, while those who had been put in prison for a minor and commonplace offense he released after accepting money.[397] Thus the prison was cleared of inmates while the countryside was filled with brigands.

*Commentary.* Lucceius Albinus was procurator from A.D. 62–64, succeeded by Gessius Florus (A.D. 64–66) whose governorship ended at the outbreak of the Jewish War against Rome. He was of equestrian rank and held office in Judea "either as *praefectus* under the control of the governor of Syria or already as independent presidial procurator."[398] A positive interpretation of Josephus' account in *A. J.* 20.215 suggests, "he cleared up legal business still pending in Jerusalem by executing people who were in prison for capita offenses (largely terrorists) and releasing those awaiting trial on merely trivial offences (bribery of course being alleged in the latter cases)."[399]

This text is sometimes cited to demonstrate that the Roman governors of Judea had total authority over Jews who had committed a capital offense: they could execute them, or they could release them.[400] This is plausible only if the

---

made it save for the laborers who had asked for higher wages to return to the city, and also to Pliny, *Ep.* 10.32 (No. 105).

[397] L. H. FELDMAN translates χρήματα λαμβάνων as "for a personal consideration" (LCL).

[398] ECK, L. Albinus. On Gessius Florus cf. IRINA WANDREY, Gessius Florus, BNP 5 (2004): 826–827, on both governors SCHÜRER, History, 1:468–70; SMALLWOOD, Jews, 271.

[399] SMALLWOOD, Jews, 282; she correctly points out that the last sentence in the paragraph does not follow logically on what precedes (ibid. n. 88): if Albinus released people who had committed minor offenses, why is the countryside filling with "brigands" (or "revolutionaries")? For a source-critical discussion of the text cf. COHEN, Josephus in Galilee and Rome, 60–62. For a discussion of the self-contradictory elements in Josephus' portrayal of Albinus cf. SCHWARTZ, Reading, 150–51.

[400] MERKEL, Begnadigung, 303; cf. BLINZLER, Prozeß, 301–2 with n. 4, with reference to John 19:10: οὐκ οἶδας ὅτι ἐξουσίαν ἔχω ἀπολῦσαί σε καὶ ἐξουσίαν ἔχω σταυρῶσαί σε; ("do you not know that I have power to release you, and power to crucify you?"). Cf. WALDSTEIN, Begnadigungsrecht, 42 n. 7 (mistakenly citing *A. J.* 20.205), who refers to this and other texts to document the caprice of many Roman governors.

phrase ἐκ μικρᾶς καὶ τῆς τυχούσης αἰτίας ("for a minor and commonplace offense") is an apologetic version of the misdeeds of these released prisoners: according to the version in *B. J.* 2.274–276, Albinus regularly released brigands and revolutionaries from prison accepting bribes.[401]

**(105)** Plinius, *Epistulae* 10.31–32

C. PLINIUS TRAIANO IMPERATORI. [1] Salva magnitudine tua, domine, descendas oportet ad meas curas, cum ius mihi dederis referendi ad te, de quibus dubito. [2] in plerisque civitatibus, maxime Nicomediae et Nicaeae, quidam vel in opus damnati vel in ludum similiaque his genera poenarum publicorum servorum officio ministerioque funguntur, atque etiam ut publici servi annua accipiunt. quod ego cum audissem, diu multumque haesitavi, quid facere deberem. [3] nam et reddere poenae post longum tempus plerosque iam senes et, quantum adfirmatur, frugaliter modesteque viventes nimis severum arbitrabar, et in publicis officiis retinere damnatos non satis honestum putabam; eosdem rursus a re publica pasci otiosos inutile, non pasci etiam periculosum existimabam. [4] necessario ergo rem totam, dum te consulerem, in suspenso reliqui. quaeres fortasse, quem ad modum evenerit, ut poenis in quas damnati erant, exsolverentur: et ego quaesii, sed nihil comperi, quod affirmare tibi possim. ut decreta quibus damnati erant, proferebantur, ita nulla monumenta quibus liberati probarentur. [5] erant tamen, qui dicerent deprecantes iussu proconsulum legatorumve dimissos. addebat fidem, quod credibile erat neminem hoc ausum sine auctore.

32 TRAIANUS PLINIO [1] Meminerimus idcirco te in istam provinciam missum, quoniam multa in ea emendanda apparuerint. erit autem vel hoc maxime corrigendum, quod, qui damnati ad poenam erant, non modo ea sine auctore, ut scribis, liberati sunt, sed etiam in condicionem proborum ministrorum retrahuntur. [2] qui igitur intra hos proximos decem annos damnati nec ullo idoneo auctore liberati sunt, hos oportebit poenae suae reddi; si qui vetustiores invenientur et senes ante annos decem damnati, distribuamus illos in ea ministeria, quae non longe a poena sint. solent enim eius modi ad balineum, ad purgationes cloacarum, item munitiones viarum et vicorum dari.[402]

*Translation.* C. Plinius to Emperor Trajan. (1) Without prejudice to your eminent position, Lord, it is expedient that you deign to consider my problems,

---

[401] Cf. COHEN, Josephus in Galilee and Rome, 61–62.

[402] ELMER T. MERRILL, C. Plini Caecili Secundi Epistularum Libri Decem (Leipzig: Teubner, 1922), 275, reads at the beginning of the last sentence: "solent et ad balineum"; thus also Budé and Oxoniensis. The reading leaves the sense slightly obscure; cf. ADRIAN NICOLAS SHERWIN-WHITE, The Letters of Pliny: A Historical and Social Commentary (orig. 1966; repr., Oxford: Clarendon, 1985), 606.

since you granted me the right to refer to you in doubtful cases. (2) In most cities, particularly in Nicomedia and Nicaea, there are people who were sentenced to forced labor, to fight as gladiators, or to similar punishments, but are now performing the duties and services of public slaves and who are receiving an annual salary for their work. When I heard about this, I pondered for a long time what to do. (3) Because many are already old and lead, as I have been assured, quiet and honest lives, I felt it was too harsh to send them back to serve their sentences after much time has passed; on the other hand, I believed that it is not quite fitting to retain criminals in public service; to support them at public expense even if they do not work seemed to me useless, not to feed them outright dangerous. (4) By necessity I left the whole matter undecided until I could consult you. You may perhaps ask how they came to be released from the punishments to which they had been sentenced. I have asked this myself, but have not been able to establish anything for certain that I could report to you. The rulings about their sentences were produced, but no documents that would have proven their release. [5] Some maintain that they were released on account of an appeal for clemency by order of the proconsuls (governors) or legates (deputies). This appears credible because surely nobody would have done something like this without authorization.

Trajan to Plinius. (1) Let us not forget that the reason for sending you to your province was the fact many matters had arisen in the province that needed to be rectified. First and foremost among the matters that need to be corrected is the situation where people who had been sentenced to punishments, as you write, have been released not only without authorization but are actually restored to the status of honorable servants. (2) Therefore, those who were sentenced within the last ten years and released without proper authorization must be returned to their punishments. If older and elderly people are found who were sentenced over ten years ago, we want to employ them in work which is not far removed from penal labor. Such people are mostly used for the baths, for the cleaning of the latrines, and for repairing streets and highways

*Commentary.*[403] The problem that Pliny wants the emperor to address in this exchange of letters, dated A.D. 99,[404] concerns people who had been convicted

---

[403] Text: MAURIZ SCHUSTER / RUDOLPH HANSLIK, C. Plini Caecili Secundi Epistularum libri novem, Epistularum ad Traianum liber, Panegyricus (3. Auflage; orig. 1958; repr., BSGRT; Stuttgart / Leipzig: Teubner, 1992); for other text editions and translations cf. HELMUT KASTEN, Gaius Plinius Caecilius Secundus. Briefe: Epistularum libri decem (Lateinisch und deutsch. 7. Auflage; Sammlung Tusculum; München / Zürich: Artemis & Winkler, 1995); ROGER A. B. MYNORS, C. Plinius Caecilius Secundus: Epistularum libri decem (Scriptorum Classicorum Bibliotheca Oxoniensis; Oxford: Oxford University Press, 1963); BETTY RADICE, Pliny the Younger: Letters and Panegyricus of Pliny (2 vols.; LCL; Cambridge: Harvard University Press, 1969).

[404] Cf. SHERWIN-WHITE, Letters, 63.

of crimes and sentenced to severe punishments – the punishment of having to fight in the arena was tantamount to a death sentence – and who were subsequently released and employed in public service. The problem was not the release of convicted criminals as such but the fact that no proper documentation could be found which would explain the circumstances of their release. A Roman governor had the authority to resolve this matter on the spot. Pliny consults the emperor because he wants to innovate: rather than apply the rigor of the law, he wants do deal gently with these cases.[405] The reference to "similar punishments" (*similaque*) refers to hard labor in mines (*damnatio ad medallum*); together with service in the amphitheater (*damnatio in ludum, damnatio ad gladium*), this type of hard labor "replaced the capital sentence, and entailed perpetual sentence and loss of civic rights. The condemned person was defined in status, ultimately, as *servus poenae* ... Condemnation *in opus publicum*, either *in tempus* or perpetual, was less severe, since the prisoner did not lose his civic status."[406] The phrase *in opus damnati* ("sentenced to forced labor") seems to refer to all forms of *damnatio in metallum*. Retaining condemned men in public service is problematic on account of the often confidential nature of the work that was performed by public slaves. The reason why Pliny did not find the documents (*monumenta*) regarding legal decisions of earlier governors is perhaps due to the possibility that proconsuls took their records back to Rome where they were filed in the senatorial archives; at the same time, the spoken word (*iussu*) of a governor with *imperium* "sufficed for action without the need for documentation."[407] The fact that convicted criminals were "released without proper authorization" (*nec ullo idoneo auctore liberati sunt*) suggests that it was possible to be released *with* proper authorization.

W. WALDSTEIN regards the text as evidence for the authority of a provincial governor to grant a pardon.[408] C. A. EVANS refers to the text as corroborating evidence for the historicity of Mark's report of Pilatus' custom of the release of prisoners.[409]

---

[405] SHERWIN-WHITE, Letters, 602. The verb *dubitare* is used here as a reference to Pliny's right to refer legal matters that are doubtful to the emperor Trajan; cf. COOK, Attitudes, 158 n. 120.

[406] SHERWIN-WHITE, Letters, 602–3; for the following comment cf. ibid.

[407] Cf. SHERWIN-WHITE, Letters, 605; for proconsuls filing their "acts" in the senatorial archives at Rome cf. THEODOR MOMMSEN, Gesammelte Schriften (8 vols.; Berlin: Weidmann, 1905–1913), 5:343–44.

[408] WALDSTEIN, Begnadigungsrecht, 31 n. 56; SHERWIN-WHITE, Letters, 605–6, does not comment on the phrase.

[409] EVANS, Mark, 480. BROWN, Death, 1:816, remains unconvinced: this example, as well as P. Flor I 61 and Josephus, *A. J.* 20.215 "tell us nothing about a regular custom on a feast; at most they are isolated instances of humane behavior".

**(106)** *m. Pesaḥim* 8:6

הָאוֹנֵן וְהַמְפַקֵּחַ בַּגַּל וְכֵן מִי שֶׁהִבְטִיחוּהוּ לְהוֹצִיאוֹ מִבֵּית הָאֲסוּרִים הַחוֹלֶה וְהַזָּקֵן שֶׁהֵן יְכוֹלִין לֶאֱכֹל
כַּזַּיִת שׁוֹחֲטִין עֲלֵיהֶם וְעַל־כֻּלָּם אֵין שׁוֹחֲטִין עֲלֵיהֶם בִּפְנֵי עַצְמָן שֶׁלֹּא יְבִיאוּהוּ לִידֵי פָסוּל

*Translation.* They may slaughter (a Passover offering) for one who mourns (a close relative), and for one who digs in a heap of debris, and one whom they have promised to free from prison, and for a sick person and an aged person, who are able to eat on olive's bulk (of the Passover offering); but as regards these cases, they do not slaughter (a Passover offering) on their behalf alone, lest they cause the Passover offering to become invalid.

*Commentary.*[410] This and the previous mishnah explain that if a person's impurity – for example, impurity contracted by contact with a corpse in connection with the death of a close relative, or contracted by clearing away debris in a ruin where a dead body may be located[411] – ends on the 14th of Nisan, they prepare a Passover offering on their behalf and they eat it in the evening when their impurity is ended (through immersion). According to this mishnah, one does not prepare a Passover offering on behalf of a person if that person may not be able to eat from the offering due to sickness or impurity. Among the people to whom this ruling applies is "one whom they have promised to free from prison" (מִי שֶׁהִבְטִיחוּהוּ לְהוֹצִיאוֹ מִבֵּית הָאֲסוּרִים): one shall not prepare a Passover offering for a prisoner who has been promised freedom because he may not be released in time (for whatever reason[412]) for eating the Passover.

Scholars refer to this mishnah as evidence for the Passover amnesty mentioned by Pilatus (John 18:39; Mark 15:6).[413] J. BLINZLER summarizes, "An

---

[410] Text: GEORG BEER, Pesachim (Die Mischna II/3; Gießen: Töpelmann, 1912); cf. HERMANN L. STRACK, Pᵉsaḥim. Der Mišnatraktat Passafest (Mit Berücksichtigung des Neuen Testaments und der jetzigen Passafeier der Juden. Nach Handschriften und alten Drucken herausgegeben, übersetzt und erläutert; Schriften des Institutum Judaicum in Berlin 40; Leipzig: Hinrichs, 1911).

[411] Cf. JASTROW s.v. פקח pi. "esp. (with גל) to open a heap of debris; to attempt to rescue a person supposed to be buried in debris . . . הַמְפַקֵּחַ he who digs among debris (not knowing certainly that a corpse is buried there)"; cf. BEER, Pesachim, 173.

[412] STRACK, Pᵉsaḥim, 26 n. 15, suggests that the Jewish prisoner may be incarcerated in a pagan prison or in a prison outside of Jerusalem: in these cases, one cannot be certain that the prisoner is released. As regards a prisoner who is incarcerated in a Jewish prison in Jerusalem, his relatives can take a portion of the Passover lamb to him in prison.

[413] CHRISTIAN SCHÖTTGEN, Horae Hebraicae et Talmudicae in universum Novum Testamentum (2 vols.; Dresden / Leipzig: Hekel, 1733–1942), 1:235; BEER, Pesachim, 55, 173; CHARLES B. CHAVEL, "The Releasing of a Prisoner on the Eve of Passover in Ancient Jerusalem," JBL 60 (1941): 273–278; STAUFFER, Jesusforschung, 464; BLINZLER, Prozeß, 317–19, with a discussion of the arguments of J. JEREMIAS against the proposal of CHAVEL; STROBEL, Stunde, 121–22; PESCH, Markusevangelium, 2:462; GUNDRY, Mark, 935; EVANS, Mark, 480.

Israelite who is a prisoner in a Roman prison in Jerusalem has the well-founded prospect, although no certainty, that he might be released from prison shortly before the evening of the Passover festival. This case must have been a regular occurrence which normally took place every year before the 15th of Nisan, since it is connected in the Pesaḥim Tractate with constantly reoccurring cases of different kinds."[414] E. BAMMEL points out that the text, while not confirming a regular custom of a Passover amnesty, indicates the Jewish desire to free Jewish prisoners at this time.[415] R. T. FRANCE argues that *m. Pesaḥ.* 8:6 "is too unspecific to provide confirmation, and too late to be used as evidence specifically for the custom followed by Pilate."[416] In his discussion of *m. Pesaḥ.* 8:8 which treats the period of impurity after circumcision in connection with the eating of the Passover,[417] D. INSTONE-BREWER suggests that the priests' refusal to enter Pilatus' residence for the trial of Jesus (John 18:28) might have been related to corpse impurity, although he acknowledges that we do not know in what way the priests thought that they might contract impurity.[418] John's description of the priests refusal to go inside the praetorium (αὐτοὶ οὐκ εἰσῆλθον εἰς τὸ πραιτώριον) seems to imply that the priests thought that the building itself imparted impurity. According to rabbinic law, this happens only if there is a corpse inside the building at the time: a house, made of stone or mud, does not carry impurity (unlike a tent which is made of fabric). However, according to Qumran law, a "house" was interpreted as a type of "tent" which according to Num 19:14 transmits corpse impurity. If the priests followed the latter interpretation, they would have regarded any Gentile building as permanently impure; in this case "they were afraid of contracting *corpse impurity* from the building itself, and this *impurity* would last for 7 days so they would miss the Passover."[419]

*Amnesty and Acclamatio Populi.* The texts discussed in 2.6 do not provide evidence for a regular practice of either Pilatus or other prefects of Judea releasing a prisoner on the occasion of the Jewish Passover festival. But they

---

[414] BLINZLER, Prozeß, 319.

[415] ERNST BAMMEL, The Trial before Pilate, in Jesus and the Politics of His Day (ed. E. Bammel and C.F.D. Moule; Cambridge: Cambridge University Press, 1984), 415–451, 427; followed by KEENER, Gospel of Matthew, 669 n. 181.

[416] R. T. FRANCE, The Gospel of Matthew (NICNT; Grand Rapids: Eerdmans, 2007), 1052 n. 26; cf. DAVIES / ALLISON, Matthew, 3:583 n. 16; BROWN, Death, 1:818.

[417] *m. Pesaḥ.* 8:8: "A mourner immerses (to cleanse himself from corpse impurity) and (then) eats his Passover in the evening, but (he does) not (eat) holy things (i.e. festival sacrifices). He who hears (news) of his (relative's) death or who is gathering up bones (into an ossuary) immerses and eats holy things (in the evening)." Translation D. INSTONE-BREWER.

[418] DAVID INSTONE-BREWER, Traditions of the Rabbis from the Era of the New Testament. Vol. 2A: Feasts and Sabbaths: Passover and Atonement (Grand Rapids: Eerdmans, 2011), 163; the following discussion ibid.

[419] INSTONE-BREWER, Traditions of the Rabbis IIA, 163.

do provide evidence for the possibility that Pilatus indeed wanted to release Jesus. The latter is emphasized not only by John (18:38; 19:12), but also by Luke (23:13–16, 17, 20, 22). In the context of Pilatus' plan to release Jesus, it makes sense to describe Pilatus as concluding that Jesus is innocent of the charge of *seditio* or *crimen maiestatis*. Pilatus' decision to have Herod Antipas, the *tetrarch* of Galilee, decide the case (Luke 23:7) makes sense in this context: in Galilee Antipas had jurisdiction in capital cases, and Pilatus grants him the exercise of this right in Jerusalem in the case of Jesus, surely aware of the fact that his order to end the court session and have Jesus transferred to Antipas renders the trial an informal action.[420] When the case is referred back to Pilatus (Luke 23:11), Pilatus opens a second hearing in which the chief priests and the leaders of the Sanhedrin (οἱ ἀρχιερεῖς καὶ οἱ ἄρχοντες) appear again, but now also the people (ὁ λαός). In contrast to the role of the people in Roman criminal trials in which the *provocatio ad populum* is directed against the guilty verdict of the magistrates, the crowd in front of Pilatus' praetorium votes, with heated shouts and without arguments, against the position of Pilatus, for the execution of the accused.[421] Livius 8.35.6 and *P. Flor.* I 61 line 60 demonstrate how the participation of the people in a legal case leads to amnesty. But not in Jesus' trial: the crowd demands Jesus' crucifixion. M. SCHUOL asserts: "Die Öffentlichkeit wird also – entgegen der ihr zugedachten Rolle als mögliches Rechtsmittel der Gnadeninstanz im römischen Kapitalverfahren – Jesus zum Verhängnis. Ebenso wie im römischen Verfahren vor dem *concilium plebis* (Multklage) oder vor den Zenturiatskomitien (Kapitalklage) spricht die Volksversammlung im Prozeß gegen Jesus ihr Urteil, ohne an bestehende Gesetze oder Gewohnheiten gebunden zu sein und schafft damit Recht für diesen zur Abstimmung stehenden Einzelfall."[422]

## 2.7  Abuse of Convicted Criminals

The Gospels relate that Jesus was mocked and beaten after Pontius Pilatus had sentenced him to execution by crucifixion. The prefect's soldiers clothed Jesus in a purple cloak, placed a crown woven of thorns on his head, saluted

---

[420] SCHUOL, Augustus, 190, 200; cf. HEUSLER, Kapitalprozesse, 93–99, 106–10, 116–26, who emphasizes that Luke 23:6–12 describes a trial as a stage in the trial against Jesus which moved through several levels of jurisdiction.

[421] On the participation of the people in trial proceedings cf. BAUMAN, Crimen Maiestatis, 23–33; WOLFGANG KUNKEL and ROLAND WITTMANN, Staatsordnung und Staatspraxis der römischen Republik. Zweiter Abschnitt: Die Magistratur (HdA X/3.2.2; München: Beck, 1995), 266–67.

[422] SCHUOL, Augustus, 201; cf. HEUSLER, Kapitalprozesse, 213–66, on the application of Roman criminal law by Pilatus in Jesus' trial, assuming the criminal procedure of the *ordo*.

him as "King of the Jews," struck his head with a reed symbolizing a scepter, spit at him, and kneeled before him in mock homage (Mark 15:16–20; Matt 27:28–31; cf. John 19:2–3).[423] Then Pilatus ordered Jesus to be flogged (Mark 15:15; Matt 27:26; cf. John 19:1). Both Jewish and Roman sources illustrate that people who had been convicted were mocked and tortured.

**(107)** Titus Livius, *Ab urbe condita* 24.5.10–14

index unum ex coniuratis Theodotum, a quo ipse appellatus erat, nominare potuit, qui conprensus extemplo traditusque Adranodoro torquendus de se ipse haud cunctanter fassus conscios celabat. postremo, cum omnibus intolerandis patientiae humanae cruciatibus laceraretur, victum malis se simulans avertit ab consciis in insontes indicium, Thrasonem esse auctorem consilii mentitus, nec nisi tam potenti duce confisos rem tantam ausuros *fuisse; addit nonnullos* ab latere tyranni, quorum capita vilissima fingenti inter dolores gemitusque occurrere. maxime animo tyranni credibile indicium Thraso nominatus fecit; itaque extemplo traditur ad supplicium, adiectique poenae ceteri iuxta inson-tes. consciorum nemo, cum diu socius consilii torqueretur, aut latuit aut fugit; tantum illis in virtute ac fide Theodoti fiduciae fuit tantumque ipsi Theodoto virium ad arcana occultanda.

*Translation.* The informer was able to name only one of the conspirators, Theodotus, by whom he had been approached. And Theodotus, who was immediately seized and handed over for torture to Adranodorus, confessed without hesitation with regard to himself, but did not reveal his accomplices. Finally, racked by all the tortures which go beyond human endurance, pretended to be overcome by his sufferings and turned informer against the innocent instead of against his accomplices. He falsely stated that Thraso was responsible for the plan: that they would not have ventured upon such an undertaking if they had not relied upon so powerful a leader. He also named attendants of the tyrant as associates, men whose lives, it occurred to him as he was fabricating between pains and groans, were of the least account. His reference to Thraso made the information particularly credible to the tyrant. Accordingly, Thraso was handed over for execution, and the rest, equally innocent, shared his punishment. Not one of the accomplices either hid himself or fled, though their partner in the plot was under torture for a long time. Such was their confidence in the courage and loyalty of Theodotus, and such was Theodotus' will-power to keep secrets that he possessed.

*Commentary.* Hieronymus of Syracuse succeeded his grandfather Hieron II and became king of Sicily in 215 B.C. at the age of fifteen.[424] Soon after his

---

[423] Luke 23:11 links a scene of mocking to Jesus' encounter with Herod Antipas.
[424] Cf. KLAUS MEISTER, Hieronymus [3] H. of Syracus, BNP 6 (2005): 315; HELMUT

accession, pro-Roman officials attempted a coup, which was exposed. An informer named Theodotus,[425] who betrayed Thraso, the leading pro-Roman politician (cf. Polybius 7.2.1). He gave up Thraso's name after he was handed over to Adranodorus, son-in-law of Hieron II and one of Hieronymus' guardians, who was responsible for the radical turn of Syracusian politics to the Carthaginians.[426] The verb describing torture (*torqueo*) generally means "turn, twist, bend" and is used here and in many other texts for twisting the limbs of a person with the goal of extracting information. Torture is used in the repression of the *crimen maiestatis*, as this example demonstrates. The emperor Tiberius tortured Clemes, a libertus of Agrippa: ὁ Τιβέριος σοφίᾳ αὐτὸν διά τινων ὡς καὶ τὰ ἐκείνου φρονούντων ἐχειρώσατο, καὶ μετὰ τοῦτο βασανίσας ἵνα τι περὶ τῶν συνεγνωκότων αὐτῷ μάθῃ, ἔπειτ᾿ ἐπειδὴ μηδὲν ἐξελάλησεν, ἐπύθετο αὐτοῦ "πῶς ᾿Αγρίππας ἐγένου"· καὶ ὃς ἀπεκρίνατο ὅτι "οὕτως ὡς καὶ σὺ Καῖσαρ" (Tiberius, however, got him in his hands by a clever device and through the agency of certain persons who pretended to sympathize with the upstart. Then he tortured the prisoner in order to learn something about his fellow conspirators, but when the victim uttered not a word the emperor asked him, "How did you get to be Agrippa?" And he replied, "In the same way as you got to be Caesar;" Dio 57.16.4). Quintilian writes in a passage about the rhetorical figure of insinuation: Tyrannidis adfectatae damnatus torqueatur, ut conscios indicet; accusator eius optet, quod volet. Patrem quidam damnavit, optat, ne is torqueator; pater ei contra dicit ("A man condemned for attempting to establish himself as tyrant shall be tortured to make him reveal the names of his accomplices. The accuser shall choose what reward he pleases. A certain man has secured the condemnation of his father and demands as his reward that he should not be tortured. The father opposes his choice" (*Inst.* 9.2.81.6–7).

## (108) Philo, *In Flaccum* 36–40

ἦν τις μεμηνὼς ὄνομα Καραβᾶς οὐ τὴν ἀγρίαν καὶ θηριώδη μανίαν ἄσκηπτος γὰρ αὕτη γε καὶ τοῖς ἔχουσι καὶ τοῖς πλησιάζουσιν, ἀλλὰ τὴν ἀνειμένην καὶ μαλακωτέραν οὗτος διημέρευε καὶ διενυκτέρευε γυμνὸς ἐν ταῖς ὁδοῖς οὔτε θάλπος οὔτε κρυμὸν ἐκτρεπόμενος, ἄθυρμα νηπίων καὶ μειρακίων σχολαζόν-των [37] συνελάσαντες τὸν ἄθλιον ἄχρι τοῦ γυμνασίου καὶ στήσαντες μετέω-

---

BERVE, Die Tyrannis bei den Griechen (2 vols.; München: Beck, 1967), 1:471–75, 2:735–36; ARTHUR M. ECKSTEIN, Senate and General: Individual Decision-Making and Roman Foreign Relations 264–194 B.C. (Berkeley: University of California Press, 1987), 136–38.

[425] Cf. LINDA-MARIE GÜNTHER, Theodotos [5], BNP 14 (2009): 478. Theodotus was involved in a successful coup against Hieronymus in 214 B.C., and was elected *strategos* by the people, together with Andranodorus and others.

[426] KLAUS MEISTER, Adranodorus, BNP 1 (2002): 153; cf. WERNER HUSS, Geschichte der Karthager (HdA III.8; München: Beck, 1985), 350–53.

ρον, ἵνα καθορῷτο πρὸς πάντων, βύβλον μὲν εὐρύναντες ἀντὶ διαδήματος
ἐπιτιθέασιν αὐτοῦ τῇ κεφαλῇ, χαμαιστρώτῳ δὲ τὸ ἄλλο σῶμα περιβάλλουσιν
ἀντὶ χλαμύδος, ἀντὶ δὲ σκήπτρου βραχύ τι παπύρου τμῆμα τῆς ἐγχωρίου καθ᾽
ὁδὸν ἐρριμμένον ἰδών τις ἀναδίδωσιν ³⁸ ἐπεὶ δὲ ὡς ἐν θεατρικοῖς μίμοις τὰ
παράσημα τῆς βασιλείας ἀνειλήφει καὶ διεκεκόσμητο εἰς βασιλέα, νεανίαι
ῥάβδους ἐπὶ τῶν ὤμων φέροντες ἀντὶ λογχοφόρων ἑκατέρωθεν εἱστήκεσαν
μιμούμενοι δορυφόρους εἶθ᾽ ἕτεροι προσῄεσαν, οἱ μὲν ὡς ἀσπασόμενοι, οἱ δὲ
ὡς δικασόμενοι, οἱ δ᾽ ὡς ἐντευξόμενοι περὶ κοινῶν πραγμάτων. ³⁹ εἶτ᾽ ἐκ τοῦ
περιεστῶτος ἐν κύκλῳ πλήθους ἐξήχει βοή τις ἄτοπος Μάριν ἀποκαλούντων
οὕτως δέ φασι τὸν κύριον ὀνομάζεσθαι παρὰ Σύροις· ᾔδεσαν γὰρ Ἀγρίππαν
καὶ γένει Σύρον καὶ Συρίας μεγάλην ἀποτομὴν ἔχοντα, ἧς ἐβασίλευε ⁴⁰ ταῦτα
δὲ ἀκούων, μᾶλλον δὲ ὁρῶν ὁ Φλάκκος, δεόντως ἂν καὶ τὸν μεμηνότα συλλαβὼν καὶ καθείρξας, ἵνα μὴ παρέχῃ τοῖς κατακερτομοῦσιν ἀφορμὴν εἰς ὕβριν
τῶν βελτιόνων, καὶ τοὺς ἐνσκευάσαντας τιμωρησάμενος, ὅτι γε βασιλέα καὶ
φίλον Καίσαρος καὶ ὑπὸ τῆς Ῥωμαίων βουλῆς τετιμημένον στρατηγικαῖς
τιμαῖς ἐτόλμησαν καὶ ἔργοις καὶ λόγοις καὶ φανερῶς καὶ πλαγίως ὑβρίζειν, οὐ
μόνον οὐκ ἐπέπληξεν, ἀλλ᾽ οὐδ᾽ ἐπισχεῖν ἠξίωσεν ἄδειαν καὶ ἐκεχειρίαν
διδοὺς τοῖς ἐθελοκακοῦσι καὶ ἐθελέχθρως ἔχουσι, προσποιούμενος ἅ τε ἑώρα
μὴ ὁρᾶν καὶ ὧν ἤκουε μὴ ἀκούειν.

*Translation.* There was a certain madman named Karabas whose madness was
not the wild and savage kind which is dangerous both to the madmen themselves and to those who are near them, but of a more relaxed and gentler type.
He spent day and night naked in the streets, mindful of neither hear or cold,
the toy of the children and the youngsters who had nothing to do. ³⁷ They
drove the pitiful man to the gymnasium and raised him off the ground so that
he could be seen by all. They spread a leaf of papyrus on his head for a diadem and clothed the rest of his body with a doormat for a robe and for a scepter they gave him a small piece of native papyrus which they had found
thrown away in the street. ³⁸ And when he had received the insignia of royal
authority and when he had been adorned as a king, as in some theatrical spectacle,⁴²⁷ the young men carrying rods on their shoulders stood, as if they were
carrying spears, on each side of him in imitation of bodyguards. Then others
approached him, some who pretended to salute him, others as though they
were pleading their cause before him, and others to consult him about affairs
of the state. ³⁹ Then there arose a paradoxical⁴²⁸ shout from among the multitude of people standing around him, calling him "Marin," which is said to be
the word for "Lord" among the Syrians; for they knew that Agrippa was both

---

⁴²⁷ F. H. COLSON translates ὡς ἐν θεατρικοῖς μίμοις "as in some theatrical farce;" note that
μῖμος has the neutral sense of "mime, character-sketch" (LSJ s.v. μῖμος II.1). Of course, the
action of the Alexandrian youth was not a "neutral" play.

⁴²⁸ The adjective ἄτοπος is translated as "tremendous" (COLSON), "wonderful" (YONGE),
"strange" (HORST).

a Syrian by birth and also ruled as king over a great part of Syria.[40] When Flaccus heard, or rather saw all this, he should have arrested the madman and put him in prison, to prevent him from giving an opportunity to the violent mob to insult their superiors, and he should have punished those responsible for dressing him up like that, because they had dared both in word and deed, both openly and indirectly, to insult someone who was a king and a friend of Caesar, someone who had been honored by the Senate of Rome with the praetorian insignia. Instead, he did not merely not punish them, he did not even restrain them, thus giving license and impunity to those who were evil and malicious, pretending not to see what he saw and not to hear what he heard.

*Commentary.* The context of this passage is the visit of king Agrippa I, the grandson of king Herod, in Alexandria in the summer of A.D. 38, and the anti-Jewish violence that erupted in the city.[429] Philo levels massive accusations against the Egyptians, charging them with being jealous, envious, and innately hostile to the Jews (*Flacc.* 29). He regards the attacks against the Jews in Alexandria as an escalation of the traditional conflict between Jews and Egyptians. The episode of Karabas relates an incident in which the enemies of the Jews staged a mocking ceremony for Agrippa: they take a local madman named Karabas and dress him up as king in one of the gymnasia of the city. By hailing a madman as a Syrian (Aramaic) king, they caricature Agrippa, whose territory was mostly located in the mountains of Lebanon (which belonged to Syria) and his claim to royal power as the king of the Jews.[430] The non-interference of Flaccus, the Roman governor in Egypt, encouraged Alexandrians who hated the Jews to go a step further and engage in violent actions against the Jews of the city, e.g. erecting statues of the emperor in the synagogue thus desecrating them (*Flacc.* 41–44). Karabas was probably Jewish. This has been inferred from the name Καραβᾶς, which has been interpreted as Barab(b)as, the Aramaic name known from Mark 15:11, 15; Matt 27:16, 17, 20, 21, 26; Luke 23:18; John 18:40, or from the Aramaic term for "cabbage," used here as a nickname. Others argue for a Greek derivation of the name: since καραβᾶς also refers to a beetle or crayfish, the name of the man could be a nickname based on his way of walking.[431] A more likely basis for assuming that the insane man was Jewish is the phrase ἵνα καθορῷτο πρὸς πάντων ("so that he could be seen by all"): since Philo relates in *Spec.* 1.1–2 that many Alexandrians were ridiculing the Jewish practice of circumcision,

---

[429] Cf. SCHWARTZ, Agrippa I, 74–77; LOUIS H. FELDMAN, Jew and Gentile in the Ancient World: Attitudes and Interactions from Alexander to Justinian (Princeton: Princeton University Press, 1993), 113–17. For the historical context of Philo's *In Flaccum* cf. PIETER W. VAN DER HORST, Philo's Flaccus: The First Pogrom. Introduction, Translation, and Commentary (Philo of Alexandria Commentary 2; Leiden: Brill, 2003), 1–4, 18–38.

[430] Cf. SCHIMANOWSKI, Juden und Nichtjuden in Alexandrien, 113–114.

[431] Cf. HORST, Philo's Flaccus, 128. For the following point cf. ibid. 129.

the hostile crowd may have displayed Karabas, who walked around naked, with his circumcised member exposed to public ridicule. A. KERKESLAGER comments, "In the athletic context of the gymnasium the circumcision of the mock Jewish king presented a visible contrast with the uncircumsized young men that made up his bodyguard."[432] Karabas is given a mock diadem (a sheet of papyrus), a mock royal purple robe (a doormat probably made of papyrus), a mock scepter (made of papyrus), mock bodyguards, and a mock salute as kind: they hail him with the word Μάριν, the Aramaic word for "our Lord."[433] L. H. FELDMAN suggests that "the use of the Aramaic word would seem to be intended to emphasize the allegation that the Jews' first loyalty was to the Aramaic-speaking ruler of Palestine" rather than to the Roman emperor. [434]

The scene of Karabas being mocked as a king is regarded as "strongly reminiscent of the story of the mocking of Jesus as a dressed-up king."[435] Joel Marcus comments, "The mockery of Jesus, which was so similar to that of Carabas, may also have been a response to a local event, an insurrection ... with which the soldiers probably linked the so-called king of the Jews. What better way to obtain revenge for past revolutionary violence and deter future activity of the same sort than by torturing and mocking its supposed ringleaders, thereby exposing the emptiness of his pretensions to kingship?"[436]

## (109)  P. Louvre 68 (CPJ II 158a)

I

[Πα]ῦλος πε[ρὶ τ]οῦ βασιλέως ἐν[ ...]
[.]ο ὡς προήγαγον καὶ ἐτοσα[...
[.]ο ἀνηγ[όρε]υσε, καὶ Θέω[ν
[π]ερὶ τούτ[ου] διάταγμα ἀνέγνω [τοῦ?
[Λ]ούπου, ὡς προάγειν αὐ[τ]οὺς
[ἐ]κέλευε χλευάζων τὸν [ἀ]πὸ

---

[432] ALLEN KERKESLAGER, Maintaining Jewish Identity in the Greek Gymnasium: A 'Jewish Load' in CPJ 3.519 (= P. Schub. 37 = P. Berol. 13406, JSJ 28 (2011): 12–33, 32, in a study of CPJ III 519 which mentions laughter, in an athletic context, about a man bearing "a Jewish burden."

[433] Cf. JACOB HOFTIJZER and KAREL JONGELING, Dictionary of the North-West Semitic Inscriptions (Boston: Brill, 2003), s.v. *mar* 2.a: title of a king; the king of Aram was called *ma-ri-ʾ mrʾy mlk* "my Lord the king" (2:687). See HORST, Philo's Flaccus, 130.

[434] FELDMAN, Jew and Gentile, 115, also quoted by HORST, Philo's Flaccus, 131.

[435] HORST, Philo's Flaccus, 129, with reference to M. EUGENE BORING, KLAUS BERGER, and CARSTEN COLPE, Hellenistic Commentary to the New Testament (Nashville: Abingdon, 1995), 303–4; SCHWEMER, Passion des Messias, 160–61; WINTER, Trial, 147–49. See also BLINZLER, Prozeß, 327 n. 30; BROWN, Death, 1:812–13, 874; CHILTON / BOCK, Mark, 501.

[436] MARCUS, Mark, 2:1047, with reference to Mark 14:48. Cf. EVANS, Mark, 488, who argues that the close parallels do not "require us to conclude that Mark is dependent in some way on this incident or on Philo's work itself."

[σ]κηνῆς καὶ ἐκ μείμου βασιλέα.
[ο]ὕτως ἡμων καὶ ὁ αὐτοκράτωρ
[ἐ]σχεδίασεν εἰπὼν πρὸς
[Π]αῦλον καὶ τοὺς ἡμετέρου[ς
[πά]ντα[ς]· ἐν ταῖς τ[οι]αύταις πα
[ρα]τάξεσ[ι] γίνεται ἐμοὶ .η
[..] ἐν τῶι Δακικῶι πολέμ[ω]ι
....

*Translation.* Paulus (spoke) about the king / how they brought him forth and / (mocked him?); and Theon / read the edict of / Lupus ordering them to lead him forth / in order to make fun of / the king in the stage-mime. / After we had thus (testified?), the emperor / took occasion to remark to / Paulus and our people / as follows: "During such / disturbances ... / during the war in Dacia"

*Commentary.*[437] This papyrus, with at least eight columns and dating to the early second century A.D., relates a dispute between a Greek and a Jewish embassy before the emperor, identified as Hadrian (A.D. 117–138).[438] Paulus and Theon were among the leading members of the Alexandrian embassy to the emperor. Theon reads an edict (διάταγμα) of Lupus, who is identified with M. Rutilius Lupus, the *praefectus Aegypti* from A.D. 112–117.[439]

Some scholars refer to this text as illustrative of the soldiers' mocking of Jesus as would-be king.[440] The term βασιλεύς in the phrase τὸν ἀπὸ σκηνῆς καὶ ἐκ μείμου βασιλέα (line 7) has been interpreted as referring to the hero of a theatrical mime which the Alexandrians enacted in order to mock the Jews and their would-be king.[441] This interpretation is implausible, however, since

---

[437] Editio princeps: WLADIMIR BRUNET DE PRESLE, Notices et extraits des manuscrits de la Bibliothèque Impériale XVIII, Seconde Partie (Paris: Imprimerie Impériale, 1865), 383–90; definitive edition by ULRICH WILCKEN, Ein Aktenstück zum jüdischen Kriege Trajans, Hermes 27 (1892): 464–480; ULRICH WILCKEN, Zum alexandrinischen Antisemitismus, in Abhandlungen der königlich-sächsischen Gesellschaft der Wissenschaften (Band 27/23; Leipzig: Teubner, 1909), 781–839, 807–22; ERNST VON DOBSCHÜTZ, Jews and Anti-Semites in Ancient Alexandria, AJT 8 (1904): 728–755, 738–47; ANTON VON PREMERSTEIN, Alexandrinische und jüdische Gesandte vor Kaiser Hadrian, Hermes 57 (1922): 266–316; VICTOR A. TCHERIKOVER and ALEXANDER FUKS, eds., Corpus Papyrorum Judaicarum (3 vols.; Cambridge: Harvard University Press, 1957–1964), 87–99 (CPJ II 158a); HERBERT MUSURILLO, The Acts of the Pagan Martyrs I: Acta Alexandrinorum (orig. 1954; repr., Oxford: Clarendon, 2000), 49–59 (No. 9A, Acta Pauli et Antonini).

[438] WILCKEN had suggested Trajan.

[439] CHRISTINA WALDE, Rutilus [II 4] M. R. Lupus, BNP 12 (2009): 797; cf. SCHÜRER, History, 1:530.

[440] DAVID FLUSSER, Jesus in Selbstzeugnissen und Bilddokumenten (Hamburg: Rowohlt, 1968), 131–32; DAVID FLUSSER, The Sage from Galilee: Rediscovering Jesus' Genius (Grand Rapids: Eerdmans, 2007), 158; BLINZLER, Prozeß, 327 n. 30; EVANS, Mark, 488.

[441] WILHELM WEBER, Eine Gerichtsverhandlung vor Kaiser Traian, Hermes 50 (1915): 47–92, 81–83; PREMERSTEIN, Gesandte, 277; MUSURILLO, Acts of the Pagan Martyrs I, 248.

it has to assume that the Roman governor willingly participated in a play performed by the mob of Alexandria, and it leaves open the question as to the content of the edict mentioned in line 4. It seems preferable to identify the βασιλεύς directly with Loukuas, the messianic pretender of the Jews of Cyrene and leader of an armed revolt against the Romans: he would have been a prisoner in the hand of the Romans, who ruthlessly crushed the revolt, rather than in the hands of the Alexandrians.[442]

## 2.8 Requisitioning of Provincials

The Gospels relate that the soldiers who took Jesus to Golgotha compelled a certain Simon from Cyrene to carry the cross: "they forced him to carry the cross" (ἀγγαρεύουσιν ... ἵνα ἄρη τὸν σταυρὸν αὐτοῦ (Mark 15:21; Matt 27:32: τοῦτον ἠγγάρευσαν ἵνα ἄρη τὸν σταυρὸν αὐτοῦ; cf. Luke 23:26). Compulsory public service, known as ἀγγαρεία (Lat. *angaria*), imposed on the local population, was known in Persia, in Ptolemaic Egypt, and in the Roman empire.[443] The jurists of the third century used the term *angaria* (or *angarium*) for means of transport.[444] The following papyri and inscriptions illustrate the practice.

---

[442] TCHERIKOVER / FUKS, Corpus Papyrorum Judaicarum, II, 95, comment on line 7; they add: "And why would Hadrian be so angry with the Alexandrians ... when the object of their mockeries was the Jewish king, certainly a criminal in the eyes of the Romans?" On Lukuas, who is mentioned in Eusebius, *Hist. eccl.* 4.1.2, cf. MARTIN HENGEL, Messianische Hoffnung und politischer 'Radikalismus' in der 'jüdischen-hellenistischen Diaspora'. Zur Frage der Voraussetzungen des jüdischen Aufstandes unter Trajan 115–117 n.Chr. [1983], in Judaica et Hellenistica. Kleine Schriften I (WUNT 90; Tübingen: Mohr-Siebeck, 1996), 314–343, 322–23; JOHN M. G. BARCLAY, Jews in the Mediterranean Diaspora: From Alexander to Trajan (323 BCE – 117 CE) (Edinburgh: T & T Clark, 1996), 78–79; J. CARLETON PAGET, Messianism and Resistance amongst Jews and Christians in Egypt, in Jews [2007], Christians and Jewish Christians in Antiquity (WUNT 251; Tübingen: Mohr Siebeck, 2010), 103–122, 111–112. Dio Cassius 58.32 mentions a certain Andreas, whom some identify with Lukuas.

[443] Cf. MICHAEL ROSTOWZEW, Angariae, Klio 6 (1906): 249–258, on Matt 27:32 / Mark 15:21; Luke 23:26 cf. ibid. 251; STEPHEN MITCHELL, Requisitioned Transport in the Roman Empire: A New Inscription from Pisidia, JRS 66 (1976): 106–131; J. BRIAN CAMPBELL, The Emperor and the Roman Army, 31 BC – AD 235 (New York: Clarendon/Oxford University Press, 1984), 246–53; PETER HERRMANN, Hilferufe aus römischen Provinzen. Ein Aspekt der Krise des römischen Reiches im 3. Jhdt. n. Chr. (BSJJGW 8/4; Hamburg / Göttingen: Vandenhoeck & Ruprecht, 1990), 43–49; NAPHTALI LEWIS, The Compulsory Public Services of Roman Egypt (orig. 1982; repr., Papyrologica Florentina 28; Florence: Gonnelli, 1997); HORSLEY and LLEWELYN, New Documents, 7:58–92; ANNE KOLB, Angaria, BNP 1 (2002): 693. For Persia, cf. Herodotus 3.126.2; 8.98.2; Xenophon, *Cyr.* 8.6.17. On the petition from Aragua in Phrygia to the emperor Philippus Arabs (CIL III 14191; OGIS II 519; IGR IV 598), cf. HERRMANN, ibid. 28–33; TOR HAUKEN, Petition and Response: An Epigraphic Study of the Petitions to Roman Emperors, 181–249 (Monographs from the Norwegian Institute at Athens 2; Bergen: Norwegian Institute at Athens, 1998), 140–61.

[444] Cf. *Dig.* 50.4.18.4; 50.4.18.21; 50.4.18.29; 50.5.10.2; 50.5.10.11.

**(110)** *SEG* XXVI 1392

Sex(tus) Sotidius Strabo Libuscidianus leg(atus)
Ti(beri) Caesaris Augusti pro pr(aetore) dic(it)

Est quidem omnium iniquissimum me edicto meo adstringere id quod
Augusti alter deorum alter principum

maximus diligentissime caverunt ne quis gratuitis vehiculis utatur sed
quoniam licentia quorundam

5 praes(e)ntem vindictam desiderat formulam eorum quae [pra]estari iudico
oportere in singulis civitatibus

et vicis proposui servaturus eam aut si neglecta erit vindicaturus non mea
tantum potestate sed

principis optimi a quo id ip[s]um in mandatis accepti maiestate. (*vac*)

Sagalassenos{o} ministerium carrorum decem et mulorum totidem
praestare debent ad usus neces-

sarios transe/untium et accipere in singula carra et in singulos schoenos ab
iis qui utentur aeris denos in mulos autem singulos

10 et schoenos singulos aeris quaternos quod si asinos malent eodem pretio
duos pro uno mulo dent.

Aut si malent in singulos mulos et in singula carra id quod accepturi erant
si ipsi praeberent (*vac*)

dare praestent iis qui alterius civitatis aut vici munere fungentur ut idem
procedant.

Praestare autem debebunt vehicula usque Cormasa et Conanam. Neque
tamen omnibus

huius rei ius erit sed procuratori principis optimi filioque eius usu da[to
us]que ad carra decem aut

15 pro singulis carris mulorum trium aut pro singulis mulis asinorum binorum
quibus eodem

tempore utentur soluturi pretium a me constitutum praeterea militantibus et
iis qui diplomum hab-

ebunt et iis qui ex aliis provincis militantes commeabunt ita ut senatori
populi Romani non plus quam

decem carra aut pro singulis carris muli terni aut pro singulis mulis asini
bini praestentur soluturis id quod

praescripsi equiti Romano cuius officio princeps optimus utitur ter carra
aut in singula terni muli aut

20 in singulos [mu]los bini asini dari debebunt eadem condicione si quo
amplius quis desiderabit conducet

arbitrio locantis centurioni carrum aut tres muli aut asini sexs eadem
condicione. Iis qui frumen-

tum aut aliudq<u>id tale vel quaestus sui cau{s}sa vel usus portant

praestari nihil volo neque cuiquam p-
ro suo aut suorum libertorum aut servorum iumentu mansionem omnibus
    qui erunt ex
comitatu nostro et militantibus ex omnibus provincis et principis optimi
    libertis et servis et iumentis
eorum gratuitam praestari oportet ita ut reliqua ab invitis gratuita non
    e(x)sigant (*vac*)

*Translation*. Sextus Sotidius Strabo Libuscidianus, legate of Tiberius Caesar Augustus acting as praetor, declares: It is indeed of all things most inequitable that I should be tightening up by my edict what the two Augustuses, the one the greatest of gods, the other the greatest of leaders, most carefully guarded against, namely that no one should make use of transport free, but since the licence of certain people // demands immediate action, I have promulgated in the individual cities and villages a schedule of what I judge desirable to be supplied, it being my intention to maintain it or if neglected enforce it not merely by my own powers but by the supremacy of the excellent leader from which I accept this very thing in my mandate. The Sagalassenes are obligated to supply a service of ten carts and as many mules for the necessary uses of those passing through, and to accept ten bronze (asses) per cart per schoenus from those who use them, or per mule // per schoenus, four, but if they prefer donkeys they are to supply two for one mule at the same rate. Of if they prefer they are to pay over what they would have received per mule and per cart, if they themselves had provided them, to those who perform the obligation of another city or village, so that they can fulfill it. They shall be obliged, moreover, to supply transport as far as Cormasa and Conana. However, not everyone has the right to this, but to the procurator of the excellent leader and to his son is granted the use of it up to ten carts, or // three mules in place of a cart, or two donkeys in place of a mule when used at the same time, subject to their paying the price established by me; and likewise, to those on military service, or who hold a certificate, and to those who are travelling from other provinces on military service, on the basis that to a senator of the Roman people are supplied no more than ten carts or three mules in place of a cart or two donkeys in place of a mule subject to their paying what I have prescribed; to a Roman knight whose services the excellent leader is using three carts or three mules for a cart or // two donkeys for a mule must be given on the same terms, while anyone who desires more shall have it at the contractor's discretion; to a centurion a cart or three mules or six donkeys on the same terms. To those who carry grain or any such thing for their own profit or use I do not wish anything to be supplied, nor (anything) for anyone for his own beasts of burden or those of his freedmen or slaves. Accommodation for all those who belong to my staff and for those on military service from all provinces and for the freedmen and slaves of the excellent leader and their beasts // ought to be supplied free, but without their demanding the rest (of their costs) free from those who are unwilling (to supply them).

*Commentary*.[445] The inscription is a bilingual edict of Sextus Sotidius Strabo Libuscidianus, discovered in Burdur in Pisidia, and dated to A.D. 18/19, issued when he was *legatus pro praeatore* of the province of Galatia early in the reign of emperor Tiberius. The edict applies a complex set of rules, drawn up by the emperor, relating to the right of official travellers to requisition transport at fixed prices and to demand free accommodation up to specific limits to the city of Sagalassos.[446] The text provides the earliest epigraphical evidence for the system of imposing transport and billeting services on local communities in the Roman empire, which constantly gave rise to problems.[447] The *primus optimus* is the emperor Tiberius.[448] E. A. JUDGE infers from the frustrated *iniquissimum* ("most inequitable," line 3) in the preamble the possibility that "Tiberius had given him only general *mandata* (3) / *adikon* (27) on the subject, perhaps refusing to supply such specific advice as Augustus had to the proconsuls in the Cyrene edicts[449] or Trajan to Pliny (*Ep.* 10), but had left open the possibility of his seeking help if he failed to assert control on his own authority."[450] It should be noted that the governor invokes the *maiestas* (line 7; Greek: θειότης) of the emperor, i.e., of Tiberius, as the reason for punishment if the stipulations of the edict are not obeyed. The term *schoenos* (Greek σχοῖνος) is a measure of travel time, perhaps corresponding to *parasang* of the

---

[445] Editio princeps: MITCHELL, Requisitioned Transport; with corrections in STEPHEN MITCHELL, The Requisitioning Edict of Sex. Sotidius Strabo Libuscidianus, ZPE 45 (1982): 99–100. AE 1976 653 = SEG XXVI 1392; E. A. JUDGE, in HORSLEY and LLEWELYN, New Documents, 1:36–45 (No. 9) = EDWIN A. JUDGE, The Regional *kanōn* for Requisitioned Transport [1981], in The First Christians in the Roman World: Augustan and New Testament Essays (ed. J. R. Harrison; WUNT 229; Tübingen: Mohr Siebeck, 2008), 348–359; ROBERT K. SHERK, ed, The Roman Empire: Augustus to Hadrian (Translated Documents of Greece and Rome 6; Cambridge: Cambridge University Press, 1988), 55–56 (No. 29). We print only the Latin text; the Greek texts occupies lines 26–52. The translation follows JUDGE, omitting the Greek variations.

[446] FERGUS MILLAR, State and Subject: The Impact of Monarch [1984], in Rome, the Greek World, and the East. Vol. 1: The Roman Republic and the Augustan Revolution (ed. G. M. Rogers H. M. Cotton; Chapel Hill: University of North Carolina Press, 2002), 292–313, 303–4. Cf. ANNE KOLB, Transport und Nachrichtentransfer im Römischen Reich (Klio Beihefte NF 2; Berlin: Akademie Verlag, 2000), 54–62.

[447] Cf. MITCHELL, Requisitioned Transport, 111–12, who lists 21 documents.

[448] Cf. JUDGE, Transport, 353–54, against MITCHELL, Requisitioned Transport, 113, who argues that the phrase refers to Augustus, who must have appointed Sotidius. JUDGE points out that the reference to the procurator's son (lines 14, 37) fits the year A.D. 18 when Germanicus, the son of Tiberius, shared the consulship with him and was sent to take control of the eastern provinces, formally on the same legal terms with his father.

[449] EHRENBERG / JONES, Documents, No. 311.

[450] JUDGE, Transport, 352.

Persian system. E. A. JUDGE links the text with Simon of Cyrene being required to carry Jesus' cross (Matt 27:32; Mark 15:21).[451]

**(111)** P. London III 1171

Λεύκιος Αἰμίλλις Ῥῆκτος λέγει·
μηδενὶ ἐξέστω ἐνγαρευειν τοὺς ἐπὶ τῆς χώρας
μηδὲ ἐφόδια ἢ ἄλλο τι δωρεὰν αἰτεῖν ἄτερ
ἐμο[ῦ] διπλώματος, λαμ[β]άνειν δὲ ἕκας[το]ν τῶν
5  ἐχ[όν]των ἐμὸν δίπλωμα τὰ αὐταάρκει ἐπιδήτια
τιμὴν ἀποδιδόντας αὐτῶν. ἐὰν δέ τις
μηνυθῆ ἢ τῶν στρατευομένων ἢ τῶν μαχαιροφόρω(ν)
ἢ ὅστις οὖν τῶν ὑπηρετῶν τῶ[ν ἐν τ]αῖς δημοσ[ίαις]
χρήαις παρ[ὰ τ]ὸ ἐμὸν διάτα[γμ]α πεποηκὼς ἢ βεβισ-
10  μένος τινὰ τῶν ἀπὸ τῆς χώρας ἢ ἀργυρολογήσας,
κατὰ τούτου τῇ ἀνωτάτω χρήσομαι τειμωρίᾳ
(Ἔτους) β̄ Τιβερίου Κλαυδίου Καίσαρος Σεβαστοῦ Αὐτοκράτορος
Γερμανικείου δ̄

*Translation.* Lucius Aemilius Rectus declares: / No one is permitted to requisition those in the chora (i.e., country districts) / or to ask for travelling provisions or anything else free of charge without / my diploma, but each person // holding my diploma should take sufficient provisions / paying their price. If any soldier or policeman / or servant of public services is informed against / as having acted against my order or as having forced // any of those from the chora or as having levied money, / I will use the severest punishment against him. / Year 2 of Tiberius Claudius Caesar Augustus Imperator, / on the 4th of Germanikeios.[452]

*Commentary.*[453] The papyrus, dated to A.D. 42, records an edict of Lucius Aemilius Rectus, the *praefectus Aegypti.*[454] The edict prohibits traveling offi-

---

[451] JUDGE, Transport, 355; cf. Matt 5:41; Matt 21:2–7 / Mark 11:2–6 / Luke 19:30–34; Acts 27:2, 6; 28:11, and to 2 Cor 10:13–16 with respect to the meaning of the term κανῶν.

[452] Germanikeios is the Egyptian month Pachon (April 26 – May 25), probably renamed in honor of the emperor Claudius.

[453] Editio princeps: FREDERIC G. KENYON and H. IDRIS BELL, Greek Papyri in the British Museum: Catalogue Vol. III (London: Frowde, 1907), 105–107 (No. 1171); cf. MITTEIS / WILCKEN, Chrestomathie, No. 439; STEPHEN R. LLEWELYN in HORSLEY and LLEWELYN, New Documents, 7:66–67; translation from LLEWELYN, with some modifications; cf. the translations of NAPHTALI LEWIS and MEYER REINHOLD, eds., Roman Civilization. Selected Readings (2 vols. Third ed.; New York: Columbia University Press, 1990), 2:320; KOLB, Transport, 76.

[454] Lucius Aemilius Rectus is known for the letter of emperor Claudius which he posted in Alexandria in A.D. 41 (P. London VI 1912 = CPJ II 153), warning of possible imperial intervention if the Jews of Alexandria dared to entertain fellow Jews from Syria or Egypt fomenting "what is a general plague infecting the whole world."

cials of the provincial (and presumably imperial) Roman administration – soldiers (στρατευόμενοι), policemen (μαχαιροφόροι) or "servants of public services" (ᾧστις τῶν ὑπηρετῶν τῶν ἐν ταῖς δημοσίαις χρήαις) – from unauthorized or excessive demands on the local population. Requisitioning local people or provisions requires a "diploma" (διπλώμα), i.e., a permit from the prefect.

**(112)** *PSI* V 446

   Μᾶρκος Πετρώνιος Μαμερτῖνος
   ἔπαρχος Αἰγύπτου λέγει·
   ἐπέγνων πολλοὺς τῶν στρατ[ι]ωτῶν ἄνευ διπλῆς
   διὰ τῆς χώρας πορευομένους πλοῖα καὶ κτήνη καὶ
5  ἀνθρώπους αἰτεῖν παρὰ τὸ προσῆκον, τὰ μὲν αὐτοὺς π[ρ]ὸς βίαν ἀποσπῶντας, τὰ δὲ καὶ κατὰ χάριν
   ἢ θεραπείαν π[α]ρὰ τῶν στρατηγῶν λαμβάνοντας,
   ἐξ οὗ τοῖς μὲν ἰδιώταις ὕβρις[455] τε καὶ ἐπηρείας γείνε -
   σθαι, τὸ δὲ στρατ[ι]ωτικὸν ἐπὶ πλεονεξίᾳ καὶ ἀδικίᾳ
10 λαμβά[ν]εσθαι[456] συνβέβηκε. παραγγέλλω δὴ τοῖς στρα-
   τηγοῖς καὶ βασιλικοῖς ἀπαξαπλῶς μηδενὶ παρέχειν ἄν[ε]υ διπλῆς μηθὲ ἕν τῶν ἱς παραπομπὴν-
   διδο[μέ]νων μήτε πλέοντι μήτε πεζῇ βαδί[ζον-]
   τι, ὡς [ἐμ]οῦ κο[λ]άσοντος ἐρρωμένως ἐάν τις ἁλῷ
15 μετὰ τ[οῦτο] τὸ διάταγμα λαμβάνων ἢ διδούς
   τι τῶν [προειρη]μένων.
   [("Ετους) .. ] Ἀδριαγοῦ Καίσαρος τοῦ
      κυρίου, . [ . ] ..

*Translation.* Marcus Petronius Mamertinus / prefect of Egypt, says: / I have discovered that many of the soldiers travelling without a diploma / through the chora (i.e., country districts) requisition boats, animals, and // people contrary to what is proper, some / they drag away forcibly, others pursuant to a favor / or receiving help from the *strategoi*, / whence it happens that private persons suffer outrages and insults / and the army on account of its greed and wrongdoing // acquires a bad name. I give orders to the *strategoi* and *basilikogrammateis* absolutely not to provide anyone / without a diploma any means of transport / whether he is sailing or travelling on foot, / since I will exact vigorous punishment if anyone is caught // taking or giving after this order / any of the aforementioned. / [Year ?]of Hadrian, Caesar, the lord, [month and day].

---

[455] ὕβρεις.
[456] διαβά[λλ]εσθαι.

*Commentary.*[457] The reference to emperor Hadrian in line 17 dates the papyrus to between A.D. 133–137. This edict of Marcus Petronius Mamertinus, the prefect of Egypt,[458] orders the *strategoi* and *basilikogrammateis* – officials who were responsible for the financial administration of a nome – not to provide transport to people travelling without a *diploma*. Only those officials who hold *diplomata* from the prefect are entitled to use transport provided by the public. Nothing is said regarding financial compensation to the owners of the requisitioned transport. S. L. WALLACE suggests that in Egypt a capitation tax (μερισμὸς διπλῶν) was raised by the Romans from the second century A.D. onwards to defray the cost of billeting officials and soldiers.[459]

## 2.9 Carrying the Crossbeam

The Synoptic Gospels relate that the soldiers forced Simon from Cyrene to carry the cross on which Jesus was to be executed. Mark 15:21: ἀγγαρεύουσιν παράγοντά τινα Σίμωνα Κυρηναῖον ἐρχόμενον ἀπ' ἀγροῦ ... ἵνα ἄρῃ τὸν σταυρὸν αὐτοῦ ("they compelled a passer-by, who was coming in from the country, to carry his cross; it was Simon of Cyrene"); Matt 27:32: τοῦτον ἠγγάρευσαν ἵνα ἄρῃ τὸν σταυρὸν αὐτοῦ ("they compelled this man to carry his cross"); Luke 23:26: ἐπέθηκαν αὐτῷ τὸν σταυρὸν φέρειν ὄπισθεν τοῦ Ἰησοῦ). According to John 19:17, Jesus carried the cross himself: καὶ βαστά-ζων ἑαυτῷ τὸν σταυρὸν ἐξῆλθεν εἰς τὸν λεγόμενον Κρανίου Τόπον, ὃ λέγεται Ἑβραϊστὶ Γολγοθα ("and carrying the cross by himself, he went out to what is called The Place of the Skull, which in Hebrew is called Golgotha"). This is a reference to the *patibulum*, the heavy horizontal beam or crossbar to which the outstretched arms of the convicted criminal were attached with nails or ropes, then hoisted upright on a post so that the convict could be exposed to the public until he died.[460] The following texts are often cited in New Testament commentaries as illustrative of Jesus (or Simon of Cyrene) carrying the cross to the place of execution.[461]

---

[457] Editio princeps: GIROLAMO VITELLI, MEDEA NORSA, and VITTORIO BARTOLETTI, eds., Papiri greci e latini (Società Italiana per la ricerca dei Papiri greci e latini in Egitto; 15 vols.; Florence: Ariani, 1912–2008), Vol. V (1917), 1–2 (No. 446); cf. STEPHEN R. LLEWELYN in HORSLEY and LLEWELYN, New Documents, 7:70-71, with translation, which is adopted here with minor modifications; see ibid. for the commentary.

[458] MISCHA MEIER, Petronius [7] M. P. Mamertinus, BNP 10 (2007): 880; he was prefect of the praetorian guard under Antoninus Pius.

[459] SHERMAN L. WALLACE, Taxation in Egypt from Augustus to Diocletian (orig. 1938; repr., Princeton: Princeton University Press, 1969), 153–54; WALLACE, Taxation; WALLACE, Taxationcf. HORSLEY and LLEWELYN, New Documents, 7:71.

[460] Cf. CHRISTOPH H. BRECHT, Patibulum, RE XVIII/4 (1949): 2167–2169.

[461] Cf. LUZ, Matthäus, 4:312 n. 23; EVANS, Mark, 499; MICHAEL WOLTER, Das Lukasevangelium (HNT 5; Tübingen: Mohr Siebeck, 2008), 752; RUDOLF BULTMANN, Das

**(113)**  Plautus, *Miles Gloriosus* 358–360

Pal. [358] quid ais tu, Sceledre?
Scel. Hanc rem gero. habeo auris, loquere quidvis.
Pal. [359] Credo ego istoc extemplo tibi esse eundum actutum extra portam,
[360] dispessis manibus, patibulum quom habebis.

*Translation*. Palaestrio: [358] What do you say, Sceledrus? Scel.: I am doing my job.[462] I have ears, just speak your wishes. Pal.: [359] You will have to go through the gate [360] with hands spread out, when you will have the crossbar.

*Commentary*.[463] Titus Maccius Plautus (c. 250–184 B.C.)[464] wrote twenty-one comedies, whose 21,500 verses represent the largest corpus in Latin literature before Cicero. On account of the reference to Cn. Naevius in lines 211–212, the play *Miles gloriosus* ("The braggart soldier") is generally dated to 206/204 B.C.[465] With 1431 lines, *Miles gloriosus* is the longest Roman comedy. The swaggeringly vainglorious mercenary soldier Pyrgopolinices has abducted the

---

Evangelium des Johannes (21. Auflage; orig. 1941; repr., KEK II; Göttingen: Vandenhoeck & Ruprecht, 1986), 517 n. 4.

[462] Following MASON HAMMOND, ARTHUR M. MACK, and WALTER MOSKALEW, T. Macci Plauti Miles Gloriosus (Edited with an Introduction and Notes; orig. 1963; repr., Cambridge: Harvard University Press, 1997), 109.

[463] Text: WALLACE M. LINDSAY, T. Macci Plauti Comoediae (2 vols.; orig. 1903; repr., Oxford Classical Texts; Oxford: Clarendon, 1910); for other text editions and translations cf. GUSTAV LÖWE, GEORG GÖTZ, and FRIEDRICH SCHÖLL, T. Macci Plauti Comoediae. Recensuit, Instrumento Critico et Prolegomenis. Tom. IV. Casina, Miles gloriosus, Persa, Mostellaria, Cistellaria, Fragmenta (BSGRT; Leipzig: Teubner, 1890); FRIEDRICH LEO, T. Macci Plauti Comoediae (2 vols.; orig. 1895–1896; repr., Berlin: Weidmann, 1958); PAUL NIXON, Plautus (5 vols.; LCL; Cambridge: Harvard University Press, 1916–1938), 3:120–285; HAMMOND / MACK / MOSKALEW, Miles Gloriosus ; PETER RAU, T. Maccius Plautus. Miles gloriosus. Der glorreiche Hauptmann (Lateinisch / Deutsch; Stuttgart: Reclam, 1984); PETER L. SMITH, Plautus. Three Comedies: Miles Gloriosus, Pseudolus, Rudens. Translated and with an Introduction (Ithaca: Cornell University Press, 1991); ERICH SEGAL, The Braggart Soldier *(Miles Gloriosus)*, in Plautus. The Comedies. Volume I (ed. David R. Slavitt and P. Bovie; Complete Roman Drama in Translation; Baltimore: Johns Hopkins University Press, 1995), 65–179; DEENA BERG and DOUGLASS PARKER, Plautus and Terence. Five Comedies. Miles Gloriosus. Menaechmi. Bacchides. Hecyra. Adelphoe (Indianapolis: Hackett, 1999); WOLFGANG DE MELO, Plautus. The Merchant. The Braggart Soldier. The Ghost. The Persian (LCL; Cambridge: Harvard University Press, 2011).

[464] Cf. ECKHARD LEFÈVRE, Plautus, BNP 11 (2007): 361–366; MICHAEL VON ALBRECHT and GARETH SCHMELING, A History of Roman Literature: From Livius Andronicus to Boethius (2 vols.; Mnemosyne Sup 165; Leiden: Brill, 1996), 163–205; WERNER SUERBAUM, Die archaische Literatur von den Anfängen bis Sullas Tod. Die vorliterarische Periode und die Zeit von 240 bis 78 v. Chr. (HdA VIII.1; München: Beck, 2002), 183–228.

[465] Cf. SUERBAUM, Archaische Literatur, 187; cf. LOTHAR SCHAAF, Der Miles Gloriosus des Plautus und sein griechisches Original. Ein Beitrag zur Kontaminationsfrage (München: Fink, 1977), 373–77.

hetaira Philocomasium, the lover of the young Athenian Pleusicles, to Ephesus. Palaestrio, Pleusicles' brilliant slave-strategist,[466] has also been abducted and sold to Pyrgopolinices. Palaestrio informed his master of the whereabouts of Philocomasium and, after his arrival in Ephesus, manages to accommodate him next door in the house of the bachelor Periplectomenus. Sceledrus, a slave of Pyrgopolinices, is Philocomasium's guard. The ultimate aim of the plot is the rescue of Philocomasium from Pyrgopolinices and her reunion with Pleusicles. At the end of Act II Scene 3, the slave Sceledrus stations himself in front of Periplectomenus' house, evidently with his arms spread out to block the door. At the beginning of Act II Scene 4, Palaestrio emerges from Pyrgopolinices' house, bringing with him Philocomasium. Palaestrio taunts Sceledrus with a reference to crucifixion, a punishment often inflicted on slaves for serious dereliction of duty: if he neglects his duty guarding Philocomasium, he might have to walk through the gate "with hands spread out" (dispessis manibus), with the crossbeam of the cross on his back (patibulum quom habebis). The gate is probably a reference to the Esquiline gate in Rome outside of which public executions took place and where the poor were buried.[467] The crucifixion taunt is coined for the purpose of humor, grim though it may be,[468] taking for granted that slaves are punished by having their outstretched arms tied to a crossbeam which they then have to carry to the place of their execution.[469]

## (114)  Plautus, *Carbonaria*, Frag. 2

patibulum ferat per urbem, deinde offigitur cruci.

*Translation.* He carries the crossbeam through the city, then he is affixed to the cross.

*Commentary.*[470] Besides Plautus' 21 comedies that have been preserved, there are fragments of 32 comedies whose names are of uncertain authenticity.

---

[466] ERICH SEGAL, Roman Laughter: The Comedy of Plautus (Second ed.; orig. 1968; repr., Oxford: Oxford University Press, 1987), 126.

[467] Cf. HAMMOND / MACK / MOSKALEW, Miles Gloriosus , 109, adding the comment: "Crucifixion seems not to have been practiced in Greece at this time, and its mention may therefore be taken as a distinctly Roman addition by Plautus."

[468] Cf. HENGEL, Mors Turpissima Crucis (cf. HENGEL, Crucifixion, 52) who speaks of "gallows humor."

[469] SEGAL, Laughter, points out that "Plautus mentions an astonishing number of torture devices, including iron chains, hot tar, burning clothes, restraining collars, the rack, the pillory, and the mill." For the *patibulum* cf. Plautus, *Mostellaria* 55–57 (below No. 303).

[470] The fragment is found in Nonius Marcellus, *De compendiosa doctrina* 221; cf. WILLIAM M. LINDSAY, Nonius Marcellus. De Conpendiosa Doctrina (3 vols.; orig. 1903; repr., Bibliotheca Teubneriana; München / Leipzig: Saur, 2003), 327.

Three brief one-line fragments of the play *Carbonaria* ("The Charcoal Woman") are known.

Fragment 2 is often cited to illustrate Simon of Cyrene carrying the cross on which Jesus was executed through the city of Jerusalem: "it was usual for condemned criminals to carry the crossbeam through the city to the place of crucifixion."[471]

**(115)** Dionysius Halicarnassus, *Antiquitates Romanae* 7.69.1–2

ἀνὴρ Ῥωμαῖος οὐκ ἀφανὴς θεράποντα ἴδιον ἐπὶ τιμωρίᾳ θανάτου παραδοὺς τοῖς ὁμοδούλοις ἄγειν, ἵνα δὴ περιφανὴς ἡ τιμωρία τοῦ ἀνθρώπου γένηται, δι' ἀγορᾶς αὐτὸν ἐκέλευσε μαστιγούμενον ἕλκειν καὶ εἴ τις ἄλλος ἦν τῆς πόλεως τόπος ἐπιφανὴς ἡγούμενον τῆς πομπῆς, ἣν ἔστελλε τῷ θεῷ κατ' ἐκεῖνον τὸν καιρὸν ἡ πόλις. ² οἱ δ' ἄγοντες τὸν θεράποντα ἐπὶ τὴν τιμωρίαν τὰς χεῖρας ἀποτείναντες ἀμφοτέρας καὶ ξύλῳ προσδήσαντες παρὰ τὰ στέρνα τε καὶ τοὺς ὤμους καὶ μέχρι τῶν καρπῶν διήκοντι παρηκολούθουν ξαίνοντες μάστιξι γυμνὸν ὄντα. ὁ δ' ἐν τοιᾷδε ἀνάγκῃ κρατούμενος ἐβόα τε φωνὰς δυσφήμους, ἃς ἡ ἀλγηδὼν ἐβούλετο, καὶ κινήσεις διὰ τὴν αἰκίαν ἀσχήμονας ἐκινεῖτο. τοῦτον δὴ πάντες ἐνόμισαν εἶναι τὸν ὑπὸ τοῦ θεοῦ μηνυόμενον ὀρχηστὴν οὐ' καλόν.

*Translation.* A Roman citizen of no uncertain status had ordered one of his slaves to be put to death. He handed him over to his fellow-slaves to be led away and, in order that his punishment could be witnessed by all, ordered them to drag him through the forum and every other prominent place in the city as they whipped him, and that he should go in front of the procession that the Romans were conducting at that time in honor of the god. ² The men who had been ordered to lead the slave to his punishment stretched out both his arms and affixed them to a piece of wood which extended across his chest and shoulders as far as his wrists; they followed him, thrashing his naked body with whips. The culprit, overcome by such cruelty, not only shouted shameful expressions, forced forth by the pain, but he also made indecent movements under the blows.

---

[471] JUSTIN TAYLOR, The Role of Rhetorical Elaboration in the Formation of Mark's Passion Narrative (Mark 14:43–16:8): An Enquiry, in Greco-Roman Culture and the New Testament (Studies Commemorating the Centennial of the Pontifical Biblical Institute; ed. D. E. Aune and F. E. Brenk; NovTSup 143; Leiden: Brill, 2012), 11–26; cf. HENGEL, Mors Turpissima Crucis, 631; HENGEL, Crucifixion, 62; BROWN, Death, 2:912.

*Commentary*.[472] Dionysius of Halicarnassus, in Rome since about 30 B.C., published the first of 20 books of his "Roman History" (Ῥωμαικὴ ἀρχαιολο-γία, Lat. *Antiquitates Romanae*) in 8/7 B.C.[473] The historical context of *Ant. Rom.* 7.69.1–2 is the election of magistrates, when Quintus Sulpicius Camerinus (Cornutus)[474] and Spurius Larcius Flavus were elected consuls, the latter for the second time (7.68.1). Spurius Larcius Flavus (or Rufus), whose identity is uncertain, was consul in 506 and 490 B.C.; he is said to have been commander in a war against the Etruscans (Livius 2.11.7–10).[475] In the year of the consulship, various disturbances occurred, unusual sights appeared to many, voices were heard, abnormal children and cattle were born, oracles were uttered, women foretold dreadful misfortunes, great numbers of cattle perished in a pestilence, and many people became sick. Some thought that these events were the will of the god who was angry with them, others thought that they were pure change (7.68.1–2). Then a sick, old farmer named Titus Latinius was brought before the senate on a litter; he told the senators of a dream, repeated three times because he did not believe it, in which Jupiter Capitolinus appeared to him, telling him to inform his fellow citizens that "in the recent procession they did not give me an acceptable leader of the dance, in order that they may renew the rites and perform them over again, for I have not accepted these" (7.68.3). When the farmer got well after telling his dream, the senators were speechless, unable to discern what the god's message meant, until one of them recalled the incident of the slave who had been condemned to death and who, on orders of his master, had been walking in front of the procession (7.69.1–2) The slave was dragged (ἕλκειν) through the forum (δι' ἀγορᾶς) and every other prominent place in the city (τῆς πόλεως τόπος ἐπιφανής), being whipped (μαστιγούμενον). His fellow slaves had forced him to stretch out his arms (τὰς χεῖρας ἀποτείναντες ἀμφοτέρας), which they affixed to a piece of wood (ξύλῳ προσδήσαντες παρὰ τὰ στέρνα) that ex-

---

[472] Text: KARL JACOBY, Dionysius Halicarnaseus. Antiquitates Romanae (4 vols.; orig. 1888–1905; repr., Bibliotheca Scriptorum Graecorum et Romanorum Teubneriana; Stuttgart / Leipzig: Teubner, 1997); for other editions and translations cf. EARNEST CARY, Dionysius of Halicarnassus. Roman Antiquities (8 vols.; LCL; Cambridge: Harvard University Press, 1937–1950); VALÉRIE FROMENTIN and JACQUES-HUBERT SAUTEL, Denys d' Halicarnasse. Antiquités Romaines (Collection Budé; Paris: Les Belles Lettres, 1998).

[473] SOTERA FORNARO, Dionysius [18] D. of Halicarnassus, BNP 4 (2004): 480–484, 480.

[474] Cf. WALTER EDER and JOHANNES RENGER, Chronologies of the Ancient World: Names, Dates and Dynasties (Brill's New Pauly Supplements; Brill: Leiden, 2007), 200 (No. 264); ROBERT WERNER, Der Beginn der römischen Republik. Historisch-chronologische Untersuchungen über die Anfangszeit der libera res publica (München: Oldenbourg, 1963), 145, 157, 264.

[475] CHRISTIAN MÜLLER, Larcius [I 2] L. (Flavius?), Sp., BNP 7 (2005): 245. WERNER, Beginn, 266, accepts Spurius Larcius as a historical person since Larcius is the name of a *gens* of Etruscan origin whose members are mentioned only in the context of the early phase of the Republic.

tended across his chest (παρὰ τὰ στέρνα) and shoulders (τοὺς ὤμους) as far as his wrists (μέχρι τῶν καρπῶν). As he walked in front of the procession, they followed him (παρηκολούθουν) and thrashed his naked body with whips (ξαίνοντες μάστιξι γυμνὸν ὄντα). The condemned slave shouted shameful words and made indecent movements, which was now interpreted in terms of the man being "the unacceptable dancer signified by the god" (7.69.2). The story is often discussed by New Testament scholars in the context of miracle narratives and dream vision.[476] J. BLINZLER and others cite this text for the nudity of the convicted criminal who is led to execution.[477] C. S. KEENER refers to this text for scourging that preceded crucifixion,[478] M. WOLTER for condemned criminals carrying the crossbeam to the place of execution.[479]

**(116)**  Chariton, *Chaereas and Callirhoe* 4.2.6–7

κἀκεῖνος οὐδὲ ἰδὼν αὐτοὺς οὐδὲ ἀπολογουμένων ἀκούσας εὐθὺς ἐκέλευσε τοὺς ἑξκαίδεκα τοὺς ὁμοσκήνους ἀνασταυρῶσαι. [7] προήχθησαν οὖν πόδας τε καὶ τραχήλους συνδεδεμένοι, καὶ ἕκαστος αὐτῶν τὸν σταυρὸν ἔφερε· τῇ γὰρ ἀναγκαίᾳ τιμωρίᾳ καὶ τὴν ἔξωθεν φαντασίαν σκυθρωπὴν προσέθεσαν οἱ κολάζοντες εἰς φόβου παράδειγμα τοῖς ὁμοίοις. Χαιρέας μὲν οὖν συναπαγόμενος ἐσίγα, Πολύχαρμος δὲ τὸν σταυρὸν βαστάσας[480] "διὰ σὲ" φησίν, "ὦ Καλλιρόη, ταῦτα πάσχομεν. σὺ πάντων ἡμῖν τῶν κακῶν αἰτία."

*Translation.* Without seeing them or hearing their defense, the master (Mithridates) immediately ordered the crucifixion of the sixteen cellmates. They were brought out, chained together at the foot and the neck, each carrying his cross. The men who executed the sentence added this grim public spectacle to the inevitable punishment as an example to frighten the other

---

[476] Cf. REINHARD VON BENDEMANN, 'Many-Colored Illnesses' (Mk 1:34): On the Significance of Illnesses in New Testament Therapy Narratives, in Wonders Never Cease: The Purpose of Narrating Miracle Stories in the New Testament and its Religious Environment (ed. B. J. Lietaert Peerbolte and M. Labahn; LNTS 288; London / New York: T&T Clark, 2006), 100–124, 117 n. 60; and RICHARD E. STRELAN, Strange Acts: Studies in the Cultural World of the Acts of the Apostles (BZNW 126; Berlin: De Gruyter, 2004), 162; JOHN B. F. MILLER, Convinced that God had Called Us: Dreams, Visions, and the Perception of God's Will in Luke-Acts (Biblical Interpretation 85; Leiden/Boston: Brill, 2007), 35.

[477] BLINZLER, Prozeß, 345 with n. 26; cf. Valerius Maximus 1.7.4; Josephus, *A. J.* 19.270. Cf. DAVIES / ALLISON, Matthew, 3:605; MARCUS, Mark, 2:1040, who suggest that "it may be that in Palestine the Romans avoided nudity, even in condemned prisoners, out of consideration for Jewish sensibilities" (with reference to *Jub.* 3:30–31; *m. Sanh.* 6:3); cf. BROWN, Death, 2:953; CRAIG S. KEENER, The Historical Jesus of the Gospels (Grand Rapids: Eerdmans, 2009), 575 n. 287.

[478] KEENER, Gospel of Matthew, 672.

[479] WOLTER, Lukasevangelium, 752.

[480] Following the reading of Π[2] (*P. Oxy.* 1019); F (Codex Florentinus Laurentianus Conventi Soppressi 627) reads βαστάζων (thus older editions).

prisoners. Chaereas said nothing when he was led off with the others, but Polycharmus, as he carried his cross, said: "Callirhoe, it is because of you that we are suffering like this! You are the cause of all our troubles."

*Commentary*.[481] Chariton of Aphrosidias wrote what is regarded as the earliest work of Greek prose fiction, written in the middle of the first century A.D.,[482] set at least four hundred years before his own time in the context of the Athenians' defeat when they invaded Sicily in 415–413 B.C. during the Peloponnesian War. Callirhoe, the heroine of the novel, is the daughter of Hermocrates, the *strategos* of Syracuse, famous for his victory over Athen's army.[483] The novel tells the story of Chaereas and Callirhoe, two children of rival families who fall in love and, after a plebiscite, marry. Callirhoe, kicked by the jealous Chaeras, apparently dies, and, after being abducted, is sold in Miletus. For the sake of the child she is expecting by Chaereas she consents to marry the noble Dionysius (Books 1.1–3.1). Chaereas searches for his wife in Miletus and in the region of Caria, where is serves as slave of the satrap Mithridates, who is also in love with Callirhoe (Books 3.2–5.10). The action then moves to Babylon and ends with the couple's reunion and return to Syracus (Books 6–7). While Chaereas has to work as a slave in Caria, some of the slaves chained with him break their chains at night, kill the foreman, run away, but are caught again (4.2.5). When Mithridates hears about the escape attempt, he orders that the sixteen prisoners be crucified (ἀνασταυρῶσαι). As deterrence for similar attempts to escape, the men in charge of the punishment (οἱ κολάζοντες) made a "grim public spectacle" (τὴν ἔξωθεν φαντασίαν σκυθρωπήν) of the condemned to be crucified: they were brought out (προήχθησαν), chained together (συνδεδεμένοι) at the foot and the neck (πόδας τε καὶ τραχήλους),

---

[481] Text: BRYAN P. REARDON, Chariton Aphrodisiensis. De Callirhoe narrationes amatoriae (Bibliotheca Scriptorum Graecorum et Romanorum Teubneriana; München / Leipzig: Saur, 2004); for other text editions and translations cf. WARREN E. BLAKE, Charitonis Aphrodisiensis de Chaerea et Callirhoe Amatoriarum Narrationum Libri Octo (Oxford: Clarendon, 1938); GEORGES MOLINIÉ, Chariton. Le romain de Chairéas et Callirhoé (orig. 1979; repr., Collection Budé; Paris: Les Belles Lettres, 1989); GEORGE P. GOOLD, Chariton. Callirhoe (LCL; Cambridge: Harvard University Press, 1995); KARL PLEPELITS, Chariton von Aphrodisias: Kallirhoe (Eingeleitet, übersetzt und erläutert; Bibliothek der griechischen Literatur 6; Stuttgart: Hiersemann, 1976); BRYAN P. REARDON, Chariton: Chaereas and Callirhoe, in Collected Ancient Greek Novels (orig. 1989; repr., Berkeley: University of California Press, 2008), 17–124; STEPHEN M. TRZASKOMA, Two Novels from Ancient Greece: *Callirhoe* and *An Ephesian Story* (Translated, with Introduction and Notes; Indianapolis: Hackett, 2010).

[482] Cf. REARDON, Chariton, 17; PLEPELITS, Chariton, 4–9; CONSUELO RUIZ MONTERO, Chariton von Aphrodisias: Ein Überblick, ANRW II.34.2 (1994): 1006–1054.

[483] Cf. RICHARD HUNTER, History and Historicity in the Romance of Chariton [1994], in On Coming After: Studies in Post-Classical Greek Literature and Its Reception. Part 2: Comedy and Performance, Greek Poetry of the Roman Empire, the Ancient Novel (Trends in Classics Sup 3/2; Berlin: De Gruyter, 2008), 737–774, for a discussion of historical anachronisms.

and each was forced to carry his cross (ἕκαστος αὐτῶν τὸν σταυρὸν ἔφερε) as they marched from Miltiades' house to the place of execution (4.2.7). Chaereas, who is crucified, is taken down from the cross when Miltiades hears the story of Chaereas and Callirhoe (4.2.8–4.3.12).

**(117)** Plutarch, *De sera numinis vindicta* 9 (554A–B)

"Ἀλλὰ ταῦτα μέν" ἔφην "ἡμεῖς λέγομεν, ὥσπερ ἠξίωται, γίγνεσθαί τινα τῆς τιμωρίας ἀναβολὴν ὑποθέμενοι τοῖς πονηροῖς· τὰ λοιπὰ δ᾽ Ἡσιόδου χρὴ νομίζειν ἀκροᾶσθαι, λέγοντος οὐχ Πλάτων ἀκόλουθον εἶναι τιμωρίαν ἀδικίας πάθην· ἀλλ᾽ ἡλικιῶτιν ἐκ τῆς αὐτῆς ὁμόθεν χώρας καὶ ῥίζης συνυποφυομένην· ἡ᾽ γὰρ ᾽κακή᾽ φησὶ ᾽βουλὴ τῷ βουλεύσαντι κακίστη᾽ καὶ ὃς δ᾽ ἄλλῳ κακὰ τεύχει, ἐῷ κακὸν ἥπατι τεύχει. ἡ μὲν γὰρ κανθαρὶς ἐν αὐτῇ λέγεται τὸ βοηθητικὸν ἔκ τινος ἀντιπαθείας ἔχειν συγκεκραμένον ἡ δὲ πονηρία συγγεννῶσα τὸ λυποῦν ἑαυτῇ καὶ κολάζον, οὐχ ὕστερον ἀλλ᾽ ἐν αὐτῇ τῇ ὕβρει τὴν δίκην τοῦ ἀδικεῖν δίδωσι· (B) καὶ τῷ μὲν σώματι τῶν κολαζομένων ἕκαστος κακούργων ἐκφέρει τὸν αὐτοῦ σταυρόν· ἡ δὲ κακία τῶν κολαστηρίων ἐφ᾽ ἑαυτὴν ἕκαστον ἐξ αὐτῆς τεκταίνεται, δεινοῦ τις οὖσα βίου δημιουργὸς οἴκτους σὺν αἰσχύνῃ φόβους τε πολλοὺς καὶ πάθη χαλεπὰ καὶ μεταμελείας καὶ ταραχὰς ἀπαύστους ἔχοντος. ἀλλ᾽ οὐδὲν ἔνιοι διαφέρουσι παιδαρίων, ἃ τοὺς κακούργους ἐν τοῖς θεάτροις θεώμενα πολλάκις ἐν χιτῶσι διαχρύσοις καὶ χλαμυδίοις ἁλουργοῖς ἐστεφανωμένους καὶ πυρριχίζοντας ἄγαται καὶ τέθηπεν ὡς μακαρίους ἄχρι οὗ κεντούμενοι καὶ μαστιγούμενοι καὶ πῦρ ἀνιέντες ἐκ τῆς ἀνθινῆς ἐκείνης καὶ πολυτελοῦς ἐσθῆτος ὀφθῶσιν.

*Translation.* "But so far," I said, "the arguments have been our own. They rest on the assumption that the punishment of the wicked is deferred. What remains to be said we must imagine hearing from Hesiod, who does not say with Plato that punishment is a suffering following injustice, but holds it to be from the same source as injustice, springing up together with it from the same soil and root. Thus he says, 'The evil plan is worst for him who planned it,'[484] and 'He who devises evil for others, devises evil for his own liver.'[485] For while the blister beetle is reported to contain, mixed with itself, its own remedy, which operates by a sort of counteraction, wickedness engenders with itself its pain and punishment, and thus pays the penalty of its wrongdoing not later, but at the very moment of commission. (B) And while every criminal who is executed carries his own cross on his back, evil devises out of itself each instrument of its own punishment, cunning artisan that it is of a life of

---

[484] Hesiod, *Opera et dies* 266.
[485] Not in Hesiod, but from Lucillius, cf. *Anthologia Palatina* 11.183.5; cf. PHILLIP H. DE LACY and BENEDICT EINARSON, Plutarch. Moralia VII (LCL; Cambridge: Harvard University Press, 1959), 214–15 note c.

wretchedness, containing with infamy a host of terrors, regrets, cruel passions, and never ending anxieties. Yet some are no wiser than little children, who see criminals in the amphitheater, often clad in tunics of gold cloth and purple mantles, wearing chaplets and dancing Pyrrhic measures, and struck with awe and wonderment suppose them supremely happy, till the moment when before their eyes the criminals are stabbed and scourged and that happy and sumptuous garment bursts into flame

*Commentary.*[486] Plutarch (c. A.D. 45–125), who accepted posts for several Pythiads in Delphi, in *De sera numinis vindicta* ("On the delays of divine vengeance"), gives an account to Quietus of a discussion at Delphi which included himself, his brother Timon, Patrocleas, Olympichus, and a certain Epicurus.[487] Epicurus, who has already departed from the group, objected against the notion of divine providence by arguing that the god seems to delay his punishment of the wicked. Plutarch's rejoinder to this and other arguments raised by his discussion partners focuses on the problem how the common belief that the god rewards people who do good and punishes those who do evil can be meaningfully explained. In the first part of the treatise Plutarch shows that many problems involving the deity can be solved by reason, examining the relevant traditions and using analogies. He reaffirms the notion of the survival of the soul after death and argues that this helps us understand even the most puzzling forms of divine response to human conduct. At the end Plutarch abandons the concept of divine punishment and replaces it with a process of therapy for the soul: what people call "divine punishments" are corrective and preventive measures which derive from the divine therapy for the soul. In *Sera* 9 (554A) Plutarch quotes Hesiod to show that evil generates its own punishment.[488] He explains this principle with two analogies. First, the blister beetle (κανθαρίς; Lat. *Cantharis vesicatoria*), which is used as a medicine, is at the same time poisonous when taken internally. Second, every criminal (ἕκαστος κακούργων) who is being executed (κολαζομένων) "carries his own cross on his back" (τῷ μὲν σώματι ... ἐκφέρει τὸν αὐτοῦ σταυρόν), which

---

[486] Text: WILLIAM R. PATON, MAX POHLENZ, and WILLIAM SIEVEKING, Plutarchus Moralia III (orig. 1929; repr., Bibliotheca Teubneriana; München / Leipzig: Saur, 2001), 394–444; for other text editions and translations cf. LACY / EINARSON, Plutarch. Moralia VII, 169–299; ROBERT KLAERR and YVONNE VERNIÈRE, Plutarque: Œuvres morales. Vol. VII/2 (Paris: Les Belles Lettres, 1974); HERWIG GÖRGEMANNS, Plutarch. Drei religionsphilosophische Schriften. Über den Aberglauben. Über die späte Strafe der Gottheit. Über Isis und Osiris (Griechisch-deutsch; Sammlung Tusculum; Düsseldorf /Zürich, 2003). The translation follows LACY / EINARSON, with some modifications.

[487] Cf. HANS DIETER BETZ, PETER A. DIRKSE, and EDGAR W. SMITH, De sera numinis vindicta (Moralia 548A – 568A), in Plutarch's Theological Writings and Early Christian Literature (ed. H. D. Betz; Leiden: Brill, 1975), 181–236, 181; cf. ibid. 181–82 for the following summary.

[488] BETZ / DIRKSE / SMITH, De sera numinis vindicta, 204.

illustrates the principle that "evil devises out of itself each instrument of its own punishment." This statement reflects the historical reality of criminals condemned to death by crucifixion carry the crossbeam, from the court, or the prison in which they had been held, to the place of execution.[489]

**(118)** Artemidorus, *Oneirocritica* 2.56

Βαστάζειν τινὰ τῶν δαιμόνων τῶν χθονίων, ἢ αὐτὸν τὸν Πλούτωνα ἢ τὸν Κέρβερον ἢ ἄλλον τινὰ τῶν ἐν Ἅιδου, κακούργῳ μὲν ἰδόντι σταυρὸν βαστάσαι σημαίνει· ἔοικε γὰρ καὶ ὁ σταυρὸς θανάτῳ, καὶ ὁ μέλλων αὐτῷ προσηλοῦσθαι πρότερον αὐτὸν βαστάζει· ἀνδρὶ δὲ μὴ κακούργῳ θηρίον βαστάσαι σημαίνει, καὶ εἰ μὲν βαρύνοιτο, δηχθῆναι καὶ ἀποθανεῖν· εἰ δὲ μή, αἰσθόμενον ἀποθέσθαι καὶ μὴ διαφθαρῆναι.

*Translation.* If an evildoer dreams that he carries one of the gods beneath the earth, Pluto himself or Cerberus or someone else in Hades, it signifies that he will carry a cross. For the cross leads to death, and the man who will be nailed to it carries it beforehand. For a man who is not an evildoer (the dream) signifies that he will carry a wild animal and, if he feels depressed by his burden, that he will be bitten and die. If this is not the case, he will notice it and cast it down, and he will not perish.

*Commentary.*[490] Artemidorus of Daldis, also known as Artemidorus of Ephesus, lived in the 2nd century A.D.[491] The *Oneirocritica* (Ὀνειροκριτικά) is the only treatise on dream interpretation that has been completely preserved. Artemidorus is mostly interested in prophetic dreams (ὄνειροι) that have meaning, in contrast to dreams which reflect only momentary physical and mental conditions (ἐνύπνια; 1.1; 4.praef.). The event that a dream predicts can be represented either directly (ὄνειροι θεωρηματικοί), or they can be represented symbolically (ὄνειροι ἀλληγορικοί), in which case they require an

---

[489] Cf. HELGE ALMQVIST, Plutarch und das Neue Testament. Ein Beitrag zum Corpus Hellenisticum Novi Testamenti (Acta Seminarii Neotestamentici Upsaliensis 15; Uppsala: Appelbergs Boktryckeri, 1946), 76; WOLTER, Lukasevangelium, 752.

[490] Text: ROGER A. PACK, Artemidori Daldiani Onirocriticon Libri V (BSGRT; Leipzig: Teubner, 1963); for further text editions and translations cf. FRIEDRICH S. KRAUSS, Artemidor von Daldis. Traumbuch (Bearbeitet und ergänzt von Martin Kaiser; Basel / Stuttgart: Schwabe, 1965); ANDRÉ JEAN FESTUGIÈRE, Artemidore. La clef des songes: Onirocriticon (Collection Bibliothèque des textes philosophiques; Paris: Librairie Philosophique J. Vrin, 1975); KARL BRACKERTZ, Artemidorus von Daldis. Das Traumbuch (München: Artemis, 1979); ROBERT J. WHITE, Artemidorus. Oneirocritica. The Interpretation of Dreams. Translation and Commentary (Second Edition, Revised and enlarged; orig. 1975; repr., Torrance, Calif.: Original Books, 1990); DANIEL E. HARRIS-MCCOY, Artemidorus' Oneirocritica: Text, Translation, and Commentary (Oxford: Oxford University Press, 2012).

[491] Cf. MICHAEL TRAPP, Artemidorus [6] of Daldis, BNP 2 (2003): 60–61. Artemidorus was born in Ephesus, but called himself "of Daldis" after his mother's native city in Lydia.

experienced interpreter. The evildoer's dream of carrying one of the deities of the underworld is interpreted in terms of the evildoer passing into Hades by carrying the means why which he dies: since convicted criminals who were given the death penalty, were either beheaded (*decollatio*), burned to death (*crematio*), or crucified,[492] a dream that involves carrying something as one enters Hades is rather plausibly interpreted in terms of carrying the cross (σταυρὸν βαστάσαι). Artemidorus links the cross and death (ὁ σταυρὸς θανάτῳ), and he knows that people who are going to be nailed (προσηλοῦσ-θαι) to a cross first carry it (αὐτὸν βαστάζει) to the place of execution.[493]

## 2.10  Titulus

John informs his readers that Pilatus had the reason for Jesus' death sentence written on a titulus in three languages: ἔγραψεν δὲ καὶ τίτλον ὁ Πιλᾶτος καὶ ἔθηκεν ἐπὶ τοῦ σταυροῦ ("Pilatus also had an inscription written and put on the cross," John 19:19).[494] The term τίτλος refers here not to a text engraved on a stone or bronze tablet but to a text written on perishable material such as wood (*tabula albata*) or papyrus.[495] John adds that the titulus was written in three languages: καὶ ἦν γεγραμμένον Ἑβραϊστί, Ῥωμαϊστί, Ἑλληνιστί ("and it was written in Hebrew, in Latin, and in Greek," John 20:20). The term Ἑβραϊστί can also refer to Aramaic, the more commonly spoken language in Judea in the first century. Assuming that this Johannine tradition is reliable, this was an "unparalleled case of a quasi-official (but ironical) use by the Romans of a vernacular language (an act of offensive accommodation ... meant to annoy the Jews)."[496] The Gospels provide the following versions of the titulus:

---

[492] Cf. GOTTFRIED SCHIEMANN, Death Penalty, BNP 4 (2004): 136–137, 137.

[493] KRAUSS, Artemidor. Traumbuch, 211 n. 1, compares with John 19:17; Mark 15:21.

[494] NRSV; TNIV: "Pilate had a notice prepared and fastened to the cross;" Luther: "Pilatus aber schrieb eine Aufschrift und setzte sie auf das Kreuz;" GNB: "Pilatus ließ ein Schild am Kreuz anbringen;" ZB: "Pilatus liess auch eine Tafel beschriften und sie oben am Kreuz anbringen." The titulus on the cross of Jesus is discussed as inscription No. 15 by WERNER ECK in CIIP I/1, 62. For a visual representation see the relief from Miletus (2nd/3rd cent.) representing a warder and three prisoners, the first of which carries a placard which presumably identified the miscreants and their crime: REBECCA BENEFIEL / KATHLEEN COLEMAN, Graffiti, in Excavations at Zeugma Conducted by Oxford Archaeology (3 vols.; ed. W. Aylward; Los Altos: Packard Humanities Institute, 2013), 1:178–191, here 183 Fig. 11.

[495] Cf. WERNER ECK, Kaiserliches Handeln in italienischen Städten, in L'Italie d'Auguste à Dioclétien (Actes du colloque international organisé par l'École française de Rome (25–28 Mars 1992); Rome: École Française de Rome, 1994), 329–351, 348; ECK, Spiegel der Macht, 47–48; also JOSEPH GEIGER, Titulus crucis, SCI 15 (1996): 202–207; PAUL L. MAIER, The Inscription on the Cross of Jesus of Nazareth, Hermes 124 (1996): 58–75. Cf. W. ECK, in CIIP I.1, 62: "Such texts were not engraved at all, but painted on a tabula albata."

[496] ADAMS, Bilingualism, 268.

(1) Matt 27:37 ΟΥΤΟΣ ΕΣΤΙΝ ΙΗΣΟΥΣ Ο ΒΑΣΙΛΕΨΣ ΤΩΝ ΙΟΥΔΑΙΩΝ
(2) Mark 15:26 Ο ΒΑΣΙΛΕΥΣ ΤΩΝ ΙΟΥΔΑΙΩΝ
(3) Luke 23:38 Ο ΒΑΣΙΛΕΥΣ ΤΩΝ ΙΟΥΔΑΙΩΝ ΟΥΤΟΣ
(4) John 19:19 ΙΗΣΟΥΣ Ο ΝΑΖΩΡΑΙΟΣ Ο ΒΑΣΙΛΕΥΣ ΤΥΝ ΙΟΥΔΑΙΩΝ

(1) οὗτός ἐστιν Ἰησοῦς ὁ βασιλεὺς τῶν Ἰουδαίων
(2) ὁ βασιλεὺς τῶν Ἰουδαίων
(3) ὁ βασιλεὺς τῶν Ἰουδαίων οὗτος
(4) Ἰησοῦς ὁ Ναζωραῖος ὁ βασιλεὺς τῶν Ἰουδαίων

(1) This is Jesus, the king of the Jews
(2) The king of the Jews
(3) This is the king of the Jews
(4) Jesus of Nazareth, the king of the Jews

WERNER Eck comments, "According to Roman practice the reason for the punishment of a condemned person could be shown on a tabula albata. Therefore there is no reason to doubt the tradition that a titulus with the reason for his condemnation by Pilatus was affixed on Jesus' cross."[497]

**(119)** Suetonius, *Gaius Caligula* 32.1–2

Animum quoque remittenti ludoque et epulis dedito eadem factorum dictorumque saevitia aderat. Saepe in conspectu prandentis vel comisantis seriae quaestiones per tormenta habebantur, miles decollandi artifex quibuscumque e custodia capita amputabat. Puteolis dedicatione pontis, quem excogitatum ab eo significavimus, cum multos e litore invitasset ad se, repente omnis praecipitavit, quosdam gubernacula apprehendentes contis remisque detrusit in mare. ² Romae publico epulo servum ob detractam lectis argenteam laminam carnifici confestim tradidit, ut manibus abscisis atque ante pectus e collo pendentibus, praecedente titulo qui causam poenae indicaret, per coetus epulantium circumduceretur.

*Translation.* Even when he was relaxing and taken up with entertainment and feasting, his words and his actions were equally cruel. Often, while he was

---

[497] W. ECK, in CIIP I.1, 62. ECK rejects as inauthentic the fourth century story that the titulus was shown in Jerusalem to the pilgrims (Egeria, *Itineratio* 37.1), and as a later fabrication the fragment in Santa Croce in Gerusalemme in Rome; contra MARIA-LUISA RIGATO, Il Titolo della Croce di Gesù. Confronto tra i Vangeli e la Tavoletta-reliquia della Basilica Eleniana a Roma (Second ed.; Tesi gregoriana. Serie teologia 100; Rome: Gregorian University Press, 2005), cf. MARIA-LUISA RIGATO, I.N.R.I. Il titolo della Croce (Biblica; Bologna: Edizioni Dehoniane Bologna, 2010). On the historicity of the titulus see now also WEBB, Roman Examination, 747–48; KEENER, Historical Jesus, 323–24.

having lunch or enjoying himself, investigations in capital cases by torture were conducted in his presence; a soldier, who was adept at decapitation, cut off the heads of a number of prisoners. When his bridge at Puteoli, the design of which I recounted above,[498] was being dedicated, he invited a large number of people who were on the shore to come out to him, then pushed them all into the sea. When some caught hold of the rudders of the ships, he pushed them back into the sea with boat hooks and oars. [2] At a public banquet in Rome he handed a slave over to executioners for stealing a strip of silver from the couches, with orders that his hands be cut off and hung from his neck on his chest, and that he be led around among the guests, preceded by a placard giving the reason for his punishment.

*Commentary*.[499] Emperor Gaius Caligula (A.D. 37–41) is known not for significant political actions, but for his erratic decisions, often quickly repealed, and for the instability of his character which resulted, among other excesses, in numerous executions.[500] He suspended the *maiestas* law at the beginning of his reign, but changed his mind two years later when "the emperor was replaced by the monster" (*Cal.* 22.1).[501] In *Cal.* 22–49, Suetonius describes Caligula's actions as those of a *monstrum*: his *impietas* ("irreverence, disloyalty") towards the gods, his family, his wives, his friends, and the *ordines* (22–26); his *saevitia* ("cruelty," 27–35); his *impudicitia* ("shamelessness," 36), *nepotatus* ("debauchery," 37), *rapinae* ("robbery," 38–42), and *militia* ("warfare," 43–49).[502] In *Cal.* 32–33, Suetonius details the emperor's cruelty in actions and words during inappropriate situations of leisure. Torture sessions during meals are a regular element in literary works as an example of tyranny.[503] The occasion of the incident related in 32.2 is unknown. The cruel punishment exemplified a master's power of his slaves, and was meant to

---

[498] Suetonius, *Cal.* 19.

[499] On Suetonius' use of sources for his biography of Caligula cf. DAVID WARDLE, Suetonius' Life of Caligula. A Commentary (Collection Latomus 225; Bruxelles: Latomus / Revue d'études latines, 1994), 30–95, who concludes, "*Caligula* is a subtle, complex creation which succeeds in leaving the reader with a powerful, lasting impression of its subject. Its affinities are far closer to the mainstream of ancient historiography than its form would suggest, its origins and techniques owe more to rhetoric than to antiquarian scholarship, and its content must be approached with caution" (ibid. 94–95).

[500] Cf. WERNER ECK, Caligula, BNP 2 (2003): 955–957, 956; ANTHONY A. BARRETT, Caligula: The Corruption of Power (New Haven: Yale University Press, 1990), 73–90, 242.

[501] Cf. BAUMANN, Impietas in Principem, 204–10; BAUMANN, Crime and Punishment, 66.

[502] WARDLE, Suetonius' Life of Caligula, 20–21; the following comment ibid. 260.

[503] Cf. Seneca, *Contr.* 9.2; Livius 39.42–43; Cicero, *Sen.* 42. WARDLE, Suetonius' Life of Caligula, 72. For the use of an expert for decapitations cf. JEAN-LOUIS VOISIN, Les Romains, chasseurs de têtes, in Du châtiment dans la cité. Supplices corporels et peine de mort dans le monde antique (Table Ronde, Rome 9–11 novembre 1982; Collection de l'École Française de Rome 79; Rome: École française de Rome, 1984), 241–292, 243–44, 258.

serve as an example to the other slaves.[504] Caligula had the slave who was sentenced to death because he had stolen a strip of silver, paraded among the guests of a public banquet (*publicum epulum*), with his cut off hands hanging from his neck and a placard (*titulus*)[505] carried in front of him "giving the reason for his punishment" (*qui causam poenae indicaret*).

**(120)** Suetonius, *Domitianus* 10.1

Sed neque in clementiae neque in abstinentiae tenore permansit, et tamen aliquanto celerius ad saevitiam descivit quam ad cupiditatem. Discipulum Paridis pantomimi impuberem adhuc et cum maxime aegrum, quod arte formaque non absimilis magistro videbatur, occidit; item Hermogenem Tarsensem propter quasdam in historia figuras, librariis etiam, qui eam descripserat, cruci fixis. Patrem familias, quod Thraecem myrmilloni parem, munerario imparem dixerat, detractum e spectaculis in harenam, canibus obiecit, cum hoc titulo: Impie locutus parmularius.

*Translation*. But he did not continue this course of mercy and integrity, but turned to cruelty somewhat more speedily than to avarice. He killed a student of the pantomime Paris who was still a boy without a beard and ill at the time, because he seemed not unlike his master in skill and appearance. He also killed Hermogenes of Tarsus because of some allusions in his History, and he even crucified the slaves who had written it out. He ordered that a family man who had said that a *thrax* was a match for the *myrmillo*, but not for the *munerarius*, be dragged from his seat and thrown into the arena to the dogs, with this placard: "A *parmularius* who spoke impiously."

*Commentary*. Emperor Domitian (A.D. 81–96) is traditionally regarded as *tyrannus* on account of the dominance of senatorial sources, which view him negatively, and the fact that he was one of the greatest persecutors of the church.[506] Dio Cassius depends on sources hostile to Domitian, Suetonius adopts the largely negative assessment of Rome's senators, but is less hostile than Dio or Tacitus. Domitian had considerable military successes and subjected the governors of the provinces to strict regulations, which prompts Suetonius to state that "at no time they were more honest or just" (8.20). In *Dom*. 10.1, Suetonius gives three examples of his cruelty. He killed a boy who studied with Paris to be a mime. Paris was a famous *pantomimus* whose fame

---

[504] WARDLE, Suetonius' Life of Caligula, 261, refers for the "extreme and exemplary" punishment to Plautus, *Capt.* 668 and Suetonius, *Dom.* 10.5.

[505] The OLD defines *titulus* as a "flat piece of wood or other material inscribed with a notice, identification or other information."

[506] Cf. WERNER ECK, Domitianus, BNP 4 (2004): 635–639, 639; cf. BRIAN W. JONES, The Emperor Domitian (London: Routledge, 1992).

spread beyond Rome; graffitti from Pompeii mention the *Paridiani*, his local fan club.[507] He killed the historian Hermogenes because of some "allusions" (*figurae*), i.e., indirect attacks against him, even crucifying the slaves who had written out Hermogenes' work. This is not Hermogenes of Tarsus but perhaps the Hermogenes (date uncertain) who wrote a mythological account of Phrygia.[508] R. A. BAUMAN suggests, on the basis of Quintilian's example for *figurae* (innuendos, indirect attacks) in which he uses the phrase *duxi uxorem, quae patri placuit* ("I married the wife who pleased by father"),[509] with *patri* being Quintilian's "discreet emendation of a *fratri* in Hermogenes' history," the allusion referring to Titus' alleged affair with Domitia.[510] And Domitian killed a family man who had implied unfairness on the part of Domitian who favored the *thrax* in gladiatorial contests. The *thrax* (or *thraex*) was a "Thracian" gladiator who, like the *retiarius* (fighter with a net), fought with a net and trident, lightly armed with a small round shield (*parma*) and a short, sometimes curved sword (*scutum*), which were, perhaps, originally "Thracian" weapons; the *myrmillo* (or *murmillo*) was a "Gallic" gladiator who was heavily armed with a rectangular shield and a visored helmet which had a symbolic fish (*mormyr*) on the top.[511] A *munerarius* is the organizer of a *munus*, a gladiatorial contest; a *parmularius* is a supporter of the Thracian gladiators armed with a *parma*, a small round shield. Domitian made fun of the unfortunate family man who had made the mistake of supporting the Thracians whom Domitian despised, "and then compounded his error by claiming that the *munerarius* was biased," who, on this occasion, may have been the emperor himself.[512] The man who was condemned to die in the arena fighting dogs was made to carry a "placard" (*titulus*) that recorded the reason for his execution: he had refused to show due *pietas* to the emperor.

---

[507] CIL IV 7919; cf. BRIAN W. JONES, Suetonius. Domitian (Edited with Introduction, Commentary and Bibliography; Bristol: Bristol Classical Press, 1996), 31. According to Dio, Domitian had Paris murdered because of his adultery with Domitia, and then killed several of his supporters who commemorated his death (Dio 67.3.1).

[508] JONES, Suetonius. Domitian, 84.

[509] Quintilian 9.2.69.

[510] BAUMANN, Impietas in Principem, 162; cf. JONES, Suetonius. Domitian, 85, who adds that "Domitian was notoriously sensitive to attacks on his wife."

[511] Cf. AUGUSTA HÖNLE, Munus, Munera, BNP 9 (2006): 301–312, 311; THOMAS E. J. WIEDEMANN, Emperors and Gladiators (orig. 1992; repr., London: Routledge, 1995), 185–86; BAUMANN, Impietas in Principem, 85.

[512] JONES, Emperor Domitian, 124, with reference to *Dom.* 4.1: Domitian could be "persuaded" to provide gladiators, at his own expense, for the last event of the day; cf. Pliny, *Pan.* 33.3–4, who writes that at the time of Trajan "no one risked the old charge of *impietas* if he disliked a gladiator," and who accuses Domitian of "using the arena to collect charges of *maiestas*." Cf. BAUMANN, Impietas in Principem, 86, 163–65.

**(121)** Dio Cassius, *Historia Romana* 54.3.7

τοῦ γοῦν πατρὸς τοῦ Καιπίωνος τὸν μὲν ἕτερον τῶν δούλων τῶν συμφυγόν-
των τῷ υἱεῖ ἐλευθερώσαντος, ὅτι ἀμῦναί οἱ θνήσκοντι ἠθέλησε, τὸν δὲ ἕτερον
τὸν προδόντα αὐτὸν διά τε τῆς ἀγορᾶς μέσης μετὰ γραμμάτων τὴν αἰτίαν τῆς
θανατώσεως αὐτοῦ δηλούντων διαγαγόντος καὶ μετὰ ταῦτα ἀνασταυρώσαντος, οὐκ ἠγανάκτησε.

*Translation.* When Caepio's father freed one of the two slaves who had
accompanied his son in his flight, because this slave had wished to defend his
young master when he met his death, but led the second slave, who had
deserted his son, through the center of the forum with an inscription that made
known the reason why he was to be put to death, and then he crucified him,
the emperor was not irritated.

*Commentary.*[513] Dio Cassius Cocceianus, born A.D. 164 in Nicaea in Bithynia,
held high state offices; of his work "Roman History" (Ῥωμαϊκὴ ἱστορία),
books 36–60 (on events between 68 B.C. and A.D. 47) and books 78–79 (A.D.
216–218) are extant.[514] In the context of comments on Augustus' moderate
administration and readiness to help friends, Cassius Dio relates how Fannius
Caepio instigated a conspiracy against Augustus in 22 B.C., was convicted
without standing trial on the supposition that he intended to flee, and executed
when trying to escape arrest (54.3.4–5).[515] Suetonius relates that the prosecution *in absentia* was supervised by Tiberius, Augustus' stepson and later
emperor, under the charge of *crimen maiestatis* (*Tib.* 8.1).[516] According to
Cassius Dio, Augustus passed a law that in trials, where the defendant was not
present, the vote should not be secret and conviction had to be by unanimous
vote (54.3.6), and he agreed with the release of one of Caepio's slaves who
had stayed with him until his execution (54.3.7). When Caepio fled before his

---

[513] URSULUS PHILIPPUS BOISSEVAIN, Cassii Dionis Cocceiani Historiarum Romanarum
quae supersunt (5 vols.; Berlin: Weidmann, 1895–1931); for other editions and translations cf.
HERBERT B. FOSTER and EARNEST CARY, Dio's Roman History (9 vols.; LCL; Cambridge:
Harvard University Press, 1914–1927); OTTO VEH, Cassius Dio. Römische Geschichte (5
vols. 2., überarbeitete Auflage; orig. 1985–1987; repr., Bibliothek der Alten Welt; Berlin:
Akademie Verlag, 2012); IAN SCOTT-KILVERT, Cassius Dio. The Roman History: The Reign
of Augustus (Penguin Classics; London: Penguin, 1989).

[514] ANTHONY R. BIRLEY, Cassius [III 1] L. Cl(audius) C. Dio Cocceianus, BNP 2
(2003): 1171–1172.

[515] Cf. WERNER ECK, Fannius [II 1] F. Caepio, BNP 5 (2004): 351; RONALD SYME, The
Augustan Aristocracy (orig. 1986; repr., Oxford: Clarendon, 1989), 40, 384, 387–89;
MELISSA BARDEN DOWLING, Clemency and Cruelty in the Roman World (Ann Arbor, MI:
University of Michigan Press, 2006), 65. According to SYME, ibid. 40 n. 47, Fannius Caepio
was probably the son of C. Fannius, a Republican among the last companions of Sextus
Pompeius in 35 B.C. (Appian, *Bell. civ.* 5.139.579).

[516] Cf. BAUMANN, Crime and Punishment, 55.

arrest, he had been accompanied by two slaves. Caepio's father freed the one slave who stayed with Caepio until the end. The slave who had deserted Caepio was led (διαγαγόντος) "through the center of the forum" (διά τε τῆς ἀγορᾶς μέσης), accompanied by an "inscription" (μετὰ γραμμάτων) which "made known the reason why he as to be put to death" (τὴν αἰτίαν τῆς θανατώσεως αὐτοῦ), and then he was crucified (ἀνασταυρώσαντος; 54.3.7).

Part 3

# Crucifixion

## 3.1 Introduction to the Study of Crucifixions

The modern academic study of crucifixion has historically engaged in a variety of questions, some of which relate only tangentially to Jesus' death on a cross: When was crucifixion first employed? How did Roman crucifixion relate to other forms of penal bodily suspension? Did Jewish leaders accept and promote crucifixion? What kinds of people were crucified? What crimes merited the cross? How was crucifixion performed? How did people perceive the cross and its victims in antiquity? When did crucifixion cease being practiced by the Romans? Most such historical queries, when conducted properly, merit complex answers. In subsequent sections, an array of sources has been produced to engage these and other questions.

While this book does not seek to present a fully comprehensive collection, most sources that have been employed in past scholarly research are found here (without prejudice in the selection process against more debatable instances of crucifixion). Because of the importance of the Judaean context for understanding Jesus' death, the reader will find more emphasis on the Jewish experience of crucifixion than in many other studies. And special effort has been made to study the role of human bodily suspension in the centuries prior to the Roman Empire (especially in the ancient Near East). The commentary, in addition to providing a sense of context, investigates the relevance of each text to the understanding of crucifixion within its broader conceptual field of penal human bodily suspension.

The Graeco-Roman context of Jesus' crucifixion has been studied in monographs since J. LIPSIUS and H. FULDA.[1] In the twentieth century, H.-W. KUHN and M. HENGEL performed especially notable analyses.[2] HENGEL

---

[1] JUSTUS LIPSIUS, De cruce libri tres ad sacram profanamque historiam utiles (Editio ultima; orig. 1594; repr., Paris: Beys, 1598); HERMANN FULDA, Das Kreuz und die Kreuzigung. Eine antiquarische Untersuchung nebst Nachweis der vielen seit Lipsius verbreiteten Irrthümer: zugleich vier Excurse über verwandte Gegenstände (Breslau: Koebner, 1878).

[2] HEINZ-WOLFGANG KUHN, Die Kreuzesstrafe während der frühen Kaiserzeit. Ihre Wirklichkeit und Wertung in der Umwelt des Urchristentums, ANRW II/25.1 (1982): 648–793; HENGEL, Mors Turpissima Crucis, enlarged into a short English monograph: HENGEL, Crucifixion; reprinted in MARTIN HENGEL, The Cross of the Son of God (London: SCM,

famously emphasized that crucifixion was a painful form of execution, the origins of which were thought to be barbarian; such a punishment was not typically practiced against Roman citizens but reserved instead for bandits, rebels, and slaves. Subsequent articles and studies are often quite indebted to the works of KUHN and HENGEL.[3]

The Jewish context of Jesus' crucifixion has received more attention of late, with substantial contributions by L. DÍEZ MERINO and D. W. CHAPMAN. DÍEZ MERINO argued that some Jewish groups (notably the Sadducees and Essenes) accepted crucifixion *ante mortem* as a legitimate Jewish penalty, while others (particularly the Pharisees) believed such practices exceeded the bounds of Jewish law.[4] Many shorter articles have engaged this question of whether Jewish people or sects in antiquity practiced or endorsed crucifixion.[5] Meanwhile, CHAPMAN pursued a somewhat different line of inquiry in order to emphasize that a range of "perceptions" about the cross can be found within Second Temple and early Rabbinic sources; many of these viewpoints about crucifixion and its victims overlap with their contemporary Graeco-Roman concepts, but Jewish literature also evidences distinctive perceptions due to its connection to the Jewish Scriptures and to Jewish experience of Roman crucifixion during Roman military actions.[6]

In the twenty-first century, some voices have challenged the way in which the ancient sources have been studied by modern scholarship on crucifixion. In particular, G. SAMUELSSON has built upon concerns raised by other scholars

---

1976), and slightly expanded into French: MARTIN HENGEL, La crucifixion dans l'antiquité et la folie du message de la croix (Translated by Albert Chazelle; LD 105; Paris: Cerf, 1981). Given the widespread use of the English monograph, it will most often be cited below, except when particular points are significant from Hengel's German or French versions.

[3] E.g., DAVID G. BURKE and HENRY E. DOSKER, "Cross, Crucify," in The International Standard Bible Encyclopedia (ed. G. W. Bromiley; Grand Rapids: Eerdmans, 1979–1988), 1:825–830; GERALD G. O'COLLINS, Crucifixion, ABD 1 (1992): 1207–1210.

[4] The fullest exposition of this thesis is found in LUIS DÍEZ MERINO, El suplicio de la cruz en la literatura Judia intertestamental, LASBF 26 (1976): 31–120, abbreviated in two other publications: LUIS DÍEZ MERINO, La crucifixión en la antigua literatura judía (Periodo intertestamental), EstEcl 51 (1976): 5–27; LUIS DÍEZ MERINO, La crocifissione nella letteratura ebrea antica (Periodo intertestamentale), in La Sapienza Della Croce Oggi (Atti del Congresso internazionale Roma, 13–18 ottobre 1975; La Sapienza Della Croce Nella Rivelazione e Nell'Ecumenismo; Turin: Leumann, 1976), 1:61–68.

[5] Key voices in this debate include SAMUEL ROSENBLATT, The Crucifixion of Jesus from the Standpoint of Pharisaic Law, JBL 75 (1956): 315–321; ETHELBERT STAUFFER, Jerusalem und Rom im Zeitalter Jesu Christi (Dalp Taschenbücher 331; Bern: Francke, 1957), esp. 123–127; ERNST BAMMEL, Crucifixion as a Punishment in Palestine [1970], in Judaica: Kleine Schriften I (WUNT 37; Tübingen: Mohr, 1986), 76–78; JOSEPH A. FITZMYER, Crucifixion in Ancient Palestine, Qumran Literature, and the New Testament, CBQ 40 (1978): 493–513; HENGEL, Rabbinische Legende. The debate has especially involved issues arising from the Nahum Pesher and the Temple Scroll from Qumran; see below 3.5.

[6] CHAPMAN, Crucifixion; reprinted as DAVID W. CHAPMAN, Ancient Jewish and Christian Perceptions of Crucifixion (Paperback Edition; Grand Rapids: Baker, 2010).

in asserting that our primary sources often do not provide enough information to know whether the reported incidents of bodily suspension were performed as the actual means of execution through long public exposure with arms spread out on a cross.[7] In response, a substantial theme in J. G. COOK's recent monograph has been an extended argument that many more sources convey notions of crucifixion than SAMUELSSON allows.[8] More than anyone to date, COOK has developed a comprehensive catalog of ancient sources that depict the use of the cross in antiquity. More importantly, this debate between SAMUELSSON and his respondents broaches the issue of how one ought to define "crucifixion," and it also raises the corollary question of just how many of our sources are truly pertinent to studying the concepts that the ancients associated with crucifixion. Thus we first turn to issues of definition.

### 3.1.1 Crucifixion, Bodily Suspension, and Issues of Definition

The definition of "crucifixion" remains key to many debates concerning the study of the cross in antiquity. This section introduces several of the issues involved. As the reader engages Part 3, it will become clear that many (if not most) passages from ancient writers do not portray the precise mode of death of a person attached to a cross. In fact, the precise shape of the "cross" (*crux*, σταυρός, etc.) was only very rarely depicted in antiquity. Moreover, many ancient sources conflate the same terminology (be it Greek, Latin, Hebrew, Aramaic, etc.) for *ante mortem* suspension as a means of execution with *post mortem* suspension as a means of publicly displaying a corpse.[9] Therefore,

---

[7] A printed version of Samuelsson's dissertation appeared as GUNNAR SAMUELSSON, Crucifixion in Antiquity: An Inquiry into the Background of the New Testament Terminology of Crucifixion (Skrifter utgivna av institutionen för litteratur, idéhistoria och religion, Göteborgs universitet; Göteborg: University of Gothenburg, 2010). This work was subsequently published by Mohr Siebeck, and it is currently in a second edition (which will be the edition cited in the following pages): GUNNAR SAMUELSSON, Crucifixion in Antiquity: An Inquiry into the Background and Significance of the New Testament Terminology of Crucifixion (Second Revised ed.; WUNT 2/310; Tübingen: Mohr Siebeck, 2013). This critique of modern studies was anticipated in a more radical way in a short article by Guillet though Samuelsson does not cite Guillet, cf. P.-E. GUILLET, Les 800 'Crucifiés' d'Alexandre Jannée, Cahiers du Cercle Ernest Renan 25 (1977): 11–16.

[8] JOHN GRANGER COOK, Crucifixion in the Mediterranean World (WUNT 327; Tübingen: Mohr Siebeck, 2014). Cook's monograph appeared fairly late in the production of this volume, and an attempt has been made to incorporate it where possible (but less so than it undoubtedly deserves). As of the time of writing, a summary of some of Cook's key findings (with drawings and brief bibliography) can be found at JOHN GRANGER COOK, Crucifixion in the Ancient Mediterranean World, Bibleinterp.com. June 2014. Accessed October 12, 2014. http://www.bibleinterp.com/PDFs/CrucifixionAncientMed.pdf.

[9] On the way Latin, Greek, Hebrew, and Aramaic all employ the same terminology for *post*- and *ante-mortem* human bodily suspension, cf. CHAPMAN, Crucifixion, 7–33. Similar

unless the passage includes unambiguous contextual clues, it is often unclear whether the victim's body was suspended before or after death.

Hence the question arises about how one should define crucifixion in antiquity. Certainly, most moderns assume (often under the influence of Christian iconography) that crucifixion must involve a wooden cross-shaped object with vertical and horizontal poles against which a person is suspended by nails or rope in order to affect a lengthy execution. With that in mind, scholars have followed at least four academic approaches to the issue of definition. First, some minimalist scholars demand we employ a similar modern definition in determining whether any one ancient text indicates crucifixion.[10] However, such an insistence on the modern use of the term invariably rules out many (if not most) ancient passages that mention human suspension since these individual texts typically do not clearly signal in context the particulars of how the person was suspended.[11] Second, some have countered with ancient literary

---

issues occur with *ṣalb* (the crucifixion term found in Umayyad-era Arabic sources), as recognized in SEAN W. ANTHONY, Crucifixion and Death as Spectacle: Umayyad Crucifixion in its Late Antique Context (AOS 96; New Haven: American Oriental Society, 2014), 4–5, 6–7.

[10] This is especially true in GUILLET, Les 800. A more nuanced, but still fairly limiting approach is found in SAMUELSSON, who notes the following definition of what can properly be called crucifixion: "An attempted or completed execution by suspension, in which the victim is nailed or tied with his limbs to a vertical execution tool, usually a pole, with or without crossbeam, and thereby publicly displayed, in order to be subjected to an extended, painful death struggle" (SAMUELSSON, Crucifixion, 29, 270). Very rarely does any one ancient text on its own supply sufficient detail to meet simultaneously all the points of this criteria. SAMUELSSON further limits his field of study of Greek texts to those that occur "until the turn of the first century [A.D.]" (p. 37), on the grounds that authors after the first century could be influenced by Christianity. Apart from overestimating the likely effect of early Christianity on second-century pagan literature, this rules out a substantial number of important data points. Some useful reviews of Samuelsson include: PAUL FOSTER, Do we know how Jesus died? ExpT 123 (2011): 122–124, and especially the well-considered critical analyses by BRIAN POUNDS, Review of Crucifixion in Antiquity, by Gunnar Samuelsson, JSNT 33 (2011): 398–405; JOHN GRANGER COOK, Review of Crucifixion in Antiquity, by Gunnar Samuelsson, RBL (2014); http://www.bookreviews.org/pdf/9718_10735.pdf.

[11] Such "minimalistic" conclusions are evident in SAMUELSSON, Crucifixion, esp. 147–150, 202–207, 257–260. SAMUELSSON determines that prior to the second century A.D., the only extant Greek literature to support his definition of crucifixion is Herodotus, *Hist.* 7.33.1; 9.120.4; 9.122.1 (though even here, the suspension tool was a "plank" and not a cross); Diodorus Siculus, *Bib. hist.* 20.54.7; and Chariton, *Chaer.* 3.4.18; 4.2.6–7 (with recapitulations in 4.3.3–10; 8.7.8; 8.8.2–4). Yet, SAMUELSSON qualifies even this by saying that Chariton comes the "closest" to supporting a crucifixion identification (see ibid., p. 150), implying that no potential ancient Greek text (prior to the second century) provides all the hallmarks needed for a definite identification. Further, SAMUELSSON employs his definition and analysis to conclude that no Latin literature up to the beginning of the second century A.D. clearly conveyed the notion of crucifixion (ibid., p. 205; though a page later he seems to allow Seneca, *Dial.* 1.3.9–10). And even the NT texts do not provide sufficient evidence that Jesus' execution fits this understanding of crucifixion. Thus SAMUELSSON can assert that "there was no defined punishment called crucifixion before the execution of Jesus" and that "[t]he shapes of the crucifixion punishment familiar to the present-day reader appear to be formed after

and graffito examples to contend that there was actually more standardization to the Roman form of the cross than the "minimalist" may assume; thus even where the ancient texts do not provide clear indicators of the specific form and application of the cross, one should typically assume that crucifixion on a cross-shaped object is intended, unless context indicates differently.[12] Third, other scholars, noting the ancient terminology encapsulates a broader range of punishments than is typically included in our modern assumptions about "crucifixion," have argued we should broaden our modern terminology so that all human bodily suspensions depicted in ancient sources with typical crucifixion terms should be considered events of "crucifixion." That is to say, this third group of scholars redefines "crucifixion" to include the full range of suspension penalties found in antiquity.[13] Fourth, it has also been argued that because the ancients appear to have lumped together a variety of suspension penalties into a general category (delineated by terms such as *crucifigo* or σταυρόω), all these penalties appear to share similar conceptual fields; therefore, since the modern scholar is often most interested in what the ancients thought about crucifixion (rather than the precise methodology employed in every event), we should consider "crucifixion" (according to our modern understanding) to be a subset of the broader conceptual field of "penal human bodily suspension."[14] In this last viewpoint, while we moderns may desire to restrict the term "crucifixion" to *ante mortem* suspensions, we cannot study such ancient crucifixions apart from all other human bodily suspensions (including *post mortem* suspensions).

The reader should keep in mind these options as we begin to discuss examples of crucifixion and bodily suspension terminology and as we examine the complex variations in bodily suspension practices found in antiquity. We begin with examples of Greek and Latin terms for crucifixion because the majority of texts cited in Part 3 have come from texts in these languages. Discussions of Semitic terms for the cross will be left for later sections.

---

Jesus' death" (both quotes on p. 205). With such negative conclusions, one might ponder whether the problem lies with the ancient literature or with SAMUELSSON's modern stipulations (and threshold of evidence) concerning what can be considered a "crucifixion." Note again the critical reviews of these conclusions by POUNDS and COOK.

[12] We may note the helpful discussion of ancient terminology in COOK, Crucifixion, 2–50.

[13] E.g., DÍEZ MERINO, El suplicio de la cruz, 44–47; note 44: "Existen diversos términos que se refieren a un único suplicio, y que reviste distintas formas; con frecuencia las antiguas lenguas no tienen vocablos que los distingan, pues todos ellos vienen a significar 'suspender en un madero', 'colgar', 'subir al patíbulo', etc.; per con tales términos a menudo no se puede especificar qué forma de crucifixión denotan." HENGEL also recognized that the form of crucifixion "varied greatly" and that similar terminology was employed for both *post-* and *ante-mortem* suspensions on a stake; cf. HENGEL, Crucifixion, 24.

[14] CHAPMAN, Crucifixion, 7–33, esp. 30–33.

### 3.1.2 Greek Terminology

**(122)** Lucian, *Prometheus* 1–2

[Ἑρμῆς] ὁ μὲν Καύκασος, ὦ Ἥφαιστε, οὗτος, ᾧ τὸν ἄθλιον τουτονὶ Τιτᾶνα προσηλῶσθαι δεήσει· περισκοπῶμεν δὲ ἤδη κρημνόν τινα ἐπιτήδειον, εἴ που τῆς χιόνος τι γυμνόν ἐστιν, ὡς βεβαιότερον καταπαγείη τὰ δεσμὰ καὶ οὗτος ἅπασι περιφανὴς εἴη κρεμάμενος.

[Ἥφαιστος] Περισκοπῶμεν, ὦ Ἑρμῆ· οὔτε γὰρ ταπεινὸν καὶ πρόσγειον ἐσταυρῶσθαι[15] χρή, ὡς μὴ ἐπαμύνοιεν αὐτῷ τὰ πλάσματα αὐτοῦ οἱ ἄνθρωποι, οὔτε μὴν κατὰ τὸ ἄκρον – ἀφανὴς γὰρ ἂν εἴη τοῖς κάτω – ἀλλ᾽ εἰ δοκεῖ κατὰ μέσον ἐνταῦθά που ὑπὲρ τῆς φάραγγος ἀνεσταυρώσθω ἐκπετασθεὶς τὼ χεῖρε ἀπὸ τουτουὶ τοῦ κρημνοῦ πρὸς τὸν ἐναντίον.

[Ἑρμῆς] Εὖ λέγεις· ἀπόξυροί τε γὰρ αἱ πέτραι καὶ ἀπρόσβατοι πανταχόθεν, ἠρέμα ἐπινενευκυῖαι, καὶ τῷ ποδὶ στενὴν ταύτην ὁ κρημνὸς ἔχει τὴν ἐπίβασιν, ὡς ἀκροποδητὶ μόλις ἑστάναι, καὶ ὅλως ἐπικαιρότατος ἂν ὁ σταυρὸς γένοιτο. μὴ μέλλε οὖν, ὦ Προμηθεῦ, ἀλλ᾽ ἀνάβαινε καὶ πάρεχε σεαυτὸν καταπαγησό-μενον πρὸς τὸ ὄρος.

[2] [Προμηθεύς] Ἀλλὰ κἂν ὑμεῖς γε, ὦ Ἥφαιστε καὶ Ἑρμῆ, κατελεήσατέ με παρὰ τὴν ἀξίαν δυστυχοῦντα.

[Ἑρμῆς] Τοῦτ᾽ ἔφης, ὦ Προμηθεῦ, [τὸ κατελεήσατε] ἀντὶ σοῦ ἀνασκολοπισ-θῆναι αὐτίκα μάλα παρακούσαντας τοῦ ἐπιτάγματος· ἢ οὐχ ἱκανὸς εἶναί σοι δοκεῖ ὁ Καύκασος καὶ ἄλλους χωρῆσαι δύο προσπατταλευθέντας[16]; ἀλλ᾽ ὄρεγε τὴν δεξιάν· σὺ δέ, ὦ Ἥφαιστε, κατάκλειε καὶ προσήλου καὶ τὴν σφῦραν ἐρρωμένως κατάφερε. δὸς καὶ τὴν ἑτέραν· κατειλήφθω εὖ μάλα καὶ αὕτη. εὖ ἔχει. καταπτήσεται δὲ ἤδη καὶ ὁ ἀετὸς ἀποκερῶν τὸ ἧπαρ, ὡς πάντα ἔχοις ἀντὶ τῆς καλῆς καὶ εὐμηχάνου πλαστικῆς.

*Translation.* [Hermes] This is the Caucasus, O Hephaestus, where this wretched Titan will need to be pinned up. And let us now look around for some service-able cliff where there is some place bare of snow so the bonds may be more securely stuck fast and this god may be clearly seen by all while he is hanging. [Hephaestus] Let us look around, O Hermes. For it is necessary neither to cru-cify him low and near the ground, lest his human creations might come to his aid, nor indeed to crucify him upon the peak, for then he would be unseen by those below. But consider whether we should let him be crucified somewhere

---

[15] The JACOBITZ edition here follows one group of manuscripts (which MACLEOD labels as the â tradition) in reading ἀνεσταυρῶσθαι instead of ἐσταυρῶσθαι.

[16] MATTHEW D. MACLEOD, *Luciani Opera* (4 vols.; Scriptorum classicorum bibliotheca Oxoniensis; Oxford: Clarendon, 1972–1987), 279 observes that the γ tradition reads προσ-πατταλευθῆναι in place of προσπατταλευθέντας (found in MACLEOD and JACOBITZ). JACOBITZ reads ἂν after ἄλλους.

here in the middle over the ravine, spreading out his hands from this cliff to the opposite one.

[Hermes] You speak well, for the rocks are both sheer and inaccessible from all around, slightly overhanging, and the cliff has this narrow foothold for the feet, so one can barely stand on tiptoe, and this cross seems wholly advantageous. Therefore, O Prometheus, do not delay, but ascend and offer yourself to be affixed to the mountain.

[2] [Prometheus] But perhaps you, O Hephaestus and Hermes, might have mercy on me concerning my undeserved misfortune.

[Hermes] You say this, O Prometheus, so we (instead of you)[17] would be crucified forthwith for plainly disobeying the order. Or would it not appear sufficient to you that the Caucasus also holds two others who have been pinned to it? But stretch out your right hand; and you, Hephaestus, clamp it down, and nail it, and bear down your hammer vigorously. Also give me the other. Let it also be bound very well. It is done well. And even now the eagle flies down in order to cut out your liver, so you might have all these things done in return for your pretty and ingenious creation.

*Commentary.*[18] Lucian retells the myth of Prometheus, who, having created humankind and having stolen fire to give to humanity, faced the wrath of Zeus. In the myth, Zeus orders Hephaestus and Hermes to affix Prometheus to the Caucasus Mountains in order that an eagle might daily devour his intestines in the sight of all. Lucian, critical of the classic mythology and the ethics it implies, displays throughout this dialogue both the uncontrolled wrath of Zeus (see also Lucian's *Juppiter Tragoedus* and *Juppiter Confutatis*) and the cruel irony found in Prometheus' judicial penalty. The gods themselves have benefitted by Prometheus' creations since, among other matters, they enjoy the daily burnt sacrifices offered by humanity in temples fashioned by human hands. In order to emphasize the cruelty of the punishment enforced on Prometheus, Lucian describes it with the same terminology typical of crucifixion in his day (see also Lucian, *Jupp. Conf.* 8; *Sacr.* 6).

There are several intriguing features to this passage. First, several standard crucifixion terms are employed, which provides an introduction to Greek cru-

---

[17] The translation does not include τὸ κατελεήσατε. If those awkward words were included, one would probably have to render the phrase: "you would have compassion, so that we (instead of you) would be crucified".

[18] Text: MACLEOD, Luciani Opera, 1:278–279 (τὸ κατελεήσατε appears in brackets, reporting that HEMSTERHUYS conjectures its deletion). Compared with KARL JACOBITZ, Luciani Samosatensis opera (3 vols.; orig. 1903–1905; repr., Bibliotheca scriptorum Graecorum et Romanorum Teubneriana; Leipzig: Teubner, 1913–1921), 1:62–63 (in the last speech from Hermes, JACOBITZ includes the bracketed words and reads Τοῦτο φῇς in place of Τοῦτ' ἔφης). Text has been checked against AUSTIN M. HARMON, Lucian (8 vols.; LCL; Cambridge: Harvard University Press, 1913–1967), 2:242–244 (HARMON omits τὸ κατελεήσατε).

cifixion/suspension vocabulary.[19] In the section cited above note σταυρός, σταυρόω, ἀνασταυρόω, ἀνασκολοπίζω (cf. *Prom.* 4, 7, 9, 10, 15, 17). Many of these terms clearly apply to crucifixions elsewhere in Lucian (cf. *Cat.* 6; *Jupp. Trag.* 19; *Peregr.* 11, 13, 34, 45; *Philops.* 29; *Pisc.* 2).[20] Other, less-technical verbs are also used to speak of how he will be affixed to the "cross" of the Caucasus: προσηλόω ("nail, fix to"), καταπήγνυμι ("stick fast, plant firmly"), κρεμάννυμι/κρεμάω ("hang up"), προσπατταλεύω ("nail fast to, nail up").

Second, to the extent Lucian intentionally mimics the crucifixions of his day, we learn something of how he expected them to be performed. The arms are outstretched (ἀπὸ τουτουὶ τοῦ κρημνοῦ πρὸς τὸν ἐναντίον, "from this cliff to the opposite one"). There is a "narrow foothold for the feet" that allows one to "barely stand on tiptoe." While it is possible that this "foot-hold" describes the executioners' access point to the place of execution, it seems more likely the foothold was in place for Prometheus to stand on tiptoe while appended to the "cross"/Caucasus. The executioners expect a bird (here an eagle) will attack the suspended body. There is also a concern that the victim be publicly viewable but not able to be easily removed. Of course, the mention of the eagle and the public viewing are part of the original myth and thus may not have direct ties to Lucian's addition of crucifixion language. However, many texts discussed below indicate that crucifixions are typically public events, often ending in decomposed bodies mutilated by birds, and officials are frequently concerned to prevent bystanders from removing the bodies early. So it appears most likely that Lucian's connection of Prometheus' punishment with crucifixion relies not merely on the penal suspension of the body in the original myth but also on the prolonged, public nature of the sentence.

Third, Lucian's approach serves as a *metaphorical* exposition of the original mythic torture of Prometheus. The educated ancient reader would know Prometheus, being a god, is ultimately not going to die from this punishment. Also, obviously no wooden "cross" is involved. However, we need not, for these reasons, discard the very present crucifixion imagery Lucian intentionally employs in order to shock his readers.[21]

Finally, we note again the simple fact that Lucian can apply crucifixion terminology to a mythological event that originally did not bear such connotations. This serves as an example of "actualizing" an ancient myth in order to bring it alive to the author's contemporary readers. More instances of this will be observed below (see 3.9). The effectiveness of employing crucifixion language for Lucian's satirical purposes relies in part on the way in which cruci-

---

[19] HENGEL, Crucifixion, 11 notes that "Lucian uses all the technical terms of a crucifixion".

[20] These terms have been studied in multiple theological dictionaries and lexicons. See especially: JOHANNES SCHNEIDER, σταυρός, σταυρόω, ἀνασταυρόω, TDNT 7 (1971): 572–584; HEINZ-WOLFGANG KUHN, σταυρός, σταυρόω, EDNT 3 (1993): 267–272.

[21] As does SAMUELSSON, Crucifixion, 234–235, 268.

fixion was viewed with dread in antiquity. Further citations from this dialogue are found below in 3.9.

### 3.1.3 Latin Terminology

**(123)** Seneca, *Epistulae* 101.14

Invenitur aliquis qui velit inter supplicia tabescere et perire membratim et totiens per stilicidia emittere animam quam semel exhalare? Invenitur qui velit adactus ad illud infelix lignum, iam debilis, iam pravus et in foedum scapularum ac pectoris tuber elisus, cui multae moriendi causae etiam citra crucem fuerant, trahere animam tot tormenta tracturam?

*Translation.* Can anyone be found who would want to waste away amid punishments and to perish limb by limb and to emit his soul (as so often occurs) by dripping bodily fluids, rather than to expire at once? Can he be found who – having been driven to that cursed tree, already weak, already deformed and in an abominable way thrusting out swellings from his shoulders and chest, for whom many causes of death would have be even nearer than a cross – would want to drag out a soul that has been dealt so many torments?

*Commentary.*[22] Seneca argues the Stoic position that suicide remains sometimes the best option for freedom from suffering. Whereas Maecenas had previously contended that every breath of life should be sustained, even if one were sitting on a cross (*si sedeam cruce* in 101.11), Seneca graphically depicts the agony that crucifixion involves, and he considers death the wiser option.

The death portrayed here is clearly one of living torment while still attached to a *crux*. The term *crux* also appears alongside the *infelix lignum* ("cursed tree") as references to the wooden object against which the person has been affixed. The fact he is "already weak" and "already deformed" likely indicates that Seneca presumes some torture (perhaps scourging) has preceded the actual crucifixion. Seneca felt no need to depict the exact shape of the device to which the man has been attached (whether because he assumed his readers would know or because he did not think the precise contours formed a relevant detail).

---

[22] Text: LEIGHTON DURHAM REYNOLDS, L. Annaei Senecae Ad Lucilium epistulae morales (2 vols.; Scriptorum classicorum bibliotheca Oxoniensis; Oxford: Clarendon, 1965), 2:424. Same text (with slightly different punctuation) in RICHARD M. GUMMERE, Seneca. Ad Lucilium epistulae morales (3 vols; LCL; London: Heineman, 1917–1925), 3:166. HENSE follows BUECHELER in conjecturing *potius* in place of *totiens*; cf. OTTO HENSE, L. Annaei Senecae ad Lucilium epistularum moralium quae supersunt (L. Annaei Senecae opera quae supersunt 3; Leipzig: Teubner, 1898), 470–471.

## 3.1.4 Ante mortem and post mortem Suspension

Though we have observed some typical crucifixion terminology, it should also be noted that Greek and Latin authors were content to apply these same terms to both executionary suspensions (*ante mortem*) and *post mortem* bodily suspensions. An example of each is provided below (both from Polybius), and many others from both categories will be found in the pages to follow. It appears then that many authors were seemingly unconcerned whether the person was alive or dead when pinned to a cross. Indeed, more often than not, the context cannot be fully determinative whether the crucifixion serves as a means of execution or as a *post mortem* event.

**(124)** Polybius, *Historiae* 1.86.4–7

μετὰ δὲ ταῦτα προσαγαγόντες πρὸς τὰ τείχη τοὺς περὶ τὸν Σπένδιον αἰχμαλώ-τους ἐσταύρωσαν ἐπιφανῶς. ⁵ οἱ δὲ περὶ τὸν Μάθω κατανοήσαντες τὸν Ἀννίβαν ῥᾳθύμως καὶ κατατεθαρρηκότως ἀναστρεφόμενον, ἐπιθέμενοι τῷ χάρακι πολλοὺς μὲν τῶν Καρχηδονίων ἀπέκτειναν, πάντας δ᾽ ἐξέβαλον ἐκ τῆς στρατοπεδείας, ἐκυρίευσαν δὲ καὶ τῆς ἀποσκευῆς ἁπάσης, ἔλαβον δὲ καὶ τὸν στρατηγὸν Ἀννίβαν ζωγρίᾳ. ⁶ τοῦτον μὲν οὖν παραχρῆμα πρὸς τὸν τοῦ Σπεν-δίου σταυρὸν ἀγαγόντες καὶ τιμωρησάμενοι πικρῶς, ἐκεῖνον μὲν καθεῖλον, τοῦτον δ᾽ ἀνέθεσαν ζῶντα καὶ περικατέσφαξαν τριάκοντα τῶν Καρχηδονίων τοὺς ἐπιφανεστάτους περὶ τὸ τοῦ Σπενδίου σῶμα, ⁷ τῆς τύχης ὥσπερ ἐπίτηδες ἐκ παραθέσεως ἀμφοτέροις ἐναλλὰξ διδούσης ἀφορμὰς εἰς ὑπερβολὴν τῆς κατ᾽ ἀλλήλων τιμωρίας.

*Translation.* And after these things they [the Carthaginians] led those who had been taken prisoner with Spendius to the walls, and crucified them for all to see. ⁵ But those who were with Mathos observed Hannibal behaving indifferently and boldly; and, setting upon his palisaded camp, they slew many of the Carthaginians, and cast out all of them from the encampment. And they took possession of all the [Carthaginian] baggage. And they also took Hannibal, the general, alive. ⁶ Therefore, leading him immediately to Spendius' cross, and harshly taking vengeance against him, they took down that person [Spendius] and hung up this one [Hannibal] alive, and they slaughtered around the body of Spendius thirty of the most illustrious among the Carthaginians, ⁷ even as fortune, cunningly from their juxtaposition, gave to both [opponents] in inverted order their occasions for excessive vengeance against the other.

*Commentary.*[23] Shortly after the First Punic War, the Carthaginians have to deal with a revolt by their mercenaries (cf. Polybius, *Hist.* 1.65ff.) – known as the Mercenary War (or the Libyan War, 241–237 B.C.). Spendius and Mathos had joined forces with the Libyan mercenaries. Spendius was said to be a runaway Roman slave from Campania (1.69.4). At this stage in the revolt, Spendius has been captured by the Carthaginians, who are under the leadership of Hamilcar and of one of his generals named Hannibal (though not the famed Hannibal of the Second Punic War). The exchange of crucifixions mentioned above, in keeping with a major theme in Polybius, occurs according to machinations of Fate/Fortune. This same event is recorded, likely with strong reference to Polybius' account, in Diodorus Siculus, *Bib. hist.* 25.5.1–2 (analyzed in No. 231). Polybius wrote *Histories* in the late second century B.C.

Above we read of an *ante mortem* suspension of the living Hannibal (ἀνέθεσαν ζῶντα), presumably on the very σταυρός once occupied by Spendius. It is less certain in Polybius' text whether Spendius was alive when "crucified" (ἐσταύρωσαν). Several features of this passage echo recurring themes in many crucifixion sources: The place of suspension is very public (ἐπιφανῶς, "for all to see"), it is performed outside the walls of a city, and the context is one of extremely harsh treatment by (non-Roman) barbarians during war. Though Polybius does not highlight this fact, it is ironic that Spendius, an escaped slave, meets a slave's punishment in the end. Polybius does imply that, in his estimation, this exchange of penalties was excessive (εἰς ὑπερβολὴν). In sum, Polybius represents Hannibal's death clearly as an *ante mortem* crucifixion, and Spendius' end also involved a suspension (whether *ante* or *post mortem*, Polybius does not feel the need to inform his readers).

## (125) Polybius, *Historiae* 5.54.3,6–7

ὁ δὲ Μόλων συννοήσας τὸ γεγονὸς καὶ πανταχόθεν ἤδη κυκλούμενος, λαβὼν πρὸ ὀφθαλμῶν τὰς ἐσομένας περὶ αὐτὸν αἰκίας, ἐὰν ὑποχείριος γένηται καὶ ζωγρίᾳ ληφθῇ, προσήνεγκε τὰς χεῖρας ἑαυτῷ ... [6] ὁ δὲ βασιλεὺς διαρπάσας τὴν παρεμβολὴν τῶν πολεμίων, τὸ μὲν σῶμα τοῦ Μόλωνος ἀνασταυρῶσαι προσέταξε κατὰ τὸν ἐπιφανέστατον τόπον τῆς Μηδίας. [7] ὃ καὶ παραχρῆμα συνετέλεσαν οἱ πρὸς τούτοις τεταγμένοι· διακομίσαντες γὰρ εἰς τὴν Καλλωνῖτιν πρὸς αὐταῖς ἀνεσταύρωσαν ταῖς εἰς τὸν Ζάγρον ἀναβολαῖς.

*Translation.* And Molon, after having reflected on what had occurred, and being already encircled on every side, and after having before his mind's eye the torments that were about to happen concerning him if he were made cap-

---

[23] Text: THEODOR BÜTTNER-WOBST, Polybius. Historiae (5 vols.; Stuttgart: Teubner, 1893–1904), 1:117–118; checked against WILLIAM R. PATON, Polybius: Histories (6 vols.; LCL; London: Heinemann, 1922–1927), 1:232.

tive and was caught alive, brought his own hand against himself ... [6] The king, having plundered the camp of his enemies, commanded that the body of Molon be crucified on the most conspicuous place in Media. [7] Which deed those appointed to these matters also immediately completed, for they carried the body across to the Callonitis and crucified it before the territories that ascend unto the Zagros Mountain.

*Commentary.*[24] Molon, satrap of Media, revolts against Antiochus the Great, who has just inherited the Seleucid throne (Polybius, *Hist.* 5.40.4ff.). Ultimately, the battle reverses against Molon, and he commits suicide (thus "he brought his own hand against himself" in 5.54.3). Antiochus orders a *post mortem* suspension/crucifixion of Molon's body. The precise shape and material of the suspension device is not described. However, there is substantial emphasis on the public nature of the suspension: it occurs in "the most conspicuous place" (τὸν ἐπιφανέστατον τόπον). Notably, Polybius applies standard bodily-suspension / crucifixion terminology (ἀνασταυρῶσαι) to this *post mortem* event. The Seleucid king clearly desired for the suspension to be conducted in a prominent public location.

### 3.1.5 Shape of the Cross

Surprisingly few texts provide any indication about the shape of the device employed in crucifixion. In a passage cited above (Lucian, *Prom.* 1), Lucian in the second century A.D. intentionally mimicked crucifixion practice when he applied cross terminology to the myth of Prometheus. Lucian indicated that the god's arms would be spread out and that he would barely be able to stand on tiptoe on a narrow ledge. That text apparently presumes crucifixion involved extended arms and a footrest that remains just scarcely in reach. Below are two other texts that provide us with some indication of the shape of the cross. The first appears in the standard corpus of Lucian's writings but apparently actually stems from a later hand; the second is found in the Stoic lectures of Epictetus (mid-first to second century A.D.) as collected by Arrian.

**(126)** [Pseudo-] Lucian, *Iudicium vocalium* 12

Οὕτω μὲν οὖν ὅσον ἐς φωνὴν ἀνθρώπους ἀδικεῖ· ἔργῳ δὲ πῶς; κλάουσιν ἄνθρωποι καὶ τὴν αὑτῶν τύχην ὀδύρονται καὶ Κάδμῳ καταρῶνται πολλάκις, ὅτι τὸ Ταῦ ἐς τὸ τῶν στοιχείων γένος παρήγαγε· τῷ γὰρ τούτου σώματί φασι τοὺς τυράννους ἀκολουθήσαντας καὶ μιμησαμένους αὐτοῦ τὸ πλάσμα ἔπειτα

---

[24] Text: BÜTTNER-WOBST, Polybius. Historiae 2:171–172; same text, with slight punctuation variation, in PATON, Polybius: Histories, 2:132.

σχήματι τοιούτῳ ξύλα τεκτήναντας ἀνθρώπους ἀνασκολοπίζειν ἐπ' αὐτά· ἀπὸ δὲ τούτου καὶ τῷ τεχνήματι τῷ πονηρῷ τὴν πονηρὰν ἐπωνυμίαν συνελθεῖν. Τούτων οὖν ἀπάντων ἕνεκα πόσων θανάτων τὸ Ταῦ ἄξιον εἶναι νομίζετε; ἐγὼ μὲν γὰρ οἶμαι δικαίως τοῦτο μόνον ἐς τὴν τοῦ Ταῦ τιμωρίαν ὑπολείπεσθαι, τὸ τῷ σχήματι τῷ αὐτοῦ τὴν δίκην ὑποσχεῖν, [ὃ δὴ σταυρὸς εἶναι ἀπὸ τούτου ἐδημιουργήθη, ὑπὸ δὲ ἀνθρώπων ὀνομάζεται.]

*Translation.* Therefore, thus much by [his] voice he [Tau] injures men, but how about by [his] work? Men weep and mourn their fortune, and frequently utter imprecations against Cadmus because he placed the Tau in the offspring of the letters. For, it is said that tyrants, having followed Tau's body and having imitated his form, then having devised wooden beams in such a form, crucify men on them; and from him [Tau] and by his evil handiwork the evil device even comes to its surname. Therefore, on account of all this, do you consider the Tau to be worthy of many deaths? For I think it right to leave him behind alone unto the vengeance of the Tau, to undergo the judgment which accords to his own form, [which certainly was fabricated to be a cross from this one, but was named by men.]

*Commentary.*[25] HARMON contends that this work was not penned by Lucian but is "much later than his time."[26] In this mock court battle, the alphabetic letter Sigma prosecutes the letter Tau before a jury consisting of the Vowels. Tau has been supplanting Sigma in a host of Greek words, and Sigma asks that Tau be condemned for his actions. Modern grammarians of late Hellenistic Greek do indeed attest to the tendency of Greek speakers and authors to write *tau* in place of *sigma* in many Greek words during this (and later) periods. The vital material comes at the end of the dialogue, where the Sigma presses home his point that Tau, beyond injuring the voice/speech of humanity (since Tau has supplanted other letters), has also injured humankind physically by serving as the form of the cross employed in crucifixion (note ἀνασκολοπίζειν). By way of punishment, Sigma calls for Tau to be crucified on a Tau-shaped cross. Certainly this short ironic discourse implies that its author believed it common practice to attach a crossbar to an upright pole in order to crucify those condemned by a court of law.

---

[25] Text (also known as *Lis Consonantium*) in MACLEOD, Luciani Opera, 1:143. Brackets are mine, indicating text that HARMON, Lucian, 1:406–408 deletes, though the material is (probably rightly) included in MACLEOD's edition. HARMON follows a conjecture by SOMMERBRODT, but the bracketed text appears in the extant manuscripts.

[26] HARMON, Lucian, 1:395.

**(127)** Epictetus, *Diatribes* 3.26.21–22

Εἶτα φοβῇ λιμόν, ὡς δοκεῖς. σὺ δ' οὐ λιμὸν φοβῇ, ἀλλὰ δέδοικας μὴ οὐ σχῇς μάγειρον, μὴ οὐ σχῇς ἄλλον ὀψωνητήν, ἄλλον τὸν ὑποδήσοντα, ἄλλον τὸν ἐνδύσοντα, ἄλλους τοὺς τρίψοντας, ἄλλους τοὺς ἀκολουθήσοντας, ²² ἵν' ἐν τῷ βαλανείῳ ἐκδυσάμενος καὶ ἐκτείνας σεαυτὸν ὡς οἱ ἐσταυρωμένοι τρίβῃ ἔνθεν καὶ ἔνθεν, εἶθ' ὁ ἀλείπτης ἐπιστὰς λέγῃ 'μετάβηθι, δὸς πλευρόν, κεφαλὴν αὐτοῦ λάβε, παράθες τὸν ὦμον', εἶτ' ἐλθὼν ἐκ τοῦ βαλανείου εἰς οἶκον κραυγάσῃς 'οὐδεὶς φέρει φαγεῖν;' εἶτ' 'ἆρον τὰς τραπέζας, σπόγγισον'.

*Translation.* Then you fear hunger, as you consider it. Yet you do not fear hunger, but you are alarmed that you might not have a cook, you might not have another [slave] who buys your fish, another who puts on your shoes, another who dresses you, others who massage you, others who follow you, ²² in order that after you have undressed in a bath and stretched yourself out as those who have been crucified are pressed out on this side and on that, then the bath-attendant standing near might say, 'Turn him, give me his side, take his head, provide me his shoulder." Then, after you come out of the bath into your house, you might cry, "Will no one bring me something to eat?" Then, "Take up the tables, and sponge them!".

*Commentary.*²⁷ In this discourse on "those who fear want," the early-second-century A.D. Stoic philosopher Epictetus belittles those of the privileged classes who demand so much from others with the result that they become incapable of providing for themselves. Here, he imagines a man who, though wealthy enough to be accompanied by his various specialized slaves, fears what would happen should he loose these privileges. At the bath, the man lays out for a massage, and the process of stretching him out is ironically compared to crucifixion. The crucified person is portrayed as one who has been pressed out "on this side and on that" (ἔνθεν καὶ ἔνθεν), implying that he has been forced to stretch out his appendages. This can be compared to Prometheus stretched from one cliff face to another in Lucian's dialogue (*Prom.* 1). And we can well imagine this would have occurred on a cross shaped much like the Tau mentioned earlier by Pseudo-Lucian (*Iud. voc.* 12).

---

²⁷ Text: Henricus Schenkl, Epicteti Dissertationes ab Arriano digestae (BSGRT; Leipzig: Teubner, 1916), 310; checked against William Abbott Oldfather, Epictetus: The Discourses as Reported by Arrian, the Manual, and Fragments (2 vols.; LCL; Cambridge: Harvard University Press, 1928), 232–234.

## 3.1.6 Variations in Crucifixion Practices

While there are a few texts that signal some expected shape to the cross (at least by the first or second century A.D.), a handful of others also indicate the shape of the cross could vary, especially when the executioners decide to engage in cruel creativity.

**(128)** Seneca, *De consolatione ad Marciam* (*Dialogue* 6) 20.3

Video istic cruces non unius quidem generis sed aliter ab aliis fabricatas: capite quidam conuersos in terram suspendere, alii per obscena stipitem egerunt, alii brachia patibulo explicuerunt; uideo fidiculas, uideo uerbera, et membris singulis articulis singula docuerunt machinamenta: sed uideo et mortem.

*Translation.* I see there crosses, not merely of one kind, but fashioned differently by different people: a certain one suspends [a person] with his head upside down towards the ground, others impale a stake through the sexual organs, others extend the victim's arms by a yoke [*patibulum*]. I see instruments of torture; I see whips, and for individual limbs and parts of the body, individual machines have acted as a teacher. But I also see death!

*Commentary.*[28] Seneca the Younger writes in the mid-first-century A.D. to console Marcia in her grief over the death of her son. The genre of *consolatio* was previously known in Latin and Greek literature, and Seneca himself authored three such treatises, all from his Stoic viewpoint. In this context, he praises death, which benefits the deceased as a cessation of earthly troubles. For instance, earlier he notes the example of cruelly-treated slaves who are released from their bonds by death. Here, he provides extreme illustrations of how death frees one from torture and even from crucifixion. Death should thus be welcomed. The term *cruces* has been translated "instruments of torture" by BASORE, which is possible but unlikely.[29] A *crux*, while it can designate "torture" or a "torment," most often refers to a "cross."[30] Moreover, Seneca describes three forms of *cruces* in the following clauses: the third (with the extended arms of the victim) clearly indicates a death on a cross, and

---

[28] Text: LEIGHTON DURHAM REYNOLDS, L. Annaei Senecae dialogorum libri duodecim (Scriptorum classicorum bibliotheca Oxoniensis; Oxford: Clarendoni, 1977) 155. For the awkward *docuerunt* ("have acted as a teacher"), which is found in the manuscripts, other editors have suggested the more sensible *nocuerunt* ("have created injury"); see e.g., BASORE, Seneca. Moral Essays, 68. According to REYNOLDS, other editors have proposed deleting *docuerunt* or conjectured instead *admouerunt, adplicuerunt,* or *aptauerunt.*

[29] BASORE, Seneca. Moral Essays, 69.

[30] See the range of meanings given in P. G. W. GLARE, Oxford Latin Dictionary (Oxford: Oxford University Press, 1982), 463.

the first (with the person crucified upside down) is also a known use of the cross in antiquity (at least in early Christian tradition; cf. Eusebius, *Hist. eccl.* 3.1.2;[31] 8.8.2). The second form is admittedly shocking,[32] but variation on an expected form is, in fact, the point of Seneca's emphasis on "difference" in the first clause. Notably here the victims must clearly be alive while on the *cruces*, otherwise the rhetoric makes no sense. Just as death provides relief from the tortures mentioned in the sentences preceding the text quoted above, so death also provides welcome release to the living victims attached to these various types of *crux*.

Observe from this text that Seneca certainly recognized the person could be attached to a cross in a variety of manners. However, the fact he goes out of his way to first say "not merely of one kind" (*non unius quidem generis*) likely indicates that he assumes his reader will anticipate a particular typical style of cross; it is this presupposition Seneca challenges. Therefore, he testifies to a diversity of forms of execution that could be met on a cross, even while he also admits there may be "one kind" of cross that most of his contemporaries expected. Given the frequent mention of slavery and of enemies in the context surrounding this passage, we could speculate that Seneca believed the *crux* to be a punishment reserved for slaves and/or meted out in war to enemies. However, he is not clear here on this point.

## (129) Josephus, *Bellum Judaicum* 5.451

προσήλουν δὲ οἱ στρατιῶται δι' ὀργὴν καὶ μῖσος τοὺς ἁλόντας ἄλλον ἄλλῳ σχήματι πρὸς χλεύην, καὶ διὰ τὸ πλῆθος χώρα τε ἐνέλειπε τοῖς σταυροῖς καὶ σταυροὶ τοῖς σώμασιν.[33]

*Translation.* The soldiers, on account of anger and hatred, for a joke nailed in various forms those who had been captured; and because of the multitude, both the space was lacking for the crosses and crosses were lacking for the bodies.

---

[31] This is one of several references to the Apostle Peter being crucified upside down. The accuracy of this tradition has been disputed on the grounds that Tertullian does not mention the inverted nature of Peter's crucifixion. On the complexity of this issue, see e.g., MATTHEW C. BALDWIN, Whose Acts of Peter? Text and Historical Context of the Actus Vercellenses (WUNT 2/196; Tübingen: Mohr-Siebeck, 2005), 70–76.

[32] SAMUELSSON, Crucifixion, 188 suggests this may have involved a "rectal impaling". Assyrian reliefs (albeit from a much earlier period) could potentially portray how such a horrible suspension would work (see below 3.2 on the Balawat Gate reliefs of Shalmaneser III).

[33] NIESE indicates that καὶ σταυροὶ was omitted in one manuscript (MS R). Were only σταυροί omitted, then this could be for sake of parallelism ("and also the space was lacking for the crosses and the bodies"), but the omission of καί with σταυροί (and the τε in the text) makes it most likely that this is a case of haplography due to *homoiïarcton* with the first σταυροῖς.

*Commentary.*[34] During the first Jewish revolt (A.D. 66–73/74), the Romans besieged Jerusalem and crucified those Jewish inhabitants who attempted to escape to find food. This passage will be analyzed more fully later, and an argument will be made that at least some of those crucified were still alive when pinned to the σταυρός (see 3.7.3).[35] However, for now, observe the intentional variations (ἄλλον ἄλλῳ σχήματι "in various forms") introduced by the Roman soldiers. While this may assume a standard crucifixion form existed, it certainly shows that soldiers could, given sufficient opportunity and rage, develop a variety of ways to attach people to the cross. Josephus still describes all of these suspensions with terms here such as σταυρός (cf. ἀνασταυρόω in 5.449).

**(130)** Tacitus, *Annales* 15.44

et pereuntibus addita ludibria, ut ferarum tergis contecti laniatu canum interirent, aut crucibus adfixi, ut flammandi, atque ubi defecisset dies, in usum nocturni luminis urerentur.

*Translation.* And mockeries had been added to those who were passing away, so that they, having been covered with the skins of wild beasts, died by the lacerations of dogs; or so that, having been affixed to crosses or having been set aflame, when the daylight withdrew, they were burned for light in the enjoyment of the night.

*Commentary.*[36] In this famous incident, Nero, having blamed the Roman Christians for setting fire to Rome, has the Christians condemned (for "hatred of the human race") to extremely harsh means of execution. A fuller account of this text appeared earlier in 2.1. For now, let us focus on the means of execution. The Latin text here is difficult; it is unclear whether the crosses and the "having been set aflame" are overlapping penalties, as implied by the one subjunctive verb *urerentur* uniting them, or whether they are separate punishments, as suggested by the *aut...[a]ut* construction. In the translation, we sug-

---

[34] Text: NIESE, Flavii Josephi Opera, 6:496.

[35] On this passage cf. CHAPMAN, Crucifixion, 84–86; note the contrasting views between SAMUELSSON, Crucifixion, 107, and COOK, Crucifixion, 197–198.

[36] Text: ERICH KOESTERMANN, STEPHANUS BORZSÁK, and KENNETH WELLESLEY, P. Cornelii Taciti libri qui supersunt (2 vols.; Bibliotheca Scriptorum Graecorum et Romanorum Teubneriana; Leipzig: Teubner, 1965–1962), I/2 (ed. K. WELLESLEY), 115; note the useful apparatus on p. 157–158 concerning varying views among modern editors about *aut crucibus adfixi, ut flammandi, atque ubi.* These variations primarily concern the conjunctions (especially whether to read *aut* or *ut* before *flammandi*), though some editors (without textual evidence) will bracket the reference to *ut flammandi.* Text compared with CHARLES D. FISHER, Cornelii Taciti Annalium ab excessu divi Augusti libri (Scriptorum classicorum bibliotheca Oxoniensis; Oxford: Clarendon, 1906), loc. cit. (no page numbers in this edition). Also compared with MOORE and JACKSON, Tacitus, 4:284.

gest the same victims are both affixed to crosses and burned (given that both participles *adfixi* and *flammandi* are syntactically dependent upon *urerentur*).

This then represents a variation in crucifixion practice. Christians are crucified (possibly in mockery of their crucified Lord) and then burned while on the cross (likely in "retribution" for the burning of Rome).

### 3.1.7 Summary and Note on Translations

This section has briefly discussed some of the complexities involved in the study of perceptions of crucifixion in antiquity. Some key Greek and Latin terms for the cross have been observed. However, it also has become clear that none of this ancient terminology overlaps at all times in a one-for-one correspondence with many modern definitions of "crucifixion." Indeed, the ancient texts often represent both *ante mortem* and *post mortem* suspensions in similar ways. Furthermore, while there exist a few key passages that indicate a standard form of crucifixion (at least in the first century A.D. and afterwards),[37] other passages from the same time frame indicate that executioners felt free to play with the form of cross-suspension in cruel ways. Most often, the ancient texts do not provide sufficient contextual clues to pronounce definitively on how any one penal bodily suspension occurred or even whether it was *post* or *ante mortem*.

At the very least, this should caution the modern reader to recognize that the ancients often lumped all such suspensions into a single broad category, with overlapping perceptions between the many actual forms of suspension. However, it is these very broad perceptions of human bodily suspension that most concern the scholar of antiquity since crucifixion, as a subcategory of

---

[37] To the passages from Lucian, [Pseudo-] Lucian, and Epictetus cited above, all of which depict a person suspended with arms spread out, we could add Artemidorus, *Oneir.* 2.53; and at least the following passages (from Christian sources) discussed in COOK, Crucifixion, 2–50, esp. 2–8, 26–28, 33–37, 49–50, that indicate a *tau*-shaped cross: *Barn.* 9:8; Justin, *1 Apol.* 55.1–8; *Dial.* 91.1–2; Tertullian, *Apol.* 16.6–7; *Adv. Jud.* 10.7; 13.21; *Nat.* 1.12.3–4; *Marc.* 3.18.3–4; Minucius Felix, *Oct.* 29.7–8; and Eusebius, *Hist. eccl.* 8.9.4. Cook additionally notes that the *tau*-shaped cross appears on graffiti from Puteoli and from the Palatine Hill (and that a *patibulum* cross-bar for torture is pictured in the Arieti tomb). See further: JOHN GRANGER COOK, Crucifixion as Spectacle in Roman Campania, NovT 54 (2012): 68–100; JOHN GRANGER COOK, John 19:17 and the Man on the *Patibulum* in the Arieti Tomb, Early Christianity 4 (2013): 427–453. One could also reference many other examples of an extended death by suspension (as Cook does in Crucifixion, 9–13), though the precise form of the suspension device, i.e. whether it is in the shape of a *tau*, cannot be proven based on these texts. Eusebius also indicates that there was a standard method of crucifixion "according to the custom for criminals" (κατὰ τὸ σύνηθες τοῖς κακούργοις), from which the executioners could also vary by inverting the cross for some Christians (*Hist. eccl.* 8.8.2; cf. our discussion of Seneca, *Marc.* 20.3 [*Dial.* 6] above).

human bodily suspension, likely partook of most (if not all) of the perceptions commonly associated with any penal bodily suspension.

If we develop too tight a definition of what properly constitutes "crucifixion" to the modern reader and attempt to read ancient texts through the filter of just such a modern definition, we may find ourselves erring simultaneously in two different directions. First, we may rule out data (which would have been deemed pertinent by the ancients) on the grounds that it does not cohere with our modern definition. Second, we could well be requiring from the ancient writers a level of detail in their descriptions of execution procedure that they felt was irrelevant to their task. Most importantly, perceptions of the cross in antiquity appear inextricably connected to perceptions of human bodily suspension; thus if we are properly to understand the former, we must also study the latter. For these reasons, below we shall cast a rather broad net in the study of public bodily suspensions, including those that do not bear clear contextual evidence of the shape of the device or even of the *ante* versus *post mortem* nature of the suspension.

The commentaries in this section will indeed observe (when available) particular textual features that most approximate the form of *ante mortem* suspension known today as crucifixion. In addition to textual hints at the shape of the device, one helpful clue will be when the ancient author implies that the victim was "alive" on the suspension device, especially for a longer period of time.[38] There remains very little reason to believe that the ancients regularly practiced hanging someone from the neck,[39] thus impalement served as the other major means (besides crucifixion) of executing someone on an upright pole in antiquity. Impalement, however, would typically produce a very speedy death.[40] Therefore, a prolonged death on an upright device (whether shaped like a *tau* or not), would essentially constitute an *ante mortem* crucifixion.

Nevertheless, since many passages will not provide sufficient context to

---

[38] Some texts will indicate this directly, by referring to the "living" person(s) on the cross. Other passages may provide indirect clues, such as when the crucifixion victim sees, speaks, or gestures from the cross.

[39] Below, we shall encounter the occasional suicide produced by suspension from the neck (e.g., Plautus, *Casina* 111–113, 424; *Persa* 815; Philo, *Mut.* 62; *Spec. Leg.* 3.161; *Bereshit Rabbah* 65:22). The use of a noose does not appear in antiquity as a widely-performed form of official penal or military suspension (especially not by the Romans before Constantine). A similar opinion appears in HEINZ-WOLFGANG KUHN, Die Bedeutung der Qumrantexte für das Verständnis des Galaterbriefes aus dem Münchener Projekt: Qumran und das Neue Testament, in New Qumran Texts and Studies (Proceedings of the First Meeting of the International Organization for Qumran Studies, Paris 1992; ed. G. J. Brooke and F. García Martínez; STDJ 15; Leiden: Brill, 1994), 169–221, esp. 180. On this matter, especially note the extensive footnote in COOK, Crucifixion, 3–4, with the comment that, aside from a later reference to the use of a noose by the barbarian Cimbri people (in 105 B.C.), the earliest Roman evidence he could find for hanging someone else on a noose occurs in the time of Constantine.

[40] Similarly COOK, Crucifixion, 3, 50.

determine the exact means of suspension employed, this still leaves a difficult translational choice before us. How ought the translator convey into simple English diction nouns such as *crux*, σταυρός, etc.? To translate these nouns as "a device for human bodily suspension" appears far too pedantic when compared with the more modest "cross," even if it might at times be more accurate. Yet, other concise expressions, such as "gallows" or "stake," are typically misleading in their own ways since they unduly distance such translated passages from our study of crucifixion. This is especially true with a term such as "gallows" (which often conjures up "hanging from a noose" for an English reader) since there is very little evidence that public "hangings" from the neck were practiced in antiquity. Similarly, a "stake" can easily invoke among English readers images of a device used for public burnings or whippings rather than an instrument for bodily suspension. Moreover, there exists a long legacy among English translators of rendering these Greek and Latin nouns (*crux*, σταυρός, etc.) with the word "cross." Indeed, few modern readers can empathize much with a person who has been "suspended," but we typically understand "crucified" with the same kind of horror and disgust frequently expressed by the ancient authors. Similar points could be made concerning verbal forms such as *crucifigo*, ἀνασταυρόω, and ἀνασκολοπίζω. Finally, the English reader is again reminded that the fine distinctions between crucifixion and other forms of bodily suspension seemed to matter little to most ancient readers. Therefore, it is important that modern readers correctly comprehend the ancient import of a text, and this might be obscured if our translations too precisely isolate only some few texts as clear examples of "crucifixion," while others are left to the vagaries of "suspension" language.

During the writing of this book, numerous tragic accounts have appeared in the American and British press of Islamic militants in Syria and Iraq "crucifying" their opponents.[41] Upon analyzing these news reports, it becomes evident that these militants are often executing such victims first, usually by beheading, and only then raising them up on "crosses." Though we often imagine the term "crucifixion" to refer solely to a means of execution by suspension on a cross-shaped object, these reports indicate that the contemporary English term itself actually has a greater semantic range than some might realize.

For these many reasons, we shall often follow the historical precedent of most English translations and render such Greek and Latin words below with English crucifixion vocabulary, especially where an execution associated with a prolonged suspension on a wooden device is intended.[42] However, the

---

[41] E.g., ALISON GEE, "Crucifixion from ancient Rome to modern Syria," *BBC News Magazine*, BBC.com, May 7, 2014, http://www.bbc.com/news/magazine-27245852.

[42] Thus we will often work with a definition similar to what ANTHONY, Crucifixion, 5 calls the "very literal understanding of *crucifigo*": "to fasten a body, living or dead, to a piece of wood fashioned for the purpose of execution and/or suspension for ignominious display".

reader has been duly cautioned about the complexity of the terminological issues. And the commentaries on the texts below will often attempt to clarify as much as possible from the context of any one passage what that author says about precisely how the reported bodily suspension took place.

### 3.1.8 Human Bodily Suspension in Broader Context

Certainly, as we acknowledged above, crucifixion (narrowly defined) served as a subset of a broader array of human bodily suspension penalties (both *ante* and *post mortem*). Indeed, ancient authors often do not clearly distinguish the subset from the set. Yet even this circle could potentially be broadened to include a further array of punishments. For example, one facet of crucifixion involves the prolonged exposure of the body, and yet there were many ways to expose a body/corpse without suspending it. Thus ancient sources of multiple nationalities frequently mention the penalty of refusing to bury the bodies of military opponents or those of heinous criminals (quite apart from suspension).[43] Some texts depict a beheaded body being suspended, or conversely, the decapitated head of a victim could be hung aloft. Torture, which often preceded crucifixion, could also occur prior to other means of execution that did not involve suspension. And excruciating means of prolonged executions in antiquity were not limited to the cross. So, without making any attempt to be comprehensive, it is certainly appropriate to consider here very briefly some related penalties from antiquity in order to begin to envision the broader resonances that potentially overlap with crucifixion. However, we will conclude by noting that, especially in the territory of the Roman Empire, crucifixion/bodily-suspension had its own terminology and its own specific legal sanction; thus the ancients themselves do typically distinguish crucifixion and bodily suspension from these other broadly related punishments.

Ancient cultures commonly evidence profound commitment to the proper disposal of corpses. The actual mechanism of disposal could vary across cultures and times (e.g., cremation versus inhumation, and various shapes of tombs, sepulchers, reburial devices, etc.). However, most societies projected certain norms concerning the disposal of bodies, and this was regularly connected with religious notions of piety.[44] Thus, to leave a body unburied was

---

[43] A special case of death by torturous public exposure is the Greek practice of *apotympanismos*, which HENGEL (among others) claims as a forerunner of crucifixion in Greece (HENGEL, Crucifixion, 70–72). This will be further addressed below in 3.4.

[44] Cf. VALERIE M. HOPE, Death in Ancient Rome: A Source Book (Routledge Sourcebooks for the Ancient World; London/New York: Routledge, 2007). For Graeco-Roman funerary practices cf. DONNA C. KURTZ and JOHN BOARDMAN, Greek Burial Customs (Ithaca: Cornell University Press, 1971); JOCELYN M. C. TOYNBEE, Death and Burial in the Roman World (Aspects of Greek and Roman life; London: Thames & Hudson, 1971); ROBERT GAR-

often a great insult to the deceased and potentially a great religious sacrilege.[45] Nevertheless, bodies of conquered victims in war were often deliberately exposed to the elements, sometimes as a kind of intentional revenge upon the opponent. Some legal penalties involved long, public exposure of the criminal's corpse. Note how the bodies of the sons of Saul were reportedly left unburied by the Gibeonites for many days (2 Sam 21:6–10).[46] Particularly illuminating are texts that require burial of a corpse, even after a limited period of penal public exposure (Deut 21:22–23). In the rest of this volume, we shall observe many instances in which the lack of burial in crucifixion and other related suspension penalties invokes the horror associated with maltreating a human body by refusing it proper and religiously-sanctioned funerary rites.

Decapitation was a common method of execution in antiquity, and beheadings could also occur in the course of war. Decapitated heads might even be carried some distance as retribution on the deceased or to prove to a ruler that someone had died.[47] Authors report headless bodies being suspended (see 1 Sam 31:10; 2 Sam 21:12; also Herodotus, *Hist.* 6.30.1). It is also notable that other body parts could be cut off prior to publicly hanging up a body (e.g., hands and feet in 2 Sam 4:12). Conversely, the ancients could also display various body parts apart from the torso of the conquered victim.[48] In particular, Greek- and Roman-era historians record many instances in which decapi-

---

LAND, The Greek Way of Death (Ithaca: Cornell University Press, 1985); VALERIE M. HOPE, Roman Death: Dying and the Dead in Ancient Rome (London/New York: Continuum, 2009). For Judaism cf. RACHEL S. HALLOTE, Death, Burial, and Afterlife in the Biblical World: How the Israelites and Their Neighbors Treated the Dead (Chicago: Dee, 2001); RACHEL HACHLILI, Jewish Funerary Customs, Practices and Rites in the Second Temple Period (JSJSup 94; Leiden: Brill, 2005).

[45] There are exceptions to this since some ancient cultures engaged in "excarnation" – the practice of regularly exposing deceased bodies so that birds and other animals would devour the flesh. However, in the time period and geographic locales that concern us, the evidence highly favors an almost universal insistence on cremation or inhumation of the corpse. For example, ARAV has argued that some Chalcolithic sites in the Levant (esp. Rogem Hiri) testify to peoples there following the Neolithic and Chalcolithic practice of excarnation found in Anatolia; see his popular-level discussion, RAMI ARAV, Excarnation: Food for Vultures, BAR 37.6 (2011): 40–49, 17. This thesis, while worthy of further consideration, speaks of Chalcolithic structures that precede by a few millennia the time-period we are discussing.

[46] On this text and later Jewish traditions see CHAPMAN, Crucifixion, 154–157.

[47] For an extensive collection of evidence (both literary and visual) for the public display of decapitated heads by Romans in times of war cf. VOISIN, Chasseurs. Such employment of decapitation is also known in the ANE, and thus the sons of Rimmon bring the head of Ish-bosheth to King David (2 Sam 4:5–12).

[48] As when Ashurbanipal refuses burial to Nabû-kâtâ-sabat, and has his decapitated head hung from the neck of his brother; Rassam Cylinder, col. VII, lines 45–50; DANIEL DAVID LUCKENBILL, Ancient Records of Assyria and Babylonia (2 vols.; Chicago: University of Chicago Press, 1926–1927), §815; MAXIMILIAN STRECK, Assurbanipal und die letzten assyrischen Könige bis zum Untergange Niniveh's (3 vols.; Vorderasiatische Bibliothek 7; Leipzig: Hinrichs, 1916), 62–63.

tated heads are publicly suspended (often on posts) to dishonor defeated foes and warn others.[49] To list just a few examples: Herodotus announces that the Tauri regularly suspended the heads of captured Greeks up on poles (*Hist.* 4.103.2) and that the Persians hung up the head of the Spartan general Leonidas at Thermopylae (*Hist.* 7.238.1; 9.78.3). The Maccabean leader Judas ordered Nicanor's head displayed at the citadel in Jerusalem (1 Macc 7:47; 2 Macc 15:28–35). The Romans suspended heads in the forum on (or near) the rostra in Rome.[50] After the battle in Britain at Lugdunum in A.D. 197, Emperor Severus receives the head of Albinus and sends it to Rome to be hung up in public.[51]

Sometimes suspensions of decapitated heads can employ the same terminology (such as ἀνασταυρόω) used to depict suspension/crucifixion of the whole body (e.g., Herodotus, *Hist.* 9.78.3; Herodian, *Hist.* 3.8.1). However, contextual indicators are typically present to distinguish the hanging up of heads from the suspension of entire human bodies. There is, nevertheless, undoubtedly some conceptual overlap in terms of how ancients thought about such practices. The choice to limit ourselves to human bodily suspension (and not to broaden this even further to the suspension of body parts) is thus in some measure a practical one – the data must be limited in some fashion. Perhaps others can pursue even broader associations in their research. Still, the suspension of a whole (or largely-intact) human body appears to form a special class of penalty in antiquity.

When studying ANE and Classical-era sources, it becomes frankly impossible to read for long without realizing that ancient people developed some truly horrible ways to torture and execute their fellow human beings. While scourging often preceded crucifixion in the Roman Empire, such scourging (along with beating and other methods of torture) could similarly preface many forms of execution in antiquity. In this way, other executions could also intentionally be incredibly painful and humiliating. Crucifixion is not alone in this respect. Below, we shall observe that the cross could be called "the most

---

[49] Sometimes other ways of displaying the head were deemed more *apropos* than suspension on a pole, as when Appian reports that Dolabella had the decapitated head of the praetor Trebonius (who had been involved in Caesar's assassination) displayed on his praetor's chair (*Bella Civilia* 3.3.26) – later the soldiers played ball with it.

[50] Thus in the second century A.D., Appian employs ἀποκρεμάννυμι and κρεμάννυμι to depict the hanging up of heads in the Roman forum, especially the head of Cicero (by Antony in Appian, *Bella Civilia* 4.4.20) and (shockingly) the heads of the senatorial consuls and other leading figures (under Octavian in *Bella Civilia* 1.8.71). Appian's usage has additional interest because he also frequently employs κρεμάννυμι for bodily suspensions (likely crucifixions), e.g., *Bella Civilia* 1.14.119; 1.14.120; 2.13.90; 3.1.3; 4.4.29; 4.5.35; 4.10.81.

[51] Cf. δημοσίᾳ ἀνασταυρωθῆναι in Herodian, *Hist.* 3.8.1; cf. 3.7.7; cf. Niger in Cassius Dio, *Hist. Rom.* 75.8.3 (employing ἀνασταύρωσεν). For a further public display of a decapitated head see Cassius Dio, *Hist. Rom.* 74.10.2; and *Historia Augusta* 8 [Pertinax] 14.7 (death and decapitation of Pertinax).

cruel" way to die. Nevertheless, the ancient Roman elite could be quite creative in developing horrendous methods of execution. For example, victims were often made to face ravenous beasts, and this could be taken to horrible extremes, such as in the widely circulated report that Vedius Pollio in the late first century B.C. would on occasion cast his slaves into pools he kept full of hungry lampreys (or eels, lat. *murena*; cf. Cassius Dio, 54.23.1–4; Pliny, *Nat. hist.* 9.39; Seneca, *De Ira* 3.40.2–4).

While admitting there existed this large sphere of torturous execution methods, it must still be said that human bodily suspension (including crucifixion) formed its own category in antiquity. Such suspensions have their own terminology, especially by the Roman period. Moreover, under the Romans, crucifixion/suspension was an officially accepted procedure that could be repeated empire-wide (as opposed to some of the more creative forms of execution individual Romans seem to have conjured up on their own). Although it would be difficult to measure which means of death was truly the most horrible (who would want to contemplate that for long!), crucifixion was likely widely perceived to be the most extreme among the main official penalties of Rome.[52] Also, as shall be observed in the next few sections, human bodily suspension had a long legacy of being practiced in a variety of forms prior to the Roman institutionalization of the penalty.

## 3.2  Bodily Suspension in the Ancient Near East

Scholars of crucifixion commonly discuss the practice of human bodily suspension in the ancient Near East for two reasons. First, they desire to trace the historical origins of Roman crucifixion from earlier ANE practices. Second, Roman-era sources (including those from Jesus' own day) repeatedly connect the cross with ANE barbarians, so these ANE texts help us understand the barbarous connotations associated with crucifixion in later eras. To these rea-

---

[52] See below on the *summa supplicia* (esp. in 3.10). One potential caveat may be observed concerning the Roman punishment of parricide (the murder of parents, grandparents, siblings, children, and other near family members), which was punished by drowning the offender in a sack (vicious animals appear to have been added to the sack in later periods; cf. Justinian, *Institutes* 4.18.6, which claims this form of execution removes the person from contact with "every element," including sky and land). The severity of this extraordinary crime may well indicate that its punishment was considered more strict than others (including possibly the *crux*); however, parricide appears to be a rare and exceptional issue in Roman law; cf. OLIVIA F. ROBINSON, Criminal Trials, in A Companion to Justinian's Institutes (ed. E. Metzger; Ithaca: Cornell University Press, 1998), 229–242, 234–235; ANDRÉ MAGDELAIN, Paricidas, in Du châtiment dans la cité. Supplices corporels et peine de mort dans le monde antique (Table ronde organisée par l'École française de Rome avec le concours du Centre national de la recherche scientifique (Rome 9.-11. novembre 1982); Collection de l'École Française de Rome 79; Rome: École française de Rome, 1984), 549–571.

sons, we can add at least two others: First, as we shall observe in §3.9, Jewish people in the time of Jesus could interpret the many bodily suspensions recorded in the Hebrew Bible as crucifixions; thus we should first understand these OT texts in their own ANE contexts before proceeding to later Jewish interpretations.[53] Second, while, at the end of the day, the historical origins of cross-shaped execution devices may remain murky, we can still observe that many first-century perceptions associated with crucifixion actually have their origins in the preceding centuries, which also practiced the suspension of human bodies (both before and after death) on upright posts and other objects.

The question is often asked: When and where was crucifixion first practiced? Sadly, our primary sources are less clear on this issue than we might wish. It is commonly suggested that crucifixion was first employed in ancient Persia, with Romans later imitating the Persian practice.[54] Greek and Roman authors do indeed associate bodily suspension (even "crucifixion" language) with Persian (and also Assyrian) military activity, and Graeco-Roman authors occasionally criticize these Near Eastern practices. Monumental texts from ancient Persia more directly testify to Persian willingness to suspend opposing military leaders. However, from our extant sources, it is difficult to ascertain the precise shape of the Persian suspension devices (though they may well have mimicked Assyrian impalements).

More importantly, the Persian actions were preceded by a long history of ancient Near Eastern civilizations engaging in bodily suspension. The terminology can vary between these accounts, so some have postulated careful distinctions between forms of punishment (e.g., between "impalement" and "hanging someone up"), but all of these reports intend some form of public suspension. Babylonian, Assyrian, and Egyptian texts record bodily suspensions in legal codes and in military histories. Assyrian reliefs visually portray

---

[53] Concerning these OT passages, commentators on the Hebrew Bible, in their search for ANE parallels, typically only reference the few pictorial representations found in ANEP alongside the incidents recorded in Hammurabi's Code (conveniently found in ANET), all of which are Babylonian or Assyrian in origin (see below). This has unfortunately skewed their use of the parallel data. One particular example can be found in an article by Nili Wazana, who draws conclusions concerning the aims of the book of Joshua solely in light of Assyrian practices, without first considering whether bodily suspension was actually a more widespread feature throughout the ANE lands (beyond Assyria); see NILI WAZANA, 'For an Impaled Body is a Curse of God' (Deut 21:23): Impaled Bodies in Biblical Law and Conquest Narratives, in Law and Narrative in the Bible and in Neighbouring Ancient Cultures (ed. K. P. Adam, F. Avemarie, and N. Wazana; Forschungen zum Alten Testament 2/54; Tübingen: Mohr Siebeck, 2012), 69–98. Perhaps this section will help broaden the horizons of future OT scholarship on such matters.

[54] Cf. DONALD G. KYLE, Spectacles of Death in Ancient Rome (London/New York: Routledge, 1998), 53 ("Used earlier in the Near East and probably invented by Persia"). SCHIEMANN suggests a much broader set of possible forerunners to the Roman cross: "*Damnatio in crucem* was perhaps based on Oriental and Punic precedents"; GOTTFRIED SCHIEMANN, Damnatio in crucem, BNP 4 (2004): 59.

public impalements on upright poles, thus testifying to this form of Assyrian practice during military conquest. The Hebrew Bible also recounts bodily suspensions in Egyptian and Persian contexts, and it lays down rules concerning the appropriate employment of such practices among the Israelites themselves. Suspension penalties against both heinous criminals and military opponents appear throughout these ANE sources, demonstrating that human bodily suspension during executions was widespread and practiced in most ancient Near Eastern cultures.[55] By studying this material and comparing it to later practices, we can observe how the broader study of suspension in the ANE forms an important backdrop to analyzing the more specific use of crucifixion in later periods.[56]

### 3.2.1 Old Babylonia

Hammurabi's Code mentions three legal cases that involve forms of execution that are connected with human bodily suspension. Two different terms are used for suspending the body – one is applied to a *post mortem* hanging up of the body (in §§21 and 227) and the other likely refers to impaling the victim aloft (in §153). This evidence is significant for its testimony both to general Old Babylonian legal procedures in the eighteenth century B.C. and to the influence Hammurabi's Code had on later ANE legal practices.

**(131)** *Code of Hammurabi* §21 [col. 9a, lines 14–21]

[14] *šum-ma a-wi-lum* [15] *bi-tam* [16] *ip-lu-uš* [17] *i-na pa-ni* [18] *pí-il-ši-im* [19] *šu-a-ti* [20] *i-du-uk-ku-šu-ma* [21] *i-ḫa-al-la-lu-šu*

*Translation.* [14] If a man has broken into a house, [17] they shall put him to death and hang him before the breach which he has made.

*Commentary.*[57] In this famous eighteenth-century Old Babylonian law code,

---

[55] For summaries of the range of evidence included here cf. CHAPMAN, Crucifixion, 99–101; COOK, Crucifixion, 312–315; DAVID W. CHAPMAN, Hanging and Impalement. Hebrew Bible/Old Testament, EBR (Forthcoming).

[56] This section does not seek to generate a comprehensive list of all extant materials about human suspension in the ANE. However, its findings are intended to be illustrative of the range and potential frequency of ANE practices. Translations in this section typically defer to experts in the various Akkadian, Egyptian, Persian, and Ugaritic languages.

[57] The text and translation of the Code of Hammurabi [CH] follows GODFREY R. DRIVER and JOHN C. MILES, The Babylonian Laws (2 vols.; Ancient Codes and Laws of the Near East; Oxford: Clarendon, 1952–1955), here 2:20–21. The format of line numbering in all CH passages follows HUGO WINCKLER, Die Gesetze Hammurabis in Umschrift und Übersetzung (Leipzig: Hinrichs, 1904), against which the text has also been checked. The text has further

three passages call for the suspension of a criminal. Hammurabi (who reigned 1792–1750 B.C.) had his Code inscribed on a tall, black diorite stele. This stele was unearthed during early twentieth-century French excavations at Susa (where it had been relocated in antiquity from Babylonia by the Elamites). The stele invokes the sanction of the deity Shamash over the king's edicts – both in its famous pictorial relief at the top of the stele and in the text itself. Within the midst of several passages that pronounce penalties for robbery, this one contains the most severe sentence. The "breach" would likely result from digging through the mud-brick walls in order to enter the house.

The method of punishment hinges on the meaning of *i-ḫa-al-la-lu-šu* in the last line. A footnote in the DRIVER / MILES translation provides the alternative "transfix" in place of "hang", and they elsewhere allow possible derivations either from *ḫalālu* and the adjective *ḫalilu* ("pierced") or from the verb *ḫalālu* ("to immure/incarcerate"). DRIVER / MILES nevertheless argue that *iḫallalušu* means "they shall hang him up" on the strength of a proposed lexical root from *alālu* and in comparison with the Hittite punishment of hanging someone in front of his own door.[58] The main lexicons follow this same derivation.[59] Moreover, the sequence of verbs likely implies that the person is executed prior to being suspended (*idukkušuma iḫallalušu*).[60] Whether this involved impalement or some other form of suspension, the criminal's body was left as a warning to others never to attempt such a brash form of thievery.

**(132)** *Code of Hammurabi* §153 [col. 9b, lines 61–66]

[61] *šum-ma aš-ša-at a-wi-lim* [62] *aš-šum zi-ka-ri-im* [63] *ša-ni-im* [64] *mu-sà uš-di-ik* [65] SAL *šu-a-ti i-na ga-ši-ši-im* [66] *i-ša-ak-ka-nu-ši*

---

been verified with MARTHA T. ROTH, Law Collections from Mesopotamia and Asia Minor (Second ed.; SBL Writings from the Ancient World 6; Altanta: Scholars Press, 1997), 85; M. E. J. RICHARDSON, Hammurabi's Laws: Text, Translation and Glossary (Sheffield: Sheffield Academic Press, 2000); HANS-DIETER VIEL, ed., The Complete Code of Hammurabi (2 vols.; München: LINCOM Europa, 2005).

[58] DRIVER and MILES, Babylonian Laws, 2:158–159. Similar conclusions are found in *CAD* 1/1, 330. Elsewhere DRIVER and MILES will distinguish this from *išakkanuši* in §153 (which they understand to be impalement), and they will compare the penalty here to the Hebrew suspension practice of Josh 10:26 and 2 Sam 4:12 (cf. ibid. 1:108–109). RICHARDSON, Hammurabi's Laws, 142, 356 similarly derives *iḫallalušu* in §§21 and 227 (along with *ittaḫlalū* in §58) from *alālu*. In contrast, WINCKLER, Gesetze Hammurabis, 15 has the man killed and buried.

[59] See *CAD* 1.1:330 (s.v. *alālu*), which renders §21 as "if a man breaks into a house, they kill him and hang him in front of that very breach." Also *AHw* 1:34 (s.v. *alālu(m)* II), which provides the gloss "aufhängen".

[60] So also DRIVER and MILES, Babylonian Laws, 1:108. A contrary position is held by RICHARDSON, who translates "they shall kill him by hanging him just where he broke in" ARDSON, Hammurabi's Laws, 49, also 142 where he defines *alālu* as "to execute by hanging"); similarly see VIEL, Complete Code of Hammurabi, 2:420, 427.

*Translation.* [61] If a woman has procured the death of her husband on account of another man, [65] they shall impale that woman.

*Commentary.*[61] Within a series of marital laws, suddenly one is confronted with this murderous act and its dreadful penalty. The woman was to be impaled, but no mention is made of punishing her lover; this likely implies that the murder of her husband was assumed to have been produced by her own hand or at her instigation.[62] DRIVERS / MILES argue for a distinction between *ina gašiši šakānu* (or *šitkunu*) and *ina gašiši alālu*, with the former implying "to impale" (often while still alive) and the latter "to hang on a stake" the corpse as a warning to others.[63] On this accounting, here the woman has been has been impaled aloft. Hammurabi's code typically does not specify the precise form of execution, except for matters of adultery and other sexual sins (drowning) and for a few penalties that deserve death by fire.[64] This is the

---

[61] Text and translation from DRIVER and MILES, Babylonian Laws, 2:58–59. Cf. RICHARD-SON, Hammurabi's Laws, 88; VIEL, Complete Code of Hammurabi, 2:565–566; ROTH, Law Collections, 110.

[62] So also DRIVER and MILES, Babylonian Laws, 1:313. Note further ROTH's translation: "If a man's wife *has her husband killed* on account of (her relationship with) another male, they shall impale that woman"; ROTH, Law Collections, 110, emphasis mine). Naturally, were a man also involved in the act of murder, his execution would be presumed. Contrast RICHARD-SON, Hammurabi's Laws, 89 and VIEL, Complete Code of Hammurabi, 2:573: "If a woman *has let her husband be killed* because of another man they shall stick that woman on a stake" (emphasis mine). However, VERSTEEG argues that the woman has murdered her husband or has caused him to be murdered (possibly by poison): RUSS VERSTEEG, Early Mesopotamian Law (Durham, N.C.: Carolina Academic Press, 2000), 109–110. VERSTEEG also mentions an ancient Nippur account in which a woman is accused of conspiring to kill her husband; however, this early second-millennium account actually just represents the wife covering up the deed after the fact – she is put to death along with the three male murderers; for this account see MARTHA T. ROTH, Gender and Law: A Case Study from Ancient Mesopotamia, in Gender and Law in the Hebrew Bible and the Ancient Near East (ed. V. H. Matthews, B. M. Levinson, and T. Frymer-Kensky; JSOTSup 262; Sheffield: Sheffield Academic Press, 1998), 173–184 (translation 176–77).

[63] DRIVER and MILES, Babylonian Laws, 2:230; also 1:313–314, 496. This is consistent with WINCKLER's assessment, cf. the extended note in WINCKLER, Gesetze Hammurabis, 44.

[64] General references to execution (without precise means specified) in Hammurabi's Code can be found in cases involving murder, stealing from a temple, general thievery, kidnapping, freeing another's slave, refusing military service, abusing military command, harboring criminals, killing a debtor's son, causing death by poor construction practices, and bearing false witness in cases leading to execution (§§1, 2, 3, 6, 7, 8, 9, 10, 11, 14, 15, 16, 19, 22, 26, 33, 34, 109, 116, 210, 229, 230). Further generic execution references can be found in the fragmentary "gap" passages between §65 and §100 (§m, n, and bb, following ROTH's numbering (ROTH, Law Collections, 94–99). Note also the passages from §21 and §§227 discussed in this section; both involve a generic reference to execution followed by the public suspension of the body. People who steal while assisting in the rescue of someone from a fire are burned in §25. Also burned are those who break into an innkeeper's storage (§110) and sons/mothers who commit incest (§157). Adulterers, rapists and other sexual offenders are drowned (§§129, 130, 133, 155), as are women who disparage their husbands (§143) and women innkeepers who

only passage that calls for impalement, setting apart both this penalty and the crime. Compare further the impalement of the woman who procures her own abortion in the Middle Assyrian Laws (Tablet A §53; see below).

**(133)** *Code of Hammurabi §§226–227 [col. 19b, lines 36–55]*

[§226] ³⁶ *šum-ma ŠU.I* ³⁷ *ba-lum be-el ERU(M)* ³⁸ *ab-bu-ti* ³⁹ *ERU(M) la še-e-im* ⁴⁰ *ú-gal-li-ib* ⁴¹ *ŠID.LAL ŠU.I šu-a-ti* ⁴² *i-na-ak-ki-sú* [§227] ⁴³ *šum-ma a-wi-lum* ⁴⁴ *ŠU.I i-da-aṣ-ma* ⁴⁵ *ab-bu-ti* ⁴⁶ *ERU(M) la še-e-im* ⁴⁷ *ug-tá-al-li-ib* ⁴⁸ *a-wi-lam* *šu-a-ti* ⁴⁹ *i-du-uk-ku-šu-ma* ⁵⁰ *i-na KÁ-šu* ⁵¹ *i-ḫa-al-la-lu-šu* ⁵² *ŠU.I i-na i-du-ú* ⁵³ *la ú-gal-li-bu* ⁵⁴ *i-tam-ma-ma* ⁵⁵ *ú-ta-aš-šar*

*Translation.* [§226] ³⁶ If a barber has excised a slave's mark without (the knowledge of) his owner so that he cannot be traced, ⁴¹ they shall cut off the fore-hand of that barber. [§227] ⁴³ If a man has constrained the barber and he excises the slave's mark so that he cannot be traced, ⁴⁸ they shall put that man to death and shall hang him at his (own) door; ⁵² the barber may swear 'Surely I excised (it) unwittingly', and he then goes free.

*Commentary.*[65] A "barber" in antiquity was in possession of knives and other surgical-type implements and could produce (as well as remove) slave marks.[66] The preceding legal sections in the Code of Hammurabi concerned physicians/surgeons and (often) slaves/masters (see Code of Hammurabi §§215–225), so there is a natural transition here to the surgical "barber" who defaces slave marks. The barber here removes or renders unrecognizable the mark of ownership identification applied to the skin of a slave.[67] In the first instance (§226), the barber does so with full intent and thus receives the whole punishment (i.e., removing the hand, which was the barber's body part involved in removing the slave-mark). In the second instance (§227), another

---

falsely inflate the cost of beer (§108). ROTH's index also lists dragging by cattle as a possible cause of death (§256).

[65] Text and translation from DRIVER and MILES, Babylonian Laws, 2:82–83. Cf. ROTH, Law Collections, 124; RICHARDSON, Hammurabi's Laws, 106; VIEL, Complete Code of Hammurabi, 2:655–658.

[66] Thus MEEK translates this person with the title "brander"; cf. THEOPHILE J. MEEK, The Code of Hammurabi, in Ancient Near Eastern Texts Relating to the Old Testament (Second ed.; ed. J. B. Pritchard; Princeton: Princeton University Press, 1969), 163–180, here 176. It is unlikely that the barber simply cut off the lock of hair that identified a slave, a position held by ROTH, Law Collections, 124; cf. MARTHA T. ROTH, The Laws of Hammurabi (2.131), in The Context of Scripture. Vol. 2: Monumental Inscriptions from the Biblical World (ed. W. W. Hallo and K. L. Younger; Leiden: Brill, 2003), 335–353, here 349; STEPHEN BERTMAN, Handbook, to Life in Ancient Mesopotamia (New York: Oxford University Press, 2003), 275.

[67] Modern scholars debate whether this mark was a brand, a tattoo, or something else. For an extensive treatment of the complex lexical considerations here, see DRIVER and MILES, Babylonian Laws, 2:253–255, also 1:421–425.

person compels the services of the barber, probably through deception. Here, the barber can be considered innocent since his action was unintentional (cf. §206), but the person who coerced the barber is executed.

This criminal act can best be compared to the person who breaks into a house in Code of Hammurabi §21 (cited above), for both criminal acts involve a highly deliberate attempt at stealing the property of another. Also, both felons are put to death prior to suspension.[68] Furthermore, the same lexical question occurs here as was discussed in Code of Hammurabi §21 above: Does *i-ḥa-al-la-lu-šu* imply the perpetrator is "hung up" or that he is "transfixed" through impalement? The former is more likely.[69] In any case, as in §21 the punishment in §227 concerns the public *post mortem* suspension of the guilty.

### 3.2.2 Mari

At least one text found at Mari testifies to the use of bodily suspension toward the end of the royal ascendancy of this famous Mesopotamian city. Unfortunately the text is quite fragmentary, but it remains useful for us to examine.

**(134)** Letter of Kibri-Dagan to Zimri-Lin (*ARM* 13.108) lines 12'–16'

$^{12'}$*[a-na ba-za]-ḫa-[ti-i]a dan-na-tim aš-ku-un* $^{13'}$*[šum-ma awîlam] ša-a-tu i-ṣa-ba-tu-nim* $^{14'}$*[i-na] gi-ši-ši - im* $^{15'}$*[li-iš-š]a-ki-in - ma* $^{16'}$[   ]X *it-ti - šu*

*Translation.* $^{12'}$ [To my guard forces] I have given these harsh orders. $^{13'}$ If they seize that [man], $^{14'}$ [he shall be] impaled on a stake and $^{15'}$ […] with him.

*Commentary.*[70] Among the many letters found in chamber 115 at Mari, this text appears on lines 12'–16' of the reverse of a letter from Kibri-Dagan, governor of Terqa, to "my lord" Zimri-Lin (cf. recto line 1). The date would be roughly contemporary with the eighteenth-century B.C. Hammurabi materials above (since Hammurabi famously attacked Zimri-Lin and destroyed Mari). In this letter, though Kibri-Dagan begins by reporting that all is well in Terqa, the main discussion on the reverse focuses on escaped fugitives. The text is

---

[68] Contrast the DRIVER / MILES translation (cited above) with RICHARDSON, Hammurabi's Laws, 107 and VIEL, Complete Code of Hammurabi, 2:671: "they shall kill that man by hanging him in his doorway." See fuller discussion above concerning Hammurabi's Code §21.

[69] Thus also *CAD* I/1, 330; *AHw* I, 34.

[70] Text and French translation by JEAN-ROBERT KUPPER in GEORGES DOSSIN, ed., Archives royales de Mari. Vol. 13, Textes divers (Paris: Geuthner, 1964), 115–116 (No. 108). The English translation above is my rendering of KUPPER's French translation, which reads: "[A mes forces de gendarmerie] j'ai donné des ordres sévères. [S']ils s'emparent de cet [homme], [il sera] empalé [sur] un pieu et [   ] avec lui".

fragmentary and difficult to reconstruct fully, and Sasson suggests these fugitives may refer to people fleeing the military draft.[71] In this passage, Kibri-Dagan promises that when a fugitive has been seized, the governor has decreed that fugitive will be punished with impalement. Notably, this edict is described as a "severe command" or "harsh order" (*dannatim*).[72]

### 3.2.3 Egypt (Second Intermediate, New Kingdom, and Ptolemaic Periods)

Egyptian texts repeatedly testify to the penalty of "placing someone on a stake" in the New Kingdom period. As several Egyptologists have argued, this is a likely reference to impalement.[73] Rebellious foreign troops could be impaled, as could people who stole sacrifices from the temples and those who raided royal tombs. Frequently, those charged with tomb robbery invoke the threat of impalement upon themselves as they take oaths not to give false witness before judicial authorities. In light of this broader context, the mention in Genesis 40–41 of "hanging on a tree/post" in the Egypt of Joseph's day, though prior to the New Kingdom era, may cohere with established Egyptian practices. Because biblical scholars often appear unaware of the Egyptian use of suspension penalties and because most works in Egyptology do not represent the extent of the use of "impalement" in legal oaths, this section will present multiple examples of these human bodily suspension practices.[74] The

---

[71] JACK M. SASSON, Treatment of Criminals at Mari, Journal of the Economic and Social History of the Orient 20 (1977): 90–113, here 94, 109. SASSON notes that other forms of execution are recorded in Mari texts, including burnings, beheadings, and also "executions" without specific description (ibid. 109–110). I am grateful to J. G. COOK this reference.

[72] JEREMY BLACK, ANDREW GEORGE, and NICHOLAS POSTGATE, A Concise Dictionary of Akkadian (Second Corrected Printing; Wiesbaden: Harrassowitz, 2000), 56, s.v. *dannatu(m)*.

[73] See especially WOLFGANG BOOCHS, Über den Strafzweck des Pfählens, Göttinger Miszellen 69 (1983): 7–10, esp. 7. I was directed to many of the ancient texts in this section via BOOCHS' brief article. BOOCHS himself lists impalement as an Egyptian penalty for these crimes and military acts: "Grabraub, Meineid, Unterschlagung und Veruntreuung von Tempelvermögen sowie Strafe für Kriegsgefangene und Rebellen" (ibid. 7).

[74] In addition to the texts cited below, further Egyptian texts refer to impalement as a means of criminal punishment. Thus LORTON mentions P. Berlin 10496 (verso 1–4) as another example from Deir-el-Medina where a person must swear in court that, if he has robbed a tomb, he will have his nose and ears cut off and shall be impaled; see DAVID LORTON, The Treatment of Criminals in Ancient Egypt: Through the New Kingdom, Journal of the Economic and Social History of the Orient 20 (1977): 2–64, here 40. Another twentieth-dynasty text (P. Mayer) records a similar penalty for tomb robbery (see LORTON, ibid. 31 n. 141); the hieroglyphic text of P. Mayer (A13, B1) may be found in THOMAS ERIC PEET, The Great Tomb-Robberies of the Twentieth Egyptian Dynasty (orig. 1930; repr., Hildesheim: Olms, 1977), Vol. 2, pl. 24. For such a punishment cf. RICHARD JASNOW, Egypt: New Kingdom, in A History of Ancient Near Eastern Law (ed. R. Westbrook; Handbook of Oriental Studies: The Near and Middle East 72; Leiden: Brill, 2003), 289–356, here 344.

constant recurrence emphasizes the reality of the threat of impalement in this period.

**(135)** Genesis 40:18–22; 41:12–13

וַיַּעַן יוֹסֵף וַיֹּאמֶר זֶה פִּתְרֹנוֹ שְׁלֹשֶׁת הַסַּלִּים שְׁלֹשֶׁת יָמִים הֵם: ¹⁹ בְּעוֹד שְׁלֹשֶׁת יָמִים יִשָּׂא פַרְעֹה
אֶת־רֹאשְׁךָ מֵעָלֶיךָ וְתָלָה אוֹתְךָ עַל־עֵץ וְאָכַל הָעוֹף אֶת־בְּשָׂרְךָ מֵעָלֶיךָ: ²⁰ וַיְהִי בַּיּוֹם הַשְּׁלִישִׁי יוֹם
הֻלֶּדֶת אֶת־פַּרְעֹה וַיַּעַשׂ מִשְׁתֶּה לְכָל־עֲבָדָיו וַיִּשָּׂא אֶת־רֹאשׁ שַׂר הַמַּשְׁקִים וְאֶת־רֹאשׁ שַׂר הָאֹפִים
בְּתוֹךְ עֲבָדָיו: ²¹ וַיָּשֶׁב אֶת־שַׂר הַמַּשְׁקִים עַל־מַשְׁקֵהוּ וַיִּתֵּן הַכּוֹס עַל־כַּף פַּרְעֹה: ²² וְאֵת שַׂר הָאֹפִים
תָּלָה כַּאֲשֶׁר פָּתַר לָהֶם יוֹסֵף:
⁴¹:¹² וְשָׁם אִתָּנוּ נַעַר עִבְרִי עֶבֶד לְשַׂר הַטַּבָּחִים וַנְּסַפֶּר־לוֹ וַיִּפְתָּר־לָנוּ אֶת־חֲלֹמֹתֵינוּ אִישׁ כַּחֲלֹמוֹ
פָּתָר: ¹³ וַיְהִי כַּאֲשֶׁר פָּתַר־לָנוּ כֵּן הָיָה אֹתִי הֵשִׁיב עַל־כַּנִּי וְאֹתוֹ תָלָה:

*Translation.* ⁴⁰:¹⁸ Joseph answered and said, "This is its interpretation: The three baskets are three days; ¹⁹ within yet three days Pharaoh will lift up your head from upon you, and he will hang you on a tree, and the birds will eat your flesh from upon you." ²⁰ And it came to pass on the third day, which was Pharaoh's birthday, he made a feast for all his servants. And he lifted up the head of the chief cupbearer and the head of the chief baker in the midst of his servants. ²¹ He returned the chief cupbearer unto his cupbearing; and [the chief cupbearer] placed the cup in the hand of Pharaoh. ²² But the chief baker he hung up, just as Joseph had interpreted to them.
⁴¹:¹² "And there with us was a Hebrew young man, a servant to the captain of the guards. And we recounted to him [our dreams], and he interpreted for us our dreams – he interpreted each according to his dream. ¹³ And it came to pass; as he interpreted to us, thus it happened. He [i.e., Pharaoh] returned me to my place, but him he hung up."

*Commentary.*[75] A recurring theme in the Joseph narratives of Genesis concerns Joseph's ability to see and/or interpret dreams. Here, while imprisoned with these two servants of Pharaoh, Joseph interprets the chief cupbearer's dream positively and warns the chief baker of his coming demise. The baker's head is to be removed,[76] and he is to be hung aloft. The sequence of verbs in 40:19 (ישא "will lift up [your head]" followed by ותלה "and he will hang [you]") implies that the chief baker was beheaded prior to being suspended.[77]

---

[75] Unless otherwise noted, all texts from the Hebrew Bible are from BHS.

[76] Decapitation is especially implied by how Pharaoh "will lift up your head *from upon you.*" The מעליך is omitted in two manuscripts and in the Vulgate, but the majority of older manuscripts include מעליך as does the rest of the versional evidence. Its inclusion is thus highly probable, and this would imply that the chief baker's head was removed from him, i.e. that he was beheaded. Some commentators argue, however, that the inclusion of מעליך resulted from a scribal blunder. For a detailed discussion see CHAPMAN, Crucifixion, 102–103.

[77] Commentators disagree on this point. Some choose not to translate the first מעליך ("from upon you") in 40:19, thus understanding the "lifting up" of each servant to be an invitation

Nevertheless, the suspension of the body is emphasized more than the beheading, for "hanging up" receives repeated mention in 40:19, 22; 41:13, and the suspension is recorded by itself (without mention of beheading) in 40:22 and 41:13. The use of "lift up" (נשׂא) permits the wordplay in 40:20, where both servants have their heads "lifted up", the cupbearer being exalted back to his position, but the baker being beheaded. The retrospective account in 41:12–13 results from the chief cupbearer eventually relating the story to the Pharaoh.

The reported event is projected into the time of Joseph, with the specific implied dating of the event thus dependent on the dating of the Exodus and (more specifically) the arrival of the Patriarchs into Egypt – in general terms, this text would refer either to the late Middle Kingdom or to the Second Intermediate period in Egyptian history. The actual date of composition depends on which source theory seems most compelling for Genesis (with commentators arguing for dates anywhere from the time of Moses to the post-exilic period). Relatively few Genesis commentators reference any ancient parallels for this penal use of bodily suspension, and those who do seek out parallels often find connections here with Mesopotamian (esp. Assyrian) suspension texts and reliefs.[78] However, we shall observe below that there are also multi-

---

into Pharaoh's presence (cf. also 40:13, 20). Among proponents of the "invitation" approach (with some variations) see ANTHONY PHILLIPS, Ancient Israel's Criminal Law: A New Approach to the Decalogue (Oxford: Blackwell, 1970), 27; G. R. DRIVER, Review of Ancient Israel's Criminal Law: A New Approach to the Decalogue, by Anthony Phillips, JTS 23 (1972): 160–164, 161; CLAUS WESTERMANN, Genesis: A Commentary (Translated by John J. Scullion; 3 vols.; Minneapolis: Augsburg, 1984–1986), 3:77; NAHUM M. SARNA, Genesis (JPS Torah Commentary; Philadelphia: Jewish Publication Society, 1989), 279–280; VICTOR P. HAMILTON, The Book of Genesis (2 vols.; NICOT; Grand Rapids: Eerdmans, 1990–1995), 2:483. On the other hand, for the understanding "beheading" see, in addition to the ancient treatment by Ibn Ezra: FRANZ DELITZSCH, A New Commentary on Genesis (Translated by Sophia Taylor; 2 vols.; Edinburgh: T.& T. Clark, 1888–1989), 2:291–92; AUGUST DILLMANN, Genesis: Critically and Exegetically Expounded (Translated by Wm. B. Stevenson. 2 vols.; Edinburgh: T.& T. Clark, 1897), 2:364; EPHRAIM A. SPEISER, Genesis (AB 1; Garden City, NY: Doubleday, 1964), 307–308; CHAPMAN, Crucifixion, also compare GERHARD VON RAD, Das erste Buch Mose: Genesis (Zehnte Auflage; Alte Testament Deutsch 2/4; Göttingen: Vandenhoeck & Ruprecht, 1976), 304; DAVID MARCUS, 'Lifting up the Head': On the Trail of a Word Play in Genesis 40, Prooftexts 10 (1990): 17–27, here 18.

[78] For example, I found no reference to extra-biblical parallels from other ancient suspension accounts in the commentaries by BRUEGGEMANN, DELITZSCH, HAMILTON, SARNA, WENHAM, or WESTERMANN; yet SARNA, Genesis, 280 does rightly indicate that impaling was a widespread mode of execution in the ANE (citing only biblical examples). WALTKE at least remarks on the three Assyrian examples of impalement found in *ANEP*; BRUCE K. WALTKE and CATHI J. FREDRICKS, Genesis: A Commentary (Grand Rapids: Zondervan, 2001), 527. Even the newer "background commentaries" are rather sparse on the subject, with no explicit references to ancient extra-biblical sources; cf. JOHN H. WALTON, ed., Zondervan Illustrated Bible Backgrounds Commentary (5 vols.; Grand Rapids: Zondervan, 2009), 1:129. JOHN H. WALTON and VICTOR H. MATTHEWS, The IVP Bible Background Commentary: Genesis–Deuteronomy (Downers Grove: InterVarsity Press, 1997), unfortunately suggests that this could "involve suspension on a rope by the neck" in addition to impalement.

ple Egyptian examples of bodily suspension penalties (especially from the New Kingdom period), so this Joseph narrative could well have drawn on memories of ancient Egyptian practices. In Second Temple and early Rabbinic Judaism, this passage was increasingly actualized by employing later suspension (and crucifixion) terms; cf. Philo, *Jos.* 96–98, 156; *Som.* 2.213; Josephus, *A. J.* 2.72–73, 77; the Genesis Targumim (discussed below in 3.9).[79]

**(136)** Stele of Akhenaten at Buhen no. 1595, lines 6–12

[6] *wn-in hm·f ḥr rdi(t) m ḥr n p₃ s₃-nsw (n Kš imy-r ḫ₃swt rswt Ḏḥwty-ms r ḏd(?)… ḥr)* [7] *-w n ḫ₃st 'Ik₃yt₃ iṯ₃* (…) [8] *i(t)rw ḥr mḥtt n (.?.)yḫyt* (…) [9] *ḥr ḫ₃st ḥ·n p₃ wtḫ* (…) [10] *…n nḫtw m ibw·sn m₃i* (…) *sm₃* (…) [11] (…) *ḳn(t) n* (…)*tt* (…) *rḫt (n ḥrw) (n) 'Ik₃yt₃ nḥsy ʿnḫ 80 (?…)* [12] *(…(wr?)) -w ·sn 12 dmḏ tp ʿnḫ 145 nty ḥr ḫt(w…)* [13] (…) *dmḏ 225 sm₃w 361*

*Translation.* [6] Thereupon His Majesty commissioned the viceroy (of Kush and overseer of southern countries Thutmose saying: 'Crush and destroy?) [7] the enemies belonging to the country of Ikayta; seize (…) [8] the river (?) to the north of (…) *yḫyt* (…) [9] upon the upland. The fugitive rejoiced (?) (…) [10] the (paean?) of victory being in their hearts, the Lion (…) slaying (…) [11] valour (…) List (of the enemy belonging to) Ikayta: living Nehesi 80+?; (…) [12] (…) their (chiefs?) 12; total of live captives 145; those who were impaled (…) [13] (…) total 225; beasts 361.

*Commentary.*[80] This triumphal stele likely stems from years 10–12 of the reign of Akhenaten (i.e., Amenophis IV, or Amenhotep IV, mid-fourteenth century B.C.).[81] The editor suggests the stele was intentionally shattered during the persecution of Akhenaten's name at the transition between the Eighteenth and Nineteenth Dynasties.[82] The resulting fragments are housed in the collections of the Universities of Durham and Pennsylvania. The text depicts a campaign

---

[79] These passages are also discussed in Chapman, *Crucifixion*, 104–109.

[80] HARRY S. SMITH, Fortress of Buhen: The Inscriptions (London: Egypt Exploration Society, 1976), 124–129 (transcription 125, translation 125–126, photographic plate LXXV). For purposes of printing, we have shifted the consonantal "i" to the current form. SMITH offers the following conjectures for filling in the *lacunae* in lines 6–11: "Thereupon His Majesty commissioned the Viceroy of Kush and overseer of foreign countries saying: 'Crush and destroy the enemies belonging to the land of Ikayta. Seize all their goods and cattle. Burn their encampments.' The army of His Majesty crossed the river north of ·yḫyt, and destroyed the enemy at ... and put them to flight upon the upland. The fugitive rejoiced when he was offered the breath of life. His Majesty's army pursued them and slew them, the paean of victory being in their hearts, the Lion himself (i.e. the Pharaoh) inspiring them to slay and to capture. The army returned safely in valour and victory and triumph. List of the enemy belonging to Ikayta (etc., etc.)." (ibid. 127 n.9).

[81] So SMITH, Fortress of Buhen: The Inscriptions, 126 n.1 and 129.

[82] SMITH, Fortress of Buhen: The Inscriptions, 125.

in Lower Nubia carried out by the viceroy of Kush (probably Thutmose, though the text is fragmentary here) against the Ikayta people, who likely sought to capture the gold mines of Wadi el-Allaqi. The editor concludes that the number 225 includes all conquered human enemies (including the 145 living captives), and thus 80 enemies were killed – at least some of whom had been impaled (ibid., p. 129). That impalements occurred is based on a likely reconstruction of the several fragments that make up line 12.[83]

**(137)** Abydos Decree of Seti I at Nauri lines 74–80

*Translation.* [74] And as to any keeper of cattle, any keeper of hounds (?), any herdsman [75] belonging to the House (etc.) who shall give any head of animals belonging to the House (etc.) [76] by defalcation to another; likewi[se] he who shall cause it to be offered on another direction (?), and not be offered [77] to Osiris his Lord in the House (etc.), punishment shall be done to him by casting him down and placing him on [78] the end of a stake, forfeiting (?) his wife and children and all his property to the House (etc.) [79] and exacting the head of animals from him to whom he shall have [given] it as stolen from the House (etc., full name) [80] at the rate of a hundred to one.

*Commentary.*[84] This Abydos Decree appears upon a nine-foot high stele (in conjunction with text on the surrounding rock) that had been inserted upon a large 300-foot-tall rock outcrop found at Nauri (about halfway between the Third Cataract and the Kagbar Cataract of the Nile River). The text of the inscription primarily records a decree of Seti I (or Sethos I) regarding the Temple of Osiris at Abydos (i.e., the "House" mentioned above).[85] Seti I was a Nineteenth Dynasty pharaoh at the beginning of the thirteenth century – the decree stems from his fourth year (cf. line 1). A substantial part of the decree is given over to making sure that provisions for the temple would not be hin-

---

[83] SMITH, Fortress of Buhen: The Inscriptions, 127 n. 15: "Though Blackman superfluously supplied [the letter 's'] and read *sḥt*, I think the sense of *nty ḥr ḥtw* 'those who are on the stakes' cannot be mistaken; the evidence for the Egyptians impaling their enemies is far too strong to be doubted. Säve-Söderbergh's 'die unterstellt waren' will not fit the traces."

[84] Translation from FRANCIS L. GRIFFITH, The Abydos Decree of Seti I at Nauri, Journal of Egyptian Archaeology 13 (1927): 193–208, here 203 (hieroglyphic text in Plate XLII). The difficulty of reproducing hieroglyphs will prevent us from representing this text, as well as subsequent hieroglyphic texts below.

[85] The decree appears on lines 29–118 after laudatory words about Seti I and his piety toward the house of Osiris. GRIFFITH "to save wearisome repetitions" abbreviates the titles of the House so that "the House (etc.)" stands for "the House of Men-ma-re 'Heart's ease' in Abydos" and "the House (etc. full name)" refers to "the House of Millions of Years of the Rush and the Bee-King Men-ma-re, 'The Heart is at Ease in Abydos'"; see GRIFFITH, Abydos Decree, 200 n.9 and discussion ibid. 205–206. GRIFFITH suggests this "House" was an earlier temple that Seti rebuilt and refurnished rather than the famous temple begun under Seti I and completed by Ramesses II (ibid. 206).

dered and that theft from the temple would be deterred. The rules above were intended to dissuade temple personnel from stealing the temple's animal sacrifices for sake of embezzlement ("defalcation") or in order to present them at another temple. The temple personnel responsible for stealing sacrificial animals are to be executed and impaled ("casting him down and placing him on the end of a stake")[86] while all his household (both his family and his possessions) becomes the property of the temple. Lorton is among those who argue that this "placing on the wood" is an example of impalement.[87] The one who received the stolen animals must pay back the temple a hundred-fold. This crime must have been viewed as particularly heinous due to the involvement of temple personnel because a lesser punishment (mutilation and enslavement of the thief and his family) is mentioned earlier in the decree for people not in the temple's employ who steal from Osiris' house (lines 71–74).

**(138)**  Abydos Decree of Seti I at Nauri lines 104–109

*Translation.* [104] [and if] any person belonging to the House (etc.) [complain] [105] [to any council that is in any city? saying] a certain [inspect]or, a certain equerry, a certain chief of stables, [a certain] officer [106] [hath interfered with me, and hath taken my goods from me, they shall exact] the things which shall be deficient from him, [107] [and he shall recover the goods from the man who has] interfered with him. But his majesty hath avoided causing [108] [him that molested them to be cast on the ground and] put on the end of a stake, desiring to let him be convicted in any council [109] of any city to which they go.

*Commentary.*[88] In this section, Seti's decree dictates laws that are intended to prevent district officials from inhibiting the work of the Osiris Temple personnel. In this case, when the temple personnel have evidence that district officials have interfered with their work and have taken goods from the temple personnel, those personnel "belonging to the House" of Osiris are instructed to go to the local council to seek retribution. Seti's decree mandates that the property taken be returned, and it leaves any further punishment up to the local council. The last two lines specifically state that Seti I ("his majesty") does not mandate that the offenders be executed and impaled ("put on the end of a stake"). The likely rationale stems from the legal tradition that such a form of execution was reserved for Pharaoh himself, and thus any trial that

---

[86] GRIFFITH, Abydos Decree, 203 n. 5 argues that impalement is the best translation, based on parallels in the Abbott Papyrus and in the Rosetta Stone inscription; for these, see below.

[87] LORTON, Treatment, 26-27.

[88] Translation from GRIFFITH, Abydos Decree, 204.

could result in impalement ultimately had to be referred to Pharaoh's court.[89] Here Seti would rather that the crime be judged at the local council level. Nevertheless, despite Seti's decision to not mandate impalement for this particular offense, this passage (in connection with lines 74–80 above) indicates that execution followed by impalement could be an officially sanctioned legal procedure for some particularly odious crimes in New Kingdom Egypt.

**(139)** Merenptah Nubian War Stele

*Translation.* One came to inform His Majesty (that) the fallen ones of Wawat had transgressed in the South. Now, it happened in Year 5, 3rd Month of Shomu, Day 1, – just when the valiant army of His Majesty came (to) overthrow the despicable chief of the Libyans (*Libu*). Never shall they leave any people for the Libu, any who shall bring them up in their land! They are cast to the ground, (?) by hundred-thousands and ten-thousands, the remainder being impaled ('put to the stake') on the South of Memphis. All their property was plundered, being brought back to Egypt.

*Commentary.*[90] Merenptah (*aka* Merneptah) was a New Kingdom (Nineteenth Dynasty) Pharaoh for ten years at the close of the thirteenth century B.C. He engaged in a number of celebrated military endeavors (including a famous conquest of much of Canaan when "Israel" was in the land). Year 5 of Merenptah's reign (1209/1208 B.C.)[91] saw him fighting on multiple fronts: with the Libyans and Sea Peoples in the north and the Nubians in the south. In this passage from a stele erected during Merenptah's reign, the Nubians (i.e., the people of Wawat) "transgress" in the southern Upper Nile region by attacking while Merenptah's forces are engaged with the Libyans in the north. This may have been a coordinated strategy between Egypt's enemies; on the other hand, the forces in one region might have seen their opportunity once Egypt was engaged elsewhere. Nevertheless, according to this stele, Egypt was triumphant in the north, and most of the Libyans were "cast to the ground" south of Memphis, with the remaining survivors being "put to the

---

[89] Note how the various tomb-robbery papyri from the Twentieth Dynasty presume that death sentences must be referred to Pharaoh for confirmation before the executions occur; see PEET, Tomb-Robberies, 1:26 (and the multiple tomb-robbery papryi discussed below).

[90] KENNETH A. KITCHEN, Ramesside Inscriptions Translated and Annotated. Series A: Translations (8 vols.; Oxford: Blackwell, 2000–2014), 4:1. Due to the difficulty of representing hieroglyphs, KITCHEN's edition of the text of this inscription is not presented here (this will also be true for texts below). J. G. COOK provided my initial entry point into this and other Egyptian traditions; I am most grateful for his assistance.

[91] For the date see KITCHEN, Ramesside Inscriptions Series A: Translations, 4:xxv.

stake."[92] In the translation above, Kitchen understands this to represent mass impalement of the survivors.

**(140)** The Abbott Papyrus (B.M. 10221) 6.9–20

*Translation.* [9] [Pewero reports:] And this prince of Nō [i.e., Pesiūr] said to him again a second time, 'The scribe Horisheri son of Amennakht of the Necropolis of Khenkheni [10] came to this great side of Nō to where I was to make to me three [11] very serious charges, and my scribe and the two scribes of the quarter of Nō wrote them down. And the scribe of the Necropolis Pebes made to me two further [12] charges, total five, and they wrote those down likewise, it being impossible to suppress them, for they are serious charges involving mutilation or [13] impaling or the severest penalties. And I am writing about them to Pharaoh my Lord [14] to cause him to send servants of Pharaoh to deal with you.' So said he [Pesiūr] to them, this prince of Nō. And he made ten oaths saying, [15] 'Verily I will do it'. I [Pewero] heard the words which this prince of Nō spoke to the people of the Great and Noble Necropolis of Millions of Years of [16] Pharaoh on the West of Thebes, and I report them to my Lord. For it would be sin in one in my position [17] to hear a thing and to conceal it. Now I do not know the bearing of the very serious charges which the prince of Nō says [18] the scribes of the Necropolis of Kheni who move among the men made to him: truly I cannot [19] fathom them. But I report them to my lord, that my lord may get to the bottom of these charges which this prince of Nō said that [20] the scribes of the Necropolis made to him, and that he was writing concerning them to Pharaoh.

*Commentary.*[93] This is part of a scroll depicting investigations into tomb robberies during the 16th regnal year of the 20th Dynasty pharaoh Ramesses IX (Neferkare setepenre) at the end of the twelfth century B.C.[94] These concern the Necropolis to the west of Thebes, including the Valley of the Kings and the Valley of the Queens. The people of the Necropolis would likely be those who lived in Deir el-Medina (the place where the necropolis workmen were housed in antiquity and the site of substantial archaeological discoveries over

---

[92] K. L. YOUNGER also considers the text to refer to a mass impalement of Libyan adversaries; see K. LAWSON YOUNGER, Ancient Conquest Accounts: A Study in Ancient Near Eastern and Biblical History Writing (JSOTSup 98; Sheffield: JSOT Press, 1990), 317 n. 88.

[93] Translation from PEET, Tomb-Robberies, 1:41; hieroglyphic text Vol. 2, plates III–IV.

[94] Lines 1.1–2 ascribe the investigation to the reign of Neferkerē Setpenrē. Hornung dates his reign to 1127–1108 B.C.; see ERIK HORNUNG, History of Ancient Egypt (Translated by David Lorton; Ithaca: Cornell University Press, 1999), xvii, 122. Note HORNUNG's comment: "The long reign of Ramesses IX … was filled with economic and political difficulties. Symptomatic were the tomb robberies in the Theban necropolis, which for a long time were quietly tolerated; when a judicial investigation finally occurred, it uncovered an overwhelming amount of corruption and neglect extending to the very top of the administration" (ibid. 122).

the past century). This portion of the text represents a deposition sent to the vizier from Pewero the "prince of the West of Nō and chief of Mazoi of the Necropolis" (5.19). Pewero obviously is at enmity with Pesiūr "the prince of Nō", who is leveling charges of permitting tomb robbery against the people of the Theban Necropolis and against its many administrators, over whom Pewero is in charge. Although the tomb of King Sebekemsaf was found to have been violated, most of the rest of Pesiūr's accusations are refuted, and the whole of this papyrus appears slanted to Pewero's view that very little robbery has actually occurred.[95] In this particular passage, Pewero depicts Pesiūr (the prince of Nō) as referencing five "very serious charges" that two scribes have brought to him. Pewero does not specify the charges leveled, but evidently they involved robbery from the royal tombs of the necropolis. Pewero cleverly alludes to his doubt about the charges (note lines 17–19: "Now I do not know the bearing of the very serious charges... truly I cannot fathom them. But I report them to my lord, that my lord may get to the bottom of these charges..."). For our purposes, note that mutilation and impaling are specifically listed as possible penalties for these crimes, alongside the "severest penalties." The translation "impalement" is defended by PEET in his introduction based on the various uses of "on the stake" and "top of the wood" in this papyrus, in Mayer Papyri A and B, and in Papyrus BM 10052.[96]

**(141)**  The Abbott Papyrus (B.M. 10221) 5.5–8

*Translation.* [5] The notables caused this coppersmith to be examined in most severe examination in the Great Valley, but it could not be [6] found that he knew of any place there save the two places he had pointed out. He took an oath on pain of being beaten, of having his nose [7] and ears cut off, and of being impaled, saying, I know of no place here among these tombs except this tomb which is open and [8] this house which I pointed out to you.

---

[95] On the political tensions and machinations between Pewero and Pesiūr cf. PEET, Tomb-Robberies, 1:32–37; PASCAL VERNUS, Affairs and Scandals in Ancient Egypt (Translated by D. Lorton; Ithaca, N.Y.: Cornell University Press, 2003), 7–19 (passage above p. 8).

[96] Thus PEET, Tomb-Robberies, 1:27: "The evidence of Mayer A, 13 B. I is therefore important on this point. We are told that seven men had previously been put to death 'on the stake', *ḥr tp ḫt*. This punishment is often referred to in the oath, the phrase being 'If I be found to have spoken untruth may I be placed upon the *tp ḫt*', *didi·tw r or ḥr tp ḫt*' (10052, 7.3, 8.26, &c.; the preposition *r* or *ḥr* is often omitted). Now *tp ḫt* must be a compound noun meaning literally the 'top of the wood', and judging by the variant *mnit* 'stake' or 'peg' in ABBOTT, 6.13 the punishment intended must be that of impaling." PEET finishes this argument with a statement that is now outdated by Kitchen's edition of the Merenptah Nubian War Stele mentioned above: "We have no other evidence from Egyptian literature for this cruel practice, which was common enough in Mesopotamia." (ibid. 1:27).

*Commentary.*[97] This is slightly earlier in the Abbott Papyrus than the preceding text. Here the papyrus again sides with Pewero to the effect that Pesiūr's
charges of massive tomb robbery in the Theban Necropolis are falling flat.
Even the coppersmith Peikharu, who had previously confessed to robbing the
royal tombs, is unable to locate an actual royal tomb worthy of being robbed
(the "two places" mentioned in 5.6 refer to an empty, unused tomb and to the
house of a workman). "Severe examination" (i.e., severe tortures) is applied to
Peikharu (5.5), and he is made to swear an oath. The oath formula in 5.6–7 is
what most interests us. Should Peikharu be caught in deceit, the oath specifies
a form of mutilation (cutting off the nose and ears) and a means of death
(impalement). Subsequent examples below will make repeated use of analogous oaths involving mutilation and impalement.

**(142)** Papyrus B.M. 10053 3.3–5

*Translation.* [3] Now after some days we went to the door of the gateway of
stone of Elephantine and brought away the 40½ … and we put them ‹in›
our…s [4] The attendant Nekhtamenwēse took 7 *deben* of copper, the foreigner
Ptahkhau took 3 *deben* of copper and the young priest Paherer ½ a *deben* of
copper. There remained to us 30 *deben* of copper. [5] He took an oath by the
Ruler, If all that I say is not true may I be placed on the stake.

*Commentary.*[98] The trial represented on this text is dated to "Year 9" (in line
2.1), which Peet argues refers to the 9th year of the *whm mswt* from the era of
Ramesses XI (beginning of the eleventh century B.C.). PEET also reasons that
it concerns trials for those caught stripping precious decorations from the
Ramesseum of Ramesses II.[99] Unfortunately, the fragmentary text preceding
the lines quoted above does not provide the name of the individual being
examined. The lines above also contain some fragmentation (represented in
the ellipses). Note how, at the conclusion of his testimony, this man vouched
for the trustworthiness of his account by taking "an oath by the Ruler" that
invokes the punishment of being "placed on the stake" (i.e., impaled) should
his statement be proven false.

---

[97] Translation from PEET, Tomb-Robberies, 1:40; hieroglyphic text Vol. 2, plate III.

[98] Translation from PEET, Tomb-Robberies, 1:117–118; hieroglyphic text Vol. 2, plate XX.

[99] PEET, Tomb-Robberies, 1:113–114 (for the Ramesseum identification) and ibid. 114–
116 for the date (cf. p. 7 for the locating of the *whm mswt* to the time of Ramesses XI).
HORNUNG, History, xvii, 123–124 dates Ramesses XI to 1104–1075 B.C.

**(143)** Papyrus B.M. 10052 7.1–8

*Translation.* [1] Fourth month of summer day 7. [2] Examination. Pneferahau was brought, the slave of the singer Mutemhab of the temple of Mut. He was made to take the oath by the Ruler saying, if [I] [3] speak falsehood let me be mutilated and placed on the stake. <He said>, Amenkhau the son of Mutemhab was an accomplice of Bukhaaf and the gang who [4] were with him. He came from the house of the herdsman Bukhaaf bringing a *dꜣiw*-garment of good Upper Egyptian cloth. He gave it to me. [5] I washed it and he went downstream in the 'Noble Staff' taking it with him. He was examined with the stick. [6] They said to him, Tell the story of the silver which you saw in the possession of this master of yours. He said, I saw some silver [7] in his possession as thick as *theb*-vases of copper, but I did not set foot in this tomb. I only saw it with my eye [8] in the possession of Amenkhau this son of Mutemhab my mistress.

*Commentary.*[100] Papyrus B.M. 10052 concerns a series of examinations over the course of five days in Year 1 of the *whm mswt* (renaissance) of Ramesses XI.[101] These examinations apparently implicated two groups of thieves – those associated with Bukhaaf (in lines 1.1–7.8 and 13.10 to end) and those associated with Efnamūn (in lines 7.9–13.9). Amenkhau son of Mutemhab is not only identified by Pneferahau as an accomplice of Bukhaaf in the passage above, but Bukhaaf himself lists Amenkhau son of Mutemhab as one of his thirteen gang members who entered the tombs (cf. line 2.8, where Amenkhau is also called a "young slave"; also 16.12).[102] The scribe of this papyrus was the same as that of Papyrus Mayer A, which also contains references to impalement.

Papyrus B.M. 10052 includes dozens of descriptions of people being "examined." These often explicitly involved the person swearing an oath prior to the judicial oral examination and then being beaten in an effort to exact the truth, after which the person either confessed or refused to admit to the charges. In the following pages, we shall list the cases in which the oaths include references to being "placed on the stake" (i.e., impaled) – often in concert with being "mutilated". Based on the Abbott Papyrus (B.M. 10221) 5.5–8 (quoted above) and on B.M. 10052 14.24 (in this papyrus see below), mutilations likely involved cutting off the individual's ears and nose. While there are several instances of the oath invoking impalement, there are other

---

[100] Translation from PEET, Tomb-Robberies, 1:149; hieroglyphic text Vol. 2, plate XXIX.

[101] For the dating cf. PEET, Tomb-Robberies, 1:128–130 (cf. p. 7). This places the events either at the end of the 12th century or the beginning of the 11th century B.C., depending on whether the *whm mswt* begins with the reign of Ramesses XI or starts later in his reign.

[102] A different man named Amenkhau ("the son of Hori") was accused by the conspirator Perpethew (3.22–28). That Amenkhau was found innocent and freed after successfully convincing the judges that he had been falsely accused by Perpethew (4.6–14). Note that text clearly assumes that "death" is the fate which awaits tomb-robbers (esp. 4.9–10).

forms of such oaths, especially "may I be mutilated and sent to Ethiopia."[103] It is not altogether self-evident why some of the accused take one form of the oath as opposed to the other.[104] Clearly these oaths are meant to convince the accused of the gravity of their testimony.

**(144)** Papyrus B.M. 10052 8.25–26

*Translation.* [25] Examination. The foreigner Pentewere of the battalion of Ethiopia was brought. He was given [the oath by the Ruler, saying, If I speak untruth, may I be mutilated] [26] and placed on the stake. The vizier said to him what is the story of … (*Some lines lost*)

*Commentary.*[105] These final lines of page 8 present a more fragmentary version of the oath found in 7.2–3. Again, the witness is threatened with mutilation and the stake if he lies. This passage is found in the midst of an examination of a different group of thieves (i.e., those associated with Efnamun rather than Bukhaaf), though it is likely that the same set of examiners and the same scribe are involved in the investigations of both groups.

---

[103] Other "oath by the Ruler" forms include "may I be mutilated and sent to Ethiopia" (3.22; 5.5; 5.25; 7.10; 8.18; 11.2; 11.9–10; 11.23) or simply "not to speak falsehood on pain of being sent to Ethiopia" (4.22; cf. 11.4). PEET suggests this would require the person either to be sent to the garrison in remote Cush or to serve in "perhaps a troop of conscripted labourers who worked in the Nubian gold mines" (ibid., p. 23). In any case, this was a highly feared consequence. "Mutilation" can also be invoked by itself, as occurs in other papyri. Sometimes reference is made simply to an oath "not to speak falsehood" (e.g., 12.13; 12.24; 13.1; 13.11; 13.23; 14.2; 14.10; 15.1; 15.5; cf. 15.19; fragmentary in 16.1; 16.18). In some cases, this may just be scribal shorthand for a longer oath (e.g., one that would invoke mutilation, deportation to Ethiopia, or impalement). In several examination accounts, the scribe omits record of the oath-taking altogether (e.g., 4.6; 4.15; 12.1–2; 12.22; 13.15; 15.10–11; 15.21), though it may well be that the reader should assume oaths were nevertheless invoked. Note also that Bukhaaf swears "if there be found a man who was with me and whom I have concealed let his punishment be done to me" (2.15–16).

[104] The oath-forms do not appear to correlate with the presumed guiltiness or innocence of the accused, or with gender of the person, or with day of trial. Even the social status of the person does not appear determinative (though this would require more study). This lack of obvious correlation is especially true of oaths that invoke mutilation, deportation or impalement. However, the examinations toward the end of the papyrus are typically briefer than those in the first two-thirds, and these briefer accounts often contain less-complex oaths (simple mentions of oath-taking, or oaths "not to speak falsehood"). This may be due to the accused being relatively minor characters in the tomb-robberies and/or it may simply be the result of the scribe's choice to generate a shorter record of later trials (whether due to space, laziness, or feeling them to be less important).

[105] Translation PEET, Tomb-Robberies, 1:151; hieroglyphic text Vol. 2, plates XXX–XXXI.

**(145)** Papyrus B.M. 10052 10.1–4

*Translation.* [1] Examination. There was brought the gardener Pei[kha]ru the younger, son of Amen[emhab of the temple of] Khonsu of Amenōpe. [2] There was given to him the oath by the Ruler, saying, If I speak falsehood let me be mutilated and placed [on] the stake. The vizier said to him, [3] What about the matter of the Great Tombs which you attacked along with the men who were with you? [4] He said, I never went: let <me?> tell you the story (?).

*Commentary.*[106] Peikharu is made to swear the form of the oath that invokes impalement if he were to testify falsely. The text continues with Peikharu's story that he accompanied his father when they came across priests in possession of an inner coffin. Though the priests claim the coffin is theirs, they appear to bribe Peikharu and his father by giving them a garment. Consequently, Peikharu's mother says to his father, "Silly old man that you are, what you have done is committing a theft." Presumably their "theft" is really colluding with thieves. Peikharu refuses any further confession, even after being examined "with a stick."

**(146)** Papyrus B.M. 10052 10.11–19

*Translation.* [11] Examination. The citizeness Ēse was brought, the wife of the gardener Ker of the funerary chapel of Ramōse. [12] There was give to her the oath by the Ruler to the effect that if she spoke falsehood she should be mutilated and placed on the stake. [13] The vizier said to her, What is the story of this silver which your husband brought away from the Great Tombs? [14] She said, I did not see it. The scribe Dhutmōse said to her, How did you buy the servants [15] which you bought? She said, I bought them in exchange for crops (?) from my garden. The vizier [16] said, Let Painekh her servant be brought that he may accuse her. The slave Painekh was brought. [17] He was made to take oath by the Ruler in the same way. They said to him, What have you to say? He said, (*sic*) What is the story of this silver which your master brought away? [18] He said, When Peinehesi destroyed Hartai the young Nubian Butehamūn bought me, and the foreigner [19] Pentesekhenu bought <me> from him: he gave two *deben* of silver for me. Now when he was killed the [20] gardener Ker bought me.

---

[106] Translation PEET, Tomb-Robberies, 1:151–152; hieroglyphic text Vol. 2, plate XXXI.

*Commentary.*[107] In line 12, Ēse takes the oath that threatens impalement if she were to lie.[108] The mention in lines 16–17 of Painekh taking the oath "in the same way" may indicate that he, too, took the oath form that threatened impalement. The court officials clearly did not believe Ēse's story that she had been able to purchase the slave Painekh without using the silver from her husband's tomb-robbing, thus implying her guilt as well as her husband's. It is unclear whether Painekh's testimony was sufficient to prove her guilt.

**(147)** Papyrus B.M. 10052 11.14–22

*Translation.* [14] Examination. The inspector Pairsekher of the temple of Amūn was brought. They gave him the oath by the Ruler, saying, If I speak falsehood may I be mutilated [15] and placed on the stake. They said to him, What is the story of your going to attack the Great Tombs? He said, Far be it from me, far be it [16] from me. He was examined with the stick. He said, Let be, I will speak. But he did not confess. [17] Examination. The priest Pewensh of the temple of Mut, was brought. They gave him the oath by the Ruler, saying, If I speak falsehood may I be mutilated and placed on the stake. [18] They said to him, what have you to say? He said, I saw no one; I lived on a small house (?) belonging to the temple of Mut. He was examined with the stick [19] but he would not confess. [20] Examination. There was brought the sailor Khonsmōse son of Painōzem of the temple of Amūn. They gave him the oath in the same way. They said to him, What have you to say about the matter of this [21] silver which the sailor Pewerro says you bought? He was examined with the stick. He said, Do not tell lies; it is quite untrue. He was again [22] examined with the stick, but he would not confess.

*Commentary.*[109] In two more examinations, the oath-form invokes impalement ("placed on the stake" in lines 15, 17). The third examination may also involve this form of the oath ("in the same way" in line 20). Even with torture ("examined with the stick"), the accused appear able to endure without confessing to the crime.

**(148)** Papyrus B.M. 10052 13.10–14

*Translation.* [10] Examination. There was brought the servant Pekeneny son of Wennefer of the temple of Amūn. He was given [11] the oath by the Ruler not to

---

[107] Translation from PEET, Tomb-Robberies, 1:152; hieroglyphic text Vol. 2, plate XXXI.

[108] The status of "citizeness" does not seem to directly influence which form of the oath Ēse was made to take, for in 11.4 the citeness Irinūfer took the form of the oath: "If I speak falsehood may I be sent to Ethiopia."

[109] Translation PEET, Tomb-Robberies, 1:153; hieroglyphic text Vol. 2, plate XXXII.

speak falsehood. They said to him, What have you to say concerning the affair of the Tombs? [12] He said, As Amūn lives and as the Ruler lives if it be found that I had to do with the men [13] or that they gave me a *kite* of silver or a *kite* of gold let me be mutilated and placed on the stake. He was examined with the stick. Said (*end, sic*).[110]

*Commentary.*[111] We return to the examinations of individuals associated with Bukhaaf and his fellow thieves. Bukhaaf had listed Pekeneny among those who had received a portion of "Bukhaaf's share of precious metal" in the form of two *deben* of silver (2.17–18), though Bukhaaf did not name him as one of his fellow thieves who entered the tomb. A *kite* is a tenth of a *deben*, so Pekeneny claims he did not even receive a twentieth of the portion Bukhaaf alleges. In this text, the form of the "oath by the Ruler" that is recorded as administered initially is simply "not to speak falsehood" (13.11). Pekeneny is represented as voluntarily invoking an oath later in the examination in the name of Amūn and of the Ruler to the effect that he is willing to be "mutilated and placed on the stake" should his testimony be proven false (13.13).

### (149) Papyrus B.M. 10052 14.1–5

*Translation.* [1] Examination. There was brought the servant Painozem of the temple of Amūn in consequence (?) of the deposition of the slave Degay. [2] He was given the oath not to speak falsehood. They said to him, What have you to say concerning the affair of the vessels of [3] silver which they say were lying in the basket (?) together with the vessels of alabaster (?) on the flats? [4] He made an oath saying, If I be found to have set foot on this stone [5] may I be placed on the stake. He said, Let there be brought a man to accuse me.

*Commentary.*[112] Like the text just quoted earlier (Papyrus B.M. 10052 13.10–14), here the defendant is required to give a simple "oath not to speak false-hood" but later voluntarily asserts his honesty by making an oath that invokes the penalty of being "placed on a stake" (14.4–5). Degay had been previously examined over the course of two days according to 4.15–31.[113] Apparently he had named Painozem as a co-conspirator with Bukhaaf, and perhaps this was

---

[110] The ending "Said (*end, sic*)" is precisely how PEET's translation concludes. The scribe apparently did not fully record the closing interactions with Pekeneny.

[111] Translation PEET, Tomb-Robberies, 1:155; hieroglyphic text Vol. 2, plate XXXIII.

[112] Translation PEET, Tomb-Robberies, 1:155; hieroglyphic text Vol. 2, plate XXXIV.

[113] Degay is called "the slave of the servant Shedbeg, who was in the employ of the herds-man Bukhaaf" (4.15). Bukhaaf alleged that he left 2 *deben* of silver and 60 *deben* of copper (among other items) in payment with Shedbeg for the services of Degay (2.23). The examination of Degay was apparently prolonged by his initial refusal to confess knowledge of the events, followed by a period of torture resulting in him showing the path to the tomb at night and in him providing a long list of Bukhaaf's confederates (4.15–31).

recorded in the lost lines at the end of page 4 of this papyrus. After Painozem
challenges the court to bring a "man to accuse me" (14.5), they recall Degay to
make more specific allegations (14.5–9). However, Degay's testimony was
later viewed as less reliable than the actual examinations of Painozem since
Painozem was set at liberty (14.19–21). Yet, after this time of liberty, Painozem will again be examined by the court – in that passage he is declared innocent (see below Papyrus B.M. 10052 15.16–18).

**(150)**  Papyrus B.M. 10052 14.22–25

*Translation.* [22] Examination. The scribe Paoemtaumt was brought. [23] He was
given the oath not to speak falsehood. He said, As Amūn lives and as the
Ruler lives, if I be found [24] to have had anything to do with any one of the
thieves may I be mutilated in nose and ears and placed on the stake. He was
examined [25] with the stick. He was found to have been arrested on account of
the measurer Paoemtaumt son of Ḳaḳa.

*Commentary.*[114] This appears to be a case of mistaken identity in which one
Paoemtaumt (the scribe) was confused with another man of the same name
(the measurer Paoemtaumt son of Ḳaḳa, who is mentioned in 2.12 and
3.12).[115] Nevertheless, he went through a full examination involving both a
simplified oath not to speak falsehood and a period of torture. As in 13.12–13
and 14.4–5 quoted above, Paoemtaumt puts forth his own oath to protest his
innocence. This oath form specifies the kind of mutilation ("in nose and
ears"), which may be a clue to other imprecise mutilation formulas cited
above. Paoemtaumt's own oath also invokes being "placed on the stake."

**(151)**  Papyrus B.M. 10052 15.16–18

*Translation.* [16] Examination. There was brought the servant Painōzem of the
temple of Amūn. [17] He took an oath by the Ruler saying, If I be found to have
had anything to do with the thieves may I be placed on the stake. [18] He was
examined and found innocent with regard to the thieves.

*Commentary.*[116] Painōzem is likely the father of Khonsmōse, who is mentioned in 11.20 (quoted above), and he would be the person accused by Degay
the slave in 14.1–5 (see above). It is unclear why, having been set at liberty in
14.21, he was reexamined and finally proclaimed "innocent" in this passage
(15.18). The oath form in 15.17 is slightly different than previous exemplars

---

[114] Translation PEET, Tomb-Robberies, 1:156; hieroglyphic text Vol. 2, plate XXXIV.
[115] Concerning the Abbott Dockets col. B line 5, cf. PEET, Tomb-Robberies, 1:133.
[116] Translation PEET, Tomb-Robberies, 1:157; hieroglyphic text Vol. 2, plate XXXV.

("If I be found to have had anything to do with the thieves…"), but it also invokes being "placed on the stake." This passage is located within a series of examinations in which the accused is "found innocent" (e.g. 15.3; 15.15; 15.23).

**(152)** Papyrus B.M. 10403 2.2–5

*Translation.* [2] The scribe Dhutmōse and the scribe Hori son of Seni stole for themselves the [3] copper casing of this chest, the two of them together. He took [4] an oath by the Ruler saying, All that I say is true, and if I be found [5] to have spoken falsehood let me be placed on the wood.

*Commentary.* [117] This papyrus stems from a period slightly later than B.M. 10052 (which was quoted repeatedly above) since B.M. 10403 locates itself in Year 2 of the *whm mswt* (B.M. 10403 1.1); thus both papyri come from the era of Ramesses XI at the juncture of the twelfth and eleventh centuries B.C.[118] This passage occurs at the conclusion of a long record of the testimony of Pentehetnakht (1.9–2.5), who had rallied ten men in order to plunder the chest of Ramessesnakht, chief priest of Amun (1.13–19). At the beginning of Pentehetnakht's examination, he was "given the oath by the Ruler on pain of mutilation not to speak falsehood" (1.10–11; cf. 3.24–25). At the end of his examination (quoted above), he takes a second oath, requiring him to be "placed on the wood" if he is found to have committed false testimony.

**(153)** Memphis Decree of Ptolemy V Epiphanes (Rosetta Stone)

*Translation of Demotic Text §16.*[119] … (as for) the rebels who had gathered

---

[117] Translation PEET, Tomb-Robberies, 1:172; text Vol. 2, plates XXXVI–XXXVII.

[118] For date see discussion in PEET, Tomb-Robberies, 1:128–130, 169.

[119] This translation is the revised version of R. S. SIMPSON's that appears in RICHARD PARKINSON, The Rosetta Stone (London: British Museum Press, 2005), 57–60, here 58. SIMPSON's initial translation appears in ROBERT S. SIMPSON, Demotic Grammar in the Ptolemaic Sacerdotal Decrees (Oxford: Griffith Institute, Ashmolean Museum, 1996). This can be compared with the translation (and transliterated Demotic text) in E. A. WALLIS BUDGE, The Rosetta Stone in the British Museum. The Greek, Demotic and Hieroglyphic Texts (London: Religious Tract Society, 1929), 85, 97. BUDGE translates the final phrase as: "and he had them slain by means of the wood [*i.e.* he either crucified them or impaled them]" (ibid. 85). A transcription of the Demotic text (and transliteration) can be found in WILHELM SPIEGELBERG, Der demotische Text der Priesterdekrete von Kanopus und Memphis (Rosettana) mit den hieroglyphischen und griechischen Fassungen und deutscher Übersetzung nebst demotischem Glossar (Heidelberg: Winters Universitätsbuchhandlung, 1922), 50–51. SPIEGELBERG translates the last phrase as: "Er liess sie an das Holz schlagen(?)"; this he compares to the hieroglypic text: "Er tötete (sie), indem er sie auf das Holz spiesste(?)" (ibid. 81); and he comments "Die Übersetzung sowohl der demotischen wie der hierogl. Fassung ist nur geraten. Handelt es sich etwa um ein 'Pfählen' nach assyrischer Art?" (ibid. 94).

armies and led them to disturb the nomes, harming the temples and abandoning the way of the King and his father, the gods let him overcome them at Memphis during the festival of the Reception of the Rulership which he did from his father, and he had them slain on the wood.

*Translation of Hieroglyphic Text §§R1 and N23.*[120] [R1] Behold, the enemy had gathered together the soldiers, and they were at their head, and they led astray [the people] in the [other] nomes, and looted the Horus Lands (i.e., the temples and their estates). They transgressed the way of His Majesty and his august father. The gods bestowed victory upon him, and some of them were brought into Aneb Ḥetcht-t (i.e., White Wall or, Memphis) [N23] at the time of the celebration of the festival whereat he received the kingdom from his father. He slaughtered them by setting them up upon wood (*i.e.* he either crucified or impaled them).

*Commentary.* With this passage, we skip several centuries into the Ptolemaic era. The Memphis Decree was copied and distributed throughout Ptolemaic Egypt, and a few extant copies have surfaced in modern times. However, it received its now most-renowned impression in the trilingual inscription on the fragmentary stele known as the Rosetta Stone (in Egyptian hieroglyphs, Demotic, and Greek), which permitted the earliest modern decipherment and translation of Egyptian hieroglyphs. This decree represents an edict from the priestly elite in 196 B.C. honoring the formal ascension of Ptolemy V (Epiphanes) to the Pharaonic crown at the age of 13 (in reality he had been "ruling" already for about eight years). The decree recounts some of the previous successes and benefactions under the rule of Ptolemy V. Among these was the conquest in Lycopolis in the Nile Delta of rebels, some of whom were later punished with impalement during Ptolemy's coronation festival. The Demotic and the Hieroglyphic texts record that these individuals were "slain/set up on the wood", while the Greek text is more circumspect and does not record the method of execution.[121] The Hieroglyphic text on the Rosetta stone is fragmentary on the crucial line, but, fortunately, a parallel passage in the Nubayrah/Damanhur stele provides the missing text of the Memphis Decree (above "R1" indicates the fragmentary first extant line of the Rosetta Stone text and "N23" indicates the twenty-third line of the Nubayrah text). Though human

---

[120] Translation from BUDGE, Rosetta Stone, 113. BUDGE provides a transcription and transliteration of the hieroglyphic text (ibid. 146–147). The parenthetical comment at the end "(*i.e.* he either crucified or impaled them)" represents BUDGE's interpretation of the phrase "setting them up upon wood."

[121] For the corresponding Greek text (§§27–28) cf. BUDGE, Rosetta Stone, 59, 71; SPIEGELBERG, Priesterdekrete, 81. Both read the crucial clause in §28 as "πάντας ἐκόλασεν καθηκόντως", which we would translate as "he properly punished all"). Convenient English translation of the Greek can be found in CAROL ANDREWS, The Rosetta Stone (London: British Museum Publications, 1981), 26.

bodily suspension was known in the Hellenistic period, the fact that this inscription is most direct about these public suspensions in its two native Egyptian language versions (Hieroglyphic and Demotic) might imply that Ptolemy was following Egyptian precedent. It is striking that this delayed form of execution, coming as it did during his coronation festivities, celebrated Ptolemy's victory over the rebels of Lycopolis in this particularly gruesome and public way.

## 3.2.4 Ugarit

At least one text from Ras Shamra (RS 86.2221) deserves mention here.[122] D. ARNAUD, the editor with access to the unpublished original text, has variously described the text as representing a crucifixion or impalement. Following the interpretation in ARNAUD's publications,[123] this Ugarit Akkadian text (found in the house of Urtenu on the southern side of Ras Shamra) speaks of a charge of blasphemy from Sidonians against some residents of Ugarit, who had defiled the temple of the Sidonian storm-god. A subsequent plague in Sidon was interpreted to indicate that this blasphemous act required atonement. The perpetrators were required to bring a considerable sacrifice, but at least one failed to do so. Therefore, the people of Sidon called for the malefactor's execution itself to serve as a form of expiation, by first stoning him (casting him down from a high place while inebriated) and then suspending his body. ARNAUD understands the crucial lines to indicate that though only one person was to be executed in this manner (as indicated by singular suffixes), the suspension device for this individual was built from at least two pieces of wood (plural, hence implying a cross).[124] Nevertheless, ARNAUD

---

[122] The text appears to remain unpublished. Since I have been unable to find either a complete textual edition or translation, the description here is intended to summarize preliminary references to the text by D. ARNAUD and others.

[123] See esp. DANIEL ARNAUD, Les ports de la «Phénicie» à la fin de l'âge du Bronze récent (XIV-XIII siècles) d'après les textes cunéiformes de Syrie, Studi Micenei ed Egeo-Anatolici 30 (1992): 179–194. Also note his brief description of the text in the exhibition volume Syrie, mémoire et civilisation (Paris: Institut du monde arabe: Flammarion, 1993), 246 (concerning item 215 "Lettre du roi de Sidon au roi d'Ugarit"); there ARNAUD dates the work to the end of the thirteenth or beginning of the twelfth century B.C.

[124] ARNAUD's most complete account of this is found in two footnotes, which reference lines 33–34 and 79 of the Ugarit Akkadian text; see ARNAUD, Ports, 191 n. 65, 68. Note 65 reads: "Car le texte 5.12, ll. 33–34 n'est pas clair. Les Sidoniens auraient déclaré au roi: «Nous voul[ons installer des bois] et nous voulons le planter sur des bois» (*lu na-ša-k*[*a-an* giš.meš] *ù i-na* giš.meš *lu ni-iz-qu-up-šu*). Les premiers «bois» (on notera le pluriel à chaque fois) sont-ils un échafaud ou déjà la croix?" Note 68 reports that line 79 reads: "'[et] ils veulent le pl<a>nter [sur] des bois' ([*ù i-na*] giš.meš *li-<iz>-qu-pu-uš*)." That note (p. 191 n. 68) continues by spelling out Arnaud's argument: "Le pluriel giš.meš suppose au moins

carefully distinguishes this *post mortem* suspension, which he calls a "crucifixion," from the kinds of crucifixions the Romans performed.[125] CLEMENS,
while acknowledging the need to wait for final publication, nonetheless suggests that the singular (3ms) suffixes referencing the victim(s) may constitute
a generic reference to the suspension of a group, and thus the multiple pieces
of wood may have been used to impale (rather than crucify) more than one
malefactor.[126] CLEMENS thus compares this Sidonian (and possibly also
Ugaritic) penalty with Middle Assyrian public impalements. This use of *post
mortem* suspension on a wooden device after stoning strongly resembles some
key biblical passages cited below (a fact not lost on ARNAUD or CLEMENS).[127]


## 3.2.5 Assyria


Texts and reliefs from ancient Assyria present numerous instances of impalement and bodily suspension. Legal documents endorse such a penalty for
women who procure their own abortions (in the Middle Assyrian Laws) and
for property owners who infringe on the royal road (in a relief from Sennacherib). Yet, most Assyrian examples appear in military accounts from the historical royal inscriptions and reliefs of Assyrian rulers. These military cases of
impalement/suspension typically refer to the punishment of civic and military
leaders whose cities have rebelled against their Assyrian overlords. Such suspensions occur amid the many savage acts Assyrians committed (especially in
siege warfare) against their opponents, including rape, enslavement, deportation, dismemberment, flaying victims alive, burning captive cities, as well as
decapitating, blinding, and defacing their victims. These constitute acts of

---

deux éléments, donc une croix. Le verbe *zaqāpu* signifie 'planter'; dans les textes néo-
assyriens, il est traduit couramment par 'empaler', et cette interprétation a pour elle les
représentations des reliefs contemporains mais, en syriaque, ce verbe a bien le sens de 'cruci-
fier'." In context (ibid. 190–191), Arnaud compares this with the Jewish talmudic means of
executing blasphemers by stoning (via throwing from a height) and subsequent suspension "…
sur une croix, faite, sans doute, de deux planches."

[125] This is especially evident in ARNAUD's brief reference to the matter in Syrie, mémoire
et civilisation, 246: "Les coupables ont à choisir entre fournir des sacrifices ou être mis à mort
par crucifixion. La description de ce supplice montre l'ancienneté de la tradition sémitique et
sa différence totale avec le supplice romain du même nom: le condamné est d'abord tué par
précipitation et lapidation, avant que son cadavre ne soit exposé sur des bois."

[126] DAVID M. CLEMENS, Sources for Ugaritic Ritual and Sacrifice (Alter Orient und Altes
Testament 284/1; Münster: Ugarit-Verlag, 2001), 1034–1041, esp. 1039–1040. Certainly
CLEMENS correctly rejects ARNAUD's dependence on later Syriac parallels (ibid. 1039). This
section in CLEMENS also provides a useful English summary of ARNAUD's various publications on the matter. I remain indebted to ROBERT VASHOLZ, who several years ago drew my
attention to these pages in CLEMENS.

[127] Thus CLEMENS, Sources, 639 notes comparisons with Deut 21:22–23; Josh 8:29;
10:26–27; 2 Sam 18:9,17.

public humility and cruelty designed, in part, to warn others against opposing the Assyrian rulers.[128]

**(154)** Middle Assyrian Laws – Tablet A (§53, column 7, lines 92–105)

[92] *šum-ma* SAL *i-na ra-mi-ni-ša* [93] *ša ŠÀ^{bi}-ša ta-aṣ-ṣi-li* [94] *ub-ta-e-ru-ú-ši* [95] *uk-ta-i-nu-ú-ši* [96] *i-na* GIŠ.MEŠ *i-za-qu-pu-ú-ši* [97] *la-a i-qa-ab-bi-ru-ši* [98] *šum-ma ša-a ŠÀ^{bi}-ša* [99] *i-na ṣa-li-e mi-ta-a-at* [100] *i-na* GIŠ.MEŠ *i-za-qu-pu-ú-ši* [101] *la-a i-qa-ab-bi-ru-ši* [102] *šum-ma* SAL *ši-it ki-i ša ŠÀ^{bi}-ša* [103] *ta-aṣ-li-ú-ni* [104] *up-[ta]-zi-ru-ú-ši* [105] *[a-na* LUGAL *la-a] iq-bi-ú*

*Translation.* [92] If a woman has cast the fruit of her womb by her own act [94] (and) charge (and) proof have been brought against her, [96] she shall be impaled [97] (and) shall not be buried. [98] If she has died in casting the fruit of her womb, [100] she shall be impaled [101] (and) shall not be buried. [102] If that woman was concealed(?) when she cast the fruit of her womb [105] (and) it was not told to the king.

*Commentary.*[129] Tablet A of the Middle Assyrian Laws dates to the eleventh century B.C., though the laws themselves are thought to have been composed perhaps three centuries earlier.[130] Lines 103–105 are difficult to read, and the concluding lines (106ff.) of this column of text are illegible.[131] The preceding sections in Tablet A (§§50–52) concern cases in which someone strikes a pregnant woman and causes an abortion (cf. Exod 21:22–25). In this text, the woman procures her own abortion and thus is held liable. The combined penalty involves impalement and a lack of burial (lines 96–97 and 100–101). The verb *zaqāpu* (here *i-za-qu-pu-ú-ši*) and its derivatives also indicate bodily impalement in many other Assyrian texts below.[132] The punishment of prolonged public impalement is enacted even if the woman has died in the course of the abortion (lines 98–101). In the event she was still living, the impalement may well have been the means of execution since the text does not mention a prior form of capital punishment. Driver and Miles argue that the "sav-

---

[128] BOYD SEEVERS, Warfare in the Old Testament: The Organization, Weapons, and Tactics of Ancient Near Eastern Armies (Grand Rapids: Kregel, 2013), 239–241 labels these tactics instances of "psychological warfare and cruelty".

[129] Text and translation from GODFREY R. DRIVER and JOHN C. MILES, The Assyrian Laws (Ancient Codes and Laws of the Near East; Oxford: Clarendon Press, 1935), 420–421.

[130] MARTHA T. ROTH, The Middle Assyrian Laws (2.132) (Tablet A), in The Context of Scripture. Vol. 2: Monumental Inscriptions from the Biblical World (ed. W. W. Hallo and K. L. Younger; Leiden: Brill, 2003), 353–360, 353. MEEK dates the tablets to the twelfth century, and the laws to the fifteenth; THEOPHILE J. MEEK, The Middle Assyrian Laws, in Ancient Near Eastern Texts Relating to the Old Testament (Second Edition.; ed. J. B. Pritchard; Princeton: Princeton University Press, 1969), 180–188, 180.

[131] On the reconstruction of lines 102–105, cf. DRIVER and MILES, Assyrian Laws, 118.

[132] For *zaqāpu* cf. CAD 21:51–55 (esp. 1.d and 3.c). Also see *zaqīpu* in CAD 21:58.

agery of the punishment" indicates this act of aborting the sacred blood of the family would be "regarded as a most heinous and presumably sacrilegious offence."[133] The text is emphatic that the woman not be buried, and a lack of burial may well have been assumed in many of the other occasions when Assyrians impaled their victims (e.g., in times of war – see below). Modern scholars have commonly associated the lack of burial with dishonoring the body, summoning public shame, serving as a warning to others, and invoking religious horror against remaining unburied.

**(155)** Annals A (A.0.101.1) of Ashurnasirpal II [col. I, lines 89–94]

[89]...ᵐ*a-zi*-DINGER LÚ.GAR-*nu šá ra-ma-ni-ia* UGU-*šú-nu aš-kun a-si-tu ina pu-ut* KÁ.GAL-*šú ar-ṣip* LÚ.GAL.MEŠ *am-mar* [90] *ib-bal-ki-tu-ni a-ku-ṣu* KUŠ.MEŠ-*šú-nu a-si-tu ú-ḫal-lip a-nu-te ina lìb-bi a-si-te ú-ma-gigi a-nu-te ina* UGU [91] *i-si-te ina zi-qi-be ú-za-qip an-nu-te ina bat-tu-bat-ti šá a-si-te ina zi-qi-be ú-šal-bi ma-a᾿-du-te ina pi-rík* KUR-*ia* [92] *a-ku-ṣu* KUŠ.MEŠ-*šú-nu* BÀD.MEŠ-*ni ú-ḫal-lip šá* LÚ.*šá*-SAG.MEŠ *šá* LÚ.*šá*-SAG MAN.MEŠ-*ni* EN *ḫi-i-tí* UZU.MEŠ-*šú-nu ú-ba-tiq* [93] ᵐ*a-ḫi-ia-ba-ba ana* URU *ni-nu-a ub-la-šu a-ku-su* KUŠ-*šú* BÀD *šá* URU *ni-nu-a ú-ḫal-lip li-ta ù dan-na-ni* [94] UGU KUR *la-qe-e al-ta-kan*

*Translation.* I appointed Azi-ili as my own governor over them. I erected a pile in front of his gate; I flayed as many nobles as had rebelled against me (and) draped their skins over the pile; some I spread out within the pile, some I erected on stakes upon the pile, (and) some I placed on stakes around about the pile. I flayed many right through my land (and) draped their skins over the walls. I slashed the flesh of the eunuchs (and) of the royal eunuchs who were guilty. I brought Aḫi-iababa to Nineveh, flayed him, (and) draped his skin over the wall of Nineveh. (Thus) have I constantly established my victory and strength over the land Laqû.

*Commentary.*[134] Ashurnasirpal II reigned from 883–859 B.C. The events of this text are apparently dated in his accession year (cf. i.43–44 and i.69) or at least toward the beginning of his reign. While he was away on campaign, the city of Sūru rebelled, killing its governor Ḫamatāiia and appointing Aḫi-iababa ("the son of a nobody") as king (see i.74–76). Ashurnasirpal turned to

---

[133] DRIVER and MILES, Assyrian Laws, 116–117.

[134] Text and translation from ALBERT KIRK GRAYSON, Assyrian Rulers of the Early First Millennium BC I (1114–859 BC) (The Royal Inscriptions of Mesopotamia 2; Toronto: University of Toronto Press, 1991), 199–200. Essentially the same translation can be found in ALBERT KIRK GRAYSON, Assyrian Royal Inscriptions (2 vols.; Records of the Ancient Near East; Wiesbaden: Harrassowitz, 1972), 2:124–125. Cf. E. A. WALLIS BUDGE and LEONARD W. KING, eds., Annals of the Kings of Assyria: The Cuneiform Texts with Translations, Transliterations, etc., from the Original Documents in the British Museum (London: British Museum, 1902), 1:285.

attack Sūru with the aid of the gods Ashur and Adad. Some nobles of Sūru submissively entreated with him. Nonetheless, Ashurnasirpal besieged the city, capturing both it and the rebellious Aḫi-iababa. In addition to recounting Ashurnasirpal's reception of a massive tribute, the above text details his harsh vengeance on the rebellious nobles. Ashurnasirpal repeatedly reports flaying the skin off the nobles (a theme repeated throughout his annals). The *annute…* *annute… annute…* ("some… some… some…") construct in lines 90–91 is somewhat ambiguous, making it unclear whether the nobles' bodies were impaled on the stakes or whether only their skins were so attached.[135] In any case, this provides a vivid introduction to the extremely harsh measures Ashurnasirpal was willing to employ against rebellious vassals.

**(156)** Annals A (A.0.101.1) of Ashurnasirpal II [col. II, lines 103b–110a]

[103] *ina* GIŠ.*tukul-ti aš-šur* EN-*ia* TA URU *tu-uš-ḫa-an a-tú-muš* GIŠ.GIGIR.MEŠ KAL-*tu pit-ḫal-lu* SAG-*su i-si-ia a-se-qe ina rak-su-te* [104] ÍD.IDIGNA *e-te-bir* DÙ *mu-ši-ti ar-te-di a-na* URU *pi-tu-ra* URU *dan-nu-ti-šú-nu šá* KUR *di-ir-ra-a-ia aq-ṭí-rib* URU GIG *dan-niš* [105] 2 BÀD.MEŠ-*ni la-a-bi kir-ḫu-šu* GIM ŠU.SI KUR-*e šá-qi ina* Á.MEŠ MAḪ.MEŠ *šá aš-šur* EN-*ia ina gi-piš* ÉRIN.ḪI.A.MEŠ-*a* MÈ-*ia šit-mu-ri* [106] *it-ti-šú-nu am-da-ḫi-iṣ ina* 2 *u-me la-am* UTU *na-pa-ḫi* GIM IŠKUR *šá* GÌR.BAL UGU-*šú-nu áš-gu-um nab-lu* UGU-*šú-nu ú-šá-za-nin ina šip-ṣi* [107] *u da-na-ni mun-daḫ-ṣi-a* GIM *an-ze-e.* MUŠEN UGU-*šú-nu i-še-ʾu* URU KUR-*ad* 8 ME ÉRIN.MEŠ *mun-daḫ-ṣi-šú-nu ina* GIŠ.TUKUL.MEŠ *ú-šam-qit* SAG.DU.MEŠ-*šú-nu* [108] KUD-*is* ÉRIN.MEŠ TI.LA.MEŠ ḪI.A.MEŠ *ina* ŠU DIB-*ta si-ta-ti-šú-nu ina* IZI.MEŠ GÍBIL-*up šal-la-su-nu* DUGUD-*ta aš-lul a-si-tu šá* TI.LA.MEŠ *šá* SAG.DU.MEŠ [109] *ina pu-ut* KÁ.GAL-*šú ar-ṣip* 7 ME ÉRIN.MEŠ *ina pu-ut* KÁ.GAL-*šú-nu a-na* GIŠ *zi-qi-pi ú-za-qip* URU *a-púl a-qur ana* DU *u kar-me* GUR-*er* LÚ *ba-tu-li-šú-nu* [110] MUNUS *ba-tu-la-ti-šú-nu ana* GÍBIL-*te* GÍBIL

*Translation.* With the support of Aššur, my lord, I moved on from the city Tušḫa. I took with me strong chariots, cavalry, (and) crack troops. I crossed the Tigris by means of a bridge of rafts. Travelling all night I approached the city Pitura, the fortified city of the Dirru. The city was exceptionally difficult; it was surrounded by two walls; its citadel was lofty like a mountain peak. With the exalted strength of Aššur, my lord, with my massive troops, and with my fierce battle I fought with them. On the second day, before sunrise, I thundered against them like the god Adad-of-the-Devastation (and) rained down flames upon them. With might and main my combat troops flew against them like the Storm Bird. I conquered the city. I felled 800 of their combat troops

---

[135] All translations maintain this ambiguity, though GRAYSON seems to favor the skins being "spread out", while other translations could more easily imply that the people were impaled; BUDGE / KING, Annals, 285; LUCKENBILL, Records, 1:145 (§443).

with the sword (and) cut off their heads. I captured many soldiers alive. The rest of them I burnt. I carried off valuable tribute from them. I built a pile of live (men and) of heads before his gate. I impaled on stakes 700 soldiers before their gate. I razed, destroyed, (and) turned into ruin hills the city. I burnt their adolescent boys (and) girls.

*Commentary.*[136] In his fifth campaign, Ashurnasirpal II captured the heavily fortified city of Pitura. The speed with which he conquered the city (two days, if we are to believe his annals) is remarkable. For our purposes, note especially that (among his many other gruesome boasts) Ashurnasirpal claims to have impaled 700 soldiers before the gate of the city (line 109). The impalement terminology is also found in many other royal inscriptions below.[137]

Two other monolithic stone stelae from Ashurnasirpal's reign also record this event with some slight variations. Lines 70–77a of the Kurkh Monolith recounts the conquest of Pitura, deleting the reference to adolescent girls (maidens) being burnt alongside the young boys.[138] The Nimrud Monolith (or "Great Monolith") also reproduces the account (in column IV, lines 60–83a);[139] it likewise limits the recorded burning of adolescents to boys, and notably indicates that "500" were impaled (as opposed to the "700" recorded in Annals A and in the Kurkh Monolith).[140] The precise number of impaled victims is of secondary interest, since we can be certain that the king desired others to *think* he had impaled a vast number of people outside the city walls.

**(157)** Annals A (A.0.101.1) of Ashurnasirpal II [col. III, lines 31b–33a]

[31] *a-púl a-qur ina* IZI.MEŠ *áš-ru-up ina ger-ri-ia-ma a-su-uḫ-ra* TA *pi-a-te šá* ÍD *ḫa-bur a-di* [32] URU *ṣi-ḫa-te šá* KUR *su-ḫi* URU.DIDLI.MEŠ *šá* GÌR *an-nu-te šú* ÍD *pu-rat-te šá* KUR *la-qe-e šá* KUR *su-ḫi ap-púl a-qur ina* IZI.MEŠ *áš-ru-up* BURU.MEŠ-*šú-nu e-ṣi-di* 4 ME 70 ÉRIN.MEŠ [33] *ti-du-ki-šú-nu ina* GIŠ.TUKUL.MEŠ *ú-šam-qit* 30 TI.LA.MEŠ *ú-ṣab-bi-ta ina* GIŠ *zi-qi-be ú-ze-qi-be*

---

[136] Text and translation: GRAYSON, Assyrian Rulers II, 210. Cf. BUDGE / KING, Annals, 334–337; LUCKENBILL, Records, 1:156 (§463); GRAYSON, Assyrian Royal Inscriptions, 2:134–135 (which strangely reads "300" combat troops in line 107 rather than "800").

[137] On this terminology see *zaqīpu* in CAD 21:58.

[138] Text and translation of the Kurkh Monolith (A.0.101.19) can be found in A. Kirk Grayson, *Assyrian Rulers of the Early First Millennium BC I (1114–859 BC)*, 260. Cf. E. A. WALLIS BUDGE and L. W. KING, eds., *Annals of the Kings of Assyria*, 233–234 (who list the text as rev. 21–28); LUCKENBILL, *Ancient Records*, 1:180 (§499); GRAYSON, *Assyrian Royal Inscriptions*, 2:160–161 (§638). Among the orthographical variations in the Kurkh Monolith note *ana zi-qi-bi ú-za-qi-bi* (in line 76) for *ana zi-qi-pi ú-za-qip* (in Annals A, ii.109).

[139] See text and translation in GRAYSON, Assyrian Rulers II, 250–251.

[140] The reference to 500 is in col. IV, line 80. Among the orthographical variants in the Nimrud Monolith note *ana* GIŠ *zi-qi-pi ú-za-qi-pi* in iv.81; GRAYSON, Assyrian Rulers II, 251.

*Translation.* In (the course of) my campaign I turned (aside and) razed, destroyed, (and) burnt the cities which are on this bank of the Euphrates (and) which (belong to) the land Laqû (and) the land Suḫu, from the mouth of the River Ḫabur as far as the city Ṣibatu of the land Suḫu. I reaped their harvests. I felled with the sword 470 of their fighting-men. I captured 30 alive (and) erected (them) on stakes.

*Commentary.*[141] Here, Ashurnasirpal reacts to the rebellion of the land Laqû while he was in Calah. He crosses the Tigris and makes his way along the Euphrates, conquering the cities in the lands of Laqû and Suḫu. This short excerpt above precedes a longer narrative of Ashurnasirpal's victorious, larger battles with these rebels. Here, he briefly mentions his impalement of 30 living soldiers.

**(158)** Annals A (A.0.101.1) of Ashurnasirpal II [col. III, lines 83b–84a]

[83] *ki-i ina* URU *a-ri-bu-a us-ba-ku-ni* URU.MEŠ-*ni šá* KUR *lu-ḫu-ti* KUR-*ad* GAZ.MEŠ-*šú-nu* ḪI.A.MEŠ-*šú-nu a-duk ap-púl aq-qur ina* IZI.MEŠ [84] *áš-ru-up* ÉRIN.MEŠ TI.LA.MEŠ *ina* ŠU *ú-ṣab-bi-ta ina* GIŠ *zi-qi-bi ina pu-ut* URU.DIDLI-*šú-nu ú-za-qib*

*Translation.* While I was in the city Aribua I conquered the cities of the land Luḫutu. I massacred many of their (inhabitants), I razed, destroyed, (and) burnt. I captured soldiers alive (and) impaled (them) on stakes before their cities.

*Commentary.*[142] Aribua is the "fortified city of Lubarna", which was captured by Ashurnasirpal II (iii.78–79). Ashurnasirpal brings grain into Aribua, settles Assyrians in the city, and uses it as a base for attacking the surrounding land of Luḫutu. The numbers of cities and inhabitants attacked in the surrounding territory are left unspecified in the above text. To the standard formula "I razed, destroyed, (and) burnt" Ashurnasirpal's scribes add the reference to impaling the soldiers that had been captured alive. As elsewhere in these annals, this is done "before the cities."

---

[141] Text and translation from GRAYSON, *Assyrian Rulers II*, 214; translation also appears in GRAYSON, *Assyrian Royal Inscriptions*, 2:139 (§579). Cf. BUDGE / KING, *Annals*, 354–355 (who follow the variant "20" for those who were captured and impaled); LUCKENBILL, *Records*, 1:161 (§472) also reads "twenty".

[142] Text and translation from GRAYSON, *Assyrian Rulers II*, 218; slightly different translation in GRAYSON, *Assyrian Royal Inscriptions*, 2:143 (§585). Cf. BUDGE / KING, *Annals*, 372 ("Some men I took alive and impaled them on stakes over against their cities"). Translation also in LUCKENBILL, *Records*, 1:166 (§478).

**(159)** Annals A (A.0.101.1) of Ashurnasirpal II [col. III, lines 105–113a]

¹⁰⁵ *a-na* URU *dam-dam-mu-sa* URU *dan-nu-ti-šú šá* ᵐ*i-la-a-ni* DUMU *za-ma-ni aq-ṭí-rib* URU *a-si-bi qu-ra-di-ia ki-ma* MUŠEN UGU-*šú-nu i-še-* ʾ*i* ¹⁰⁶ 6 ME ÉRIN.MEŠ *mun-daḫ-ṣi-šú-nu ina* GIŠ.TUKUL.MEŠ *ú-šam-qit* SAG.DU.MEŠ-*šú-nu ú-na-kis* 4 ME ÉRIN.MEŠ TI.LA.MEŠ *ina* ŠU.MEŠ *ú-ṣab-bi-ta* ¹⁰⁷ 3 LIM *šal-la-su-nu ú-še-ṣi-a* URU *šu-a-tú a-na ra-ma-ni-a aṣ-bat* LÚ.ÉRIN.MEŠ TI.LA.MEŠ SAG.DU.MEŠ *a-na* URU *a-me-di* URU MAN-*ti-šú lu ú-bi-il* ¹⁰⁸ *a-si-tu šá* SAG.DU.MEŠ *ina pu-ut* KÁ.GAL-*šú lu ar-ṣip* LÚ.ÉRIN.MEŠ TI.LA.MEŠ *ina ba-at-tu-ba-at-te šá* URU-*šú a-na* GIŠ *zi-qi-pi lu ú-za-qi-pi* ¹⁰⁹ *me-et-ḫu-ṣi ina* ŠÀ KÁ.GAL-*šú áš-kun* GIŠ.KIRI.MEŠ-*šú a-kis iš-tu* URU *a-me-di at-tum-šá ina né-re-be šá* KUR *kaš-ia-ri šá* URU *al-la ab-si-a* ¹¹⁰ *šá ina* MAN.MEŠ-*ni* AD.MEŠ-*a ma-am-ma kib-su ù me-tu-qu ina lìb-be la-a iš-kun-na* KU-*ub a-na* URU *ú-da* URU *dan-nu-ti-šú šá* ᵐ*lab-ṭu-ri* DUMU *ṭu-pu-si* ¹¹¹ *aq-ṭí-rib* URU *a-si-bi ina píl-ši* GIŠ *ṣa-pi-te ù né-pe-še* URU KUR-*ud* 1 LIM 4 ME [...] ÉRIN.MEŠ [...]-*šú-nu ina* GIŠ.TUKUL.MEŠ *ú-šam-qit* 7 ME 80 LÚ.ÉRIN.MEŠ TI.MEŠ ¹¹² *ina* ŠU *ú-ṣa-bi-it* 3 LIM *šal-la-su-nu ú-še-ṣi-a* LÚ.ÉRIN.MEŠ TI.LA.MEŠ *ina ba-tu-bat-te* [UR]U-*šú a-na* GIŠ *zi-qi-pi ú-za-qi-pi an-nu-te* ¹¹³ IGI.II.MEŠ-*šú-nu ú-na-píl si-ta-ti-šú-nu as-su-ḫa a-na* KUR *aš-šur ub-la* URU *a-na* [N]Í-*ia aṣ-bat*

*Translation.* I approached the city Damdammusa, the fortified city of Ilānu, a man of Bīt-Zamāni. I besieged the city. My warriors flew like bird(s) against them. I felled 600 of their combat troops with the sword (and) cut off their heads. I captured 400 of their soldiers alive. I brought out 3,000 captives from them. I took that city in hand for myself. I took the live soldiers (and) the heads to the city Amedu, his royal city, (and) built a pile of heads before his gate. I impaled the live soldiers on stakes around about his city. I fought my way inside his gate (and) cut down his orchards. Moving on from the city Amedu I entered the pass of Mount Kašiiari at the city Allabsia wherein none of the kings my fathers had ever set foot. I approached the city Udu, the fortified city of Labṭuru, son of Ṭupusu. I besieged the city (and) conquered it by means of tunnels, siege-towers, (and) battering-rams. I felled with the sword 1,400 [...] of their [fighting] men. I captured 780 soldiers alive. I brought out 3,000 captives from them. I impaled the live soldiers on stakes around about his city. I gouged out the eyes of some (and) the remainder I uprooted (and) brought to Assyria. I took the city in hand [for myself].

*Commentary.*¹⁴³ Thus concludes the final campaign of Ashurnasirpal II as reported in these annals. The text that follows this passage serves as a sum-

---

¹⁴³ Text and translation from GRAYSON, Assyrian Rulers II, 220–221. In his earlier translation, Grayson reads "I hung the live soldiers on stakes" rather than the "I impaled the live soldiers on stakes" found above (GRAYSON, Assyrian Royal Inscriptions, 2:144–145 [§587]). Both BUDGE / KING and LUCKENBILL follow the variant reading "580" for the number "780" in line 111; BUDGE / KING, Annals, 378–380; LUCKENBILL, Records, 1:168–169 (§480).

mary of his accomplishments, titles, and building projects. In the text quoted above, two mentions of impalement appear (lines 108, 112), corresponding to the capture of the cities of Amedu and Udu. Both episodes reference the impaling of live soldiers on stakes around the cities. Intriguingly, the first episode indicates Ashurnasirpal brought with him captives from the city of Damdammusa in order to impale them around the "royal city" of Amedu during his siege. Presumably, this was intended as a gruesome warning to the inhabitants of Amedu concerning their fate should they fail to submit.

**(160)** Shalmaneser III – Bronze Gates of Balawat (Band IV; BM 124658)

*Illustration* (Fig. 1)

*Commentary.*[144] This relief comes from a series of bronze bands, now housed in the British Museum, that once adorned the gates of a palace of Shalmaneser III (who reigned 858–824 B.C.). They in all probability come from Tell Balawat, though a century ago some disputed this provenance.[145] Balawat was a smaller

---

[144] Drawing by Karis Chapman based on photograph in ANEP 126 (No. 362). A photograph of the bands of the Shalmaneser III Balawat Gates housed in the British Museum is provided in RICHARD BARNETT, JOHN E. CURTIS, and NIGEL TALLIS, The Balawat Gates of Ashurnasirpal II (London: British Museum Press, 2008), 211 (plate 5); although this book primarily describes the corresponding gates of Ashurnasirpal II, it provides useful information on the Shalmaneser era find as well. This band is labelled BM 124658 in Barnett (who notes that the British Museum arranged the bands in his picture in "random order," so the number four on Band IV does not here refer to the original position, but to its displayed position). Currently the British Museum displays this as the third band from the top of this gate.

[145] Cf. BARNETT, CURTIS, and TALLIS, The Balawat Gates, 11–15, 17–18, who argue that these gates were indeed found by Hormuzd Rassam at Balawat in 1878, refuting BUDGE's claims to the contrary.

Assyrian city a days-march northeast of Nimrud. The gates themselves were
made of huge cedar doors, each with eight bronze bands mounted across the
outside of the door. The bands portray a series of military campaigns by
Shalmaneser III. The upper register in Band IV bears the inscription "Smiting
of Dabigu, the city of Ahuni, son of Adini."[146] This event is dated to 858 B.C.
The lower register may portray another city since the towers are shaped differently (the city in the upper register has crenelated towers while the city below
has towers with "beehive" roofs that match the house within the walls).[147] In
the lower register (portrayed in Fig. 1), as Assyrians continue to advance on
the city, they have also impaled six people on the ramp leading to the upper
town. The arms and legs of these victims appear to be hanging freely. Either
(as seems likely) the stakes have pierced the victims between the legs, or the
victims have somehow been attached to the outside of the poles (note how this
contrasts with the form of suspension on the reliefs below from Tiglath-
pileser III and Sennacherib). The feet of the victims appear to be intact (contrast with Fig. 2). Certainly this testifies to public suspension as a tactic of
ninth-century B.C. Assyrian siege warfare.

**(161)** Shalmaneser III – Bronze Gates of Balawat (BM 124656)

*Illustration* (Fig. 2)

*Commentary.*[148] This further scene from Shalmaneser's Balawat Gates bronze

---

[146] Translation from LUCKENBILL, Records, 1:226 (§614); note also his description of the
find in ibid. 224–227 (§§612–615).

[147] So the description of No. 362 in ANEP 292, which labels the city an "unnamed Syrian
town."

[148] Drawing by Karis Chapman based on photographs of this image from the British
Museum (available at britishmuseum.org) and from TODD BOLEN and A. D. RIDDLE, Pictorial
Library of Bible Lands: The Museum Collection (DVD; 2012), images entitled Balawat Gates
of Shalmaneser III, adr090506028.jpg and adr090506029.jpg. For the location of this
embossed picture on its bronze band, cf. BARNETT, CURTIS, and TALLIS, The Balawat Gates,

bands occurs on the portion of this band that once wrapped around the sizable cedar hinge post. Moving across the bottom register of this band: A kneeling naked man is in the process of being slain by an Assyrian soldier, another Assyrian warrior has severed the hands and feet from his clothed victim (see also below on 2 Sam 4:12; cf. Xenophon, *Anabasis* 3.1.17; Ctesias, *Persica*, FGH 3c 688 Frag. 16.66), hands and feet also lie strewn on the ground around him, and a man has been impaled naked outside the gates of the city (which gates are themselves covered with decapitated heads). The impaled person has been attached to the device in a manner reminiscent of the preceding image from these same gates, and he has likely been impaled through the buttocks and up his spine. However, unlike in the preceding image, here his feet and hands have clearly been cut off.

**(162)**  Tiglath-pileser III – Relief from Nimrud (BM 118903)

*Illustration* (Fig. 3)

*Commentary.*[149] This relief on gypsum from Nimrud in the time of Tiglath-pileser III (who reigned from 744–727 B.C.) depicts a sieged town. Assyrian

---

210 (plate 4); note the left-hand side of the bottom register of the second band from top. However, the current display in the British Museum represents this as the bottom band (of eight). This band is labelled BM 124656 in BARNETT.

[149] Drawing by Karis Chapman. Photograph in ANEP 128, No. 368. HUGO GRESSMANN, Altorientalische Bilder zum Alten Testament (Zweite, völlig neugestaltete und stark vermehrte Auflage; Berlin/Leipzig: De Gruyter, 1927), No. 132.

bowmen fire on the city while a siege engine approaches the walls. A fallen soldier is visible on the ground (not pictured), while a person on the wall raises his arms in surrender.[150] The left edge of the drawing represents the edge of the panel, though an extant connecting left-hand panel continues the scene. Observe the three suspended townspeople outside the city. Three poles have been erected, and each victim has been impaled through the chest by the top of the pole. Such impalement could have caused their deaths, or it may have been *post mortem*. They are apparently suspended naked with at least a meter/yard of the poles remaining between their feet and the ground. The relief is currently in the holdings of the British Museum.

**(163)** Kalḫu Annals of Tiglath-pileser III [text 8, lines 4b–8a]

4 ᵐ*tu-ni-i* KUR.*su-mur-za-a-a* x[…] ⁵ *ak-šud* LÚ.*mun-daḫ-ṣe-šú a-na* GIŠ.⟨*za*⟩-*qi-pa-ni ú-še-li* […] ⁶ KUR.*su-mur-zu* KUR.É-*ḫa-am-ban a-na mi-ṣir* KUR *aš-šur ú-*[*ter-ra* (…) UN.MEŠ KUR.KUR *ki-šit-ti* ŠU.II-*ia i-na lìb-bi*] ⁷ *ú-še-šib* LÚ.*šu-ut* SAG-*ia* LÚ.EN.NAM UGU-*šú-nu áš-kun* […] ⁸ *a-na aš-šur* EN-*ia ar-ku-us*

*Translation.* Tunî of the land Sumurzu …[…]. I captured […]. I impaled his warriors, […]. I an[nexed] the lands Sumurzu (and) Bīt-Ḫamban to Assyria. [(…)] I settled [the people of (foreign) lands conquered by me therein] (and) placed a eunuch of mine as provincial governor over them. I apportioned […] to (the god) Aššur, my lord.

*Commentary.*[151] This fragmentary text records Tiglath-pileser III campaigning in the Zagros Mountains during his second period of office. It makes brief mention in line 5 of his impaling the warriors of Tunî on a *zaqipa*.

**(164)** Kalḫu Annals of Tiglath-pileser III [text 20, lines 8′b–12′]

8 *šu-ú a-na šu-zu-ub* ZI.MEŠ-*šú e-de-nu-uš-šu ip-par-ši-id-ma* ⁹ [*ki-ma*] ᵈNIN.KILIM KÁ.GAL URU-*šú* KU-*ub* LÚ.SAG.KAL.MEŠ-*šú bal-ṭu-us-su-nu* ¹⁰ [*a-na* GIŠ].*za-qi-pa-a-ni ú-še-li-ma ú-šad-gi-la* KUR-*su* 40.ÀM 5 UD.MEŠ *uš-ma-ni* ¹¹ [*i-na i-ta*]-*at* URU-*šu ak-ṣur-ma* GIM *iṣ-ṣur qu-up-pi e-sir-šú* GIŠ.KIRI.MEŠ-*šú* ¹² […]-*nu* ⟨*ṣip*⟩-*pa-a-te ša ni-i-ba la i-šu-ú ak-kis-ma* 1-*en ul e-zib*

---

[150] The interpretation of raised arms as indicating surrender is suggested by Pritchard in ANEP, 293 (description of No. 368).

[151] Text and translation from HAYIM TADMOR and SHIGEO YAMADA, The Royal Inscriptions of Tiglath-pileser III (744–727 BC) and Shalmaneser V (726–722 BC), Kings of Assyria (The Royal Inscriptions of the Neo-Assyrian Period 1; Winona Lake, Ind.: Eisenbrauns, 2011), 32–33. Compare with HAYIM TADMOR, The Inscriptions of Tiglath-pileser III, King of Assyria: Critical Edition, with Introductions, Translations, and Commentary (Jerusalem: Israel Academy of Sciences and Humanities, 1994), 48–51 (listed as Ann. 12; cf. Plate VIII).

*Translation.* In order to save his life, he (Raḫiānu) fled alone and entered the gate of his city [like] a mongoose. I [im]paled his foremost men alive while making (the people of) his land watch. For forty-five days I set up my camp [aro]und his city and confined him (there) like a bird in a cage. I cut down his plantations, [...] (and) orchards, which were without number; I did not leave a single one (standing).

*Commentary.*[152] Recounting his thirteenth year of office (733 B.C.), Tiglath-pileser III boasts of his devastating blows against Raḫiānu (Rezin), the king of Damascus. Tiglath-pileser pursues Raḫiānu to "his city" and besieges Damascus for 45 days. TADMOR notes that line 11 (with its reference to "confined him there like a bird in a cage") implies that Tiglath-pileser blockaded Damascus but failed to capture the city. He would only succeed in capturing Damascus during his next campaign in 732 B.C. (cf. 2 Kings 16:9).[153] Among his recorded boasts against Raḫiānu, Tiglath-pileser emphasizes that he impaled Raḫiānu's "foremost men." Significantly, these impalements likely served as a grave embarrassment to his opponent since Raḫiānu's people are watching this gruesome spectacle while Raḫiānu is proven to be powerless to intervene.

**(165)** Summary Inscription 1 of Tiglath-pileser III [text 39, lines 8–11a]

[8] KUR.É-ᵐ*ši-la-a-ni a-na si-ḫir-ti-šú ki-ma ḫaṣ-bat-ti ú-daq-qi-iq* URU.*sa-ar-ra-ba-a-nu* [9] URU LUGAL-*ti-šú-nu* GAL-*a* GIM DU *a-bu-bi ú-ab-bit-ma* [*šal*]-*la-su áš-lu-la* ᵐᵈMUATI-*ú-šab-ši* LUGAL-*šú-nu* [10] *mé-eḫ-ret* KÁ.GAL URU-*šú a-na* GIŠ.*za-qi-pi ú-še-li-ma* ⟨*ú-šad-gi-la*⟩ KUR-*su* DAM-*su* DUMU.MEŠ-*šú* DUMU.MUNUS.MEŠ-*šú* NÍG.GA-*šu* [11] *ni-ṣir-ti*-⟨⟨*šú*⟩⟩ É.GAL-*šú áš-lu-la*

*Translation.* I smashed the land Bīt-Šilāni in its entirety like a pot. I destroyed the city Sarrabānu, its (text: "their") great royal city, (making it) like a *tell* after the Deluge and I [plun]dered it. I impaled Nabû-ušabši, their king, before the gate of his city ⟨while making⟩ (the people of) his land ⟨watch⟩. I carried off his wife, his sons, his daughters, his possessions, (and) the treasures of his palace.

---

[152] Text and translation from TADMOR and YAMADA, Royal Inscriptions, 59. Cf. edition and notes in TADMOR, Inscriptions of Tiglath-pileser, 78–81, Ann. 23; note Plates XX–XXII.

[153] Cf. TADMOR, Inscriptions of Tiglath-pileser, 79 (notes 11′–12′), who compares with the Annals of Sennacherib and other inscriptions of Tiglath-pileser III and Shalmaneser III.

*Commentary.*[154] This text, which once likely served as a pavement slab at Tiglath-pileser's palace at Kalḫu, would have been the first in a series of slabs summarizing his achievements. This early section concerns his conquest of Chaldea. Though it does not explicitly mention its date of composition, TADMOR suggests that it must have been written c.731–730 B.C.[155] The text provides evocative comparisons with shattered pots and even with the devastation of the great Flood. The remarkable feature for our purposes is Tiglath-pileser's boast that he impaled the king of Bīt-Šilāni before the gate of his royal city Sarrabānu. Certainly, the royal social status of opponents did not save them from such a fate, indeed the very status of king likely called for such harsh treatment by the Assyrians. Others are compelled to view the spectacle, thus cementing the finality of Tiglath-pileser's conquest and adding to the humiliation of Nabû-ušabši's death.

**(166)**  Sennacherib's Capture of Lachish (BM 124906)

*Illustration* (Fig. 4)

*Commentary.*[156] The Lachish Reliefs, housed in the British Museum, repre-

---

[154] Text and translation from TADMOR and YAMADA, Royal Inscriptions, 97. Cf. TADMOR, Inscriptions of Tiglath-pileser, 122–123 (listed as "Summ. 1"; note Plates XLII–XLIV).

[155] Cf. TADMOR and YAMADA, Royal Inscriptions, 95–96.

[156] Drawing by Karis Chapman. Photograph may be found in ANEP 131, No. 373. Drawing is included in GRESSMANN, Altorientalische Bilder, No. 141. Further photographs (by AVRAHAM HAY) and drawings (by JUDITH DEKEL) are included in DAVID USSISHKIN, The Conquest of Lachish by Sennacherib (Publications of the Institute of Archaeology 6; Tel

sent Sennacherib's own perspective on the siege and capture of the fortified Judean city of Lachish (cf. 2 Kings 18:13–14, 17; 2 Chron 32:9; Isa 36:1–2). Lachish lies approximately 27 miles (44 km) southwest of Jerusalem. Sennacherib reigned from 704–681 B.C. Carved into gypsum, these reliefs were excavated by AUSTEN HENRY LAYARD in the mid-nineteenth century from Sennacherib's palace at Kuyunjik (ancient Nineveh). They provide a central visual corpus for the study of Assyrian siege tactics. Beyond the visual reference to impalement (discussed here), the reliefs also represent Assyrian archers stretching out naked captives on the ground, which SEEVERS suggests may be prior to flaying off their skin (as is mentioned in other Assyrian annals).[157] This section of the relief portrays the Assyrian forces advancing on a tower. Four men atop the tower are firing arrows and throwing down firebrands. The siege engine has a lance protruding from it. Bowmen accompany the siege machine, and one man pours water to extinguish fire before the engine. Men and women are exiting the city with their possessions. Fig. 4 highlights a single scene: two soldiers are in the process of impaling three nude men on poles that pierce through their chest cavities.[158]

**(167)** Sennacherib Oriental Institute Prism $H_2$ [col. III, lines 8–17]

[8] *ak-rib-ma $^{am}$šakkanakê$^{pl}$ $^{am}$rubûte$^{pl}$ šá ḫi-iṭ-ṭu* [9] *ú-šab-šú-ú a-duk-ma i-na di-ma-a-ti* [10] *si-ḫir-ti ali a-lul pag-ri-šu-un mâre$^{pl}$ ali* [11] *e-piš an-ni ù ḳil-la-ti a-*

---

Aviv: Tel Aviv University, Institute of Archaeology, 1982), 75, 77, 82–83, 121. USSISHKIN compares the Sennacherib's Reliefs to the archaeological site of Lachish, and notes the overall accuracy of the portrayal in the Reliefs (see esp. ibid. 99–102 for this particular segment/slab).

[157] SEEVERS, Warfare, 239–240 (and Fig. 7.13). Photographs and drawings in USSISHKIN, Conquest of Lachish, 86–87 (who also interprets this as flaying alive, ibid. 109). Texts in Part 3 that mention such flayings include 'Annals A' (A.0.101.1) of Ashurnasirpal II [col. I, lines 89–94]; Cylinder B of Ashurbanipal (col. I, line 95 – col. II, line 6).

[158] USSISHKIN, Conquest of Lachish, 102 provides the following description: "At the bottom of the siege ramp in front of the gate, three prisoners, stripped naked, are impaled on stakes … All appear to be men, although a fan-shaped object above the head of the impaled prisoner at the right might perhaps be interpreted as strands of long hair tied together. The heads of the impaled prisoners are sagging forward, indicating that they are already dead. Two Assyrian spearmen with crested helmets are securing in the ground the stake on which the prisoner at the right has just been impaled. Although this cruel scene appears at the bottom of the siege ramp, it seems more logical to associate it with the events that transpire after the battle, when the captives and the deportees are forced to leave the city, rather than with the actual attack on the walls." USSISHKIN's observations are accurate, though one may wonder whether the impalements outside the city might well occur *during* a battle in order to motivate surrender of the city's occupants (as occurs in several literary passages from antiquity). In a similar fashion, the reliefs of Shalmaneser III and Tiglath-pileser III (both above) each represent impalements occurring during the active siege of a city. Still, we must admit that portrayed nearby on the same slab in the Lachish Reliefs are deportees being escorted into exile away from the city, an event that could well presage consequences after the battle.

*na šal-la-ti am-nu* [12] *si-it-tu-te-šu-nu la ba-bil ḫi-ṭi-ti* [13] *ù ḳul-lul-ti šá a-ra-an-šu-nu la ib-šú-ú* [14] *uš-šur-šu-un aḳbi* ᵐ*Pa-di-I šarra-šu-nu* [15] *ul-tu ki-rib* ᶜ*Ur-sa-li-im-mu ú-še-ṣa-am-ma* [16] *i-na* ʷ*kussi be-lu-ti eli-šu-un ú-še-šib-ma* [17] *man-da-at-tu be-lu-ti-ia ú-kin ṣi-ru-uš-šu*

*Translation.* [8] I drew near to Ekron and slew the governors and nobles [9] who had committed sin (that is, rebelled), and [10] hung their bodies on stakes around the city. The citizens [11] who sinned and treated (Assyria) lightly, I counted as spoil. [12] The rest of them, who were not guilty (carriers) of sin [13] and contempt, for whom there was no punishment,– [14] I spoke their pardon. Padi, their king, [15] I brought out of Jerusalem, [16] set him on the royal throne over them and [17] imposed upon him my kingly tribute.

*Commentary.*[159] This annalistic account portrays Sennacherib recording the events of his third campaign (col. II, line 37 – col. III, line 49). The campaign focuses on Syria (called "the Hittite-land" in ii.37) and the Philistine coastland. The nobles of Ekron had expelled Padi, the Assyrian vassal-king of Ekron, and sent him to captivity in Hezekiah's Jerusalem (ii.73–77). Even though the people of Ekron called upon Egyptian and Ethiopian support (ii.79–81), Sennacherib claims to have conquered them all by the aid of Assur (iii.1–17). Famously, he proceeds to attack the Judean fortified cities and besieges Jerusalem, coercing tribute from Hezekiah (iii.18–49; cf. 2 Kings 18–19; 2 Chron 32; Isa 36–37). In the passage above, the rebellious "governors and nobles" of Ekron are slain, and the Assyrian forces hang their bodies on stakes surrounding the city.

**(168)** Stele Inscription of Sennacherib concerning the Royal Road [ll. 23–26]

[23] *ma-ti-ma niše a-ši-bu-ut ali ša-a-šu ša bît-su* [24] *la-bi-ru i-naq-qa-ru-ma eš-šu i-ba-nu-u* [25] *ša uš-še bîti-šu a-na gir-ri šarri ir-ru-ba* [26] *ṣi-ir bîti-šu a-na ga-ši-ši il-la-lu-šu*

*Translation.* If ever (anyone of) the people who dwell in that city tears down his old house and builds a new one, and the foundation of his house encroaches upon the royal road, they shall hang him upon a stake (crucify him)[160] over his (own) house.

---

[159] Text and translation from DANIEL DAVID LUCKENBILL, The Annals of Sennacherib (Oriental Institute Publications 2; Chicago: University of Chicago Press, 1924), 32. Also see OPPENHEIMER's translation in ANET, 288.

[160] The parenthetic alternative translation "crucify him" is in LUCKENBILL's original translation.

*Commentary.*[161] A stele from Nineveh announces that Sennacherib ("the mighty king", "king of Assyria," and "king of the four regions of the world"), having conquered the whole earth through the favor of Assur and Ishtar, has enlarged Nineveh and made its market street wide enough for a royal road (52 cubits wide). In order to prevent anyone from narrowing the road, Sennacherib has ordered that two stelae be erected opposite one another and the above penalty be inscribed on them. The locale chosen for suspending any violator is at "his house," which would also be the place where the crime occurs (compare the location of the suspension here with the thief who "breaks-in" to a house and with the person who conspires to remove a slave mark – see above in the Code of Hammurabi §21 and §227). In the translation above, LUCKENBILL suggests this constitutes crucifixion, but his interpretation likely projects later terminology and procedures back onto this Assyrian law. However, it is notable that there is no indication in the law itself that the person would have been executed prior to being affixed to the stake.

**(169)** Esarhaddon "Tablet 2" K 2852 + K 9662 (obverse, col. II, lines 10–13)

[10] [...] *x-šú-nu-ma gul-gul-li-šú-nu ir-ṣi-pu di-ma-ti-iš* [11] [...]*-nu e-lu-lu-ma il-mu-u si-ḫi-ir-ti* URU-*šú-un* [12] [*ul-tu er*]-*ni-it-ti-ia ak-šu-du-ma am-ṣu-u mal* ŠÀ-*ia* [13] [...] *al-qam-ma* UGU URU.*up-pu-me áš-ta-kan uš-man-ni*

*Translation.* [...] ... them and they built towers of their skulls; they hung [th]eir [... on stakes] and completely surrounded their city (with them). [After] I achieved my [vi]ctory and did everything I pleased, I took [...] and set up my camp by the city Uppume.

*Commentary.*[162] In this tablet from Nineveh, Esarhaddon, who reigned 680–669 B.C., recounts (in the form of a letter to the god Assur) his expedition against the land of Šubria in 673 B.C. In these lines, he mentions the close of his siege of Uppume (see i.36 – ii.13). After entering the burning city, his guards set up the pile of skulls and begin suspending people around the city. The key text is fragmentary in the line 11, but it likely references suspension of bodies (as in other Assyrian texts).

---

[161] Text from JEAN-VINCENT SCHEIL, La stèle de la chaussée royale du Roi Sennachérib, Revue d'Assyriologie 40 (1914): 188–192, 191. Translation from LUCKENBILL, Records, 2:195 (§476). Compare SCHEIL's translation: "A l'avenir, des habitants de cette ville lorsque quelqu'un sa maison vieillie restaurera ou bâtira à neuf, – si les fondations de sa maison empiétaient sur la chaussée royale, au haut de sa proper maison à la potence on le pendra!"

[162] Text and translation from ERLE LEICHTY, ed., The Royal Inscriptions of Esarhaddon, King of Assyria (680–669 BC) (The Royal Inscriptions of the Neo-Assyrian Period 4; Winona Lake, Ind.: Eisenbrauns, 2011), 83.

**(170)** Rassam Cylinder of Ashurbanipal (col. I, line 134 – col. II, line 7)

[col. I] $^{134}$ *du-un-ku ù niše$^{meš}$ $^{alu}$sa-a-a $^{alu}$pi-in-di-di $^{alu}$si-'-nu* [col. II] $^1$ *ù si-it-ti alâni$^{meš}$ ma-la it-ti-šu-nu šak-nu ik-pu-du limuttu$^{tú}$* $^2$ *ṣiḫir u rabi ina $^{iṣu}$kakkê$^{meš}$ ú-šam-ki-tu e-du a-me-lum la e-zi-bu ina libbi$^{bi}$ $^{3amêlu}$pagrê $^{meš}$-šunu i-lu-lu ina $^{iṣu}$ga-ši-ši* $^4$ *maškê $^m[^{eš}]$-šunu iš-ḫ]u-ṭu ú-ḫal-li-pu dûr ali* $^5$ *šarrâni$^{meš}$ an-nu-ti ša limuttu$^{tu}$ iš-te-ni-'-u* $^6$ *a-na ummânât $^{mâtu}$aššur$^{ki}$ bal-ṭu-us-su-nu* $^7$ *a-na ninua$^{ki}$ a-di maḫ-ri-ia ú-bil-u-ni*

*Translation.* And the people of Sais, Pintiti, Si'nu and the rest of the cities, as many as had joined with them in plotting evil, they struck down with the sword, both great and small, — not a man among them escaped. Their corpses they hung on stakes, they stripped off their skins and covered the city wall(s) with them. These kings, who had planned evil against the armies of Assyria, they brought before me, alive, to Nineveh.

*Commentary.*[163] The Rassam Cylinder is dated between 644–636 B.C. It chronicles much of Ashurbanipal's reign (668–c.627 B.C.) and here speaks of events after his first campaign in Egypt. According to the Cylinder, this first campaign was against Tarkû, king of Egypt and Cush, who revolted against the Assyrian governors installed by Esarhaddon (Ashurbanipal's father). Ashurbanipal claims the assistance of the deities Assur, Bel, Nabû, and Ishtar. After Ashurbanipal's successful campaign, Tarkû was still able to rally some of Assyria's vassal cities to rebel again. The text quoted above records how Ashurbanipal's loyal officials crushed this rebellion and punished the perpetrators. The hyperbolic statement records the suspension of the corpses of the slain rebels with the additional flaying of corpses (and draping of their skins on the city walls).

**(171)** Cylinder B of Ashurbanipal (col. I, line 95 – col. II, line 6)

$^{95}$ *(âlu)sa-a-a (âlu)bi-in-ṭi-ṭi (âlu)sa-'-nu* $^{96}$ *ša ib-bal-ki-tu* $^{97}$ *it-ti (I)tar-qu-u iš-ku-nu pi-i-šu-un* $^{98}$ *âlâni (meš) ša-a-tu-nu ak-šu-ud* $^{99}$ *nišê (meš) a-šib lìb-bi-šu-nu a-ni-ir ina (iṣu)kakkê(meš)* $^1$ *(amêlu) pagrê(meš)-šu-nu ina (iṣu)ga-ši-ši a-lul* $^2$ *maškê(meš)-šu-nu áš-ḫu-uṭ dûr âli ú-ḫal-lip* $^3$ *(I)šarru-lu-dá-ri ša abu-u-a ina (mâtu)mu-ṣur* $^4$ *iš-ku-nu-uš a-na šarru-u-ti* $^5$ *ša limuttu(tu) iq-pu-du a-na mârê(meš) (mâtu)aš-šur(ki)* $^6$ *ina qa-ti aṣ-bat ú-ra-a a-na (mâtu)aš-šur(ki)*

---

[163] Transliterated text from STRECK, *Assurbanipal*, 2:12–14 (STRECK translates lines 3 and 4 as "Ihre Leichname hingen sie auf Stangen auf, zogen ihnen die Haut ab (und) bekleideten die Stadtmauer damit"; ibid. 15). English translation from LUCKENBILL, *Records*, 2:294–295 (§§773–774). Another translation can be found by A. LEO OPPENHEIM in ANET, 295.

*Translation.* [95] Sais, Binṭiṭi, Sa'nu, [96] which had revolted, [97] had made common cause (lit. set their mouth) with Taharka – [98] those cities I conquered, [99] the people dwelling in them I slaughtered with weapons. [1] Their corpses I hung on poles, [2] flayed, covered the wall of the city (therewith). [3] Šarrulûdâri, whom my father [4] had made king in Egypt, [5] who had plotted evil against the Assyrians, [6] I captured with (my) hands, I brought to Assyria.[164]

*Commentary.*[165] Cylinder B is dated to c. 649–648 B.C.[166] It provides an abbreviated account of many of the same events from Ashurbanipal's reign as are chronicled in the later Rassam Cylinder. Cylinder B likewise recalls the revolt of Ashurbanipal's Egyptian and Cushite vassals (Taharka is the king of Ethiopia/Cush) during the period of his first campaign against Egypt. It similarly records the suspension of the rebels on stakes, along with their flaying and the covering of the wall with their skins. Unfortunately the text in the original Cylinder B is somewhat fragmentary, making some of the important lines (notably those about suspension) less certain to earlier translators.[167] The fuller text above from Piepkorn represents his extensive study of several parallel "Edition B" traditions. Strikingly, this account appears in the first person ("I"), with Ashurbanipal claiming credit for the victory, whereas the parallel report in the Rassam Cylinder implies in the third person that Ashurbanipal's loyal officials were the ones to suppress the revolt and bring the captives back to him.

---

[164] The translation of LUCKENBILL, Records, 2:324, though based on lesser epigraphic evidence than PIEPKORN's, can still be usefully compared with his translation of the passage from the Rassam Cylinder (quoted in the preceding passage): "[The people] of Sais, Bintiti, Sa'nu, who had revolted, who had made common cause with [Tarkû, king of Ethiopia], I captured. [Great and small] I cut down with the sword. [Their corpses] I hung on stakes. [I tore off their skins] and covered the [wall] of the city (with them). [Those kings whom] I had [set up] in Egypt as rulers, [who planned evil against] the Assyrians, [I seized and brought] to Assyria."

[165] Transcription and translation (and line numbers) from ARTHUR CARL PIEPKORN, Historical Prism Inscriptions of Ashurbanipal. Vol. 1: Editions E, B$_{1-5}$, D and K (Assyriological Studies 5; Chicago: University of Chicago Press, 1933), 34–37. A transcription, transliteration, and translation can also be found in GEORGE SMITH, History of Assurbanipal, Translated from the Cuneiform Inscriptions (London: Williams and Norgate, 1871), 32–33. Translation also in LUCKENBILL, Records, 2:324 (§844). SMITH and LUCKENBILL both cite the text as column 2, lines 1–11. Cuneiform text can be found (partially rendered) in HENRY C. RAWLINSON, The Cuneiform Inscriptions of Western Asia (5 vols.; 1861–1884), Vol. 3, plate 29 (in parallel with texts from Cylinder E).

[166] On this date see PIEPKORN, Prism Inscriptions I, 19–20, and compare LUCKENBILL, Records, 2:323.

[167] Thus SMITH represents the plight of their corpses as: "[their corpses in] the dust I threw down", and this appears to be mostly due to his reconstruction of line 1 and his rendering of the crucial *(iṣu)ga-ši-ši a-lul* in that line; cf. SMITH, History of Assurbanipal, 33. However, note the similar wording in the next passage from the Rassam Cylinder.

**(172)** Rassam Cylinder of Ashurbanipal (col. IX, lines 122–128)

[122] *nišê^{meš} ^{alu}ak-ku-u la kan-šú-ti a-nir* [123] *^{amêlu}pagrê^{meš}-šu-nu ina ^{išu}ga-ši-ši a-lul* [124] *si-ḫir-ti ali ú-šal- mi* [125] *si-it-tu-ti-šu-nu al-ḳa-a a-na ^{mâtu-ilu} aššur^{ki}* [126] *a-na ki-ṣir ak-ṣur-ma* [127] *eli ummânâte-ia ma-'-da-a-ti* [128] *ša ^{ilu}aššur i-ḳí-ša ú-rad-di*

*Translation.* The insubmissive people of Akkû (Acre) I slaughtered. Their corpses I hung on stakes, surrounding the city (with them). Those who were left I carried away to Assyria, joined them to (my) military organization, adding them to the many troops which Assur had given me.

*Commentary.*[168] Another event in Ashurbanipal's reign is recorded on the Rassam Cylinder. Here, he is campaigning along the Levantine coast. Since Ushu had failed to continue paying tribute to Assyria, Ashurbanipal conquers this coastal city that lay near Tyre – carrying away its inhabitants and its gods (lines 115–121). Then the text above continues the narrative as Ashurbanipal heads south to Akkû. The text vividly depicts a city encircled with the suspended corpses of its populace while others are carried away and impressed into Assyrian military service. Another fragmentary historical text from this era (K 2802) contains wording similar to line 123 above.[169]

## 3.2.6 Assyria in Greek and Roman Sources

Sources from later eras occasionally narrate acts of crucifixion performed by the Assyrian kings. However, these sources exhibit confused memories of the long-extinct Neo-Assyrian Empire, so we should not assume they provide reliable historical evidence that Assyrians actually engaged in crucifixion in the same way it was later practiced in the Roman Empire. These Greek and Roman sources may, however, be informed by a broad ancient memory that the Assyrians did suspend (especially impale) people in time of war. More importantly, the following sources display limited evidence that the Greeks

---

[168] Text from STRECK, Assurbanipal, 2:80–82. Translation from LUCKENBILL, Records, 2:319 (§830). The crucial lines 123–124 are translated by STRECK as "[123]Ihre Leichname hing ich auf Stangen auf [124](und) ließ sie die Stadt im Kreise umgeben" (ibid. 2:83). Another translation can be found by A. LEO OPPENHEIM in ANET, 300.

[169] See STRECK, Assurbanipal, 2:196–197. K 2802 col. II, line 1 reads: *ina ^{išu}ga-ši-ši ^{amêlu}pagrê-šu-nu a-lul*. Note, aside from change in word order, the pertinent clause is essentially the same. STRECK, ibid. 197 translates this: "Auf Stangen hing ich ihre Leichname auf". Also compare the highly fragmentary text of K 2846 line 25 in STRECK, ibid. 2:208: *[ina ga-ši-ši] i-lu-ul-ma ala ú-šal-mi* (with translation p. 209: "hing er [auf Stangen] auf und ließ die Stadt (damit) umgeben").

and Romans later *believed* crucifixion had been practiced by the barbarous Assyrians.

**(173)** Diodorus Siculus, *Bibliotheca Historica* 2.1.9–10 [Ctesias, FGH 3c 688 Frag. 1b 2.1.9–10]

ἀεὶ δὲ μᾶλλον αὐξόμενος ἐστράτευσεν εἰς τὴν Μηδίαν. [10] ὁ δὲ ταύτης βασιλεὺς Φάρνος παραταξάμενος ἀξιολόγῳ δυνάμει καὶ λειφθείς, τῶν τε στρατιωτῶν τοὺς πλείους ἀπέβαλε καὶ αὐτὸς μετὰ τέκνων ἑπτὰ καὶ γυναικὸς αἰχμάλωτος ληφθεὶς ἀνεσταυρώθη.

*Translation.* And, as he [i.e., Ninus] was ever growing stronger, he waged war against Media. [10] The king of this land, Pharnos, having drawn up in battle with a remarkable force and having been defeated, both lost most of his soldiers, and he himself was taken as a captive, along with seven of his children and his wife, and was crucified.

*Commentary.*[170] Diodorus of Sicily, writing in the mid-first century B.C., recounts world history up until his day. Ninus, called "king of the Assyrians" (e.g., 2.1.4,7), brought Babylon and Armenia under his authority (2.1.7–9) and here turns to battle Media. Later, he is said to have conquered Egypt, the Levant, and much of Asia Minor (2.2.1–4); Ninus followed that by founding the city of Nineveh, which is named after him (2.3.2–4). Diodorus claims the authority of the fifth-century B.C. historian Ctesias of Cnidus for this material (2.2.2), and thus this passage is typically attributed as a fragment from Ctesias' *Persica.*[171] Much of this account appears legendary, and the acts of different Assyrian kings may have been combined to create this "history".

For present purposes, note that Pharnos is said to have been "crucified" (ἀνεσταυρώθη) by this Assyrian king. The text in Ctesias/Diodorus does not mention any form of execution prior to this suspension, likely implying that it

---

[170] Text: CURTIUS THEODOR FISCHER and FRIEDRICH VOGEL, Diodori bibliotheca historica (6 vols.; Bibliothea Scriptorum Graecorum et Romanorum Teubneriana; Leipzig: Teubner, 1888–1906), 1:171; compared with CHARLES HENRY OLDFATHER, CHARLES L. SHERMAN, RUSSEL M. GEER, and FRANCIS R. WALTON, Diodorus of Sicily (12 vols.; LCL; Cambridge: Harvard University Press, 1933–1967), 1:352.

[171] This text is attributed to Ctesias in J. JACOBY, FGH 3c 688 Frag. 1b. Cf. DOMINIQUE LENFANT, Ctésias de Cnide. La Perse, l'Inde, autres fragments (Collection des universités de France 435; Paris: Belles lettres, 2004), 24 (French translation and Greek text, which is identical to the Diodorus text reproduced above except for capitalization). Text and English translation in JAN P. STRONK, Ctesias's Persian History. Vol. 1: Introduction, Text, Translation (Reihe Geschichte 2; Düsseldorf: Wellem, 2010), 204–205 (who translates ἀνεσταυρώθη as "he was personally impaled as well"). English translation in LLOYD LLEWELLYN-JONES and JAMES ROBSON, Ctesias' History of Persia: Tales of the Orient (Routledge Classical Translations; London / New York: Routledge, 2010), 114 (who translate ἀνεσταυρώθη as "was crucified"). Texts in these editions are all identical to the Diodorus text cited above.

was the cause of Pharnos' death. Ctesias himself (insofar as we can recreate his *Persica*) can use ἀνασταυρόω in reference to impalements.[172] Diodorus frequently alleges the use of this penalty (ἀνασταυρόω) by other barbarian races (see below repeatedly in 3.3). Still, the precise form this punishment took is more assumed than described. As this text was passed on by Diodorus in the first century B.C. (and as Diodorus' text continued to be read in subsequent centuries), this word usage would have reminded his readers of the kinds of crucifixion and suspension penalties that were practiced in their day.

**(174)** Lucian, *Juppiter confutatus* 16

καὶ πάλιν Σωκράτης μὲν παρεδόθη τοῖς ἕνδεκα, Μέλητος δὲ οὐ παρεδόθη, καὶ Σαρδανάπαλλος μὲν ἐβασίλευε θῆλυς ὤν, Γώχης δὲ ἀνὴρ ἐνάρετος ἀνεσκολοπίσθη πρὸς αὐτοῦ, διότι μὴ ἠρέσκετο τοῖς γιγνομένοις ...

*Translation.* And again, Socrates was handed over to the Eleven, but Meletus was not handed over. And Sardanapallus ruled even though he was effeminate, but Goches, a virtuous man, was crucified before him, because he was not pleased by the things that occurred.

*Commentary.*[173] Lucian's sarcastic voice turns against Zeus in this dialogue as Cyniscus argues that righteous people frequently suffer in this world, while unworthy persons often profit. In the brief sample quoted above, Cyniscus presents two paired examples of such injustices. The great philosopher Socrates ultimately is condemned to commit suicide, while his own prosecutor (Meletus) suffers nothing, even though Meletus' arguments for Socrates' guilt had been proven to be false by Socrates himself (cf. Plato, *Apol.* 24b–28b).[174]

---

[172] SAMUELSSON's treatment of Ctesias does rightly suggest that "impalement" may have been what Ctesias was envisioning, especially in Ctesias, FGH 3c 688 Frag. 14.39 (in Photius). Cf. SAMUELSSON, Crucifixion, 61–62. Further, ἀνασταυρόω in Ctesias may well be post-mortem (depending on how serious the flaying is of the victim) in Ctesias, FGH 3c 688 Frag. 9.6 (in Photius); Frag. 16.66 (in Photius); and Frag. 26.17.7 (Plutarch, *Art.* 17.5, if the specifics are properly attributed to Ctesias; see below). Commentators on Ctesias also suggest parallels to the Assyrian reliefs that depict impalement (namely those by Sennacherib and others discussed above): cf. LENFANT, Ctésias de Cnide, 24 n. 91, with translation "avant d'être empalé"; compare with JANICK AUBERGER, Ctésias. Histoires de l'Orient (Roue à Livres 11; Paris: Les Belles Lettres, 1991), 30, 143 n. 6, with translation "il mourut sur la croix" (the note suggests either impalement or crucifixion are acceptable translations).

[173] Text: MACLEOD, Luciani Opera, 1:211. Also in HARMON, Lucian, 2:80. The text from Γώχης to ἠρέσκετο is represented in MACLEOD's β family, while the γ family has instead: Περσῶν δὲ τοσοῦτοι καλοί τε κἀγαθοὶ ἄνδρες ἀνεσκολοπίζοντο πρὸς αὐτοῦ ὅτι μὴ ἠρέσκοντο τοῖς γιγνομένοις ("but such noble and good Persian men were crucified by him because they were not pleased by the things that had occurred").

[174] According to Plato, Socrates actually charges Meletus with being "guilty" (ἀδικεῖν) of treating a serious issue with extreme haste (*Apology* 24c). Thus the guilty one goes free, and Socrates is compelled to take his own life.

The second pair concerns Sardanapallus and Goches. In the Greek histories of Diodorus Siculus (and Ctesias before him), Sardanapallus was the last king of Assyria.[175] According to Diodorus (and Ctesias), his famed effeminacy included dressing up and speaking as a woman and also engaging in transgendered sexual acts.[176] Lucian contrasts Sardanapallus' effeminacy (θῆλυς ὤν) with Goches manly *virtus* (ἀνὴρ ἐνάρετος).

Goches is apparently otherwise unknown in our extant records, though the above text would imply that Sardanapallus had him crucified (ἀνεσκολοπίσ-θη).[177] Lucian's use of ἀνεσκολοπίσθη elsewhere, especially concerning Prometheus earlier in this same dialogue (see *Iupp. conf.* 8; cf. *Prom.* 2, 7), would strongly imply that Lucian intends this term here to designate crucifixion, despite the lack of clear description in this passage as to how the execution was performed. There is evident confusion in this later Greek tradition over Sardanapallus, whose description does not clearly match any known Assyrian king. This makes the historical reliability of the above crucifixion account also significantly suspect. Nevertheless, this text does testify to later Graeco-Roman perceptions of the Assyrian kings as crucifiers.

## 3.2.7 Israel

The Hebrew Bible records instances in which the Israelites employed bodily suspension (typically *post mortem*). Amidst the laws of Deuteronomy is an intriguing (if complicated) text that limits criminal suspensions to only the daylight hours of the execution day. Two passages mention that Joshua suspended conquered kings, and in both cases, Joshua is said to have followed the stipulations of Deuteronomy 21 (despite the military, rather than penal,

---

[175] See Diodorus Siculus, *Bib. hist.* 2.23.1; 2.27.2; 2.28.8. Each of these passages is thought to originate in Ctesias; see JACOBY, FGH 3c 688 Frag. 1b passim; LENFANT, Ctésias de Cnide, 54–55, 62, 64; STRONK, Ctesias's Persian History, 236–239, 244–247, 248–249. Also note the brief reference to Sardanapallus' wealth in Herodotus, *Hist.* 2.150.3.

[176] Diodorus Siculus, *Bib. hist.* 2.23.1–2 (in a section attributed to Ctesias' influence, cf. Ctesias, FGH 3c 688 Frag. 1b 23.1–2); so Diodorus states: "he lived the life of a woman" (βίον ἔζησε γυναικός in 23.2.1).

[177] HARMON, Lucian, 2:81 asserts that Goches is otherwise unknown. Indeed, a Thesaurus Linguae Graecae search discovered only two mentions of this name in the TLG corpus (here and in the scholia on Lucian). On the other hand, Sardanapallus became a familiar example among the philosophers of intemperance (e.g., Aristotle, *Eth. Nic.* 1095b; *Pol.* 1312a; Dio Chrysostom, *Or.* 1.3 [*Peri Basileias A*]; 62.5; Epictetus, *Diatr.* 3.22.30 [On the Cynic Calling]; Philo, *Spec. Leg.* 4.122) as well as the historians (e.g., Polybius, *Hist.* 8.10.3; 36.15.6). Obviously, Socrates and Meletus were also famous. Thus it is likely that Lucian here is drawing on relatively well-known contrasting pairs for the sake of his argument (even if our own contemporary knowledge of Goches is severely limited).

context of his actions). The followers of King David also suspended the bodies (or at least members of the bodies) of military foes.

**(175)** Deuteronomy 21:22–23

וְכִי־יִהְיֶה בְאִישׁ חֵטְא מִשְׁפַּט־מָוֶת וְהוּמָת וְתָלִיתָ אֹתוֹ עַל־עֵץ: [23] לֹא־תָלִין נִבְלָתוֹ עַל־הָעֵץ כִּי־קָבוֹר
תִּקְבְּרֶנּוּ בַּיּוֹם הַהוּא כִּי־קִלְלַת אֱלֹהִים תָּלוּי וְלֹא תְטַמֵּא אֶת־אַדְמָתְךָ אֲשֶׁר יְהוָה אֱלֹהֶיךָ נֹתֵן לְךָ נַחֲלָה:

*Translation.* [22]And when there is in a man a sin bearing a judgment of death, and he is executed, and you hang him on a tree, [23] his corpse shall not spend the night on the tree, but you shall surely bury him in that day, for a curse of God is the one who is hung, and you shall not defile your land, which the Lord your God gives to you as an inheritance.

*Commentary.* This OT legal text assumes that at least some capital offenses should lead to a short *post mortem* suspension. This suspension is referred to as being "hung on [the] tree" – terminology used exclusively in the Hebrew Bible for penal human bodily suspension (cf. Gen 40:19; Josh 8:29; 10:26; Esth 2:23; 5:14; 6:4; 7:9–10; 8:7; 9:13, 25). The central point of this law is actually to promote burial and to limit the duration of the suspension to the day of execution. The rationale that undergirds this burial mandate concerns the "curse of God" and the avoidance of defiling the land.

This text unfortunately does not: define which offenses merit such a punishment, specify the precise means of execution, clarify how precisely "one who is hung" is a "curse of God", or explain how the land would be defiled should this law not be heeded. Each of these issues has thus been much debated among commentators and translators, both ancient and modern.[178]

The order of verbs וְהוּמָת ("and he is executed") followed by וְתָלִיתָ ("and you hang [him]") would likely imply that the criminal has been put to death before being hung (as also found in *Sifre Dev.* 221; *b. Sanh.* 46b). However, some ancient readers appear to have assumed that the suspension was actually the means of execution (e.g., 11QTemple LXIV, 6–13; and in the Peshiṭta). Indeed, a few Second Temple Jewish sources explicitly associate this passage with crucifixion (Philo, *Spec. Leg.* 3.151–152; cf. Josephus, *B. J.* 4.317; for these see 3.5.1 and 3.5.4 below).

The genitive construct "curse of God" could be taken objectively or subjectively – in other words, "curse of God" could either imply that the criminal had in some way "cursed God" (e.g., through blasphemy) or that the person had been "cursed by God." Both options are evidenced in early Jewish interpretation.[179] Modern commentators often fail to mention ANE parallels to

---

[178] Cf. CHAPMAN, *Crucifixion*, 117–149.

[179] The person is deemed "cursed by God" (subjective genitive) in the Septuagint and *Targum Neofiti* (as well as in the Old Latin and Vulgate). The objective genitive (with its

such a penal suspension, and when they do so, they commonly only reference a limited range of evidence.[180] This law is best seen in the context of the broad range of suspension procedures employed by multiple cultures in antiquity.

**(176)** Joshua 8:29

וְאֶת־מֶלֶךְ הָעַי תָּלָה עַל־הָעֵץ עַד־עֵת הָעָרֶב וּכְבוֹא הַשֶּׁמֶשׁ צִוָּה יְהוֹשֻׁעַ וַיֹּרִידוּ אֶת־נִבְלָתוֹ מִן־הָעֵץ וַיַּשְׁלִיכוּ אוֹתָהּ אֶל־פֶּתַח שַׁעַר הָעִיר וַיָּקִימוּ עָלָיו גַּל־אֲבָנִים גָּדוֹל עַד הַיּוֹם הַזֶּה:

*Translation.* But he hung the king of Ai on the tree until the evening time; and, as the sun was setting, Joshua commanded, and they took down his corpse from the tree. And they flung it into the opening of the gate of the city. And they erected over him a great heap of stones, [which stands] until this day.

*Commentary.* This chapter of Joshua records the Israelite battle against the king and town of Ai. Joshua's activities are situated in the Late Bronze Age, with the precise date being disputed. He craftily convinces the men of Ai to pursue the apparently retreating Israelite forces, while the remaining Israelite army ambushes the vacated town.[181] The king is taken alive (Josh 8:23), the city destroyed (8:28), and thousands are slain and devoted to the ban (8:25). The Hebrew "hung on the tree" again links to other bodily suspension passages throughout the Hebrew Bible (see No. 175 on Deut 21:22–23). The narrator may have considered the suspension of a city's conquered king to be a standard military procedure since a similar action is also reported in Josh

---

notion of blasphemy) is clearly found in Symmachus' Greek translation, in the Peshiṭta, in Josephus, *A. J.* 4.202, and in several rabbinic texts. An alternative objective genitive interpretation involves the derision of the suspended person (created in the image of God), which in turn brings derision on God's name (see the Rabbi Meir traditions in *m. Sanh.* 6:5; *t. Sanh.* 9:7; *b. Sanh.* 46b).

[180] I could find no reference to extra-biblical examples of suspension in the commentaries by S. R. DRIVER, J. G. MCCONVILLE, E. H. MERRILL, P. D. MILLER, and G. E. WRIGHT. JACK R. LUNDBOM, Deuteronomy: A Commentary (Grand Rapids: Eerdmans, 2013), 609, does note Hammurabi's Code and a few biblical parallels. JEFFREY H. TIGAY, Deuteronomy (Philadelphia: Jewish Publication Society, 1996), 383 n. 61 references Hammurabi and the Middle Assyrian Laws (with the unfortunate statement these are "the only certain cases of impaling in Mesopotamian law"). DUANE L. CHRISTENSEN, Deuteronomy (WBC 6b; Nashville: Nelson, 1991–2002), 2:489 represents the fullest range of such ANE examples (though still limited to Mesopotamian and Graeco-Roman examples and broadened to include texts that simply refer to a refusal of burial). The "background commentaries" (see bibliography under J. WALTON) provide a quite limited array of (entirely Mesopotamian-based) evidence.

[181] Locating the city of Ai has become a famous conundrum in Levantine archaeology, with some suggesting it may actually have been a relatively small town that moved locations in antiquity. The size of the town of Ai appears to have been smaller than Gibeon (Josh 10:2), and the population is initially described as "few" (מעט; 7:3). Still, the narrator also recollects the initial attack of the Israelites was thwarted by the people of Ai, and the number of non-Israelites slain in this encounter is later described as many thousand (8:25).

10:26–27 (see below).[182] This suspension of the conquered king is reminiscent of other ANE conquest accounts (as illustrated above). What distinguishes this text from other ANE reports is the explicit mention of the king being taken down from the tree before sunset. This appears to comply with the commandment in Deut 21:22–23, even though the Deuteronomy text speaks to capital punishment rather than military conquest. Still, there is no great attempt to honor the body, which the Israelites merely "flung" (וישליכו) into the city gate.[183] Burial is produced by a heap of stones rather than any other formal honorific Bronze Age burial (note also Josh 7:26). The burial here at the gate of the city reminds us that suspensions frequently occur at the gates of cities in Assyrian annals and reliefs (and even in Babylonian law codes). As with regard to other biblical texts above, the commentators often do not cite ANE parallels, and where they do, they tend to focus on a limited array of Assyrian examples (easily accessible in ANET and ANEP).[184] NILI WAZANA has recently argued that by penning a reference to Joshua's burial of the king, the Deuteronomic author of Joshua reacted to the experience of Judah as it suffered under the Assyrian war machine (with its vicious custom of impaling bodies), thus calling for a reassessment of common Assyrian practices and offering a humane alternative to the Assyrian claim to have control over life and death (an alternative that speaks to the sanctity of the human body made in God's image).[185] This intriguing proposal suffers from a lack of awareness of the widespread nature of bodily suspension in the ANE (as evidenced throughout this section 3.2), thus skewing the biblical parallel solely in favor of Assyrian practices. Rather, the text of Joshua (like Deuteronomy before it), with its emphasis on burial within the day, stands in stark contrast to the widespread use of suspension throughout antiquity as a means of long-term public exposure of the body.

---

[182] Also note the curious mention in Josh 10:1 of how "…as he did to Jericho and its king, thus he did to Ai and its king." Though the king of Ai is executed and hung up (8:29), the demise of the king of Jericho is not explicitly depicted earlier in the text (cf. 6:2, 21).

[183] LXX reads ἔρριψαν αὐτὸν εἰς τὸν βόθρον ("they cast him into the trench").

[184] There appears to be no reference to extra-biblical parallels in the commentaries by T. C. BUTLER, R. D. NELSON, P. PITKÄNEN or M. H. WOUDSTRA. DAVID M. HOWARD, Joshua (NAC 5; Nashville: Broadman & Holman, 1998) references YOUNGER, Ancient Conquest Accounts. Limited evidence (from Sennacherib and Tiglath-pileser III) is also noted in WALTON, ed., Zondervan Illustrated Bible Backgrounds Commentary, 2:38.

[185] WAZANA, Impaled Body, 92–96. For parallel evidence, WAZANA cites only annals from Ashurnasirpal II, Tiglath-pileser III, and Sennacherib (along with his Lachish Reliefs).

**(177)** Joshua 10:26–27

וַיֵּהִי 27 :וַיַּכֵּם יְהוֹשֻׁעַ אַחֲרֵי־כֵן וַיְמִיתֵם וַיִּתְלֵם עַל חֲמִשָּׁה עֵצִים וַיִּהְיוּ תְּלוּיִם עַל־הָעֵצִים עַד־הָעָרֶב:
לְעֵת בּוֹא הַשֶּׁמֶשׁ צִוָּה יְהוֹשֻׁעַ וַיֹּרִידוּם מֵעַל הָעֵצִים וַיַּשְׁלִכֻם אֶל־הַמְּעָרָה אֲשֶׁר נֶחְבְּאוּ־שָׁם וַיָּשִׂמוּ
אֲבָנִים גְּדֹלוֹת עַל־פִּי הַמְּעָרָה עַד־עֶצֶם הַיּוֹם הַזֶּה:

*Translation.* And Joshua struck them afterwards, and he put them to death,[186] and he hung them on five trees; and they were hanging on the trees until the evening. [27] And it happened at the time the sun was setting, Joshua commanded and they took them down from upon the trees. And they flung them into the cave where they [i.e., the kings] had hid themselves. And they placed great stones over the mouth of the cave, [which remain] until this selfsame day.

*Commentary.* The "five kings" of the Amorite cities of Jerusalem, Hebron, Jarmuth, Lachish, and Eglon (Josh 10:3, 5–6) are executed and hung up. They had attacked Gibeon because of their fear of Israel and its alliance with Gibeon, yet Joshua honored the alliance and used the attack as an opportunity to battle these kings. Military tactics and miraculous intervention combined to rout the enemy (10:8–21). The kings hid themselves in a cave at Makkedah, which Joshua sealed. He then later brought the kings out alive, and the Israelites put their feet on the kings' necks as a sign of victory (10:24–25). Then they executed all five kings and hung them up.[187] As in 8:29, these kings are apparently executed prior to being hung up – note the sequence of verbs in 10:26: ויכם ("struck"), followed by וימיתם ("he put them to death"), followed by ויתלם ("and he hung them"). Each receives his own "tree" (עץ, likely an upright pole) for his suspension (10:26).[188] And, as in 8:29, each is taken down before sunset and given a humble burial (10:27) in compliance with Deut 21:22–23.

Intriguingly, later Jewish tradition rarely expounds on Joshua's suspension of his opponents; Josephus, in particular, downplays these episodes with the consequence that he does not mention at all that this Jewish hero (Joshua) hung his victims aloft (as was commonly done by the Romans in Josephus' day).[189] This appears to be an intentional omission.

---

[186] LXX abridges ויכם ... וימיתם: καὶ ἀπέκτεινεν αὐτοὺς Ἰησοῦς ("and Joshua killed them").

[187] YOUNGER, *Ancient Conquest Accounts*, 223, 317 n.88 notes that this feature of suspending foreign leaders corresponds well with Assyrian and Egyptian practices.

[188] The upright nature of the pole is indicated not merely by the word עץ but also by the fact that the kings are "hung on" these poles and then later "taken down" (ויורידום) from them.

[189] Cf. CHAPMAN, *Crucifixion*, 152.

**(178)**  2 Samuel 4:9–12

וַיַּעַן דָּוִד אֶת־רֵכָב וְאֶת־בַּעֲנָה אָחִיו בְּנֵי רִמּוֹן הַבְּאֵרֹתִי וַיֹּאמֶר לָהֶם חַי־יְהוָה אֲשֶׁר־פָּדָה אֶת־נַפְשִׁי
מִכָּל־צָרָה: <sup>10</sup> כִּי הַמַּגִּיד לִי לֵאמֹר הִנֵּה־מֵת שָׁאוּל וְהוּא־הָיָה כִמְבַשֵּׂר בְּעֵינָיו וָאֹחֲזָה בוֹ וָאֶהְרְגֵהוּ
בְּצִקְלָג אֲשֶׁר לְתִתִּי־לוֹ בְּשֹׂרָה: <sup>11</sup> אַף כִּי־אֲנָשִׁים רְשָׁעִים הָרְגוּ אֶת־אִישׁ־צַדִּיק בְּבֵיתוֹ עַל־מִשְׁכָּבוֹ
וְעַתָּה הֲלוֹא אֲבַקֵּשׁ אֶת־דָּמוֹ מִיֶּדְכֶם וּבִעַרְתִּי אֶתְכֶם מִן־הָאָרֶץ: <sup>12</sup> וַיְצַו דָּוִד אֶת־הַנְּעָרִים וַיַּהַרְגוּם
וַיְקַצְּצוּ אֶת־יְדֵיהֶם וְאֶת־רַגְלֵיהֶם וַיִּתְלוּ עַל־הַבְּרֵכָה בְּחֶבְרוֹן וְאֵת רֹאשׁ אִישׁ־בֹּשֶׁת לָקָחוּ וַיִּקְבְּרוּ
בְקֶבֶר־אַבְנֵר בְּחֶבְרוֹן:

*Translation.* But David answered Rechab and Baanah his brother, the sons of
Rimmon the Beerothite, and he said to them, "As the Lord lives, who redeemed
my life from every distress, <sup>10</sup> when someone declared to me, 'Behold, Saul is
dead', he was as one bringing good news in his own eyes. But I seized him
and slew him in Ziklag, which [response] I gave him for his good news.
<sup>11</sup> Indeed when wicked men have slain a man of righteousness in his house on
his bed, shall I not now seek his blood from your hand? And I shall purge you
from the earth." <sup>12</sup> And David commanded his young men, and they slew them
and cut off their hands and their feet, and they hung them beside the pool at
Hebron. But the head of Ish-bosheth they took and buried in the tomb of
Abner at Hebron.

*Commentary.* The people of Beeroth were counted among the tribe of Benjamin, which was Saul's tribe. After the death of Saul (1 Sam. 31:6), Abner, the
commander of the army, made Ish-bosheth son of Saul the king over Israel
(2 Sam 2:8–10). Ish-bosheth and David thus became opposing kings of Israel
and Judah (2 Sam 2:10–11; 3:1). Abner switched sides and ultimately was
killed, much to Ish-bosheth's dismay. Rechab and Baanah took advantage of
their standing as captains in order to enter Ish-bosheth's house during his mid-
day nap and kill him.[190] They beheaded his corpse and brought the head to
David, expecting to be rewarded for assassinating David's foe (2 Sam 4:8).[191]
In this passage, before pronouncing judgment upon Rechab and Baanah, David
recaps his earlier verdict against the Amalekite who had claimed responsibility for having mercifully killed the dying Saul – David had him slain for killing "the Lord's anointed" (2 Sam 1:2–16).

David likely viewed Ish-bosheth as Saul's royal heir and understood his
beheading as a horrendous act. Thus David's response here is even stronger
than to the man who claimed to have killed Saul. David deems Rechab and
Baanah to be "wicked men" (4:11), and he vows to purge them from the earth.
The cutting off of hands and feet disfigures the body and may well remove the

---

[190] The MT text is difficult to comprehend in 2 Sam 4:6–7, since the brothers appear to
enter twice in order to kill Ish-bosheth. The LXX has additional complexities.

[191] Note how this beheading echoes the demise of Saul himself, whose corpse is beheaded
by Philistines in 1 Sam 31:9 (see below).

body parts (especially the hands) that were most guilty for having stabbed Ish-bosheth. Such disfigurements are common in ANE law codes and historical documents (cf. Fig. 2 from the Balawat Gates of Shalmaneser III; and below on Xenophon, *Anabasis* 3.1.17; Ctesias, *Persica*, FGH 3c 688, Frag. 16.66). After executing the men, David had their bodies suspended, without mention of burial. The author appears to favor David's righteous stance in opposing wickedness, even if David may well have exceeded the parameters of the OT laws of execution (both by disfiguring the bodies and likely by leaving them unburied).

## *3.2.8 Philistia*

Some texts in the Hebrew Bible accuse the Philistines of engaging in *post mortem* suspension against Hebrew militants. Given the widespread use of suspension in the ANE, especially in relatively nearby Mari and Ugarit, these events are certainly plausible, even if they are only evidenced in the literature of their opponents.

**(179)**  1 Samuel 31:8–13; 2 Samuel 21:12

1 Samuel 31:8 וַיְהִי מִמָּחֳרָת וַיָּבֹאוּ פְלִשְׁתִּים לְפַשֵּׁט אֶת־הַחֲלָלִים וַיִּמְצְאוּ אֶת־שָׁאוּל וְאֶת־שְׁלֹשֶׁת בָּנָיו נֹפְלִים בְּהַר הַגִּלְבֹּעַ: 9 וַיִּכְרְתוּ אֶת־רֹאשׁוֹ וַיַּפְשִׁיטוּ אֶת־כֵּלָיו וַיְשַׁלְּחוּ בְאֶרֶץ־פְּלִשְׁתִּים סָבִיב לְבַשֵּׂר בֵּית עֲצַבֵּיהֶם וְאֶת־הָעָם: 10 וַיָּשִׂמוּ אֶת־כֵּלָיו בֵּית עַשְׁתָּרוֹת וְאֶת־גְּוִיָּתוֹ תָּקְעוּ בְּחוֹמַת בֵּית שָׁן: 11 וַיִּשְׁמְעוּ אֵלָיו יֹשְׁבֵי יָבֵישׁ גִּלְעָד אֵת אֲשֶׁר־עָשׂוּ פְלִשְׁתִּים לְשָׁאוּל: 12 וַיָּקוּמוּ כָּל־אִישׁ חַיִל וַיֵּלְכוּ כָל־הַלַּיְלָה וַיִּקְחוּ אֶת־גְּוִיַּת שָׁאוּל וְאֵת גְּוִיֹּת בָּנָיו מֵחוֹמַת בֵּית שָׁן וַיָּבֹאוּ יָבֵשָׁה וַיִּשְׂרְפוּ אֹתָם שָׁם: 13 וַיִּקְחוּ אֶת־עַצְמֹתֵיהֶם וַיִּקְבְּרוּ תַחַת־הָאֶשֶׁל בְּיָבֵשָׁה וַיָּצֻמוּ שִׁבְעַת יָמִים:

2 Samuel 21:12 וַיֵּלֶךְ דָּוִד וַיִּקַּח אֶת־עַצְמוֹת שָׁאוּל וְאֶת־עַצְמוֹת יְהוֹנָתָן בְּנוֹ מֵאֵת בַּעֲלֵי יָבֵישׁ גִּלְעָד אֲשֶׁר גָּנְבוּ אֹתָם מֵרְחֹב בֵּית־שַׁן אֲשֶׁר תָּלוּם שָׁם [Qere תְּלָאוּם] הַפְּלִשְׁתִּים שָׁמָּה פְּלִשְׁתִּים בְּיוֹם הַכּוֹת פְּלִשְׁתִּים אֶת־שָׁאוּל בַּגִּלְבֹּעַ:

*Translation.* 1 Samuel 31:8 And it came to pass on the next day Philistines came to strip the slain, and they found Saul and his three sons fallen on Mount Gilboa. 9 And they cut off his head and stripped away his weapons, and they sent out in the land of the Philistines all around to bear news both to the house of their idols and to the people. 10 And they set his weapons in the house of Ashtaroth, but his body they fastened on the wall of Beth Shean. 11 But when the inhabitants of Jabesh-gilead heard what Philistines had done to Saul, 12 each strong man arose, and walked all night, and took the body of Saul and the bodies of his sons from the wall of Beth Shean. And they came to Jabesh, and they burned them there. 13 And they took their bones and buried them under the Tamarisk in Jabesh. And they fasted seven days.

2 Samuel 21:12: And David went and took the bones of Saul and the bones of Jonathan his son from the masters of Jabesh-gilead, which they stole from the public square of Beth Shean, where the Philistines had hung them up on the day when Philistines struck Saul in Gilboa.

*Commentary.* Saul's death is reported in 1 Sam 31:6 and here the maltreatment of his corpse is recounted. In keeping with the trajectory of Saul's downfall in 1 Samuel, this whole incident emphasizes the dishonorable death of Saul (his slow suicide, the beheading, the distribution of his weapons and head as Philistine spoils, and the suspension of his body on the wall). The deaths of Saul and his sons also increasingly made possible David's claim to the throne of Israel. The author of the books of Samuel repeatedly mentions beheadings (see also 1 Sam 17:46, 51 [Goliath]; 2 Sam 4:7 [Ish-bosheth]; 20:22 [Sheba the son of Bichri]). According to the text, the Philistines offer their deity weapons from their fallen opponent; such a practice was common in antiquity, though here it also serves to remind the reader of the pagan nature of the Philistines. In the passage, the suspension of Saul's beheaded body and his lack of burial were viewed with such horror that the men of Jabesh-gilead valiantly risked their lives to provide some burial rites for the bodies of Saul and his sons. David later provides these bones proper burial (2 Sam 21:12).

Saul's body was said in 1 Sam 31:10 to be "fastened" (תקעו) on the wall, employing a verb (תקע) that indicates a thrusting blow like the kind used to erect a tent, or blow a horn, or thrust a sword or javelin into someone (cf. Gen 31:25; Num 10:3; Josh 6:4; Judg 3:21; 4:21; 1 Sam 13:3; 2 Sam 18:14). This likely indicates that Saul's body was pinned to the wall in some manner (cf. LXX κατέπηξαν). However, the retrospective mention of this event in 2 Sam 21:12 has Saul "hung" (Kethibh תלום; Qere תלאום; contrast LXX ἔστησαν "stood") in the public square (מרחב) of Beth Shean; this clearly assumes that the pinning of these corpses to the wall involved a public suspension of Saul and his sons.

### 3.2.9 Persia and Media

This famous ancient tri-literal Persian inscription from Behistûn provides multiple instances of Darius proudly asserting that he had impaled/suspended his opponents. The Hebrew Bible also indicates that the Persians practiced such policies.

**(180)** Behistûn Inscription of Darius the Great (Babylonian version ll. 57–61)

<sup>57</sup> <sup>m</sup>*da-ri-ia-muš* LUGAL *ki-a-am i-qab-bi ár-ki ul-tu* DIN.TIR.KI *ana-ku ú-ṣa-am-ma at-ta-lak a-na* KUR *ma-da-a-a a-na ka-šá-di a-na* KUR *ma-da-a-a ina* URU *ku-un-du-ur šu-um-šú ina* KUR *ma-da-a-a* <sup>58</sup> *a-na tar-ṣi-iá* <sup>m</sup>*pa-ar-ú-mar-ti-iš a-ga-šu-u šá iq-bu-u um-ma a-na-ku* <sup>m</sup>*ḫa-šá-at-ri-it-ti* NUMUN *šá* <sup>m</sup>*ú-ma-ku-iš-tar* LUGAL KUR *ma-da-a-a it-ti ú-qu it-ta-lak a-na e-peš* MÈ *ár-ki ni-te-pu-uš ṣal-tu₄* <sup>d</sup>*ú-ra-mi-iz-da is-se-dan-nu ina* GIŠ.MI *šá* <sup>d</sup>*ú-ra-mi-iz-da ú-qu šá* <sup>m</sup>*pa-ar-ú-mar-ti-iš* <sup>59</sup> *[ni]-du-uk* UD 25 KAM *šá* ITI BÁR *ni-te-pu-uš ṣa-[al-tu₄] ni-du-uk ina lib-bi-šú-nu* 34? LIM 4? ME 25 *u bal-ṭu-tú uṣ-ṣab-bi-tú      ár-ki* <sup>m</sup>*pa-ar-ú-mar-ti-iš a-ga-šu-u it-ti* LÚ ÉRIN.MEŠ *i-ṣu-tú e-li* EDIN *šá* ANŠE.KUR.RA.MEŠ ZÁḪ-*ma il-lik-ma ina* KUR *ra-ga-' šu-um-šú ina* KUR *ma-da-a-a ár-ki a-na-ku ú-qu* <sup>60</sup> *a-na tar-ṣi-šú-nu aš-pur-ma* <sup>m</sup>*pa-ar-ú-mar-ti-iš a-ga-šu-u u* LÚ ERIN.MEŠ *šá it-ti-šú iṣ-ṣab-tu-ma a-na pa-ni-iá iš-pu-ru ár-ki ana-ku ap-pi-šú* GESTU<sup>II</sup>-*šú li-ša-an-šú ú-bat-tiq* I-*en* IGI-*šú ú-nap-pil šu-ú ṣab-tu ku-ul-lu ina* KÁ-*iá ú-qu gab-bi im-ma-ru-uš ár-ki ina za-qi-pi ina* URU *a-ga-ma-ta-nu al-ta-kan-šú* <sup>61</sup> LÚ DUMU.DÙ.MEŠ-*šú ad-du-uk* PAP 47 *[bi]-rit* URU *a-ga-ma-ta-nu* SAG.DU.MEŠ-*šu-nu a-lu-ul ul-tu ki-li-li [šá] bir-tu*

*Translation.* <sup>57</sup> King Darius states: Then I went out from Babylon and proceeded to Media. When I reached Media, in the town Kundur, by name, in Media, <sup>58</sup> that Fravartish who said, "I am Khashatritti, a descendant of Cyaxares, king of Media," went toward me with troops to attack. Then we fought the battle. Ahura Mazda supported me. Under the protection of Ahura Mazda, the army of Fravartish <sup>59</sup> we defeated. On the 25<sup>th</sup> day of Nisannu we fought the battle. We killed 34425? of them and took prisoner (number illegible).    Then that Fravartish fled with a few soldiers mounted on horseback and came to the territory of Ragā, by name, in Media. Then I <sup>60</sup> sent troops after him. They captured that Fravartish and the soldiers who were with him and sent (them) to me. Then I cut off his nose, his two ears, his tongue (and) blinded one eye of his. He was held in fetters at my gate. All the people could see him. Then I impaled him at Ecbatana. <sup>61</sup> I executed his nobles, a total of 47. I hung their heads inside Ecbatana from the battlements of the fortress.

*Commentary.*<sup>192</sup> This is the first of four occasions in the Behistûn Inscription in which Darius boasts of suspending the body of someone who had revolted

---

<sup>192</sup> Text and translation from ELIZABETH N. VOIGTLANDER, The Bisitun Inscription of Darius the Great: Babylonian Version (Corpus Inscriptionum Iranicarum II.1; London: Lund Humphries, 1978), 27–28, 57–58 (Section 25). For purposes of printing, it has been necessary to remove the raised angle brackets that Voigtlander employs to indicate levels of confidence in the text. Compared with text and translation in LEONARD WILLIAM KING and REGINALD CAMPBELL THOMPSON, The Sculptures and Inscription of Darius the Great, on the Rock of Behistûn in Persia. A new collation of the Persian, Susian, and Babylonian Texts, with English Translations (London: Harrison, 1907), 181–182 (§26).

against his rule. The monumental cliff-side, trilingual, inscription of Darius the Great at Behistûn/Bisitun in western Iran became instrumental in the transliteration and translation of cuneiform in the nineteenth century. It recounts in Babylonian, Elamite (or Susian), and Old Persian Darius' exploits in suppressing rebellion against his rule of Persia following the deaths of Cyrus and Cambyses II. The text purports to focus on his military victories over the course of one year from early in Darius' reign. The text would thus originate from some time in the late sixth or possibly early fifth century B.C. The Babylonian text is cited and translated above. Earlier in the Babylonian inscription, Darius indicates that the lands of Persia, Elam, Media, Assyria, Egypt, Parthia, Margiana, Sattagydia, and Scythia had rebelled against him while he was conducting military operations in Babylon (§20, lines 40–41). The grand bas-relief in the center of these inscriptions represents a giant Darius standing triumphant over ten bound foes. The image of each foe receives a brief identifying inscription (thus Fravartish/Phraortes is the third standing figure). Fravar-tish the Mede (in other translations: Phraortes) is introduced in §22 (Babylonian text lines 43ff.) as a man who sought to be king of Media, and Darius acknowledges that others supported his claim since the Parthians and Margians also "stood with Fravartish" (§§28–30, lines 64–68). In the passage cited above, Darius conquers Fravartish, mutilates him, puts him on public display, and eventually impales him on a *zaqipi*. Earlier translators rendered this as an act of crucifixion,[193] but the precise form of bodily suspension is not fully described. Impalement would be more probable, given the precursors evident on Assyrian reliefs (discussed above). Nevertheless, this serves as another example of the widespread military use in the ANE of human bodily suspension against conquered enemies. The Elamite and Old Persian inscriptions similarly reference this event and the bodily suspension of Fravartish.[194] This text is further known from an Aramaic copy found at Elephantine, proving that Darius wished his exploits to be broadly published; however, the Elephantine Aramaic text is unfortunately fragmentary in this section.[195]

---

[193] KING and THOMPSON, Sculptures and Inscription of Darius the Great, 182: "Then did I crucify him in Ecbatana".

[194] For transcriptions and translations of the Old Persian and Elamite/Susian texts see KING and THOMPSON, Sculptures and Inscription of Darius the Great, 34–37 (Old Persian §§31–32, lines ii.64–78), 121–123 (Elamite/Susian §25, lines ii.48–58). Both of these texts they render as they do the Babylonian: "Then did I crucify him in Ecbatana" (ibid. 37, 123).

[195] Cf. ARTHUR E. COWLEY, Aramaic Papyri of the Fifth Century B.C. (Oxford: Clarendon, 1923; repr., Osnabrück: Zeller, 1967), 258.

**(181)** Behistûn Inscription of Darius the Great (Babylonian version ll. 61–64)

⁶¹ ᵐ*da-ri-ia-muš* LUGAL *ki-a-am i-qab-bi ár-ki* I-*en* LÚ ᵐ*ši-it-ra-an-taḫ-ma* LÚ
*sa-ga-ar-ta-a-a it-ba-am-ma i-qab-bi a-na ú-qu um-ma ana-ku* LUGAL NUMUN
*šá* ᵐ*ú-ma-ku-iš-tar ár-ki ana-ku ú-qu* KUR *ma-da-a-a* ⁶² [*u*] KUR *par-su áš-
pur-ma* ᵐ*taḫ-ma-as-pa-da* MU-*šú* LÚ *qal-la-a* LÚ *ma-da-a-a* GAL-*ú ina* UGU-
[*šú-nu*] *al-ta-par um-ma al-ka-ma du-ka-*' *ni-ik-ru-tú šá la i-šem-mu-*'*-in-ni
ár-ki* ᵐ*taḫ-ma-as-pa-da it-ta-lak it-ti ú-qu ṣa-al-tu₄ it-ti* ᵐ*ši-it-ra-an-taḫ-ma i-
pu-uš-ma* ᵈ*ú-ra-mi-iz-da is-se-dan-nu ina* GIŠ.MI *ša* ᵈ*ú-ra-mi-iz-da* ⁶³ *ú-qu at-
tu-u-a a-na ni-ik-ru-tu id-du-ku* UD 5 KAM *šá* ITI DU₆ [*i-te*]-*ep-šú ṣal-tú* ᵐ*ši-it-
ra-an-taḫ-ma iṣ-ṣab-tú-ma a-na pa-ni-iá iš-pu-ru ár-ki a-na-ku ap-pi-šu*
GESTU^II-*šu li-šá-an-šu ú-*[*bat*]-*tiq* I-*en* IGI-*šu* [*ú*]-*nap-pil šu-ú ṣab-tu ku-ul-lu
ina* KÁ-*iá ú-qu gab-bi im-ma-ru-uš ár-ki ina* URU *ar-ba-*'*-il ina za-qi-pi áš-ku-
un-šú* PAP *di-i-ki u bal-ṭu* ⁶⁴ [*šá*] *ú-qu ni-ik-ru-tú* 4 ME 47   ᵐ*da-ri-ia-muš*
LUGAL *ki-a-am i-qab-bi a-ga-a šá a-na-ku ina* KUR *ma-da-a-a e-pu-šú*

*Translation.* ⁶¹ King Darius states: Next a certain man, Shitrantakhma, a Sa-
gartian, arose saying to the people, "I am the king, a descendant of Cyaxares."
Then I sent out Median ⁶² and Persian troops. Takhmaspāda, by name, my
subject, a Mede, was in command of them. I sent (them) an order: "Go and
defeat the rebels who do not obey me." Then Takhmaspāda went out with the
troops. He fought a battle with Shitrantakhma. Ahura Mazda supported me.
Under the protection of Ahura Mazda ⁶³ my troops defeated the rebels. On the
5th day of Tashrītu they fought the battle. They captured Shitrantakhma and
sent him to me. Then I cut off his nose, his two ears, his tongue, (and) blinded
one eye of his. He was held in fetters at my gate. All the people could see him.
Then I impaled him at Arbela. The total dead and surviving ⁶⁴ of the rebel
force was 447? King Darius states: This is what I did in Media.

*Commentary.*¹⁹⁶ This text immediately follows the previous passage from the
Behistûn inscription. Although Darius calls Shitrantakhma a member of the
ancient Iranian tribe of the Sagartians, Shitrantakhma lays claim to the Median
crown through Cyaxares (line 61), and Darius includes this section among the
acts he "did in Media" (line 64). From this we learn that there were two claim-
ants competing with Darius for the kingdom of the Medes (Fravartish mentioned in the previous passage and Shitrantakhma recorded here). As Darius
did with Fravartish, so here he mutilates the captured Shitrantakhma, displays
him publicly, and then impales him aloft (again mentioning the *za-qi-pi*). This
public humiliation of Shitrantakhma again serves to bring his rebellion to a
decisive halt, and it warns off others from engaging in such a revolt. The com-

---

¹⁹⁶ Text and translation from VOIGTLANDER, *Bisitun Inscription*, 28–29, 58 (Sections 26–
27). Compared with text and translation in KING and THOMPSON, *Sculptures and Inscription
of Darius the Great*, 181–182 (§§27–228).

panion Old Persian and Elamite/Susian versions provide parallel evidence of Shitrantakhma's suspended body.[197]

**(182)** Behistûn Inscription of Darius the Great (Babylonian version ll. 71–72, 75–78)

[71] ᵐ*da-ri-ia-muš* LUGAL *ki-a-am i-qab-bi* 1-*en* LÚ ᵐ*ú-mi-iz-da-a-tu₄ šu-um-šú* LÚ *par-sa-a-a* [*ina*] URU *ta-ar-ma šu-um-šú* [*ina* KUR] *ia-ú-ti-ia šu-um-šú ina* KUR *par-su a-ši-ib šu-ú it-ba-am-ma ina* KUR *par-su i-qab-bi a-na ú-qu* [72] *um-ma a-na-ku* ᵐ*bar-zi-ia* DUMU-[*šú šá*] ᵐ*ku-ra-áš* LUGAL KUR.[KUR] *ár-ki ú-qu šá* KUR *par-su* [*ma-la*] *ina* É DIN.TIR.KI *maḫ-ru-ú ul-tu* [KUR] *an-za-an* KI *a-na pa-ni-ia il-li-ku-' it-te-ek-ru-' la-pa-ni-ia a-na* UGU ᵐ*ú-mi-iz-da-a-tu₄ it-tal-ku-' šu-ú a-na* LUGAL KUR *par-su it-tur* ... [75] *ár-ki* ᵐ*ú-mi-iz-da-a-tu₄ a-ga-šu-u it-ti ú-qu i-ṣi e-li* EDIN *šá* ANŠE.KUR.RA.MEŠ *iḫ-liq-ma a-na* [76] KUR *pi-ši-'-ḫu-ma-da il-lik-ma ul-tu lìb-bi-šá id-ki-e-ma ú-qu it-[ta]-lak a-na tar-ṣi* ᵐ*ar-ta-mar-zi-ia a-na e-peš* MÈ KUR *pa-ar-ga-' šu-um-šú* KUR-*ú* [*ina*] KUR *par-su ina lìb-bi i-te-ep-šú ṣa-al-tu₄* ᵈ*ú-ra-ma-az-da is-se-dan-nu ina* GIŠ.MI *šá* ᵈ*ú-ra-ma-az-da ú-qu at-tu-u-a id-du-ku a-na ú-qu šá* ᵐ*ú-mi-iz-da-a-ti* [77] UD 5 KAM *šá* ITI ŠU *i-te-ep-šu ṣa-al-tu₄ id-du-ku ina lìb-bi-šú-nu* 6 LIM 2 ME 46 *ù bal-ṭu-tu₄ uṣ-ṣab-bi-tu* 4 LIM 4 ME 64 ᵐ*ú-[mi]-iz-da-a-tu₄ ù* LÚ DUMU.DÙ.MEŠ *šá it-ti-šú uṣ-ṣab-bi-tu ṣab-tu* ᵐ*da-ri-ia-muš* LUGAL *ki-a-am i-qab-bi ár-ki ana-ku* ᵐ*ú-mi-iz-da-a-tú a-ga-šu-ú ù* LÚ DUMU.DÙ.MEŠ *šá it-ti-šú gab-bi ina za-qí-pi* [78] *áš-ku-un ina* URU *ú-ba-da-sa-ia šu-um-šú ina* KUR *par-su ina lìb-bi ad-du-uk* PAP [5]2 ᵐ*da-ri-ia-muš* LUGAL *ki-a-am i-qab-bi ár-ki* MA.DA *a-ga-ta a-na at-tu-u-a ta-at-tur a-ga-a šá a-na-ku ina* KUR *par-su e-pu-šú*

*Translation.* [§33] [71] King Darius states: There was a certain man, Vahyaz-dāta, by name, a Persian, residing in Tarma in the territory Yautiya, by name, in Persia. He arose in Persia saying to the people, [72] "I am Barziya, the son of Cyrus, king of lands." Then all the Persian troops who had previously come to me to the palace of Babylon from Anshan revolted from me and went over to Vahyazdāta. He became king of Persia ... [§34] [75] Then that Vahyazdāta fled with a small force mounted on horseback and [76] arrived in the territory of Pishīkhumada. From thence he called up troops and went toward Artamarziya to attack. Mt. Parga, by name, a mountain in Persia – there they fought the battle. Ahura Mazda supported me. Under the protection of Ahura Mazda my troops defeated the troops of Vahyazdāta. [77] On the 5th day of Du'ūzu they

---

[197] For the Old Persian and Elamite/Susian texts see KING and THOMPSON, Sculptures and Inscription of Darius the Great, 37–40 (Old Persian §§33–34, lines ii.78–91), 123–125 (Elamite/Susian §§26–27, lines ii.58–67). They render the Old Persian text as, "Afterwards did I crucify him in Arbela" (ibid. 39), and the Susian version as "Then did I crucify him in Arbela" (ibid. 125). The Elephantine Aramaic papyrus is entirely missing this section among the extant remains.

fought the battle. They killed 6246? of them and took prisoner 4464?. They took captive Vahyazdāta and the nobles who were with him. [§35] King Darius states: Then I impaled that Vahyazdāta and all the nobles who were with him [78] in the town Ubadasaya by name, in Persia – there. (*sic*) I executed a total of 52? [§36] King Darius states: Then this land became mine. This is what I did in Persia.

*Commentary.*[198] After mentioning rebellions among the Parthians and Margians (who had joined Fravartish of Media in revolt against Darius),[199] Darius' annalistic account now continues with the "revolt" of Vahyazdāta in Persia itself. This appears to have been a particularly serious event for Darius, for he is forced to acknowledge (in addition to Vahyazdāta's claim to be a son of Cyrus in line 72) that Vahyazdāta succeeded in becoming "king of Persia" (line 72) and that other territories joined Vahyazdāta in his "revolt" (lines 78–84). The above passage has been abbreviated for sake of space, with the omitted lines (72–75) recording Darius' call upon the "small Persian force which had not revolted from me and the Median forces" under the command of Artamarziya to do battle against Vahyazdāta. Artamarziya's initial success in this battle allowed him to continue to pursue Vahyazdāta, with the results recorded above in lines 75–78. Like the preceding accounts above of Darius impaling both Fravartish the Mede and Shitrantakhma of Sargatia/Media, here Darius impales Vahyazdāta. There are, however, two distinctions in the language used here: first, there is no mention of mutilating the bodies, and second, the "nobles" are impaled alongside Vahyazdāta. It is certainly possible (even likely?) that Darius mutilated Vahyazdāta and his comrades prior to suspending them, but Darius chooses to emphasize the most important humiliation upon them – their impalement/suspension aloft. Also, the seriousness of this particular rebellion explains why Darius here chose to impale/suspend the whole host of captured "nobles" alongside Vahyazdāta. Again the Elamite / Susian version and the Old Persian versions repeat these same suspension penalties against Vahyazdāta and his supporters, whereas the Elephantine Aramaic text, though extant for this section, is fragmentary in the crucial line.[200]

---

[198] Text and translation from VOIGTLANDER, Bisitun Inscription, 31–34, 58–59 (Sections 33–36). Compared with text and translation in KING and THOMPSON, Sculptures and Inscription of Darius the Great, 187–191 (§§34–37).

[199] See the Babylonian text lines 64–71 (VOIGTLANDER §§28–32, translation p. 58).

[200] For the Old Persian and Elamite/Susian texts see KING and THOMPSON, Sculptures and Inscription of Darius the Great, 46–51 (Old Persian §§40–44, lines iii.21–53), 129–134 (Elamite/Susian §§33–36, lines ii.85–iii.20). Most of the line is missing in the Elephantine Aramaic papyrus where it would speak of Vahyazdāta's suspension. COWLEY, Aramaic Papyri, 253 (text line iii.35) and 258 (translation), reconstructs the missing portion to indicate that Darius "crucified" (צלבת) the rebellious Vahyazdāta. BEZALEL PORTEN and ADA YARDENI, Textbook of Aramaic Documents from Ancient Egypt (4 vols.; Winona Lake, Ind.: Eisenbrauns, 1986–1993), 3:68–69 reconstruct the text to suggest that Darius impaled

**(183)**  Behistûn Inscription of Darius the Great (Babylonian version ll. 84–89)

$^{84}$ $^{m}$*da-ri-{ia-muš* LUGAL *ki-a-am i-qab-bi a-di* UGU *šá a-na-ku ina* KUR *par-su u* KUR *ma-da-a-a}* $^{85}$ *at-tu-ru* LÚ DIN.TIR.KI-*a-a*MEŠ *la-pa-ni-ia it-te-ek-ru-' I-en* LÚ $^{m}$*a-ra-ḫu šu-um-šú* LÚ *ú-ra-aš-ṭa-a-[a* A]-*šú [šá* $^{m}$] *ḫal-di-ta it-ba-am-ma* ⟨⟨ŠEŠ⟩⟩ *ina* ŠEŠ.UNUG.KI *šu-um-šú ina* DIN.TIR.KI [*ina*] *lìb-bi a-na ú-qu i-par-ra-{aṣ um-ma a-na-ku* $^{md}$MUATI.NÍG.DU.ÙRU A-*šú šá* $^{md}$MUATI.I *ár-ki ú-qu šá* DIN.TIR.KI *la-pa-ni-iá}* $^{86}$ *it-te-ek-ru-' a-na* UGU $^{m}$*a-ra-ḫu a-ga-šu-ú it-tal-ku-'* DIN.TIR.KI [*iṣ*]- *ṣab-tu-' [šu*]-*ú ana* LUGAL DIN.TIR.KI *it-tur ár-ki ú-qu ana* DIN.TIR.KI *áš-pur* $^{m}$*ú-mi-in-ta-pa-ar-na-' šu-um-šú* LÚ *qal-la-a* LÚ *par-sa-a-a ra-bu-[ú] {ina* [UGU]- *šú-nu al-ta-par um-ma a-lik-ma du-ú-ku a-na ú-qu ni-ik-ru-tú}* $^{87}$ [*šá*] DIN.TIR.KI *šá la i-šem-mu-'-in-ni ár-ki* $^{m}$*ú-mi-in-ta-pa-ar-na-' it-ti ú-qu a-na* DIN.TIR.KI *it-ta-lak* $^{d}$*ú-ra-ma-az-da is-se-dan-nu ina* GIŠ.MI *šá* $^{d}$*ú-ra-ma-az-da* $^{m}$*ú-mi-in-ta-pa-ar-{na-' ú-qu šá* E.KI *ni-ik-ru-tú id-duk u uṣ-ṣab-bit-su-nu-tu ú-qu šá ina lìb-bi-šú-nu}* $^{88}$ *ni-ik-ru-tu gab-bi* UD 22 KAM *šá* ITI APIN *i-te-ep-šu ṣa-al-tu$_4$ ina u$_4$-mu-šu-ma* $^{m}$*a-ra-ḫu a-ga-šu-ú šá i-par-ra-ṣu um-ma a-na-ku* $^{md}$MUATI.NÍG.DU.ÙRU [A-*šú*] *šá* $^{md}$MUATI.NÍ.TUK *ṣu-ub-bu-tu [u]* LÚ DUMU.DÙ.MEŠ *šá it-ti-šú* KI-*šú ṣu-{ub-bu-tu-' ár-ki a-na-ku ṭè-e-me al-ta-kan um-ma* $^{m}$*a-ra-ḫu u* LÚ DUMU.DÙ.MEŠ}* $^{89}$ *šá it-ti-šú šu-uk-na-'-šu-nu-tu [ina] za-qi-pi ár-ki* $^{m}$*a-ra-ḫu a-ga-šu-ú u* LÚ DUMU.DÙ.MEŠ *šá it-ti-šú ina za-qi-pi ina* DIN.TIR.KI *iš-ku-un* PAP [*di*]-*i-ku u bal-ṭu šá ú-qu šá* $^{m}$*a-ra-ḫu* 2 LIM 4 ME 97 $^{m}$*da-ri-ia-muš* LUGAL *ki-a-am {i-qab-bi a-ga-a šá ana-ku ina* E.KI *e-pu-šú …}*

*Translation.* [§39] $^{84}$ King Darius states: When I was back in Persia and Media $^{85}$ the Babylonians revolted from me. A certain man, Arakhu, by name, an Urartian, a son of Haldita, arose in Ur, by name, in Babylonia. There he lied to the people, "I am Nebuchadnezzar, a son of Nabū-na'id." Then the army of Babylonia revolted from me. $^{86}$ They went over to that Arakhu. They took possession of Babylon. He became king of Babylonia. Then I sent troops to Babylon. Vindafarna, by name, my subject, a Persian, was in command of them. I sent (him) an order: "Go and defeat the rebel troops $^{87}$ of Babylonia who do not obey me." Then Vindafarna went to Babylon with troops. Ahura Mazda supported me. Under the protection of Ahura Mazda Vindafarna defeated the rebel troops of Babylonia and took them prisoner – all the rebel troops who were among them. $^{88}$ On the 22$^{nd}$ day of Arahsamnu they fought the battle. At that time that Arakhu who had lied, "I am Nebuchadnezzar, a son of Nabū-na'id" was taken prisoner, and the nobles who were with him were taken prisoner with him. Then I decreed, "As to Arakhu and the nobles $^{89}$ who were with him, impale them." Then he impaled that Arakhu and the

---

Vahyazdāta: "all (of them) on the stake [בזקיפא] I put" (who label it column vii, line 49). Neither Aramaic reconstruction can be strongly endorsed over the other, given the extent of fragmentation in the Elephantine papyrus.

nobles who were with him in Babylon. The total dead and surviving of the army of Arakhu was 2497. [§40] King Darius states: This is what I did in Babylon.

*Commentary.*[201] Darius here records another serious challenge to his rule, this time coming from Arakhu in Babylon. As in other places on this inscription, Darius alleges that Arakhu lied about his (supposedly royal) family lineage, and provides an alternative genealogy that supports his claim that Arakhu was a mere usurper. Again, we see that Arakhu was so successful that Darius grudgingly refers to him as "king of Babylon." Like Vahyazdāta in the preceding text, Darius demanded impalement of both Arakhu and the nobility that supported him, though the Babylonian text is fragmentary on this point.[202]

## (184) Ezra 6:11–12

וּמִנִּי שִׂים טְעֵם דִּי כָל־אֱנָשׁ דִּי יְהַשְׁנֵא פִּתְגָמָא דְנָה יִתְנְסַח אָע מִן־בַּיְתֵהּ וּזְקִיף יִתְמְחֵא עֲלֹהִי וּבַיְתֵהּ
נְוָלוּ יִתְעֲבֵד עַל־דְּנָה: ¹² וֵאלָהָא דִּי שַׁכִּן שְׁמֵהּ תַּמָּה יְמַגַּר כָּל־מֶלֶךְ וְעַם דִּי יִשְׁלַח יְדֵהּ לְהַשְׁנָיָה
לְחַבָּלָה בֵּית־אֱלָהָא דֵךְ דִּי בִירוּשְׁלֶם אֲנָה דָרְיָוֶשׁ שָׂמֶת טְעֵם אָסְפַּרְנָא יִתְעֲבִד:

*Translation.* "And a decree was issued by me that for every man who alters this command, a beam shall be pulled up from his house, and being raised up he shall be smitten on it, and his house will be made as a dunghill on account of this. ¹² And may the God, who made his name dwell there, overthrow every king and people who will send out his hand to alter this and to destroy this house of God which is in Jerusalem. I, Darius, made a decree. Let it be performed diligently."

*Commentary.* Ezra 6 begins during the reign of Darius (6:1–2) with the rediscovery of a decree instituted by his predecessor Cyrus (6:3). Cyrus had commanded that provision be made for the rebuilding of the Jerusalem Temple. Then 6:6–12 continues to issue specific instructions that called for royal funds to be provided for the Temple, which was to be reconstructed, along with a reinstatement of sacrifices, by the local Jewish population. The text 6:1–12 is somewhat difficult because, by the end of the account, the decree is said to

---

[201] Text and translation from VOIGTLANDER, Bisitun Inscription, 37–39, 60 (Section 39). The portions in {}-brackets are readings taken from KING / THOMPSON (the British Museum squeeze ended with line 78, so VOIGTLANDER had to resort to KING and THOMPSON's publication to fill out the material that was illegible at the time of her own direct work with the inscription). Compared with text and translation in KING and THOMPSON, Sculptures and Inscription of Darius the Great, 194–196 (§§40–41).

[202] Fortunately the text is more complete in the Old Persian and Susian versions. For the Old Persian and Elamite/Susian texts see KING and THOMPSON, Sculptures and Inscription of Darius the Great, 56–60 (Old Persian §§49–51, lines iii.77–iv.2), 138–140 (Elamite/Susian §§39–40, lines iii.35–47).

have come from Darius (cf. 6:1, 12), while Cyrus is mentioned in 6:2–3. One solution is to accord 6:3–5 to Cyrus' initial edict and assign 6:6–12 to Darius' decree, which implements Cyrus' edict.[203]

The Aramaic is not entirely clear about the form of the penalty for altering and/or violating the edict. It certainly involves a "tree" (אָע, or better a "beam") from the offender's house. Then the person undergoes וְזָקִיף (translated above as "being raised up") followed by יִתְמְחֵא ("he shall be smitten"). The first verb (*zqp*) is strongly reminiscent of the Assyrian and Persian terminology of *zaqāpu* found in texts above (e.g., the Middle Assyrian Laws – Tablet A; cf. *zaqipi* in Darius' Behistûn Inscription), where it probably indicates some form of impalement. This, combined with יִתְמְחֵא, would suggest that the person was to be suspended alongside the beam and then be impaled upon it.[204] The later Greek traditions render this punishment either with suspension terminology or even with crucifixion vocabulary.[205]

The king's edict demonstrates how seriously he took its implementation and also may testify to the desire to honor foreign gods in the hopes that those deities would also be benefactors of Persia. Notably, the idea of connecting this suspension penalty to the (beam of the) offender's house is strongly reminiscent of Sennacherib's inscription concerning infringing upon the royal road (discussed above in 3.2.5) – both warn against violating a royal edict, which would result in public suspension/impalement, with the suspension being connected in some manner to the violator's house. This suggests the punishment mentioned in this account is historically plausible.

---

[203] This would also explain why Tattenai is named in Darius' implementation decree in Ezra 6:6 and then actually performs the action during Darius' reign in Ezra 6:13. Confusion over this matter is evident among the ancient interpreters, especially in Josephus, who twice attributes the decree of Ezra 6:6–12 to Cyrus (*A. J.* 11.12–18; 11.99–103). In contrast, 1 Esdras 6:33 (RSV translation 6:34) likely assigns the material in Ezra 6:6–12 to Darius.

[204] The range of options here are discussed in CHAPMAN, Crucifixion, 170–171. HUGH G. M. WILLIAMSON, Ezra, Nehemiah (WBC 16; Dallas: Word, 1985), 69, 72, 83 suggests that this indicates a public flogging. Others follow the interpretation above; see BDB 1091b; F. CHARLES FENSHAM, The Books of Ezra and Nehemiah (NICOT; Grand Rapids: Eerdmans, 1982), 90–91. Also note JACOB M. MYERS, Ezra, Nehemiah (AB 14; New York: Doubleday, 1965), who translates "be impaled" though he argues for "crucify".

[205] Note λημφθῆναι ξύλον ἐκ τῶν ἰδίων αὐτοῦ καὶ ἐπὶ τούτου κρεμασθῆναι (1 Esdras 6:31 [RSV 6:32]). 2 Esdras 6:11 in most manuscripts employs the verbs ὠρθωμένος παγήσεται ("being set upright he was affixed" on the beam). Most remarkably, Josephus translates this passage with ἀνασταυρόω in *A. J.* 11.17 and 11.103. All this testifies to how early readers of the Aramaic understood the Aramaic verbs in question.

**(185)** Esther 2:21–23

בַּיָּמִים הָהֵם וּמָרְדֳּכַי יֹשֵׁב בְּשַׁעַר־הַמֶּלֶךְ קָצַף בִּגְתָן וָתֶרֶשׁ שְׁנֵי־סָרִיסֵי הַמֶּלֶךְ מִשֹּׁמְרֵי הַסַּף וַיְבַקְשׁוּ
לִשְׁלֹחַ יָד בַּמֶּלֶךְ אֲחַשְׁוֵרֹשׁ: <sup>22</sup> וַיִּוָּדַע הַדָּבָר לְמָרְדֳּכַי וַיַּגֵּד לְאֶסְתֵּר הַמַּלְכָּה וַתֹּאמֶר אֶסְתֵּר לַמֶּלֶךְ בְּשֵׁם
מָרְדֳּכָי: <sup>23</sup> וַיְבֻקַּשׁ הַדָּבָר וַיִּמָּצֵא וַיִּתָּלוּ שְׁנֵיהֶם עַל־עֵץ וַיִּכָּתֵב בְּסֵפֶר דִּבְרֵי הַיָּמִים לִפְנֵי הַמֶּלֶךְ:

*Translation.* In those days, when Mordecai was sitting in the gate of the king, Bigthan and Teresh, two of the king's eunuchs who guarded the threshold, were angry. And they sought to stretch out a hand against King Ahasuerus. <sup>22</sup> And the matter became known to Mordecai, and he declared it to Esther the Queen; and Esther told it to the king in the name of Mordecai. <sup>23</sup> The matter was sought out, and it was found [true]. So the two of them were hung on a tree. And it was written in the book of the chronicles before the king.

*Commentary.* Several key verses in the book of Esther recount the idea of someone being "hung on a tree" (Esth 2:23; 5:14; 6:4; 7:9–10; 8:7; 9:13–14, 25). This book provides a single, continuous narrative about how the Persian diaspora community of Jewish people came to be severely threatened by Haman and other Persians and how Mordecai and Queen Esther (both of Jewish stock) saved their people through gaining the ear of King Ahasuerus in the Persian capital of Susa. The narrative climax is driven by a reversal upon Haman and his associates of all the evils they had sought to perform against Mordecai and the whole diaspora Jewish nation. The Hebrew text famously does not mention the name of God, though its events do seem governed by divine providence; the Greek versions make up for this omission (and others) by adding several lengthy passages throughout the course of the book.

In this text, Mordecai preserves the life of the king, and this deed is recorded for future reference. This brief event serves an important function later in the book as Mordecai is exalted because of this deed even as Haman seeks his death (cf. Esth 6:1–12). Here, we are most concerned with how the narrator describes the fate of Bigthan and Teresh, who are "hung on a tree." There is no mention of their deaths prior to this suspension, so it could well have been the means of execution. Yet later in Esther, similar terminology is used of the *post mortem* suspension of Haman's sons and possibly of Haman himself (see discussion below of Esther 9:12–14 and 7:8–10). Many English translations render this "tree" with the word "gallows" (e.g., KJV, RSV, NASB, NIV, NRSV, ESV – though the ESV provides the alternative "stake" in its footnotes). The two main interpretations of the method of suspension involve either impalement (in the fashion depicted in the Assyrian reliefs) or "hanging" on the gallows (from the neck). The former interpretation has the distinct advantage of clear ANE precedent. Despite the prevalence of bodily suspension in the famous Behistûn inscription, when commentators cite ANE parallels, they rarely reference actual Persian texts.<sup>206</sup> One might observe that the text only mentions one tree, but the syntax may well permit the view that both men were individually delivered to the penalty of being "hung on a tree" (i.e., that there were consequently two trees involved), and/or it could also be that the phrase "hung on a tree" had become a set phrase for public suspension (note the lack of article) which does not intend to designate the number of poles involved.

**(186)** Esther 5:11–14

וַיְסַפֵּר לָהֶם הָמָן אֶת־כְּבוֹד עָשְׁרוֹ וְרֹב בָּנָיו וְאֵת כָּל־אֲשֶׁר גִּדְּלוֹ הַמֶּלֶךְ וְאֵת אֲשֶׁר נִשְּׂאוֹ עַל־הַשָּׂרִים וְעַבְדֵי הַמֶּלֶךְ: 12 וַיֹּאמֶר הָמָן אַף לֹא־הֵבִיאָה אֶסְתֵּר הַמַּלְכָּה עִם־הַמֶּלֶךְ אֶל־הַמִּשְׁתֶּה אֲשֶׁר־עָשָׂתָה כִּי אִם־אוֹתִי וְגַם־לְמָחָר אֲנִי קָרוּא־לָהּ עִם־הַמֶּלֶךְ: 13 וְכָל־זֶה אֵינֶנּוּ שֹׁוֶה לִי בְּכָל־עֵת אֲשֶׁר אֲנִי רֹאֶה אֶת־מָרְדֳּכַי הַיְּהוּדִי יוֹשֵׁב בְּשַׁעַר הַמֶּלֶךְ: 14 וַתֹּאמֶר לוֹ זֶרֶשׁ אִשְׁתּוֹ וְכָל־אֹהֲבָיו יַעֲשׂוּ־עֵץ גָּבֹהַּ חֲמִשִּׁים אַמָּה וּבַבֹּקֶר אֱמֹר לַמֶּלֶךְ וְיִתְלוּ אֶת־מָרְדֳּכַי עָלָיו וּבֹא־עִם־הַמֶּלֶךְ אֶל־הַמִּשְׁתֶּה שָׂמֵחַ וַיִּיטַב הַדָּבָר לִפְנֵי הָמָן וַיַּעַשׂ הָעֵץ:

*Translation.* And Haman recounted to them the glory of his riches, and the multitude of his sons, and every way by which the king had make him great, and by which he had raised him over the officials and the servants of the king. 12 And Haman said, "Even Esther the queen did not have anyone brought in to the banquet with the king which she made, except me. And also tomorrow I am summoned to her along with the king. 13 But all this is not enough for me on every occasion when I see Mordecai the Judean sitting at the gate of the king." 14 Then Zeresh his wife and all his friends said to him, "Let them construct a great tree fifty cubits high, and in the morning speak to the king, and let them hang Mordecai on it. And then go with the king to the banquet rejoicing." And the matter was pleasing before Haman, and he constructed the tree.

*Commentary.* Haman is over all the officials in Persia (Esth 3:1–2), but Mordecai refuses to pay him homage (3:3–5). Consequently, Haman desires Mordecai's death and the slaughter of all of the Judeans along with him (3:5–6), and Haman is able to convince the king to assent to such a decree (3:8–11). Mordecai learns of this and, along with Esther, schemes to invite the king and Haman to a banquet with Esther at which she would ask the king to rescind the decree (4:1–5:8). The passage above narrates part of Haman's report back to his wife and friends. Vainly, Haman recounts his status and wealth and also affirms how irate he is at Mordecai. His wife and friends respond by suggesting that Haman have Mordecai "hung on a tree" (much as Bigthan and Teresh had met their doom in Esth 2:21–23). The height that the narrator attributes to this pole is particularly striking – 50 cubits (approximately 25 meters or 75

---

[206] However, some commentators do at least cite Persian examples in Herodotus (in addition to Assyrian parallels); cf. KAREN H. JOBES, Esther (NIVAC; Grand Rapids: Zondervan, 1999), 166; WALTON, ed., Zondervan Illustrated Bible Backgrounds Commentary, 3:486, 504.

feet). It is also clear that this device is at least partially man-made (it is "constructed"). Once again, there is no mention of Mordecai being put to death prior to being hung up, so it may well be a means of execution (though note the caveats mentioned concerning Esth 2:21–23 above).

**(187)  Esther 6:4**

וַיֹּאמֶר הַמֶּלֶךְ מִי בֶחָצֵר וְהָמָן בָּא לַחֲצַר בֵּית־הַמֶּלֶךְ הַחִיצוֹנָה לֵאמֹר לַמֶּלֶךְ לִתְלוֹת אֶת־מָרְדֳּכַי
עַל־הָעֵץ אֲשֶׁר־הֵכִין לוֹ:

*Translation.* And the king said, "Who is in the court?" Now Haman had gone to the outer court of the king's house to talk to the king in order to hang Mordecai on the tree which he had prepared for him.

*Commentary.* As the story progresses, King Ahasuerus learns from the book of chronicles that he had not properly rewarded Mordecai for saving him from the clutches of Bigthan and Teresh (see Esth 2:21–23 above). Thus the king seeks advice as to how best to reward Mordecai. Ironically, he turns to Haman, who has just planned Mordecai's demise. In subsequent verses, Haman unwittingly designs for the king a grand reward for Mordecai. This verse also serves to reemphasize Haman's desire to "hang Mordecai on the tree."

**(188)  Esther 7:8–10**

וְהַמֶּלֶךְ שָׁב מִגִּנַּת הַבִּיתָן אֶל־בֵּית מִשְׁתֵּה הַיַּיִן וְהָמָן נֹפֵל עַל־הַמִּטָּה אֲשֶׁר אֶסְתֵּר עָלֶיהָ וַיֹּאמֶר הַמֶּלֶךְ
הֲגַם לִכְבּוֹשׁ אֶת־הַמַּלְכָּה עִמִּי בַּבָּיִת הַדָּבָר יָצָא מִפִּי הַמֶּלֶךְ וּפְנֵי הָמָן חָפוּ: ס 9 וַיֹּאמֶר חַרְבוֹנָה אֶחָד
מִן־הַסָּרִיסִים לִפְנֵי הַמֶּלֶךְ גַּם הִנֵּה־הָעֵץ אֲשֶׁר־עָשָׂה הָמָן לְמָרְדֳּכַי אֲשֶׁר דִּבֶּר־טוֹב עַל־הַמֶּלֶךְ עֹמֵד
בְּבֵית הָמָן גָּבֹהַּ חֲמִשִּׁים אַמָּה וַיֹּאמֶר הַמֶּלֶךְ תְּלֻהוּ עָלָיו: 10 וַיִּתְלוּ אֶת־הָמָן עַל־הָעֵץ אֲשֶׁר־הֵכִין
לְמָרְדֳּכָי וַחֲמַת הַמֶּלֶךְ שָׁכָכָה:

*Translation.* And the king returned from the garden of his house to the place of the drinking of wine. And Haman was falling on the couch on which Esther lay. And the king said, "Will he even subdue the queen alongside me in my house?" The word went out from the mouth of the king, and they covered the face of Haman. 9 And Harbona, one of the eunuchs before the king, said, "Moreover, behold the tree which Haman constructed for Mordecai, who spoke well concerning the king; it is standing in the house of Haman fifty cubits high." And the king said, "Hang him on it." 10 And they hung Haman on the tree which he had prepared for Mordecai. And the wrath of the king abated.

*Commentary.* In these verses, we encounter the greatest ironic reversal in the book of Esther. Haman had planned this suspension for Mordecai, but instead it falls upon Haman himself. In the preceding verses, Esther used the second day of feasting to request of King Ahasuerus that her people (the Judeans) not be slaughtered. The king then learns that Haman had been the cause of the decree against the Judeans. The angry king leaves the banquet to go into the garden. In his absence, Haman begs Esther for his life, but he does so in such a way that the king, on his return, believes Haman is assaulting Esther. Haman's demise is then depicted above. Harbona is also mentioned in 1:10 as one of the seven eunuchs "who serve before the king."

The mode of death is perplexing here. In verse 8, they "covered the face of Haman." This could indicate he had already expired (and they covered the face of his corpse), or it could indicate that it was "covered" to await further judgment. In any case, Haman is suspended on the "tree" – likely a large wooden pole – that he had erected. This is clearly meant to dishonor his body, as is further evidenced in the suspension of his sons.

## (189) Esther 8:7

וַיֹּאמֶר הַמֶּלֶךְ אֲחַשְׁוֵרֹשׁ לְאֶסְתֵּר הַמַּלְכָּה וּלְמָרְדֳּכַי הַיְּהוּדִי הִנֵּה בֵית־הָמָן נָתַתִּי לְאֶסְתֵּר וְאֹתוֹ תָּלוּ
עַל־הָעֵץ עַל אֲשֶׁר־שָׁלַח יָדוֹ בַּיְּהוּדִיים [Qere] בַּיְּהוּדִים:

*Translation.* And King Ahasuerus said to Esther the queen and to Mordecai the Judean, "Behold, the house of Haman I gave to Esther, but they have hung him on the tree because he stretched out his hand against the Judeans."

*Commentary.* In Esth 8:1–2, the king grants Haman's house (likely including all his property) to Queen Esther, who, in turn, sets Mordecai over Haman's house. In 8:4–6 Esther pleads for the lives of the Jewish people and for a reversal of Haman's letters calling for their slaughter. The king responds positively to her request in 8:7–8. Verse 8 above thus serves as a retrospective mention of Haman's suspension and of the disposition of his land.

## (190) Esther 9:12–14, 25

וַיֹּאמֶר הַמֶּלֶךְ לְאֶסְתֵּר הַמַּלְכָּה בְּשׁוּשַׁן הַבִּירָה הָרְגוּ הַיְּהוּדִים וְאַבֵּד חֲמֵשׁ מֵאוֹת אִישׁ וְאֵת עֲשֶׂרֶת
בְּנֵי־הָמָן בִּשְׁאָר מְדִינוֹת הַמֶּלֶךְ מֶה עָשׂוּ וּמַה־שְּׁאֵלָתֵךְ וְיִנָּתֵן לָךְ וּמַה־בַּקָּשָׁתֵךְ עוֹד וְתֵעָשׂ׃ 13 וַתֹּאמֶר
אֶסְתֵּר אִם־עַל־הַמֶּלֶךְ טוֹב יִנָּתֵן גַּם־מָחָר לַיְּהוּדִים אֲשֶׁר בְּשׁוּשָׁן לַעֲשׂוֹת כְּדָת הַיּוֹם וְאֵת עֲשֶׂרֶת
בְּנֵי־הָמָן יִתְלוּ עַל־הָעֵץ׃ 14 וַיֹּאמֶר הַמֶּלֶךְ לְהֵעָשׂוֹת כֵּן וַתִּנָּתֵן דָּת בְּשׁוּשָׁן וְאֵת עֲשֶׂרֶת בְּנֵי־הָמָן תָּלוּ׃
25 ... וּבְבֹאָהּ לִפְנֵי הַמֶּלֶךְ אָמַר עִם־הַסֵּפֶר יָשׁוּב מַחֲשַׁבְתּוֹ הָרָעָה אֲשֶׁר־חָשַׁב עַל־הַיְּהוּדִים עַל־רֹאשׁוֹ
וְתָלוּ אֹתוֹ וְאֶת־בָּנָיו עַל־הָעֵץ׃

*Translation.* And the king said to Esther the queen, "In Susa the fortress the Judeans have slain and destroyed 500 men and the ten sons of Haman. In the remainder of the provinces of the king what have they done?! What do you ask? It will be given to you. And what do you still request? It will be done.

[13] And Esther said, "If it seems good to the king, let even tomorrow be given to the Judeans who are in Susa to do according to the decree of the day; and let them hang the ten sons of Haman on the tree." [14] And the king said for this to be done, and a decree was given in Susa, and they hung the ten sons of Haman ... [25] But, when she [Esther] came before the king, he said with the written decree: "His [Haman's] evil plan which he devised against the Judeans will return on his own head." And they hung him and his sons on the tree.

*Commentary.* The theme of dramatic reversal continues in Esther chapters 8–9. Mordecai is granted the authority to rescind Haman's letters that called for the Judeans to be slaughtered, and instead he orders the slaughter of those in the kingdom who were to carry out Haman's plan. For one day, the Jewish people are given the right to kill their opponents, which they did throughout the land. In Susa alone 500 of the opponents were killed (9:6–10).

According to 9:10, Haman's ten sons are among those slain in Susa (this is also reaffirmed above in 9:12). Thus, when those sons are hung up in 9:13–14, the narrative clearly indicates this was a *post mortem* suspension performed to dishonor the corpses of Haman's lineage. Esther passionately appeals for this to occur – showing that she (probably along with Mordecai) felt no hesitation in employing such a Persian penalty. From the standpoint of the Hebrew Bible, the executionary suspension of a person on a tree (especially *post mortem*) is entirely legitimate (cf. Deut 21:22–23; Josh 8:29; 10:26–27 – see above). Nonetheless, in this context, there is no mention of burial (which runs counter to Deut 21:22–23), though from this alone, we cannot ascertain the final disposition of the bodies.

Esther also asks for another day of slaughter (9:13). The king, though already expressing some shock at the numbers slain (9:12), grants her request (9:14–15), with the result that another 300 are killed in Susa and 75,000 are slain throughout the empire (9:14–15). Jewish feasts are celebrated throughout the land (8:17; 9:17–19), and Mordecai orders this to become an annual time of Jewish feasting – thus resulting in the festival of Purim (9:20–32). The last verse translated above (9:25) represents the final retrospective mention of the suspension of Haman and his sons.

The book of Esther was quite famous in Second Temple and early Rabbinic Judaism, especially since it was central to the annual Purim festival. It is not surprising then to find this story repeatedly retold in our extant sources. Notably, however, this text is often combined with language and imagery of crucifixion; to this we shall return below in 3.9.

## 3.2.10 Persia and Media in Greek and Roman Sources

The early Greek authors lived as contemporaries of the Persian Empire, especially Herodotus, Ctesias, Thucydides, and Xenophon. The Greeks were repeatedly engaged in war against the Persians, employed in mercenary forces that supported Persian causes, and involved in international commerce with the Persians.[207] Thus Greek historical narratives about Persia have a greater plausibility to them than the more chronologically remote rumors about Assyria in the Roman-era sources we studied above. In addition to texts in this section, note also the reference to Cyrus' death at the hands of a Scythian queen in Diodorus Siculus (*Bib. hist.* 2.44.1–2; discussed in No. 223).

**(191)**  Herodotus, *Historiae* 1.128.1–2

Διαλυθέντος δὲ τοῦ Μηδικοῦ στρατεύματος αἰσχρῶς, ὡς ἐπύθετο τάχιστα ὁ Ἀστυάγης, ἔφη ἀπειλέων τῷ Κύρῳ· "Ἀλλ' οὐδ' ὣς Κῦρός γε χαιρήσει."
[2] Τοσαῦτα εἴπας πρῶτον μὲν τῶν μάγων τοὺς ὀνειροπόλους, οἵ μιν ἀνέγνωσαν μετεῖναι τὸν Κῦρον, τούτους ἀνεσκολόπισε.

*Translation.* And after the Median army had been shamefully dispersed, as soon as Astyages learned of this, he spoke and threatened Cyrus: "Nevertheless, Cyrus will not rejoice!" [2] He [Astyages] first denounced the dream interpreters of the Magi (those who read to him [the dream] to ignore Cyrus) – these interpreters he impaled.

*Commentary.*[208] Herodotus lived and wrote in the mid-fifth century B.C. In 1.120, Magi assure Astyages, king of the Medes, that he need not concern himself any more with the dream that Cyrus will be made king. The battle in 1.127, in which Cyrus is victorious, proves them wrong. Astyages has the dream interpreters impaled (ἀνεσκολόπισε) prior to engaging in one final fiasco of a battle with Cyrus. This impalement certainly comes with the fury

---

[207] The military encounters between Greece and Persia are quite well known. Yet archaeology is increasingly evidencing extensive commercial contact as well, especially at the border regions, such as Palestine. See e.g., ERIC M. MEYERS and MARK A. CHANCEY, Alexander to Constantine: Archaeology of the Land of the Bible (Anchor Bible Reference Library; New Haven: Yale University Press, 2014), 3–7.

[208] Text: CARL HUDE, Herodoti Historiae (Editio tertia. 2 vols.; Scriptorum classicorum bibliotheca Oxoniensis; Oxford: Clarendon, 1927); page numbers are not provided in this edition. I have provided quotation marks and capitalization that are not in Hude's edition. The same text appears (with punctuation and capitalization variation) in HAIIM B. ROSÉN, Herodoti historiae [2 vols.; Bibliotheca Scriptorum Graecorum et Romanorum Teubneriana; Leipzig: Teubner, 1987–1989], 1:86; Rosén notes a reversal in word order in τούτους ἀνεσκολόπισε in one manuscript and substitution of πάντας for τούτους in another MS).

of the king amidst war, but it might also have been deemed justified by the religious failure of these particular Magi to understand the portents correctly.

The translation "impaled" is common in English translations, though perhaps "fix upon a stake" would be closer to the etymology of ἀνασκολοπίζω.[209] The precise type of penalty that Herodotus invokes here cannot be inferred from the word alone. It is likely that this would have involved putting the person "up" somewhere for public view, as implied by the prefix ἀνα and also as indicated by other uses elsewhere in Herodotus that imply public venues with a massive number of people affixed to stakes (3.159.1; 4.202.1 – see below). Since the pictorial representation we have of Assyrian practice in the Lachish reliefs implies impalement of the chest cavity (as seen above), one might assume a similar posture (though the instances are separated by a century and by different nationalities).

**(192)** Ctesias, *Persica*, FGH 3c 688 Frag. 9.6 (from Photius, *Bibliotheca* 72)

ἔτι διαλαμβάνει ὡς ἀποστέλλει Κῦρος ἐν Περσίδι Πετησάκαν τὸν εὐνοῦχον, μέγα παρ' αὐτῶι δυνάμενον, ἐνέγκαι ἀπὸ Βαρκανίων Ἀστυίγαν· ἐπόθει γὰρ αὐτός τε καὶ ἡ θυγάτηρ Ἄμυτις τὸν πατέρα ἰδεῖν· καὶ ὡς Οἰβάρας βουλεύει Πετησάκαι ἐν ἐρήμωι τόπωι καταλιπόντα Ἀστυίγαν λιμῶι καὶ δίψει ἀπολέσαι· ὃ καὶ γέγονε· δι' ἐνυπνίων δὲ τοῦ μιάσματος μηνυθέντος, Πετησάκας πολλάκις αἰτησαμένης Ἀμύτιος εἰς τιμωρίαν παρὰ Κύρου ἐκδίδοται· ἡ δὲ τοὺς ὀφθαλμοὺς ἐξορύξασα καὶ τὸ δέρμα περιδείρασα ἀνεσταύρισεν. Οἰβάρας δὲ δεδιὼς μὴ τὰ ὅμοια πείσεται, καίτοι Κύρου μηδὲν τοιοῦτον ἰσχυριζομένου παραχωρῆσαι, αὐτὸς μὲν ἀποκαρτερήσας δι' ἡμερῶν δέκα ἑαυτὸν ἐξήγαγεν. Ἀστυίγας δὲ μεγαλοπρεπῶς ἐτάφη· καὶ ἐν τῆι ἐρήμηι δὲ ἄβρωτος αὐτοῦ διέμεινεν ὁ νεκρός· λέοντες γὰρ αὐτοῦ (φησίν), μέχρι Πετησάκαν πάλιν ἐλθεῖν καὶ ἀναλαβεῖν, ἐφύλαττον τὸν νεκρόν.

*Translation.* He [i.e., Ctesias] further distinguishes how Cyrus in Persia dispatched Petesacas the eunuch, who had great influence with him, to bring back Astyigas from the Barcanians; for, both [Cyrus] himself and [Astyigas'] daughter Amytis desired to see her father. And how Oebaras wished Petesacas, by leaving Astyigas in a deserted place, to kill [Astyigas] with hunger and thirst – which also came to pass. But since through a dream [his] guilt was

---

[209] See LSJ s.v. ἀνασκολοπίζω, which defines the word as "fix on a pole or stake, impale" in reference to Herodotus. A σκόλοψ in Herodotus can also be a sharp stake driven into the ground to create a defensive fortification (*Hist.* 9.97). English editions regularly translate ἀνεσκολόπισε as "impaled" in this passage; cf. ALRED D. GODLEY, Herodotus (4 vols.; orig. 1920–1925; repr., LCL; Cambridge: Harvard University Press, 1963), 1:167; GEORGE RAWLINSON, Herodotus: The Histories (ed. Hugh Bowden; London: Everyman, 1992), 71; ROBERT B. STRASSLER, ed., The Landmark Herodotus: The Histories (Translated by A. L. Purvis; New York: Pantheon, 2007), 70.

disclosed, Petesacas (due to Amytis' frequent petitioning) was handed over by Cyrus unto punishment. And she, after gouging out his eyes and flaying his skin, affixed him up on a *stauros*. And Oebaras, since he had become afraid lest he suffer the same things, although Cyrus stiffly maintained that he would permit no such occurrence, he [Oebaras] on the one hand starved himself for ten days and passed away. But on the other hand, Astyigas was buried magnificently; and his corpse even remained uneaten in the desert, for (Ctesias says) the lions, until Petesakas again came and retrieved it, guarded his corpse.

*Commentary.*[210] In the late fifth or (more likely) early fourth century B.C., Ctesias of Cnidus wrote the *Persica*,[211] which is now extant only in fragmentary excerpts from later authors. This passage comes from Photius' ninth-century A.D. *Bibliotheca*, which spends all of codex 72 summarizing, and occasionally commenting on, Ctesias' *Persica* and his *Indica*. Photius, Patriarch of Constantinople, produced his *Library* as a series of his personal notes on earlier authors (many of whose works are no longer extant), and he thus offers an uneven recollection of what he had read. One must be careful, therefore, to recognize that such an epitome may not be completely accurate (especially in the details of word choice).[212]

The events here would have occurred sometime in the mid-sixth century B.C. (Cyrus ruled Media from 550–530 B.C.). Astyigas is the same king of Media as the one mentioned in the previous selection from Herodotus (there spelled Astyages). According to Ctesias, once Cyrus had defeated Astyigas and thus captured Media, he freed Astyigas and "honored him as a father" (FGH 3c 688 Frag. 9.1). The same fragment also reports that Cyrus married Astyigas' daughter Amytis after her husband was killed (while hiding Astyigas); Photius notes there that this varies from Herodotus' account. Oebaras was an important Persian advisor and general to Cyrus (cf. Ctesias in FGH 3c 688 Frag. 8d.11–19, 8d.27, 8d.32, and 8d.39–40, all attributed to Nicolas of Damascus). Oebaras assisted in the capture of Astyigas (Ctesias in FGH 3c 688 Frag. 9.1), and he may well have suspected Astyigas to be still dangerous. There are some reasons to question the historicity on some specifics of these events: The text above certainly has legendary elements (e.g.,

---

[210] Text from JACOBY, FGH 3c 688 Frag. 9.6. Compared with LENFANT, Ctésias de Cnide, 314–316 (English translation ibid. 315–317). Further English translation in LLEWELLYN-JONES and ROBSON, Ctesias' History of Persia, 172–173. One manuscript in the family A tradition reads ἀνεσταύρωσεν for ἀνεσταύρισεν (see apparatus in LENFANT, ibid. 111).

[211] While occasionally one will see this work dated to the 5th century, LLEWELLYN-JONES and ROBSON, Ctesias' History of Persia, 17–18, date his writings to after the 394 B.C. defeat of the Spartans. STRONK, Ctesias's Persian History, 11, suggests a *terminus post quem* to 393/392 B.C. based on Ctesias' reference in Photius to Clearchus' grave from that year.

[212] Cf. LLEWELLYN-JONES and ROBSON, Ctesias' History of Persia, 43–44 and particularly STRONK, Ctesias's Persian History, 107–148, esp. 130–146 for evaluations of Photius' usefulness in reconstructing Ctesias' original.

lions guarding the corpse of Astyigas), and it perhaps too neatly parallels
Oebaras' death (by voluntary starvation) with the means of execution he com-
mended as Astyigas' fate (starvation and thirst) and too deftly contrasts the
reversal of the fortunes of Astyigas and Oebaras in death (via the μὲν... δὲ
construction). Further, while Herodotus corroborates Ctesias' *Persica* concerning Cyrus' honorable treatment of Astyigas, he certainly does not mention
Astyigas' cruel death (cf. Herodotus, *Historiae* 1.130.3). The central lines for
our purposes concern how Amytis was given free reign to vindicate her father
by executing Petesacas by first gouging out his eyes and flaying his skin (τοὺς
ὀφθαλμοὺς ἐξορύξασα καὶ τὸ δέρμα περιδείρασα), then affixing him up on a
*stauros* (ἀνεσταύρισεν).[213] The means of attaching him to the *stauros* is not
clearly depicted in Ctesias/Photius, and Ctesias' other uses of ἀνασταυρόω
(combined with images from the Assyrian reliefs) might well argue for impalement.[214] Depending on how severely Petesacas was injured during the gouging and flaying process, it is quite possible that this suspension was *post
mortem*. However, Photius may well have understood this to be crucifixion
since, as a Byzantine Christian patriarch, he often employed especially the
terms σταυρόω and σταυρός in reference to Jesus' crucifixion (e.g., Photius,
*Bibliotheca* codices 46 [10b]; 107 [88a]; 114 [90b]; 162 [106b]; 177 [123a];
179 [124b]; 232 [290b and 291a]). The next passage also summarizes this
same story from Ctesias.

**(193)** Ctesias, *Persica*, FGH 3c 688 Frag. 9a, lines 6–12 (from Joannes
Tzetzes, *Chiliades*, 1.1.97–103)

Πρὸς Ἀστυάγη πέπομφεν ὁ Κῦρος Πετησάκαν,
ὅπως ἐλθὼν τὴν Ἄμυτιν ἴδη σὺν Ἀστυάγει.
Ἡ Ἄμυτις ὑπάρχουσα δὲ παῖς τοῦ Ἀστυάγους
τοῦτον τὸν πρωτοεύνουχον ἄθλιον Πετησάκαν,
ἐπίβουλον νοήσασα τούτου τοῦ Ἀστυάγους,
τοὺς ὀφθαλμοὺς ἐξώρυξεν ἐκδείρασά τε ζῶντα.
Ἀνεσκολόπισε σταυρῷ θεῖσα βορὰν ὀρνέοις.

---

[213] SAMUELSSON, Crucifixion, 61 suggests the text here is ambiguous, allowing either
Petesacas himself *or his skin* to be suspended. However, the syntax of the passage would
strongly imply that Petesacas himself was suspended, since the preceding participles have different direct objects (eyes/skin), so there is no reason to assume just one of these objects
(skin) also serves as the object of the main verb. The same point is all the more obvious in
Ctesias, *Persica*, FGH 3c 688 Frag. 9a, lines 6–12 below.

[214] See above in comments on Diodorus Siculus, *Bib. hist.* 2.1.9–10 [Ctesias, FGH 3c 688
Frag. 1b 2.1.9–10], where we note SAMUELSSON's argument that the passage in Ctesias, FGH
3c 688 Frag. 14.39 (also from Photius) would imply impaling a person against three *stauroi*;
cf. SAMUELSSON, Crucifixion, 61–62.

*Translation.* Cyrus had sent Petesakas to Astyages,
in order that, after [Cyrus] came, he would see Amytis with Astyages.
And Amytis, being the daughter of Astyages,
after perceiving that this wretched chief-eunuch Petesakas
had plotted against this Astyages,
she gouged out his eyes and flayed him alive.
She impaled him up on a cross, setting him as food for birds.

*Commentary.*[215] Joannes Tzetzes of Constantinople (12th century A.D.) wrote
his *Histories* (known as the *Chiliades*) in poetic verse based on summaries of
over 400 items from Greek literature. This passage here abridges the same
events found in the previous text from Ctesias. It is unclear whether Tzetzes
had direct access to a manuscript of Ctesias.[216] JACOBY does not include this
passage amid the fragments of Ctesias, but both LENFANT and STRONK do cite
it based on the reference (in *Chiliades* 1.1.85–89) to Ctesias the physician as
Tzetzes' source for the material in lines 90ff. Tzetzes' paraphrase of Ctesias
also mentions the demise of "Astyages" in terms of gouged eyes, flaying alive,
and impalement upon a cross. Note the change in bodily suspension verb from
ἀνεσταύρισεν in Photius to ἀνεσκολόπισε σταυρῷ in Tzetzes. It is difficult to
be certain whether the additional feature in Tzetzes' account of Astyages'
execution ("setting him as food for birds") was based on Ctesias (and omitted
in Photius) or was due (as is perhaps likely) to Tzetzes' own poetic flair.[217]

## (194) Herodotus, *Historiae* 3.125.2–4

Ἀπικόμενος δὲ ἐς τὴν Μαγνησίην ὁ Πολυκράτης διεφθάρη κακῶς, οὔτε
ἑωυτοῦ ἀξίως οὔτε τῶν ἑωυτοῦ φρονημάτων· ὅτι γὰρ μὴ οἱ Συρηκοσίων
γενόμενοι τύραννοι, οὐδὲ εἷς τῶν ἄλλων Ἑλληνικῶν τυράννων ἄξιός ἐστι
Πολυκράτεϊ μεγαλοπρεπείην συμβληθῆναι. ³ Ἀποκτείνας δέ μιν οὐκ ἀξίως
ἀπηγήσιος Ὀροίτης ἀνεσταύρωσε·[218] τῶν δέ οἱ ἐπομένων ὅσοι μὲν ἦσαν

---

[215] Text: LENFANT, Ctésias de Cnide, 113; compared with STRONK, Ctesias's Persian History, 318 (with minor capitalization differences; English translation ibid. 319). Further English translation in LLEWELLYN-JONES and ROBSON, Ctesias' History of Persia, 174.

[216] Note the conclusion of STRONK, Ctesias's Persian History, 149–150: "Tzetzes' references are too indirect to conclude with certainty that the work still survived in his day, though he obviously was aware of relevant data: we therefore certainly cannot exclude the possibility that it did, whether or not fragmentarily."

[217] In light of the lack of reference to these birds in Photius' account of Ctesias, the questions concerning whether Tzetzes was working from an actual manuscript of Ctesias (or from memory or from someone else's account), and Tzetzes' renown for adding poetic flourishes, it seems likely that Tzetzes added the reference to fowl, in which case he (rather than Ctesias) was drawing on other ancient accounts of suspended victims becoming food for birds.

[218] The corrector to one manuscript reads the considerably less likely ἀνεσταύροσε.

Σάμιοι, ἀπῆκε, κελεύων σφέας ἑωυτῷ χάριν εἰδέναι ἐόντας ἐλευθέρους, ὅσοι δὲ ἦσαν ξεῖνοί τε καὶ δοῦλοι τῶν ἑπομένων, ἐν ἀνδραπόδων λόγῳ ποιεύμενος εἶχε. ⁴ Πολυκράτης δὲ ἀνακρεμάμενος²¹⁹ ἐπετέλεε πᾶσαν τὴν ὄψιν τῆς θυγατρός· ἐλοῦτο μὲν γὰρ ὑπὸ τοῦ Διός, ὅκως ὕοι, ἐχρίετο δὲ ὑπὸ τοῦ ἡλίου ἀνιεὶς αὐτὸς ἐκ τοῦ σώματος ἰκμάδα.

*Translation.* And after Polycrates arrived at Magnesia, he was wickedly murdered, in a manner neither worthy of himself nor of his proud designs. For, except for those who were tyrants of the Syracusans, none of the other Hellenic tyrants was worthy to be compared with Polycrates for magnificence. ³ And after putting him to death in a way not fit to be told,²²⁰ Oroetes suspended him on a stake. But of all those Samians who had followed [Polycrates], he [Oroetes] forgave them, commanding them to make known their thanks to him for their being free. But, as many of the foreigners and slaves who followed him, he had them placed in slavery by his command. ⁴ But when Polycrates was hung up, he fulfilled every part of the vision of his daughter, for he was washed by Zeus, in the form of rain, and he was anointed by the sun while letting loose moisture from his body.

*Commentary.*²²¹ This passage records the rather famous demise of Polycrates, who, in later ancient authors, becomes an archetype of the fate awaiting the covetous and over-indulgent. Whereas later texts often represent Polycrates' suspension as the means of his execution,²²² Herodotus appears to report the suspension here as *post mortem* (following the order of verbs ἀποκτείνας ... ἀνεσταύρωσε). Still, the suspension can be depicted both with ἀνεσταύρωσε (translated as "suspended on a stake") and with ἀνακρεμάμενος ("hung up"). This is a strong indicator that ἀνασταυρόω in Herodotus' day must have involved hanging someone aloft, and thus it complements the etymological argument that ἀνασταυρόω would have implied placing someone up (ἀνα) on a σταυρός ("pole"). GODLEY translates ἀνεσταύρωσε here as "crucified him", but it is not entirely clear in the context the precise way that Herodotus understood Polycrates to have been hung on the stake.²²³ HENGEL contends: "As a rule, Herodotus uses the verb ἀνασκολοπίζειν of living men and ἀνασταυροῦν

---

²¹⁹ As reported by both HUDE and ROSÉN, one manuscript has ἀνακρεκράμενος and two manuscripts contain ἀνακεκράμενος; both readings must be due to confused scribes.

²²⁰ For οὐκ ἀξίως ἀπηγήσιος see LSJ s.v. ἀφηγήσις.

²²¹ Text: HUDE, Herodoti Historiae, with capitalization here provided at the beginning of each sentence. Same text appears, with minor punctuation differences except for omission of τύραννοι, in ROSÉN, Herodoti historiae, 1:332.

²²² For example, observe the way Polycrates is treated in Dio Chrysostom, *Orationes* 17.15 ("On Covetousness"); Lucian, *Cont.* 14; Philo, *Prov.* 2.24–25 (Eusebius, *Praep.* 8.14.24–25). On all these texts see 3.9.

²²³ GODLEY, Herodotus, 2:155. Cf. RAWLINSON, Herodotus, 278 ("hung his dead body upon a cross"); PURVIS in STRASSLER, Herodotus, 265 has "hung his body from a stake".

of corpses."[224] This is possible, though most of the instances of ἀνασκολοπί-ζειν in Herodotus do not overtly indicate in context whether that penalty was the cause of death or was performed after death (1.128.2; 3.132.2; 3.159.1; 4.43.2,6; 4.202.1; 9.78.3; see the discussion on *Hist.* 9.78–79 in 3.4 below).

While Polycrates was a Hellenic tyrant over Samos, Oroetes is described as the Persian governor of Sardis sent by Cyrus (3.120.1). Thus we should consider this to be a Persian manner of dealing with Polycrates' body. Herodotus has heard two possible stories for why Oroetes so vehemently determined to kill Polycrates: a desire for revenge since Oroetes had been demeaned by others for failing to capture Samos from Polycrates (3.120.3–4) or retaliation for Polycrates' scorning the herald from Oroetes (3.121.1–2). Herodotus seems personally to favor the first explanation (cf. 3.120 and 3.126.2; though note 3.122.1). Herodotus appears quite critical of Oroetes' vicious actions here: He calls the incident an "unholy act" (πρήγματος οὐκ ὁσίου; 3.120.1), speaks of Polycrates as being "wickedly murdered" (διεφθάρη κακῶς; 3.125.2), refers to the manner of death prior to suspension as "in a way not fit to be told" (οὐκ ἀξίως ἀπηγήσιος; 3.125.3), and calls Oroetes' own execution a retribution (τίσιες) for his treatment of Polycrates (3.126.1; 3.128.5).

Oroetes actually lured Polycrates into a trap by offering him great wealth and the ability to become ruler of all Hellas (3.122.3–4). Herodotus declares that Polycrates "greatly longed for money" (3.123.1) and that he ambitiously desired to rule the seas (3.122.2–3), especially around Ionia. Thus, Polycrates' greed becomes a famous cautionary tale among later authors (see below 3.9). The intensity of Polycrates' greed is magnified by how, in falling for Oroetes' trap, Polycrates had refused to heed the counsel of family and friends, even ignoring oracles that cautioned him against sailing to meet Oroetes (3.124.1–3.125.1; cf. 3.40–43). In particular, his own daughter forewarned Polycrates of her dream that "she saw her father raised in the air, being washed by Zeus and anointed by the sun" (ἐδόκεέ οἱ τὸν πατέρα ἐν τῷ ἠέρι μετέωρον ἐόντα λοῦσθαι μὲν ὑπὸ τοῦ Διός, χρίεσθαι δὲ ὑπὸ τοῦ ἡλίου; 3.124.1). It is this dream that was fulfilled at the conclusion of the passage cited above.

**(195)** Herodotus, *Historiae* 3.132.1–2

Τότε δὴ ὁ Δημοκήδης ἐν τοῖσι Σούσοισι ἐξιησάμενος Δαρεῖον οἶκόν τε μέγιστον εἶχε καὶ ὁμοτράπεζος βασιλέϊ ἐγεγόνεε, πλήν τε ἑνός τοῦ ἐς Ἕλληνας ἀπιέναι πάντα τἆλλά οἱ παρῆν. ² Καὶ τοῦτο μὲν τοὺς Αἰγυπτίους ἰητρούς, οἳ βασιλέα πρότερον ἰῶντο, μέλλοντας ἀνασκολοπιεῖσθαι[225] διότι ὑπὸ Ἕλληνος ἰητροῦ ἐσσώθησαν, τούτους βασιλέα παραιτησάμενος ἐρρύσατο.

---

[224] HENGEL, Crucifixion, 24 (HENGEL, Cross, 116).

[225] Several manuscripts read ἀνασκολοπίζεσθαι, which does not dramatically alter the meaning of the clause; see HUDE, Herodoti Historiae, 1:337.

*Translation.* At that very time Democedes, having cured Darius at Susa, had a great house and became one who ate at table with the king. Except for one matter (being allowed to depart back to Greece) they presented him with everything else. [2] And, when the Egyptian physicians, who earlier had cared for the king, were about to be impaled because they were proven inferior by the Greek physician, he appealed to the king and delivered them.

*Commentary.*[226] When Darius the Persian sprained his foot leaping from his horse, his Egyptian physicians were unable to heal him (and actually made the pain worse; see 3.129–130). Democedes (the famous Greek physician) was brought out from his slavery and healed the king. In return, Democedes receives great wealth. He even has sufficient influence at court to prevent the Egyptian physicians from being impaled (ἀνασκολοπιεῖσθαι) for their quackery.

**(196)** Herodotus, *Historiae* 3.159.1

Δαρεῖος δὲ ἐπείτε ἐκράτησε τῶν Βαβυλωνίων, τοῦτο μέν σφεων τὸ τεῖχος περιεῖλε καὶ τὰς πύλας πάσας ἀπέσπασε (τὸ γὰρ πρότερον ἑλὼν Κῦρος τὴν Βαβυλῶνα ἐποίησε τούτων οὐδέτερον), τοῦτο δὲ ὁ Δαρεῖος τῶν ἀνδρῶν τοὺς κορυφαίους μάλιστα ἐς τρισχιλίους ἀνεσκολόπισε, τοῖσι δὲ λοιποῖσι Βαβυλω-νίοισι ἀπέδωκε τὴν πόλιν οἰκέειν.

*Translation.* And when Darius conquered the Babylonians, he removed their city-wall and tore down all the gates (for when Cyrus first took Babylon he did neither of these things); and Darius impaled as many as three thousand leaders of the men; but to the remaining Babylonians he returned the city for them to inhabit.

*Commentary.*[227] At the conclusion of this very costly second Persian conquest of Babylon, Darius goes to great lengths to prevent a third conflict. Thus he destroys the city defenses and impales (ἀνεσκολόπισε) the city's leadership. Elsewhere, however, Darius displays his mercy by allowing citizens to return to Babylon and by providing wives for the men of the city. The bodily suspensions here are notable for two factors: the use of this penalty at the conclusion of a difficult siege and for the number of people who suffered this means of execution (as many as 3000 according to Herodotus).

---

[226] Text: HUDE, Herodoti Historiae, with capitalization here provided at the beginning of each sentence; also in ROSÉN, Herodoti historiae, 1:337.

[227] Text: HUDE, Herodoti Historiae; cf. ROSÉN, Herodoti historiae, 1: 351–352 (who reads instead τοῖσδε [λοιποῖσι Βαβυλωνίοις]).

**(197)** Herodotus, *Historiae* 4.43.2–3, 6

Θυγατέρα γὰρ Ζωπύρου τοῦ Μεγαβύζου ἐβιήσατο παρθένον· ἔπειτα μέλλον-
τος [αὐτοῦ] διὰ ταύτην τὴν αἰτίην ἀνασκολοπιεῖσθαι ὑπὸ Ξέρξεω βασιλέος ἡ
μήτηρ τοῦ Σατάσπεος ἐοῦσα Δαρείου ἀδελφεὴ παραιτήσατο, φᾶσά οἱ αὐτὴ
μέζω ζημίην ἐπιθήσειν ἤ περ ἐκεῖνον· ³ Λιβύην γάρ οἱ ἀνάγκην ἔσεσθαι
περιπλέειν, ἐς ὃ ἂν ἀπίκηται περιπλέων αὐτὴν ἐς τὸν Ἀράβιον κόλπον ...
⁶ Τοῦ δὲ μὴ περιπλῶσαι Λιβύην παντελέως αἴτιον τόδε ἔλεγε, τὸ πλοῖον τὸ
πρόσω οὐ δυνατὸν ἔτι εἶναι προβαίνειν ἀλλ᾽ ἐνίσχεσθαι. Ξέρξης δὲ οὐ οἱ²²⁸
συγγινώσκων λέγειν ἀληθέα, οὐκ ἐπιτελέσαντά γε τὸν προκείμενον ἄεθλον,
ἀνεσκολόπισε, τὴν ἀρχαίην δίκην ἐπιτιμῶν.

*Translation.* For he [i.e., Sataspes] had ravished the virgin daughter of Zopyrus
son of Megabyzus. Then, when he was about to be impaled because of this
charge by Xerxes the king, Sataspes' mother (being the sister of Darius)
entreated, saying that she would lay upon him a greater penalty than even that.
³ For his requirement would be to circumnavigate Libya, until which point,
having circumnavigated it, he arrived in the Arabian Gulf ... [Intervening text
tells of Sataspes giving up in his quest to sail around Africa.] ⁶ And for not
completely circumnavigating Libya [Sataspes] spoke this reason: The boat
was not able to go forward anymore but was held back. Yet Xerxes did not
acknowledge that he spoke the truth, and since he did not complete the
appointed contest, [Xerxes] impaled him, making the original trial the ground
of punishment.

*Commentary.*²²⁹ In a section depicting the geography of the known world,
Herodotus recounts two attempts to sail around Libya (i.e., the whole of
Africa). The first was sponsored by Nechos king of Egypt, involved Phoenici-
ans, and was successful. The second was attempted by Sataspes on behalf of
the Persians in lieu of his punishment for raping the daughter of Zopyrus.
Sataspes is said to have made it past the Pillars of Herakles (i.e., the Straits of
Gibraltar) and travelled several months south down the western coast of
Africa. Seeing only further ocean ahead, he gave up and returned home with
tales of pygmies and forbidding seas. With Sataspes having failed to accomplish his set task, Darius orders the original penalty to be carried out against
Sataspes.

Since Herodotus records impalement (ἀνεσκολόπισε) to have been the
mandated punishment for this rape, he likely testifies to revulsion at Sataspes'
actions, especially carried out against such a noble daughter of Persia. Her

---

²²⁸ Some manuscripts read οἱ οὐ.

²²⁹ Text: HUDE, *Herodoti Historiae*, with some capitalization added. Similar text in ROSÉN,
*Herodoti historiae*, 1:374–375 (though with variations in the inflection of παραιτήσατο and
περιπλέειν, and with the bracketing of the beginning of 4.43.6 through ἔλεγε; none of these
will drastically affect the sense of the whole).

father, Zopyrus, had previously mutilated himself in order to allow Darius to conquer Babylon, and he was one of the most honored men among all of Darius' friends (3.153–160; cf. Diodorus Siculus, *Bib. hist.* 10.19).[230]

**(198)** Herodotus, *Historiae* 4.202.1–2

Τοὺς μέν νυν αἰτιωτάτους τῶν Βαρκαίων ἡ Φερετίμη, ἐπείτε οἱ ἐκ τῶν Περ-σέων παρεδόθησαν, ἀνεσκολόπισε κύκλῳ τοῦ τείχεος, τῶν δέ σφι γυναικῶν τοὺς μαζοὺς ἀποταμοῦσα περιέστιξε καὶ τούτοισι τὸ τεῖχος. ² Τοὺς δὲ λοιποὺς τῶν Βαρκαίων ληίην ἐκέλευσε θέσθαι τοὺς Πέρσας, πλὴν ὅσοι αὐτῶν ἦσαν Βαττιάδαι τε καὶ τοῦ φόνου οὐ μεταίτιοι· τούτοισι δὲ τὴν πόλιν ἐπέτρεψε ἡ Φερετίμη.

*Translation.* Now the most culpable of the Barcaeans, when they had been handed over by the Persians, Pheretime impaled around the walls; and the breasts of their wives she had cut off and also stuck them around the walls. ² The remainder of the Barcaeans she ordered to be given the Persians as plunder. But as many of those who were Battiadai and not accessories to the murder, to those Pheretime entrusted the city.

*Commentary.*[231] Pheretime was the wife of Battus the lame, the king of the Greek colony of Cyrene in Libya (4.161–162). Their son Arcesilaüs attempted to regain some of the privileges lost during his father's reign, but after multiple battles and his own cruelly authoritarian rule, he was later murdered while in exile in the nearby city of Barca (4.164). His mother, Pheretime, sought to avenge the death of her son upon the Barcaean citizens and the Cyrenaean exiles who lived in Barca. She requested troops from Aryandes, the Persian governor of Egypt, which he granted with the goal of capturing this part of Libya for Persia (4.165–167).

The above narrative records the events once the Persians, after enduring a difficult nine-month siege of Barca, finally gained control of the city through devious means. The Battiadai would be trusted members of Pheretime's own household of Battus.

Pheretime was likely of Greek ancestry in a Hellenic colony, so we might be inclined to list this an early instance of a Greek performing impalement (ἀνεσκολόπισε) among other forms of butchery. However, the greater portion of the conquering force was Persian, and the penalty accords with the many Persian acts already recorded in Herodotus.[232] So from Herodotus' perspec-

---

[230] The trick is strikingly reminscent of Odysseus in Homer, *Od.* 4.245ff. Zopyros' famed act was much later remembered in Ammianus Marcellinus, *Rerum Gestarum* 18.5.3.

[231] Text: HUDE, Herodoti Historiae, with capitalization added at the beginning of each sentence. Same text with minor variations in ROSÉN, Herodoti historiae, 1:456–457.

[232] In addition to the impalements listed here, the other occasion in Herodotus that invol-

tive, Pheretime appears to be permitting (or perhaps imitating) the kinds of battlefield acts in which the Persians engaged. Though this particular mass impalement is not actually depicted in detail, it was certainly a public event that involved exposing the bodies of the impaled all around the city walls. It is likely that the leadership of the city was impaled, while the citizenry was led off to Persian slavery (4.203–204). The penalty signals military revenge at the end of a bitter conflict, which had undoubtedly angered the Persians greatly.

Herodotus' own verdict on Pheretime's actions comes at the very close of *Historiae* Book Four, where he notes that she "died horribly" (ἀπέθανε κακῶς; 4.205) – her body was swarmed with worms that ate her flesh while she still lived (cf. Acts 12:23). Herodotus believes this gruesome demise of Pheretime manifested the anger of the gods against her excessive vengeance on Barca.[233]

**(199)** Herodotus, *Historiae* 6.30.1–2

Εἰ μέν νυν, ὡς ἐζωγρήθη, ἄχθη[234] ἀγόμενος παρὰ βασιλέα Δαρεῖον, ὁ δὲ οὔτ' ἂν ἔπαθε κακὸν οὐδέν, δοκέειν ἐμοί, ἀπῆκέ τ' ἂν αὐτῷ τὴν αἰτίην· νῦν δέ μιν αὐτῶν τε τούτων εἵνεκα καὶ ἵνα μὴ διαφυγὼν αὖτις μέγας παρὰ βασιλέϊ γένηται, Ἀρταφρένης τε ὁ Σαρδίων ὕπαρχος καὶ ὁ λαβὼν Ἅρπαγος, ὡς ἀπίκετο ἀγόμενος ἐς [τὰς] Σάρδις, τὸ μὲν αὐτοῦ σῶμα αὐτοῦ ταύτη ἀνεσταύρωσαν, τὴν δὲ κεφαλὴν ταριχεύσαντες ἀνήνεικαν παρὰ βασιλέα Δαρεῖον ἐς Σοῦσα. ² Δαρεῖος δὲ πυθόμενος ταῦτα καὶ ἐπαιτιησάμενος τοὺς ταῦτα ποιήσαντας ὅτι μιν οὐ ζώοντα ἀνήγαγον ἐς ὄψιν τὴν ἑωυτοῦ, τὴν κεφαλὴν τὴν Ἱστιαίου λούσαντάς τε καὶ περιστείλαντας εὖ ἐνετείλατο θάψαι ὡς ἀνδρὸς μεγάλως ἑωυτῷ τε καὶ Πέρσῃσι εὐεργέτεω. Τὰ μὲν περὶ Ἱστιαῖον οὕτω ἔσχε.[235]

*Translation.* Since he was taken alive, if he [i.e., Histiaeus] had been brought to King Darius, then he would not have suffered any harm (it seems to me) and [Darius] would have forgiven his offense. But now, since on account of these things [which he had done] and in order that he not escape again and become great beside the king, Artaphrenes, the viceroy of Sardis, and Harpagus, who captured Histiaeus, as he arrived in Sardis, suspended his very body

---

ved the cutting off of a woman's breast is recorded as a vengeful act by Amestris of the Persian royal household, who had the king's bodyguard mutilate her rival by cutting off her breasts (and throwing them to dogs), as well as cutting her nose, ears, lips, and tongue (9.112).

[233] 4.205: ὡς ἄρα ἀνθρώποισι αἱ λίην ἰσχυραὶ τιμωρίαι πρὸς θεῶν ἐπίφθονοι γίνονται. Ἡ μὲν δὴ Φερετίμης τῆς Βάττου τοιαύτη τε καὶ τοσαύτη τιμωρίη ἐγένετο ἐς Βαρκαίους ("Thus to men, exceedingly severe acts of vengeance become odious with the gods. So then, both such kind of and such magnitude of vengeance came from Pheretime, wife of Battus, against the Barcaeans."

[234] One manuscript reads ἔχθη; Bredow conjectures ἀνήχθη.

[235] The LCL edition by GODLEY along with ROSÉN labels this last clause as part of 6.31; the OCT text by HUDE reads it with 6.30.

up on a pole in that place. And having embalmed his head, they brought it to King Darius in Susa. ² But Darius, after learning these things and blaming those who did them (because they did not bring [Histiaeus] alive into his presence), ordered the head of Histiaeus washed, wrapped well, and buried as a man who had performed much good for Darius himself and for the Persians. These events concerning Histiaeus happened in this way.

*Commentary.*²³⁶ This marks the second instance in Herodotus in which ἀνασταυρόω indicates the putting up of a body on a σταυρός ("pole"; see also 3.125 above).²³⁷ While elsewhere in *Historiae* ἀνασταυρόω can be used with κεφαλή to indicate the *post mortem* suspension of a head on a pole (4.103.2; cf. 7.238.1; 9.78.3),²³⁸ here the headless body is suspended. In this passage, it is unclear whether Histiaeus' body was suspended before or after his death, and also the text does not depict when he was beheaded relative to the time of his bodily suspension.

Histiaeus of Miletus, though initially helpful to the Persian cause (4.141), began scheming to take portions of Greece and Asia Minor for himself (e.g., 5.35–36; 6.4–5; 6.26–28). Though Histiaeus is able to fool Darius concerning his designs (5.106–107), Artaphrenes sees through his ambitions (6.1–4). Harpagus manages to capture Histiaeus (6.28–29), and they execute him as recorded in the text quoted above. Artaphrenes and Harpagus likely understood their suspension (ἀνεσταύρωσαν) of Histiaeus to be in keeping with typical military procedure since he had sought (as a Greek) to oppose Persian rule in the war. However, the timing of the execution preceded the judgment of Darius, in whose court Histiaeus once resided. This angered Darius, likely validating Artaphrenes' fears that Darius might still favor Histiaeus, even despite his rebellious tendencies.

**(200)** Aristotle, *Politica* 5.1311b (lines 35–39)

ὁμοίως δὲ καὶ διὰ φόβον· ἓν γάρ τι τοῦτο τῶν αἰτίων ἦν, ὥσπερ καὶ περὶ τὰς πολιτείας καὶ περὶ τὰς μοναρχίας· οἷον Ξέρξην Ἀρταπάνης φοβούμενος τὴν διαβολὴν τὴν περὶ Δαρεῖον, ὅτι ἐκρέμασεν οὐ κελεύσαντος Ξέρξου, ἀλλ᾽ οἰόμενος [40] συγγνώσεσθαι ὡς ἀμνημονοῦντα διὰ τὸ δειπνεῖν.

---

²³⁶ Text: HUDE, Herodoti Historiae, vol. 2, with some capitalization added. The awkward repeated αὐτοῦ (in τὸ μὲν αὐτοῦ σῶμα αὐτοῦ ταύτῃ ἀνεσταύρωσαν) is correct, though some have suggested its deletion. ROSÉN, Herodoti historiae, 2:92–93 deletes the ταύτῃ.

²³⁷ Note that σταυρός is clearly used of poles to hold platforms in Herodotus, *Hist.* 5.16.

²³⁸ The Greek in *Hist.* 4.103.2 (τὴν δὲ κεφαλὴν ἀνασταυροῦσι) is clear (as is especially its context) that the head is hung up, while the body is disposed of otherwise. The Greek is slightly less definitive in 7.238.1 (ἐκέλευσε ἀποταμόντας τὴν κεφαλὴν ἀνασταυρῶσαι) and in 9.78.3 (ἀποταμόντες τὴν κεφαλὴν ἀνεσταύρωσαν), both in reference to Xerxes' decapitation of Leonidas' corpse and his suspension of Leonidas' head (or, less plausibly, the body).

*Translation*. And likewise also on account of fear. For this was one of the causes [listed above], just as [it was] concerning both constitutional governments and monarchies. Such as Xerxes, [who was murdered] when Artapanus feared accusation concerning Darius, because he had hung [Darius] even though Xerxes had not commanded it, but [Artapanus] supposed [Xerxes] to have consented since [Xerxes] was unmindful because he was dining.

*Commentary*.[239] Aristotle (384–322 B.C.) writes here about the death of Xerxes (465 B.C.) following his substantial loss to the Greeks. This section in the *Politics* (beginning in 1309b) concerns the causes of the destruction and preservation of monarchies (both royal rules and tyrannies). In these lines, by the example of Xerxes' death, fear is shown to be one cause of insurrection against a monarchy (just as earlier it was revealed to similarly imperil constitutional governments – see 1302b).

The episode is briefly stated, and the intended historical details are not entirely clear. Aristotle apparently claims that Artapanus (also called Artabanus by others) had previously hung Darius (Xerxes' son) without proper orders from the king, and therefore Artapanus feared punishment. The suspension is recorded without clear markers concerning its method. Artapanus is known to have been a chief official of the king, possibly a member of the king's bodyguard. Significantly, though other Greek historians have varying accounts of this episode, they all agree (against Aristotle) that Darius was killed only after Artabanus had assassinated Xerxes (cf. Ctesias, *Persica*, FGH 3c 688 Frag. 13.33 and 14.34; Justin, *Epitome* 3.1.2–4; Diodorus Siculus, *Bib. hist.* 11.69.2–5). In fact, these other accounts all assert Artabanus claimed that Darius had killed his own father (Xerxes), thus convincing Artaxerxes to kill his brother Darius as recompense for their father's death. All are agreed that Artabanus met his end when Artaxerxes later slew him.

Even though Aristotle's account could well be inaccurate, it does testify to Greek belief in the fourth century B.C. that Persians could execute others by bodily suspension.

**(201)** Thucydides, *Historiae* 1.110.2–3

Αἴγυπτος δὲ πάλιν ὑπὸ βασιλέα ἐγένετο πλὴν Ἀμυρταίου τοῦ ἐν τοῖς ἕλεσι βασιλέως· τοῦτον δὲ διὰ μέγεθός τε τοῦ ἕλους οὐκ ἐδύναντο ἑλεῖν, καὶ ἅμα μαχιμώτατοί εἰσι τῶν Αἰγυπτίων οἱ ἕλειοι. ³ Ἰνάρως δὲ ὁ Λιβύων βασιλεύς, ὃς τὰ πάντα ἔπραξε περὶ τῆς Αἰγύπτου, προδοσίᾳ ληφθεὶς ἀνεσταυρώθη.

*Translation*. And Egypt again came under the king [i.e., Artaxerxes], except for Amyrtaeus who was king in the marshes. And they were not able to capture

---

[239] Text: WILLIAM DAVID ROSS, *Aristotelis politica* (Oxford: Clarendon, 1957).

him [Amyrtaeus] both on account of the magnitude of the marshes together with the fact that the marsh-dwellers are the most warlike of the Egyptians. [3] But Inaros, the king of the Libyans, who began practicing all these things regarding Egypt, was taken by betrayal and suspended on a *stauros*.

*Commentary.*[240] Thucydides wrote in the late fifth century about these events that occurred c. 454 B.C. Inaros had conspired to overthrow the Persian rule of Egypt under Artaxerxes, and he requested Athenian assistance in this endeavor (*Hist.* 1.104). He and his Athenian allies are conquered by the Persians, and Inaros meets his end in this passage. According to Thucydides, his execution involved ἀνεσταυρώθη, which likely means that he was hung up on a pole; the etymology favors this, especially given Thucydides frequent use of σταυρός for pointed poles.[241] How precisely Thucydides pictures this suspension, and whether any crossbeam was involved cannot be stated with certainty.[242] There is no other means of death mentioned, so the suspension could likely have led to his demise.

In the context of this passage, the Persians are the likely actors in suspending Inaros. They would have considered this action justified since he was both a military opponent and a rebel leader. A varying (though perhaps complementary) account of this event is found in the Ctesias fragment next below, where we further assess the historicity of the event.

**(202)** Ctesias, *Persica*, FGH 3c 688 Frag. 14.39 (from Photius, *Bibliotheca* 72)

Ἀμῆστρις δὲ ὑπὲρ τοῦ παιδὸς Ἀχαιμενίδου δεινὰ ἐποιεῖτο, εἰ μὴ τιμωρήσαιτο Ἴναρον καὶ τοὺς Ἕλληνας, καὶ αἰτεῖται ταῦτα βασιλεῖ, ὁ δὲ οὐκ ἐνδίδωσιν· εἶτα Μεγαβύζῳ· ὁ δὲ ἀποπέμπεται. εἶτα ἐπεὶ διώχλει τὸν υἱόν, κατειργάσατο· καὶ πέντε παρελθόντων ἐτῶν λαμβάνει τὸν Ἴναρον παρὰ βασιλέως καὶ τοὺς

---

[240] Text: HENRY STUART JONES and JOHN ENOCH POWELL, Thucydidis Historiae (2 vols.; Scriptorum classicorum bibliotheca Oxoniensis; Oxford: Clarendon, 1942); there are no page numbers in this edition. The same text, with slight punctuation differences, occurs in CARL HUDE, Thucydidis Historiae (Editio Minor; Leipzig: Teubner, 1903), 1:85.

[241] A σταυρός is a fortification stake in Thucydides, *Hist.* 4.90.2; 6.99.2; 6.100.3; 7.25.5–7. Moreover, Thucydides employs several cognate terms for building palisades (or similar military enclosures constructed of poles): σταυρόω (6.100.1; 7.25.7), διασταυρόω (6.97.2), περισταυρόω (2.75.1), προσταυρόω (6.75.1), προσσταυρόω (4.9.1), ἀποσταυρόω (4.69.2; 6.101.2; 7.80.6). A σταύρωμα is a "palisade" or stockade (5.10.6; 6.64.3; 6.66.2; 6.74.2; 6.100.1–3; 6.101.3; 7.25.7; 7.38.2; 7.53.1). This provides considerable support for ἀνασταυρόω to maintain its connection to "suspend on a pole" since all other uses of σταυρός cognates in Thucydides retain their relationship to poles stuck in the ground.

[242] Some English translations render ἀνεσταυρώθη as "crucified"; cf. RICHARD CRAWLEY, Thucydides. The Peloponnesian War (New ed.; ed. W. Robert Connor; London: Dent, 1993), 52. The same CRAWLEY translation also appears in STRASSLER, Thucydides. CHARLES FOSTER SMITH, Thucydides (4 vols.; LCL; Cambridge: Harvard University Press, 1919–1930), 1:185 reads "impaled".

Ἕλληνας. καὶ ἀνεσταύρισεν μὲν ἐπὶ τρισὶ σταυροῖς· πεντήκοντα δὲ Ἑλλήνων, ὅσους λαβεῖν ἴσχυσε, τούτων ἔτεμε τὰς κεφαλάς.

*Translation.* But Amestris was making complaints on account of her son Achaemenides, [fearful] she would not be able to avenge herself on Inaros and the Greeks. And she requested these [acts of vengeance] from the king, but he did not give in; then [she requested these things] from Megabyzus, but he sent [her] away. Then after she wearied her son [i.e., king Artaxerxes], she pre-vailed upon him. And after five years had passed, she procured Inaros and the Greeks from the king. And she affixed [Inaros] up on three *stauroi*; but fifty Greeks (as many as she had the influence to procure) – she cut off their heads.

*Commentary.*[243] Ctesias' *Persica* is only extant in excerpts from later authors (such as the ninth-century A.D. patriarch Photius of Constantinople, here in his *Bibliotheca* codex 72).[244] Ctesias was a contemporary of Thucydides. Ctesias provides a much more detailed account of Inaros' death than does Thucydi-des' account above (*Hist.* 1.110.2–3). Also, Thucydides' narrative focuses on the Greek forces in Egypt (*Hist.* 1.104.1–2; 1.109.1–110.4), as does that of Diodorus Siculus (*Bib. hist.* 11.71.3–6; 11.74.1–75.6; 11.77.1–5). In contrast, Ctesias provides more space for depicting the Persians. Earlier, Photius recorded Ctesias as saying that the Libyan Inaros had led an Egyptian revolt against Artaxerxes,[245] who sent his brother Achaemenides with a force of 400,000 to battle Inaros. Achaemenides was killed by Inaros, who sent his corpse back to Artaxerxes (FGH 3c 688 Frag. 14.36).[246] Megabyzus was then dispatched with 200,000 more men; he engaged Inaros and injured him. Inaros escapes to Byblos, where Megabyzus makes a treaty with him. Megabyzus appealed to Artaxerxes to guarantee the safety of Inaros (and the more than 6,000 Greeks who were among his forces), and Artaxerxes consented (FGH 3c 688 Frag. 14.38). Here, we rejoin the narrative above in which Amestris

---

[243] Text: LENFANT, Ctésias de Cnide, 131; STRONK, Ctesias's Persian History, 340, transla-tion 341. Cf. LLEWELLYN-JONES and ROBSON, Ctesias' History of Persia, 189. LENFANT, ibid. 268, n. 557 (also apparatus p. 131) observes that the manuscripts read "Amytis" rather than "Amestris", though the latter is clearly correct (and it is Ἀμῆστρις that appears in the texts of JACOBY, LENFANT, and STRONK). As in Frag. 9.6 one manuscript in the family A tradition reads ἀνεσταύρωσεν for ἀνεσταύρισεν (see apparatus in LENFANT, 131).

[244] On concerns about Photius' accuracy cf. No. 192 (Ctesias, FGH 3c 688 Frag. 9.6).

[245] In addition to Ctesias and Thucydides, Diodorus references Inaros by name (*Bib. hist.* 11.71.3–4), though he does not record Inaros' death.

[246] Thucydides's brief account does not mention the role and death of Achaemenides. Herodotus instead mentions Achaemenes, son of Darius (and brother of Xerxes), in *Hist.* 3.12.4 and 7.7 (also cf. 7.97; 7.236–237). Diodorus Siculus similarly recollects the name as Achaemenes, son of Darius and *uncle* (rather than "son," as in Ctesias) of Artaxerxes (*Bib. hist.* 11.74.1). JOAN M. BIGWOOD, Ctesias' Account of the Revolt of Inarus, Phoenix 30 (1976): 1–24, 7-9 argues cogently that Ctesias (rather than Photius or a copiest) must have been confused about the name (and parentage) of Achaemenides.

(the mother of both Artaxerxes and Achaemenides), in contrast to Artaxerxes' promises, desires vengeance on Inaros for Achaemenides' death. She eventually pro-cures this vengeance from Artaxerxes after five years of pleading both with Artaxerxes (her son, the king) and with Megabyzus (who had promised Inaros safety). In contrast to Thucydides (*Hist.* 1.110.3), Ctesias claims that Inaros entered into an agreement with Megabyzus (rather than being betrayed) and that an extended five-year time elapsed before Inaros was suspended by the Persians. In Ctesias, the suspension occurs at the command of Amestris, who is not mentioned by Thucydides. Most significantly, where Thucydides merely declares that Inaros was suspended on a *stauros* (ἀνεσταυρώθη), here in Ctesias, Amestris affixes Inaros up on three such *stauroi* (καὶ ἀνεσταύρισεν μὲν ἐπὶ τρισὶ σταυροῖς). SAMUELSSON concludes that such a procedure must involve impalement (rather than crucifixion), given the use of three poles.[247] In truth, it is difficult to be sure exactly what kind of suspension Ctesias / Photius imagines here, though it should likely be compared to the reference in Plutarch (who may well also be indebted to Ctesias for the information) to three *stauroi* employed to transfix Masabates' body sideways (Plutarch, *Art.* 17.5; Ctesias, FGH 3c 688 Frag. 26.17.7; see below).[248] For another possibili-ty, COOK helpfully compares Inaros' death to the portrayal on a bronze *cista* (lidded box) of the mythical Andromeda attached to three poles, with the horizontal cross beam supported on either side by an upright pole (forming a kind of half rectangle) – her arms are tied to the crossbeam.[249] There are reasons to be suspicious of some of the details in Ctesias, especially since this episode plays into a theme in Ctesias / Photius of mothers (or grandmothers) wreaking vengeance on an assailant of their sons/grandsons.[250] In

---

[247] SAMUELSSON, Crucifixion, 62.

[248] The commentators also note this comparison, including AUBERGER, Ctésias, 159 n. 7 and LENFANT, Ctésias de Cnide, 268 n. 558.

[249] COOK, Crucifixion, 222 (image ibid. 455; discussion ibid. 33). COOK rightly notes that Marcus Manilius speaks of Andromeda "hung on the virgin cross" (*cruce virginea ... pependit*; Manilius, *Astrol.* 5.552), ibid. 117. Cf. COOK, Patibulum, 445–446.

[250] Observe how Amestris later procured the death on a *stauros* of a Caunian man who killed her grandson Zopyros (Frag. 14.45 from Photius; see below) and how she buried alive (after two months of punishment) the doctor who took sexual advantage of her daughter (Frag. 14.44). Compare this with the involvement of Parysatis in beguiling Artaxerxes II to permit her to suspend on three *stauroi* Masabates for his role in the death of her son Cyrus (Ctesias, FGH 3c 688 Frag. 26.17.1–7 from Plutarch; see below; compare and contrast the same episode in Frag. 16.66 from Photius; also below). Parysatis played an earlier role in killing the Carian, who claimed to have executed Cyrus (Frag. 26.14.9–10 also from Plutarch). Also note how Amytis attempted to convince Cambyses to allow her vengeance on the murderer of her son (Frag. 13.13 from Photius). Joan Bigwood also observes Ctesias' tendency to produce examples of vengeful mothers, and she questions the accuracy of the earlier accounts in Ctesias in part on the basis of these and other such recurring themes in Ctesias' *Persica*, as well as on Ctesias' mistaken use of names and questionable numbers for soldiers/ships (BIGWOOD, Ctesias' Account, 19). BIGWOOD ultimately accuses Ctesias of reshaping past

any case, it appears that in Thucydides and in Ctesias, we have two (apparently independent) witnesses to the bodily suspension of Inaros. After Amestris' actions in the passage above, Ctesias goes on to recount that Megabyzus grieved for the Persian's broken promises to Inaros and the Greeks; consequently Megabyzus sent the other Greek captives to Syria where he met them and launched a successful rebellion (Ctesias, FGH 3c 688 Frag. 9.40–43).

**(203)** Ctesias, *Persica*, FGH 3c 688 Frag. 14.45 (from Photius, *Bibliotheca* 72)

Ζώπυρος δὲ ὁ Μεγαβύζου καὶ Ἀμύτιος παῖς, ἐπεὶ αὐτῷ ὅ τε πατὴρ καὶ ἡ μήτηρ ἐτελεύτησαν, ἀπέστη βασιλέως, καὶ εἰς Ἀθήνας ἀφίκετο, κατὰ τὴν τῆς μητρὸς εἰς αὐτοὺς εὐεργεσίαν. Εἰς Καῦνον δὲ ἅμα τῶν ἑπομένων εἰσέπλευσε, καὶ ἐκέλευσε παραδιδόναι τὴν πόλιν· Καύνιοι δὲ αὐτῷ μὲν παραδιδόναι τὴν πόλιν ἔφασκον, Ἀθηναίοις δὲ τοῖς συνεπομένοις οὐκέτι. Εἰσιόντι δὲ Ζωπύρῳ εἰς τὸ τεῖχος, λίθον Ἀλκίδης Καύνιος ἐμβάλλει εἰς τὴν κεφαλὴν καὶ οὕτω Ζώπυρος ἀποθνῄσκει. Ἀμῆστρις δὲ ἡ μάμμη τὸν Καύνιον ἀνεσταύρισεν.

*Translation.* And Zopyros, the son of Megabyzus and Amytis, after both his father and mother died, deserted the king, and he came into Athens, on account of the kindness of his mother to them. And he sailed into Caunos with his followers, and he ordered [them] to hand over the city. And the Caunians affirmed that they would hand over the city to him, but no longer to his Athenian followers. And as Zopyros was entering into the city wall, Alcides (a Caunian) threw a stone onto his head, and thus Zopyros died. But Amestris, his grandmother, affixed up the Caunian on a *stauros*.

*Commentary.*[251] Ctesias (as extant in Photius' summary) pens another episode in which Amestris has a person fixed up on a *stauros* (ἀνεσταύρισεν; cf. FGH 3c 688 Frag. 14.39 above), this time for the murder of her grandson. The precise date of such an event is unclear, but it would presumably be in the later half of the fifth century B.C.,[252] after Zopyros' father (Megabyzus) had made

---

events to conform to the events of Ctesias' own lifetime (ibid. 20–21), such as conflating the deaths on three *stauroi* of Inaros (at the instigation of Amestris) with the death of Masabates / Bagapates (at the hand of Parysatis) on three *stauroi* from the time of Ctesias' own experience of Artaxerxes II (ibid., 19). BIGWOOD's skeptical conclusions are warranted but perhaps excessive since Ctesias may well have been emphasizing a pattern that did indeed re-occur in the Persian court; it is difficult to be sure. In any case, Ctesias (and his readers) could easily imagine powerful Persian women calling for the bodily suspension of their enemies.

[251] Text: LENFANT, Ctésias de Cnide, 134; compared with STRONK, Ctesias's Persian History, 344, translation ibid. 345; cf. LLEWELLYN-JONES and ROBSON, Ctesias' History of Persia, 191. LENFANT notes that the two main Photius MSS read various forms for ἀνεσταύρισεν (in the 12th c. M/451, while the 10th c. A/450 reads ἀνεσταύρωσεν); meaning is unchanged; further variation in ἅμα τῶν ἑπομένων (A/450), ἅμα τοῖς ἑπομένοις (M/451) and ἅμ᾿ αὐτῶν ἑπομένων (conjecture JACOBY, following BEKKER); STRONK suggests ἅμ᾿ αὐτοῖς ἑπομένοις.

[252] So AUBERGER, Ctésias, 160 n. 13; also LENFANT, Ctésias de Cnide, 270 n. 580.

allegiances with the Athenians with whom he had made a treaty in Egypt (see our preceding discussion of Frag. 14.39). However, this passage implies that it was Zopyros' mother (Amytis), rather than his father, whose patronage ("kindness") had won the Athenians to the side of their family. That both Megabyzus and Amytis had positive relations with Athens is possible (even likely given Amytis' royal parentage), but Ctesias could possibly be confused. Zopyros son of Megabyzus is also mentioned in Herodotus (*Hist.* 3.160.2), where Zopyros is said to have "deserted Persia, and gone over to the Athenians," though Herodotus does not mention Zopyros' death.[253] Caunos / Caunus is a coastal city in Caria (southwest Anatolia; Strabo, *Geogr.* 14.2.2–3).[254]

**(204)** Xenophon, *Anabasis* 3.1.17–18

καὶ μὴν εἰ ὑφησόμεθα καὶ ἐπὶ βασιλεῖ γενησόμεθα, τί οἰόμεθα πείσεσθαι; ὃς καὶ τοῦ ὁμομητρίου καὶ ὁμοπατρίου ἀδελφοῦ καὶ τεθνηκότος ἤδη ἀποτεμὼν τὴν κεφαλὴν καὶ τὴν χεῖρα ἀνεσταύρωσεν· ἡμᾶς δέ, οἷς κηδεμὼν μὲν οὐδεὶς πάρεστιν, ἐστρατεύσαμεν δὲ ἐπ' αὐτὸν ὡς δοῦλον ἀντὶ βασιλέως ποιήσοντες καὶ ἀποκτενοῦντες εἰ δυναίμεθα, τί ἂν οἰόμεθα παθεῖν; ¹⁸ ἆρ' οὐκ ἂν ἐπὶ πᾶν ἔλθοι ὡς ἡμᾶς τὰ ἔσχατα αἰκισάμενος πᾶσιν ἀνθρώποις φόβον παράσχοι τοῦ στρατεῦσαί ποτε ἐπ' αὐτόν;

*Translation.* And yet if we were to give up and were to come upon the king, what do we suppose would happen? Who even concerning his already-dead brother (born of the same mother and same father) cut off his head and hand and crucified him. But we, who have no one to appear as protector, and we who waged war against him, seeking to make [him] as a slave rather than a king and seeking to kill [him] if we were able, what do we suppose would happen [to us]? ¹⁸ So then would he not come against everyone, so by torturing us with extreme means he might deliver fear to all men that have ever sought to wage war against him?

---

[253] Herodotus here helpfully distinguishes between the Zopyros son of Megabyzus, whom Herodotus had earlier discussed in 3.154–160 (and whom we encountered above in this chapter) from the later Zopyros in 3.160.2. That older Zopyros had a son named Megabyzus, and a grandson named Zopyros; it is this grandson who Ctesias is talking about in this fragment from Photius.

[254] The Caunians are also mentioned in Herodotus (*Hist.* 1.171.1; 1.172.1–2; 1.176.2), where they fought harshly against the Persian forces of Harpagos. They are referenced repeatedly in Thucydides, where they were subjugated to Athenian forces (esp. 1.116.3) and where they (after the events in our text) made a harbor for the Spartan forces who opposed Athens in the Peloponnesian War (8.39.3–4; 8.41.1; etc.). Concerning the Caunian desire here not to have Athenian forces enter their city, see LENFANT, Ctésias de Cnide, 270 n. 581: "Ils préféraient donc être sous contrôle perse plutôt que retomber sous la domination d'Athènes".

*Commentary.*[255] Writing in the fourth century B.C., Xenophon the Athenian recounts his personal memories of the Greek mercenary expedition on behalf of Cyrus. At this stage in Xenophon's narrative, Cyrus' expedition against his brother Darius has failed (401 B.C.), and his Greek mercenaries are left in Persian land without generals and without any hope of protection. Xenophon has a dream that warns him of their danger, and he responds by delivering the above speech to the remaining captains of the Greek expedition. In it, he recounts the death of Darius and how Cyrus had maltreated his brother's corpse by beheading it, removing its hands, and suspending it aloft. The detail about cutting off the hand may well remind the reader of the image above (Fig. 2) from Shalmaneser's Balawat Gates as well as the texts from 2 Sam 4:12 and Ctesias (*Persica* FGH 3c 688 Frag. 16.66; see below). Xenophon rightly concludes that his colleagues can only expect similar (or possibly worse) treatment from their Persian foes.

**(205)** Plutarch, *Artaxerxes* 17.5 [Ctesias, FGH 3c 688 Frag. 26.17.7]

καὶ πρὶν ἐν ὑποψίᾳ γενέσθαι βασιλέα τοῦ πράγματος, ἐγχειρίσασα τοῖς ἐπὶ τῶν τιμωριῶν προσέταξεν ἐκδεῖραι ζῶντα, καὶ τὸ μὲν σῶμα πλάγιον διὰ τριῶν σταυρῶν ἀναπῆξαι, τὸ δὲ δέρμα χωρὶς διαπατταλεῦσαι.

*Translation.* And before the king became suspicious of her deed, she put [Masabates] into the hands of those who are over the state-punishments, and she ordered [them] to strip off his skin while he was living, and to transfix his body sideways through three crosses, and to peg up his skin separately.

*Commentary.*[256] Plutarch here represents Parysatis as taking gruesome revenge on the eunuch Masabates, who had decapitated the corpse of her son Cyrus (cf. *Artaxerxes* 13.2; 17.1). This section (from 14.1–17.9) of Plutarch is often attributed by modern scholars as originating from Ctesias' *Persica* based on Plutarch's reference to Ctesias being rewarded for his involvement in the battle recorded in *Artaxerxes* 14.1.[257] In the excerpt above, the Persian "king"

---

[255] Text: CARL HUDE, Xenophontis Expeditio Cyri: Anabasis (Editionem correctiorem curavit J. Peters; Bibliotheca scriptorum Graecorum et Romanorum Teubneriana; Leipzig: Teubner, 1972), 84. Essentially the same text appears, with omission of καὶ ὁμοπατρίου, in EDGAR C. MARCHANT, Xenophontis Opera omnia (5 vols.; Scriptorum classicorum bibliotheca Oxoniensis; Oxford: Clarendon, 1900–1920), Vol. 3 (no page numbers in this edition); CARLETON L. BROWNSON, Xenophon. Anabasis (LCL; Cambridge: Harvard University Press, 1998), 422–424.

[256] Text: KONRAT ZIEGLER, Plutarchi vitae parallelae (Zweite Auflage; Bibliotheca Scriptorum Graecorum et Romanorum Teubneriana; Leipzig: Teubner, 1971), III/1, 335. ZIEGLER labels this passage 17.7; we follow the LCL numbering; cf. BERNADOTTE PERRIN, Plutarch's Lives (11 vols.; LCL; Cambridge: Harvard University Press, 1914–1926), 11:166.

[257] Thus it appears (in addition to appearing in reduced fontsize in JACOBY, FGH 3c 688 Frag. 26) in LENFANT, Ctésias de Cnide, 157; STRONK, Ctesias's Persian History, 376–377;

now is Artaxerxes II, whose brother Cyrus also aspired to the throne. "She" refers to Parysatis, the mother of both Artaxerxes II and Cyrus (being the daughter of Artaxerxes I and wife of Darius; cf. 1.1). Though Artaxerxes II was the eldest, Parysatis favored Cyrus for king (2.2–3). Yet, Darius still passed the monarchy down to his eldest son Artaxerxes.[258] When Cyrus later revolted (6.1–11.6), Parysatis likely preferred his cause (6.4–5; cf. 17.6; 18.2), and after Cyrus' death, she cunningly sought retaliation against those most responsible for his demise (14.5; 16.1; 17.1–5; cf. 6.5; 18.4; 19.1–6). Plutarch vividly describes each of Parysatis' acts of vengeance in horrific detail – for example, one man was tortured for ten days and then killed by having molten bronze poured into his head (14.5).

Plutarch appears enthralled with Parysatis' cruel creativity, as evidenced in the passage above. After Parysatis won control over Masabates through betting at a dice game with her oblivious son Artaxerxes (17.1–5), she called for Masabates' skinned body to be transfixed through three σταυροί. Presumably, this was fashioned as a variation on impalement. Given Parysatis' creativity in Plutarch's *Life of Artaxerxes*, there is no reason to assume this was a common form of suspension (either in Persia or in Plutarch's day). Plutarch's vivid description and overly enthusiastic portrayal of the brutality of Parysatis may call into question the accuracy of his account. However, Plutarch does repeatedly reference his sources (Ctesias, Deinon, and Xenophon's *Anabasis*), and Plutarch repeatedly claims to take an evaluative and critical stance toward that source material (e.g., 1.2; 6.5–6; 7.1; 9.4; 11.6; 13.3–4; 18.4–5; 19.3–4). The relationship of his account to Ctesias can be furthered by next studying a later summary of Ctesias.

**(206)** Ctesias, *Persica*, FGH 3c 688 Frag. 16.66 (from Photius, *Bibliotheca* 72)

Ὡς Παρύσατις εἰς Βαβυλῶνα ἀφίκετο πενθοῦσα Κῦρον, καὶ μόλις ἐκομίσατο τὴν κεφαλὴν αὐτοῦ καὶ τὴν χεῖρα, καὶ ἔθαψεν καὶ ἀπέστειλεν εἰς Σοῦσα. Τὰ περὶ Βαγαπάτου, τοῦ ἀποτεμόντος προστάξει βασιλέως τὴν κεφαλὴν ἀπὸ τοῦ σώματος Κύρου· ὅπως ἡ μήτηρ μετὰ βασιλέως κύβοις ἐπὶ συνθήκαις παίξασα καὶ νικήσασα, ἔλαβε Βαγαπάτην· καὶ ὃν τρόπον τὸ δέρμα περιαιρεθεὶς ἀνε-

LLEWELLYN-JONES and ROBSON, Ctesias' History of Persia, 208. For a helpful discussion of Plutarch's dependency on Ctesias, see STRONK, ibid. esp. 99–103, 187–188. Even in 14.1, Plutarch is (at best) indirect about attributing Ctesias as his source for this material, and other ancient authors may have influenced Plutarch here. Moreover, Plutarch inserts his own moral framework into the way he tells a story. In light of those issues, this text is addressed, for our purposes, in terms of how it works in Plutarch's narrative (rather than emphasizing a specific word-for-word attribution to Ctesias, of which we can be less certain).

[258] These events form the backdrop to Xenophon's *Anabasis* (cf. *Anab.* 1.1). Other events involving Parysatis and Artaxerxes II are recounted in Diodorus Siculus, *Bib. hist.* 14.80.6–8.

σταυρίσθη ὑπὸ Παρυσάτιδος, ὅτε καὶ τὸ πολὺ ἐπὶ Κύρῳ πένθος αὐτῇ ἐπαύσα-
το διὰ τὴν πολλὴν τοῦ Ἀρτοξέρξου δέησιν.

*Translation.* [Ctesias records] how Parysatis arrived in Babylon while grie-
ving for Cyrus, and she was scarcely able to carry away his head and hand [for
burial]. And she rendered funeral rites and sent [these remains] to Susa.
[Ctesias further records] the events concerning Bagapates, who by order of the
king had cut off the head from Cyrus' body. [Ctesias tells] how [Cyrus']
mother [Parysatis], by playing dice with the king upon his agreements and by
winning, acquired Bagapates. And [Ctesias says] by which manner, after
[Bagapates'] flesh was stripped off, he was fixed up on a *stauros* by Parysatis;
when also her great grief for Cyrus was brought to an end through the many
entreaties of Artaxerxes.

*Commentary.*[259] Here, the ninth-century Byzantine author Photius provides his
summary of Ctesias' accounts of Parysatis' efforts at revenge against those
who sought the death of her son, Cyrus. This text above is followed in Photius
(Frag. 16.67) by stories of two other occasions when Parysatis wrought vengeance on Cyrus' assailants (the Carian is tortured and killed, and the boastful
Mitradates is harshly killed); these vary in some respects from the longer
account in Plutarch (*Art.* 14.5–16.7).[260] Similarly Photius' version of the death
of Bagapates is briefer than Plutarch's longer account (*Art.* 17.1–5, and summarized above), though both cover essentially the same ground.

The name of Cyrus' decapitator varies between these authors (Masabates in
Plutarch, Bagapates in Photius),[261] showing some confusion in our extant
sources; but otherwise in both cases, he acts at the behest of king Artaxerxes,
who later must give him up due to losing at a dice game to Parysatis. Most

---

[259] Text: LENFANT, Ctésias de Cnide, 144; compared with STRONK, Ctesias's Persian History, 358 (with punctuation variations only; English translation ibid. 359). Further English
translation in LLEWELLYN-JONES and ROBSON, Ctesias' History of Persia, 199.

[260] As noted above, Plutarch's *Art.* 14.1–17.9 is also often attributed to Ctesias, and thus
appears (albeit in reduced print) under the Ctesias fragments in FGH 3c 688 Frag. 26. The
variations are noted in LENFANT, Ctésias de Cnide, 278 n. 662–663. The order of executions
is different between the Photius and Plutarch records. Artaxerxes II wanted the credit himself
for killing Cyrus in battle, though Mithridates and the Carian had both struck Cyrus first
(Plutarch, *Art.* 14.5–6). In the Plutarch account, the Carian had reportedly struck Cyrus in the
knee (but not finished him off) and is given gifts for having reported Cyrus' death but later
claims full responsibility for the death. Artaxerxes permits Parysatis to have him tortured for
ten days, his eyes gouged out, and molten bronze poured into his ears (Plutarch, *Art.* 14.7–10).
In Plutarch, Mithridates (note the spelling differs from Photius), while drunk at a banquet (as
in Photius), insists he killed Cyrus, and he receives death by the "Torture of the Boats"
(described in gruesome detail in *Art.* 16.3–7).

[261] Also note in this account that Parysatis had possession not only of her son's decapitated
head, but also his "hand." This reminds us of the severing of limbs mentioned elsewhere as a
means of maltreating the dead (cf. Fig. 2 of Shalmaneser's Balawat Gates; 2 Sam 4:12; and
Xenophon, *Anab.* 3.1.17).

importantly, in both accounts, Masabates/Bagapates endures an execution connected with the *stauros*. It is thus reasonable to assume that both stories share a common origin and that not only does Photius explicitly epitomize Ctesias, but Plutarch's account also stems from Ctesias' report. However, Plutarch (*Art.* 17.5) specifies in detail Parysatis' employment of three *stauroi* on which Masabates was pinned, a version which strikingly parallels Photius' summation of Ctesias on Amestris' earlier vengeful execution of Inaros (see above Ctesias, *Persica*, FGH 3c 688 Frag. 14.39; whereas Thucydides does not mention three such *stauroi* in his Inaros account). Here, we can envision at least two possibilities: Ctesias mentioned three *stauroi* in both places (but Thucydides in his history and Photius in his summary of Ctesias in Frag. 16.66 omit such details), or Ctesias only records three *stauroi* in one of the two accounts and someone (either Photius in Frag. 14.39, or Plutarch in *Art.* 17.5) has displaced that detail to another story of a mother's vengeance.

It is difficult to decide with certainty on the matter. However, we can observe that Photius does speak here in a very summative tone about the "manner" (ὃν τρόπον) with which Ctesias states that Parysatis employed the *stauros*, perhaps as a clue that Photius is not describing that manner of death found in Ctesias in all its grim details. In any case, we can see that both Plutarch and Photius agree (likely both due in some manner to Ctesias) that Parysatis made use of (at least one) *stauros* in her act of revenge. Readers of these later authors would naturally associate such a penalty with the crosses of their day, even if Ctesias may have intended something more resembling an impalement.

## 3.3 Barbarians and Crucifixion according to Graeco-Roman Sources

The Greek and Latin sources associate crucifixion (and related suspension penalties) with various barbarian nations. Roman authors especially emphasize reports about crucifixions at the hands of the Carthaginians, against whom the Romans fought epic wars. This section provides evidence of barbarian crucifixions and suspensions from Graeco-Roman reports, beginning with those concerning the lands north of Italy and working east and south. Often such accounts cannot be independently verified by sources more indigenous to these ancient cultures, though they may well have some basis in fact. However, these narratives do provide evidence that Greek and Roman authors viewed crucifixion as a barbarous act.

### 3.3.1 Gauls, Germani, Brittani

**(207)** Diodorus Siculus, *Bibliotheca Historica* 5.32.6

ἀκολούθως δὲ τῇ κατ' αὐτοὺς ἀγριότητι καὶ περὶ τὰς θυσίας ἐκτόπως ἀσεβοῦσι· τοὺς γὰρ κακούργους κατὰ πενταετηρίδα φυλάξαντες ἀνασκολοπίζουσι τοῖς θεοῖς καὶ μετ' ἄλλων πολλῶν ἀπαρχῶν καθαγίζουσι, πυρὰς παμμεγέθεις κατασκευάζοντες. χρῶνται δὲ καὶ τοῖς αἰχμαλώτοις ὡς ἱερείοις πρὸς τὰς τῶν θεῶν τιμάς. τινὲς δ' αὐτῶν καὶ τὰ κατὰ πόλεμον ληφθέντα ζῷα μετὰ τῶν ἀνθρώπων ἀποκτείνουσιν ἢ κατακάουσιν ἤ τισιν ἄλλαις τιμωρίαις ἀφανίζουσι.

*Translation.* And following on their own savagery, they also are extraordinarily impious concerning their sacrifices. For, after imprisoning criminals for five years, they impale them up unto their gods and burn them with many other first-fruit offerings, constructing immense pyres. And they also use captives as sacrificial victims for the honor of the gods. And some of them also slay those animals taken in war along with the humans, or burn them, or do away with them by some other punishments.

*Commentary.*[262] In the first century B.C., Diodorus of Sicily writes concerning the savagery of the Gauls. Diodorus had earlier reminded the reader that the Gauls had attacked and captured Rome, plundered the sanctuary of Delphi, intermixed at times with the Greeks, and destroyed many Roman armies. Here, he emphasizes the impiety of their savage ways by describing how they offer to the gods human sacrifices of their criminals and war captives. The verbs ἀνασκολοπίζουσι (translated as "they impaled them up") followed by καθαγίζουσι imply that the criminals were impaled/suspended and then burned along with other offerings.

**(208)** Cassius Dio, *Historiae Romanae* 54.20.4–5

ὁ δὲ δὴ μέγιστος τῶν τότε συμβάντων τοῖς Ῥωμαίοις πολέμων, ὅσπερ που καὶ τὸν Αὔγουστον ἐκ τῆς πόλεως ἐξήγαγε, πρὸς τοὺς Κελτοὺς ἐγένετο. Σύγαμβροί τε γὰρ καὶ Οὐσιπέται καὶ Τέγκτηροι τὸ μὲν πρῶτον ἐν τῇ σφετέρᾳ τινὰς αὐτῶν συλλαβόντες ἀνεσταύρωσαν, [5] ἔπειτα δὲ καὶ τὸν Ῥῆνον διαβάντες τήν τε Γερμανίαν καὶ τὴν Γαλατίαν ἐληλάτησαν.

*Translation.* But now the greatest of the wars which then befell the Romans – the very one which brought Augustus out from the city – came against the Celts. For even the Sugambri, Usipetes, and Tencteri, having first seized some

---

[262] Text from FISCHER and VOGEL, Diodori bibliotheca historica, 2:46. Also compared with OLDFATHER, SHERMAN, GEER, and WALTON, Diodorus, 3:182.

of them [i.e., Romans] in their own territory, crucified them. ⁵ And then also, crossing the Rhine, they plundered both Germania and Galatia.

*Commentary.*²⁶³ Cassius Dio, writing in the early third century A.D., mentions that during the reign of Augustus, barbarians used the cross in raids that apparently began in the Celtic lands and then spread across the Rhine. He does not detail the method used in such "crucifixions" (ἀνεσταύρωσαν), though his other uses of ἀνασταυρόω in his *Historiae Romanae* imply that he perceived this penalty to be similar to the crucifixions of his day. A few lines later, Dio styles these Celts as "barbarians" (βάρβαροι in 54.20.6). The victims of the cross are not specified, but the context indicates "them" (αὐτῶν) in 54.20.4 has its most likely antecedent in the Romans (τοῖς Ῥωμαίοις), whose military forces were by this means drawn into the battle.²⁶⁴

**(209)** Florus, *Epitome* 2.30 [4.12.24]

Inde validissimas nationes Cheruscos Suebosque et Sicambros pariter adgressus est, qui viginti centurionibus in crucem actis hoc velut sacramento sumpserant bellum, adeo certa victoriae spe, ut praedam in anticessum pactione diviserint.

*Translation.* Thence he [i.e., Drusus] assaulted the most formidable races of the Cherusci, Suebi, and Sicambri simultaneously, who, once twenty centurions had been led out to the cross, had taken up this war as though it were an oath, with such a sure hope of victory that they had divided up the plunder in terms made in advance.

*Commentary.*²⁶⁵ Precisely which Florus wrote this *Epitome bellorum omnium annorum DCC* ("Epitome of All the Wars of 700 Years") is debated even among the manuscript copyists, though the author himself dates his work to sometime in the second century A.D. (some "two hundred years" after Augustus Caesar; cf. *Epitome* 1 Intro. 8). He provides a condensed overview of Roman history (especially Roman wars) until his time. Florus considers the Germanic wars to have been unwise (2.30.21–22), for though Drusus conquered much territory, the Roman leaders who followed him (especially Quintillius Varus) engaged in cruel practices, and thus the Romans were later embarrassed by the loss of the Germanic lands (2.30.29–39). In this selection concerning the *bellum Germanicum*, Florus represents Nero Claudius Drusus (the younger brother of Tiberius Caesar) as fighting three united Germanic tribes. The event is to be dated to approximately 9 B.C. Florus indicates the

---

²⁶³ Text: FOSTER / CARY, Dio's Roman History, 6:332.

²⁶⁴ Thus too the translation of E. Cary in FOSTER / CARY, Dio's Roman History, 6:333.

²⁶⁵ Text: EDWARD SEYMOUR FORSTER, Lucius Annaeus Florus. Epitome of Roman History (orig. 1929; repr., LCL; Cambridge: Harvard University Press, 1984), 336.

tribes engaged in initial hostilities against the Romans, likely subsequent to Drusus' conquest of other Germanic nations. These hostilities included the use of the *crux* against 20 Roman centurions. Writing in the second century A.D., Florus and his audience likely conceived of this *crux* in the crucifixion terms common in their day. Florus' readership certainly would have taken offense at the crucifixion of Roman centurions. Drusus, in turn, defeated these three Germanic tribes and sold them into slavery.

**(210)** Tacitus, *Germania* 12.1–2

Licet apud concilium accusare quoque et discrimen capitis intendere. distinctio poenarum ex delicto: proditores et transfugas arboribus suspendunt, ignavos et imbelles et corpore Infames caeno ac palude, iniecta insuper crate, mergunt. ² diversitas supplicii illuc respicit, tamquam scelera ostendi oporteat dum puniuntur, flagitia abscondi.

*Translation.* It is also permitted at this assembly to accuse others and to bring a capital charge.[266] The distinction of the penalties stems from the offense: traitors and deserters are suspended from trees; they plunge those who are cowardly, unwarlike and disgraced-in-body into mud and swamp with a frame thrown over him. ² The diversity of punishment reflects this: just as it is proper for crimes to be exposed while they are punished, shameful actions should be concealed.

*Commentary.*[267] Toward the end of the first century A.D., Cornelius Tacitus penned this volume on the German tribes. Having introduced their political assemblies (which meet on appointed days according to the lunar cycle; cf. *Germ.* 11), he describes here the judicial authority these assemblies have. He first describes capital punishments (in the selection above) before going on to depict lesser penalties for lesser crimes. The passage above indicates traitors and deserters (*proditores et transfugas*) are "suspended from trees" (*arboribus suspendunt*). Tacitus does not describe the mechanism used, though it is clear that part of the rationale for this penalty is that both the criminal and his crime (*scelera*) be exposed (*ostendi*). On the other hand, perpetrators of shameful crimes (cowardliness, refusal of military service, and disgraceful actions) are put to death in a way so as to hide them (by plunging them beneath a muddy swamp).

---

[266] For *discrimen capitis intendere* as "bring a capital charge" see OLD s.v. *discrimen*.

[267] Text: KOESTERMANN, BORZSÁK, and WELLESLEY, P. Cornelii Taciti libri, II/2 (ed. ALF ÖNNERFORS), 10; compared with WILLIAM PETERSON and MAURICE HUTTON, Cornelius Tacitus. Dialogus; Agricola; Germania (LCL; Cambridge: Harvard University Press, 1914), 280.

**(211)** Tacitus, *Annales* 1.61.2–4

prima Vari castra lato ambitu et dimensis principiis trium legionum manus ostentabant; dein semiruto uallo, humili fossa accisae iam reliquiae consedisse intellegebantur. medio campi albentia ossa, ut fugerant, ut restiterant, disiecta uel aggerata. ³ adiacebant fragmina telorum equorumque artus, simul truncis arborum antefixa ora. lucis propinquis barbarae arae, apud quas tribunos ac primorum ordinum centuriones mactauerant. ⁴ et cladis eius superstites, pugnam aut uincula elapsi, referebant hic cecidisse legatos, illic raptas aquilas; primum ubi uulnus Varo adactum, ubi infelici dextera et suo ictu mortem inuenerit; quo tribunali contionatus Arminius, quot patibula captiuis, quae scrobes, utque signis et aquilis per superbiam inluserit.

*Translation*. Varus' first camp, with its large extent and measured headquarters, displayed the handiwork of three legions; afterwards by means of a half-ruined palisade [and] insignificant trench the weakened remnant now were perceived to have taken cover. In the midst of the camp courtyard whitened bones were dispersed or heaped up as they had fled or as they had offered resistance. ³ Fragments of spears and limbs of horses lay adjacent; at the same time faces [i.e., skulls] were nailed to the front of the treetrunks. In nearby groves there were barbarous altars, on which they had slain tribunes and centurions of the first ranks. ⁴ And survivors of this disaster, who had escaped the battle or fetters, repeated these matters: how here legates fell and there eagles were seized, where the first wound came to Varus, where he found death by his miserable hand and by his own [suicidal] blow, from which tribunal Arminius delivered his harangue, how many *patibula* for the prisoners, which pits, and how with arrogance the standards and the eagles were ridiculed.

*Commentary*.[268] Writing in the early second century A.D., Tacitus depicts the discovery by Caesar and his troops of the locale in the Teutoburgian Forest where the Germans (led by Arminius) had conquered P. Quintilius Varus' Roman camp some six years earlier (cf. *Ann.* 1.60.3–1.62.1). Varus' defeat is repeatedly mentioned by Tacitus as one of the greatest Roman military disgraces to befall the Augustan era (note *infamiae* in *Ann.* 1.3.6; also see 1.10.4; cf. 1.43.1; 1.55.2–3; 1.58.2; etc.).[269] Tacitus provides a vivid description of the battleground, including Roman skulls nailed to trees (*truncis arborum antefixa ora*) and the remains of Romans sacrificed on German altars. Such "barbarous altars" for human sacrifice remind us of Diodorus Siculus' passage

---

[268] Text: KOESTERMANN, BORZSÁK, and WELLESLEY, P. Cornelii Taciti libri, I/1 (ed. BORZSÁK), 26–27; cf. FISHER, Cornelii Taciti Annalium (except for capitalizations and consonantal "u"); MOORE and JACKSON, Tacitus, 2:346–348.

[269] Tacitus' disgust at Varus' defeat was similarly shared by Florus, who blamed the German revolt on Varus' licentiousness and cruelty (*Epitome* 2.30.29–39).

cited above about the Gauls (*Bib. hist.* 5.32.6). The "pits" (*scrobes*) in the last two lines likely refers to pits/graves used to bury captured Romans alive.[270]

In *Annals* 1.60.4, the survivors[271] describe the disaster and mention that prisoners faced the *patibula* (*quot patibula captivis*). The context is not sufficient to indicate that crucifixion on a *patibulum* is implied, but such a term used elsewhere in Tacitus indicates a device on which a body is suspended (*Ann.* 4.72.3; 14.33.6; *Hist.* 4.3).

## (212) Tacitus, *Annales* 4.72.1–3

Eodem anno Frisii, Transrhenanus populus, pacem exuere nostra magis auaritia quam obsequii impatientes. tributum iis Drusus iusserat modicum pro angustia rerum, ut in usus militaris coria boum penderent, non intenta cuiusquam cura, quae firmitudo, quae mensura, donec Olennius e primipilaribus, regendis Frisiis impositus, terga urorum delegit, quorum ad formam acciperentur. ² id, aliis quoque nationibus arduum, apud Germanos difficilius tolerabatur, quis ingentium beluarum feraces saltus, modica domi armenta sunt. ac primo boves ipsos, mox agros, postremo corpora coniugum aut liberorum seruitio tradebant. ³ hinc ira et questus et postquam non subueniebatur, remedium ex bello. rapti, qui tributo aderant, milites et patibulo adfixi; Olennius infensos fuga praeuenit, receptus castello, cui nomen Fleuum, et haud spernenda illic ciuium sociorumque manus litora Oceani praesidebat.

*Translation.* In that same year, the Frisians, a people living east of the Rhine River, set aside the peace – due more to our great avarice than from being impatient at their submission. Drusus had commanded a moderate tribute for them in proportion to their limited circumstances, so that they paid hides of oxen for military use, without anyone's attention directed as to the firmness or measurement [of the hides] – until Olennius, appointed from the chief centurions who ruled the Frisians, assigned the hides of the long-horned wild ox as the form which would be accepted. ² This requirement, which would also be arduous for other nations, was tolerated with difficulty by the Germans, whose forests are fertile with huge beasts but whose domestic herds are moderate. And so at first the cattle alone, soon their fields, and afterward the bodies of their wives and children were handed over to servitude. ³ Hence anger and complaint, then (after it was not alleviated) remedy by war. Soldiers who were present at the tribute were seized and fixed to the *patibulum*. Olennius forestalled their hostile actions by fleeing, being received by a fortress with the name Flevum, and there an armed force (which was by no means to be disdained) of citizens and allies guarded the Ocean shores.

---

[270] See note in MILLER, Annals Book 1, 185.

[271] Survivors of this disaster are also depicted in Cassius Dio, *Hist. Rom.* 56.22.

*Commentary.*[272] Tacitus reports the revolt of the Germanic tribe of the Frisians during the reign of Tiberius (c. A.D. 29). He blames the revolt in part on the avarice (*avaritia*) of the Romans, in particular due to Olennius' onerous interpretation of an otherwise moderate tribute. Olennius required the Frisians to pay with hides of the auroch (a now extinct large wild European ox),[273] even though their domesticated herds were smaller. The Frisians' inability to comply apparently led to confiscation of property and servitude of their wives and children. After the Frisians revolted, they seized the soldiers who were in charge of implementing the tribute and *patibulo adfixi* (fixed them to the *patibulum*). Tacitus elsewhere employs the verb *adfigo* in a similar context of brutal punishment with *crux* in *Ann.* 15.44 (*crucibus adfixi*; for full text and discussion see 2.1 above). As with *Ann.* 1.61.4 (see above), this use of the *patibulum* would imply some form of bodily suspension, would connect the *patibulum* with a barbarian revolt, and would likely remind Roman readers of crucifixion. The Frisian revolt was not readily suppressed (cf. *Ann.* 4.73.1– 4.74.1; cf. 13.54).

**(213)** Tacitus, *Annales* 14.33.2

eadem clades municipio Verulamio fuit, quia barbari omissis castellis praesidiisque militarium, quod uberrimum spolianti et defendentibus intutum, laeti praeda et laborum segnes petebant. ad septuaginta milia ciuium et sociorum iis, quae memoraui, locis cecidisse constitit. neque enim capere aut uenundare aliudue quod belli commercium, sed caedes patibula, ignes cruces, tamquam reddituri supplicium, ac praerepta interim ultione, festinabant.

*Translation.* The same disaster came upon the municipality of Verulamium, since the barbarians (delighting in loot and slothful regarding labor) attacked, after the fortified outposts and military encampments had been ignored [by the barbarians] because of the great abundance of [other] things to pillage and because of the areas unprotected by the defenses. Up to seventy thousand citizens and their allies remained together to be killed in those places that I have mentioned. For [the barbarians] made haste, neither to capture nor to sell [captives] nor other exchanges due to war, but massacre, cross-beams, fires, crosses – just as those who will be appointed to punishment, but meanwhile first seize their vengeance.

---

[272] Text: KOESTERMANN, BORZSÁK, and WELLESLEY, P. Cornelii Taciti libri, I/1 (ed. BORZSÁK), 128; text is the same (except for consonantal "u" and punctuation) in FISHER, Cornelii Taciti Annalium; MOORE and JACKSON, Tacitus, 3:126–128.

[273] See note in MOORE and JACKSON, Tacitus, 3:127; cf. OLD s.v. *urus*.

*Commentary.*[274] This section of Tacitus' *Annals* concerns the famous revolt of British tribes under Boudicca, the queen of the Iceni, largely in response to Roman attrocities (14.29ff.). Gaius Suetonius Paulinus returned from his battles on the Isle of Mona to take charge of the Roman army, whose ninth legion had already been routed by the Britons. Suetonius cautiously chose not to defend Londinium and Verulamium (modern London and St. Albans). Consequently, those who remained in these cities were pillaged and slaughtered by the Britons (A.D. 60/61). The text above (by inserting a comma before the *quia barbari* ... clause) understands the pillaging of the barbarians to refer especially to the *municipium* of Verulamium, though the plural "outposts and military encampments" (*castellis praesidiisque militarium*) may indicate a broader area.[275] Nonetheless, the total number (up to 70,000!)[276] of those who remained together (*constitit*) and were killed (literally "to have fallen", cf. *cecidisse*) would include both residents of Londinium and Verulamium since those were the "places" Tacitus mentioned (*iis quae memoravi locis*). Tacitus certainly represents the Britons as barbarians (*barbari*), who conducted war more for plunder than for military advantage. They slaughter "citizens" and others who remain behind, whom Tacitus identifies just prior to the passage cited above as "attached to the place on account of weakness of sex, or frailty of age, or the delights of the place."[277] In particular, rather than engaging in the normal slave-trade with their war captives (or even perhaps the ransoming of the prisoners back to the Romans), the Britons instead brought harsh means of execution on their captives. Tacitus describes these as if they presaged the kind of punishment (*supplicium*) to which the Britons themselves would be properly appointed (*reddituri*) – they anticipated the vengeance due them by practicing it first (*praerepta interim ultione*). Noticeably the list of harsh forms of execution distinguishes the "cross-beams" (*patibula*) from the "crosses" (*cruces*). We could wish to know more about how Tacitus separated these modes of death, yet we can clearly conclude that (whatever the precise forms of death) the terms *patibulum* and *crux* could be associated with war atrocities at the hands of barbarians in Briton.

---

[274] Text: KOESTERMANN, BORZSÁK, and WELLESLEY, P. Cornelii Taciti libri, I/2 (ed. K. WELLESLEY), 85. Text compared with MOORE and JACKSON, Tacitus, 4:162 (with minor differences in punctuation).

[275] In his translation, GRANT keeps the *eadem clades municipio Verulamio fuit* clause with the preceding material about Londinium, but he begins a new paragraph with the *quia barbari* clause, thus implying that everything from *quia barbari* on refers to the populations of both Londinium and Verulamium. Cf. MICHAEL GRANT, Tacitus: The Annals of Imperial Rome (London: Penguin, 1996), 329.

[276] JACKSON contends that the "estimate" of 70,000 is "probably valueless" (MOORE and JACKSON, Tacitus, 4:162).

[277] *quos imbellis sexus aut fessa aetas vel loci dulcedo attinuerat.*

**(214)** Cassius Dio, *Historiae Romanae* 62.7.1–3

Τοιαῦτ' ἄττα ἡ Βουδουῖκα δημηγορήσασα ἐπῆγε τοῖς Ῥωμαίοις τὴν στρατιάν· ἔτυχον γὰρ ἄναρχοι ὄντες διὰ τὸ Παυλῖνον τὸν ἡγεμόνα σφῶν εἰς νῆσόν τινα Μῶνναν ἀγχοῦ τῆς Βρεττανίας κειμένην ἐπιστρατεῦσαι. διὰ τοῦτο πόλεις τε δύο Ῥωμαϊκὰς ἐξεπόρθησε καὶ διήρπασε καὶ φόνον ἀμύθητον, ὡς ἔφην, εἰργάσατο· τοῖς τε ἁλισκομένοις ἀνθρώποις ὑπ' αὐτῶν οὐδὲν τῶν δεινοτάτων ἔστιν ὅ τι οὐκ ἐγίνετο. ² καὶ ὃ δὴ δεινότατον καὶ θηριωδέστατον ἔπραξαν· τὰς γὰρ γυναῖκας τὰς εὐγενεστάτας καὶ εὐπρεπεστάτας γυμνὰς ἐκρέμασαν, καὶ τούς τε μαστοὺς αὐτῶν περιέτεμον καὶ τοῖς στόμασί σφων προσέρραπτον, ὅπως ὡς καὶ ἐσθίουσαι αὐτοὺς ὁρῶντο, καὶ μετὰ τοῦτο πασσάλοις ὀξέσι διὰ παντὸς τοῦ σώματος κατὰ μῆκος ἀνέπειραν. ³ καὶ ταῦτα πάντα, θύοντές τε ἅμα καὶ ἑστιώμενοι καὶ ὑβρίζοντες, ἔν τε τοῖς ἄλλοις σφῶν ἱεροῖς καὶ ἐν τῷ τῆς Ἀνδάτης μάλιστα ἄλσει ἐποίουν. οὕτω τε γὰρ τὴν Νίκην ὠνόμαζον, καὶ ἔσεβον αὐτὴν περιττότατα.

*Translation.* Boudicca, having publicly spoken some such things, led out the army against the Romans. For, it happened that these [Romans] were leaderless because Paulinus, their commander, had gone on an expedition against a certain island named Mona, which lay near Britannia. On account of this she pillaged and plundered two Roman cities, and she performed inexpressible slaughter, as I said; and to those people seized by them, there are none of the most awful things which did not occur against them. ² And they did that which now is the most awful and most bestial, for they hung up naked the most noble and most comely women, and they cut off their breasts and stitched them to their mouths, in order that they may be seen as if they were eating them; and after this they pierced them with sharp stakes lengthwise through their whole body. ³ And they performed all these things while sacrificing, banqueting, and doing outrageous things both in their own sacred places and especially in the sacred precincts of Andate, for thus they name Nike and worship her exceedingly.

*Commentary.*[278] Dio's account of Boudicca's famous revolt in southern Britain (c. A.D. 60/61) permits him the opportunity to describe the horrendous actions that Romans attributed to the British tribes. His portrait is even more harsh than is Tacitus' (*Ann.* 14.33; see above). In this epitome of Dio's *Roman History*, Boudicca delivers a fiery speech to the goddess Andraste, proclaiming the Brittains to be men of war (in contrast to the effeminate Romans), and then launches war on Roman cities (presumably modern Colchester and London). To highlight the barbaric nature of the Britanni, Dio details their treatment of captured Roman women. The womens' torturous deaths involve bodily suspension (ἐκρέμασαν), breast mutilation, and a particularly cruel

---

[278] Text: CARY, Dionysius of Halicarnassus. Roman Antiquities, 8:94.

form of impalement. Dio portrays these "awful" and "bestial" actions as examples of barbarian religious sacrifices since he records them amidst the simultaneous worship of deities (among whom he singles out Andate, i.e., Victory).

**(215)** Cassius Dio, *Historiae Romanae* 62.11.4–5

ἂν δὲ δὴ παρ' ἐλπίδα τι συμβῇ (οὐδὲ γὰρ οὐδὲ τοῦτ' εἰπεῖν ὀκνήσω), ἄμεινόν ἐστι μαχομένους ἡμᾶς ἀνδρείως πεσεῖν ἢ ἁλόντας ἀνασκολοπισθῆναι, τὰ σπλάγχνα τὰ ἑαυτῶν ἐκτμηθέντα ἰδεῖν, πασσάλοις διαπύροις ἀναπαρῆναι καὶ ὕδατι ζέοντι τηκομένους ἀπολέσθαι, καθάπερ ἐς θηρία τινὰ ἄγρια ἄνομα ἀνόσια ἐμπεπτωκότας. ⁵ ἢ οὖν περιγενώμεθα αὐτῶν, ἢ ἐνταῦθα ἀποθάνωμεν.

*Translation.* But now, should something come to pass contrary to hope (for I will not hesitate to speak even about this), it would be better for us, fighting, to fall like men, rather than, being seized, to be impaled, to see our own bowels being cut out, to be pierced with fiery stakes, and to be killed by melting with boiling water, as those who fall among certain wild, lawless, and unholy beasts. ⁵ Therefore, let us either overcome them or let us die here!

*Commentary.*[279] According to Dio, Paulinus (i.e., Gaius Suetonius Paulinus, i.e., "Suetonius" in Tacitus) returns to Britain, having subdued the island of Mona, and successfully battles Boudicca's forces. This text provides a short excerpt of one of his three exhortations to the British troops (cf. 62.9.1–62.11.5).[280] While the general tenor of his third exhortation is hope of victory, Paulinus warns the soldiers that they should die fighting rather than allow themselves to be captured by the barbarian tribes, which would be far worse. The term ἀνασκολοπισθῆναι depicts a public suspension/crucifixion (likely by impaling them aloft). Paulinus goes on through a string of infinitives to depict other horrendous consequences should they be captured. One possible reading would understand each to apply to distinct groups of captives (e.g., some are impaled, some are disemboweled, others are pierced with stakes, etc.). However, given the parallels with the plight of the Roman women in *Hist. Rom.* 62.7.2 (see above), it is also possible that Dio (in the guise of Paulinus) envisions those who are being impaled aloft as also being disemboweled alive, pierced with stakes, and then killed with boiling water.[281]

---

[279] Text: CARY, Dionysius of Halicarnassus. Roman Antiquities, 8:100.

[280] One could contrast Tacitus' much shorter record of Paulinus' (= Suetonius') speech (*Ann.* 14.36), where Tacitus makes no mention of such brutal consequences of a Roman loss.

[281] Like the women in 62.7.2, Paulinus describes people being impaled aloft (ἀνασκολοπισθῆναι; cf. ἐκρέμασαν in 62.7.2) and then in danger of being pierced with stakes (ἀναπείρω and πασσάλοι as in 62.7.2; note that 62.11.4 represents the stakes as fiery hot with διαπύροις). The disemboweling of the living victims in 62.11.4 would correspond to the cutting off of the living women's breasts in 62.7.2, also horribly maiming the bodies. Then the only distinct feature in 62.11.4 would be the use of boiling water to "melt" the suspended victims to death.

## 3.3.2 Thracians and Pontians

**(216)** Diodorus Siculus, *Bibliotheca Historica* 33.15.1

῞Οτι ὁ ῎Ατταλος ἀκούων τὸν Διήγυλιν παρὰ τοῖς ὑποτεταγμένοις διαβεβλῆσθαι διά τε τὴν πλεονεξίαν καὶ τὴν ὑπερβολὴν τῆς ὠμότητος ἐζήλωσε τὴν ἐναντίαν προαίρεσιν. διὸ καὶ τοὺς ἁλισκομένους τῶν Θρακῶν ἀπολύων μετὰ φιλανθρωπίας, πολλοὺς ἔσχε κήρυκας τῆς ἰδίας ἐπιεικείας. ἃ δὴ πυνθανόμενος ὁ Διήγυλις τῶν μὲν ἀποχωρούντων τοὺς ὁμήρους δειναῖς ὕβρεσι καὶ παρανόμοις αἰκίαις περιέβαλλεν, ὧν ἦσάν τινες τῶν ἀσθενεστάτων παίδων ἡλικίᾳ καὶ φύσει. καὶ γὰρ τούτων οἱ μὲν διαμεμελισμένοι τὰ σώματα ποικίλως, οἱ δὲ κεφαλὰς καὶ χεῖρας καὶ πόδας ἀφῃρημένοι· καὶ τούτων οἱ μὲν ἐπὶ σκόλοψιν, οἱ δὲ ἐπὶ δένδρεσιν ἀνήρτηντο.

*Translation.* Thus Attalus, when he heard that Diegylis was resented by his subjects on account of his greediness and the extremity of his savagery, emulated the opposite policy. Wherefore, as he even released with philanthropy many Thracian captives, he had heralds of his clemency. Which things Diegylis learned and then encompassed the hostages of the departed with fearful assaults and lawless outrages, among whom were children who were most feeble in age and nature, for even of these were those who were variously dismembered in body and who were deprived of heads and hands and feet; and of these were those who were hung on posts and those hung on trees.

*Commentary.*[282] Among the fragmentary remains of the concluding books of Diodorus' *Bibliotheca Historica* we encounter this depiction of the Thracian ruler Diegylis in the second century B.C.[283] Diodorus emphasizes the harshness of Diegylis' rule beginning in 33.14.1 (including many gruesome descriptions in 33.14.3–5). After the text quoted above, Diodorus continues to portray Diegylis' shameful treatment of women and depicts these actions as performed according to "the arrogance of Barbarians" (ὑπερηφανίας βαρβάρων) and as "demonstrations of a shameless savagery" (ὠμότητος ἀναισχύντου δεῖγμα). In the above passage, Diegylis' actions are contrasted with those of Attalus II (Philadelphus) of Pergamum (160–138 B.C.), who showed "philanthropy". Diegylis instead dismembered children and/or hung them aloft (ἀνήρτηντο). While Diodorus does not describe the precise method of suspension, the Greek indicates these suspensions occurred both on "posts" (ἐπὶ σκόλοψιν)

---

[282] Text: FISCHER and VOGEL, Diodori bibliotheca historica, 6:76.

[283] WALTON dates these events to about 144 B.C. (OLDFATHER, SHERMAN, GEER, and WALTON, Diodorus, 12:27). The numbering of the fragments from books 21–32 follows DINDORF's Teubner edition (also in the VOGEL and FISCHER revision), which, in turn, was followed by WALTON.

and on "trees" (ἐπὶ δένδρεσιν) – the distinction likely being that the posts were constructed by men.

**(217)** Diodorus Siculus, *Bibliotheca Historica* 34/35.12.1

Ὅτι ὁ τοῦ Διηγύλιος υἱὸς Ζιβέλμιος, ἐζηλωκὼς τὰς τοῦ πατρὸς μιαιφονίας, μνησικακῶν δὲ ὑπὲρ τῶν εἰς Διήγυλιν τοῖς Θρᾳξὶ πραχθέντων, ἐπὶ τοσοῦτον προῆλθεν ὠμότητος καὶ παρανομίας ὥστε τοὺς προσκόψαντας πανοικίους τιμωρεῖσθαι. ἐπὶ γὰρ ταῖς τυχούσαις αἰτίαις τοὺς μὲν διεμέλιζε, τοὺς δὲ ἀνεσταύρου, τοὺς δὲ καὶ ζῶντας ἐνεπύριζε. γονέων δὲ ἐν ὄμμασι καὶ κόλποις ἐγκατέσφαζε τέκνα, καὶ κρεανομῶν τὰ σώματα παρετίθει τοῖς συγγενεστάτοις, ἀνανεούμενος τὰς παλαιὰς ἐκείνας Τηρέως ἢ Θυέστου θοινάς.

*Translation.* That Zibelmius, the son of Diegylis, having emulated his father's bloodthirsty nature and bearing malice about that which had been done by the Thracians unto Diegylis, advanced unto such savagery and lawlessness so that he took vengeance against the whole house of those who had offended him. For upon any opportune reason he dismembered some men, he crucified some, and some he even burnt alive. And in the eyes and laps of parents he slaughtered children; and, dividing their flesh, he placed their bodies before their closest kinsmen, reviving those ancient feasts of Tereus and Thyestes.

*Commentary.*[284] Later in the fragments of Diodorus, we now encounter Diegylis' son, Zibelmius. Some of the key terms used of the Thracian father in 33.15.1–2 (cited earlier) are also applied to the son, especially "savagery" (ὠμότης) and "lawlessness" (παρανομία). Among the horrors Zibelmius performs is that he "crucified" (ἀνεσταύρου) others. This is clearly viewed with great dread, though it is not the worst of his deeds. The precise form of "crucifixion" is not described, so we can assume little more than that this was a bodily suspension in the same category as the crucifixions/suspensions Diodorus himself would have pictured in his own day.

**(218)** Appian, *Mithridatica* 15.97 (§§449–451)

Πομπήιος μὲν οὖν εὐθὺς ἐκ τῆς Ἀσίας στρατὸν ἀγείρας μετεστρατοπέδευεν ἐπὶ τοὺς ὅρους τοῦ Μιθριδάτου· Μιθριδάτῃ δὲ ἦν ἐπίλεκτος οἰκεῖος στρατός, τρισμύριοι πεζοὶ καὶ ἱππεῖς τρισχίλιοι, καὶ προυκάθητο τῆς χώρας. [450] ἄρτι δ' αὐτὴν Λουκούλλου διεφθαρκότος ἀπόρως εἶχεν ἀγορᾶς· ὅθεν αὐτομολίαις ἐπετίθεντο πολλοί. καὶ τούσδε μὲν ὁ Μιθριδάτης ἐρευνώμενος ἐκρήμνη καὶ ὀφθαλμοὺς ἀνώρυττε καὶ ἔκαιε. [451] καὶ τὰ μὲν τῶν αὐτομολιῶν ἧσσον ἠνώχλει διὰ φόβον τῶν κολάσεων, ἐπέτριβε δ' ἡ ἀπορία.

---

[284] Text in FISCHER and VOGEL, Diodori bibliotheca historica, 6:105.

*Translation.* Therefore Pompey, immediately collecting his army from Asia, moved camp unto Mithridates' borders. But Mithridates had a chosen private army which was 30,000 foot-soldiers and 3,000 horse, and he defended his land. [450] Yet now since Lucullus had ruined that land, he [Mithridates] scarcely had provisions, whence many attempted desertions. And Mithridates having sought these deserters, he hung them up, and gouged out their eyes and burnt them. [451] And these actions addressed the lessening of the deserters through fear of punishment, but poverty was afflicting [his forces].

*Commentary.*[285] Appian of Alexandria wrote his *Roman History*, including Book 12 on the Mithridatic Wars, during the mid-second century A.D. According to Appian, during the Third Mithridatic war (73–63 B.C.), Pompey was assigned to battle Pontian king Mithridates VI after successfully suppressing pirates in the eastern Mediterranean. He moves swiftly against Mithridates, whose troops are deserting because the territory can no longer support them all. As punishment for these deserters, Appian says, Mithridates "hung them up [ἐκρήμνη], and gouged out their eyes and burnt them." It is unclear from the Greek whether these represent three separate penalties applied variously to deserters, or whether all three penalties were applied to each. The precise nature of the suspension is also not described. However, these actions were enough to persuade Mithridates' soldiers not to abandon their posts.

**(219)** Valerius Maximus, *Facta et Dicta Memorabilia* 9.2 ext. 3

Tam hercule quam Mithridatem regem, qui una epistola octoginta milia ciuium Romanorum in Asia per urbes negotiandi gratia dispersa interemit, tantaeque prouinciae hospitalis deos iniusto sed non inulto cruore respersit, quoniam cum maximo cruciatu ueneno repugnantem spiritum suum tandem succumbere coegit, simulque piacula crucibus illis dedit, quibus illos amicos suos auctore Gauro spadone, libidinosus obsequio scelestus imperio, adfecerat.

*Translation.* So too, by Hercules!, king Mithridates, who with one epistle killed 80,000 Roman citizens (dispersed on account of business throughout cities in Asia), and who splattered the gods of hospitality of such a great province with unmerited, but not unavenged, blood – because with extreme agony he compelled his obstinate soul at last to submit to poison, and at the

---

[285] Text: PAUL VIERECK, ANTOON GERARD ROOS, and EMILIO GABBA, Appiani Historia romana (Editio stereotypa correctior. Addenda et corrigenda adiecit E. Gabba. 2 vols.; Bibliotheca Scriptorum Graecorum et Romanorum Teubneriana; Leipzig, 1939–1962), 1:507–508 (who note that ἐκρήμνη is spelled ἐκρήμνει in the Vaticanus manuscript). They list the cited passage as §§449–451. The text has been checked against HORACE WHITE, Appian's Roman History (4 vols.; LCL; Cambridge: Harvard University Press, 1912–1913), 2:424 (where the text is listed as §97 at the beginning of chapter 15).

same time he paid atonement for those crosses, with which he – licentious in servility, villainous in rule – caused those friends of his to suffer, with Gaurus the eunuch as the authority.

*Commentary.*[286] Valerius Maximus composed his *Memorable Deeds and Sayings* while Tiberius was emperor in the first century A.D., and he dedicated the volume to Tiberius in his preface to the first Book. This work consists of thematic collections of material about Roman luminaries, often followed by briefer "external" (non-Roman) examples. Section 2 of Book 9 concerns *De Crudelitate* ("On Cruelty"). While Sulla, Marius, Damasippus, and Munatius Flaccus provide examples of cruel Roman leaders, Valerius manages to trot out many more "external" cases of brutality, among whom is Mithridates VI (Eupator Dionysius) of Pontus, the great Asian arch-rival of Rome in the first century B.C. This whole passage is effectively one long series of clauses connected to the opening sentence fragment (*tam ... quam Mitridatem regem,* "so too ... King Mithridates"); that fragment assumes its subject and predicate from the preceding sentence (9.2 ext. 2), indicating that the senate was justified (if slow) in acting against Mithridates.[287] Valerius especially focuses on the "Asian Vespers" of 88 B.C. during the First Mithridatic War (89–85 B.C.), when Mithridates ordered the massacre of all Romans and Italians resident in Asia Minor. Appian's account of these events mentions many instances of Romans or Italians claiming sanctuary in temples, only to be slaughtered in the sacred precincts (cf. Appian, *Mithr.* 4.22–23). Valerius believes it fitting that Mithridates died in agony (by extreme torment while taking poison) so as to avenge his own deeds. Actually, Mithridates was believed to have accustomed himself to various poisons by taking them daily (e.g., Pliny, *Nat. hist.* 25.3; Celsus, *De medicina* 5.23). Toward the conclusion of the Third Mithridatic War, Mithridates' own son Pharnaces led a revolt against him (63 B.C.). Finding himself likely to be captured and turned over to the Romans, Mithridates attempted to commit suicide by taking poison, but found himself immune to its effects; thus he had to ask one of his officers to slay him instead (cf.

---

[286] Text: JOHN BRISCOE, Valeri Maximi Facta et Dicta Memorabilia (2 vols.; Stuttgart / Leipzig: Teubner, 1998), 2:581. The principle textual variant concerns *illos* (before *amicos*), with other editors reading *alios* or *ipsos*; this does not effect our study. Text also compared with KARL F. B. KEMPF, Valeri Maximi Factorum et dictorum memorabilium libri novem. Cum incerti auctoris fragmento De praenominibus (Berlin: Reimer, 1854), 686; KARL HALM, Valeri Maximi Factorum et dictorum memorabilium libri novem (Leipzig: Teubner, 1865), 440 (with only punctuation differences in KEMPF and HALM).

[287] The preceding clause refers to Hannibal, and intones: *iusto ergo illum odio, uerum tamen tardo supplicio senatus ... ad uoluntariam mortem compulit* ("Therefore, the senate with justified hatred, yet at the same time with a tardy punishment ... compelled that man to suicide"). The parallels between Hannibal and Mithridates are striking: the senate (and the Romans) despised both men, the Romans took a long time (decades) in conquering these two foes, and both men finally were compelled to suicide to prevent Roman capture.

Appian, *Mith.* 16.111; Livius 102). Valerius also understands Mithridates' death as an "atonement" (*piacula ... dedit*) for the "crosses" (*crucibus*) he employed against even his own friends.[288] It is rather remarkable that Valerius, in picking out examples of "cruelty" in the reign of Mithridates, would pair his use of the cross against friends with the massacre of thousands of Romans.

### 3.3.3 Taurians, Armenians, Scythians, and Indians

**(220)** Euripides, *Iphigenia in Tauris* 1422–1430

1422   ὦ πάντες ἀστοὶ τῆσδε βαρβάρου χθονός,
       οὐκ εἶα πώλοις ἐμβαλόντες ἡνίας
       παράκτιοι δραμεῖσθε κἀκβολὰς νεὼς
1425   Ἑλληνίδος δέξεσθε, σὺν δὲ τῆι θεῶι
       σπεύδοντες ἄνδρας δυσσεβεῖς θηράσετε,
       οἱ δ' ὠκυπόμπους ἕλξετ' ἐς πόντον πλάτας,
       ὡς ἐκ θαλάσσης ἔκ τε γῆς ἱππεύμασιν
       λαβόντες αὐτοὺς ἢ κατὰ στύφλου πέτρας
1430   ῥίψωμεν ἢ σκόλοψι πήξωμεν δέμας.

*Translation.*
1422   O! All citizens of this barbarian land,
       Are you not up! Bridle reins on your horses,
       Gallop on the seaside, and anything thrown out of the Hellenic ship
1425   take!, and with the goddess
       hasten and hunt the impious men!
       And draw rapid oar-planks in the sea,
       so that from sea and from land by horseback
       capturing them, either against the rough rock
1430   we may hurl them, or we may nail their living body to stakes.

*Commentary.*[289] In Euripides' play *Iphigenia in Tauris* from the fifth century B.C., he tells the story of Iphigenia being transported to the Taurian region north of the Black Sea to serve as priestess of Artemis. There she presides over the sacrificial execution of all strangers to the Taurian land, until her brother Orestes arrives to help her escape. The passage quoted above comes toward the end of the play, after Orestes and Iphigenia have escaped to a ship

---

[288] According to DAVID R. SHACKLETON BAILEY, Valerius Maximus. Memorable Doings and Sayings (2 vols.; LCL; Cambridge: Harvard University Press, 2000), 2:315, Gaurus is "[n]ot mentioned elsewhere".

[289] Text: JAMES DIGGLE, Euripidis fabulae (3 vols.; Scriptorum classicorum bibliotheca Oxoniensis; Oxford: Clarendon, 1981–1994), 2:300–301.

and taken with them the cult statue of Artemis (e.g., 1358–1360). Thoas, the king of the Thracians, speaks these lines to his people when he learns the ship is caught near the shore. Immediately after his speech the goddess Athena will intervene and instruct him to let Orestes and Iphigenia return to Greece.

Euripides depicts the Taurians as a savage race that sacrifices humans to the gods.[290] In this passage, even their king calls them by the Greek epithet βάρβαροι ("barbarians"). His goal will be to catch the fleeing ship and send its crew members to their deaths, either by hurling them from a cliff or by nailing their living bodies to stakes (σκόλοψι πήξωμεν δέμας). The latter penalty receives scant description, yet it does appear to assume some bodily suspension of a (likely living) human body (δέμας)[291] on one (or more) wooden stakes (σκόλοψι). Although Euripides views this as the intended action of barbarians, he also allows that they felt that by these means, they would be executing "impious men" (ἄνδρας δυσσεβεῖς) who had sought to steal the cult statue of Artemis.

## (221) Appian, *Mithridatica* 12.84 (§378)

Τιγράνη δ᾽ οὐδεὶς ἐμήνυεν ἐπιόντα Λεύκολλον· ὁ γάρ τοι πρῶτος εἰπὼν ἐκεκρέμαστο ὑπ᾽ αὐτοῦ, συνταράσσειν αὐτὸν τὰς πόλεις νομίσαντος. ὡς δέ ποτε ᾔσθετο, Μιθροβαρζάνην προύπεμπε μετὰ δισχιλίων ἱππέων, Λούκουλλον ἐπισχεῖν τοῦ δρόμου.

*Translation.* But no one informed Tigranes that Lucullus was at hand, for the first who said, "let me tell you," had been hung up by him [Tigranes], since [Tigranes] considered him to have thrown the city into confusion. But when [Tigranes] perceived [the danger], he sent forward Mithrobarzanes with two thousand horse in order to restrain Lucullus' quick advance.

*Commentary.*[292] At this point (69 B.C.) in the Third Mithridatic War (as recorded in Book 12 of Appian's *Roman History*), Mithridates VI of Pontus is on the run from the Romans. Tigranes of Armenia is harboring Mithridates. Lucullus, the Roman general, consequently attacks Tigranes (especially his city of Tigranocerta). The first person to report the threat of Lucullus' advance

---

[290] This charge of human sacrifice, perhaps promulgated in part through Euripides, does function as a continuing literary motif in later authors (e.g., Tertullian, *Marc.* 1.1.3 mentions "*de sacrificiis Taurorum*" alongside "*amoribus Colchorum et crucibus Caucasorum*", with these latter two also traceable back to plays by Euripides and Aeschylus).

[291] According to LSJ s.v. δέμας, the term properly refers to a living body, but it can be used of corpses.

[292] Text: VIERECK, ROOS, and GABBA, Appiani Historia romana, 1:494 (where it is §378); compared with text in WHITE, Appian's Roman History, 2:398 (who reads Λεύκολλον for both instances of Λεύκουλλον, and ἐκεκρέμαστο for κεκρέμαστο; both changes are essentially orthographic discrepancies).

to Tigranes had been "hung up" (κεκρέμαστο) by him, using terminology that implies that his execution involved bodily suspension (Appian often employs this verb for events resembling crucifixions).[293] The actual verbal report that angered Tigranes is stated all too briefly in this account (merely the enclitic word τοι, indicating "let me tell you"), though that brisk report also appears to have been rather brash (τοι is not something one should say to one's superior). In any case, Tigranes apparently feared that the city would be disturbed by the way the news was being delivered, so he hung the informer up. The result was that others were afraid to notify Tigranes of the impending danger from Lucullus, until it was almost too late.

**(222)**  Justin, *Epitome* of Pompeius Trogus, *Historiae Philippicae* 2.5.1–7

Scythae autem tertia expeditione Asiana cum annis octo a coniugibus et liberis afuissent, servili bello domi excipiuntur: [2] quippe coniuges eorum longa expectatione virorum fessae nec iam teneri bello, sed deletos ratae servis ad custodiam pecorum relictis nubunt, [3] qui reversos cum victoria dominos velut advenas armati finibus prohibent. [4] Quibus cum varia victoria fuisset, admonentur Scythae mutare genus pugnae, memores non cum hostibus, sed cum servis proeliandum, nec armorum, sed dominorum iure vincendos: verbera in aciem, non arma adferenda, omissoque ferro virgas et flagella ceteraque servilis metus paranda instrumenta. [5] Probato omnes consilio instructi, sicut praeceptum erat, postquam ad hostem accessere, inopinantibus verbera intenta: adeoque illos perculerunt, ut quos ferro non poterant, metu verberum vincerent, fugamque non ut hostes victi, sed ut fugitivi servi capesserent. [6] Quicumque capi potuerunt, supplicia crucibus luerunt. [7] Mulieres quoque male sibi consciae partim ferro, partim suspendio vitam finierunt.

*Translation.* Moreover, the Scythians, during their third Asian expedition, when on the eighth year they had come near [back home] to their wives and freemen, they were greeted with war by the slaves at home: [2] The reason was

---

[293] Appian typically uses κρεμάννυμι in reference to human bodily suspension (often crucifixion), as can be observed in the multiple texts from Appian below in section 3.6. A contrasting form of death is found a few sections earlier in Appian's *Mithridatica* (12.82), where Mithridates despairs of his life and kingdom, and thus he orders his sisters, wives and concubines killed. They are murdered with "swords, poisons, and neck-halters" (διεφθείροντο ξίφεσι καὶ φαρμάκοις καὶ βρόχοις; i.e., stabbed/beheaded, poisoned, and strangled). Notably, although WHITE's translation (2:395) renders the last method of execution as "hanged," Appian's language actually varies substantially here from the form of human bodily suspension ("hanging up") that he references elsewhere as with κρεμάννυμι. Therefore in contrast to 12.82, it is likely that "hanging up" (κρεμάννυμι) in 12.84 does not refer to strangulation of the throat (whether by gallows or some other form), but to some other form of suspension – namely impalement, or quite possibly crucifixion (for the latter see especially our discussion in section 3.6.1 concerning Appian, *Bella Civilia* 3.1.3).

that their wives, having become weary of the long wait for their husbands and supposing [the husbands] to no longer be held back by war but annihilated, married the slaves who were left behind for the custody of the cattle, [3] which slaves stopped their masters (who had returned victoriously) at the borders with arms as if they were foreigners. [4] Concerning whom, when the victories had varied [between masters and slaves], the Scythians were prompted to change their method of combat, remembering they were contending not with foreign enemies but with slaves, who will be conquered not with military arms but with the lawful means of masters: bearing whips into the fray, not weapons, and leaving behind the sword [they would bear] rods and lashes and other instruments that produce fear in slaves. [5] With this advice deemed acceptable, all were equipped just as it had been ordered, and after they advanced against the enemy, whips were exerted against those not expecting it: even to such a degree that they overcame those [slaves] so that those whom they were not able [to defeat] with the sword, they conquered by fear of whips, and so that [the slaves] took to flight not as conquered enemies but as fugitive slaves. [6] Anyone whom [the Scythians] were able to seize they made pay their punishments with crosses. [7] The wives also, conscious of their own wickedness, ended their life – some by the sword and others by suspending themselves.

*Commentary.*[294] Marcus Junianius Justinus produced in the second century A.D. (or possibly later)[295] an *Epitome* (i.e., summary abridgment) of Pompeius Trogus' *Philippic Histories* (which is otherwise lost to us). Trogus likely lived during the Augustan period (cf. *Epitome* 43.5.11–12) and thus completed his work by the early first century A.D. Scholars debate the degree to which Justin (aside from selection of material for inclusion) interpolated his own thoughts into Trogus' text. This passage recounts a rather well-known story concerning the Scythians (also found in Herodotus, *Hist.* 4.1–4), though the important lines 6–7 in Justin are not found in Herodotus. The Scythians were nomadic peoples who lived primarily north and east of the Black Sea.[296] In the Roman era, this story of slaves taking over their former masters' houses/wives would have sounded much like a slave-revolt. The punishment for such revolts was crucifixion (see 3.6.3), so there would presumably have been some concurrence among Justin/Trogus' Roman readers with the Scythian use of the *crux* to punish such rebellious slaves (*supplicia crucibus luerunt* in line 6).

---

[294] Text: JUSTUS W. L. JEEP, Iustinus. Trogi Pompei Historiarum Philippicarum epitoma (Bibliotheca scriptorum Graecorum et Romanorum Teubneriana; Leipzig: Teubner, 1859), 2: 17–18; cf. JOHN C. YARDLEY, Justin. Epitome of the Philippic History of Pompeius Trogus (American Philological Association Classical Resources 3; Atlanta: Scholars Press, 1994).

[295] Dates have varied for Justin from the second century until the late fourth century. Cf. YARDLEY, Justin. Epitome, 4 who argues for a late second-century date.

[296] Justin defines their territory as flanked by Pontus, the Riphaean Mountains, and Asia to the Phasis river (*Epitome* 2.1.1).

**(223)** Diodorus Siculus, *Bibliotheca Historica* 2.44.1–2

μετὰ δὲ ταῦτα ἀναρχίας γενομένης κατὰ τὴν Σκυθίαν, ἐβασίλευσαν γυναῖκες ἀλκῇ διαφέρουσαι. ἐν τούτοις γὰρ τοῖς ἔθνεσιν αἱ γυναῖκες γυμνάζονται πρὸς πόλεμον παραπλησίως τοῖς ἀνδράσι καὶ ταῖς ἀνδρείαις οὐδὲν λείπονται τῶν ἀνδρῶν. διὸ καὶ γυναικῶν ἐπιφανῶν πολλαὶ καὶ μεγάλαι πράξεις ἐπετελέσθη-σαν οὐ μόνον κατὰ τὴν Σκυθίαν, ἀλλὰ καὶ κατὰ τὴν ὅμορον ταύτης χώραν. ² Κύρου μὲν γὰρ τοῦ Περσῶν βασιλέως πλεῖστον ἰσχύσαντος τῶν καθ' αὑτὸν καὶ στρατεύσαντος ἀξιολόγοις δυνάμεσιν εἰς τὴν Σκυθίαν, ἡ βασίλισσα τῶν Σκυθῶν τό τε στρατόπεδον τῶν Περσῶν κατέκοψε καὶ τὸν Κῦρον αἰχμάλωτον γενόμενον ἀνεσταύρωσε· τό τε συσταθὲν ἔθνος τῶν Ἀμαζόνων τοσοῦτον ἀνδρείᾳ διήνεγκεν ὥστε μὴ μόνον πολλὴν χώραν ὅμορον καταδραμεῖν, ἀλλὰ καὶ πολλὴν τῆς Εὐρώπης καὶ τῆς Ἀσίας καταστρέψασθαι.

*Translation.* And after these things anarchy came throughout Scythia, and women ruled who were distinguished in strength. For among these nations women train for war alongside men, and in manly deeds they are in no way inferior to men. Wherefore also many great deeds of renowned women have been accomplished, not only throughout Scythia but also throughout the land that borders it. ² For, when Cyrus, the Persian king, was the strongest of his times, and he with a remarkable force battled against Scythia, the queen of the Scythians both cut his camp into pieces and crucified the captured Cyrus. And the national league of the Amazons were distinguished with such manly deeds that they overran not only much of their bordering lands but also subdued much of Europe and Asia.

*Commentary.*[297] Diodorus begins to discuss the Scythians in *Bib. hist.* 2.43.1. According to him, they inhabit the country near India, and their lands once extended as far west as up to Egypt. The text quoted above appears in the *Bibliotheca* as a literary aside on militaristic women in the region of Scythia, but (at least with regard to the Scythian queen) it also occurs "after these things" (i.e., after the Medians had ravaged much of Scythia; 2.43.7). Diodo-rus provides two examples of lands with militaristic women: one of the Scythian queen and another of the Amazonian women. Thus Diodorus later will go on to discuss the Amazons (2.44.2–2.46.6). For our purposes, note that Diodorus here recounts the matriarchal rule of Scythia, whose queen was of such valor that she destroyed the remarkable forces of Cyrus and crucified (ἀνεσταύρωσε) king Cyrus himself. The actual punishment she enacted against Cyrus comes down differently to us in various sources: thus both in Herodotus' *Histories* (1.214.4) and in Justin's *Epitome* of Pompeius Trogus (1.8.13), queen Tamyris decapitates Cyrus and inserts his head into a wineskin filled with blood.[298] In any case, this Diodorus passage testifies to how some

---

[297] Text: FISCHER and VOGEL, Diodori bibliotheca historica, 1:241.

Romans believed Cyrus had been crucified by the Scythian queen. The nature of this crucifixion penalty against a Persian ruler reminds us that the Persians themselves engaged in acts of suspending the bodies of their victims – events that Roman writers also associated with the term ἀνασταυρόω (see section 3.2.10). From Diodorus' perspective, the Scythians may have simply been repaying the Persians in kind. Certainly the Romans would have understood these barbarians to be acting out of their barbarous natures.

**(224)** Diodorus Siculus, *Bibliotheca Historica* 2.18.1–2 [Ctesias, FGH 3c 688 Frag. 1b. 18.1–2)

Ἐπεὶ δ᾽ αὐτῷ πάντα τὰ πρὸς τὸν πόλεμον κατεσκεύαστο, πρὸς τὴν Σεμίραμιν καθ᾽ ὁδὸν οὖσαν ἀπέστειλεν ἀγγέλους, ἐγκαλῶν ὅτι προκατάρχεται τοῦ πολέμου μηδὲν ἀδικηθεῖσα· πολλὰ δὲ καὶ ἄρρητα κατ᾽ αὐτῆς ὡς ἑταίρας βλασφημήσας διὰ τῶν γραμμάτων καὶ θεοὺς ἐπιμαρτυράμενος, ἠπείλει καταπολεμήσας αὐτὴν σταυρῷ προσηλώσειν. ² ἡ δὲ Σεμίραμις ἀναγνοῦσα τὴν ἐπιστολὴν καὶ καταγελάσασα τῶν γεγραμμένων, διὰ τῶν ἔργων ἔφησε τὸν Ἰνδὸν πειράσεσθαι τῆς περὶ αὐτὴν ἀρετῆς.

*Translation.* And when he [i.e., the Indian ruler Stabrobates] had prepared for himself everything for the war, he sent messengers to Semiramis, who was on the road, indicting her that she first began the war, though she had been wronged in no way; and with many shameful words against her he defamed her through the letter as a harlot, he appealed to the gods, and threatened her that after subduing her in war he would nail her to a cross. ² But Semiramis, after reading the letter and mocking what had been written, said that through deeds the Indian will test her virtue.

*Commentary.*[299] According to this legendary account in Diodorus, Semiramis ruled as queen of Assyria upon the death of her husband, king Ninus (2.7.1–2; cf. Justin, *Epitome* 1.2.1–10). During her rule of 42 years (2.20.2) she built great monuments and conquered many distant lands, including Egypt and Ethiopia (2.14.3–4; cf. Strabo, *Geog.* 16.1.2; Pliny, *Nat.* 6.25; Ovid, *Metam.* 4.57–58). Diodorus records that Semiramis was personally compelled to "attempt great things and be ambitious to surpass the glory of the one who had ruled before her."[300] However, Semiramis' Indian campaign (2.16.1–2.19.10) ultimately ended in defeat, with her having lost approximately two-thirds of her forces and barely escaping with her own life (2.19.10). Semiramis had pre-

---

[298] Herodotus himself remarks on the "many biographical stories told of Cyrus' death" and claims to have followed the most reliable one (*Hist.* 1.214.4, Τὰ μὲν δὴ κατὰ τὴν Κύρου τελευτὴν τοῦ βίου πολλῶν λόγων λεγομένων ὅδε μοι ὁ πιθανώτατος εἴρηται.).

[299] Text: FISCHER and VOGEL, Diodori bibliotheca historica, 1:198–199.

[300] Diodorus, *Bib. hist.* 2.7.2: οὖσα φύσει μεγαλεπίβολος καὶ φιλοτιμουμένη τῇ δόξῃ τὸν βεβασιλευκότα πρὸ αὐτῆς ὑπερθέσθαι.

pared for many months for this war (2.16.5–2.17.2), and Stabrobates, in turn, had also gathered an immense army (2.17.4–8). Diodorus frequently appeals to the authority of Ctesias for his information on Semiramis, consequently all of *Bib. hist.* 2.1.4–2.28.7 appears commonly listed as fragmentary testimony to Ctesias' lost *Persica* (including this passage).[301]

A play on words likely occurs at the very end of this passage since ἀρετῆς can refer to brave deeds in battle as well as to virtuous conduct. Thus Semiramis claims that she will show the greater courage and also that her virtue will be proven even amidst the Indian's defamatory assertions that she is a harlot. However, it seems that Diodorus (and Ctesias) himself likely agreed with Stabrobates since Diodorus explicitly states Semiramis initiated the war without provocation (2.16.4) and that she also took many men as concubines to herself (killing them once she was done with their services; 2.13.4).[302]

In the Ctesias/Diodorus account the Indian threatens to nail Semiramis to a cross (σταυρῷ προσηλώσειν).[303] As is often the case, the precise method of execution is not detailed; yet Diodorus does indicate that Semiramis would be pinned (προσηλώσειν) to the device, and this would have easily been associated with crucifixion by Diodorus' readers. Although Semiramis mockingly laughed off the threat, the Indian clearly intended that the prospect of facing a σταυρός would stir up great fear in Semiramis. As in Diodorus' reference to the Scythian crucifixion of Cyrus (see *Bib. hist.* 2.44.2 above), his Roman audience would likely believe that Stabrobates was pledging to apply a standard Assyrian punishment against his Assyrian provocateur (see 3.2.10 on Graeco-Roman accounts of Assyrian suspensions).

## 3.3.4 Carthaginians

**(225)** Justin, *Epitome* of Pompeius Trogus, *Historiae Philippicae* 18.7.9–15

Interiectis deinde diebus Carthalo petito commeatu a populo cum reversus ad patrem esset ornatusque purpura et infulis sacerdotii omnium se oculis ingereret, tum in secretum abducto pater ait: [10] 'aususne es, nefandissimum caput, ista purpura et auro ornatus in conspectum tot miserorum civium venire et

---

[301] Thus this identical Greek text appears in LENFANT, Ctésias de Cnide, 46; STRONK, Ctesias's Persian History, 228 (who brackets the τὰ in the first line). English translation in STRONK, ibid. 229 and in LLEWELLYN-JONES and ROBSON, Ctesias' History of Persia, 128.

[302] It may also be pertinent to note that Semiramis came to be queen when king Ninus, infatuated by her beauty and impressed with her military leadership abilities, insisted that her first husband Onnes give her up (even threatening Onnes until he committed suicide; 2.6.9–10). Semiramis is also charged with sexual deviance with her son in Justin, *Epitome* 1.2.10.

[303] AUBERGER, Ctésias, 149 n. 37 comments: "Ces messages d'insultes font encore partie du roman, bien sûr!"

maesta ac lugentia castra circumfluentibus quietae felicitatis insignibus velut exultabundus intrare? Nusquamne te aliis iactare potuisti? [11] Nullus locus aptior quam sordes patris et exilii infelicis aerumnae fuerunt? [12] Quid, quod paulo ante vocatus, non dico patrem, ducem certe civium superbe sprevisti? [13] Quid porro tu in purpura ista coronisque aliud quam victoriarum mearum titulos geris? [14] Quoniam in patre igitur nihil nisi exulis nomen agnoscis, ego quoque imperatorem me magis quam patrem iudicabo statuamque in te exemplum, ne quis posthac infelicibus miseriis patris inludat.' [15] Atque ita eum cum ornatu suo in altissimam crucem in conspectu urbis suffigi iussit.

*Translation.* After some intervening days, with leave of absence requested from the people, when Carthalo had returned to his father [i.e., Malchus] and appeared before the eyes of everyone adorned with purple and his priestly headwear, then, once he had been secretly led away, his father said to him: [10] Were you not brash, most impious leader, to come adorned with that purple and gold of yours in the view of so many miserable citizens, and to enter a grim and mourning camp while surrounded by the insignia of quiescent good fortune just like someone rejoicing? Were you not able to flaunt yourself around elsewhere before others? [11] Was there no place more suitable than the squalor of your father and the afflictions of his unfortunate exile? [12] What! Because having been summoned a short while ago, did you disdainfully spurn your – I do not say your father, but certainly the leader of the citizens? [13] Furthermore, in that purple and the wreaths of yours what honors do you bear other than my victories? [14] Therefore, in view of the fact that in your father you recognize nothing except the name of an exile, I likewise will pronounce myself authority greater than a father, and I will set up an example in you, so that afterwards no one will trifle against his unfortunate and miserable father. [15] And so [Malchus] ordered him to be hung up with his adornment on the highest cross in the view of the city.

*Commentary.*[304] In Book 18 of Justin's second-century A.D. *Epitome* of the first-century A.D. *Philippic History* of Pompeius Trogus,[305] Justin/Trogus provides a brief history of the Carthaginians. Prior to the text cited above, Justin/ Trogus recounts how in the sixth-century B.C., the Carthaginians, led by their general Malchus, lost a key battle against the Sardinians after a series of successes in Sicily (*Epitome* 18.7.1). The author attributes this loss to the disfavor of the gods, who had been angered by the Carthaginian practice of child sacrifice to ward off a plague on the city (18.6.11–12).[306] The Carthaginians

---

[304] Text: JEEP, Iustinus, 2:119–120.

[305] As noted earlier, the date of Justin's *Epitome* is debated (with scholars suggesting dates ranging from the second to the fourth centuries A.D.). Our view follows Develin in his introduction to Justin, *Epitome*, trans. J. C. Yardley, pp. 3–4.

[306] Archaeologists continue to debate LARRY STAGER's identification of a "tophet" (burial ground for child sacrifices) at Carthage, though this certainly coheres with ancient records

respond to this military defeat by exiling Malchus and his remaining troops (18.7.2). Malchus, in turn, launches a war against his own city and besieges Carthage. Meanwhile, Malchus' son, Carthalo, who served as priest of Carthage, had been sent to the temple of Hercules in Tyre with spoils from his father's Sicilian campaign to honor the god. Upon Carthalo's return from Tyre, his father summoned him, but Carthalo replied that he must first enter into Carthage in fulfillment of his civic duty. Malchus' motives in summoning Carthalo may well have been to remind his son and the city that he was the cause of their Sicilian victory (if also of the Sardinian defeat). In any case, Malchus believed he had been spurned by his son, and in the text above, we witness the resulting interaction once Carthalo finally visited his father.

Observe above how the author indicates that, in the very spoils Carthalo had carried to Hercules, he was bearing the victories of Malchus (*victoriarum mearum*) from the Sicilian war. There are many wordplays in the Latin, including the terms for fortune/misfortune, the frequent use of "father", and the recurring references to adornment. Malchus calls his priestly son, who should be the most "pious" of Carthaginians, the "most impious leader" (*nefandissimum caput*). For our purposes, one very intriguing wordplay involves Malchus' declaration to his son: *statuamque in te exemplum* ("and I will set up an example in you"), for indeed Carthalo is "set up" when his "hung up on the cross" (*crucem ... suffigi*). This suspension is conceived as a warning/example to the city itself (*urbis*), who looks on (*conspectu*) as the father/ruler Malchus crucifies his own son – How then will he treat us? they might well wonder. The cross is also said to be "extremely high" (*altissimam crucem*), adding to the very public nature of this suspension. Within a few days, Malchus will capture Carthage and execute ten civic leaders, though he will otherwise not punish the city. Still, Justin later describes Malchus' own death as a penalty for attempting to become king,[307] and for his double crimes against his son and his fatherland (*Nec multo post ipse adfectati regni accusatus duplicis et in filio et in patria*; 18.7.18). Malchus consequently "pays the penalty of a parricide" (*parricidii poenas dedit*). Thus Justin's *Epitome* judges as excessive Malchus' actions against Carthage and against his own son

**(226)** Polybius, *Historiae* 1.11.4–5

οἱ δὲ Μαμερτῖνοι τὸν μὲν τῶν Καρχηδονίων στρατηγὸν ἤδη κατέχοντα τὴν ἄκραν ἐξέβαλον, τὰ μὲν καταπληξάμενοι, τὰ δὲ παραλογισάμενοι· τὸν δ'

---

(such as this one). Cf. PATRICIA SMITH, LAWRENCE E. STAGER, JOSEPH A.GREENE, and GAL AVISHAI, Age Estimations Attest to Infant Sacrifice at the Carthage Tophet, Antiquity 87.338 (2013): 1191–1199.

[307] Here it should be noted that the name "Malchus" may itself be a corruption of the Semitic term for king (*mlk*); see note in YARDLEY, Justin. Epitome, 159.

Ἄππιον ἐπεσπῶντο καὶ τούτῳ τὴν πόλιν ἐνεχείριζον. ⁵ Καρχηδόνιοι δὲ τὸν μὲν στρατηγὸν αὐτῶν ἀνεσταύρωσαν, νομίσαντες αὐτὸν ἀβούλως, ἅμα δ' ἀνάνδρως προέσθαι τὴν ἀκρόπολιν.

*Translation.* And the Mamertines cast the Carthaginian commander out of the citadel, which he had already occupied, both by confounding and by defrauding him; and they welcomed Appius and placed the city in his hands. ⁵ But the Carthaginians crucified their commander, considering it ill-advised and unmanly for him to let go of the acropolis.

*Commentary.*[308] Writing in the mid-second century B.C., Polybius provides an account of Rome's military rise in the Mediterranean. In this opening text, Polybius introduces the proximate cause of the First Punic War between Rome and Carthage. The Mamertines are Italic (Campanian) mercenaries who settled in the town of Messana in Sicily, which lies just across the Sicilian Straits from Rhegium in Italy. The Mamertines eventually took harsh military control of Messana (Polybius, *Hist.* 1.7). When they began to fear the Syracusans might assist the native Sicilians in removing their Mamertine overlords, some Mamertines called for Carthage to protect them while others asked Rome to come to their aid (*Hist.* 1.10). After some debate, the Roman populace votes to assist the Mamertines, largely with the concern that Carthage will otherwise have a foothold from which to attack Italy. In about 264 B.C., those Mamertines allied with Rome to remove the Carthaginian commander (Hanno)[309] and install the Roman consul (Appius Claudius). The fiercesome Carthaginians punish the foolish and "unmanly" action of Hanno, who relinquished the citadel that gave them claim to Messana. Their method of punishment involved bodily suspension (ἀνεσταύρωσαν – above translated "crucified"). Polybius employs his first of many uses of ἀνασταυρόω to depict Carthaginian actions. The Carthaginians are as likely to employ ἀνασταυρόω against their own ("unmanly") failed generals as they are to use it against their adversaries.

**(227)** Polybius, *Historiae* 1.24.5–6

μετὰ δὲ ταύτην τὴν πρᾶξιν ὁ μὲν Ἀννίβας ἔχων τὰς διασωθείσας ναῦς ἀπέπλευσεν εἰς τὴν Καρχηδόνα, μετ' οὐ πολὺ δ' ἐκεῖθεν εἰς Σαρδόνα διῆρε, προσλαβὼν ναῦς καί τινας τῶν ἐνδόξων τριηράρχων. ⁶ χρόνοις δ' οὐ πολλοῖς κατόπιν ἐν τῇ Σαρδόνι συγκλεισθεὶς ὑπὸ Ῥωμαίων ἔν τινι λιμένι καὶ πολλὰς

---

[308] Text: BÜTTNER-WOBST, Polybius. Historiae, 1:13. Same text (with slight punctuation difference) in PATON, Polybius: Histories, 1:26.

[309] Several Carthaginians are known to history by the name "Hanno." This one appears only briefly here at the inception of the conflict before he is crucified.

ἀποβαλὼν τῶν νεῶν, παραυτίκα συλληφθεὶς ὑπὸ τῶν διασωθέντων Καρχηδονίων ἀνεσταυρώθη.

*Translation*. And after these deeds Hannibal, who held the ships which had been preserved, sailed unto Carthage, and after not many days he crossed over from there unto Sardinia, taking ships and some of the esteemed trireme captains. ⁶ But in not much time afterwards in Sardinia, having been blockaded in a certain harbor by the Romans and having lost many ships, immediately he was seized by the preserved Carthaginians and crucified.

*Commentary*.[310] Polybius recounts the demise of one of several Carthaginian leaders named Hannibal (not the famous antagonist from the Second Punic War). This Hannibal had led the Carthaginians through several forced retreats (see *Hist*. 1.18–19, 1.23–24), but in his last battle, Hannibal was deemed guilty by the Carthaginian soldiers of having been responsible for too many losses. They thus suspended his body (ἀνεσταυρώθη) circa 260 B.C. Most translators render Hannibal's demise with "crucifixion" language, though the precise means of such suspension is not detailed. Certainly, this suspension is associated with his death; moreover, it is clearly the most important penalty applied to him since it is the only punishment against Hannibal that Polybius explicitly recalls. Again, we witness the Carthaginians suspending one of their own generals after he proved to be insufficient to the task (cf. Polybius, *Hist*. 1.11.5 above). This action penalized the offending general, but it also undoubtedly served as cautionary motivation to other Carthaginian leaders.

## (228) Appian, *Sicelica* 2.7–8 [2.3]

καταλυθέντος δὲ τοῦ πολέμου τοῦδε Κελτοὶ Καρχηδονίους τόν τε μισθὸν ᾔτουν τὸν ἔτι ὀφειλόμενον σφίσιν ἐκ Σικελίας καὶ δωρεὰς, ὅσας ὑπέσχητο αὐτοῖς δώσειν Ἀμίλχας. ᾔτουν δὲ καὶ Λίβυες, ὑπήκοοι μὲν ὄντες οἴδε Καρχηδονίων, ἀπὸ δὲ τῆς ἐν Σικελίᾳ στρατείας ἐπὶ φρονήματος γεγονότες καὶ τοὺς Καρχηδονίους ἀσθενεῖς καὶ ταπεινοὺς ὁρῶντες, ἐχαλέπαινόν τε αὐτοῖς τῆς ἀναιρέσεως τῶν τρισχιλίων, οὓς ἐσταυρώκεσαν τῆς ἐς Ῥωμαίους μεταβολῆς οὕνεκα.

*Translation*. And after this war had ended, the Gauls asked the Carthaginians both for the payment still owed them from [the war in] Sicily and for the gifts – as much as Hamilcar had promised to give them. And the Libyans also asked [for such pay], though these were subjects of the Carthaginians, but they had become presumptuous from the campaign in Sicily and had seen the Carthaginians weak and humble; and [the Libyans] were angry with them [the

---

[310] Text: BÜTTNER-WOBST, Polybius. Historiae, 1:33–34; same text in PATON, Polybius: Histories, 1:66.

Carthaginians] concerning the slaying of the three thousand, whom [the Carthaginians] had crucified on account of their going over to the Romans.

*Commentary.*[311] At the close of the First Punic War, after paying a huge tribute to Rome, Carthage still had substantial debts owed to their Celtic mercenary force from Gaul and to their African (Libyan) colleagues. Carthage was unable to pay, which led to a revolt of their former mercenaries (who quickly capture Tunis and Utica), and thus was launched the Mercenary War (of 241–237 B.C.) between Carthage and these former mercenaries. Appian implies that the Libyans did not actually deserve such pay, since they were subjects of Carthage, but presumption (ἐπὶ φρονήματος) had led to their demands, along with an awareness that the Carthaginians were too weak to deny their request. Appian adds the detail that the Libyan forces, beyond feeling that they deserved pay, also wished some recompense on the Carthaginians, who had suspended 3,000 of their Libyan colleagues on *stauroi* after they had deserted to Rome. This mass suspension, as recollected by Appian in the mid-second century A.D., does not occur in the earlier account by Polybius,[312] which diminishes our ability to assert absolute confidence in the historical details. Still, as penned by a learned Roman citizen from Alexandria, this account exhibits an influential second-century perspective concerning Carthaginian military practices. It is relatively rare for Appian to employ this verb (ἐσταυρώκεσαν) for such a suspension (more often he uses κρεμάννυμι), though he also utilizes σταυρόω in reference to human suspension in *Bell. civ.* 5.8.70.[313]

## (229) Polybius, *Historiae* 1.79.3–4

αὖθις δὲ τῶν Καρχηδονίων στρατηγὸν ἐξαποστειλάντων μετὰ δυνάμεως
Ἄννωνα, κἄπειτα καὶ τούτων τῶν δυνάμεων ἐγκαταλιπουσῶν τὸν Ἄννωνα
⁴ καὶ μεταθεμένων πρὸς σφᾶς, γενόμενοι ζωγρίᾳ κύριοι τοῦ προειρημένου,

---

[311] Text: VIERECK, ROOS, and GABBA, *Appiani Historia romana*, 1:59 (text at 2.7–8). The same text, with only differences in punctuation, appears in WHITE, *Appian's Roman History*, 1:130 (text at 2.3).

[312] Polybius does not mention the Libyan anger over such a mass suspension as a cause of this war. Instead, he notes among the causes the failure of the Carthaginians to conduct their negotiations wisely with the mercenaries (Polybius, 1.67), the instigation of the self-promoting mercenaries Spendius and Matho amidst the Libyans (1.69), the Carthaginian (especially Gesco's) refusal to pay the Libyan soldiers (1.69–70), and the excessive taxation of the Libyan countryside (1.72). However, Polybius does detail the presumption of the mercenaries in demanding pay (beyond even what was promised and was reasonable), due to the evident weakness of the Carthaginians without their mercenary troops (1.68).

[313] Like many earlier authors, in addition to depicting human bodily suspension with σταυρόω, Appian also uses the verb for the construction of a palisade (made of σταυροί or ξύλοι); e.g., *Punica* (*Libyca*) 18.119. For more on Appian's suspension vocabulary, see the commentary on Appian, *Bell. civ.* 3.1.3 (below in No. 300).

παραυτίκα τοῦτον μὲν ἀνεσταύρωσαν, μετὰ δὲ ταῦτα παρηλλαγμένας ἐπινο-
οῦντες τιμωρίας, πάντας τοὺς ἐν τῇ νήσῳ Καρχηδονίους στρεβλοῦντες ἀπέκτειναν.

*Translation.* Again when the Carthaginians sent the general Hanno with a
force, and then when even these forces abandoned Hanno [4] and changed sides
to them, the masters of those spoken above took him alive and immediately
crucified him, and after these things they contrived alternating punishments
for, tortured, and killed all the Carthaginians on the island.

*Commentary.*[314] After the First Punic War, the city of Carthage was unable to
pay the debts it owed to its multitude of hired mercenaries. The mercenaries
revolted, and the resulting Mercenary War (the Libyan War, 241–237 B.C.)
compelled the Carthaginians to do battle with them (*Hist.* 1.66ff.). Polybius
emphasizes events that directly affected the city of Carthage (especially the
wars during the mercenary leadership of Spendius and Manno), though in this
passage he briefly notes that the revolt spread to other communities that were
guarded by mercenaries under Carthage, allowing Polybius tangentially to
explain the Carthaginian loss of the island of Sardinia.

　　According to Polybius, this particular Hanno met his demise by bodily suspension. His death is commonly considered a reference to crucifixion by the
translators, though the specific method of execution by suspension is not fully
detailed and must be inferred from Polybius' use of ἀνασταυρόω.[315] Hanno's
execution initiates the first of many torturous deaths that are mentioned here
against the Carthaginians on the island of Sardinia. However, it appears that
some of the Carthaginian military force became turncoats (μεταθεμένων πρὸς
σφᾶς) and allied themselves with those mercenaries who initiated the Sardinian revolt against Carthage. Thus it seems unlikely that "all the Carthaginians
on the island" were actually killed. Indeed, these turncoat Carthaginians could
well have suggested the means of dealing death to their own general (in keeping with Carthaginian practice noted above). Nevertheless, the "masters" in
this context appear to be the mercenaries In the Sardinian garrison mentioned
in 1.79.1; their explicit nationalities are not mentioned, although Polybius testifies generally to mercenaries primarily from Libya and also to those from
Iberia, Celtic lands, Liguria and the Balearic Islands, along with a considerable number of Greeks (whom he claims were "mostly deserters and slaves";
see *Hist.* 1.67.7).

---

[314] Text: BÜTTNER-WOBST, Polybius. Historiae, 1:107–108; the omission of the comma
before πάντας appears to be a printing error, corrected by PATON). Same text in PATON,
Polybius: Histories, 1:212.

[315] Especially relevant would be how ἀνασταυρόω is applied to the living Hannibal in
Polybius 1.86.3–7 (see above 3.1), thus indicating that for Polybius, it is a means of execution
that involves the victim being alive during the procedure.

**(230)**  Polybius, *Historiae* 1.86.3–7

This passage was discussed in No. 124. Spendius, one of the instigators of the
Mercenary War, is crucified by the Carthaginians, and his death is avenged by
his Libyan compatriot Matho, who crucifies Hannibal "alive," along with
thirty of his leading men. For further comments see No. 124.


**(231)**  Diodorus Siculus, *Bibliotheca Historica* 25.5.1–2

Τὸ γὰρ δαιμόνιον, ὡς ἔοικε, ταύτην ἀμοιβὴν τῶν ἀσεβημάτων αὐτοῖς ἐδικαίωσεν. ² Ὅτι τὸν Σπόνδιον ἀνεσταύρωσεν Ἀμίλκας. ὁ δὲ Μάθως Ἀννίβαν εἰς
τὸν αὐτὸν σταυρὸν αἰχμάλωτον λαβὼν προσήλωσεν, ὥστε δοκεῖν τὴν τύχην
ὥσπερ ἐπίτηδες ἐναλλὰξ τὰς εὐημερίας καὶ τὰς ἥττας ἀπονέμειν τοῖς περὶ τὴν
ἀνθρωπίνην φύσιν ἠσεβηκόσιν.

*Translation.* For the *daemon*, as it seemed, claimed this recompense against
them for their impieties. ² Because Hamilcar crucified Spendius, but Mathos,
taking Hannibal prisoner, nailed him unto the same cross, so that it seemed
that Fortune as it were cunningly assigned alternatingly prosperity and defeat
against those who had committed impiety against human nature.

*Commentary.*[316] This provides another reference to the paired deaths on a
σταυρός of the mercenary leader Spendius and the Carthaginian commander
Hannibal (mentioned above in Polybius, *Hist.* 1.86). This section of the first-
century B.C. historian Diodorus is no longer fully extant; it only comes to us in
the form of later summaries of his work. Even in this epitomized episode,
there is a strong verbal echo of Polybius in the phrase τὴν τύχην ὥσπερ
ἐπίτηδες ἐναλλὰξ (cf. τῆς τύχης ὥσπερ ἐπίτηδες ἐκ παραθέσεως ἀμφοτέροις
ἐναλλὰξ, Polybius 1.86.7); thus in his original, Diodorus was likely following
Polybius. Notably, Diodorus depicts Hannibal as being "nailed" (προσήλωσεν)
to the cross. As one would rightly expect, ἀνασταυρόω appears to be the verbal equivalent of an expression with its cognate noun σταυρός ("εἰς τὸν αὐτὸν
σταυρὸν προσήλωσεν"). Diodorus believed that in the broad sweep of fate, it
was appropriate for Fortune to assign these penalties to these men since both
had committed "impiety against human nature" (τοῖς περὶ τὴν ἀνθρωπίνην
φύσιν ἠσεβηκόσιν). Diodorus also refers to these events as having been under
the influence of a *daemon* (δαιμόνιον), which appears to be a deity figure,[317]
possibly Fortune herself. This *daemon*-deity claims "recompense against
them for their impieties" (ταύτην ἀμοιβὴν τῶν ἀσεβημάτων αὐτοῖς ἐδικαίωσεν). So

---

[316] Text: FISCHER and VOGEL, Diodori bibliotheca historica, 5:343.

[317] WALTON, in OLDFATHER, SHERMAN, GEER, and WALTON, Diodorus, 12:149, translates
as "higher power".

the very cruel demise of Spendius and Hannibal, even on the "same cross" (εἰς τὸν αὐτὸν σταυρὸν), is shown to be a just punishment for their actions.

**(232)** Diodorus Siculus, *Bibliotheca Historica* 25.10.2

Ἰνδόρτης δὲ πάλιν ἀθροίσας πεντακισμυρίους, καὶ πρὶν πολέμου τραπεὶς καὶ φυγὼν εἰς λόφον τινά, καὶ πολιορκηθεὶς ὑπ᾽ Ἀμίλκα καὶ νυκτὸς πάλιν φυγών, τὸ πλεῖστον αὐτοῦ κατεκόπη, αὐτὸς δὲ Ἰνδόρτης καὶ ζωγρίας ἐλήφθη. ὃν τυφλώσας Ἀμίλκας καὶ τὸ σῶμα αἰκισάμενος ἀνεσταύρωσε· τοὺς δὲ ἄλλους αἰχμαλώτους, ὄντας μυρίων πλείους, ἀπέλυσε.

*Translation*. And again Indortes mustered fifty thousand, but before the battle he turned and fled onto a certain ridge; and being besieged by Hamilcar, he again fled during the night. The majority of his troops were cut in pieces, but Indortes himself was also taken as a prisoner, whom Hamilcar (after blinding him and torturing his body) crucified; but the other prisoners, being many myriads, he released.

*Commentary*.[318] After Hamilcar Barca (and Hanno) suppressed the Mercenary War (c. 237 B.C., cf. Diodorus Siculus, *Bib. hist.* 25.8), this Hamilcar took leadership of Carthaginian forces in Spain, seeking to expand Carthaginian control over its key resources, with the possible goal of preparing for another war against Rome (cf. Polybius 2.1.5–8; Livius 21.1.4–21.2.3). In these fragments of the *Library of History*, Diodorus appears to alternate between a general admiration of Hamilcar and an occasional attack upon his character.[319] In Spain, Hamilcar makes war on the Iberians, Tartessians, and Celts. After defeating a large force under Istolatius (*Bib. hist.* 25.10.1), Hamilcar now faces monumental odds against Indortes. When the text above states, "he [Indortes] fled," we should likely imagine Indortes retreating with his army. The specifics of the battle are largely missing, but the text does emphasize Indortes' demise. Hamilcar demands Indortes be blinded, tortured, and then crucified (ὃν τυφλώσας Ἀμίλκας καὶ τὸ σῶμα αἰκισάμενος ἀνεσταύρωσε). Given that Indortes would have been living while he was blinded and tortured, the reader naturally assumes the cross was itself the means of execution. Hamilcar's clemency is otherwise shown to the remaining "myriads" of prisoners. His sons Hannibal and Hasdrubal were key Carthaginian leaders during

---

[318] Text: FISCHER and VOGEL, Diodori bibliotheca historica, 5:345.

[319] Thus Diodorus will speak of Hamilcar's "many great deeds for his fatherland" and his "prudent" conduct of the Libyan Wars (25.8), of his bravery alongside his troops (25.9), and of his sacrificial death (25.10.4). Yet, Diodorus also criticizes Hamilcar's choice of the "most wicked men" as compatriots after the Libyan War, and of his accumulation of wealth and popular acclaim (25.8). Nonetheless, Diodorus' final word is that Hamilcar deserves praise as his epitaph (25.10.5; also cf. Polybius 2.1.7–8).

the Second Punic War, and we shall soon observe how the son imitated his father's use of the cross.

**(233)** Diodorus Siculus, *Bibliotheca Historica* 26.23.1

"Ότι Καρχηδόνιοι καταλύσαντες τὸν Λιβυκὸν πόλεμον, τὸ τῶν Μικατανῶν Νομάδων ἔθνος σὺν γυναιξὶ καὶ τέκνοις τιμωρησάμενοι πάντας τοὺς συλληφ-θέντας ἀνεσταύρωσαν. διόπερ οἱ τούτων ἀπόγονοι τῆς εἰς τοὺς πατέρας ὠμότητος ἀναμιμνησκόμενοι χαλεπώτατοι τοῖς Καρχηδονίοις πολέμιοι καθει-στήκεισαν.

*Translation.* That the Carthaginians, after the Libyan War ceased, exacted vengeance on the nation of the Numidian Micatani along with their women and children, and they crucified all those who were captured. Wherefore, their descendants, remembering the savagery unto their fathers, were established as the most dangerous enemies against the Carthaginians.

*Commentary.*[320] This passage is unfortunately only known in fragmentary excerpts from Diodorus (sequences of which begin with ὅτι, "that"),[321] and thus we have no real immediate context for this passage. However, the historical referent is clear enough. The close of the Mercenary (or "Libyan") War (c. 237 B.C.) brought with it Carthaginian recompense on the Numidians who had joined the mercenaries in their war against Carthage.[322] According to Diodorus, it was Hasdrubal (Hamilcar Barca's son-in-law) who prosecuted the war against the Numidians, "cutting down" 8,000 (κατέκοψεν ὀκτακισχιλίους) and enslaving many more (*Bib. hist.* 25.10.3). In contrast, the fragment above would imply (contrary to *Bib. hist.* 25.10.3) that *all* the captured Carthaginians (even women and children!) were crucified (πάντας τοὺς συλληφθέντας ἀνεσταύρωσαν), which seems a case of literary hyperbole either by Diodorus or by his epitomist (especially in light of Diodorus' earlier statement in 25.10.3).[323] Certainly, the cruel actions of the Carthaginians against these Numidians can

---

[320] Text: FISCHER and VOGEL, Diodori bibliotheca historica, 5:362.

[321] Numidians later in the Second Punic War again served both as allies of Carthage and as allies of Rome under Scipio (e.g., Polybius 14.1–9). The Numidian Syphax actually changes allegiances to join Rome (Livius 24.48–49). The fact that Scipio made Numidian allies likely explains the location of this fragment after other fragments speaking of Scipio (*Bib. hist.* 26.21–22). In fact, the "Numidians" constituted various tribes (as Diodorus seems to know in his reference to the "Numidian Micatani"), whose fighting among themselves could lead to different tribes joining Carthage or Rome to counter the allegiances of an opposing tribe.

[322] Numidians had also been involved as mercenaries of Carthage in the First Punic War (cf. Polybius 1.19), though some had also acted on behalf of Rome (cf. Polybius 1.31).

[323] Admittedly, it is conceivable that here Diodorus just refers to the fate of one tribe of Numidians (the Micatani), and that in 25.10.3 he considers a broader landscape of Numidians. So, the passages may not be completely at odds. But, the scale of mass executions/crucifixions in this passage certainly appears excessive.

explain why a longstanding hatred would have endured. Further, we can observe that the Roman author (again either Diodorus or his epitomist) could conceive of Carthaginian barbarism extending to mass executions on crosses of whole tribes, even including women and children.

**(234)**  Titus Livius, *Ab urbe condita* 22.13.7–9

ubi cum montibus fluminibusque clausam regionem circumspexisset, vocatum ducem percunctatur, ubi terrarum esset. [8] cum is Casilini eo die mansurum eum dixisset, tum demum cognitus est error, et Casinum longe inde alia regione esse; [9] virgisque caeso duce et ad reliquorum terrorem in crucem sublato, castris communitis, Maharbalem cum equitibus in agrum Falernum praedatum dimisit.

*Translation.* Where he [Hannibal] looked around the enclosed territory with its mountains and rivers, called the guide, and inquired where on earth he was. [8] When he [the guide] said to him that he shall remain in Casilinum that day, then at last was known the mistake and that Casinum was a long way from there in another territory; [9] and after the guide had been beaten with a rod and (so as to promote fear among the others) raised on a cross, and after the encampment was fortified on all sides, he dispatched Maharbal with horses in order to plunder in the fields of Falernus.

*Commentary.*[324] During the Second Punic War,[325] this famous Hannibal was led astray by his guide (presumably by accident), who had confused the words "Casinum" and "Casilinum" due to Carthaginian difficulties in pronouncing Latin (22.13.6). Hannibal's intent had been to capture the pass of Casinum (22.13.5), but the guide instead led him to Casilinum. The enclosed territory of Casilinum must have not looked at all like a pass, thus Hannibal became aware of the error and harshly punished the guide. Though the shape of the "cross" (*crux*) is not defined, Livy implies that the guide was raised on the cross (*in crucem sublato*) in order to produce death. This crucifixion is preceded by a beating (*virgisque caeso duce*). And Livy clearly states that this suspension was for the purpose of terrifying the others who were there (*ad reliquorum terrorem*), presumably so they would be particularly careful in their military service.

---

[324] Text: THOMAS ALAN DOREY, Titi Livi Ab urbe condita libri XXI-XXII (Bibliotheca Scriptorum Graecorum et Romanorum Teubneriana; Stuttgart: Teubner, 1971), 1:81. Same text in WEISSENBORN, Titi Livi Ab urbe condita libri , 2:274.

[325] MOORE dates this event to 217 B.C.; cf. BENJAMIN O. FOSTER, FRANK GARDNER MOORE, EVAN TAYLOR SAGE, ALFRED C. SCHLESINGER, and RUSSEL M. GEER, Livy (14 vols.; LCL; Cambridge: Harvard University Press, 1919–1957), 5:245.

**(235)** Titus Livius, *Ab urbe condita* 28.37.1–2

Mago cum Gades repetisset, exclusus inde ad Cimbios – haud procul a Gadibus is locus abest – classe adpulsa, mittendis legatis querendoque, quod portae sibi socio atque amico clausae forent, [2] purgantibus iis multitudinis concursu factum infestae ob direpta quaedam ab conscendentibus naves militibus, ad colloquium sufetes eorum, qui summus Poenis est magistratus, cum quaestore elicuit, laceratosque verberibus cruci adfigi iussit.

*Translation.* Mago, when he again made for Gades and had been shut out from there, his fleet put in to Cimbii (this place is not far from Gades), so that a delegation could be sent and a protest made because the ports had been shut against him though he was an ally and friend. [2] [The Gaditani] made their excuses due to the assembly of the multitude, which was hostile [to Mago's soldiers] on account of certain plunderings by the soldiers as they embarked the ships. [Mago] lured to a conference their *sufetes*, who are the highest Phoenician magistrates, with the *quaestor*, and, having lacerated them with whips, he ordered them to be affixed to the cross.

*Commentary.*[326] This single complex sentence in Latin emphasizes by grammar and position Mago's treatment of the civic leaders of Gades – he commanded them to be affixed to the cross (*cruci adfigi iussit*). Hannibal repeatedly entrusted his brother Mago with a substantial force during the Second Punic War (e.g., Livius 21.54–55; 22.46; 23.1) and also with occasionally serving as his delegate to the Carthaginian senate (23.11–13). Gades (modern Cadiz) is a port city on the southwestern coast of Spain; it figures heavily into Carthaginian naval planning throughout Livy's account. Livy records this event from 206 B.C.. A plot to defect to Rome had previously been discovered by Mago at Gades (28.30.4), so he may have had some reason to suspect the Gaditani of favoring the Romans. Indeed, shortly after Magos' crucifixion of the leaders and his defeat in the Balearic Islands, the city of Gades surrendered to the Romans (28.37.10). The people of Gades, for their part, had indeed been pillaged by Mago at his previous visit (28.36.3),[327] so the reader can well sympathize with their desire to shut the gates against Mago's sol-

---

[326] Text: PATRICK G. WALSH, Titi Livi Ab Urbe Condita Libri XXVIII-XXX (Bibliotheca Scriptorum Graecorum et Romanorum Teubneriana; Stuttgart: Teubner, 1986), 41 (consonantal "u" here "v"). Same text, with slight variations in punctuation, in WEISSENBORN, Titi Livi Ab urbe condita libri, 3:262; WALTERS and CONWAY, Titi Livi Ab urbe condita. Tomus II (no page numbers in this edition).

[327] Thus AUBREY DE SÉLINCOURT, Livy. The War with Hannibal. Books XXI-XXX of The History of Rome From its Foundation (Penguin Classics; London/New York: Penguin Books, 1965), 545, translates 28.36.3 as: "and he himself [i.e., Mago] wrung all he could from the people of Gades, not only emptying their treasury but robbing the temples and forcing every individual to contribute such gold and silver as he possessed."

diers. It is not entirely obvious in this passage whether the leadership of Gades agreed with the multitude in repulsing the Carthaginian ships, but Mago holds the leaders responsible for the people's action and makes an example of them as well. Note here that, as is frequently the case in battle (especially in Carthaginian warfare), the obstructionist city is taught a lesson by having its leadership cruelly suspended. Also, as elsewhere, the victims are first beaten before being suspended on the *crux*.

**(236)**  Titus Livius, *Ab urbe condita* 38.48.13

Nunc, quoniam suscepti belli purgatum est crimen, gesti reddenda est ratio. in quo confiderem equidem causae meae etiam si non apud Romanum sed apud Carthaginiensem senatum agerem, ubi in crucem tolli imperatores dicuntur, si prospero eventu pravo consilio rem gesserunt.

*Translation.* Now, since the accusation has been cleared that I undertook the war, it must be sustained that reason [for the war] be given in explanation. In which I, for my part, would trust my cause, even if I were dealing, not with the Roman, but with the Carthaginian senate, where generals are said to be raised on the cross if they conduct a matter with favorable fortune but with a misguided plan.

*Commentary.*[328] This is a section from a speech by Gnaeus Manlius Volso (38.47–49) from 187 B.C. in which he sought the favor of a triumphal procession from the Roman senate for his battle victories against the Gauls of Asia Minor. He must respond to the charges of two of his subordinates (Lucius Furius Purpurio and Lucius Aemilius Paulus) that he had rushed headlong into war for purposes of personal gain and that he had won the war more by good luck than by superior tactics (38.44–46). In its depiction of Manlius' response to these two charges, this passage transitions from an apologetic for his initiating the war to a reply to the charge that he used poor tactics. Livy records that despite the fervency of Manlius' speech, it took the intervention of others on his behalf for him to be granted the triumph (38.50.1–3). Manlius makes passing rhetorical appeal to his confidence being such that he would be willing to pass the test of the Carthaginian senate (rather than the pious Romans). In Carthage, he alledges, they hang on the cross generals who happen to win, though with deficient tactics. By this rhetorical move, Manlius hopes to begin to counter the second charge of Furius and Aemilius (i.e., that he conducted the war poorly). E. T. SAGE notes that Valerius Maximus

---

[328] Text: JOHN BRISCOE, Titi Livi Ab urbe condita. Libri XXXI-XL (2 vols.; Bibliotheca Scriptorum Graecorum et Romanorum Teubneriana; Stuttgart: Teubner, 1991), 2:588 (consonantal "u" here "v"). Same text in WEISSENBORN, Titi Livi Ab urbe condita libri, 4:364, with slight punctuation variations.

records a similar claim (cf. *Facta et Dicta Memorabilia* 2.7 ext. 1 below), though "extant cases seem to illustrate only crucifixion after defeat."[329] SAGE's comment is consistent with our previous findings that, though Carthaginians would suspend their generals on a cross, they did so only after significant losses. Thus it is difficult to know whether Manlius' assertion is accurate or mere hyperbole. In either case, it would appear that some Romans *thought* the Carthaginians were capable of holding their generals to such a strict standard of combined success and excellent tactics, with failure entailing suspension on a Carthaginian *crux*.

**(237)** Valerius Maximus, *Facta et Dicta Memorabilia* 2.7 ext. 1

Leniter hoc patres conscripti, si Carthaginiensium senatus in militiae negotiis procurandis uiolentiam intueri uelimus; a quo duces bella prauo consilio gerentes, etiam si prospera fortuna subsecuta esset, cruci tamen suffigebantur, quod bene gesserant deorum immortalium adiutorio, quod male commiserant ipsorum culpae imputantes.

*Translation.* The senate did this moderately: if we want to inspect the ferocity of the Carthaginian senate in administering the work of the military, by whom leaders who conducted wars with misguided plans, even though prosperous fortune followed, were nevertheless fastened to the cross, because though they conducted [wars] well with the help of the immortal gods, they engaged in battle poorly, thus being charged with the blame of those very ones [i.e., the gods].

*Commentary.*[330] Valerius alleges the same charge against the Carthaginian senate as was found just above in Livy's account of Manlius' speech (Livius 38.48.13) – the Carthaginians would affix to a cross even their own successful generals whose victories stemmed more from luck than careful scheming. Livy is a commonly recognized source for Valerius' writing, so it may be that Valerius was here dependent on Livy (note "*prauo consilio*"). Valerius wrote

---

[329] EVAN T. SAGE in FOSTER, MOORE, SAGE, SCHLESINGER, and GEER, Livy, 11:169. BRISCOE remarks that, other than in Valerius Maximus 2.7 ext. 1 (which he believes derives from here in Livy), no other evidence exists for such Carthaginian practice; JOHN BRISCOE, A Commentary on Livy, Books 38–40 (Oxford: Oxford University Press, 2008), 167.

[330] Text: BRISCOE, Titi Livi Ab urbe condita. Libri XXXI-XL, 1:130–131; the principal textual issue concerns the ending on *imputantes*. Compared with text of KEMPF, Valeri Maximi Factorum et dictorum memorabilium libri, 219–220; HALM, Valeri Maximi Factorum et dictorum memorabilium libri, 94; CHARLES BENOÎT HASE, Valerius Maximus De dictis factisque memorabilibus et Jul. Obsequens de prodigiis cum supplementis Conradi Lycosthenis (2 vols.; Bibliotheca classica latina; Paris: Lemaire, 1822–1823), 1:152; in HASE the differences are primarily in punctuation and spelling, e.g. *subsequuta* for *subsecuta*. HALM thinks that this passage did not make it into the c. fourth-century epitome by Iulius Paris.

in the early first century A.D., during the reign of Tiberius. Here he illustrates his discussion of military discipline by appealing to non-Roman examples (*De Disciplina Militari Observata ab Externis*), which juxtapose the many more examples he provides earlier of domestic Roman military practice. The opening words (*leniter hoc patres conscripti*) contrast the moderation of the Roman senate (here called *patres conscripti*, "conscript fathers"; cf. 2.1.9; 2.7.15; etc.)[331] with the ferocity of the Carthaginian *senatus*. Unlike Livy, Valerius likely provides the reason for this fierce treatment of foolish generals: the gods themselves (though they aided in the victory) held the generals blameworthy for their poor conduct, and thus the senate is merely concurring with the gods.[332] As we noted with Livy, there is insufficient corroboration from other historical accounts to insist that the Carthaginian senate actually did crucify *successful* generals. However, even if Valerius is merely relying on Livy, this passage does support the notion that at least some Romans believed the Carthaginians were capable of such barbarian ferocity.

**(238)** Silius Italicus, *Punica* 1.144–154

144    Interea rerum Hasdrubali traduntur habenae,
145    occidui qui solis opes et vulgus Hiberum
       Baeticolasque viros furiis agitabat iniquis.
       tristia corda ducis, simul immedicabilis ira,
       et fructus regni feritas erat. asper amore
       sanguinis, et metui demens credebat honorem;
150    nec nota docilis poena satiare furores.
       ore excellentem et spectatum fortibus ausis
       antiqua de stirpe Tagum, superumque hominumque
       immemor, erecto suffossum [*or* suffixum] robore maestis
       ostentabat ovans populis sine funere regem.

---

[331] Cf. OLD s.v. "conscriptus".

[332] This assumes that *ipsorum* in *ipsorum culpae* is a subjective genitive (similar to *deorum* in the preceding clause with *deorum immortalium adiutorio*) and that *ipsorum* refers to the gods themselves from the preceding clause (*deorum*). It is also grammatically possible that *ipsorum* functions instead as an objective genitive, refering reflexively to the blameworthiness of the leaders ("their own blame"); thus the SHACKLETON BAILEY and WALKER translations ("It attributed their success to the aid of the immortal gods, their mistakes to their own fault"); cf. SHACKLETON BAILEY, Valerius Maximus, 199; HENRY JOHN WALKER, Valerius Maximus. Memorable Deeds and Sayings: One Thousand Tales from Ancient Rome (Indianapolis: Hackett, 2004), 68. Latin grammarians recognize that *ipse* can be used either as a personal pronoun or as a substitute reflexive pronoun; see JAMES B. GREENOUGH, G. L. KITTREDGE, A. A. HOWARD, and B. L. D'OOGE, Allen and Greenough's New Latin Grammar for Schools and Colleges, Founded on Comparative Grammar (College Classical Series; New Rochelle: Caratzas, 1983), §§298.d.1, 300.b.

*Translation.*

144    Meanwhile, the reins of affairs were handed over to Hasdrubal;
145    and concerning the Western regions, which are the resources and peo-
          ple of Spain
          and Baetis, [Hasdrubal] harassed those men with harsh fury.
          This leader's heart was harsh, simultaneously his anger incurable,
          and the fruit of his reign was savagery. Bitter with the love
          of blood and also insane, he believed honor came by fear;
150    nor with well-known penalties were his furies apt to be satisfied.
          Regarding [king] Tagus, who was outstanding in countenance and dis-
              tinguished by mighty exploits
          and from ancient ancestral stock, [Hasdrubal], who was being heedless
              of both celestial beings and humanity,
          by means of an erected oak-post exhibited to a mournful people
          their pierced [*or* suspended] king [i.e., Tagus], exulting over him with-
              out burial.

*Commentary.*[333] Silius Italicus (Tiberius Catius Asconius Silius) wrote this epic historical poem in the late first century A.D. In addition to portraying the Punic Wars as an outworking of the goddess Juno's enmity against Rome, the *Punica* repeatedly represents the barbarous and savage Carthaginians as Juno's vindictive tool. Hasdrubal was the son-in-law of Hamilcar and served as Carthaginian general for approximately eight years (cf. Livius 21.2.3). The textual issue concerning *suffossum* in line 153 is of some import. DELZ follows a handful of manuscripts/marginal notes in reading *suffossum* ("pierced"), but there is roughly similar manuscript support for *suffixum* ("fixed aloft") or *suspensum* ("suspended").[334] In any of these three cases, a death by suspension is implied, but with *suffossum,* an impalement becomes more likely.[335] The gist of lines 151–154 concerns Hasdrubal's public exhibition of king Tagus by having him publicly suspended aloft (*suffossum* [or *suffixum*]... *ostentabat*) by means of an erected oaken post (*erecto ... robore*) before a watching, mourning multitude (*maestis ... populis*). Tagus is portrayed as a king

---

[333] Text: JOSEPH DELZ, ed., Sili Italici Punica (Stuttgart: Teubner, 1987), 6 (revised to include consonantal "v" and some added punctuation). Text compared with JAMES D. DUFF, Silius Italicus. Punica (2 vols.; LCL; Cambridge: Harvard University Press, 1927–1934), 1:14. The principal textual variant – *suffixum* or *suspensum* for *suffossum* – is discussed below.

[334] Cf. DELZ, Sili Italici Punica, 6 note. DUFF, Silius Italicus. Punica, 14 reads *suffixum.*

[335] Yet even with *suffossum*, such "piercing" could also refer to being beaten, prodded, stabbed, or poked from underneath while affixed to the *robur* (for *suffodere* in beatings with hands cf. Apuleius, *Met.* 2.26; for stabbing with a knife see Suetonius, *Dom.* 17.1; for horses being pierced from underneath see Tacitus, *Ann.* 1.65; 2.11).

who is admirable both in appearance and in rule,[336] and Silius follows the above passage with an encomium for Tagus (1.155–164). In contrast, Hasdrubal is depicted as an irate and savage man. Hasdrubal's suspension of Tagus thus illustrates Hasdrubal's savage nature as he refuses to heed both divine and human customs (*superumque hominumque immemor*), engaging in furious punishments that exceeded the established penalties (*nota poena*). In No. 239, Silius will refer to this same "oak-post" as a *crux* (1.181).

**(239)** Silius Italicus, *Punica* 1.165–184

165     quem postquam diro suspensum robore vidit
          deformem leti famulus, clam corripit ensem
          dilectum domino pernixque inrumpit in aulam
          atque immite ferit geminato vulnere pectus.
          at Poeni, succensa ira turbataque luctu
170     et saevis gens laeta, ruunt tormentaque portant.
          non ignes candensque chalybs, non verbera passim
          ictibus innumeris lacerum scindentia corpus,
          carnificaeve manus penitusve infusa medullis
          pestis et in medio lucentes vulnere flammae
175     cessavere. ferum visu dictuque, per artem
          saevitiae extenti, quantum tormenta iubebant,
          creverunt artus, atque omni sanguine rupto
          ossa liquefactis fumarunt fervida membris.
          mens intacta manet. superat ridetque dolores
180     spectanti similis fessosque labore ministros
          increpitat dominique crucem clamore reposcit.
          Haec inter spretae miseranda piacula poenae
          erepto trepidus ductore exercitus una
          Hannibalem voce atque alacri certamine poscit.

*Translation.*

165     Whom after his slave saw him suspended on the dreadful oak-post –
              disfigured in death, [the slave] secretly snatched up the sword
          that was dear to his master, and swiftly burst into the palace
          and mercilessly smote [Hasdrubal's] breast with repeated wounds.
          But the Carthaginians, with inflamed anger and stirred up grief
170     and being a people delighting in savagery, rushed in and brought their
              tortures.

---

[336] It is possible that Silius made an intentional wordplay when he states that Tagus, who is of "ancient ancestral stock" (*antiqua de stirpe*), met his end on a "oak-post" (*robur*), since *stirps* ("stem of a tree" or "ancestral stock") can also be used to refer to a wooden cross.

Not fire and gleaming hot iron, nor indiscriminate scourgings
with innumerable blows rending the lacerated body,
[but] either the hand of the butcherer, or the plague poured deep to the
     marrow,
and the alight flames rested in the midst of the wound.
175      Uncivilized to see and to speak about, through savage guile
[joints] had been stretched and so many tortures ordered,
that joints were separated, and with all the blood having burst out
the burning bones smoked with melted limbs.
[Yet the slave's] mind remained intact. He overcame and laughed at
     his distress
180      similar to a spectator, and the exhausted servants in their labor
he chided, and he demanded with a shout the cross of his master.
Between these deplorable expiations of this disdained penalty,
the soldiers, anxious with their general being snatched away, with one
voice and eager contention demanded Hannibal [be general].

*Commentary*.[337] This text continues the previous narrative in 1.144–154 (after
lines in honor of king Tagus in 1.155–164) by relating how Tagus' slave
avenged his death. The slave brutally kills Hasdrubal but is, in turn, viciously
tortured by the Carthaginians. The tortures are depicted in gruesome detail,
yet, and here is the most pertinent matter, Tagus' slave mockingly requests to
be crucified like Tagus. From this we learn four things. First, Silius considers
the erected oak-post (*erecto ... robore*, 1.153; cf. *diro robore*, "dreadful oak-
post", 1.165) on which Tagus had been suspended to be the equivalent of a
*crux*.[338] Second, Tagus' slave seemingly taunts the torturers to even greater

---

[337] Text: DELZ, Sili Italici Punica, 7, revised to include consonantal "v". Text compared
with DUFF, Silius Italicus. Punica, 1:16. Some other editors read *rapto* ("stolen away") in line
177 instead of *rupto* ("having burst out") in Delz; the issue is of no real concern here.

[338] Thus a *crux/robur* here is certainly a wooden device, erected by human hands, for the
purpose of suspending someone. Silius also identifies the *robur* and the *crux* elsewhere
(*Punica*, 2.343; see below in §3.6). The shape of the *crux* is not delineated in Silius. The use
of *robur* here might be compared with the kind of "oak post" to which criminals were chained
(see OLD, s.v. *robur* 2c), though the texts cited in OLD do not all convey the notion of a
"post" and all such parallels come from outside Silius himself. Silius uses *robur* to depict a
wooden club (*Punica* 2.244, 267; 5.243; 8.584; cf. Statius, *Thebaid* 2.619), a wooden spear
(4.282, 540), or a large wooden beam used as a fiery missile (*Punica* 1.350–364, esp. 352).
Further uses of *robur* in Silius include: as a metaphor for staunch-as-oak strength (*Punica*
1.664; 3.603; 5.435, 572; 8.446, 586; 9.106; 11.157; 15.412, 655; 16.669), as branches of an
oak tree (5.484, 512), and as mere wood, wooden timbers, wooden oars, or the trees themselves (2.471; 3.189, 638, 688; 4.23; 6.192; 13.104; 14.311, 328, 381, 390, 417, 543;
15.389). The obvious unifying feature of all these instances (even likely including the metaphorical ones) is that they all concern wood (esp. oak). Still, the non-metaphorical uses mostly
invoke essentially straight wooden objects (club, spear, beam, oars, etc.). Thus in connecting
*robur* and *crux*, Silius may have been identifying the *crux* with an upright stake, although it is
equally possible that he was merely focusing on the wooden nature of the *crux* without indi-

labors, with the *crux* being the culmination of their work (1.179–181). Third, Silius considers all this to be the butcherous (*carnificae*, 1.173), savage (*saeuitiae*, 1.176), uncivilized (*ferum*, 1.175), and deplorable (*miseranda*, 1.182) work of a barbarian people who "delight in savagery" (*saeuis gens laeta*, 1.170). Fourth, the slave heroically disdains their efforts, even mocking the potential eventuality of being suspended on a *crux* (cf. 1.179–181; *spretae ... poenae*, 1.182). This demonstrates that despite the cruel horror of the *crux*, the Romans could admire a man who laughingly embraces such an end, especially as the consequence of exacting just vengeance on a barbarous Carthaginian (see further Silius Italicus, *Punica* 2.340–344, 435–436; and other examples of "Heroes and Martyrs" in 3.6 below).

## *3.3.5 Numidians*

**(240)** Sallust, *Bellum Iugurthinum* 14.15

quid agam? aut quo potissumum infelix adcedam? generis praesidia omnia extincta sunt. pater, uti necesse erat, naturae concessit. fratri, quem minume decuit, propinquos per scelus vitam eripuit. affinis amicos propinquos ceteros meos alium alia clades oppressit: capti ab Iugurtha pars in crucem acti, pars bestiis obiecti sunt, pauci, quibus relicta est anima, clausi in tenebris cum maerore et luctu morte graviorem vitam exigunt.

*Translation.* What shall I do? Or whom may I approach regarding my special misfortune? All the protections of my family are obliterated. My father, as was inevitable, surrendered to nature. My brother, for whom it was least proper, a kinsman snatched his life through villainy.[339] Other calamities overwhelmed the rest of my other in-laws, friends and kinsmen: having be captured by Jugurtha, a portion had been compelled to the cross, a portion had been cast to the beasts, and a few, for whom their souls were permitted to survive, because they had been confined in darkness with grief and lament led out their life in ways more oppressive than death.

---

cating that he conceived of it as a single upright pole. It might be worth remarking that a century later Tertullian insisted that the *robur* was the upright pole fixed into the ground that was "always a part of the cross" (*Apol.* 16.5/6: *pars crucis est omne robur quod erecta statione defigitur*). The context in Tertullian implies that the *crux* also had a crossbar attached to the *robur*.

[339] This translation takes *propinquos* as the subject of *eripuit*, following the form *propincus* found in JOHN C. ROLFE, Sallust (LCL; Cambridge: Harvard University Press, 1931), 160. The term *propinquos* in this sentence may be a scribal blunder based on *propinquos* in the following clause.

*Commentary.*[340] Writing in the middle of the first century B.C., Sallust records events toward the end of the second century B.C. The Numidian king Micipsa had adopted Jugurtha and had given him preeminence of place over Micipsa's sons, Hiempsal and Adherbal (10.1–8). After the king's death and various offenses by Hiempsal, Jugurtha has Hiempsal murdered (cf. 12.5). Following a brief battle between Adherbal and Jugurtha, Adherbal flees to Rome to request assistance in gaining the Numidian throne, while Jugurtha's delegates argued the contrary. This section recalls Adherbal's speech to the Roman senate (14.1–25). Adherbal mentions the death of his brother Hiempsal (Jugurtha is the "kinsman who snatched [Hiempsal's] life through villainy"). Adherbal further recounts what has happened to the rest of his kinsmen; at least a portion of these were "compelled to the *crux*." [341] Sallust provides no independent verification of Adherbal's claims. The Romans would have likely viewed as unbecoming to the royal family and friends of Adherbal both the use of the *crux* and the employment of wild beasts as means of execution.

## (241)  Caesar, *Bellum Africum* 66

Postero die Iuba Numidas eos qui loco amisso fuga se receperant in castra in cruce omnis suffixit.

*Translation.* On the next day Juba fastened to a cross of every kind those Numidians, who, having relinquished their position by flight, had retreated to the military camp.

*Commentary.*[342] The author of this work (likely one of Caesar's soldiers)[343] recounts Julius Caesar's victory over his foes (most notably Metullus Scipio and Cato the Younger) in Africa, which amounted to a continuation of the Civil War between Caesar/Antony and the Roman republican forces. Juba of Numidia allied with Scipio and brought a large number of troops to the war. In this section, Labienus' republican/Numidian troops set an ambush for Caesar by employing two legions in wait for him (*Bell. afr.* 65). However, Caesar learned of the trap via deserters, and he instead surprised the concealed troops with a calvary attack. Labienus consequently lost about 500 troops, and Caesar "threw the rest into the most shameful flight" (*reliquos in fugam turpissimam coniecit*; earlier in *Bell. afr.* 66). Labienus managed to come to

---

[340] Text: AXEL W. AHLBERG, C. Sallusti Crispi: Catalina, Iugurtha, Orationes et epistulae excerptae de Historiis (Bibliotheca scriptorum Graecorum et Romanorum; Leipzig: Teubner, 1919), 64–65.

[341] For *in crucem agere* meaning "to crucify" see OLD s.v. *ago* 16b.

[342] Text: A. G. WAY, Caesar. Alexandrian War. African War. Spanish War (LCL; Cambridge: Harvard University Press, 1955), 248.

[343] On authorship cf. WAY, Caesar. Alexandrian War. African War. Spanish War, 141–143.

the aid of these routed soldiers, but Juba believed their action in fleeing the scene sufficiently shameful to fasten up the Numidian soldiers on crosses.[344] If the above translation is correct for *in cruce omnis* ("to a cross *of every kind*"), then the author may have intended to depict more than one form of cross. This passage recalls the Carthaginian use of the *crux* to punish soldiers whose conduct in war is viewed as dishonorable. Certainly the goal would have been to use fear and shame to spur others on to more arduous militancy.

# 3.4 Suspension and Crucifixion in Classical and Hellenistic Greece

Previous pages observed Greek authors recounting suspensions performed by non-Greek "barbarians" (whether in the ANE or further afield). This chapter now turns to the Greeks themselves. These sources below are selected from a broader range of reports concerning Greek use of suspension.[345] The picture is not always as clear as we might hope, especially in the Greek classical era. However, though the Greeks associated penal bodily suspension with barbarians, they too practiced execution forms that required extended exposure, lack of burial, and bodily suspension. It is difficult to ascertain whether these were internal Greek developments, or whether they found themselves mimicking the surrounding cultures. As both archaeological and literary sources attest, Ancient Greece, beginning at least with the Bronze Age, had long been in contact with other lands via far-flung colonies, Ionian settlements on the coast of Anatolia, maritime trade, international war, and Greek mercenary service. The inevitable intermingling of cultures impacted Greece, even as she influenced her neighbors. We begin with a brief précis to one of the more controversial issues, the role of *apotympanismos*. Data points multiply as we progress further toward the Hellenistic age, though then these memories become intermingled with later Roman-era reflection on earlier periods of Greek life.

## 3.4.1 Suspension and Apotympanismos

The verb ἀποτυμπανίζω and cognate noun ἀποτυμπανισμός fundamentally refer to employing a τύμπανον in torture or execution.[346] Yet the range of

---

[344] OLD s.v. *suffigo* 2b refers to *in cruce suffigere* as "to fasten to a cross or other instrument of punishment, crucify". Note it is only the Numidian soldiers whom he punished in this way; it is unclear what proportion this would have been of the overall routed force.

[345] For more complete lists of sources on Greek suspension in the classical, Hellenistic, and Roman eras cf. HENGEL, Crucifixion; SAMUELSSON, Crucifixion, 37–150; COOK, Crucifixion, 218–294.

meanings of these cognates terms is complex and likely changed over time. There is potential overlap with crucifixion in the Greek classical and Roman eras, although the whole issue requires further study. Rather than engage in that study here, a brief summary of previous discussion is provided.

Ancient references to ἀποτυμπανίζω that are cited in the lexicons usually provide little help as to what that penalty entailed since, though those sources typically signal that this penalty leads to death, they do not actually provide clear indications as to how the procedure was conducted (Demosthenes, *Orat.* 8.61; 9.61; 19.137; Lysias 13.56; Aristotle, *Rhet.* 1383a.5; Josephus, *C. Ap.* 1.148; *P. Oxy.* 1798.1.7).[347] Thus although the ninth edition of LSJ specified that the verb ἀποτυμπανίζω denotes "crucify on a plank," the evidential basis in that edition was wanting. The Revised Supplement of LSJ now reads instead: "*put to death, execute* (whether by judicial sentence or less formally; perh[aps] originally *cudgel to death*, but this is not specified in the quot[-ations])."[348] This is a substantive change, and one that hints at the complexities of attempting to identify this elusive verb. The evidential basis in the Revised Supplement also displays a broader interaction with the ancient sources than in the original ninth edition.

Ever since the early twentieth-century studies by M. KERAMOPOULOS and L. GERNET, scholars have worked with the conception of ἀποτυμπανισμός as a formal punishment that involved attaching a criminal to planks with bonds around their necks, wrists, and ankles for the purpose of prolonged exposure leading to death (presumably these planks were simply laid out on the earth). Hengel was certainly impacted by this view in his study of crucifixion, and portrayed ἀποτυμπανισμός as a potential Greek forerunner of the cross.[349] However, many of the ancient texts HENGEL cites do not actually employ the term ἀποτυμπανισμός; indeed, many of those texts often use simple suspension language, which may be otherwise useful to the study of crucifixion (and

---

[346] Aside from references to an ancient drum, cf. LSJ s.v. τύμπανον for this definition of τύμπανον: "name of some instrument of torture or execution". This definition is certainly vague. LSJ cite: Aristophanes (*Plutus* 476) places the term in parallel with κύφωνες (a yoke or pillory); Sextus Empiricus (*Math.* 2.30) collocates it with a prison; 2 Macc 6:19, 28 would indicate that the τύμπανον was a device upon which someone was beaten and whipped (note use of πληγαῖς and μαστιγούμενος in 2 Macc 6:30).

[347] All these references are from LSJ s.v. ἀποτυμπανίζω. In contrast to the LSJ gloss, many English translations (especially older ones) often render these passages with "cudgel to death" or "flog." In contrast, Lysias 13.56, has been rendered into English with "death on the plank" in the LAMB LCL translation, but there the context truly does not make the punishment clear.

[348] LSJ, Revised Supplement 1996, s.v. ἀποτυμπανίζω, p. 47.

[349] HENGEL, Crucifixion, 69–72.

its forerunners) but may not all relate to ἀποτυμπανισμός.[350] The central evidence for this punishment is actually archaeological. Thus HENGEL, following KERAMOPOULOS and GERNET, remarks on the osteological evidence from Phaleron, where seventeen skeletons were discovered with evidence of rings around their necks and with hooks around their hands and feet.[351] To this archaeological example, COOK adds the evidence of two skeletons from Delos, which were discovered with nails and staples immediately adjacent to the legs and ankles and possible rust stains near the hands; one skeleton was decapitated.[352]

Nevertheless, a very useful lexical study by C. BALAMOSHEV has noted that the papyri and many literary sources indicate that ἀποτυμπανισμός often involved a beating (with or without death) or some further means of capital punishment other than exposure on planks.[353] COOK, aware of BALAMOSHEV's work, ultimately notes the "multivalence of the term" and suggests that it became "polysemic."[354] Yet, COOK also helpfully observes two texts from the second century A.D. philosopher Lucian where τύμπανον or τυμπανίζω can appear in association with crucifixion terminology (Lucian, *Jupp. trag.* 19; *Cat.* 6).[355] However, in these two passages we can also observe that the penalties (crucifixion and τυμπανίζω) are distinct from one another, even if they still overlap in that they both entail repulsive means of death.

In close, it would appear that more study here would be fruitful. One can certainly observe that the Greeks did readily employ brutal methods of torture and execution, sometimes involving prolonged *ante mortem* (or possibly *post mortem*) exposure. Now we turn to terminology and passages more directly associated with crucifixion.

---

[350] Cf. HENGEL, Crucifixion, 71–72. HENGEL's references to Aristophanes (*Thesmophoriazusai*, 930ff.) and Plutarch (*Pericles* 28.3) are indeed worth further study, whether or not they directly entail ἀποτυμπανισμός. It is worth further noting that even HENGEL allows that such allusions "may only depict a pillory" (ibid. 70).

[351] HENGEL, Crucifixion, 70.

[352] COOK, Crucifixion, 14–15.

[353] See CONSTANTINOS BALAMOSHEV, ΑΠΟΤΥΜΠΑΝΙΣΜΟΣ: Just Death by Exposing on the Plank? JJP 41 (2011): 15–33. BALAMOSHEV notes evidence for beating associated with ἀποτυμπανισμός in *P. Enteux.* 86; he compares this with beatings in *P. Mich.* inv. 6979 (*SB* XX 15001; use of προσαποτυμπανίσωσιν) and *UPZ* I 119 (employing ἀκποτυπανισθῶσιν). He presents arguments against prolonged exposure from Plutarch, *Sol.* 968E and from several other important texts (many of which are, admittedly, later), cf. ibid. 26–33.

[354] COOK, Crucifixion, 15; note further ibid. 13–15; for the following comment cf. ibid. 13.

[355] Texts from the HARMON edition with COOK's translations (COOK, Crucifixion, 13): Lucian, *Jupp. trag.* 19: καὶ τοὺς μὲν ἱεροσύλους οὐ κολαζομένους ἀλλὰ διαλανθάνοντας, ἀνασκολοπιζομένους δὲ καὶ τυμπανιζομένους ἐνίοτε τοὺς οὐδὲν ἀδικοῦντας; ("and temple robbers are not punished but are forgotten, while people who have done no wrong are sometimes crucified or exposed on a plank?"). Lucian, *Cat.* 6.: τοὺς ἐκ δικαστηρίων δῆτα παράγαγε, λέγω δὲ τοὺς ἐκ τυμπάνου καὶ τοὺς ἀνεσκολοπισμένους ("Bring in now the people from the courts, I mean those from the plank [tympanum] and those who were crucified").

## 3.4.2 Classical Greece

Several key texts are involved in discussions about crucifixion in classical Greek lands. Many of these (especially in Plato and Demosthenes) are more safely situated within the broader category of human bodily suspension, though the reader may well notice that the perceptions of suspension involved overlap substantially with passages that are more securely known to refer to *ante mortem* suspension on a cross. Herodotus provides a particularly interesting author, since he can indicate both Greek opposition to bodily suspension (*Hist.* 9.78–79) and Greek practice of the same (*Hist.* 7.33; 9.120).

**(242)** Herodotus, *Historiae* 9.78–79

¹ Ἐν δὲ Πλαταιῆσι ἐν τῷ στρατοπέδῳ τῶν Αἰγινητέων ἦν Λάμπων ὁ Πυθέω, Αἰγινητέων ‹ἐὼν› τὰ πρῶτα· ὃς ἀνοσιώτατον ἔχων λόγον ἵετο πρὸς Παυσανίην, ἀπικόμενος δὲ σπουδῇ ἔλεγε τάδε· ² "Ὦ παῖ Κλεομβρότου, ἔργον ἔργασταί τοι ὑπερφυὲς μέγαθός τε καὶ κάλλος, καί τοι θεὸς παρέδωκε ῥυσάμενον τὴν Ἑλλάδα κλέος καταθέσθαι μέγιστον Ἑλλήνων τῶν ἡμεῖς ἴδμεν. Σὺ δὲ καὶ τὰ λοιπὰ τὰ ἐπὶ τούτοισι ποίησον, ὅκως λόγος τέ σε ἔχῃ ἔτι μέζων καί τις ὕστερον φυλάσσηται τῶν βαρβάρων μὴ ὑπάρχειν ἔργα ἀτάσθαλα ποιέων ἐς τοὺς Ἕλληνας. ³ Λεωνίδεω γὰρ ἀποθανόντος ἐν Θερμοπύλῃσι Μαρδόνιός τε καὶ Ξέρξης ἀποταμόντες τὴν κεφαλὴν ἀνεσταύρωσαν· τῷ σὺ τὴν ὁμοίην ἀποδιδοὺς ἔπαινον ἕξεις πρῶτα μὲν ὑπὸ πάντων Σπαρτιητέων, αὖτις δὲ καὶ πρὸς τῶν ἄλλων Ἑλλήνων· Μαρδόνιον γὰρ ἀνασκολοπίσας τετιμωρήσεαι ἐς πάτρων τὸν σὸν Λεωνίδην." Ὁ μὲν δοκέων χαρίζεσθαι ἔλεγε τάδε, ὁ δ᾽ ἀνταμείβετο τοῖσδε·³⁵⁶

(79) ¹ "Ὦ ξεῖνε Αἰγινῆτα, τὸ μὲν εὐνοέειν τε καὶ προορᾶν ἄγαμαί σευ, γνώμης μέντοι ἡμάρτηκας χρηστῆς· ἐξάρας γάρ με ὑψοῦ καὶ τὴν πάτρην καὶ τὸ ἔργον, ἐς τὸ μηδὲν κατέβαλες παραινέων νεκρῷ λυμαίνεσθαι, καὶ ἢν ταῦτα ποιέω, φὰς ἄμεινόν με ἀκούσεσθαι· τὰ πρέπει μᾶλλον βαρβάροισι ποιέειν ἤ περ Ἕλλησι, κἀκείνοισι³⁵⁷ δὲ ἐπιφθονέομεν. ² Ἐγὼ δ᾽ ὦν τούτου εἵνεκα μήτε Αἰγινήτῃσι ἄδοιμι μήτε τοῖσι ταῦτα ἀρέσκεται, ἀποχρᾷ δέ μοι Σπαρτιήτῃσι ἀρεσκόμενον ὅσια μὲν ποιέειν, ὅσια δὲ καὶ λέγειν. Λεωνίδῃ δέ, τῷ με κελεύεις τιμωρῆσαι, φημὶ μεγάλως τετιμωρῆσθαι, ψυχῇσί τε τῇσι τῶνδε ἀναριθμήτοισι τετίμηται αὐτός τε καὶ οἱ ἄλλοι οἱ ἐν Θερμοπύλῃσι τελευτήσαντες. Σὺ μέντοι ἔτι ἔχων λόγον τοιόνδε μήτε προσέλθῃς ἔμοιγε μήτε συμβουλεύσῃς, χάριν τε ἴσθι ἐὼν ἀπαθής."

---

³⁵⁶ We follow HUDE's Oxford edition and ROSÉN's Teubner edition in including with 9.78.3 the sentence beginning with Ὁ μὲν. GODLEY (LCL) attaches this to 9.79.1.

³⁵⁷ A few manuscripts read: καὶ ἐκείνοισι for κἀκείνοισι.

*Translation.* [1] At Plataea in the army of the Aeginetans there was Lampon son of Pythea, who was among the leading Aeginetans, who having the most profane thought hastened to Pausanias, and after reaching him he spoke this in haste: [2] "O son of Cleombrotus, a marvelous work has been performed by you that is both great and a thing of beauty, and god has handed over to you the delivering of Hellas in order to place upon you a renown that is greatest among the Greeks whom we have known. But you also must perform that which remains against these men, so that this report may hold you even greater and so that some remainder of the barbarians may be restrained in order not to begin performing reckless works among the Greeks. [3] For after Leonidas was slain in Thermopylae, both Mardonius and Xerxes had his head cut off and suspended. Repay a similar penalty to such men and you will have praise first by all the Spartans and again also among the other Greeks. For after impaling Mardonius you will have avenged Leonidas who was your father's brother." Lampon, considering this to be pleasing, spoke these things, but Pausanias answered with this:

(79) [1] "O guest-friend Aeginetan, I wonder at both your well-wishing and thoughtfulness; however, you have missed the mark of right knowledge. For having exalted me on high along with my fatherland and my deed, then you cast me down into nothing by advising me to inflict indignities upon the dead; and concerning which, if I do these things, you say I will hear myself called for the better. These things are more fitting for barbarians to do than for a Greek, and we even begrudge those. [2] And if I were [to do this] on account of this I would neither delight the Aeginetans nor those who are pleased by such things, but it is enough for me to please the Spartans by doing holy things and also speaking holy things. And as for Leonidas, whom you command me to avenge, I say he has been more greatly avenged; and both he and the others who died at Thermopylae have been avenged by these uncounted souls. However you, receive such a warning that you neither come to me again nor counsel me, and be thankful that you are permitted to go unpunished."

*Commentary.*[358] Herodotus of Halicarnassus, writing in the fifth century B.C., continues his praise of Pausanias (cf. 9.64), who with his Spartan army conquered the Persians. Here Pausanias' good character is revealed as he refuses to stoop to Persian cruelty in impaling their opponents.

According to Herodotus, the Medes and the Persians frequently impaled (ἀνασκολοπίζειν) their opponents (1.128; 3.132; 3.159; 4.43; 4.202; cf. 6.30); see No. 191, especially on ἀνασκολοπίζειν in reference to 1.128). Lampon the Aeginetan counsels Pausanias to imitate this penalty as repayment for the way the Persians had dealt with Leonidas, who had been beheaded and then had his

---

[358] Text: HUDE, *Herodoti Historiae*, vol. 2. Cf. ROSÉN, *Herodoti historiae*, 2:429–430, with minor punctuation and capitalization differences. A few manuscripts read ἐσταύρωσαν instead of ἀνεσταύρωσαν.

head suspended (7.238). Lampon also intended such an impalement to warn the Persians against attempting such aggressive military acts again (9.78).

Note that the action of ἀνασκολοπίζειν (to impale) can be considered a penalty in the same class as suspending a head (τὴν κεφαλὴν ἀνεσταύρωσαν; 9.78). To perform ἀνασκολοπίζειν could be considered an act of "repaying with a similar penalty" for ἀνασταυροῦν (see τοῖσι σὺ τὴν ὁμοίην ἀποδιδοὺς in 9.78). Thus there must be some conceptual overlap for Herodotus between ἀνασκολοπίζειν and ἀνασταυροῦν. Although there is little detailed description of the precise procedures that both these terms implied in Herodotus, it is likely that they both involve some form of suspension, as is otherwise implied by the preposition ἀνα prefixed within each word.

Lampon's counsel was deemed by Herodotus himself to have been "most profane" (ἀνοσιώτατον). Herodotus thus approves of Pausanias' refusal to countenance Lampon's advice. To impale an opponent is to inflict indignities upon the dead (νεκρῷ λυμαίνεσθαι; 9.79).[359] It is an act that barbarians rather than Greeks perform (τὰ πρέπει μᾶλλον βαρβάροισι ποιέειν ἤ περ Ἕλλησι; 9.79), and the Greeks consider such people all the more barbarous as a result. Thus, the good thinking Greeks would not be pleased by such an action. In contrast to Lampon's counsel, Pausanias resolves to perform and speak "holy things" (ὅσια). The death of the uncounted numbers of Persians is vengeance enough for the fallen Spartans. Lampon's counsel is never again welcome in Pausanias' presence. Combined with ἀνοσιώτατον ("most profane"), his contrasting reference to ὅσια ("holy thing") indicates that Herodotus (via Pausanias) considered the Persian practice of ἀνασκολοπίζειν to fall afoul of Hellenic religious and legal principles.

It would have been difficult for Herodotus to say any more clearly that Greeks should oppose the barbarous Persian practice of ἀνασκολοπίζειν. However, it must be allowed that Lampon himself hailed from the Greek island of Aegina. His advice may certainly have been one of imitating a Persian practice, but it does signal that (even in Herodotus) perhaps some Greeks thought that it was justifiable to let the Persians have a taste of their own medicine. Moreover, elsewhere Herodotus records that Pheretime, the deposed queen of the Hellenistic colony of Cyrene, called for impalement of her opponents at the hands of the Persians among her other atrocities (4.202; see No. 198). And we shall see that the Athenians engage in a related suspension penalty against Artaÿctes in our next two sources from Herodotus.

---

[359] On the translation "inflict indignities or outrages upon" the dead for νεκρῷ λυμαίνεσθαι see LSJ s.v. λυμαίνομαι.

**(243)** Herodotus, *Historiae* 7.33

Ἔστι δὲ τῆς Χερσονήσου τῆς ἐν Ἑλλησπόντῳ, Σηστοῦ τε πόλιος μεταξὺ καὶ Μαδύτου, ἀκτὴ τρηχέα ἐς θάλασσαν κατήκουσα Ἀβύδῳ καταντίον, ἔνθα μετὰ ταῦτα, χρόνῳ ὕστερον οὐ πολλῷ, ἐπὶ Ξανθίππου τοῦ Ἀρίφρονος στρατηγοῦ Ἀθηναίων, Ἀρταΰκτην ἄνδρα Πέρσην λαβόντες Σηστοῦ ὕπαρχον ζώοντα πρὸς σανίδα διεπασσάλευσαν, ὃς καὶ ἐς τοῦ Πρωτεσίλεω τὸ ἱρὸν ἐς Ἐλαιοῦντα ἀγινεόμενος γυναῖκας ἀθέμιστα [ἔργα] ἔρδεσκε.

*Translation.* And on the Chersonese at the Hellespont, between Sestos the city and Madytus, there is a rocky promontory projecting into the sea before Abydos. There after these things, though not much later, upon the orders of the Athenian general Xanthippus son of Ariphron, they took Artaÿctes the Persian (satrap of Sestos) and nailed him still living to a plank. He [Artaÿctes] was the one who also, while conducting women into the temple of Protesiläus in Elaeus, practiced lawless deeds.

*Commentary.*[360] In the context of the passage (7.33) Xerxes is about to bridge the Hellespont in order to attack Abydos (the bridge succeeds, but a storm destroys it, prompting Xerxes famously to order the Hellespont to be whipped). Herodotus provides a geographical connection then with the story that is more fully told in 9.120 (see below). The Athenian Greeks are the ones to execute Artaÿctes in this manner.[361] In this passage, Artaÿctes is certainly alive (ζώοντα) when he is nailed (διεπασσάλευσαν) to a plank (σανίδα).[362] GODLEY directly calls this a crucifixion,[363] though only in 9.120 does it become clear that the plank was raised aloft.

---

[360] Text: HUDE, Herodoti Historiae, vol. 2. Text compared with ROSÉN, Herodoti historiae, 2:188–189. A few minor differences occur in ROSÉN: τραχέα for τρηχέα, ἱερὸν for ἱρὸν, and omission of the bracketed [ἔργα]); the most substantive difference for our purposes is προσδιεπασσάλευσαν for διεπασσάλευσαν (with little distinction in meaning, but a key term).

[361] This is most clear in the LEGRAND edition, which follows STEIN in asserting that the text should read Ἀθηναῖοι (in the nominative); PHILIPPE-ERNEST LEGRAND, Hérodote: Histoires (11 vols.; Collection des universités de France; Paris: Belles Lettres, 1932–1954), ad loc. However, the manuscripts read Ἀθηναίων, as does HUDE, Herodoti Historiae, ad loc.; thus Xanthippus is the general *of the Athenians*.

[362] Some manuscripts read προσδιεπασσάλευσαν. In reference to this passage, LSJ defines διαπασσαλεύω as "stretch out by nailing the extremities", and notes other uses of the term in depicting an animal hide pegged out for tanning. They do not provide a separate definition for προσδιαπασσαλεύω, though likely it is just a slightly more emphatic form of διαπασσαλεύω.

[363] GODLEY, Herodotus, 3:347. Other translators simply say they "nailed him alive to a wooden plank"; cf. STRASSLER, Herodotus, 510; RAWLINSON, Herodotus, 518.

**(244)** Herodotus, *Historiae* 9.120.4

Ταῦτα ὑπισχόμενος τὸν στρατηγὸν Ξάνθιππον οὐκ ἔπειθε· οἱ γὰρ Ἐλαιούσιοι τῷ Πρωτεσίλεῳ τιμωρέοντες ἐδέοντό μιν καταχρησθῆναι, καὶ αὐτοῦ τοῦ στρατηγοῦ ταύτῃ ὁ νόος ἔφερε. Ἀπαγαγόντες δὲ αὐτὸν ἐς τὴν ἀκτὴν ἐς τὴν Ξέρξης ἔζευξε τὸν πόρον, οἱ δὲ λέγουσι ἐπὶ τὸν κολωνὸν τὸν ὑπὲρ Μαδύτου πόλιος, πρὸς σανίδας προσπασσαλεύσαντες ἀνεκρέμασαν, τὸν δὲ παῖδα ἐν ὀφθαλμοῖσι τοῦ Ἀρταΰκτεω κατέλευσαν.

*Translation.* Although he [Artaÿctes] promised these things, he did not persuade general Xanthippus. For the men of Elaeus, seeking to avenge Protesiläus, pleaded for him to be killed, and the mind of the general himself was brought to this purpose. And they led him [Artaÿctes] onto the promontory at which Xerxes joined the strait (but some say on the hill which is above the city of Madytus), and after they nailed him to planks, they hung him up. And before the eyes of Artaÿctes they stoned his child.

*Commentary.*[364] At the conclusion of his *Histories*, Herodotus more fully records the events mentioned in our previous source (7.33). Artaÿctes, while satrap of the district, pilfered the tomb and sacred precinct of Protesiläus and repeatedly engaged in intercourse with women in the shrine. Later, while escaping the Athenian siege of Sestos, Artaÿctes is captured by the Athenians. While under guard, Artaÿctes witnesses a portent that leads him to confess his defiling of the temple of Protesiläus of Elaeus. Artaÿctes offers to pay a large ransom to the god of Protesiläus and to the Athenians. However in the passage before us, Xanthippus refuses this offer and puts Artaÿctes to death by suspending him alive on planks.

If we follow the text above, then this particular passage varies from 7.33 in indicating that Artaÿctes was nailed to multiple planks (σανίδας in 9.120) whereas in 7.33 Herodotus only mentions one plank (σανίδα).[365] All manuscripts agree that Herodotus relates that Artaÿctes was hung aloft (ἀνεκρέμασαν). A few sentences later Herodotus will again mention that Artaÿctes was suspended (see ἀνακρεμασθέντος in 9.122).[366] Herodotus portrays Artaÿctes as being alive while suspended (also in 7.33), as is evident here from how his son is put to death in front of his eyes.[367]

---

[364] The text follows the HUDE edition except for the words πρὸς σανίδας (on which see below) and for the ὁ before νόος (HUDE brackets the ὁ, ROSÉN omits). Text compared with ROSÉN, Herodoti historiae, 2:454.

[365] The words πρὸς σανίδας are found in the LEGRAND edition and in GODLEY's LCL text. HUDE reads simply σανίδι (following a conjecture by REISKE), which would obviate the point above. However, the majority of manuscripts (except for S and V) contain the plural σανίδας. See further the apparatus in ROSÉN, Herodoti historiae, 454.

[366] GODLEY, Herodotus, 4:299, again, refers to this execution as a crucifixion.

[367] HENGEL, Crucifixion, 24 refers to this as "the only detailed account of a crucifixion

The specific reason for Artaÿctes' harsh treatment can only be inferred from the context. Certainly he was a despised opponent in a difficult war, but he had also acted wickedly against the sacred precinct and its god (something that likely increased the pious anger of the people of Elaeus).

**(245)** Plato, *Republic* 361e–362a

λεκτέον οὖν: καὶ δὴ κᾶν ἀγροικοτέρως λέγηται, μὴ ἐμὲ οἴου λέγειν, ὦ Σώκρατες, ἀλλὰ τοὺς ἐπαινοῦντας πρὸ δικαιοσύνης ἀδικίαν. ἐροῦσι δὲ τάδε, ὅτι
οὕτω διακείμενος ὁ δίκαιος μαστιγώσεται, στρεβλώσεται, δεδήσεται, ἐκκαυ-
θήσεται τὠφθαλμώ, τελευτῶν πάντα κακὰ παθὼν ἀνασχινδυλευθήσεται καὶ
γνώσεται ὅτι οὐκ εἶναι δίκαιον ἀλλὰ δοκεῖν δεῖ ἐθέλειν.

*Translation.* Therefore it must be said, even if it was spoken rather boorishly, that I did not speak of such things, O Socrates, but those who praise injustice above righteousness [speak thus]. And they will say these things: That thus the one well-disposed to justice will be whipped, racked, bound, and burned in the eye;[368] while dying and suffering all wicked things, he will be impaled and he will know that it is not to be just, but to seem [to be just], that one must desire.

*Commentary.*[369] Plato (c. 429–347 B.C.) was the famed student of Socrates, and he later incorporated his venerable teacher as a character in his philosophical dialogues. The *Republic* is commonly believed to stem from Plato's "middle period," in which Socrates' character more often sets out his own positive views (as opposed to merely critically undermining others in the earlier dialogues). In this renowned dialogue, Socrates defends the position that justice and virtue are worth seeking in themselves (apart from any earthly consequences that one achieves from acting justly). Here in the second book, Plato represents Glaucon arguing the contrary view (albeit more strongly than Glaucon himself would be willing to support): The truly unjust man will seek

---

given by Herodotus" (cf. HENGEL, Cross, 116). Later HENGEL admits that "the phrase 'nail to planks', which appears only here, suggests that a real cross was not used in this case, but the '*tympanum*', which was familiar from their own penal law. This was a flat board made up of planks (σανίδες) on which criminals were fastened for public display, torture or execution" HENGEL, Cross (HENGEL, Crucifixion, 69–70; idem, Cross, 161–162). This is one of the very few texts that SAMUELSSON is willing to label a crucifixion (SAMUELSSON, Crucifixion, 57), due to the "fatal nailing to an execution tool with a likewise outdrawn death struggle" (ibid.), though he later allows that the device employed is a plank not a cross (ibid. 149).

[368] "Burned in the eye" may well involve the use of a hot metal rod (as some translators suggest). In any case, as noted by ADAM, compare Plato, *Gorgias* 473 (see below) and Herodotus, *Hist.* 7.18.1; JAMES ADAM, The Republic of Plato: Edited with Critical Notes, Commentary and Appendices (2 vols.; Cambridge: Cambridge University Press, 1902), 1:75.

[369] Text: JOHN BURNET, Platonis opera (5 vols.; orig. ; 1900–1907; repr., Scriptorum Classicorum Bibliotheca Oxoniensis.; Oxford: Clarendon, 1959–1962), vol. 2 ad loc.

(unjustly) to appear just, and thus will win all accolades; but the truly just man would avoid all such honors (since he is most just when he acts righteously without proper reward), and instead the just man will content himself with being misjudged as a wrongdoer. Thus the most unjust man will appear to all as the most just, while the most just man will be perceived by society to be the most blameworthy and will suffer accordingly. Those sufferings are then detailed in the passage above. The vital element concerns how his sufferings will culminate in being impaled (ἀνασχινδυλευθήσεται) – this Greek term is relatively understudied in the lexicons (LSJ simply pronounces that its meaning equals ἀνασκολοπίζειν), which is largely due to the scant early references in Greek outside of Plato (all of which according to the TLG are mentioned in footnotes here). The term clearly involves a dreaded means of death that is likely associated with suspension.[370] However, even HENGEL and COOK note that this may well not be a crucifixion.[371] Still, the medieval *etymologica* tradition consistently equates ἀνασχινδυλεύω with ἀνασκολοπίζω and even with ἀνασταυρόω.[372] This Platonic account served early Christians as a paradigm

---

[370] Given the paucity of evidence outside Plato, one is left to the medieval lexica and etymology. The stem is perhaps most akin to σχινδυλ-, σκινδαλ-, or σκινδυλ- (all of which refer to splintered wood and similar), which when combined with ἀνα would likely indicate a person impaled up on some wooden device. Etymologies must be viewed with some hesitancy, though here they do line up with the medieval lexical tradition. Cf. SAMUELSSON, Crucifixion, 66, tending toward "impaling", though he is properly cautious.

[371] Despite observing early Christian interpretation of this as referencing the cross, HENGEL, Crucifixion, 27–28, ultimately considers the word in Plato to be likely a "particularly cruel form of '*apotympanismos*'" (ibid. 28n). COOK, Crucifixion, 272, noting the early association of ἀνασχινδυλευθῆναι (*sic*; this is ἀνασχινδαλευθῆναι in Timaeus) with ἀνασκολοπισθῆναι and ἀνασταυρωθῆναι in Timaeus' *Lexicon Platonicum* (and in Suda) as well as Atticus' 2nd cent. A.D. interpretation of Plato's argument to refer to a cross (σταυρός). nevertheless suggests (like HENGEL) that this may be an example of *apotympanismos*.

[372] To the data from COOK noted above, a TLG search shows that the etymological treatments of this term are fairly consistent, though likely at times dependent on one another: Hesychius in the fifth century A.D. defines ἀνασκινδυλεύεσθαι (note the change from χ to κ) in his entry 4583 as ἀνασκολοπισθῆναι (in reference to this passage in the *Republic*; the *Lexicon Patmense* follows similar lines). Photius in his *Lexicon* writes in the ninth-century A.D. (in entry 1662): "Ἀνασκινδυλευθῆναι· ἀνασκολοπισθῆναι, ἀνασταυρωθῆναι. κέχρηται τῇ λέξει Πλάτων ἐν Πολιτείᾳ (2, 362a)." By comparison Photius also states of the cognate verb: "Σκινδαλεύειν: ἀνασταυροῦν." The *Suda* indicates (entry 2071): "Ἀνασκινδυλευθῆναι: ἀνασκολοπισθῆναι, ἀνασταυρωθῆναι. ὁ ἐνεστὼς Ἀνασκολοπίζω." The twelfth-century *Etymologicum* of Symeon reads: "ἀνασκινδυλεῦσαι· τὸ ἀνασκολοπίσαι, τὸ σταυρῶσαι." And the twelfth-century *Etymologicum magnum* states (for its definition of Ἀνασκολοπισθῆναι): "Ἀνασκολοπισθῆναι: Ἀνασταυρωθῆναι. Σκόλοπες γὰρ ξύλα ὀξέα. Παρὰ τὸ σκέλλω [τὸ ξηραίνω,] σκέλλῳ καὶ σκόλῳ. Λέγεται καὶ ἀνασκινδυλευθῆναι." Similarly the TLG indicates that the *scholia* on Plato also associate ἀνασχινδυλευθήσεται with ἀνασκολοπισθήσεται; see WILLIAM CASWELL GREENE, Scholia Platonica (Philological Monographs 8; Haverford: American Philological Association, 1938). The only other instance of ἀνασχινδαλευθῆναι in the TLG search yields a rather uninformative reference to this passage from Plato in (the 2nd cent. A.D. Atticist) Phrynicus Arabius, *Praeparatio sophistica* (ἀνασχινδαλευθῆναι).

of the sufferings of Christ (the just man who suffers unjustly), and thus subsequent Christian authors do interpret this passage as a reference to the cross, and they further employ Plato's key verb (ἀνασχινδυλεύω) in contexts of martyrdom.[373] Christians were not the only ones to interpret Plato's verb as a reference to the cross.[374] In any case, this passage indicates classical Greek awareness of penal suspension for sake of execution (most plausibly an impalement),[375] and this passage also displays the philosophical use of such punishments to represent an extreme case in an ethical argument.

(246) Plato, *Gorgias* 473b–d

[Σωκράτης] Ἴσως. σὺ δέ γε εὐδαίμονας αὖ τοὺς ἀδικοῦντας, ἐὰν μὴ διδῶσι δίκην.
[Πῶλος] Πάνυ μὲν οὖν.
[Σωκράτης] Ἐγὼ δέ γε αὐτοὺς ἀθλιωτάτους φημί, τοὺς δὲ διδόντας δίκην ἧττον. βούλει καὶ τοῦτο ἐλέγχειν;
[Πῶλος] Ἀλλ᾽ ἔτι τοῦτ᾽ ἐκείνου χαλεπώτερόν ἐστιν, ὦ Σώκρατες, ἐξελέγξαι.
[Σωκράτης] Οὐ δῆτα, ὦ Πῶλε, ἀλλ᾽ ἀδύνατον· τὸ γὰρ ἀληθὲς οὐδέποτε ἐλέγχεται.
[Πῶλος] Πῶς λέγεις; ἐὰν ἀδικῶν ἄνθρωπος ληφθῇ τυραννίδι ἐπιβουλεύων, καὶ ληφθεὶς στρεβλῶται καὶ ἐκτέμνηται καὶ τοὺς ὀφθαλμοὺς ἐκκάηται, καὶ ἄλλας πολλὰς καὶ μεγάλας καὶ παντοδαπὰς λώβας αὐτός τε λωβηθεὶς καὶ τοὺς αὐτοῦ ἐπιδὼν παῖδάς τε καὶ γυναῖκα τὸ ἔσχατον ἀνασταυρωθῇ ἢ καταπιττωθῇ, οὗτος εὐδαιμονέστερος ἔσται ἢ ἐὰν διαφυγὼν τύραννος καταστῇ καὶ ἄρχων

---

[373] Note especially Clement of Alexandria, *Strom.* 5.14.108 (where Plato in *Republic* 361–362 essentially acts as a prophet): "ὁ Πλάτων μονονουχὶ προφητεύων τὴν σωτήριον οἰκονομίαν ἐν τῷ δευτέρῳ τῆς Πολιτείας." Clement's text is also quoted in Eusebius, *Praep. ev.* 13.13.35. Also note Eusebius, *Praep. ev.* 12.10.4 (see 12.10.1ff.); Theodoret, *Graecarum affectionum curatio* 8.50; and the *Acta Apollonius* 40 (Musurillo, *Acts of the Christian Martyrs*, p. 100). Clement of Alexandria will also employ ἀνασκινδυλευομένων of Christian martyrs (*Strom.* 2.20.125): "ἡμῖν δὲ ἄφθονοι μαρτύρων πηγαὶ ἑκάστης ἡμέρας ἐν ὀφθαλμοῖς ἡμῶν θεωρούμεναι παροπτωμένων ἀνασκινδυλευομένων τὰς κεφαλὰς ἀποτεμνομένων" ("But to us bounteous springs of martyrs each day are being beheld by our eyes who are roasted, impaled, and decapitated."). Similarly, on Christian martyrs see Clement, *Strom.* 4.11.78: "ὡς διὰ τὸ ὄνομα αὐτοῦ διωχθησόμεθα, φονευθησόμεθα, ἀνασκινδυλευθησόμεθα" ("how on account of his name we have been persecuted, slaughtered, and impaled"). Also note Theodoret, *Graecarum affectionum curatio* 8.9.

[374] Thus Atticus, the second century (A.D. 150–200) Platonist, will employ σταυρούς in a parallel context; cf. COOK, *Crucifixion*, 273.

[375] Among the English translators note: PAUL SHOREY, Plato. The Republic (2 vols.; orig. 1930; repr., LCL; Cambridge: Harvard University Press, 1969), 1:125 reads "crucified", though with a footnote saying "Or strictly 'impaled'". This footnote is unfortunately omitted in PAUL SHOREY, "Republic," in EDITH HAMILTON and HUNTINGTON CAIRNS, The Collected Dialogues of Plato (Princeton: Princeton University Press, 1961), 609. GEORGE M. A. GRUBE, Plato's Republic (Indianapolis: Hackett, 1974), 33, translates with "impaled".

ἐν τῇ πόλει διαβιῷ ποιῶν ὅτι ἂν βούληται, ζηλωτὸς ὢν καὶ εὐδαιμονιζόμενος ὑπὸ τῶν πολιτῶν καὶ τῶν ἄλλων ξένων; ταῦτα λέγεις ἀδύνατον εἶναι ἐξελέγχειν.

*Translation.* [Socrates] Perhaps. But you indeed further [suppose] that those who act unjustly are truly happy if they do not pay the penalty.
[Polus] By all means!
[Socrates] But I indeed say that they are the most wretched, and that those who pay the penalty are less so. Do you also wish to refute this?
[Polus] But this is still more difficult to refute than that, O Socrates.
[Socrates] Not merely [more difficult], O Polus, but impossible: for the truth is never refuted.
[Polus] How do you say so? If a man, acting unjustly, was captured plotting tyranny, and after being captured, he was racked and castrated and had his eyes burnt out, and many other great and manifold mutilations, and after he was mutilated and after they delivered over both his children and wife, he was finally either crucified or tarred and burned, then would this one be more truly happy than if after he fled, he established himself as a tyrant, and if, while he ruled over the city, he spent his life doing whatever he wished, being envied and made happy by the citizens and the other foreigners? Do you say these things are impossible to refute?

*Commentary.*[376] Likely written a bit earlier than the *Republic*, this dialogue represents Socrates debating the rhetoricians of his day (in the form of Gorgias and his followers) in order to establish the superiority of philosophy over politics (and consequently over rhetoric as politics' handmaiden). Here Socrates seeks to establish that it is best to choose justice, but if one were to have acted unjustly, it is then still better to bear one's punishment than to go through life unpunished. Polus, a pupil of the rhetorician Gorgias, here proposes an extreme counterexample against Socrates' view, arguing that punishment is the worst option, and that unpunished political tyranny actually is the best route to happiness. This extreme counterexample, like the one in the episode above from the *Republic* (361e–362a), speaks of racks, the burning of eyes, and death by suspension.[377] Here the term for suspension is the much more common ἀνασταυρόω (rendered above as "crucified"), though the context provides little clue about how this suspension on a σταυρός would have been performed in Plato's day.[378] Given the parallels, this penalty could well have

---

[376] Text: BURNET, Platonis opera, vol. 3, ad loc. The names of the characters are spelled out for clarity.

[377] Differences between the two passages include the mention of castration, and the possibility of death by burning. Still the overall arc of the narrative is strikingly parallel. DODDS mentions that "ἐπιδεῖν is the *vox propria* for witnessing calamities" and how he compares the list of tortures here to Plato, *Rep.* 361e and Aeschylus, *Eum.* 186–90; ERIC R. DODDS, Plato. Gorgias. A Revised Text with Introduction and Commentary (Oxford: Clarendon, 1959), 246.

been much the same as the form of execution in the *Republic* (earlier translated as "impaled").[379] Yet, ἀνασταυρόω is also not the only extreme way to die in this passage since καταπισσόω (being covered with tar and set alight) is set as a parallel egregious form of execution. The text implies that this sequence of penalties was an expected method of dealing with those who wished to become tyrants (the Greek tyrants having been fairly recently expelled and still hated in Plato's day).[380]

**(247)** Demosthenes, *Oratio* 21 (*In Midiam*) 105

ἀλλ' οὐδὲ πρὸς οὓς ἔλεγεν αὐτοὺς ἠσχύνθη, εἰ τοιοῦτο κακὸν καὶ τηλικοῦτον ἀδίκως ἐπάγει τῳ, ἀλλ' ἕν' ὅρον θέμενος παντὶ τρόπῳ μ' ἀνελεῖν, οὐδὲν ἐλλείπειν ᾤετο δεῖν, ὡς δέον, εἴ τις ὑβρισθεὶς ὑπὸ τούτου δίκης ἀξιοῖ τυχεῖν καὶ μὴ σιωπᾷ, τοῦτον ἐξόριστον ἀνῃρῆσθαι καὶ μηδαμῇ παρεθῆναι, ἀλλὰ καὶ λιποταξίου γραφὴν ἑαλωκέναι καὶ ἐφ' αἵματι φεύγειν καὶ μόνον οὐ προσηλῶσθαι.

*Translation.* But neither was he ashamed before those to whom he spoke these [words], when he then unjustly brought such a wicked and great matter [against me]. But, having established as his one aim that by any manner he might destroy me, in order that he may leave out nothing he supposed to be necessary; as if it were necessary, when someone who had been insulted by this man thought it worthy to obtain satisfaction and not remain silent, for this person to be banished in order to be destroyed and to be nowhere present, but even to be condemned to a prosecution of desertion, and to flee [trial] for murder merely so as not to be fastened by nails.

*Commentary.*[381] Demosthenes (384–322 B.C.) penned the speech *Against Meidias* in preparation for his prosecution of Meidias before the Athenian courts for crimes and insults against himself. The speech was apparently never

---

[378] SAMUELSSON, Crucifixion, 65, observes that this is the only instance of ἀνασταυρόω in Plato, so the means of execution here is "difficult to determine".

[379] COOK, Crucifixion, 271 considers this *Gorgias* text a case of *apotympanismos*, and objects to suggestions that this could refer to impalement because "impalement was not used in ancient Greece". He argues that it is probably best to say that ἀνασταυρόω does not mean "impale" in classical Greek literature (ibid. 8–10) though on the very next page after discussing *Gorgias* he knows of respected scholars who present reasons that *Republic* 361e–362a is a likely instance of impalement (272 n.). In any case, ἀνασταυρόω does refer to the impaling of heads (as COOK allows; ibid. 8–9), so the impaling of bodies likely cannot be ruled out at this classical period of Greek.

[380] HENGEL, Crucifixion, 27: this is "probably based on the political realities of the time."

[381] Text: SAMUEL H. BUTCHER and WILLIAMS RENNIE, Demosthenis Orationes (3 vols.; Scriptorum classicorum bibliotheca Oxoniensis; Oxford: Clarendon, 1903–1931), II/1, 547–548.

delivered since Meidias settled out of court.[382] Meidias had long been at enmity with Demosthenes, and Demosthenes lists throughout a series of his insults. Some of Meidias' offenses, which had previously gained Demosthenes a unanimous vote against Meidias from the Assembly, concerned how Meidias actively inhibited Demosthenes in his role as the chorus-master for one of the Athenian tribes at the Dionysia festival (e.g., Demosthenes, *Mid.* 11–21). Meidias even struck Demosthenes during the festival. However, Demosthenes further alleges that Meidias had circulated trumped-up charges which claim Demosthenes had committed desertion, and that Meidias had attempted to pay relatives of a murder-victim to accuse Demosthenes (*Mid.* 102–104). Concerning these last two attacks, Demosthenes believes that Meidias essentially acted as a murderer, since such trumped-up charges of desertion and murder, in addition to assaulting Demosthenes' integrity, also could have led to his banishment or execution. It is these last most dangerous charges that Demosthenes alludes to in the text above. The form of execution here employs προσηλόω ("be fastened by nails" or "crucified", LSJ). Such a term was certainly associated with crucifixion in later authors, but it is difficult to ascertain the precise form of execution intended here.

### 3.4.3 Examples from the Hellenistic Period

Some (especially Roman) authors represent Alexander the Great, or one of his generals and/or successors, suspending others up on a *stauros*. These Macedonian militants share Greek values, though they could well also have been more inclined to such penal measures against enemies in battle due to Persian (and other Eastern) practices. The sources below are selected from an array of suspension reports in Greek and Latin literature on the lives of Alexander and his successors.[383] At the same time, some of these sources are quite chronologically removed from the events, so their accuracy could be challenged, even if they certainly represent perspectives from their own day about these earlier events.

---

[382] JAMES H. VINCE, Demosthenes (7 vols.; LCL; Cambridge: Harvard University Press, 1926–1949), 3:2–5.

[383] Arrian provides the reader occasional insight into his use of sources, permitting some greater confidence in the antiquity of his material, thus this section consistently addresses Arrian's references to the hanging up of a person. Plutarch, Diodorus, and Appian provide an intriguing dialogue with Arrian. On the other hand, with some regret due to space, only two texts are translated below from Curtius Rufus (see further his *Hist. Alex.* 6.3.14; 7.5.40; 7.11.28), and there are no quotations of the Alexander-Romance of Pseudo-Callistenes (for a fuller account of both, see COOK, Crucifixion, 124–125, 266–268). See further Diodorus Siculus, *Bibl. hist.* 16.35.6; 16.61.2.

**(248)** Q. Curtius Rufus, *Historiae Alexandri Magni* 4.4.17

Triste deinde spectaculum victoribus ira praebuit regis; II milia, in quibus occidendis defecerat rabies, crucibus adfixi per ingens litoris spatium pependerunt.

*Translation.* Sadly then, the anger of the king presented a spectacle to the victors. Two thousand, in whose dying [the king's] rage fell away, had been fixed up on crosses and hung along a huge length of the seashore.

*Commentary.*[384] Quintus Curtius Rufus authored his ten books on Alexander the Great during the late first or early second century A.D. He is famous for his rhetorical style and his lack of attributing his sources. This passage comes from the close of the seven-month siege of the island city-fortress of Tyre. Alexander famously conquered Tyre by building a land bridge to the island, which lay just off the coast of Phoenicia, but he also made extensive use of ship warfare. The battle was hard and slow, leading to great animosity toward the Tyrians. Curtius earlier records that Alexander ordered all the city's inhabitants to be slain except those who took refuge in the temples, and he calculates that 6,000 Tyrian soldiers died. Alexander's anger gave vent to a mass use of the *crux* along the Phoenician shore, thus dispatching 2,000 more. Diodorus also reports a mass "hanging up" (ἐκρέμασε) of not less than 2,000.[385] In comparison, Arrian merely reports that 8,000 Tyrians died, without noting Alexander's rage or the mass crucifixion (Arrian, *Anab.* 2.24.4). This mention of the *crux* in Curtius' day would have encouraged his Roman audience to associate these events under Alexander with mass employment of the *crux* in Roman military campaigns (note section 3.6–7). Justin's summary report of these crucifixions is given below.

**(249)** Justin, *Epitome* of Pompeius Trogus 18.3.18–19

Itaque Alexander Magnus, cum interiecto tempore in Oriente bellum gereret, velut ultor publicae securitatis, expugnata eorum urbe omnes, qui proelio superfuerant, ob memoriam veteris caedis crucibus adfixit: [19] genus tantum Stratonis inviolatum servavit regnumque stirpi eius restituit.

*Translation.* So, when after an interval of time Alexander the Great had brought war in the East (as though an avenger of public security), and once all their city was captured, those who had remained alive from the battle, as in mem-

---

[384] Text: JOHN C. ROLFE, Quintus Curtius (2 vols.; LCL; Cambridge: Harvard University Press, 1946), 1:204.

[385] Diodorus Siculus, *Bibl. hist.* 17.46.4: ὁ δὲ βασιλεὺς τέκνα μὲν καὶ γυναῖκας ἐξηνδραποδίσατο, τοὺς δὲ νέους πάντας, ὄντας οὐκ ἐλάττους τῶν δισχιλίων, ἐκρέμασε.

ory of the old slaughter, he had fixed up on crosses; [19] the family of Strato however he preserved unharmed and restored the king's office to his family line.

*Commentary.*[386] Pompeius Trogus wrote his *Historiae Philippicae* in the first
century B.C., but its contents come to us primarily through Justin's *Epitome*
from the late Roman period. The context here is quite different than in Curtius
or Arrian. He first narrates the ancient history of Tyre, a city that was captured
by slaves who slaughtered their masters, accidentally leaving only Strato, who
later came to be king. Justin follows Pompcius Trogus in seeing Alexander's
conquest of Tyre as a just recompense on the city for this slave revolt in their
distant past. The crucifixion serves to equal the mass slaughter during that
slave revolt, and Alexander reestablishes the royal place of Strato's line. Crucifixion was a common Roman penalty employed during the suppression of
slave revolts (see 3.6), which makes even more fitting the analogy Justin (and
Pompeius Trogus before him) draws here.

**(250)** Arrian, *Anabasis* 4.14.3–4

Καλλισθένην δὲ Ἀριστόβουλος μὲν λέγει δεδεμένον ἐν πέδαις ξυμπεριάγεσθαι
τῇ στρατιᾷ, ἔπειτα νόσῳ τελευτῆσαι, Πτολεμαῖος δὲ ὁ Λάγου στρεβλωθέντα
καὶ κρεμασθέντα ἀποθανεῖν. οὕτως οὐδὲ οἱ πάνυ πιστοὶ ἐς τὴν ἀφήγησιν καὶ
ξυγγενόμενοι ἐν τῷ τότε Ἀλεξάνδρῳ ὑπὲρ τῶν γνωρίμων τε καὶ οὐ λαθόντων
σφᾶς ὅπως ἐπράχθη ξύμφωνα ἀνέγραψαν. [4] πολλὰ δὲ καὶ ἄλλα ὑπὲρ τούτων
αὐτῶν ἄλλοι ἄλλως ἀφηγήσαντο, ἀλλ᾽ ἐμοὶ ταῦτα ἀποχρῶντα ἔστω ἀναγε-
γραμμένα.

*Translation.* On the one hand, Aristobulus says that Callisthenes, having been
bound with fetters, was carried around with the army, then he died by a disease; but on the other hand, Ptolemy son of Lagos [says that], after being
racked and hung up, he was put to death. Thus neither of these [witnesses],
who are exceedingly trustworthy in their report and who kept company with
Alexander at the time, concerning both well known and not unseen [events],
recorded these matters so that it can be studied harmoniously. [4] And others
otherwise relate even many other things beyond these, but let these be sufficient for me to have recorded.

*Commentary.*[387] Arrian (c. A.D. 86–160) provides another of our earliest
extant accounts of the fourth-century B.C. life and military exploits of Alexander the Great. Among options for source material in his day, Arrian drew

---

[386] Text: JEEP, Iustinus, 116.
[387] Text: ANTOON G. ROOS and GERHARD WIRTH, Flavii Arriani quae exstant omnia (2
vols.; orig. 1967–1968; repr., Bibliotheca Scriptorum Graecorum et Romanorum Teubneriana;
Leipzig: Teubner, 1907–1928), 1:200; cf. PETER A. BRUNT, Arrian (2 vols.; LCL; Cambridge:
Harvard University Press, 1976), 1:386.

especially on Ptolemy son of Lagos and Aristobulus son of Aristobulus, both of whom he regards as the most trustworthy of sources in his day because both took part in Alexander's expedition and because Ptolemy was later a king, for whom it would be shameful to lie (see esp. Arrian, *Anab*. Preface 1–3; some of this is also reflected in the passage here). In his preface, Arrian informs the reader that he will commonly record material as true when these esteemed two predecessors agree; but if there is disagreement, Arrian will choose the version that appears more trustworthy and that reads as the one most worth telling (τούτων τὰ πιστότερα ἐμοὶ φαινόμενα καὶ ἅμα ἀξιαφηγητότερα ἐπιλεξάμενος; *Anab*. Pref. 1). Nevertheless, in the sections of the Anabasis around 4.14, Arrian repeatedly contrasts the varying accounts that have come down to him. Concerning the "many other things" mentioned in the sentence from 4.14.4 above, it is clear that Arrian is also selecting a subset of material from a broader array of stories about this period in Alexander's expedition (and per-haps even from other narratives that speak to Callisthenes' demise).

Callisthenes of Olynthus was a past pupil of Aristotle and a historian who wrote eulogistically of Alexander's early expedition even as he served in it, only to find himself at odds with Alexander over the king's tendency to accommodate and embrace Mesopotamian ruler-deity expectations, especially by requiring the obeisance of prostrating oneself on the ground before Alexan-der (cf. Arrian, *Anab*. 4.10.1–4.12.7). In any case, according to Arrian, Callis-thenes' enemies implicated him in a plot by Alexander's pages to assassinate him (ibid. 4.12.7–4.14.2); both Aristobulus and Ptolemy believe Callisthenes was involved in the plot, but Arrian seems to follow the view of others that Alexander was simply willing to believe the worst of Callisthenes (4.14.1–2). Subsequent to the plot being discovered, some were stoned, but Callisthenes was treated differently. The varying accounts of Callisthenes' fate in the pas-sage here pit Aristobulus against Ptolemy, and it appears difficult from a dis-tance to vouch for who was right. In any case, Ptolemy's fourth-century B.C. account would indicate that rumors circulated shortly after Alexander's death about Alexander's own use of public bodily suspension. The verb employed here is the standard term in Arrian for suspending a human body,[388] which in the second-century A.D. would likely invoke notions of the cross. In this case, the sequence of verbs would indicate (according to Arrian's summary of Ptol-emy) both that torture preceded the suspension and that the suspension was *ante mortem* (and was the likely cause of death).

---

[388] See also Arrian, *Anab*. 6.17.2; 6.30.2; 7.14.4; *Indica* 5.11; *Historia successorum Alexandri* (FGH 2b 156) Fragments 1.11; 1.18; *Periplus ponti Euxini* 11.5.

**(251)** Plutarch, *Alexander* 55.9

ἀποθανεῖν δ' αὐτὸν οἱ μὲν ὑπ' Ἀλεξάνδρου κρεμασθέντα λέγουσιν, οἱ δ' ἐν πέδαις δεδεμένον καὶ νοσήσαντα, Χάρης δὲ μετὰ τὴν σύλληψιν ἑπτὰ μῆνας φυλάττεσθαι δεδεμένον, ὡς ἐν τῷ συνεδρίῳ κριθείη παρόντος Ἀριστοτέλους· ἐν αἷς δ' ἡμέραις Ἀλέξανδρος [ἐν Μαλλοῖς Ὀξυδράκαις] ἐτρώθη περὶ τὴν Ἰνδίαν, ἀποθανεῖν ὑπέρπαχυν γενόμενον καὶ φθειριάσαντα.

*Translation.* Some say that he [Callisthenes] died by being hung up by Alexander, and some that he had been bound by the feet and became ill, and Chares [says that] after his arrest he, having been bound, was guarded for seven months, so in the council he might be judged while Aristotle was present, but in those days when Alexander was wounded around India, he [Callisthenes] died since he was exceedingly fat and lice-infected.

*Commentary.*[389] Plutarch's concerns about the stories surrounding Callisthenes' death appear tied to the author's philosophical motives. Plutarch repeatedly observes that Callisthenes was a sophist and student of Aristotle, such that even Alexander is made to say that he himself had the youths (responsible for the insurrection) stoned, while he planned a different punishment for "the sophist"; this admission by Alexander reveals (in Plutarch's estimation) Alexander's opposition to Aristotle, who was his own tutor (*Alex.* 55.7–8). This apparently exemplifies Alexander's immoderate rejection of philosophy. It also would imply that Plutarch likely preferred the final possible account given above of Callisthenes' demise (perhaps more because of what it illustrated about Alexander and philosophy than due to any actual evidence). Yet Plutarch is able to name his source for the information as Chares of Mytilene, who served as chamberlain to Alexander and wrote a history of Alexander.[390] On the other hand, the two other possible modes of Callisthenes' demise overlap with those recorded by Arrian (*Anab.* 4.14.3–4; No. 250). One of these modes uses a verb (κρεμασθέντα) that is cognate to the one Arrian employed in talking about Callisthenes' death by suspension. Nevertheless, the range of possibilities for Callisthenes' death should caution us from stating firm historical conclusions, even if we can again acknowledge that the rumor of a death by suspension must have circulated widely for many centuries.

---

[389] Text: CLAES LINDSKOG and KONRAT ZIEGLER, Plutarchi Vitae parallelae (4 vols.; Bibliotheca Scriptorum Graecorum et Romanorum Teubneriana; Leipzig: Teubner, 1957–80), II/2, 226–227. Should the bracketed words (ἐν Μαλλοῖς Ὀξυδράκαις) be read, they would remind the reader that Alexander was injured while attacking the lands of the Mallians and Oxydracae (see Arrian, *Anab.* 6.11.1–8; cf. *Anab.* 6.4.3–6.5.4).

[390] Cf. Chares in FGH 125 Frag. 15.

**(252)** Arrian, *Anabasis* 6.17.2

ἔνθα δὴ Μουσικανός τε ξυλληφθεὶς ἄγεται πρὸς Πείθωνος, καὶ τοῦτον κρεμάσαι κελεύει Ἀλέξανδρος ἐν τῇ αὐτοῦ γῇ, καὶ τῶν Βραχμάνων ὅσοι αἴτιοι τῆς ἀποστάσεως τῷ Μουσικανῷ κατέστησαν.

*Translation.* At this point Musicanus, having been taken captive, was led by Peitho; and Alexander ordered this man to be hung in his own land, along with as many of the Brachmans as who had been guilty of the revolt and had been arrayed with Musicanus.

*Commentary.*[391] Musicanus was an Indian rajah, whose kingdom is described as the "wealthiest of all India" (Arrian, *Anab.* 6.15.5). He initially ignored Alexander, but once Alexander came suddenly into his territory, Musicanus brought gifts and promised allegiance (6.15.6–7). Alexander granted him continued sovereignty over his land, yet he here rebels again. The Brachmans are described by Arrian as the σοφισταί ("the sages") of India, some of whom had previously been put to death for opposing Alexander's conquest (6.16.5). When Musicanus revolted, Alexander directed Peitho to put down the insurrection, which he did by attacking the cities and establishing garrisons. Apparently, Peitho brought Musicanus captive back to Alexander, who commanded him to be hung. This suspension was quite likely his cause of death (no other cause is mentioned in the text). In any case, the location must have been chosen to make a public display of Musicanus in his own land and before his countrymen. A number of the Brachman sages were apparently suspended as well, joining their leader in his death, much as they had been arrayed with him in his revolt.

**(253)** Q. Curtius Rufus, *Historiae Alexandri Magni* 9.8.16

Rursus Musicani defecerunt; ad quos opprimendos missus est Pithon, qui captum principem gentis, eundemque defectionis auctorem, adduxit ad regem. Quo Alexander in crucem sublato, rursus amnem, in quo classem expectare se iusserat, repetit.

*Translation.* Again the Musicani revolted; to their suppression Pithon had been sent, who led to the king the captured chief of the race (the very same author of their defection). In consequence, after [the chief] had been raised up on a cross, Alexander again returned to the river, at which he had ordered the army to await him.

---

[391] Text: ROOS and WIRTH, *Flavii Arriani quae exstant omnia*, 1:312–313; cf. BRUNT, *Arrian*, 2:150.

*Commentary*.[392] This text provides Curtius' parallel account to the preceding text by Arrian. It appears that Curtius here has transferred the name of the Indian rajah (Musicanus) to the people of the rajah's land (Musicani). Curtius mentions their initial conquest by Alexander in 9.8.10. Pithon's leadership is equivalent to the role of Peitho in Arrian. The most striking feature in Curtius concerns his clear application of the language of the cross (*in crucem sublato*), corresponding to Arrian's "hanging up" (κρεμάσαι) of Musicanus.

**(254)** Arrian, *Anabasis* 6.30.1–2

καὶ μὲν δὴ καὶ κατὰ Ὀρξίνου πολλοὶ λόγοι ἐλέχθησαν πρὸς Περσῶν, ὃς ἦρξε Περσῶν ἐπειδὴ Φρασαόρτης ἐτελεύτησε. ² καὶ ἐξηλέγχθη Ὀρξίνης ἱερά τε ὅτι σεσυλήκει καὶ τάφους βασιλικούς, καὶ Περσῶν πολλοὺς ὅτι οὐ ξὺν δίκῃ ἀπέκτεινε. τοῦτον μὲν δὴ οἷς ἐτάχθη ὑπὸ Ἀλεξάνδρου ἐκρέμασαν.

*Translation.* And then many accusations were also spoken by the Persians against Orxines, who ruled the Persians after Phrasaortes died. ² And Orxines was convicted because he had pillaged both temples and royal tombs, and because he had killed many Persians without cause. Thus those who were appointed by Alexander hung this man.

*Commentary*.[393] When Alexander returns to Persia, he finds her changed since his previous conquests. Earlier in the narrative, Arrian had observed how Orxines usurped control over Persian territory after the terminal illness of Phrasaortes, who had earlier been appointed Satrap by Alexander (*Anab.* 6.29.2; cf. 3.18.11). Arrian says relatively little about Orxines beyond what we find above.[394] The plundering of temples and royal tombs would have been viewed as a great sacrilege in addition to its obvious destructive effect.[395] Orxines' killing of Persians "without cause" (οὐ ξὺν δίκῃ), likely comments on the lack of legal procedure accorded the victims. In contrast, Orxines receives a formal conviction and punishment. His suspension is recorded without details, though other texts in Arrian employ this verb as a mode of execution (cf. 4.14.3; No. 250).

---

[392] Text: ROLFE, *Quintus Curtius* , 2:436.

[393] Text: ROOS and WIRTH, *Flavii Arriani quae exstant omnia*, 1:337. ROOS reports that KRÜGER conjectured προσετάχθη for ἐτάχθη (with little difference in meaning). Cf. BRUNT, *Arrian*, 2:196.

[394] And a TLG search of this specific term turns up no other hits in Greek literature, save to a reference to a Red Sea tribe by the same name in Arrian, *Anab.* 3.8.5.

[395] One might think here of Cicero's charges against Verres for using his official capacity to plunder temples, which will be mentioned below.

**(255)** Arrian, *Anabasis* 7.14.2–4

Ἔνθα δὴ καὶ ἄλλοι ἄλλα ἀνέγραψαν ὑπὲρ τοῦ πένθους τοῦ Ἀλεξάνδρου·
μέγα μὲν γενέσθαι αὐτῷ τὸ πένθος, πάντες τοῦτο ἀνέγραψαν, τὰ δὲ πραχθέντα
ἐπ᾽ αὐτῷ ἄλλοι ἄλλα, ὡς ἕκαστος ἢ εὐνοίας πρὸς Ἡφαιστίωνα ἢ φθόνου εἶχεν
ἢ καὶ πρὸς αὐτὸν Ἀλέξανδρον ... ³ οἱ μέν, τὸ πολὺ μέρος τῆς ἡμέρας ἐκείνης
ἐρριμμένον ἐπὶ τοῦ σώματος τοῦ ἑταίρου ὀδύρεσθαι οὐδ᾽ ἐθέλειν ἀπαλλαγῆ-
ναι, πρίν γε δὴ πρὸς βίαν ἀπηνέχθη πρὸς τῶν ἑταίρων· ⁴ οἱ δέ, τήν τε ἡμέραν
ὅλην καὶ τὴν νύκτα ὅλην ἐρρῖφθαι ἐπὶ τῷ σώματι· οἱ δὲ καί, τὸν ἰατρὸν
Γλαυκίαν ὅτι ἐκρέμασε, καὶ τοῦτο[ν] ὡς ἐπὶ φαρμάκῳ κακῶς δοθέντι, οἱ δέ,
ὅτι οἴνου περιεῖδεν ἐμπλησθέντα θεωρῶν αὐτός.

*Translation.* At this point others record different things concerning Alexander's grief: That his grief was great – all record this. But his other actions
other [authors record] as each [bears] good-will toward Hephaestion, or ill-
will [toward him] or toward Alexander himself ... ³ Some [say] the greater
portion of that day [Alexander] lamented, prostrate on the body of his companion, and did not wish to be removed, before he was taken away by force by
his companions; ⁴ but some [say] he was prostrate on the body the whole day
and the whole night. And some even [say] that he hung the physician
Glaucias, and this on account of a drug that had been poorly administered; but
some [say] that he himself well-knew that [Hephaestion] had been quite full
of wine, since he observed [him].

*Commentary.*³⁹⁶ The events depicted above concern Alexander's grief at the
death of Hephaestion, who in Arrian's account died subsequent to a seven-day
long illness (*Anab.* 7.14.1). Hephaestion was the most beloved of Alexander's
companions, and he appears throughout Arrian's *Anabasis* as Alexander's
friend and military leader. Modern scholars debate whether this was a sexual
relationship, although Arrian does not present that opinion, and above he uses
the same terminology for Hephaestion (ἑταίρου) as for the rest of Alexander's
companions/comrades (ἑταίρων). After this passage Arrian continues to narrate other scenes of Alexander's grief (7.14.5–10), and the ellipsis above
omits how Arrian juxtaposes contrary views as to whether Alexander's level
of grief displays either the merit of his affection or the shameful excess that
was not commendable for a king. Among the many stories Arrian has heard
concerns one about Alexander having Hephaestion's physician (Glaucias) put
to death for badly administering the medication. It would appear that this story
was not universally recorded by other historians (note that only in 7.14.8 does
Arrian mention areas of general agreement among the earlier accounts), and
Arrian does not commit to whether or not he believes the story. The execution

---

³⁹⁶ Text: Roos and Wirth, Flavii Arriani quae exstant omnia, 1:361–362; cf. Brunt,
Arrian, 2:248–250.

of incompetent physicians is a theme in Graeco-Roman literature. Here Alexander's method of execution involved suspension, though without accompanying details as to the precise method employed. The translation above varies from some published translations concerning the final phrases above about Hephaestion's drinking, for it appears that these refer not to *Glaucias'* awareness of Hephaestion's drunken excesses while ill, but to *Alexander's* awareness of this unwise behavior.[397]

**(256)** Plutarch, *Alexander* 72.3

τοῦτο οὐδενὶ λογισμῷ τὸ πάθος Ἀλέξανδρος ἤνεγκεν, ἀλλ᾽ εὐθὺς μὲν ἵππους τε κεῖραι πάντας ἐπὶ πένθει καὶ ἡμιόνους ἐκέλευσε, καὶ τῶν πέριξ πόλεων ἀφεῖλε τὰς ἐπάλξεις, τὸν δὲ ἄθλιον ἰατρὸν ἀνεσταύρωσεν, αὐλοὺς δὲ κατέπαυσε καὶ μουσικὴν πᾶσαν ἐν τῷ στρατοπέδῳ πολὺν χρόνον, ἕως ἐξ Ἄμμωνος ἦλθε μαντεία τιμᾶν Ἡφαιστίωνα καὶ θύειν ὡς ἥρωϊ παρακελεύουσα.

*Translation.* This emotion of Alexander admitted no reason, but immediately he ordered all the horses and mules sheared on account of mourning, and he took away the battlements around the city, and the wretched physician he crucified, and he made flutes and all music stop in the encampment for a long time, until an oracle came from Ammon prescribing [him] to honor Hephaestion and to sacrifice [to him] as to a hero.

*Commentary.*[398] Plutarch pens an account of Hephaestion's death that concurs with the story in Arrian that Alexander suspended Hephaestion's physician (earlier identified as Glaucus in *Alex.* 72.2). Plutarch employs language common to second-century A.D. crucifixions (ἀνεσταύρωσεν). Throughout his *Parallel Lives*, Plutarch recounts biographies for the purpose of illustrating proper and improper behavior. Plutarch is inclined to blame Hephaestion's death on the youth's own immoderate behavior – while he was still sick, he waited for Glaucus to go to the theater, had a huge meal (consisting of wine and fowl), and subsequently died (*Alex.* 72.2). Similarly, Alexander in this

---

[397] Thus I respectfully disagree with the (typically excellent) ROBSON / BLUNT translation, which reads: "or alternatively because Glaudias had seen Hephaestion drinking most immoderately and had not stopped him" (BRUNT, Arrian, 2:251). BRUNT's translation is a revision of the earlier (1933) LCL edition of E. ILIFF ROBSON, Arrian [2 vols.; Cambridge: Harvard University Press, 1929–1933], 2:251, which reads virtually the same, except without the words "or alternatively". These are my reasons for disagreement: 1) ROBSON / BLUNT's "and had not stopped him" has no equivalent in the Greek text; 2) throughout the reports of the "others" recorded here by Arrian, Alexander commonly serves as their subject; 3) in parallel with the preceding phrase (concerning the hanging of Glaucias) the ὅτι is not causal, but introduces the indirect discourse of the report; and 4) with that parallelism established (in the ὅτι clauses) it is most natural to assume they have a common subject (Alexander), which is made more emphatic by the inclusion of αὐτός at the close of the phrase under discussion.

[398] Text: LINDSKOG and ZIEGLER, Plutarchi Vitae parallelae, II/2, 246–247.

passage shows the kind of capitulation to his passions that Stoic-influenced second-century philosophers found improper; note especially that Alexander's emotion "admitted no reason" (τοῦτο οὐδενὶ λογισμῷ τὸ πάθος Ἀλέξανδρος ἤνεγκεν). The list of mourning procedures likely further illustrates Alexander's unreasoning surrender to his passions. The shearing of horses is mentioned as a sign of Persian grief in Herodotus (*Hist.* 9.24 – where the Persian army cuts their own hair and shears the horses upon the death of Masistios). Certainly, it seems irrational for Alexander to have removed the battlements and forbidden music (even the music of mourning). Consequently, Plutarch may well allude to the irrationality of crucifying the physician (especially when Hephaestion caused his own death).

**(257)** Appian, *Mithridates* 2.8

Περδίκκας δέ, ὃς ἐπὶ Ἀλεξάνδρῳ τῆς Μακεδόνων ἦρχεν, Ἀριαράθην Καππαδοκίας ἡγούμενον, εἴτε ἀφιστάμενον εἴτε τὴν ἀρχὴν αὐτοῦ περιποιούμενος Μακεδόσιν, εἷλε καὶ ἐκρέμασε· καὶ ἐπέστησε τοῖς ἔθνεσιν Εὐμένη τὸν Καρδιανόν.

*Translation.* But Perdiccas, who ruled the Macedonians after Alexander, seized and hung up Ariarathes, the leader of Cappadocia, whether because [Ariarathes] revolted or because [Perdiccas] was acquiring his realm for the Macedonians; and he appointed Eumenes of Cardia over those nations.

*Commentary.*[399] Appian of Alexandria wrote his *Roman History* during the second century A.D. Upon the death of Alexander the Great in 323 B.C., we enter into the era of the Diadochoi, Alexander's competing successors. Perdiccas was one of Alexander's generals, a son of Orontes (Arrian in FGH 2b 156 Frag. 1.2), and thus a man reportedly of Macedonian descent from Orestis. Upon Alexander's death, Perdiccas served as *chiliarch* and was effectively guardian of the whole empire while Philip III (Alexander's "dim-witted" half-brother) was king and while Alexander's children were still in their youth.[400] Arrian, Diodorus, and Plutarch also record Perdiccas' appoint-

---

[399] Text: VIERECK, ROOS, and GABBA, Appiani Historia romana, 1:424. The punctuation after ἐκρέμασε was added by me.

[400] Perdiccas is mentioned in several sources, including repeatedly in Arrian, Diodorus Siculus and also on the inscription of the Parian Marble; for the latter cf. MICHEL M. AUSTIN, The Hellenistic World from Alexander to the Roman Conquest: A Selection of Ancient Sources in Translation [Cambridge: Cambridge University Press, 1981], 39 No. 21; also see ibid. pp. 41–43 No. 22, for the fragments of Arrian. The reference to Perdiccas' initial leadership over the whole empire can be found in Appian, *Syr.* 9.52; in Arrian (FGH 156 Frag. 1.3–7); and in Diodorus Siculus (*Bibl. hist.* 18.2.4–18.3.5). This incident should not be confused with the relationship over a century later between Eumenes II of Pergamum and another Ariarathes (IV), king of Cappadocia (cf. Livius 42.29–30).

ment of Eumenes over Cappadocia and Paphlagonia (e.g., Arrian FGH 156 Frag. 1.5; Diodorus, *Bibl. hist.* 18.22.1; Plutarch, *Eumenes* 3.2; 5.1), and Eumenes will later valiantly serve Perdiccas when warfare increased among the Diadochoi (Diodorus, *Bibl. hist.* 18.29.1–37.2; Plutarch, *Eumenes* passim). Perdiccas himself was assassinated in 320 B.C. (cf. e.g., Diodorus, *Bibl. hist.* 18.36.1–5). Ariarathes was granted the satrapy of Cappadocia by the Persians c. 350 B.C., and continued to rule it, even after the Persians were defeated in Anatolia in 331 B.C. Ariarathes' death must have occurred between those of Alexander and Perdiccas (i.e., between 323 and 320 B.C.); a date of c. 322 B.C. is likely. Others provide reference to Ariarathes' defeat and execution; see especially Diodorus, Arrian, and Lucian in the next three texts. In this passage, Appian employs the verb ἐκρέμασε ("hung up") to depict Ariarathes' fate; this is standard vocabulary in Appian for human bodily suspension, including incidents that likely reference crucifixion.[401]

**(258)** Diodorus Siculus, *Bibliotheca Historica* 18.16.2–3

ὁ δὲ Περδίκκας συνάψας αὐτῷ μάχην καὶ τῇ παρατάξει νικήσας ἀνεῖλε μὲν εἰς τετρακισχιλίους, ἐζώγρησε δὲ ὑπὲρ τοὺς πεντακισχιλίους, ἐν οἷς ἦν καὶ αὐτὸς ὁ Ἀριαράθης. ³ τοῦτον μὲν οὖν καὶ τοὺς συγγενεῖς αὐτοῦ πάντας αἰκισάμενος ἀνεσταύρωσε· τοῖς δ᾽ ἡττηθεῖσι συγχωρήσας τὴν ἀσφάλειαν καὶ καταστήσας τὰ κατὰ τὴν Καππαδοκίαν παρέδωκε τὴν σατραπείαν Εὐμενεῖ τῷ Καρδιανῷ, καθάπερ ἐξ ἀρχῆς ἦν μεμερισμένος.

*Translation.* And Perdiccas joined against him [Ariarathes] in battle; and after conquering [Ariarathes'] battle line, he killed as many as four thousand, and took as live captives more than five thousand, among whom also was Ariarathes himself. ³ Therefore, after torturing this man and all his relatives, [Perdiccas] crucified them. And, after conceding safety to those who had been defeated and after restoring affairs concerning Cappadocia, [Perdiccas] handed over the satrapy to Eumenes the Cardian, just as it had been apportioned from the beginning.

*Commentary.*[402] This Diodorus passage provides further detail to the episode found in Appian (*Mith.* 2.8). Diodorus had immediately previously recorded that Ariarathes, though failing to follow Macedonian orders, was still nevertheless left to his own devices in Cappadocia while Alexander was fighting with Persia. During that time, Ariarathes amassed fortune and soldiers, being prepared (according to Diodorus) to field 30,000 infantry and 15,000 cavalrymen (Diodorus, *Bibl. hist.* 18.16.1–2) in the conflict with Perdiccas. The text before us depicts Perdiccas' victory and its aftermath. Of particular interest is

---

[401] See the discussion of Appian's use of κρεμάννυμι in *Bella Civilia* 3.1.3 below in 3.6.1.
[402] Text: FISCHER and VOGEL, Diodori bibliotheca historica, 4:343.

how Diodorus describes Ariarathes' fate (as well as those of his family) as torture followed by being hung up on *stauroi* (ἀνεσταύρωσε). The episode clearly mirrors Appian's "hanging up" (ἐκρέμασε) of Ariarathes.

Unlike Appian, Diodorus, and Arrian (below), Justin's epitome of Trogus only records Ariarathes' defeat by Perdiccas (not his execution) and the subsequent mass suicide (and property-burning) of his followers (Justin, *Epitome* 13.6.1–3), which is somewhat at odds with Diodorus' statement of Perdiccas' generosity to guarantee safety to the survivors. Plutarch mentions that Perdiccas was directly involved in the military actions against Ariarathes, but only states that Ariarathes was "taken prisoner" (*Eumenes* 3.6). Yet, Diodorus himself, who does mention Ariarathes' execution by suspension in this passage (*Bibl. hist.* 18.16.3), also can summarize Ariarathes' death with "he was defeated and fell in battle" (*Bibl. hist.* 31.19.4); so, (assuming some consistency in Diodorus' thought) we should not infer that a mere statement of defeat (or of death in battle) necessarily rules out that the author believed that demise to have ultimately concluded on a *stauros*. Such a death would have readily been understood in Diodorus' day to look like other crucifixions.

**(259)** Arrian, *Historia successorum Alexandri* (FGH 2b 156) Frag. 1.11 (from Photius, *Bibliotheca* 92)

πολεμεῖ δὲ καὶ Περδίκκας Ἀριαράθηι τῶι Καππαδοκίας, ὅτι Εὐμένει ἄρχειν ἐπιτετραμμένωι τῆς ἀρχῆς οὐκ ἐξίστατο· καὶ δυσὶ νικήσας μάχαις καὶ συλλαβὼν ἐκρέμασεν, Εὐμένει τὴν ἀρχὴν ἀποκαταστήσας.

*Translation.* And Perdiccas also warred against Ariarathes of Cappadocia, because he would not abandon his rule to Eumenes, who had been entrusted to rule. And, after conquering [Ariarathes] in two battles and capturing [him], [Perdiccas] hung him up, reinstating the rule to Eumenes.

*Commentary.*[403] The ninth-century A.D. Byzantine scholar Photius in codex 92 of his *Library* summarizes the ten books of Arrian's *History of the Successors to Alexander*, written c. 150 A.D. The text appears toward the end of books 1–5, where Arrian lists various wars fought by the Diadochoi. The text agrees with other traditions concerning Perdiccas' defeat of Ariarathes, though it adds a reference to *two* battles fought before Ariarathes was captured. Like Appian, Arrian employs his typical verb ἐκρέμασεν to depict the bodily suspension of Ariarathes (note previous examples from Appian).[404]

---

[403] Text: Roos and Wirth, Flavii Arriani quae exstant omnia, 2:259, which includes, in brackets after Καππαδοκίας, the word δυνάστῃ, which I omitted above.

[404] ἐκρέμασεν could have come from Photius' hand rather than Arrian's. The widespread use of this verb by Arrian in similar contexts points to it originating with Arrian himself.

**(260)** [Pseudo-] Lucian, *Macrobii* 13

Ἀριαράθης δὲ ὁ Καππαδοκῶν βασιλεὺς δύο μὲν καὶ ὀγδοήκοντα ἔζησεν ἔτη, ὡς Ἱερώνυμος ἱστορεῖ· ἐδυνήθη δὲ ἴσως καὶ ἐπὶ πλέον διαγενέσθαι, ἀλλ' ἐν τῇ πρὸς Περδίκκαν μάχῃ ζωγρηθεὶς ἀνεσκολοπίσθη.

*Translation.* And Ariarathes, the king of the Cappadocians, lived 82 years, as Hieronymos records; but it was perhaps possible [for him] to have lived even more, except, after having been captured alive in the battle with Perdiccas, he was crucified.

*Commentary.* [405] There is some question about the authorship of this treatise, since it lacks the typical form and thoroughgoing sarcasm of Lucian' authentic writings. The author certainly claims residence in Rome (*Macr.* 9), and addresses his brief treatise to Quintillus on his birthday (*Macr.* 1–2). The *Macrobii* (Greek Μακρόβιοι) concerns a list of ancient historical figures (especially kings and literary men) with "Long Lives" (hence the title). These are intended to encourage Quintillus that he may well have many years left. The author lists many examples over 80 years of age, and some over 90 (beyond that age he tends to be suspicious of the historians such as Herodotus). Ariarathes, as a man who passed 80, provides an example among the kings of Anatolia. The tradition of Ariarathes being "captured alive" (ζωγρηθεὶς) is reminiscent of the same occurrence/verb in Diodorus on Ariarathes (*Bibl. Hist.* 18.6.3). This could well be due to common source material in Hieronymos of Cardia (fourth–third century B.C.), in which case the tradition may be more reliable (or at least more ancient) than the later date of this treatise might otherwise imply. Lucian (as well as his pseudepigraphers) tends to use ἀνασκολοπίζω interchangeably with ἀνασταυρόω, thus equating the *skolops* with the *stauros* as an implement upon which one suspends a human body (likely a cross in Lucian's second-century A.D. world and later).

To summarize these Ariarathes traditions, we have four sources, all second century A.D. (or possibly later in the case of [Pseudo-]Lucian), who represent the bodily suspension of Ariarathes. While the verbs employed can vary from κρεμάννυμι (Appian and Arrian) to ἀνασταυρόω (Diodorus) to ἀνασκολοπίζω ([Pseudo-]Lucian), all clearly depict him hung aloft. While other sources do not mention this suspension, it is likely that this common tradition about his execution was widespread among the Roman *literati* by the second century. It also seems probable that, in that era of Roman rule, many readers (and plausibly the authors themselves) would have associated Ariarathes' demise with the use of the suspension devices (i.e., crosses) from their own day.

---

[405] Text: HARMON, Lucian, 1:232. There the work appears under the title *Octogenarians* (*Longaevi*). HARMON, ibid. 1:221 also disavows Lucian as the actual author.

# 3.5  Jewish Suspension and Crucifixion in the Hellenistic and Roman Eras

One of the most debated topics in the current academic study of crucifixion concerns the question of whether Jewish people in antiquity ever employed the cross as a means of execution. This debate stems in part from the relative paucity of the conflicting data points. Rabbinic sources repeatedly disavow crucifixion as a penalty available to the Sanhedrin, while they simultaneously affirm *post mortem* suspension based on Deut 21:22–23. However, ancient literature attests that some Jewish leaders practiced suspension as a form of execution, and other texts suggest that rabbinic opposition to the cross was not a settled conclusion until later in antiquity. Key evidence for these conflicting viewpoints will be provided below.[406]

In addition to the conflicting testimony from antiquity, the potential consequences of the conclusions have also lent urgency to the debate. On the one hand, the issue affects the perceived accuracy of the canonical Gospels, which indicate both that the Jewish leadership in first-century Jerusalem actively sought a guilty verdict against Jesus from Pilatus, thus essentially condemning Jesus to the cross, and that the crowds cried out directly for Jesus' crucifixion. The Gospels point to Jewish leadership seeking Jesus' death in many places, including: Matt 26:4, 59, 66; 27:20; Mark 11:18; 14:1, 55, 64; Luke 19:47; 22:2 (cf. 23:10); 23:18–25; John 11:45–53; 18:14, 28–32. However, these do not typically refer to an interest in Jesus being crucified *per se*. The populace of Jerusalem calls for Jesus to be crucified, instead of Barabbas (Matt 27:22–25; Mark 15:13–15; Luke 23:16–25) under the presumed instigation of the chief priests and elders (cf. Matt 27:20; Mark 15:11; Luke 23:13; cf. John 18:40). A direct call for crucifixion, especially from chief priests and officers, is related in John 19:6–7, 12–16. Luke states that "our high priests and leaders" are responsible for Jesus' death and crucifixion (Luke 24:20). Further, the leaders show no sympathy to (in fact, they revile) Jesus and the two robbers who are crucified (Matt 27:41–44; Mark 15:31–32; Luke 23:35: just Jesus). The crowds also deride Jesus while he is on the cross (Matt 27:39–40; Mark 15:29–30). In Matthew, Jesus accuses the scribes and Pharisees of killing and crucifying prophets and wise men (Matt 23:34). Further NT texts also point to Jewish instigation in Jesus' death (note esp. Acts 2:23, 36; 4:10).[407] Of course, most of these NT texts were written by Jewish Christians who likely had no

---

[406] See also CHAPMAN, Ancient Jewish and Christian Perceptions of Crucifixion, esp. 33–39; many translations below are from that volume. Cf. the very brief summary in DAVID W. CHAPMAN, Crucifixion II. Judaism, EBR 5 (2012): 1087–1088.

[407] The literature on potential anti-Semitism in the NT is extensive; a useful starting point can be found in CRAIG A. EVANS and DONALD A. HAGNER, eds., Anti-Semitism and Early Christianity: Issues of Polemic and Faith (Minneapolis: Fortress, 1993).

anti-Semitic motives but rather saw themselves as engaging in an intra-Jewish prophetic struggle for the identity of the Jewish nation (along the model of OT prophets), while also accepting the many Gentiles who had joined the early *ecclesia*. Thus these NT authors presumably would have found immensely disconcerting the frequent use of their writings in anti-Semitic harangues (and worse) from antiquity until the present.

Were the Jewish leadership in the first century to have consistently and actively opposed crucifixion in their teachings and practice, then the Gospel accounts would appear implausible on this measure. The array of scholarly positions on the matter can be outlined as follows. Some believe that Jewish people in antiquity, with the possible exception of some exceedingly helle-nized Hasmonean leaders, did not advocate or practice crucifixion, which was instead a Roman (i.e., Gentile) penalty that Jewish leaders rejected as alien to their ancient practices.[408] Others contend that Jewish leaders accepted cruci-fixion but that later rabbinic pronouncements, perhaps influenced by the rising tide of Christianity which proclaimed a crucified Christ, sought to curtail this acceptance.[409] Still others suggest that a halakic divide existed among differ-ent Jewish factions in antiquity, with the Sadducees and Essenes advocating crucifixion but the Pharisees rejecting it.[410] HENGEL modifies this position by contending that the Pharisees also accepted crucifixion at an earlier stage in their history.[411] The publication of the Temple Scroll by YADIN has resulted in a particularly contentious scholarly debate since he argued that 11QTemple LXIV, 6–13, in connection with the Nahum Pesher (4QpNah 3–4 i 6–8), points to the Essene acceptance of *ante mortem* suspension, even crucifixion.

---

[408] See esp. ROSENBLATT, Crucifixion. Variations on this position occur in EMIL G. HIRSCH, Crucifixion, in The Jewish Encyclopedia (New York: Funk and Wagnalls, 1903), 4:373–374; SOLOMON ZEITLIN, The Crucifixion of Jesus Re-examined, JQR 31 (1941): 327–369; WINTER, Trial, 90–96. The Qumran documents in this view do not represent crucifixion (or they are exceptional); cf. JOSEPH M. BAUMGARTEN, Does *TLH* in the Temple Scroll Refer to Crucifixion? JBL 91 (1972): 472–481; JOSEPH M. BAUMGARTEN, Hanging and Treason in Qumran and Roman Law, Eretz Yisrael 16 (1982): 7*–16*.

[409] DAVID J. HALPERIN, Crucifixion, the Nahum Pesher, and the Rabbinic Penalty of Stran-gulation, JJS 32 (1981): 32–46. Another factor, perhaps not sufficiently considered in modern scholarship, that may have led to a change in views toward crucifixion among rabbinic author-ities would be the Jewish experience of persecution via the Roman use of the cross, especially during the Jewish Revolt; see examples below in 3.7.

[410] The most substantial argument for this position is found in DÍEZ MERINO, El suplicio de la cruz; cf. DÍEZ MERINO, Crucifixión; DÍEZ MERINO, Crocifissione. See further J. MASSYNGBERDE FORD, 'Crucify him, Crucify him' and the Temple Scroll, ExpTim 87 (1975–1976): 275–278; FITZMYER, Crucifixion, esp. 498–507. Related views earlier in STAUFFER, Jerusalem und Rom, 123–127; BAMMEL, Crucifixion; originally published in ERNST BAMMEL, Crucifixion as a Punishment in Palestine, in The Trial of Jesus (FS C.F.D.Moule; ed. E. Bammel; London: SCM, 1970), 162–165.

[411] HENGEL, Rabbinische Legende.

Many have engaged Yadin's conclusions, both pro and con.[412] The following discussion lays out the key texts involved; some of the evidence has appeared earlier in this volume, especially the discussion of 11QTemple LXIV, 6–13, which shall only be supplemented below.

### 3.5.1 Jewish Suspension and Deuteronomy 21:22–23

Before directly engaging the question of whether any Jewish use of crucifixion occurred in antiquity, it is best to explore what basis there may have been in the Hebrew Bible for Roman-era Jewish religious leaders to consider its permissibility. We shall soon observe that the main text in this ancient discussion was Deut 21:22–23. However, let us first recall the broad array of passages in the Hebrew Bible that mention human bodily suspension.

As was examined above (see 3.2), several passages in the Hebrew Bible mention the bodily suspension of a human being, most often with the phrase "hung upon a tree." Some of these report the actions of a non-Jewish person, usually a ruler, who suspends criminals or captured prisoners-of-war: Gen 40:19, 22; 41:13 (Pharaoh suspends the baker); 2 Sam 21:12 (cf. 1 Sam 31:10; Saul and his sons are hung/fastened to the city-wall by Philistines); Lam 5:12–13 (princes of Israel are hung up by Israel's enemies); Esther 2:23 (the Persian king hangs up his attempted-murderers); Esth 5:14; 6:4; 7:9–10 (Haman plans to suspend Mordecai on a very tall, purpose-built, wooden device); Esth 7:9–10; 8:7; 9:13, 14, 25 (Haman and his sons are instead hung up by order of the king); Ezra 6:11 (the Persian king threatens suspension against any who disobey his order).

On other occasions, Jewish leaders are directly involved in suspending others: Josh 8:29 (Joshua hangs up the king of Ai); Josh 10:26–27 (Joshua suspends the corpses of five kings on a tree); 2 Sam 4:12 (David hangs up Ishbosheth's murderers). Other texts, though not directly mentioning suspension, are associated with public bodily suspension in Second Temple and/or early rabbinic Jewish literature, note especially Num 25:4 (Moses slays the idolaters of Israel); and 2 Sam 21:6, 9–10 (Saul's sons are executed by the Gibeonites with David's permission). Finally, it should be observed that one of the central Jewish protagonists of the book of Esther, Esther herself, actively sought the king's permission to have Haman's sons hung up (Esth 9:13–14).

It is probable in some of these cases that the person was dead before being hung up (e.g., Josh 10:26–27; also see 1 Sam 31:10; likely Gen 40:19), but in most other instances, no direct mention is made of whether the suspension was *ante mortem* or *post mortem*. As we shall see below (3.9), all of these

---

[412] Cf. YIGAEL YADIN, Pesher Nahum (4QpNahum) Reconsidered, IEJ 21 (1971): 1–12; also YADIN, Temple Scroll, 1:378n.

passages receive at least some expansion (or "actualization") in the Second Temple and Rabbinic eras, usually toward connecting the text with terminology commonly used of crosses and crucifixion in contemporaneous Jewish literature (e.g., σταυρόω, צלב or their respective cognates).[413] It is conceivable that many of these passages (especially those in which Jewish actors performed the suspensions) would have influenced Roman-era Jewish legal discussions about the permissibility of crucifixion. However, it is striking that none of these texts seem to have been directly brought into extant Jewish legal discussions in classical antiquity concerning whether crucifixion was a legitimate means of execution.[414]

The primary OT halakic basis for any ancient Jewish legal discussion of penal bodily suspension is Deut 21:22–23, which has been discussed above in its ANE context (section 3.2). For sake of comparison, that text is also presented here. This will be followed by a series of Jewish ancient translations/paraphrases that represent the "actualization" of this foundational text into later Jewish tradition. Then we shall examine some rabbinic interpretations that most relate to the matters that concern us in this study. Other subsections here in 3.5 will also include material that directly ties back to this passage.

**(261)** Deuteronomy 21:22–23

וְכִי־יִהְיֶה בְאִישׁ חֵטְא מִשְׁפַּט־מָוֶת וְהוּמָת וְתָלִיתָ אֹתוֹ עַל־עֵץ: ‏23 לֹא־תָלִין נִבְלָתוֹ עַל־הָעֵץ כִּי־קָבוֹר תִּקְבְּרֶנּוּ בַּיּוֹם הַהוּא כִּי־קִלְלַת אֱלֹהִים תָּלוּי וְלֹא תְטַמֵּא אֶת־אַדְמָתְךָ אֲשֶׁר יְהוָה אֱלֹהֶיךָ נֹתֵן לְךָ נַחֲלָה:

*Translation.* And when there is in a man a sin bearing a judgment of death, and he is executed, and you hang him on a tree, ²³ his corpse shall not spend the night on the tree, but you shall surely bury him in that day, for a curse of God is the one who is hung, and you shall not defile your land, which the Lord your God gives to you as an inheritance.

---

[413] For extensive discussion of these OT texts and their development in subsequent Jewish literature (up to the codification of the Babylonian Talmud), see esp. CHAPMAN, Crucifixion, 97–177. Many of the translations below come from that volume.

[414] Perhaps the closest example to halakic interpretation of these passages (in ways that could overlap with Jewish use of the cross) concerns how Targumim on Num 25:4 (especially the Palestinian Targumim of Neofiti, Pseudo-Jonathan, and the Fragment Targum) incorporated Deut 21:22–23 into their expansion of the original Hebrew text. The effect is to portray Moses as obeying the Deuteronomic law as he calls for the idolaters to be hung up (employing צלב). However, though we may wish to draw ramifications from this for the question under discussion – whether crucifixion was considered a legal form of Jewish execution – the Targumim do not overtly draw out any such consequences for us.

*Note.* A fuller commentary on the passage is found above in No. 175. Here, we merely recall that the Hebrew text is vague on several key points: What crimes deserve this punishment? What is the "sin bearing a judgment of death"? Further, how precisely is the person to be executed (and can his execution be produced by the suspension device itself)? Does the "curse of God" represent a subjective genitive (God cursing the person) or an objective genitive (God being cursed in some way by the person, possibly through blasphemy or through being associated with his crime)? And why does this defile the land?

Later Jewish traditions expand on the meaning of this passage, often seeking to answer the questions just raised. These expansions (especially as they are incorporated into translations, paraphrases, and retellings of the text) serve to actualize the text by re-reading it in terms of the questions (and the answers) of later generations of readers. In section 3.9 we shall observe that such forms of actualization occur in antiquity for all the suspension texts in the Hebrew Bible mentioned above in this section. Here we provide examples of how the interpretation of Deuteronomy 21 developed in Second Temple and early rabbinic thought, focusing on matters most pertinent to this source-book.

**(262)** Early Greek Translations of Deuteronomy 21:22–23

*Septuagint*[415]

ἐὰν δὲ γένηται ἔν <u>τινι</u> ἁμαρτία κρίμα θανάτου καὶ ἀποθάνῃ καὶ κρεμάσητε αὐτὸν ἐπὶ ξύλου [23] οὐκ ἐπικοιμηθήσεται τὸ σῶμα αὐτοῦ ἐπὶ τοῦ ξύλου <u>ἀλλὰ</u> ταφῇ θάψετε αὐτὸν ἐν τῇ ἡμέρᾳ ἐκείνῃ <u>ὅτι</u> <u>κεκατηραμένος</u> <u>ὑπὸ</u> θεοῦ <u>πᾶς</u> κρεμάμενος <u>ἐπὶ ξύλου</u> καὶ οὐ μιανεῖτε τὴν γῆν ἣν κύριος ὁ θεός σου δίδωσίν σοι ἐν κλήρῳ

*Translation.* And if there is in <u>someone</u> a sin bearing a judgment of death, and he is executed, and you [<u>plural</u>] hang him on a tree, [23] his body shall not lay[416] on the tree, <u>but</u> you [pl.] shall surely bury him in that day, <u>for</u> <u>everyone</u> who hangs <u>on a tree</u> <u>has been cursed by</u> God, and you [pl.] shall not defile the land, which the Lord your God gives to you in inheritance.

---

[415] Text: WEVERS, Deuteronomium.
[416] For the translation of ἐπικοιμηθήσεται, see CHAPMAN, Crucifixion, 120.

*Aquila*[417]

Et cum <u>fuerit</u> in viro peccatum <u>in</u> iudicium mortis, et occisus fuerit, et suspenderis eum super lignum, [23] non commorabitur (οὐκ αὐλισθήσεται) morticinium eius super lignum, sed sepeliens sepelies eum in die illa, quia maledictio Dei est, qui suspensus est (κατάρα θεοῦ κρεμάμενος): et non contaminabis humum tuam quam Dominus Deus tuus dabit tibi haereditatem.

*Translation.* And when there <u>has been</u> in a man a sin [leading] <u>to</u> a judgment of death, and he had been executed, and you have hung him upon the wood, [23] his corpse shall not remain upon the wood, but you shall surely bury him in that day, because a curse of God is he who has been hung, and you shall not defile your ground, which the Lord your God gave to you as an inheritance.

*Symmachus*[418]

<u>Si autem fuerit</u> homini peccatum <u>ad</u> iudicium mortis, et occisus fuerit, et suspenderis eum super lignum, [23] non pernoctabit cadaver ipsius super lignum, sed sepultura sepelies eum in die ipsa, quia <u>propter blasphemiam</u> Dei suspensus est (ὅτι διὰ βλασφημίαν θεοῦ ἐκρεμάσθη) et non contaminabis terram tuam quam Dominus Deus tuus dabit tibi ad haereditatem.

*Translation.* <u>However, if</u> there <u>has been</u> in a man a sin [leading] <u>to</u> a judgment of death, and he had been executed, and you have hung him upon the wood, [23] his own corpse shall not spend the night upon the wood, but you shall surely bury him in that day, because <u>on account of the blasphemy of</u> God he has been hung, and you shall not defile your land, which the Lord your God gave to you for an inheritance.

*Theodotion*

Et <u>quia erit</u> in viro peccatum <u>in</u> iudicium mortis, et <u>morietur</u>, et suspendes eum in ligno, [23] non <u>dormiet</u> morticinium eius super lignum, quia sepultura sepelies eum in die ipsa, quia maledictio Dei est suspensus (κατάρα θεοῦ κρεμάμενος): et non contaminabis adama tuam quam Dominus Deus tuus dederit tibi haereditatem.

*Translation.* And <u>because there was</u> in a man a sin [leading] <u>to</u> a judgment of death, and he <u>is dead</u>, and you hang him upon the wood, [23] his corpse <u>shall not sleep</u> upon the wood, because you shall surely bury him in that day, because a

---

[417] Text of Aquila, Symmachus, and Theodotion in Jerome, *Comm. Gal.* 2 (on Gal 3:12–14) in Migne, *Patrologia Latina*, vol. 26, 386C–387B. FIELD also provides text and attempted retroversion back into Greek; FRIDERICUS FIELD, Origenis Hexaplorum quae supersunt (2 vols.; Oxford: Clarendon, 1875), 1:304–305.

[418] Cf. ALISON SALVESEN, Symmachus in the Pentateuch (JSS Monograph 15; Manchester: University of Manchester, 1991), 124–125.

curse of God is the one who has been hung, and you shall not defile your *'adamah*, which the Lord your God has given to you as an inheritance.

*Commentary.* Above are represented the extant ancient Greek translations, with underlining in order to highlight key variations from the Hebrew original. The Septuagint of Deuteronomy dates to about two hundred years B.C., and it certainly represents an early Jewish translation. Aquila, Symmachus, and Theodotion, transmitted in Origen's *Hexapla,* were authored in the second (or early third) century A.D. The text of Deut 21:22–23 in these hexaplaric Three, aside from isolated fragments of the Greek text (in parentheses above), are primarily known from short quotations translated into Latin by Jerome in his *Commentary on Galatians.*[419] The nuanced differences between the Three in Jerome's translation primarily concern verb tenses and the proper way to render the Hebrew particle כִּי (whether causal or conditional); additionally, each of the Three has its own words in 21:23 for "land" (*humum, terram, adama*)[420] and for the command not to "spend the night" (*commorabitur, pernoctabit, dormiet*).

The key matter here concerns how the Greek translators rendered the "curse of God" phrase in V. 23. Aquila and Theodotion translated it fairly literally into Greek (κατάρα θεοῦ κρεμάμενος). The Septuagint translators understand the Hebrew construct to represent a subjective genitive – the person "has been cursed by God" (κεκατηραμένος ὑπὸ θεοῦ). Among others, the apostle Paul follows the Septuagint's understanding in Gal 3:13.[421] On the other hand, Symmachus interprets the Hebrew construct as an objective genitive – the person committed "blasphemy of God" (βλασφημίαν θεοῦ) by cursing God. Symmachus' religious background is debated (some argue he was an Ebionite Christian, others that he was Jewish), but the Jewish-inspired, Semitic influence in his translation is well known, and it is striking how his

---

[419] Despite not containing most of the original Greek, Jerome's Latin translations of these passages (in Aquila, Symmachus, and Theodotian) are likely fairly reliable (apart from some potentially lesser matters involving verb tense, etc.) as can be seen by comparing his Latin translation of the Septuagint with its Greek text; on this see CHAPMAN, Crucifixion, 122–123.

[420] The use of *adama* in Theodotion is a Latin transliteration of the Hebrew (or Aramaic) word for "land," with Jerome presumably following Theodotion's own Greek transliteration of the Semitic word. Theodotion is known for including such Semitic transliterations in his Greek; see e.g., KAREN H. JOBES and MOISÉS SILVA, Invitation to the Septuagint (Grand Rapids: Baker, 2000), 41.

[421] Gal 3:13: Χριστὸς ἡμᾶς ἐξηγόρασεν ἐκ τῆς κατάρας τοῦ νόμου γενόμενος ὑπὲρ ἡμῶν κατάρα, ὅτι γέγραπται· *ἐπικατάρατος πᾶς ὁ κρεμάμενος ἐπὶ ξύλου* ("Christ redeemed us from the curse of the Law by becoming a curse on behalf of us, because it has been written: 'Cursed is everyone who hangs on a tree'"). Though Paul does not explicitly state that the person has been cursed by God, he does clearly assume that the person is himself cursed (rather than cursing/blaspheming God), and the context implies that the cursing has been performed by God (or at least under God's sovereign behest).

interpretation here ("blasphemy") overlaps with that of Josephus and with some key rabbinic and targumic traditions (see below)

Not surprisingly, the Old Latin traditions follow the Septuagint fairly closely, particularly in presenting the suspended person as *maledictus a Deo* "(cursed by God")," as does Jerome's Vulgate.[422] More notable is how the Syriac Peshiṭta instead states that the suspended person has "reviled God," thus following the objective-genitive interpretation that we witnessed in Symmachus and that appears later in rabbinic authorities; the Peshiṭta on this point may well represent traditional Jewish influence.[423]

**(263)** Targumim on Deuteronomy 21:22–23

*Tg. Onq.*

‏<sup>22</sup> וארי יהי בגבר חובת דין דקטול ויתקטיל <u>ותצלוב</u> יתיה על <u>צליבא</u>: <sup>23</sup> לא תבית נבילתיה על
<u>צליבא</u> ארי מקבר תקבריניה ביומא ההוא ארי <u>על דחב קדם יוי אצטליב</u> ולא תסאיב ית ארעך
דיוי אלהך יהיב לך אחסנא:

*Tg. Neof.*

‏<sup>22</sup> וארום יהווי בגברא <u>סדר</u> חובת דין דקטולין ויתקטל <u>ותצלבון</u> יתיה על קיסה: <sup>23</sup> לא תבית
נבלתיה על קיסה ארום מקבר תקברון יתיה ביומה ההוא ארום <u>ליט קדם ייי כל דצליב</u> ולא
תסאבון ית ארע<u>כון</u> דייי אלה<u>כון</u> יהיב ל<u>כון</u> אחסנה:

*Tg. Ps.-J.*

‏<sup>22</sup> וארום <u>אין</u> יהוי בגבר חובת דין קטול <u>ויתחייב אטלות אבנין ובתר כדין יצלבון</u> יתיה על קיסא:
<sup>23</sup> לא תבית ניבלת <u>גושמיה</u> על קיסא ארום מקבר תקברו<u>ניה</u> ביומה ההוא ארום <u>קילותא קדם</u>
<u>אילקא למצלוב גבר אלהן חובוי גרמו ליה ומן־בגלל דבדיוקנא דייי אתעבד</u> תקברו<u>ניה</u> <u>עם</u>
<u>מטמוע שימשא דלא יקילון ברייתא ביה</u> ולא תטנפון <u>בנבילתהון דחייביא</u> ית ארע<u>כון</u> דייי אלק<u>כון</u>
יהיב ל<u>כון</u> :

*Frg. Tg.*

‏על עץ: <u>ותצלבון</u> יתיה על קייסא

---

[422] The text of the Latin can be found in PIERRE SABATIER, Bibliorum Sacrorum Latinae versiones antiquae (3 vols.; Rheims: Florentain, 1733–1749). It reads: (22) Si autem fuerit in aliquo delicto ita ut judicium mortis sit, & morietur & suspendetis eum in ligno: (23) sed & sepultura sepelietis eum ipsa die: quoniam maledictus a Deo est omnis qui suspensus fuerit in ligno: & non inquinabitis terram, quam Dominus Deus tuus dabit tibi in forte.

[423] For a fuller analysis of traditions on Deut 21:22–23 see CHAPMAN, Crucifixion, 117–149. The Syriac text and discussion appears ibid. 124–125 with the following translation: "(22) And if a man is condemned on account of a sin bearing the judgment of death, and he is hung on the tree and he is killed, (23) his corpse shall not spend the night on the tree, but you [pl.] shall bury him in that day, because one who reviles God is hung, and you shall not defile your land, which the Lord your God gave to you [as] a possession."

*Tg. Onq.* And if there is in a man a sin bearing a judgment of death, and he is executed, and you <u>suspend</u> him on <u>the cross</u>, [23] his corpse shall not spend the night[424] on the <u>cross</u>, but you [pl.] shall surely bury him in that day, because <u>on account of his having sinned before the Lord he was suspended</u>; and you shall not defile your land, which the Lord your God <u>will</u> give to you as an inheritance.

*Tg. Neof.* And if there is <u>arranged</u> in <u>the</u> man a sin bearing a judgment of death<u>s</u>, and he is executed, and you [pl.] <u>suspend</u> him on a tree, [23] his corpse shall not spend the night on <u>a</u> tree, but you [pl.] shall surely bury him in that day, because cursed [<u>participle</u>] <u>before the Lord</u> is <u>everyone who is suspended</u>, and you [pl.] shall not defile your [pl.] land, which the Lord your [pl.] God <u>will</u> give to you [pl.] as an inheritance.

*Tg. Ps.-J.* And if <u>indeed</u> there is in a man a sin bearing a judgment of death, <u>and he is convicted [to] a casting of stones [= a stoning]</u>, and <u>after this they</u> <u>suspend</u> him on the tree; [23] the corpse <u>of his body</u> shall not spend the night on a tree, but you [pl.] shall surely bury him in that day, because <u>it is a disgrace</u> <u>before the Lord to suspend a man, unless his sins caused it. And because in</u> <u>the image of the Lord he was made</u>, you [pl.] shall bury him <u>with the setting</u> <u>of the sun, so that the creatures will not treat him improperly</u>; and you [pl.] shall not defile <u>with the corpses of the guilty</u> your [pl.] land, which the Lord your [pl.] God <u>will</u> give to you [pl.].

*Frg. Tg.* on Deut 21:22 *On a tree:* And you [pl.] shall <u>suspend</u> him on <u>the</u> tree.

*Commentary.*[425] These targumim are Aramaic translations (or paraphrases) of the Pentateuch. Onqelos employs Babylonian Aramaic, while the other targumim (Neofiti, Pseudo-Jonathan, and the Fragment Targum) are considered Palestinian. The origins of such targumim appear to be in the synagogue, where the Jewish populace needed the Hebrew Bible to be conveyed to them (and interpreted) in their native Aramaic. The dates for these traditions (espe-

---

[424] Concerning the translation of תבית as *peal*, rather than *aphel* as pointed in SPERBER, see CHAPMAN, Crucifixion, 138 nn. 152, 154; cf. ibid. for *Neofiti* marginal readings.

[425] Texts: ALEXANDER SPERBER, The Bible in Aramaic Based on Old Manuscripts and Printed Texts (4 vols.; 1959–1973; repr., Leiden: Brill, 1992), 1:326–327 (*Tg. Onq.*); ALEJANDRO DÍEZ MACHO, Neophyti I. Targum Palestinense MS de la Biblioteca Vaticana (6 vols.; Textos y Estudios Cardinal Cisneros 7–11.20; Madrid / Barcelona: Consejo Superior de Investigaciones Cientificas, 1968–1979) (*Tg. Neof.*); MOSES GINSBURGER, Pseudo-Jonathan (Thargum Jonathan ben Usiel zum Pentateuch). Nach der Londoner Handschrift (Brit. Mus. add. 27031) (orig. 1903; repr., New York: Hildesheim, 1966) (*Tg. Ps.-J.*); MICHAEL L. KLEIN, The Fragment-Targums of the Pentateuch According to their Extant Sources (2 vols.; AnBib 76; Rom: Biblical Institute Press, 1980) (*Frag. Tg.*). Palestinian traditions compared with ALEJANDO DÍEZ MACHO, LUIS DIEZ MERINO, EMILIANO MARTÍNEZ BOROBIO, and TERESA MARTÍNEZ SÁIZ. Biblia Polyglotta Matritensia IV: Targum Palestinense in Pentateuchum (5 vols.; Madrid: Consejo Superior de Investigaciones Cientificas, 1977–1988).

cially for the Palestinian targumim) are widely debated among scholars, though we shall consider them to represent the period of the Amoraim (after the Mishnah but before the Talmud) with many traditions they contain likely stemming from the earlier Tannaitic age. In the texts and translations above, we have underlined the areas where the targumim are most clearly interpreting/paraphrasing the Hebrew.[426]

For this study, the most substantial feature of all these targumim concerns how they have chosen to translate the Hebrew verb תלה ("hang up") into Aramaic. Although Aramaic has an equivalent generic verb for "to hang [something] up" in תלא, all these targumim instead substitute the verb צלב in place of the Hebrew תלה. In addition, while the Palestinian targumim all render the Hebrew word for tree/wood (עץ) with a roughly synonymous Aramaic word (קיסה), Targum Onqelos calls the device on which the person is suspended by the term צליבא. As will be observed below (section 3.9), similar shifts occur in the targumim to all those OT texts that mention a person being hung on a tree. In fact, both צלב and צליבא are employed exclusively to designate human bodily suspension in this era (both in Jewish targumic Aramaic and in Rabbinic Hebrew). Further, there are many clear examples in which צלב and its nominal cognates depict events that can only be understood as crucifixions.[427]

Does this mean (as some have asserted) that these targumim have shifted the meaning of Deuteronomy 21 to reference crucifixion as a form of executing a live human being? In fact, no. The texts retain the order of verbs found in the Hebrew text, which likely implies that the person was first executed and then his body was suspended. Moreover, Targum Pseudo-Jonathan clearly adds to the text of verse 22 the notion that the person is first stoned to death and then suspended aloft (a view that strikingly aligns with rabbinic procedures we shall analyze further below). Although these passages likely refer to *post mortem* suspension, the shift in terminology to צלב does do two things. First, it makes this Deuteronomic passage refer even more technically to human bodily suspension, and second, in doing so, it also correlates this passage with terminology that is easily associated with the cross.

However, Targum Pseudo-Jonathan particularly goes out of its way to distinguish this penalty from crucifixion. Not only does it mention the sequence of stoning then suspension (as noted already), but Pseudo-Jonathan also adds a reference to the danger of animals maltreating the corpses of suspension victims as an argument for burying the body within the day. References to prolonged suspensions and to animal scavengers occur in many ancient crucifixion accounts. So it is likely that this Targum was actively distinguishing the

---

[426] This follows the procedure established in CHAPMAN, *Crucifixion*, 138.

[427] Discussion of the semantic range of צלב (and cognates) appears in CHAPMAN, *Crucifixion*, 14–26 (note further bibliography there); COOK, *Crucifixion*, 326–355.

Jewish punishment of Deuteronomy from the *ante mortem* (and prolonged) crucifixion practices of the Romans.

In these targumic traditions, we again encounter conflicting interpretations of the Hebrew "curse of God." The subjective genitive interpretation appears in Targum Neofiti, where the person is "cursed before the Lord." Onqelos refers to the person "sinning before the Lord," which seems to be a tamed-down version of the objective genitive (in which the sin, though not actually blaspheming God, is still deemed to be directed at the Lord). Finally, Pseudo-Jonathan parallels Onqelos in putting the onus on the person whose "sins caused" his suspension. Yet, Pseudo-Jonathan also adds an allusive reference to the "image of the Lord," which may simultaneously point to the concept (known in rabbinic sayings) that when a human being (created in the divine image as per Gen 1:26–28) is suspended in an accursed way, this in some way becomes a cursing of the Divine himself. So, Pseudo-Jonathan simultaneously represents two different (but parallel) objective-genitive interpretations (the sin/curse is against God, and the curse is also against the divine image). In this, Pseudo-Jonathan finds itself more aligned with Onqelos (a Babylonian targum) than with the subjective genitive interpretation found in its fellow Palestinian targum (Neofiti).

**(264)** Josephus, *Antiquitates judaicae* 4.264–265

οὐδ' ἂν οἱ λόγοι καὶ ἡ παρ' αὐτῶν διδασκαλία τοῦ σωφρονεῖν τὸ μηδὲν εἶναι φανῶσιν, ἐχθροὺς δ' ἀσπόνδους αὐτῷ ποιῇ τοὺς νόμους τοῖς συνεχέσι κατὰ τῶν γονέων τολμήμασι, προαχθεὶς ὑπ' αὐτῶν τούτων ἔξω τῆς πόλεως τοῦ πλήθους ἑπομένου καταλευέσθω καὶ μείνας δι' ὅλης τῆς ἡμέρας εἰς θέαν τὴν ἁπάντων θαπτέσθω νυκτός. ²⁶⁵ οὕτως δὲ καὶ οἱ ὁπωσοῦν ὑπὸ τῶν νόμων ἀναιρεθῆναι κατακριθέντες. θαπτέσθωσαν δὲ καὶ οἱ πολέμιοι καὶ νεκρὸς μηδὲ εἰς ἄμοιρος γῆς κείσθω περαιτέρω τοῦ δικαίου τιμωρίαν ἐκτίνων.

*Translation.* But should neither these words, and the teaching from them, appear to bring any moderation [to him], and should he make the laws implacable enemies against himself by continuous shameless acts against his parents, then after having been brought forth by these very ones [= his parents] outside the city while the multitude follows, let him be stoned to death, and after remaining through the whole day in the sight of all, let him be buried during the night. ²⁶⁵ And thus also those who have been condemned by the laws to be put to death in any way. And let even the military enemies be buried, and do not let even a single corpse lie without a lot of ground, paying punishment further than is just.

*Commentary.*[428] In much of *Antiquities* Book 4, Josephus provides an extensive interpretation of the Torah laws, likely with an apologetic eye toward
explaining them and showing their reasonableness to his readers.[429] Here,
Josephus brings together two contiguous laws in Deuteronomy 21: one concerning the stubborn and rebellious son (Deut 21:18–21) and another concerning burial for the executed and suspended man (21:22–23). We may recall that
Deut 21:22 is unclear as to what crimes constitute "a sin bearing a judgment
of death" (and thus what sins merit suspension); here, it is apparent that
Josephus believed the death penalty in the immediately preceding verse (Deut
21:21) against the rebellious son suggests that such rebelliousness constitutes
one such sin (cf. *b. Sanh.* 46a). The son is first to be stoned (as in Deut 21:21)
and then left exposed. Josephus makes no direct mention of hanging up the
corpse on a tree (as per Deut 21:22), but he clearly invokes Deuteronomy
21:23 in calling for a burial during the night.[430] Lack of burial is deemed by
him to be a punishment that goes beyond what is just (περαιτέρω τοῦ δικαίου
in *A. J.* 4.265). Instead, each corpse deserves its allotment of land (ἄμοιρος
γῆς). The opening reference in *A. J.* 4.264 to "these words" (οἱ λόγοι) and
their teaching refers back to an extensive monologue from the parents to the
rebellious child (in *A. J.* 4.260–263) not reflected in the biblical text.[431] The
goal was to call the child to moderate (σωφρονεῖν in 4.264) his behavior. The
references to "laws" above refer to the Torah precepts, particularly to those
whose violation brings shame on the parents. As in Deut 21:18–20, the parents initiate the execution procedure. Elsewhere, Josephus will appear to limit

---

[428] Text: NIESE, Flavii Josephi Opera, 1:277–278. Numerous variations occur in the
manuscripts and modern editions for the opening words οὐδ' ἄν, though the overall meaning is
not substantially affected. Commentary on this passage, often comparing it with rabbinic texts,
can be found in FELDMAN, Judean Antiquities 1–4, 434–436.

[429] In the beginning of Josephus' legal exposition, he appears to focus on a Gentile audience to whom he will describe the Jewish form of government (*A. J.* 4.196). Yet he also antic-
ipates some Jewish readers to whom he gives an apologetic for putting the Mosaic laws into a
logical system (4.197).

[430] The genitive of time ("time within which") applied to νυκτός (at the end of Josephus,
*A. J.* 4.264) would indicate that the body is buried "during the night" (i.e., once night has
started). This would certainly comply with the command not to let the corpse "spend the
night" on the tree in Deut 21:23, but it may be at odds with the parallel command in 21:23 that
"you shall surely bury him in that day" (since a new day starts with nightfall).

[431] Rather, recalling the Mosaic procedure of the parents bringing the child before the
elders of the city (Deut 21:19–21), Josephus represents a long, thoughtful appeal from the parents to the child to reform his (or her, cf. *A. J.* 2.263) ways (*A. J.* 2.260–263). Perhaps the
most intriguing dimension of this appeal concerns the reference to God as the Father of the
whole human race, who also appears to suffer dishonor when the rebellious children disobey
earthly fathers (who share this paternal role with the heavenly Father; *A. J.* 2.262). Such logic
could stem from a belief that the rebellious son indirectly curses God by rebelling/cursing
against his parents. Thus Josephus may have in mind a further connection to Deut 21:22–23,
allowing its application to such a son.

the practice of bodily suspension to blasphemy (as do many rabbinic traditions), but this passage requires us to add at least one more category of sin (rebellion against one's parents) that deserves such a suspension.

It is particularly intriguing how Josephus in *A. J.* 4.265 broadens the requirement of burial to include two groups: those who have been condemned to any form (ὁπωσοῦν) of execution by the laws, and those who were military enemies (οἱ πολέμιοι) of Israel. The latter could well have a biblical reference to Josh 8:29 and 10:26–27, where Joshua hangs aloft the conquered king of Ai and the five Amorite kings, only to bury them within the day; yet Josephus never recounts these penal suspensions by Joshua.[432] The mention of those "condemned by the laws to be put to death in any way" likely simply insists on universal burial (perhaps cf. Josephus, *B. J.* 3.377), though it may be a reference to all those who are suspended (implying that these may have first been executed with methods other than stoning).

**(265)**   Josephus, *Antiquitates judaicae* 4.202

Ὁ δὲ βλασφημήσας θεὸν καταλευσθεὶς κρεμάσθω δι᾽ ἡμέρας καὶ ἀτίμως καὶ ἀφανῶς θαπτέσθω.

*Translation.* And the one who blasphemes God – after being stoned, let him be hung up through the day, and let him be buried dishonorably and obscurely.

*Commentary.*[433] Here, we have a clear reference to Deut 21:22–23 earlier in the *Antiquities*. It comes fairly early in Josephus' explication of the Mosaic constitution in the midst of references to the construction of the single Jewish Temple and the worship of God (*A. J.* 4.199–204). The reference to Deut 21 is again obvious by the command to bury the corpse, but also by the reference to hanging up (κρεμάσθω) the body. Observe that the person to be punished has "blasphemed God," which likely is predicated on an objective-genitive interpretation of "curse of God" in Deut 21:23, as we saw above in Symmachus and will encounter below in the Rabbis. The man is first executed, here by stoning, which is the Levitical punishment for blasphemers (Lev 24:16) also found in rabbinic law. In contrast to the Deuteronomy 21 text (which does not actually require suspension but legislates burial *if* suspension has occurred), Josephus makes the suspension a requisite part of the command to stone and

---

[432] Perhaps Josephus desires to distance any respected OT Jewish leader from use of suspension (even crucifixion). Notably, this passage here (*A. J.* 4.265) may indicate that Josephus was well aware of OT (or other Jewish) figures who did suspend military enemies but that he intentionally did not record such episodes in his *Jewish Antiquities*.

[433] Text: NIESE, Flavii Josephi Opera, 1:265. Textual variations are incidental, including how some mss read κρεμνάσθω for κρεμάσθω (one ms makes the phonological error of reading κριμνάσθω). See the commentary by FELDMAN, Judean Antiquities 1–4, 400–402.

hang blasphemers.[434] The *post mortem* hanging is "through the day" (δι' ἡμέρας),[435] which likely implies burial at nightfall, as we saw above in *A.J.* 4.264–265.[436] Josephus here does not follow Deuteronomy in providing a reason for the necessity of burial (as does Josephus in 4.265 and Deuteronomy in 21:23); rather, in this passage, Josephus insists the burial be dishonorable and obscure, perhaps a reference to the rabbinic burial locations reserved for executed criminals (*m. Sanh.* 6:7 [DANBY 6:5]; *t. Sanh.* 9:8–9).

**(266)** Josephus, *Bellum judaicum* 4.317

προῆλθον δὲ εἰς τοσοῦτον ἀσεβείας ὥστε καὶ ἀτάφους ῥῖψαι, καίτοι τοσαύτην Ἰουδαίων περὶ τὰς ταφὰς πρόνοιαν ποιουμένων, ὥστε καὶ τοὺς ἐκ καταδίκης ἀνεσταυρωμένους πρὸ δύντος ἡλίου καθελεῖν τε καὶ θάπτειν.

*Translation.* And they [the Idumaeans] advanced unto so much impiety that they even threw away the unburied bodies, although Jews perform so much forethought concerning burials that even those who have been crucified because of a legal sentence are both taken down and buried before the sun sets.

*Commentary.*[437] Josephus' passing reference here to Jewish burial law stemming from Deut 21:22–23 comes in the midst of his account of the brutalities of the Jewish revolt in Jerusalem. Jewish zealots have let the Idumaeans into Jerusalem, seeking comrades-in-arms against the priestly leadership of the city (*B. J.* 4.300–313). Josephus depicts the Idumaeans as "the most savage" people (ὠμότατοι in *B. J.* 4.310). Once they had plundered the houses and murdered many, the Idumaeans slaughtered the high priest, Ananus, and the elder priest, Jesus, and stood afterwards on their dead bodies (*B. J.* 4.315–316). It is likely their bodies are those Josephus describes in the passage above as having been left unburied. He considers this act – the slaying of the high priest – as the true beginning of Jerusalem's destruction (*B. J.* 4.318–325). He will later speak of the bodies of Ananus and Jesus as "thrown away naked" and as "food of dogs and beasts" (*B. J.* 4.324), in stark contrast to their having been covered in priestly garments and deemed worthy of veneration just a short time before. In this passage, Josephus considers the refusal of burial a great

---

[434] In fact, one could argue the grammatical emphasis lies on the command to hang the blasphemer (which is a Greek imperative) as opposed to the lesser verb for stoning (which is a participle that has less force than the imperative).

[435] Two important 11th century manuscripts read here δι' ὅλης ἡμέρας.

[436] This is at variance from those rabbis who insist the person is hung up and immediately taken down; cf. *m. Sanh.* 6:6 [DANBY 6:4]; see No. 35. *Sifre Dev.* §221 indicates the suspension should happen at dusk, and then the body should be released (presumably shortly afterwards) at night; see No. 62.

[437] Text: NIESE, Flavii Josephi Opera, 6:388. Several manuscripts read ἀνασταυρουμένους ("those who are crucified") for ἀνεσταυρωμένους ("those who have been crucified").

impiety (ἀσεβείας), perhaps worse given the status of the victims involved. He also contrasts the ungodly act of the Idumaeans with the Jewish practice of requiring burial before sunset, even for convicted felons who have been "crucified" (ἀνεσταυρωμένους). This term is typical in Josephus for bodily suspension, and in most contexts (especially in the *Jewish War*), it refers to the kinds of suspensions/crucifixions the Romans performed (see esp. section 3.7), including those in which the person is executed by a prolonged suspension on the cross. We observed earlier that in his presentation of the Jewish Law (both in *A. J.* 4.202 and 4.264–265 above), Josephus is careful to distinguish Deut 21:22–23 from crucifixion – clearly indicating in both places that any such suspension is subsequent to a death by stoning. This distinction accords with much rabbinic teaching, and it may even be attributable to Josephus' Pharisaic training and allegiance (cf. Josephus, *Vita* 12). However, in this context, he indicates a belief that Deuteronomy 21 applies even to those who are suspended on a *stauros* (a connection made most natural by viewing ἀνασταυρόω as a type of suspension, analogous in some ways to the suspension of Deut 21:23).[438]

### (267) *m. Sanhedrin* 6:4–6 and *Sifre Devarim* §221

*Additional Notes.* These passages were covered in detail above in No. 35 and No. 62 respectively; see there for texts and translations. Yet it is important to recall here a few key points relevant to this discussion. Both passages concern the penalty of suspension, drawing heavily on Deut 21:22–23 for these rabbinic discussions.

The Mishnah reports a debate concerning who is suspended. R. Eliezer advocates for everyone who is stoned to be hung up, while the Sages limit the penalty to the blasphemer and the idol-worshipper (*m. Sanh.* 6:5 [DANBY 6:4]; see further *y. Sanh.* 6:7). This reminds us that the "sin bearing a judgment of death" in Deut 21:22 is not clearly defined in context. The (majority) position

---

[438] Another intriguing statement about burial by sunset is found in Josephus, *B. J.* 3.377: τοὺς γοῦν ἀναιροῦντας ἑαυτοὺς παρὰ μὲν ἡμῖν μέχρις ἡλίου δύσεως ἀτάφους ἐκρίπτειν ἔκριναν καίτοι καὶ πολεμίους θάπτειν θεμιτὸν ἡγούμενοι ("[Our laws] then judged that those who kill themselves be cast out by us unburied until the setting of the sun, and yet they command it lawful for enemies to be buried"). In context, Josephus records his speech to the army in an (unsuccessful) attempt to dissuade them from a mass suicide (*B. J.* 3.361–382). In this speech, Josephus, acting as a philosopher, presents various arguments for why it is best not to commit suicide. In 3.377 he observes that the Jewish laws themselves accord a better lot to Israel's enemies (burial) than to her own suicides (no burial until sunset). This appears informed by Deuteronomy 21 (concerning burial at the setting of the sun; esp. cf. Josephus, *A. J.* 4.265 above) and by various OT military narratives; however, it does not mention bodily suspension, so it seems to stem from Deuteronomy 21 by implication (even heinous criminals are buried by sunset, therefore all should be) rather than by specific application to the suspended person (in contrast to *B. J.* 4.317 above).

of the Sages, which by default the Mishnah accepts over R. Eliezer, obviously hinges on the objective-genitive interpretation of "curse of God" – the man has cursed God by blasphemy or idolatry. We noted earlier that both Symmachus and Josephus assume the blasphemer interpretation, both with possible ties to Pharisaic or rabbinic Judaism. Rabbi Eliezer's position would open up bodily suspension to include all those who are stoned to death, presumably because all such offenders have committed a "sin bearing a judgment of death",[439] with the probable list of such offenses appearing in *m. Sanh.* 7.4 (see text and commentary above in No. 36): incest, homosexuality, bestiality, blasphemy, idolatry, child-sacrifice, divination, Sabbath-profanation, cursing of parents, adultery with a betrothed woman, enticing others to idolatry, leading others astray, sorcery, and stubborn and rebellious sons. That last item (stubborn and rebellious sons) reminds us that Josephus, who was especially influenced by Pharisaic Judaism, also considered this category of offenders as worthy of suspension, despite his official connection of Deut 21:22–23 with blasphemers.

There is a further reported disagreement between R. Eliezer and the Sages concerning who can be hung up (*m Sanh.* 6:5 [DANBY 6:4]; *Sifre Dev.* 221; also *b. Sanh.* 46a). Eliezer permits both men and women to be suspended, while the Sages limit the penalty to men only.[440] Eliezer argues from the example of Simeon b. Shetach (on which see below in 3.5.5). The *Sifre* spells out the rabbinic argument to limit suspension to men[441]: Deut 21:22 says, "if there is in *a man* [בְאִישׁ] a sin" – thus it must refer to men (not women) receiving such a punishment. According to the *Sifre*, one can deduce by a similar examination of "you shall hang *him*" (אתו) in the singular that only one man is hung in a day, that false witnesses are not hung (who would otherwise be put to death in place of the "him"), and that the man is hung naked ("him" does not include his clothes). The last point is particularly striking since the Romans appear to have typically hung up a person naked on a cross as well.

The Mishnah orders that the suspension device be planted in the ground, but R. Yose has the device leaning up against a wall. So the precise form of the device (though established for later generations by the Mishnaic acceptance of the majority position) appears to have been in flux in the early rabbinic period (and likely before). Both the Mishnah and the *Sifre* are clear that burial must happen before the day is over.

---

[439] R. Eliezer's argumentation as reported in *Sifre Dev.* §221 is a bit different: He draws an analogy between the blasphemer (who is stoned and hanged) and all those who are stoned and hanged. This would imply Eliezer accepted the objective-genitive interpretation ("curse of God", i.e. blaspheme) and simply extended from that crime to all analogous crimes, analogous because their punishment is the same, viz. stoning.

[440] R. Judah follows R. Eliezer in permitting women to be hung up; see below in 3.5.5 concerning Simeon b. Shetach traditions.

[441] Similar arguments occur in *b. Sanh.* 46a.

Finally, the rabbis clarify why the person was hanged: "because he cursed [lit. 'blessed'] the name" (*m. Sanh.* 6:6 [DANBY 6:4]; and *Sifre Dev.* §221). This was a circumspect way to say he blasphemed God. Again, this testifies to the objective-genitive interpretation of "curse of God" (in Deut 21:23).

The study of rabbinic traditions could further progress to the Tosefta and the talmudic literature, and these texts have been studied elsewhere.[442] To mention two key passages: (1) The Tosefta also records many of the bodily suspension procedures known in the Mishnah and Sifre, adding that the *mitzvah* concerning suspension necessitates a period short enough that one person should tie the suspended person up, while another unties him (*t. Sanh.* 9:6) – note the use of rope rather than nails, and the fact that the suspending of a person is called a commandment. (2) The Tosefta and Bavli both contain versions of a parable from R. Meir about a crucified brigand (who is the twin brother of the king); this parable compares the "curse of God" in Deut 21:23 with how a person hung aloft (i.e., crucified) is nevertheless in the image of the "king", i.e., in the image of God (*t. Sanh.* 9:7; *b. Sanh.* 46b).

### 3.5.2 Opposition to Crucifixion in Jewish Sources

Three brief statements in rabbinic literature represent the most explicit opposition to crucifixion being permitted as a Jewish capital penalty. These are closely related and all are predicated on Deut 21:22–23. They also all purport to represent Tannaitic opinions from the rabbinic generations dating from before the early third-century Mishnah (even the Talmud reports its statement as a *baraita*). However, more specific dates cannot be given, in part since no rabbinic authorities are named. Such opposition to crucifixion should also be connected with the passages above, in which Josephus, the targumim, and other rabbinic texts clearly portray the criminal of Deuteronomy 21 as being executed (usually by stoning) prior to suspension (i.e., *post mortem* rather than *ante mortem*).

**(268)** *Sifre Devarim* §221 on Deuteronomy 21:22

יכול יהו תולים אותו חי כדרך שהמלכות עושה תלמוד לומר והומת ותלית אותו על עץ.

*Translation.* One might think that they will hang him alive, as in the manner that the [Roman] government does. Scripture says, "and he was put to death, and you hung him on a tree.

---

[442] CHAPMAN, Crucifixion, 144–147.

*Commentary*.[443] The *Sifre Devarim* is a midrashic composition that collates rabbinic stories and opinions with the text of Deuteronomy from (at least largely) the age of the Tannaim (pre-Mishnaic rabbis).[444] Here the rabbis consider whether an *ante mortem* suspension is legally permissible. The phrase "as is the practice of the state" does not appear in all manuscripts, but it does have substantial textual support and is included in Finkelstein's edition. The "state" (המלכות) here refers (as often elsewhere in Rabbinic Hebrew) to the Roman government. The penalty considered, being *ante-mortem* in Roman style, would thus appear to be crucifixion. This is rejected on the basis of the order of the verbs in Deut 21:22 ("put to death" precedes "hang").

## (269) *Midrash Tannaim* p. 132, lines 7–8

והומת ותלית יכול יהוא תולין אותו חי כדרך שהמלכות עושה ת"ל והומת ממיתין אותו ואחר כך
תולין אתו.

*Translation.* "And he was put to death, and you hung [him]": One might think that they will hang him alive, as in the manner that the [Roman] government does. Scripture says, "and he was put to death …" [So] they put him to death and afterwards they hang him.

*Commentary*.[445] The *Midrash Tannaim* represents an alternative halakhic midrash on Deuteronomy, roughly parallel to *Sifre Devarim* (and likely from the same era). It is known primarily through fragments of Genizah manuscripts and through quotations in later rabbinic sources, which have been collected into the current HOFFMAN edition.[446] As HOFFMAN reconstructs the passage, the first half of the text is virtually identical to *Sifre Dev.* §221, save for essentially orthographic matters. The second half of the text is found in *b. Sanh.* 46b (see No. 270). The argumentation is the same as in the *Sifre*; the order of verbs in Deut 21:22–23 would imply a *post mortem* suspension, unlike the Roman method of executing a person via the cross.

## (270) *b. Sanhedrin* 46b

תנו רבנן אילו נאמר חטא ותלית היתי אומר תולין אותו ואחר כך ממיתין אותו כדרך שהמלכות
עושה תלמוד לומר והומת ותלית ממיתין אותו ואח"כ תולין אותו

---

[443] Text: FINKELSTEIN, Sifre ad Deuteronomium.

[444] See STRACK / STEMBERGER / BOCKMUEHL, Introduction, 270–273.

[445] Text: DAVID HOFFMANN, Midrasch Tannaïm zum Deuteronomium (2 vols.; Berlin: Poppelauer, 1908–1909), 2:132 (lines 7–8). There appears to be a printing error on והומת after ת"ל (the printed edition reads וחומת), which has been corrected here.

[446] For an introduction see STRACK / STEMBERGER / BOCKMUEHL, Introduction, 273–275.

*Translation.* The Rabbis taught, "If it were to say, 'He sinned, and you hanged [him],' then I would have said, 'They hang him and afterwards they put him to death, as in the manner which the [Roman] government does.' Scripture says, 'And he is put to death and you hang [him].' [So] they put him to death and afterwards they hang him."

*Commentary.*[447] The Babylonian Talmud presents this text as a *baraita* (a Tannaitic passage from the era of the Mishnah or before). Certainly, the concluding sentence is worded identically to the *Midrash Tannaim*, and the first part effectively paraphrases the passage common to the *Sifre Dev.* and the *Midrash Tannaim*. Thus the argument is essentially the same. Here the author spells out more clearly that had the clause "hanged [him]" in Deut 21:22 preceded the clause "put to death," then the suspension would be the evident cause of his death. Such an *ante mortem* suspension would be similar to the Roman method of crucifixion. But the Deuteronomy passage places the death prior to the suspension, so crucifixion is rejected.

### 3.5.3 Transitions in Jewish Capital Law

The Mishnah enumerates four accepted methods of execution, and suspension/crucifixion is not among them. This would add weight to the argument from the rabbinic texts cited in the previous subsection that crucifixion was not a sanctioned form of execution, at least in rabbinic Judaism. However, some variation occurs in the fourfold list, as noted in the Targum on Ruth, with "hanging" being substituted for the Mishnah's "strangling." This may indicate that the rabbinic laws on execution were still developing. Three key sources are presented below. It should be acknowledged that only stoning and burning are clearly established as death penalties in the Hebrew Bible,[448] so the four-fold list must be a development from a later stage in early Judaism.

---

[447] Text from the Soncino Talmud; ISIDORE EPSTEIN, ed., Hebrew-English Edition of the Babylonian Talmud (New Edition in 30 vols.; London: Soncino, 1967–1989), IV/4, loc.cit.

[448] A similar view (with list) in ROLAND DE VAUX, Ancient Israel: Its Life and Institutions (2nd ed.; London: Darton, Longman & Todd, 1961), 158–159. The Yerushalmi bravely acknowledges that strangling is not found in Scripture (*y. Sanh.* 7:1 and 7:4). The beheading of Ish-bosheth is viewed with some alarm (2 Sam 4:7) and thus does not serve as a model execution. However, HYMAN E. GOLDIN, Hebrew Criminal Law and Procedure: Mishnah: Sanhedrin–Makkot (New York: Twayne, 1952), 28, 36 also notes the putting to the sword of a whole town for apostasy (Deut 13:12–16). This Deut 13 passage seems to underlie the reasoning of *m. Sanh.* 9:1 concerning beheading residents of apostate towns (*b. Sanh.* 52b); but it is otherwise unclear which OT rationales motivated the distribution of other crimes to the Mishnaic penalties of beheading and strangling (cf. *m. Sanh.* 9:1; 11:1). Most OT texts DANBY cites as Mishnaic justification only state that the offender shall die, without specifying means; though note the argument (and the confusion) in *y. Sanh.* 7:1; *b. Sanh.* 52b–53a.

Though there is insufficient space here to present a full account, it is also worth observing that the actual procedures for performing the four Mishnaic methods of execution appear to be in transition in the Roman period. In particular, most Mishnaic-approved methods look to be late: (1) This was noted already concerning *stoning* (in the discussion of *m. Sanh.* 6:4 in No. 35). While (in the first instance) the Mishnah pronounces that stoning is produced by throwing the offender off a precipice and then tossing stones on him if he is not yet dead, there are in fact several examples of stoning in the first century being performed by crowds throwing stones at a person, without indication of a precipice, which also would appear the more natural way to read the Torah laws.[449] Josephus repeatedly records stone throwing.[450] (2) Similarly, the Mishnah itself reports disagreement concerning the method of *beheading*; the general view is that the victim should be decapitated with a sword ("in the manner of the [Roman] government"), but the highly respected R. Judah b. Ilai (even differing in opinion in the mid-second century) says they beheaded him with an axe on a block (*m. Sanh.* 7:3; cf. *t. Sanh.* 9:11; the response to Judah differs between *y. Sanh.* 7:3 and *b. Sanh.* 52b). (3) The official Mishnaic method of *burning* requires burying the victim in dung to his or her knees, compelling him to open his mouth by coercing it open with a cloth around his neck, and then throwing a heated strip/wick down his throat

---

[449] People pick up stones to stone Jesus in John 8:59; 10:31 (cf. 8:7, albeit textually suspect), though they attempt to throw him off a precipice in Luke 4:29. Stoning by throwing stones appears likely in the case of Stephen (Acts 7:58–60) and certain in the case of the mob-stoning feared in Acts 5:26. The same Greek verbs are used of pagan-stoning (with tossed stones) in Acts 14:5, 19. In the Hebrew Bible, the phrase "they shall stone him with [a] stone" (e.g., Lev 20:2, 27; 24:23; cf. 1 Kings 12:18; 2 Chron 10:18; 24:21) is somewhat ambiguous as to how many stones are involved – "stone" is in the anarthrous singular in Hebrew, likely designating a generic use of the word rather than indicating that a single stone is to be used for the procedure (note that in the LXX, most of these texts render "stone" as plural, clarifying that multiple stones were to be employed). Numbers 15:35–36 certainly indicates multiple stones were used to execute the Sabbath-breaker, and this is also consistently true of stoning in Deuteronomy (Deut 13:11; 17:5; 21:21; 22:21, 24; cf. Josh 7:25; and 1 Kings 21:13 concerning Naboth). The LXX also interprets Shimei throwing stones at David as an attempted stoning (2 Sam 16:6, 13). An intriguing parallel can be made between the later Mishnaic method for stoning (throwing from a precipice) and the Roman use of the Tarpeian rock, from whence criminals were cast down to their death (found as early as the Twelve Tables 8.14; 8.23; see CARL GEORG BRUNS, ed., Fontes Iuris Romani Antiqui [Post curas Theodori Mommseni editionibus quintae et sextae adhibitas septimum edidit Otto Gradenwitz. 2 vols.; Tübingen: Mohr Siebeck, 1909], 1:32–33; and also see discussion below in 3.6).

[450] E.g., Josephus, *A. J.* 2.327 (mob throws stones at Moses); 7.207 (Shimei throws stones at David); 8.220–221 (Adoram is stoned); 9.168 (Zechariah the high priest is stoned); *B. J.* 1.550 (offenders are stoned after an assembly of the people – with stones and sticks); 2.9,11 (stones are thrown at Archelaus and his soldiers). Cf. the throwing of stones in battles with similar terminology in (for example) *A. J.* 13.90; 14.456; 20.176, 180; *B. J.* 2.492; 3.525; 4.200; 5.111; 6.67. On the other hand, the mob can also stone someone by throwing that person off a precipice and then pelting him or her with stones (e.g., *B. J.* 2.534).

(*m. Sanh.* 7:2; the makeup of the wick is debated, whether lead, tin or oil – see *y. Sanh.* 7:2). The Mishnah reports this procedure of burning received a slight disagreement from R. Judah (who required tongs be used to open the mouth) and a strong counter-argument from the second-generation *tanna* R. Eliezer b. Zadok (who noted that historically, a defiled priest's daughter had been burned by being encompassed with lit kindling). The Mishnah (*Sanh.* 7:2) responds to R. Eliezer: "that *Beth-din* was not well-versed in the law"; and such a statement strikingly indicates the standpoint of a later rabbinic perspective critiquing the formal practice of an earlier rabbinic court. [451] Certainly, R. Eliezer's approach would be the more expected method, especially based on OT exemplars.[452] (4) The Mishnaic method of *strangulation* is also surprisingly complex: The convict is buried in dung to his knees, a cloth-wrapped cord is looped around his neck and drawn tight by the two witnesses pulling on the cord's ends (*m. Sanh.* 7:3).[453] Likely such complexity developed over time. (5) We shall note further below that R. Simeon b. Shetach departed from the *post mortem* bodily suspension procedure later sanctioned by the Mishnah. (6) Finally, the rabbis openly sanction exceptions to their approved procedures "when the times require it."[454]

---

[451] In the *Bavli*, R. Joseph responds that the court was made up of Sadducees (*b. Sanh.* 52b). The Sages in the *Tosefta* (*t. Sanh.* 9:11; also *y. Sanh.* 7:2) responds more disparagingly to R. Eliezer (or Eleazar) by claiming he was too young at the time for his testimony to count (the *Bavli* reconciles the two responses to Eliezer by claiming these were two different historical examples he put forth – in *b. Sanh.* 52b). For various attempts to found the Mishnaic penalty in Scripture and continued discussion of objections, see *b. Sanh.* 52a–b.

[452] Death by burning in the OT (Lev 20:14; 21:9) uses the same terminology as burning up a sacrifice with fire (Lev 16:27; 19:6), so it would be surprising if the procedure for the one (sacrifices burned over an open fire) varied markedly from the procedure for the other. Joshua commands that the person who takes things devoted to destruction be burned with fire along with all he has (Josh 7:15), which indicates the use of open flame. So the OT death penalty of burning likely involved burning the offender over lit kindling. Cf. Josephus, *B. J.* 2.624 (in war, of burning houses and families); less clear in (for example) *A. J.* 4.248; *B. J.* 2.599.

[453] Once during a private conversation with NICHOLAS DE LANGE, who was kindly instructing a few of us in Rabbinic Hebrew at Cambridge, he wondered aloud whether most of these Mishnaic methods of execution, with the likely exception of beheading, actually made it difficult for any Roman officials to ascertain mode of death: cloth-wrapped cords leave lighter marks, burning lead inserted in the mouth may not be obvious externally, and a person thrown off a precipice could have potentially fallen accidentally. Thus these punishments could plausibly be carried out surreptitiously without the consent of the Romans. This intriguing suggestion is worth further consideration.

[454] Such an exception is discussed below regarding Simeon b. Shetach using suspension to put witches to death, and there we shall observe that *y. Ḥag.* 2:2 [78a] widens that talmudic conversation to include other examples of rabbinic procedures being abandoned "when the times require it" (including a second-century debate about accepting perjured testimony and a statement that some people could be put to death for non-capital crimes).

This variation, some of it represented by the rabbinic documents themselves, should caution us from assuming that later rabbinic procedures accurately reflect the full range of earlier Jewish practice (even among key rabbinic leaders).

**(271)** *m. Sanhedrin* 7:1

ארבע מיתות נמסרו לבית דין, סקילה שריפה הרג וחנק; ר' שמעון אומר שריפה סקילה חנק
והרג. זו מצות הנסקלין.

*Translation.* Four death penalties were delivered to the *Beth-din*: stoning, burning, beheading, and strangling. Rabbi Simeon says: burning, stoning, strangling, and beheading. This is the commandment of those who are to be stoned.

*Commentary.*[455] The *Beth-din* (lit. "house of judgment") is the Sanhedrin
court that has authority to hear capital cases. Four forms of capital punishment
are permitted here, and other rabbinic works follow this tradition.[456] The
Mishnah indicates that these penalties were "delivered" (נמסרו) to the court,
implying the legacy of earlier rabbinic tradition (and the authority of God in
handing down these punishments through that tradition).[457] According to
R. Simeon b. Yohai, the four penalties remain the same but appear in a variant
order; this signifies that Simeon believed the order of severity should be different than the ranking implied by the general position accepted by the
Mishnah (cf. *m. Sanh.* 9:3, where Simeon debates just this issue; and see
*y. Sanh.* 7:1; *b. Sanh.* 49b–50b). This certainly represents only a slight disagreement, but it is another indication that the rabbis actively continued to discuss capital penalties after the destruction of the Temple (R. Simeon b. Yohai
was active in the mid-second century A.D.). The final clause ("this is the commandment") likely associates *m. Sanh.* 7:1 with the preceding legislation on
stoning in *m. Sanh.* 6:1–8, including the suspension of the stoned corpses,
since the next clause (*m. Sanh.* 7:2) moves immediately to the discussion of
those who are burned (though *m. Sanh.* 7:4–8:7 will return to the topic of
stoning). While *post mortem* suspension is indeed accepted (even required)
earlier in *m. Sanh.* 6:5–6 (6:4 in DANBY), certainly the Mishnah does not list
any form of bodily suspension among the four accepted methods of accomplishing the execution itself.

---

[455] Text: KRAUSS, Mishnah Treatise Sanhedrin, 16; compared with KRAUSS, Sanhedrin–
Makkot.

[456] See e.g., *t. Sanh.* 9:10 (which mentions "four" forms without listing them, though the
civil government is only granted beheading); *y. Sanh.* 7:1; *b. Sanh.* 49b.

[457] For נמסרו in a similar context see *m. Abot* 8:7 [8:8 in DANBY], where pestilence comes
because capital offenses are left unpunished even though they belong to those crimes "delivered" to the *Beth-din*.

**(272)** *Targum Ruth* 1:17

אמר' נעמי אית לנא ארבע דיני מותא לחייביא רגימת אבנין ויקידת נורא וקטילת סייפא וצליבת
קיסא

*Translation.* Naomi said, "We have four kinds of deaths for guilty people: being stoned of stones, and burned of fire, and slain of the sword, and suspended of the tree."

*Commentary.*[458] This Aramaic paraphrase of Ruth is particularly interesting in the way Ruth serves as a model of a Gentile proselyte to Judaism. Ruth, though from Moab and her Hebrew husband dead, refuses to turn back to her people and their Moabite gods, proclaiming "your God will be my God" (1:15–17). In this expansive insertion into Ruth, Naomi engages in the kind of challenge that the rabbis prescribed all proselytes be offered.[459] Naomi warns Ruth that once she enters into Judaism, all the law becomes obligatory for her, even those commandments that invoke the death penalty.[460] Thus Naomi lists the four forms of capital punishment. The list is noticeably similar to the Mishnah (*m. Sanh.* 7:1) in respect to the four penalties and their order, but it is also strikingly different in the fourth item ("suspended of the tree").

Some have argued that, substituting as this does for "strangulation" in the Mishnaic list, this must be a reference to a hanging by the neck on the tree (another form of strangulation).[461] This is certainly possible, but it is equally

---

[458] Text, with pointing removed, from ÉTAN LEVINE, The Aramaic Version of Ruth (AnBib 58; Rome: Biblical Institute Press, 1973).

[459] E.g., proselytes are to be warned of the death penalties for not keeping the Torah in a *baraita* in *b. Yeb.* 47a.

[460] For legal distinctions between proselytes and Gentiles concerning the death penalties, see also *m. Ketub.* 4:3

[461] See especially BAUMGARTEN, Crucifixion, 472–474. BAUMGARTEN bases his conclusion on these items: that one manuscript of the Ruth Targum (MS De Rossi 31) includes "strangulation of the scarf" in the place of "suspended of the tree"; that *Ruth Rabbah* 2:24 (on Ruth 1:17) similarly references strangulation; that Simeon b. Shetach "hung up" witches in Ashkelon (presuming they were hung from the neck); and that Jaķim of Zeroroth, when he committed suicide by simultaneously performing all four capital penalties on himself, hanged himself by the neck (*Gen. Rab.* 65:22; *Midr. Psa.* 11:7; see *Gen. Rab.* text and discussion below in 3.5.5). In response, it should be observed that both MS De Rossi 31 and *Ruth Rabbah* are best understood as seeking to bring the divergent *Ruth Targum* tradition in line with Mishnaic practice, so they do not prove strangulation was the original intent, rather they highlight the deviation in the *Ruth Targum* on just this very point. The Simeon b. Shetach episode could involve crucifixion or impalement rather than hanging from the neck (see below). And the Jaķim tradition is driven by Jaķim's need of a means of accomplishing all four Mishnaic penalties (stoning, burning, sword, and strangulation) *simultaneously* and *by himself.* In order to do so, Jaķim obviously must vary from the accepted methods of each, so the Jaķim tradition does testify to the four-fold list, but it cannot be used to define the manner in which each method should be done. After all, how else was Jaķim to strangle himself? For a fuller engagement with BAUMGARTEN's thesis, see CHAPMAN, Crucifixion, 16–26.

plausible that some other suspension penalty is entailed. The essential point is that this method of execution varies from the Mishnaic practice of *post mortem* suspension; such variation implies that the later rabbinic viewpoint was not universally embraced in early Judaism, and thus some groups might well have viewed one (or more) suspension forms as a means of execution. Many have also argued, based on the principle "that which is anti-Mishnaic must be pre-Mishnaic," that this Targum encodes an earlier form of the capital punishment list than we have in the Mishnah.[462] Indeed, without endorsing every use of that principle in contemporary scholarship, it is difficult to conceive in this instance how the variation from Mishnaic norm here can be anything other than evidence for a variation in ancient halakic viewpoints about the appropriateness of Jewish practice of *ante mortem* suspension. In any case, it does indicate that in rabbinic circles, the accepted practices of capital punishment were not fully settled in the early Roman period.

## (273) Philo, *De Aeternitate Mundi* 20

ὁμοιοτρόπως δὲ καὶ ζῴοις ἐπιγίνεται τελευτὴ νοσήσασι μὲν ἐξ ἑαυτῶν, ὑπὸ δὲ τῶν ἐκτὸς σφαττομένοις ἢ καταλευομένοις ἢ ἐμπιπραμένοις ἢ θάνατον οὐ καθαρὸν τὸν δι' ἀγχόνης ὑπομένουσιν.

*Translation.* And in like fashion, death also comes at the end for living things either from themselves by being sick, or by things from without – by being slain (with the sword), or by being stoned, or by being burnt, or by suffering the unclean death that comes through [hanging on] a halter.

*Commentary.*[463] Writing in the first half of the first century A.D., Philo investigates the question of the origin and destructibility of the world.[464] He will ultimately contend the world is created and indestructible, yet in much of the essay (including here), Philo will lay out arguments for the opposing view that

---

[462] This is especially asserted by Díez Merino, El suplicio de la cruz, 86–98. Arguments for the pre-Mishnaic antiquity of this text can also be found in Joseph Heinemann, Early Halakhah in the Palestinian Targumim, JJS 25 (1974): 114–122; Joseph Heinemann, The Targum of Ex. XXII,4 and the Ancient Halakha [Hebrew], Tarbis 38 (1969): 294–296 (English summary p. v). Also see Levine, Aramaic Version of Ruth, 60–62.

[463] Text: Cohn / Wendland / Reiter, Philonis Alexandrini opera, 6:79. They report some variation in the manuscripts concerning καταλευομένοις.

[464] The attribution to Philo has been questioned, but most authorities accept this work as Philonic; cf. Colson / Whitaker / Marcus, Philo, 9:171–77; Roger Arnaldez / Jean Pouilloux, De Aeternitate Mundi (Les oeuvres de Philon d'Alexandrie 30; Paris: Cerf, 1969), 12–37; David T. Runia, Philo's *De aeternitate mundi*: The Problem of its Interpretation, VC 35 (1981): 105–151. Cf. James R. Royse, The Spurious Texts of Philo of Alexandria. A Study of Textual Transmission and Corruption with Indexes to the Major Collections to Greek Fragments (ALGH 22; Leiden: Brill, 1991), 145, who considers the text to be authentic, and thus does not treat it.

the world is uncreated and indestructible.[465] This opposing argument proceeds from the way in which things are destroyed – either by internal forces (such as rust on iron) or by external forces (such as cities by fire; see earlier in *Aet.* 20). In similar fashion (as quoted above), humans and other animals die either from internal forces (disease) or external forces (sword, stoning, burning, halter). That list of external causes of death is strikingly similar to the accepted death penalties in the Mishnah (beheading, stoning, burning), save for the last member (hanging on the halter). Philo's other references to a "halter" in contexts of human death implies this comprises a form of suicide by hanging oneself from the neck on a halter/noose.[466] As is the case here, such a suicidal death is also deemed unclean in Philo's *De Mutatione Nominum* 62. Given the striking parallel of three of the four external means of death to the rabbinic capital penalties, one might argue that Philo here imagines hanging from a halter to be a form of capital punishment. However, given the other uses of ἀγχόνη in contexts of suicide, he could equally be imagining a four-fold set of categories concerning the way in which people die (by other's hands and/or by their own). In any case, this text could well show that the four categories of death cataloged by the rabbis had a striking precursor in first-century diaspora Judaism, though with an important variation in the fourth member of the set.

### 3.5.4 Ante Mortem Suspension in Jewish Sources

While some key rabbinic passages oppose "hanging him alive" in the manner employed by the Roman government, still other Jewish texts apparently consider *ante mortem* suspension (in some cases explicitly "crucifixion") to be an acceptable Jewish penalty. These also often connect to Deut 21.

---

[465] That Philo is considering here the views of others is evident from the opening lines of *Aet.* 20 and from the final paragraph in *Aet.* 150 where he states that in later treatises, he plans to refute these positions he just finished describing in this treatise. RUNIA, *Philo's De aeternitate mundi*, 139 also views §§20–149 as depicting views contrary to Philo's own, yet still expressed in Philo's own manner.

[466] The suicide connection is evident in *Mut.* 62; *Spec. Leg.* 3.161. For ἀγχόνη meaning a "halter" that can be used for hanging a person (or a person's soul metaphorically) see also *Post.* 27; *Praem.* 151; *Quis Her.* 269; *Jos.* 150; *Som.* 2.44. Cf. the definition in GEOFFREY W. H. LAMPE, *A Patristic Greek Lexicon* (Oxford: Clarendon, 1961–1968), s.v. Such matters are also discussed in CHAPMAN, *Crucifixion*, 36–37.

## (274) 11QTemple LXIV, 6–13

*Further Notes.* Text, translation and commentary on this second-century B.C. document can be found in No. 22.[467] Here we shall focus on matters that connect with *ante mortem* suspension. As an overview, recall that the tradition of Deut 21:22–23 is modified by the Temple Scroll in four major respects.[468]

First, the types of crime meriting suspension are spelled out in the Temple Scroll in two parallel conditional clauses (either treason involving slandering Israel, surrendering Israel to foreign powers, and evil-doing against Israel; or a Judean abandoning Israel and cursing Israel among the nations for sake of escaping a capital judgment back home). The details of the offense in the second conditional clause has received discussion. Did the person receive the death penalty first and then escape Israel to a foreign land (in short, does the sequence of *wayyiqtol* forms in lines 9–10 present the order of events)? Or does the death penalty clause with its "sin requiring a judgment of death" (albeit listed first in line 9) state the penalty for the following offense (of escaping to the nations and cursing Israel)? The latter option requires that the *waw* on ויברח in line 9 be considered an explicative *waw*. YADIN initially held the first option but later switched to the second.[469] BERNSTEIN argues the second.[470] If the first option is upheld, which seems grammatically more natural for the sequence of *wayyiqtol* forms, then the capital punishment of suspension in 11QTemple LXIV, 10–11 is levied at the offender as a more strenuous form of execution than he was originally to undergo before he escaped and cursed Israel. Thus *ante mortem* suspension would be a very severe (perhaps the most severe) form of Jewish capital punishment known to this author.

Second, following OT precedent (cf. Deut 17:6; 19:15), the number of witnesses is stated (at least two or three are required for a conviction).

Third, the "curse of God" from Deuteronomy 21:23 receives interpretation as a subjective genitive, and possibly as an objective genitive as well. Line 12 says, "those hanged on a tree are cursed by God *and the people*." This would imply a subjective-genitive interpretation to the "curse of God" construct in Deut 21:23, with the remarkable addition of God's people Israel also cursing the suspended person. Yet, it is also notable in line 10 that the offender "curses

---

[467] The passage also occurs in the fragmentary version of the Temple Scroll labeled 4Q524, without significant variation.

[468] A more minor difference between Deut 21:22–23 and 11QTemple concerns the way "you" has shifted from a second person singular ("*you* shall hang him") to a plural; this alters the directive to suspend the criminal towards an even more clearly communal practice. Similarly, there is a shift from Deuteronomy's singular ("you shall not leave *his corpse* on the tree") to 11QTemple's plural ("you shall not leave their corpses on the tree"); this likely stems from how 11QTemple now contains two conditional clauses (rather than the one in Deuteronomy) that combine to depict two types of criminals deserving said punishment.

[469] YADIN, Pesher Nahum, 7; YADIN, Temple Scroll, 1:374.

[470] BERNSTEIN, *Midrash Halakhah* at Qumran?, 149.

my people", and similarly speaks against Israel in line 7. This might imply that the cursing of God's people was essentially a cursing of God himself, i.e., an objective-genitive interpretation. Thus we find evidence that the author overtly follows a subjective-genitive interpretation but may well have simultaneously accepted the objective genitive as a means of determining the criminal act that deserves such a demise. YADIN's later publication suggests something similar.[471] An intriguing and carefully argued proposal from SCHWARTZ contends there is no subjective genitive interpretation in line 12.[472]

Fourth (and most important for our discussion), the order of phrases is switched from Deuteronomy's "he is executed and you hang him on the tree" to "you shall hang him on a tree, and he shall die" (in both lines 8 and 10–11).

That last matter (concerning switching the Deuteronomic phrases) is especially striking in light of the rabbinic tendency to argue that penal suspensions must be *post mortem* based on the phrase order in Deuteronomy (as noted above). Such a switch in order would strongly indicate that the author of the Temple Scroll (and his community) believed hanging up the criminal on a wooden device should be the means of execution. This indeed was the position taken by YADIN when he first published this text.[473] Yet substantial discussion has occurred about this since YADIN's edition. Many see this as a reference to *ante mortem* suspension, even to crucifixion, arising out of an interpretation of Deuteronomy 21.[474] However, there are two major counter-arguments to YADIN's position. First, BAUMGARTEN, drawing on the presumed development of the rabbinic four-fold order of capital punishments, argues in detail that what is intended here is not crucifixion but hanging the

---

[471] YADIN, Temple Scroll, 1:379.

[472] DANIEL R. SCHWARTZ, The Contemners of Judges and Men' (11Q Temple 64:12) [1982–1983], in Studies in the Jewish Background of Christianity (WUNT 60; Tübingen: Mohr Siebeck, 1992), 81–88; originally published in Leshonenu 47 (1982–1983): 18–24. For a brief, though detailed, refutation of SCHWARTZ see CHAPMAN, Crucifixion, 130–132.

[473] YADIN, Pesher Nahum, 9; and YADIN, Temple Scroll, 1:374–378.

[474] Concerning the view that this is *ante mortem* suspension see the earlier references LUIS DÍEZ MERINO, J. MASSYNGBERDE FORD, JOSEPH A. FITZMYER, MARTIN HENGEL, and DAVID J. HALPERIN. Add to these OTTO BETZ, The Death of Choni-Onias in the Light of the Temple Scroll from Qumran, in Jerusalem in the Second Temple Period (FS A. Schalit; ed. A. Oppenheimer, U. Rappaport, and M. Stern; Library of the history of the Yishuv in Eretz-Yisrael; Jerusalem: Yad Izhak Ben-Zvi, 1980), 84–97 (English summary, p. v); OTTO BETZ, Der Tod des Choni-Onias im Licht der Tempelrolle von Qumran: Bemerkungen zu Josephus Antiquitates 14,22–24 [1980], in Jesus der Messias Israels: Aufsätze zur biblischen Theologie (WUNT 42; Tübingen: Mohr Siebeck, 1987), 59–74 ; ÉMILE PUECH, Die Kreuzigung und die altjüdische Tradition, Welt und Umwelt der Bibel 9 (1998): 73–75.

offender on a noose.[475] Note that BAUMGARTEN is not attempting to claim 11QTemple LXIV, 6–13 does not concern *ante mortem* suspension; he instead sets out to discover the precise method of *ante mortem* suspension the author intends. However, BAUMGARTEN's lexical attempt to limit תלה (when used as an *ante mortem* penalty) to "hanging on a noose" involves several problematic steps.[476] (1) As BAUMGARTEN himself observes, צלב is often used in the targumim and rabbinic literature as an equivalent of תלה, yet later Aramaic dialects (esp. Syriac, Christian Palestinian Aramaic, and Mandaic) display how cognates of צלב commonly refer to crucifixion; in fact צלב is only used in the targumim and rabbinic literature for human bodily suspension, and there are many cases where צלב in the rabbinic texts must designate crucifixion (e.g., *m. Yeb.* 16:3; *t. Sanh.* 9:7; *t. Giṭ.* 7[5]:1; *m. Šabb.* 6:10; *m. Ohol.* 3:5; and targumic parallels to each of these). Thus תלה can be rendered with a term (צלב) that often denotes crucifixion. (2) Later Jewish renderings of OT תלה passages often employ crucifixion terminology (e.g., Old Greek of Esth 7:9; Philo, *Jos.* 96–98; *Som.* 2.213; Josephus, *A. J.* 2.73, 77; 11.208, 246, 261, 266–267, 280). (3) Indeed, some key texts that BAUMGARTEN cites for "hanging from a noose" are most plausibly instances of crucifixion (e.g., *b. Sanh.* 34b–35a; 67a). Note also the abbreviated discussion above concerning BAUMGARTEN's views on *Targum Ruth* 1:17. Rather, it is best to understand that the author affirms that some form of *ante mortem* suspension is required, with the precise method (hanging on a noose, impalement, crucifixion) not being sufficiently defined by the context (literary or historical). Second, BERNSTEIN contends that the author of the Temple Scroll was not actually engaging in "halakhic exegesis" of Deuteronomy 21:22–23 but that this text "replaces" Deuteronomy 21 with a legal interpolation drawn from other sources.[477] The degree of continuity with Deut 21:22–23 makes BERNSTEIN's point difficult to sustain, especially because the most expansive material here (in lines 6–10) overtly attempts to define the otherwise vague reference in Deut 21:22 to a "sin bearing a judgment of death."[478] We might well conclude

---

[475] Cf. BAUMGARTEN, Crucifixion; BAUMGARTEN, Hanging. BAUMGARTEN also assumes that Romans employed hanging on a noose and that the Temple Scroll was copying Roman practice. However, it is difficult to adduce examples of Roman use of a noose, aside from cases of suicide, and thus KUHN flatly denies such a Roman practice; KUHN, Bedeutung der Qumrantexte, esp. 180.

[476] For the following see CHAPMAN, Crucifixion, 16–26, 128–129.

[477] BERNSTEIN, *Midrash Halakhah* at Qumran?. See further MOSHE J. BERNSTEIN, כי קללת אלהים תלוי (Deut 21.23): A Study in Early Jewish Exegesis, JQR 74 (1983): 21–45.

[478] See CHAPMAN, Crucifixion, 129–130. Part of the issue here concerns the threshold required to depict an ancient pre-rabbinic author as engaging in "halakhic exegesis." Despite disagreement with SCHWARTZ registered above, SCHWARTZ has usefully sought to spell out how the author of 11QTemple (as do later rabbis) has brought to bear other OT passages (esp. Exod 22:27; Lev 19:16) in his halakic conclusions on Deut 21:22–23 (cf. SCHWARTZ, Contemners).

that the Temple Scroll, written a few centuries before the Tannaitic pronouncements against Jewish practice of *ante mortem* suspension, indicates that the
author (and his audience) readily accepted suspension as a viable means of
execution for the kinds of treasons it describes. This might well find its historical context in Josephus' account that several key Jewish leaders during the
Hasmonean times sought foreign help to attempt to regain (or hold onto) positions of status in Judea.[479]

Given the character of the halakic decisions in the Temple Scroll and the
halakic material in, for example, 4QMMT, some suggest the Temple Scroll is
of Sadducean/Zadokite origin.[480] Yet, scholarly consensus, though not without
significant detractors, has tended to view the Qumran corpus as an Essene collection of documents. With multiple copies of the Temple Scroll now known
at Qumran (and with the care taken to preserve the copy among the relatively
few documents in cave 11), we may assume such sectarians found the Temple
Scroll valuable. The sectarian dimension to this document has led some to
conclude that the legislation in 11QTemple LXIV, which accepts *ante mortem*
suspension, is itself sectarian. We should certainly be cautious about generali-
zing any conclusions here to the whole of early Judaism. More data points are
needed.

**(275)** Philo, *De Specialibus Legibus* 3.151–152

ἐπεὶ δ᾽ ὅρον οὐκ ἔχουσιν οἱ πονηροὶ τὰς φύσεις τοῦ πλημμελεῖν, ἀλλ᾽ ἀεὶ
μεγαλουργοῦσι προσυπερβάλλοντες καὶ τὰς κακίας ἐπιτείνουσι καὶ διαίρουσι
πρὸς τὸ ἄμετρον καὶ ἀπερίγραφον, μυρίους μὲν θανάτους, εἴπερ οἷόν τε ἦν,
ὥρισεν ἂν κατ᾽ αὐτῶν ὁ νομοθέτης· ἐπεὶ δὲ τοῦτ᾽ οὐκ ἐνεδέχετο, τιμωρίαν
ἄλλην προσδιατάττεται κελεύων τοὺς ἀνελόντας ἀνασκολοπίζεσθαι. [152] καὶ
τοῦτο προστάξας ἀνατρέχει πάλιν ἐπὶ τὴν αὐτοῦ φιλανθρωπίαν, ἡμερούμενος
πρὸς τοὺς ἀνήμερα εἰργασμένους, καί φησι· μὴ ἐπιδυέτω ὁ ἥλιος ἀνεσκολο-
πισμένοις, ἀλλ᾽ ἐπικρυπτέσθωσαν γῇ πρὸ δύσεως καθαιρεθέντες. ἦν γὰρ
ἀναγκαῖον τοὺς ἅπασι τοῖς μέρεσι τοῦ κόσμου πολεμίους μετεωρίσαντας εἰς
τοὐμφανὲς ἐπιδείξασθαι μὲν αὐτοὺς ἡλίῳ καὶ οὐρανῷ καὶ ἀέρι καὶ ὕδατι καὶ
γῇ κολασθέντας, πάλιν δὲ εἰς τὸν νεκρῶν χῶρον ὑποσῦραί τε καὶ καταχῶσαι,
ὅπως μὴ τὰ ὑπὲρ γῆν μιαίνωσι.

---

[479] Commentators will occasionally correlate the historical context of 11QTemple LXIV
with crucifixions under Alexander Jannaeus (along with 4QpNahum) or possibly the persecutions by Alcimus; on these episodes, see further below. Such a correlation is possible (especially in the case of 4QpNahum), but one can also recall the attempted alignments of many
other Jewish leaders with Seleucid and/or Ptolemaic powers going back to before the
Maccabean revolt and afterwards.

[480] Note the references to SCHIFFMAN in the discussion of the several 11QTemple passages
discussed in section 1.3.

*Translation.* And, since evil-doers do not limit their natures to offend, but they always perform immense things by exceeding [the bounds], and their wickedness they heighten and determine beyond any measure and limit, the lawgiver (if indeed it was possible) would on the one hand appoint myriads of deaths against them; but, since this was not possible, He ordained besides another punishment, commanding those who took human life to be crucified. [152] And, after ordering this, He hastens again to his philanthropy, being subdued toward those who had worked savage acts; and He says, "Do not let the sun set upon those who have been crucified, but let them be concealed in the earth, having been taken down before sunset." For it was necessary to raise up the enemies with respect to all the parts of the cosmos, in order that they on the one hand be displayed publicly to sun and heaven and air and water and earth as punished, and again to drag [them] down to the place of the dead and also to bury [them], in order that they not defile the things above the earth.

*Commentary.*[481] Philo of Alexandria was famed for his use of Stoic categories in his efforts to explain the reasonableness, even rational perfection, of the Jewish Scriptures. In *De Specialibus Legibus,* he is explaining the profound logic of the divine Lawgiver, who presented the Israelites with his Law. Although the text here only rarely copies verbatim the LXX Greek of Deut 21:22–23, it is nevertheless clear that the Deuteronomic text serves as the basis for Philo's exposition as he defends the justice and philanthropy of God; note the references to the need to bury before sunset, the context of public suspension, and the concern not to defile the land. Philo employs ἀνασκολοπίζω (translated as "crucify") as the verb depicting the suspension of the criminals.[482] This verb is Philo's standard vocabulary for crucifixion (e.g., *Flacc.* 83–84). In any case, it would appear this suspension is the means of execution, substituting for the "myriad of deaths" that would otherwise be justified (were such a repetition of deaths possible). Crucifixion here works particularly well since its prolonged and painful nature makes it seem as though the criminal is suffering many deaths at once. Hence Philo interprets Deut 21:22–23 as God commanding (κελεύων) that criminals be crucified. The specific nature of the crime of the πονηροί ("evil-doers") is further delimited by τοὺς ἀνελόντας ("those who take human life") at the end of 3.151 and by the discussion of the sixth commandment against murder in the surrounding context (3.150,153). Thus Philo believes murderers deserve such a demise. He depicts the rational purpose of such a suspension: It displays to the heavens and the earthly ele-

---

[481] Text: COHN / WENDLAND / REITER, Philonis Alexandrini opera, 5:192–193.

[482] In contrast to the view argued here, DOGNIEZ and HARL, without argument, distance this verb in Philo's text from meaning "crucifixion"; GILLES DOGNIEZ and MARGUERITE HARL, La Bible d'Alexandrie. Vol. 5: Le Deutéronome. Traduction du texte grec de la Septante, introduction et notes (Paris: Cerf, 1992), 248.

ments the just execution of the criminal. And Philo conceives of such suspensions as public, not just so people will look on them but so that creation itself will witness the person hung aloft. Yet burial too is necessary because the corpse bears some kind of contagion (perhaps the curse of God) that could defile everything above the earth unless it is contained underground.

### 3.5.5 Historical Examples

There are several clear examples of Jewish leaders engaging in *ante mortem* suspension, especially Alexander Jannaeus and Simeon b. Shetach, and of others, looking on such suspensions with some approval (4QpNahum) or even handing the person over to Roman officials who will execute them on a cross (R. Eleazar b. Simeon). Alexander Jannaeus, despite his unpopularity, was nevertheless both high priest and king. And Simeon b. Shetach was viewed as an honored forerunner of rabbinic Judaism (even one of the *Zugot*).

We might add that various Jewish authors recount the lives of others of Jewish descent who employed or endorsed such methods of execution, yet these individuals are often considered to have rejected their Jewish heritage. Here, we might especially point to Tiberius Iulius Alexander, a nephew of Philo of Alexandria and a man who, while serving as procurator of Judea (c. A.D. 46–48), crucified the sons of Judas the Galilean (Josephus, *A. J.* 20.102). However, Tiberius is portrayed in Josephus as having left his Jewish roots and having become essentially Roman (see discussion in section 3.7). More pertinent to our study, later rabbinic texts portray Jaķim of Ẓeroroth mocking Jose b. Joezer as Jose was led to the cross. In any case, these individuals (standing as they do on the periphery of Judaism at best) can only be tangential to other examples of Jewish suspensions.

### (276) *Bereshit Rabbah* 65:22

יקים איש צרורות היה בן אחותו של ר' יוסי בן יועזר איש צרידה והוה רכיב סוסיה, אזל קמי
שריתא אזל למצטלבה, אמר ליה חמי סוסי דארכבי מרי וחמי סוסך דארכבך מרך, אמר ליה אם
כך למכעיסיו קל וחומר לעושי רצונו, אמר לו ועשה אדם רצונו יותר ממך, אמר לו ואם כך
לעושי רצונו קל וחומר למכעיסיו, נכנס בו הדבר כארס שלחכנה, הלך וקיים בו ארבע מיתות
בית דין סקילה שריפה הרג וחנק, מה עשה הביא קורה ונעצה בארץ ועשה סביבה גדר וקשר בה
נינייא [ועשה מדורה לפניה ונעץ את החרב באמצע נתלה בקורה נפסקה נינייא] ונחנק, קידמתו
החרב ונהפך עליו גדר ונשרף, נתנמנם יוסי בן יועזר וראה את מיטתו פורחה באויר, אמר בשעה
קלה קידמני זה לגן עדן

*Translation.* Jaķim of Ẓeroroth was the nephew of R. Jose b. Joezer of Ẓere-
dah. Riding on a horse he [Jaķim] went before the beam on which he [R. Jose]

was to be hanged [i.e., crucified], and taunted him: 'See the horse on which my master has let me ride, and the horse upon which your Master has made you ride.' 'If it is so with those who anger Him, how much more with those who do His will,' he [R. Jose] replied. 'Has then any man done His will more than thou?' he [Jakim] jeered. 'If it is thus with those who do His will, how much more with those who anger Him,' he [R. Jose] retorted.

This pierced him [Jakim] like the poison of a snake, and he went and subjected himself to the four modes of execution inflicted by the Beth Din: stoning, burning, decapitation, and strangulation. What did he do? He took a post and planted it in the earth, raised a wall of stones around it and tied a cord to it. He made a fire in front of it and fixed a sword in the middle [of the post]. He hanged himself on the post, the cord was burnt through and he was strangled. The sword caught him, while the wall [of stones] fell upon him and he was burnt. Jose b. Joezer of Zeredah fell into a doze and saw his [Jakim's] bier flying in the air. 'By a little while he has preceded me into the Garden of Eden,' said he.

*Commentary*.[483] This is a later rabbinic tradition, appearing in the c. fifth-century A.D. *Genesis Rabbah* (at least 500 years after the purported events). A similar text occurs in the medieval *Midrash Tehillim* (on Psalm 11:7).[484] This narrative depicts the suspension death of the esteemed rabbi Jose b. Joezer (one of the first rabbis listed among the *zugot*, cf. *m. Abot* 1:4), his being mocked by his nephew Jakim, and Jakim's subsequent penitent suicide by means of all four of the sanctioned rabbinic means of execution. Each of these features deserves some comment.

The execution of Jose b. Joezer appears in this source as a prolonged *ante mortem* suspension, likely a crucifixion. The midrash employs צלב,[485] a term used exclusively in early rabbinic writings for human bodily suspension (and often associated with crucifixion in rabbinic writing). The author depicts a procession to the place of execution with beam in tow (again, a common feature of crucifixions). Jakim puns that Jose will "ride" that beam. Moreover, the final sentences likely portray Jose falling in and out of a doze while still attached to the beam, thus implying the suspension was prolonged and *ante mortem*. In the context of Late Antiquity, the audience would naturally pre-

---

[483] Text: J. THEODOR ALBECK and HANOKH ALBECK, Midrash Bereshit Rabba. Critical Edition with Notes and Commentary (3 vols.; Berlin: Poppelauer, 1912–1936), 742–44. Translation HARRY FREEDMAN, Midrash Rabbah: Genesis (2 vols.; London: Soncino, 1939).

[484] A convenient translation of the *Midrash Tehillim* text may be found in WILLIAM G. BRAUDE, The Midrash on Psalms (Yale Judaica 13; New Haven: Yale University Press, 1959), 1:166–167.

[485] The *hithpael* (with metathesis of the sibilant) form למצטלבה or למצטלבא here was confused in the manuscripts (see Theodore and ALBECK and ALBECK, Midrash Bereshit Rabba, 742), but the meaning and origin of the word in צלב is clear enough; see JASTROW, Dictionary, s.v. מצטבלה.

sume such a death occurred on something shaped like a Roman *crux* (or perhaps a Byzantine *furca*). The source is late, and the current version has legendary elements, but it could plausibly represent the kind of death the Seleucids were known to inflict on Jewish leaders who did not support their regime.

Jakim's Jewish lineage is clear in this passage – after all he is the nephew of Jose. Jakim (*aka* Jakum) may well refer to the Jewish high-priest Alcimus, who aligned himself with the Seleucids in opposition to the Hasmoneans.[486] Alcimus was appointed under Demetrius I Soter, and a Seleucid army under Bacchides guaranteed his installment in office (1 Macc 7:5–11). After initially making a peaceful appeal to the scribes and Hasideans, he then slaughtered 60 of them in a single day (1 Macc 7:12–18). A second army under Nicanor also was required to assert Alcimus' priestly control (1 Macc 7:21ff.; cf. slightly varying traditions in 2 Macc 14:3–14; 14:26) and a further Seleucid expedition on behalf of Alcimus was made in 1 Macc 9:1ff. However, in contrast to the text above, the death of Alcimus is depicted in 1 Maccabees as a death of great agony after being struck by God with dumbness and paralysis as divine recompense for his attempt to destroy a wall of the Temple (1 Macc 9:54–57).[487] Therefore, if Jakim = Alcimus, then Jakim's mode of death described in *Bereshit Rabbah* would presumably be a later invention, albeit one that trades on the tradition that Jakim was a vicious opponent of the faithful Hasideans (the group with whom the rabbis identified).

E. STAUFFER has intriguingly argued that this represents the first recorded crucifixion ordered by a Jewish leader (Alcimus), with Jakim's mocking of Jose indicating Alcimus' initiation of the penalty.[488] However, the legendary aspect of Jakim's death (and the late date of the text) makes it likely that legendary material has informed this story, so it is difficult to vouch for the historicity of the details of Jakim's actions. Our earliest sources (1–2 Macc and Josephus' *Antiquities*) certainly do not record any such crucifixion initiated by Alcimus.[489] Also, the text itself does not say Jakim ordered the punishment

---

[486] See Josephus, *A. J.* 12.385: "And the high priest after the death of Menelaus was Alcimus, who was also called Jakimos" (ἀρχιερεὺς δὲ ἐγένετο μετὰ τὸν Μενελάου θάνατον Ἄλκιμος ὁ καὶ Ἰάκιμος κληθείς). Josephus elsewhere says that this "Jakimos was of the Aaronic line but not of the high priestly house (*A. J.* 20.235; cf. 12.386). See further 1 Macc 7–9; 2 Macc 14. The revised SCHÜRER argues the connection of Alcimus and Jakim (also with reference to those manuscripts of 1 and 2 Maccabees that insert ὁ καὶ Ἰάκιμος); see SCHÜRER, History, 1:168. NEUSNER rejects the identification (but without argument); NEUSNER, Rabbinic Traditions about the Pharisees, 1:77. The identification is, however, assumed in the articles on "Alcimus" in the Jewish Encyclopedia and the Encyclopaedia Judaica.

[487] Josephus also, likely drawing on 1 Maccabees, says Alcimus was struck by God, unable to speak, and died in torment after several days (*A. J.* 12.413). Alcimus' death is further mentioned, without elaboration, in Josephus, *A. J.* 20.237.

[488] Cf. STAUFFER, Jerusalem und Rom, 124–125, 128–132. STAUFFER connects this passage with Alcimus' execution of 60 Hasideans, and he correlates the crucifixions in the Nahum Pesher with this event.

(even if he enjoyed the event). What can be said with greater certainty is that later rabbinic tradition had no difficulty portraying a famous Jewish heretical high priest as readily endorsing the Seleucid-era crucifixion of a fellow countryman. The text also points to the possibility of entering into the heavenly world to come for a penitent person (even for one as awful as Jaḳim).

It is striking how this rabbinic text from Late Antiquity makes the story cohere with the four accepted methods of rabbinic capital punishment. Jaḳim's suicide is depicted as a creative attempt to implement all four methods simultaneously. Nevertheless (as noted in a footnote above), the creativity required for such a single-handed simultaneous suicide will naturally necessitate that Jaḳim's methods diverge from the accepted forms of each of the four punishments.[490] Therefore, one should not conclude from this creative account that the rabbinic penalty of strangulation was originally produced by hanging from the neck while attached to a post.[491]

Finally, we should observe key perceptions of suspension/crucifixion embedded in the passage. Such suspensions are public activities that are cause for mocking and derision. The person spent considerable time hung up on the device, even falling in and out of consciousness. Finally, in the case of such a respected rabbinic figure, such an undeserved harsh death becomes an instance of martyrdom.[492]

**(277)** Josephus, *Antiquitates judaicae* 13.380–381, 383

κατακλείσας δὲ τοὺς δυνατωτάτους αὐτῶν ἐν Βαιθομμει πόλει ἐπολιόρκει, λαβὼν δὲ τὴν πόλιν καὶ γενόμενος ἐγκρατὴς αὐτῶν ἀνήγαγεν εἰς Ἱεροσόλυμα καὶ πάντων ὠμότατον ἔργον ἔδρασεν· ἑστιώμενος γὰρ ἐν ἀπόπτῳ μετὰ τῶν παλλακίδων ἀνασταυρῶσαι προσέταξεν αὐτῶν ὡς ὀκτακοσίους, τοὺς δὲ παῖδας αὐτῶν καὶ τὰς γυναῖκας ἔτι ζώντων παρὰ τὰς ἐκείνων ὄψεις ἀπέσφαττεν, [381]ὑπὲρ μὲν ὧν ἠδίκητο ἀμυνόμενος, ἄλλως δὲ ὑπὲρ ἄνθρωπον ταύτην εἰσ-

---

[489] This observation is made more significant when we consider that these sources "show no fondness for Alcimus and thus have no reason to hide his atrocities" (CHAPMAN, Crucifixion, 52). Note especially that Josephus records just such crucifixions at the hand of Alexander Jannaeus (see *A. J.* 13.380–381 below), though not in *A. J.* 12.399–400 concerning Alcimus.

[490] Thus in this passage: stoning comes by stones collapsing onto him rather than being thrown off a precipice; burning does not involve a burning piece of metal inserted in his mouth, as in the rabbinic method; the sword cuts or pierces him as he falls, not a beheading; and he is strangled via the cord on a post, not one pulled by the two witnesses.

[491] Note the interaction above concerning BAUMGARTEN's views on *Targum Ruth* 1:17.

[492] Observe that in the medieval *Midrash Tehillim* text, the above passage is prefaced by a remark that this occurred in a time of "religious persecution." Such martyrdom implications are also observed by NEUSNER, Rabbinic Traditions about the Pharisees, 1:77; JAN W. VAN HENTEN and FRIEDRICH AVEMARIE, Martyrdom and Noble Death: Selected Texts from Graeco-Roman, Jewish, and Christian Antiquity (Context of Early Christianity; London: Routledge, 2002), 134–135, 142–144.

πραττόμενος τὴν δίκην ... ³⁸³ἀλλ' [οὖν οὐκ] ἐπιτηδείως δοκεῖ ταῦτα δρᾶσαι, ὥστε διὰ τὴν τῆς ὠμότητος ὑπερβολὴν ἐπικληθῆναι αὐτὸν ὑπὸ τῶν Ἰουδαίων Θρακίδαν. οἱ δ' ἀντιστασιῶται αὐτοῦ τὸ πλῆθος ὄντες περὶ ὀκτακισχιλίους φεύγουσιν νυκτὸς καὶ παρ' ὃν ἔζη χρόνον Ἀλέξανδρος ἦσαν ἐν τῇ φυγῇ.

*Translation.* And having shut up the most powerful of these in the city of Bethome, he [Alexander Jannaeus] besieged it; and after taking the city and coming in possession of them, he led them up to Jerusalem and did the most savage work of all. For, while feasting in a conspicuous place with his concubines, he ordered approximately eight hundred of them to be crucified, and he cut the throats of their children and wives before the eyes of those who were still living, ³⁸¹on account of whom he had on the one hand been injured while defending himself, but otherwise he inhumanely exacted for himself this punishment ... ³⁸³But still, it does not seem that he did these things suitably, so that on account of the excess of this most savage act, he is called Thracidas by the Jews. And the multitude, those who had opposed him, being around eight thousand, fled during the night; and during the time Alexander lived they were in exile.

*Commentary.*⁴⁹³ This represents our first certain post-biblical account of a Jewish person employing *ante mortem* suspension, here on a reportedly mammoth scale.⁴⁹⁴ Josephus, writing at the turn of the first to second century A.D., records these events from the reign of the Hasmonean king Alexander Jannaeus (103–76 B.C.).⁴⁹⁵ A parallel account appears in Josephus, *B. J.* 1.96– 97 (see No. 30), and Josephus makes retrospective mention of the public *ante mortem* suspension of these 800 (in *B. J.* 1.113 and *A. J.* 13.410). Preceding our passage, Josephus narrated the seditious nature (στασιασάντων) of the Jewish people against Alexander (*A. J.* 13.372ff.): They pelted him with citrons at the Festival of Sukkoth (Booths/Tabernacles)⁴⁹⁶ and reviled his ancestry, to which he responded by slaying 6,000 (*A. J.* 13.372–373; *B. J.* 1.88–89). The reviling of Alexander's ancestry deserves some comment since

---

⁴⁹³ Text: NIESE, Flavii Josephi Opera, 3:221–222. Multiple spellings for Βαιθομμει (sic) appear in the manuscripts.

⁴⁹⁴ As noted earlier here in 3.5.5, STAUFFER argues that the high priest Alcimus crucified others; STAUFFER, Jerusalem und Rom, 124–125, 128–32. We suggested that any such connection between Alcimus and crucifixion is uncertain.

⁴⁹⁵ On the life of Alexander Jannaeus, and these events, cf. SCHÜRER, History, 1:219–228.

⁴⁹⁶ *m. Sukk.* 4:9 recalls that citrons were thrown at a high priest, quite possibly Alexander, for pouring the water-libation of Sukkoth on his feet. This may represent a halakic difference or a simple error on the priest's part. The Bavli in a *baraita* attributes the same act to a Boethusian (*b. Sukk.* 48b–49a), which may imply a halakic difference was at stake; the Boethusians in rabbinic tradition being a heretical group associated with the Sadducees. Such groups are confused at times in rabbinic tradition. The Yerushalmi recalls rabbinic authorities attributing this act of water pouring on the feet to the same Sadducean priest who wrongly performed the burning of the red cow and the rites of the Day of Atonement (*y. Sukk.* 4:6 [54d]).

this would be of great consequence for whether he could have validly served as high priest. High priests had to be fully Jewish and of the priestly line of Aaron; some would further say of the line of Zadok. Josephus does not mention this issue in *B. J.* 1.88, but he does recollect the following concerning Alexander in *A. J.* 13.372: προσεξελοιδόρησαν δ' αὐτὸν ὡς ἐξ αἰχμαλώτων γεγονότα καὶ τῆς τιμῆς καὶ τοῦ θύειν ἀνάξιον ("and they reviled him as having been from captives and unworthy of honor and unworthy to make sacrifice"). A much later tradition in the Bavli (*b. Qidd.* 66a), yet also a *baraita* attributed to pre-Mishnaic authorities, says of King Yannai that while feasting after conquering 60 towns, he was encouraged by a worthless fellow (Eleazar b. Poirah) to challenge the Pharisees to see whether they believed him worthy of serving as both priest and king. To this challenge, Judah b. Gedidiah replied that Yannai could be king but not high priest since his mother had been a captive in Modiim. Captive women were considered to have been raped, and their offspring were suspect, unless testimony could be made to the contrary; cf. *m. Ketub.* 2:5–6. This tradition is strikingly similar to Josephus' statement that the Jews reviled Alexander's ancestry as "from captives." The Bavli (*b. Qidd.* 66a) continues the story by recording that the worthless Eleazar consequently counseled Yannai to destroy the Sages who opposed his high priesthood. Alexander did indeed sorely oppress them until Simeon b. Shetach came and restored the Torah. According to Josephus, similar questions arose from a man named Eleazar concerning the ancestry of John Hyrcanus I (*A. J.* 13.288–298), which Hyrcanus (mis-)attributed to the common opinion of the Pharisees; this caused Hyrcanus to join the Sadducees. SCHÜRER suggests that *b. Qidd.* 66a then mistakenly ascribes earlier events under Hyrcanus to Yannai.[497] Rabbinic tradition in *b. Qidd.* 66a is firm on the attribution to Yannai, mentioning not only his name but also that of Simeon b. Shetach.

After Alexander's loss in battle against Obedas and retreat to Jerusalem, the people insulted him; in the ensuing battles with his fellow Jews, Alexander (according to Josephus) slew "no less than 50,000" of them over the course of six years (*B. J.* 1.90–91; cf. *A. J.* 13.375–376). Finally, many of his Jewish opponents aligned with Demetrius III Eucaerus, who had substantial initial success against Alexander but later abandoned the field when he saw Jews flock back to Alexander's side (*A. J.* 13.376–379; *B. J.* 1.92–95).[498] In return, Alexander slew "many" (πολλοί) of his fellow Jews in the ensuing battles (*A. J.* 13.379).[499]

---

[497] SCHÜRER, History, 1:214n, 223n.

[498] Based on existing coinage of Demetrius, which was replaced in 87/6 B.C. by the coins of Antiochus XII, the revised SCHÜRER dates this event to about 88 B.C.; SCHÜRER, History, 1:224. Josephus cynically calls Demetrius Ἄκαιρον ("the Ill-timed") instead of Εὔκαιρος ("the Well-timed"); cf. *B. J.* 1.92 and *A. J.* 13.376.

[499] Josephus states in *B. J.* 1.96 that he slew most of those remaining (μέχρι πλείστους ἀποκτείνας τοὺς λοιπούς) during the course of the war after Demetrius left.

The text records how Alexander besieged his remaining Jewish opponents,[500] eventually capturing them and leading them back to Jerusalem for a mass crucifixion. Some have questioned whether ἀνασταυρῶσαι should be translated as "crucify".[501] Yet this does appear to be the best translation given that many of the suspended victims apparently were still alive to see their wives and children slain (also in *B. J*. 1.97), the text refers solely to their suspension (implying it was the means of death since no other form of execution is mentioned), and this is Josephus' typical word for the comparable Roman penalty.[502] Thus Josephus' Roman readers would likely have envisioned suspension on the kind of cross/*stauros* in use in their day.

Josephus' perspective on these executions is fairly vehement. This was "the most savage" of all Alexander's acts (πάντων ὠμότατον ἔργον in *A. J*. 13.380) and it was "on account of the excess of this most savage act" (διὰ τὴν τῆς ὠμότητος ὑπερβολὴν in *A. J*. 13.383) that Alexander came to be called Thracidas (Θρακίδαν).[503] The act was inhumane (ὑπὲρ ἄνθρωπον in 13.380).

---

[500] The name of the besieged city is Bemeselis (Βεμέσελιν πόλιν) in *B. J*. 1.96 and Bethome (Βαιθομμει πόλει) in *A. J*. 13.380. SCHÜRER, History, 1:224n suggests this may have been located at Beth ha-Melekh approximately 10 miles north-east of Samaria.

[501] See esp. GUILLET, Les 800, who argues that impalement is more likely based on similar vocabulary in Herodotus, Thucydides and Plato. Yet even GUILLET concedes Polybius and Plutarch employ such terminology for crucifixion (and these authors are closer to the era of Josephus). SAMUELSSON, Crucifixion, 95–111, though he states there are "no firm crucifixion accounts in the *corpus Josepheum*" (111), apparently does allow that the reference to still-living suspension victims in this passage *may* count toward information about crucifixion (111, cf. 102–103).

[502] Other suspension penalties, esp. hanging and impalement, should have produced quick deaths, not allowing the "living" suspended victims to see their loved ones be slaughtered. While Josephus can speak of the dead suspended on crosses (e.g., *A. J*. 6.374), other key accounts in Josephus inform us of living persons suspended for extended times until dead (e.g., *Vita* 420–421; *A. J*. 12.256; also cf. *A. J*. 11.267; 19.94; *B. J*. 3.321). Multiple examples from Josephus of Roman suspensions are found below (3.7). Such reports would have certainly been deemed to be "crucifixions" by the Romans, whether or not they completely conform to our modern preconceptions of the cross.

[503] From context, this term is clearly intended as a slur referring to Alexander's savagery. Others have suggested its connection to the Thracians. However, only limited data exists on the term outside this passage. TLG offers four other items: Diodorus Siculus speaks to a group at Delphi who are known by this eponym (τούς τε Θρακίδας καλουμένους τῶν Δελφῶν in *Bib. hist*. 16.24.3); Aelius Herodianus (second-century A.D. grammarian) includes it twice in a list of names, in *De prosodia catholica* (AUGUST LENTZ, Herodian De Prosodia Catholica [Grammatici Graeci III.1; Leipzig: Teubner, 1867], 54) and in Περὶ κλίσεως ὀ νομάτων (AUGUST LENTZ, Herodian Περὶ Κλίσεως Ὀνομάτων [Grammatici Graeci III.2; Leipzig: Teubner, 1870], 636); and the 8–9th century A.D. chronicler Georgius Syncellus (*Ecloga chronographica*; ALDEN A. MOSSHAMMER, Georgii Syncelli Ecloga chronographica [Bibliotheca Scriptorum Graecorum et Romanorum Teubneriana; Leipzig: Teubner, 1984], 354), presumably indebted to Josephus, either directly or through his sources, says of Alexander Jannaeus: οἱ δὲ μισοῦντες Θρᾳκιδᾶν ὡς ἀδικώτατον ("Those who hated [him called him] Thrakidas as the most unjust"; bracketed words supplied from previous clause).

And in Josephus' *Jewish War* he intones that Alexander's "fury became so extreme that his savagery progressed to impiety" (προύκοψεν δὲ αὐτῷ δι' ὑπερβολὴν ὀργῆς εἰς ἀσέβειαν τὸ τῆς ὠμότητος in *B. J.* 1.97). The word "impiety" (ἀσέβεια) was an especially caustic anti-religious remark in both Roman and Jewish thought. And Josephus further implicitly critiques Alexander, who was looking down upon the scene (as *B. J.* 1.97 states; cf. *A. J.* 13.380) "while drinking and reclining with his concubines" (καὶ ταῦτα πίνων καὶ συγκατακείμενος ταῖς παλλακίσιν ἀφεώρα).

Nevertheless, in *Antiquities* (though less so in the *Jewish War*) Josephus can also convey Alexander's viewpoint concerning why Alexander may have felt justified to exact such vengeance against his Jewish enemies: He had after all "been injured" (*A. J.* 13.381), his life and kingdom had been imperiled (13.381), they had called upon Judea's enemy Demetrius (and perhaps others) in their fight with him (13.381), they had made him give up territory (which he had previously won) to other nations (13.382), and they had brought upon him a "myriad" of outrages and abuse (13.382). Still, even given these offenses, Josephus' final verdict is that such a mass crucifixion was "the most savage" act imaginable.

A substantial scholarly discussion has gone into determining who were the "approximately 800" victims of crucifixion. Often they have been considered Pharisees,[504] and this has become important for the study of the Nahum Pesher (see next text below). Josephus himself, however, never makes that identification in the passages under discussion; rather, he just calls them "the rest of the multitude" (τό γε λοιπὸν πλῆθος; *B. J.* 1.96) and "the most powerful" (τοὺς δυνατωτάτους; *A. J.* 13.380), and he indicates their Jewish descent (cf. *A. J.* 13.376, 379; cf. *B. J.* 1.92).[505] Nevertheless, Josephus portrays the Hasmonean kings, starting with John Hyrcanus I (Alexander's father), as siding with the Sadducees and opposing the Pharisees, who nevertheless have the multitude on their side (*A. J.* 13.288–298).[506] Josephus also recalls that on his deathbed, Alexander instructed his wife Alexandra to make friends with his enemies the Pharisees, and thus win over the populace (*A. J.* 13.400–406; *B. J.* 1.107–108).[507] Alexandra follows his advice, and the Pharisees, having

---

[504] Thus HENGEL, Crucifixion, 84 will simply speak of Alexander's crucifixion of "800 Pharisees" although he is more guarded in the later French edition ("probablement Pharisiens"; HENGEL, La crucifixion, 106).

[505] On this basis, RABIN rejects an identification of the 800 with the Pharisees; CHAIM RABIN, Alexander Jannaeus and the Pharisees, JJS 7 (1956): 3–11.

[506] In Herod's day, the Pharisees were also said to oppose kings to the point of battle (Josephus, *A. J.* 17.41), with the result that Herod slaughtered many of them (17.44, 46).

[507] Pharisees" (τοῖς Φαρισαίοις ἐξουσίαν τινὰ παρασχεῖν; *A. J.* 13.401) since they have the ability to hinder whom they hate and to help their friends, especially because the multitude believes the bad things they say about others. Most importantly, "and [Alexander] stated that he had given offense to the nation on account of these [Pharisees], who had been injured by him" (αὐτόν τε προσκροῦσαι τῷ ἔθνει διὰ τούτους ἔλεγεν ὑβρισθέντας ὑπ' αὐτοῦ; *A. J.*

been granted immense power by Alexandra, inflict vengeance by executing those who had previously counseled Alexander to crucify the 800 (*B. J.* 1.113; *A. J.* 13. 410).[508] Later rabbinic traditions further portray King Yannai (Jannaeus) as putting to death the rabbinic sages (who are at times strongly connected to the Pharisees) and allying himself with the Sadducees.[509] Nevertheless, the numbers killed by Alexander are formidable, not just the 800 but also the 6,000 and the 50,000. Even given Josephus' tendency to inflate such figures, it is unlikely the Pharisees constituted all (or even a substantial portion) of those slaughtered by Alexander. Rather, the Pharisees are presented in Josephus as relatively small in number,[510] but they are nonetheless large in their influence over the people (e.g. *A. J.* 13.288, 298). This presentation is also evident in his account of Alexander's deathbed advice; it is what the Pharisees *say* that gives them such sway over the populace (*A. J.* 13.402; cf. 18.15). So, we can fairly definitively conclude that the Pharisees strongly sympathized with the crucified 800 (cf. *A.J.* 13.410), and we can likely presume that some (maybe many) of these 800 had official allegiance to the Phar-

---

13.402). Cf. CHAPMAN, Crucifixion, 56 regarding the reason for Alexander's counsel to Alexandra that she should offer to leave his body unburied (13.403). This could be a *quid pro quo* reference to the 800 crucified (and presumably unburied); in return Alexandra offers to leave unburied their executioner. Yet in Josephus, Alexander is confident the Pharisees will still bury him, possibly because he knew of the Pharisee's legal insistence on burial and understood that their lust for power would lead them to eulogize him instead, as they did in 13.406.

[508] *B. J.* 1.113: Διογένην γοῦν τινα τῶν ἐπισήμων φίλον Ἀλεξάνδρῳ γεγενημένον κτείνουσιν αὐτοὶ σύμβουλον ἐγκαλοῦντες γεγονέναι περὶ τῶν ἀνασταυρωθέντων ὑπὸ τοῦ βασιλέως ὀκτακοσίων. ἐνῆγον δὲ τὴν Ἀλεξάνδραν εἰς τὸ καὶ τοὺς ἄλλους διαχειρίσασθαι τῶν παροξυνάντων ἐπ’ ἐκείνους τὸν Ἀλέξανδρον· ἐνδιδούσης δ’ ὑπὸ δεισιδαιμονίας ἀνήρουν οὓς ἐθέλοιεν αὐτοί. "Thus at least they slew Diogenes, one of the distinguished men (having been a friend to Alexander), charging him with having been an advisor concerning the 800 who had been crucified by the king. And they urged Alexandra in order that the others also may be slain who had provoked Alexander against them; and [as she] under religious feeling permitted [this], they killed whom they wished." *A. J.* 13.410: ἠρέμει δ’ ἡ χώρα πᾶσα πάρεξ τῶν Φαρισαίων· οὗτοι γὰρ ἐπετάρασσον τὴν βασίλειαν πείθοντες, ὅπως κτείνειεν τοὺς Ἀλεξάνδρῳ παραινέσαντας ἀνελεῖν τοὺς ὀκτακοσίους. εἶτα αὐτοὶ τούτων ἕνα σφάττουσιν Διογένην καὶ μετ’ αὐτὸν ἄλλους ἐπ’ ἄλλοις ("And all the country was quiet except the Pharisees: for these were troubling the queen by prevailing upon [her], in order that she might kill those who advised Alexander to kill the 800. Then they slew one of these, Diogenes, and after him others upon others"). Josephus later suggests that women are particularly susceptible to the Pharisees' religious teaching (*A. J.* 17.41).

[509] Note the earlier footnote on the *baraita* in *b. Qidd.* 66a, which records the Pharisaic rejection of Yannai and his putting the Sages to death. In *b. Ber.* 48a and b. *Soṭah* 47a there is also mention of Yannai killing the rabbis. For Yannai's association with the Sadducees, this is a probable inference from *b. Ber.* 29a. Schiffman argues *m. Sukk.* 4:9 and *b. Qidd.* 66a (which he mislabels 61a) help connect the 800 to the Pharisees; see LAWRENCE H. SCHIFFMAN, Pharisees and Sadducees in *Pesher Nahum*, in Minḥah le-Naḥum. Biblical and Other Studies (FS Nahum M. Sarna; ed. M. Brettler and M. Fishbane; JSOTSup 154; Sheffield: JSOT Press, 1993), 272–290, esp. 275–279.

[510] In *A. J.* 17.42 he puts their numbers at 6,000 total under the time of Herod the Great.

isees. But that number may well have included Jewish people who simply were happy to act in rebellion against Alexander without a formal affiliation to the Pharisees. Yet from afar (say from the standpoint of 4QpNahum), it would have been possible to assume some connection between the Pharisees and the crucified.

According to Josephus, Alexander certainly did not act on his own in producing such crucifixions, rather he was advised to do so (cf. *A. J.* 13.410; *B. J.* 1.113). Thus Alexander, the Jewish high priest and king, and his party clearly viewed such a mass crucifixion as an expedient measure to end the war. And, we must admit, it achieved the desired outcome – the remaining opponents of Alexander (numbered around 8,000) fled to exile, and peace returned to Alexander's realm until his death (*A. J.* 13.383; *B. J.* 1.98).

**(278)** 4QpNahum 3–4 i 1–9

| | |
|---|---|
| [ מדור לרשעי גוים אשר הלך ארי לבוא שם גור ארי] [ | 1 [ |
| [טרוס מלך יון אשר בקש לבוא ירושלים בעצת דורשי החלקות | 2 [ |
| [ביד מלכי יון מאנתיכוס עד עמוד מושלי כתיים ואחר תרמס | 3 [ |
| [ ארי טורף בדי גוריו ומחנק ללביותיו טרף | 4 [ |
| [ על כפיר החרון אשר יכה בגדוליו ואנשי עצתו | 5 [ |
| [חורה ומעונתו טרפה        פשרו על כפיר החרון | 6 [ |
| [מות בדורשי החלקות אשר יתלה אנשים חיים | 7 [ |
| [ בישראל מלפנים כי לתלוי חי על העץ [יק]רא הנני אלי[כה | 8 [ |
| נא[ם יהוה צבאות והבערתי בעשן רובכ]ה וכפיריכה תאכל חרב והכר[תי מארץ ט]רפה | 9 [ |

*Translation.*

1 […] dwelling for the wicked ones of the nations. *Where the lion went to enter, there the cub of the lion…*(Nah 2:12)

2 [… Deme]trios king of Javan, who sought to enter Jerusalem with the counsel of the Seekers-of-Smooth-Things

3 […] into the hand of the kings of Javan from Antikos until the rise of the rulers of the Kittim; but after(wards) […] will be trampled

4 […] *Lion tears enough for his cubs and strangles prey for his lionesses* (Nah 2:13a)

5 […] on account of the Angry Young Lion, who would strike with his great ones and men of his counsel

6 […*and fill*] *cave and his lair [with] prey.* (Nah 2:13b). Its interpretation concerns the Angry Young Lion

7 […]*mwt* in the Seekers-of-Smooth-Things; who will hang up living men

8 […] in Israel before, for concerning one hanged alive upon the tree [it] reads, *Behold I am against you,*

*9 say[s the Lord of hosts, and I shall burn your abundance with smoke] and a sword will eat your young lions, and I shall cut off from the earth (its) prey.* (Nah 2:14)

*Commentary.*[511] As one of the first published Qumran texts referring to historical figures and events, the Nahum Pesher has remained a disputed text in Qumran studies even as scholars attempt to understand the nature of the community behind this document. As a *pesher* document, it is formatted as a running commentary on the text of Nahum, especially applying that prophetic Hebrew text to events contemporary to the era of the Qumran community. Each verse from Nahum is quoted, followed by an interpretation (often introduced by פשרו "its interpretation", cf. line 6 above). A blank space typically separates the verse from its explication (also cf. line 6).[512] Orthographic analysis of the script indicates that the scroll was written in the late Hasmonean or early Herodian period,[513] which would weigh heavily against any attempt to date the scroll later than the Herodian age.[514]

This text is fragmentary, with ca. forty percent of this column missing. This results in disputes regarding both the reconstruction of these substantial lacunae and the translation of the existing text.[515] Concerning the lacunae, the best

---

[511] The text combines the *editio princeps* of JOHN MARCO ALLEGRO, Qumran Cave 4.I (4Q158–4Q186) (DJD 5; Oxford: Clarendon Press, 1968), 37–42 (plates xii–xiv); with the meticulous textual suggestions of JOHN STRUGNELL, Notes en marge du volume V des 'Discoveries in the Judaean Desert of Jordan', RdQ 7 (1970): 163–276, esp. 204–210; and with my own evaluation of the plates. Originally the text as edited here appeared in CHAPMAN, Crucifixion, 58, with close attention there to spacing based on the alignment of Frag. 3 and 4 in line 9. Other important editions consulted include JOHN MARCO ALLEGRO, Further Light on the History of the Qumran Sect, JBL 75 (1956): 89–95; MAURYA P. HORGAN, Pesharim: Qumran Interpretations of Biblical Books (CBQMS 8; Washington: Catholic Biblical Association, 1979); MAURYA P. HORGAN, Nahum Pesher (4Q169 = 4QpNah), in Pesharim, Other Commentaries, and Related Documents (ed. J. H. Charlesworth; The Dead Sea Scrolls 6B; Tübingen: Mohr Siebeck, 2002), 144–155; GREGORY L. DOUDNA, 4Q Pesher Nahum: A Critical Edition (JSPSup 35; London: Sheffield Academic Press, 2001); SHANI L. BERRIN, The Pesher Nahum Scroll from Qumran: An Exegetical Study of 4Q169 (Leiden: Brill, 2004).

[512] The fact that blank spaces frequently precede the interpretation would affect the number of characters allowed in any reconstruction of the lacunae in lines 2 and 5.

[513] STRUGNELL, Notes en marge, 205; BERRIN, Pesher Nahum Scroll, 8; DOUDNA, 4Q Pesher Nahum, 675–682.

[514] Particularly it would work against the creative suggestions of SOLOMON ZEITLIN, The Dead Sea Scrolls: A Travesty of Scholarship, JQR 47 (1956–57): 1–36, esp. 31–36; ARTHUR E. PALUMBO, A New Interpretation of the Nahum Commentary, FO 29 (1992–93): 153–162.

[515] Regarding the translation of the text, some of the key issues concern: (1) Whether in line 1 to read לביא ("to make enter" or "lion[ess]" as per ALLEGRO, DOUDNA, and BERRIN based on MT) or לבוא ("to enter" as per STRUGNELL and HORGAN); the latter seems more likely, comparing the plates with לבוא in line 2. (2) Should גור in line 1 be understood as "cub" (as most scholars and here) or as "sojourning" (infinitive construct, thus DOUDNA)? (3) The spelling of [Deme]trios in line 2. (4) Whether the "and" (Hebrew *waw*) in line 4 is present in the scroll. (5) The best way to render אשר in line 7 (above translated as "who"). (6) The recon-

way to estimate the amount of missing text is to assume line 9 contains a full citation of Nah 2:14. This permits one to infer the number of characters missing in that line, and thus to calculate an approximate distance from the (missing) right margin (found only in the tiny fragment 3) to the extant letters (in the left-hand side represented by fragment 4). With such an estimate in hand, a better reconstruction can be attempted; note that most early reconstruction proposals of these lines tended to have too few characters.

The text clearly refers to historical figures: "king(s) of Javan" (lines 2, 3) would imply Greek (i.e., Seleucid) monarchs, "Antikos" (line 3) would be Antiochus, the "Kittim" (line 3) are likely the Romans, and [Deme]trios king of Javan would be one of the Seleucid rulers named Demetrius. The pejorative term "Seekers-of-Smooth-Things" (lines 2, 7) is best interpreted as referring to the Pharisees, who are generally viewed negatively throughout the Qumran documents.[516] The identity of the Lion of Wrath hinges on the historical context of the other figures. The key identification concerns Demetrius: Is he Demetrius I Soter (in which case the Lion is Alcimus or Antiochus IV Epiphanes),[517] or is he Demetrius III Eucaerus, in which case the Lion is Alexander Jannaeus?[518] The latter is more commonly accepted and more probable: As we observed above, Josephus (*A. J.* 13.380–381; *B. J.* 1.96–97) records crucifixions under Alexander Jannaeus (but not under Alcimus, and Antiochus IV is otherwise problematic here), the scrolls elsewhere refer to events during the reign of Alexander's queen Salome Alexandra (Shelamzion in 4Q332 Frag. 2)[519] and the Pharisees (Seekers-of-Smooth-Things) are prominently opposed by Alexander Jannaeus in Josephus' account (and plausibly included among the crucified 800). Assuming this historical backdrop, the scroll depicts events that happened after Antiochus III won Judea in his 198 B.C. battle with the Ptolemies[520] but before the Romans had taken a key interest in the land (line

---

struction in line 7 of ‏קר[יא‏ ("[it] reads") – most follow this (as also above), but GARCÍA MARTÍNEZ suggests ‏נו[רא‏ ("it is horrible"; see commentary below).

[516] See further 4QpNah 3–4 ii 3–6; 4QpNah 3–4 iii 1–8; also e.g., CD I, 18–II, 1; 4QpIsa[c] [4Q163] II, 10–11; 1QH X, 15–19 [*aka* II, 15–19]; 1QH XII, 7–12 [*aka* IV, 7–12]. Further, some halakic positions supported by Pharisees are explicitly rejected in 4QMMT. "Seekers-of-Smooth-Things" is commonly held to be connected with "do not prophesy to us what is right, speak to us *smooth things*" in Isa 30:10.

[517] As noted above concerning Jose b. Joezer and Jaķim, STAUFFER, Jerusalem und Rom, 124–25, 128–132 supported this identification with Demetrius I and Alcimus. HAROLD H. ROWLEY, 4QpNahum and the Teacher of Righteousness, JBL 75 (1956): 188–193, argues for Antiochus IV as the crucifying Lion of Wrath.

[518] For an extensive argument cf. BERRIN, Pesher Nahum Scroll, 87–130. Perhaps too specific is IGOR R. TANTLEVSKIJ, The Reflection of the Political Situation in Judaea in 88 B.C.E. in the Qumran Commentary on Nahum (4QpNah, Columns 1–4), St. Petersburg Journal of Oriental Studies 6 (1994): 221–231.

[519] Cf. GEZA VERMES, The Complete Dead Sea Scrolls in English (Fiftieth Anniversary ed.; London: New York: Penguin, 2011), 405 (translation with introduction).

[520] Antikos in line 3 could be Antiochus IV Epiphanes, but his father, Antiochus III ("the

3).[521] Demetrius III had been called upon by the rebellious Jews (with the instigation of some Pharisees) in order to attempt to dethrone Alexander Jannaeus, but the war ultimately went to Alexander, and he crucified many of his opponents (as noted above concerning Josephus, *A. J.* 13.380–381).

The key phrase for our study concerns the men in line 7 who are hung (יתלה) while still living (חיים). The initial debates (concerning whether this could refer to crucifixion) have been largely resolved by noting that a similar reference to "hang him alive" appears with clear application to crucifixion in *Sifre Dev.* §221, where, in most key *Sifre* manuscripts, such hanging alive refers to being hanged in a manner "like the [Roman] government does" (see No. 268).[522] Scholars thus generally accept that line 7 refers to *ante mortem* suspension on a cross.[523]

The translation here does not attempt to fill in the missing lacunae (except in line 9). However, the reconstruction of the lacunae is primarily what is at issue in interpreting this text. With these events referring to the mass crucifixion of the 800 under Alexander Jannaeus, how are these crucifixions viewed by the author? There is not space for a full accounting of the issues,[524] but the key concerns are: (1) Does the אשר in line 7 function as a relative pronoun ("who") or a temporal conjunction ("when")? (2) If אשר in line 7 is a relative pronoun, then does it refer (as an antecedent) to the Seekers-of-Smooth-Things or to someone else? (3) How should one reconstruct the beginning of line 8 (and does it speak positively or negatively of the Lion and his actions)? (4) How does the citation of Nahum 2:14 in lines 8–9 relate to the suspension mentioned in line 8?

One quick approach to these questions would be to note that אשר most typically is used as a relative pronoun in the *pesharim*. The antecedent of such a relative pronoun (אשר) in line 7 is most likely singular (since the subject of the masculine singular verb יתלה in the אשר clause would be singular), and this would rule against the plural "Seekers-of-Smooth-Things" as antecedent. Further the prefixed preposition ב ("in," "by," "against," etc.) on "Seekers"

---

Great"), actually was the first Antiochus to have a significant footprint in Judea with his conquest of Syria and Judea in 198 B.C. against Ptolemy V Epiphanes.

[521] Though many Hasmonean rulers sent embassies to Rome in the first and second centuries B.C., the reference here plausibly refers to Pompey entering Jerusalem (63 B.C.). Thus line 3 refers to events occurring between 198 and 63 B.C.

[522] For the earlier debates about the meaning of יתלה see NAPHTALI WIEDER, Notes on the New Documents from the Fourth Cave of Qumran, JJS 7 (1956): 71–76; SOLOMON ZEITLIN, The Phrase יתלה אנשים חיים, JJS 8 (1957): 117–118; NAPHTALI WIEDER, Rejoinder, JJS 8 (1957): 119–121.

[523] SAMUELSSON, Crucifixion, 229 merely acknowledges that it refers to "some kind of an ante-mortem suspension," but the text "does not reveal *which* kind." COOK, Crucifixion, 317–318 counters that both impalement and crucifixion are culturally more likely execution forms than hanging on a noose, and the Josephus parallels would argue for crucifixion.

[524] For a somewhat fuller analysis see CHAPMAN, Crucifixion, 57–66.

(בדורשי) indicates that "Seekers-of-Smooth-Things" is subsidiary to another noun (missing in the lacunae of line 7), and that noun would likely serve as the antecedent of אשר. From what we have in the extant text, the most likely antecedent of אשר, and thus the effective subject of יתלה, would be the "Lion of Wrath," who hangs living men (i.e., crucifies them). This is consistent with the "Lion of Wrath" being Alexander Jannaeus.

Multiple reconstructions have been attempted for line 8; here are three of the more prominent earlier attempts:[525]

ALLEGRO: [...which was never done (?)] before in Israel, for it (the Scripture) calls the one hanged alive on the tree – *Behold, I am against* [*thee,*

YADIN: [*on the tree as this is the law*] *in Israel as of old since the* hanged one is called alive on the tree.

BAUMGARTEN: (1) [Such a thing had never] before [been done] in Israel, for he (the Young Lion of Wrath) took "hanged" (Deut 21:23) to mean "alive on a tree."

All three of these proposals are too short; they do not include enough Hebrew letters to fill the lacunae at the beginning of the line. It is important to note that the first and third proposal assume the author was stating an objection to the crucifixions (they break with Israelite tradition), while YADIN's proposal contends the author viewed such suspensions as being in accord with Jewish law. For this conclusion, YADIN drew on the institution of *ante mortem* suspension in the Temple Scroll (11QTemple LXIV, 6–13; vgl. No. 274), and he further argued that "wrath" (in reference to the "Lion of Wrath") is a positive trait shared with God and that the Pharisees were despised by the Qumran community. YADIN thus argues the author believed Alexander Jannaeus showed righteous anger when he legally put to death his Pharisaic opponents by hanging them up. BAUMGARTEN counters that "wrath" is not always a positive trait associated with God in the Qumran scrolls (cf. 1QpHab iii 12) and that later in the scrolls Gentiles punish the Seekers-of-Smooth-Things (4QpNah 3–4 ii 4–5), so not all opponents of the Pharisees are admired by the author of 4QpNahum. BAUMGARTEN also rightly observes that our passage in 4QpNahum developed from an essentially negative portrayal of the (Assyrian) lion in Nah 2:12–14.

Many other reconstructions have been suggested, but these have been cited to lay out some of the central disputes about this crucial line. In reality, the

---

[525] See ALLEGRO, Light, 91; YADIN, Pesher Nahum, 11–12; BAUMGARTEN, Crucifixion, 481. Note that BAUMGARTEN's translation omits the last two Hebrew words; he later suggested (without translating the first two Hebrew words): "for regarding one who *hangs* a living man upon a tree (Scripture) reads: Behold I am against you, says the Lord of hosts" (BAUMGARTEN, Hanging, 14*). This later translation of BAUMGARTEN has the unfortunate default of requiring לתלוי to be an active verb rather than the passive it clearly is.

modern scholar must first decide whether the author of the *Nahum Pesher* believed the Lion of Wrath had done an admirable thing in crucifying the Seekers-of-Smooth-Things, then only after that decision can one attempt to find an appropriate length of text to fill the lacuna. For our purposes, it is enough to simply decide whether the *Pesher's* author approved of Alexander's practice of crucifixion (leaving a full textual reconstruction to others). Here, we simply cannot pronounce with absolute certainty. However, BAUMGARTEN does validly observe that "wrath" is *not* always a positive trait in this scroll and in acknowledging that not everyone who opposed the Pharisees was esteemed by the Qumran community. Further, the "Lion" is viewed negatively both in Nahum and here in the scroll as well (see 4QpNah 3–4 i 9ff.). Thus it appears that although the author was glad for the Pharisees to receive their punishment, he does not view the agent of that punishment positively. Furthermore, the Qumran community, with its focus on a pure lineage of Zadokite high priests, would likely have held Alexander Jannaeus to be an improper candidate for the high priesthood. This gives us warrant for viewing the "Lion of wrath" negatively but not necessarily his action.

Investigating the conclusion of line 8 might provide further assistance. Most scholars believe that the text of Nah 2:14 (beginning with הנני) is first introduced by יק[רא ("[it] reads"). However, GARCÍA MARTÍNEZ argues the two fragmentary letters of יק[רא could instead be reconstructed as נו]רא ("it is horrible"), lending to the following translation: "for it is [hor]rible for the one suspended alive on the tree." This would imply a negative comment on the action of Alexander, who has delivered these people over to a horrible and fearful death.[526] On the other hand, if one were to follow the reading of the majority, then the יקרא likely introduces (in a way that is admittedly unusual for this Pesher) Nah 2:14 as a judgment upon the crucified: "for concerning one hanged alive upon a tree [Scripture] reads, 'Behold I am against you, says the Lord of hosts." The crucifixions here, then, would be evidence of God's providential punishment upon the Pharisees (even through an unrighteous Lion of wrath). In either case, line 8 would show that the death of the Pharisees is either "horrible" or represents providential judgment from God.[527]

---

[526] FLORENTINO GARCÍA MARTÍNEZ, 4QpNah y la Crucifixión: Nueva hipótesis de reconstrucción de 4Q 169 3–4 i, 4–8, EstBib 38 (1979–80): 221–235, esp. 228, 230–232, with fuller translation of line 8 ibid. 232 (parentheses indicating reconstructed text): "(en el árbol, cometiendo una abominación que no se cometía) en Israel desde antiguo, pues (es terri)ble para el colgado vivo en el árbol (Sigue Nah 2,14)." GARCÍA MARTÍNEZ notes that few other verbs in the Dead Sea Scrolls end in רא- and that a similar use of נורא appears in Ps 76:13. The Psalm reference is intriguing, well representing the Niphal of נורא along with a prepositional phrase introduced by ל; however, some differences are apparent (esp. word order and the participial phrase in the psalm versus the relative clause in the *pesher*). The English translation of his position in the main text above is from GARCÍA MARTÍNEZ and TIGCHELAAR, Dead Sea Scrolls Study Edition, 1:337.

[527] Intriguingly, both options (especially perhaps the one reading יקרא) would also cohere

This brief commentary has not sought to resolve all disputed matters, nor is there space to delve deeply into the reconstruction of the several important lacunae in the passage. It is hoped the reader is now sufficiently oriented to pursue the minutiae further should he or she wish. Nonetheless, we have argued these results: The text most plausibly refers to events during the time of Alexander Jannaeus, when the Pharisees sought the help of Demetrius III in overthrowing Alexander; in this they were unsuccessful, and Alexander crucified many of the instigators (likely including many Seekers-of-Smooth-Things). Yet in this context, the author of the scroll does not actually admire the person of Alexander ("the Lion of Wrath"), and thus this author may not have condoned Alexander's use of crucifixion. The author of the *Nahum Pesher* does, however, believe either that these crucifixions are horrible or that they prove God providentially opposed the Seekers-of-Smooth-Things.

### (279) Simeon b. Shetach Traditions

*Translation of m. Sanh. 6:5.* All those who are stoned are hanged. These are the words of Rabbi Eliezer. But the Sages say, "Only the blasphemer and the one who worships an idol are hanged." A man is hanged with the face towards the people, and a woman is hanged with the face towards the wood. These are the words of Rabbi Eliezer. But the sages say, "The man is hanged, but the woman is not hanged." Rabbi Eliezer said to them, "Did not Simeon ben Shetach hang eighty women in Ashkelon?" The sages answered, "He hanged eighty women, and they ought not to judge not even two (persons) on a single day!"

*Commentary.* The text and translation of *m. Sanh.* 6:4–6 (6:4 in the DANBY translation) is found above in No. 35; this translation excerpt is provided here for sake of convenience. While earlier this text was discussed in reference to its interpretation of Deut 21:22–23 (see No. 267), our focus here is on the connection to Simeon b. Shetach. In this passage, the opinion of R. Eliezer b. Hyrcanus, who is widely quoted in the Mishnah and is an important second-generation Tannaitic authority of the first and second century A.D., varies in two respects from the majority view concerning proper application of Deut 21. He considers more offenses worthy of suspension, and he would hang up both men and women, also providing descriptions of which way they would face, presumably to prevent women's frontal regions from being prominently dis-

---

with a subjective-genitive understanding of "curse of God" in Deut 21:23; the suspended person receives either a terrifying/cursed death or one that is providentially from God's judgment. Such a subjective genitive is found in the interpretation of Deut 21:23 in 11QTemple LXIV (see No. 274).

played.[528] In order to defend his stance on suspending women, Eliezer appeals to the historical precedent of the renowned rabbinic predecessor Simeon b. Shetach, who is numbered among the *zugot* (the "pairs" of respected early rabbis in *m. Abot* 1:8–9) and was active in the first half of the first century B.C.[529] Simeon hung up 80 *women*. The majority view retorts that this case was exceptional, not only because he hung up women but because rabbinic procedures require that only one capital case be heard per day (while Simeon hung up *80* in one day).[530]

*Sifre Dev.* §221 (text and translation No. 62) also records this dispute between R. Eliezer and the Sages, dropping the reference to the direction of suspension,[531] with the additional comment that Simeon's case "was an emergency intended as a lesson to others."[532] This may well be, but Simeon's actions certainly indicate that earlier rabbis believed certain cases existed in which one could depart from the later codified rabbinic norms of capital penalties and suspension – here, concerning both the gender and the number who could be executed in a day. Further, the fact that such events are recorded even while contrary to rabbinic norms would indicate a firm memory in the rabbinic tradition that Simeon performed such suspensions.

Neither the Mishnah nor the Sifre specifies whether these women were suspended *ante mortem* or *post mortem*, and that too becomes a point of departure from rabbinic norms in the talmudic tradition. In two locations, the Yerushalmi contains expansive haggadic treatments of the Simeon b. Shetach story (*y. Sanh.* 6:9 [23c–d];[533] *y. Ḥag.* 2:2 [77d–78a]). The core narrative is the

---

[528] Elsewhere, the rabbis determine that people are suspended naked. On the concerns of Eliezer to avoid prurient interest in the deceased, see note 531.

[529] Evidence of respect for Simeon b. Shetach abounds, especially concerning his reverence for the Torah and for the profundity of his legal decisions, e.g., *t. Sanh.* 6:6; 8:3; cf. *b. Qidd.* 66a.

[530] See also *b. Sanh.* 46a, where it is acknowledged that this creates further legal disagreement since some rabbinical authorities suggest multiple executions are permitted in one day if they are all for the same charge.

[531] Note in the bracketed section of *Sifre Dev.* §221 (missing in some key manuscripts) quoted in No. 62 that R. Judah (not Eliezer) reportedly stated that both men and women are hanged, with women hung facing the "tree" and with both having strategically placed strips of cloth covering their private parts. In the *Tosefta* (*t. Sanh.* 9:6), this statement in the *Sifre* is also attributed to R. Judah, which he spoke "in the name of R. Eliezer," thus it is likely that two famous rabbis disagreed with the majority position. For R. Judah, see also *y. Sanh.* 6:4, which overtly portrays R. Judah as concerned to avoid generating lust among the bystanders.

[532] This additional phrase is also represented in the way in which the Yerushalmi quotes the Mishnah here in some places since the Yerushalmi ends the text found in *m. Sanh.* 6:5 with "but the times required it"; see *y. Sanh.* 6:9 [23c], end of 6:6 in Neusner's translation; *y Ḥag.* 2:2 [78a].

[533] In the NEUSNER translation, this text appears as *y. Sanh.* 6:6 (despite the Leiden manuscript and the *editio princeps* listing it as 6:9); JACOB NEUSNER, The Talmud of the Land of Israel (35 vols.; Chicago: University of Chicago Press, 1982–1994), 31:180–184. A very useful edition of the *y. Sanhedrin* text, presenting the Leiden manuscript and the *editio princeps*

same between these two talmudic accounts, though their respective contexts alter some of the more tangential features.[534] Simeon is challenged by a holy man's heavenly vision to keep his promise to dispatch witches from Israel. He goes to Ashkelon, accompanied by a group of eighty men, in the guise of a sorcerer. Simeon approaches the group of eighty witches there and offers to magically provide for them men with whom they may have pleasure. They gladly accept, and Simeon signals for the men to appear, who lift the witches from the ground. No longer in contact with the earth, the witches loose their magical powers,[535] and they are then suspended to death by being hung up one by one. This highly legendary account, again occurring twice in the Yerushalmi, would indicate the talmudic charge against the women was performing magic (they are now called "witches") and (more importantly) that their executions were carried out by *ante mortem* suspension on the order of the great rabbi Simeon.

M. HENGEL has argued that the Simeon b. Shetach episode here represents an encrypted memory that Simeon took vengeance on those who allied with Alexander Jannaeus against the Pharisees.[536] Simeon was remembered to have been a contemporary of Alexander (Yannai),[537] and the *Bavli* claims that after Yannai had destroyed the Sages of Israel, the Torah was only restored by the hand of Simeon b. Shetach (*b. Qidd.* 66a). HENGEL's argument draws these traditions together with Josephus' depiction of Alexander Jannaeus crucifying of the 800 and the portrayal of that event in the Nahum Pesher. HENGEL further remarks that the story about the witches in the Yerushalmi is not only legendary, it is patently impossible: How was a rabbinic leader to gain sufficient authority in a non-Jewish territory ("Ashkelon") to be able to kill several dozen of its inhabitants? Rather, as Alexander crucified 800 Pharisees, so

---

in synopsis form, can be found in PETER SCHÄFER and HANS-JÜRGEN BECKER, Synopse zum Talmud Yerushalmi (Tübingen: Mohr Siebeck, 1991), 4:181–182.

[534] The preface to the narrative in each account adopts this story to the concerns of that tractate: Sanhedrin aims to explicate R. Eliezer's appeal to the narrative, Ḥagigah is most concerned with how this story helps determine which of the contemporary *zugot* (Judah b. Tabbai or Simeon b. Shetach) was the *nasi* ("patriarch") at the time. Yet within the common story, *y. Ḥag.* 2:2 additionally indicates it was raining when Simeon approached the witches. Simeon presented himself to them wearing dry clothes despite the rain and claimed to have "run between the raindrops", adding to the witches' belief that he was one of them. The Ḥagigah text also mentions earlier in the narrative that the witches' magic would not work unless they were in contact with the ground, thus better preparing the reader for this key plot point.

[535] On the theme of magicians needing contact with earth in order to perform magic see HENGEL, Rabbinische Legende, 19–20.

[536] HENGEL, Rabbinische Legende, 11–62, esp. 48–57. HENGEL anticipated that much longer argument in HENGEL, Crucifixion, 84–85; HENGEL, La crucifixion, 106–107.

[537] Both *b. Ber* 48a and *b. Sotah* 47a indicate that Simeon's sister was Alexander's wife. Highly legendary episodes in the talmudic traditions are also associated with King Yannai (e.g., *b. Git.* 57a), especially some that illustrate Yannai's belligerent interactions with Simeon b. Shetach (*y. Ber.* 7:2 = *y. Naz.* 5:3; *b. Sanh.* 19a–b).

after Alexander's death, Simeon crucified eighty of his cronies. The talmudic legend then encodes this episode with humorously ironic terminology. The term "witches" is a slander against the irreligious nature of the suspended companions of Alexander, "Ashkelon" speaks of the moral failure of Jerusalem in falling under their spell, "eighty" is related etymologically to "eight hundred", and the eighty men who assisted him in "hanging up" these "witches" were fellow Pharisees who helped crucify their foes.

HENGEL's argumentation is learned and thorough. At the same time, it is difficult to refute, or substantiate; it is a thesis that requires all the key terms (women, witches, eighty, Ashkelon) to mean something ironically different than their normal referents. When Josephus records that the Pharisees slaughtered Alexander's former associates (Diogenes and others) after Alexander's death, he employs verbs that would imply slayings and beheadings (such as σφάττουσιν in *A. J.* 13.410) rather than crucifixions.[538] It is conceivable that Josephus may have wished to protect the Pharisees from such charges, but this certainly does not lend support to HENGEL's thesis. More importantly, the rabbinic tradition is highly dependent on Simeon hanging up *women*. This is the reason R. Eliezer makes reference to Simeon in order to substantiate that *women* (as well as men) can be suspended, in keeping with Deuteronomy 21. If the term "witches" or "women" were really an encrypted reference to Alexander's (male) cronies, then Eliezer's argument would, at best, appear to be a joke, and perhaps one he himself is not in on. So, on balance, HENGEL's argument is worth considering, but a more straightforward reading, at least of the Mishnah, appears to be a wise choice.

The conclusion, nonetheless, is that a rabbi/Pharisee was remembered in the Tannaitic era for engaging in a mass suspension of women, and in the Amoraic era, this *ante mortem* suspension could even be portrayed as the means of the execution of those women (or "witches"). All of this is at substantial variance from accepted rabbinic norms, thus indicating either that those norms were not widely established in this earlier period or that respected rabbis could depart from such norms if the circumstances required. Both the Sifre and the talmudic tradition assert that Simeon's actions were exceptional because of the circumstances, along with other historical examples of exceptions being acknowledged in the talmudic material.[539]

---

[538] Beheading also makes the analogy in *A. J.* 13.412 stronger with them being "cut of" (κόπτεσθαι) in the manner of cattle. Still, the words ἀνῃρημένοις in *A. J.* 13.413, as well as κτείνουσιν, διαχειρίσασθαι and ἀνῇρουν in *B. J.* 1.113, are admittedly vague on the form(s) of slaying involved.

[539] Simeon's actions are acknowledged as exceptional in *Sifre Dev.* §221 (this "was needed of the moment to teach others by it"); and in *y. Ḥag.* 2:2 [78a] ("the times required it"; also *y. Sanh.* 6:9 [23c]). Note that *y. Ḥag.* 2:2 [78a] (with general parallel in *b. Yeb.* 90b; *b. Sanh.* 46a) goes on to discuss under what circumstances "the times require it" is sufficient excuse to vary from accepted rabbinic legal procedure: R. Eliezar b. Jacob and R. Jose [b. Halafta], both

## (280) *b. Baba Meṣ'ia* 83b

אתיוה לרבי אלעזר ברבי שמעון וקא תפיס גנבי ואזיל שלח ליה ר' יהושע בן קרחה חומץ בן יין
עד מתי אתה מוסר עמו של אלהינו להריגה שלח ליה קוצים אני מכלה מן הכרם שלח ליה יבא
בעל הכרם ויכלה את קוציו יומא חד פגע ביה ההוא כובס קרייה חומץ בן יין אמר מדחציף כולי
האי שמע מינה רשיעא הוא אמר להו תפסוהו תפסוהו לבתר דנח דעתיה אזל בתריה לפרוקיה
ולא מצי קרי עליה שומר פיו ולשונו שומר מצרות נפשו זקפוהו קם תותי זקיפא וקא בכי אמרו
ליה רבי אל ירע בעיניך שהוא ובנו בעלו נערה מאורסה ביום הכפורים הניח ידו על בני מעיו
אמר שישו בני מעי שישו ומה ספיקות שלכם כך ודאית שלכם על אחת כמה

*Translation.* R. Eleazar, son of R. Simeon, was accordingly sent for, and he proceeded to arrest the thieves. Thereupon R. Joshua, son of Ḳarḥah, sent word to him, "Vinegar, son of wine! How long will you deliver up the people of our God for slaughter!" Back came the reply: "I weed out thorns from the vineyard." Whereupon R. Joshua retorted: "Let the owner of the vineyard himself [God] come and weed out the thorns."

One day a fuller met him [R. Eleazar], and dubbed him "Vinegar, son of wine." Said the Rabbi to himself, "Since he is so insolent, he is certainly a culprit." So he gave the order to his attendant: "Arrest him! Arrest him!" When his anger cooled, he went after him in order to secure his release, but did not succeed. Thereupon he applied to him [the fuller], the verse: *Whoso keepeth his mouth and his tongue, keepeth his soul from troubles.* Then they hanged him, and he [R. Eleazar son of R. Simeon] stood under the gallows and wept. Said they [his disciples] to him: "Master, do not grieve; for he and his son seduced a betrothed maiden on the Day of Atonement." [On hearing this,] he laid his hand upon his heart and exclaimed: "Rejoice, my heart! If matters on which thou [sc. the heart] art doubtful are thus, how much more so those on which thou art certain!

*Commentary.*[540] Rabbi Eleazar [son of R. Simeon b. Yohai] was a fourth generation Tanna active at the end of the second century A.D.[541] He was famous

---

third generation Tannaim of the mid–second century, disagree whether perjured testimony can be ignored, and cases are cited of a person put to death for riding his horse on the Sabbath and for a man flogged for having sex with his wife outside his home. Those two cited exceptional cases (not clearly attributed in the Yerushalmi) are specifically attributed to R. Eliezer b. Jacob in *b. Yeb.* 90b, with his stated goal of establishing a "fence around the Torah"; cf. this as a *baraita* in *b. Sanh.* 46a.

[540] Text and translation: EPSTEIN, ed., Hebrew-English Edition of the Babylonian Talmud, IV/2, *loc. cit.*

[541] "Fourth" generation according to STRACK / STEMBERGER / BOCKMUEHL, Introduction, 79), "fifth" generation following the order of *tannaim* in HERBERT DANBY, The Mishnah. Translated from the Hebrew with Introduction and Brief Explanatory Notes (Oxford: University Press, 1933), 800. At least three Mishnaic rulings are attributed to him: *m. Beṣah* 4:5 (leading out cattle on a Festival day); *m. Tem.* 4:4 (concerning atonement offerings); *m. Neg.* 12:3 (on leprosy signs).

for collaborating with the Roman government. He was also renowned for his extreme girth.[542] The above passage is preceded by an account of R. Eleazar's coming across an officer hunting thieves and suggesting to him a wiser way of catching them (by going into the tavern at mid-morning and inquiring about the jobs of its sleepy customers). The royal court then summons Eleazar to use his own approach to arrest thieves. The above text then records an instance that reassures R. Eleazar (and the readers of the *Bavli*) that he had been righteous in his decisions (especially in his willingness to collaborate with the Roman government). First, we hear the challenge from R. Joshua ("vinegar son of wine" meaning that he was far less than his famed rabbinic father), but this is countered with a story of Eleazar's right judgment. That story takes an example in which Eleazar could be most wrong (offended, and thus biased, as he was at the fuller's insolence) but then shows that his judgment was certainly correct. Intriguingly, the fuller taunts Eleazar with the very same phrase that R. Joshua spoke ("vinegar son of wine"), thus Eleazar's right judgment concerning the fuller doubly undermines Joshua's challenge. The guilt of this fuller is portrayed as overwhelming – engaging in sex with a betrothed woman (due the penalty of stoning in *m. Sanh.* 7:4; cf. 7:9) along with his son (due stoning for being guilty of laws against father and son having sex with same woman in *m. Sanh.* 7:4) and doing so on the holy Day of Atonement (when any sexual act is forbidden in *m. Yoma* 8:1). While the common view in the Mishnah is that only blasphemers and idolaters are suspended after stoning, a reported minority view held that all who are stoned are hung (*m. Sanh.* 6:5; 6:4 in DANBY); that minority view would then apply here to this fuller (who deserves stoning and thus deserves being suspended).

This passage shows that "thieves" were commonly hung up on wooden devices in this era. More importantly, it illustrates how an important rabbinic figure could collude with the "government" (i.e., the Roman authorities) in order to bring such brigands to execution by *ante mortem* suspension. Such a suspension at the hands of the Romans in the second century would surely have been presumed to be a crucifixion. Earlier in this commentary, it was suggested that the origins of this tradition about Eleazar and the fuller likely stemmed from those who wished to defend R. Eleazar b. Simeon from charges against his character.[543] That such a story can vouch for his character implies

---

[542] Just after the passage quoted above, R. Eleazar b. R. Simeon is further proven to be righteous, for after an operation in which they remove "baskets" of fat from him, that fat does not decay, calling forth from R. Eleazar a quotation of Ps 16:9 ("also my flesh dwells securely"), a Psalm whose context guarantees the psalmist of life everlasting.

[543] CHAPMAN, *Crucifixion*, 93–94, postulating either that the whole text initiated with R. Eleazar's supporters, or that the R. Joshua references initiated with R. Eleazar's detractors, only to receive response from Eleazar's supporters via the narrative about the fuller. This is not to deny some historical event underlying the passage (this may or may not be the case), but it is to explain why the story continued to be told in rabbinic circles.

not only that a rabbi could conceivably collude with the Romans in crucifying a criminal, but also that other rabbinic figures (those passing down this tradition as favorable to Eleazar) would similarly have believed such a means of death to have been just recompense on the criminal.

### 3.5.6 Summary of Evidence and the Question of Jesus' Crucifixion

The sources support a complex picture concerning the relationship of Roman-era Jewish leaders to *ante mortem* suspension. There are a few key rabbinic texts that specifically distinguish Jewish penal *post mortem* suspension practice from the form of suspension practiced by the Roman government. The rabbinic and targumic documents commonly recognize that proper Jewish suspensions occur after the person is already dead (and more specifically after he has been stoned). Josephus evidences similar assumptions about the *post mortem* nature of biblically sanctioned suspensions against blasphemers (and, intriguingly, also against the stubborn and rebellious child), therefore such rabbinic tradition plausibly dates into the first century A.D., possibly before.

While rabbinic opposition to *ante mortem* suspension may have increased over time, due to such factors as the rise of Christianity and as the harsh experience of Jewish persecution on the cross at the hands of the Romans, such data would suggest that some sectors of Judaism were in the first century already emphasizing the application of Deut 21:22–23 to *post mortem* suspension. Similarly, the rabbinic list of four accepted death penalties in its Mishnaic and talmudic forms does not include execution by suspension.

However, one should not assume that later rabbinic conclusions represent the practice of all Judaism (or even of all earlier rabbis). Significant evidence supports the claim that the four-fold means of capital punishment were in continued discussion (even transition) during the Second Temple and early Rabbinic periods. In that context, the Ruth Targum may well indicate that some early Jewish halakah supported suspension as an acceptable means of death.

Outside Pharisaic circles, the halakic retelling of Deuteronomy in the Temple Scroll seems to indicate that its author and his sectarian community accepted such *ante mortem* hanging for certain particularly heinous crimes against Israel, the people of God. Philo discusses Deut 21:22–23 with regard to the death by crucifixion to which murderers are sentenced. And even Josephus allows that Deut 21 applies to crucified persons, at least with respect to the need to bury the body.

Historical examples demonstrate that Alexander Jannaeus, the Hasmonean high priest and king, followed his advisors' counsel by publicly crucifying a large number of his opponents; such an impious and savage act, while condemned by many (including Josephus), nevertheless accomplished its purpose of achieving peace from civil war. The stance of the Nahum Pesher on such a mass execution is debated, but it is likely the author felt little sympathy for the Pharisee-led rebels who opposed the Lion of Wrath. Later rabbis would also tell of Jaḳim, who can plausibly be identified with the high-priest Alcimus, dancing in mockery of the crucifixion of his uncle (and famed rabbi) Jose b. Joezer; this episode displays (from later rabbinic perspective) Jaḳim's initial willing acceptance of (if not his initiating hand in) such a crucifixion death. From the age of the *zugot* also originates the story of Simeon b. Shetach suspending eighty women in ways that contravene later rabbinic rulings about the gender and number of those who can be so punished; indeed, this event may further contravene (if the *Yerushalmi* accounts are to be trusted in some measure) the rabbinic ruling against *ante mortem* suspension – later generations of rabbis certainly believed so. The rabbinic response to the Simeon account is ultimately: "the times required it", a response that can occasionally justify other unsanctioned penal procedures. Finally, we have witnessed at least one example of a rabbi (R. Eleazar b. R. Simeon) whose collusion with the Roman government resulted in his actively and deliberately catching brigands, who then would ultimately be crucified by the Romans. In the midst of such complicity with the government, the vivid narrative about R. Eleazar's sagaciously initiating the crucifixion of a horribly licentious fuller proves to later rabbinic generations that Eleazar's actions were just.

The picture thus is a complex one, attesting to rejection of *ante mortem* suspension by some key lines of tradition but also testifying to its acceptance at other times, by other sectarians, and even by its normal detractors in moments of great urgency. When we inquire about the legal acceptability of the crucifixion of Jesus in his day, such complexity gives us pause to think of an equally multifaceted set of ways halakic authorities (alongside illiterate masses) may have approached the question. Some might well have objected to such a punishment, yet the complexity of halakic possibilities that would permit a Jewish call for Jesus' crucifixion might include: belief that *ante mortem* suspension was acceptable for certain crimes, or belief that collaborating with the Romans in such cases was permissible, or conviction that the severity of the times required unusual action. Of course, these various possibilities may have worked to influence different members of the crowd in different ways as many collectively cried out for his crucifixion.

Finally, while there is not space here to develop properly one other key line of argument, perhaps it is suggestive that while some modern authors have strongly asserted that Jewish religious leaders in antiquity could not have supported any call to crucify Jesus, ancient post-NT sources, both Christian and Jewish, appear ready to accept the willingness of Jewish leaders and the crowds in demanding Jesus' execution (even one via the cross).[544] Although the *Testimonium Flavianum* (Josephus, *A. J.* 18.63–64; see No. 67) certainly bears Christian interpolations, the historical core to the document, written by a man who self-identified as a Pharisee, most plausibly accepts that Jesus was crucified by Pilatus with some Jewish involvement. Some consider the whole *Testimonium* to be a Christian insertion, but it seems wiser to envision an original core of material from Josephus that was later expanded by Christian scribes into different recensions in the Greek manuscripts and in other language traditions, especially the Arabic tradition in Agapius mentioned below. It would be especially pertinent if one could establish whether one particular phrase in *A. J.* 18.64 goes back to Josephus (as opposed to a Christian interpolator), namely that Jesus was accused by the "first men among us" (ἐνδείξει τῶν πρώτων ἀνδρῶν παρ' ἡμῖν) and that Pilatus, on that basis, condemned him. This phrase is accepted as authentic, for example, in the carefully considered work of J. P. MEIER,[545] who rightly points to how this phraseology overlaps well with Josephus' own language elsewhere. Still, the so-called "Arabic version" (really a quotation of Josephus in the tenth-century Arabic Christian work of Agapius) does not contain the phrase, which diminishes this line of potential corroborating external evidence.[546] The original *Testimonium* (prior to Christian interpolation) almost certainly contained a reference to crucifixion because: (1) Josephus elsewhere frequently recounts such Roman execution forms, (2) reference to Jesus' crucifixion appears in the Greek text and in the "Arabic Version," (3) Jesus' crucifixion remains one of the central facts of his life that is consistently recorded in Roman literature (e.g., in Tacitus, Lucian, and Celsus via Origen), and (4) that reference to crucifixion creates a key thematic narrative link between the *Testimonium* (*A. J.* 18.63–64) and the episode in Egypt that immediately follows it (*A. J.* 18.65–80; esp. 18.79).

Christian *Adversus Iudaeos* literature (especially the dialogue genre) consistently represents the Jewish interlocutors in these dialogues as readily allowing that Jesus was crucified and that Jewish leaders shared some complicity in his death. In the *Altercatio Simonis et Theophili* 2.4 (BRATKE edition; 6.22 IN HARNACK / VARNER), Simon the Jew says Jesus was "fastened by our fathers upon the patibulum of a cross" and thus cursed like Haman.[547]

---

[544] These sources receive some analysis, though toward answering a different set of questions, in CHAPMAN, Crucifixion, 223–262.

[545] MEIER, Jesus in Josephus, esp. 85n, 87–88, 102.

[546] See SHLOMO PINES, An Arabic Version of the Testimonium Flavanium and its Implications (Jerusalem: The Israel Academy of Sciences and Humanities, 1971), 16.

[547] EDWARD BRATKE, Scriptores ecclesiastici minores saeculorum IV. V. VI., Fasciculus I: Evagrii Altercatio legis inter Simonem Iudaeum et Theophilum Christianum (CSEL 45; Wien / Leipzig: Tempsky / Freytag, 1904), 25; WILLIAM VARNER, Ancient Jewish-Christian Dialogues. Athanasius and Zacchaeus, Simon and Theophilus, Timothy and Aquila: Introductions, Texts, and Translations (Studies in the Bible and Early Christianity 58; Lewiston, N.Y.: Mellen, 2004), 112–113.

The crucifixion of Jesus is a substantial stumbling-block for Trypho, who applies Deut 21:22–23 to suggest Jesus was cursed (cf. Justin, *Dial.* 32; 38; 89; 90), yet Trypho accepts without refutation Justin's charge that Jesus "was crucified under Pontius Pilatus by your people" (*Dial.* 85.2; cf. 108.2). Further study could surface similar tendencies in the *Dialogue of Timothy and Aquila* and in the *Dialogue of Athanasius and Zacchaeus*. Albeit noted for some strikingly anti-Semitic statements, John Chrysostom also testifies that Jewish people respond to the question of why they crucified the Christ with the response: "as being one who leads astray and practices magic" (*Expositio in Psalmum* 8.3; PG 55.110). The *Martyrium Pionii* (13.3–9)[548] implies that Jewish people of Pionius' day considered Jesus a (merely) human criminal and magician, which likely offered a rationale for accepting Jesus' criminal punishment as just (also *Martyrium Cononi* 4.6–7).[549] Similarly, Origen represents Celsus' Jewish source as accusing Jesus of being a brigand (*Contra Celsum* 2.44).

Of course, there are multiple reasons for being suspicious of the accuracy of the Christian portrayal of the Jewish position in such literature, but it is striking that at least on this point, the Christian literature aligns with the limited array we have of extant Jewish *adversus Christianos* literature concerning the involvement of the Jewish populace of Jerusalem in these events e.g., *b. Sanh.* 43a (see No. 70) and many *Toledoth Jeshu* texts. The censored passage of *b. Sanh.* 43a is illustrative of two tendencies in such *adversus Christianos* texts. (1) The Jewish leaders actively seek to execute and suspend Jesus for stated offenses – here, for sorcery as well as for misleading and enticing Israel; such charges also occur in *b. Sanh.* 107b (see No. 71). (2) The passage seeks to make the execution conform in some respects to rabbinic norms (note Yeshu is to be stoned as well as hung), often in fanciful ways (for *forty days* they announce his upcoming execution on the eve of Passover!). The *Toledoth Jeshu*, which constitute medieval Jewish anti-Christian gospels of Jesus' life and death, likely with some lineage from Late Antiquity, evidence very similar tendencies. Indeed some *Toledoth Jeshu* texts represent Jesus (or even his disciples) as having been hung on the cross for his use of magic and then stoned while thus hanging.[550] Such *adversus Christianos* writings typically accept with little hesitation the direct involvement of the first-century Jewish leaders in putting Jesus to death (even at times assuming a level of Jewish legal condemnation more direct than that found in the Gospels). In most such cases the Jewish sources imply Jesus' guilt in contravening biblical law and

---

[548] HERBERT MUSURILLO, The Acts of the Christian Martyrs (Oxford: Clarendon, 1972), 152–155.

[549] MUSURILLO, Acts of the Christian Martyrs, 188–191.

[550] See references in CHAPMAN, Crucifixion, 231n; HILLEL NEWMAN, The Death of Jesus in the *Toledot Yeshu* Literature, JTS 50 (1999): 59–79.

thus justify his execution.[551] Nearly every one of these ancient works has difficult and complex issues involved in its analysis, but the overall picture appears strikingly in favor of Jewish generations in the Roman and the Late Antique periods accepting that first-century Jewish crowds and authorities were involved in supporting the public suspension of Jesus. We would hasten to add that, on any sane response to history, this rightly provides no excuse at all for any of the horrendous tyrannies of anti-Semitism in the many centuries past! Among other matters, the earliest church documents actually represent all in charge in first-century Jerusalem – Jew and Gentile alike – as complicit in the judgment against Jesus. Yet, here is a question ancient historians might well ponder: If both ancient Jewish and Christian documents fairly consistently allow that first-century Jewish leaders found the crucifixion of Jesus expedient, then might modern objections to Jewish involvement by those very leaders be making too much of one line of evidence? The issue, as we said at the start, is complex.

## 3.6  Victims of Crucifixion in the Roman Period

This section includes an array of sources that illustrate the kinds of people who would face the cross during Roman republican and imperial rule. Romans applied bodily suspension principally to the public execution of slaves, brigands, and rebels, and occasionally to conquered enemy generals. Roman citizens (esp. *honestiores*) were typically exempt from such punishments, except in cases of high treason. The few historical exceptions to this citizenship exemption were often met with great opposition in the republican period to the Roman governor who had pronounced such an order. In stark contrast to the privileges of the Roman citizen, Plautus (among our earliest extant Roman sources on the *crux*) repeatedly employs the motif of the slave who fears that his life will end on a cross. Slaves were indeed often crucified, according to our extant sources. And one should not overlook the occasional ancient record of innocent sufferers, heroes and martyrs encountering the cross. Although the literary evidence is extensive, we should remember that we actually only have records of a small portion of crucifixions that were performed in antiquity.[552]

---

[551] This line of investigation could further proceed into medieval *adversus Christianos* Jewish texts, and into accounts of medieval Jewish-Christian disputations, though that would take us even further afield. For some orientation to these possible resources see SAMUEL KRAUSS, The Jewish-Christian Controversy from the Earliest Times to 1789. Volume I: History (ed. W. Horbury; TSAJ 56; Tübingen: Mohr Siebeck, 1996).

[552] This point is aptly made by JOHN GRANGER COOK, Crucifixion I. Greco-Roman Antiquity, EBR 5 (2012): 1085–1086, who also cites HENGEL, Crucifixion, 47. COOK, following HENGEL, notes that while Titus "crucified up to 500 Jews a day during the siege of Jerusa-

Crucifixion served as one of the most (if not *the* most) terrible punishments in the standard arsenal of judicial penalties available to the Roman senate and provincial governors. Thus the Romans typically reserved the cross for the crimes they feared most undermined Roman rule and society – hence its use against rebels who directly sought to overthrow Roman dominion, against brigands who endangered the Roman peace and economic trade, and against slaves whose disobedient and rebellious ways undermined a chief aspect of the Roman economy. Similarly, conquered foreign military commanders could face the cross, though most reported cases were those in which the cross was deemed just retribution for previous severe treatment of Roman captives (especially against enemy commanders who had crucified Roman citizens and soldiers). In times of war, Roman military deserters also could be threatened with the cross, largely in order to discourage others from deserting their posts.

Yet modern readers should remember that every revolution or social movement has at least two sides. While the Roman citizenry often considered the victims of crucifixion to be enemies of Rome, those who disagreed with Roman rule may well have looked on the crucified revolutionary (or even the crucified brigand) as a hero to their cause. A further case in point involves Christians crucified under imperial rule. Many outside the Christian church may have considered their deaths justified, if perhaps at times unduly harsh, while those inside the *ecclesia* looked on their suspended comrades as martyrs.

Specific episodes of Roman crucifixion in the region of Judea-Palestine will appear in section 3.7, which will further fill out the picture of the kinds of victims who went to the Roman *crux*.

## 3.6.1 Social Class

From its earliest known history, Roman law imposed different penalties for citizens than for non-citizens, especially slaves. There was a further distinction between citizens, styled in terms of *honestiores* and *humiliores*, that had to do with economical, political, and social status.[553] Especially as more free-

---

lem," our only knowledge of these crosses comes exclusively from Josephus (*B. J.* 5.449–451), with Tacitus (in *Hist.* 5.8–13) not even mentioning these crucifixions; therefore, awareness of a mass crucifixion such as this comes to us only through the happenstance of possessing extant manuscripts of a single author who was willing to record the atrocious event (rather than overlook it in politically convenient silence). Similarly, the geographical extent of crucifixion can only be deduced by patching together testimony from our extant sources.

[553] The legal juxtaposition of *honestiores/humiliores* is especially witnessed after the Severan period (third century A.D.). However, references to the *persona, dignitas*, and *condicio* of the defendant appeared earlier. The term *humiliores* encompassed the *plebeii* and the *tenuiores* (that is the lower citizen classes); *honestiores* certainly included the senatorial class, as well as other high-status citizens (including veterans, and the decurions who consti-

men of the empire were incorporated into the Roman citizenry, this distinction between *honestiores* and *humiliores* became more significant in Roman law.

As Cicero repeatedly testifies for the era of the Late Republic, typically a convicted Roman citizen might face (at worse) exile or beheading, while the non-citizen convicted of a heinous crime might well be delivered to slavery in the mines/quarries or handed over for crucifixion. For the Romans of Cicero's day, suspension on a *crux* was not properly a penalty to be employed against citizens. However, the crime of high treason against the state appears to have merited death on a *crux*, even for a Roman citizen (and despite Cicero's objections noted below). Still, a few accounts indicate that some Roman provincial governors occasionally brought citizens to the *crux*, though in the late republican and early imperial periods such an action would be cause for complaint against such a governor. In the first century B.C., the great Roman republican orator Cicero made robust use of such accusations, especially in his prosecution against Verres, the former Roman governor of Sicily. In the extensive selections below, Cicero speaks with such passion that it is easy to assume all Romans would have agreed with his assessment that a Roman citizen should never be threatened with the cross. But while Cicero may have had popular sentiment on his side, our sources do not actually provide us with conclusive evidence that all Romans would have concurred (especially in the post-republican empire). Nevertheless, in the two centuries after Cicero, a similar concern that citizens not face the cross can also be found in the writings of Josephus and Suetonius (for Josephus, *B. J.* 2.308 see 3.7). By the time imperial rule was well underway, the *Pauli Sententiae* prevent the application of crucifixion against *honestiores* while simultaneously advocating use of the *crux* against both *humiliores* and (especially) slaves for certain heinous crimes; for evidence of this, see repeatedly in section 3.6.4 on criminals.

**(281)** Cicero, *In Verrem* 2.5.165–166

Adhuc enim testes ex eo genere a me sunt dati, non qui novisse Gavium, sed se vidisse dicerent, cum is, qui se civem Romanum esse clamaret, in crucem ageretur. Hoc tu, Verres, idem dicis, hoc tu confiteris, illum clamitasse se civem esse Romanum; apud te nomen civitatis ne tantum quidem valuisse ut dubitationem aliquam [crucis], ut crudelissimi taeterrimique supplici aliquam parvam moram saltem posset adferre. [166] Hoc teneo, hic haereo, iudices, hoc sum contentus uno, omitto ac neglego cetera; sua confessione induatur ac iuguletur necesse est. Qui esset ignorabas, speculatorem esse suspicabare; non quaero qua suspicione, tua te accuso oratione: civem Romanum se esse dicebat.

---

tuted local municipal leadership). See PETER GARNSEY, Social Status and Legal Privilege in the Roman Empire (Oxford: Clarendon, 1970), 221–223.

*Translation.* For, up to now the witnesses concerning this matter that have been presented by me are not those who said they knew Gavius but those who said they saw him when he, who declared himself to be a Roman citizen, was led to the cross. This, Verres, you say yourself. This you concede: that man declared himself to be a Roman citizen; with you the name of citizen is admittedly not even of such strength that it at least would have been able to bring a fair amount of hesitation [of the cross] or a fair amount of short delay of this cruelest and vilest penalty. [166] This I hold. To this I adhere, judges. With this one matter I am content. I would omit and neglect other matters. By his own confession it is necessary that [Verres] be caught and his throat be slit. You [Verres] were ignorant who [Gavius] was; you suspected [him] to be a spy. I do not inquire what grounds [you had] for suspicion. I accuse you by your own oration: he said he was a Roman citizen.

*Commentary.*[554] Cicero' reputation was greatly increased by his success as the prosecutor of the trial of Verres, which occurred in 70 B.C. The trial took place before the Extortion Court of Rome, which was charged with examining extortion claims against Roman provincial governors and which was temporarily in the hands of senatorial judges. The court had previously been under equestrian control, but Sulla had handed it over to senatorial control about 81 B.C. In the same year as Verres' trial (70 B.C.), a popular movement was seeking to return control of the Extortion Court to the *equites*, and we shall see in the selections below that Cicero occasionally warns the senatorial judges that popular sentiment may strip them of their judicial role (and return the court to the *equites*) should they fail to convict Verres. Cicero was called to serve as prosecutor in this trial on behalf of Sicily (with the notable exception of the Sicilian cities of Messana/Messina and Syracuse, which favored Verres). Sicily was asking for Verres to be prosecuted for actions he had taken during his rule as Roman governor (proconsul) there in 73–71 B.C. Verres was charged with abusing his power in order to: (1) extort great sums from the populace, (2) rob the Sicilian temples of their furnishings, and (3) mistreat the citizens, even to the point of crucifying a Roman citizen named Gavius. The court was effectively a civilian, not a criminal court, and Sicily's goal was to recover a large sum of money from Verres. The form of trial involved two *actiones* (series of speeches and witnesses) separated by a multi-day break in

---

[554] Text: ALBERT CURTIS CLARK and WILLIAM PETERSON, eds., M. Tulli Ciceronis Orationes (Second Edition. 6 vols.; Scriptorum Classicorum Bibliotheca Oxoniensis; Oxford: Clarendon, 1905–1918), vol. 3 ad loc.; the 1948 reprint Clarendon edition does not have page numbers. The bracketed word *crucis* appears in some medieval codices, though alongside further (questionable) alterations to the text; reference to the cross in that line is certainly implied, even if *crucis* was not in the original text. Following recent conventions of citation for this work, the reference above (2.5.165–166) refers to *actio secunda*, i.e. the second series of speeches by Cicero), Book 5. This particular section is also listed under Chapter 64, so a fuller accounting would be: 2.5.64.165–166.

proceedings (*comperendinatio*). After the first *actio*, Verres voluntarily withdrew into exile, thus the case against him was effectively won before a formal judgment could be rendered. The five speeches here, collected under the *actio secunda*, were drafted by Cicero for use in court but were never actually delivered due to Verres' exile; nevertheless, they likely represent Cicero's planned prosecution speeches, which he later published. This famed series of Verrine Orations brought great renown to Cicero: Not only did Cicero's resolve in prosecuting Verres result in Verres' exile (and his *de facto* admission of guilt), but they eloquently bested the arguments of another illustrious orator of the day, Hortensius, who was defending Verres and who had long held sway over Roman judicial proceedings (cf. 2.5.174–176).

At the very culmination of his fifth and final oratory in his second sequence (*actio*) of speeches, Cicero highlights the evidence that Verres crucified a Roman citizen. The text of *In Verrem* 2.5.169 (No. 284) implies Gavius was alive for a period of time while affixed to the freshly-constructed *crux*, so (though Cicero may not describe the precise shape of the *crux*) we shall refer to this as a crucifixion in the discussion below.

For some time in this speech prior to the passage cited above (2.5.165–166), Cicero has been accusing Verres of intentionally executing Roman citizens in Sicily, even hiding some citizens among the imprisoned pirates heading to execution so that no one would know or object (2.5.156–157; cf. 2.5.72–74,77). Cicero then emphasizes the particular case of Publius Gavius, a citizen of the Roman municipality of Cosa/Consa (2.5.158ff.). Gavius was among other Roman citizens whom Verres had earlier imprisoned in the quarries, but Gavius had managed to escape (2.5.160; cf. 2.5.164). When Gavius arrived in Messana, he announced his intent to complain at Rome of his imprisonment as a Roman citizen (2.5.160). But Verres recaptures Gavius and has him stripped in preparation for being beaten. In such a state in the forum of Messana, Gavius publicly declares he is a Roman citizen and proclaims that Lucius Raecius of Panhormus can vouch for his identity (2.5.161). However, Verres (without witnesses) declares him to be a spy, working for escaped slaves (2.5.161). Gavius is scourged, all the while insisting he is a Roman citizen, and then Verres orders a cross for his execution (2.5.162).[555] Throughout this section of the speech, Cicero will take umbrage at the imprisonment of the Roman citizen Gavius and at his scourging and torture; however, it is especially the crucifixion of a Roman citizen that Cicero finds most horrific. And Cicero hopes the Roman judges (themselves citizens) will join him in his

---

[555] *sed cum imploraret saepius usurparetque nomen civitatis, crux – crux, inquam – infelici et aerumnoso, qui numquam istam pestem viderat, comparabatur.* "But, when he repeatedly invoked and asserted the name of citizen, a cross – a cross, I say! – was prepared for this misfortunate and miserable man, who had never seen that instrument of death" (2.5.162). Some "inferior" manuscripts read *potestatem* instead of *pestem* ("instrument of death"); CLARK / PETERSON, M. Tulli Ciceronis Orationes, ad loc.

indignation against Verres. Cicero has already promised to bring witnesses who can prove the crucified Gavius was indeed a citizen (2.5.164).[556] At this stage in the text above, Cicero seeks to convince the jury, simply on the basis of Verres' own testimony, that Verres knew Gavius was claiming citizenship but had, nonetheless, refused to delay his execution to allow time for the claim to be substantiated.[557] Cicero argues that the citizenship claim should have caused hesitation and delay, given that Gavius was facing the "cruelest and vilest penalty" (*crudelissimi taeterrimique supplici*).

The short passage above neatly summarizes the key planks at this stage in Cicero's argument, so we have cited it first. However, Cicero repeatedly returns to Gavius' execution on the cross in his oratory, and thus it is worth quoting below the other passages that emphasize how strongly he (and others) felt about the injury caused to the Roman people by having one of their fellow citizens crucified.[558]

**(282)**  Cicero, *In Verrem* 2.5.163

O nomen dulce libertatis! o ius eximium nostrae civitatis! o lex Porcia legesque Semproniae! o graviter desiderata et aliquando reddita plebi Romanae tribunicia potestas! Hucine tandem haec omnia reciderunt ut civis Romanus in provincia populi Romani, in oppido foederatorum, ab eo qui beneficio populi Romani fascis et securis haberet deligatus in foro virgis caederetur? Quid? cum ignes ardentesque laminae ceterique cruciatus admovebantur, si te illius acerba imploratio et vox miserabilis non inhibebat, ne civium quidem Romanorum qui tum aderant fletu et gemitu maximo commovebare? In crucem tu agere ausus es quemquam qui se civem Romanum esse diceret? Nolui tam vehementer agere hoc prima actione, iudices, nolui; vidistis enim ut animi multitudinis in istum dolore et odio et communis periculi metu concitarentur.

---

[556] *Producam etiam Consanos municipes illius ac necessarios, qui te nunc sero doceant, iudices non sero, illum P. Gavium quem tu in crucem egisti civem Romanum et municipem Consanum, non speculatorem fugitivorum fuisse.* "I will also produce Cosani (municipal citizens of that place) and close relations, who will teach you (now that it is too late) and the judges (for whom it is not too late), that the very Publius Gavius, whom you crucified [*quem tu in crucem egisti*], was a Roman citizen and a municipal citizen of Cosa, and not a spy of fugitive slaves" (2.5.164).

[557] Cicero presses this again a bit later in 2.5.166: *ille, quisquis erat, quem tu in crucem rapiebas, qui tibi esset ignotus, cum civem se Romanum esse diceret, apud te praetorem si non effugium ne moram quidem mortis mentione atque usurpatione civitatis adsequi potuit?* "That man, whoever he was, whom you raced to the cross [and] who was unknown to you, when he said he was a Roman, was it possible to attain with you as praetor, if not an escape, at least a delay of death at the mention and assertion of citizenship?"

[558] Thus a full accounting of Cicero's crucifixion language in *Against Verres* will be found in sections 3.6.1 and 3.6.2.

*Translation.* O sweet name of liberty! O exceptional right of our citizenship! O Porcian Law and the Sempronian Laws! O tribunal power, which had been sorely missed and at long last restored to the Roman plebeians! Have not all these things lapsed to such a degree that a Roman citizen – in the provinces of the Roman people, in a town of our federated peoples, by him who by the beneficence of the Roman people had the *fasces* and *securis* – [that such a citizen] had been tied up in the forum and beaten with rods? What? When fire and burning objects of metal and other torture devices are applied, if the bitter entreaty and miserable cry of that man did not restrain you, will not even those [entreaties and cries] of the Roman citizens who at that time attended with tears and were shaking with intense moaning? Are you one who dares to compel anyone to the cross who has said he is a Roman citizen? I was not so willing to push this vigorously in the first trial, judges – I was not willing. For you saw that the high spirits of the multitude were incited against that man by their indignation and antipathy and fear of public harm.

*Commentary.* This passage is found a few paragraphs earlier than our previous text. It represents Cicero's appeal to Roman legal precedents (and to the anger of the multitude) against Verres' act of publicly beating, torturing and suspending on a *crux* a Roman citizen (i.e., Gavius). He lists the laws of freemen and of citizens, the precedents of Cato (i.e., the Porcian Law of Marcus Porcius Cato) and of the Gracchi (i.e., Sempronian Laws of Tiberius and Gaius Sempronius Gracchus), and the tribunal power that had been granted to the plebeians (i.e., the non-patrician Roman citizens), implying that all these precedents would have opposed this form of executing a Roman citizen.[559] In doing so, Cicero also subtly invokes class animosity within the Roman citizenry between plebeians and patricians, perhaps as a warning against those senators who might conspire with Verres to see him acquitted for their own gain. Cicero emphasizes that the location where Gavius was beaten and crucified was a Roman provincial town (i.e., Messana), surrounded by many Roman citizens; he was a citizen maltreated within Roman territory among other citizens. The sequence of punishments is typical of such suspensions: beating and torture followed by suspension on a *crux*. Cicero has previously not highlighted that torture had been applied to Gavius (in addition to the beating and especially to the affixing to a *crux*). Cicero observes the irony that the very citizens who had granted Verres the visible emblems of provincial rule (the *fasces* and *securis*) were now mournfully witnessing the illegal public suspension of a fellow citizen on the *crux*. According to Cicero, Verres is unmoved by the tears of anyone. Finally, Cicero alludes to the public anger that (as he writes in the sentence immediately following the passage cited above) might have sparked vigilante justice at the first *actio* had Cicero not

---

[559] Cicero makes a similar appeal in *Pro Rabirio Perduellionis Reo* 3.12; 4.13; see below.

checked the testimony at that previous portion of the trial and had he not concurred with the judge, who quickly dismissed Cicero's *eques*-witness (who was testifying to this treatment of a Roman citizen).

**(283)** Cicero, *In Verrem* 2.5.168

Quid? si L. Raecium,[560] equitem Romanum, qui tum erat in Sicilia, nominabat, etiamne id magnum fuit, Panhormum litteras mittere? Adservasses hominem custodiis Mamertinorum tuorum, vinctum clausum habuisses, dum Panhormo Raecius veniret; cognosceret hominem, aliquid de summo supplicio remitteres; si ignoraret, tum, si ita tibi videretur, hoc iuris in omnis constitueres, ut, qui neque tibi notus esset neque cognitorem locupletem daret, quamvis civis Romanus esset, in crucem tolleretur.

*Translation.* What? If [Gavius] named [as guarantor of his citizenship] Lucius Raecius, a Roman *eques*, who was then in Sicily, was it actually a great matter to send a letter to Panhormus? You might have guarded the man in the garrison of your Mamertines; you might have had him fettered in an inaccessible place, until Raecius came from Panhormus. Would he have known the man, then you could relax the most extreme penalty in some way; if he did not know him, then if it appeared to you best, you would establish this for a law among all: that, he who neither was known to you nor could provide a guarantor who could give security, even though he was a Roman citizen, he was to be raised on a cross.

*Commentary.* Here, Cicero drives home his point that it would have been very little trouble to have verified Gavius' citizenship claim. In the process, Cicero refers to the *crux* as the "most extreme penalty" (cf. *de summo supplicio remitteres*). Even allowing for some rhetorical flourish, Cicero appears serious in his charge that no other standard Roman legal penalty was worse for a person (especially a citizen!) to endure.[561] This passage is preceded by a long sentence arguing that it would undermine the protections of every Roman citizen were a precedent established requiring citizens to be ready at any time to produce proof of citizenship. In antiquity there was no standard documentation for people to carry with them. With that in mind, the final clauses above appear to be ironic: Verres could have established a law enabling the accused to avoid the cross if he had a guarantor, and even that abhorrent outcome would be better than the injustice administered to Gavius.[562]

---

[560] For *Raecium* the codices also read *Recium* or *Pretium*.

[561] Concerning *summum supplicium*, see further the discussion of the *Pauli Sententiae* in section 3.6.4, and the analysis of such terminology in 3.10.3.

[562] The notion of "guarantor" (*cognitor*), here combined with *locuples* ("able to give security"), may be a reference to a person of sufficient wealth to pay for the release of the accused

**(284)** Cicero, *In Verrem* 2.5.169

Sed quid ego plura de Gavio? quasi tu Gavio tum fueris infestus ac non nomini generi iuri civium hostis. Non illi, inquam, homini sed causae communi libertatis inimicus fuisti. Quid enim attinuit, cum Mamertini more atque instituto suo crucem fixissent post urbem in via Pompeia, te iubere in ea parte figere quae ad fretum spectaret, et hoc addere, – quod negare nullo modo potes, quod omnibus audientibus dixisti palam, – te idcirco illum locum deligere, ut ille, quoniam se civem Romanum esse diceret, ex cruce Italiam cernere ac domum suam prospicere posset? Itaque illa crux sola, iudices, post conditam Messa-nam illo in loco fixa est. Italiae conspectus ad eam rem ab isto delectus est, ut ille in dolore cruciatuque moriens perangusto fretu divisa servitutis ac libertatis iura cognosceret, Italia autem alumnum suum servitutis extremo summoque supplicio adfixum[563] videret.

*Translation*. But what more shall I [say] concerning Gavius? As if you [Verres] then were hostile to Gavius and not an enemy to the name, to the class, and to the law of the citizen. Not that, I say, you had been an opponent to men, but to the common cause of freedom. For, what was important such that, when the Mamertines by custom and by their own established practice had fastened up a cross outside the city on the Pompeian road, you [instead] ordered [the cross] to be fastened up in that part [of the city] which looks on the straits, and that you added this – which you are by no means able to deny, because you spoke openly among all who heard – that you for that reason chose that place, so that that man, since he said that he was a Roman citizen, would be able to discern Italy from the cross and to look before him at his own home? Accordingly, that cross alone, judges, subsequent to the founding of Messana has been fastened in that place. The view of Italy had been chosen by *that* man [Verres][564] for this purpose, so that that man [i.e., Gavius] who was dying in grief and torture would know that by a very narrow strait the laws of slavery and freedom have been divided, while Italy saw her own son fastened upon the desperate and most extreme punishment of slaves.

*Commentary*. Cicero continues his oratory by asserting that Verres' crucifixion of a single Roman citizen was effectively an attack on the very nature of citizenship. Verres' intentional disregard of Gavius' claim to citizenship is further heightened by his decision to break with Sicilian custom and have Gavius

---

(cf. OLD s.v. *locuples*). This, too, may be a subtle jab at Verres' lust for wealth, such that he would require the person (despite his citizenship) to be bought out of his punishment.

[563] *adfixum* is proposed by Naugerius; codices read *defixum*, *fixum*, or *ea fixum*; the essential meaning remains unchanged.

[564] Among Cicero's many rhetorical subtleties, note how Cicero employs the more perjorative *ab isto* ["by *that* man"] in reference to Verres (contrast the more neutral *ille* as "that man" for Gavius).

affixed to a *crux* in a location across the Straits of Messana overlooking Rome. Cicero's language indicates that this new *crux* was a device constructed according to Verres' command. Cicero assumes previous crucifixions had occurred in Messana, where "the Mamertines by custom and by their own established practice had fastened up a cross outside the city on the Pompeian road." The reference to "Mamertines" refers to the people of Messana, who were ruled in the third century B.C. by a warlike race of Campanian mercenaries known as "Mamertines." These mercenaries plundered the rest of Sicily and set Carthage and Rome at odds (events that led to the First Punic War). The term not only invokes the heritage of the people of Messana but also may imply some level of barbarity.

This passage strongly implies Gavius was alive when he was affixed to the *crux*, since he could "discern Italy from the cross" (*ex cruce Italiam cernere*) and "look before him at his home" (*domum suam prospicere*), and since as he "was dying in grief and torture" (*in dolore cruciatuque moriens*), he "would know" (*cognosceret*) that he was separated from the privileges of freedom by a narrow strait of water.[565] Such an *ante-mortem* execution on a *crux* could hardly remind Cicero's readers of anything other than crucifixion.[566] Cicero describes affixing someone to such a cross as "the desperate and most extreme punishment of slaves" (*servitutis extremo summoque supplicio*).

## (285) Cicero, *In Verrem* 2.5.170–171

Facinus est vincire civem Romanum, scelus verberare, prope parricidium necare: quid dicam in crucem tollere? Verbo satis digno tam nefaria res appellari nullo modo potest. Non fuit his omnibus iste contentus; 'spectet,' inquit, 'patriam; in conspectu legum libertatisque moriatur.' Non tu hoc loco Gavium, non unum hominem nescio quem, sed communem libertatis et civitatis causam in illum cruciatum et crucem egisti. Iam vero videte hominis audaciam! Nonne eum graviter tulisse arbitramini quod illam civibus Romanis crucem non posset in foro, non in comitio, non in rostris defigere? Quod enim his locis in provincia sua celebritate simillimum, regione proximum potuit, elegit; monumentum sceleris audaciaeque suae voluit esse in conspectu Italiae, vestibulo Siciliae, praetervectione omnium qui ultro citroque navigarent. [171] Si haec non ad civis Romanos, non ad aliquos amicos nostrae civitatis, non

---

[565] It is theoretically possible that Cicero here speaks in poetical exaggeration and that Gavius' lifeless body was merely hanging in such a way as to face (or "look at") Italy, much as when Italy "saw her son" facing this dread end at the end of 2.5.169. However, the rhetoric, with its repeated emphasis on Gavius conscious viewing of Italy, pushes the reader to the conclusion that this execution was all the more poignant because Gavius truly did expire while witnessing the freedoms of Italy not far off.

[566] Certainly this could not refer to impalement (let alone to hanging on a noose), since that would have constituted a fairly instantaneous death, while Gavius' death was prolonged.

ad eos qui populi Romani nomen audissent, denique si non ad homines verum ad bestias, aut etiam, ut longius progrediar, si in aliqua desertissima solitudine ad saxa et ad scopulos haec conqueri ac deplorare vellem, tamen omnia muta atque inanima tanta et tam indigna rerum acerbitate commoverentur. Nunc vero cum loquar apud senatores populi Romani, legum et iudiciorum et iuris auctores, timere non debeo ne non unus iste civis Romanus illa cruce dignus, ceteri omnes simili periculo indignissimi iudicentur.

*Translation.* It is a crime to fetter a Roman citizen, wickedness to flog him, nearly parricide to kill him: what would I call 'to raise him on a cross'? Such a vile thing can by no means be named by a sufficiently suitable word. That man there [Verres] was not content with all this: "Let him look on the fatherland," he said, "[and] in the view of laws and freedom let him die." You [Verres] have not in this place [driven to torture and the cross] Gavium, nor a single unknown man, but you drove the common cause of freedom and citizenship onto that torture and cross. Now truly look at the audacity of this man! Did you [Verres] not think to take offense that it was impossible to embed that cross of Roman citizens in the forum, nor in the place of assembly, nor in the rostrum? For, to the extent that he chose the area in his crowded province that he was able [to consider] most similar to these places and the nearest territory, he wished the monument of his wickedness and audacity to be in the view of Italy, at the entrance to Sicily, to the place where all who navigated on both sides sailed past. [171] If these matters – not to Roman citizens, nor to some friends of our citizenship, nor to those who have heard the renown of the Roman people, even if not to true men but to beasts, or (yet that I might go further) if in some deserted wasteland to boulders and crags – if I wanted to bewail and lament these matters, nevertheless all mute and inanimate things would be moved by so great and such undeserved bitterness of deed. Now truly when I speak with senators of the Roman people, authors of laws and judgments and a legal code, I ought not fear lest that one Roman citizen there [will] not [be judged as] deserving that cross, and all others will be judged as most undeserving a similar harm.

*Commentary.* As Cicero brings this discussion of Gavius' crucifixion to a close, he emphasizes the "audacity" and "wickedness" of Verres, whose wanton act effectively undid the special prerogatives of citizenship. The *crux* is here also identified with torture (perhaps due to the tortures that preceded being pinned to a *crux* but also likely because the *crux* was itself a torturous way to die). The *crux* is certainly represented as a public means of death – so that even people at sea could witness the event as they looked upon the island. Cicero's rhetoric in the complex final sentence implies that Verres himself was actually the only Roman citizen truly deserving of death on the *crux*, and all other Roman citizens are undeserving of being crucified. Finally, we should return to the first sentence in this passage (2.5.170), which evidences the Ciceronian passion against crucifying Roman citizens; this is likely best comprehended in the loose translation by GREENWOOD: "To bind a Roman citizen is a crime, to flog him is an abomination, to slay him is almost an act of murder: to crucify him is – what? There is no fitting word that can possibly describe so horrible a deed."[567]

**(286)** Cicero, *In Verrem* 2.1.6–7

Tametsi de absolutione istius neque ipse iam sperat nec populus Romanus metuit: de impudentia singulari, quod adest, quod respondet, sunt qui mirentur. Mihi pro cetera eius audacia atque amentia ne hoc quidem mirandum videtur; multa enim et in deos et in homines impie nefarieque commisit, quorum scelerum poenis agitatur et a mente consilioque deducitur. [7] Agunt eum praecipitem poenae civium Romanorum, quos partim securi percussit, partim in vinculis necavit, partim implorantis iura libertatis et civitatis in crucem sustulit.

*Translation.* Yet, concerning that man's acquittal neither he himself now hopes [for it], nor the Roman people fear [it]: concerning this effrontery alone – that he is present, that he speaks in his defense – these are what bewilder. To me, in view of his other audacities and insane acts, this does not even appear strange. For he impiously and wickedly committed many things against both gods and men, for which wickedness he is being troubled by the penalties and is being weighed down by his mind and his inner deliberation. [7] The penalties of the Roman citizens drive him to the brink, some of whom he beheaded, some he killed in captivity, [and] some while they invoked the law of freedom and citizenship he raised up on the cross.

*Commentary.* Having just examined several passages from the end of Cicero's second series of orations against Verres (Book 5), we now return to the beginning of those speeches (Book 1). In these opening paragraphs, Cicero lays the groundwork for his whole series of speeches by surveying the arguments to which he will return throughout. Although Verres' voluntary exile preempted

---

[567] GREENWOOD, Verrine Orations, 2:655, 657. GREENWOOD, who argues that *parricidium* in this context simply means "murder" and not actually "parricide", states ibid. 654: "The actions *vincire, verberare, necare* are spoken of as the actions of a *magistrate*. That a magistrate should officially execute a Roman citizen in any manner is, Cicero says, nearly as bad as that one private person should murder another. Cicero does not mean us to think of Roman citizens actually convicted of crime: but even such persons were not normally bound, flogged or executed, so that even applied to them the dictum is not a gross or obvious exaggeration." Yet, it should be remembered that "parricide" in Roman law extended beyond killing parents to the killing of siblings and children; parricide was a particularly atrocious form of murder that was punished more harshly than other acts of homicide; thus "parricide" fits well here with the Ciceronian exaggerated rhetoric.

the actual delivery of the speeches in this second *actio*, Cicero wrote this speech anticipating Verres' appearance in court. In this passage, Cicero seems to diminish the impact of Verres' appearance, holding it up to contempt and attributing it to insanity, saying there is no way Verres can hope to gain a positive outcome. Verres, Cicero says, is troubled by the penalties his wickedness deserves. His mind and inner thoughts are weighing him down as he finds himself contemplating his wickedness and its inevitable result. What is driving him to the brink of insanity? For a start, his overly harsh penalties against Roman citizens. Cicero then begins to list Verres' wicked acts, starting with his executions of Roman citizens. He will later go on to list other offenses, including Verres' defiling of the sanctuaries of the gods. Here in 2.1.7, Cicero briefly catalogues the manner in which Verres executed Roman citizens. Note that "raised up on the cross" (*in crucem sustulit*) culminates the list. Even as they are being hung up on the *crux,* these citizens are said to have "invoked the law of freedom and citizenship" (*implorantis iura libertatis et civitatis*). This is certainly reminiscent of the Gavius account above (2.5.163–171). It is unclear whether Cicero believes other citizens (in addition to Gavius) were crucified by Verres (note the use of *partim,* "some"), or whether he is merely overstating the case.

**(287)** Cicero, *In Verrem* 2.1.9

Nam quis hoc non intellegit, istum absolutum dis hominibusque invitis tamen ex manibus populi Romani eripi nullo modo posse? Quis hoc non perspicit, praeclare nobiscum actum iri si populus Romanus istius unius supplicio contentus fuerit, ac non sic statuerit, non istum maius in sese scelus concepisse, – cum fana spoliarit, cum tot homines innocentis necarit, cum civis Romanos morte, cruciatu, cruce adfecerit, cum praedonum duces accepta pecunia dimiserit,[568] – quam eos, si qui istum tot tantis tam nefariis sceleribus coopertum iurati sententia sua liberarint?

*Translation.* For who does not understand this: although that man were acquitted against the wishes of the gods and men, nevertheless he would by no means be able to be snatched away from the hands of the Roman people? Who does not perceive this: it would work out splendid for us if the Roman people were content with the punishment of that one man, and not determined as follows: that very man has not produced a greater wickedness in himself than those – when he despoiled temples, when he killed so many innocent men, when he visited Roman citizens with death, torture and the cross, and when he released the leaders of the pirates by accepting a bribe – if those, con-

---

[568] The phrase *cum praedonum ... dimiserti* is omitted in some manuscripts.

spiring by their own sentence, let that one free who is so deep in so very many nefarious wicked deeds.

*Commentary.* In this passage, Cicero implies that even an acquittal would not avail Verres, for the citizens of Rome would still seek justice. Indeed – and this is the point of the long final sentence – were the senators to acquit Verres, they would be deemed as wicked conspirators with him, and the masses would not be at all content. In our first of many selections from this oration (see above commentary on *In Verrem* 2.5.165–166), we noted that the historical context of this trial places it during a tenuous time for the Roman senate. Under Sulla, the senate had exerted greater authority over Roman politics, including the acquisition from the *equites* of control of the Extortion Court, which heard all judicial charges of extortion against Roman provincial governors. However, in the year of this trial (70 B.C.), the lesser ranks of Roman society were reasserting their political leverage, including seeking the return of the Extortion Court to the *equites*. Cicero recognizes that bribes from Verres to the senators might well result in his acquittal. To counter that possibility, Cicero implies that a "not guilty" vote would likely result in popular insurrection against the senate, leading perhaps to a loss of senatorial control over the Extortion Court. In the center of this long sentence above, through a series of *cum* clauses, Cicero inserts evidence for Verres' excessive number of nefarious wicked deeds (*tantis tam nefariis sceleribus*). These include robbing temples, killing innocent people, and accepting bribes from pirates/brigands (*praedones*). They also include visiting Roman citizens with death, torture, and the cross (*cum civis Romanos morte, cruciatu, cruce adfecerit*).[569]

## (288) Cicero, *In Verrem* 2.1.12–13

Ex hoc quoque evaserit: proficiscar eo quo me iam pridem vocat populus Romanus; [13]de iure enim libertatis et civitatis suum putat esse iudicium, et recte putat. Confringat iste sane vi sua consilia senatoria, quaestiones omnium perrumpat, evolet ex vestra severitate: mihi credite, artioribus apud populum Romanum laqueis tenebitur. Credet his[570] equitibus Romanis populus Romanus qui ad vos antea producti testes ipsis inspectantibus ab isto civem Romanum, qui cognitores homines honestos daret, sublatum esse in crucem dixerunt.

---

[569] The reader will note this provides yet another opportunity to distinguish *cruciatus* ("torture") from the *crux* ("cross"); cf. OLD and LEWIS-SHORT on these terms. Though *cruciatus* and *crux* share lexical stems, they must have different senses and referents, as is evident from the tri-fold escalation in punishments implied by *cum civis Romanos morte, cruciatu, cruce adfecerit* in the sentence above.

[570] For *his*, many editions read *iis*.

*Translation.* Should he [Verres] also have escaped from this [charge]: I would proceed there to the place where the Roman people long ago called me; [13]for, concerning the law of liberty and citizenship, [the people] suppose that the jurisdiction is theirs, and they suppose rightly. Let that man [Verres] soundly subvert by his force the senatorial councils, let him force a way through everyone's inquiries, and let him fly away from your severity: believe me, he will be held with firmer bonds in the custody of the Roman people. The Roman people will believe those Roman *equites* (having been previously produced for you as witnesses, since those very actions had been observed), who have spoken about how a Roman citizen (who could give honorable men as guarantors) had been raised up on a cross by that man.

*Commentary.* The section that began in the previous text (2.1.9) now proceeds more directly to Cicero's warning. Even should Verres elude punishment by the senate's Extortion Court for his many extortive acts while a provincial governor (enumerated again by Cicero in 2.1.9–12), the Roman people would still cry out for justice against his persecution of fellow citizens. The Extortion Court, before whom Cicero speaks, technically can only consider the financial charges against Verres. However, Cicero all along has portrayed Verres' cruelty to citizens. Though Verres' friends had sought to shield him from a trial before the Roman tribunes, such a trial could still be demanded by the Roman populace (were the Extortion Court to fail in its duties). After this passage, Cicero will go on to summarize the many acts that could impeach Verres before the tribunal (2.1.13–14), including his beheading of Roman citizens and his sentencing of citizens to the quarries. However, Cicero begins that list with the most shocking crime against civic liberty: the raising of a citizen on a cross (*sublatum esse in crucem*). This presumably refers to the crucifixion of Gavius, to which Cicero will return repeatedly throughout the prosecution.

**(289)** Cicero, *In Verrem* 2.3.6

qui civium Romanorum iura ac libertatem sanctam apud omnis haberi velit, is non tibi plus etiam quam inimicus esse debeat, cum tua verbera, cum securis, cum cruces ad civium Romanorum supplicia fixas recordetur?

*Translation.* He who wishes the laws and freedom of Roman citizens to be sacred before all men – ought he not be to you even more than an enemy, when he calls to mind your whips, the axes for execution, and the crosses erected for the punishment of Roman citizens?

*Commentary.* It appears that Hortensius, in Verres' defense, attempted to impeach Cicero's motives in acting as prosecutor, likely by insinuating that Cicero bore personal enmity against Verres (see earlier in 2.3.6).[571] Cicero begins this third oratory by stating that he concurs that prosecutors should not act out of a personal grudge or for the sake of reward (2.3.1). In this paragraph, Cicero contends that if he has enmity against Verres, it is not because of personal injury; rather, it stems from conflicting views of loyalty to Rome, and especially from Verres' willingness to rob others, commit adultery, plunder sanctuaries, and to commit continuous judicial injustices. At the culmination of a series of rhetorical questions concerning enmity against Verres' crimes, the above passage concludes with a reminder that Verres had erected *cruces* for the punishment of Roman citizens. Again, the plural *civium Romanorum* implies that Cicero believes Verres crucified (or at least intended to crucify) other citizens besides Gavius.

**(290)** Cicero, *In Verrem* 2.3.58–59

Contempsit Siculos; non duxit homines nec ipsos ad persequendum vehementis fore, et vos eorum iniurias leviter laturos existimavit. [59] Esto; falsam de illis habuit opinionem, malam de vobis; verum tamen, cum de Siculis male mereretur, civis Romanos coluit, iis indulsit, eorum voluntati et gratiae deditus fuit. Iste civis Romanos? At nullis inimicior aut infestior fuit. Mitto vincla, mitto carcerem, mitto verbera, mitto securis, crucem denique illam praetermitto quam iste civibus Romanis testem humanitatis in eos ac benivolentiae suae voluit esse – mitto, inquam, haec omnia atque in aliud dicendi tempus reicio; de decumis, de civium Romanorum condicione in arationibus disputo; qui quem ad modum essent accepti, iudices, audistis ex ipsis; bona sibi erepta esse dixerunt.[572]

*Translation.* He despised the Sicilians. He did not consider them men – he did not suppose they would be vigorous in seeking restitution, and he supposed you would endure their injustices lightly. [59] So be it! He had a false opinion of them, and an evil one of you; however, [we might think that] while he behaved badly among the Sicilians, he fostered Roman citizens, he was lenient to them, [and] he was devoted to their goodwill and favor. That man foster Roman citizens?! Rather, to none was he more ill-disposed or hostile. I pass over the fetters, I pass over the prison, I pass over the whips, I pass over the executioner's axes, I further omit to mention that cross which that man wanted to be the proof to Roman citizens of his humanity to them and of his benevolence – I pass over, I say, all these matters, and I postpone to speak [about them] to another time. Concerning the tithes – concerning the condition of Roman citizens in the estates – I examine. How they were greeted – you, judges, heard from them. They well said that [their property] was seized from them.

---

[571] Presumably this had occurred in the first *actio*. Alternatively, Cicero was anticipating that Hortensius would make such a charge during the second *actio*.

[572] Many manuscripts read the more difficult *dixere*.

*Commentary*. Cicero argues that while Verres despised the native Sicilians, he also treated harshly even the Roman citizens under his provincial rule. At this point in the argument, Cicero is presenting evidence that Verres encouraged a system of tax-farming that was not content with the mere "tenth" (*decumus*) due from the citizens who were working the estates (*arationes*) farmed out in return for a tithe of the produce. Much greater taxes were required, and the punishments for failure to pay were severe (e.g., 2.3.48–57). Even Roman *equites* were made to suffer such injustices (cf. 2.3.60–63). Yet in the midst of this argument, Cicero cannot help but digress and sarcastically point out that Verres also applied worse injustices to Roman citizens – chains, prison, scourgings, and executions – with this list culminating with the *crux*. To these injustices he promises to return later in his orations; and indeed he does so in 2.5.163–171, as we saw above. Here, the term for cross is singular (*crucem*), implying one of three things: Verres used only one such device to crucify many citizens; he performed only one actual act of crucifixion against a citizen (i.e., Gavius); or Cicero is using "cross" here generically for the punishment of crucifixion Verres repeatedly applied. These options cause us to struggle again with the tension between Cicero's initial implication that Verres crucified many citizens (2.1.7; 2.3.6; and possibly 2.1.9; 2.3.70, 112) and his naming only Gavius as a crucified Roman citizen (2.5.163–171).

**(291)**  Cicero, *In Verrem* 2.3.70

Haec condicio fuit isto praetore aratorum, ut secum praeclare agi arbitrarentur si vacuos agros Apronio tradere liceret; multas enim cruces propositas effugere cupiebant.

*Translation*. This was the situation of the farmers while that one was *praetor*, with the result that they imagined it to go very successfully with themselves if he fetched vacant farms to hand over to Apronius; for they desired to flee from the many crosses that were being exhibited.

*Commentary*. During Verres' praetorship, he contracted much of his tax-farming out to Apronius for sums of produce the territory itself could not sustain. Here, Cicero depicts the farmers (*aratores*) in Sicily as being glad for Verres to merely take control of vacated farms. Their worse fear was to be sent to the *cruces* that were on show. It is possible this refers to mere tortures, but the frequent use of *crux* elsewhere in this work makes it probable that Cicero alludes to crosses.[573]

---

[573] OLD s.v. *crux*: *cruces* can refer to tortures, though it more commonly references the cross and "any wooden frame on which criminals were exposed to die." GREENWOOD, Verrine Orations, 2:83 translates the *multas enim cruces propositas effugere cupiebant* clause as "they were only too eager to escape the numerous sufferings they saw in front of them". On the

**(292)** Cicero, *In Verrem* 2.3.112

Iugera professi sunt aratores omnes imperio atque instituto tuo: non opinor quemquam minus esse professum quam quantum arasset, cum tot cruces, tot supplicia,[574] tot ex cohorte recuperatores proponerentur.

*Translation.* All the farmers made a return of their acreage to your command and program: I do not suppose anyone returned less than the amount he ploughed, when so many crosses, so many punishments, and so many assessors from [your] staff were being exhibited.

*Commentary.* Cicero continues to charge Verres with harshness in his tax farming via Apronius. Apronius kept no records of his receipts, which Cicero finds highly suspicious. Cicero notes that the farmers (*aratores*) certainly complied with Verres' program but did so under duress. Cicero may even be insinuating that they were made to pay everything they cultivated (*quam quantum arasset*) – much more than a mere tenth![575] In the following paragraphs, Cicero will contend that Apronius actually promised to collect more "tithes" than the land could produce (e.g., 2.3.112–119). The means of gaining compliance involved the "crosses, penalties and assessors," who were continually in the public view. As with the previous selection from Cicero, *cruces* could potentially refer to "tortures" but more likely implies public crosses that were used to threaten local farmers into submission.[576]

**(293)** Cicero, *In Verrem* 2.4.24

Hinc illa Verria nata sunt, quod in convivium Sex. Cominium protrahi iussit, in quem scyphum de manu iacere conatus est, quem obtorta gula de convivio in vincla atque in tenebras abripi iussit; hinc illa crux in quam iste civem Romanum multis inspectantibus sustulit, quam non ausus est usquam defigere nisi apud eos quibuscum omnia scelera sua ac latrocinia communicavit.

---

other hand, JAMES WHITE, The Orations of Marcus Tullius Cicero against Caius Cornelius Verres, Translated from the Original (London: Cadell, 1787), 213 translates as, "It was their object to escape crucifixion."

[574] For *supplicia* one important codex reads *iudicia*.

[575] Cf. esp. 2.3.114: *multis autem non modo granum nullum, sed ne paleae quidem ex omni fructu atque ex annuo labore relinquerentur* ("for many however in no way had a single grain of corn, but they did not even leave behind the chaff of wheat out of all their yield and yearlong labor").

[576] While GREENWOOD renders *cruces* as "tortures", CHARLES DUKE YONGE, The Orations of Marcus Tullius Cicero, literally translated (London: Bell, 1903), translates with "crosses". Since *cruces* is earlier in the list here, and not at its normal culmination of punishments, it is more possible here to conceive it merely means "tortures"; however, the usage elsewhere in Cicero still favors *crux* meaning "cross."

*Translation.* From here [Messana] that Verrean festival was born, because at a banquet he [Verres] ordered Sextus Cominius dragged forward, at whom by his own hand he had endeavored to throw a goblet, and whom with a noose around the throat he ordered to be snatched away from the banquet into fetters and darkness. From here [Messana] was that cross, on which that man there [Verres] hung up a Roman citizen while many watched, which [cross] he had not dared to plant anywhere except among them, with whom he shared all his villainy and brigandage.

*Commentary.* In this section, Cicero counters the fact that the city of Messana had sent a delegation to Rome to praise Verres. Messana was the Sicilian city from which Verres ruled the island. Earlier in this oration, Cicero demonstrated that Gaius Heius, the lead eulogizer from Messana, had essentially admitted Verres had stolen art from him (2.4.3–19; 2.4.27–28; cf. 2.2.13); thus even Verres' friends inadvertently provide evidence to condemn him. Cicero then accuses the city populace of complicity in Verres' outrages, for they themselves benefitted from his crimes, especially as Verres, without approval of the senate, made them exempt from their dutiful fiscal obligations to Rome (2.4.20–23). In the passage above, Cicero insinuates that the people of Messana were well aware of Verres' criminal acts against respectable citizens. They stood by when Verres publicly humiliated Sextus Cominius at a banquet and threw him into prison (the place of fetters and darkness). Verres himself apparently instigated the Verrean festival in Messana, at which he claimed divine honors, though the people of Sicily discontinued it after he left the island.[577] Cicero charges the people of Messana with sharing in Verres' criminal behavior, which Cicero describes in some of the strongest possible terms for forceful robbery (*omnia scelera sua ac latrocinia*, "all his villainy and brigandage"). More importantly, this passage alludes to the crucifixion of Gavius, and observes that the people of Messana not only watched (*multis inspectantibus*) this outrage against a Roman citizen but served as the only populace among whom Verres would dare to commit such an act.

## (294) Cicero, *In Verrem* 2.4.26

In populi Romani quidem conspectum quo ore vos commisistis? nec prius illam crucem, quae etiam nunc civis Romani sanguine redundat, quae fixa est

---

[577] On the Verrean Festival, see OLD, 2039. Cicero elsewhere describes the festival as "shameful" (*flagitiosa*) and says, "for it would be least fitting if the honor of the gods would be had by him who carried off the images of the gods" (2.4.151), a reference to Verres robbing temples. See further 2.2.52; 2.2.114; 2.2.154.

ad portum urbemque vestram, revellistis neque in profundum abiecistis locumque illum omnem expiastis, quam Romam atque in horum conventum adiretis? In Mamertinorum solo foederato atque pacato monumentum istius crudelitatis constitutum est. Vestrane urbs electa est ad quam cum adirent ex Italia cives crucem civis Romani prius quam quemquam amicum populi Romani viderent? quam vos Reginis, quorum civitati invidetis, itemque incolis vestris, civibus Romanis, ostendere soletis, quo minus sibi adrogent minusque vos despiciant, cum videant ius civitatis illo supplicio esse mactatum.

*Translation.* With what countenance did you [people of Messana] present yourselves in the very view of the Roman people? Neither did you first tear down that cross, which even now runs with the blood of a Roman citizen and which has been fastened up near your port and city, nor did you throw it down into the deep sea and ritually purify that whole place, [so] how did you approach Rome and this assembly here? In only the federated and peaceful land of the Mamertines has a monument of that cruelty been erected? Has not your city been chosen for the one which, when citizens approach from Italy, they see the cross of a Roman citizen before seeing any friend of the Roman people? Which thing [the cross] you are accustomed to display to the people of Rhegium, whose citizenship you envy, and likewise to your own inhabitants who are Roman citizens, by which they adjudge themselves less and regard you less, when they see the law of citizenship has been afflicted with that punishment.

*Commentary.* Cicero presses his case that the eulogies sent from Messana to Rome on Verres' behalf should be disregarded. Earlier, Cicero had observed that the people of Messana had so benefitted from Verres' excesses that they continued to favor him. Here, he emphasizes that they have allowed Gavius' cross to remain standing in public view, rather than being ashamed of it. Thus Gavius' cross remains a testimony to Verres' savagery against Roman citizens and a witness to the Mamertines' (people of Messana) own complicity in his actions. Cicero's language continues to imply that the cross was a purposely erected (*fixa est*) device in view of both land and sea. Rhegium lies in Italy just across the Strait of Messina from Sicily and (in particular) across from the city of Messana. So the Roman citizens of Rhegium, as well as those Romans dwelling in the provincial city of Messana itself, are left to consider their citizenship privileges to be of lesser value in Messana; hence these citizens also view the people of Messana as a less-worthy lot.[578] Even were the cross re-

---

[578] This represents an interpretation of *minusque vos despiciant* in which the phrase refers to a reduction in the Roman citizens' positive regard for the people of Messana. Alternatively, *despicio* could bear its more common meaning of "despise" (cf. YONGE and GREENWOOD), in which case the people of Messana are "less despised" by Roman citizens, presumably because the Mamertines, due to their savagery, have generated dismay among the Roman citizens, which causes the Mamertines to be more respected (at least out of fear).

moved, Cicero insinuates that the surrounding land would need to undergo ritual purification, since Verres' sinful act requires expiation (note *expiastis*).

**(295)** Cicero *Pro Rabirio Perduellionis Reo* 3.10

Nam de perduellionis iudicio, quod a me sublatum esse criminari soles, meum crimen est, non Rabiri. quod utinam, Quirites, ego id aut primus aut solus ex hac re publica sustulissem! utinam hoc, quod ille crimen esse volt, proprium testimonium meae laudis esset. Quid enim optari potest quod ego mallem quam me in consulatu meo carnificem de foro, crucem de campo sustulisse? Sed ista laus primum est maiorum nostrorum, Quirites, qui expulsis regibus nullum in libero populo vestigium crudelitatis regiae retinuerunt, deinde multorum virorum fortium qui vestram libertatem non acerbitate suppliciorum infestam sed lenitate legum munitam esse voluerunt.

*Translation.* For, concerning the trial for treason, which you are accustomed to accuse me for having eliminated – that is an accusation against me, not against Rabirius. O Citizens, if only I was the first person or the only one to abolish it from this Republic. If only this: the matter which that man [Labienus] wishes to be an accusation, may it be a particular testimony of my praise. For what could be desired most would be that I chose in my consulship to eliminate the executioner from the forum and the cross from the Campus [Martius]. But, Citizens, that praise belongs first to our ancestors, who during the expulsion of the kings retained among a free people no vestige of the cruelty of kingship, and then [second it belongs] to the many courageous men who wished your freedom not to be infested with the harshness of punishments but to be secured by the mildness of laws.

*Commentary.*[579] In this speech from 63 B.C. (known as *In Defense of Gaius Rabirius on the Charge of Treason*), Cicero defends Rabirius, an elderly senator charged with murdering Saturninus thirty-six years earlier. In reality, this trial represents the machinations of the tribunes and their party (including Julius Caesar) to diminish the senate's authority. Saturninus had been killed in 100 B.C., when the senate had authorized the use of force to suppress his and his associates' increasingly demagogic actions (in their response to the murder of a senator and to later public riots). Rabirius was one of many senators and prominent men who rallied to the senatorial decree and were involved in the deaths of Saturninus and his associates, although, according to Cicero, Rabirius was not actually the person who had killed Saturninus (cf. *Rab. Perd.* 6.18; 11.31). This trial was an attempt to overturn the senatorial edict of *senatus consultum ultimum,* which had enacted a state of emergency in 100 B.C., plac-

---

[579] Text: HUMFREY G. HODGE, Cicero. The Speeches (LCL; Cambridge: Harvard University Press, 1927), 460.

ing Rome further under senatorial control and providing a legal cover for those who sought Saturninus' death. In this trial, in which Cicero delivered the speech *Pro Rabirio Perduellionis*, Titus Labienus (as tribune) served as prosecutor against Rabirius, and Cicero, as consul in 63 B.C. (and as a friend of the senate), came to Rabirius' defense. Cicero recognizes that should Labienus be successful and Rabirius be condemned, the authority of the senate and of the consuls would ultimately be greatly diminished (cf. *Rab. Perd.* 1.2–3) because future senates could not proclaim the *senatus consultum ultimum* without fear of their edict being overturned.[580]

Prior to this trial, Labienus was able to pass a resolution instituting a board of *duumviri* (two chief men) to adjudicate any charge of *perduellio* (high treason) arising from an inquiry into Saturninus' death. The senate was outmaneuvered in this regard but was able (upon Cicero's insistence as consul) to have the penalty for this crime reduced from crucifixion to exile. In the paragraph cited above, Cicero acknowledges his achievement at reducing the penalty, and he also employs that action as a point of allegation against Labienus, for Labienus had wished to crucify a Roman citizen on a cross set up in the Campus Martius. Cicero notes that Labienus' desire to establish such a cross flies in the face of Roman tradition and instead belongs to the kinds of acts that speak of unduly harsh punishments (*acerbitate suppliciorum*) and of the cruel tyrants of Rome's distant past (*vestigium crudelitatis regiae*).

**(296)** Cicero *Pro Rabirio Perduellionis Reo* 4.11

Quam ob rem uter nostrum tandem, Labiene, popularis est, tune qui civibus Romanis in contione ipsa carnificem, qui vincla adhiberi putas oportere, qui in campo Martio comitiis centuriatis auspicato in loco crucem ad civium supplicium defigi et constitui iubes, an ego qui funestari contionem contagione carnificis veto, qui expiandum forum populi Romani ab illis nefarii sceleris vestigiis esse dico, qui castam contionem, sanctum campum, inviolatum corpus omnium civium Romanorum, integrum ius libertatis defendo servari oportere?

*Translation.* Wherefore, Labienus, which of either of us after all is the people's choice? Is it you, who considers it right to apply the executioner against Roman citizens in their own assembly, and who considers it correct to apply chains, and who in the Campus Martius by the Comitia Centuriata – in that hallowed place – ordered a cross to be fixed in the ground and planted for the punishment of citizens? Or is it I, who prohibits the assembly to be stained with blood by contact with the executioner, who speaks in order to expiate the forum of the Roman people from those traces of [your] vile crime, and who

---

[580] Cf. HODGE, Cicero. Speeches, 444–451 for an introduction to the historical context.

argues in defense that it is right to preserve the assembly as pure, the Campus as holy, the body of all Roman citizens as inviolable, and the law of liberty as unimpaired?

*Commentary.* This passage immediately follows 3.10. Here, Cicero claims he is a better representative of the Roman people than is Labienus (despite the latter being a tribune in the popular assembly). Cicero repeatedly highlights that a Roman *citizen* would have faced crucifixion had Labienus had his way. Similarly, Cicero observes that Labienus had wished this execution to take place in the Campus Martius, which was a central, open area just outside the sacred boundaries of republican Rome, filled with temples and space for assembly. In that famous Campus met the Comitia Centuriata, an assembly of Roman citizens (divided by property classes) responsible for enacting laws and hearing the appeals of certain high-profile cases against citizens, such as that against Rabirius. Certainly, Cicero objects to the sacred Campus Martius being defiled by a *crux*. He also appears concerned that the penalty of crucifixion would violate the rights of a Roman citizen and transgress the laws of free men.

After this passage (in 4.12), Cicero will proceed to contrast Labienus' tribuneship with the traditions of Roman law. The Porcian laws forbade the beating of Roman citizens, but Labienus has brought in both the scourge and the executioner. Gaius Gracchus had required the consent of the Assembly to execute a Roman citizen, but Labienus had championed a resolution that would permit the *duumviri* to condemn Rabirius to death without a specific hearing before the Assembly. As we shall see in the next passage, this then leads Cicero to criticize Labienus' willingness to apply cruel language in his treatment of Roman citizens.

**(297)** Cicero *Pro Rabirio Perduellionis Reo* 4.13

Tu mihi etiam legis Porciae, tu C. Gracchi, tu horum libertatis, tu cuiusquam denique hominis popularis mentionem facis, qui non modo suppliciis invisi-tatis[581] sed etiam verborum crudelitate inaudita violare libertatem huius populi, temptare mansuetudinem, commutare disciplinam conatus es? Namque haec tua, quae te, hominem clementem popularemque, delectant, 'I, "LICTOR", "CONLIGA MANVS",' non modo huius libertatis mansuetudinisque non sunt sed ne Romuli quidem aut Numae Pompili; Tarquini, superbissimi atque crudelissimi regis, ista sunt cruciatus carmina quae tu, homo lenis ac popularis, libentissime commemoras: '"CAPVT OBNVBITO", "ARBORI INFELICI SVSPENDITO",' quae verba, Quirites, iam pridem in hac re publica non solum tenebris vetustatis verum etiam luce libertatis oppressa sunt.

---

[581] HODGE reads *inusitatis*.

*Translation.* Do you still make mention to me of the Porcian Law, you of Gaius Gracchus, you of their liberty, you indeed of any such man of the people – you who have attempted, not only with unfamiliar punishments but even with the unheard of cruelty of your words, to violate the liberty of this people, to test their clemency, and to transform their system of conduct? For these are your words which delight you, O merciful and popular man: "Go, lictor, bind the hands!" – which not only are not words of freedom and clemency, but also certainly are not the words of Romulus or of Numa Pompilius. To Tarquinius, the proudest and cruelest of kings, belong those songs of torture which you, gentle and popular man, commemorate most cheerfully: "Veil the head! Suspend him on the unlucky tree!" – which words, Citizens, long ago had been extinguished in this republic not only due to the darkness of antiquity but also due to the light of liberty.

*Commentary.* Continuing with Cicero's argument, here he criticizes not only the actions of Labienus but also his willingness to give oral commands that counteract the liberty and traditions of the laws of Roman citizens. Cicero singles out two commands in particular – the employment of the lictor[582] to bind a Roman citizen and the execution of a citizen with a veiled head on the *arbor infelix*. The *arbor infelix* ("unlucky tree") was one "consecrated to the gods of the underworld (Macr. 3.20.3) on which in primitive law condemned criminals were hung."[583] Cicero is clearly associating that *arbor infelix* with the *crux* Labienus desires to apply against Rabirius. Whatever the form of suspension implied by the ancient Roman penalty of *arbor infelix*, Cicero believes crucifixion to be its analog; he thus reads each penalty (the ancient *arbor infelix* and the cross of Labienus) in light of the other.

In contrast, Cicero insists that such commands would not be heard from the great founder of Rome (Romulus) and Rome's legendary second ruler (Numa Pompilius, to whom were credited the laws and practices of Roman religion). The laws instituted for the benefit of the common citizens – those of Porcius and the practices of Gaius Gracchus – would not sanction Labienus' demands.[584] Indeed, Cicero claims Labienus brought in "unfamiliar punishments" (*suppliciis invisitatis*) and "unheard of cruelty" (*crudelitate inaudita*). This is certainly hyperbole – such penalties were regularly practiced against non-citizens and could be occasioned against citizens who became enemies of the state. Nevertheless, Cicero claims the last time such penalties were sanctioned against citizens was during the cruel days of Lucius Tarquinius Superbus (534–510 B.C.), the notorious ancient arch-tyrant whose overthrow estab-

---

[582] The *lictores* were attendants of magistrates. They carried the magistrate's sign of office (*fasces*), announced his approach, cleared his path, and implemented his command to summon or arrest others. They could sometimes perform their duties with violence.

[583] See OLD s.v. *infelix*.

[584] Cicero also referenced these laws to similar purpose; *Verr.* 2.5.163 (No. 282).

lished the Roman republic. The irony is palpable here,[585] and it is particularly remarkable that Cicero repeatedly charges Labienus with acting less like a tribune (who appropriately would be a man of the people) and more like a royal despot, such as the cruelest of tyrant-kings, Tarquinius.

**(298)** Cicero *Pro Rabirio Perduellionis Reo* 5.16–17

Misera est ignominia iudiciorum publicorum, misera multatio bonorum, miserum exsilium; sed tamen in omni calamitate retinetur aliquod vestigium libertatis. Mors denique si proponitur, in libertate moriamur, carnifex vero et obductio capitis et nomen ipsum crucis absit non modo a corpore civium Romanorum sed etiam a cogitatione, oculis, auribus. Harum enim omnium rerum non solum eventus atque perpessio sed etiam condicio, exspectatio, mentio ipsa denique indigna cive Romano atque homine libero est. An vero servos nostros horum suppliciorum omnium metu dominorum benignitas vindicta una liberat; nos a verberibus, ab unco, a crucis denique terrore neque res gestae neque acta aetas neque vestri honores vindicabunt? [17] Quam ob rem fateor atque etiam, Labiene, profiteor et prae me fero te ex illa crudeli, importuna, non tribunicia actione sed regia, meo consilio, virtute, auctoritate esse depulsum. Qua tu in actione quamquam omnia exempla maiorum, omnis leges, omnem auctoritatem senatus, omnis religiones atque auspiciorum publica iura neglexisti, tamen a me haec in hoc tam exiguo meo tempore non audies; liberum tempus nobis dabitur ad istam disceptationem.

*Translation.* Wretched is the disgrace of public trials, wretched is the imposition of a property fine, wretched is exile; nevertheless, in every such calamity some trace of liberty is retained. Even if death is appointed, we should die in liberty; certainly the executioner, and the veiling of the head, and that name of the cross should be absent – not only from the body of Roman citizens, but also from their thought, eyes, and ears. For, the occurrence and suffering endurance of not only all these things, but also their own character, expectation, and even the mention of them is shameful for a Roman citizen and free man. Or certainly, when the benevolence of masters frees our slaves from the fear of all these punishments by one act of manumission, will neither our deeds, nor our lives we have led, nor your honors manumit us from the scourgings, from the executioner's hook, and even from the terror of the cross? [17] Wherefore, I admit and even, Labienus, avow and affirm that you were forced to desist from that cruel, perverse action (which was not characteristic of the power of a tribune but of kingly power) by my counsel, virtue, and authority. Concerning which, however much you neglected in your action

---

[585] Among other features, note how L. Tarquinius *Superbus* is labelled *superbissimi atque crudelissimi regis.*

all the precedents of the ancestors, all the laws, all the authority of the senate, all religious principles and states laws concerning the auspices, still you will not hear from me these matters in this my scanty time. Spare time will be provided for us for that dispute.

*Commentary.* Cicero begins this passage by laying out penalties typical of condemned citizens (trials, property fines, and even exile), which he asserts are wretched enough. Then he contrasts those standard penalties with Labienus' call for Rabirius to be crucified publicly. Cicero acknowledges the death penalty can indeed be appointed against a Roman citizen (*mors denique si proponitur*) but insists citizens should die as men who possess *libertas* (perhaps this references enforced suicide, in which the citizen "freely" takes his own life). In contrast, there is "the executioner and the veiling of the head and that name of the cross" (*carnifex vero et obductio capitis et nomen ipsum crucis*). These should be "absent from the body of Roman citizens" (hinting at Cicero's opposition to the *crux* ever being employed against a Roman citizen) as well as absent from "their thought, eyes, and ears" (indicating Cicero's disapproval of Labienus' attempt to set up the *crux* in the very public Campus Martius for all citizens to view; note *Rab. Perd.* 4.11; No. 296). The very "occurrence and suffering endurance" (*eventus atque perpessio*) of such punishments is wrong for a Roman citizen, and so is their "character, expectation and mention". This again serves to denigrate Labienus' desire for a public crucifixion, during which all citizens would see the character of the punishment, fear that it might be applied to them, and talk about it openly. Most significantly, the very mention of this form of execution is itself "shameful" (*indigna*); this serves as one of many indications that in a society so concerned with honor, crucifixion was viewed as a shameful way to die.

Cicero notes that slaves, upon manumission, are freed from the fear of such punishments – an indication that this form of execution was especially reserved for slaves (on this, see more below in section 3.6.2). In light of that, Cicero insists all the more that a citizen's honorable acts on behalf of the state should serve as a bulwark against such a slave-like punishment. "Scourgings" (*verberes*) typically precede crucifixion in the sources. The "executioner's hook" (*uncus*) was employed in the dragging of dead bodies throughout the city as a form of public condemnation. It is unclear whether the threefold sequence "scourgings, hook, cross" represents a rhetorical escalation (with the *crux* being the most severe of the three penalties) or an actual order of punishments.[586]

---

[586] It seems more likely that this sequence is rhetorical, especially since in the *Pro Rabirio,* Cicero has rhetorically consistently emphasized the *crux* last as the most dreaded of penalties that should not be applied to Roman citizens. However, if the alternate view is taken that the three items here ("scourgings, hook, cross") appear in the order they would have been applied, then Cicero may be speaking of a *postmortem* application of the *crux* (since the person would

In the second paragraph (5.17), Cicero again counts it to his own virtue that during these trials, he has successfully opposed Labienus' attempt to impose the *crux* as the penalty for treason. He calls the attempt to institute this penalty "cruel and perverse" (*crudeli, importuna*) and again implies Labienus' tyrannical actions are more suited to the ancient Roman tyrant-kings than they are to a tribune and man of the people (cf. 4.13 above). Cicero asserts in the strongest possible way that Labienus' actions constituted a break with previous Roman law and precedent. The reference to "state laws concerning the auspices" may allude to Cicero's observation that the Campus Martius in particular had been set aside for certain holy purposes according to the auspices of generations past (see *auspicato in loco* in 4.11, translated above as "that hallowed place"). The last two sentences quoted above refer to the limited time provided to Cicero for his defense: Labienus had broken with tradition and restricted Cicero's oration to 30 minutes (cf. 2.6; 13.38). Cicero hopes to address that wrong at a different time (though it is difficult to discern whether he intends to do so informally or by way of a formal legal charge).[587]

**(299)**  Cicero *Pro Rabirio Perduellionis Reo* 10.28

Etenim si C. Rabirio, quod iit ad arma, crucem T. Labienus in campo Martio defigendam putavit quod tandem excogitabitur in eum supplicium qui vocavit?

*Translation.* For indeed, if Titus Labienus supposed that for Gaius Rabirius (because he took up arms) a cross should be planted in the Campus Martius, what penalty after all should be invented for him who called [for him to take up arms]?

*Commentary.* In context, Cicero argues that Rabirius' action (of supporting with arms the senate's call to suppress Saturninus) was much less consequential than were the actions of other highly respected officials of the day. In particular, Gaius Marius (titled "father of his country"; cf. 10.27) had given the summons to citizens to aid the senate. Marius was consul in 100 B.C. during Saturninus' tribuneship and had initially been in league with Saturninus until Saturninus went too far in his bid to reform the state. Once the senate issued the *senatus consultum ultimum*, Marius acted to suppress Saturninus, driving him and his supporters to the Capitol, where later they were killed.[588] Ironi-

---

be scourged and killed, with the dead body being dragged through the city before being hung on the *crux*). However, other Roman legal sources do not appear to follow such an order of punishments, so the rhetorical sequencing is the more probable.

[587] HODGE, Cicero. Speeches, 468n. suggests: "This may hint either at a further hearing of Rabirius's case or at Cicero's intention to bring Labienus to trial subsequently".

[588] Cicero may seem to be overreaching since, although Marius did act on behalf of the senate to suppress Saturninus and his colleagues, there is no evidence he ordered them to be slaughtered once they retreated to the Capitol. Nonetheless, Marius' opposition to Saturninus,

cally, Marius was also the uncle of Julius Caesar, so invoking his name allowed Cicero to turn the tables on Caesar (whose hand lay behind Labienus' actions in Cicero's day). Marius' stature remained so great in 63 B.C. that it would have been appalling to suggest he should be punished for supporting the senate, despite the fact that he was much more responsible for the violence against Saturninus and his associates than Rabirius (see 10.28–30). The rhetoric again emphasizes the severity of crucifixion: To develop a worse penalty than the cross Labienus threatened against Rabirius would require invention (*excogitabitur*). Cicero thus implies that no such penalty against citizens already stood in Labienus' arsenal, and thus, among the penalties allowed under the laws of the Roman republic, there was none worse than the *crux*.

**(300)** Appian, *Bella Civilia* 3.1.3 [3.9]

ὡς δέ τις αὐτοῖς ἔφη καὶ τὸ ἐργαστήριον, ἔνθα οἱ ἀνδριάντες ἀνεσκευάζοντο, δείξειν, εὐθὺς εἵποντο καὶ ἰδόντες ἐνεπίμπρασαν, ἕως ἑτέρων ἐπιπεμφθέντων ἐξ Ἀντωνίου ἀμυνόμενοί τε ἀνηρέθησαν ἔνιοι καὶ συλληφθέντες ἕτεροι ἐκρεμάσθησαν, ὅσοι θεράποντες ἦσαν, οἱ δὲ ἐλεύθεροι κατὰ τοῦ κρημνοῦ κατερρίφησαν.

*Translation.* And when someone said he would also show them the workshop where the statues were being dismantled, immediately they followed; and upon seeing [the place] they set it on fire, until others had been sent by Antony, and some who were defending themselves were killed, and others who were seized were hung up (as many as were servants), but the free men were thrown down the cliff.

*Commentary.*[589] Appian of Alexandria, having moved to Rome as a citizen, was befriended by Fronto and served as a procurator under Antoninus Pius. In the middle second century A.D., he authored his twenty-four book *Roman History* (*Bell. civ.* Book 4 is *Hist. rom.* Book 16). Appian is clearly dependent on earlier sources. This particular text provides another example of different treatments for various classes of the Roman populace, as well as a significant indication that servants/slaves were treated more harshly than freemen (even in identical cases of guilt). This episode in Appian occurs shortly after Julius Caesar's assassination. Mark Antony, whose funeral oration had incited the

---

his willingness to take up arms to defend the senate, and his obedience to the *senatus consultum ultimum* put him in the same situation as Rabirius. If Rabirius did not personally murder Saturninus (as Cicero claims is widely known), he can only be guilty of conspiring to support the cause of the senate which led to Saturninus' demise; but Marius did precisely the same.

[589] Text: LUDWIG MENDELSSOHN, Appiani Historia Romana (Editio altera correctior; Leipzig: Teubner, 1905), 295 [where it is 3.9]. Same text in WHITE, Appian's Roman History, 3:522, where the text is listed as 3.1.3.

people to violence against Caesar's assassins (who were senators), was taking steps to re-ingratiate himself to the senate. Antony had put to death Amatius (who had alleged himself to be a descendant of Marius and a relative of Caesar; see *Bell. civ.* 3.1.2). Amatius had been inflaming the multitudes and leading gangs in search of Brutus, Cassius, and other assassins. However, Amatius was still admired by the populace, and his former followers captured the forum and opposed Antony (3.1.3). Antony's soldiers responded by driving these firebrands out of the forum, which only angered them further. They went searching for the individuals who were destroying statues of Julius Caesar. Arson within the city of Rome was an especially provocative act and one that received harsh punishment in antiquity since fires potentially imperiled the whole city.[590] Therefore, the death penalties described above likely would have been viewed as appropriate to the case. Here the freedmen are "thrown down the cliff" (κατὰ τοῦ κρημνοῦ κατερρίφησαν) – a reference to the traditional penalty of throwing the guilty off the Tarpeian rock in Rome.[591] The servants/slaves are instead "hung up" (ἐκρεμάσθησαν).

Because we shall encounter Appian several times in this chapter, it would be helpful to offer some brief observations about his vocabulary for penal bodily suspension. In two cases, Appian invokes σταυρόω: first, in reference to the suspension/crucifixion of slaves (*Bell. civ.* 5.8.70), and second, concerning the Carthaginian use of the *stauros* against defecting African mercenaries (*Sicily* 2.3). However, Appian (like Arrian) more frequently employs κρεμάννυμι in his references to human bodily suspension (likely crucifixion), such as against slaves (cf. *Mithr.* 5.29 [§114]; *Bell. civ.* 3.1.3; 4.5.35; 4.10.81; cf. Theodotus the tutor in *Bell. civ.* 2.13.90), or in war (*Mithr.* 2.8 [§25]; 5.29 [§114]; 12.84 [§378]), and especially in response to a slave revolt (*Bell. civ.* 1.14.119; 1.14.120). Appian also uses cognate forms of κρήμνημι/ κρημνάω to portray individuals being hung up (see *Mithr* 15.97 [ §§449–451] above in 3.3.2). The heads of slain men can be "hung up", employing κρεμάννυμι in *Bell. civ.* 1.8.71 (of senators' heads suspended in the forum during Octavian's time) and ἀποκρεμάννυμι in *Bell. civ.* 4.4.20 (of Cicero's head suspended

---

[590] E.g., in a later century see *Pauli Sententiae* 5.20.1 (*incendiarii, qui quid in oppido praedandi causa faciunt, capite puniuntur*, "Those who set fires, who do this in a town for the purpose of acquiring loot, are punished with capital punishment").

[591] Reference to execution by being thrown off the Tarpeian Rock can be found as early as the Twelve Tables 8.14 (slaves commiting theft) and 8.23 (false witness); see text in BRUNS, Fontes Iuris Romani Antiqui, 1:32–33. An intriguing comparison of execution by Tarpeian Rock and death by incarceration (with helpful examples of the former) in JEAN-MICHEL DAVID, Du *comitium* à la roche Tarpéienne. Sur certains rituels d'exécution capitale sous la République, les règnes d'Auguste et de Tibère, in Du châtiment dans la cité: Supplices corporels et peine de mort dans le monde antique (Table ronde organisée par l'École française de Rome avec le concours du Centre national de la recherche scientifique [Rome 9.-11. novembre 1982]; ed. Y. Thomas; Collection de l'École française de Rome 79; Rome / Paris: École francaise de Rome / Boccard, 1984) 131–176, esp. 134–139, 168–170.

from the rostra by Antony). Yet Appian also depicts with κρεμάννυμι the hanging up of objects such as a diadem (*Syriaca* 9.56 [§288]) and a cloak (hung up as a war trophy in *Bell. civ.* 2.13.90). Thus κρεμάννυμι is not a mere technical term for bodily suspension in Appian, though it is his most common means of referencing the "hanging up" of a human body during Roman executions. In Appian's era, this would most plausibly have been understood as crucifixion, and in any case it would definitely have been associated with the range of suspension punishments that included the cross.

**(301)** Suetonius, *Galba* 9.1

Per octo annos varie et inaequabiliter provinciam rexit, primo acer et vehemens et in coercendis quidem delictis vel immodicus. Nam et nummulario non ex fide versanti pecunias manus amputavit mensaeque eius adfixit, et tutorem, quod pupillum, cui substitutus heres erat, veneno necasset, cruce adfecit; implorantique leges et civem Romanum se testificanti, quasi solacio et honore aliquo poenam levaturus, mutari multoque praeter ceteras altiorem et dealbatam statui crucem iussit.

*Translation.* For eight years he [Galba] ruled the province inconsistently and unevenly; indeed at first he was severe and violent and even excessive in punishing offenses. For, when a banker was not faithful in transacting money, he amputated his hands and fixed them to the man's table; and he fixed up on a cross a guardian because he had murdered with poison his ward, for whom he was an alternate heir. When [the tutor] invoked the laws and testified that he was a Roman citizen, [Galba], as if relieving the penalty by some solace and honor, ordered the cross to be changed out and another to be stood up that was much higher (so as to surpass the others) and that was whitewashed.

*Commentary.*[592] In this paragraph from his biography of Servius Sulpicius Galba (3 B.C.–A.D. 69), Suetonius depicts the kind of provincial governor Galba was in Tarraconensian Spain (c. A.D. 61–68) before he seized imperial control. Suetonius charges Galba with inconsistency in his judicial decisions. Galba was harsh in the beginning (represented in the passage above)[593] but became apathetic, a fact that Suetonius will report in the sentence following

---

[592] Text: ROLFE, Suetonius, 2:204.

[593] The three adjectives that Suetonius uses to describe Galba's initial rule in Spain (*acer et vehemens et ... vel immodicus*, "severe and violent and ... even excessive") actually begin somewhat ambiguously: *acer* can mean "keen" and "vigilant" as well as "strict" and "severe", and *vehemens* can indicate "energetic" and "strenuous" as well as "violent" and "excessive in zeal." However, the translation above follows the clearly negative connotation of the third adjective (*immodicus*, "immoderate; excessive in degree") in implying that all three adjectives should be understood to depict Galba being more harsh than was necessary. The two examples Suetonius cites also incline the reader to view Galba's actions as unduly severe and violent.

the text above. The second example above of Galba's initial excess in handing out punishments concerns the crucifixion of a legal guardian (*tutor*) who had murdered his own underage ward (*pupillus*) to receive the ward's inheritance, which apparently had been willed to the guardian should the ward die. After Galba decreed crucifixion for the guardian, the murderous guardian was still able to appeal to his Roman citizenship, with Suetonius here assuming this should have called for a lesser punishment (even for such a cold-blooded crime). Galba's severity is illustrated by his refusal to take proper account of the citizen's status, commanding instead that a special prominent cross be erected (one that is very high and white). The irony of Galba's decision appears in the "solace and honor" (*solacio et honore*) he claimed to have accorded the guardian and also in how his penalty was "relieved" (*levaturus*, from *levo* meaning "raise up") by the elevating of his *crux*. The text implies that other crosses (*praeter ceteras*) were also present at the place of execution; thus though Suetonius remains silent about who inhabited those crosses, he indirectly testifies to the many other crucifixions that occurred during Galba's provincial reign. Suetonius must have viewed these other crucifixions as sufficiently commonplace so as to overlook them.

## *3.6.2 Slaves*

There is widespread evidence in the extant sources that the *crux* was a means of punishing slaves.[594] This occurs in Latin literature at least as early as Plautus. We have already encountered the association of the cross with the punishment for slaves in Cicero's *In Verrem* (2.5.169; cf. 3.6.1): "while Italy saw her own son fastened upon the desperate and most extreme punishment of slaves" (*Italia autem alumnum suum servitutis extremo summoque supplicio adfixum videret*). Note further: Cassius Dio's record of the crucifixion (ἀνα-σταυρώσαντος) of a slave in the Augustan era (*Hist. rom.* 54.3.7; see above in section 2.10); Domitian's crucifixion of slave-scribes who had assisted in penning an unflattering history (Suetonius, *Dom.* 10.1; cf. No. 120); and the contrast between penalties due Roman citizens and those due slaves in both Cicero's *Rab. Perd.* 5.16–17 (No. 298) and Appian's *Bella Civilia* 3.1.3 (No. 300). In addition, see Dionysius of Halicarnassus, *Ant. Rom.* 7.69.1–2 (No. 115), which mentions outstretched arms but not specifically a cross. We should also call attention to examples in texts that will be discussed in later

---

[594] On the crucifixion of slaves cf. KUHN, Die Kreuzesstrafe, 719–723; HENGEL, Crucifixion, 51–63. Although SCHIEMANN suggests that the Roman legal penalty of crucifixion probably originated as a deterrence against slaves (SCHIEMANN, Damnatio in crucem), this claim may be difficult to verify with confidence, especially given the widespread exposure of Romans to its neighbors' use of suspension in war.

sections, such as repeatedly in the *Pauli Sententiae* (below in 3.6.4), in the *Historia Augusta* 6 [Avidius Cassius] 4.6, which equates being hung up on a cross (*in crucem tolli*) with being "fixed up in the punishment of slaves" (*servilique supplicio adfici*), and in *Hist. Aug.* 15 [Opellius Macrinus] 12.2, which parallels the crucifixion of soldiers with the "punishments of slaves" (*servilibus suppliciis*; also cf. Valerius Maximus, in No. 355). Many further instances are adduced in this section, and a separate section will be devoted to the *crux* as the principal punishment against slave revolts.

**(302)** Plautus, *Mostellaria* 348–361

Iuppiter supremus summis opibus atque industriis
me periisse et Philolachetem cupit erilem filium.
occidit Spes nostra, nusquam stabulum est Confidentiae,
nec Salus nobis saluti iam esse, si cupiat, potest:
ita mali, maeroris montem maximum ad portum modo
conspicatus sum: erus advenit peregre, periit Tranio.
ecquis homo est, qui facere argenti cupiat aliquantum lucri,
qui hodie sese excruciari meam vicem possit pati?
ubi sunt isti plagipatidae, ferritribaces viri,
vel isti qui hosticas trium nummum causa subeunt sub falas,
ubi quinis aut denis hastis corpus transfigi solet?
ego dabo ei talentum, primus qui in crucem excucurrerit;
sed ea lege, ut offigantur bis pedes, bis bracchia.
ubi id erit factum, a me argentum petito praesentarium.

*Translation.* Jupiter Most Exalted, with all his might and diligence,
desires me and Philolaches, the master's son, to perish.
Our Spes [Hope] dies, Confidence is nowhere a shelter,
nor is Salus [Salvation] able now to save us, even if she desires to:
Such a great mountain of calamity and grief at the harbor
have I just now seen: The master arrives from abroad; Tranio will perish.
[*To the audience*] Is there any man [out there] who might desire to enrich himself with a bit of silver,
who today might be able to endure my turn to be tormented?
Where are those well-beaten guys, men who exhaust iron chains,
or those who for three small coins take on enemy siege towers,
where five or ten spears are accustomed to pierce your body?
I will give a silver talent to him who is the first to rush out to the cross;
but with this rule: twice his feet should be nailed, and twice his forearms.
When that has been accomplished, the silver will be paid on the spot by soliciting it from me.

*Commentary.*[595] Titus Maccius Plautus (c. 255–184 B.C.) composed Latin comedies, which appeared mostly in the early second century B.C. Plautus typically models his farces on earlier Greek New Comedy plays, updating them for his Roman audience and employing many Latin turns of phrase. The Greek original of the *Mostellaria* is likely to have been the *Phasma* of Philemon (dated to the third century B.C.).[596] A stock character in Plautus' comedies is the shrewd slave who saves his rash master from various social perils.[597] Such a slave often worries aloud about going to the cross should he be caught in his cunning. Since Plautus' works are indebted to Greek New Comedy archetypes, we may well wonder whether there was not an analogous slave penalty in the original Greek plays. Less speculatively, both Plautus and his Roman audience obviously could readily imagine slaves of their own era being so cruelly executed, and his Roman audience must have assumed Athenian Greeks had practiced similar penalties.

Act Two of *Mostellaria* ("The Haunted House") begins with this poetic speech from the slave Tranio. He has just learned that his *pater familias,* Theopropides, has returned to Athens after a three-year absence (cf. *Most.* 79) during which his son, Philolaches, whom Tranio has been serving, has been holding drunken revelries at their house and squandering his father's money. Tranio himself is fond of wine, women and food, and he has apparently been leading Philolaches astray (see lines 11–83). Tranio assumes that once Theopropides finds out, he will discipline his son and have Tranio nailed to the *crux* (others have warned him of such an outcome, cf. *Mostellaria* 56, 69). Tranio attributes this sudden peril to the hand of Jupiter and asserts that even the minor goddesses of protection (*Spes, Confidentiae,* and *Salus,* i.e., Hope, Confidence and Salvation) will not avert Jupiter's will. The play will continue with a series of Tranio's schemes for protecting himself and his young master, Philolaches; most famously Tranio warns off Theopropides from entering the family house (where the drunken revelers are hiding), telling him it is haunted. The reader should especially observe Tranio's meta-theatrical comic appeal to the audience for someone to take his place at the *crux.* While hard-bitten army troops earn a mere few coins per day risking their lives, Tranio is glad to pay the much larger sum of a silver talent, but only to the person who will "rush out to the cross" (*qui in crucem excucurrerit*). Ironically, Tranio states he will withhold the proffered pay until the person is fully fastened to cross and thus barely able to "solicit" the silver from him, let alone "chase" or "fetch" it (which may be the actual connotation of *petito* in *a me argentum petito*

---

[595] Text: LEO, Plautus Comoediae, 2:94–95; compared with NIXON, Plautus, 3:324.

[596] See NIXON, Plautus, 3:ix.

[597] Plautus' use of this motif has famously influenced such later authors as SHAKESPEARE, MOLIÈRE, and P. G. WODEHOUSE (think Jeeves and Wooster), as well as the STEPHEN SONDHEIM musical *A Funny Thing Happened on the Way to the Forum*.

*praesentarium*). Thus Tranio's schemes include fleecing members of the audience even as they are crucified on his behalf! Though the passage does not fully describe this manner of execution or the device on which it is performed, note two important features: First, the person is presumed to be alive while affixed to the *crux* (how else could they even attempt to "solicit" the money); second, the person is attached to the cross by the nailing of each foot and forearm (*offigantur bis pedes, bis bracchia*).[598] Crucifixion (even in the modern sense of the term) of a living person nailed by his appendages to a wooden device is thus strongly assumed, and the many other references in Plautus to the use of a *crux* in execution can best be understood in light of this brief depiction.

**(303)** Plautus, *Mostellaria* 55–57

O carnuficium cribrum, quod credo fore,
ita te forabunt patibulatum per vias
stimulis <carnufices>, si huc reveniat senex.

*Translation.* O executioners' sieve!, which I believe will be your state as, fastened to the *patibulum* [while carrying it] through the streets, executioners will perforate you with pointed sticks, should the old man return here.

*Commentary.* This takes us back to the opening scene of the play, where Grumio (a country slave in the house of Theopropides) is gleefully threatening Tranio, claiming Tranio's cavorting with the master's wealth as an urban slave will lead to his demise once the master returns from his three-year absence. Grumio vividly conjures up the idea of a cook's sieve, which is poked full of holes so liquid can run out. Thus will Tranio be led through the streets carrying a *patibulum* as the executioners stick him with pointed goads while his bodily fluids leak out.

The reference to the *patibulum* in all probability indicates the crossbar which criminals carried on their way to the cross (as it clearly does in Plautus, *Miles Gloriosus* 358–360; and in his *Carbonaria*, Frag. 2; cf. No. 113,

---

[598] This phrase *offigantur bis pedes, bis bracchia* ("twice his feet should be nailed, and twice his forearms") is best understood as indicating that two nails are applied among his two feet (one apiece) and two among the forearms. The RILEY translation agrees, saying: "Some suppose that by 'bis pedes, bis brachia,' he means that two nails were to be driven into each leg and foot. It seems more probable that he means two for the feet and two for the hands." Cf. HENRY THOMAS RILEY, The Comedies of Plautus: Literally Translated into English Prose, with Notes (2 vols.; London: Bell, 1882), 2:475 (RILEY lists this as Act 1, Scene 5). See OLD s.v. *offigo* for the meaning "to drive in" (a stake or something similar) or "to fasten (one thing against another) by nailing".

114).[599] One may well recall Jesus carrying his crossbar to the place of his execution (John 19:17; cf. Mark 15:21; Matt 27:32; Luke 23:26). Grumio's suggestion is one of several foreboding images early in *Mostellaria* that precede Tranio's own vivid fear of the cross in 348–361 (cited above). In the moment, Tranio's retort to his fellow slave is, "How do you know that this will not happen to you before it happens to me?" (line 58). Grumio's rejoinder is telling: It simply will not happen to him first because he does not deserve it (line 59); slaves certainly face the threat of an execution suspended from a *patibulum* on a *crux*, but only those slaves who warrant such a punishment.

Grumio and Tranio trade insults throughout this first scene, and Grumio's barbs frequently return to the theme of anticipating the harsh punishment properly due Tranio. Thus Grumio calls Tranio *mastigia* ("one who deserves a whipping")[600] in line 1.[601] Tranio also gives back in kind, as when he says "*abi dierecte*" ("go away and be hung up" in line 8).[602] One final exchange between these two is worth quoting in the next selection.

---

[599] NIXON, Plautus, 3:295 thus translates *patibulatum* as "with your arms on a cross". Some translations prefer to render *patibulum* as "gibbet" (a definition also found in OLD), which misleads some modern readers to think of a beam of a hangman's apparatus. However, RILEY, Comedies, 2:463, who employs "gibbet", includes the helpful footnote: "Bearing his own cross; a refinement of torture which was too often employed upon malefactors."

[600] Cf. OLD s.v. *mastigia*, which refers to the whips of Greek parlance: μαστιγίας. NIXON's translation ("ropes-end") likely refers to such a whipping, but some readers might be confused into thinking "hanging" is implied by "ropes-end." RILEY reads "whip-scoundrel." See also *Casina* 361, *Amphitryon* 1034A.

[601] Grumio suggests lesser (but still harsh) punishments when he claims Tranio knows he will be traded off "to the mill" (*quod te in pistrinum scis actutum tradier*, line 17) or will soon add to the numbers on the farm in the manacled service of the *genus ferratile* ("chained race").

[602] OLD s.v. *dierectus* states that *dierectus* is of "uncertain etymology", yet the *erectus* stem would indicate some manner of suspension, and English translations tend to imply suspension (often hanging, which is improbable unless Tranio is commanding Grumio to commit suicide). Plautus employs *dierectus* similarly in *Trin.* 457 (*abin hinc dierecte?*; spoken to a slave). Suicide is mentioned with other terminology in Plautus, where it apparently involves a man hanging himself from the neck and certainly involves the use of rope, see *Cas.* 424 (*Si nunc me suspendam, meam operam luserim et praeter operam restim sumpti fecerim*, "If now I were to hang myself, I would have made a jest of my work, and, besides the work, I would have to take to procuring a rope"). See further: *Cas.* 111–113, 392 (*laqueum* in a possible reference to suicide with a "noose"); *Cist.* 250 (amidst the fragments of the play); *Pers.* 815 (employing a "stout rope", *restim crassam*); *Poen.* 795; *Trin.* 536. Thus hanging by the neck is known in Plautus, but only in cases of suicide. Other suspension terms can be employed for hanging someone in order to apply torture to them: see *pendentem* in *Men.* 951, referring to hanging someone in order to stick them with goads over the period of 30 days.

**(304)** Plautus, *Mostellaria* 69–71

*Tr.*     quid est? quid tu me nunc optuere, furcifer?
*Gr.*     Pol tibi istuc credo nomen actutum fore.
*Tr.*     Dum interea sic sit, istuc actutum sino.

*Translation.*
*Tr.*     What is it? What are you looking at me for now, *furcifer*?
*Gr.*     By Pollux, I believe that name will be yours straightaway.
*Tr.*     While in the meantime this may be so, I shall let that straightaway pass.

*Commentary.* In one of the final exchanges between Tranio and Grumio, Tranio labels his fellow slave a *furcifer*. This could be a mere profane epithet for a scoundrel (as readers of the beginning *Cambridge Latin Course* may well recall), but Grumio's response in line 70 indicates that he recognizes some actual punishment implied in the term since he contends it is a more appropriate name for Tranio. *Furcifer* is often translated as a "gallows-bird" (cf. OLD), which notes its derivation from the noun *furca*, a "Y-shaped piece of wood" used for a yoke or for a cross/gallows.[603] Given the theme of Tranio being threatened with the *crux*, it seems likely that *furcifer* here insinuates Tranio's looming fate as a crucified slave. If so, then perhaps *furcifer* throughout Plautus often bears implications of "one who deserves to face the *furca*."[604]

The use of the *crux* in curses and vulgar taunts will be dealt with more fully in section 3.10. For now, note Tranio's cavalier attitude in response (line 71): He is happy for the time to pass before the threat of that name (*furcifer*) becomes imminent. With comedic irony, that threat has "straightaway" arrived a few minutes later in the play, and (as we have seen in *Most.* 348–361 at the

---

[603] The word *furca* is further used interchangeably with *crux* in *Pers.* 854–855 (see below 3.10). *Furca* also refers to a device for hanging up a person unto death (or possibly torture) in *Cist.* 248, and it is employed as part of a profanity in *Cas.* 388–390 (*tu hodie canem et furcam feras*, "you today will be carrying a chain and a yoke"). Nonetheless, *furca* can merely imply a "yoke" or a device for carrying burdens (i.e., the charcoal of a *carbonarius*) in *Cas.* 438 (though even here it may have overtones of torture, if not crucifixion, see line 445). Finally, *furca* refers to a place where someone was bound and scourged in *Men.* 943, without any clear indication of execution.

[604] In Plautus, *furcifer* appears as a profanity against slaves in *Amphitryon* 285, 539 (with the god Mercury feigning to be a slave); *Asinaria* 677; *Capitivi* 562; *Casina* 139; *Miles Gloriosus* 545; *Mostellaria* 1172; and *Rudens* 996. All these instances could easily connote the *crux/furca* as a fitting death of a scandalous slave. It is employed similarly against pimps in *Poenulus* 784 (in context of *crux* in 789, 799) and in *Pseudolus* 193, 360. Although the scoundrel slave Leonida refers to a free-trader as a *verbero* ("whipping-post") and a *furcifer* in *Asinaria* 484–485, Leonida's very tendency to treat a freeman as a slave actually evidences Leonida's poor character (cf. lines 477–478). Thus we can fairly affirm that *furcifer* is a term properly reserved for swearing at slaves and pimps in Plautus (with *Asinaria* 484–485 being the exception that proves the rule).

beginning of Act 2) Tranio faces the impending wrath of his *pater familias*, who has just disembarked at the harbor, along with the threat of the *crux*.

**(305)** Plautus, *Mostellaria* 741–744/745

*Si.* Vellem ut tu velles, Tranio. sed quid est negoti? *Tr.* Eloquar.
erus peregre venit. *Si.* Tunc <tibi>[605] portenditur,
inde ferriterium, postea <crux. *Tr.* Per tua te g>enua obsecro,
ne indicium ero facias meo. *Si.* E me, ne quid metuas, nil sciet.

*Translation.*
| | |
|---|---|
| *Si.* | I would want what you want, Tranio. But what is the matter? |
| *Tr.* | I will tell [you]. |
| | The master comes from abroad. |
| *Si.* | Then that portends for you [first the whip], |
| | then iron-chafery, later the cross. |
| *Tr.* | By your knees I beseech you, |
| | do not give away the secret to my master. |
| *Si.* | From me he will get to know nothing, you need not fear that. |

*Commentary.* Here in Act 3, Scene 2, yet another character cautions the slave Tranio that his less-than-admirable lifestyle will eventually lead him to the cross. Tranio approaches Simo, an elderly and wealthy free citizen, as a humble supplicant in order to borrow the use of Simo's home. Tranio actually schemes to show the home to Theopropides as if it were Theopropides' new family home, though Tranio does not inform Simo of his nefarious plan. Nonetheless, Simo is cognizant that plenty of cavorting has been going on at Theopropides' home while he was out of the country. Simo actually at some level admires the elegant excess of Philolaches and Tranio; however, Simo also recognizes that Theopropides will not be at all happy to learn of his son's dissipation. As Tranio grasps Simo's knees in humble supplication, Simo promises to keep the secret. Nonetheless, Simo also predicts Tranio will soon be punished through increasingly harsh measures. The text unfortunately evidences a lacuna in lines 742–743 (with the editor's suggestion supplied in brackets), but the cross is likely the final (and most severe) punishment on the list (*postea crux*).

---

[605] NIXON, Plautus, 3:364 inserts at the asterisk in line 742 "[primum flagrum]" following the suggestion of LEO on the supposition that there is a lacuna in this line (note the meter would be broken without the emendation). This bracketed text will be translated above. Also, the material in line 743 is supplied by LEO (and NIXON), who follows USSING and CAMERARIUS.

**(306)** Plautus, *Mostellaria* 1128–1134

*Call.* iubeo te salvere et salvos cum advenis, Theopropides,
peregre, gaudeo. hic apud nos hodie cenes, sic face.
*Th.* Callidamates, dei te ament. de cena facio gratiam.
*Call.* Quin venis? *Tr.* Promitte: ego ibo pro te, si tibi non libet.
*Th.* Verbero, etiam inrides? *Tr.* Quian me pro te ire ad cenam autumo?
*Th.* Non enim ibis. ego ferare faxo, ut meruisti, in crucem.
*Call.* Age mitte ista ac te ad me ad cenam dic venturum.

*Translation.*

| | |
|---|---|
| *Call.* | I welcome you, and I rejoice that you are well on your return from abroad, Theopropides. You should dine with us here today, please! |
| *Th.* | Callidamates, gods love you! Regarding dinner: I thank you. |
| *Call.* | Why not come? |
| *Tr.* | Accept. I'll go for you, if you don't feel like it. |
| *Th.* | Whipping-post, do you still mock? |
| *Tr.* | Is this because I mention that I will go to dinner in your place? |
| *Th.* | To be sure you will not go! I shall have you carried to the cross, as you deserve. |
| *Call.* | Come! Abandon that, and say that you will come to dinner with me. |

*Commentary.* In this final scene from *Mostellaria*, Callidamates, a drinking-friend of Philolaches, is attempting to soothe the wrath of Theopropides, who has only recently discerned that his slave Tranio has been making a fool of him, convincing him that his house is haunted, that he now owns a new house, that he should inspect it, etc., and has been hiding the fact that Theopropides' son (Philolaches) is drinking away his money with courtesans. In the play, Tranio has just sat on an altar and thus is claiming sanctuary from punishment as long as he remains there. Meanwhile, Tranio continues to throw humorous taunting jabs at Theopropides. Theopropides threatens Tranio with a variety of punishments,[606] calling him a "whipping-post" (*verbero*) and menacing him with the possibility of the *crux*. As to the comedic conclusion, at length Callidamates succeeds in winning a reprieve for all.[607]

---

[606] In the preceding scene, Theopropides plans to manacle Tranio (1065), beat him (1067), and employ a hook in the process (1070). Once Tranio has taken his seat on the altar, Theopropides suggests he should have Tranio burned alive (1114; note Tranio's artful response: "I am sweeter broiled than roasted"). Theopropides calls for Tranio to be cut to pieces with whips while being hung up (*verberibus caedere multum pendens* in line 1167; cf. 1174).

[607] Cf. *Most.* 849–851 for a further use of *crux* in a vulgar curse formula; cf. below 3.10.

**(307)** Plautus, *Aulularia* 56–59

istic astato. si hercle tu ex istoc loco
digitum transvorsum aut unguem latum excesseris
aut si respexis, donicum ego te iussero,
continuo hercle ego te dedam discipulam cruci.

*Translation.* Stand still there! If, by Hercules, you from that place
go beyond an extended finger or a raised finger-nail,
or if you look around, until I command you,
then, by Hercules, I will immediately deliver you over as a pupil for the cross.

*Commentary.* At the beginning of Act 1 of *The Pot of Gold*, the elderly miser
Euclio commands the old slave-woman Staphyla not to spy on him. Euclio has
a pot of gold hidden in his house, and he fears that she (or someone else) will
find it. As he goes to double-check that the pot of gold is still there, he threatens Staphyla not to move, lest she become a *discipulam cruci*. This strange
epithet would imply that the cross, as her teacher, would educate her.[608]

**(308)** Plautus, *Bacchides* 358–365

sed quid futurumst, cum hoc senex resciverit,
cum se excucurrisse illuc frustra sciverit
nosque aurum abusos? quid mihi fiet postea?
credo hercle adveniens nomen mutabit mihi
facietque extemplo Crucisalum me ex Chrysalo.
aufugero hercle, si magis usus venerit.
si ero reprehensus, macto ego illum infortunio:
si illi sunt virgae ruri, at mihi tergum domist.

*Translation.* But what is the future when this old man wises up,
and when he ascertains that he has needlessly made an expedition there,
and we have squandered the gold? What will he do to me then?
By Hercules, I believe when he arrives, he will change my name
and immediately will make me Crucisalus [Cross-dancer] instead of Chrysalus.
By Hercules, I will have fled, if the need has greatly arisen.
If I am retrieved, I will vex that man with this misfortune:
if he has rods on his estate, nevertheless my back is here at home.

*Commentary.* At the close of Act 2, the slave Chrysalus has just managed to
trick his master's father, Nicobulus, into traveling from Athens to Ephesus in
order to retrieve gold that was supposedly left in the care of the Temple of

---

[608] Two further mentions of the *crux* in the *Aulularia* (522, 631) appear in section 3.10.

Artemis/Diana. The real aim of this deceit is to get Nicobulus out of town so Chrysalus' master, Mnesilochus, can spend the real money on his love for Bacchis, a beautiful courtesan. After Chrysalus initially rejoices in his successful scheme, he worries about what will happen when Nicobulus returns. Humorously, he imagines Nicobulus will change his name from Chrysalus to "Crucisalus" (meaning "one who dances on the *crux*"),[609] an indication that unfaithful slaves could face the *crux*. Note how this notion of dancing might imply Chrysalus would be hung up alive while attached to the *crux*.[610] Instead, Chrysalus decides he will escape as soon as he learns Nicobulus has returned, although even then, he jokes that his recapture would actually be an unfortunate inconvenience for Nicobulus since Nicobulus would have to travel to his country estate in order to retrieve the rods required to beat him.

**(309)** Plautus, *Miles Gloriosus* 368–374

*Ph.* Tun me vidisti? *Scel.* Atque his quidem hercle oculis. *Phil.* Carebis, credo,
qui plus vident quam quod vident. *Scel.* Numquam hercle deterrebor
quin viderim id quod viderim. *Phil.* Ego stulta et mora multum,
quae cum hoc insano fabuler, quem pol ego capitis perdam.
*Scel.* Noli minitari: scio crucem futuram mihi sepulcrum;
ibi mei sunt maiores siti, pater, avos, proavos, abavos.
non possunt mihi minaciis tuis hisce oculi exfodiri.

*Translation.*

*Phil.* You saw me?
*Scel.* And indeed, by Hercules, with these eyes.
*Phil.* You will be deprived [of those eyes], I believe,
which see more than what they [actually] see.
*Scel.* Never, by Hercules, will I be frightened off, but I saw what I saw.
*Phil.* I suffer much with this fool and with this delay when I converse with
this madman, whom, by Pollux, I will injure in the head.
*Scel.* Do not threaten: I know a cross is my future tomb.
That was the place that had been permitted my ancestors – my father,
grandfathers, great-grandfathers, and great-great-grandfathers.
My eyes are not able to be dug out from me by those threats of yours.

---

[609] Cf. OLD s.v. *Crucisalus*; LEWIS and SHORT, Latin Dictionary, s.v. Chrysalus plays an earlier game with his name in *Bacch.* 240.

[610] Alternatively, the body could "dance" by swaying in the breeze; or, if the *crux* is a mere device on which he would be scourged (see *Asinaria* 545–557 below), then his body might convulse and contort at the beating. However, the majority of references to the *crux* as a place of punishing slaves in Plautus appears to indicate a place of execution (e.g., note passages from *Mostellaria* and *Miles Gloriosus* in this section), and the idea of dancing would indicate a person being alive to "perform" for others even as he suffers his own prolonged execution.

*Commentary.* In Act 2, Scene 4 of *Miles Gloriosus* ("The Braggart Warrior"),
the slave Sceledrus asserts he has witnessed his master's female courtesan,
Philocomasium (whom his master had taken from Athens to Ephesus), kissing
a man in the Ephesian house next door. In fact, Philocomasium did indeed
meet there with her Athenian lover via a hole cut between the houses, but in
this passage, she denies it. Soon she will claim her twin sister was the person
Sceledrus saw next door. Plautus loves the ironic turn of phrase, so when
Philocomasium swears "by Pollux" (the famous twin of Castor), the idea of
twins is already subtly anticipated. Sceledrus appears immune to threats, in
large measure because he has already predicted he will meet a slave's death on
a *crux*. That the *crux* would be his tomb (*sepulcrum*) likely indicates that, for
Plautus, a body suspended on a *crux* was expected to decompose on the cross
(and potentially was never formally buried). Plautus' hyperbolic language
implies Sceledrus' ancestors (at least to four generations) have already suffered the *crux,* and thus the penalty was an ancient one (and one very typical
of the slave).[611] Also note how this passage follows a few lines after the mention of Sceledrus having to carry a *patibulum* (crossbar) outside the gate of the
city (*Mil. glor.* 359–360; No. 113): "You will have to go through the gate with
hands spread out, when you will have the crossbar (*patibulum quom habebis*)."

**(310)** Plautus, *Miles Gloriosus* 182–184

I sis, iube transire huc quantum possit, se ut videant domi
familiares, nisi quidem illa nos volt, qui servi sumus,
propter amorem suom omnes crucibus contubernales dari.

*Translation.*
Go please, command [her] to go across to that [house] with the greatest speed
she can, so that the members of the household might see [her] at home,
unless indeed she wishes us, who are slaves,
on account of her love affair, all to be given over to crosses as slave-mates.

*Commentary.* At this point in the play (Act 2, Scene 2), the slave Palaestrio
(who is speaking in this passage) has just observed Sceledrus spying on the

---

[611] HENGEL, Crucifixion, 52, vividly suggests: "For Plautus, slaves have been executed on
the cross 'from time immemorial'." *Mil. glor.* 547–548 (Act 2, Scene 6) may also hint at the
*crux*, when Sceledrus the slave, having been utterly fooled by Palaestrio and Philocomasium,
admits his "error" at seeing Philocomasium with another man: "*meruisse equidem me
maxumum fateor malum, et tuae fecisse me hospitae aio iniuriam*" ("I confess that I truly
deserve the greatest possible misfortune, and I affirm that I did an injury to your female
guest"). Elsewhere Plautus employs the phrase *maxumum malum crucem* (e.g., *Capt.* 469,
*Cas.* 612; *Men.* 66, 328; *Pers.* 352; *Rud.* 518; *Trin.* 598; for all these texts see section 3.10);
thus such a *crux* might be inferred in *Mil. glor.* 547 in the words *maxumum malum*, especially
in light of Sceledrus' expectation in 368–374 that he will eventually face the *crux*.

slave-courtesan Philocomasium during her rendezvous next door with her Athenian lover at the house of Periplectomenus. Palaestrio is afraid Philocomasium's tryst will be reported to her owner (Pyrgopolynices, the "braggart soldier") and that all the slaves involved will be harshly punished. Here, Palaestrio begins to save the situation by asking Periplectomenus to direct Philocomasium to return home through the hole cut in the wall between the houses. These three lines are brimming with slave imagery, not just in the mention of *servi* ("slaves") but also concerning the *familiares* (the "members of the household," which primarily refers to slaves) and the *contubernales* ("slave-mates").[612] Palaestrio's principal fear is that he and his fellow slaves (likely including Philocomasium herself) will all share a home on a series of crosses.

**(311)** Plautus, *Miles Gloriosus* 305–312

quid ego nunc faciam? custodem me illi miles addidit:
nunc si indicium facio, interii; si taceo, <interii> tamen,
si hoc palam fuerit. quid peius muliere aut audacius?
dum ego in tegulis sum, illaec sese ex hospitio edit foras;
edepol facinus fecit audax. hocine si miles sciat,
credo hercle has sustollat aedis totas atque hunc in crucem.
hercle quidquid est, mussitabo potius quam inteream male;
non ego possum quae ipsa sese venditat tutarier.

*Translation.*
What should I do now? The soldier assigned me as a guardian for her:
now, if I give away the secret, I'm dead; if I remain quiet, I'm nevertheless dead
if this becomes generally known. What is worse or more audacious than a woman?
While I was on the roof-tiles, she slipped outside from her lodging;
by Pollux, she performed an audacious misdeed. If the soldier should get to know this,
by Hercules, I believe he will raise up this whole household and this man here [i.e., me] on the cross.
By Hercules, whatever happens, I shall keep quiet rather than die wickedly;
I am not able to protect a woman who offers herself for sale.

---

[612] Cf. OLD s.v. *familiaris*, a substantive referring to "a member of a household (esp. a slave)"; s.v. *contubernalis*, meaning "one who shares the same tent, a comrade-in-arms" but also having special reference to slaves as "a slave's 'mate' (having the relationship but not the status of a husband or wife)." In context of Philocomasium's amorous behavior, Plautus seems to have produced a pun with *contubernales*, as she and he (and likely other slaves) will be given the "same tent" and will be "mates" as they mount their respective crosses.

*Commentary.* Here the slave Sceledrus conveys angst about his situation. At this point in the play (Act 2, Scene 3), Sceledrus believes that while he was chasing a monkey across the roof, he saw Philocomasium (his master's slave-courtesan) kissing a man next door. And the slave Palestrio has not yet been able to fool him to the contrary. Sceledrus well recognizes that his master (the "braggart soldier" Pyrgopolynices) will hold him responsible for Philocomasium's misdeeds since Sceledrus was designated to be her *custos*. Sceledrus worries aloud that he and the rest of the household slaves will consequently be hung up on a cross. In this context, the cross involves a mass suspension of its victims (*sustollat... in crucem*) and constitutes a wicked death (cf. *inteream male*) that should be avoided at all cost.

**(312)** Plautus, *Asinaria* 545–557

Perfidiae laudes gratiasque habemus merito magnas,
quom nostris sycophantiis, dolis astutiisque,
[scapularum confidentia, virtute ulmorum freti]
qui advorsum stimulos,[613] lamminas, crucesque compedesque,
nervos, catenas, carceres, numellas, pedicas, boias
indoctoresque acerrumos gnarosque nostri tergi,
[qui saepe ante in nostras scapulas cicatrices indiderunt] [...]
eae nunc legiones, copiae exercitusque eorum
vi pugnando periuriis nostris fugae potiti.
id virtute huius collegae meaque comitate
factumst. qui me vir fortior ad sufferundas plagas?

*Translation.*
We give great praises and thanks to Perfidy just as she deserves,
since [relying on] our deceptions, trickeries, and stratagems,
[the audacity of our upper back and the valor that comes from the elm-wood]
which had been inflicted: goads, red-hot irons, and crosses, and shackles,
bonds, chains, prisons, collars, fetters, yokes,
and painters,[614] who are most severe and are knowledgeable about our backs,
[who often previously introduced scars to our backs] [...]
Now, these legions, troops, and their army,
after fighting by force, have been seized with flight by our perjuries.
This has been done by the merit of this colleague and by my companionship.
Who is a braver man than me at suffering blows?

---

[613] NIXON, Plautus, 1:182, following USSING, suggests *advorsum stetimus* ("we have stood against"); manuscript tradition: *qui advorsum stimulos* ("which had been inflicted: goads").

[614] The translation ("and painters") follows NIXON in translating *inductoresque* although the manuscripts read *indoctoresque* (perhaps "and the anti-trainers"?). LEO suggests *virgatoresque* ("and the one who wields the rod").

*Commentary.*[615] At the beginning of Act 3, Scene 2, the audience is privy to a happy-go-lucky conversation between two slaves, and here, Libanus shares with Leonida the secret of their success. The goddess Perfidy (Treachery) is on their side, as is evident in their own tricks and guile, which have helped them escape the various punishments often accorded to slaves. The text is likely corrupt, leading to various suggestions about what should be deleted, included, and emended. In any case, the *crux* appears on the list of punishments, but here, it does not seem to reference a means of death since it is listed among various tortures and blows Libanus claims they have survived.[616] Though not a form of execution, it is important to include this text to balance out our presentation of Plautus. Concerning the instances of *crux* in Plautus that refer to an actual punishment (as opposed to a mere vulgar taunt or curse formula, on which see section 3.10), most indicate a means of death (note especially the instances in *Mostellaria* and in *Miles Gloriosus* above), whereas here the *crux* appears to be a device upon which someone is tortured.[617]

**(313)** Terence, *Andria* 616–625

| | |
|---|---|
| *Pam.* | ehodum, bone vir, quid ais? viden me consiliis tuis miserum impeditum esse? |
| *Davus* | at iam expediam. |
| *Pam.* | expedies? |
| *Davus* | certe, Pamphile. |
| *Pam.* | nempe ut modo. |
| *Davus* | immo melius spero. |
| *Pam.* | oh, tibi ego ut credam furcifer? tu rem impeditam et perditam restituas? em quo fretus sim, qui me hodie ex tranquillissuma re coniecisti in nuptias. an non dixi esse hoc futurum? |
| *Davus* | dixti. |

---

[615] Text: Leo, Plautus Comoediae, 1:74. This has been compared with Nixon, Plautus, 1:180–182. The text appears to have been corrupted, and the brackets above represent lines that Leo believed are suspect, and that do not appear in Nixon's edition; this includes the possible missing line represented in the bracketed ellipsis.

[616] Their ability to weather such torture appears even more clearly in the text, if one includes the two lines that are not in Nixon; Leo also finds those lines suspicious. Those two lines boast of backs that are scarred but audaciously and valorously able to confront the elm-wood and other devices the "painters" and others throw at them.

[617] It is intriguing to note that when Plautus employs the *crux* in vulgar taunts between characters in his play, the recipient of the taunt is almost always a slave; cf. *Cas.* 611; *Men.* 849; *Pers.* 352; *Rud.* 518; *Trin.* 598). The primary exception here is a "parasite" (i.e., a guest who sponges meals off his patron in exchange for being witty company), but such an exception may well be comedic, given the patron's jests that his client deserves the same treatment as a slave (*Stich.* 625; cf. *Capt.* 469). All these texts are discussed in section 3.10.

| | |
|---|---|
| *Pam.* | quid meritu's? |
| *Davus* | crucem. |
| | sed sine paululum ad me redeam: iam aliquid dispiciam. |
| *Pam.* | ei mihi, |
| | quom non habeo spatium, ut de te sumam supplicium ut volo! |
| | namque hoc tempus praecavere mihi me haud te ulcisci sinit. |

*Translation.*

| | |
|---|---|
| *Pam.* | Hey now! good man, what do you say? Do you not see that by your council misery has entangled me. |
| *Davus* | But now I shall extricate [you]. |
| *Pam.* | You will extricate [me]? |
| *Davus* | Certainly, Pamphilus. |
| *Pam.* | No doubt, as [you did] just recently. |
| *Davus* | Rather, better I hope. |
| *Pam.* | Oh, how shall I believe you, *furcifer*? |
| | Will you reverse an entangled and desperate situation? Look at this one whom I am relying on, |
| | who hurled me today from an extremely tranquil state into marriage. |
| | Didn't I say this would be the future? |
| *Davus* | You said [so]. |
| *Pam.* | What do you deserve? |
| *Davus* | The cross. |
| | But allow me a little bit, I'll recover my senses: by then I shall think up something. |
| *Pam.* | Ah me! |
| | On every occasion when I do not have a break, so that I may exact the punishment from you that I want! |
| | For, this present time allows me [only] to take care for myself, not to take vengeance on you. |

*Commentary.*[618] Based on the opening superscription, Publius Terentius Afer authored *The Lady of Andros* in 166 B.C., adapting it from two Greek New Comedy plays of Menander. The interaction between masters and slaves is similar to Plautus, though perhaps a bit less bawdy in style. Pamphilus is in love with a woman down the street (by whom he secretly has a child), who appears to be a courtesan's friend, but who will ultimately turn out to be an Athenian citizen. Meanwhile, his father has pledged him to be married to another woman, a marriage to which Pamphilus assents because his slave (Davus) has assured him it will never happen. At this stage in the play (Act 3,

---

[618] Text: JOHN SARGEAUNT, Terence (2 vols.; LCL; Cambridge: Harvard University Press, 1912), 1:66.

Scene 5), Davus has been proven wrong, and thus Pamphilus is soon to be married to a woman he does not love. Both men know this and thus Pamphilus sarcastically addresses his slave as *bone vir* ("good man") and then proceeds to lambast him. Typically, derogative epithets are addressed to slaves in this play, especially those that speak of a cruel torture or death.[619] For our purposes, note two items above: First, the slave Davus acknowledges he deserves (*meritu*) the cross (*crucem*) for the evil he has brought on his master; second, even prior to that acknowledgment (and perhaps suggesting Davus' mention of the *crux*), Pamphilus addresses Davus as a *furcifer*, which may (as above in Plautus) reference a slave's death upon a *furca*.[620]

**(314)** Appian, *Bella Civilia* 4.4.29 [4.125–126]

ἔπαυλιν ἕτερος εἶχε περικαλλῆ καὶ σύσκιον, ἄντρον τε καλὸν ἦν ἐν αὐτῇ καὶ βαθύ, καὶ τάχα διὰ ταῦτα καὶ προυγράφη. ἔτυχε δὲ ἀναψύχων κατὰ τὸ ἄντρον, καὶ αὐτῷ τῶν σφαγέων ἔτι μακρόθεν ἐπιθεόντων θεράπων αὐτὸν ἐς τὸν μυχὸν τοῦ ἄντρου προπέμψας ἐνέδυ τὸν τοῦ δεσπότου χιτωνίσκον καὶ ὑπεκρίνετο ἐκεῖνος εἶναι καὶ δεδιέναι· καὶ τάχα ἂν ἐπέτυχεν ἀναιρεθείς, εἰ μὴ τῶν ὁμοδούλων τις ἐνέφηνε τὴν ἐνέδραν. ἀναιρεθέντος δὲ ὧδε τοῦ δεσπότου, ὁ δῆμος ἀγανακτῶν παρὰ τοῖς ἄρχουσιν οὐκ ἐπαύετο, μέχρι τὸν μὲν ἐνδείξαντα κρεμασθῆναι, τὸν δὲ περισώσαντα ἐλευθερῶσαι ἐποίησεν.

*Translation.* Another man had a very beautiful and thickly-shaded country house (there was a pretty and deep cavern on its property), and perhaps on account of this he also was proscribed. But he happened to be cooling off in the cavern; and while the cut-throats were running after him from still far away, a servant conducted him into the inmost part of the cavern, put on the short frock of his master, and pretended to be that man and to flee. And perhaps [the servant] would have succeeded in being slain, except a certain one of the fellow-slaves informed about the trick. But after the master had been slain in this manner, the populace did not cease being displeased with the

---

[619] For example, Davus is repeatedly called a *carnufex* ("scoundrel," or more literally "one to be executed") by his masters (*Andr.* 183, 651, 852). He is also imprecated with a curse from the gods (*O scelus at tibi di dignum factis exitium duint!*; 665–666). As in Plautus, Terence's characters can speak from their difficult situations in terms of their needing to commit suicide by "hanging yourself" (e.g., *suspende te*; *Andr.* 255). The term *cruciatus* also appears in this play: *em scelera: hanc iam oportet in cruciatum hinc abripi* ("Here you are, villainess: it is right that this woman now be carried off from here to torture;" *Andr.* 786–787). Though the context is not determinative, *cruciatus* there should likely be considered a reference to "torture" (following OLD s.v. *cruciatus*) rather than "crucifixion" (contra the translation "she ought to be dragged off and crucified" in SARGEAUNT, Terence, 1:85). Other words from the same stem also indicate "torture", cf. *excrucio me* for "I torture myself" in 886.

[620] See commentary in No. 304 on Plautus, *Most.* 69–71. For other instances of *furcifer* in Terence see *Eun.* 798, 862, 989.

leaders, until [the triumvir] caused the one who informed to be hung up, and the one who [attempted to] save [his master's] life to be freed.

*Commentary.*[621] Throughout this chapter, Appian (writing in the second century A.D.) depicts the time under the Second Triumvirate in 43–42 B.C. when Mark Antony, M. Aemilius Lepidus and Octavian instituted proscriptions against supposed enemies of the state, largely in an effort to remove their enemies and to garner funds for their forces (and for their own purses). Such proscriptions were notices calling for the execution of various members of the Roman elite (often senators) and for the commandeering of their property for sake of the state coffers. Squads of soldiers were sent to capture the proscribed men, and the public, along with slaves and other members of the victim's families, was encouraged by offer of financial reward to assist in putting them to death. In that context, the above episode contrasts two slaves – the faithful slave, who willingly offers his life to protect his master, and the greedy slave, who betrays his master, presumably in hopes of fiscal gain. The episode is likely located in Appian here thematically. The preceding subject in 4.4.29 concerns a man proscribed for sake of his property, and the event following this passage depicts a slave who greedily revealed his master's hiding place. In this text, the public, upon learning of these events, instead insists that the triumvirs do the just thing, providing the traditional reward for the faithful slave (his freedom) and the traditional penalty to the slave who sought his master's demise (public suspension/crucifixion).[622] The terminology for this suspension (κρεμασθῆναι, "to be hung up") only vaguely depicts the means of the slave's execution, but Appian's readers would likely presume a *crux* had been employed. For more on Appian's vocabulary for penal bodily suspension, see the extended discussion above on Appian, *Bell. civ.* 3.1.3 (No. 300).

**(315)** Appian, *Bella Civilia* 4.5.35 [4.148]

ὁ δὲ τῶν μὲν ὁπλιτῶν ἔδεισεν ἅψασθαι, μὴ σφᾶς ἐφ᾽ ἑαυτὸν παροξύνῃ, τῶν δὲ θεραπόντων τινάς, οἳ σχήματι στρατιωτῶν συνεξημάρτανον ἐκείνοις, λαβὼν ἐκρέμασε.

*Translation.* Yet he [the consul] was afraid to lay hands on the soldiers, lest he provoke their [anger] against himself; but after capturing some of the servants, who in the guise of soldiers shared in the fault with those [soldiers], he hung them up.

---

[621] Text: VIERECK, ROOS, and GABBA, *Appiani Historia romana*, 2:415–416 (where it is 4.125–126). Same text appears in WHITE, *Appian's Roman History*, 4:188–190 (as 4.4.29).

[622] In the *Pauli Sententiae* (3.5.1–12), slaves are to be tortured for any remotely potential complicity in the homicide of their masters. If a slave abandons his master when his master is murdered by brigands, the slave should suffer death by the *summum supplicium* (3.5.8).

*Commentary.* Appian continues to relate the "extreme misfortunes" (*Bell. civ.* 4.6.36) that occurred against the proscribed during the Second Triumvirate. He indicates in 4.5.35 that the soldiers often exceeded their mandate – executing people not proscribed and confiscating their property, as well as demanding a share in any impounded estates, and insisting on being adopted as heirs of the rich. In response, the triumviri eventually issued edicts empowering the consuls to rein in the soldiers. Nevertheless, the text insists that the consuls were too afraid of the soldiers to act in keeping with these edicts. They did, however, punish the slaves who had joined the soldiers in pillaging the proscribed. Appian commonly uses θεράπων ("servants") for "slaves" (cf. *Bell. civ.* 4.4.29, No. 314; also see 4.10.81; 5.8.70 in No. 316, 317). Appian (following his typical suspension/crucifixion terminology) reports that the consuls suspended (ἐκρέμασε) these slaves as the central element in their execution.

**(316)** Appian, *Bella Civilia* 4.10.81 [4.341–343]

ὁ δ᾽ ἐσελθὼν ἔκτεινε μὲν οὐδένα οὐδ᾽ ἐξήλασε, χρυσὸν δὲ καὶ ἄργυρον, ὅσον ἡ πόλις εἶχε, συνενεγκὼν ἐκέλευε καὶ τὸν ἰδιωτικὸν ἑκάστους ἐσφέρειν ὑπὸ ζημίαις καὶ μηνύμασιν, οἵοις καὶ Κάσσιος ἐκήρυξεν ἐν Ῥόδῳ. [342] καὶ οἱ μὲν ἐσέφερον, θεράπων δὲ τὸν δεσπότην ἐμήνυσε χρυσίον κρύψαι καὶ πεμφθέντι λοχαγῷ τὸ χρυσίον ἔδειξεν. ἀγομένων δὲ ἁπάντων ὁ μὲν δεσπότης ἐσιώπα, ἡ δὲ ἐκείνου μήτηρ περισῴζουσα τὸν υἱὸν εἵπετο, βοῶσα αὐτὴ τὸ χρυσίον κρύψαι. ὁ δὲ οἰκέτης, οὐδὲ ἀνερωτώμενος, τὴν μὲν ἤλεγχε ψευδομένην, τὸν δὲ κρύψαντα. [343] καὶ ὁ Βροῦτος τὸν μὲν νεανίαν ἀπεδέξατο τῆς σιωπῆς καὶ τὴν μητέρα τοῦ πάθους καὶ μεθῆκεν ἀμφοτέρους ἀπαθεῖς ἀπιέναι τὸ χρυσίον φερομένους, τὸν δὲ οἰκέτην ὡς πέρα τοῦ προστάγματος ἐπιβουλεύσαντα τοῖς δεσπόταις ἐκρέμασε.

*Translation.* And upon entering [the city of Patara], [Brutus] killed no one, nor did he banish [anyone]; yet, the gold and silver, as much as the city had, he ordered brought together and each person to bring in his private wealth under the penalties and rewards for information that Cassius had also proclaimed in Rhodes. [342] And they brought in [the monies], but a servant informed that his master had hidden gold and showed the gold to the centurion who had been sent. And when all were led [to Brutus], the master was silent, but his mother, attempting to save her son from death, followed, crying out that she had hidden the gold. But the household slave, though he was not being questioned, rebuked [the mother's] lying and [the master's] hiding. [343] And Brutus approved the young man's silence and the mother's passion, and he set both free unpunished, with the result that he sent them away carrying their gold; but, the household slave, since he had plotted against his masters beyond the proscription, Brutus hung up.

*Commentary.* As Appian's *Civil Wars* progresses, Brutus and Cassius (with other colleagues) attempt to solidify territory on the island of Rhodes and in coastal Lycia (modern southwest Turkey). Brutus had just captured the Lycian city of Xanthus (where the inhabitants, after a spirited defense, committed mass suicide rather than be captured; *Bell. civ.* 4.10.80). In this passage, Brutus has moved south to the port city of Patara,[623] where he besieges the town and offers the Patarans terms (using surviving Xanthians as heralds to testify to the hazards of fighting the Romans). Patara opens its gates to Brutus, and he enacts the same program Cassius had employed at Rhodes for exacting the needed funds for the war against Antony and Octavian (cf. *Bell. civ.* 4.9.73). In contrast to Cassius, Brutus, upon capturing the city, shows leniency by not executing or banishing the prominent citizens (contrast 4.9.73).[624] If the "penalties and rewards for information" (ὑπὸ ζημίαις καὶ μηνύμασιν) were indeed the same as Cassius' at Rhodes, then, according to Appian, these would have required the penalty of death for citizens who hid their money and the reward of a tenth of the plunder for informants who revealed the secret, with slave informants also receiving their freedom (4.9.73). Thus, in the narrative above, the master and his mother could expect death, while the informing slave/servant (θεράπων) should have received freedom and a portion of the proceeds. Yet the slave overplayed his hand, while the master was honorable and the mother pitiable. Thus the faithless slave was "hung up" (ἐκρέμασε), employing Appian's typical term for human bodily suspension (quite plausibly crucifixion). This brief story sounds similar to the reversal enacted upon the traitorous slave during the proscriptions in 4.4.29 (No. 314), which also involved the suspension of the faithless slave; so we may be encountering a motif in Appian that serves his literary (as much as his historical) purposes.

**(317)**   Appian, *Bella Civilia* 5.8.70 [5.295]

ὁ δὲ χιλίαρχον καὶ λοχαγὸν αὐτοῦ Μούρκου διαφθείρας ἔπεμψεν ἀνελεῖν αὐτὸν καὶ φάσκειν ὑπὸ θεραπόντων ἀνῃρῆσθαι· ἔς τε πίστιν τῆς ὑποκρίσεως τοὺς θεράποντας ἐσταύρου.

---

[623] Excavations in Patara have yielded substantial remains from the Roman-era city.

[624] Plutarch explicitly contrasts Brutus' actions in Patara with Cassius' harsher measures in Rhodes, noting the difference in monies exacted from the citizens (*Brut.* 32.2). Cassius Dio records that Brutus only imposed a fine on Patara, without engaging in more vehement penalties (*Hist. rom.* 47.34.6). Both attribute the opening of the Pataran gates to the Patarans' response to a different act of Brutus' clemency than Appian records (Plutarch to Brutus' release of Lycian women without ransom, and Dio to Brutus' refusal to complete the threatened auction of citizens before the Pataran gates). Neither corroborates the story.

*Translation.* And, after corrupting Murcus' own tribune and centurion, [Sextus Pompeius] sent them to kill him and to affirm that he had been killed by servants; and for the credence of playing the part, he crucified the servants.

*Commentary.* As the war has progressed, Cassius and Brutus were defeated at Philippi, but Sextus Pompeius remained an antagonist of the now-united Antony and Octavian. Sextus and his forces have been disrupting the grain supply to Rome, and in 39 B.C. pressures are coming upon the multiple sides to reconcile. In Appian's account, Menodorus, one of Sextus' inner circle, counsels him to remain at war (with the famine in Rome on his side) and spurs on distrust against Sextus' ally Lucius Staius Murcus, who had advised reconciliation.[625] Under Menodorus' influence, Sextus Pompeius severs contact with Murcus, and eventually Murcus retires to Syracuse, insulting Sextus to his guards. In light of these events, Sextus schemes to murder Murcus and blame it on his slaves/servants (whom Appian again designates with θεράπων). For the purpose of adding believability to his plan, Sextus also sends the accused slaves to the fate that would rightly have been theirs had they truly put their master to death. Notably, Dio's account includes no mention of blaming the slaves. Lucius Staius is simply put to death by Sextus' command on charges of treachery (ἔγκλημα αὐτῷ προδοσίας; Cassius Dio, *Hist. rom.* 48.19). The historicity of Appian's account is thus somewhat murky, though his is the more detailed. In any case, we witness from Appian that σταυρόω was the kind of punishment he (and his second-century A.D. readers) viewed as commonly applied against treacherous slaves. Appian employs σταυρόω more rarely than κρεμάννυμι in depicting human bodily suspension (cf. *Sic.* 2.3 of the crucifying Carthaginians).[626] However, the interchangeability of these suspension terms is implied by the matter-of-fact way Appian implies in all such instances that σταυρόω/κρεμάννυμι is a common punishment for a treacherous slave (θεράπων) who sought his master's demise.

### (318) Tacitus, *Historiae* 4.3

viso milite quies et minoribus coloniis impunitas: Capuae legio tertia hiemandi causa locatur et domus inlustres adflictae, cum contra Tarracinenses nulla ope iuvarentur. tanto proclivius est iniuriae quam beneficio vicem exolvere, quia gratia oneri, ultio in quaestu habetur. solacio fuit servus Vergilii Capitonis,

---

[625] Menodorus is known in other ancient sources as Menas (e.g., Cassius Dio, *Hist. rom.* 48.30.4–8; Plutarch, *Ant.* 32.1–5). Dio records the reconciliation (albeit a temporary one) between Sextus and Antony/Octavian in *Hist. rom.* 48.36.1–6 (cf. Plutarch, *Ant.* 32.1–5), which here occurs in Appian (*Bell. civ.* 5.8.71–73).

[626] Other than *Sic.* 2.3, all selections from Appian in this chapter involve κρεμάννυμι rather than σταυρόω. Like other authors, Appian can also employ σταυρόω for the putting up of a palisade (made of σταυροί or ξύλοι); cf. *Pun.* 18.119.

quem proditorem Tarracinensium diximus, patibulo adfixus in isdem anulis quos acceptos a Vitellio gestabat.

*Translation*. After the military appeared, there was calm, and for the smaller colonies there was exemption from punishment: At Capua the Third Legion was located for the sake of wintering [there], and the illustrious houses were afflicted, while on the other hand the Tarracines were given no assistance. Such is the greater inclination to award repayment for injury rather than for kindness, because [while] gratitude is considered something onerous, vengeance derives a profit. For consolation, the slave of Vergilius Capito, whom we said was the betrayer of the Tarracines, was fastened to a *patibulum* wearing the same rings that he had received from Vitellius.

*Commentary*.[627] Tacitus' *Histories* were likely composed in the first decade of the second century, and the extant Books 1–5 cover only A.D. 69–70. At the close of the "year of four emperors" (A.D. 69), Vespasian's troops have conquered Vitellius, and Lucilius Bassus has been sent to restore peace in Campania. Tacitus records that the city of Capua (which had supported Vitellius) was forced to quarter the Third Legion for the winter (to the financial destruction of the noble families of the host city). Meanwhile, Tarracina (which supported Vespasian; cf. *Hist*. 3.57) was given nothing in return for its previous loyalty. This is the reason for Tacitus' comment that there is a greater proclivity to "repayment for injury" (*iniuriae ... vicem*; concerning Capua) than to "repayment for kindness" (*iniuriae beneficio*; concerning Tarracina); note the implicit wordplay with *vicis*. According to Tacitus, the only consolation the Tarracines received was the public punishment of Vergilius Capito's slave, who had previously guided Vitellius' forces through the weak defenses of Tarracina, enabling them to massacre the city's pro-Vespasian (but poorly-organized) inhabitants (cf. *Hist*. 3.76–77). Apparently this slave had received finger-rings of honor for his treacherous service, and many interpret these rings as implying that Vitellius had granted the slave equestrian rank (in addition to his freedom).[628] The form of punishment Involves affixing him to a *patibulum* (*patibulo adfixus*).[629] The context makes it likely this was a public penalty (with the rings being worn for all to see). Suspension is also likely, though the precise form cannot be determined with certainty. Other Latin

---

[627] Text: CHARLES D. FISHER, Cornelii Taciti Historiarum libri (Scriptorum classicorum bibliotheca Oxoniensis; Oxford: Clarendon, 1911); cf. MOORE and JACKSON, Tacitus, 2:6. The only difference of note in the manuscripts concerns the name *Verginii* or *Vergilii*.

[628] OLD s.v. *anulus* indicates that *anulus* can stand for the sign of senatorial or equestrian rank. Cf. Tacitus, *Hist*. 2.57 where he indicates that Vitellius had granted the freedman Asiaticus the *anuli* of the equestrian class. Concerning 4.3, HENGEL, Crucifixion, 60 calls this "the insignia of the equestrian order."

[629] For all further instances of *patibulum* in Tacitus, cf. *Ann*. 1.61; 4.72; 14.33 (No. 211, 212, 213).

*patibulum* accounts would indicate out-stretched arms. This text could well belong in another section (e.g., note the use of suspension in war below), but the fact that the victim was a former *servus* (slave) of Vergilius Capito makes the *patibulum* penalty particularly apropos.

**(319)** Tacitus, *Historiae* 4.11

Iulius Priscus praetoriarum sub Vitellio cohortium praefectus se ipse interfecit, pudore magis quam necessitate. Alfenus Varus ignaviae infamiaeque suae superfuit. Asiaticus (is enim libertus)[630] malam potentiam servili supplicio expiavit.

*Translation.* Julius Priscus, prefect of the praetorian cohorts under Vitellius, killed himself, due to feeling shame rather than due to necessity. Alfenus Varus survived his cowardice and disgrace. Asiaticus (because he was a freedman) atoned for his wicked influence by the slave's punishment.

*Commentary.* Explicit references to crucifixion are even less certain in this passage and in the next one below (*Hist.* 2.72). HENGEL argues that the "slave's punishment" (*servili supplicio*, above) refers to the standard application of crucifixion against slaves,[631] while SAMUELSSON questions this reasoning.[632] Crucifixion is quite possible here, but not certain; in any case, these passages are included for sake of exhaustiveness. In this brief selection, Tacitus informs us of the fate of some of Vitellius' key leaders after his demise. As their troops fled to join Vespasian, both Julius Priscus and Alfenus Varus had abandoned their command over the field of battle in the Apennines and returned to Rome (*Hist.* 3.61; cf. 3.55), hence Tacitus' reference to their

---

[630] The key manuscript reads *enim is libertus,* where FISHER's text reads *is enim libertus* ("because he was a freedman"), and MOORE / JACKSON suggest *etenim is libertus* ("for he was a freedman"); all authorities thus agree on the essential meaning of the phrase.

[631] HENGEL, Crucifixion, 51n, 60; HENGEL, Cross, 143n, 152. HENGEL's argument is strengthened by parallel mention of a "slave penalty" in connection with crucifixion in, especially, *Scriptores Historiae Augustae* 6.4.6 (Vulcacius Gallicanus, *Avidius Cassius*). HENGEL further notes references to the "slave penalty" in tandem with the cross in: Valerius Maximus 2.7.12; Horace, *Sat.* 1.8.32; Tacitus, *Hist.* 4.11; *Scriptores Historiae Augustae* 15.12.2 (Julius Capitolinus, *Macrinus*). These texts should be distinguished from *Scriptores Historiae Augustae* 6.4.6 because in each, the Latin grammar could suggest the crucifixion and the "slave penalty" are not identical. Finally, HENGEL notes the "punishment of slaves" connected with a lack of burial afterward in Livius 29.9.10; 29.18.14. In HENGEL's favor, we can also note that slaves, and occasionally *humiliores* as opposed to *honestiores*, repeatedly face the cross in the *Pauli Sententiae*; see repeatedly in section 3.6.4.

[632] SAMUELSSON, Crucifixion, 163, in reference to *Hist.* 2.72 and 4.11 says: "neither text shows what kind of punishment a 'slave punishment' was in Tacitus' eyes." SAMUELSSON, perhaps too quickly, discounts HENGEL's appeal to Valerius Maximus and Livius, both of whom connect *crux* with slave punishments (see previous note).

shame, cowardice and disgrace. Our focus is on Asiaticus, who as a *libertus* (a freed former slave) nevertheless met a slave's demise. Tacitus clearly believes this a suitable atoning (cf. *expiavit*) for his "wicked influence" (*malam potentiam*). Earlier in *Hist.* 2.72, Tacitus mentioned that Vitellius' soldiers had asked from the emperor that the freedman Asiaticus be granted equestrian dignity (*ut libertum suum Asiaticum equesti dignitate donaret*), which Tacitus calls a "shameful adulation" (*inhonestam adulationem*). Vitellius initially refuses this request but later grants it in private, giving Asiaticus the *anuli* (rings) of the equestrian class. Tacitus refers to Asiaticus as "a repugnant slave and one who gains favor by wicked arts" (*foedum mancipium et malis artibus ambitiosum*; 2.72; cf. 2.95). In short, Tacitus likely wished Asiaticus good riddance, and thus approved of his slave-style demise.

**(320)** Tacitus, *Historiae* 2.72

Non ultra paucos dies quamquam acribus initiis coeptum mendacium valuit. extiterat quidam Scribonianum se Camerinum ferens, Neronianorum temporum metu in Histria occultatum, quod illic clientelae et agri veterum Crassorum ac nominis favor manebat. igitur deterrimo quoque in argumentum fabulae adsumpto vulgus credulum et quidam militum, errore veri seu turbarum studio, certatim adgregabantur, cum pertractus ad Vitellium interrogatusque quisnam mortalium esset. postquam nulla dictis fides et a domino noscebatur condicione fugitivus, nomine Geta, sumptum de eo supplicium in servilem modum.

*Translation.* A false scheme, albeit with a bitter initial phase, succeeded for no more than a few days. [A man] claimed attention, alleging he was a certain Scribonianus Camerinus, having been concealed in Histria for fear of the Neronian times, because in that place remained the support of the clientship, land, and renown of the old Crassi. Therefore, after the least desirable men also were enlisted in the story of his fable, the credulous commoners and some soldiers, whether by straying from truth or by zeal of the crowds, began eagerly flocking [to him], when he was hauled to Vitellius and interrogated as to just what mortal he was. After no faith [was accorded] to his utterances and he was acknowledged by [his] master as a fugitive slave by status, Geta by name, punishment was exacted from him in the manner of slaves.

*Commentary.* We are now earlier in Tacitus' *Histories*, in the midst of the narrative of Vitellius' brief imperial reign. Here, we learn of this fleeting challenge to his rule. The text implies that the Scriboniani were a famous family (related to the Crassi), whose members had been oppressed under Nero.[633]

---

[633] MOORE and JACKSON, Tacitus, 1:274 references "Dio Cass. lxiii.18" [*sic*] and Plinius, *Ep.* 1.5 to the effect that Nero's slave Helios had Scribonianus and his father murdered. However, the Cassius Dio text (actually 62.18) refers instead to *Sulpicius* Camerinus (Σουλπίκιον

Histria/Istria was a peninsula in the north-eastern Adriatic. The pretender's story appears to have caught on, with commoners and soldiers alike joining in his support. Sufficient concern must have arisen for him to be dragged before Vitellius for trial, where he was examined as to "just what mortal he was" (*quisnam mortalium*; i.e., who is he?). Tacitus appears to affirm the interrogator's conclusion, premised on the testimony of a *dominus* (a "master", quite possibly the pretender's master), that this pretender was an escaped slave who impersonated a renowned citizen in order to foment revolt. With those charges, and especially with the rather vicious Vitellius in charge, the death penalty is not unexpected. Hence, it is likely that the "punishment ... in the manner of slaves" (*supplicium in servilem modum*) involved the kind of *death* typically applied to slaves. HENGEL's inference that this was crucifixion cannot be proven, but remains a distinct possibility.[634]

Perhaps this is the best location to note that HENGEL further extends this notion that crucifixion was connected to a slave's penalty when he suggests the "place chosen for the slaves' penalties" (*locum servilibus poenis sepositum*; Tacitus, *Ann.* 15.60.1) was "outside the Esquiline Gate" (*extra portam Esquilinam*; Tacitus, *Ann.* 2.32.2), contending this was the area where slaves were crucified outside Rome.[635] Admittedly, neither of these Tacitus texts specifically refers to crucifixion (or even to the execution of slaves, since they respectively concern the executions of the consul-designate Plautius Lateranus and the astrologer/magician Publius Marcius). Actually, the use of this Esquiline region was more complex than HENGEL allows since that area was once known for its pits for the disposal of the corpses of commoners (see Varro, *Ling.* 5.25 on *puticuli*; also Horace, *Sat.* 1.8.14–16), while the Campus Esquilinus housed sepulchres of nobles (cf. Cicero, *Phil.* 9.7.17). Gaius Maecenas famously built gardens in the vicinity in the first century B.C. Occasionally, famous Roman citizens were dishonored by being left unburied there, including Galba's head (Plutarch, *Galb.* 28.3, where Σεσσώριον is an area past the Esquiline gate). Under Claudius, foreigners who usurped rights of Roman citizens (including, most likely, falsely claiming Roman *nomina*) were beheaded (*securi percussit*) in the Campus Esquilinus (Suetonius, *Claud.* 25.3). Though scavenger birds were associated (along with wolves) with the Esquiline (Horace, *Epod.* 5.99–100), and vultures were indeed drawn to devour

---

Καμερῖνον) and son as having been killed, and the Pliny text (*numquid ego Crasso aut Camerino molestus sum?*) does not mention the *nomen* Scribonianus. On the other hand, the renown of other Scriboniani is well testified, and they typically appear in opposition to the emperor of the day (e.g., M. Furius Camillus Scribonianus in Tacitus, *Ann.* 6.1, 12.52, *Hist.* 1.89, 2.75; Suetonius, *Claud.* 13; his son Furius Camillus Scribonianus in Tacitus, *Ann.* 12.52; and Licinius Crassus Scribonianus in Tacitus, *Hist.* 4.39; cf. 1.47; note Licinius can trace his family lineage both to the Crassi and the Scriboniani).

[634] HENGEL, Crucifixion, 51n, 60. SAMUELSSON, Crucifixion, 163 rejects this claim.

[635] HENGEL, Crucifixion, 146.

the flesh of crucifixion victims (Juvenal, *Sat.* 14.77–80), it should not be
assumed that such birds were only attracted to crosses; the burial pits in the
region likely also attracted scavengers. Indeed, the Horace text HENGEL cites
does not imply crucifixion of witches, but stoning (*Epod.* 5.97–100). HENGEL's
other references to Tacitus (*Ann.* 15.40) and Catullus (*Car.* 108) are not pertinent. It thus seems preferable to say that the *extra portam Esquilinam* was at
one time a disposal location for common corpses, and consequently, it also
served as a place where people could be executed using a variety of means,
especially if one wished to humiliate one's victim; crucifixion would likely
have been one of those means, but the evidence is not certain.

In any case, we observe here that certain punishments could readily be
associated with the class of slaves.

**(321)**  Juvenal, *Saturae* 6.219–224

"Pone crucem servo." "meruit quo crimine servus
supplicium? quis testis adest? quis detulit? audi;
nulla umquam de morte hominis cunctatio longa est."
"o demens, ita servus homo est? nil fecerit, esto:
hoc volo, sic iubeo, sit pro ratione voluntas."
imperat ergo viro.

*Translation.*
[The wife says:] "Erect a cross for the slave."
[The husband replies:] "For what charge did the slave deserve punishment?
Who is present as a witness? Who accused [him]? Listen; no delay is ever too
long concerning the death of a man."
[The wife retorts:] "O madman, so is a slave a man? He did nothing, suppose
that is so: I wish this; thus I command; let [my] wish be in place of a reason."
Thus she rules over the husband.

*Commentary.*[636] Despite possible personal allusions in the *Saturae* by Decimus
Iunius Iuvenalis, little is known about the author. He appears to have written
in the first third of the second century A.D. (during the reigns of Trajan and
Hadrian). In Book 2 (*Sat.* 6), Juvenal depicts at some length the perils of mat-
rimony in an attempt to dissuade men from marrying, often deriding any
potential Roman bride in what appears to us as unmitigated sexism. The selection above provides an extreme example of the control a wife exerts over a
husband (*imperat ergo viro*). She wishes a slave to be executed on the cross,
and (even without any charge, testimony, or conviction) she insists that her
desire be carried out. In the process, the wife questions whether a slave should

---

[636] Text: GEORGE GILBERT RAMSAY, *Juvenal and Persius* (LCL; Cambridge: Harvard University Press, 1918), 100.

truly be classified as a man. The *crux* here is clearly a device that must be erected (*pone crucem*) as a punishment (*supplicium*) for the purpose of putting a man to death (cf. *de morte hominis*). The precise form and manner of execution is assumed rather than given full description. The text presupposes that a slave-owner could willfully execute his slave on a *crux* without appeal to a judicial authority, though Juvenal certainly implies that properly the slave should be chargeable for a crime.

**(322)** *Historia Augusta* 8 [Pertinax] 9.10

eos qui calumniis adpetiti per servos fuerant damnatis severius delatoribus liberavit, in crucem sublatis talibus servis; aliquos etiam mortuos vindicavit.

*Translation.* Those, who had been assailed with false accusations by the agency of slaves, he [Pertinax] freed, while the accusers were condemned to more severe treatment, such slaves being lifted up on a cross; he even avenged some who had died.

*Commentary.*[637] The *Historia Augusta* contains thirty biographical books of Roman emperors and imperial pretenders from the second and third centuries A.D. Although six authors are named as contributors, the current form shows evidence of considerable redaction in the fourth century, and some of the authorship notations may be spurious.[638] This book on Pertinax (who ruled in A.D. 193) is attributed to Julius Capitolinus, who reportedly planned to write a series of such biographies dedicated to Constantine (cf. *Historia Augusta* 19 [Maximini Duo] 1.1–3; and 20 [Gordiani Tres] 1.1–5); he is asserted as the author of nine biographies appearing in the *Historia Augusta*. Pertinax was hailed as emperor after the murder of Commodus, and he may well have conspired with the murderers, though only after the deed (*Historia Augusta* 8.4.4–11; Herodian, *Hist.* 2.1.5–10; Cassius Dio, *Hist. Rom.* 74.1.1). Pertinax's short reign was generally viewed positively (despite his miserliness and rigor), although he was considered to have too hastily enacted much-needed reforms and thus to have angered his murderous soldiers (e.g., Cassius Dio, *Hist. rom.* 74.10.2–3; cf. Herodian, *Hist.* 2.4.1–5.1). The present author asserts that Pertinax was himself murdered because of his integrity (*Historia Augusta* 8.10.8). The passage above is collected (in a fashion reminiscent of Suetonius) in a series of Pertinax's admirable actions (8.9.8–10), hence there can be no doubt that the author viewed as a commendable and judicious measure Pertinax's punishment of the dishonest slaves on the cross.[639]

---

[637] Text: DAVID MAGIE, The Scriptores Historiae Augustae (3 vols.; LCL; Cambridge: Harvard University Press, 1922–1932), 1:334.

[638] A helpful summary of the issues involved can be found in the introductions to volumes one and (especially) two of MAGIE, Scriptores Historiae Augustae.

**(323)**  *Historia Augusta* 18 [Severus Alexander] 23.7–8

idem tertium genus hominum eunuchos esse dicebat nec videndum nec in usu habendum a viris sed vix a feminis nobilibus. [8] qui de eo fumos[640] vendiderat et a quodam militari centum aureos acceperat, in crucem tolli iussit per eam viam qua esset servis suis ad suburbana imperatoria iter frequentissimum.

*Translation.* That same man [Severus Alexander] would say that eunuchs were a third race of humans, neither to be seen nor to be kept in use by men, but reluctantly [they may be kept in use] by noble women. [8] When one of these [eunuchs] sold empty promises and acquired a hundred gold coins from a certain soldier, he commanded [him] to be hung on a cross along that road which was the route to the imperial suburban estates most crowded by his slaves.

*Commentary.* This book in the *Historia Augusta*, attributed to Aelius Lampridius and purporting to be written to Constantine,[641] reports on the reign of emperor Marcus Aurelius Severus Alexander (A.D. 222–235). The passage comes in the midst of notable imperial decisions and actions by Alexander, most of which appear to have been agreeable to the author. Such eunuchs were slaves (cf. e.g., 18.66.3–4), and Alexander acted to decrease the influence eunuchs had at court (in contrast to his predecessor Elagabalus; cf. 18.23.4–6). Elsewhere, the author notes that court eunuchs were in the habit of selling imperial plans and profiteering in other ways from their positions (18.45.4–5; 18.66.3–4). He further observes that Severus Alexander enjoined the death penalty (even without a court trial) against eunuchs who misused their position (18.34.3). In this passage, one such eunuch reportedly sold rumors to a military man for 100 *aurei* (gold coins). The slave-eunuch's punishment was to be hung on a cross (*in crucem tolli*). Notably, the place of execution was a very public venue, and the locale especially permitted this suspension to serve as a warning to other slaves. The passage above is not paralleled in Cassius Dio or Herodian, though it is consistent with some of Herodian's statements.[642] In any case, it certainly represents the author's view (even in the 4th century A.D.) that slaves could justifiably merit the cross.[643]

---

[639] Neither Cassius Dio nor Herodian report this event, though Herodian does note that Pertinax took precautions against false informants (*Hist. rom.* 2.4.8).

[640] For *fumos*, the manuscript tradition also reads *fumus*, and an editor suggests *fumum*; either accusative option (singular or plural) makes good sense, and both convey the same essential meaning.

[641] For the attribution of authorship, see the title of the work. For its dedication to Constantine, compare *Historia Augusta* 17 [Elagabalus] 35.1–7 with 18 [Severus Alexander] 67.1.

[642] Cassius Dio (in Book 80 of his *Roman History*) only briefly covers Severus Alexander's reign, which is a sad omission, since he was an eyewitness during this period. Although Herodian notes that the youthful Alexander was overly controlled by the women around him, he generally speaks admiringly of Alexander's constraint in using the death penalty (Herodian,

### 3.6.3 Slave Revolts

Closely related to the punishment of slaves on the *crux*, the main conspirators of slave revolts were often caught and suspended on such a device. As will be noted below, other (non-slave) rebel leaders could face similar punishment, but here, we focus on the special case of fugitive slaves seeking to capture Roman territory from their former masters. Although modern estimates vary substantially, Rome's economy was certainly heavily dependent on slavery, with many suggesting that 25 percent or more of the population were enslaved, constituting millions of people. The peril to the economy of slaves fleeing *en masse* from their masters would have been a sufficient concern. Moreover, one can only imagine the potential danger from the sheer numbers of adversaries should those slaves have taken up arms. Thus the Romans imposed extremely harsh measures in suppressing such revolts and in punishing the culpable afterwards (also cf. Livy in Nos. 352, 353).

**(324)** Dionysius of Halicarnassus, *Antiquitates romanae* 5.51.3

Ἐν ᾧ δὲ ταῦτ' ἐπράττετο χρόνῳ, συνωμοσία κατὰ τῆς πόλεως ἐγένετο δούλων συχνῶν συνειπαμένων τάς τ' ἄκρας καταλαβέσθαι καὶ κατὰ πολλοὺς ἐμπρῆσαι τόπους τὴν πόλιν. μηνύσεως δὲ γενομένης ὑπὸ τῶν συνειδότων ⟨αἱ⟩ πύλαι τ' ὑπὸ τῶν ὑπάτων εὐθὺς ἐκλείοντο, καὶ πάντα τὰ ἐρύματα τῆς πόλεως ὑπὸ τῶν ἱππέων κατείληπτο· καὶ αὐτίκα οἱ μὲν ἐκ τῶν οἰκιῶν συλληφθέντες, οἱ δ' ἐκ τῶν ἀγρῶν ἀναχθέντες,[644] ὅσους ἀπέφαινον οἱ μηνυταὶ μετασχεῖν τῆς συνωμοσίας, μάστιξι καὶ βασάνοις αἰκισθέντες ἀνεσκολοπίσθησαν ἅπαντες. ταῦτ' ἐπὶ τούτων ἐπράχθη τῶν ὑπάτων.

*Translation.* And at the time these matters were being managed, a conspiracy against the city occurred when many slaves agreed both to seize the highest points and to set the city on fire in many places. But, when information came via [their] accomplices, the gates were immediately shut by the consuls, and all the guard-points of the city were seized by the *equites*; and at once those who had been arrested from the houses, and those who had been led up from the fields, as many as the informers denounced for partaking in the conspiracy – all these, after being tortured with whips and [other] tortures, were crucified. These events were managed at the time of these consuls.

---

*Hist. rom.* 6.1.7). Significantly, Herodian records (in a way reminiscent of the *Historia Augusta*) that Severus Alexander removed from prestigious positions in the government the unqualified and the notoriously wicked men (cf. τούς τε ὑπ' ἐκείνου ἀλόγως ἢ ἐφ' οἷς εὐδοκιμήκεσαν ἁμαρτήμασιν) whom Elagabalus had appointed (Herodian, *Hist. rom.* 6.1.3).

[643] The author apparently appreciated Alexander's use of the *crux* to punish a thieving military-man, who had formerly held office (18 [Severus Alexander] 28.4–5); see No. 345.

[644] CARY reads ἀπαχθέντες, following KIESSLING; the JACOBY text is printed above.

*Commentary.*[645] The events are dated to the consulship of Postumus Cominius and Titus Larcius (499 B.C.; cf. *Ant. Rom.* 5.50.1).[646] Dionysius, an advocate of the Attic revival of Greek rhetoric, is writing in Rome during the Augustan period. His account of this consulship is more detailed than Livy's (cf. 2.18), who does not there mention this revolt. The "city" (πόλις) concerned is un-doubtedly Rome, and the suppression of the revolt is attributed to the city leadership – consuls and *equites* ( "knights") – acting on information from unnamed sources. These sources identified household slaves working in city homes and in country fields. The conspirators were first flayed and tortured, and then they were crucified (ἀνεσκολοπίσθησαν) to death, i.e., they were sus-pended up on a σόλοψ. While specific description of the form of ἀνεσκολο-πίσθησαν is not provided, it clearly represents an extreme form of death-by-suspension for rebellious slaves.[647] Dionysius is sufficiently removed from the events that one may question his accuracy on the details; however, one cannot doubt that Dionysius' first-century B.C. Roman audience would have consid-ered such a punishment of rebellious slaves to be justified.

**(325)** Dionysius of Halicarnassus, *Antiquitates romanae* 12.6.4–6

Ἀγρίππας Μενήνιος καὶ Πόπλιος Λουκρήτιος καὶ Σερούιος Ναύτιος, χιλίαρχοι τιμηθέντες, ἐπίθεσίν τινα κατὰ τῆς πόλεως γενομένην ὑπὸ δούλων ἐφώρασαν. ⁵ ἔμελλον δὲ οἱ μετέχοντες τῆς συνωμοσίας πῦρ ἐμβαλόντες ταῖς οἰκίαις κατὰ πολλοὺς ἅμα τόπους νύκτωρ, ὁπότε μάθοιεν ἐπὶ τὴν τῶν καιομένων βοηθείαν ὡρμηκότας ἅπαντας τό τε Καπιτώλιον καὶ τοὺς ἄλλους ἐρυμνοὺς καταλαμβά-νεσθαι τόπους, ἐγκρατεῖς δὲ γενόμενοι τῶν καρτερῶν τῆς πόλεως, ἐπὶ τὴν ἐλευθερίαν τοὺς ἄλλους δούλους παρακαλεῖν, καὶ σὺν ἐκείνοις ἀποκτείναντες τοὺς δεσπότας τὰς τῶν πεφονευμένων γυναῖκάς τε καὶ κτήσεις παραλαμβά-νειν. ⁶ τῆς δὲ πράξεως περιφανοῦς γενομένης συλληφθέντες οἱ πρῶτοι συν-θέντες τὴν ἐπιβουλὴν καὶ μαστιγωθέντες ἐπὶ τοὺς σταυροὺς ἀπήχθησαν· τῶν δὲ μηνυσάντων αὐτούς, ὄντων δυεῖν, ἐλευθερίαν τε καὶ δραχμὰς [χιλίας]⁶⁴⁸ ἑκάτερος ἔλαβεν ἐκ τοῦ δημοσίου.

---

[645] Text: JACOBY, Dionysius Halicarnaseus. Antiquitates Romanae, 2:215. Compared with CARY, Dionysius of Halicarnassus. Roman Antiquities, 3:152.

[646] For the date cf. CARY, Dionysius of Halicarnassus. Roman Antiquities, 3:147.

[647] For another text from Dionysius Halicarnassus potentially pertinent to this study see *Ant. Rom.* 7.69.1–2 (No. 115), where a Roman master has his slave put to death after first hav-ing him dragged through the forum during a festival with his arms stretched out on a piece of wood while being whipped; note that crucifixion is not explicitly mentioned.

[648] χιλίας ("thousand") is not in the manuscripts, but was added by the editors on the sug-gestion that it had been omitted by the copyists and complies with Livy (who reads *dena milia gravis aeris*, "10,000 of bronze weight"). ROBERT M. OGILVIE, A Commentary on Livy. Books 1–5 (Oxford: Clarendon, 1965), 603 suggests Livy's sum was "over-schematic" and would not have been paid in this era from the city treasury (*aerarium*).

*Translation.* Agrippa Menenius, Publius Lucretius, and Servius Nautius, after being honored as military tribunes, detected a particular attack taking place against the city by slaves. [5] Those who were partaking in the conspiracy were about to set fire to the houses in many places at the same time during the night, in order that, when it was learned that all people had hastened to the aid of that which was burning, [the conspirators] would seize the Capitol and the other fortified places, and in order that, having come in possession of the strong places of the city, they would exhort the other slaves unto freedom, and in order that along with them, after slaying the masters, they would seize both the wives of those who had been slain and [their] possessions. [6] But, after the treachery became conspicuous, the leaders who put together the plot were apprehended; and, after being scourged, they were led away to the crosses. And those who informed on them, being two, each received both freedom and a [thousand] drachmas from the state treasury.

*Commentary.*[649] The later books of *Antiquitates Romanae* are only known from excerpts in subsequent authors (this text comes from excerpts in the fifteenth-century manuscript Ambrosianus Q 13 sup.), so the fuller original context is somewhat lost to us. The city (πόλις) is again Rome. Livy provides a more condensed account of this same slave revolt of 419–418 B.C. (4.44.13–4.45.2), naming the tribunes as Agrippa Menenius Lanatus, Publius Lucretius Tricipitinus, and Spurius Nautius [Rutulus].[650] The accounts of Livy and Dionysius essentially agree (though Livy attributes the revolt's discovery to Jupiter), but the shorter Livy text is vague about the penalties meted out to the conspirators.[651] Dionysius represents the goals of the conspiracy in three successive infinitival purpose clauses (each beginning with "in order that" in the translation). These purpose clauses well represent the significant perils of a slave revolt to Roman society: Not only was the society economically dependent on a slave-based economy, but (given the number of slaves in Rome) a

---

[649] Text: JACOBY, Dionysius Halicarnaseus. Antiquitates Romanae, 4:225–226 (as 12.6.6). Compared with CARY, Dionysius of Halicarnassus. Roman Antiquities, 7:218–220. Note the variation in subsection numbering between these editions (JACOBY 12.6.6 = CARY 12.6.5–6); otherwise, the differences are limited to the minor shifting of two commas after ἅπαντας and παρακαλεῖν, neither of which affects the sense of the passage.

[650] Note the shift between *Spurius* Nautius in Livy and *Servius* Nautius in Dionysius; the difference in abbreviated praenomen being two letters or less and thus ultimately a minor error in transmission. The date for these events comes from FOSTER, MOORE, SAGE, SCHLESINGER, and GEER, Livy, 2:403. The cognomen "Rutulus" for Spurius Nautius is missing in the manuscripts.

[651] Thus Livius 4.45.2: *Avertit nefanda consilia Iuppiter, indicioque duorum comprehensi sontes poenas dederunt* ("Jupiter repelled [their] heinous schemes, and by the evidence of two men, after the guilty were arrested, they were handed over to punishments"). OGILVIE, Commentary, 603 contends that the mention of Jupiter is "not a personal confession of belief in divine intervention by [Livy] himself ... but represents an adaptation of the entry in the Annales referring to the preservation of the temple of Juppiter [*sic*] Capitolinus."

revolt could quickly spread among the populace. Rebellious slaves were also likely to kill their masters, despoil the masters' wives, and seize their property. Dionysius certainly represents the memory in his day that such slave revolts were punished with scourging (μαστιγωθέντες), followed by taking the miscreants out to crosses (ἐπὶ τοὺς σταυροὺς ἀπήχθησαν) – the use of the article (τούς) with σταυρούς may also imply that such crosses were well-known in Dionysius' day and were fully expected by his readership as the rebels' final destination.[652]

## (326) Appian, *Bella Civilia* 1.14.119 [1.553]

Σπάρτακος δὲ ἱππέας ποθὲν προσιόντας αὐτῷ περιμένων οὐκέτι μὲν ἐς μάχην ᾔει τῷ στρατῷ παντί, πολλὰ δ' ἠνώχλει τοῖς περικαθημένοις ἀνὰ μέρος, ἄφνω τε καὶ συνεχῶς αὐτοῖς ἐπιπίπτων, φακέλους τε ξύλων ἐς τὴν τάφρον ἐμβάλλων κατέκαιε καὶ τὸν πόνον αὐτοῖς δύσεργον ἐποίει. αἰχμάλωτόν τε Ῥωμαῖον ἐκρέμασεν ἐν τῷ μεταιχμίῳ, δεικνὺς τοῖς ἰδίοις τὴν ὄψιν ὧν πείσονται, μὴ κρατοῦντες.

*Translation.* But Spartacus, as he awaited cavalry to come to him from somewhere, on the one hand no longer went into combat with the whole army, but was very much annoying the besieging force in turn – both falling upon them unawares and unremittingly, and, as he threw bundles of wood into the trench, he burned [the bundles] and made the labor difficult for them. And he hung up a Roman captive in the space between the two armies, showing his own [troops] the vision of what will befall [them], if they do not prevail.

*Commentary.* Writing in the mid-second century A.D., Appian recounts the famous slave revolt of 73–71 B.C., which is most associated with the instigation of Spartacus (a gladiator of Thracian origin), although other leaders were involved. The revolt was of sufficient importance to be recorded by numerous ancient authors.[653] It began with the escape of Spartacus and other gladiators

---

[652] Given Livy's mere mention that the rebels faced "punishments" (*poenas*), it could be debated whether Dionysius' more specific details of those penalties were his fabrication (or that of another) or whether they represent authentic historical memory. However, the point is that for Dionysius (and his audience) in the few decades preceding Christ's death, the punishment of rebellious slaves on σταυροί was entirely expected. Though Dionysius does not depict the precise shape or use of the σταυροί, this too is largely irrelevant for the current study since the mention of σταυροί in the Christian message was likely sufficient to invoke memories of other contemporary uses of σταυροί, including those for punishing rebellious slaves.

[653] On Spartacus' revolt see Florus, *Epitome* 2.8.1–14 [3.20.1–14]; Livius 95.2–97.1 (from the fragmentary epitomes known as "Periochae"); Plutarch, *Crass.* 8.1–11.7; Sallust, *Hist.*, fragments from book 3 (3.96; 3.98 in BERTOLD MAURENBRECHER, C. Sallusti Crispi Historiarum reliquiae [2 vols.; Leipzig: Teubner, 1891–1893], 149–153). Also compare the briefer accounts in Velleius Paterculus, *Hist. rom.* 2.30.5–6; and Plutarch, *Pomp.* 21.1–2. And note the later traditions in Eutropius, *Breviarium ab urbe condita* 6.7; Orosius, *Historiae Adversum*

(the exact number varies in the sources from "more than 30" to "78") from the gladiatorial school of Lentulus in Capua. When they had shown some success in assaulting the Roman countryside, tens of thousands of escaped slaves (and others from the countryside) then rallied to their side. They attacked army camps, country houses, villages and towns throughout Italy. Spartacus showed himself to be an able leader.[654] After the death of thousands of Roman soldiers, Marcus Licinius Crassus managed to suppress the revolt (along with the threat of Pompey's troops – with both Crassus and Pompey vying for a share of the glory). Scholars debate the reasons for the revolt: although a Marxist-style proletarian revolt is unlikely (as is a freedom-garnering revolution designed to utterly abolish slavery), clearly some socio-economic forces must have made it an attractive proposition for slaves and others to join the marauding band in massive numbers. Appian calls Spartacus a man "who was considered worthy by no one" (ἀνδρὶ ἐπ' οὐδεμιᾶς ἀξιώσεως ὄντι; *Mithr.* 16.109).[655]

In the passage above, the war is beginning to go badly for Spartacus and the rebels. Prior to Crassus' involvement, nearly every military engagement went in favor of the rebels (cf. Appian, *Bell. civ.* 1.14.116–117). Once Crassus was assigned the command, he re-instilled discipline in the Roman ranks by the shocking act of decimating the legions (putting to death one in ten troops for poor conduct on the battlefield; cf. 1.14.118). Crassus then marches on Spartacus in southwest Italy, prevents him from passing over to Sicily, and hems in the rebels by means of a huge ditch that circumvallated Spartacus' forces. Spartacus attempted to break through but (if we are to follow Appian's rather implausible numbers) lost six thousand men, while the Romans only lost three. That is where our passage begins: Spartacus has now resolved to wait for cavalry reinforcements (which arrive later in 1.14.120) before attempting a field battle. He instead engages in various forms of irritating the

---

*Paganos* 5.24.1–8. Less relevant for our analysis is Frontinus, *Strategemata* 2.4.7; 2.5.34 (both focusing on Crassus' moves); also Plutarch, *Comp. Nic. Crass.* 3.2 (on Crassus); and Plutarch, *Cat. Min.* 8.1–2 (Cato's minimal involvement). In the early third century A.D., Athenaeus (*Deipnosophistai* 6.104) portrays Laurentius remembering the revolt of Spartacus alongside other famous slave revolts. Spartacus' name eventually became a perjorative invective against others, and his reputation served as a point of comparison and contrast for other dastardly foes of Rome (cf. Cicero, *Phil.* 3.8.20; 13.10.22; Tacitus, *Ann.* 3.73; 15.46; even in the fourth century with Ammianus Marcellinus, *Rerum Gestarum* 14.11.33). In contrast, Crassus' conquest of Spartacus is remembered with admiration (cf. Lucan, *Phars.* 2.552–554). Augustine (*De Civitate Dei* 3.26) mentions this Servile War among those military conflicts that proved, despite pagan claims that worshipping the gods brought safety to the city, that the Roman founding of the Temple of Concord garnered no subsequent pagan peace.

[654] In addition to other ancient texts noted here, see also Frontinus, *Strategemata* 1.5.20–22; 1.7.6 for some of Spartacus' brilliant military moves.

[655] Florus argued that a slave revolt is a tolerable "dishonor" (*dedecus*), since slaves are an inferior class of humans (*quasi secundum hominum genus*), but the war led by Spartacus was worse because it was fought not only against the most humble (*infimus*) men (slaves) but also against the most wicked (*pessumus*) men (the gladiator leadership); Florus, *Epitome* 2.8.1–2.

enemy. The key episode concerns Spartacus "hanging up" (ἐκρέμασεν) a Roman captive between the two camps, with the purpose of warning his fellow rebels (many of whom are escaped slaves) what awaits them if caught. This appears to be our only early extant ancient source that mentions this act of Spartacus in crucifying a Roman soldier. In the *Roman History,* this event serves to foreshadow the mass crucifixion of the rebels at the conclusion of Appian's account of the war in 1.14.120.

**(327)** Appian, *Bella Civilia* 1.14.120 [1.557–559]

ὡς δὲ καὶ Λεύκολλον ἔμαθεν ὁ Σπάρτακος ἐς τὸ Βρεντέσιον, ἀπὸ τῆς ἐπὶ Μιθριδάτῃ νίκης ἐπανιόντα, εἶναι, πάντων ἀπογνοὺς ἐς χεῖρας ᾔει τῷ Κράσσῳ μετὰ πολλοῦ καὶ τότε πλήθους· γενομένης δὲ τῆς μάχης μακρᾶς τε καὶ καρτερᾶς ὡς ἐν ἀπογνώσει τοσῶνδε μυριάδων, τιτρώσκεται ἐς τὸν μηρὸν ὁ Σπάρτακος δορατίῳ καὶ συγκάμψας τὸ γόνυ καὶ προβαλὼν τὴν ἀσπίδα πρὸς τοὺς ἐπιόντας ἀπεμάχετο, μέχρι καὶ αὐτὸς καὶ πολὺ πλῆθος ἀμφ᾽ αὐτὸν κυκλωθέντες ἔπεσον. ὅ τε λοιπὸς αὐτοῦ στρατὸς ἀκόσμως ἤδη κατεκόπτοντο κατὰ πλῆθος, ὡς φόνον γενέσθαι τῶν μὲν οὐδ᾽ εὐαρίθμητον, Ῥωμαίων δὲ ἐς χιλίους ἄνδρας, καὶ τὸν Σπαρτάκου νέκυν οὐχ εὑρεθῆναι. πολὺ δ᾽ ἔτι πλῆθος ἦν ἐν τοῖς ὄρεσιν, ἐκ τῆς μάχης διαφυγόν· ἐφ᾽ οὓς ὁ Κράσσος ἀνέβαινεν. οἱ δὲ διελόντες ἑαυτοὺς ἐς τέσσαρα μέρη ἀπεμάχοντο, μέχρι πάντες ἀπώλοντο πλὴν ἑξακισχιλίων, οἳ ληφθέντες ἐκρεμάσθησαν ἀνὰ ὅλην τὴν ἐς Ῥώμην ἀπὸ Καπύης ὁδόν.

*Translation.* But when Spartacus also learned that Lucullus was in Brundisium (returning from the victory over Mithridates), he despaired of all things and went in close against Crassus with many men and then with a multitude. And as the combat was both long and severe (since so many myriads [of men] were in despair), Spartacus was wounded in the thigh with a spear; and by bending his knee and sticking out his shield, he fought against those who came against him, until both he and the great multitude about him, after being encircled, fell. And the remainder of his army was already cut in disorderly pieces a large number at a time, so that the slaughter of these was not countable (but [the slaughter] of the Romans was about 1000 men), and so that Spartacus' corpse was not found. But a great multitude was still in the mountains after having escaped from the combat. Crassus went up against them. But they, dividing themselves into four parts, continued fighting, until all perished except 6000; those captives were hung up along the whole road into Rome from Capua.

*Commentary.* The city of Rome became sufficiently concerned with Spartacus' revolt to further assign the legions under Pompey (with troops from Spain) and L. Licinius Lucullus (with troops from the Third Mithridatic War against Mithridates Eupator in Asia Minor). Crassus was jealous that the victory be his alone and sought to conquer Spartacus before Pompey arrived. Spartacus managed to break through Crassus' siege and headed toward Brundisium. However, joining our story above, once Spartacus learned that Lucullus' army was likely to meet him in Brundisium, Spartacus decided to engage in close-combat against Crassus' troops. Appian's history speaks of Spartacus bravely fighting while injured. Nevertheless, the Romans conquered the rebel force (largely due to Crassus, though Pompey was happy to received his undue share of the credit; cf. 1.14.121). The extent of the slaughter (with massive quantities of body parts strewn disorderly on the field) had two consequences according to Appian: The numbers of the rebels could not be counted with certainty, and Spartacus' body could not be located.[656]

The ancient road from Brundisium in southern Italy to Rome also ran through Capua; it was known as the *Via Appia*, named after the fourth-century B.C. patrician Appius Claudius Caecus, who conceived of the project. Modern historians frequently refer to this image of six thousand slaves (and other rebels) being crucified all along the approximately 200 km (ca. 120 miles) of the Appian Way from Capua to Rome. If evenly distributed in a line, this would mean that a cross appeared roughly every 35 meters (100 ft.). Capua was where Spartacus' revolt began, with the escape of Spartacus and his fellow gladiators. As he commonly does, Appian chooses to use the less-specific term ἐκρεμάσθησαν (cf. *Bell. civ.* 1.14.119, No. 326) to depict these public suspensions. While one may wish more information on the precise form of suspension Appian implies by this term, it is difficult to conceive of the Romans performing something other than crucifixion; and, in any case, Appian clearly intends a public suspension of the sort we are studying (cf. his similar employment of κρεμάννυμι in *Bell. civ.* 1.14.119; 4.4.29, No. 314, 326).[657] More remarkably, the final massive crucifixion of rebels during this slave revolt led by Spartacus is not mentioned in the extant works of Livy, Plutarch, or Florus (though it should be allowed that Livy here exists currently only in epitome),[658] nor does this mass crucifixion appear in any of the other texts about Spartacus noted above in the commentary on *Bell. civ.* 1.14.119.[659]

---

[656] The translation above observes that two infinitival result clauses hang on the main clause. This feature is unfortunately not as evident in other translations.

[657] For Appian's use of κρεμάννυμι see the extended discussion in No. 300.

[658] The mass crucifixion is not mentioned in Florus, *Epitome* 2.8.13–14; Livius 97.1 (fragmentary from an epitome known as the "Periochae"); Plutarch, *Crass.* 11.6–7 (nor in *Pomp.* 21.2). Sadly, Sallust's fragmentary *History* is missing its record of Spartacus' demise; see fragment 3.98 C–D in MAURENBRECHER, C. Sallusti Crispi Historiarum reliquiae, 153.

[659] This crucifixion of captives also receives no record in any of the above-listed sources

Thus the extant support for the historicity of this mass crucifixion event is certainly less than is commonly assumed. In contrast to the conclusion of the Stanley Kubrick movie *Spartacus* starring Kirk Douglas, Spartacus' actual demise is never said to have occurred on a cross since he is consistently recorded as having been slain on the battlefield,[660] although Appian does allow above that Spartacus' body was never identified.

**(328)**  Cicero, *In Verrem* 2.5.7

Contagio autem ista servilis belli cur abs te potius quam ab iis omnibus qui ceteras provincias obtinuerunt praedicatur? An quod in Sicilia iam antea bella fugitivorum fuerunt? at ea ipsa causa est cur ista provincia minimo in periculo sit et fuerit. Nam posteaquam illinc M. Aquilius decessit, omnium instituta atque edicta praetorum fuerunt eius modi ut ne quis cum telo servus esset. Vetus est quod dicam, et propter severitatem exempli nemini fortasse vestrum inauditum, L. Domitium praetorem in Sicilia, cum aper ingens ad eum adlatus esset, admiratum requisisse quis eum percussisset; cum audisset pastorem cuiusdam fuisse, eum vocari ad se iussisse; illum cupide ad praetorem quasi ad laudem atque ad praemium accucurrisse; quaesisse Domitium qui tantam bestiam percussisset; illum respondisse, venabulo; statim deinde iussu praetoris in crucem esse sublatum. Durum hoc fortasse videatur, neque ego ullam in partem disputo: tantum intellego, maluisse Domitium crudelem in animadvertendo quam in praetermittendo dissolutum videri.

*Translation.* But [concerning] that contagion from the Slave War, why is it mentioned by you more than by all those who governed the other provinces? Is it because in Sicily already in the past there had been wars against fugitive slaves? But, that very reason is why that province is, and has been, least in danger. For, after Manius Aquilius resigned from there, the institutes and edicts of all [its] governors were of this kind: that there would not be a slave who had a weapon. There is an old story that I will tell, and on account of the severity of its example perhaps none of you have not heard it: Lucius Domitius was governor in Sicily – when a huge bull was served to him, astonished he

---

(in notes concerning Appian, *Bell. civ.* 1.4.119–120) on this Servile War with Spartacus. Admittedly, the capture of 6,000 rebels is mentioned, though without reference to crucifixion, in the fifth-century work by Orosius (*Historiae Adversum Paganos* 5.24.7). Notably, the numbers given for the dead also vary substantially in the sources. Appian, in the text *Bell. civ.* 1.14.120, seems to know this confusion and refuses to count. It is certainly unlikely that every rebel was killed or captured by Crassus and Pompey (cf. Cicero, *Verr.* 2.5.15.6; also Orosius, *Historiae Adversum Paganos* 5.24.8), as Suetonius also implies when he recalls that Gaius Octavius continued to deal with brigands in Macedonia who were remnants of the wars against Spartacus and Catiline (Suetonius, *Aug.* 3.1).

[660] In addition to Appian, see Florus, *Epitome* 2.8.14; Plutarch, *Crass.* 11.7; cf. Livius, 97.1; Athenaeus, *Deipnosophistai* 6.104; later Orosius, *Historiae Adversum Paganos* 5.24.7.

inquired about who had struck it dead; when he heard it had been someone's shepherd, he ordered him to be summoned to him. That [shepherd] eagerly hastened to the governor as if to praise and to reward. Domitius inquired how he had struck dead such a beast. That one responded, "With a hunting spear." Immediately then, by the order of the governor [the shepherd] was raised up on a cross. This is perhaps seen as harsh, nor do I for my part examine any of this: I only deduce that Domitius had preferred to be seen as cruel in inflicting punishment than to be seen as lax in letting [the crime] slip.

*Commentary.* Returning again to Cicero's *Against Verres* (see the extensive treatment in section 3.6.1), Cicero undermines here any attempt to defend Verres before the Extortion Court by claiming Verres deserved to be released from any other charges simply because of his military exploits on behalf of Rome (cf. 2.5.1–4). The specific claim Cicero refutes concerns whether Verres managed to prevent the "contagion" of the famous Slave Revolt of Spartacus (73–71 B.C.) from spreading to Sicily during Verres' provincial governorship (also 73–71 B.C.). The defense tactic may have had some popular resonance in Rome given that: (1) Spartacus' infamous and vicious revolt (having ended only a couple years prior to this trial) would have been fresh in Roman memory, (2) the rebel slaves under Spartacus had apparently intended to move on Sicily but failed to for lack of ships,[661] and (3) there had indeed been two famous earlier slave revolts in Sicily (c. 135–132, 104–100 B.C.),[662] which consequently might have caused Romans to view Sicily as prone to such wars.[663] However, Cicero observes there is no actual evidence for any attempted revolt in Sicily during Verres' tenure (2.5.5, 2.5.9), that Spartacus' rebels were prevented from traveling from Italy to Sicily by others and not by any move on Verres' part (2.5.5–6), and that the earlier revolts in Sicily had resulted in effective anti-revolt laws that antedated Verres (2.5.7–8). Concerning that last matter, Cicero recounts the story above to impress on his audience that, long preceding Verres, forceful laws and harsh governors had made sure that slave revolts were not likely to happen in Sicily. The shepherd in the story above was a slave (cf. *pastorem cuiusdam,* "someone's shepherd") who killed a giant boar "with a hunting spear" (*venabulo*), despite the laws that no

---

[661] Florus records that they could not obtain ships, but attempted to make their own rafts to cross the strait (Florus, *Epitome* 2.8.13). Plutarch indicates Cilician pirates deceived Spartacus into thinking they would supply him with ships (Plutarch, *Cras.* 10.3–4).

[662] For these dates see A. MOMIGLIANO, A. G. WOODHEAD, R. J. W. WILSON, Art. Sicily, OCD, 1361–63.

[663] Significantly, Plutarch, *Crass.* 10.3 claims Spartacus hoped to advance on Sicily with 2000 men in order to "rekindle the slave war there, which had not yet for much time been quenched and which needed again [only] a little fuel" (καὶ δισχιλίους ἄνδρας ἐμβαλὼν εἰς τὴν νῆσον αὖθις ἐκζωπυρῆσαι τὸν δουλικὸν ἐκεῖ πόλεμον, οὔπω πολὺν χρόνον ἀπεσβηκότα καὶ μικρῶν πάλιν ὑπεκκαυμάτων δεόμενον). The Romans may well have felt that Sicily was a slave tinderbox ready to ignite again into revolt at any time.

slave should have a weapon (*ut ne quis cum telo servus esset*). It was for this reason that this shepherd was sentenced by the order of Lucius Domitius to being raised up on a cross (*iussu praetoris in crucem esse sublatum*). Cicero himself allows that this action may have been harsh (*durum*) and cruel (*crudelem*), though he avoids investigating Lucius Domitius since Cicero's point here is to prove that previous governors had not been lax in overlooking slave crimes (*in praetermittendo dissolutum*) and thus that slaves were not in a place to revolt in Sicily long before Verres governed there. The *crux* was part of the arsenal that helped keep rebellious slaves in check.

**(329)** Cicero, *In Verrem* 2.5.10–11

In Triocalino, quem locum fugitivi iam ante tenuerunt, Leonidae cuiusdam Siculi familia in suspicionem est vocata coniurationis. Res delata ad istum. Statim, ut par fuit, iussu eius homines qui fuerant nominati comprehensi sunt adductique Lilybaeum; domino denuntiatum est, causa dicta, damnati ... damnatis quidem servis quae praedandi potest esse ratio? produci ad supplici-um necesse est. Testes enim sunt qui in consilio fuerunt, testes publicae tabulae, testis splendidissima civitas Lilybitana, testis honestissimus maximus-que conventus civium Romanorum: fieri nihil potest, producendi sunt. Itaque producuntur et ad palum alligantur. [11] Etiam nunc mihi exspectare videmini, iudices, quid deinde factum sit, quod iste nihil umquam fecit sine aliquo quaestu atque praeda. Quid in eius modi re fieri potuit? Quod commodum est,[664] exspectate facinus quam vultis improbum; vincam tamen exspectati-onem omnium. Homines sceleris coniurationisque damnati, ad supplicium tra-diti, ad palum alligati, repente multis milibus hominum inspectantibus soluti sunt et Triocalino illi domino redditi.

*Translation.* In Triocalino, which was a place fugitive slaves had held in the past, the household slaves of a certain Leonidas of Sicily had been summoned upon suspicion of conspiracy. The matter had been reported to that man [Verres]. Immediately, as was reasonable, by his command the men who had been accused had been seized and brought to Lilybaeum; a summons had been served to their master, the case had been pled, they had been condemned ... Certainly, since the slaves had been condemned, what reason for acquiring loot was possible [for Verres]? It is necessary to lead [them] out to punish-ment. For, there are witnesses who had been in the court, witnesses of public record, the most splendid city of Lilybaeum is witness, the most honorable and largest community of Roman citizens is witness: nothing else was able to occur, they must be lead out. Accordingly, they are lead out and bound to the stake. [11] Even now, judges, you appear to me to look forward to what he had

---

[664] Some editions locate this comma after *exspectate*; GREENWOOD, Verrine Orations, 478.

done next, since that man never did anything without some profit and booty. What was he able to do in a situation of that kind? What is [his] reward? Expect the rascally misdeed you want; nevertheless I shall overcome the expectation of all. The men had been condemned of villainy and conspiracy, handed over to punishment, bound to the stake, and suddenly (while many thousand men were looking on) they were released and restored to that master from Triocala.

*Commentary*. Cicero continues to undermine Verres' appeal to his military service, especially to his supposed suppression of slave revolts in Sicily. Cicero begins to adduce examples of masters whose slaves were initially charged with conspiracy against the state, then let off when the master paid extortion money to Verres (cf. 2.5.9–24). This first example (in 2.5.10–14) is the most pertinent for our purposes. The slaves of Leonidas were condemned but then suddenly set free and returned to Leonidas, even as their punishments were about to occur. Slaves were obviously expensive and valuable assets, and thus the remission of penalties against them (especially the death penalty) benefitted their owners enough that they would be willing to pay extortion. Cicero apparently does not have physical evidence of extortion payments in this case, so he focuses instead on the fact that the slaves were unlawfully freed, despite the decision of the court. The lines omitted above from 2.5.10, speak to the ways in which Verres could have accomplished their release (and the exchange of monies) more covertly. In contrast, Verres' brash release of the slaves, even after they had been condemned and bound to the stake, clearly contravenes their formal sentence by the court. The punishment these slaves were due to receive includes being "bound to a pole" (*ad palum alligantur* in 2.5.10 and *ad palum alligati* in 2.5.11). It is not clear whether this refers to torture/scourging on a whipping-post prior to being put to death (on a *crux*) or whether *palus* ("pole") here is another term for the *crux*; the former alternative seems more likely, as will be obvious in the next two selections.

## (330)  Cicero, *In Verrem* 2.5.12

Quid ais, bone custos defensorque provinciae? Tu quos servos arma capere et bellum facere in Sicilia voluisse cognoras et de consili sententia iudicaras, hos ad supplicium iam more maiorum traditos[665] ex media morte eripere ac liberare ausus es, ut, quam damnatis crucem servis fixeras, hanc indemnatis videlicet civibus Romanis reservares?

---

[665] Some editions insert *et ad palum alligatos* ("and having been bound to the post") here. PETERSON considers this a defective reading (likely due to a similar clause in 2.5.10) and instead follows the main manuscripts in deleting it (as does the GREENWOOD text). Were one to concur with this unlikely reading, it would bring *palum* and *crux* even closer in proximity.

*Translation.* What do you say, O good guardian and defender of the province? You had investigated which slaves wanted to take up arms and to make war in Sicily, and you had decreed according to the sentence of the jury. [Concerning] these, after they had already been handed over by inherited custom to punishment, did you dare to snatch them from the midst of death and to liberate them – doubtlessly so that the cross, which you had fastened up for condemned slaves, you might reserve for uncondemned Roman citizens?

*Commentary.* Cicero continues to discuss the freeing of Leonidas' slaves, whom Verres had released even after assenting to the guilty verdict. Cicero's rhetoric drips with sarcasm, as is especially evident both in the opening vocative title for Verres ("O good guardian and defender of the province") and in the use of *videlicet* ("doubtlessly") in the concluding result clause. A good provincial governor would not discharge rebellious slaves from the *crux*, nor would he reserve the *crux* for uncondemned Roman citizens. Cicero, of course, returns to Verres' use of the *crux* against a citizen repeatedly in Book 5 (see section 3.6.1). Also observe how the "handing over" (*traditos*) of slaves to such a punishment (*ad supplicium*) follows a long-accepted tradition of the Roman ancestors (*more maiorum*). Cicero accepts the harsh punishment of rebellious slaves (even on the *crux*) as a laudable action of a provincial governor in keeping with Roman tradition.

**(331)**  Cicero, *In Verrem* 2.5.14

Cum servitiorum animos in Sicilia suspensos propter bellum Italiae fugitivorum videret, ne quis se commovere auderet, quantum terroris iniecit! Comprendi iussit; quis non pertimescat? causam dicere dominos; quid servo tam formidolosum? FECISSE VIDERI pronuntiat; exortam videtur flammam paucorum dolore ac morte restinxisse. Quid deinde sequitur? Verbera atque ignes et illa extrema ad supplicium damnatorum, metum ceterorum, cruciatus et crux.[666] Hisce omnibus suppliciis sunt liberati. Quis dubitet quin servorum animos summa formidine oppresserit, cum viderent ea facilitate praetorem ut ab eo servorum sceleris coniurationisque damnatorum vita vel ipso carnifice internuntio redimeretur?

*Translation.* When he [Verres] saw the animosity of the slaves in Sicily heightened on account of the war of fugitive slaves in Italy, lest some [slave] should dare to take action, how much terror did he inject! He ordered them to be seized; who would not be terribly frightened? [He ordered] masters to

---

[666] A few early important manuscripts read *et cruciatus et crux*, which produces little change in the sense (though it may slightly heighten the distinction between *cruciatus* and *crux*: "both torture and the cross"). See the PETERSON edition, which presumably omits the first *et* on internal grounds, in addition to the support of an 11th c. codex.

plead the case; what [causes] so much alarm for a slave? He pronounced: "It appears they have done it" [i.e., they appear guilty]; [thus] he appears to have quenched the emerging flame by the anguish and death of a few. What then comes next? Whippings, and fires, and those final stages for the punishment of the condemned and for the fear of the rest: torture and the cross. From all these punishments they had been set free! Who would doubt but that he suppressed the animosity of slaves with the utmost alarm, when they saw the governor with that indulgence, so that the lives of slaves condemned of villainy and conspiracy could be ransomed by him, even with the executioner himself being the intermediary [in the negotiations].

*Commentary.* In our final selection from *Against Verres*, Cicero again applies sarcasm to insinuate that Verres, who claimed to be the great suppressor of the slave revolt in Sicily, actually probably fanned the flames of revolt, if anything, by his willingness to take payments in exchange for freeing convicted slaves. Granted Verres' guilty verdict (*fecisse videri*, "It appears they have done it") was a bit weak-kneed,[667] but the proper trajectory of merited punishment is clear enough: from scourging, to "fires" (perhaps being administered with white-hot iron), to torture, and finally to the cross.[668] Note that *cruciatus* and *crux*, as elsewhere, are properly distinguished from one another, with *cruciatus* depicting the further torture that precedes death on the *crux*.[669] Again, Cicero assumes such punishment of rebellious slaves is indeed proper, and here he further notes such gruesome retribution should rightly result in the rest of the slave population being afraid to engage in such rebellious activity (*metum ceterorum*). Thus the cross is a public act intended to instill fear. However, Verres instead sets them free, apparently involving the executioner himself as an intermediary (*internuntius*) in the financial negotiations with the slave owners to ransom (*redimere*) the slaves. Cicero's sarcasm is especially

---

[667] See C.T. Lewis Short, *A Latin Dictionary*, s.v. *video* II.B.7.δ.b ("in official decisions, as a guarded opinion instead of a positive declaration"); cf. OLD s.v. *video* 22 ("to appear after due consideration, or sim., be deemed").

[668] The sense of escalation in this series of punishments is increased if we correctly understand *et illa extrema ad supplicium damnatorum, metum ceterorum* as rendered above ("and those final stages for the punishment of the condemned and for the fear of the rest"), where *extrema* is derived from the noun *extremum* (meaning "the final part or stage" in OLD, s.v. *extremum* 2a). YONGE's translation requires *extrema* to come from the adjective *extremus*, and he follows a much more idiomatic interpretation (necessitating insertion of words not evidenced in the Latin): "and all those extreme agonies which are part of the punishment of condemned criminals, and which strike terror into the rest."

[669] Contrast this with GREENWOOD's translation of *cruciatus et crux*, which appears to take these two nouns as a hendiadys: "the torments of crucifixion". Our translation is to be preferred since it maintains the distinct meanings of the two nouns and makes best sense of the plural use of *illa extrema* ("those final stages") in apposition to *cruciatus et crux*. Finally, if the earliest manuscripts are followed (*et cruciatus et crux*), the "both ... and" structure is best maintained by viewing these as separate stages of punishment; cf. note above on the Latin text.

evident at the beginning ("how much terror did he inject") and end ("who would doubt but that he suppressed the animosity of slaves with the utmost alarm") of the passage.

## 3.6.4 Criminals – General

While the cross is often associated with the suppression of rebellion or the punishment of treacherous slaves, other crimes were punished with the *crux* in Roman law. Substantial testimony for this is especially found in the *Pauli Sententiae* from the third century A.D., but other passages confirm this broader use of the cross in state executions. For example, we can recall Plutarch's (likely hyperbolic) statement that "every criminal who is executed carries his own cross on his back."[670] According to the texts below (many from the third century A.D.), a list of offenses that merited the cross would include: slaves who set fire to their domicile and kill their master, slaves who consult divination regarding their masters' health, stealing from the state mines or sacred mint, authors and instigators of sedition and rebellion, intentional homicide or planned homicide, abetting in homicide, giving false testimony in a capital case, provision of magical potions that (intentionally or unintentionally) lead to death, engaging in magic in order to bewitch another person, being "privy to the magical art," fraud in the case of wills or state coinage, and (from evidence in later eras) concealing, selling, or fettering a person who ought not be enslaved (or who actually belonged to another slave owner).[671]

The cross may well have been among the most feared of the standard Roman penal procedures. However, there were certainly other forms of execution that were viewed as "extreme." Thus the *crux* is listed among the *summa supplicia* ("extreme punishments") alongside burning someone alive and beheading (cf. Paulus, *Sent.* 5.17.2), and in other places it appears somewhat interchangeably with being thrown to wild beasts (e.g., Paulus, *Sent.* 5.23.14–17). Yet the cross can also be singled out as the principal *summum supplicium*, especially concerning slaves (5.21.4). Nevertheless, Roman law in the *Lex Pompeia* also knew a special level of punishment for parricides, involving tying them in a sack and throwing them into the sea.[672] This was later changed

---

[670] Plutarch, *Mor.* 554B [*De sera numinis vindicta* 9]: καὶ τῷ μὲν σώματι τῶν κολαζομένων ἕκαστος κακούργων ἐκφέρει τὸν αὑτοῦ σταυρόν. For full text and discussion of 554A–B, see above No. 117. Here, note that the "criminals" are not defined beyond the rather vague term κακοῦργοι, which leaves a number of possible capital crimes that Plutarch might have thought deserved the cross.

[671] And possibly the theft of someone's crops, if *suspensum* in the *Leges XII Tabularum* 8.5 (in Pliny, *Nat. hist.* 18.3.12) was ever interpreted to include crucifixion at some stage in Roman law. Note also the later report that Severus Alexander crucified at least one thief (*Hist. Aug.* 18 [Severus Alexander] 28.4–5).

to being burned alive or thrown to wild beasts (5.24.1). Such a punishment was more rare than the cross, yet it was viewed as particularly severe. We can rightly conclude that the cross was one of the harshest standard Roman punishments, and perhaps the most severe of all if we exclude the penalty against parricides. In addition, the texts below will provide further evidence of how the *crux* was typically reserved for members of the lesser classes of society (*humiliores*, and especially slaves; cf. sections 3.6.1–3)

**(332)** *Leges XII Tabularum* 8.5 (Plinius, *Nat. hist.* 18.3.12)

Frugem quidem aratro quaesitam noctu pavisse ac secuisse puberi XII tabulis capital erat, suspensumque Cereri necari iubebant, gravius quam in homicidio convictum, impubem praetoris arbitratu verberari noxiamve duplionemve decerni.

*Translation.* Crops certainly, had they been intended for the plow, [if someone were] to have grazed them or reaped them by night, it was a capital offense for an adult according to the Twelve Tables; and after he had been hung up, they commanded [him] to be put to death for Ceres – [a penalty] more severe than for a man found guilty of homicide. For someone below the age of puberty, at the discretion of the *praetor* [he was] to be scourged or to be decreed damages or double damages.

*Commentary.*[673] The Twelve Tables formed the historic basis for statutory laws in Rome. The origins were said to stem from ten citizens appointed to the task in 451–450 B.C., with some later revisions in the middle republic. We possess fragmentary testimony to this important law code, often in the form of citations from Roman authors and from the (fragmentary) commentary by Gaius. The Tables were posted in Rome, so citations by Roman authors (such as Pliny) could well indeed represent the ancient law accurately. This statute

---

[672] The penalty is further described in Justinian's *Institutes* 4.18.6 as tying the parricide into a sack with a dog, a cock, a snake, and a monkey, and then throwing the sack into the river or sea; this mode of execution was said to have separated the offender in his death from contact with all the "elements" (esp. sky and land); see text and translation in BIRKS / MCLEOD, Justinian's Institutes, 144–145. However, ROBINSON notes that this aggravated penalty was likely only imposed against those who murdered their parents or grandparents (while the Pompeian law against parricides also condemned the murder of step-parents, children or siblings). Robinson further suggests that the addition of animals to the sack was "probably the work of the emperor Constantine (A.D. 312–37) or his sons"; ROBINSON, Criminal Trials, 234–235, 236–237.

[673] Text: MICHAEL H. CRAWFORD, ed., Roman Statutes (2 vols.; Bulletin of the Institute of Classical Studies Supplement 64; London: Institute of Classical Studies, University of London, 1996), 2:684. The edition in BRUNS (listing this text as *Leges XII Tabularum* 8.9, as does FIRA 1; Schoell lists as 8.8) omits the following words: *quidem* and *gravius quam in homicidio convictum*; cf. BRUNS, Fontes Iuris Romani Antiqui, 1:31.

from the *Twelve Tables* is known from its citation by Pliny the Elder (A.D. 23/24–79) in the context of his discussion of the importance of agriculture in early Rome.[674] Table VIII discusses torts and delicts, several of which involve subjects arising from agriculture. Here the issue concerns stealing from someone else's crops (ones that had been "intended for the plow" and thus set aside for income or self-sustenance). The manner of stealing includes both the surreptitious grazing of a flock on someone else's land or the actual reaping of their crops from the land. Two sets of punishments are listed – for adults and for children (prior to puberty).[675] The adult receives a capital punishment that requires him first to have been "hung up" (*suspensum*) and then concludes in him being "put to death" (*necari*). The means of death is not specified, nor is the precise means of suspension – though it would appear that the person has been suspended alive (prior to death). Some modern scholars have suggested this refers to crucifixion or to a hanging, while others presume the person was scourged to death while suspended.[676] Strikingly, such a death has sacrificial elements since it is performed on behalf of the goddess of crops (Ceres).[677] Pliny, from his standpoint in the first century B.C., likely inserted the comment that this manner of execution was more severe than the penalties applied against a murderer.[678]

## (333) Epitaph from Amyzon

Δημήτριος Παγκράτου.
Πᾶσιν δακρυτὸς Δημήτριος, ὅγ γλυκὺς ὕπνος
εἶχεν καὶ Βρομίου νεκτάρεαι προπόσεις·
δούλου δ' ἐκ χειρῶν [σ]φαγισθεὶς καὶ πυρὶ πολλῶι

---

[674] CRAWFORD, Roman Statutes, 2:684 attributes the following words to Pliny (as alterations to the original *Twelve Tables*): *decerni* (for *decidi*), *noxiam* (for *damnum*), *frugem aratro quaesitam* (a "piece of literary embellishment"), *furtim*, and *praetoris arbitratu* (an "inference from the text"). Nonetheless, even if these conjectural emendations to the text in Pliny are correct, still this leaves intact in the ancient *Twelve Tables*: the key dimensions of the crime, the separate punishments for adults and youths, and the suspension of adults.

[675] Concerning the child (*impubes*), the "damages" (*noxia*) to be paid involves recompense from the father for the harm caused by a dependent child. The legalities are further discussed in Gaius' *Institutes* (4.75–79; text in FIRA 2:169–170) under the category of *noxales actiones* with special reference to the Twelve Tables (likely to this statute) in 4.76. In Paulus, *Sent.* 2.31.24(25) (for text see FIRA 2:355) only the repayment of double damages is mentioned concerning this crime, omitting any distinction between adult and youth, and without reference to the suspension and execution required of adults in the *XII Tabulae*.

[676] Cf. COOK, Crucifixion, 47–48, esp. n 235. COOK argues it could not have been a death by hanging since such a penalty was not performed in republican or imperial times.

[677] Thus CRAWFORD, Roman Statutes, 2:685 states, "The penalty of hanging 'for Ceres' is presumably one transferred from the sacral to the public domain."

[678] Hence *gravius quam in homicidio convictum* is omitted in BRUNS' edition.

⁵ φλεχθεὶς σὺμ μελάθροις ἤλυθον εἰς ᾽Αΐδην,
ὄφρα πατὴρ καὶ ὅμαιμοι ἐμοὶ καὶ πρέσβεα μήτηρ
δέξαντ᾽ εἰς κόλπους ὄστεα καὶ σποδιήν·
ἀλλὰ πολῖται ἐμοὶ τὸν ἐμὲ ῥέξαντα τοιαῦτα
θηρσὶ καὶ οἰωνοῖς ζωὸν ἀνεκρέμασαν.

*Translation.* Demetrios son of Pankrates.
Demetrios, mourned by all, whom sweet sleep
held and the nectarous drink of Bromios;
slain by the hands of a slave and in a great conflagration
⁵ burnt together with the house, I came to Hades,
whilst my father, siblings and elderly mother
received to their bosoms bones and ashes;
but the one who did such things to me my fellow-citizens
crucified alive for the wild beasts and birds.

*Commentary.*[679] This striking funerary epitaph depicts a dead master, murdered by the hand of his own slave, and the consequent *ante mortem* suspension of the slave. Amyzon was an important Seleucid city in Caria in south-western Anatolia in the third century B.C. LLEWELYN dates the inscription not later than the second century B.C.[680] Although the Romans were active in Asia Minor at the time, this form of execution could well be a legacy of Hellenistic practices (even if it overlaps with Roman procedure). Lines 2–3 indicate that Demetrios was in a deep sleep after a period of drinking when the unnamed slave first slayed him (σφαγισθείς) and then set the house on fire (lines 4–5), likely with the intent of concealing his crime. Brief mention is made of the man's relatives, and their grief receives a touching picture that invokes the bones and ash of the deceased (lines 6–7). The concluding lines (8–9) contrast the mourning for Demetrios with the actions of the civic population (πολῖται) in punishing the slave: They hung him up alive (ζωὸν ἀνεκρέμασαν), knowing that his body would be assaulted by wild beasts and birds. The imagery is typical of crucifixion texts, though here without a definitive depiction of the method of suspension. Yet the *ante mortem* suspension, along with the long-term public exposure, places this inscription firmly within our field of study.

---

[679] Text and translation: S. R. LLEWELYN, in HORSLEY and LLEWELYN, New Documents, 8:1. It would be difficult to improve on this fine translation, though I might have chosen "hung up" rather the "crucified" for ἀνεκρέμασαν. Editio princeps: JEANNE ROBERT and LOUIS ROBERT, Fouilles d' Amyzon en Carie. Tome 1, Exploration, histoire, monnaies et inscriptions (Paris: Boccard, 1983), 259–263.

[680] LLEWELLYN, in HORSLEY and LLEWELYN, New Documents, 1; see the analysis ibid. 1–3 where LLEWELYN discusses date and possible Roman influence, disagreeing with HENGEL's willingness to date this even into the first century B.C. (HENGEL, Crucifixion, 76). Note the discussion of COOK, Crucifixion, 230–231, suggesting a possible connection to the revolt of Aristonicus (133–129 B.C.), the conclusion of which led to direct Roman control of the region.

**(334)** *Lex Libitinaria* from Puteoli (*AE* 1971, 88) 2.8–14

Qui supplic(ium) de ser(uo) seruaue priuatim sumer(e) uolet, uti is {qui} sumi
uolet, ita supplic(ium) sumet; si in cruc(em) / [9] patibul(...) agere uolet, redemp-
t(or) asser(es uincul(a) restes uerberatorib(us) et uerberator(es) praeber (e)
d(ebeto), et / [10] quisq(uis) supplic(ium) sumet pro oper(is) sing(ulis) quae
patibul(um) ferunt uerberatorib(us)q(ue) item carnif(ice) HS IIII d(are) d(ebeto). *uacat* [11] Quot(iens) supplic(ium) magistrat(us) public(e) sumet, ita impe-
rat(o); quotienscumq(ue) imperat(um) er(it), praestu esse su- / [12] plicium
sumer(e) cruces statuere clauos pecem ceram candel(as) quaeq(ue) ad eas res
opus erunt red(emptor) / [13] gratis praest(are) d(ebeto); item si u[n]co extrahere
iussus erit, oper(is) russat(is) id cadauer ubi plura / [14] cadauera erunt cum tin-
tinnabulo extrahere debebit. *uacat*

*Translation.* He who will want privately to procure the punishment of his slave
or female slave – as he wants it to be procured, so he will procure the punishment [thus]: if he wants to lead [the slave] to the cross with a patibulum, the
contractor will be under obligation to supply wooden beams, chains, cords for
the floggers, and the floggers; and whoever procures the punishment will be
under obligation to pay 4 sesterces: to each of the workers who bear the patibulum, and to the floggers, as well as to the executioner. [11] Whenever the magistrate will procure a punishment for the public, thus [he does] by decree; and
whenever there will be a decree, the contractor will be under obligation to be
ready to procure the punishment, to fix upright the crosses, and to provide free
of charge the nails, pitch, wax, candles, and whatever work will be [needed]
for this matter; in addition, if he will have been commanded to drag [the victim's corpse] with a hook, then, with workers clad in red, he will be obligated
with a bell [ringing] to drag that corpse to where there are many corpses.

*Commentary.*[681] This inscription from Puteoli (mod. Puzzuoli in the Campania
region of Italy) provides evidence that the execution of slaves and criminals
was contracted out to local executioners, who often hired others in the process. Based on orthography, morphological forms, and content, the inscription
has been variously dated from the first century B.C. to the early first century

---

[681] Text: FRANÇOIS HINARD and JEAN-CHRISTIAN DUMONT, Libitina: Pompes funèbres et
supplices en Campanie à l'époque d'Auguste. Édition, traduction et commentaire de la Lex
Libitinae Puteolana (Paris: Boccard, 2003), 18 (cf. "diplomatic text" transcribed ibid. 12;
plates at the book's end). Their text expands the original Latin abbreviations in parentheses,
while less certain matters are put in brackets. Note especially the analysis of these punishments ibid. 89–95 and their commentary ibid. 116–122. Essentially the same text of lines 11–
14 appears in an appendix in JOHN BODEL, Graveyards and Groves: A Study of the *Lex
Lucerina*, AJAH 11 (1986): 1–133, here 77; however, BODEL (following BOVE) reads
*impera<bi>t* for *imperat(o)*, *reo* for *red(emptor)*, and *oper(a) russat(a)* for *oper(is) russat(is)*.
Note also plate 4 in BODEL for a partial photograph of this text. BODEL's work provides a useful point of comparison in Roman burial law with the *Lex Lucerina*.

A.D.[682] The extant text is three columns long (each with 25–34 lines); it was written on a single large slab, but it only survives as three contiguous (though incomplete) fragments. At the top of the original inscription, the word "Libitina" was written, indicating that this inscription concerns statutes about burial. The second column stipulates regulations for the staffing requirements of the contracting undertaker (among other matters, he and his staff must live outside of town and identify themselves clearly when they come into town), and then it proceeds in the lines above to discuss the equipment and personnel that must be supplied for any execution. The slave's master pays for private executions of slaves, while public executions sanctioned by the magistrate must be performed free of charge. Thus here we have evidence both of slaves and criminals being condemned to death on a *crux*. The masters are presumed to have control over the lives (and deaths) of their slaves. Intriguingly, it would appear that both male and female slaves could be attached to a *crux*. Concerning slaves, the cross requires beams and scourging. Likely, such items are also needed for the executions of criminals, but added in line 12 are further implements of torture (pitch, wax and candles) as well as nails (which probably served to attach the victims to the *cruces*). The "hook" is a device known elsewhere – by it the corpses of criminals are dishonored by being pierced by the hook and then dragged through the city to the place where criminals are discarded. COOK provides a helpful analysis of the details, along with parallel evidence for the particulars.[683] SAMUELSSON argues that the use of "pitch, wax and candles" would indicate some form of torture applied as part of the experience on the *crux*, thus perhaps distancing the cross here from modern views of crucifixion.[684] However, the lists of supplies (and personnel) required in both lines 9 and 12 could well apply to the whole process of execution, with the person being tortured (by scourging and/or fire) before being appended to the *crux*. Certainly the mention of "hook" and the overall context would imply the *crux* is a means of penal execution. One key debate concerns the relationship of the word "patibul(...)" at the beginning of line 9 to its surroundings. SAMUELSSON argues that the slave is brought to the *patibulum*, reading *patibulatum* in line 9 as the victim who is brought.[685] Most recently, COOK has responded that *patibulatum*, as he too reconstructs the abbreviated text, references the victim being "patibulated", that is, attached to the *patibulum* while led through the city streets.[686] The translation above suggests instead

---

[682] Contrast HINARD and DUMONT who date it to the Augustan age with BODEL who contends for a date in the first half of the first century B.C.; see esp. BODEL, *Lex Lucerina*, 74–76.

[683] This is neatly summarized in COOK, Crucifixion, 370–387. See further JOHN GRANGER COOK, Envisioning Crucifixion: Light from Several Inscriptions and the Palatine Graffito, NovT 50 (2008): 262–285, esp. 264–282; Cook, "Crucifixion as Spectacle in Roman Campania", 82–85.

[684] SAMUELSSON, Crucifixion, 199–201.

[685] SAMUELSSON, Crucifixion, 200–201.

that we should read "by or with a *patibulum*" (i.e., *patibulo*).[687] In any case, this passage serves as striking epigraphic testimony to the use of the *crux* against both slaves and criminals. It also provides fascinating insight into some key legal mechanisms concerning the executioner's role.

**(335)** Seneca, *De Clementia* [*Dialogue* 6] 1.23

Pater tuus plures intra quinquennium culleo insuit, quam omnibus saeculis insutos accepimus ... pessimo vero loco pietas fuit, postquam saepius culleos vidimus quam cruces.

*Translation.* Your father [Claudius] had sewn up more men in a sack within five years than we understood to have been sewn up in all [other] generations ... Piety [toward parents] was without doubt in its worst place, after we saw sacks more often than crosses.

*Commentary.*[688] In this essay Lucius Annaeus Seneca (the Younger) argues before Nero that extreme penalties should be used more rarely, and that the ruler/judge should be known most for his clemency. In this context Seneca provides several examples where overuse of harsh punishment actual increased the number of crimes (because people became hardened to the fear of those punishments, and because the public nature of the punishments increased an awareness of the crime, with more people consequently imitating that criminal act). According to Seneca, one typically would see crosses employed more often in the first century A.D. than the sack, which was the punishment for parricides (those who put parents, or other family members, to death).[689] Yet under the rule of Claudius, who was avid in employing the sack against parricides, the number of parricides actually Increased under his rule (rivaling, at least in Seneca's rhetoric, the number of crucifixions). Here Seneca is undoubtedly comparing two of most severe penalties in the law (the sack and the *crux*). The cross appears to have been somewhat common in Seneca's Roman experience, but the sack less so, at least until the time of Claudius.

---

[686] COOK, Crucifixion, 370 n.69, 374–376.

[687] This suggestion follows a path previously taken by BODEL and DUMONT. It could potentially imply either that the workers carry the *patibulum* (as in line 10) as they convey the criminal to the place of execution, or that the criminal is led with/by (ablative of instrument) the *patibulum* (on his back) to the upright cross (the *patibulum* having been first brought to him by the workers). I favor the latter as making most sense of this text and as following other known mentions of *patibulum*-carrying.

[688] In Seneca, *De Clementia* 23.1. Text: BASORE, Seneca. Moral Essays, 1:420; FRANÇOIS PRÉCHAC, Sénèque. De la clémence (orig. 1921; repr., Budé; Paris: Belles Lettres, 2005), 43 (under XXI.1 = 1.23).

[689] Again, the "sack" involved tying the offender in a sack and throwing them into a body of water; see footnote above at the beginning of this section on "Criminals–General".

**(336)** *Pauli Sententiae* 5.17.2

Summa supplicia sunt crux crematio decollatio: mediocrium autem delictorum poenae sunt metallum ludus deportatio: minimae relegatio exilium opus publicum vincula. Sane qui ad gladium dantur, intra annum consumendi sunt.

*Translation.* The extreme punishments are the cross, burning, and beheading; but the penalties of moderate offenses are the mine, the [gladiatorial] school, and deportation [to an island]; the least [penalties are] banishment, exile, public work, and chains. Certainly, those who are sentenced to capital punishment are to be killed within the year.

*Commentary.*[690] Julius Paulus was a famed Roman lawyer of the Severan Age (early third century A.D.) and contemporary of Ulpian. The *Sententiae* purportedly represent a collection of his juristic viewpoints (written to his son), but likely this work stems from the late third century. Paulus' views, often directly attributed to the *Sententiae* in his name, are frequently cited in Justinian's sixth-century *Digesta*, as well as in the fourth-century *Collatio Legum Mosaicarum et Romanarum* and in the fifth century *Consultatio veteris cuiusdam iurisconsulti*. Further, the Breviary of Alaric, known as the *Lex Romana Visigothorum*, and the *Epitoma Vaticana*, provide a summary of titles and contents for the *Sententiae*, assisting in the full reconstruction of the text. Certainly, though not all of the *Sententiae* can with confidence be said to originate in Paulus' writings, it does represent a constant witness to pre-Constantinian legal opinion.[691]

In this passage we observe a three-fold gradation of punishments that correspond to the class of crime. Among the *summa supplicia* (extreme punishments) are three forms of execution (cross, burning, and beheading). The middle category of "moderate offenses" receives one of two forms of enslavement (mines or gladiatorial school) or deportation. The distinction between deportation, banishment, and exile likely has to do with how far away one is removed from home, and the degree of contact one is permitted with others. The penalties within each category may be distributed according to the social class of

---

[690] Text: SALVATOR RICCOBONO, et al., Fontes iuris romani antejustiniani in usum scholarum (3 vols.; 1940–1943; repr., Florence: Barbera, 1968–1969), 2:405. Throughout this chapter, I have altered the text from FIRA by rendering consonantal "u" as "v".

[691] Caution must be exercised since the possibility also exists that the extant references to the *Pauli Sententiae* date to revisions that post-date the original compilation. Thus, in examining book 1 of the *Sententiae*, Levy has attempted to trace traditions that stem from the late third-century author, or from alterations to the original that date into layers of tradition from the fourth, fifth, or even sixth century. Levy personally concluded that the bulk of material stems from the late third century, though alterations also come from later layers in about a third of the cases. See ERNST LEVY, Pauli Sententie: A Palingenesia of the Opening Titles as a Specimen of Research in West Roman Vulgar Law (Ithaca: Cornell University Press, 1945; repr. New York: Kelley, 1969).

the criminal. Thus concerning perpetrators who commit acts deserving punishment from the middle category: Slaves or *humiliores* would be sent to the mines, while *honestiores* are more likely to face deportation.

**(337)** *Pauli Sententiae* 5.21.4

Non tantum divinatione quis, sed ipsa scientia eiusque libris melius fecerit abstinere. Quod si servi de salute dominorum consuluerint, summo supplicio, id est cruce, adficiuntur: consulti autem si responsa dederint, aut in metallum damnantur aut in insulam relegantur.

*Translation.* Not only should a person abstain from divination, but also more fittingly from the books with its own particular knowledge. Wherefore, if slaves have consulted [divination] concerning the well being of their masters, they shall be made to suffer the extreme punishment – that is, the cross. But, if the people consulted have given a reply, [those diviners] either will be condemned to the mine or they will be banished to an island.

*Commentary.*[692] This section is from the *Sententiae* group of sayings that have to do with divination and its practitioners. Given the frequent use of haruspices and other forms of foretelling the future in Roman society, this must be set in its context. The concern seems to be with *individuals* who (in a non-official capacity) consult soothsayers, especially concerning the health of their superior. In 5.21.3 the death penalty (*capite punitur*) is prescribed against those who seek to divine the health of the emperor or of the Roman state (and against those diviners who respond). The idea appears to be to squash any suspicion of those wishing for (or even contemplating) the death of the emperor or the collapse of the state. In a similar way, the above passage, though it makes broad pronouncements against divination as a whole (such a pronouncement may even be a post-Constantinian interpolation), ultimately concerns slaves who seek to divine the health of their masters, a concern that likely goes back early in Roman history. Those who assist the errant slaves receive medium-level penalties, but the slaves receive the extreme punishment of crucifixion. That the (singular) *summum supplicium* can be solely identified with the cross, even though the preceding text above (5.17.2) lists three varieties of *summa supplicia*, is likely due to the status of the individuals here under discussion – they are slaves and therefore the *crux* is the form of *summa supplicia* that is appropriate to them.

---

[692] Text: FIRA 2:407.

**(338)** *Pauli Sententiae* 5.21a.1–2 [Justinian, *Digesta* 48.19.38.pr–1]

Si quis aliquid ex metallo principis vel ex moneta sacra furatus sit, poena metalli et exilii punitur. ² Transfugae ad hostes vel consiliorum nostrorum renuntiatiores aut vivi exuruntur aut furcae suspenduntur.

*Translation.* If someone has stolen something from a mine of the *princeps* or from the sacred mint, he is punished by the mine and exile. ² Deserters to the enemies, or informers about our strategies, either are burnt alive or are hung up on a *furca*.

*Commentary.*⁶⁹³ The text of *Pauli Sententiae* 5.21a.1–2 appears in asterisks in FIRA since it does not occur in the main extant manuscript tradition, but it is known to have been in the *Sententiae* on the textual witness of Justinian's *Digesta* in 48.19.38.pr–1 (the whole of 48.19.38.1–12 is attributed in the *Digesta* to book 5 of the *Pauli Sententiae*). These represent two paired sets of crimes against the Roman state. In 5.21a.1 the concern is theft from the imperial mines or from the temple of Moneta at Rome, where money was coined.⁶⁹⁴ In 5.21a.2 the crimes involve desertion to the enemies of Rome, especially if that involves being an informer. For the latter set of crimes two forms of execution are prescribed (burning and suspension). Since "burning alive" (*vivi exuruntur*) is elsewhere in the *Pauli Sententiae* paired with suspension on the *crux* as constituting *summa supplicia*,⁶⁹⁵ it seems reasonable to think either that the *furca* and the *crux* are being employed interchangeably by the author of the *Sententiae* or, perhaps more likely, that the tradition in Justinian's *Digesta* has altered an original *cruci* (in the *Sententiae*) to read *furcae* (in the *Digesta*, which is our only extant textual witness).⁶⁹⁶

---

⁶⁹³ Text: FIRA 2:407. Compared with the text from Justinian's *Digesta* as it appears in Paul Krüger and Theodor Mommsen, Corpus iuris civilis (Editio stereotypa quinta. 3 vols.; Berlin: Weidmann, 1889), 1:817.

⁶⁹⁴ For the meaning of *moneta sacra*, see OLD s.v. *moneta*.

⁶⁹⁵ Note the threefold *summa supplicia* of 5.17.2 (see above): *crux*, *crematio*, and *decollatio*. Here *crematio* is likely synonymous with *vivi exuruntur*, and this further proves that this author can use synonymous terms for the same penalty and that he pairs "burning" with the *crux*. However, *vivi exuruntur* is applied to magicians, while the *crux* (and being thrown to wild beasts) is applied to those who are merely privy to the magician's work (see below on 5.23.17).

⁶⁹⁶ Note the comparison immediately below, where *Pauli Sententiae* 5.22.1 reads *in crucem tolluntur*, while the parallel passage in Justinian's *Digesta* (48.19.38.2) reads *in furcae tolluntur*. By Justinian's time, the *crux* was no longer an official punishment, but the *furca* was still in use as a form of suspension, so it would be natural to substitute *furca* for an earlier *crux*.

**(339)**  *Pauli Sententiae* 5.22.1

Auctores seditionis et tumultus vel concitatores populi pro qualitate dignitatis aut in crucem tolluntur aut bestiis obiciuntur aut in insulam deportantur.

*Translation.* The authors of sedition and rebellion, or the instigators of the people, according to the character of their dignity, are raised up on a cross, or are thrown to wild beasts, or are deported to an island.

*Commentary.*[697] This text lays out punishments for those who seek to undermine the state. All of 5.22.1–6 appears under the heading *De seditiosis*. Such *seditio* concerns violent political discord and (especially) rebellion or mutiny. *Tumultus* would refer to a sudden outbreak of violence or more particularly to a state of rebellion.[698] It is intriguing that the degree of penalty is not here tied to the degree of sedition, but to the dignity of the person's status (*pro qualitate dignitatis*). This text by itself does not specify which social status receives which penalty, but the preceding context in *Pauli Sententiae* would certainly indicate that slaves would merit the *crux* (5.21.4; No. 337). It could well be argued that *humiliores* would face the *crux* as well (cf. 5.23.1; 5.25.1; 5.30b.1 below). However, the very next law in 5.22.2 (against those who destroy property markers) has a similar tripartite division of penalties, though with a stated division of the populace into slaves-*humiliores*-*honestiores*, and 5.22.2 gives the middle penalty to the *humiliores*. On analogy then in 5.22.1, it could be that the slaves receive the *crux*, the *humiliores* are thrown to the wild beasts, and the *honestiores* face deportation. Two sections below will be devoted to the way that revolts (3.6.6), especially Jewish revolts (3.7), were suppressed by crucifying the ringleaders.

**(340)**  *Digesta* 48.19.38.2

Actores seditionis et tumultus populo concitato pro qualitate dignitatis aut in furcam tolluntur aut bestiis obiciuntur aut in insulam deportantur.

*Translation.* The agents of sedition and rebellion, once the people have been incited, according to the character of their dignity, are raised up on a *furca*, or are thrown to wild beasts, or are deported to an island.

---

[697] Text: FIRA 2:407. The text can also be found in the *Lex Romana Visigothorum* (concerning the *Pauli Sententiae*, lib. 5, tit. 24); it is especially important to note that *crux* appears here in the *Lex Romana Visigothorum* manuscript and in two of its epitomes (since *furca* will appear in the parallel passage from Justinian's *Digesta* 48.19.38.2 discussed below); text in GUSTAV HAENEL, Lex Romana Visigothorum (Leipzig: Teubner, 1849), 434–435.

[698] See definitions in OLD s.v. *tumultus*.

*Commentary.*[699] All of Justinian's *Digesta* 48.19.38 appears under the heading *Idem* [*Paulus*] *libro quinto sententiarum* (48.19.38.pr), and thus this selection is also attributed to *Sententiae* book 5. The text here is indeed virtually identical to the passage we cited just above (*Pauli Sententiae* 5.22.1; No. 339). There are some minor variations from the extant *Sententiae* text: *auctores* ("authors") is here *actores* ("agents"; likely a case of a single letter being omitted) and *vel concitatores populi* ("or the instigators of the people") is here *populo concitato* ("once the people have been incited"). The most noteworthy change concerns how *in crucem tolluntur* ("are raised up on a *crux*") in the *Sententiae* text appears as *in furcam tolluntur* ("are raised up on a *furca*") in the *Digesta*. By the time of Justinian, the *crux* had long fallen out of official use (due to Christian religious objections).[700] However, penal public suspension continued, albeit with a different form for the suspension device – the *furca* (a two-pronged, Y-shaped piece of wood). The *furca* was also known in earlier Roman texts,[701] where it might even be used interchangeably with *crux*, so this appears to revive a long-standing name for Roman penal suspension. The post-Constantinian change in official procedure may well explain how a statement from the second-century jurist *Paulus* (as remembered in the third-century document *Pauli Sententiae*) could now appear in the sixth-century *Digesta* with the term *furca* in place of the *crux*. Given that such a change of terms likely occurs here, other texts in the *Digesta* that attribute the use of the *furca* to pre-Constantinian jurists may well have originally referred to the *crux* (some of these will be studied further below).[702]

**(341)** *Pauli Sententiae* 5.23.1 (*Collatio* 1.2.1–2; 8.4.1–2)

Lex Cornelia poenam deportationis infligit ei qui hominem occiderit eiusve rei causa furtive faciendi cum telo fuerit, et qui venenum hominis necandi causa habuerit vendiderit paraverit, falsum testimonium dixerit, quo quis periret, mortisve causam praestiterit. Quae omnia facinora in honestiores poena capitis vindicari placuit, humiliores vero in crucem tolluntur aut bestiis obiciuntur.

*Translation.* The *Lex Cornelia* inflicts the penalty of deportation if someone has killed a man, or if because of this thing [because he was seeking to murder] he has been acting furtively with a weapon, and [if] someone has

---

[699] Text: KRÜGER and MOMMSEN, Corpus iuris civilis, 1:817. MOMMSEN's footnotes, in addition to comparing this text to the *Pauli Sententiae*, also notes that manuscript F reads the concluding clause as *aut insulam deportatur*.

[700] Christian sources could attribute the cessation of crucifixion to the emperor Constantine, e.g., Sozomon, *Hist. eccl.* 1.8.

[701] Note the discussion of *furca* concerning Plautus, *Persa* 853–857 in section 3.10.11, and especially the observations on *furca* and *furcifer* in No. 304 on Plautus, *Most.* 69–71.

[702] Cf. COOK, Crucifixion, 393. Also note comments above on *Pauli Sententiae* 5.21a.1–2.

owned, sold, or prepared a poison for the purpose of killing a man, [if] he has spoken false testimony on account of which someone perished, or [if] he has furnished the cause of death. It has been resolved that all such deeds are punished on *honestiores* by the capital penalty, *humiliores* on the other hand are raised up on a cross or are thrown to wild beasts.

*Commentary.*[703] Lucius Cornelius Sulla Felix instituted the *Lex Cornelia* in 82–81 B.C. Sulla had engaged in a series of legal reforms (especially focused on increasing the power of the senate). This passage is a summary of a section from the *Lex Cornelia de Sicariis et Veneficis* (Cornelian Law concerning Assassins and Poisoners). This text groups together murder, attempted murder, and abetting in murder – the homicidal intent is the same, so all receive the same penalty. A similar death awaits those convicted of false testimony that led to an execution in a capital case. There is some tension between the opening penalty (deportation) and the later forms of execution applied against the *humiliores* and the *honestiores*.[704] Nonetheless, it is clear that the author of the *Pauli Sententiae* believed that *humiliores* who engage in acts of murder could legally be sentenced to the *crux*.[705] The same text is found (attributed to the *Pauli Sententiae*) in the *Collatio Legum Mosaicarum et Romanorum* (1.2.1–2 and 8.4.1–2), a fourth-century A.D. comparison of Roman legal practice with the Mosaic Law, where the Cornelian Law is compared to an abbreviated form of Numbers 35:16–21.[706]

---

[703] Text: FIRA 2:408. Contrast some differences between our translation and the translation by SCOTT, Civil Law: I read *mortisve causam praestiterit* as its own conditional clause (thus separate from the false testimony charge), and similarly I understand *eiusve rei causa ... fuerit* to be a separate chargeable offense (attempted murder, as opposed to a qualifier on the intent of the murderer in the opening *Lex Cornelia ... occiderit* clause).

[704] Yet note that OLD s.v. *caput* suggests that "through most of the classical period exile commonly took the place of the death penalty for Roman citizens."

[705] Perhaps this should be contrasted with the opinion of the jurist Marcianus concerning the *Lex Cornelia* in Justinian's *Digesta* 48.8.3.5: *Legis corneliae de sicariis et veneficis poena insulae deportatio est et omnium bonorum ademptio. sed solent hodie capite puniri, nisi honestiore loco positi fuerint, ut poenam legis sustineant: humiliores enim solent vel bestiis subici, altiores vero deportantur in insulam.* "The penalty of the Cornelian Law concerning Assassins and Poisoners is deportation and removal from all good men. But they are accustomed today to be punished capitally, unless their positions are in the place of the *honestior*, so that they preserve the penalty of the law: for *humiliores* are accustomed to be thrown to wild beasts, however others are deported to an island." Also compare how *Pauli Sententiae* 5.25.2 (also in *Collatio* 8.5.1), concerning paying for false witnesses, merely prescribes "capital punishment" (*capite puniuntur*) to the *humiliores* and deportation to an island (*in insulam deportantur*) for *honestiores* (though this law does not specifically refer to the death of the person falsely accused, and it is discussing the ones paying the witnesses or judges, and not the witnesses themselves).

[706] For text and translation of the *Collatio*, see FIRA 2:544, 564; cf. MOSES HYAMSON, Mosaicarum et romanarum legum collatio (With Introduction, Facsimile and Transcription of the Berlin Codex, Translation, Notes and Appendices; London: Oxford University Press, 1913), 2, 56–57, 98–99 (variants ibid. 173, 211). Aside from minor punctuation differences,

**(342)** *Pauli Sententiae* 5.23.14–17

Qui abortionis aut amatorium poculum dant, etsi id dolo non faciant, tamen quia mali exempli res est, humiliores in metallum, honestiores in insulam amissa parte bonorum relegantur: quod si ex hoc mulier aut homo perierit, summo supplicio adficiuntur. [15] Qui sacra impia nocturnave, ut quem obcantarent defigerent obligarent, fecerint faciendave curaverint, aut cruci suffiguntur aut bestiis obiciuntur. [16] Qui hominem immolaverint exve eius sanguine litaverint, fanum templumve, polluerint, bestiis obiciuntur, vel si honestiores sint, capite puniuntur. [17] Magicae artis conscios summo supplicio adfici placuit, idest bestiis obici aut cruci suffigi. Ipsi autem magi vivi exuruntur.

*Translation.* Those who provide a draught for abortion or for love potions, even if they do not do it with malice, nevertheless it is a bad example: *humiliores* are banished to the mine, and *honestiores* are banished to an island after their share of possessions has been forfeited. Wherefore if the woman or the man has died from this, they suffer the extreme punishment. [15] Those who have performed or have undertaken to perform impious or nocturnal sacred rites, in order that they may enchant, bewitch, and spellbind someone, they are either fastened to a cross or thrown to wild beasts. [16] Those who have sacrificed a man, or have obtained favorable omens from his blood, [or] have polluted a shrine or a temple, are thrown to wild beasts, or if they are *honestiores* they are punished with capital punishment. [17] It has been resolved that those privy to the magical art will be visited with the extreme punishment – that is, to be thrown to wild beasts or to be fastened to the cross. However, the magicians themselves are burned alive.

*Commentary.*[707] As we continue here further down in the section on the *Lex Cornelia Sicariis et Veneficis* in the *Pauli Sententiae*, there are a series of laws condemning magical practices (especially those which harm other people). Two of the laws above prescribe the *summum supplicium* ("extreme punishment") for producing the death of someone with a magic potion (albeit with the plan to produce love or an abortion; 5.23.14) of for being "privy to the magical art" (*magicae artis conscios*; 5.23.17).[708] The first of these does not

---

the text of the *Collatio* is the same as *Pauli Sententiae* except for the addition of *–ve* on *falsum* in the *Collatio*, which makes for a more clear clausal connection. The *Collatio* (1.3.1–2) notes that Ulpian interprets the *Lex Cornelia* to refer just to the execution of "slaves and foreigners" (*servum et peregrinum*).

[707] Text: FIRA 2:409. The text of 5.23.14, attributed to book 5 of the *Sententiae*, also appears in Justinian's *Digesta* 48.19.38.5, where the variants are slight (omission of *id* after *etsi*; and *quod si eo mulier* in place of *quod si ex hoc mulier*); see the MOMMSEN edition of the *Digesta* in KRÜGER and MOMMSEN, Corpus iuris civilis, 1:817.

[708] The person "privy to the magical art" must be different than the magician mentioned later in 5.23.17 who is burned. Could this be an assistant? Or a frequent client of the magician?

further define what is meant by the *summum supplicium*. Earlier in the *Sententiae* (5.17.2), the *summa supplicia* were defined as the "cross, burning or beheading" (*crux crematio decollatio*), but the second mention of *summum supplicium* in the passage above (5.23.17) identifies the "extreme punishment" as either the *crux* or the wild beasts. Thus the cross is certainly among the most extreme penalties in the regular Roman judicial system, and likely can be inferred as a possible demise in the *Sententiae* for those criminals whose execution by *summum supplicium* is otherwise not defined (as in 5.23.14).[709] Similarly, explicitly in this passage (5.23.15) the cross is the place of death for the person who acts to bewitch another. We must acknowledge that in 5.23.17 burning appears to be an even more severe death (for the magician who produced the magic) than the *crux*, which is applied against those who were merely "privy" to the magical acts. However, this may well have to do with the need to fully consume the magician so as to destroy his or her power, and thus we need not always assume that burning alive is more severe than the *crux*.

## (343) *Pauli Sententiae* 5.25.1

Lege Cornelia testamentaria [tenentur]: qui testamentum quodve aliud instrumentum falsum sciens dolo malo scripserit recitaverit subiecerit suppresserit amoverit resignaverit deleverit, quodve signum adulterinum sculpserit fecerit expresserit amoverit reseraverit, quive nummos aureos argenteos adulteraverit laverit conflaverit raserit corruperit vitiaverit, vultuve principum signatam monetam praeter adulterinam reprobaverit: honestiores quidem in insulam deportantur, humiliores autem aut in metallum dantur aut in crucem tolluntur: servi autem post admissum manumissi capite puniuntur.

---

[709] This is a convenient place to list other texts in the *Pauli Sententiae* that mention the *summum supplicium* (notably all in the singular) without explicitly delineating which "extreme punishment" is intended: 2.24.9: *Obstetricem, quae partum alienum attulit, ut supponi possit, summo supplicio adfici placuit.* 3.5.8 *Servos, qui in itinere circumdatum a latronibus dominum per fugam deseruerunt, apprehensos et torqueri et summo supplicio adfici placuit.* 5.3.6: *Incendiarii, qui consulto incendium inferunt, summo supplicio adficiuntur.* 5.4.14: *Qui puero praetextato stuprum aliudve flagitium abducto ab eo vel corrupto comite persuaserit, mulierem puellamve interpellaverit, quidve pudicitiae corrumpendae gratia fecerit, donum praebuerit pretiumve, quo id persuadeat, dederit, perfecto flagitio capite punitur, imperfecto in insulam deportatur: corrupti comites summo supplicio adficiuntur.* 5.12.12: *Eius bona, qui falsam monetam percussisse dicitur, fisco vindicantur. Quod si servi ignorante domino id fecisse dicantur, ipsi quidem summo supplicio adficiuntur, domino tamen nihil aufertur, quia peiorem domini causam servi facere, nisi forte scierit, omnino non possunt.* 5.19a.1: *Rei sepulchrorum violatorum, si corpora ipsa extraxerint vel ossa eruerint, humilioris quidem fortunae summo supplicio adficiuntur, honestiores in insulam deportantur: alias autem relegantur aut in metallum damnantur.*

*Translation.* He is liable to the Cornelian Law relating to wills: who, knowingly with malice aforethought, has written, publicly recited, fraudulently introduced, suppressed, removed, unsealed, or erased a will or some other false document; or [who] has engraved, made, stamped, removed, or displayed, some counterfeit seal; or who has counterfeited, extracted metal from, melted down, reduced by scraping, damaged, or caused defects in, gold [and] silver coins; or [who] has rejected money stamped with the face of the emperor, unless it is counterfeit – *honestiores* are certainly deported to an island, while *humiliores* are either given over to the mine or raised up on a cross, while those slaves who have been manumitted after the crime are punished with capital punishment.

*Commentary.*[710] Another aspect of the extensive legal reforms of Lucius Cornelius Sulla Felix (in 81–80 B.C.) involved laws concerning wills and other sealed items.[711] This selection further encompasses the penalties for damaging money (the value of which in antiquity continued in large measure to rest on the weight and purity of metal in the coin, so that there must have been temptation to remove metal from coins). And finally, it insists on the acceptance of imperial coinage. This last matter, though it could be a logical extension of the *Lex Cornelia*, could not actually have dated in its present form back to republican times (prior to the imperial face on the coin). The severity of the penalties, as in other texts above, distinguishes between the classes of society. Yet in these cases, the law apparently granted some leeway with *humiliores* to determine whether the lesser or greater punishment is deserved (i.e., being given to the mines, or raised up on a cross). As elsewhere in Latin, the use of *tollo* with *in crucem* shows that suspension ("raising up") on the *crux*-device is intended. It is striking here how the freed slaves in the final clause receive a less specified form of capital punishment (*capite puniuntur*) than the *crux* option for the *humiliores* in the preceding clause.[712] It may well be that the notion of "capital punishment" could be assumed to include hanging up on a *crux*, and that this was so obvious that it need not have been stated for the case of slaves. Or perhaps their new status as freedmen has already granted them a lesser gradation of execution in this instance. However, as one proceeds

---

[710] Text: FIRA 2:410.

[711] The lines concerning wills have some grammatical awkwardness, due in some measure to the contrastable direct objects, which involve both true wills and false documents/wills. The suppression or erasure of a true will is clearly a crime, while it is the promulgation of false documents and wills (through writing, reciting, fraudulent introducing, etc.) that is the related (albeit contrary) evil.

[712] Contrast the translation by S. P. SCOTT, which reverses the "punished capitally" and the "crucified," so that the former refers to those "of inferior station" and the latter refers to slaves. Perhaps SCOTT assumes some confusion in the manuscripts themselves; and this possibility must be considered, given the observation in the next note concerning *humiliores* in the rest of 5.25 never being directly punished with the *crux*.

through related cases in the *Pauli Sententiae* 5.25, it is striking how repeatedly the application to *honestiores* remains the same (deportation), while *humiliores* are fairly consistently given over to the mines without mention of a crucifixion option.[713] Moreover, there is some tension between this recollection of the *Lex Cornelia testamentaria* in book 5, and an earlier account of the *Lex Cornelia* in book 4 (*Paulus Sententiae* 4.7.1), which is briefer and which only mentions the penalty of deportation to an island.[714] One could tentatively suggest that 5.25.1, in addition to reporting on the *Lex Cornelia*, incorporates some of the author's own extended understanding of the ramifications of the law (e.g., the mention of *imperial* coinage), while the briefer citation in 4.7.1 may represent a more strict citation of the Cornelian original. In this case, it is hard to know if the mention of the *crux* was of republican (or early imperial) legacy, or if the author of the *Sententiae* (or perhaps Paulus himself) was elaborating on the Cornelian law in light of the assumption that such significant capital crimes require a harsher penalty for *humiliores* than for the *honestiores*.

**(344)** *Pauli Sententiae* 5.30b.1 (*Collatio* 14.2.1–2)

Lege Fabia tenetur, qui civem Romanum ingenuum, libertinum servumve alienum celaverit vendiderit vinxerit comparaverit. Et olim quidem huius legis poena nummaria fuit, sed translata est cognitio in praefectum urbis, itemque praesidis provinciae extra ordinem meruit aniumdversionem. Ideoque humi-

---

[713] *Humiliores* are "generally" (*plerumque*) given over to the mines (while *honestiores* are deported) in 5.25.7 (regarding reading wills of people who are still living). Similarly, there is only mention of mines for *humiliores* (no crosses) in 5.25.8 and 5.25.9 (both concerning people who betray contents of wills to the testator's enemies) and in 5.25.10 (concerning people who used forged documents). However, *humiliores* receive capital punishment (*capite punitur*, without specifying the *crux*) in 5.25.2 (those who pay for false testimony or seek to corrupt judges) and in 5.25.12–13 (misuse of military standing and selling decisions of judges). Generic reference to people subject to the penalty for forgery (*falsi poena coercetur*), without any further detail, can be found in 5.25.5 (also see 5.25.11).

[714] Thus *Pauli Sententiae* 4.7.1 (in FIRA 2:376): *Qui testamentum falsum scripserit recitaverit subiecerit signaverit suppresserit amoverit resignaverit deleverit, poena legis Corneliae de falsis tenebitur, id est in insulam deportatur* ("The one who has written, publicly recited, fraudulently introduced, sealed, suppressed, removed, unsealed, or erased a false will, he is liable to the penalty of the Cornelian law concerning false [wills] – that is, he is deported to an island"). The list of verbs and other aspects of this text are strikingly similar to 5.25.1, such that they clearly reference the same rule. However, in contrast to 5.25.1, this text in 4.7.1: (1) omits mention of *quodve aliud instrumentum* [*falsum*] ("or some other false document") so that now *falsum* modifies *testamentum*, (2) omits *sciens dolo malo* ("knowingly with malice aforethought"), (3) adds *signaverit* ("has sealed") in place of the extended clauses concerning seals in 5.25.1 (*quodve signum ... reseraverit*), (4) omits references to coins, (5) and most importantly only discusses deportation without separately including harsher penalties for *humiliores* and slaves. The remainder of 4.7.2–6 apparently comments on, and clarifies, the Cornelian law.

liores aut in metallum dantur aut in crucem tolluntur, honestiores adempta dimidia parte bonorum in perpetuum relegantur.

*Translation.* He is liable to the Fabian Law who has concealed, sold, fettered, or purchased a free-born Roman citizen, a freedman, or someone else's slave. And formerly the penalty of this law was admittedly financial, but the judicial inquiry has been transferred to the *praefectus* of the city, and correspondingly it has incurred extraordinary punishment from the governor of the province. And therefore *humiliores* are either given over to the mine or are raised up on a cross; *honestiores*, after a half portion of their possessions has been confiscated, are banished for life.

*Commentary.*[715] The *Lex Fabia* concerns kidnapping (*de plagiariis*). It is also evidenced in Cicero (*Pro Rabirio* 3.8) and especially in Justinian's *Institutes* (4.18.10), *Digest* (48.15.1–7), and *Code* (9.20.1–16). The precise beginning of the *Lex Fabia* is debated, with origins suggested as early as the late third century B.C., though a later date B.C. is certainly possible.[716] This passage appears in the FIRA edition of *Pauli Sententiae*, but with asterisks to indicate its omission from the *Epitoma Vaticana* and from the *Lex Romana Visigothorum*. It is included in FIRA on the evidence of the *Collatio Legum Mosaicarum et Romanarum* 14.2.1–2, where it is cited in full, with the statement that it appears in the fifth book of *Pauli Sententiae*.[717] The text acknowledges the growing severity of the penalty for infringement of the Fabian Law from its origins in the Republic,[718] especially now that the procedure of *cognitio* (judicial inquiry) has come under the control of Roman prefects, who had greater latitude in dispensing punishments. While in an earlier era a financial penalty

---

[715] Text: FIRA 2:414 (*Sententiae*). Compared with the *Collatio* text (FIRA 2:577) and HYAMSON, Mosaicarum et romanarum legum collatio, 122. The *Collatio* reads *libertinumve* for *libertinum*, and *animadversionem* for *aniumdversionem*; neither variant effects the meaning. In *Sententiae*, *aniumdversionem* appears to be a defective spelling of *animumadversionem*.

[716] ROBINSON, Criminal Trials, 235 suggests a date in the late third or early second century.

[717] Further testimony in the early sixth-century A.D. collection (under King Gundobad) of earlier Roman laws known as the *Lex Romana Burgundionum* 20 (FIRA 2:732): *Si quis ingenuum natum ligauerit, uindiderit, honestiores persone damnantur exilio, uiliores uero metallis deputantur; exceptis his, qui captiuitatis iugo tenentur obnoxii, secundum speciem Pauli sententiarum libro V, sub titulo: [Ad legem Fabiam]* ("If someone has bound [or] sold a freeborn child – *honestiores* are condemned to resounding exile, *humiliores* on the other hand are assigned to the mines; with these exceptions: those who are held liable to the yoke of bondage, in accordance with the legal precedent of the *Pauli Sententiae* book 5, under the title: On the Fabian Law").

[718] Similarly, note Justinian's *Digesta* 48.15.7 (KRÜGER and MOMMSEN, Corpus iuris civilis, 1:808), where in the late third century A.D. the jurist Hermogenianus states: *Poena pecuniaria statuta lege Fabia in usu esse desiit: nam in hoc crimine detecti pro delicti modo coercentur et plerumque in metallum damnantur* ("The financial penalty appointed by the Fabian law ceased to be in use; for, those who have been detected in this crime are punished in proportion to the offence, and mostly they are condemned to the mine").

was imposed, by the imperial period the punishment could even include being raised on a cross (*in crucem tolluntur*) for *humiliores*. Yet later generations of jurists preferred to focus on the condemnation to the mines,[719] and the following sentences in the *Pauli Sententiae* (5.30b.2) assert that those slaves who infringe this law are (merely) to be sent to the mines.[720]

**(345)** *Historia Augusta* 18 [Severus Alexander] 28.4–5

cum quidam ex honoratis vitae sordidae et aliquando furtorum reus per ambitionem nimiam ad militiam adspirasset, idcirco quod per reges amicos ambierat admissus, statim in furto praesentibus patronis detectus est iussusque a regibus audiri damnatus est re probata. ⁵ et cum quaereretur a regibus, quid apud eos paterentur fures, illi responderunt "crucem." ad eorum responsum in crucem sublatus est. ita et patronis auctoribus damnatus ambitor est et Alexandri quam praecipue tuebatur servata clementia est.

*Translation.* When a certain man (from honored [ancestors], yet guilty of a sordid life and sometimes guilty of theft) had aspired to military office by means of excessive solicitation, after he had been admitted because he had solicited friends by means of the kings, right from the start he had been detected in theft while his patrons were present; and after he had been ordered to be heard by the kings, he had been condemned when the matter had been proved. ⁵And when it was sought from the kings what thieves would suffer among them, they responded, "The cross." At that response, he had been raised up on a cross. Accordingly, both the one who solicited [military office] had been condemned by his patron-supporters, and Alexander's clemency had been preserved, which [Alexander] was especially protecting.

*Commentary.*[721] This is another account from the biography of emperor Severus Alexander attributed to Aelius Lampridius and purporting to be written for Constantine (see comments in No. 323 on *Historia Augusta* 18 [Severus Alexander] 23.7–8). In this section (18.28.2–5) the author provides illustrations of Alexander's extreme severity (*severissimus* in 18.28.2) against thieves. Earlier the author had suggested that Alexander condemned such thieves most bitterly (*acerrime*) because he believed them to be the special enemies and

---

[719] Thus Hermongenianus in *Dig.* 48.15.7 and the *Lex Romana Burgundionum* 20 (both quoted in previous footnotes).

[720] *Si servus sciente domino alienum servum subtraxerit vendiderit celaverit, in ipsum dominum animadvertitur. Quod si id domino ignorante commiserit, in metallum datur.* Note the distinction between those slaves who commit this crime with their master's knowledge (even likely at their master's instigation) and those who do not – only the latter slaves (who are more culpable) are sent to the mine.

[721] Text: MAGIE, Scriptores Historiae Augustae, 2:232.

foes of the state (*solos hostes inimicosque rei publicae* in 18.28.2).[722] The case above likely presented some difficulty for Alexander, since the thief had eminent friends among the "kings." In the immediate context, it is not entirely clear who these "kings" would be; however elsewhere in the various authors of the *Historia Augusta*, the term *reges* applies to barbarian kings; and (in particular) the other occurrences of *rex* in this biography of Severus Alexander would likely point to Persian (or other barbarian) nobility, whom Alexander fought and conquered (18.55.1–57.3).[723] Alexander's solution to this case was to involve these barbarian kings both in adjudicating the man's guilt and in determining the standard punishment for theft. The punishment was crucifixion, and its harshness likely accords with Alexander's own proclivity to extreme severity against thieves. Yet, Alexander also manages to maintain the image of a *princeps* inclined to clemency by attributing this extreme punishment to the decision of others.[724]

## 3.6.5 Bandits and Brigands

From the previous section, it is evident (especially in the later empire) that a relatively wide range of heinous crimes could merit the cross. Yet one class of

---

[722] See further *Historia Augusta* 18.17.1, 3–4 (desiring to tear out eyes of thieving judges); 18.18.2–5 (where Alexander threatens capital punishment against thieves who come before the emperor, and where he passes on pejorative sayings about thieves).

[723] For *rex* in this biography (all in reference to Persian kings), see: 18.18.3; 18.55.1–57.3 (repeatedly); and 18.66.3. Also note 18.38.4–6. On the historical events of Alexander's conquest of the Persian army, note the helpful summary and notes by MAGIE, Scriptores Historiae Augustae, 2:288–291, of Alexander's military engagement with Ardashir (Artaxerxes) in A.D. 231. He also did battle with Parthia (18.50.1; 18.60.3 – with possible confusion with Persia), Germany (18.59.1–5), Britain and Gaul (18.59.6); meanwhile, other of his commanders did battle elsewhere (18.58.1). If it is the Persian (or other barbarian) kings who are the *reges* in this account, then we have another example where a Roman author indicates that the Persians (or other barbarians) readily employed the *crux* (here for the punishment of thieves). For the use of *reges* concerning barbarian kings among the various authors of the *Historia Augusta* note: the reference to "toparchs and kings" in 1 [Hadrian] 13.8 (with special reference to Parthia); 1.17.10; 1.20.13–14 (Albanian, Hiberian, and Bactrian kings); 22 [Valeriani Duo] 4.3; 27 [Tacitus] 12.1 ("barbarian kings"); 28 [Probus] 12.5 ("kings of other nations"); 28.14.6 (of Germans); 28.15.2 (Germans). Also observe the general references to kings of other lands with whom the emperor is in contact in 3 [Antonius Pius] 12.8; 4 [Marcus Antoninus] 14.2; 4.26.1 (with special reference to Persia); 5 [Varus] 7.8; 11 [Pescinnius Niger] 12.6; 25 [Divus Claudius] 9.4. Note especially the reference to Persian kings in 4 [Marcus Antoninus] 26.1 (Persian kings in plural, alongside other kings); 20 [Gordiani Tres] 27.5; 24 [Tyranni Triginta] 30.13. For the plural of *rex* elsewhere in the *Scriptores Historiae Augustae*, see also: 1 [Hadrian] 17.8; 10 [Severus] 17.2; 17 [Elagabalus] 34.5; 22 [Valeriani Duo] 1.1; 25 [Divus Claudius] 10.3.

[724] Clemency was one of the virtues that a Roman ruler, especially an emperor, was supposed to display; cf. Seneca, *De Clementia*.

criminal eventually becomes particularly associated with the *crux* – the *latrones*. While early Roman comedy would emphasize the slave as the chief inhabitant of the cross, in later Roman novels and in Jewish rabbinic stories the brigand becomes its primary resident. Often translated "thieves," in reality the *latrones* are typically much more violent in their actions – hence "bandits" or "brigands" is frequently the better translation. These are no mere pickpockets. In the city the *latrones* endanger the good order of the civic body. In the countryside *latrones* commonly attack travelers, and thus they potentially inhibit trade, upset the confidence people have in the Roman constabularies, and generally threaten the *pax Romana*. Brigandage and piracy are effectively flip sides of the same coin, with the main difference being their criminal venue (i.e., land or water). For those reasons, and because of the frequent deaths associated with the brigand's actions, the brigand was punished most harshly. We remember that Jesus was crucified amidst two such brigands, and thus he was numbered among them in his crucifixion (Matt 27:38, 44; Mark 15:27; cf. Matt 26:55; Mark 14:48; Luke 22:52).

The passages below form a very brief testimony to this theme in Roman-era literature. Texts that appear elsewhere in this volume also witness to the application of the cross against brigands. Thus below we shall encounter a tale told by Petronius: "the governor of the province ordered brigands [*latrones*] fixed up on crosses" (*imperator provinciae latrones iussit crucibus affigi*; in *Satyricon* 111; see No. 384). And the theme of brigandage is closely intertwined with rebellious behavior in some crucifixion accounts from Josephus (see below 3.7). Notably, several rabbinic anecdotes and parables make reference to brigands being crucified in Judea-Palestine (see 3.7.2).

H.-W. KUHN has argued that there is little testimony to *latrones* being crucified simply for having engaged in brigandage (apart from rebellion). Rather, he contends that (especially in Palestine) such "brigands" were typically involved in political insurrection and were crucified for their opposition to the Roman state. He believes this informs how one should understand Jesus' crucifixion, namely that he was crucified on charges of being a political revolutionary.[725] HENGEL concurs that rebels could be styled as "bandits"; yet by examining popular stories and dream handbooks, Hengel also effectively broadens the idea of banditry to include criminals who do not express revolutionary motives.[726] Granted, some of HENGEL's textual evidence includes passages that refer more generally to criminals and less specifically to brigandage.[727] Nevertheless, especially if the rabbinic evidence from Judea-Palestine is taken into account (see 3.7.2), it still appears plausible in some contexts to speak of

---

[725] KUHN, Die Kreuzesstrafe, 724–736.

[726] HENGEL, Crucifixion, 46–50.

[727] E.g., passages from Artemidorus (*Oneirocriticon* 1.76; 2.56; 2.68) refer to the criminal as κακοῦργος or πανοῦργος; and Quintillian (*Declamationes* 274) calls them *noxii*.

brigands who are only seeking financial gain through violent robbery, even if other brigands could also be drawn into full-scale rebellion.

**(346)**  *Digesta* 48.19.28.15

Famosos latrones in his locis, ubi grassati sunt, furca figendos compluribus placuit, ut et conspectu deterreantur alii ab isdem facinoribus et solacio sit cognatis et adfinibus interemptorum eodem loco poena reddita, in quo latrones homicidia fecissent: nonnulli etiam ad bestias hos damnaverunt.

*Translation*. It is agreed by many that famous brigands, in the very place where they had prowled, are to be affixed to the furca, so that others may be deterred by the sight from those same misdeeds, and so that there may be solace to the kinsmen and relatives of those killed in the same place (once the penalty has been exacted) in which the brigands had performed the homicides; yet some have condemned these to the beasts.

*Commentary*.[728] Although Justinian's *Digesta* is later than our period, it nevertheless provides one of the best extant points of contact with earlier law. Note here the brigands (*latrones*) are clearly violent actors, who prowl in search of victims (*grassati sunt*)[729] and then murder them (cf. *interemptorum* and *homicidia fecissent*). Yet there is no indication of instigation of a rebellion. The point of the passage is twofold: To present the manner of execution (most say execution occurs by affixing them to the *furca*, though some would condemn them to the beasts), and to insist that the place of execution should be back at the place where the brigands murdered their victims. The penalty and location are chosen both as a deterrent to future crime in the region and as a means of solace to those closest to the brigands' victims. The *furca* at this period would likely have been distinguished from the *crux*, since the cross was no longer supposed to be employed in Byzantine law. However, above we observed that the pre-Constantinian passages in the *Pauli Sententiae* that mention the *crux* had been intentionally changed in the *Digesta* to read *furca*. Therefore, to the extent this passage may refer to pre-Constantinian practice, it likely testifies to the use of the *crux* against *latrones* in the Roman Empire.

**(347)**  Apuleius, *Metamorphoses* 3.9.1–3

Nec mora, cum ritu Graeciensi ignis et rota, tum omne flagrorum genus inferuntur. Augetur oppido, immo duplicatur mihi maestitia quod integro saltem

---

[728] Text: KRÜGER and MOMMSEN, Corpus iuris civilis, 1:817 (MOMMSEN).

[729] Cf. OLD s.v. *grassor*, meaning "to roam in search of victims, etc., prowl" in the case of robbers, pirates, etc.

mori non licuerit. Sed anus illa, quae fletibus cuncta turbaverat, "Prius" inquit "Optimi cives, quam latronem istum miserorum pignorum meorum peremptorem cruci affigatis, permittite corpora necatorum revelari, ut et formae simul et aetatis contemplatione magis magisque ad iustam indignationem arrecti pro modo facinoris saeviatis."

*Translation*. Neither was there a delay, when (by Greek custom) fire and wheel, then every kind of lash, were inflicted. Grief was exceedingly intensified against me – in reality it was doubled – because it would not be permitted [for me] at least to die uninjured. But that old woman, who had troubled all by her weeping, said, "Before, excellent citizens, you affix to a cross that brigand, that destroyer of my wretched child-guarantees, allow the bodies of the dead to be revealed, so that as soon as, by the contemplation of their form and youth, you have been more and more aroused to just indignation, you might be enraged by the manner of the misdeed.

*Commentary*.[730] Apuleius wrote in the mid-second century A.D. The novel's narrator (Lucius) believed himself to be under attack by three men, whom he assumed were thieves, just as he was about to enter his lodging at night (2.32). He defends himself with his sword, slaying all three of his assailants. The next morning he awakes, afraid of who might judge him for this deed. He is indeed led to prison, and then brought to the theater for judgment, being accused of homicide. After he completes his account before the judges, an old woman approaches weeping, beseeching his conviction. The use of the fire, wheel, and lash (mentioned above) are performed with the intent of making him reveal anyone else who may have assisted him in the murders (cf. 3.8). Note how he is called a *latro* ("brigand"), which is evidently the charge against him. Thus they believe him not just guilty of murder but of conspiring with others in the process of murderous robbery. There is certainly no assumption of insurrection, simply of brigandage. The *crux* is his intended form of execution (*cruci affigatis*), at least according to the old woman. She claims the three murdered youths were her "child-guarantees" (*pignorum meorum*), thus implying that they were to stand as her assurance throughout her marriage and into her old age.[731] As the story continues, they uncover the "bodies" only to discover that they were actually just three large bladders that he had stabbed in the night (he was undoubtedly drunk at the time). Everyone has a good laugh about the prank that had been played on him by the town during the festival day in honor of the god *Risui* ("laughter"). In recompense, they grant him the honor of becoming a patron of the city. This is one of many like instances of crucifixion being threatened against criminals in Apuleius' story.[732]

---

[730] Text: WILLIAM ADLINGTON and STEPHEN GASELEE, The Golden Ass: Being the Metamorphoses of Lucius Apuleius (LCL; Cambridge: Harvard University Press, 1915), 112–114.

[731] OLD s.v. *pignus*, "applied to children as the guarantee of the reality of a marriage".

**(348)** Firmicus Maternus, *Mathesis* 8.22.3

Quodsi Lunam et horoscopum Mars radiatione aliqua aspexerit, latrocinantes crudeli feritate grassantur. Sed hi aut in crucem tolluntur, aut publica animadversione peribunt.

*Translation*. But if Mars somehow catches sight of the moon and the horoscope while gleaming, then those who engage in brigandage will prowl with cruel brutality. But these will either be hung on the cross, or they will die by a public punishment.

*Commentary*.[733] Julius Firmicus Maternus wrote this astrological treatise in A.D. 334–337; he later converted to the Christian religion. Section 8.22 concerns the horoscope relative to Cancer. Here he betrays a sense that brigands are potentially bound for the cross. The fact that he is writing this in the Constantinian age is of some interest, since Constantine was believed to have abolished crucifixion, and yet Firmicus continues to act as if crucifixion was still a continuing punishment for brigandage. Indeed he associates it with several classes of criminals.[734] COOK counters this by observing that Firmicus also mentions the potential of being condemned to gladiatorial combat, even though Constantine likely did away with gladiatorial shows; hence Firmicus' material may be more traditional than up-to-date.[735] In any case, this passage continues the traditional association of brigandage with crucifixion.

### 3.6.6 Conquered Peoples in War

While the Romans often associated the use of the cross with the military exploits of foreign countries (sections 3.2–4), the Roman military also practiced similar gruesome execution measures. Many literary examples occur of Roman crucifixion during times of combat. Some of these have received attention under the narrower categories of Slave Revolts (3.6.3) or Rebels (3.6.7; 3.7.3). Some brigandage accounts, especially in Judea (3.7.2), also required official Roman military intervention. Given the large number of potential other examples, just a few selections are made below.[736]

---

[732] See Apuleius, *Met*. 1.14.2; 1.15.6; 3.17.4–5; 4.10.3–4; 6.31.1–3; 6.32.1; 10.12.4. Note comments in HENGEL, Crucifixion, 140; COOK, Crucifixion, 129–132.

[733] Text: WILHELM KROLL and FRANZ SKUTSCH, Iulii Firmici Materni Matheseos libri VIII (2 vols.; Bibliotheca Scriptorum Graecorum et Romanorum Teubneriana; Leipzig: Teubner, 1897–1913), 2:327. Note HENGEL, Crucifixion, 49.

[734] See Firmicus Maternus, *Mathesis* 6.31.58–59; 6.31.73; 8.6.11; 8.17.2; 8.25.6. For all these texts cf. HENGEL, Crucifixion, 78n.; COOK, Crucifixion, 147–149.

[735] COOK, Crucifixion, 406–407, 149.

[736] On this matter, note COOK, Crucifixion, 161–179, which is principally concerned with

**(349)**  Appian, *Mithridatic Wars* 5.29 [113–114]

καὶ Βρύττιος, ἐκ Μακεδονίας ἐπελθὼν σὺν ὀλίγῳ στρατῷ, διεναυμάχησέ τε αὐτῷ καὶ καταποντώσας τι πλοῖον καὶ ἡμιολίαν ἔκτεινε πάντας τοὺς ἐν αὐτοῖς, ἐφορῶντος τοῦ Μητροφάνους. ¹¹⁴ ὃ δὲ καταπλαγεὶς ἔφευγε, καὶ αὐτόν, αἰσίῳ ἀνέμῳ χρώμενον, ὁ Βρύττιος οὐ καταλαβὼν Σκίαθον ἐξεῖλεν, ἣ τῆς λείας τοῖς βαρβάροις ταμιεῖον ἦν, καὶ δούλους τινὰς αὐτῶν ἐκρέμασε καὶ ἐλευθέρων ἀπέτεμε τὰς χεῖρας.

*Translation.* And Bruttius came out from Macedon with a small army and engaged in naval battle with him [Metrophanes]; and by drowning a certain boat and a *hemiolia*, he killed all those in them, while Metrophanes watched. ¹¹⁴ And panic-struck, [Metrophanes] fled. And Bruttius, being unable to catch him while he was experiencing an opportune wind, demolished Skiathos, which was a store of plunder for the barbarians; and some of their slaves he hung up, and he cut off the hands of the freemen.

*Commentary.*⁷³⁷ During the First Mithridatic War (89–85 B.C.) between Rome and Mithridates VI of Pontus, Metrophanes had been sent in 87 B.C. by Mithridates to ravage Euboea, Demetrias and Magnesia in Thessaly (all allies of Rome). According to Plutarch, Bruttius Sura was the Roman lieutenant of Sentius (who was the praetor of Macedonia); Bruttius engaged in subsequent further brilliant battles against Mithridates' general, Archelaus (Plutarch, *Sulla* 11.4–5). In this passage Bruttius pursues Metrophanes to put an end to his raids. After a brief conflict, the wind favors Metrophanes, so Bruttius breaks off the pursuit and instead attacks the small Aegean island of Skiathos, where Mithridates' forces stored the loot from their plunderings. In Skiathos, Bruttius punishes those in charge of the stores – noticeably dealing out different penalties to slave and free (as we have already seen repeatedly above). Bruttius orders the slaves "hung up" (ἐκρέμασε), which verb appears throughout Appian's work to refer to human bodily suspension associated with execution (probably something akin to crucifixion in this Roman context; see No. 300 on Appian, *Bell. civ.* 3.1.3).

---

wars and slave revolts in republican Rome. Many of his examples from imperial Rome also concern military affairs (ibid. 180–214). These sections in his book were anticipated by JOHN GRANGER COOK, Roman Crucifixions: From the Second Punic War to Constantine, ZNW 104 (2013): 1–32. Sometimes the mere threat of crucifixion is of military value, see, e.g., Cicero, *Phil.* 13.21; Lucan, *Bell. civ.* 7.303–304; Frontinus, *Str.* 4.7.24.

⁷³⁷ Text: VIERECK, ROOS, and GABBA, Appiani Historia romana, 1:443–444. Compared with WHITE, Appian's Roman History, 2:290–292 (where Βρύττιος is not spelled consistently throughout the passage).

**(350)** Appian, *Bella Civilia* 2.13.90 [377]

Ἐπεὶ δ' ὁ στρατὸς αὐτῷ κατέπλευσε, Ποθεινὸν μὲν καὶ Ἀχιλλᾶν ἐκόλασε θανάτῳ τῆς ἐς τὸν Πομπήιον παρανομίας, Θεόδοτον δὲ διαδράντα Κάσσιος ὕστερον ἐκρέμασεν, εὑρὼν ἐν Ἀσίᾳ.

*Translation.* And when the army sailed down to him [Caesar], he punished Pothinus and Achillas with death for the transgression in regard to Pompey; but Cassius later hung up Theodotus (who had escaped), after finding [him] in Asia.

*Commentary.*[738] Toward the end of the Civil War between the forces of Pompey and Julius Caesar, Pompey fled toward Alexandria (in September of 48 B.C.). Arriving in Egypt, Pompey petitioned the young Ptolemy for friendship and sanctuary. Appian records that Ptolemy received advice to assassinate Pompey from Achillas (his army commander), from the eunuch Pothinus (in charge of the treasury), and especially from his tutor Theodotus (*Bell. civ.* 2.12.84–85). Plutarch also credits Theodotus the sophist with convincing Ptolemy to kill Pompey, even recording the essence of Theodotus' argument (cf. Plutarch, *Pomp.* 77.4). Ultimately Ptolemy's officials do have Pompey assassinated, and Appian asserts that the "associates of Pothinus" decapitated the body (*Bell. civ.* 2.12.86), retaining Pompey's head to present to Caesar in hopes of a reward. According to Appian, Caesar instead orders Pothinus and Achillas executed (important earlier Roman sources vary from Appian on this matter).[739] In the passage above, Theodotus' escape is cut short by Cassius, who "hangs up" (ἐκρέμασεν) Theodotus in Asia. As we witnessed repeatedly above (esp. in the commentary on Appian, *Bell. civ.* 3.1.3), κρεμάννυμι is commonly employed by Appian as a term for human bodily suspension, appearing to indicate something much akin to crucifixion. Theodotus' demise in Asia is also reported in Plutarch, though with some important differences in detail (including a lack of mentioning bodily suspension).[740] We could wish for more agreement in the sources concerning this demise of Theodotus, but

---

[738] Text: VIERECK, ROOS, and GABBA, Appiani Historia romana, 2:226. Checked with WHITE, Appian's Roman History, 3:392.

[739] Plutarch, *Pomp.* 80.5 agrees with Appian here. However, contrast this with Caesar, *Bell. civ.* 112 and Caesar, *Bell. Alex.* 4, where Pothinus is also said to have been captured and killed by Caesar, but Achillas was known to have been assassinated by Arsinoë (who plays a similar role in Dionysius Halicarnassus, *Ant. Rom.* 42.40.1).

[740] So Plutarch, *Pomp.* 80.6 credits the capture of Theodotus instead to Marcus Brutus (after Caesar had been slain), and claims that Brutus put Theodotus to death after having tortured him "with every torture" (πᾶσαν αἰκίαν αἰκισάμενος ἀπέκτεινεν). Caesar himself focuses his account on Achillas as the man especially responsible for Ptolemy's death (*Bell. civ.* 3.104), omitting any mention of Theodotus (perhaps Caesar does so in order to not permit his autobiographical works to stray too much from his own deeds of renown). Cassius Dio also omits reference to Theodotus (cf. 42.3.3–4).

certainly Appian represents the belief in the second century A.D. that such a man, who had caused the downfall of one of Rome's most illustrious generals, would rightly meet his end by being suspended before his Roman captors.

**(351)** [Pseudo-] Caesar, *De Bello Hispaniensi* 20.5

Ea nocte speculatores prensi servi III et unus ex legione vernacula. Servi sunt in crucem sublati, militi cervices abscisae.

*Translation.* In that night, spies had been caught – three slaves and one from a locally-levied legion. The slaves were hung up on the cross; the soldier's neck was cut off.

*Commentary.*[741] The *Spanish Wars* is not likely to have been authored by Caesar himself, but could potentially have been penned by one of his military men. This brief account is situated during the battles between Caesar and Pompey (and likely dated to 45–44 B.C.). Pompey had taken refuge near the town of Ucubi (a Roman colony southeast of Cordoba), but several of his military personnel are deserting to Caesar. In the midst of these events, four spies are captured in Caesar's camp. One is from a "locally-levied legion" (*ex legione vernacula*); such legions receive repeated mention in the context. The distinction in penalties follows the trend we have witnessed earlier in terms of social categories: The slaves are crucified (*sunt in crucem sublati*), but the soldier is beheaded. This distinction might imply an intentional military judgment has been rendered, following Roman precedent in distribution of capital punishment.

### 3.6.7 Rebels

While crucifixion could generally be employed in times of war, it was especially used in the suppression of anti-Roman revolutionary movements. A selection from the *Pauli Sententiae* (5.22.1; see No. 339) laid out the legal basis for the use of the cross against *auctores seditionis et tumultus vel concitatores populi* ("the authors of sedition and rebellion, or the instigators of the people"), especially against those who belonged to the lower classes of society. Earlier we examined the use of the cross in quelling slave revolts (3.6.3; e.g., Appian, *Bell. civ.* 1.14.119–120; Cicero, *Verr.* 2.5.7–14), with some later Roman authors envisioning the use of the cross in the earliest known Roman slave uprisings (e.g., Dionysius of Halicarnassus, *Ant. rom.*

---

[741] Text: RENATUS DU PONTET, C. Iuli Caesaris commentariorum (2 vols.; Scriptorum classicorum bibliotheca Oxoniensis; Oxford: Clarendon, 1900), vol. 2, ad loc.

5.51.3; 12.6.6).[742] Other instances that represent suppression of slave revolts are also reported in this section below. Further, in 3.7.3 multiple examples will be provided from Roman conduct during the First Jewish Revolt.

**(352)** Titus Livius, *Ab urbe condita* 22.33.1–2

Per eosdem dies speculator Carthaginiensis qui per biennium fefellerat Romae deprensus praecisisque manibus dimissus, ² et servi quinque et viginti in crucem acti, quod in campo Martio coniurassent. Indici data libertas et aeris gravis viginti milia.

*Translation*. Around those days, a Carthaginian spy, who had escaped notice for two years, was caught in Rome, and after his hands were cut off, he was sent away, ² and twenty-five slaves were led to the cross because they had formed a conspiracy in the Campus Martius. Freedom was given to the informer, and twenty thousand weight of copper coins.

*Commentary*.[743] The events here occur during the consulship of Atilius and Geminus Servilius in 217 B.C. (cf. 22.32.1). Hannibal remains with his Carthaginian army in Italy, but Rome has resorted to cutting off his supplies rather than direct attack. Livy makes passing mention of a slave revolt that resulted in its twenty-five instigators facing the cross. This continues the theme we observed earlier of slave revolts calling forth suspension on a *crux* (3.6.3). The manuscripts vary in their location of the phrase *in campo Martio*, some locating it after the *quod* (as above) and others before the *quod*; if one were to follow the latter reading, then it would be clear that the crucifixions occurred in the Campus Martius (as they often did in this period) rather than the conspiracy being formed in that precinct. The informer was evidently a slave himself (he was granted freedom and a substantial sum).

**(353)** Titus Livius, *Ab urbe condita* 33.36.1–3

Cum haec in Graecia Macedoniaque et Asia gererentur, Etruriam infestam prope coniuratio seruorum fecit. ² ad quaerendam opprimendamque eam M'. Acilius Glabrio praetor, cui inter civis peregrinosque iurisdictio obtigerat, cum una ex duabus legione urbana est missus, alios < ... alios> iam congregatos pugnando uicit: ³ ex his multi occisi, multi capti; alios uerberatos crucibus adfixit, qui principes coniurationis fuerant, alios dominis restituit.

---

[742] From the standpoint of Late Antiquity, we could add others, e.g., Orosius, *Historiae Adversum Paganos* 5.9.4. For the earlier period, also see Florus, *Epitome* 2.7 [3.19.8].

[743] Text: FOSTER, MOORE, SAGE, SCHLESINGER, and GEER, Livy, 5:308–310. The manuscripts vary in the spelling of *speculator* and in the location of the phrase *in campo Martio*.

*Translation*. While these things had been occurring in Greece, Macedonia, and Asia, a conspiracy of slaves almost made Etruria insecure. ² In order to seek out and suppress it, M. Acilius Glabrio as praetor, to whom jurisdiction had been given for [cases] between citizens and foreigners, was sent with one of two city legions. Others ..., others who had gathered together he now conquered by fighting. ³ From these many had been killed, many captured; others, after being scourged, he fixed to crosses (namely those who had been the leaders of the conspiracy), and others he restored to their masters.

*Commentary*.[744] Livy is writing during the era of Augustus (first century B.C. – first century A.D.) about events that occurred in 196 B.C. Here is another account of a slave revolt that was suppressed with crosses being applied to the chief instigators. The ellipses represent the editor's understanding that the text is faulty.

### 3.6.8 Military Deserters

Roman authors claim that various barbarians would crucify/suspend deserters. This is especially a theme in Roman accounts about Carthage (above in 3.3). Also note Appian's claim that Mithridates VI of Pontus "hung up" deserters in his battle against Pompey (Appian, *Mithr.* 15.97; cf. No. 218).

Valerius Maximus indicates below some opposition to the crucifixion of deserters, while Livy merely reports the same example. Above it was observed how desertion is punished with the *furca* in Justinian's *Digesta* (48.19.38.1), and this may be one of several passages that originally read *crux* in the *Pauli Sententiae* (*Pauli Sententiae* 5.21a.1–2; see No. 338) since Justinian's corpus typically changes *crux* to *furca* when they quote earlier sources. Other Roman acts of extreme military discipline are recorded in literature from the Constantinian age.[745]

**(354)**  Titus Livius, *Ab urbe condita* 30.43.10–13

Ita dimissi ab Roma Carthaginienses cum in Africam uenissent ad Scipionem, quibus ante dictum est legibus pacem fecerunt. ¹¹ naues longas elephantos perfugas fugitiuos, captiuorum quattuor milia tradiderunt ... ¹³ de perfugis grauius quam de fugitiuis consultum: nominis Latini qui erant, securi percussi, Romani in crucem sublati.

---

[744] Text: BRISCOE, Titi Livi Ab urbe condita. Libri XXXI–XL, 1:175.

[745] See further *Historia Augusta* 6 [Avidius Cassius] 4.1–6; 15 [Opellius Macrinus] 12.2; 19 [Maximini Duo] 8.6–7.

*Translation.* The Carthaginians, having been thus sent away from Rome, once they had come to Scipio in Africa, made peace according to those agreements that have been recorded earlier. [11] The long boats, elephants, deserters, fugitive slaves, and four thousand captives were handed over ... [13] The decree was more severe concerning deserters than concerning fugitive slaves: those who were Latin by nationality were beheaded with the axe, Romans were hung up on the cross.

*Commentary.*[746] At the close of the Second Punic War (201 B.C.) the Roman senate granted to Publius Cornelius Scipio Africanus the responsibility of settling the peace and setting the terms. Meanwhile, the Carthaginians have admitted defeat and accede to Rome's demands (30.43.1–9). The short list of items "handed over" from the Carthaginians to the Romans (30.43.11) includes their Punic long boats. In the text omitted above (in the ellipses), those boats are said to have been burned (500 of them), much to the dismay of the Carthaginians, whose fleet had been the core of their economic (as well as military) livelihood. Also in this list are the military deserters (*perfugae*) and the fugitive slaves (*fugitivi*) who had fled to Carthage's side. Livy begins in 30.43.13 by comparing the greater severity of punishment that befell the military deserters with that of the fugitive slaves, but the final clauses (*nominis ... sublati*) appear to just focus on the means of execution accorded to the deserters (leaving aside the issue of fugitive slaves). The distinction in punishments has to do with the nationality of these military deserters: Those Latin citizens (who are Italian, but not Roman, citizens) are beheaded, while the Roman citizens are crucified. The *crux* here clearly involves a device on which someone is hung up (*sublati*). Though the precise method of suspension is not detailed, the parallel clause with "beheading" would indicate that both beheading and suspension on the cross were the actual means of execution. Livy reports the crucifixion of Roman citizen military deserters as a mere fact, without stating whether he thought this an appropriate form of discipline or not.

## (355) Valerius Maximus, *Facta et Dicta Memorabilia* 2.7.12

Nihil mitius superiore Africano. is tamen ad firmandam disciplinam militarem aliquid ab alienissima sibi crudelitate amaritudinis mutuandum existimauit: si quidem deuicta Carthagine, cum omnes qui ex nostris exercitibus ad Poenos transierant, in suam potestatem redegisset, grauius in Romanos quam in Latinos transfugas animaduertit: hos enim tamquam patriae fugitiuos crucibus adfixit, illos tamquam perfidos socios securi percussit. non prosequar hoc factum ulterius, et quia Scipionis est et quia Romano sanguini, quamuis

---

[746] Text: WALSH, *Titi Livi Ab Urbe Condita Libri XXVIII–XXX*, 146.

merito, perpesso seruile supplicium insultare non attinet, cum praesertim transire ad ea liceat quae sine domestico uolnere gesta narrari possunt.

*Translation*. There was nothing of mildness with the elder Africanus. Nevertheless he, in order that military discipline be somewhat strengthened, considered borrowing bitterness from a cruelty most alien to himself: If indeed the Carthaginians had been subdued, when all who had transferred allegiance from our army to the Carthaginians had been brought back under his control, he paid attention more severely to the Roman deserters than to the Latin ones: these he fixed up on crosses just like fugitives from the fatherland, those he beheaded with an axe just like treacherous allies. Permit me to not pursue this deed further, both because it is Scipio's [deed] and because it is not proper to mock at the punishment for slaves endured by Roman blood, however much deserved, particularly when it is permissible to pass over to those deeds which are able to be narrated without wounding the domestic [esteem].

*Commentary*.[747] Valerius, writing during Tiberius' reign, has in this chapter collected examples of military discipline, which he describes as "the principal dignity and stability of the Roman empire" (2.7.praef.). Thus, in general terms, Valerius sets out admirable instances of Roman military discipline, though he appears less enthused about this case from Publius Cornelius Scipio Africanus' conduct of the Second Punic War at the end of the third century. In context, Valerius reports that Q. Fabius Maximus had cut off the hands of deserters (2.7.11) and that the younger Africanus (Scipio's adopted son) threw non-Roman deserters to the beasts (2.7.13). Here, Valerius turns to an event from Scipio's conduct of the Punic War, which concerns the same instance of crucifixion as in the example we just studied in Livy (30.43.13). There are some intriguing lexical connections between these passages in Valerius and Livy (especially *gravius, securi percussi,* and *in crucem*), which may testify to Valerius' source material (perhaps either Livy or some derivative tradition from Livy). However, while the comparative *gravius* in Livy contrasts the penalties accorded the deserters and fugitive slaves, Valerius makes the *gravius* comparison between the nationalities of the deserters themselves, thus adding clarity to the contrasting penalties that is otherwise a bit muddled in Livy. Valerius depicts the crucifixion of Roman deserters as attaining a level of severity unusual even for Scipio.[748] Valerius emphasizes this severity:

---

[747] Text: BRISCOE, Valeri Maximi Facta et Dicta Memorabilia, 1:126. The text in the SHACKLETON BAILEY edition is essentially the same (save for punctuation and for *uolnere* spelled *vulnere*); cf. SHACKLETON BAILEY, Valerius Maximus, 1:190.

[748] Note that the translation above of *nihil mitius superiore Africano* ("there was nothing of mildness with the elder Africanus") would imply that Scipio Africanus was already a severe person, who exceeded his own severity with this punishment of deserters. Contrast the translation by SHACKLETON BAILEY, Valerius Maximus, 1:191: "The elder Africanus was the mildest of men."

Scipio had to borrow the "bitterness" (*amaritudinis*) from "cruelty" (*crudelitate*) that was "most alien" (*alienissima*) and hence effectively barbaric. Valerius asserts his authorial refusal to pursue the issue further (out of respect for Scipio and for the Roman blood that was shed), and he expresses concern that such a discussion could potentially injure Roman domestic pride. Valerius' record indicates that this event was still known in the first century A.D., and that some people viewed it as an example of excessive (if still necessary) military discipline. Note also how Valerius provides further indirect testimony to crucifixion being associated with the punishment of slaves (*seruile supplicium*).

**(356)** *Digesta* 49.16.3.10

Is, qui ad hostem confugit et rediit, torquebitur ad bestiasque vel in furcam damnabitur, quamvis milites nihil eorum patiantur.

*Translation.* The one who flees for refuge to the enemy and returns, he will be racked and condemned to beasts or on a furca; however, soldiers will be subject to none of these.

*Commentary.*[749] Section 49.16 concerns matters of military law, with 49.16.3 collecting statements attributed to book four of Herennius Modestinus' *On Punishments* (early third century A.D.). Just prior to this passage, Modestinus indicates that those who desert to the enemy are granted a window of time to return and suffer a mere drop in rank or even potentially a pardon (see 49.16.3.9). Yet those who are actively scheming to desert to the enemy are to suffer capital punishment (49.16.3.11). In this passage here, those who have previously deserted and then returned (presumably after the window for clemency has passed) are handed over to the harshest means of death – either thrown to the beasts or placed on a *furca*. This is similar to the passage from the *Pauli Sententiae* (5.21a.1–2) concerning the placing of deserters on the *furca*, which was studied in section 3.6.5 and is found in the *Digesta* (48.19.38.1).[750] Because Justinian's jurists typically altered *crux* to *furca* in their selections from the *Pauli Sententiae*, it is also possible that the suspension penalty here in Modestinus would originally have been on a *crux* rather than on a Byzantine *furca*.

---

[749] Text: KRÜGER and MOMMSEN, Corpus iuris civilis, 1:836 (MOMMSEN).

[750] See No. 338, where the translation reads: "Deserters to the enemies, or informers about our strategies, either are burnt alive or are hung up on a *furca*."

## 3.6.9 Innocents, Heroes and Martyrs

Even according to the standards of Roman law, not everyone who went to the cross deserved his or her fate. Cicero's argument proceeds from that premise in his *In Verrem*, in which he indicts Verres for unjustly sentencing a Roman citizen to the cross, and in his *Pro Rabirio*, in which he accuses Labienus and his ilk of seeking to crucify a guiltless Roman senator (see 3.6.1). In mass military executions, it also becomes possible for innocent sufferers to be crucified, even as they are captured in the midst of more deserving rebels and brigands.

Innocence can also be a matter of perspective. The standpoint of the audience affects the presumption of innocence of the crucifixion victim (especially in times of war). Thus the Romans readily reproach the Carthaginians for crucifying Roman soldiers, and then the Romans employ like forms of bodily suspension against their own foes. If you are Roman, then a crucified Roman constitutes an injustice, while a dead Carthaginian deserved what he got. Meanwhile, the Carthaginians likely believed just the opposite. Thus as the Romans frequently applied crucifixion to suppress rebellions, likely the colleagues, neighbors, and family of the victims may well have thought such a crucifixion undeserved. For some, a crucifixion might actually have represented a badge of honor for the deceased.

It is a slight step then to speak of crucified heroes or (even) martyrs. Thus the Roman general Regulus, who sacrificially endured the Carthaginian cross with confidence, became a beacon for future generations who wished to emulate his faithfulness to the Roman state. The Romans especially admired endurance amidst strife and torture. Such heroic fortitude in facing the cross has already been witnessed in the slave who smote Hasdrubal in recompense for the cruel execution of his master (Silius Italicus, *Punica* 1.165–184; No. 239). In like manner, as will be observed further below in section 3.7, Jewish literature can portray Jews who endured the Seleucid or Roman cross to have been innocent sufferers (or even heroes). Only two examples are provided below, though others exist.

**(357)** Florus, *Epitome* 1.18 (2.2.25)

Sed nec illo voluntario ad hostis suos reditu nec ultimo sive carceris seu crucis supplicio deformata maiestas; immo his omnibus admirabilior quid aliud quam victor de victoribus atque etiam, quia Carthago non cesserat, de fortuna triumphavit? Populus autem Romanus multo acrior intentiorque pro ultione Reguli quam pro victoria fuit.

*Translation.* But neither by his [Regulus'] voluntary return to his enemy nor by [his] ultimate punishment, whether of prison or of the cross, had his dignity been marred; rather, by all this being more worthy of admiration, what did he do other than become a victor over the victors and even, since Carthage did not desist, triumph over fortune? However, the Roman people were much more diligent and more intent for the avenging of Regulus than for victory.

*Commentary.*[751] Marcus Atilius Regulus had long been considered a hero of the First Punic War. He was successful in battle, although when he was sent to settle terms for the Carthaginian surrender, he demanded too much, so they continued to fight (cf. Polybius, *Hist.* 1.31). Ultimately Regulus lost in a key encounter with Xanthippus and was captured. Though Polybius only knew of his capture (1.34), later traditions expanded on the legend that the Carthaginians sent Regulus back to Rome to encourage Roman surrender and that he first made a promise to return to Carthage. Regulus went to Rome as pledged, but instead spoke against the Carthaginian terms for peace. Having accomplished his delegation to Rome (though simultaneously undermining its goal), he then kept his promise and returned to Carthage, where he was tortured to death. Florus is a representative of the tradition that Regulus may have died on the cross, though Florus also simultaneously seems to allow for a death in prison. Other authors make Regulus' willing return to a cross serve as a point of great honor for Regulus and the Roman people (e.g., Seneca, *Ep.* 98.12; *Prov.* 3.9), and the encomiums can become quite excessive (e.g., Silius Italicus, *Punica* 2.340–344, 435–436; though cf. 6.529–551). In any case, we witness in Florus how Regulus has become a hero (and perhaps even a martyr to the Roman cause).

**(358)** Strabo, *Geographia* 3.4.18

τῆς δ' ἀπονοίας καὶ τοῦτο λέγεται τῆς Καντάβρων, ὅτι ἁλόντες τινές, ἀναπε-πηγότες ἐπὶ τῶν σταυρῶν, ἐπαιώνιζον. τὰ μὲν οὖν τοιαῦτα τῶν ἠθῶν ἀγριότη-τός τινος παραδείγματ' ἂν εἴη.

*Translation.* And concerning the madness of the Cantabrians, this also is told: that some captives, after being nailed up on crosses, chanted the song of victory. Thus such matters might be an example of a certain savageness of their customs.

*Commentary.*[752] Strabo of Amaseia, writing in the Augustan period, here records tales he knows concerning the Cantabrians of northwest Spain. In Strabo's day, the Cantabrians would have only recently been conquered (dur-

---

[751] Text: FORSTER, Lucius Annaeus Florus. Epitome, 84.
[752] Text: HORACE LEONARD JONES, The Geography of Strabo (8 vols.; LCL; London/Cambridge: Heinemann/Harvard University Press, 1917–1932), 2:114. Other editions read ἐπαιάνιζον for ἐπαιώνιζον (the meaning is the same).

ing 26–19 B.C.), thus the account may represent contemporary memory of the event. The word ἀπονοίας can convey a certain "loss of good sense," leading to "madness" or "rebellion"; perhaps each of these glosses could fit well here. Similarly, earlier Strabo had recounted examples of the Cantabrians possessing a "senseless" bestial and ferocious nature (3.4.17). There he illustrates that claim by mentioning how Cantabrian mothers would kill their own children rather than let them be taken captive. However, Strabo is also able to recognize courage in their manners (3.4.17), and he will follow the passage above with a brief note about their occasional civility. In any case, Strabo finds the story above an example of madness and senselessness, and he suggests that it exemplifies a backwoodsy savageness (ἀγριότητός). In this, Strabo undoubtedly portrays the Roman viewpoint on such matters. However, from the point of view of the Cantabrians, these singing victims of the cross may well represent the pride and fortitude of their heroic opposition to Rome.[753]

## 3.6.10 Christians

Several Christian sources record Christian martyrdoms on the cross. It is intriguing to compare these to a pagan report such as Tacitus, *An.* 15.44.4 (No. 84). Tacitus records Nero's application of torture and mass crucifixion against Christians (and his lighting the crosses on fire) under the accusation of their having begun the great Roman conflagration. Tacitus does not doubt the victims' guilt, at least regarding their superstition, if not the actual fire; yet even he finds Nero's spectacle cruel, and he observes that popular sentiment began to sympathize, at least in some measure, with the crucified. Roman law prescribed the death penalty for anyone who sought to set fire to a city (*Pauli Sententiae* 5.20.1),[754] thus from the Roman legal perspective these executions may have had some merit. Nonetheless, the remaining Christians viewed their suffering colleagues as innocents, perhaps even as heroes or martyrs. Most of our sources concerning Christian crucifixions stem from Christian authors, and thus the martyr perspective naturally prevails. Two brief examples of Christians being crucified are provided below, though certainly more exist.[755]

---

[753] Similar fortitude in facing the cross can be found in other accounts of non-Roman sufferers, such as in Valerius Maximus 6.2 ext. 3.

[754] *Incendiarii, qui quid in oppido praedandi causa faciunt, capite puniuntur* ("Those who set fires, who do this in a town for the purpose of acquiring loot, are punished with capital punishment"). Note there is no distinction between social status here, although presumably the form of the death penalty could vary depending on the class of the person. This can be contrasted with those who engage in arson against a house or villa: They are merely sentenced to the mine or public works (if they are *humiliores*) or banished to an island (if they are *honestiores*). Similar punishments and distinctions are in place for those who set fire to fields of growing crops (5.20.5).

**(359)** Justin, *Dialogus cum Tryphone* 110.4

κεφαλοτομούμενοι γὰρ καὶ σταυρούμενοι καὶ θηρίοις παραβαλλόμενοι καὶ δεσμοῖς καὶ πυρὶ καὶ πάσαις ταῖς ἄλλαις βασάνοις ὅτι οὐκ ἀφιστάμεθα τῆς ὁμολογίας, δῆλόν ἐστιν, ἀλλ᾽ ὅσῳπερ ἂν τοιαῦτά τινα γίνηται, τοσούτῳ μᾶλλον ἄλλοι πλείονες πιστοὶ καὶ θεοσεβεῖς διὰ τοῦ ὀνόματος τοῦ Ἰησοῦ γίνονται.

*Translation.* For, though being beheaded and crucified and thrown to beasts, chains, fire and all other tortures, it is clear that we do not depart from the confession, but in so long as such things occur, to so great an extent many others rather become believers and God-worshipers through the name of Jesus.

*Commentary.*[756] Writing in the mid-second century A.D., Justin engages in a prolonged dialogical debate with Trypho the Jew. Justin is in the midst of applying Micah 4 to the two advents of the Christ. Here, he references the Christian response to suffering in his own day as evidence that the church will endure until the Messiah's second coming. The list of sufferings, including σταυρούμενοι, should now be familiar to the reader as a standard catalog of Roman punishments and capital penalties. These punishments presumably were tied to Roman legal procedure applied against various members of the church.

**(360)** Tertullian, *Ad nationes* 1.18.1

Reliquum obstinationis in illo capitulo collocatis, quod neque gladios neque cruces neque bestias vestras, non ignem, non tormenta ob duritatem ac contemptum mortis animo recusemus.

*Translation.* You assemble the remainder of [our] obstinacy in that heading, that with spirit we refuse neither swords, nor crosses, nor your beasts, not fire, and not torment, on account of hardness and contempt of death.

*Commentary.*[757] Tertullian writes as an apologist before the Romans, arguing that Christians ought to be admired rather than chastised. The charge of obstinacy against Christians comes up in 1.17.1, there for refusal to worship Caesar. In the passage here, a different obstinacy is in view, namely the refusal to

---

[755] E.g., Tertullian, *Apol.* 12.3; 50.12; *Nat.* 1.3.8; 1.6.6; 1.18.1; *An.* 1.6; 56.8; Eusebius, *Hist. eccl.* 2.25.5; 3.32.6; 5.1.41; 8.8.10.

[756] Text: EDGAR J. GOODSPEED, Die ältesten Apologeten. Texte mir kurzen Einleitungen (orig. 1914; repr., Göttingen: Vandenhoeck & Ruprecht, 1984), 226.

[757] Text: FRANZ OEHLER, Qu. Septimii Florentis Tertulliani Apologeticum et Ad nationes libri duo, ex fide optimorum codicum manuscriptorum aut primum aut denuo collatorum cum adnotatione perpetua et indicibus (Halle: Anton, 1849), 325.

recant when faced with the various resources of the Roman legal system. Tertullian observes the kinds of penalties that are applied against Christians, *cruces* being one. He will go on to argue that this brave endurance of penalty has in the Roman past been an admirable virtue. In this regard, he will cite the example of the Roman hero Regulus, who himself endured the cross (1.18.3; see No. 357 and other texts noted there).

## 3.7 Crucifixion in Roman Judea–Palestine

When the Romans established their military and provincial administration in Judea-Palestine, they also imported their conventions of law and combat. This naturally extended to their employment of the cross. In this respect, Judea does not truly present a special case among other Roman provinces and regions. However, given our interest in understanding the specific context of the Roman crucifixion of Jesus, it is especially relevant to provide focused analysis of crucifixion in this region during Roman rule. This period was frequently marked by Roman suppression of brigandage and rebellion, with the prime examples of the latter being found in the First and Second Jewish Revolts, which the Romans crushed with vicious efficiency.

Most of the victims of the cross in this section are Jewish or Samaritan. The regions covered here include Judea, Samaria, and Galilee. This region later became part of the Roman/Byzantine provinces of Palestine (*Palaestina Prima* and *Secunda*). The chapter employs interchangeably the shorthand of calling this area Judea / Palestine.[758] As in many matters of Jewish history for this period, Josephus serves as the major witness. He often supplies personal testimony in addition to passing on secondhand reports (cf. *Vita* 420–421 in 3.8). The frequency of the cross in this region led to its repeated mention in rabbinic stories and case law. Undoubtedly Jewish sympathy could be accorded in antiquity toward the many Jewish people who were executed on the cross, thus there are reported incidents of innocent sufferers, heroes, and even martyrs undergoing crucifixion. It has been argued elsewhere that while Jews in the first century shared many of the perceptions of the cross that were widespread in the Roman empire, their understanding of the cross would also have been distinctly affected by their special experience of enduring Roman oppression, which was often most manifest in the fields of crucified Judeans.[759]

---

[758] The territory thus mostly corresponds to modern Israel and the West Bank. The interchangeable labels used are ancient and not intended to align with conflicting modern parties.

[759] Cf. CHAPMAN, Crucifixion, 210–219, esp. 218–219.

## 3.7.1 Suspension in Ancient Judea-Palestine

Centuries before the Romans were in Judea, suspension penalties (both legal and military) had been practiced in this region. The textual and visual evidence for this has been covered above, but it is fitting here to remind ourselves of this context before proceeding to Roman-era accounts.

The texts in section 3.2 illustrated the widespread use of suspension procedures in Egypt and the ancient Near East. Assyrian sources, especially Sennacherib's Lachish reliefs, explicitly testify to the employment of suspension/impalement during times of Assyrian siege warfare within the realm of Judah itself. The Hebrew Bible acknowledges Jewish contact with such penalties among especially the Egyptians, Philistines, and Persians (Gen 40:19, 23; 41:13; 1 Sam 31:8–13; 2 Sam 21:12; Ezra 6:11–12; Esth 2:23; 5:14; 6:4; 7:9–10; 8:7; 9:13–14, 25). Indeed, the OT also indicates that ancient Jewish leaders sanctioned the use of suspension – albeit for a relatively brief duration, in most instances, and likely as a *post mortem* dishonoring of the corpse (Deut 21:22–23; Josh 8:29; 10:26–27; 2 Sam 4:12). From the examples available in the limited repertoire of extant ANE visual representations (all Assyrian) and from the Egyptian terminology (of placing someone on the "tip" of a wooden device), these suspensions were most likely impalements. Nevertheless, Jewish interpreters in the Roman period were well aware of these OT texts, and (as will be observed below in section 3.9) they often actualized them by applying to those biblical passages contemporary Roman-era language for suspension (language that overlaps with the terminology of crucifixion).

Moving into the Hellenistic period, evidence exists for continued use of suspension by the Ptolemies, Seleucids, and other Hellenized (as well as barbarian) peoples (see above in sections 3.3–4). Thus Judea continued to be surrounded by (and often under the control of) civilizations that practiced human bodily suspension.[760] In section 3.5 we discussed evidence for and against the Jewish practice of suspension in the Hellenistic and Roman periods. At least some of these, by mentioning prolonged suspensions of living victims, overlap profoundly with Roman-era notions of crucifixion (note the death of Jose b. Joezer, and the suspension of 800 by Alexander Jannaeus). Despite rabbinic objections in Late Antiquity to Jewish employment of crucifixion (see section 3.5.2), and notwithstanding some earlier indications of Jewish rejection of such a capital penalty,[761] in the Hellenistic era there remain a few clear examples of Jewish authors approving *ante mortem* suspension (11QTemple and

---

[760] One striking example of this in Judea is Josephus' account of Antiochus Epiphanes suspending living victims on *stauroi*; see discussion below in 3.7.6.

[761] Note the analysis of the rabbinic list of four accepted means of capital punishment (3.5.3), and observe how Josephus typically distances crucifixion from Jewish suspension practices (also noted in 3.5).

Philo) and of Jewish leaders practicing *ante mortem* suspension on a massive scale (800 under Alexander Jannaeus, eighty under Simeon b. Shetach).

All this provides a backdrop to suspensions/crucifixions in Roman-era Judea-Palestine. The Romans were certainly not the first to practice suspension in this territory. And the perceptions of Roman penalties would have been informed by previous Jewish experience with human bodily suspension in Judea and neighboring territories.

### 3.7.2 Brigands in Judea

Though often translated as thief or robber, the terminology of brigandage (ληστής, *latro*, ליסטס, ליסטאה) typically conveys a more violent offender – one who employs battery and murder (often in group raids) in order to steal from others (cf. 3.6.5 above). Brigandage in Judea-Palestine receives its typical punishment through crucifixion, as is evident in both history and tales. Rabbinic sources occasionally make the crucified brigand a stock character in the service of some broader story. Earlier we read how R. Eleazar collaborated with the Romans in capturing brigands (*b. B. Meṣ.* 83b; No. 280); the context clearly implies those criminals were crucified, and Eleazar weeps at the foot of one of their crosses (only later to be vindicated in his judgment). Also, mention was made of R. Meir's parable of the twins, one of whom was a king and the other a brigand; in the parable the brigand is crucified, but the onlookers mistakenly imagine that the king has been hung up (*t. Sanh.* 9:7; *b. Sanh.* 46b; cf. No. 267). Jesus' parable of the Good Samaritan depicts the victim being attacked by λῃσταί on the highway between Jerusalem and Jericho (Luke 10:30, 36): he is beaten, robbed of all his valuables including his clothes, and left for dead. The Gospels' accounts of Jesus' death in Jerusalem portray him as crucified between two λῃσταί (Matt 27:38, 44; Mark 15:27; cf. Matt 26:55; Mark 14:48; Luke 22:52). And the man who was released in Jesus' stead (Barabbas) was likewise called a λῃστής (John 18:40) in addition to δέσμιον ("prisoner" in Matt 27:16). Intriguingly, Barabbas is said in Mark 15:7 to have committed murder during the insurrection (οἵτινες ἐν τῇ στάσει φόνον πεποιήκεισαν), and thus he is labeled μετὰ τῶν στασιαστῶν ("among the insurrectionists"). Thus the same man can be described both as an "insurrectionist" and as a "brigand." Similarly the account below from Josephus (*B. J.* 2.253) reminds us that the nefarious occupation of brigand often overlapped with the sentiments of a revolutionary. Some of the accounts of "rebels" in section 3.7.3 will also mention brigandage in their contexts (e.g., *B. J.* 2.241; cf. 2.235, 238). The list of rabbinic passages below is particularly selective.[762]

---

[762] For some further instances, as well as fuller analysis of the texts below, cf. CHAPMAN, Crucifixion, 188–195.

**(361)** Josephus, *Bellum judaicum* 2.253

οὗτος τόν τε ἀρχιληστὴν Ἐλεάζαρον ἔτεσιν εἴκοσι τὴν χώραν λησάμενον καὶ πολλοὺς τῶν σὺν αὐτῷ ζωγρήσας ἀνέπεμψεν εἰς Ῥώμην· τῶν δ' ἀνασταυρω-θέντων ὑπ' αὐτοῦ λῃστῶν καὶ τῶν ἐπὶ κοινωνίᾳ φωραθέντων δημοτῶν οὓς ἐκόλασεν, ἄπειρόν τι πλῆθος ἦν.

*Translation.* This man [Felix] took captive and remitted to Rome both the chief-brigand Eleazar, who had plundered the country for twenty years, and many of those with him; but of those brigands crucified by him, and of those commoners detected in [their] association whom he punished – such was a countless multitude.

*Commentary.*[763] Josephus reports that Nero made Felix procurator (ἐπίτροπον) over Judea (*B. J.* 2.252; cf. 2.247). The account above highlights Felix's deeds at suppressing brigandage. As noted in section 3.6.5, the term λῃστής and its cognates certainly designates robbery,[764] but it most often also bears indications of violence along with such thievery; hence we prefer the translation "brigand." The notion of violence in λῃστής is all the more obvious in the very next sentence after this passage, where Josephus calls the Sicarii assassins "another form of brigands" (ἕτερον εἶδος λῃστῶν; *B. J.* 2.254). Indeed, Eleazar appears earlier in Josephus' narrative (*B. J.* 2.235–236) as a leader in the Jewish popular uprising against the Samaritans who had slain a Galilean pilgrim en route to Jerusalem; such an uprising degenerated into brigandage and general insurrection (2.238). Such deeds remind us that there was often an overlap between Jewish brigands and leaders of Jewish nationalist movements. KUHN highlights the insurrectionist element in this episode (and in other instances of brigandage in Josephus), and he concludes that the Romans primarily viewed these men as rebels, applying crucifixion to them more to quash revolt than to suppress robbery.[765] Nevertheless, rabbinic crucifixion tales (see below) can focus on Roman opposition to brigandage as robbery apart from revolutionary notions, so perhaps it is best to see a dual motive in this Roman mass crucifixion of "brigands", both to oppose violent crime and to inhibit revolt.

Josephus elsewhere reports that Felix captured Eleazar by subterfuge; Felix promised Eleazar safe passage, but instead captured and bound him for deportation to Rome (*A. J.* 20.160–161).[766] While Eleazar was led away for punishment in Rome, a countless multitude of his associates were punished, with many being crucified at Felix's command (ἀνασταυρωθέντων ὑπ'

---

[763] Text: NIESE, Flavii Josephi Opera, 6:202.

[764] Note that LSJ s.v. λῃστής supplies both "robber" and "pirate" as definitions.

[765] Cf. KUHN, Die Kreuzesstrafe, 724–736, esp. 724–727.

[766] This corresponding text in *A. J.* 20.160–161 does not mention crucifixion, but indicates that Felix "put to death" (ἀνῄρει) many magicians and brigands, who had filled the country.

αὐτοῦ). The precise details of these suspensions are not outlined, but presumably these conform both to standard Roman military procedure and with the other Roman executions reported by Josephus via this verb (ἀνασταυρόω).[767]

## (362) *Mekilta*, Shirata 7

מושלו משל למה הדבר דומה ללסטים שהיה עומד ומנאץ אחר פלטרין של מלך אומר אם אמצא
את בן המלך אני תופשו והורגו וצולבו וממית אותו מיתות חמורות כך היה פרעה הרשע עומד
ומנאץ בתוך ארץ מצרים אמר אויב ארדוף אשיג וגו' ורוח הקדש מלעגת עליו ואומרת נשפת
ברוחך

*Translation.* To give a parable, to what is this matter compared? To a brigand[768] who was standing and threatening behind a king's palace, saying: "If I find the king's son, I shall seize him, and slay him, and crucify him, and make him die most severe deaths." So also was wicked Pharaoh standing and threatening in the midst of the land of Egypt: "An enemy said: 'I will pursue, I will overtake, etc.'" [Exod 15:9] But the Holy Spirit mocks him and says: "You blew with Your wind ..." [Exod 15:10 – in reference to God's Red Sea destruction of Pharaoh's army].

*Commentary.*[769] This parable, along with the next few passages, indicates that the connection between brigandage and crucifixion became a standard one in rabbinic literature, even after crucifixion had officially ceased in the Roman

---

[767] Note the many examples of Roman use of the *stauros* further below in section 3.7. The semantic range of ἀνασταυρόω in Josephus has been discussed in No. 277 (*A. J.* 13.380–381, 383). Josephus can employ the term to refer to the *post mortem* suspension of Saul and his sons on the walls of Beth Shean (Scythopolis) in *A. J.* 6.374. However, Josephus also typically uses the term to refer to the extended suspension of victims as a means of execution (*B. J.* 1.97, 113; *A. J.* 11.267; 12.256; 13.380, 410). While most Roman examples from Josephus (mentioned further below) similarly do not depict the precise mode of suspension and/or death, the Roman cases that do provide more details certainly imply that the Romans hung up people alive (esp. *Vita* 420–421; cf. *B. J.* 3.321) with much blood expected from living victims during such suspensions (*A. J.* 19.94). This, of course, lines up with Jewish expectations (noted above in §3.5.2) that the Roman government did indeed hang people up alive (*Sifre Dev.* §221; *Midrash Tannaim* 132, lines 7–8; *b. Sanh.* 46b). If one were to accept the reference to σταυρός as being within a non-interpolated clause in the *Testimonium Flavianum* (*A. J.* 18.64), then this σταυρός device is also the one used against Jesus.

[768] The noun is plural, but the sense throughout is singular.

[769] Text: JACOB Z. LAUTERBACH, Mekilta de-Rabbi Ishmael: A Critical Edition on the Basis of Manuscripts and Early Editions with an English Translation, Introduction and Notes (3 vols.; Library of Jewish Classics; Philadelphia: Jewish Publication Society, 1933–1935), 2:57–58 (lines 57–63). Compared with HAIM SAUL HOROVITZ and ISRAEL ABRAHAM RABIN, Mechilta d'Rabbi Ismael (orig. 1931; repr., Corpus Tannaiticum 3.1(3); Jerusalem: Bamberger & Wahrmann, 1960), 1931, p. 141 (lines 1–3). These texts vary on whether "most severe deaths" should be plural or singular. The translations of rabbinic passages below reflect those in CHAPMAN, Crucifixion.

Empire. This parable in the halakic midrash on Exodus known as the *Mekilta de-Rabbi Ishmael* is preceded by a reference to Pharaoh declaring the five boasts of the enemy, as remembered in Exodus 15:9 (in Moses' song). This text above then mocks Pharaoh's boasting as if he were a mere brigand, stating grandiose plans to crucify the king's son. Israel (God's son) is clearly analogous to the king's son in the parable. The fact that the Exodus story concludes with Pharaoh's demise, may indicate that the parable leaves unstated the obvious reversal: the brigand (i.e., Pharaoh) will instead be captured and crucified, as is appropriate to all brigands. In addition to threatening to crucify the son, the brigand also promises "most severe deaths" – could this be analogous to the *summa supplicia* of Roman law? The brigand in this parable appears more concerned with murder than with plunder, and thus he may be more on the insurrectionist side of brigandage than on the pillaging side.

**(363)** *Mekilta,* Shirata 10

יי ימלוך אימתי תבינהו בשתי ידיך. משל למה הדבר דומה ללסטים שנכנסו לפלטין של מלך בזזו נכסיו והרגו פמליא של מלך והחריבו פלטרין של מלך לאחר זמן ישב עליהן המלך בדין תפש מהם הרג מהם צלב מהם וישב בפלטין שלו ואחר כך נתודעה מלכותו בעולם לכך נאמר מקדש יי כוננו ידיך יי ימלוך לעולם ועד.

*Translation.* "The Lord will reign." (Exod 15:18) When? [When] you [God] will build it [the Temple] with your two hands. To give a parable, to what is this matter compared? To brigands who entered the palace of a king, plundered his property, slew the king's *familia* and destroyed the king's residence. After a time, the king sat over them in judgment – he imprisoned some of them, he slew some of them, he crucified some of them – and he dwelt in his palace. And afterwards his reign was made known in the world. Thus it is said: "The sanctuary, O Lord, your hands established. The Lord will reign forever and ever" (Exod 15:17–18).

*Commentary.*[770] In this early rabbinic commentary on Exodus 15:18, the eschatological question is posed regarding when God will reign again in his Temple. The parable compares God's judgment of the nations to the king who imprisons, slays, and crucifies brigands. In this parable the brigands have gone so far as to attack the king's family and plunder his property, though the parable does not delineate whether the brigand's actions were accomplished purely for profit or from some revolutionary impetus. The analog to these brigands must be the Gentile nations, especially Rome (which destroyed the "king's residence"). The penal actions of the king would have paralleled the Gentile (esp. Rome's) use of such penalties against brigands. Ironically, God now

---

[770] Text: LAUTERBACH, Mekilta de-Rabbi Ishmael, 2:79–80 (lines 42–49). Compared with HOROVITZ and RABIN, Mechilta d'Rabbi Ismael, 150 (lines 11–14) on [*Beshallaḥ*] *Shirata* 10.

serves as the one who will bring such penalties on the oppressive rulers who have captured his land and Temple. This selection from *Mekilta* produced by Rabbi Ishmael, receives a parallel (with some variations) in the *Mekilta de-Rabbi Shimon bar Yohai*.[771]

**(364)** *Pesikta de-Rab Kahana*, suppl. ii.2

א"ר שמואל בר' נחמני במקום שקיפה הליסטים שם צולבין אותו, מן ירושלים קפחו ושבו
לפיכך יצלבו בירושלם

*Translation.* R. Samuel bar Naḥmani said: "In the place where the brigands rob, there they crucify him. From Jerusalem they [the nations] robbed and then returned; therefore they will be crucified in Jerusalem."

*Commentary.*[772] The *PRK* likely stems from around the fifth century A.D., though some date it later.[773] R. Samuel bar Naḥmani was a third generation Palestinian *Amora*. This passage contains one of a few occurrences of the aphorism "where the brigands rob, there he is crucified" (see further *Esth. Rab.* 3.14 [7d] on Esth 1:12 with a parallel text to that above; also note a related aphorism in *Eccl. Rab.* 7.37 [2c] on Eccl 7:26).[774] The text focuses on the plundering dimension of brigandage ("where the brigands rob"), but the brigand's use of violence is certainly assumed (especially on analogy to the nations who robbed Jerusalem). Here, the notion is that the Gentile nations despoiled Jerusalem, and thus they shall meet their eschatological fate there. Remarkably, the recompense on the nations is found here in God performing a kind of "crucifixion" on the sinful nations. Another eschatological text in *PRK* suggests that the people of God will crucify those who crucified them.[775]

**(365)** *Ecclesiastes Rabbah* 7.37 [21c] on Eccl 7:26

נפק בההוא ליליא נפק ליסטאה ותקין תזקיטא בתריהון. דין דהוה חכים שביליא ערק ואישתיזב.
ודין לא הוה חכים שביליא איתצייד ואיצטלב. וקרון עלוי לקיש לסטים בכיר לצלובים:

---

[771] See *Mekilta de-Rabbi Shimon bar Yohai* 36.2 in W. DAVID NELSON, Mekhilta de-Rabbi Shimon bar Yohai (Philadelphia: Jewish Publication Society, 2006), 157. For an analysis of this text, with attention to its variations from the *Mekilta* above, cf. CHAPMAN, Crucifixion, 190–191.

[772] Text: BERNARD MANDELBAUM, Pesikta de Rav Kahana: According to an Oxford Manuscript with Variants from all Known Manuscripts and Genizoth Fragments and Parallel Passages with Commentary and Introduction (Second Edition. 2 vols.; New York: Jewish Theological Seminary of America, 1987), 2:453 (lines 19–21).

[773] Cf. STRACK / STEMBERGER / BOCKMUEHL, Introduction, 295.

[774] For these other passages cf. CHAPMAN, Crucifixion, 191–193.

[775] *Pesikta de-Rab Kahana* 9.2; cf. CHAPMAN, Crucifixion, 193 for text and translation.

*Translation.* He [the husband] went out in that night, the brigand went out [i.e., with his gang], but the sergeant arranged [to go out] after them. This one [i.e., the brigand] who recognized the paths fled, and he was saved. But this one [who] did not recognize the paths [i.e., the husband] was caught, and he was crucified. And they applied to him [the proverb], "The latest of the brigands is the first of the crucified."

*Commentary.* This rabbinic commentary is often dated to the early medieval era (sixth–eighth centuries A.D.), so it definitely extends beyond our normal focal period. Yet presumably the aphorism in the passage above ("the latest of the brigands is the first of the crucified"), on which the episode hangs, would have been in previous existence. This text also continues to illustrate the connection between brigandage and crucifixion, with brigandage here entirely focused on monetary gain. In the early context of the parable (not quoted above), a man's wife insists that he join the thieving band of the local brigand since she was jealous of the wealth to be had in such criminal endeavors. However, due to his ignorance of the ways of the brigand, the man is instead caught and crucified.

## 3.7.3 Rebels in Judea

Josephus frequently records instances of Roman use of crucifixion to suppress Jewish rebellion. Such accounts occur before the First Revolt (A.D. 66–73/74), but they are also prominent during that Revolt itself. Many of these narratives indicate immense numbers suspended up on crosses simultaneously, with consequently large death tolls. To the passages below we could add *B. J.* 3.320–321; *Vita* 420 (see Nos. 382, 386 below).

**(366)** Josephus, *Bellum judaicum* 2.75; *Antiquitates judaicae* 17.295

[*B. J.* 2.75] Οὔαρος δὲ κατὰ μοῖραν τῆς στρατιᾶς ἐπὶ τοὺς αἰτίους τοῦ κινήματος ἔπεμψεν περὶ τὴν χώραν, καὶ πολλῶν ἀγομένων τοὺς μὲν ἧττον θορυβώδεις φανέντας ἐφρούρει, τοὺς δὲ αἰτιωτάτους ἀνεσταύρωσεν περὶ δισχιλίους.

*Translation.* And Varus sent around the country a portion of the army against those culpable for the political uproar; and once many had been captured, he kept guard over those who appeared less turbulent, but the most culpable he crucified (approximately two thousand).

[*A. J.* 17.295] Οὖαρος δὲ κατὰ τὴν χώραν πέμψας τοῦ στρατοῦ μέρος ἐπεζήτει τοὺς αἰτίους τῆς ἀποστάσεως. καὶ σημαινομένων τοὺς μὲν ἐκόλασεν ὡς αἰτιωτάτους, εἰσὶ δ' οὓς καὶ ἀφῆκεν· ἐγίνοντο δὲ οἱ διὰ ταύτην τὴν αἰτίαν σταυρωθέντες δισχίλιοι.

*Translation.* And Varus, having sent throughout the country a portion of the army, sought out those culpable for the revolt. And when some were indicated as the most culpable, he punished them; but there were also those whom he released. And those who were crucified on account of this charge were two thousand.

*Commentary.*[776] A substantial series of local Judean insurrections resulted from the Jewish power vacuum in Palestine subsequent to Herod's death in 4 B.C. (*B. J.* 2.39–79; *A. J.* 17.250–298). Sabinus, the Roman procurator in Judea, was overzealous in how he suppressed a local revolt during Pentecost in Jerusalem, and he greedily pilfered the Temple (whose very precincts were also burnt by the Romans during the conflict). The result was even more tumult throughout the land, with various men taking charge of Jewish rebel groups (e.g., Judas, Simon, Athronges, and others). Varus ruled as the Roman governor over Syria (*A. J.* 17.89), and he comes to suppress the revolts (*B. J.* 2.66–79; *A. J.* 17.286–298). After initially staging his troops in Ptolemais (two legions plus horsemen and auxiliaries), Varus marched upon Galilee, Samaria, and Jerusalem. Having secured the major urban centers, he then (above) turns to mopping up the countryside. The results in both accounts display simultaneously Varus' leniency (in guarding or releasing the lesser offenders) and his severity. Josephus indicates that severe treatment was only accorded the most culpable; approximately 2,000 of these face the cross (ἀνεσταύρωσεν in the *War*, σταυρωθέντες in the *Antiquities*). He reports the event without any negative statements against Varus (though earlier he was quite harsh on Sabinus), thus Josephus chose to remain neutral here, or perhaps he even felt the Roman actions necessary. Likely, the immediate relatives and friends of these ragtag Jewish insurrectionists might have felt more sympathy for their gruesome deaths (cf. *As. Mos.* 6:7–9 below).

## (367) Josephus, *Antiquitates judaicae* 20.102

πρὸς τούτοις δὲ καὶ οἱ παῖδες Ἰούδα τοῦ Γαλιλαίου ἀνήχθησαν τοῦ τὸν λαὸν ἀπὸ Ῥωμαίων ἀποστήσαντος Κυρινίου τῆς Ἰουδαίας τιμητεύοντος, ὡς ἐν τοῖς πρὸ τούτων δεδηλώκαμεν, Ἰάκωβος καὶ Σίμων, οὓς ἀνασταυρῶσαι προσέταξεν Ἀλέξανδρος.

---

[776] Text: NIESE, Flavii Josephi Opera, 6:168 (*B. J.* 2.75); 4:126 (*A. J.* 17.295).

*Translation.* And besides these things, the sons of Judas the Galilean (which man caused the people to revolt from the Romans when Quirinius was performing the census of Judea, as we have made clear in the chapters before these) were also brought up [for trial] – namely James and Simon, whom Alexander ordered to be crucified.

*Commentary.*[777] Tiberius Alexander was procurator of Judea (c. A.D. 46–48). He came from an eminent and wealthy Jewish family of Alexandria (*A. J.* 20.100). However, Josephus states that Alexander "did not remain in the customs of his fathers" (τοῖς γὰρ πατρίοις οὐκ ἐνέμεινεν οὗτος ἔθεσιν) and that his own father surpassed him in godliness (20.101). He was also a nephew of Philo. Josephus earlier had asserted that Judas the Galilean was the author of the "fourth philosophy" of Zealots, who were like the Pharisees except for their desire for liberty through revolt (*A. J.* 18.9, 23–25). It appears his sons also were disposed to this philosophy. Alexander, despite his Jewish roots, ordered James and Simon to be stationed up on the cross (ἀνασταυρῶσαι).

**(368)** Josephus, *Bellum judaicum* 2.241; *Antiquitates judaicae* 20.129

[*B. J.* 2.241] Κουαδρᾶτος δὲ τότε μὲν ἑκατέρους ὑπερτίθεται φήσας, ἐπειδὰν εἰς τοὺς τόπους παραγένηται, διερευνήσειν ἕκαστα, αὖθις δὲ παρελθὼν εἰς Καισάρειαν τοὺς ὑπὸ Κουμανοῦ ζωγρηθέντας ἀνεσταύρωσεν πάντας.

*Translation.* And Quadratus then deferred either party by saying that whenever he came to these locales, he would examine each matter; and after arriving at Caesarea, he crucified all those captured alive by Cumanus.

[*A. J.* 20.129] μετ' οὐ πολὺν δὲ χρόνον ὁ Κουαδρᾶτος ἧκεν εἰς Σαμάρειαν, ἔνθα διακούσας αἰτίους τῆς ταραχῆς ὑπέλαβε γεγονέναι τοὺς Σαμαρεῖς. Σαμαρέων δὲ καὶ Ἰουδαίων οὕστινας νεωτερίσαντας ἔμαθεν ἀνεσταύρωσεν οὓς Κουμανὸς ἔλαβεν αἰχμαλώτους.

*Translation.* And not much later, Quadratus came into Samaria, where after hearing the trial, he suspected those culpable of the tumult to have been the Samaritans. And he crucified those of the Samaritans and Judeans whom he learned had attempted revolution and whom Cumanus had taken captive.

*Commentary.*[778] Cumanus was the procurator of Judea subsequent to Tiberius Alexander. Josephus records that under Cumanus, the troubles began and the ruin of the Jews ensued (*B. J.* 2.223; ἐφ' οὗ θόρυβοί τε ἤρξαντο καὶ φθορὰ πάλιν Ἰουδαίων ἐγένετο). Among the many causes for popular disturbance, the Samaritans of the village Geman/Ginae slayed a Galilean Jew on pilgrim-

---

[777] Text: NIESE, Flavii Josephi Opera, 4:293.
[778] Text: NIESE, Flavii Josephi Opera, 6:200 (*B. J.* 2.241); 4:298 (*A. J.* 20.129).

age to Jerusalem (*B. J.* 2.232; or even "many" pilgrim Jews in *A. J.* 20.118). The Galileans subsequently engaged in battle with the Samaritans, but Cumanus was slow to react to the Jewish leadership, who had requested his intervention. Instead, a Jewish multitude from the festival in Jerusalem joined the onslaught, destroying Samaritan towns and slaughtering all their inhabitants under the leadership of Eleazar son of Dineus. Cumanus finally takes troops from Caesarea to suppress Eleazar's followers, while the Jerusalem leadership successfully begs their countrymen to desist. Though clearly antagonistic toward the Samaritans, Josephus also claims that the Jewish instigators (for whom he has little sympathy) were motivated by a mixture of revenge, revolutionary action, and self-seeking brigandage (e.g., *B. J.* 2.235, 238). Ultimately, the Samaritans and Jews both send delegations to Quadratus, governor of Syria, who decides (in addition to the text above): to further slay eighteen Jewish instigators (according to *B. J.* 2.242; only five are mentioned in *A. J.* 20.130), to send the illustrious Samaritan and Jewish leaders (including the Jewish high priests) before Caesar, and to command that Cumanus account for his actions before Caesar as well.

The two texts above provide essentially the same story arc, resulting in the crucifixion of the culprits caught by Cumanus (note ἀνεσταύρωσεν in both texts). However, there are differences in detail, such as the reference to Caesarea in the *War*. Most of these differences in the texts above seem to play to the favor of the Jews in the *Antiquities*. For example, in the *Antiquities* Quadratus suspects the Samaritans to be culpable, and Josephus is at pains to note both Jews and Samaritans were crucified. Similar observations of greater favoritism toward the Jewish story in the *Antiquities* can be made in the surrounding context: In *Antiquities* Josephus more directly asserts that Cumanus was bribed by the Samaritans (*A. J.* 20.119, 127), the numbers initially slain by the Samaritans in Geman/Ginae are much higher in *Antiquities* (contrast *A. J.* 20.118 with *B. J.* 2.232), and the subsequent trial of Jewish instigators in *Antiquities* is limited to five, with only one leading Jewish individual named, as if there were really only a few revolutionaries that set off the others (*A. J.* 20.130–131). Nevertheless, in both accounts the resulting decision of Claudius in Rome, with some influence from Agrippa, came hard against the Samaritans and against Cumanus (*B. J.* 2.245–246; *A. J.* 20.134–136).

Josephus apparently presumes that Quadratus acted justly in meting out the various punishments. Quadratus certainly followed typical Roman provincial procedure in directing the leaders of the Jewish and Samaritan communities (as well as the failed Roman official, Cumanus) to go before Caesar. It is further striking that, in addition to the crucified individuals mentioned above, the key Jewish leaders, who were subsequently captured and judged, were apparently not crucified but beheaded (esp. πελέκει διεχειρίσατο in *B. J.* 2.242, though only ἀνελεῖν in *A. J.* 20.130–131). This could plausibly be accounted for by their higher social status; note that Doëtus is described as "one of the chief of the Jews" (τῶν Ἰουδαίων τις πρῶτος) in *A. J.* 20.130. Thus, Quadratus appears in all places here to follow typical Roman procedure. Josephus, for his part, does not censure Quadratus, but instead reserves his invective for the Samaritans, for the Jewish brigand-rebels, and for Cumanus.

**(369)** Josephus, *Bellum judaicum* 2.306–308

φυγὴ δ᾽ ἦν ἐκ τῶν στενωπῶν καὶ φόνος τῶν καταλαμβανομένων, τρόπος τε ἁρπαγῆς οὐδεὶς παρελείπετο, καὶ πολλοὺς τῶν μετρίων συλλαβόντες ἐπὶ τὸν Φλῶρον ἀνῆγον· οὓς μάστιξιν προαικισάμενος ἀνεσταύρωσεν. [307] ὁ δὲ σύμπας τῶν ἐκείνης ἀπολομένων τῆς ἡμέρας ἀριθμὸς σὺν γυναιξὶν καὶ τέκνοις, οὐδὲ γὰρ νηπίων ἀπέσχοντο, περὶ τριάκοντα καὶ ἑξακοσίους συνήχθη. [308] βαρυτέραν τε ἐποίει τὴν συμφορὰν τὸ καινὸν τῆς Ῥωμαίων ὠμότητος· ὃ γὰρ μηδεὶς πρότερον τότε Φλῶρος ἐτόλμησεν, ἄνδρας ἱππικοῦ τάγματος μαστιγῶσαί τε πρὸ τοῦ βήματος καὶ σταυρῷ προσηλῶσαι, ὧν εἰ καὶ τὸ γένος Ἰουδαίων ἀλλὰ γοῦν τὸ ἀξίωμα Ῥωμαϊκὸν ἦν.

*Translation.* And there was a flight out of the narrow lanes and there was murder of those who had been seized, and no manner of pillaging was neglected; and many of the moderate inhabitants, after being captured, were led up to Florus, whom he first maltreated with the scourge, [then] he crucified. [307] And the whole number of those killed during that day, together with women and children (for neither did they refrain from the infants), came together to about 630. [308] And the novelty of the Roman savagery performed a very oppressive misfortune, concerning which no one before Florus had dared at that time: men of the status of *equites* were scourged before the tribunal and nailed to a cross, whom even if they were of the Jewish race, yet they still at least possessed Roman rank.

*Commentary.*[779] Josephus repeatedly recounts how the Roman governors, often for sake of their own pockets, stoked the antagonism of the Jewish populace. Josephus records no good to come of Florus' reign, and he speaks of Florus as the worst of the lot of Roman procurators in Palestine (see esp. *B. J.* 2.277–279; *A. J.* 20.252–258). Among other matters, Florus refuses to hear the complaint of the Jews of Caesarea against the pagan citizens who had been taunting them (*B. J.* 2.289–292); later the First Revolt will begin in Caesarea due to just such tensions. In this context, Florus has made attempts to remove seventeen talents from the Temple treasury in Jerusalem (*B. J.* 2.293), causing a clamor in the city and motivating some to mock Florus as a beggar. Florus takes personal offense, and holds a tribunal at the palace. The high priests and city leaders come before him and beseech him not to seek the mockers (*B. J.*

---

[779] Text: NIESE, *Flavii Josephi Opera*, 6:212–213. One manuscript reads ἐσταύρωσεν for ἀνεσταύρωσεν.

2.301–304). Instead of following the leaders' advice, Florus directs the soldiers to plunder the upper market and to slay the bystanders, which they accomplish with fervor, even breaking into homes (*B. J.* 2.305).

The passage above then continues to recount the atrocities. The number of those dead varies in the manuscripts, with some reading τρισχιλίους in place of τριάκοντα (thus totaling 3600 rather than 630).[780] Crucifixion is mentioned twice; both times scourging precedes it, and in both places crucifixion is the culmination of Florus' outrages. The terminology implies that these people were "nailed" to such a cross (σταυρῷ προσηλῶσαι), and the text likely presumes this was the mode of death. Notably, Josephus focuses on the cruelties against the many "moderate inhabitants" (πολλοὺς τῶν μετρίων). This both displays Florus' excess and also leads into Josephus' distinction between the moderate faction in Judea (who tended to oppose the First Revolt) and those who fanned the flames of revolution. Florus is attacking the very people who could stem the tide against revolt. Further, Josephus carefully records that women, children, and (even) infants were victims.

Yet Josephus pours his greatest umbrage into his complaint that Florus' crucified Jewish men of Roman equestrian rank. This well reminds us of Cicero's objections to the actions of Verres – Roman citizens are not to face the cross, especially not the highest ranks of citizens (see above 3.6.1). This could also be personal for Josephus, since he likely counted himself as one with such people (i.e., moderate Jews of the elite ranks; cf. *Vita* 1–7, 414–430). Here, he shrewdly observes that Florus' actions were "novel" (καινὸν) and that no one had ever dared the like before (ὃ γὰρ μηδεὶς πρότερον τότε Φλῶρος ἐτόλμησεν). Josephus clearly seeks to win his readership to the view that Florus, due to his cruel excesses and lust for loot, was extremely culpable in instigating further troubles. Finally, in this narrative Josephus certainly depicts the Jewish victims of the cross as innocent sufferers.

### (370) Josephus, *Bellum judaicum* 5.289

συνέβη δ᾽ ἐν ταύτῃ τῇ μάχῃ καὶ ζωγρηθῆναί τινα τῶν Ἰουδαίων, ὃν ὁ Τίτος ἀνασταυρῶσαι πρὸ τοῦ τείχους ἐκέλευσεν, εἴ τι πρὸς τὴν ὄψιν ἐνδοῖεν οἱ λοιποὶ καταπλαγέντες.

*Translation.* And during this battle it also came to pass that a certain one of the Jews was captured alive, whom Titus commanded to be crucified before the wall, [in case] if any of the remaining inhabitants, because they were panic-stricken by the sight, might surrender.

---

[780] Text (and translation) follows NIESE (along with the majority of Greek manuscripts and the Latin tradition) in reading τριάκοντα. THACKERAY follows the minority (three manuscripts) in reading τρισχιλίους and translating the numbers as "three thousand six hundred."

*Commentary.*[781] During the Roman siege of Jerusalem, the Roman general Titus has managed to surround the city, and he has set siege engines to work at destroying Jerusalem's walls (*B. J.* 5.275–277). The Jews boldly sally forth and attack those guarding the siege engines outside the city. Eventually, Titus himself is forced to assist his troops with horsemen, managing to kill a dozen Jewish leaders and to force the Jews back into the city (5.287–288). The account above follows. One theme in Josephus involves Roman military leader crucifying one or more Jewish revolutionaries before a city in hopes of compelling the citizens in that besieged city to recognize their fate and to surrender the city (cf. 3.321; 5.450; see Nos. 371, 382). Sometimes this works for the Romans (7.202–203; No. 370), though it does not here.

**(371)** Josephus, *Bellum judaicum* 5.449–451

λαμβανόμενοι δὲ κατ᾽ ἀνάγκην ἠμύνοντο, καὶ μετὰ μάχην ἱκετεύειν ἄωρον ἐδόκει. μαστιγούμενοι δὴ καὶ προβασανιζόμενοι τοῦ θανάτου πᾶσαν αἰκίαν ἀνεσταυροῦντο τοῦ τείχους ἀντικρύ. ⁴⁵⁰ Τίτῳ μὲν οὖν οἰκτρὸν τὸ πάθος κατεφαίνετο πεντακοσίων ἑκάστης ἡμέρας ἔστι δὲ ὅτε καὶ πλειόνων ἁλισκομένων, οὔτε δὲ τοὺς βίᾳ ληφθέντας ἀφεῖναι ἀσφαλὲς καὶ φυλάττειν τοσούτους φρουρὰν τῶν φυλαξόντων ἑώρα· τό γε μὴν πλέον οὐκ ἐκώλυεν τάχ᾽ ἂν ἐνδοῦναι πρὸς τὴν ὄψιν ἐλπίσας αὐτούς, εἰ μὴ παραδοῖεν, ὅμοια πεισομένους. ⁴⁵¹ προσήλουν δὲ οἱ στρατιῶται δι᾽ ὀργὴν καὶ μῖσος τοὺς ἁλόντας ἄλλον ἄλλῳ σχήματι πρὸς χλεύην, καὶ διὰ τὸ πλῆθος χώρα τε ἐνέλειπε τοῖς σταυροῖς καὶ σταυροὶ τοῖς σώμασιν.

*Translation.* And as they were being captured, by necessity they defended themselves. And after a battle it seemed ill-timed to supplicate [for their lives]. They were indeed scourged and tortured prior to death with every torment, and then they were crucified opposite the wall. ⁴⁵⁰ Thus on the one hand their pitiable suffering was plain to Titus, as there were then more than five hundred seized each day, but neither did it appear secure to free those who had been captured by force, and to guard so many appeared a prison for those who would keep guard; indeed surely the greater [reason] he did not cease was that [Titus] hoped [those in the city] might quickly surrender in response to the sight, lest they be handed over, suffering a similar fate. ⁴⁵¹ The soldiers, on account of anger and hatred, for a joke nailed in various forms those who had been captured; and because of the multitude, both the space was lacking for the crosses and crosses were lacking for the bodies.

*Commentary.*[782] In one of the most vivid accounts during Titus' siege of Jerusalem, he has commanded his soldiers to set ambushes all around the city in

---

[781] Text: NIESE, Flavii Josephi Opera, 6:474.
[782] Text: NIESE, Flavii Josephi Opera, 6:496.

order to capture the starving inhabitants who leave the city to search for food (*B. J.* 5.446). Josephus claims that most of these people were the poor of the city, who felt compelled to remain with the rebels for fear of what would happen to their relatives should they attempt to flee (5.447–448). The passage above then depicts their plight. Throughout they are treated as innocent sufferers of the cross.

Josephus is careful to balance his call to pity these victims, with his desire to portray Titus in the best possible light. Thus he invites us into Titus' decision matrix. Though not without sympathy for the sufferers, Titus had three good reasons for continuing to capture, torture and execute them: the peril of releasing combatants, the difficulty of committing troops to guard them, and especially his desire to motivate Jewish surrender. Josephus' defense of his Flavian sponsor signals some of Josephus' sensitivities in writing the *Jewish War*, and his discomfort at having to justify these events also serves as an indirect testimony to the veracity of this episode. Josephus was likely present for such events (cf. 5.361–420; 6.96–118).

We have previously encountered in Josephus the idea that crucifixions outside a city could cause the inhabitants to despair and surrender (5.289; cf. 3.321; 7.202–203). The numbers crucified should not go overlooked, with Josephus essentially claiming the total was incalculable, requiring all available wood and space. Torture clearly precedes their death by crucifixion (μαστιγούμενοι δὴ καὶ προβασανιζόμενοι τοῦ θανάτου πᾶσαν αἰκίαν). In section 3.1, we made brief comments concerning the various postures the Roman guards employed in this text. Crucifixion could take many forms, though there may well have been an expected norm that these enraged soldiers were sadistically varying. Josephus wishes the reader to engage with just how cruel this scene must have been. That cruelty he puts squarely on the shoulders of the battle-maddened soldiers. It remains a realistic depiction, and one that displays the potential barbarism of crucifixion in military operations, especially when employed on a massive scale.

## (372) Josephus, *Bellum judaicum* 7.202–203

ὁ μὲν γὰρ προσέταξε καταπηγνύναι σταυρὸν ὡς αὐτίκα κρεμῶν τὸν Ἐλεάζαρον, τοῖς δὲ ἀπὸ τοῦ φρουρίου τοῦτο θεασαμένοις ὀδύνη τε πλείων προσέπεσε, καὶ διωλύγιον ἀνῴμωζον οὐκ ἀνασχετὸν εἶναι τὸ πάθος βοῶντες. [203] ἐνταῦθα δὴ τοίνυν Ἐλεάζαρος ἱκέτευεν αὐτοὺς μήτε αὐτὸν περιιδεῖν ὑπομείναντα θανάτων τὸν οἴκτιστον καὶ σφίσιν αὐτοῖς τὴν σωτηρίαν παρασχεῖν τῇ Ῥωμαίων εἴξαντας ἰσχύι καὶ τύχῃ μετὰ πάντας ἤδη κεχειρωμένους.

*Translation.* For he ordered a cross to be firmly planted, as though he would immediately hang Eleazar; and more distress fell upon those watching this from the citadel, and they wailed loudly, crying out that the calamity was not endurable. [203] Thereupon Eleazar accordingly besought them not to observe him submitting to the most pitiable of deaths and to attend to their own salvation by yielding to the strength and fortune of the Romans, with all others having already been subdued.

*Commentary.*[783] These events occur toward the end of the First Revolt, during the Roman siege of the fortress of Machaerus (east of the Dead Sea). Young Eleazar had fought bravely in defending the fortress (*B. J.* 7.196), but he was captured by the Romans (7.199). Lucilius Bassus, the Roman legate, took the opportunity to have Eleazar stripped naked and scourged before the walls (7.200). This led to such consternation in the fortress that Bassus decided to attempt what Josephus calls a "stratagem" (στρατήγημα in 7.201) in order to increase their dismay and to motivate their surrender of the city. Though Josephus reports a similar stratagem had been employed by Roman generals earlier in the Revolt (3.320–321; 5.450), this is the first time it succeeded (as Josephus himself suggests in 7.204–205). Above, the grief of the impending crucifixion receives vivid depiction. Josephus reports Eleazar's speech as indirect discourse: Eleazar does not wish to be observed in his suffering (likely suggesting that he wants the inhabitants to surrender before the crucifixion begins) and he recommends that the Jewish people seek their own safety by yielding to the Romans. Eleazar's numerous and eminent family within the fortress also sought his release through surrender. Apparently there was disagreement between the factions in the city, for some (after an agreement with Bassus) opened the city to the Romans, while others fought the Romans. Josephus records 1700 slain (7.206–208). Eleazar and his compatriots are eventually set free by Bassus, who honors his agreement (7.209). The text represents the manner of attachment to the cross (σταυρὸν) as a suspension (κρεμῶν); the resulting penalty will eventually cause his death. Indeed, Eleazar calls this "the most pitiable of deaths" (θανάτων τὸν οἴκτιστον).

### 3.7.4 Archaeology and Crucifixion

Key archaeological evidence for crucifixion in the Roman world, and especially in Roman Judea, appeared in 1968 during the excavation of a tomb-complex at Giv'at ha-Mivtar outside ancient Jerusalem. The discovery involves the human remains in the fourth of eight ossuaries found in Tomb 1.[784] Among the bones located in that limestone reburial container was a calcaneum

---

[783] Text: NIESE, Flavii Josephi Opera, 6:596–597. The most notable variant concerns κρεμῶν, which three manuscripts read as κρεμνῶν; κρεμάσων has been suggested (these variations would have no real affect on the meaning).

[784] The original overview was provided by VASSILIOS TZAFERIS, Jewish Tombs at and near Giv'at ha-Mivtar, Jerusalem, IEJ 20 (1970): 18–32.

(heal bone) with a nail still lodged into it. The excavators identified this as evidence of crucifixion. Several controversies have surrounded this find, and thus a brief summary of current scholarship is in order.

The period of ossuary usage in Judea is relatively short, usually considered to be confined to the first century B.C. until the first century A.D., with some scholars narrowing that window; and the pottery in the tomb would concur with a first-century A.D. date. TZAFERIS argues that the reburial must have occurred before the First Jewish Revolt since such reburials would have been difficult during or afterward.[785] This is possible, but one could imagine other scenarios after Jerusalem fell. In any case a first-century date is fairly secure.

The find was originally published in 1970, but the original osteological analysis was necessarily rushed (as they often are) due to Jewish religious sensitivities about leaving bodies unburied. The initial report included a description of the bones by HAAS.[786] He observes that the ossuary contained the bones of the crucified adult male (24–28 years old), along with bones of a child (3–4 years old). The adult stood approximately 167 cm (ca. 5.5 ft), and was healthy, but he showed no evidence of having ever performed "heavy corporeal labour". Haas provided the following analysis (all these items were later disputed): The nail shows evidence of two calcanei (both heels) attached together; the original length of the nail was 17–18 cm, though it later was bent to 11–12 cm; scratches inside the right radius ("on the distal third of the interosseous border") would indicate the arm had also once been nailed to a plank; comminuted (pulverized) right tibia and a broken line in the left tibia and fibula signify blows were applied to break the leg bones in order to hasten death; the man had a cleft palate and asymmetry of the cerebral cranium (plagiocephaly, i.e., his skull was flattened on one side and not evenly shaped, further indicating that his mother was unhealthy during pregnancy); and bones from just the two individuals (adult and child) were present in the ossuary. Undisputed is the evidence of a wooden plaque at the head of the nail (used to press against the heel and keep it from slipping off the nail). The wooden plaque is said by N. HAAS to be from the acacia tree (disputed below), while the wood at the tip of the nail would point to an olive tree serving as the cross. Oil spots on the bones evidenced ritual anointing from the time of reburial.

Based on this evidence, HAAS and his team developed two sketches which have been redrawn here. The first represents the man with his legs in the "open position," but they ultimately rejected this based on their restoration of the talus, navicular, and cuboid bones.[787] Thus the second drawing, also from

---

[785] TZAFERIS, Jewish Tombs, 31. He associates this crucified body with "the census revolt in A.D. 7 or the victim of some occasional crucifixion" in the 1st c. A.D. (before the First Revolt).

[786] NICO HAAS, Anthropological Observations on the Skeletal Remains from Giv'at ha-Mivtar, IEJ 20 (1970): 38–59; the following reference to "heavy corporeal labour" ibid. 55.

[787] HAAS, Observations, 57.

HAAS' publication, portrays the man with legs parallel together and at an angle. They further argue that the feet had not been sufficiently fastened to the cross to bear the weight of the individual, thus it is likely the cross had a "sedecula" or "sedile"; i.e., a small plank used as a seat.

Another stage in the scholarly debate concerned the reading of one of the inscriptions on the exterior of the ossuary.[788] It consists of two lines, and the first line clearly reads יהוחנן (Jehoḥanan). The second line begins with בן ("son") but then continues with characters that are somewhat difficult to discern. NAVEH read it as חגקול and suggested that the writer mistakenly wrote ג in place of ז, thus implying "son of Ezekiel."[789] YADIN made two suggestions over time: In the first he proposed it was a corruption of Αγκολ (a foreign name); in the second he argued that the word actually begins with a ה rather than a ח, and thus the name should be read as a variant on העקול ("the bow-legged").[790] YADIN thus suggested that this was a sarcastic comment on his manner of death (implying a straddled position on the cross). There are many problems with YADIN's proposal: It requires the inscription to be an ironic comment, the ה to be a ח, and the ג to be an unusual phonetic equivalent of ע. KUHN later suggested that the word was the Semitic equivalent of ἀγκύλος ("crooked"), also (like in YADIN) a reference to his manner of death.[791] On the whole it seems best to follow RAHMANI, who believes the best reading of the sloppy inscription is actually חזקיל (being a form of Ezekiel).[792] RAHMANI is followed by J. J. PRICE and H. MISGAV in CIIP No. 50. In this case, his name is "Jehoḥanan son of Ezekiel," and there are no indications of his manner of death to be found in the inscription.

The third drawing represents the view of V. MØLLER-CHRISTENSEN who suggests that a crude rectangular "foot-frame" would have made matters easier for those appending the man to the cross.[793] He otherwise assumed HAAS' analysis of the osteological remains. This article presents little new evidence to suggest this position is more likely. And, should the wood have varied (from acacia to olive) on either side of the nail as in the original report, it seems the "foot-frame" would have been an odd eclectic assortment of local wood.

---

[788] J. J. PRICE and H. MISGAV, in CIIP II/1, 93 (No. 50). Note the helpful photo. The other inscription (i.e., other than the one debated above) consists of a more lightly etched "Jehoḥanan" just above and to the right of the more deeply etched inscription discussed here.

[789] JOSEPH NAVEH, The Ossuary Inscriptions from Giv'at ha-Mivtar, IEJ 20 (1970): 33–37.

[790] YIGAEL YADIN, Epigraphy and Crucifixion, IEJ 23 (1973): 18–22.

[791] HEINZ-WOLFGANG KUHN, Der Gekreuzigte von Giv'at ha-Mivtar: Bilanz einer Entdeckung, in Theologia Crucis – Signum Crucis (FS E. Dinkler; ed. C. Andresen and G. Klein; Tübingen: Mohr Siebeck, 1979), 303–334.

[792] LEVI Y. RAHMANI, A Catalogue of Jewish Ossuaries in the Collections of the State of Israel (Jerusalem: The Israel Antiquities Authority, The Israel Academy of Sciences and Humanities, 1994), 130 (No. 218).

[793] VILHELM MØLLER-CHRISTENSEN, Skeletal Remains from Giv'at ha-Mivtar, IEJ 26 (1976): 35–38.

*Illustration* (Fig. 5. Four possible reconstructions of Jehoḥanan's crucifixion based on osteological analysis (all redrawn by Karis Chapman). *Top left:* HAAS' first drawing, which he later rejected; *Top right:* HAAS' second drawing; *Bottom left:* MØLLER-CHRISTENSEN's "foot-frame" suggestion; *Bottom right:* ZIAS/SEKELES proposal)

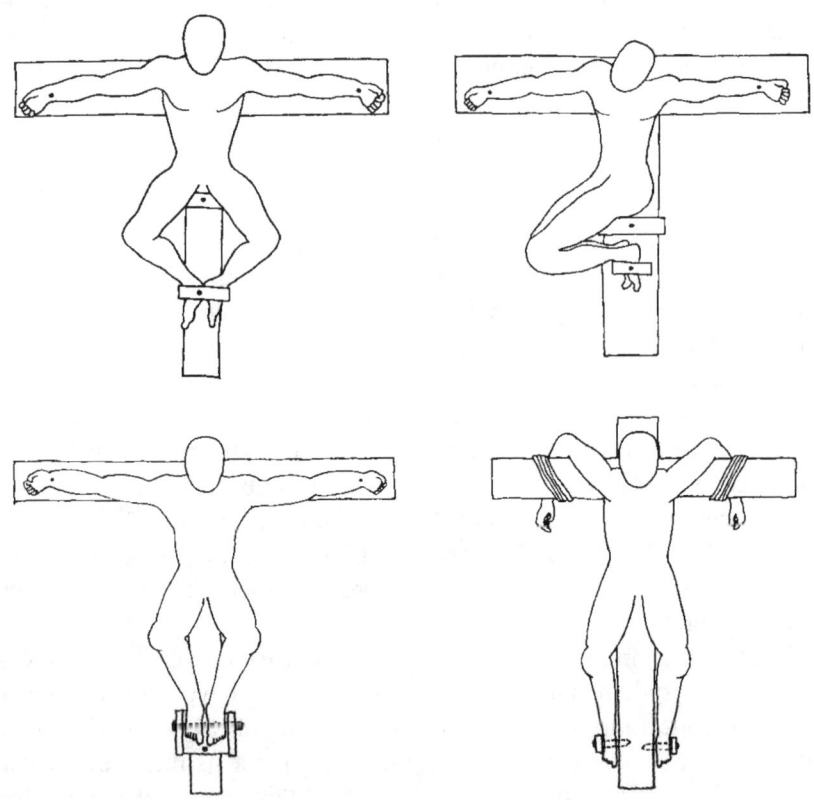

The final drawing represents a complete reassessment by JOSEPH ZIAS and ELIEZER SEKELES of the original analysis.[794] Though they were not able to say this in the article, it appears that at least some of the original bones remained available for scholarly analysis (as opposed to being buried). In fact, a realistic model of the original calcaneum and nail has been on display recently in the Israel Museum, and the actual original is rumored to still be available for analysis. ZIAS and SEKELES argue cogently that only the right calcaneum was attached to the nail, with other bone fragments being "impregnated by iron oxides" and thus coming to be attached by rust after burial. The nail was origi-

---

[794] JOSEPH ZIAS and ELIEZER SEKELES, The Crucified Man from Giv'at ha-Mivtar: A Reappraisal, IEJ 35 (1985): 22–27, plates 5–7. Cf. JOE ZIAS and JAMES H. CHARLESWORTH, Crucifixion: Archaeology, Jesus, and the Dead Sea Scrolls, in Jesus and the Dead Sea Scrolls (ed. J. H. Charlesworth; orig. 1992; repr., New York: Doubleday, 1995), 273–289.

nally 11.5 cm, and hence not long enough to attach both heels to the cross; this is also evident in all drawings and pictures of the calcaneum. The nail must have penetrated the right calcaneum from the right side (lateral as opposed to medial, which was suggested by the second HAAS drawing). The scratch on the right radius evidences common "non-traumatic" signs, so it appears no nails pierced the victim's arms. The breaks in the leg bones (tibiae and fibula) were likely produced after death. They submitted the wooden fragments for botanical analysis, with the conclusion that the wooden plaque is actually olive wood (not acacia), but that the wood at the tip was insufficient to produce a verifiable result. The foot was not amputated in order to facilitate removal before burial. All six dental experts consulted at Johns Hopkins concur that there is no evidence of a cleft palate. And finally, at least one bone from a third adult was reinterred in this ossuary. Based on these conclusions, their drawing (the fourth one in our composite) then represents each heel being affixed to the cross by its own nail (straddling the vertical beam) with the arms attached by cords (since there was no evidence of nails in the arms/hands). This position appears the most reasonable reconstruction yet (especially concerning the feet), though the precise orientation of the arms is essentially mere conjecture. It is hoped that further osteological specialists will be granted access to the data so these findings can be confirmed and evaluated.[795] We should not assume that the posture of this individual crucifixion is illustrative of all crucifixions in Judea in this era, but it does provide us with one very helpful data-point.

Before leaving this archaeological discovery, one might consider the cultural implications that come from a crucifixion victim appearing in an ossuary. Only the wealthier elite could afford an ossuary reburial (or a large family tomb for that matter), and it is reasonable to assume that this ossuary was unearthed in the family tomb of the victim. The inscription appears normal, and the body was reburied with other family members. Thus Jehoḥanan's family granted him the standard burial rites, extending even to an ossuary reburial. Previously it has been observed that this "suggests that the body of the crucified was shown a degree of sympathy, or at least non-abhorrence."[796]

### 3.7.5 Rabbinic Law and Roman Crucifixion

The rabbis repeatedly mention crucifixion in their halakic discussions. On a few occasions the cross serves to provide an extreme case for debating various

---

[795] In his popular book, SHIMON GIBSON, who is in a position to know, mentions that ISRAEL HERSHKOVITZ has performed medical scans on the calcaneum with these indicating "that the actual piecing together and gluing of the shattered heel bone (*calcaneum*) by HAAS in 1968 may have been incorrect"; cf. GIBSON, Final Days, 113.

[796] CHAPMAN, Crucifixion, 89.

issues of rabbinic law. Such passages do not mention why the person is affixed to the cross, instead they merely address issues that would arise from such crucifixions. Intriguingly, each of these passages clearly assumes the victim is alive on the cross, something that does not accord with rabbinic *post mortem* suspension practices, therefore indicating that these represent actions of the Roman government. The citizen is also warned away from magical use of nails from the cross. Elsewhere, the effects of crucifixion on Jewish burial law will be discussed (concerning *Semaḥot* 2.11 [44b]; see section 3.8). All these passages help undergird lexical arguments for this Hebrew/Aramaic vocabulary (צלב and cognates) being employed in Jewish writings to depict prolonged penal suspension of a living person upon a cross (i.e., crucifixion).[797] They likely arise from memories of Roman crucifixions in the vicinity of Palestine.

## (373) *m. Ohalot* 3:5

איזהו דם תבוסה. צלוב שדמו שותת ונמצא תחתיו רביעית דם. טמא. אבל המת שדמו מנטף
ונמצא תחתיו רביעית דם טהור. רבי יהודה אומר לא כי. אלא השותת. טהור. והמנטף. טמא.

*Translation.* What counts as 'mixed blood'? [Concerning] one who was crucified, whose blood flows out, and under whom was found a quarter [of a *log*] of blood, [that blood] is unclean. But [concerning] the corpse, whose blood drips, and under whom was found a quarter [of a *log*] of blood, [that blood] is clean. Rabbi Judah says: It is not so, but [the blood] that flows out is clean, and [the blood] that drips is unclean.

*Commentary.* The context here concerns how "mixed blood" from a dead person renders the blood of a living person unclean. The dead are ritually unclean in Levitical law, and thus their blood is too. But if a person is still living, then that blood is clean. Should a person on the cross still be dripping blood, then each drip can be understood as a discrete event, thus not enough to render everything else unclean (cf. *t. Ohal.* 4:11). Or, following R. Judah's opinion here, flowing blood shows that person is still alive, and thus that blood is still deemed to be living. Later versions of this same account attribute Judah's position here to R. Simeon, claiming instead that Judah argued that the final drop of death may have remained on the cross, so dripping blood beneath a cross is not unclean (*t. Ohal.* 4:11; *b. Nid.* 71b). The rabbis will also discuss the proportion necessary of dead blood to living that is required to invoke the laws of uncleanness. A "log" (לוג) is the equivalent of the contents of six eggs, so a quarter-log (as mentioned above) would be just under two-eggs-full in amount (note this is the same quantity of dead blood that renders a house unclean). One certain conclusion from this text is that a crucified person (צלוב)

---

[797] These traditions have been studied in more detail in CHAPMAN, Crucifixion, 21, 182–184, 195–202.

died a prolonged and bloody death on the cross. Intriguingly, their blood is not in any way cursed or particularly defiling; such blood rather is accorded the same legal conditions as that of any other person.

## (374) *t. Giṭṭin* 7[5]:1

היה צלוב או מגוייד ורמז ואמ' כתובו גט לאשתו כותבין ונותנין כל זמן בו נשמה.

*Translation.* [If] there was one being crucified or bleeding to death, and he gestures and asks him to write a writ of divorce for his wife. They write and give [it], as long as breath is in him.

*Commentary.*[798] This tractate concerns divorce law. For a divorce to be enacted, a man must deliver a writ of divorce (גט) to his wife. In this case, it would be a potentially merciful act for her to be divorced from him prior to his death. The legal question concerns how much communication is required in order for such a writ to be considered valid. Two manuscripts do not even mention his need to speak, but the Zuckermandel edition favors the textual tradition that (by including ואמ' after ורמז) requires him to both signal and speak for the writ of divorce, and this is supported in the talmudic tradition (e.g., *b. Giṭ.* 70b).[799] In any case, based on the ability of the victim to communicate, clearly this discussion assumes that such victims would suffer their actual death on the cross. Even on the cross, they possess the legal right to pursue a divorce.

## (375) *m. Yebamoth* 16:3

אין מעידין אלא עד שתצא נפשו, ואפילו ראוהו מגויד, וצלוב, והחיה אוכלת בו.

*Translation.* They do not witness [his death] except until his soul departs, even if they saw him bleeding to death, and being crucified, and the wild beast eating him.

*Commentary.* In order for a woman to remarry, the court must have a high degree of certainty concerning her husband's death. This passage indicates circumstances where the husband could still potentially live after the eyewitnesses depart. The cross is thus a means of execution. One might wonder: How is it possible to survive the cross? One suggestion was made in the later

---

[798] Text: ZUCKERMANDEL, Tosephta, 330.

[799] These same two manuscripts read "and" in place of "or" to arrive at "crucified and bleeding." The ZUCKERMANDEL edition and the talmudic traditions read "or" instead, thus likely implying two different forms of death were imagined (*y. Giṭ.* 7:1 [48c]; *b. Giṭ.* 70b): crucifixion or bleeding to death. Were the variant "and" to be accepted (perhaps as the more difficult reading since it varies from the talmudic tradition), then the Tosefta text would portray the person bleeding while on the cross.

rabbinic commentary in the Gemara on this passage in the Palestinian Talmud: "And [concerning] he who is crucified on the cross, I say the matron came upon him and redeemed him" (*y. Yeb.* 16:3). Thus his wife would have paid money for his early release. Stories of people surviving the cross are quite rare (cf. Josephus, *Vita* 420–421).

**(376)** *m. Šabbat* 6:10

יוצאין בביצת החרגול ובשן של שועל ובמסמר הצלוב משו' רפואה. דברי ר' יוסי ור' מאיר
אומר אף בחול אסור משום דרכי האמורי.

*Translation.* They may go out [on the Sabbath] with the egg of a ḥargol [a kind of locust], and with a tooth of a fox, and with the nail of the cross for the sake of healing – so says Rabbi Yose. But Rabbi Meir says even in an ordinary day it is forbidden, because of the "ways of the Amorite."

*Commentary.*[800] Here Akiba's most famed students (R. Yose b. Ḥalafta and R. Meir) debate which magical charms are permissible for healing (and thus can be carried on the Sabbath). Yose permits the use of the particular items listed above; Meir rejects them. The term "ways of the Amorite" is technical vocabulary for forbidden pagan practices of sorcery. Note that the "nail of the cross" is one such magical charm that was in use in antiquity. According to the various talmudic interpretations of this Mishnah, the crucifixion nail combats an inflammation (*b. Šabb.* 67a) or is useful for healing a spider's bite (*y. Šabb.* 6:9 [8c]). A later text from the Cairo Genizah (T-S Arabic 44.44 [2/17–20]) surprisingly suggests that such a nail be used to produce love.[801] Pliny the Elder (*Nat. hist.* 28.11.46) notes that some people use crucifixion nails to battle malaria. Lucan (*Bell. civ.* 6.543–549) knows of witches who gather parts of the cross for their witchcraft. And Lucian (*Philops.* 17) speaks of the protective qualities of a ring made from a cross.

*3.7.6 Innocents, Heroes and Martyrs*

The Jewish people at times encountered substantial oppression while under Seleucid and Roman rule. Below are found some key accounts that mention

---

[800] The manuscripts vary concerning the name of the rabbis. The text above follows ABRAHAM GOLDBERG, Commentary to the Mishna Shabbat: Critically Edited and Provided with Introduction, Commentary and Notes (Jerusalem, 1976); compared with WILHELM NOWACK, Schabbat (Sabbat) (Die Mischna II/1; Gießen: Töpelmann, 1924), 64–66.

[801] JOSEPH NAVEH and SHAUL SHAKED, Magic Spells and Formulae: Aramaic Incantations of Late Antiquity (Jerusalem: Magnes, 1993), 220–22 (No. 23); CHAPMAN, Crucifixion, 183.

innocent Jewish sufferers of the cross. At times, their plight is portrayed in more heroic terms, even as martyrdoms. Such themes parallel in some measure the innocents, heroes, and martyrs in Roman and Christian traditions (see sections 3.6.9–10). Of course, while the Jewish tradition remembers these events as unduly harsh, the governors of the land may have had an entirely different perspective. Among other material that might also have bearing on this theme (section 3.5) we observed rabbinic traditions about the heroic crucifixion of Jose b. Joezer (*Ber. Rab.* 65.22; cf. *Midrash Tehillim* on Psalm 11:7).

**(377)** Josephus, *Antiquitates judaicae* 12.255–256

καὶ πολλοὶ μὲν τῶν Ἰουδαίων οἱ μὲν ἑκοντὶ οἱ δὲ καὶ δι' εὐλάβειαν τῆς ἐπηγγελμένης τιμωρίας κατηκολούθουν οἷς ὁ βασιλεὺς διετέτακτο, οἱ δὲ δοκιμώτατοι καὶ τὰς ψυχὰς εὐγενεῖς οὐκ ἐφρόντισαν αὐτοῦ, τῶν δὲ πατρίων ἐθῶν πλείονα λόγον ἔσχον ἢ τῆς τιμωρίας, ἣν οὐ πειθομένοις ἠπείλησεν αὐτοῖς, καὶ διὰ τοῦτο κατὰ πᾶσαν ἡμέραν αἰκιζόμενοι καὶ πικρὰς βασάνους ὑπομένοντες ἀπέθνησκον. ²⁵⁶ καὶ γὰρ μαστιγούμενοι καὶ τὰ σώματα λυμαινόμενοι ζῶντες ἔτι καὶ ἐμπνέοντες ἀνεσταυροῦντο, τὰς δὲ γυναῖκας καὶ τοὺς παῖδας αὐτῶν, οὓς περιέτεμνον παρὰ τὴν τοῦ βασιλέως προαίρεσιν, ἀπῆγχον ἐκ τῶν τραχήλων αὐτοὺς τῶν ἀνεσταυρωμένων γονέων ἀπαρτῶντες. ἠφανίζετο δ' εἴ που βίβλος εὑρεθείη ἱερὰ καὶ νόμος, καὶ παρ' οἷς εὑρέθη καὶ αὐτοὶ κακοὶ κακῶς ἀπώλλυντο.

*Translation.* And many of the Jews – some willingly, others on account of timidity concerning the announced punishments – complied with those things the king ordained. But the most esteemed and the noble of soul did not give heed to it, and they held the word of their ancestral customs to be greater than the punishment, which he threatened those who did not obey. And on account of this, being tortured every day and enduring bitter torments, they died. ²⁵⁶ For, also being flogged and their bodies being maltreated, and while they were still living and breathing, they were crucified. And [Antiochus' troops] strangled their wives and their sons, whom they had circumcised against the policy of the king, hanging them up from the necks of their crucified parents. And wherever a holy book and the Law was found, it was destroyed; and also those same wretches with whom [the book] was found were wretchedly killed.

*Commentary.*[802] This is Josephus' most poignant description of the Maccabean martyrs. Though writing some 250 years after the event, he most often appears to follow the more restrained account represented in 1 Macc 1:20–64, though other sources may also have informed his writing here.[803] Other Greek

---

[802] Text: NIESE, *Flavii Josephi Opera*, 3:115–116. One manuscript adds καὶ πάντα δεινὰ καρτερήσαντες before ζῶντες in 2.256 (this reading is rightly considered improbable).

[803] E.g., Nicolaus of Damascus, Jason of Cyrene, and the *Assumption of Moses*.

and Roman authors, contemporary to the time of Josephus, also depict Antiochus' opposition to Jewish religion.[804] According to Josephus, Antiochus IV Epiphanes captured Jerusalem by treachery, plundered the Temple, pillaged the city, carried away a myriad of captives, burnt portions of the city, and built a citadel in its midst (*A. J.* 12.248–251).[805] Then he left a garrison of troops, who were allied with the strongly Hellenistic faction of Jews (whom Josephus styles as wicked and impious). Antiochus built a pagan altar in the Temple, slaying swine on it (a detail not found elsewhere) and compelling the worship of pagan idols (12.253). Leading into the text above, one learns of Antiochus' command against circumcision and his appointment of overseers to enforce the ordinances (12.254). According to the passage above, some of the Hellenistic faction of Jews "willingly" complied with the decrees, while others did so out of fear. Josephus instead admires those ("the most esteemed and the noble of soul") who endured torture and death rather than give up their ancestral customs.

The description of their gruesome manner of death goes beyond that in 1 Maccabees, especially in the mention of crucifixion. It is worth making a direct comparison to 1 Macc 1:60–61: "And they put to death, according to the ordinance, the women who had circumcised their children; and they hung the infants from their necks, also their households and those (males) who had circumcised them."[806] Although Josephus could well have drawn on other sources (written or oral) concerning these crucifixions (and note this crucifixion tradition may already appear in *As. Mos.* 8 discussed below), it seems plausible that here Josephus is interpreting the statement in Maccabees, inferring that the males were hung up (i.e., crucified) just like the infants.[807]

In any case, these deaths are clearly depicted as an *ante mortem* use of the cross since the victims are "still living and breathing" (ζῶντες ἔτι καὶ ἐμπνέοντες) as they are affixed to the device.[808] As is common in crucifixion accounts, the cross is preceded by flogging and a variety of tortures. Thus we have a remarkable Jewish view of heroes (even martyrs) enduring the cross.

---

[804] Note FERGUS MILLAR, The Background of the Maccabean Revolution: Reflections on Martin Hengel's Judaism and Hellenism, JJS 29 (1978): 1–21, 12–17. Cf. Diodorus Siculus, *Bib. hist.* 31.18a.1; 34/35.1.1–5; Tacitus, *Hist.* 5.8.2; Josephus, *C. Ap.* 2.84.

[805] Antiochus' motives are discussed in SCHÜRER, History, 1:150–156; OTTO MØRKHOLM, Antiochus IV of Syria (Classica et mediaevalia - Dissertationes 8; Copenhagen: Gyldendalske, 1966), 143–148.

[806] LXX: καὶ τὰς γυναῖκας τὰς περιτετμηκυίας τὰ τέκνα αὐτῶν ἐθανάτωσαν κατὰ τὸ πρόσταγμα [61] καὶ ἐκρέμασαν τὰ βρέφη ἐκ τῶν τραχήλων αὐτῶν καὶ τοὺς οἴκους αὐτῶν καὶ τοὺς περιτετμηκότας αὐτούς.

[807] For further discussion of this issue see CHAPMAN, Crucifixion, 48–49. Note JONATHAN A. GOLDSTEIN, I Maccabees (AB 41; Garden City: Doubleday, 1976), 227.

[808] SAMUELSSON, Crucifixion, 107–108 wisely contrasts the reference to ἀνεσταυροῦντο with the execution by hanging that is applied to the children in ἀπῆγχον ... ἀπαρτῶντες.

**(378)** *Assumption of Moses* 6.7–9

Et <p>roducit natos <su>cc?dentes sibi; breviora tempora do<mi>nabunt. [8] In par<t>es eorum chortis venient et occidentes rex potens qui expugnabit eos [9] et ducet captivos, et partem aedis ipsorum igni incendit, aliquos crucifigit circa coloniam eorum.

*Translation.* And he [the petulant king] will bring forth children who will succeed him. They will rule for shorter periods. [8] Cohorts will come into their territory, and a mighty king from the West, who will defeat them, [9] and lead them off in chains. And he will burn part of their Temple with fire, some he will crucify near their city.

*Commentary.*[809] The *Assumption of Moses* represents (from the position of Moses as prophet) an apocalyptic unveiling of key aspects of Jewish history up to the time of the author and then projecting into the future. The structure of the book is debated, but just prior to this passage there is a fairly clear reference to Herod the Great (the petulant king who ruled for 34 years and whose children succeeded him). This passage then should be compared to the events under Varus (see No. 366 concerning Josephus *B. J.* 2.75 and *A. J.* 17.295), including the partial burning of the Temple precincts and the mass crucifixion around the outside of the city (*aliquos crucifigit circa coloniam eorum*). It is thus likely that the author is writing subsequent to these events. Since he does not mention a later (and complete) destruction of the Temple, many have argued for a pre–70 date to the book. Indeed, Tromp dates the book to shortly after Varus' governorship (thus early first century A.D.). The mention of only some (*aliquos*) crucified, even while Josephus put the number in the thousands during Varus' actions, may play into the way the author escalates the events through to the severe era depicted in chapter 8.

**(379)** *Assumption of Moses* 8.1–5

Et <ci>ta <ad>veniet in eos ultio et ira quae talis non fuit in illis a saeculo usque ad illum tempus in quo suscitavit illis regem regum terrae et potestatem a potentia magna, qui confitentes circumcisionem in cruce suspendit. [2] Nam necantes torquebit, et tradi[di]t duci vinctos in custodiam, [3] et uxores eorum

---

[809] Text and translation from JOHANNES TROMP, The Assumption of Moses. A Critical Edition with Commentary (SVTP 10; Leiden: Brill, 1993), 14–17. The text of *Assumption of Moses* is dependent on a single Latin manuscript, which is not thought to be wholly accurate. The angle brackets above include conjectured additions by TROMP, while square brackets indicate text he believes should be deleted. TROMP conjectures *do<mi>nabunt* for *donarent*. And the readings *par<t>es, chortis, qui,* and *ducet* are all conjectured emendations (for *pares, mortis, quia,* and *ducent* respectively), which TROMP adopts from previous editors.

di[i]sdonabuntur gentibus. Et filii eorum pueri secabuntur a medicis [pueri] inducere acrobis<ti>am illis. [4] Nam illi in eis punientur in tormentis et igne et ferro, et cogentur palam bajulare idola eorum, inquinata quomodo sunt pariter contin<g>entibus ea. [5] Et a torquentibus illos pariter cogentur intrare in abditum locum eorum, et cogentur stimulis blasfemare verbum contumeliose. Novissime post haec et leges quod habebunt supra altarium suum.

*Translation.* And suddenly revenge and wrath will come over them, such as there will never have been over them since eternity until that time, in which he will raise for them the king of the kings of the earth, and a power with great might, who will hang on the cross those who confess circumcision, [2] but who will torture those who deny it. And he will lead them chained into captivity, [3] and their wives will be divided among the gentiles, and their sons will be operated on as children by physicians in order to put on them a foreskin. [4] But they will be punished by torments, and with fire and sword, and they will be forced to carry publicly their idols, that are defiled, just like those who touch them. [5] And they will also be forced by those who torture them to enter into their hidden place, and they will be forced with goads to disgracefully blaspheme the word. Finally, after these things (*sc.* they will be forced to blaspheme) also the laws through the things they will have upon their altar.

*Commentary.*[810] The most striking aspects of this passage involves how well it mimics the sufferings of the Maccabean martyrs during the time of Antiochus IV Epiphanes, especially as illustrated above by Josephus (*A. J.* 12.255–256). Note especially that the "king of the kings of the earth" (a very Persian/Seleucid sounding title) opposes Jewish circumcision, promotes use of idols, and requires blasphemy of the Law. Yet if *As. Mos.* 6:7–9 represents the era of Varus (and also 6:1–7 alludes to Herod the Great), then these events of chapter 8 should rightly precede those of chapter 6. Some modern scholars have suggested a transpositional error in the manuscripts or a clumsy interpolation of chapters 5 and 6 into the pre-existing document.[811] However, it seems more likely that the order represents the author's intent.[812] As the original reader moves into chapter 8 (or possibly chapter 7), one moves beyond the apocalyptic events of the author's own day (chapter 6) and into the eschatological

---

[810] Text and translation from TROMP, Assumption of Moses, 16–19.

[811] Such options are found in GEORGE W. E. NICKELSBURG, An Antiochan Date for the Testament of Moses, in Studies on the Testament of Moses (ed. G. W. E. Nickelsburg; SBLSBS 4; Cambridge: Society of Biblical Literature, 1973), 33–37; ROBERT H. CHARLES, The Assumption of Moses (London: Black, 1897), 28–30.

[812] A similar understanding can be found in JOHN J. COLLINS, The Date and Provenance of the Testament of Moses, in Studies on the Testament of Moses (ed. G. W. E. Nickelsburg; SBLSBS 4; Cambridge: Society of Biblical Literature, 1973), 15–32; JOHN PRIEST, Testament of Moses (First Century A.D.): A New Translation and Introduction, in The Old Testament Pseudepigrapha I (ed. J. H. Charlesworth; Garden City/London: Doubleday/Darton, Longman & Todd, 1983–85), 919–934; TROMP, Assumption of Moses, 116–123.

future. On this reading, chapter 8 represents a projection of the hardships under Antiochus Epiphanes into a similar time of persecution in the author's future, only to meet with final resolution from God later in the book (chapter 10) after the martyr-like sufferings of Taxo and sons in chapter 9 (taking up the Maccabean role to a higher pitch). Under this reading, then the crucifixions upon those who confess circumcision in 8:1 (*qui confitentes circumcisionem in cruce suspendit*) presents the anticipated suffering of God's people as part of the apocalyptic calamity that precedes the eschatological victory. Noticeably this text actually was written before Josephus' account of the Maccabean martyrs. While some have suggested influence on Josephus, this seems an unnecessary conjecture.[813] More likely here, we have parallel testimony to the ability of Jewish people in the first century A.D. to look back on the Maccabean period as an era when crucifixion was threatened against martyrs from the Jewish people.

**(380)** Philo, *In Flaccum* 72

καὶ οἱ μὲν ταῦτα δρῶντες ὥσπερ ἐν τοῖς θεατρικοῖς μίμοις καθυπεκρίνοντο τοὺς πάσχοντας· τῶν δ᾽ ὡς ἀληθῶς πεπονθότων φίλοι καὶ συγγενεῖς, ὅτι μόνον ταῖς τῶν προσηκόντων συμφοραῖς συνήλγησαν, ἀπήγοντο, ἐμαστιγοῦντο, ἐτροχίζοντο, καὶ μετὰ πάσας τὰς αἰκίας, ὅσας ἐδύνατο χωρῆσαι τὰ σώματα αὐτοῖς, ἡ τελευταία καὶ ἔφεδρος τιμωρία σταυρὸς ἦν.

*Translation.* And those who did these things as if in theatrical mimes were acting like those who were suffering; but friends and relatives of those who had truly suffered, merely because they sympathized with the misfortunes of their family relations, were arrested, scourged, tortured, and, after all these torments, as much as their bodies were able to hold, the last and lurking punishment was a cross.

*Commentary.*[814] Philo of Alexandria, writing in the mid-first century A.D., records here events of his own day. Alexandria had a sizeable Jewish population, spilling over more than one of the city's quarters. A. Avillius Flaccus was prefect of Alexandria and Egypt, and in A.D. 38 he conspired with the non-Jewish inhabitants of Alexandria to oppress the Jewish population (in

---

[813] For the suggestion of Josephus' dependence on *As. Mos.* see JONATHAN A. GOLDSTEIN, The Testament of Moses: Its Content, Its Origin, and Its Attestation in Josephus, in Studies on the Testament of Moses (ed. G. W. E. Nickelsburg; SBLSBS 4; Cambridge: Society of Biblical Literature, 1973), 44–52. One problem is that Josephus would have needed to read the chapters out of order in order to place the material of chapter 8 earlier than that of chapter 6. See CHAPMAN, Crucifixion, 74–75; note discussion ibid. 74 about whether the reference to *suspendere in cruce* can be plausibly traced back to the Greek original of this work.

[814] Text: COHN / WENDLAND / REITER, Philonis Alexandrini opera, 6:133. The translations follow CHAPMAN, Crucifixion, 75–78.

part for financial gain, and in part with the hope of achieving the favor of Gaius Caligula). Prior to this passage, Philo describes the forcible eviction of Jews from their homes, along with mob beatings, murders, and burnings. The mention of "mimes" above recalls that particular form of Roman theater, which often involved sensationalist comedic excess and mockery. Unlike the mob actions that precede this passage, these outrages here appear to have been conducted within a legal framework, with arrests and official punishments (leading from torture to the cross).[815] The cross is clearly depicted as the worst penalty imposed. That it was the "last" (τελευταία) penalty likely also implies that it was the means of execution, by which they met their final end. The parallel section in Philo's *Legat.* 119–137 does not discuss crucifixion, likely because that work is less concerned with illustrating Flaccus' heinous rule as prefect. Crucifixion is otherwise known in Roman Alexandria.[816]

**(381)** Philo, *In Flaccum* 83–84

ἤδη τινὰς οἶδα τῶν ἀνεσκολοπισμένων μελλούσης ἐνίστασθαι τοιαύτης ἐκεχειρίας καθαιρεθέντας καὶ τοῖς συγγενέσιν ἐπὶ τῷ ταφῇς ἀξιωθῆναι καὶ τυχεῖν τῶν νενομισμένων ἀποδοθέντας· ἔδει γὰρ καὶ νεκροὺς ἀπολαῦσαί τινος χρηστοῦ γενεθλιακαῖς αὐτοκράτορος καὶ ἅμα τὸ ἱεροπρεπὲς τῆς πανηγύρεως φυλαχθῆναι. ⁸⁴ ὁ δ᾽ οὐ τετελευτηκότας ἐπὶ σταυρῶν καθαιρεῖν, ζῶντας δ᾽ ἀνασκολοπίζεσθαι προσέταττεν, οἷς ἀμνηστίαν ἐπ᾽ ὀλίγον, οὐ τὴν εἰς ἅπαν, ὁ καιρὸς ἐδίδου πρὸς ὑπέρθεσιν τιμωρίας, οὐκ ἄφεσιν παντελῆ. καὶ ταῦτ᾽ εἰργάζετο μετὰ τὸ πληγαῖς αἰκίσασθαι ἐν μέσῳ τῷ θεάτρῳ καὶ πυρὶ καὶ σιδήρῳ βασανίσαι.

*Translation.* Already I know some individuals among the crucified who were taken down during such a holiday, which was about to arrive, and who were restored to their relatives because they were thought worthy of burial and because they gained the customary rites. For it was necessary that even the dead have the benefit of some good on birthdays of the emperor, and at the same time [it was necessary that] the sacredness of the festal assembly be guarded. ⁸⁴ But he [Flaccus] did not order [them] to take down those who had expired on a cross; rather he ordered the living to be crucified – those to whom the season used to give for a little while an incomplete amnesty toward a delay of punishment, [yet] not toward a complete discharge. And he did these things after tormenting [them] with blows in the midst of the theater and torturing [them] with fire and iron.

---

[815] HORST, Philo's Flaccus, 167–168 contends this all represents "lynch mob justice". But the progression from arrest to scourging, torture and crucifixion appears entirely in keeping with other official crucifixions studied in this volume.

[816] Note *P. Oxy.* XXII 2339; cf. HENGEL, Crucifixion, 80.

*Commentary.*[817] In the intervening text between this passage and the one previously cited from *Flacc.* 72, Philo provides an account of the vehement treatment that Flaccus brings upon the Jewish senate. They are scourged, and some die. While Philo will note the socio-economic status of the senate (e.g., *Flacc.* 81), he does not comment on the social status of the crucified (*Flacc.* 72, 83–84), so they may belong to the lower orders of society. In the passage above, Philo testifies in passing to previous examples of crucifixion that he has known, thus providing indirect witness to earlier crucifixions. (Note that, apart from this brief allusion, we would have no historical awareness of those other crosses, and that provides a tantalizing reminder of how few ancient crucifixions actually come down to us in the extant literature.)

Philo focuses on the emperor's birthday, since Flaccus' transgression of that occasion provided opportunity for some further measure of criticism against his actions. The birthday of the emperor, especially in age of Gaius Caligula, likely had sacred significance under the auspices of the imperial cult. Philo assumes that most victims of the cross are not taken down quickly, but he reminds the reader that certain special sacred occasions should not be met with a city full of crucifixion victims. One might think here of the removal of Jesus (and the two brigands) from the cross on the eve of Passover. Suspension on the cross is the means of execution here, since the "living" are due to be hung up (ζῶντας δ' ἀνασκολοπίζεσθαι) and since he explicitly speaks of those who had died on the cross (τετελευτηκότας ἐπὶ σταυρῶν). Their execution is preceded by the spectacle of public beatings and torture in the theater.

**(382)** Josephus, *Bellum judaicum* 3.320–321

τῷ δ' ἦν μὲν δι' ὑπονοίας ὁ αὐτόμολος τό τε πρὸς ἀλλήλους πιστὸν εἰδότι τῶν Ἰουδαίων καὶ τὴν πρὸς τὰς κολάσεις ὑπεροψίαν, [321] ἐπειδὴ καὶ πρότερον ληφθείς τις τῶν ἀπὸ τῆς Ἰωταπάτης πρὸς πᾶσαν αἰκίαν βασάνων ἀντέσχεν καὶ μηδὲν διὰ πυρὸς ἐξερευνῶσι τοῖς πολεμίοις περὶ τῶν ἔνδον εἰπὼν ἀνεσταυρώθη τοῦ θανάτου καταμειδιῶν.

*Translation.* But the deserter was [viewed] with suspicion by the one [Vespasian] who knew the faithfulness of the Jews to one another and their disdain for chastisement, [321] since also formerly a certain man from Jotapata had been captured and held out against every outrage from torturous tests, and having said nothing concerning those within [the city] to the enemies who examined him with fire, he was crucified while smiling at death.

---

[817] Text: COHN / WENDLAND / REITER, Philonis Alexandrini opera, 6:135. One manuscript reads ἀνασκολωπίζεσθαι for ἀνασκολοπίζεσθαι (no difference in meaning).

*Commentary.*[818] This incident occurred during the Roman siege of Jotapata (in Galilee near Sepphoris). Josephus himself was present as general in the citadel, so he reports these events from his eyewitness (if not unbiased) viewpoint. The town fought bravely, but at one point a Jewish deserter makes his way to Vespasian, the Roman general. This deserter then reports on the difficult conditions in the city and suggests a raid during the last watch of the night, when the guards often fall asleep (*B. J.* 3.317–319). The passage above conveys Vespasian's initial skepticism and its rationale: An earlier captive from the city had willingly endured extreme torture and crucifixion rather than reveal the secrets of Jotapata. However, Vespasian decides to risk the proposed night raid, and it is overwhelmingly successful, granting the Romans control of the city (3.322–339). Here, observe the typical sequence of torture preceding crucifixion. The man is almost certainly assumed to be alive on the cross since he remains capable of smiling disdainfully at his death. More importantly, such heroism against adversity, culminating in a glad embrace of death, would have served as a model of zealous fortitude to his Jewish compatriots and likely also as an example of Stoic virtue even to the Romans.

**(383)** *Mekilta*, Bachodesh 6 on Exod 20:3–6

לאוהבי ולשומרי מצותי. לאוהבי זה אברהם אבינו וכיוצא בו ולשומרי מצותי אלו הנביאים
והזקנים. רבי נתן אומר לאוהבי ולשומרי מצותי אלו שהם יושבין בארץ ישראל ונותנין נפשם
על המצות מה לך יוצא ליהרג על שמלתי את בני [ישראל] מה לך יוצא לישרף על בתורה
שקראתי מה לך יוצא ליצלב על שאכלתי את  המצה מה לך לוקה מאה פרגל  על שנטלתי את
הלולב. ואומר אשר הכתי בית מאהבי מכות אלו גרמו לי ליאהב לאבי שבשמים:

*Translation. Of Them that Love Me and Keep My Commandments*. "Of them that love Me," refers to our father Abraham and such as are like him. "And keep My commandments," refers to the prophets and the elders. R. Nathan says: "Of them that love Me and keep My commandments," refers to those who dwell in the land of Israel and risk their lives for the sake of the commandments. "Why are you being led out to be decapitated [=slain]?" "Because I circumcised my son to be an Israelite." "Why are you being led out to be burned?" "Because I read the Torah." "Why are you being led out to be crucified?" "Because I ate the unleavened bread." "Why are you getting a hundred lashes?" "Because I performed the ceremony of the Lulab." And it says: "Those with which I was wounded in the house of my friends" (Zech. 13.6). These wounds caused me to be beloved of My father in heaven.

---

[818] Text: NIESE, Flavii Josephi Opera, 6:316.

*Commentary*.[819] Rabbi Nathan was recorded to have returned to Palestine in the mid-second century A.D., just after the Bar Kochba revolt (A.D. 132–135). Thus a Hadrianic date for this tradition is a distinct possibility.[820] However, in an earlier publication I noted that although this tradition appears in both *Leviticus Rabbah* and the *Midrash Tehillim*, it is not ascribed to R. Nathan in those sources, and the persecutions vary between sources as well.[821] Neverthe-less, opposition to circumcision is key to all three traditions (note that Hadri-anic opposition to circumcision is one possible cause of the Second Revolt), and the stories most nearby this passage in *Leviticus Rabbah* and *Midrash Tehillim* also could plausibly stem from the Hadrianic period (since they are attributed to R. Nehemiah); thus a Hadrianic date remains possible. Both *Leviticus Rabbah* and the *Midrash Tehillim* omit any mention of crucifixion, so one can further attempt to trace whether such a reference was original. In any case, from the standpoint of the *Mekilta*, crucifixion was one of the penal-ties that suffering Jewish martyrs could be expected to endure.

## 3.8 Methods and Practices of Bodily Suspension in the Roman Period

This section summarizes various indications of crucifixion method that have been encountered so far, with particular reference to the Gospels' accounts of Jesus' execution. Since this section is mostly summative, fewer new sources will be presented here.

Lay literature on crucifixion, especially on Jesus' crucifixion, frequently speculates on the methods employed in suspending someone on a cross. Nor-mally, the assumption is that all ancient crucifixions were essentially per-formed on the same pattern. Thus a composite picture of the cross is drawn, often via citations from scattered ancient sources, and then this is compared to the records of Jesus' death in the New Testament. One grave difficulty with this procedure concerns the assumption that bodily suspensions followed a single set procedure in antiquity. Such a presumption is difficult to prove from the sources themselves. On the contrary, there certainly were profound varia-tions in ancient practices. For example, it was previously observed that both *post mortem* and *ante mortem* suspension employed the same terminology,

---

[819] Text and translation from LAUTERBACH, Mekilta de-Rabbi Ishmael, 2:247–248. I find it difficult to improve on this translation. Text compared with HOROVITZ and RABIN, Mechilta d'Rabbi Ismael, 227 (lines 5–10).

[820] A Hadrianic date is supported by JAKOB WINTER and AUGUST WÜNSCHE, Mechiltha. Ein tannaitischer Midrasch zu Exodus (orig. 1909; repr., Hildesheim: Olms, 1990), 213; JACOB NEUSNER, A History of the Jews in Babylonia (5 vols.; SPB; Leiden: Brill, 1965–1970), 1:78; SCHÜRER, History, 1:555.

[821] For a fuller analysis of this passage cf. CHAPMAN, Crucifixion, 90–92.

sometimes in the same author. Furthermore, Josephus and Seneca spoke directly to variations in suspension practice in their day (see section 3.1). Even if there may be indications of a certain standard expectation in Roman crucifixion practice by the first century A.D.,[822] it is likely that many local factors affected which elements would have been followed, modified, or omitted.[823]

Notably, most ancient sources do not provide enough information to ascertain the specific methods employed in the events they describe. Frequently the texts simply mention that a victim was hung up or affixed to the cross, without indicating any other penal events that preceded their suspension and without detailing the manner of suspension. And for those few passages that provide a greater level of detail, one cannot reasonably abstract from any one instance to all other cases of crucifixion. To consider one key example: A single crucified body, evidenced by archaeology in the environs of Jerusalem, may speak to general crucifixion procedures, or it may in reality just testify to the methods employed in that one event. Thus without more widespread osteological evidence, we must acknowledge limitations in our archaeological knowledge (especially remembering the continuing debates over the osteological analysis of those remains from Giv'at ha-Mivtar). Of course, ancient historians commonly encounter issues over the best use of scattered and underwhelming sources, and it is still appropriate to synthesize conclusions when the data can support them. Therefore, even as we engage in synthesis below, this is not intended to draw a conclusive universal list of crucifixion procedures in antiquity.

It has frequently been observed that the canonical Gospels present perhaps the most detailed accounts of a crucifixion from antiquity. Thus the Gospels are in many ways our best source on crucifixion methods, yet even they do not provide answers to every question. What was the precise shape of the device? How exactly was Jesus attached to that cross? Where specifically were the nails? Was he provided with a *sedile*? Where exactly on the device were his arms and legs attached? What was the manner of elevating the body? How tall was the cross? What was the precise cause of death? These are some of the questions that remain, and our best extant ancient sources for crucifixion method (i.e., the Gospels) do not provide that level of information.

Therefore, some scholars engage in the study of crucifixion method in order to answer questions that the Gospels do not address. They may wish to

---

[822] Observe how both Seneca (*Marc.* [*Dial.* 6)] 20.3) and Josephus (*B. J.* 5.451), while noting variation in postures on the cross, also infer that these departed from an expected norm. Seneca specifically informs the reader that the variety of postures he envisions is "not merely of one kind" (as if a single kind would normally be expected). In a later era, Eusebius assumes a single form with occasional cruel variation (*Hist. eccl.* 8.8.2). See section 3.1.

[823] Compare this with the assessment in HENGEL, Crucifixion, 25: "All attempts to give a perfect description of *the* crucifixion in archaeological terms are therefore in vain; there were too many different possibilities for the executioner."

fill out the Gospel accounts, perhaps to verify or adjust the mental image that we moderns have of Jesus' demise (informed as it is by crucifixes, pictures, statuary, movies, books, and popular preaching). This can be a reasonable historical enterprise, but wisdom requires us to acknowledge from the beginning that there will be questions that remain unanswerable due to limitations in sources and due to the difficulty of developing a composite picture of crucifixion in antiquity with a high degree of certainty.

Some scholars investigate crucifixion with more apologetic aims. Their hope is to verify (or deny) the Gospel accounts by the degree to which they accord with a hypothetical norm for ancient crucifixion. In addition to this being difficult (again due to the lack of detail in most ancient sources), such projects stem from faulty premises, especially by approaching these narratives with a high level of suspicion. In fact, the level of detail in the Gospel accounts likely testifies to the profound memories the eyewitnesses had of the event. Moreover, the Gospel writers would naturally wish to portray such an event in keeping with the ways that their contemporaries had experienced other crucifixions (in order that their accounts be received as accurate testimony). Given the desire for the Gospel witness to be perceived as trustworthy, it is even more likely that any variations from an assumed common crucifixion procedure were based on the earliest memories of the specifics of Jesus' death, necessitating variation from the expected norm. Thus one should likely begin with the assumption that the Gospel writers provide a reasonable account of the kind of crucifixion that someone in Jesus' day would have endured, and where they suggest a relatively distinctive event (such as early removal from the cross) those unique features also likely have specific historical merit.

Given that the Gospels provide substantial witness to ancient crucifixion methods, this section will proceed sequentially through various features of crucifixion and bodily suspension. Special attention will be accorded to the Gospels, and other selected sources, especially those covered earlier in this volume that reference Roman use of the cross, will be provided to further illustrate matters of method. Instead of following a single Gospel narrative, the procedure will be to work through a synoptic account. The goal is not to generate a composite picture of all ancient crucifixions; rather the aim is to illustrate points of contact and uniqueness between the death of Jesus and other known suspensions from antiquity.

### 3.8.1 Events Preceding the Cross

Jesus' crucifixion is clearly portrayed as his means of death. Among other matters, his dying words are uttered while he is attached to the cross. This reminds us of how other accounts that mention the cross can also be clearly *ante mortem* events, in which the cross becomes the means of execution.[824] Yet other ancient reports, employing the same terminology and often partaking of the same general angst about such a suspension, record a *post mortem* use of the cross. Such *post mortem* events more often occur in times of war, during which the despised enemy has already died, sometimes by his own hand. In these instances, *post mortem* suspensions seek to further dishonor the deceased enemy, announce the victory, motivate others to surrender, and generally serve as a warning to other rebels and foreign troops.[825] Roman accounts of the application of the cross against criminals are typically *ante mortem*, at least when these accounts include sufficient evidence to ascertain whether the cross was applied before of after death.

Jesus endured a series of trials and hearings before his final condemnation to the cross. Suspensions of criminals generally followed legal proceedings, though these proceedings were not universally recorded in the sources. Parts 1 and 2 above speak directly to Roman and Jewish legal procedure.

The Gospels depict Jesus as beaten and ridiculed, both by Jewish and Roman personnel, prior to his route to the cross (e.g., Matt 26:67–68; 27:26–31; Mark 14:65; 15:15–20; Luke 22:63–65; 23:11; John 19:1–3). The abuse of convicted criminals was standard practice in both Jewish and Roman contexts (see sections 1.8, 2.7). Other ancient sources on the cross repeatedly mention beatings and scourgings prior to the fixing up of the person on the cross.[826] Nevertheless, ancient penal suspensions can also employ even broader terminology such as "torture" and "rack", often along with beatings, prior to the actual crucifixion; such terminology goes even beyond the recorded array of

---

[824] To provide a selection of sources studied above, note: Plautus, *Most.* 348–361; *Bacch.* 358–365; Cicero, *Verr.* 2.5.169; Appian, *Bell. civ.* 3.1.3 [3.9]; also note the Epitaph from Amyzon in Caria (No. 333 above); Philo, *Flacc.* 83–84; Josephus, *B. J.* 3.320–321. Also see Josephus, *A. J.* 12.255–256 (though this concerns Seleucid actions, Josephus appears to have conformed them to the punishments of his day). Further non-Roman *ante mortem* suspensions are depicted by later Roman authors in (for example): Polybius, *Hist.* 1.86.4–7; Arrian, *Anab.* 4.14.3–4. One way to view these is to consider that, even before considering the accuracy of the extant reports, they certainly indicate that their *authors* believed the cross to be the cause of the person's death. One could also note the debate about whether Jewish people practiced *ante mortem* suspension in antiquity (section 3.5); there, the rabbis acknowledge that the Roman government hung up victims alive (*Sifre Dev.* 221; *Midrash Tannaim* p. 132, lines 7–8; *b. Sanh.* 46b), and other rabbinic case law presumes living victims of Roman crosses; cf. *m. Ohal.* 3:5; *t. Giṭ* 7[5]:1; *m. Yebam.* 16:3. Further, in any case where crucifixion is put alongside other death penalties as a form of capital punishment, as is frequently the case in the *Pauli Sententiae* passages in section 3.6, *ante mortem* suspension is rightly inferred.

[825] E.g., Polybius, *Hist.* 5.54.3,6–7. This is not to suggest that all military uses of the cross were invariably *post mortem* (cf. Polybius, *Hist.* 1.86.4–7). The non-military instance in Suetonius, *Iul.* 74.1 is portrayed as exceptional.

[826] Titus Livius, 33.36.1–3; Dionysius of Halicarnassus, *Ant. rom.* 12.6.6; Josephus, *B. J.* 2.306–308; 7.200–203.

pre-crucifixion torments mentioned in the Gospels.[827] However, many sources merely state that the victim "was crucified" without specific record of any harsh treatment of the victim prior to their cross. In such instances, where penal events preceding the cross are not described (though neither are they denied), various modern scholars have different approaches. Some might infer from the lack of explicit mention of torture preceding the cross that no such torments were applied. Most instead assume that beating and torture was so standard that it need not be recorded; the ancient reader would know to presume its use. This latter assumption seems more reasonable, but it is admittedly a difficult postulate to test with certainty. In any case, the Gospels are not alone in recording that beatings preceded the cross.

Jesus carries his cross to the place of execution (John 19:17), and he was assisted by Simon of Cyrene (Matt 27:32; Mark 15:21; Luke 23:26). A famous Jesus logion contains his invitation to his follower to "take up his cross and follow me" (Mark 8:34; cf. Matt 10:38; Luke 14:27). A procession to the cross is elsewhere known in other crucifixion accounts.[828] Other sources indicate that criminals could be required to carry their *patibulum* (likely "crossbeam") to their own execution (see section 2.9).[829] Other texts indicate people could be requisitioned (like Simon) into acts of public service, likely including assisting the condemned in carrying his cross (section 2.8).

For criminal executions, the cross commonly appears to have been located at a designated space outside the city.[830] This is typically a public locale since crucifixions were designed to serve as a public spectacle that illustrated the victory of the state over its opponents.[831] More than one cross can at times be found. In periods of war, crosses are often set up near the gates or walls of the city.[832] Jesus was crucified with two other victims at Golgotha, which was presumably outside the city (Matt 27:33; Mark 15:22; Luke 23:33; John 19:17).

Jesus was stripped before being affixed up on the cross, and his garments were divided by lot among the soldiers (Matt 27:35; Mark 15:24; Luke 23:34). There is a clear reference here to Psalm 22:18, but clothing was also one of

---

[827] E.g., Plautus, *Most.* 741–744/745; Cicero, *Verr.* 2.5.14; 2.5.163; Dionysius of Halicarnassus, *Ant. rom.* 5.51.3; *Lex Libitinaria* from Puteoli (*AE* 1971, 88) 2.8–14; *Digesta* 49.16.3.10; Philo, *Flacc.* 72, 83–84; Josephus, *B. J.* 3.320–321.

[828] Plautus, *Most.* 1128–1134.

[829] Also note Plautus, *Most.* 55–57. See discussion in No. 334 of *patibulum* in the *Lex Libitinaria* from Puteoli (*AE* 1971, 88) 2.8–14.

[830] E.g., Cicero announces that the cross in Syracuse had traditionally been located outside the city on the Pompeian road, and he complains that Verres has changed that locale to a more prominent location, likely in the city itself (*Verr.* 2.5.169). The mass crucifixion of the revolutionaries who had fought with Spartacus also reportedly occurs on the road leading between cities (Appian, *Bell. civ.* 1.14.120).

[831] Cicero, *Verr.* 2.4.24 (though judging it too public; cf. *Verr.* 2.4.26; 2.5.170–171); *Historia Augusta* 18.23.7–8; *Dig.* 48.19.28.15. Likely also Firmicus Maternus, *Mathesis* 8.22.3.

[832] Note especially the siege of Jerusalem; Josephus, *B. J.* 5.549–551; cf. 5.289; 7.202–203.

the more important possessions of the poor in antiquity (early Jewish marriage certificates often list clothing among valuable possessions), so there was reason for the soldiers to want his clothing (and John further records that Jesus' tunic was a special seamless one; John 19:23–24). However, it is unclear if any undergarment from Jesus would have been removed, so there is some debate about whether he would have been naked. Most ancient sources do not actually mention the naked (or clothed) status of the victim. A striking exception is found in Artemidorus (*Oneir.* 2.53), who assumes crucified persons are indeed "naked" (γυμνοί). COOK correctly counters that this word "naked" need not invariably imply stripped bare, so garments could have covered the male private parts.[833] However, although the crucified figure on the Palatino graffito (see section 3.10.6) may be wearing a shirt, perhaps a *colobium* or a short tunic, his buttocks also appear visible.[834]

The use of a *titulus*, which publicly announces the rationale for punishment, was studied in section 2.10.

### 3.8.2 Form and Functional Elements of the Cross

The precise form of the cross does not typically receive direct description in extant sources. This provides room for debate about the shape of the cross in antiquity and the precise form of Jesus' cross.

Some have argued that σταυρός in Greek fundamentally represents an upright pole, and thus Jesus was actually "crucified" on a post without any form of crossbeam.[835] Such a view typically entails an etymological fallacy, by assuming that the "original meaning" of the word remains fundamental to all future uses of the term (even centuries later). The word σταυρός may indeed derive in earliest Greek from upright posts. Cognate words such as σταύρωμα can designate a "palisade" of many such poles; the verb σταυρόω can even occasionally refer to the building of such a palisade. However at some point in Greek, σταυρός became associated with a T- (or t-) shaped crucifixion device. Such a shape to the cross is clearly found in [Pseudo-] Lucian *Iudicium vocalium* 12, where the *tau* (T) is equated with the σταυρός. Other Roman-era sources also imply arms outstretched during a crucifixion; e.g.,

---

[833] COOK, Crucifixion, 192–193 (concerning John 21:18–19 as an indirect reference to Peter's crucifixion).

[834] Note the analysis of this graffito in COOK, Envisioning Crucifixion, 282–285. COOK elsewhere notes that this figure "wears some kind of garment," implying that he was not therefore naked COOK, Crucifixion, 193). This is true, but it overlooks the visible buttocks in the graffito, even if COOK appears aware of this as well elsewhere (ibid., 427 n. 53).

[835] Such a view appears in WILLIAM E. VINE, An Expository Dictionary of New Testament Words with their Precise Meanings for English Readers (4 vols.; London: Oliphants, 1939), s.v. σταυρός. The Jehovah's Witnesses also put great weight on this etymological argument.

note σταυρός cognates in Lucian, *Prom.* 1–2; Epictetus, *Diatr.* 3.26.21–22; Artemidorus, *Oneir.* 2.53.[836] An important (likely second-century A.D.) graffito from Puteoli portrays a crucified person with outstretched arms.[837]

*Illustration* (Fig. 6)

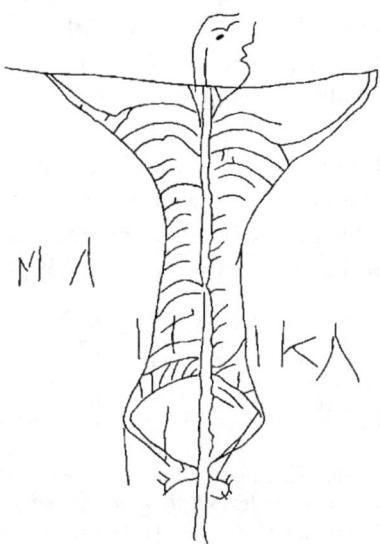

In section In section 3.10, the famed Palatino Alexamenos graffito represents a person hung up on a *tau*-shaped cross. And J. G. COOK has recently published evidence from an Arieti tomb of a man appended to a cross-shaped device.[838] Thus it is certain that many ancient people assumed that a crucifixion involved arms widespread and attached to the cross. However, since most ancient sources do not describe the precise shape the author had in mind, we should not over-assert the strength of our evidence to the point of presuming that all ancient crucifixions took on one particular form.

---

[836] In Plautus, *Most.* 348–361, the arms and legs of the crucified slave each receive a nail.

[837] The drawing in Fig. 6 is by Karis Chapman, based on a photograph in COOK, Crucifixion as Spectacle, 94 (Fig. 4); also in COOK, Crucifixion, 456. The diagram from ANTONIO LAMBATTI (ibid. 457; idem, Crucifixion as Spectacle, 95) was also consulted, but this drawing here attempts to rectify a few (minor) errant lines in the LAMBATTI rendering. COOK's informative discussion (Crucifixion as Spectacle, 92–98) presents a helpful history of scholarship on this graffito, noting among other matters: It is best dated to the time of Trajan or Hadrian; the inscribed name Alkimila to the left of the head clearly seeks to identify the victim as a woman, though it may have been added later by another hand; the lines across the back may indicate scourging or could simply be there to express the curved plane of the person's back, and the purpose of the graffito (e.g., whether it was a jest) is difficult to know for certain, but it likely depicts a historical event.

[838] COOK, Patibulum.

When it comes to the cross of Jesus, there are additional clues to take into account. A number of early Christian authors equate the cross with the *tau*, and this occurs as early as the *Epistle of Barnabas*.[839] In some of our earliest NT manuscripts (including $\mathfrak{P}^{45}$, $\mathfrak{P}^{66}$ and $\mathfrak{P}^{75}$), the *tau* and *rho* in σταυρός (and cognates) are combined to form a staurogram that looks like the head of a person astride the *tau*, implying outstretched arms. Among others, HURTADO has argued that this constitutes one of the earliest Christian artistic portrayals of the cross.[840] These memories appear quite soon in the Christian tradition, and they argue favorably for the plausibility of Jesus being crucified on a *tau*-shaped cross.[841]

Both nails and ropes are known to have been employed in instances of people attached to the *crux*.[842] Crucifixion nails receive special testimony in magical cures.[843] In Jesus' case, nails to his feet and hands are likely assumed in Luke's account of the resurrection (Luke 24:39; "see here my hands and my

---

[839] Note the following passages, many mentioned in section 3.1: *Barn.* 9:8; Justin, *1 Apol.* 55.1–8; 60.1–5; *Dial.* 40.3; 91.1–2; Irenaeus, *Haer.* 2.24.4; Tertullian, *Apol.* 16.6–7; *Adv. Jud.* 10.7; 13.21; *Nat.* 1.12.3–4; *Marc.* 3.18.3–4; 3.22; Minucius Felix, *Oct.* 29.7–8; Eusebius, *Hist. eccl.* 8.9.4.

[840] LARRY W. HURTADO, The Staurogram in Early Christian Manuscripts: The Earliest Visual Reference to the Crucified Jesus?, in New Testament Manuscripts: Their Texts and Their World (ed. T.J. Kraus and T. Nicklas; Texts and Editions for New Testament Study 2; Leiden: Brill, 2006), 207–226; LARRY W. HURTADO, The Earliest Christian Artifacts: Manuscripts and Christian Origins (Grand Rapids: Eerdmans, 2006), 135–154.

[841] An intriguing, albeit eclectic, study of cross marks in early Christianity is JACK FINEGAN, The Archeology of the New Testament: The Life of Jesus and the Beginning of the Early Church (rev. ed.; Princeton: Princeton University Press, 1992), 339–389. His discussion of cross marks on "Jewish-Christian" ossuaries does not take into sufficient account either the use of everyday hairline grid marks for use in laying out artistic design on the ossuaries, or the possibility of Christian monastics inscribing crosses on earlier ossuaries. See the discussion in CHAPMAN, Crucifixion, 178–182, which also references the contrasting views of DINKLER and GOODENOUGH; see ERICH DINKLER, "Zur Geschichte des Kreuzsymbols," *ZTK* 48 (1951): 148–72; ERICH DINKLER, "Kreuzzeichen und Kreuz – Tau, Chi und Stauros," *JAC* 5 (1962): 26–54; ERWIN R. GOODENOUGH, *Jewish Symbols in the Greco-Roman Period* (13 vols.; Bollingen Series 47; New York: Pantheon, 1953–68), 1:132; 2:254.

[842] E.g., Plautus, *Most.* 348–361; also note nails in the Prometheus myth (adapted into a crucifixion) in Lucian, *Prom.* 1–2. The nails mentioned in the *Lex Libitinaria* from Puteoli (2.8–14) are likely for use in attaching the person to the cross. The body from Giv'at ha-Mivtar was identified as a crucifixion due to the nail in his heel. See further Joseph W. Hewitt, "The Use of Nails in the Crucifixion," *HTR* 25 (1932): 29–45; however, in light of the archaeological find at Giv'at ha-Mivtar, we must reject HEWITT's claim that such nails could only have been used in hands and not in feet.

[843] Pliny the Elder, *Nat. hist.* 28.11.46, who reports both nails and cords; Lucan, *Bell.* 6.543–549; Lucian, *Philops.* 17; *m. Šabb.* 6:10; *y. Šabb.* 6:9 [8c]; *b Šabb.* 67a; and T-S Arabic 44.44 [2/17–20] from the Cairo Genizah. It is conceivable that these nails were used in the construction of the cross, but given the special magical powers attributed to these nails, it is more likely that they were in direct contact with death (and its associated power) through attaching the person to the cross.

feet") and the piercing of his hands is also mentioned in John 20:20 ("he showed them his hands and side"). Paul employs the imagery of Jesus nailing the record of debt to his cross (Col 2:14; προσηλώσας αὐτὸ τῷ σταυρῷ), thus indicating that Paul believed Jesus had been attached to the cross with nails.

Blood is also commonly associated with the cross.[844] This could be due to the various scourgings and tortures that preceded the cross, or to the application of nails to the victim; perhaps most likely it was due to both. The height of the cross can sometimes be quite elevated, in order to increase the prominence of the execution, but this appears unusual enough that the sources specifically remark about it.[845]

During the last century, the means of death has been debated. All key writings on this issue assume that outstretched arms and the application of nails were standard. Some have argued that the weight of the body pulling on the outstretched arms would immobilize the chest, resulting eventually in asphyxiation.[846] F. T. Zugibe, after significant experimentation with live volunteers, contends that a crucifixion posture does not create the conditions necessary for asphyxiation; instead death was caused by cardiac and respiratory arrest due to hypovolemic shock.[847] Others conclude that the cause was "multifactorial", including asphyxiation, hypovolemic shock, and acute heart failure as possibilities.[848] A recent article proposes that past research has been inconclusive on the matter.[849]

---

[844] Cicero, *Verr.* 2.5.170–171; Seneca, *Ep.* 101.14; Suetonius, *Cal.* 57.3–4; *m. Ohal.* 3:5.

[845] Suetonius, *Galb.* 9; cf. *Anthologia Graeca* 11.192; Plautus, *Stichus* 625–629.

[846] This is especially associated with Pierre Barbet, A Doctor at Calvary: The Passion of Our Lord Jesus Christ as Described by a Surgeon (trans. Earl of Wicklow; New York: Kennedy, 1953). This was anticipated by A. LeBec, Physiological Study of the Passion of Our Lord Jesus Christ, Catholic Medical Guardian 3 (1925): 126–132.

[847] Frederick T. Zugibe, The Crucifixion of Jesus: A Forensic Inquiry (New York: Evans, 2005); his conclusions are most succinctly stated ibid. 135 in this edition (his previous 1988 edition was entitled The Cross and the Shroud). Condensed in Frederick T. Zugibe, Two Questions About Crucifixion. Does the Victim Die of Asphyxiation? Would Nails in the Hand Hold the Weight of the Body? BRev 5 (1989): 34–43. Zugibe also spends a good deal of his book discussing the Shroud of Turin, which is a potential distraction from the other issues he writes about. Other popular-level books could be mentioned here as well.

[848] Willilam D. Edwards, Floyd E. Hosmer, and Wesley J. Gabel, On the Physical Death of Jesus Christ, Journal of the American Medical Association 255 (1986): 1455–1463; they state: "it remains unsettled whether Jesus died of cardiac rupture or of cardiorespiratory failure" (1463).

[849] Matthew W. Maslen and Piers D. Mitchell, Medical Theories on the Cause of Death in Crucifixion, Journal of the Royal Society of Medicine 99 (2006): 185–188, reviewed over forty studies by physicians, focusing on ten views, and concluded that there has been "suboptimal use" of historical sources in past publications, that humane modern re-enactments cannot fully simulate torturous ancient conditions, that there is "insufficient evidence to safely state exactly how people did die from crucifixion in Roman times," and that it is likely "different individuals died from different physiological causes" depending on their orientation on a cross. See also Cook, Crucifixion, 430–435.

### 3.8.3 Prolonged Suspension and Early Removal

When employed for *ante mortem* suspensions, the sources often assume a pro-tracted death of pain and suffering.[850] Corpses can be left on the cross long after the victim expires. A prolonged suspension of the body is also implied when the bodies are left as food for the wild beasts and birds.[851] In some cases, after death the body is eventually dragged (perhaps on a hook through the streets) to the place where corpses of criminals are discarded.[852]

   The Gospels highlight as unusual two aspects of Jesus' crucifixion. First, Pilate allowed the disposal of all the victims' bodies prior to the Day of Prepa-ration. Second, Jesus' death came more quickly than expected (Mark 15:44–45; cf. John 19:31–37). Since bodies are typically left up on the cross for a prolonged period of time, it is helpful to recall the discussion concerning Philo, *Flacc.* 83–84 (No. 381). Philo remarks, in contrast to Flaccus' cruelty, that he has seen in the past bodies taken down for burial from the cross in anticipation of an emperor's birthday, the concern being that the "sacredness of the festal assembly be guarded." Such imperial birthdays were likely key festivals for the imperial cult, and thus sacred. The Gospels testify to a parallel willingness from Pilate (at what seems to have been a tenuous time in his long career in Judea) to honor the sacredness of the Passover week festivities.

   The following three sources bring into sharper focus matters concerning prolonged suspension and the removal of living bodies from the cross.

### (384) Petronius, *Satyricon* 112

Itaque unius cruciarii parentes ut viderunt laxatam custodiam, detraxere nocte pendentem supremoque mandaverunt officio. At miles circumscriptus dum desidet, ut postero die vidit unam sine cadavere crucem, veritus supplicium, mulieri quid accidisset exponit.

*Translation.* Accordingly, the parents of one of the crucified saw the guard being lax, and removed during the night [their son] who was hanging, and committed him to the last rite. But the soldier, who had been circumvented [by the parents] while he was loitering, the next day saw one cross without a corpse; and having become afraid of punishment, he explained to the woman what had occurred.

---

[850] See especially Seneca, *Ep.* 101.14; also Cicero, *Verr.* 2.5.169.

[851] Lucian, *Prom.* 2.

[852] This may also be the intent of the hook procession in the *Lex Libitinaria* from Puteoli (*AE* 1971, 88) 2.8–14.

*Commentary.*[853] In this amusing (though unsettling) tale, Petronius' character Eumolpus tells the story of a beautiful woman whose husband died. Her grief will not allow her to leave his grave, even as she wastes away. Meanwhile, the provincial governor sentences some brigands (*latrones*) to be crucified (*crucibus affigi* in *Satyr.* 111) near her deceased husband's funeral chamber. One of the soldiers, who was tasked with guarding the crosses to prevent people burying the bodies (*qui cruces asservabat, ne quis ad sepulturam corpus detraheret*), falls in love with the woman, and he successfully courts her. While the soldier is with his new "wife" in the funeral chamber, shirking his duty, the events of the passage above occur. One of the crucified corpses is stolen from the cross and buried. The soldier is so distraught at his impending punishment for negligence of duty that he plans to take his own life, but the woman instead orders her dead husband's corpse to be hung up on the cross to replace the missing body. Observers are surprised to see the different person on the cross. Those listening to Eumolpus' tale laugh uproariously, except for Lichas, who angrily insists that the governor in the story should have the woman fixed up on the cross in place of her husband (*mulierem affigere cruci*). For present purposes, we shall observe three quick matters. First, the crucifixion victim was a *latrones* (brigand), thus continuing that theme which we observed in sections 3.6.5 and 3.7.2. Second, if Lichas' conclusion states a possible judgment on the woman, then it is noticeable that a female can be attached to the cross. Third, the prolonged exposure of crucified corpses could necessitate guards in order to prevent family members from burying their dead.

## (385) *Semaḥot* 2.11 [44b]

מי שהיה בעלה צלוב עמה בעיר, אשתו צלובה עמו בעיר, אביו ואמו צלובין עמו: לא ישרה באותה העיר אלא אם כן היתה עיר גדולה כאנטוכיא. לא ישרה בצד זה, אבל ישרה בצד אחר. עד מתי הוא אסור עד שיכלה הבשר, ואין הצורה ניכרת בעצמות

*Translation.* [A wife] whose husband was crucified[854] in her city, [a man] whose wife is crucified in his city, [a person] whose father and his mother are crucified [in] his [city] – [such a person] should not dwell in that city, unless it is a city as large as Antioch. He [whose family member was crucified] should not dwell within this border; rather, [such a] mourner should dwell

---

[853] Text: MICHAEL HESELTINE and WILLIAM H. D. ROUSE, Petronius; Seneca: Apocolocyntosis (orig. 1930; repr., LCL; Cambridge: Harvard University Press, 1987), 234.

[854] RABBINOWITZ translates צלוב as "impaled," although he acknowledges that this passage envisions a penalty enacted by the Roman authorities during which a person would be suspended for view. See J. RABBINOWITZ, Ebel Rabbathi Named Masseketh Semahoth: Tractate on Mourning, in The Minor Tractates of the Talmud: Massekthoth Ketannoth (2 vols. Second Edition; ed. Abraham Cohen; orig. 1965; repr., London: Soncino, 1971), 1:325–400, 334.

within another border. Until when is this forbidden? Until the flesh was consumed, and there is not the form [of the person] remembered in the bones.

*Commentary.*[855] The extra-canonical tractate *Semaḥot* is likely post-Mishnaic. It concerns Jewish burial law. Here, it instructs the family of the crucified to move away from where their crucified family member has been suspended. They should change towns, unless they are in a large enough urban center to shift "borders" within the city. The context assumes that the body will fully decay in public view on the cross. This appears an attempt to save the family the shame associated with crucifixion. Note again how women as well as men could face the cross.

Another passage from *Semaḥot* (2.9 [44b]), which does not directly mention crucifixion, forbids the stealing (for purposes of burial) of a corpse from where it had been executed by the Roman government. The person who steals such a corpse is compared to a murderer, idolater, adulterer, and Sabbathbreaker. Likely this rabbinic dictate stems from the fear of the wrath that the whole Jewish community would face from the Roman government, should a corpse be removed from the cross.[856]

## (386) Josephus, *Vita* 420–421

πεμφθεὶς δ᾽ ὑπὸ Τίτου Καίσαρος σὺν Κερεαλίῳ καὶ χιλίοις ἱππεῦσιν εἰς κώμην τινὰ Θεκῶαν λεγομένην προκατανοήσων, εἰ τόπος ἐπιτήδειός ἐστιν χάρακα δέξασθαι, ὡς ἐκεῖθεν ὑποστρέφων εἶδον πολλοὺς αἰχμαλώτους ἀνεσταυρωμένους καὶ τρεῖς ἐγνώρισα συνήθεις μοι γενομένους, ἤλγησά τε τὴν ψυχὴν καὶ μετὰ δακρύων προσελθὼν Τίτῳ εἶπον. [421] ὁ δ᾽ εὐθὺς ἐκέλευσεν καθαιρεθέντας αὐτοὺς θεραπείας ἐπιμελεστάτης τυχεῖν. καὶ οἱ μὲν δύο τελευτῶσιν θεραπευόμενοι, ὁ δὲ τρίτος ἔζησεν.

*Translation.* After being sent by Titus Caesar with Cerealius and a thousand horses to a certain town called Tekoa, [so that I might] observe beforehand whether there was a serviceable place to receive a fortified camp; as I was returning from there, I saw many captives who had been crucified, and I knew three who were my acquaintances. And I grieved in my soul; and, approaching with tears, I asked Titus. [421] And he immediately commanded them to be taken down in order to receive the most careful medical treatment. And two of them, though being treated, died; the third lived.

---

[855] Text: DOV ZLOTNICK, The Tractate "Mourning" (Regulations Relating to Death, Burial, and Mourning) (Translated from the Hebrew, with Introduction and Notes; Yale Judaica 17; New Haven: Yale University Press, 1966), 4 (with pointing removed).

[856] On both texts from *Semaḥot*, see CHAPMAN, Crucifixion, 199–202.

*Commentary.*[857] Josephus conveys here his compassionate side as part of his self-defense against charges from his countrymen. At this point in the First Revolt, he is already in the service of the Romans (having been captured as a former Jewish general). For purposes of this study, the account is notable for the number being crucified, the willingness to take down from the cross a revolutionary at Josephus' request, and especially for the resulting condition of the crucified. The Romans were fairly adept at medicine for their day, especially in treating battle-related injuries. Yet even with "the most careful medical treatment" (θεραπείας ἐπιμελεστάτης) being applied to three living victims of the cross, only one managed to survive. The toll of crucifixion on their bodies was too great for the other two. This could be compared to the remote possibility in the Mishnah (*m. Yeb.* 16:3 in No. 375; cf. *y. Yeb.* 16:3) of a crucified person surviving the cross. Sometimes people inquire if it was possible for a person to endure the cross and live. The answer based on this passage would be: It is unlikely. Assuming the victim was clearly alive when he or she was taken down from the cross, and assuming the person received the best possible medical care, then he or she had only a slight chance of surviving.

## 3.9 Crucifixion and the Actualization of Previous History and Myth

As famous historical narratives or fabulous legends are retold, new generations of authors often apply more contemporary terminology to ancient stories. This is certainly the case with bodily suspension accounts. While the earlier narratives may refer to human bodily suspension in relatively vague terms, later generations may employ the more specific suspension vocabulary of their day. Thus κρεμάννυμι becomes ἀνασταυρόω or *in crucem adfixi*, or תלה becomes צלב. The shift in terminology, especially to idioms that have ongoing resonance in the new author's era, lead to slight (or even large) retellings of the previous narrative. For example, if in the original account the person was vaguely "hung up", in a retelling they may well be "fixed on a cross" much like the ones the author (and his readers) would see everyday. Such processes have been labeled "actualization" by Septuagint scholars.[858] Beyond these subtle translational developments, sometimes new material is simply interpo-

---

[857] Text: NIESE, Flavii Josephi Opera, 4:388. There are no variants of great importance.

[858] Cf. ARIE VAN DER KOOIJ, Isaiah in the Septuagint, in Writing and Reading the Scroll of Isaiah: Studies of an Interpretive Tradition (2 vols.; VTSup 70; Leiden: Brill, 1997), 513–529. See further discussion in CHAPMAN, Crucifixion, 98. Actualization is here intended to imply the way a translation or interpretation of a previous text (or oral tradition) views those events through the cultural assumptions of the interpreter's day. For a visual example, one could think of how Renaissance art often portrays biblical figures in European countrysides, wearing European apparel and sitting amidst European furniture.

lated into the old. The result is a dynamic interchange between the past and its present interpretation.

In previous publications, the term "actualization" has been specifically applied to how later Jewish traditions render biblical narratives with contemporary language about bodily suspension.[859] Some of that evidence will be duplicated below. Yet, similar dynamics were at work in famous Graeco-Roman accounts of historical figures and mythic heroes. To cite an example from earlier in this volume (section 3.6.9), consider how the historical figure of Regulus received increasing attention in later Roman histories. In Polybius, Regulus' heroic return to Carthage is viewed as ending in imprisonment; in Appian, Silius Italicus, and other authors, Regulus returns to Carthage to face the cross as the reward for his bravery. This chapter is suggestive and selective, rather than comprehensive, since there are many older narratives that receive increasing use of crucifixion language in the late-Republican or Imperial periods. Below we examine one historical example (Polycrates), one mythic illustration (Prometheus), and numerous cases from the Old Testament.

### 3.9.1 Polycrates

Polycrates was the tyrant of Samos, whom Herodotus tells us was so jealous for wealth and power that he allowed himself to be lured into a deathtrap by Oroetes, the Persian governor of Sardis (see Herodotus, *Hist.* 3.125.2–4, in No. 194). Polycrates' greed became his most well-known attribute, and thus it invited others, especially philosophers, to refer to his demise as a cautionary tale. Prior to his death, evidence for Polycrates' good fortune abounded, especially in a scene when he threw his most-prized ring into the sea, only to have it returned to him in the belly of a fish (3.40–43). Note that in Herodotus' narrative (3.125.3), Polycrates was put to death first, albeit in a horrible fashion, before he was hung up *post mortem*.[860] Herodotus emphasizes Polycrates' suspension by employing both ἀνεσταύρωσε and ἀνακρεμάμενος and by telling the story of Polycrates' daughter who saw a vision of him being "washed by Zeus" (in the form of rain) and "anointed by the sun" as he was hung aloft (3.125.4; cf. 3.124.1). Later authors often overlook Polycrates' execution prior to his suspension. Instead, they will concisely speak of his execution itself as a suspension/crucifixion, and some will expand on that crucifixion imagery.

---

[859] See DAVID W. CHAPMAN, Crucifixion, Bodily Suspension, and Jewish Interpretations of the Hebrew Bible in Antiquity, in Beyond the Jordan (FS W. Harold Mare; ed. G. A. Carnagey, G. A. Carnagey, and K. N. Schoville; Eugene, Oreg.: Wipf & Stock, 2005) 37–48; also in CHAPMAN, Crucifixion, 97–177.

[860] "And after putting him to death in a way not fit to be told, Oroetes suspended him on a stake" (᾽Αποκτείνας δέ μιν οὐκ ἀξίως ἀπηγήσιος ᾽Οροίτης ἀνεσταύρωσε).

**(387)** Cicero, *De Finibus* 5.30.92

Ille vero si insipiens (quod certe, quoniam tyrannus), numquam beatus; si sapiens, ne tum quidem miser cum ab Oroete praetore Darei in crucem actus est. 'At multis malis affectus.' Quis negat? sed ea mala virtutis magnitudine obruebantur.

*Translation.* Truly, that man, if he were foolish (which he certainly was, since he was a tyrant), then he was never blessed; if he were wise, then assuredly he was never a wretch, [even] when by Oroetes, the praetor of Darius, he had been led to the cross. 'But [one might counter] he had been visited with many evils.' Who denies that? But these evils [would have been] overwhelmed by the magnitude of [his] virtue.

*Commentary.*[861] In the midst of a philosophical dialogue between Cicero and other philosophers in which they contrast the views of the Stoics and the Peripatetics, Cicero receives the charge of inconsistency in his understanding of virtue and blessedness. He counters here with the example of Polycrates, who was not blessed simply because he had wealth and frequent good luck. True blessing comes from acting wisely and virtuously, even despite pain and torture. Were Polycrates to have experienced that wisdom (and Cicero is inclined to believe he did not), then the evil of crucifixion would be more than countered by virtue. Here Polycrates' death is that of a person "led to the cross" (*in crucem actus est*).

**(388)** Philo, *De Providentia* 2.24 (Eusebius, *Praep.* 8.14.24–25)

Ἐπεὶ Πολυκράτει γε, ἐφ' οἷς δεινοῖς ἠδίκησε καὶ ἠσέβησε, χορηγὸς ἀπήντησε, χείρων μὲν ἡ τοῦ βίου βαρυδαιμονία· πρόσθες δ' ὡς ὑπὸ μεγάλου βασιλέως ἐκολάζετο, καὶ προσηλοῦτο, χρησμὸν ἐκπιπλάς.

*Translation.* Since Polycrates: by which terrible acts he injured and profaned, with these his patron encountered him; the grievous ill-luck of life became worse and increased as he was punished by a great king, and nailed, fulfilling an oracle.

---

[861] Text: HARRIS RACKHAM, Cicero. De finibus bonorum et malorum (LCL; Cambridge: Harvard University Press, 1931 [1923]), 496.

*Commentary.*[862] In the fragmentary remains we have of this treatise, Philo (in the mid-first century A.D.) recounts the story of Polycrates, recasting it allegorically as an instance of a person who made his soul depend entirely on his body (i.e., he gave into his bodily appetites, rather than committing to the philosophical care of his soul). Just after the text above, the "oracle" is cited from his daughter, though conveyed in Polycrates' own first-person account. Philo does mention here punishment (ἐκολάζετο) prior to the suspension, but there is no indication that this caused death. The suspension is recorded with προσηλοῦτο, which could indicate "impale" (as in COLSON's LCL translation, whereas YONGE has "crucified"); more likely this refers to being nailed to a cross-like object (cf. Philo, *Post.* 61; *Som.* 2.213). Later, Philo's interpretation of Polycrates' demise (in *Prov.* 2.25) allegorically develops the meaning of how this death was a suspension (κρεμάμενος).

**(389)** Dio Chrysostom, *Orationes* 17.15 ("On Covetousness")

καὶ μὴν Πολυκράτην φασίν, ἕως μὲν Σάμου μόνης ἦρχεν, εὐδαιμονέστατον ἁπάντων γενέσθαι· βουλόμενον δέ τι καὶ τῶν πέραν πολυπραγμονεῖν, δια-πλεύσαντα πρὸς Ὀροίτην, ὡς χρήματα λάβοι, μηδὲ ῥᾳδίου γε θανάτου τυχεῖν, ἀλλὰ ἀνασκολοπισθέντα ὑπὸ τοῦ βαρβάρου διαφθαρῆναι.

*Translation.* And further the example which is Polycrates: While he ruled over just Samos, he was the most blessed of all people, but since he also wished to meddle in something of the other side [of the sea], and since he sailed across to Oroetes so he might receive money, he did not obtain an easy death, but having been crucified by the barbarian, he was utterly destroyed.

*Commentary.*[863] In his speech "On Covetousness," Dio Cocceianus Chryso-stomos, who lived from the second half of the first century A.D. until the early second century, puts forth Polycrates as another historical example of the dangers of greed (alongside Paris, "the sons of Iocasta", and Xerxes). Dio writes as a Stoic-Cynic philosopher. He assumes that his audience will already know the story (much as they will remember the Trojan War when he mentions Helen and Menelaus), and thus he provides just the briefest of summaries. In terms of the means of death, only ἀνασκολοπισθέντα is mentioned, and the relationship of this verb to διαφθαρῆναι strongly suggests that Dio portrays the hanging up of Polycrates on the σκόλοψ as the manner of execution. He

---

[862] Text: COLSON / WHITAKER / MARCUS, Philo, 9:475. The Greek here is surprisingly condensed and difficult to render into English. One clue for the translator concerns how Polycrates is in the dative case, serving as the object of the verb ἀπαντάω.

[863] Text: GUY DE BUDÉ, Dionis Chrysostomi orationes post Ludovicum Dindorfium (2 vols.; Bibliotheca Scriptorum Graecorum et Romanorum Teubneriana; Leipzig: Teubner, 1916–1919), 2:311.

certainly betrays no awareness of a death prior to Polycrates' suspension (such as appears in Herodotus, *Hist.* 3.125.3).

**(390)** Lucian, *Contemplantes (Charon)* 14

εὖ γε παρῳδεῖς, ὦ Χάρων. ἀλλὰ Πολυκράτην ὁρᾷς τὸν Σαμίων τύραννον πανευδαίμονα ἡγούμενον εἶναι· ἀτὰρ καὶ οὗτος αὐτὸς ὑπὸ τοῦ παρεστῶτος οἰκέτου Μαιανδρίου προδοθεὶς Ὀροίτῃ τῷ σατράπῃ ἀνασκολοπισθήσεται, ἄθλιος ἐκπεσὼν τῆς εὐδαιμονίας ἐν ἀκαρεῖ τοῦ χρόνου· καὶ ταῦτα γὰρ τῆς Κλωθοῦς ἐπήκουσα.

*Translation.* You indeed parody well, O Charon. But you see Polycrates, the tyrant of Samos, who is held to be all blessed; nevertheless even he himself will be crucified, having been betrayed by Maeandrius, the servant who is standing nearby [him], to Oroetes the satrap – the pitiful man falling from blessedness in a moment of time. For even these things I heard from Clotho.

*Commentary.*[864] In this sarcastic dialogue, Lucian depicts Charon (the ferryman to the underworld) touring the earthly world of men with Hermes, so that Charon can better understand the lives of men before they go down to Hades. Charon has just spied Polycrates, who is receiving back the signet ring from the fish, which fortune designed to bring back the ring to him. Hermes tells Charon of Polycrates' impending fate. His extremely good fortune (represented in the ring incident) will quickly be reversed, and he will die by crucifixion (the term ἀνασκολοπισθήσεται clearly designates crucifixion in Lucian; cf. No. 122). Indeed, the servant assisting Polycrates with recovering the ring appears to be Maeandrius ("the servant who is standing nearby"), who will ultimately betray Polycrates to his executioner.

**(391)** Valerius Maximus, *Facta et Dicta Memorabilia* 6.9 ext. 5

sed hunc, cuius felicitas semper plenis velis prosperum cursum tenuit, Orontes, Darii regis praefectus, in excelsissimo Mycalensis montis vertice cruci adfixit, e qua putres eius artus et tabido cruore manantia membra atque illam laevam, cui Neptunus anulum piscatoris manu restituerat, situ marcidam Samos, amara servitute aliquamdiu pressa, liberis ac laetis oculis aspexit.

*Translation.* But this man [Polycrates], whose luck always held a fortunate course with full sail, Orontes, the prefect of king Darius, fixed to a cross on the highest peak of Mount Mycale. Upon which position [Polycrates'] putrid joints, and his members dripping with decaying gore, and that left hand (to which Neptune had restored a ring by the hand of a fisherman), Samos, weak-

---

[864] Text: HARMON, Lucian, 2:426.

ened by having been oppressed for a long while by bitter servitude, looked with free and cheerful eyes.

*Commentary.*[865] In 6.9, Valerius concerns himself with listing historical illustrations of changes in fortune. Polycrates serves here as a prime example among those exemplars from outside Rome. Since he views Polycrates as a tyrant (in the Roman sense), Valerius presumes Samos to have been sorely oppressed by him, such that the whole island rejoiced to look upon Polycrates crucified atop a mountain on the Ionian coast just across the strait from Samos. *Ante mortem* crucifixion is clearly indicated by the terminology (*cruci adfixit*) and by the lack of any other means of execution. The picture of Polycrates' crucified body is vividly drawn. Valerius has fully accommodated the earlier accounts (cf. Herodotus, whose portrayal is much more muted) into a vision of the cross that must have been prevalent in his own day.

### 3.9.2 Prometheus

The legend of Prometheus represents that god as attached to a cliff so that an eagle may come daily to devour his entrails (of course, since he is a god, Prometheus never dies). Such a terrible punishment resulted from how Prometheus angered Zeus by creating humankind and then by giving them fire.[866] The legend is an ancient one, known already in Hesiod's *Theogonia* 521–569, where Prometheus is bound and impaled with a shaft (521–522).[867] Aeschylus represents Hephaestus, along with the gods of Power and Force, executing Zeus' judgment against Prometheus in the Caucasus mountains; as in Hesiod, Aeschylus portrays the gods employing fetters to Prometheus' hands and feet and thrusting a shaft through his midriff (Aeschylus, *Prom.* 1–11, 52–81). HENGEL suggests that this punishment represents the ancient Greek penalty of *apotympanismos.*[868] The episode is not presented with crucifixion terminology in the earliest sources. Yet it was a small step for later authors to re-envision such a penalty with crucifixion language since it overlapped with the idea of a suspended living victim, fastened to his execution device, and left as food for

---

[865] Text: SHACKLETON BAILEY, Valerius Maximus, 2:96–98.

[866] The various accounts actually disagree somewhat on the reasons for Zeus' wrath; thus Hesiod tells a lengthy story about Prometheus attempting to deceive Zeus concerning the meat and fat on an ox; Hesiod, *Theog.* 534–555.

[867] Hesiod, *Theog.* 521–524: δῆσε δ' ἀλυκτοπέδῃσι Προμηθέα ποικιλόβουλον [522] δεσμοῖς ἀργαλέοισι μέσον διὰ κίον' ἐλάσσας· [523] καί οἱ ἐπ' αἰετὸν ὦρσε τανύπτερον· αὐτὰρ ὅ γ' ἧπαρ [524] ἤσθιεν ἀθάνατον. WHITE's LCL translation renders this as: "And ready-witted Prometheus he bound with inextricable bonds, cruel chains, and drove a shaft through his middle, and set on him a long-winged eagle, which used to eat his immortal liver."

[868] HENGEL, Crucifixion, 11 n. 1.

birds. One example from Lucian (*Prom.* 1–2) was already presented in section 3.1.2; another appears from Martial in section 3.10.4 (*Liber de spectaculis* 7.1).

**(392)** Arrian, *Indica* 5.10–11

κατάπερ ὦν καὶ τὸν Παραπάμοσον Καύκασον ἐκάλεον Μακεδόνες, οὐδέν τι προσήκοντα τοῦτον τῷ Καυκάσῳ. ¹¹ Καί τι καὶ ἄντρον ἐπιφρασθέντες ἐν Παραπαμισάδαισι, τοῦτο ἔφρασαν ἐκεῖνο εἶναι τοῦ Προμηθέος τοῦ Τιτῆνος τὸ ἄντρον, ἐν ὅτῳ ἐκρέματο ἐπὶ τῇ κλοπῇ τοῦ πυρός.

*Translation.* Just like the Macedonians also called the Parapamisus the "Caucasus," though this has nothing to do with the Caucasus. ¹¹ And some even, after noticing a cave in the Parapamisadae, said this is that cave of Prometheus the Titan, in which he was hung on account of the theft of fire.

*Commentary.*[869] Arrian reflects on the Macedonian incursion into India under Alexander the Great. He observes that Alexander is the only one to conquer India, save for the hero gods Dionysus and Heracles. While there is a locale associated with Dionysus' conquest in India, Arrian doubts the Macedonian claim that Alexander managed to conquer the very rock Heracles failed to capture (Aornos). Arrian then proceeds to explain a similar geographical error among the Macedonians – the identification of the Caucasus with the Parapamisus range. Note in Arrian that Prometheus was hung (ἐκρέματο). While this may appear a nondescript word, it is commonly employed in Arrian to refer to the bodily suspension of humans.[870] Here it must obviously refer to the *ante mortem* suspension of Prometheus. Assuming that Arrian is following the general contours of the Prometheus myth, impalement can likely be ruled out because of the role of the eagle in attacking Prometheus' midriff. A further reference in Arrian (*Anab.* 5.3.1–2) credits Eratosthenes the Cyrenaean with the report that the Macedonians identified a cave in the Parapamisadae with Prometheus' place of punishment (this text does not mention Prometheus' suspension, but emphasizes that he had been "bound" so that the eagle could attack). Compare this text with the following passage from Arrian: καὶ τοῦ Καυκάσου κορυφή τις ἐδείκνυτο – Στρόβιλος τῇ κορυφῇ ὄνομα – ἵναπερ ὁ Προμηθεὺς κρεμασθῆναι ὑπὸ Ἡφαίστου κατὰ πρόσταξιν Διὸς μυθεύεται ("And a certain peak of the Caucasus was shown – Strobilos is the name of the peak – in that place Prometheus was fabled to have been hung up by Hephaestus according to the command of Zeus").[871]

---

[869] Text: ROBSON, Arrian, 2:320.

[870] Arrian, *Anab.* 4.14.3; 6.17.2; 6.30.2; 7.14.4; *Historia successorum Alexandri* (FGH 2b 156) Fragments 1.11; 1.18; *Periplus ponti Euxini* 11.5.

[871] Arrian, *Periplus ponti Euxini* 11.5. Text: ROOS and WIRTH, Flavii Arriani quae exstant omnia, 2:20.

**(393)** Lucian, *De Sacrificiis* 6

Καίτοι τὰ μὲν Ἡφαίστου μέτρια· τὸν δὲ Προμηθέα τίς οὐκ οἶδεν οἷα ἔπαθεν, διότι καθ' ὑπερβολὴν φιλάνθρωπος ἦν; καὶ γὰρ αὖ καὶ τοῦτον εἰς τὴν Σκυθίαν ἀγαγὼν ὁ Ζεὺς ἀνεσταύρωσεν ἐπὶ τοῦ Καυκάσου, τὸν ἀετὸν αὐτῷ παρακατα-στήσας τὸ ἧπαρ ὁσημέραι κολάψοντα.

*Translation.* And yet these are moderate matters concerning Hephaestus, but who does not know what sorts of things befell Prometheus because he espe-cially was a lover-of-mankind? For again Zeus, having led him to Scythia, crucified him on the Caucasus, having stationed an eagle beside him that would daily peck at his liver.

*Commentary.*[872] Lucian is in the midst of sarcastically questioning the whole of the pagan sacrificial system, in part because the mythic stories about the gods call more for their derision than for their admiration. He has just observed that Zeus made Hephaestus lame by casting him out of heaven. Now he turns to another example of Zeus' anger, namely the penalty he applied to Prome-theus. This he encapsulates in the term ἀνεσταύρωσεν ("he crucified"), which is Lucian's standard language for the crucifixions of his day. This instance also serves to show that the gods (like Prometheus and Hephaestus) were themselves feebler than seems appropriate to deity.

Lucian makes another reference to the crucifixion of Prometheus for much the same purposes in *Jupp. conf.* 8.[873] There, Cyniscus (while "catechiz-ing" Zeus) inquires into the state of the gods, with Zeus responding that they are eternally blessed and live good lives. Then Cyniscus trots out multiple examples of gods who are injured or grieved, beginning with the crippling of Hephaestus and the crucifixion of Prometheus.

Moreover, the entirety of Lucian's dialogue *Prometheus* can be men-tioned again here. In section 3.1.2, *Prom.* 1–2 was discussed, where Lucian employs the whole range of crucifixion terms in discussing Prometheus' plight. Such crucifixion language continues throughout (e.g., *Prom.* 4, 7, 9, 10, 15, 17). That dialogue focuses more on Zeus' irrational behavior.

### 3.9.3 Biblical Suspension Narratives

Several passages in the Hebrew Bible refer to the bodily suspension of a per-son, usually employing תלה as the main verb. These were studied in their ANE

---

[872] Text: HARMON, Lucian, 3:162.

[873] The entirety of the pertinent text *Jupp. conf.* 8 is simply: ὁ Προμηθεὺς δὲ καὶ ἀνεσκο-λοπίσθη ποτέ ("And even Prometheus was once crucified"). Note the shift in crucifixion verbs between these dialogues, though both verbs are used interchangeably in Lucian, *Prom.* 1–2.

context in section 3.2. This subsection explores some of the ways those passages were reinterpreted by subsequent generations of Jewish readers. Often these later authors would translate תלה with Greek or Aramaic terms that function more like technical terms for human bodily suspension (such as σταυρόω and צלב). Such vocabulary not only feels more specific, but it also could be used by Jewish authors to depict the kinds of suspensions that the Romans were performing in their day. Thus the original readers of these translations and biblical summaries could understandably find their minds drawn toward crucifixion. Section 3.5 has presented traditions on Deut 21:22–23 in Second Temple and early rabbinic interpretation. The material below has been covered in substantial detail in other publications, so this section will cite a modicum of examples, especially omitting many rabbinic interpretations.[874] In contrast to earlier presentations, we shall proceed by corpus and author, rather than by biblical text.

I have argued that for Jewish people in the Roman empire, their perceptions of the cross largely overlapped with the experiences of their pagan neighbors except in two vital respects: First, the Jewish populace of Palestine (and of Alexandria) directly experienced crucifixion against their compatriots through (among other matters) the Roman suppression of various Jewish insurrectionist movements (see section 3.7), thus the Jewish populace could understand even better than most of their pagan counterparts the idea of a crucified innocent sufferer or national hero. Second, the authority of Scripture in the lives of Jewish people meant that they had an array of biblical narratives that provided paradigms of people who had been "hung on the tree." Most of these paradigms represent the victim of suspension negatively, especially the person "cursed of God" in Deut 21 and the figure of Haman, the archopponent of Judaism, in the book of Esther. The Christian proclamation of a crucified Messiah thus potentially encountered a significant stumbling block in explaining the cross of Jesus in the midst of biblical examples that would otherwise call for the derision of those who had been suspended. Evidence of the consequent difficulties for Gospel proclamation can be found in early Jewish and Christian interactions.[875]

**(394)** Greek Text of Esther

[Esth 7:9 B-text] εἶπεν δὲ Βουγαθαν εἷς τῶν εὐνούχων πρὸς τὸν βασιλέα ἰδοὺ καὶ ξύλον ἡτοίμασεν Αμαν Μαρδοχαίῳ τῷ λαλήσαντι περὶ τοῦ βασιλέως καὶ ὤρθωται ἐν τοῖς Αμαν ξύλον πηχῶν πεντήκοντα εἶπεν δὲ ὁ βασιλεύς σταυρωθήτω ἐπ' αὐτοῦ.

---

[874] See esp. CHAPMAN, Crucifixion, 97–177.
[875] For the development of these themes cf. CHAPMAN, Crucifixion, 215–217, 234–253.

*Translation*. [Esth 7:9] And Bougathan, one of the eunuchs, said to the king, "Behold, Haman also prepared a tree for Mordecai, who spoke concerning the king; and a tree fifty cubits high was raised up in Haman's property." And the king said, "Let him be crucified on it."

[Esth E17–18 = 16:17–18; Rahlfs 8:12ʳ B-text] καλῶς οὖν ποιήσετε μὴ προσχρησάμενοι τοῖς ὑπὸ Αμαν Αμαδαθου ἀποσταλεῖσι γράμμασιν διὰ τὸ αὐτὸν τὸν ταῦτα ἐξεργασάμενον πρὸς ταῖς Σούσων πύλαις ἐσταυρῶσθαι σὺν τῇ πανοικίᾳ τὴν καταξίαν τοῦ τὰ πάντα ἐπικρατοῦντος θεοῦ διὰ τάχους ἀποδόντος αὐτῷ κρίσιν.

*Translation*. [E17–18] Therefore, you will do well by not employing the letters that were sent out by Haman son of Hamadatha, because he who has done these things was crucified at the gates of Susa with his entire household – the worthy judgment of the God who rules over all and repaid him quickly.

*Commentary*.[876] Typically the Greek OT translations, commonly collected under the banner of the Septuagint, render the Hebrew "hang [תלה] on a tree" in reference to human bodily suspension with Greek forms from κρεμάννυμι / κρεμάζω, as one would expect (e.g., Gen 40:19, 22; 41:13; Deut 21:22–23; Josh 8:29; 10:26; 1 Esdras 6:31). However, the B-text [LXX] of Esther supplies early evidence of an OT translator employing technical bodily suspension terminology from σταυρόω. Though scholars discuss the textual relationship of the B-text to the Hebrew, here it is likely that the translator in 7:9 was rendering a text akin to the MT, and thus he actualized a form of תלה by inserting σταυρωθήτω.[877] In contrast, the Lucianic (A-text) at this very juncture (Hanhart L 7:13) employs κρεμασθήτω, which would be more expected.[878] In fact, both the B-text and A-text render all other forms of תלה in the Hebrew Esther with a form of κρεμάννυμι (note esp. ἐκρεμάσθη in the very next verse, 7:10, in the B-text; see further Esth 2:23; 5:14; 6:4; 8:7; 9:13–14, 25). Nevertheless, in the apocryphal Additions to Esther E18 both the Lucianic text (L 7:28 in Hanhart) and the B-text (cited above) agree in stating that Haman was publicly hung on a σταυρός (ἐσταυρῶσθαι) with his whole house. In reality, we cannot know if σταυρόω bears the specific sense of "crucify" here, though it clearly conveys a narrower application to suspension of human bodies than does κρεμάννυμι. One further passage in the Lucianic recension (A-

---

[876] Text: Robert Hanhart, Esther (2. Auflage; Septuaginta VIII.3; Göttingen: Vandenhoeck & Ruprecht, 2008).

[877] For textual relationships, note esp. Linda Day, Three Faces of a Queen: Characterization in the Books of Esther (JSOTSup 186; Sheffield: Sheffield Academic Press, 1995), 15–18. For this and other matters, see the extended discussion of suspension in Greek Esther in Chapman, Crucifixion, 163–165.

[878] The A-text of Esther, with translation, can also be found in David J. A. Clines, The Esther Scroll: The Story of the Story (JSOTSup 30; Sheffield: JSOT Press, 1984), 238–239 (where he labels this passage 8:13).

text 7:14; cf. MT 6:11) reads καθότι ἐκείνῃ τῇ ἡμέρᾳ ἐκεκρίκει ἀνασκολοπί-σαι αὐτόν ("just like in that day he had decided to crucify him"), employing ἀνασκολοπίζω, which is another important Greek term for bodily suspension. Certainly, later readers of the Greek OT would have been influenced by this initial foray in introducing contemporary suspension language into the biblical text. Josephus clearly expands on this throughout his retelling of the Esther narratives (see below).

**(395)** Philo, *De Josepho* 96, 98

τὰ τρία κανᾶ σύμβολον τριῶν ἡμερῶν ἐστιν· ἐπισχὼν ταύτας ὁ βασιλεὺς ἀνασκολοπισθῆναί σε καὶ τὴν κεφαλὴν ἀποτμηθῆναι κελεύσει καὶ καταπτάμε-να ὄρνεα τῶν σῶν εὐωχηθήσεται σαρκῶν, ἄχρις ἂν ὅλος ἐξαναλωθῇς ... ⁹⁸ τῶν κατὰ τὸ δεσμωτήριον εὐνούχων ὑπομνησθεὶς ἀχθῆναι κελεύει καὶ θεασάμενος τἀκ τῆς τῶν ὀνείρων διακρίσεως ἐπισφραγίζεται, προστάξας τὸν μὲν ἀνασκο-λοπισθῆναι τὴν κεφαλὴν ἀποτμηθέντα, τῷ δὲ τὴν ἀρχὴν ἣν διεῖπε πρότερον ἀπονεῖμαι.

*Translation.* The three baskets are a symbol of three days; upon reaching these, the king will command you to be crucified and your head to be cut off, and the attacking birds will feast on your flesh, until you wholly are consumed ... ⁹⁸ [the king], remembering the eunuchs in the prison, commanded them to be brought; and beholding them, he confirmed the judgment of the dreams, ordering the one to be crucified, his head being cut off, but to the other to be assigned the office that he held before.

*Commentary.*[879] This represents Philo's literal retelling of the Gen 40:18–22, where Joseph interprets the baker's dream. There is clear application of bodily suspension (even crucifixion) language (ἀνασκολοπισθῆναι). More impor-tantly, while the Hebrew text reads that the baker's head will be "lifted up" (likely decapitation) and then he will be hung *post mortem* on the tree, here in Philo the reversed order of verbs implies that the suspension precedes the decapitation (though the beheading on the cross is also more clearly indicated in Philo with τὴν κεφαλὴν ἀποτμηθέντα).[880] The birds are portrayed more aggressively here than in the MT, and they are said to devour the whole of the baker. All this must have looked similar to the Roman cross in Philo's day (note that he was a personal witness at such crucifixions, cf. Philo, *Flacc.* 72, and esp. 83–84; see No. 380, 381).

---

[879] Text: COHN / WENDLAND / REITER, Philonis Alexandrini opera, 4:81–82.

[880] This would be even more evident if one were to follow the reading (found in four man-uscripts) καὶ τὴν κεφαλὴν ἀποτμηθῆναι in place of τὴν κεφαλὴν ἀποτμηθέντα.

**(396)** Philo, *De Josepho* 156

τελευτὴ γὰρ ἕπεται σιτίων σπάνει· οὗ χάριν καὶ ὁ περὶ ταῦτ᾽ ἐξαμαρτὼν εἰκό-
τως θνῄσκει κρεμασθείς, ὅμοιον κακὸν ᾧ διέθηκε παθών· καὶ γὰρ αὐτὸς
ἀνεκρέμασε καὶ παρέτεινε τὸν πεινῶντα λιμῷ.

*Translation.* For death follows lack of bread-food, on account of which the
one who errs greatly concerning these things also properly dies by having
been hung, a similar evil to which he treated the sufferer, for indeed he had
hung up and stretched the famished man with hunger.

*Commentary.*[881] Philo follows his literal retelling with an allegorical exposition (though one he ambiguously claims to have "heard"). Here, the baker represents the one who is called to feed the mind's body (i.e., Pharaoh). When
failing at his job, he receives just recompense. The baker's demise here (previously depicted in *Jos.* 98 with ἀνασκολοπισθῆναι) apparently comes "by
having been hung" (understanding κρεμασθείς as an instrumental participle).
This death also involves being "hung up" (ἀνεκρέμασε) and "stretched"
(παρέτεινε). Could the "stretched" refer to being laid out with outstretched
arms on the suspension device?

**(397)** Philo, *De Somniis* 2.213

περισυληθεὶς οὖν ὁ νοῦς ὧν ἐδημιούργησεν, ὥσπερ τὸν αὐχένα ἀποτμηθεὶς
ἀκέφαλος καὶ νεκρὸς ἀνευρεθήσεται, προσηλωμένος ὥσπερ οἱ ἀνασκολοπισθέντες τῷ ξύλῳ τῆς ἀπόρου καὶ πενιχρᾶς ἀπαιδευσίας.

*Translation.* The mind, therefore, stripped of the things it fabricated, like one
who was severed at the neck, will be discovered headless and a corpse, nailed
like those crucified to the tree of poor and needy lack of training.

*Commentary.*[882] In his "On Dreams," Philo pens another allegorical interpretation of the Joseph narrative. The mind here is allegorically depicted as the
baker's head, while the baker is the "belly-slave" who provides for the intem-
perate desires of Pharaoh. The "lack of training" (ἀπαιδευσίας) is a well-
known philosophical term for those who lack proper training in instruction or
discipline. A poorly instructed mind is likened unto the decapitated baker,
who has been nailed to the tree of his wanton indiscipline. The imagery here
invokes crucifixion terminology of προσηλωμένος and οἱ ἀνασκολοπισθέντες
τῷ ξύλῳ.

---

[881] Text: COHN / WENDLAND / REITER, Philonis Alexandrini opera, 4:94.
[882] Text: COHN / WENDLAND / REITER, Philonis Alexandrini opera, 3:292–293.

**(398)** Josephus, *Antiquitates judaicae* 2.72–73

λέγει δύο τὰς πάσας ἔτι τοῦ ζῆν αὐτὸν ἔχειν ἡμέρας· τὰ γὰρ κανᾶ τοῦτο ση-
μαίνειν· [73] τῇ τρίτῃ δ᾽ αὐτὸν ἀνασταυρωθέντα βορὰν ἔσεσθαι πετεινοῖς οὐδὲν
ἀμύνειν αὐτῷ δυνάμενον. καὶ δὴ ταῦτα τέλος ὅμοιον οἷς ὁ Ἰώσηπος εἶπεν
ἀμφοτέροις ἔλαβε· τῇ γὰρ ἡμέρᾳ τῇ προειρημένῃ γενέθλιον τεθυκὼς ὁ
βασιλεὺς τὸν μὲν ἐπὶ τῶν σιτοποιῶν ἀνεσταύρωσε, τὸν δὲ οἰνοχόον τῶν
δεσμῶν ἀπολύσας ἐπὶ τῆς αὐτῆς ὑπηρεσίας κατέστησεν.

*Translation.* [Joseph] said that he still had two whole days to live, for the baskets signified this, [73] and on the third day he, having been crucified, will be
food for birds and not able to defend himself. And indeed these things
occurred perfectly like Joseph said to both [of them]; for on the day which had
been foretold, the king, having sacrificed for his birthday celebration, crucified the baker, but having released the cup bearer from his bond, he established him into the same service.

*Commentary.*[883] Josephus here recounts the events of Genesis 40, employing
ἀνασταυρόω ("crucify" or "hang up on a σταυρός") twice to indicate the fate
of the baker. By deleting any reference to the lifting of the baker's head prior to
his suspension (as appears in the Hebrew text and in the LXX of Gen 40:19),
there is no longer any possible inference of an initial beheading. Instead
ἀνασταυρόω must convey the baker's means of execution. Also observe here
that he is "not able to defend himself" (οὐδὲν ἀμύνειν αὐτῷ δυνάμενον),
which is Josephus' own interpretive comment (MT and LXX only mention
that he will be food for birds); this must envision the baker being suspended
aloft while alive and defenseless. The use of cross terminology, combined
with the living execution on the device, strongly points to how Josephus
understood this to mimic the crucifixions of his own day. In *A. J.* 2.77
Josephus will recap these events (following Gen 41:13) with the verb σταυρόω
(saying "that the one over the bakers was crucified on the same day").[884]

**(399)** Josephus, *Antiquitates judaicae* 6.374

καὶ τὰς μὲν πανοπλίας αὐτῶν ἀνέθηκαν εἰς τὸ Ἀστάρτειον ἱερόν, τὰ δὲ
σώματα ἀνεσταύρωσαν πρὸς τὰ τείχη τῆς Βηθσὰν πόλεως, ἣ νῦν Σκυθόπολις
καλεῖται.

---

[883] Text: NIESE, Flavii Josephi Opera, 1:97–98. Textual variants are minor (the most substantial involves the tense of τεθυκὼς, which is incidental to our study).

[884] *A. J.* 2.77: ὅτι τε σταυρωθείη κατὰ τὴν αὐτὴν ἡμέραν ὁ ἐπὶ τῶν σιτοποιῶν.

*Translation.* And they set up their armor in the Astarte temple, but the bodies they crucified to the walls of the city of Bethsan, which is now called Scythopolis.

*Commentary.*[885] This passage refers to the occasion when the Philistines, having just found the corpses of Saul and his sons, cut off their heads and perform *post mortem* suspensions of their bodies, by affixing them to the walls of Bethsan. Nysa-Scythopolis was the Hellenistic and Roman name for the Decapolis city of Beth Shean. In context, the punishment is indeed *post mortem*, and yet Josephus depicts the scene as an instance of ἀνασταυρόω. This reminds us of the semantic range of this term, and how it can include *ante* and *post mortem* suspensions. Here, the device is not a σταυρός, but the city wall (cf. Lucian, *Prom.* 1–2 for a cliff wall as the locale for ἀνασταυρόω). In any case, the idea of bodily suspension is enough to allow ἀνασταυρόω to be employed here. The fact that both Saul and his sons are all suspended in this text (while 1 Sam 31:9–10 only mentions Saul), likely stems from Josephus' synoptic reading of 1 Samuel 31 with 2 Sam 21:12, which mentions the hanging of the sons as well as Saul. Perhaps then the combination of "hanging" in 2 Samuel with being "affixed" to the wall in 1 Samuel aided in associating crucifixion vocabulary (where a person is suspended by being affixed to a device) with this episode.

Concerning suspension language in Josephus, perhaps the most striking feature in his retelling of Jewish history from Joshua to Kings concerns his omission of any mention of Joshua suspending the king of Ai (cf. Josh 8:29) or of Joshua hanging up the five kings (Josh 10:26). In fact, Josephus downplays these episodes in general (cf. *A. J.* 5.48, 61), while other OT suspension events he happily translates with ἀνασταυρόω and cognates. Elsewhere it has been suggested that this could either be an intentional attempt to attenuate before his Roman readership any harsh military actions by respected Judean leaders, or it may be that Josephus was sensitive about implying that biblical heroes could have employed crucifixion.[886] In light of Josephus' treatment of Deut 21:22–23 (see section 3.5.1), perhaps both motives may have prompted his refusal to associate Joshua with crucifixion.

## (400) Josephus, *Antiquitates judaicae* 11.103

τοὺς δὲ παραβάντας τι τῶν ἐπεσταλμένων συλληφθέντας ἐκέλευσεν ἀνασταυρωθῆναι καὶ τὴν οὐσίαν αὐτῶν εἰς τὴν βασιλικὴν καταταγῆναι κτῆσιν.

---

[885] Text: NIESE, Flavii Josephi Opera, 2:86.
[886] See fuller discussion in CHAPMAN, Crucifixion, 151–153.

*Translation.* But concerning those who transgress any of what has been commanded, after being captured, he commanded them to be crucified and their property to be paid as an acquisition into the royal treasury.

*Commentary.*[887] Cyrus' letter concerning the rebuilding of the Jerusalem Temple has just been found and is being read to Darius. The previous record in Josephus of the original writing of the letter has a similar command, also invoking ἀνασταυρωθῆναι on those who transgress the Persian king's edict (*A. J.* 11.17). This corresponds to the text in Ezra 6 or 1 Esdras 6, but substitutes ἀνασταυρόω for זְקִיף in MT and παγήσεται in the Greek (in Ezra 6:11) or for the κρεμασθῆναι in 1 Esdras 6:31.

**(401)** Josephus, *Antiquitates judaicae* 11.267

ὁ δὲ βασιλεὺς ἀκούσας οὐκ ἄλλη τιμωρίᾳ περιβάλλειν ἔκρινεν τὸν Ἀμάνην ἢ τῇ κατὰ Μαρδοχαίου νενοημένῃ, καὶ κελεύει παραχρῆμα αὐτὸν ἐξ ἐκείνου τοῦ σταυροῦ κρεμασθέντα ἀποθανεῖν.

*Translation.* And after the king heard [this], he determined to not encompass Haman with any penalty other than the one that had been devised against Mordecai. And he immediately commanded him, having been hung from that cross, to be put to death.

*Commentary.*[888] This passage is Josephus' equivalent of Esth 7:9–10. It comes at the key climax of the Esther narratives, when the penalty Haman had devised against Mordecai is instead brought down on Haman and his house. In Josephus, this penalty is described as hanging on a cross (ἐξ ἐκείνου τοῦ σταυροῦ κρεμασθέντα). Notably here, this serves as the mode of execution (note the relationship between the κρεμασθέντα participial phrase and the infinitive ἀποθανεῖν).[889] In his Esther narratives, Josephus expands the use of σταυρός cognates beyond those found in the LXX (B-text of 7:9 and E18), with the result that he commonly employs σταυρός cognates throughout the bodily suspension episodes in these narratives.[890] Typically these texts have precise parallels in the Greek OT Esther, in which κρεμάννυμι (or cognate) occurs. In those very places, Josephus has actualized the narrative by invoking the σταυρός either in its nominal or derivative verbal forms.

---

[887] Text: NIESE, Flavii Josephi Opera, 3:24.

[888] Text: NIESE, Flavii Josephi Opera, 3:55. For κρεμασθέντα, two mss read ἀνακρεμασθέντα and Zonaras has κρεμασθῆναι; these variants produce no significant change in meaning.

[889] The participial phrase is either temporal, in which case the hanging would precede the action of dying, or means, so the manner of death would be by hanging on a cross.

[890] Josephus, *A. J.* 11.208 (cf. Esth 2:23); 11.246 (cf. Esth 5:14); 11.261; 11.280 (cf. *Add. Esth.* E18 in B-text; L 7:28 in the A-text); and 11.289. In one of these locations, Josephus apparently expanded the LXX text with his own material (*A. J.* 11.260–261, cf. 11.266).

**(402)** Targumim on Genesis 40:19

(*Tg. Onq.*)

בסוף תלתה יומין יעדי פרעה ית רישך מינך <u>ויצלוב</u> יתך על <u>צליבא</u> וייכול עופא ית בסרך מינך

(*Tg. Neof.*)

לסוף תלתא יומין ירים פרעה ית ראשך מעילוך <u>ויצלב</u> יתך על <u>צליבה</u> ויאכל עופא ית בשרך מעלווי <u>ראשך</u>

(*Tg. Ps.-J.*)

בסוף תלתא יומין יעדי פרעה <u>בסיפא</u> ית רישך מעילוי <u>גופך ויצלוב</u> יתך על קיסא ויכול עופא ית בישרך מינך

*Translation.*

(*Tg. Onq.*) At the end of three days Pharaoh will <u>remove</u> your head from you, and he will <u>suspend</u> you on the <u>cross</u>,[891] and the birds will eat your flesh from you.

(*Tg. Neof.*) Toward the end of three days Pharaoh will lift your head from upon you, and he will <u>suspend</u> you on a <u>cross</u>, and the birds will eat your flesh from upon your <u>head</u>.

(*Tg. Ps.-J.*) At the end of three days Pharaoh will <u>remove by the sword</u> your head from upon <u>your body</u>, and he will <u>suspend</u> you on the tree, and the birds will eat your flesh from you.

*Commentary.*[892] Although Aramaic תלא was available as the equivalent of Hebrew תלה, the targumim commonly employed צלב in translating OT passages that mention human suspension. The terminology of צלב (and cognates) is much more exclusively focused on human bodily suspension, including crucifixion, and thus it represents a shift toward more technical terms. This is true throughout targumim on other biblical books as well as here in Genesis. Rather than pursue all these possible examples, which has been done elsewhere,[893] this sample from Genesis will serve to illustrate some key trends in

---

[891] The noun צליבא (also cf. *Tg. Neof.*) is here translated as "the cross," which is a common English equivalent for this noun, and which allows צליבא to be more clearly distinguished from the more neutral קיסא ("the tree" in *Tg. Ps.-J.*). However, this admittedly does bias the translation to a crucifixion reading. Certainly, צליבא technically designates a device intended for penal bodily suspension; and both death by crucifixion as well as a *post mortem* suspension (such as is likely here) can occur on צליבא.

[892] The following editions were consulted in order to produce the texts above: SPERBER, Bible in Aramaic, vol. 1; ALEJANDO DÍEZ MACHO, Neophyti 1: Targum Palestinense MS de la Biblioteca Vaticana (5 vols.; Madrid: Consejo Superior de Investigaciones Científicas, 1968–1979), vol. 1; GINSBURGER, Pseudo-Jonathan; DÍEZ MACHO, DÍEZ MERINO, MARTÍNEZ BOROBIO, and MARTÍNEZ SÁIZ. Biblia Polyglotta Matritensia IV, vol. 1.

the targumic traditions. First, one does observe the shift toward more technical suspension vocabulary with צלב and צליבה. These terms also served as standard Aramaic vocabulary for the kinds of crucifixions that the Romans performed. And thus by using this language, the original readers and hearers of the targumim may have felt some increased resonance between the biblical text and the suspension practices of their day. Second, in two of these targumic texts the meturgeman also clarifies that the Hebrew for "lift up your head" here means to "remove your head by the sword." Thus the suspension is even more clearly *post mortem* in Onqelos and Pseudo-Jonathan. Note how similar trends were observed above concerning targumic renderings of Deut 21:22–23 (the language becomes more technical concerning bodily suspension, but the rabbinic desire to emphasize *post mortem* suspension is also evident). Were there space, this could be compared further to targumic interpretation of Num 25:4, and contrasted with the crucifixion-like death of Haman in the Esther *targumim*.[894]

## 3.10 Perceptions of Crucifixion in Graeco-Roman Literature

Some of the most intriguing evidence for Roman perceptions of crucifixion appears in Greek and Latin philosophical treatises, novels, satires, and drama. In such literature (along with sources studied above) one witnesses the horror of the cross: The cross could be deemed "wicked,"[895] it was known to be painful and cruel,[896] it could be labeled among the "most extreme deaths,"[897] and it was employed in public in a way that invoked shame and terror.[898] This sec-

---

[893] CHAPMAN, Crucifixion, 108–109, 112–114, 138–141, 153, 155–156, 159–160, 166–168, covering bodily suspension terminology in the targumic paraphrases of Gen 40:19 (and 40:22; 41:13); Num 25:4; Deut 21:22–23; Josh 8:29; 10:26; 1 Sam 31:10; 2 Sam 21:6, 9–10, 12; Lam 5:12–13; and Esth 2:23; 5:14; 6:4; 7:9, 10; 8:7; 9:14, 24–25. Particularly intriguing is the application of צלב and cognates to Num 25:4 and 2 Sam 6:9–10 (where the Hebrew original does not have תלה).

[894] Again see CHAPMAN, Crucifixion, 112–114, 166–168.

[895] Note especially the repeated references to the *mala crux* ("wicked cross") below in Plautus and Terence.

[896] The cruelty of the cross has already been observed above, such as when Cicero contends that the delay of "the cruelest and vilest penalty" (*crudelissimi taeterrimique supplici*) should be obligatory until the facts of the case against one who claims Roman citizenship are verified (Cicero, *Verr.* 2.5.165; see No. 281). Also note below how Seneca (*Ira 3* [*Dial. 5*] 3.6) will list the cross among other penal instruments of rage. See further Apuleius, *Metam.* 1.15.4; Valerius Maximus, 9.2 ext. 3.

[897] The cross is a key component of the list of *summa supplicia* in *Pauli Sententiae* 5.17.2; 5.21.4; 5.23.14–17 (cf. Nos. 336, 337, 342). See further Cicero, *Verr.* 2.5.168–169 (Nos. 283, 284); Josephus, *B. J.* 7.202–203 ("most pitiable of deaths;" No. 372).

[898] See especially Cicero, *Pis.* 18.42: *an ego, si te et Gabinium cruci suffixos viderem, maiore adficerer laetitia ex corporis vestri laceratione quam adficior ex famae?* ("I, if I saw

tion proceeds by looking at some of these genres of literature. In most cases, the sources are selected as representatives of the use of the cross in that literature. However, given the importance of the early testimony to the cross in the playwrights Plautus and Terence, they are studied more exhaustively.

### 3.10.1 Use in Philosophical Argument

Philosophers appreciate extreme examples, especially because they permit theories of virtue to be tested most fully. Crucifixion has already served as an extreme example in writings studied earlier from Plato, Aristotle, Cicero, Philo, Seneca, Plutarch, Epictetus, and Lucian (among others). Especially useful in philosophical discourse have been historical or mythological examples of the cross, for these are often well known and engender immediate resonance with the reader; thus consider the actualization both of the historical demise of Polycrates and of the mythological overly-harsh punishment of Prometheus (section 3.9). For sake of space, just a couple more examples are mentioned below, though many others could be considered.[899]

**(403)** Seneca, *De Ira 3 (Dialogue 5)* 3.6

Ne quem fallat tamquam aliquo tempore, aliquo loco profutura, ostendenda est rabies eius effrenata et attonita apparatusque illi reddendus est suus, eculei et fidiculae et ergastula et cruces et circumdati defossis corporibus ignes et cadavera quoque trahens uncus, varia vinculorum genera, varia poenarum, lacerationes membrorum, inscriptiones frontis et bestiarum immanium caveae – inter haec instrumenta collocetur ira dirum quiddam atque horridum stridens, omnibus per quae furit taetrior.

*Translation.* Lest [anger] deceive someone as though at some time or at some place it will be beneficial, its unbridled and frenzied fury must be exposed, and its paraphernalia must be ascribed to it: horse-shaped racks and torture devices and chain-gangs and crosses and fires that surround bodies embedded in the ground and even a hook for dragging corpses, various types of fetters, various [types] of penalties, mangling of limbs, brandings of the forehead, and the cages of brutal beasts – among these instruments let anger be ascribed, while it shrieks a certain dreadful and horrible [sound], more vile than all [the instruments] through which [anger] rages.

---

Gabinius and you attached to a cross, would I be more affected by exultation by the lacerating of your body than I would be affected from your reputation").

[899] For other examples, consider Cicero, *Fin.* 5.84; *Att.* 7.11.2; *Quint. fratr.* 1.29; Epictetus, *Diatr.* 2.2.20; Seneca, *Ep.* 101.10–14; for 101.14 see No. 123.

*Commentary.*[900] Lucius Annaeus Seneca (The Younger), probably in the early part of Claudius' first-century A.D. reign, wrote this Stoic treatise *On Anger*. In opposition to some philosophers (including Aristotle), who are among those in danger of being "deceived," Seneca argues that there is no virtuous utility to anger. These other philosophers contended that anger is useful to energize a man in times of war, or while conducting state business, or for other times when some zeal (*calor*) is required (*De Ira* 3.3.5). Seneca would claim that in such moments anger actually drives a person to frenzied excess, and he supports his case by listing the kinds of "instruments" that rage employs, i.e., the instruments of severe corporal punishment. All these *instrumenta* are common in the Roman penal arsenal. The list is in some sense uneven – neither ordered based on the increasing intensity of punishment, nor grouped strictly according to capital and non-capital penalties. While *cruces* ("crosses") can occasionally be employed to hold someone up for a scourging, in this context it most likely refers to a means of execution.[901] Seneca here evidences a philosopher's critique of the angry excess of standard Roman penal methods, including the cross.

**(404)** Philo, *De Posteritate Caini* 25–27

καὶ ἔστιν αὐτῷ, ὅπερ ἔφη ὁ νομοθέτης, πᾶσα ἡ ζωὴ κρεμαμένη, βάσιν οὐκ ἔχουσα ἀκράδαντον, ἀλλὰ πρὸς τῶν ἀντισπώντων καὶ ἀντιμεθελκόντων ἀεὶ φορουμένη πραγμάτων. ²⁶ οὗ χάριν ἐν ἑτέροις „κεκατηραμένον ὑπὸ θεοῦ τὸν κρεμάμενον ἐπὶ ξύλου" φησίν (Deut 21:23), ὅτι, θεοῦ δέον ἐκκρέμασθαι, ὁ δὲ ἀπηώρησεν ἑαυτὸν σώματος, ὅς ἐστιν ἐν ἡμῖν ξύλινος ὄγκος, ἐπιθυμίαν ἐλπίδος ἀντικαταλλαξάμενος, ἀγαθοῦ τελείου μέγιστον κακόν. ἐλπὶς μὲν γὰρ τῶν ἀγαθῶν οὖσα προσδοκία ἐκ τοῦ φιλοδώρου θεοῦ τὴν διάνοιαν ἀρτᾷ, ἐπιθυμία δὲ ἀλόγους ἐμποιοῦσα ὀρέξεις ἐκ τοῦ σώματος, ὃ δεξαμενὴν καὶ χώραν ἡδονῶν ἡ φύσις ἐδημιούργησεν. ²⁷ οὗτοι μὲν οὖν ὥσπερ ἀπ' ἀγχόνης τῆς ἐπιθυμίας ἐκκρεμάσθωσαν.

*Translation.* And, wherefore, it is for him the Law-giver said, "all his life hangs," (Deut 28:66) since it does not have an unshaken foundation, but, from being drawn in a contrary direction and dragged in a different way, it is always born along by circumstances. ²⁶ On account of which in different words He says, "the one who hangs on a tree has been cursed by God" (Deut 21:23, cf. LXX). For it is necessary to be hung upon God, but this one hangs down from

---

[900] Text: BASORE, Seneca. Moral Essays, 1:260.

[901] Note the immediate proximity of *cruces* to other elements of Roman execution – namely, the *ignes* of a public burning, and the executioner's hook (*uncus*) used to drag the cadaver through the city after an execution. Also note how *cruces* is separated from the torture devices (*eculei et fidiculae*) by the exiling of someone into compulsory slavery in harsh environments (*ergastula*).

his own body, which is in us as a wooden mass, receiving desire in exchange for hope – the greatest evil for perfect good. For hope on the one hand, being the expectation of good things, fastens the intention on the bountiful God; but desire which produces unreasoning yearning [fastens the intention] on the body, which nature fabricated as the receptacle and the proper place of pleasures. [27] These, therefore, are hung as from the halter of desire.

*Commentary.*[902] Philo engages in allegorical interpretation of Deut 21:22–23, cited from LXX. The preceding context argues that those who forsake God and tie themselves to creation will have a life without rest (much like the person whose life is suspended in Deut 28:65–66), while those who follow the unwavering God will have a stable life. Deuteronomy 21 provides a similar warning for those who would hang their desires on their bodily appetites – they will be like the person attached to a cross (a "wooden mass"). Instead, one should fasten one's intention on God. Such allegorical understandings of the suspension passages from the Pentateuch can also be found in Philo, *Post.* 61; *Somn.* 2.213; *Prov.* 24–25 (see Nos. 388, 397).

## 3.10.2 Use in Epigrams, Stories and Tales

The cross can bring a good dose of gallows humor to any story or epigram (e.g., Nos. 122, 126, 347, 384, 392, 393). It can also imperil the characters, thus leading to greater narrative tension. Yet even as it serves a narrative purpose, a reference to the cross in literature can betray cultural assumptions concerning who, when, where, and why someone might be crucified.

**(405)** *Anthologia Graeca* 11.192 (from Lucillius)

μακροτέρῳ σταυρῷ σταυρούμενον ἄλλον ἑαυτοῦ
ὁ φθονερὸς Διοφῶν ἐγγὺς ἰδὼν ἐτάκη.

*Translation.* Another man being crucified on a taller cross than him –
The envious Diophon, looking on nearby, wasted away.

*Commentary.*[903] The *Greek Anthology* attributes this epigram to Lucillius (with 11.189–192), and states that it is an epigram "on envy" (εἰς φθονερούς). Lucillius was a satirical epigrammatist who wrote during the first-century A.D. reign of Nero (often dedicating his work to the emperor). The central character here, Diophon, may have referenced the famed athlete of the same name who

---

[902] Text: COHN / WENDLAND / REITER, Philonis Alexandrini opera, 2:6–7.
[903] Text: WILLIAM R. PATON, The Greek Anthology (5 vols.; LCL; Cambridge: Harvard University Press, 1918–1927), 4:162.

competed in the pentathlon[904]; however, other Diophons are also known, and Lucillius also likely invented names for his characters as well.[905] In any case, Diophon is portrayed here as an envious (and competitive) soul. Even as he was being crucified, Diophon spied another man on a higher cross and "wasted away" (ἐτάκη). That Greek verb (from τήκω) makes for a neat double entendre, since it can refer both to the decaying of a body as well as meta-phorically to a person who pines for something or who wastes away for want of something he desires.[906] We need not presume this was an actual event, though it is clearly predicated on the historic variation in the sizes of crosses in antiquity.

**(406)** Chariton, *De Chaerea et Callirhoe* 3.4.18

ἀπαγομένῳ δὲ Θήρωνι μέγα μέρος τοῦ πλήθους ἐπηκολούθησεν. ἀνεσκολο-πίσθη δὲ πρὸ τοῦ Καλλιρρόης τάφου καὶ ἔβλεπεν ἀπὸ τοῦ σταυροῦ τὴν θάλασσαν ἐκείνην, δι᾽ ἧς αἰχμάλωτον ἔφερε τὴν Ἑρμοκράτους θυγατέρα, ἣν οὐκ ἔλαβον οὐδὲ Ἀθηναῖοι.

*Translation.* And as Theron was being led away, a great portion of the multi-tude followed. And he was crucified before the tomb of Callirhoë, and he looked from his cross upon that sea, through which he brought the daughter of Hermocrates prisoner, whom not even the Athenians had captured.

*Commentary.*[907] Chariton of Aphrodisias wrote this novel sometime before the mid-second century A.D. In the story, Chaereas and Callirhoë fall in love and marry, but Chaereas is driven to jealousy and kicks his wife. Falsely assuming Callirhoë is dead, she is buried, but tomb robbers capture her and take her away. When Chaereas learns that Callirhoë is alive, he pursues her through many adventures, until they are finally reunited. Theron was among the tomb robbers who stole Callirhoë away. After crossing the Ionian sea, he was nevertheless captured and held accountable. Theron is tortured for infor-mation (3.4.12) prior to his crucifixion in this narrative. While on the cross he is portrayed as looking out over the sea, which likely indicates that he was

---

[904] Lucillius mocks an unnamed pentathlon contestant in 11.84 for being the worst in all five sports, and Fain contrasts this to an epigram of Simonides from *Anthologia Planudea* 3 (*Anthologia Graeca* 16.3) where Diophon won all five sports. FAIN suggests Simonides' epi-gram may have been the inspiration for Lucillius' work. See GORDON L. FAIN, Ancient Greek Epigrams: Major Poets in Verse Translation (Berkeley: University of California Press, 2010), 213, 223–224 (concerning his epigram number 6). Other people named Diophon occur in the *Anthologia Graeca* in 7.519; 12.175.

[905] So FAIN, Epigrams, 209–210.

[906] Cf. LSJ s.v. τήκω.

[907] Text: REARDON, Chariton. De Callirhoe narrationes amatoriae, 52.

alive while he was suspended. Multiple other examples of crucifixion occur in this novel.[908]

**(407)** Apuleius, *Metamorphoses* 1.15.4

Illud horae memini me terra dehiscente ima Tartara inque his canem Cerberum prorsus esurientem mei prospexisse: ac recordabar profecto bonam Meroen non misericordia iugulo meo pepercisse sed saevitia cruci me reservasse.

*Translation.* In that hour I remember I saw, as the earth split open, deepest Tartarus and in this the truly ravenous dog Cerberus. And I was assuredly thinking that good Meroe did not spare my throat with pity, but with cruelty she reserved me for the cross.

*Commentary.*[909] In this extended yarn, we walk with Aristomenes as he encounters various ills in life. He had just met Socrates, who warned him of two witches (one name Meroe). They suddenly come and slit the throat of Socrates, leaving Aristomenes with the body and (potentially) the blame. The stableman believes Aristomenes has killed his companion, and thus we enter into Aristomenes' vision above. He envisions his impending death and considers Meroe to blame. He knows that, as a murderer, he would face the *crux*. In fact, Socrates suddenly and miraculously awakes just in time. The cross is a recurring theme in Apuleius, and one we have met above (see *Metam.* 3.9.1 in No. 347).[910] It certainly stands in this passage for the worst possible death Aristomenes can imagine – the equivalent of falling into the jaws of Cerberus.

**(408)** *Anthologia Graeca* 9.378 (from Palladas)

Ἀνδροφόνῳ σαθρὸν παρὰ τειχίον ὑπνώοντι
        νυκτὸς ἐπιστῆναι φασὶ Σάραπιν ὄναρ,
καὶ χρησμῳδῆσαι· "Κατακείμενος οὗτος, ἀνίστω,
        καὶ κοιμῶ μεταβάς, ὦ τάλας, ἀλλαχόθι."
[5] ὃς δὲ διυπνισθεὶς μετέβη. τὸ δὲ σαθρὸν ἐκεῖνο
        τειχίον ἐξαίφνης εὐθὺς ἔκειτο χαμαί.
σῶστρα δ᾽ ἕωθεν ἔθυε θεοῖς χαίρων ὁ κακοῦργος,
        ἥδεσθαι νομίσας τὸν θεὸν ἀνδροφόνοις.
ἀλλ᾽ ὁ Σάραπις ἔχρησε πάλιν, διὰ νυκτὸς ἐπιστάς·

---

[908] See No. 117 for Chariton, *Chaer.* 4.2.6–7. See further: 4.3.3; 4.3.5–6; 4.3.8–10; 5.10.6; 6.2.10; 8.7.8; 8.8.2; 8.8.4. These texts are conveniently collected and discussed in SAMUELSSON, Crucifixion, 138–142 (he accepts at least two suspensions in Chariton as clear examples of crucifixion); COOK, Crucifixion, 260–262.

[909] Text: ADLINGTON and GASELEE, Golden Ass, 26–28.

[910] Cf. *Metam.* 1.14.2; 4.10.4; 6.31.2; 6.32.1; 10.12.3 for other occasions of the cross.

<sup>10</sup> "Κήδεσθαί με δοκεῖς, ἄθλιε, τῶν ἀδίκων;
εἰ μὴ νῦν σε μεθῆκα θανεῖν, θάνατον μὲν ἄλυπον
   νῦν ἔφυγες, σταυρῷ δ᾽ ἴσθι φυλαττόμενος."

*Translation.* It is said that, to a murderer sleeping beside an unstable wall,
   Sarapis appeared during the night in a dream,
and that he prophesied: "This man who is lying down, let him arise;
   and, O wretch, sleep after going away elsewhere."
<sup>5</sup> And he awoke and went away. And that unstable
   wall suddenly and immediately lay in ruins on the ground.
And at earliest dawn the criminal offered a thank-offering to the gods while
rejoicing,
   thinking that the god was amused with murderers.
But Serapis again warned by oracle, appearing during the night:
   <sup>10</sup> "Do you think, wretch, that I care for the unrighteous?
If I have not now permitted you to die, a painless death
   now you have fled, but know that you are being guarded for the cross."

*Commentary.*[911] This epigram is attributed in the *Greek Anthology* (along with
9.377–379) to the fourth-century A.D. Alexandrian author Palladas. The
paganism of the poem would indicate either that the author was a pagan himself, or that he was reproducing a pagan-influenced story.[912] Sarapis (Serapis
in Latin) is a god of the underworld and of healing; he had Egyptian origins,
was prevalent in Alexandria, and often worked through oracles and cures in
dreams. As in many other texts, the cross is here reserved for a criminal (see
above sections 3.6.4–5). The human in this tale is variously represented as a
murderer (ἀνδροφόνος), wretch (τάλας/ἄθλιος), and criminal (κακοῦργος); he
is also considered to be among the unrighteous (τῶν ἀδίκων). Sarapis assures
the murderer that the very thing he thought was divine favor actually will
enable his eventual punishment to be greater. He is being "guarded" (φυλαττόμενος) for the cross (σταυρῷ), much as a criminal is imprisoned prior to his
trial and execution. Such a reversal comforts the reader by revealing that the
gods will eventually repay the wicked.

---

[911] Text: PATON, Greek Anthology, 3:206–208. Besides 11.192 and 9.378, other examples
of σταυρός and its cognates in the *Anthologia Graeca* are typically Christian (1.54, 60, 111;
8.24, 29, 146; 15.28; cf. 9.655) and thus remain outside the parameters of this study.

[912] The religious background of Palladas is disputed.

## 3.10.3 Use in Drama

In addition to the comical references to the cross in ancient farces (see sections 3.6.2 and 3.10.6), there were vivid re-enactments of crucifixions in some ancient plays, as represented by Josephus and Juvenal. These provided important visual reinforcement of cultural stereotypes about the cross.

**(409)** Josephus, *Antiquities* 19.94–95

ἔνθα δὲ καὶ σημεῖα μανθάνει δύο γενέσθαι· καὶ γὰρ μῖμος εἰσάγεται, καθ' ὃν σταυροῦται ληφθεὶς ἡγεμών, ὅ τε ὀρχηστὴς δρᾶμα εἰσάγει Κινύραν, ἐν ᾧ αὐτός τε ἐκτείνετο καὶ ἡ θυγάτηρ Μύρρα, αἷμά τε ἦν τεχνητὸν πολὺ καὶ περὶ τὸν σταυρωθέντα ἐκκεχυμένον καὶ τῶν περὶ τὸν Κινύραν. ⁹⁵ ὁμολογεῖται δὲ καὶ τὴν ἡμέραν ἐκείνην γενέσθαι, ἐν ᾗ Φίλιππον τὸν Ἀμύντου Μακεδόνων βασιλέα κτείνει Παυσανίας εἷς τῶν ἑταίρων εἰς τὸ θέατρον εἰσιόντα.

*Translation.* And even there he [Gaius Caligula] noticed that there were two omens: for a mime was introduced, during which a ruler was crucified after he had been apprehended, and the pantomime dancer introduced the drama *Cinyras*, in which both he and his daughter Myrrha were slain; and much artificial blood had been spilt around both the crucified man and around Cinyras. ⁹⁵ And it is also agreed that was the day in which Pausanias, one of the guards, killed Philip, son of Amyntas and the king of the Macedonians, while entering into the theater.

*Commentary.*[913] Josephus (at the end of the first century A.D.) is in the midst of narrating the story of Gaius Caligula's assassination in January of A.D. 41. Gaius' murder is important to Josephus, in large measure because of Gaius' antagonism of the Jews and his sacrilegious desire to set up a statue of himself in the Jerusalem Temple – designs finally removed by his death (*A. J.* 18.257–309). Josephus previously recounted another omen that preceded the event (e.g., 19.87), but here he enumerates two more: the blood spilt in the theater, and the day coinciding with the anniversary of the death of Philip of Macedon. Earlier, Josephus had mentioned Pausanias' murder of Philip, who was the father of Alexander the Great (*A. J.* 11.304–305).[914] The fact that Philip himself had been assassinated in a theater makes the parallel appear an omen of Nero's demise. Nero was stabbed multiple times, and much blood accompanied his murder; thus the prodigious parallel with the day's theatrical perfor-

---

[913] Text: NIESE, *Flavii Josephi Opera*, 4:226–227.

[914] The involvement of Pausanias in Philip's death was well known, though any potential additional involvement of others (including Philip's family) in the plot seems to have been rumored and debated (e.g., Aristotle, *Pol.* 1311b; Diodorus Siculus, *Bib. hist.* 16.93.1–16.95.1; Justin, *Epitome* 9.6.1–9.7.2; Plutarch, *Alex.* 10.4).

mances. Mimes and pantomimes were often paired in theaters – the pantomime consisting of dramatic solo dance to musical accompaniment, and a
mime was an imitative play with multiple actors. Concerning the pantomime,
Cinyras was a legendary wealthy king/priest of Cyprus (cf. Homer, *Il.* 11.19–
28; Plato, *Leg.* 660E; Tacitus, *Hist.* 2.3), who was said to have committed
incest with his daughter Myrrha; she was later transformed into the myrrh tree
(e.g., Ovid, *Metam.* 11.298–518; Plutarch, *Parallela minora* 22; though see
Apollodorus, *Library* 3.14.3). Blood does not enter into many of the ancient
tales of Cinyras and Myrrha, though perhaps those traditions varied sufficiently in antiquity to have allowed a more violent conclusion to the story/play
(even in Ovid, Cinyras pursues his daughter with a sword). The mime involved
an actor feigning crucifixion with the aid of "artificial blood" (αἷμα ... τεχνη-
τόν). Josephus does not provide the title of the play/mime (though it has often
been asserted to be the *Laureolus*),[915] nor does he describe the mime sufficiently to allow us to discern the character traits of this "ruler" (ἡγεμών –
could this have been a leader of brigands?) or why he deserved to be crucified
(σταυροῦται).[916] For our purposes, it is significant to observe that flowing
blood (even quantities of blood) could be associated with crucifixion.[917] This
text can be compared and contrasted with our next passage.

## (410) Suetonius, *Gaius Caligula* 57.3–4

Prodigiorum loco habita sunt etiam, quae forte illo ipso die paulo prius acci-
derant. [4] Sacrificans respersus est phoenicopteri sanguine; et pantomimus
Mnester tragoediam saltavit, quam olim Neoptolemus tragoedus ludis, quibus
rex Macedonum Philippus occisus est, egerat; et cum in Laureolo mimo, in
quo actor proripiens se ruina sanguinem vomit, plures secundarum certatim ex-
perimentum artis darent, cruore scaena abundavit. Parabatur et in noctem
spectaculum, quo argumenta inferorum per Aegyptios et Aethiopas explica-
rentur.

---

[915] The reasons for identifying the mime with the *Laureolus* would include: the parallel in
Suetonius (*Cal.* 57.3–4; see below) gives the name of the mime on this day as *Laureolus*
(though Suetonius does not mention crucifixion in his account), Juvenal (*Sat.* 8.183–188; see
below) mentions a play by that name that involves a man attached to a cross, and Martial
records a spectacle about a crucified criminal playing Laureolus in the Colosseum during the
reign of Titus (see below, Martial, *Epigrammaton – Liber de spectaculis* 7.1–12).

[916] WHISTON's eighteenth-century translation referred to this character as "a leader of robbers"; WHISTON, Flavius Josephus, 507.

[917] Even if one were to skeptically assert, possibly in light of Suetonius' omission of crucifixion in his account of the mime, that Josephus was confused about crucifixion being part of
the play on that occasion, it still remains the case that Josephus himself believed that a play
about a cross would involve much blood. Josephus, of course, had witnessed many crucifixions in his day; e.g., *Vita* 420–421; *B. J.* 5.449–451; etc.

*Translation.* By way of prodigies, events had also been observed, which fortuitously had occurred a little before in that very day: ⁴ While sacrificing, he [Gaius Caligula] had been sprinkled with the blood of a flamingo. And the pantomime Mnester danced a tragedy, which long ago Neoptolemus the tragedian had acted during the games at which Philip, king of the Macedonians, had been killed. And when in the mime *Laureolus*, in which the main character bursts forth with a collapse and discharges blood, many of the secondary [actors] zealously gave proof of their craft, [so] the stage overflowed with blood. A spectacle was also prepared for the night, in which stories of those inhabiting the Underworld would be displayed by the agency of Egyptians and Ethiopians.

*Commentary.*[918] Notably, this text does not mention the cross, which is precisely why it is important to compare it with the preceding passage from Josephus. Suetonius (writing in the early second century A.D.) was quite fond of prodigies and portents, and he frequently included them in his writing (especially preceding the death of an emperor). He records *multa prodigia* in 57.1–4, going well beyond Josephus' short list. The portents in the selection above focus on spilt blood and omens of the Underworld.[919] In comparison, a few omens are also recorded in Cassius Dio (*Hist. rom.* 59.29.3–4), with some overlap with Suetonius, but Dio mentions nothing of the theater productions that day in his account of Gaius' assassination (59.29.1–59.30.1). It is these matters of the theater that concern us, and here it is good to compare and contrast Suetonius with his older contemporary Josephus (*A. J.* 19.94–95). Both indicate that a pantomime and a mime were performed, both connect the performance in some way to Philip of Macedon, and both mention an excess of blood on the stage. However, whereas Josephus names the pantomime (*Cinyras*), Suetonius provides the title of the mime (*Laureolus*). Concerning the pantomime, Suetonius focuses on Mnester (who was the solo dancer in the pantomime)[920] and on the previous performance by Neoptolemus. That earlier performance provides another contrast: while Josephus emphasizes that the calendar day was the same as the date of Philip's assassination, Suetonius does not mention the date, but records (with some level of detail) that the very play was the same. Suetonius does not directly associate blood with the pantomime, but with the mime and especially with the excesses of the secondary

---

[918] Text: ROLFE, Suetonius, 1:492.

[919] Flamingos, peacocks and other exotic birds were also regularly offered in the temple to Gaius; Suetonius, *Cal.* 22.3.

[920] Perhaps this detail was of import to Suetonius since he had previously implied that Mnester was one of Gaius' sexual favorites (*Cal.* 36.1; 55.1). Mnester was later beheaded by Claudius for his continued sexual favors to others in the imperial house, especially to Messalina (Seneca, *Apocol.* 13; Tacitus *Ann.* 11.36; cf. 11.4; Cassius Dio, *Hist. rom.* 60.22.3–5; 60.28.3–5; 60.31.5).

actors (*plures secundarum*).[921] Finally, though Suetonius relates that the title of the mime was *Laureolus*, which from other sources involved a crucifixion of the title character (see below Juvenal, *Sat.* 8.183–188; Martial, *Epigrammaton – Liber de spectaculis* 7.1–12), Suetonius only speaks to the blood the actor discharged, without referring to a cross. None of these contrasting details constitute an actual contradiction, so a harmony of the two accounts could be possible. Nevertheless, it is striking that Suetonius, who otherwise mentions the cross (cf. *Iul.* 74.1; *Cal.* 12.2; *Galb.* 9.1; *Dom.* 10.1; 11.1) and who typically provides more detail here than Josephus, does not mention crucifixion in this instance. His focus appears to be more on the bloodletting than on its precise means.

**(411)** Juvenal, *Saturae* 8.183–188

Quid si numquam adeo foedis adeoque pudendis
utimur exemplis, ut non peiora supersint?
consumptis opibus vocem, Damasippe, locasti
sipario, clamosum ageres ut Phasma Catulli.
Laureolum velox etiam bene Lentulus egit,
iudice me dignus vera cruce.

*Translation.* [183] What if we never employ such extremely repugnant and extremely shameful examples, so that no worse ones remain? [185] With [your] wealth exhausted, Damasippus, you hired out [your] voice to the stage-screen, playing Catullus' noisy Ghost. [187] Even fleet-footed Lentulus successfully played Laureolus, [188] by my judgment meriting a real cross.

*Commentary.*[922] In the early second century A.D. Juvenal derides members of the upper classes who seek fame and fortune from the theatre and other public spectacles.[923] Juvenal asserts in this satire that an ancient house and good pedigree is of no inherent value, but that "the one and only nobility is virtue" (8.20). According to Juvenal, these two examples from the stage are among those instances that represent exceedingly shocking and shameful behavior (*adeo foedis adeoque pudendis*) for a citizen. It must be remembered that Roman actors were often of the lowest classes (including slaves), and in any

---

[921] ROLFE, Suetonius, 1:492n. notes, "The actors *secundarum partium* entertained the spectators after a play by imitating the actions of the star." A similar note can be found in ROBERT GRAVES, Gaius Suetonius Tranquillus. The Twelve Caesars (Revised by Michael Grant; London / New York: Penguin, 1989), 182n.

[922] Text: RAMSAY, Juvenal and Persius, 172.

[923] Juvenal continues after this passage by also denigrating those upper-class members who watch their fellow citizens engage in such demeaning tomfoolery 8.188–199. He further mentions citizens volunteering as gladiators (8.199–210) and Nero as the extreme example of a patrician man putting himself on display at the theatre (8.211–230).

case their profession (while much in public attention) was often viewed as a crass one. In the first example, Damasippus earns money playing the voice of a ghost from behind a small stage-screen (*siparium*). In the second, Lentulus plays the role of Laureolus, who is famously crucified in the play. Juvenal's satirical twist would be to reward Lentulus' realistic portrayal of crucifixion by wishing him the honor of suffering on an actual cross. We should again note how Juvenal considers this role of crucified Laureolus as excessively shameful for a decent Roman citizen, though the context implies this has both to do with the very activity of serving as an actor as well as with the specifically demeaning role.

### 3.10.4 Use in Public Spectacle Entertainment

As a special case of the "public" nature of crucifixion (and related suspension penalties), the employment of the cross in public spectacular entertainment is particularly striking. Certainly societies both before and after the Romans have made executions into a kind of entertainment for the masses.[924] However, the Romans honed this into a gruesome art, especially in the arena, where masses of people around the empire would watch the execution of condemned criminals as a prelude to the popular gladiatorial combats.[925] Such executions were typically harsh (involving beasts, fire, crosses), and much creativity could be applied to the staging of such events. Martial's account of the dedicatory games at the Flavian Amphitheatre provides special insight into the use of such an arena.[926]

**(412)** Martial, *Epigrammaton – Liber de spectaculis* 7.1–12

Qualiter in Scythica religatus rupe Prometheus,
    adsiduam nimio pectore pavit avem,

---

[924] Even into the modern era, one can readily think of public hangings from a noose as well as use of the guillotine, drawing and quartering, and other communal participatory execution methods. Today Western culture typically does not condone such realism, preferring the death and mayhem to be artificially (albeit graphically) reproduced in films and books, and insisting that dangerous combat sports develop at least some rules to guard against a public death.

[925] For a useful study of such events, see KYLE, Spectacles; concerning crucifixion note especially ibid. 53–55, 168–169 (and the useful corresponding notes ibid. 72–75, 181–182).

[926] There are further clues to the use of cross in spectacles. Among those mentioned above, note that though Philo found Flaccus' treatment of the Jewish people abominable, it was predicated in part on the gruesome realties of execution as Roman spectacle (Philo, *Flacc.* 72, 83–84). The burning of Christians on crosses by Nero also drew on the imagery of spectacular executions (Tacitus, *Ann.* 15:44), and this becomes a theme in many subsequent Christian martyrdoms. See further the *Historia Augusta* 24 (Tyranni triginta) 29.3–4.

nuda Caledonia sic viscera praebuit urso,
    non falsa pendens in cruce Laureolus,
[5] vivebant laceri membris stillantibus artus
    inque omni nusquam corpore corpus erat,
denique supplicium [dignum tulit; ille parentis]
    vel domini iugulum foderat ense nocens,
templa vel arcano demens spoliaverat auro,
    [10] subdiderat saevas vel tibi, Roma, faces.
vicerat antiquae sceleratus crimina famae,
    in quo, quae fuerat fabula, poena fuit.

*Translation.* In the state which Prometheus, having been bound to a Scythian cliff, struck the unremitting bird with [his] extraordinary chest,
thus Laureolus, hanging on no counterfeit cross, presented [his] exposed internal organs to a Caledonian bear.
[5] [His] mutilated limbs lived, while the body members dripped [with blood], and in all the body there was nowhere a body.
In the end he endured a well-deserved punishment; that man had stabbed the throat of [his] parent or master, injuring [them] with a sword,
Being insane, either he had plundered temples with [their] hidden gold,
[10] or he had applied savage firebrands to you, O Rome.
The accursed man surpassed the crimes of ancient fame – in him that which had been a play became a penalty.

*Commentary.*[927] Marcus Valerius Martialis was raised in Spain but lived most of his adult life throughout the latter half of the first century A.D. in Rome and Italy. He penned his epigrams *On the Spectacles* to celebrate the opening shows / matches at the Flavian Amphitheatre (i.e., the "Colosseum") in A.D. 80.[928] These brief poetical units frequently honor the emperor Titus and his imperial sponsorship of these spectacles. Prior to the grand gladiatorial shows each day, it was common to produce public executions, and these could mimic famous myths or plays (as when a person playing wingless Daedalus attempted to escape an attacking boar, see *Spec.* 8). Here in *De spectaculis* 7.1–12, a criminal is made to play the part of the crucified Laureolus (on this play see above: Josephus, *A. J.* 19.94; Suetonius, *Cal.* 57; Juvenal, *Sat.* 8.183–188), with the added feature of "Laureolus" being devoured on the cross by a bear (thus combining a known play with the features of a wild animal show).

---

[927] Text: WALTER C. A. KER, Martial. Epigrams (2 vols.; LCL; London: Heinemann, 1919), 1:6–8. The bracketed section in line 7 is supplied by KER, who follows SCHNEIDEWIN.

[928] Though sometimes published with Martial's more famous extended 12 (or 14) books of *Epigrammaton*, technically the *Liber de spectaculis*, sometimes called just *Epigrammaton Liber*, preceded its more extensive kin by some years and should be distinguished from it; SAMUELSSON, Crucifixion, 198 mistakenly conflates these.

Given Martial's tendency to highlight the last line(s) of his epigrams, here he may well be emphasizing the audience's glee at recognizing how the "play became the penalty" – with a living criminal in the role of Laureolus truly suffering death before their very eyes on a very real (*non falsa*) cross.[929]

Note how in the opening lines Martial draws an analogy between Laureolus hanging from a cross (*crux*) and Prometheus being bound to a cliff; the resemblance of Prometheus' fate to crucifixion is also observed repeatedly in Lucian (*Sacr.* 6; *Jupp. conf.* 8; and *Prometheus* passim; see section 3.9.2). After Prometheus created humanity and gave them fire, Zeus/Jupiter famously sentenced him to be attached to a rocky promontory in the Caucasus Mountains, so that an eagle could daily devour the immortal's entrails. The analogy was heightened in Titus' arena by the added feature of the crucified criminal (in the guise of Laureolus) being hastened to his death by having his entrails devoured (though by a bear rather than a bird). Martial increases the irony in lines 1–4 by designating both Prometheus and Laureolus as the active subjects in each of their respective clauses – thus Prometheus is the one who strikes the bird with his chest (rather than the bird playing the active role) and Laureolus is the one who presents his internal organs to the bear.

Lines 5–6 graphically depict the criminal's death. The bear has apparently devoured the internal organs and torso of the criminal so that "in all the body there was nowhere a body" – i.e., he no longer looked like a whole human. At the same time, the limbs are apparently still hanging on the device and dripping blood. Martial depicts the limbs as still living (*vivebant laceri ... artus*), implying that the person was alive on the *crux* while the bear attacked his midriff. It is true that we receive no full description of the precise form of the *crux*, but SAMUELSSON, perhaps too cursorily, asserts that the text does not reveal the "kind of authentic device."[930] The *crux* here must have been an implement used to affix a still-living man by his limbs at an elevation that a bear could easily reach his entrails.

Martial seems unclear on the crime that led this particular man to be executed in the *crux*-form of Laureolus in the Colosseum before clamoring crowds; instead, he provides a range of options: parricide, murder of a master by a slave, temple-robbery, or attempted arson against the city of Rome. This likely provides us with a short list of the kinds of extreme crimes that could invite such a severe form of execution (cf. 3.6.4 above). In any case, Martial appears convinced that the punishment was "well-deserved" (*supplicium dignum*),[931] testifying to his trust in the proceedings, even though he does not

---

[929] Though *falsa* could potentially modify either *viscera* or *cruce* in this poetic sentence, here we follow KER in associating it with *cruce*. In either case Martial shares his amazement that a famous legend/play is being really enacted before everyone's eyes.

[930] SAMUELSSON, Crucifixion, 198.

[931] Again note that "*dignum*" in line 7 is among the text supplied by the editor, so we rightly can only assign limited weight to this one word. However, everything in Martial's text

seem to have been privy to the specifics of the crime. That the criminal may have been "insane" (*demens*) is no excuse – the modern insanity defense carried no weight in such a matter. Martial does deem the man "accursed" (*sceleratus*), though the text is too brief as to ascertain whether this assertion stems from the man's character, his excessive crimes, or his fateful death (or perhaps a combination of these).

### 3.10.5 Dream Interpretation

**(413)** Artemidorus, *Oneirocritica* 2.53

Σταυροῦσθαι πᾶσι μὲν τοῖς ναυτιλλομένοις ἀγαθόν· καὶ γὰρ ἐκ ξύλων καὶ ἥλων γέγονεν ὁ σταυρὸς ὡς καὶ τὸ πλοῖον, καὶ ἡ κατάρτιος αὐτοῦ ὁμοία ἐστὶ σταυρῷ. ἀγαθὸν δὲ καὶ πένητι· καὶ γὰρ ὑψηλὸς ὁ σταυρωθεὶς καὶ πολλοὺς τρέφει <οἰωνούς>. τὰ δὲ κρυπτὰ ἐλέγχει· ἐκφανὴς γὰρ ὁ σταυρωθείς. τοὺς δὲ πλουσίους βλάπτει· γυμνοὶ γὰρ σταυροῦνται καὶ τὰς σάρκας ἀπολλύουσιν οἱ σταυρωθέντες.

*Translation.* To be crucified is good for all those who sail, for the cross also has come from wood and nails, like the boat, and its mast is likened to the cross. And for the day-laborer it is also good, for the one who has been crucified is also up high and feeds many "birds". And the hidden things it exposes, for the one who has been crucified is manifest. But it damages the wealthy, for those who have been crucified are crucified naked and lose their flesh.

*Commentary.*[932] Writing in the late second century A.D., Artemidorus of Daldis (or Ephesus) depicts here the meaning of dreams that involve crucifixion. Obviously, crucifixion must have been prevalent enough in antiquity that people could experience dreams about it. One useful facet of Artemidorus' work is that it provides a rationale for each dream-interpretation. Thus we learn that a σταυρός involves "wood and nails" – either indicating that it required fixing more than one pole together, or that the person was affixed to the σταυρός by means of nails. The fact that it is shaped like a ship's mast may well indicate that Artemidorus assumes both an upright pole and a crossbeam. Similarly, we read that the cross is elevated, that its victim becomes food for birds, that it is public, that victims are crucified "naked,"[933] and that

---

implies that he admired this innovative way of putting such a man to death. Indeed, most of *De spectaculis* joins the crowds in savagely appreciating the brutal spectacles that Caesar staged.

[932] HARRIS-MCCOY, Artemidorus' Oneirocritica, 236.

[933] COOK, Crucifixion, 192–193 argues that γυμνοί does not necessarily mean the person was utterly without clothes.

they are left up long enough that eventually their flesh decays on the cross. After the paragraph above, the text proceeds to discuss the meaning of crucifixion for unmarried men (they will get married), for slaves (they will be freed), for house and farm owners (they will be ejected from their land), and for urban dwellers (they will achieve political office). In the process, we learn that binds could be involved in crucifixion, and that crosses were set up in the city vicinities. Further reference to the cross can be found in Artemidorus.[934]

### 3.10.6 Vulgar Taunts, Curses, and Jests

Closely related to, and sometimes difficult to distinguish from, some of the categories above is the way that references to the *crux* can appear in coarse language. This especially occurs in comedic plays and in satirical writing, where one finds frequent use of expletives, crass jokes, curses, and farcical (and occasionally crude) repartee. It is likely that this expresses something more akin to normal speech for most Romans than one finds in much of our extant well-crafted oratory and historical narratives. For that reason, a substantial number of passages occur below (esp. from the early Latin authors Plautus and Terence). The section concludes by examining two graffiti examples, one of which has substantial bearing on how Roman pagans viewed the Christian faith in a crucified Son of God.

**(414)** Plautus, *Stichus* 625–629

*Epig.* Di immortales, hic quidem pol summam in crucem
    cena aut prandio perduci potest.
*Gel.* Ita ingenium meumst:
    quicumvis depugno multo facilius quam cum fame.
*Epig.* Dum parasitus mi atque fratri fuisti, rem confregimus.
*Gel.* Non nego ista apud te.
*Epig.* Satis spectatast mihi iam tua felicitas;
    nunc ego nolo ex Gelasimo mihi fieri te Catagelasimum.

*Translation.*
*Epig.* Immortal gods!, By Pollux, this man can indeed be induced to the
    highest cross for dinner or for lunch.
*Gel.* Such is my natural disposition:
    With many things I can fight more easily than with hunger.
*Epig.* When you were a parasite to my brother and I, we ruined our wealth.
*Gel.* In your presence I would not deny that.

---

[934] Thus see *Oneir.* 2.56 in No. 118. Also see *Oneir.* 1.76 and 2.68.

*Epig.* I have witnessed your good-luck enough now;
Now I do not want you to be made for me from Gelasimus to Catagelasimus.

*Commentary.*[935] Previously we observed how Plautus makes frequent use of
the *crux* in his comedies, typically in reference to pimps and especially to
slaves (see section 3.6.2). Based on the title page, *Stichus* was produced in
200 B.C. and was based on the Ἀδελφοί by Menander from about a century
earlier. At the end of Act 4 of *Stichus* there is a protracted humorous interaction between Epignomus and Gelasimus. Epignomus was one of two destitute
brothers, while Gelasimus was their former "parasite" (i.e., a person who had
no real occupation, but who relied on their regular invitation to dinner in
exchange for his witty company). The comedy here revolves around Gelasimus' ravenous eating habits – these, claims Epignomus, had quite literally
eaten his brother and him out of house and home. Epignomus refuses to provide another meal for Gelasimus, lest he be made to look even more "ridiculous" – note while Gelasimus transliterates the Greek γελάσιμος ("laugh-
able"), Catagelasimus comes from καταγελάσιμος (meaning "ridiculous").

Epignomus had just previously joked that Gelasimus should go find his
meal at the local jail, to which Gelasimus replied that he would gladly do so if
it meant a meal. The opening line cited above then goes mockingly well
beyond the sufferings of a prison, when Epignomus intones that Gelasimus
would be willing to go to a cross if it meant he had a good square meal. While
a *crux* rarely can imply a place of torture in Plautus (likely an apparatus that
held someone while they are whipped; see Plautus, *Asin.* 545–557 quoted
above in No. 312), here the picture is of Gelasimus being led (*perduci*) to the
"highest cross" (*summam in crucem*). The height of such a device would not
have served well for scourging, and thus it is much more likely a place of
execution (cf. Plautus, *Most.* 55–57, 348–361, 1128–1134; and esp. *Mil. glor.*
368–374, quoted above in No. 309).

## (415) Plautus, *Captivi* 469–470

ilicet parasiticae arti maximam malam crucem,
ita iuventus iam ridiculos inopesque ab se segregat.

*Translation.* May the practices of the parasite go off to the most wicked cross,
since now the youth dissociate themselves from the jesters and the destitute.

*Commentary.*[936] At the beginning of Act 3 of *The Captives*, Ergasilus, a parasite, bemoans the state of parasites in his day. He finds himself going hungry

---

[935] Text: NIXON, Plautus, 5:74. For other editions (and translations) of Plautus cf. No. 113.
[936] Text: NIXON, Plautus, 1:506.

because the youth in his Greek community are less interested in having a witty conversationalist like a parasite (a "destitute jester," so to speak) at the table (whose reward comes only in invitations to eat and carouse). Instead those rich youths invite other wealthy friends to their tables who will later be able to return the favor. And such youths do not need a parasite acting as a mediator to arrange with a pimp for their prostitutes, since the youths brazenly now contract with the pimps directly. Plautus has Ergasilus employ the phrase *ilicet ... maximam malam crucem* ("may it go off to the most wicked cross") as a kind of curse on his parasitical profession. Since today we do not tell people or things to "go off to the wicked cross," this phrase is often rendered into English with a more natural English curse formula, like "go to the devil" or "to hell with."[937] However in Latin, clearly the *crux* itself is being employed here as a vehement and vulgar curse. Further examples of this vulgarity in Plautus will be provided below, though often with less comment.

**(416)**  Plautus, *Amphitryon* 1034A–B

*Amph.*  At ego te cruce et cruciatu mactabo, mastigia.
*Mer.*  Erus Amphitruost occupatus.

*Translation.*
*Amph.*  And I will punish you with the cross and with torture, whipping post!
*Mer.*  The master, Amphitryon, is busy.

*Commentary.*[938] Unfortunately, Act 4, Scene 2 of the *Amphitryon* has an extended section where only a few lines have been preserved. These two fragmentary lines above report a conversation between Amphitryon and the god Mercury (who has appeared in the guise of Amphitryon's slave, Sosia). Earlier in the play Jupiter has also masqueraded in the form of Amphitryon to sleep with Amphitryon's wife (Mercury/Sosia helped bring this about). The real Amphitryon has recently discovered that his wife has committed this "adultery," and he now seeks to charge her and to capture the male culprit. Throughout the play Amphitryon verbally abuses the crafty Mercury, all the while thinking he is talking to his slave (Sosia). Here Amphitryon calls Mercury/Sosia a *mastigia* ("one who deserves a whipping"), which is an epithet that appears often in Plautus when a person is angry with a slave.[939] Amphitryon

---

[937] Thus NIXON in LCL translation will typically render such phrases as he does here: "Devil take the parasitical profession!"; NIXON, Plautus, 1:507. OLD s.v. *ilicet* suggests "to hell with (so-and-so)" as the translation of *ilicet malam crucem* (citing Plautus, *Capt.* 469 as an example). Another approach is taken by RILEY: "Away with the profession of a Parasite to very utter and extreme perdition!"

[938] Text: NIXON, Plautus, 1:106 (where the fragmentary lines are accorded Roman numerals rather than letters – this being 1034 I & II).

[939] Another term that appears in the *Amphitryon* as a vulgar taunt against slaves is *furcifer*,

threatens Mercury/Sosia with the *crux* and with torture (*cruciatus*). Both punishments are fitting penalties for a slave (see section 3.6.2 above for *crux*). Though seeming to be lexical cognates, *crux* and *cruciatus* appear to be distinguished here, with the latter indicating "torture" and the former referring to an object upon which someone is hung.[940] Without proper context, we do not know the full story of this interaction. But, Mercury apparently still refuses to provide Amphitryon access to Jupiter (i.e., Amphitryon's double). Indeed, Mercury replies with the double entendre, "the master is busy" – note how the title "master" (*Erus*) works both as the slave Sosia (i.e., Mercury in disguise) addresses his "master" Amphitryon (albeit Jupiter in costume), and also as the god Mercury speaks of Jupiter as the "master" god, whom Amphitryon should worship rather than fight.

**(417)**  Plautus, *Asinaria* 940–941

*Art.*      I domum.
*Phil.*     Da savium etiam prius quam abis.
*Dem.*      I in crucem.
*Phil.*     Immo intro potius. sequere hac me, mi anime.
*Argyr.*    Ego vero sequor.

*Translation.*
*Art.*      Go home!
*Phil.*     Give [me] an erotic kiss again before you go away.
*Dem.*      Go to the cross!
*Phil.*     No, no, I rather go in. [*To Argyrippus*] Follow me there, my love.
*Argyr.*    Truly I am following!

*Commentary.*[941] At the end of the *Comedy of Asses*, the elderly Demaenetus receives his just desserts. Demaenetus has assisted his son, Argyrippus, in acquiring enough money to buy the beautiful courtesan Philaenium, but on the condition that Demaenetus gets the first night with her. Meanwhile, Demaenetus' enemy conspires to let Artemona (Demaenetus' wife) discover this ren-

---

which may have allusion (via *furca*) to something much akin to crucifixion (see footnote on *furcifer* in No. 304 in reference to Plautus, *Most.* 69–71): *ego pol te istis tuis pro dictis et male factis, furcifer, accipiam* ("By Pollux, I will receive you in keeping with this talk and wicked doings of yours, *furcifer*!"; *Amph.* 285–286); *Pergin autem? nonne ego possum, furcifer, te perdere?* ("Droning on again? Am I not able, *furcifer*, to destroy you?"; *Amph.* 539).

[940] While one might argue *crux* and *cruciatus* form a hendiadys here, these most likely are set alongside one another here as distinct punishments, which would indicate that the *crux* here is something other than an equivalent of "torture" (*cruciatus*). This is contrary to the translation of NIXON, Plautus, 1:107: "torture and torment".

[941] Text: NIXON, Plautus, 1:226.

dezvous. Artemona interrupts the banquet where Demaenetus is dallying with Philaenium (right in front of Argyrippus), and she carts her lecherous old husband away. As he leaves, Philaenium, who has all along been disgusted by Demaenetus, jokingly calls out to him for one last *savium* ("erotic kiss"; cf. his demand of her in line 891). He angrily retorts: *I in crucem* ("go to the cross"). To that she quips that she will "go in" instead, and invites Argyrippus to join her.

**(418)**  Plautus, *Aulularia* 517–522

iam hosce absolutos censeas: cedunt, petunt
treceni, cum stant thylacistae in atriis
textores limbularii, arcularii.
ducuntur, datur aes. iam absolutos censeas,
cum incedunt infectores corcotarii,
aut aliqua mala crux semper est, quae aliquid petat.

*Translation.*
Now you might suppose these [creditors] are finished: they go, yet
three hundred [more] pursue, even while the offering collectors[942] stand in the
    atrium,
weavers, fringe-makers, and chest-makers.
As they are led in, money is paid. Now you might suppose [these are] fin-
    ished,
when the dyers of saffron-colored robes step up,
or some other wicked cross is always there, who pursues something else.

*Commentary.*[943] The opening of Act 3, Scene 5 of the *Aulularia* (*The Pot of Gold*) presents an extended monologue by the Athenian gentleman Megadorus, who complains of the creditors that afflict wealthy gentlemen who marry wives with expensive tastes. Megadorus delineates a long list of tradesmen who come with their invoices and open hands; only a small selection of this text is presented above. In his frustration Megadorus calls such a creditor a *mala crux*.

**(419)**  Plautus, *Aulularia* 628–633

*Eucl.*  I foras, lumbrice, qui sub terra erepsisti modo,
        qui modo nusquam comparebas, nunc, cum compares, peris.
        ego pol te, praestrigiator, miseris iam accipiam modis.

---

[942] Some translations render *phylacistae* as "jailers".
[943] Text: NIXON, Plautus, 1:286–288.

*Strob.*  Quae te mala crux agitat? quid tibi mecum est commerci, senex?
        quid me adflictas? quid me raptas? qua me causa verberas?
*Eucl.*  Verberabilissime, etiam rogitas, non fur, sed trifur?

*Translation.*
*Eucl.*  Come outside, worm, who crawled out from under the earth just now,
        who first will not be seen anywhere, now, when you are seen, you dis-
        appear.
        By Pollux, trickster, I will now deal with you in a wretched way.
*Strob.*  What wicked cross rouses you? What is the relationship between you
        and me, old man?
        What are you striking me for? What are you grabbing me for? Why are
        you beating me?
*Eucl.*  O most-deserving-a beating! Do you still ask that? You are not a thief,
        but a triple-thief.

*Commentary.*[944] Act 4, Scene 4 recounts this interchange between Euclio, an old miserly gentleman, and Strobilus, who is a friend's slave. Throughout the play Euclio has been worried that someone will discover his hidden pot of gold, and now he believes Strobilus has stolen it. In fact, Strobilius has not yet done so, though he intends to. Euclio calls the slave multiple names (*lumbrice, praestrigiator, verberabilissime, trifur*), and he will continue to intimidate Strobilus (even threatening to hang him up).[945] The slave here retorts: *Quae te mala crux agitat?* ("What wicked cross rouses you?"),[946] using *mala crux* to represent a vulgar origin that has stimulated the old man's violent actions. This seems surprising language from a slave to a citizen, but therein lies some of the humor, and Strobilus will continue to taunt the "old man" for many more lines.

## (420)  Plautus, *Bacchides* 583–586

Quid istuc? quae istaec est pulsatio?[947]
quae te mala crux agitat, qui ad istunc modum
alieno viris tuas extentes ostio?
fores paene exfregisti. quid nunc vis tibi?

---

[944] Text: NIXON, Plautus, 1:298.

[945] See *Aul.* 643–644: *Fateor, quia non pendes, maximam. atque id quoque iam fiet, nisi fatere* ("I did a great [injury], because you are not hanging up. And that also soon will be done, if you do not make [a confession]").

[946] NIXON's translation captures the spirit of this well: "What the devil's got into you?"; NIXON, Plautus, 1:299.

[947] NIXON follows LEO in noting a possible lacuna here after this line in the text; NIXON, Plautus, 1:386.

*Translation.*
What is that? What is that pounding?
What wicked cross rouses you, such that in this manner
you fully exert your manhood against someone else's door?
You have all but broken open the double doors. What do you want now?

*Commentary.*[948] At the beginning of Act 4, Scene 2, Pistoclerus answers the pounding at the door,[949] where a man waits with the message that Pistoclerus must send his beloved courtesan off with the Captain who bought her. He responds angrily both to the knocking and to the message. Note the phrase *quae te mala crux agitat* is identical to that in Plautus, *Aul.* 631 (see above).

**(421)**  Plautus, *Bacchides* 899–904

| | |
|---|---|
| *Cleom.* | Vbi nunc Mnesilochus ergost? |
| *Chrys.* | Rus misit pater. |
| | illa autem in arcem abiit aedem visere |
| | Minervae. nunc apertast. i, vise estne ibi. |
| *Cleom.* | Abeo ad forum igitur. |
| *Chrys.* | Vel hercle in malam crucem. |
| *Cleom.* | Hodie exigam aurum hoc? |
| *Chrys.* | Exige, ac suspende te: |
| | ne supplicare hunc censeas tibi, nihili homo. |

*Translation.*

| | |
|---|---|
| *Cleom.* | Where now is Mnesilochus in that case? |
| *Chrys.* | His father sent [him] to the country. |
| | On the other hand, that lady went out to the Acropolis to behold the temple |
| | of Minerva. Now it is open. Go, see if she is not there. |
| *Cleom.* | Therefore I will go out to the forum. |
| *Chrys.* | Or, by Hercules, to the wicked cross. |
| *Cleom.* | Today will I exact the gold from this man? |
| *Chrys.* | You will exact it, and hang yourself: |
| | You should not suppose he will humbly petition you, O worthless man. |

---

[948] Text: NIXON, Plautus, 1:386.

[949] The knocking comes from a parasite of the Captain, who arrives with a page. The page raps quietly on the door, and the parasite angrily rebukes him for his wimpy knocking (saying: *recede hinc dierecte* – "go from here and be hanged" in line 579). The parasite then proceeds to pound on the door just prior to our excerpt above. The notion of being "hung up" (*dierecte*) shortly before *mala crux*, appears to be another example of Plautus' irony.

*Commentary*.[950] The slave Chrysalus here is working out a scheme to buy off Cleomachus' hold on his courtesan (one of two girls named Bacchis) for the sake of Mnesilochus, by using money from Nicobulus (Chrysalus' master and Mnesilochus' father). Cleomachus comes looking for Bacchis, and despite Chrysalus' statement above, Bacchis actually reclines in an adjacent room along with Mnesilochus. Meanwhile, Cleomachus, though a foreign captain, has agreed to let the slave Chrysalus abuse him (cf. line 875), in hopes that Cleomachus will obtain 200 gold pieces from Nicobulus via Chrysalus (who fears that Cleomachus will attack his son). In addition to *nihili homo* ("worthless man"), Chrysalus' terms of abuse here include wishing Cleomachus to go off *in malam crucem* ("unto the wicked cross") and commanding him to "hang yourself" (*suspende te*).

**(422)**  Plautus, *Casina* 89–96

*Ol.*  Non mihi licere meam rem me solum, ut volo,
       loqui atque cogitare, sine ted arbitro?
       quid tu, malum, me sequere?
*Ch.*  Quia certum est mihi,
       quasi umbra, quoquo tu ibis, te semper sequi;
       quin edepol etiam si in crucem vis pergere,
       sequi decretumst.

*Translation*.
*Ol.*  Am I not to be permitted to talk and to think alone, as I wish,
       about my own affairs, without you being a spectator?
       What the deuce are you following me for?
*Ch.*  Because I am determined,
       like a shadow, wherever you go, to follow you always;
       why, by Pollux, even if you want to hasten to the cross,
       I have decided to follow.

*Commentary*.[951] This conversation between two slaves comes from the very opening lines of *Casina* Act 1 (after an extended prologue). This Latin farce was based on an original Greek play by Diphilus. Chalinus is shadowing Olympio everywhere, for he realizes that Olympio is scheming to make Casina (a beautiful handmaid in their master's house) his wife. In a vividly humorous word picture between the two slaves, Chalinus asserts that he will even accompany Olympio as he mounts the cross (cf. section 3.6.2 for slaves and the *crux*).

---

[950] Text: Nixon, Plautus, 1:420.
[951] Text: Nixon, Plautus, 2:12.

**(423)** Plautus, *Casina* 415–416

*Ol.*       Ostende. mea haec est.
*Ch.*       Mala crux east quidem.
*Cleost.*   Victus es, Chaline.

*Translation.*
*Ol.*       Show me! This [lot] is mine!
*Ch.*       That indeed is a wicked cross!
*Cleost.*   You have been conquered, Chalinus.

*Commentary.*[952] Lysidamus, the master of the house, has also been stricken with lust for the slave-woman Casina. Here in Act 2, Scene 6, Lysidamus and Cleostrata (his wife) are drawing lots to see which slave gets to marry Casina. Lysidamus hopes that Olympio will win, since Olympio (Lysidamus' slave and overseer of his country estate) will then help arrange secret trysts for Lysidamus with Casina. Cleostrata suspects this is Lysidamus' aim, and puts forth Chalinus as the slave she thinks should have Casina's hand in marriage. In the first line quoted above, Olympio witnesses that the lot has indeed fallen to him, and Cleostrata acknowledges the defeat in the last line. In between, Chalinus (who truly wished to marry Casina) expresses his grief by comparing it to a "wicked cross" (*mala crux*). The overtones of death here have been signaled earlier in the play, where Chalinus repeatedly emotes that it would be death to him should Olympio marry Casina instead of him.[953]

**(424)** Plautus, *Casina* 611–613

*Lys.*      Quid nunc? missurusne es ad me uxorem tuam?
*Alc.*      Ducas, easque in maxumam malam crucem
            cum hac cum istac, cumque amica etiam tua.

*Translation.*
*Lys.*      What now? Will you be sending your wife to me?

---

[952] Text: NIXON, *Plautus*, 2:46.

[953] Chalinus even states: "By Hercules, it would be better for me to be dead by means of hanging myself, than for you to be made more entitled to her" (*hercle me suspendio, quam tu eius potior fias, satiust mortuom* in line 111–112). To which Olympio responded: "She is my plunder; so then you should plunge yourself on a noose" (*Mea praedast illa; proin tu te in laqueum induas* in line 113). And later Chalinus briefly considers suicide by hanging himself since he has lost Casina in this drawing of lots (in Act 2 scene 7), before he learns that he can help thwart Lysidamus' scheme. Such notions of suicide, despite showing the depth of emotion Chalinus feels and despite the repeated notions of a death by suspension, need not carry over to the precise means of death implied by *mala crux*. There is no reason to think that a *mala crux* is a device for holding a noose (i.e., a "gallows"). It is simply another epithet that calls forth notions of a death by suspension.

*Alc.* Take [her], and go unto the most wicked cross
 – with her, with that [wife] of yours, and with your girlfriend too!

*Commentary.*[954] Here in this comedy (Act 3, Scene 4) two old Athenian neighbors converse. Lysidamus, now beside himself in lust for Casina, has made arrangements to have an affair with Casina at Alcesimus' house (even on the night after her impending wedding to Olympio). In order to have Alcesimus' house empty for the affair, Lysidamus has asked Alcesimus to vacate the house with his servants and to send his wife over to Lysidamus' house to keep Lysidamus' wife company (and out of the way). However, Cleostrata (Lysidamus' wife), upon learning of the scheme, has stoked a conflict between the two elderly friends. The result is that Alcesimus speaks coarsely with his neighbor Lysidamus. Alcesimus' taunts to his friend include: "Why don't you hang yourself" (*Quin tu suspendis te?* in line 599),[955] and "Why indeed, by Hercules, don't the gods finally destroy you" (*Quin hercle di te perdant postremo quidem*, in line 609).[956] In the vulgar gibe quoted above, Alcesimus directs everyone else (his wife, Lysidamus' wife, the servant Lysidamus lusts after, and likely Lysidamus himself) to the *maxumam malam crucem*. One shockingly humorous dimension of this for the Latin audience would have been that this vulgarity comes from a land-owning citizen of Athens in reference to another citizen of the same class.

**(425)** Plautus, *Casina* 641–645

*Par.* Optine auris, amabo.
*Lys.* I in malam a me crucem,
     pectus, auris, caput teque di perduint,
     nam nisi ex te scio, quidquid hoc est, cito, hoc
     iam tibi istuc cerebrum dispercutiam, excetra tu,
     ludibrio pessuma adhuc quae me habuisti.

---

[954] Text: NIXON, Plautus, 2:66.

[955] This is an invitation to commit suicide on a noose, cf. *Cas.* 111–113, 424. To be fair to Alcesimus, Lysidamus first called Alcesimus a *vir minimi* (594).

[956] In this play, other language can also intone similar strong outbursts of passionate gallows-humor. Thus Lysidamus can deride his slave with *Vt quidem pol pereas cruciatu malo* ("Indeed, by Pollux, you will perish by wicked torture," in line 300). More pointed is the exchange between Chalinus and Olympio in lines 389–392 where they alternately invoke upon one another "hanging by the heels" (*pedibus pendens*), "blowing your eyes out of your head through the nose", and hanging on a "noose" (*laqueum*). Most pertinent for us is line 389, where Chalinus applies a curse to Olympio that: "you today will be carrying a chain and a *furca*" (*tu hodie canem et furcam feras*). This may have some relevance to our study, bearing in mind that a *furca* is a Y-shaped piece of wood used for hanging up a person much like a cross (it is also employed interchangeably with *crux* in Plautus, *Pers.* 854–855), though elsewhere in *Casina* it appears as a mere yoke used for carrying coal (line 438).

*Translation.*

Par.  Hold my ears, please.

Lys.  Go from me to the wicked cross;
      may the gods destroy your chest, ears, head, and you!
      For, unless I understand from you whatever this is, with this [staff]
      now I will smash that skull of yours, you hydra,
      villainess, who so far have taken me for a laughing-stock.

*Commentary.*[957] In Act 3, Scene 5, Pardalisca (the handmaid of Cleostrata, Lysidamus' wife) comes rushing out of Lysidamus' house in a feigned fright. At the instigation of Cleostrata (lines 685–688), Pardalisca runs to Lysidamus to recount a tale about how Casina has gone insane and plans to kill him. Before telling her story, Pardalisca toys with Lysidamus (perhaps knowing his amorous nature),[958] and asks him to assist her in her fright by holding her chest/breast, fanning her, and now by cradling her ears. He runs out of patience at her time-consuming explanation of what has frightened her, and he curses her, both by the gods and by wishing her to go off to the *malam crucem.*

**(426)** Plautus, *Casina* 973–978

Myrr.   Quid agis, dismarite?
Cleost. Mi vir, unde hoc ornatu advenis?
        quid fecisti scipione aut quod habuisti pallium?
Myrr.   In adulterio, dum moechissat Casinam, credo perdidit.
Lys.    Occidi.
Chal.   Etiamne imus cubitum? Casina sum.
Lys.    I in malam crucem.
Chal.   Non amas me?

*Translation.*

Myrr.   What are doing, O twice-married-man?
Cleost. My husband, where did you arrive from with that adornment?
        What did you do with your cane? Or what cloak did you have?
Myrr.   In the place of adultery, when he was committing adultery with
        Casina, I believe he has been deprived [of it].
Lys.    I'm dead.
Chal.   Should we again go to bed? I am Casina.

---

[957] Text: NIXON, Plautus, 2:70.

[958] Pardalisca certainly already knows that Lysidamus has amorous intentions toward Casina (cf. lines 670–675, 681, 685–688, 703–704). In this context, Pardalisca's frequent reiteration of *amabo*, which can simply mean "please" or "I would be grateful", may bear ironic coquettish hints of "I will love you". Also, she certainly asks Lysidamus to hold her in some pretty intimate places (e.g., *pectus, auris*).

*Lys.*     Go to the wicked cross!
*Chal.*    Do you not love me?

*Commentary.*[959] In the climactic final scene of the play, Lysidamus has become the brunt of all jests in his house. Chalinus, the male family slave who had originally desired to be married to Casina, has been veiled and substituted for Casina, even as "she" was due to be carted off as a bride to the neighbor's (i.e., Alcesimus') house in order for Lysidamus to have his evening with her (in the place of his bailiff Olympio). Once in the house, Chalinus instead beats Olympio, fends off Lysidamus, and steals Lysidamus' cane and cloak. In the selection above Myrrhina (Alcesimus' wife) first taunts Lysidamus as a bigamist (*dismarite*), who desired to be "married" to both Casina and to his own wife (Cleostrata). Cleostrata, for her part, inquires after his cane and cloak, while knowing full well what has gone on. The reference to *ornatu* ("adornment") may either refer to Lysidamus' disheveled state, or even to the beating that he likely received from Chalinus. Finally, Chalinus reveals himself as the stand-in for Casina (*Casina sum*), and invites Lysidamus to "go to bed" again together. Lysidamus replies to his slave, "Go to the wicked cross!"

**(427)** Plautus, *Curculio* 610–612

*Ther.*   Salvos sum, eccum quem quaerebam. quid agis, bone vir?
*Curc.*   Audio.
        si vis tribus bolis, vel in chlamydem.
*Ther.*   Quin tu is in malam crucem
        cum bolis, cum bulbis? redde mihi iam argentum aut virginem.

*Translation.*
*Ther.*   I am saved! Here he is! The man whom I have been seeking. How are you doing, good man?
*Curc.*   I am listening. If you wish ... with three casts of the dice ... perhaps for (your) military cloak.
*Ther.*   Why don't you go to the wicked cross with your casts of the dice and with your onions?![960] Restore to me now my money or the young girl.

---

[959] Text: NIXON, Plautus, 2:104.

[960] *cum bolis, cum bulbis.* NIXON, Plautus, 255 suggests that, though the first mention of *bolis* above refers to throws of dice, the second occurrence of *bolis* refers to choice morsels and *bulbis* refers to an onion; thus he translates: "with all your throes of throat and belly." RILEY, Comedies, translates "casts and catch-pennies", focusing on how *bulbis* was merely a nonsensical alliteration to *bolis*. The key to unraveling this appears to be in the word *bulbus* (in the nominative), which unfortunately appears fairly rare in extant Latin texts (I have found only about two score of examples through a Perseus search, most of them in Pliny the Elder or Celsus). Alliteration is certainly present, though I also wonder if the *bulbis* reference is not perhaps a crass allusion to Curculio's "bulbs" (perhaps this is related to how onions appear as

*Commentary.*[961] At this point in this play (Act 5, Scene 2), set in Epidaurus, the parasite Curculio has managed to trick Therapontigonus, a captain, into giving up his signet ring. With that ring, Curculio then succeeded in issuing papers in Therapontigonus' name to buy the courtesan-slave (Planesium) with whom Curculio's patron (Phaedromus) was in love. The ring, however, also ironically identifies Therapontigonus as Planesium's long-lost brother. At the beginning of this scene Phaedromus and Planesium have been questioning Curculio how he came by the ring. Just as Curculio confesses that he won it at a dice game with a captain, Therapontigonus (that very captain) comes marching up. The interchange above represents Therapontigonus' opening saluta- tion, Curculio's sly greeting back to Therapontigonus (Curculio invites him to another dice game), and Therapontigonus' angry response (he bids Curculio to go to a cross).

**(428)**  Plautus, *Curculio* 693–695

*Phaed.*    Collum obstringe, abduce istum in malam crucem.
*Ther.*    Quidquid est, ipse ibit potius.
*Ca.*    Pro deum atque hominum fidem,
         hocine pacto indemnatum atque intestatum me abripi?

*Translation.*
*Phaed.*    Constrain his neck! Lead that man out to the wicked cross!
*Ther.*    [*threatening Cappadox*] Whatever happens, he will rather go on his
         own!
*Ca.*    O trust of gods and men![962]
         Am I by this means to be snatched away without verdict and with-
         out witnesses?

*Commentary.*[963] In the concluding scene of this comedy, Therapontigonus and Phaedromus have cornered the pimp Cappadox, who had sold Planesium as a courtesan-slave under the condition that no one can prove her to be freeborn. However, the ring of Therapontigonus has shown her to be his sister (and thus freeborn), so they are now pressuring Cappadox to return the money he had received. Threats are exchanged both ways, including Phaedromus' sugges- tion that they lead Cappadox to the *malam crucem*, the wicked cross, even without a trial. The context certainly implies that a *mala crux* should properly

---

an aphrodisiac in Petronius, *Satyricon* 130.7; and are to be avoided by those who have excess semen in Celsus, *De medicina* 4.28); references to vegetable shapes as male anatomical parts occur elsewhere in Plautus (cf. radishes and cucumbers in *Cas.* 910).

[961] Latin text from *Plautus*, transl. PAUL NIXON, LCL, 2:254–256.

[962] See OLD s.v. *pro*[2]: as an interjection with *fidem*: "heaven and earth!"

[963] Text: NIXON, Plautus, 2:264.

be a judicial penalty. Eventually all works out without serious injury to anyone.

**(429)** Plautus, *Menaechmi* 63–66

nam rus ut ibat forte, ut multum pluerat,
ingressus fluvium rapidum ab urbe haud longule,
rapidus raptori pueri subduxit pedes
abstraxitque hominem in maximam malam crucem.

*Translation.*
For as he was by chance going into the country, when it had rained heavily,
while he was entering a rapid stream not a long distance from the city,
the rapids pulled away the feet of the one who had grabbed the boy
and carried the man away unto the most wicked cross.

*Commentary.*[964] The *Menaechmi* was possibly based on a (now lost) third-century Greek play by Poseidippus. It tells the story of two twins (each ultimately called Menaechmus), who were separated as young boys when one was suddenly taken into captivity (and later adopted) by a wealthy man from Epidamnus (a Greek city on the eastern Adriatic coast). Here in the prologue the narrator explains that this wealthy man met a fitting end. Just as he had been the "the boy's grabber" (*raptori pueri*) so a rapid river (note that *rapidus* is cognate with *rapto*) had grabbed him. The phrase *abstraxitque hominem in maximam malam crucem* certainly refers to carrying him away to death. But Plautus, with sardonic wit, metaphorically depicts that death as if it had been particularly proper to a kidnapper and thief – it is "unto the most wicked cross."

**(430)** Plautus, *Menaechmi* 326–330

| | |
|---|---|
| *Cyl.* | Iam ergo haec madebunt faxo, nil morabitur. |
| | proin tu ne quo abeas longius ab aedibus. |
| | numquid vis? |
| *Men. S.* | Vt eas maximam malam crucem. |
| *Cyl.* | Ire hercle meliust te interim atque accumbere, |
| | dum ego haec appono ad Volcani violentiam. |

---

[964] Text: NIXON, Plautus, 2:370.

*Translation.*

Cyl.     Now, therefore, this [food] will be cooked, I will have done it, noth-
         ing will be delayed.
         Accordingly then, you should not go away far from the house.
         Surely you don't want [anything more]?
Men. S.  That you go to the most wicked cross!
Cyl.     By Hercules, it is better for you to go meanwhile and lie down,
         while I expose this [food] to the violence of Vulcan.

*Commentary.*[965] After Menaechmus was taken into captivity, their grandfather
changes the name of Sosicles, Menaechmus' twin, to "Menaechmus" in honor
of the lost brother – in the text above this twin is distinguished by being
labeled "Men. S." (i.e., Menaechmus-Sosicles). Once grown, Menaechmus-
Sosicles spends years searching for his lost brother. He finally lands in Epidamnus, where he is constantly confused by the locals for his citizen brother
by the same name. As they say, "hilarity ensues." In Act 2, Scene 2 Cylindrus
is the cook of Menaechmus' mistress/courtesan (Erotium). Cylindrus mistakes
the twin for Erotium's lover, insists that they know one another, and reminds
Menaechmus-Sosicles that he is soon due to Erotium's house for dinner and
dalliance. Throughout the scene the twin responds confused and (often) abu-
sively, as when here he directs Cylindrus to go to the *maximam malam crucem*.

**(431)**  Plautus, *Menaechmi* 848–850

pugnis me votas in huius ore quicquam parcere,
ni a meis oculis abscedat in malam magnam crucem.
faciam quod iubes, Apollo.

*Translation.* You [Apollo] forbid me to be merciful with my fists against her,
unless she is taken away from my eyes unto a great wicked cross.
I shall do as you command, Apollo.

*Commentary.*[966] In Act 5, Scene 2 Menaechmus-Sosicles encounters his
brother's wife and her father, who both mistake him for Menaechmus and
seek to take him home. In order to escape them, he fakes insanity and acts as
if he is receiving instructions from Apollo. The feigned violence works, and
the wife runs away. Note how he not only threatens to beat her, but also pretends to abandon her to a wicked doom. Earlier he had menaced her with
burning out her eyes (840–841), and he will subsequently try to scare off her
father as well, though with less success (853–871).

---

[965] Text: NIXON, Plautus, 2:396.
[966] Text: NIXON, Plautus, 2:450.

**(432)** Plautus, *Menaechmi* 910–916

*Med.* Salvos sis, Menaechme. quaeso, cur apertas brachium?
non tu scis, quantum isti morbo nunc tuo facias mali?
*Men.* Quin tu te suspendis?
*Sen.* Ecquid sentis?
*Med.* Quidni sentiam?
non potest haec res ellebori iungere[967] optinerier.
sed quid ais, Menaechme?
*Men.* Quid vis?
*Med.* Dic mihi hoc quod te rogo:
album an atrum vinum potas?
*Men.* Quin tu is in malam crucem?
*Med.* Iam hercle occeptat insanire primulum.

*Translation.*
*Med.* May you be well, Menaechmus. I ask you, why do you expose your
arm?
Do you not know how much harm you are now doing to that malady of
yours?
*Men.* Why don't you hang yourself?
*Sen.* Surely you recognize [the ailment]?
*Med.* Why would I not recognize it?
This thing is not able to be harnessed and secured with hellebore.[968]
But what do you say, Menaechmus?
*Men.* What do you want?
*Med.* Tell me this which I ask of you:
Do you drink white or dark wine?
*Men.* Why don't you go to the wicked cross?
*Med.* Now, by Hercules, he begins to behave like a madman for the first
time.

*Commentary.*[969] After Menaechmus-Sosicles' performance as a madman before his twin brother's father-in-law (here identified as a *senex*, "old man"), the *senex* recruits a doctor (*medicus*) to examine his "son-in-law." Comically, instead of coming across Menaechmus-Sosicles, this time they encounter Menaechmus himself, whom they presume to be insane (due to his identical twin brother's antics). In this scene (Act 5, Scene 5) and in the scene before it, Plautus makes light of the medical profession of his day. Thus the medicinal

---

[967] NIXON, Plautus, 456 notes that LEO finds the text corrupt here, suggesting *uno onere* in place of *iungere*.

[968] If LEO's emendation is followed (*uno onere* instead of *iungere*), then the line would read: "This thing is not able to be secured with a mass [or "shipload"] of hellebore."

[969] Text: NIXON, Plautus, 2:456–458.

plant hellebore appears to be the *medicus'* primary cure (cf. lines 913, 950), and his diagnostic method involves asking questions of dubious value (as in his query about wine preferences above, cf. lines 914–930). Menaechmus by this point in the play has become frustrated by the backlash he has received due to people confusing him with his twin. Nonetheless he shares his brother's anger management issues, as is evident throughout this scene in the many ways Menaechmus expresses frustration with the *medicus*. In this passage, he both commends suicide to the *medicus* and also wishes him off to a *malam crucem*.

**(433)** Plautus, *Menaechmi* 1017–1020

Agite abite, fugite hinc in malam crucem.
em tibi etiam: quia postremus cedis, hoc praemi feres.
nimis bene ora commetavi atque ex mea sententia.
edepol, ere, ne tibi suppetias temperi adveni modo.

*Translation.* Come you, depart, flee from here unto the wicked cross!
Here! Again [this blow] is for you!: Because you withdraw last, you will bear
    this reward!
I have surveyed their faces very well and to my liking.
By Pollux, master, truly I have come to your assistance at just the right time.

*Commentary.*[970] Four slaves have been sent by the father-in-law to cart Menaechmus off to the *medicus*, but Menaechmus fights back. In the text above (from Act 5, Scene 7), Messano, Menaechmus-Sosicles' slave, rushes to aid the person he mistakenly believes is his master. Thus, we hear Messano's words as Messano fights daringly ("surveying their faces" with blows), and as he delivers a parting blow (a "reward") to the last slave to retreat. In the midst of the brawl, Messano curses his fellow slaves and demands that they depart "unto the wicked cross." Messano's valiant deed will eventually garner him his freedom from slavery, even as the two Menaechmus twins will soon meet for the first time and learn the reason for everyone else's confusion.

---

[970] Text: Nixon, Plautus, 2:468.

**(434)** Plautus, *Mostellaria* 849–851

*Th.* Ibo intro igitur.
*Tr.* Mane sis videam, ne canis –
*Th.* Agedum vide.
*Tr.* Est! abi, canis. est! abin dierecta? abin hinc in malam crucem?
at etiam restas? est! abi istinc.

*Translation.*
*Th.* I shall go inside then.
*Tr.* Wait please, let me look, lest there is a dog –
*Th.* Come! Look!
*Tr.* There he is! Go away, dog. There he is! Won't you go away and be
hung up? Won't you go away from here unto the wicked cross?
And do you still remain? There he is! Go away from there!

*Commentary.*[971] The humor of this interchange (from Act 3, Scene 2) is difficult to appreciate without a fuller context. The slave Tranio is about to lead
his master Theopropides into a neighbor's house, although Tranio has hood-
winked Theopropides into thinking that Theopropides now owns the house
(for more context and more selections from this play, see section 3.6.2). The
neighbor invites Theopropides to be "taken in". However, Theopropides, misunderstanding the invitation, insists that he refuses to be "taken in" (i.e.,
conned) by anyone, so he (in the first line above) resolves to go in of his own
accord. Tranio, who constantly parodies his master, even here comes up with
a comical way to "take in" his master. Just as the master is about to step in
first, Tranio suggests that there may be a vicious dog (wealthy Roman houses
commonly had guard dogs), and thus he frightens his master into letting the
servant go first and lead him around. There is a hound, though it turns out to
be "as placid as a pooch who has just given birth" (line 852). Nonetheless
Tranio acts as if he is battling Cerberus. He invites the dog to be "hung up,"
and "to go away to the wicked cross." The use of this suspension language
here does indicate that, even while *mala crux* does demonstrably in other passages still bear its lexical reference (to a cross),[972] the idiomatic curse formula
can be applied to creatures that you would not normally suspend on such a
device.

---

[971] Text: NIXON, Plautus, 3:376.

[972] Also note how all other mentions of *crux* in *Mostellaria* clearly refer to a place where
slaves are taken to be punished by being pinned to it and hung up until they die (*Most.* 348–
361 [esp. 359–360], 743–744, 1133; cf. 55–57, 69–71; for all these texts see section 3.6.2).

**(435)** Plautus, *Persa* 292–295

*Sag.*   Di deaeque me omnes perdant –
*Paeg.*  Amicus sum, eveniant volo tibi quae optas.
*Sag.*   Atque id fiat,
        nisi te hodie, si prehendero, defigam in terram colaphis.
*Paeg.*  Tun me defigas? te cruci ipsum adfigent propediem alii.

*Translation.*
*Sag.*   May the gods and goddesses all lead me to destruction ...
*Paeg.*  As I am a friend, I wish that what you pray for would turn out for you.
*Sag.*   And would that it occur,
        unless today I seize you, then pin you down to the ground with [my]
        fists.
*Paeg.*  Would you pin me down? Others will pin *you* up to a cross before long.

*Commentary.*[973] Plautus' play *The Persian* likely stems from an unknown
Greek original; it is set in an era before the fourth-century B.C. conquests of
Alexander the Great (when Persia still had control over Arabia; cf. *Pers.* 506–
507). Here (in Act 2, Scene 4) we witness the repartee between two slaves –
Paegnium, a young wit, and Sagaristio, a senior slave from a neighbor's house.
Paegnium fairly consistently gets the better of Sagaristio. Amidst their raillery
earlier in this scene occur many maledictions against one another (e.g.,
*scelerate, venefice, ulmitriba, cucule, morticine, incubitatus,* etc.).[974] Sagaristio has also been attempting to punch Paegnium, who dodges each blow. In
these lines, just as Sagaristio begins to swear by invoking the gods in a curse
formula, Paegnium interrupts with a jibe (from a "friend") that suggests that
the curse should be carried out rather than the desired outcome. Then there is
this amusing wordplay between *defigere* ("to pin down") and *affigere* ("to pin
up") – with the latter referring emphatically to Sagaristio as the person being
pinned up on a *crux*.

**(436)** Plautus, *Persa* 349–354

*Sat.*   Enim vero odiosa es.
*Vir.*   Non sum, neque me esse arbitror,

---

[973] Text: NIXON, Plautus, 3:456.

[974] Note especially: *abi in malam rem* ("go out to the wicked thing" in line 289), which
may well have reference to the *malam crucem*. Favoring that *rem = crucem* here, observe that
the next two lines continue to imply that a device is intended (*at tu domum: nam ibi tibi
parata praestost,* "and you [go out to] home: for there it is ready, having been prepared for
you") and that all this particular banter presumes a legal context (*vadatur hic me,* "this [slave
boy] has me post bail").

quom parva natu recte praecipio patri.
nam inimici famam non ita ut natast ferunt.
*Sat.*  Ferant eantque maximam malam crucem;
neque ego inimicitias omnes pluris existimo,
quam mensa inanis nunc si apponatur mihi.

*Translation.*
*Sat.*  Well! You are truly annoying.
*Vir.*  I am not, nor do I consider myself to be so,
when, though few in years, I rightly advise my father.
For enemies do not carry a rumor in the same way it arose.
*Sat.*  Let them carry it, and let them go to the most wicked cross!
I no more consider all their enmity now
than I would an empty table if it was set next to me.

*Commentary.*[975] Later in the play, the parasite Saturio, in order to get regular invitations to dinner with Toxilus, has ordered his *virgo* (i.e., his daughter) to dress up as a Persian slave-girl, with the goal of swindling the pimp Dordalus into falsely purchasing her (*Pers.* 127–165). In the conversation above between Saturio and his daughter, she objects to being treated this way, and hopes to talk her father out of it. She cautions him that this could mean a bad reputation for her and for him. Saturio, however, is more concerned about getting a square meal (note his ironic derision of an "empty table") than he is about any enemies circulating increasingly hostile rumors (the kinds that improve-in-the-telling). Saturio curses such enemies and tells them to go to the most wicked cross (*maximam malam crucem*).

**(437)** Plautus, *Persa* 794–798

*Dor.*  Ne sis me uno digito attigeris, ne te ad terram, scelus, adfligam.
*Paeg.* At tibi ego hoc continuo cyatho oculum excutiam tuum.
*Dor.*  Quid ais, crux, stimulorum tritor? quo modo me hodie versavisti,
ut me in tricas coniecisti, quo modo de Persa manus mi aditast?
*Tox.*  Iurgium hinc auferas, si sapias.

*Translation.*
*Dor.*  Don't you be laying a finger on me, lest I dash you to the ground, villain!
*Paeg.* Whereas I would immediately poke out your eye for you with this ladle!
*Dor.*  What did you say, cross, polisher of goads? In what way did you whirl me around today,

---

[975] Act 3, Scene 1. Text: NIXON, Plautus, 3:462.

when you cast me into this tangled mess? In what way did you cheat me by the hand of the Persian?

*Tox.* Remove [your] abuse from here, if you are wise.

*Commentary.*[976] In the final scene of *Persa*, Toxilus' stratagem has succeeded, and the pimp Dordalus has been swindled. After Toxilus bought the freedom of his beloved slave-prostitute (Lemniselenis) from Dordalus, they then lured Dordalus into buying Saturio's daughter from Sagaristio (Toxilus' fellow slave). Sagaristio was dressed as a Persian slave dealer (hence the name of the play, and the reference to *Persa* in the lines above). Saturio then enters and claims his daughter, with the result that Dordalus is out more money than Toxilus had paid for Lemniselenis.[977] In the lines above, Toxilus is hosting a drinking party to celebrate their success. Paegnium, a young boy slave, is serving the wine with a ladle. And Dordalus comes in to accuse Toxilus. Dordalus begins to heap expletives on Toxilus,[978] including *stimulorum tritor* ("polisher of goads"), presumably implying that the pointed goads should be applied so often to Toxilus that they are polished by the rubbing action. More to the point, Dordalus calls Toxilus a *crux* ("cross").

## (438) Plautus, *Persa* 853–857

*Dor.* Male disperii, sciunt referre probe inimico gratiam.
*Tox.* Satis sumpsimus supplici iam.
*Dor.* Fateor, manus vobis do.
*Tox.* Et post dabis sub furcis.
*Sag.* Abi intro – in crucem.
*Dor.* An me hic parum exercitum hisce habent?
*Tox.* Convenisse te Toxilum me
spectatores, bene valete. leno periit. plaudite.

*Translation.*
*Dor.* I have been wickedly destroyed; they know how thoroughly to return a favor to [their] enemy.
*Tox.* We have exacted sufficient punishment now.
*Dor.* I confess so! I offer you my hands.
*Tox.* And afterward you will offer [them] under the *furca*.
*Sag.* Go away indoors – unto a cross.

---

[976] Text: NIXON, Plautus, 3:514.

[977] Toxilus pays *nummos sescentos* (*Pers.* 37, 437), while Dordalus pays *sexaginta minae* minus *duobus nummis* (685–686). Toxilus announced that he planned to con Dordalus for more money in line 327.

[978] Such verbal insults between Dordalus and Toxilus are a recurring theme in the play; cf. 405–426.

*Dor.*     Have these men applied to me an insufficient harassment?
*Tox.*     You met me, Toxilus...
          Audience, goodbye! The pimp has been done in. Applaud!

*Commentary.*[979] These are the closing lines of the play. The pimp Dordalus is maltreated by Toxilus and Sagaristio during the final drinking party after their successful con. In the final line, as is typical in Plautus, a central character (here Toxilus) bids the audience adieu and demands their applause. Dordalus' last words are likely addressed to the audience as well, as he inquires of the spectators if his harassment has been "insufficient" (*parum* is a term that, in a likely double entendre, can also be used to call for an encore). For several pages of the script Toxilus and friends heap offense on Dordalus, and likely take physical shots at him as well (cf. 794–795, 809–818). Thus, though the physical movements are not in the Latin script above, they may well be implied – imagine Dordalus being kicked out the door by Sagaristio in line 855 above. The language of Dordalus' demise bears overtones of death (*disperii, periit*),[980] and his come-uppance is portrayed as a fitting punishment (*supplicium*). When he "offers his hands" (*manus vobis do*), Dordalus employs a phrase commonly heard from a gladiator making his last appeal to the audience to spare life. Thus the metaphorical imagery of the cross appears quite fitting in this context of punishment and death. Note how the mention of *furca* (a fork-shaped tree used for torture and execution) can be employed interchangeably with *crux*. The line "*abi intro – in crucem*" comically employs two competing prepositions (*intro* and *in*) against a verb (*abeo*) that bears its own prepositional prefix – as if in his drunkenness Sagaristio stammers "Go out ... inside ... unto the cross!" (and then gives Dordalus the boot).

**(439)** Plautus, *Poenulus* 271–274

I in malam crucem. tun audes etiam servos spernere,
propudium? quasi bella sit, quasi eampse reges ductitent,
monstrum mulieris, tantilla tanta verba funditat,
quoius ego nebulai cyatho septem noctes non emam.

*Translation.* Go to the wicked cross! Do you even dare to scorn slaves,
O shameful creature? As if she were beautiful, as if kings regularly took her
     home,
monster of a woman, so small a woman pours out such great words,
with whom I would not purchase seven nights with a ladle of mist.

---

[979] Text: NIXON, Plautus, 3:522.

[980] Note how earlier in line 814 Paegnium instructs Dordalus to commit suicide: "You, take a stout rope unto yourself and hang yourself!" (*Restim tu tibi cape crassam ac suspende te*).

*Commentary*.[981] Plautus' *Poenulus* (*Little Carthaginian*) was based on the Greek New Comedy play Καρχηδόνιος (see line 53). It was likely first performed toward the beginning of the second century B.C. The above lines (from Act 1, Scene 2) represent the slave Milphio expressing his disgust at a statement by the courtesan Adelphasium. She (Adelphasium) had just declared that she would rather wait to go to the Temple of Venus at this time on Venus' festival day (cf. 191), because this is the hour when the lowest prostitutes are there, whom sordid slaves are likely to purchase (264–270). Adelphasium and her sister, Anterastilis, were kidnapped as young girls (along with their nurse) and sold to the pimp, Lycus. This is the day for the sale of courtesans, and their pimp was awaiting them at the Temple (264, 339–340). Milphio takes offense at Adelphasium's disparagement of slaves, and wishes her to go to the *malam crucem*. The irony throughout this scene concerns how Milphio despises Adelphasium so greatly, while Milphio's master (Agorastocles) is hopelessly in love with her.

**(440)** Plautus, *Poenulus* 343–347

*Ag.*    quid ais tu? quando illi apud me mecum caput et corpus copulas?
*Ad.*    Quo die Orcus Acherunte mortuos amiserit.
*Ag.*    Sunt mihi intus nescio quot nummi aurei lymphatici.
*Ad.*    Deferto ad me, faxo actutum constiterit lymphaticum.
*Mil.*    Bellula hercle.
*Ag.*    I dierecte in maxumam malam crucem.

*Translation.*
*Ag.*    What do you say? At what time [are you going] with me to that place you will unite head and body with me?
*Ad.*    On the day which Orcus will have released the dead from Archeruns.
*Ag.*    Inside I have I don't know how many frantic gold coins.
*Ad.*    Let them be paid over to me, I will immediately make that which is frantic stand still.
*Mil.*    Pretty little woman, by Hercules!
*Ag.*    [To Milphio]   Go, be hung up on the most wicked cross!

*Commentary*.[982] Shortly later in the same scene (Act 1, Scene 2) Agorastocles (with Milphio by his side) has finally worked up the courage to approach Adelphasium. While he fawns over her, she comes off rather aloof to his amorous advances. Apparently Agorastocles has frequently promised to free her, but has never come through (359–364). Orcus was the god of the underworld, and Archeruns was his river – the expression has the same effect as "when

---

[981] Text: NIXON, Plautus, 4:26.
[982] Text: NIXON, Plautus, 4:34.

hell freezes over" (i.e., "never"). Adelphasium does perk up at the mention of money, to which the slave Milphio derisively calls her a *Bellula* ("pretty little woman"). Agorastocles responds angrily to Milphio's taunt. Note the verbs here with *maxumam malam crucem*, especially how *dierecte* ("be hung up") indicates an awareness (even in the midst of an otherwise common expletive in Plautus) that the *malam crux* entails bodily suspension.

**(441)** Plautus, *Poenulus* 491–497

| | |
|---|---|
| *Anta.* | Dum exta referuntur, volo |
| | narrare tibi etiam unam pugnam. |
| *Lyc.* | Nil moror. |
| *Anta.* | Ausculta. |
| *Lyc.* | Non hercle auscultabo. |
| *Anta.* | Quo modo? |
| | colaphis quidem hercle tuom iam dilidam caput, |
| | nisi aut auscultas aut is in malam crucem. |
| *Lyc.* | Malam crucem ibo potius. |
| *Anta.* | Certumnest tibi? |
| *Lyc.* | Certum. |

*Translation.*

| | |
|---|---|
| *Anta.* | While they are bringing back the sacrificial meat, I want |
| | to narrate to you yet one [more] battle. |
| *Lyc.* | I don't care for that. |
| *Anta.* | Listen! |
| *Lyc.* | By Hercules, I shall not listen! |
| *Anta.* | How is that possible? |
| | By Hercules, I shall now certainly batter to pieces your head with [my] |
| | fists, |
| | unless you either listen or go to the wicked cross. |
| *Lyc.* | I would rather go to the wicked cross. |
| *Anta.* | Your mind is made up? |
| *Lyc.* | Made up. |

*Commentary.*[983] At the end of Act 2, Lycus the pimp and Antamonides (a soldier) head to Lycus' house. Antamonides intends to buy Anterastilis, Adelphasium's younger sister. Meanwhile, Antamonides recounts absurdly boastful tales of his past military conquests, such as his slaying 60,000 flying men. Lycus has had enough and refuses to listen to more. Plautus quips that Lycus would even rather go to the *malam crucem*. Instead, they will soon go to dinner.

---

[983] Text: NIXON, Plautus, 4:50.

**(442)** Plautus, *Poenulus* 510–512

nequiquam hos procos mi elegi loripedis, tardissimos.
quin si ituri hodie estis, ite, aut ite hinc in malam crucem.
sicine oportet ire amicos homini amanti operam datum?

*Translation.*
Vainly have I selected for myself these club-footed suitors, the slowest possible
Indeed, if you are going today, go! Or go from here to the wicked cross!
Is this the proper way for friends to give service to a man in love?

*Commentary.*[984] At the beginning of Act 3, Agorastocles has recruited a group of *advocati* ("counselors"),[985] who will assist him in procuring Adelphasium from Lycus the pimp. However, as a man in love, he is eager to get going, but they are too slow for him. Agorastocles' larger monologue states that for a man in love "there is nothing more harsh than a slow friend" (504), and he remarks that he passed over selecting older men so they would not slow him down. For the next page of the play, their slow pace will be the brunt of jests and jabs. Here, he tells them to get a move on, or go to the *malam crucem.*[986]

**(443)** Plautus, *Poenulus* 779–795

*Adv.*   Periisti, leno. nam istest huius vilicus
          quem tibi nos esse Spartiatam diximus,
          qui ad te trecentos Philippeos modo detulit.
          idque in istoc adeo aurum inest marsuppio.
*Lyc.*   Vae vostrae aetati.
*Adv.*   Id quidem in mundo est tuae.
*Agor.*  Age omitte actutum, furcifer, marsuppium:
          manifesto fur es mihi. quaeso hercle, operam date,
          dum me videatis servom ab hoc abducere.
*Lyc.*   Nunc pol ego perii certo, haud arbitrario.

---

[984] Text: Nixon, Plautus, 4:52.

[985] Agorastocles calls them *procos*, which may either be a humorous reference to them assisting as *proci*, "suitors", although in reality they are helping him entrap Lycus; or a reference to them as *proci*, "leading citizens", though they bought their freedom and are not wealthy, cf. lines 519–520, 536–537. Perhaps a double-entendre permits both options to serve as an ironic play on *proci*.

[986] Various comedic touches likely connect in context to *malam crucem*: Two lines later (line 514) Agorastocles jokes that they learned their slow pace while on a chain-gang, implying continued reference to punishments accorded to criminals. The *advocati* will later say in reply *nos te nihili pendimus* ("we are hanging nothing for you"; line 520), which is an idiomatic way of saying "we care nothing about" (see OLD, s.v. *nihilum*) but which may potentially bear a sarcastic reference to the *mala crux* with which Agorastocles taunted them.

consulto hoc factum est, mihi ut insidiae fierent.
sed quid ego dubito fugere hinc in malam crucem,
prius quam hinc optorto collo ad praetorem trahor?
eheu, quom ego habui hariolos haruspices;
qui si quid bene promittunt, perspisso evenit,
id quod mali promittunt, praesentarium est.
nunc ibo, amicos consulam, quo me modo
suspendere aequom censeant potissimum.

*Translation.*

Adv.   You have perished, pimp. For that man is his *vilicus*
    whom we told you was a Spartan,
    who transferred to you three hundred gold coins just now.
    And that gold is moreover in the pouch in here.

Lyc.   Woe upon your life!

Adv.   This indeed is in store for you.

Agor.  Come, *furcifer*, let go of the pouch immediately:
    you are plainly a thief. [Addressing the *advocati*:] By Hercules, I
      implore you, devote your attention
    as you see me take [my] slave from this man.

Lyc.   Now, by Pollux, I have certainly perished, no doubt.
    It has occurred by a plan that laid an ambush against me.
    But why am I doubting that I should flee from here unto the wicked
      cross,
    before they drag me violently by the throat from here to the magistrate?
    Alas, when I had seers and diviners,
    who, if they had promised well, it happened very slowly,
    that which they promised evilly is paid on the spot.
    Now I will go; I will consult with friends about which means
    they advise as the favorable and best possible way to hang myself.

*Commentary.*[987] In Act 3, Scene 5 of *The Little Carthaginian*, Agorastocles has sprung a trap on Lycus the pimp. Agorastocles has schemed throughout to gain possession from Lycus of Adelphasium. Agorastocles sends his *vilicus* (his slave who oversees the farm) named Collybiscus to approach Lycus in the form of a wealthy Spartan, who seeks luxuriant housing and female company. However, once Collybiscus has handed over the money and has been led into Lycus' house, Agorastocles arrives with his *advocati* (counselors) as witnesses in order to accuse Lycus of harboring an escaped slave, who has pilfered his master's money. The passage has many ironic touches. For example, Scene 5 begins with Lycus stating that diviners can all "go hang themselves" (*suspendant omnes nunciam se haruspices* in line 746), for they had recently

---

[987] Text: NIXON, Plautus, 4:78.

interpreted the sacrificial entrails to indicate that Lycus' future was to be an evil one (cf. 449–466), whereas he had just received the biggest purse of his life; now Lycus recognizes that he should have listened to their warning, and he instead contemplates hanging himself (*me ... suspendere* in 794–795). The expletive *furcifer* in line 784 likely carries its typical referent to "one who dwells on the fork-shaped *furca*" here, especially so proximate to the mention of the *crux* in line 789 (and 799; see below).[988] In Rome a cross may actually have been considered an appropriate punishment for a person who helped an escaped slave. Some scholars might potentially argue that Lycus' mention of the *crux* (in 789) signifies in context his resolution to commit suicide by hanging himself (in 794–795), thus the *crux* would refer to a gallows on which one hangs by a noose. However, given the way Plautus frequently employs *in malam crucem* (with or without *magnam* or *maximam*) as a vulgar metaphor for death (much like the English "go to hell"), then we see here rather an ironic twist of words as Lycus chooses to "flee unto the wicked cross" by committing suicide (a death by suspension) rather than suffering the actual crucifixion of the magistrate. Further irony may be implied in this: he fears they will violently drag him to the magistrate by his throat, so instead he will hang himself by the neck in order to forestall the magistrate.

**(444)** Plautus, *Poenulus* 796–800

*Ag.*　　Age tu progredere, ut [testes] videant te ire istinc foras.
　　　　estne hic meus servos?
*Coll.*　Sum hercle vero, Agorastocles.
*Agor.*　Quid nunc, sceleste leno?
*Adv.*　Quicum litigas
　　　　apscessit.
*Agor.*　Vtinam hinc abierit malam crucem.
*Adv.*　Ita nos velle aequom est.

*Translation.*
*Ag.*　　Come you, go forwards! so that [the witnesses] see you going out the
　　　　　door from there.
　　　　Is this not my slave?
*Coll.*　By Hercules, I truly am, Agorastocles.
*Agor.*　What now, villainous pimp?
*Adv.*　The man with whom you are going to court
　　　　has gone away.
*Agor.*　If only he would have gone out from here to the wicked cross.
*Adv.*　Thus too is what we want as the favorable outcome.

---

[988] Note esp. *furcifer* in *Most.* 69–71 (extensively discussed in No. 304).

*Commentary.*[989] As Act 3 transitions to Scene 6, Agorastocles has gone into Lycus' house to retrieve his *vilicus* Collybiscus. Agorastocles returns unaware that Lycus has fled the scene; Agorastocles makes a grand show of having "discovered" his slave, even though both he and his advocates already knew that Collybiscus was in the house. After being informed that Lycus has bolted, Agorastocles pronounces his desire that Lycus ends up on a *malam crucem*, and the *advocati* concur with that desire (elsewhere they call Lycus *corruptorem civium*, a "corruptor of the citizens," line 816). The irony here stems from how Lycus had just considered the *malam crucem* to be his best choice for where to go next (line 789 just discussed earlier) – so everyone is on the same page in commending the "wicked cross" to him (but for very different reasons).

**(445)** Plautus, *Poenulus* 1306–1309

*Anta.*  quid tibi negoti est autem cum istac? dic mihi.
*Han.*  Adulescens, salve.
*Anta.*  Nolo, nihil ad te attinet.
    quid tibi hanc digito tactio est?
*Han.*  Quia mihi lubet.
*Anta.*  Lubet?
*Han.*  Ita dico.
*Anta.*  Ligula, i in malam crucem.

*Translation.*
*Anta.*  What is your business then with that woman? Speak to me!
*Han.*  Good health to you, young man.
*Anta.*  I do not want anything connected with you.
    What is this touching her with your finger?
*Han.*  Because I want to.
*Anta.*  Want?
*Han.*  So I said.
*Anta.*  Shoe-strap![990] Go to the wicked cross!

*Commentary.*[991] Antamonides, the braggart soldier from earlier in the play, here angrily approaches the newly arrived Carthaginian gentleman, Hanno. Hanno has just discovered his long-lost daughters Adelphasium and Anterasti-

---

[989] Text: Nixon, Plautus, 4:78–80.

[990] Aside from being an obvious curse, the precise referent of *ligula* is tricky. While Lewis and Short (s.v.) consider it a "term of reproach" related to "tongue of a shoe, a shoe-strap, shoe latchet"; OLD s.v. *ligula* classifies it amidst various tongue-shaped items as a "term of abuse [with] uncertain sense." The one other occurrence in Plautus is *Poen.* 1014, where it is simply an object to be sold alongside *canalis ... et nuces* (gutters/pipes and tree-nuts).

[991] Text: Nixon, Plautus, 4:102.

lis, as well as his kidnapped nephew Agorastocles. His daughters are affectionately embracing Hanno just as Antamonides happens on the scene. Antamonides has paid good money to the pimp for Anterastilis, and so he approaches Hanno as if he were a competing lover, hence his terms of abuse in the final line above (followed by others that continue to be offensive in lines not recorded above). Eventually by the end of the play all will be set right, the Carthaginians will all return home and Lycus the pimp will be compelled to hand over another courtesan-slave to Antamonides.[992]

**(446)** Plautus, *Pseudolus* 326–335

| | |
|---|---|
| *Cal.* | Pseudole, ei accerse hostias, |
| | victumas, lanios, ut ego huic sacruficem summo Iovi; |
| | nam hic mihi nunc est multo potior Iuppiter quam Iuppiter. |
| *Bal.* | Nolo victumas: agninis me extis placari volo. |
| *Cal.* | Propera, quid stas? ei accerse agnos. audin quid ait Iuppiter? |
| *Ps.* | Iam hic ero; verum extra portam mi etiam currendumst prius. |
| *Cal.* | Quid eo? |
| *Ps.* | Lanios inde accersam duo cum tintinnabulis, |
| | eadem duo greges virgarum inde ulmearum adegero, |
| | ut hodie ad litationem huic suppetat satias Iovi. |
| *Bal.* | I in malam crucem. |
| *Ps.* | Istuc ibit Iuppiter lenonius. |

*Translation.*

| | |
|---|---|
| *Cal.* | Pseudolus, go! Fetch sacrificial animals, |
| | sacrificial victims, and butchers, so that I may sacrifice to this highest Jove; |
| | for, this man is to me now a much more powerful Jupiter than Jupiter. |
| *Bal.* | I do not want victims: I want to be placated with lamb's meat. |
| *Cal.* | Hurry! Why are you standing? Go, fetch the lambs. Do you not hear what Jupiter says? |
| *Ps.* | I shall be here soon; but first I must yet again run outside the city gate. |
| *Cal.* | Why there? |
| *Ps.* | From there I shall fetch two butchers with their cow-bells; |

---

[992] Notably, in the process of Lycus getting his come-uppance, on several more occasions he will consider suicide by hanging himself (with variations on *suspendere me* in lines 1341–1343), and he will later offer his neck for punishment (1351–1354, 1401). However, Hanno's final threat to his welfare is certainly more vague than the NIXON translation would suggest (in line 1407: *ego te meruisse ut pereas scio*, "I know that you deserve that you should *be destroyed*," rather than NIXON's "I know that you have earned a *hanging*"; NIXON, Plautus, 4:141).

at the same time I shall have driven from there two troops of elm-wood rods,

so that today an abundance will support this Jove for his favorable sacrifice.

*Bal.*    Go to the wicked cross!

*Ps.*    There the pimping Jupiter goes.

*Commentary.*[993] In Act 1, Scene 3, Calidorus is a man in love, and he has been repeatedly entreating Ballio the pimp for the right to purchase the slave-courtesan Phoenicium (the object of Calidorus' affections). Ballio here makes Calidorus think there is hope. Calidorus responds by calling Ballio by the name Jupiter/Jove, since Ballio is the person who has the single authority that Calidorus craves (i.e., the power to sell Phoenicium). There is light-hearted talk of sacrifice/banquet, and Ballio (who has already shown his disdain for Jove, lines 265–269), merrily plays off such an identity with Jupiter and calls for a meal of lamb for himself. Meanwhile, the slave Pseudolus (the namesake of the play) treats Ballio with less regard. Pseudolus makes a number of puns between a religious animal sacrifice (with its butchers and victims) and a criminal execution (with its "butchers" and "rods" and "support" for the victim).[994] Ballio understands Pseudolus' double-entendre, and counters with a vulgarity: "go to the wicked cross." Pseudolus regards that as a place where pimps should go (especially a pimp who makes himself out to be Jupiter). Soon Pseudolus' disdain for Ballio will prove to be merited, since Ballio has all along concealed that he has already contracted Phoenicium to another man.

## (447) Plautus, *Pseudolus* 829–830, 836–847

*Coc.*    nam vel ducenos annos poterunt vivere
          meas qui essitabunt escas quas condivero ...

*Bal.*    At te Iuppiter
          dique omnes perdant cum condimentis tuis
          cumque tuis istis omnibus mendaciis.

*Coc.*    Sine sis loqui me.

*Bal.*    Loquere, atque i in malam crucem.

*Coc.*    Vbi omnes patinae fervont, omnis aperio:
          is odos dimissis manibus in caelum volat.

---

[993] Text: NIXON, Plautus, 4:184.

[994] Nixon notes: "Executioners lived outside the Esquiline Gate" (*Plautus*, transl. Nixon, 4:184n.), and this explains the reference to Pseudolus going outside the *portam* in line 331. Ballio had just earlier threatened one of his slave-courtesans that the craft of the butcher (*lanius*) would be applied to her (hanging her out on a meat frame; see lines 196–201). The "troops of elm-wood rods" (*greges virgarum...ulmearum*) refer in the double entendre both to fuel for a sacrificial fire and to rods used to beat a criminal.

*Bal.* Odos dimissis manibus?
*Coc.* Peccavi insciens.
*Bal.* Quidum?
*Coc.* Dimissis pedibus volui dicere.
eum odorem cenat Iuppiter cottidie.
*Bal.* Si nusquam is coctum, quidnam cenat Iuppiter?
*Coc.* It incenatus cubitum.
*Bal.* I in malam crucem.
istacine causa tibi hodie nummum dabo?

*Translation.*
*Coc.* For they will even be able to live two hundred years
who fed on food which I shall have seasoned ...
*Bal.* And may Jupiter
and all the gods destroy you with your spices
and with all those lies of yours!
*Coc.* Please allow me to speak.
*Bal.* Speak, and go to the wicked cross.
*Coc.* When all my pans are boiling hot, I open them all:
This odor with stretched-out hands flies to heaven.
*Bal.* An odor with stretched-out hands?
*Coc.* I made an ignorant slip.
*Bal.* How so?
*Coc.* I wanted to say with stretched-out feet.
On this odor Jupiter dines daily.
*Bal.* If you don't go cook anywhere, pray tell what does Jupiter dine on?
*Coc.* He goes to his bed without supper.
*Bal.* Go to the wicked cross!
For that reason shall I give you a *nummus* today?

*Commentary.*[995] On his birthday, the pimp Ballio has hired a cook (*cocus*) for the day. Ballio has already proven himself to be a cheapskate, who is obsessed with money (e.g., lines 170–229), but he was forced to hire the cook at the cost of a *nummus* (about twice the normal daily wage, cf. 808–809). When Ballio complains about the price (lines 790ff.), the cook insists that he costs more because his food is seasoned in a heavenly fashion – fit for Jupiter himself. On two occasions Ballio gets fed up with the cook's braggadocio, and instructs him to "go to the wicked cross" (lines 839, 846). In the intervening lines, the precise referent of *dimissis manibus* is difficult, but should it indicate "stretched-out hands" then there may be an ironic slip-of-the-tongue that the cook employs after having just been taunted with the *crux* (on which a person can appear with outstretched arms).[996]

---

[995] Text: NIXON, Plautus, 4:234.

**(448)** Plautus, *Pseudolus* 1179–1183

*Har.* Sanine estis?
*Bal.* Quid hoc quod te rogo?
noctu in vigiliam quando ibat miles, quom tu ibas simul,
conveniebatne in vaginam tuam machaera militis?
*Har.* I in malam crucem.
*Bal.* Ire licebit tamen tibi hodie temperi.
*Har.* Quin tu mulierem mi emittis, aut redde argentum.

*Translation.*
*Har.* Are you [two] sane?
*Bal.* What because I ask you this?
At night, at the time the soldier went on patrol, when you went at the
same time,
did the soldier's sword fit in your sheath?
*Har.* Go to the wicked cross!
*Bal.* Yet you will be permitted to go [there] at the right time today.
*Har.* Indeed you are to dispatch the woman to me. Or, return the money!

*Commentary.*[997] Near the climax of the play (Act 4, Scene 7), Harpax (a slave
in the service of the soldier who had already paid Ballio money for Phoenicium) encounters the pimp Ballio. Harpax insists on delivery of the girl. However, Pseudolus had already arranged for someone to intercept the soldier's
money and his seal; then they had submitted the money to Ballio, and thus
they earlier gained the release of Phoenicium from the pimp. As Harpax
approaches Ballio, the pimp is mistakenly convinced that Harpax is the fake
slave sent by Pseudolus to swindle him out of his money. Thus Ballio makes
many jests (some quite crude) against Harpax. In response to one of the most

---

[996] For outstretched arms, cf. Plautus, *Mil. glor.* 358–360; *Most.* 359–360 (see sections 2.9
and 3.6.2). OLD s.v. *dimitto* 5b permits the sense of "to cause or allow to extend, stretch out"
with particular reference to hands (citing Seneca, *Contr.* 9.6(29).12 [*sic* actually 8.6.12]:
*manus ad genua dimitte, rea es*). NIXON's translation of the *Pseudolus* follows this: "flies to
heaven with outstretched arms". On the other hand, LEWIS and SHORT, s.v. *dimitto* II.A.2
understand *dimitto* in this passage to stand for "with hands relaxed, i.e. in all haste." The other
similar passage in Plautus (*Epid.* 451–452 in Act 3, Scene 4) fits either definition: *si audias
meas pugnas, fugias manibus dimissis domum* ("If you heard my battles, you would flee home
with *manibus dimissis*" ['outstretched hands' *or* 'in all haste']). Finally, it is possible to derive
*dimissis* instead from *demitto* (see OLD s.v.) with the sense of "to lower" or "to hang down". I
found one possible parallel in the fourth-century A.D. work by Maurus Servius Honoratus,
*Commentary on the Aeneid of Vergil* on Vergil's line 4.205 (where Servius reads *nam inferos
demissis ad terram manibus invocamus*). This explains the RILEY translation of the *Pseudolus*
line: "with its hands hanging down" (the irony here then would concern how an odor can fly to
heaven with drooping hands). Our translation obviously favors the OLD suggestion with
*dimitto* (i.e., "stretched out"), but the precise identification of *dimissis* must be held tenuously.
[997] Text: NIXON, Plautus, 4:266–268.

obscene quips, Harpax above tells Ballio to "go to the wicked cross." Ballio, thinking Harpax a slave on a criminal mission, retorts that Harpax will soon himself end up on that *malam crucem*. The exchange of taunts will continue for a couple more pages before Ballio fathoms that he has been duped and that all along he has been insulting his client's trusted slave.

**(449)** Plautus, *Pseudolus* 1294–1295

*Sim.*   Di te ament, Pseudole. fu i in malam crucem.
*Ps.*    Cur ego adflictor?
*Sim.*   Quid tu, malum, in os igitur mi ebrius inructas?

*Translation.*
*Sim.*   May the gods love you, Pseudolus. [Pseudolus belches] Phew! Go to
         the wicked cross!
*Ps.*    Why am I to be afflicted?
*Sim.*   What then you, wickedness – do you, drunkard, belch into my face?

*Commentary.*[998] Simo, Calidorus' father, had wagered Ballio that Pseudolus would swindle the pimp. With the success of Pseudolus' scheme, Simo has thus received a big purse from Ballio. In this closing scene of the farce (Act 5, Scene 2), the merry Simo looks for Pseudolus to share the prize, and he soon discovers the inebriated slave. Apparently the pungent aroma of the Pseudolus' wine-soaked belches is sufficient cause for Simo to recommend him to the *malam crucem*. Nevertheless, Simo quickly forgives the soused slave, and they go off together at the end of the play.

**(450)** Plautus, *Rudens* 174–180

*Scep.*  desiluit haec autem altera in terram e scapha.
         ut prae timore in genua in undas concidit.
         salvast, evasit ex aqua. iam in litore est.
         sed dextrovorsum avorsa it in malam crucem.
         hem, errabit illaec hodie.
*Daem.*  Quid id refert tua?
*Scep.*  Si ad saxum quo capessit, ea deorsum cadit,
         errationis fecerit compendium.

*Translation.*
*Scep.*  This other woman, moreover, has leapt out of the lifeboat toward the
         land.
         How in the face of fear she falls down on her knees in the waves!

---

[998] Text: Nixon, Plautus, 4:280.

> She is saved! She has gone out from the water. Now she is on the
> shore.
> Oh, but having turned aside toward the right, she is going to the
> wicked cross. Alas! She will wander astray there today.

*Daem.*   Why is this important to you?

*Scep.*   If [she goes] to the rock toward which she is heading, and she falls
downwards, she will have made a short cut of her wandering.

*Commentary.*[999] Early in *The Rope* (Act 1, Scene 2) the boat has shipwrecked
on which traveled the pimp Labrax and his two courtesan-slaves. Daemones
and his witty slave Sceparnio observe the survivors coming to shore. Here
they focus on the plight of the second courtesan as she makes it to shore but
begins walking in a dangerous direction toward a cliff. The slave Sceparnio
refers to her impending death as if she were going toward a *malam crucem.*[1000]

## (451) Plautus, *Rudens* 516–518

*Charm.*   Bonam est quod habeas gratiam merito mihi,
qui te ex insulso salsum feci opera mea.

*Labr.*   Quin tu hinc is a me in maxumam malam crucem?

*Translation.*

*Charm.*   It is good that you give me thanks as I deserve,
who, by my service, made you from 'unsalted' to 'salty'.

*Labr.*   Why don't you go away from here and from me unto the most
wicked cross?

*Commentary.*[1001] At this point in *Rudens* (*The Rope*) the pimp Labrax and his
companion, Charmides have washed up on the shore of Cyrene after a ship-
wreck. As result of that wreck, Labrax has lost his traveling-trunk and two
slave-girl prostitutes, whom he was planning to sell for a high price in Sicily
at Charmides' recommendation. The conversation expresses the bitterness of
Labrax as he blames Charmides for his plight. Charmides meanwhile takes the
opportunity to make a host of nautical jokes, including the double entendre

---

[999] Text: NIXON, Plautus, 4:304.

[1000] It is difficult to know for certain, but Sceparnio may make a slight jest connecting the
criminal punishment implied by a *crux* to that of a *saxum*, since the *saxum* could refer in
Rome to a rock from which criminals were thrown down to their death (see OLD s.v. *saxum*).
For a *saxum* as a rock from which one can jump to commit suicide see Plautus, *Trinummus*
266. The expression *inter sacrum saxumque* may imply "[caught] between an altar and a cliff"
(although OLD provisionally suggests here that *saxum* in such contexts means a knife or
sword); see Plautus, *Capt.* 617; *Cas.* 971 [this line is potentially spurious]. *Saxum* refers to
mere rocks in Plautus, *Merc.* 197–198; *Mil. glor.* 1024; *Most.* 677.

[1001] Text: NIXON, Plautus, 4:336.

above that he helped Labrax go from being "unsalted" (*ex insulso*) to "salty" (*salsum*). *Insulsus* not only means "saltless" but also "unattractive, dull, boring, stupid," and *salsus* can also apply to a person's salty wit[1002]; thus Labrax is no longer a dull host, but a funny one. Labrax in turn reviles his companion with the expression "go away to the most wicked cross (*is...in maxumam malam crucem*)."[1003]

**(452)**  Plautus, *Rudens* 1065–1072

Trach.   ita ut occepi dicere, illum quem dudum e fano foras
         lenonem extrusisti, hic eius vidulum eccillum tenet.
Gr.      Non habeo.
Trach.   Negas quod oculis video?
Gr.      At ne videas velim.
         habeo, non habeo: quid tu me curas quid rerum geram?
Trach.   Quo modo habeas, id refert, iurene anne iniuria.
Gr.      Ni istum cepi, nulla causa est quin me condones cruci;
         si in mari reti prehendi, qui tuom potiust quam meum?
Trach.   Verba dat. hoc modo res gesta est ut ego dico.

*Translation.*
Trach.   As I began to say: concerning that pimp whom you previously expelled outside of the temple,
         this man [Gripus] holds his traveling-trunk over there.
Gr.      I do not have it.
Trach.   Do you deny what I see with my eyes?
Gr.      But I would wish you do not see!
         I have it, I don't have it: what do you care which deeds I do?
Trach.   How you have it, that is important, whether justly or unjustly.
Gr.      If I did not catch that [by fishing], there is no reason why you should not deliver me up to the cross;
         If I snagged [it] in the sea with a net, why is it more yours than mine?
Trach.   He deceives. The deed occurred in this way as I said.

*Commentary.*[1004]  Gripus, a fisherman and slave of Daemones, managed to catch Labrax's lost traveling-trunk in his net. Gripus plans to keep the trunk

---

[1002] See definitions for *insulsus* and *salsus* in OLD s.v.

[1003] Among the many other salty epithets that Labrax applies to Charmides in this conversation, we also find *malo cruciatu in Sicilia perbiteres* ("would that you perished in Sicily by wicked torture," line 495). The venom of the expletive, combined with the use of *malus*, shows a strong similarity to the passion of the text above (*Rud.* 518), but we should follow the lexicons in distinguishing *crux* ("cross") from *cruciatus* ("torture").

[1004] Text: NIXON, Plautus, 4:394.

and its contents for himself. However, the slave Trachalio caught Gripus in the act. In this interchange (from Act 4, Scene 4), Trachalio attempts to convince Daemones to open the trunk in order to discover evidence that Labrax's slave-courtesans were in fact freeborn. However, Gripus still attempts to hold on to the trunk. As a slave, Gripus acknowledges that, if he had come by the trunk dishonestly, then they should "deliver me up to the cross" (*me condones cruci*). This statement about the *crux* is not truly a vulgar taunt or jest, rather it is more a statement of fact; thus it might better fit under evidence that slaves could be crucified (see section 3.6.2), but it seemed best to keep the passages from *Rudens* together.

**(453)**  Plautus, *Rudens* 1160–1162

| | |
|---|---|
| *Daem.* | dic, in ensiculo quid nomen est paternum? |
| *Pal.* | Daemones. |
| *Daem.* | Di immortales, ubi loci sunt spes meae? |
| *Grip.* | Immo edepol meae? |
| *Trach.* | Pergite, opsecro, continuo. |
| *Grip.* | Placide, aut i in malam crucem. |

*Translation.*

| | |
|---|---|
| *Daem.* | Speak! On the toy sword what is the paternal name? |
| *Pal.* | Daemones. |
| *Daem.* | Immortal gods! Where are my hopes to be placed? |
| *Grip.* | Rather, by Pollux, my [hopes]? |
| *Trach.* | Go on, I implore [you], without more ado! |
| *Grip.* | Gradually, or go to the wicked cross! |

*Commentary.*[1005] In this climactic moment (from Act 4, Scene 4), Daemones has followed Trachalio's advice and summoned Palaestra to identify the contents of her childhood toys from a casket in Labrax's traveling-trunk. Gripus, who had hoped to keep the trunk for himself, realizes that the more items Palaestra identifies, the less he will be able to claim ownership of the trunk. Meanwhile, as Palaestra (who had been captured as a child and sold to Labrax the pimp) identifies the items, Daemones increasingly comes to realize that Palaestra is his long-lost daughter. Without stage directions in Plautus' own script, we are left to infer to whom Gripus addresses the final line quoted above. He could be addressing (perhaps under his breath) Palaestra or he might be speaking directly to Trachalio.[1006] In any case, Gripus is sufficiently

---

[1005] Text: Nixon, Plautus, 4:404.

[1006] In the preceding pages, Gripus has maligned both his fellow slave Trachalio (e.g., lines 938–1126, 1166–1168) and the slave-courtesan Palaestra (e.g., 1131–1147, 1170). Nixon's translation suggests Trachalio, and the Riley translation directs Gripus' words to Palaestra.

frustrated with his ever-decreasing prospects, to wish another slave to "go to the wicked cross."

**(454)** Plautus, *Trinummus* 595–599

sed id si alienatur, actumst de collo meo,
gestandust peregre clupeus, galea, sarcina:
effugiet ex urbe, ubi erunt factae nuptiae,
ibit istac, aliquo, in maximam malam crucem,
latrocinatum, aut in Asiam aut in Ciliciam.

*Translation*. But if it [the farm] is lost, it's cost me my neck,[1007] [since I'll be] bearing abroad [his] shield, helmet, and soldier's kit: he will escape from the city, after the wedding has been done, he will go that way in some direction unto the most wicked cross, plundering, whether in Asia or in Cilicia.

*Commentary*.[1008] At the end of Act 2 of *Trinummus* (*Three Coins*), Stasimus (a slave of Lesbonicus) has just fooled someone into allowing Lesbonicus to keep the family farm. However, Stasimus still worries that his master will give the farm away (likely as a dowry in marrying off his sister), and they would lose their last possessions. Should that happen, he imagines the unpleasantness of his destitute life when he will have to accompany Lesbonicus as his slave and weapon carrier, after his master has gone off into soldiering and plundering. The term *latrocinatum* ("plundering") is somewhat ambiguous. It can imply "serving as a mercenary soldier," which would be appropriate to the way Greek troops often served as mercenaries in Persian armies in Asia and Cilicia; but *latrocinatum* can also refer to "engaging in brigandage."[1009] Intriguingly, as we have already seen above (sections 3.6.5 and 3.7.2), brigands were often punished on the *crux* in later Latin literature. In any case, Stasimus compares the horror of that life to going *in maximam malam crucem*.

**(455)** Terence, *Eunuchus* 382–385

*Par.*      flagitium facimus.
*Chaer.*   an id flagitiumst, si in domum meretriciam
           deducar et illis crucibus, quae nos nostramque adolescentiam
           habent despicatam et quae nos semper omnibus cruciant modis,
           nunc referam gratiam atque eas itidem fallam, ut ab illis fallimur?

---

[1007] Note entry in LEWIS and SHORT, Latin Dictionary, s.v. *collum*.
[1008] Text: NIXON, Plautus, 5:154.
[1009] See OLD s.v. *latrocinor*.

*Translation.*

Par.      We are performing an outrage.

Chaer.    Can it really be an outrage, if into a house of a courtesan
          I am drawn, and with those crosses, which have scorn for us and our
             youth
          and which always torture us by every means,
          I now express gratitude and I deceive them in the same way that we
             are deceived by them.

*Commentary.*[1010] This brief excerpt comes from Act 2, Scene 3 of *The Eunuch* by Publius Terentius Afer, which was first performed in 161 B.C. and was based on an original Greek play by Menander. Amidst the many madcap events in the play, the young lad Chaerea has become enamored with a girl, named Pamphila, who was recently given as a slave to the courtesan Thais (with whom Chaerea's brother, Phaedria, is having an affair). Phaedria is about to send a eunuch to Thais as a present. Here Chaerea schemes with the slave Parmeno for Chaerea to substitute himself for the eunuch in order to spend time alone with the girl whom he adores (Pamphila). Parmeno labels this action an "outrage" (*flagitium*), and he recognizes it as a scheme that could well backfire and lead him (as a slave) to pay the penalty. Chaerea counters that, others would consider such a subterfuge well deserved (in line 387)[1011] – his reasoning being that young men are always being "tortured" by courtesans and thus such a subterfuge from a young man is merited. In this vulgar metaphor, courtesans are compared with crosses (*crucibus*), and Chaerea makes a Latin wordplay (based on similar lexical stems) between these crosses and the torment they bring (*cruciant*). As with other instances of *crux* in Terence (e.g., *Andria* 621; *Phormio* 368, 544), the context is insufficient to know precisely what device Terence intends by a *crux*, and whether it is a means of execution or merely one of torture.[1012] However, clearly a *crux*

---

[1010] Text: SARGEAUNT, Terence, 1:272.

[1011] The following two lines (386–387) read: [386] *an potius haec patri aequomst fieri, ut a me ludatur dolis?* [387]*quod qui rescierint, culpent; illud merito factum omnes putent.* ("or is it more right this be performed against my father, that he may be made sport of by me with my stratagems? [387] Since those who have become wise [to the stratagem against a father], would blame [me]; [but] that [eunuch scheme] all would suppose a deed with merit"). Chaerea argues that his eunuch scheme is laudable, especially in contrast to the stock-in-trade antics of most New Comedy plays, where slaves assist their young wards in stratagems designed to deceive their fathers.

[1012] The reader may initially think that the verb *cruciant* (from *crucio*), with its notions of torment and torture of the living, may well define the extent of the torment implied in *crucibus* (from *crux*). Furthermore, instances of *crux* as a place of mere torture are known in early Latin (see esp. Plautus, *Asinaria* 545–557 above in 3.6.2). However, *crux* in early Latin is more often associated with death by suspension (where the context is determinative), and the metaphor here is clearly intended to be superlative, which works all the better if these courtesans, while causing torment in the near term, are here also portrayed as the device upon which

is not a pleasant object for Terence. As is typical in such comedies, Pamphila will eventually (after many more humorous situations) be discovered to be free-born, and Chaerea can thus marry her.

**(456)**  Terence, *Phormio* 367–371

| | |
|---|---|
| *Phorm.* | at quem virum! quem ego viderim in vita optumum. |
| *Geta* | videas te atque illum ut narras! |
| *Phorm.* | in malam crucem! |
| | nam ni ita eum existumassem, numquam tam gravis |
| | ob hanc inimicitias caperem in vostram familiam, |
| | quam is aspernatur nunc tam illiberaliter. |

*Translation.*

| | |
|---|---|
| *Phorm.* | But what a man! Whom I would see as the best man [I've known] in life. |
| *Geta* | May you look to yourself and to that man as you tell your tale! |
| *Phorm.* | [Go] unto the wicked cross! For, unless I had esteemed him so, never so intense an enmity would I have incurred towards your family on behalf of this [girl], whom he [Demipho] now scorns so ungenerously. |

*Commentary.*[1013] In Act 2, Scene 3 of this play (performed first in 161 B.C. and taken from Apollodorus' *The Claimant*), Phormio (a parasite) and Geta (a slave) have assisted the young citizen Antipho in marrying a poor, but beautiful, young lady, while Antipho's father was away from Athens. Their initial scheme involved Phormio claiming that Antipho was the girl's nearest male kin (her cousin) after her mother had passed away (thus, by Athenian law, obligating Antipho to marry her for her welfare).[1014] Now Antipho's father (Demipho) has returned. The marriage angers Demipho and he argues that he should undo it. In the dialogue above, Phormio and Geta are aware that Demipho is listening in on their conversation. Phormio continues the deception of having known the girl's father ("the best man" he has ever met), while Geta (one of Demipho's slaves) pretends to antagonize Phormio on behalf of Demipho. Geta indirectly cautions Phormio above that he must present an honorable account of the story. To Geta's threat, Phormio responds with the imprecation: *in malam crucem* ("[Go] to the wicked cross").

---

young men ultimately meet their complete demise. Thus, we cannot decisively settle the matter.

[1013] Text: SARGEAUNT, Terence, 2:42.

[1014] Ironically, she actually is Antipho's cousin (due to his philandering uncle), though no one knows that yet.

**(457)** Terence, *Phormio* 542–544

sane hercle pulchre suades: etiam tu hinc abis?
non triumpho, ex nuptiis tuis si nil nanciscor mali,
ni etiam nunc me huius causa quaerere in malo iubeas crucem?

*Translation.*
By Hercules, you advocate very beautifully: will you get out of here?!
Should I not triumph, if from your marriage I acquire no amount of misfortune,
unless even now you order me for his sake to seek a cross in misfortune?

*Commentary.*[1015] Even while the slave Geta continues to scheme about how best to appease Demipho concerning Antipho's marriage, now Phaedria (Antipho's male cousin) and Antipho implore Geta to swindle money from Demipho so Phaedria can purchase a slave girl, with whom Phaedria is in love. In the words above, Geta expresses to Antipho his natural hesitation about taking on yet another escapade against Demipho, even while the first has not been achieved, though eventually Geta will agree to help. The final idiom he employs (*quaerere in malo ... crucem*) is a bit different than the idioms that we encountered above that combine *malam* and *crucem*, for here *malo* (ablative) does not agree with *crucem* (accusative) – thus the rendering above ("to seek a cross in misfortune"). Nonetheless, the sense of the idiom is tangible enough.[1016]

**(458)** *Anthologia Graeca* 11.230 (from Ammianus)

Μασταύρων ἀφελὼν δύο γράμματα, Μάρκε, τὰ πρῶτα,
ἄξιος εἶ πολλῶν τῶν ὑπολειπομένων.

*Translation.* Marcus, by taking away the two first letters of Mastauron,
you are worthy of much of those remaining.

*Commentary.*[1017] The *Greek Anthology* attributes this passage to Ammianus, who was a satirical epigrammatist active in the early second century A.D. (during the rule of Hadrian). Μασταύρων likely refers to the place where Marcus is from – he is Marcus of Mastaura.[1018] The taunt is an obvious one – remove

---

[1015] Text: SARGEAUNT, Terence, 2:62.

[1016] Idiomatic English translations include RILEY's "to be seeking risk upon risk," and SARGEAUNT's "to jump ... from the frying-pan into the fire".

[1017] Text: PATON, Greek Anthology, 4:180. HENGEL, Crucifixion, 9 n. 19 intends this passage in his reference to 9.230 [*sic*]; this is corrected to 11.230 in the French edition HENGEL, La crucifixion, 22 n. 19.

[1018] Grammatically this is indicated by the genitive form of Μασταύρων. Strabo mentions a Μάσταυρα ("Mastaura") in Asia, in the vicinity of Nysa and near the Maeander River (*Geogr.*

the first two letters from Μασταύρων ("of Mastaura") and you have σταύρων ("of crosses"), and thus Marcus becomes "Marcus of the Crosses."

**(459)** Petronius, *Satyricon* 58.2

Nescit quid faciat, crucis offla, corvorum cibaria.

*Translation.* He does not know what he should do, cross meat, food of ravens.

*Commentary.*[1019] This is in the context of a satirical conversation, in which a freedman gave a speech, only to be laughed at by Giton. The freedman then turns upon Giton and lets loose a full-page-worth of slurs and cut-downs. Among these are two parallel phrases above: *crucis offla* (lit. "meat of the cross)" and *corvorum cibaria* ("food of ravens"). Together these portray the person as attached to a cross and being devoured by birds. Certainly it served as a vulgar taunt.

**(460)** Petronius, *Satyricon* 126.9

Ego adhuc servo nunquam succubui, nec hoc dii sinant, ut amplexus meos in crucem mittam.

*Translation.* Until now I have never succumbed to a servant, nor may the gods permit this, that I would send my loving embrace to a cross.

*Commentary.*[1020] Later in the *Satyricon*, Petronius portrays a slave woman with high standards – she will only sit in the laps of knights, not of slaves (she leaves the slaves to her mistress). She speaks of her revulsion at sleeping with a slave, as if she would be embracing the cross that was the slave's destiny. This is surely another vulgar witticism tied to the cross. Meanwhile just after the text above in this satirical reversal, while the maid will only sleep with knights, her mistress longs to kiss the scars of the flogged slaves.

---

14.1.47). Further, a TLG search of Μασταύρων yielded 34 other texts, all of which imply that Μασταύρων is a place; most of these references are in lists of bishoprics. Note especially the seventh-century reference to Asia: Θεόδωρος ἐλέει θεοῦ ἐπίσκοπος Μασταύρων ἐπαρχίας Ἀσίας ὁμοίως ὑπέγραψα (in *Concilia Oecumenica*, *Concilium universale Constantinopolitanum tertium* [680–681], Concilii actiones I–XVIII, document 18, page 826).

[1019] Text: HESELTINE and ROUSE, Petronius; Seneca: Apocolocyntosis, 104. HESELTINE informs us that *nescit* was conjectured by BUECHELER.

[1020] Text: HESELTINE and ROUSE, Petronius; Seneca: Apocolocyntosis, 278.

**(461)** *Pompeii Graffito* (CIL IV, 2082)

In cruce figarus.

*Translation.* Be fixed to a cross!

*Commentary.*[1021] This graffito was discovered in the Stabian Baths at Pompeii, which were built in the first century B.C. and destroyed by the first century A.D. eruption of Vesuvius, so the inscription must date between those termini. The verb *figarus* is awkward. COOK suggests *figaris* ("get fixed/nailed"), but it could be an errant perfect participle. In any case, there is clearly an invective here that derisively invokes the cross upon the reader.

**(462)** *Palatino Graffito*

*Illustration* (Fig. 7)

*Commentary.*[1022] In the midst of a prolonged section on the mockery and derision that was commonly associated with crucifixion, this would be an appro-

---

[1021] See text and discussion in COOK, Crucifixion, 122 (also ibid. 455 Fig. 4). COOK helpfully compares this to CIL IV 1864: *Samius / Cornelio / suspend(e)re* ("Samius to Cornelius, be hanged!"). Also see COOK, Envisioning Crucifixion, 277.

[1022] Drawing by Karis Chapman based on photographs. Cf. GIULIA SACCO, Il graffito blasfemo del Paedagogium nella Domus Augustana del Palatino, in Le iscrizioni dei cristiani in Vaticano. Materiali e contributi scientifici per una mostra epigrafica (ed. I. Di Stefano Manzella; Inscriptiones Sanctae Sedis 2; Città del Vaticano Roma: Monumenti, Musei e gallerie pontificie Distribuzione esclusiva, Edizioni Quasar), 192–194; MARIA ANTONIETTA TOMEI, Museo Palatino, English Edition. Rome: Electra, 1997, No. 78.

priate place to close with the famed Alexamenos graffito from the Palatine hill. The picture represents a man with an ass's head crucified with outstretched arms (he may wear a shortened tunic, but his buttocks are visible); meanwhile, another man (dressed likely in a slave's tunic) raises his hand in honor of the crucified figure.[1023] The scrawled inscription reads "Αλεξαμενος σεβετε θεον" ("Alexamenos, worship god").[1024] There is clear mockery here, and it is almost certainly directed toward the Christian religion. COOK rightly observes that pagans accused Christians of worshipping the head of an ass, and ass-worship was a charge previously leveled at the Jewish religion.[1025] Indeed, there are a number of indications that pagans felt free to deride the Christian religion because it followed (in Lucian's words) a "crucified sophist."[1026] In this regard, HENGEL points to the "folly" of the message of the crucified Son of God (1 Cor 1:18).[1027]

---

[1023] COOK, Envisioning Crucifixion, 283 suggests the raised hand may indicate blowing a kiss .

[1024] Many conjecture that the author intended to write σεβεται, to imply "Alexamenos worships god"; cf. HORSLEY and LLEWELYN, New Documents, 4:137 (No. 34).

[1025] COOK, Envisioning Crucifixion, 283–284; cf. ibid. 282–285 for the broader context of the graffito. For the charge against Christians, COOK references Minucius Felix, *Oct.* 9.3; 28.7; Tertullian, *Apol.* 16.12; *Nat.* 1.14.1–4.

[1026] Lucian, *Pereg.* 13; cf. *Pereg.* 11. For pagan derision of Christianity, note the many passages cited by HENGEL, Crucifixion, 1–10; COOK, Crucifixion, 418–423. On Jewish views cf. CHAPMAN, Crucifixion, 223–253.

[1027] HENGEL, Crucifixion, 1.

# Bibliography

ABEGG, MARTIN G. Qumran Sectarian Manuscripts. With Morphological and Lexical Tags. Bellingham, WA: Logos Research Systems, 2003.

ABEL, KARLHANS. Seneca. Leben und Leistung. ANRW II.32.2 (1984): 653–775

ACHARD, GUY. Cicéron. De l'invention. Collection des universités de France 320. Paris: Belles Lettres, 1994

ADAM, JAMES. The Republic of Plato: Edited with Critical Notes, Commentary and Appendices. 2 vols. Cambridge: Cambridge University Press, 1902

ADAMS, JAMES N. Bilingualism and the Latin Language. Cambridge: Cambridge University Press, 2003

ADLINGTON, WILLIAM, and STEPHEN GASELEE. The Golden Ass: Being the Metamorphoses of Lucius Apuleius. LCL. Cambridge: Harvard University Press, 1915

AHLBERG, AXEL W. C. Sallusti Crispi: Catalina, Iugurtha, Orationes et epistulae excerptae de Historiis. Bibliotheca scriptorum Graecorum et Romanorum. Leipzig: Teubner, 1919

ALBECK, J. THEODOR, and HANOKH ALBECK. Midrash Bereshit Rabba. Critical Edition with Notes and Commentary. 3 vols. Berlin: Poppelauer, 1912–1936

ALBRECHT, MICHAEL VON, and GARETH SCHMELING. A History of Roman Literature: From Livius Andronicus to Boethius. 2 vols. Mnemosyne Sup 165. Leiden: Brill, 1996

ALFÖLDY, GEZA. Un celebre frammento epigraphico tiburtino anonimo (P. Sulpicius Quirinius?). Pages 199–208 in Le iscrizione dei Cristiani in Vaticano. Edited by I. Di Stefano Manzella. Inscriptiones Sanctae Sedis 2. Città del Vaticano Roma: Monumenti, Musei e gallerie pontificie Distribuzione esclusiva, Edizioni Quasar, 1997

–. Nochmals: Pontius Pilatus und das Tiberieum von Caesarea Maritima. Scripta Classica Israelica 21 (2002): 133–148

–. Pontius Pilatus und das Tiberieum von Caesarea Maritima. Scripta Classica Israelica 18 (1999): 85–108

–. Das neue Edikt des Augustus aus El Bierzo in Hispanien. ZPE 131 (2000): 177–205

ALLEGRO, JOHN MARCO. Further Light on the History of the Qumran Sect. JBL 75 (1956): 89–95

–. Qumran Cave 4.I (4Q158–4Q186). DJD 5. Oxford: Clarendon Press, 1968

ALMQVIST, HELGE. Plutarch und das Neue Testament. Ein Beitrag zum Corpus Hellenisticum Novi Testamenti. Acta Seminarii Neotestamentici Upsaliensis 15. Uppsala: Appelbergs Boktryckeri, 1946

ANAGNOSTOU-CANAS, BARBARA. Juge et sentence dans l'Égypte romaine. Études de philosophie et d'histoire du droit 6. Paris: L'Harmattan, 1991

–. La réparation du préjudice dans les papyrus grecs d'Egypte. Pages 307–26 in Symposion 2005. Vorträge zur griechischen und hellenistischen Rechtsgeschichte, Salerno, 14.–18.September 2005. Edited by E. Cantarella. Akten der Gesellschaft für griechische und hellenistische Rechtsgeschichte 19. Wien: Österreichische Akademie der Wissenschaften, 2007

ANDERSON, J. G. C. Augustan Edicts from Cyrene. JRS 17 (1927): 33–48

ANDO, CLIFFORD. Imperial Ideology and Provincial Loyalty in the Roman Empire. Classics and Contemporary Thought 6. Berkeley: University of California Press, 2000

ANDREWS, CAROL. The Rosetta Stone. London: British Museum Publications, 1981

ANTHONY, SEAN W. Crucifixion and Death as Spectacle: Umayyad Crucifixion in its Late Antique Context. AOS 96. New Haven: American Oriental Society, 2014

ARANGIO-RUIZ, VINCENZO. La Legislazione. Pages 101–146 in Augustus. Studi in occasione del bimillenario Augusteo. Edited by P. de Francisci and S. Riccobono. Rome: Accademia Nazionale dei Lincei, 1938

ARAV, RAMI. Excarnation: Food for Vultures. BAR 37.6 (2011): 40–49, 17

ARNALDEZ, ROGER, AND JEAN POUILLOUX. De Aeternitate Mundi. Les oeuvres de Philon d'Alexandrie 30. Paris: Cerf, 1969

ARNAUD, DANIEL. Les ports de la «Phénicie» à la fin de l'âge du Bronze récent (XIV-XIII siècles) d'après les textes cunéiformes de Syrie. Studi Micenei ed Egeo-Anatolici 30 (1992): 179–194

AUBERGER, JANICK. Ctésias. Histoires de l'Orient. Roue à livres 11. Paris: Les Belles Lettres, 1991

AUBERT, JEAN-JACQUES. A Double Standard in Roman Criminal Law? The Death Penalty and Social Structure in Late Republican and Early Imperial Rome. Pages 94–133 in Speculum Iuris: Roman Law as a Reflection of Social and Economic Life in Antiquity. Edited by J. J. Aubert and B. Sirks. Ann Arbor: University of Michigan Press, 2002

AUNE, DAVID E. Prophecy in Early Christianity and the Ancient Mediterranean World. Grand Rapids: Eerdmans, 1983

AUS, ROGER DAVID. The Release of Barabbas (Mark 15.6–15 par; John 18.39–40) and Judaic Traditions on the Book of Esther. Pages 1–27 in Barabbas and Esther and Other Studies in the Judaic Illumination of Earliest Christianity. SFSHJ 54. Atlanta: Scholars Press, 1992.

AUSTIN, MICHEL M. The Hellenistic World from Alexander to the Roman Conquest: A Selection of Ancient Sources in Translation. Cambridge: Cambridge University Press, 1981

BAGNALL, ROGER S. Official and Private Violence in Roman Egypt [1989]. Pages 201–16 in Later Roman Egypt: Society, Religion, Economy and Administration. Variorum Collected Studies. Aldershot: Ashgate, 2003

BALAMOSHEV, CONSTANTINOS. ΑΠΟΤΥΜΠΑΝΙΣΜΟΣ: Just Death by Exposing on the Plank? JJP 41 (2011): 15–33

BALDWIN, MATTHEW C. Whose Acts of Peter? Text and Historical Context of the Actus Vercellenses. WUNT 2/196. Tübingen: Mohr-Siebeck, 2005

BAMMEL, CAROLINE P. HAMMOND, ed. Der Römerbriefkommentar des Origenes. Kritische Ausgabe der Übersetzung Rufins. 3 vols. Vetus Latina: Aus der Geschiche der Lateinischen Bibel 16.33.34. Freiburg: Herder, 1990–98

BAMMEL, ERNST. Die Blutgerichtsbarkeit in der römischen Provinz Judäa vor dem ersten jüdischen Aufstand [1974]. Pages 59–72 in Judaica: Kleine Schriften I. WUNT 37. Tübingen: Mohr, 1986

–. Crucifixion as a Punishment in Palestine [1970]. Pages 76–78 in Judaica: Kleine Schriften I. WUNT 37. Tübingen: Mohr, 1986

–. Crucifixion as a Punishment in Palestine. Pages 162–65 in The Trial of Jesus. FS C.F.D.Moule. Edited by E. Bammel. London: SCM, 1970.

–. Philos tou Kaisaros. TLZ 77 (1952): 205–210

–. Pilate and Syrian Coinage [1951]. Pages 47–50 in Judaica: Kleine Schriften I. WUNT 37. Tübingen: Mohr, 1986

–. The Trial before Pilate. Pages 415–51 in Jesus and the Politics of His Day. Edited by E. Bammel and C.F.D. Moule. Cambridge: Cambridge University Press, 1984

–. Zum Kapitalrecht in Kyrene [1954]. Pages 73–75 in Judaica: Kleine Schriften I. WUNT 37. Tübingen: Mohr, 1986

–. Zum Testimonium Flavianum (Jos Ant 18,63–64) [1974]. Pages 177–189 in Judaica: Kleine Schriften I. WUNT 37. Tübingen: Mohr Siebeck, 1986

BARBER, KIMBERLY A. Rhetoric in Cicero's *Pro Balbo:* An Interpretation. Orig. 2004. Repr. Studies in Classics 6. London: Routledge / Taylor & Francis, 2012

BARBET, PIERRE. A Doctor at Calvary: The Passion of Our Lord Jesus Christ as Described by a Surgeon. Translated by Earl of Wicklow. New York: Kennedy, 1953

BARCLAY, JOHN M. G. Against Apion. Flavius Josephus: Translation and Commentary 10. Leiden: Brill, 2006

–. Jews in the Mediterranean Diaspora: From Alexander to Trajan (323 BCE – 117 CE). Edinburgh: T & T Clark, 1996

BARDET, SERGE. Le Testimonium Flavianum. Examen historique, considérations historiographiques. Paris: Cerf, 2002

BARNETT, RICHARD, JOHN E. CURTIS, and NIGEL TALLIS. The Balawat Gates of Ashurnasirpal II. Edited by J.E. Curtis and N. Tallis. London: British Museum Press, 2008

BARRETT, ANTHONY A. Caligula: The Corruption of Power. New Haven: Yale University Press, 1990

BARRETT, C. K. The Gospel According to St. John. Second Edition. London/Philadelphia: SPCK/Westminster, 1978.

BARTELS, JENS. Verres, C. BNP 15 (2010): 321–323

BASORE, JOHN W. Seneca. Moral Essays. 3 vols. Orig. 1928–1935. Repr. LCL. Cambridge: Harvard University Press, 1979

BASTIANINI, GUIDO. Lista dei prefetti d'Egitto dal 30ª al 299ᴾ. ZPE 17 (1975): 263–328

BAUCKHAM, RICHARD J. For What Offence Was James Put to Death? Pages 199–232 in James the Just and Christian Origins. Edited by B. D. Chilton and C. A. Evans. NTSup 98. Leiden: Brill, 1999

BAUDY, GERHARD. Hermes I. Cult and Mythology. BNP 6 (2005): 214–19

BAUMAN, RICHARD A. Crime and Punishment in Ancient Rome. London: Routledge, 1996

–. The Crimen Maiestatis in the Roman Republic and Augustan Principate. Johannesburg: Witwatersrand University Press, 1967

–. Impietas in Principem: A Study of Treason against the Roman Emperor with Special Reference to the First Century A.D. MBPRG 67. München: Beck, 1974

BAUMGARTEN, JOSEPH M. The Avoidance of the Death Penalty in Qumran Law. Pages 31–38 in Reworking the Bible: Apocryphal and Related Texts at Qumran, Proceedings of a Joint Symposium by the Orion Center for the Study of the Dead Sea Scrolls and Associated Literature and the Hebrew University Institute for Advanced Studies Research Group on Qumran, 15–17 January, 2002. Edited by E. G. Chazon, D. Dimant, and R. A. Clements. STDJ 58. Leiden: Brill, 2005

–. Damascus Document 4Q266–273 (4QDᵃ⁻ʰ). Pages 1–185 in Damascus Document II: Some Works on the Torah, and Related Documents. Edited by J. H. Charlesworth. The Dead Sea Scrolls 3. Tübingen: Mohr Siebeck, 2006.

–. Does *TLH* in the Temple Scroll Refer to Crucifixion? JBL 91 (1972): 472–481

–. Hanging and Treason in Qumran and Roman Law. Eretz Yisrael 16 (1982): 7*–16*

–. Judicial Procedures." EDNT 2:455–460

–. Qumran Cave 4.XIII: The Damascus Document (4Q266–4Q273). DJD 18. Oxford: Clarendon Press, 1996.

BAUMGARTEN, JOSEPH M. / DANIEL R. SCHWARZ. Damascus Document (CD). Pages 4–57 in Damascus Document, War Scroll, and Related Documents. Edited by J. H. Charlesworth. The Dead Sea Scrolls 2. Tübingen: Mohr Siebeck, 1995.

BECKER, ULRICH. Jesus und die Ehebrecherin. Untersuchungen zur Text- und Überlieferungsgeschichte von Joh. 7,53–8,11. BZNW 28. Berlin: Töpelmann, 1963

BEER, GEORG. Pesachim. Die Mischna II/3. Gießen: Töpelmann, 1912

BEHRENDS, OKKO, ROLF KNÜTEL, BERTHOLD KUPISCH, and HANS HERMANN SEILER. Corpus Iuris Civilis. Text und Übersetzung. Band I: Institutionen. 3. überarbeitete Auflage. Orig. 1990. Repr. Heidelberg: Müller, 2007

BEHRENDS, OKKO, ROLF KNÜTEL, BERTHOLD KUPISCH, and HANS HERMANN SEILER. Corpus Iuris Civilis. Text und Übersetzung. 5 vols. Heidelberg: Müller, 1990–2005

BELKIN, SAMUEL. Philo and the Oral Law: The Philonic Interpretation of Biblical law in Relation to the Palestinian Halakah. HSS 9. Cambridge: Harvard University Press, 1940

BENDEMANN, REINHARD VON. 'Many-Colored Illnesses' (Mk 1:34): On the Significance of Illnesses in New Testament Therapy Narratives. Pages 100–124 in Wonders Never Cease: The Purpose of Narrating Miracle Stories in the New Testament and its Religious Environment. Edited by B. J. Lietaert Peerbolte and M. Labahn. Library of New Testament Studies 288. London / New York: T&T Clark, 2006

BENEFIEL, REBECCA / KATHLEEN COLEMAN. Graffiti, in Excavations at Zeugma Conducted by Oxford Archaeology. 3 vols. Edited by W. Aylward. Los Altos: Packard Humanities Institute, 2013, 1:178–191

BENKO, STEPHEN. Pagan Criticism of Christianity During the First Two Centuries A.D. ANRW II.23.2 (1980): 1055–1118

BERG, DEENA, and DOUGLASS PARKER. Plautus and Terence. Five Comedies. Miles Gloriosus. Menaechmi. Bacchides. Hecyra. Adelphoe. Indianapolis: Hackett, 1999

BERNETT, MONIKA. Der Kaiserkult in Judäa unter den Herodiern und Römern. Untersuchungen zur politischen und religiösen Geschichte Judäas von 30 v. bis 66 n. Chr. WUNT 1.203. Tübingen: Mohr Siebeck, 2007

BERNSTEIN, MOSHE J. *Midrash Halakhah* at Qumran? 11QTemple 64:6–13 and Deuteronomy 21:22–23. Gesher 7 (1979): 145–166

–. כי קללת אלהים תלוי (Deut 21.23): A Study in Early Jewish Exegesis. JQR 74 (1983): 21–45

BERRIN, SHANI L. The Pesher Nahum Scroll from Qumran: An Exegetical Study of 4Q169. Leiden: Brill, 2004

BERTMAN, STEPHEN. Handbook to Life in Ancient Mesopotamia. New York: Oxford University Press, 2003

BERVE, HELMUT. Die Tyrannis bei den Griechen. 2 vols. München: Beck, 1967

BETZ, HANS DIETER, PETER A. DIRKSE, and EDGAR W. SMITH. De sera numinis vindicta (Moralia 548A – 568A). Pages 181–236 in Plutarch's Theological Writings and Early Christian Literature. Edited by H. D. Betz. Leiden: Brill, 1975

BETZ, OTTO. The Death of Choni-Onias in the Light of the Temple Scroll from Qumran. Pages 84–97 in Jerusalem in the Second Temple Period. FS A. Schalit. Edited by A. Oppenheimer, U. Rappaport, and M. Stern. Library of the history of the Yishuv in Eretz-Yisrael. Jerusalem: Yad Izhak Ben-Zvi, 1980

–. Probleme des Prozesses Jesu. ANRW II/25.1 (1982): 565–647

–. Der Tod des Choni-Onias im Licht der Tempelrolle von Qumran: Bemerkungen zu Josephus Antiquitates 14,22–24 [1980]. Pages 59–74 in Jesus der Messias Israels: Aufsätze zur biblischen Theologie. WUNT 42. Tübingen: Mohr Siebeck, 1987

BEYER, KLAUS. Die aramäischen Texte vom Toten Meer. 3 vols. Göttingen: Vandenhoeck & Ruprecht, 1984–2004.

BICKERMAN, ELIAS J. The Warning Inscription of Herod's Temple [1947]. Pages 1:483–96 in Studies in Jewish and Christian History. A New Edition in English. 2 vols. AGAJU 68. Leiden: Brill, 2007

–. Utilitas crucis. Observations sur les récits du procès de Jésus dans les Évangiles canoniques [1935]. Pages 1:82–138 in Studies in Jewish and Christian History. AGJU 9. Leiden: Brill, 1976

BIETENHARD, HANS. Der tannaitische Midrasch Sifre Deuteronomium. Übersetzt und erklärt. Mit einem Beitrag von Henrik Ljungman. Judaica et christiana 8. New York: Lang, 1984

BIGWOOD, JOAN M. Ctesias' Account of the Revolt of Inarus. Phoenix 30 (1976): 1–24

BILDE, PER. Flavius Josephus between Jerusalem and Rome: His Life, his Works and their Importance. JSPSup 2. Sheffield: JSOT, 1988

–. Der Konflikt zwischen Gaius Caligula und den Juden über die Aufstellung einer Kaiserstatue im Tempel von Jerusalem. Pages 9–48 in Kult und Macht. Religion und Herrschaft im syro-palästinensischen Raum. Studien zu ihrer Wechselbeziehung in hellenistisch-römischer Zeit. Edited by A. Lykke and F. T. Schipper. WUNT 2/319. Tübingen: Mohr Siebeck, 2011

BIRDSALL, J. NEVILLE. The Continuing Enigma of Josephus's Testimony about Jesus. BJRL 67 (1985): 609–622

BIRKS, PETER / GRANT MCLEOD. Justinian's Institutes. With the Latin Text of Paul Krueger. Orig. 1987. Repr. Ithaca: Cornell University Press, 1996

BIRLEY, ANTHONY R. Cassius [III 1] L. Cl(audius) C. Dio Cocceianus. BNP 2 (2003): 1171–1172

BIVILLE, FRÉDÉRIQUE. Graeco-Romans and Graeco-Latin: A Terminological Framework for Cases of Bilingualism. Pages 77–102 in Bilingualism in Ancient Society: Language Contact and the Written Text. Edited by J. N. Adams, M. Janse, and S. Swain. Oxford: Oxford University Press, 2002

BLACK, JEREMY, ANDREW GEORGE, and NICHOLAS POSTGATE. A Concise Dictionary of Akkadian. Second Corrected Printing. Wiesbaden: Harrassowitz, 2000

BLAKE, WARREN E. Charitonis Aphrodisiensis de Chaerea et Callirhoe Amatoriarum Narrationum Libri Octo. Oxford: Clarendon, 1938

BLASCHKE, ANDREAS. Beschneidung. Zeugnisse der Bibel und verwandter Texte. TANZ 28. Tübingen: Francke, 1998

BLEICKEN, JOCHEN. Augustus. Eine Biographie. Orig. 1998. Repr. Reinbek / Hamburg: Rohwolt, 2010

BLINZLER, JOSEF. Der Prozeß Jesu. Vierte, erneut revidierte Auflage. Orig. 1951. Repr. Regensburg: Pustet, 1969

–. Das Synedrium von Jerusalem und die Strafprozeßordnung der Mischna. ZNW 52 (1961): 54–65

–. The Trial of Jesus. Cork: Mercier, 1959

BOCK, DARRELL L. Blasphemy and Exaltation in Judaism: The Charge against Jesus in Mark 14:53–56. Orig. 1998. Repr. Grand Rapids: Baker, 2000

–. Blasphemy and the Jewish Examination of Jesus. Pages 589–667 in Key Events in the Life of the Historical Jesus: A Collaborative Exploration of Context and Coherence. Edited by D. L. Bock and R. L. Webb. WUNT 247. Tübingen: Mohr Siebeck, 2009

–. Crucifixion, Qumran, and the Jewish Interrogation of Jesus. Pages 3–10 in Literary Studies in Luke-Acts. FS Joseph B. Tyson. Edited by R. P. Thompson and T. E. Phillips. Macon: Mercer University Press, 1998

BODEL, JOHN. Graveyards and Groves: A Study of the *Lex Lucerina*. AJAH 11 (1986): 1–133

BOFFO, LAURA. Iscrizioni greche e latine per lo studio della Bibbia. Biblioteca di storia e storiografia dei tempi biblici 9. Brescia: Paideia, 1994

BOHEC, YANN LE. Ensigns. BNP 4 (2004): 992–996

BÖHM, MARTINA. Samarien und die Samaritai bei Lukas. WUNT 2/111. Tübingen: Mohr Siebeck, 1999

BOISSEVAIN, URSULUS PHILIPPUS. Cassii Dionis Cocceiani Historiarum Romanarum quae supersunt. 5 vols. Berlin: Weidmann, 1895–1931

BOLEN, TODD, and A. D. RIDDLE. Pictorial Library of Bible Lands: The Museum Collection. DVD, 2012

BOND, HELEN K. Caiaphas: Friend of Rome and Judge of Jesus. Louisville: Westminster John Knox Press, 2004

–. The Coins of Pontius Pilate: Part of an Attempt to Provoke the People or to Integrate Them into the Empire? JSJ 27 (1996): 241–262

–. Pontius Pilate in History and Interpretation. Orig. 1998. Repr. SNTSMS 100. Cambridge: Cambridge University Press, 2004

BOOCHS, WOLFGANG. Über den Strafzweck des Pfählens. Göttinger Miszellen 69 (1983): 7–10

BORGEN, PEDER, KÅRE FUGLSETH, and ROALD SKARSTEN. Philo Judaeus. The Works of Philo: Greek Text with Morphology. Bellingham, WA: Logos Reserach Systems, 2005

BORING, M. EUGENE, KLAUS BERGER, and CARSTEN COLPE. Hellenistic Commentary to the New Testament. Nashville: Abingdon, 1995

BÖRNER-KLEIN, DAGMAR.Der Midrasch Sifre zu Numeri. Übersetzung und Erklärung. Rabbinische Texte II/3. Stuttgart: Kohlhammer, 1997

BORRET, MARCEL. Origène, Contre Celse. 5 vols. Sources chrétiennes 132, 136, 147, 150, 227. Paris: Cerf, 1967–1969

BOYANCÉ, PIERRE. Cicéron. Discours. Tome VIII: Pour Cluentius. Collection des universités de France. Paris: Belles Lettres, 1953

BRACKERTZ, KARL. Artemidorus von Daldis. Das Traumbuch. München: Artemis, 1979

BRATKE, EDWARD, ed. Scriptores ecclesiastici minores saeculorum IV. V. VI., Fasciculus I: Evagrii Altercatio legis inter Simonem Iudaeum et Theophilum Christianum. CSEL 45. Wien / Leipzig: Tempsky / Freytag, 1904

BRAUDE, WILLIAM G. The Midrash on Psalms. Yale Judaica 13. New Haven: Yale University Press, 1959

BRECHT, CHRISTOPH H. Patibulum. RE XVIII/4 (1949): 2167–2169

–. Perduellio. Eine Studie zu ihrer begrifflichen Abgrenzung im römischen Strafrecht bis zum Ausgang der Republik. Münchener Beiträge zur Papyrusforschung und antiken Rechtsgeschichte 29. München: Beck, 1938

BRISCOE, JOHN. A Commentary on Livy, Books 38–40. Oxford: Oxford University Press, 2008

–. Titi Livi Ab urbe condita. Libri XXXI–XL. 2 vols. Bibliotheca Scriptorum Graecorum et Romanorum Teubneriana. Stuttgart: Teubner, 1991

–. Valeri Maximi Facta et Dicta Memorabilia. 2 vols. Stuttgart / Leipzig: Teubner, 1998

BROWN, RAYMOND E. The Babylonian Talmud on the Death of Jesus. NTS 43 (1997): 158–59

–. The Death of the Messiah: From Gethsemane to the Grave. A Commentary on the Passion Narratives in the Four Gospels. 2 vols. Anchor Bible Reference Library. London: Chapman, 1994

–. The Gospel According to John. 2 vols. Anchor Bible. New York: Doubleday, 1966–1970

BROWN, RAYMOND E., and JOHN P. MEIER. Antioch and Rome: New Testament Cradles of Catholic Christianity. New York: Paulist, 1983

BROWNSON, CARLETON L. Xenophon. Anabasis. LCL. Cambridge: Harvard University Press, 1998

BRUNET DE PRESLE, WLADIMIR. Notices et extraits des manuscrits de la Bibliothèque Impériale XVIII, Seconde Partie. Paris: Imprimerie Impériale, 1865

BRUNS, CARL GEORG, ed. Fontes Iuris Romani Antiqui. Post curas Theodori Mommseni editionibus quintae et sextae adhibitas septimum edidit Otto Gradenwitz. 2 vols. Tübingen: Mohr Siebeck, 1909

BRUNT, PETER A. Arrian. 2 vols. LCL. Cambridge: Harvard University Press, 1976

BUDÉ, GUY DE. Dionis Chrysostomi orationes post Ludovicum Dindorfium. 2 vols. Bibliotheca Scriptorum Graecorum et Romanorum Teubneriana. Leipzig: Teubner, 1916–1919

BUDGE, E. A. WALLIS. The Rosetta Stone in the British Museum. The Greek, Demotic and Hieroglyphic Texts. London: Religious Tract Society, 1929

BUDGE, E. A. WALLIS, and LEONARD W. KING, eds. Annals of the Kings of Assyria: The Cuneiform Texts with Translations, Transliterations, etc., from the Original Documents in the British Museum. London: British Museum, 1902

BULTMANN, RUDOLF. Das Evangelium des Johannes. 21. Auflage. Orig. 1941. Repr. KEK II. Göttingen: Vandenhoeck & Ruprecht, 1986

BURKE, DAVID G., and HENRY E. DOSKER. Cross, Crucify. Pages 1:825–30 in The International Standard Bible Encyclopedia. Edited by G. W. Bromiley. Grand Rapids: Eerdmans, 1979–1988

BURKILL, T. ALEC. The Trial of Jesus. VC 12 (1958): 1–18

BURKITT, FRANCIS C. Josephus and Christ. Theologische Tijdschrift 47 (1913): 135–144

BURNET, JOHN. Platonis opera. 5 Vols. Orig. 1900–1907. Repr. Scriptorum Classicorum Bibliotheca Oxoniensis. Oxford: Clarendon, 1959–1962

BURR, WOLFGANG. Epigraphischer Beitrag zur neueren Pontius-Pilatus-Forschung. Pages 37–41 in Vergangenheit, Gegenwart, Zukunft. Edited by W. Burr. Unitas Schriftenreihe 1. Würzburg: Verlag des Wissenschaftlichen Katholischen Studentenvereins Unitas, 1972

BURRELL, BARBARA. Palace to Praetorium: The Romanization of Caesarea. Pages 228–247 in Caesarea Maritima: A Retrospective after Two Millenia. Edited by A. Raban and K. G. Holum. Documenta et monumenta Orientis antiqui 21. Leiden: Brill, 1996

BUTCHER, KEVIN. Roman Syria and the Near East. Los Angeles: Paul Getty Museum, 2003

BUTCHER, SAMUEL H., and WILLIAMS RENNIE. Demosthenis Orationes. 3 vols. Scriptorum classicorum bibliotheca Oxoniensis. Oxford: Clarendon, 1903–1931

BUTLER, SHANE. Hand of Cicero. London: Routledge, 2002

BÜTTNER-WOBST, THEODOR. Polybius. Historiae. 5 vols. Stuttgart: Teubner, 1893–1904

CAMPBELL, J. BRIAN. The Emperor and the Roman Army, 31 BC – AD 235. New York: Clarendon/Oxford University Press, 1984

CARRIÉ, JEAN-MICHEL. "Archives municipales et distributions alimentaires dans l'Égypte romaine." Pages 271–302 in La mémoire perdue. Recherches sur l'administration Romaine. Edited by C. Moatti. Collection de l'École Française de Rome 243. Rome: École française de Rome, Palais Farnèse, 1998

CARTER, WARREN. Pontius Pilate: Portraits of a Roman Governor. Interfaces. Collegeville, MN: Liturgical Press, 2003

CARY, EARNEST. Dionysius of Halicarnassus. Roman Antiquities. 8 vols. LCL. Cambridge: Harvard University Press, 1937–1950

CATCHPOLE, DAVID R. The Trial of Jesus: A Study in the Gospels and Jewish Historiography from 1770 to the Present Day. Studia Post-Biblica 18. Leiden: Brill, 1971

–. You Have Heard His Blasphemy." TynB 16 (1965): 10–18

CHADWICK, HENRY. Origen: Contra Celsum. Orig; 1953. Repr. Cambridge: Cambridge University Press, 1980

CHAPMAN, DAVID W. Ancient Jewish and Christian Perceptions of Crucifixion. WUNT 2.244. Tübingen: Mohr Siebeck, 2008. Paperback Edition. Grand Rapids: Baker, 2010

–. Crucifixion, Bodily Suspension, and Jewish Interpretations of the Hebrew Bible in Antiquity. Pages 37–48 in Beyond the Jordan. FS W. Harold Mare. Edited by G. A. Carnagey, G. A. Carnagey, and K. N. Schoville. Eugene, Oreg.: Wipf & Stock, 2005

–. Crucifixion II. Judaism. EBR 5 (2012): 1087–1088

–. Hanging and Impalement. Hebrew Bible/Old Testament. EBR 11 (2015): 212–215

CHARLES, ROBERT H. The Assumption of Moses. London: Black, 1897

CHARLESWORTH, JAMES H., ed. Rule of the Community and Related Documents. The Dead Sea Scrolls 1. Tübingen: Mohr Siebeck, 1994

CHARLESWORTH, JAMES H., and JACOB MILGROM. Temple Scroll Defining Edition 11Q19 (11QTempleª): Translation. Pages 1–173 in Temple Scroll, and Related Documents. Edited by J. H. Charlesworth. The Dead Sea Scrolls 7. Tübingen: Mohr Siebeck, 2011

CHAUMARTIN, FRANÇOIS-RÉGIS. Les désillusions de Sénèque devant l'évolution de la politique néronienne et l'aspiration à la retraite: le 'De vita beata' et le 'De beneficiis'. ANRW II.36.3 (1989): 1686–1723

CHAVEL, CHARLES B. "The Releasing of a Prisoner on the Eve of Passover in Ancient Jerusalem." JBL 60 (1941): 273–278

CHILTON, BRUCE, and DARRELL L. BOCK. A Comparative Handbook to the Gospel of Mark: Comparisons with Pseudepigrapha, the Qumran Schrolls, and Rabbinic Literature. The New Testament Gospels in their Judaic Contexts 1. Leiden: Brill, 2010

CHRISTENSEN, DUANE L. DEUTERONOMY. WBC 6b. Nashville: Nelson, 1991–2002

CLARK, ALBERT CURTIS, and WILLIAM PETERSON, eds. M. Tulli Ciceronis Orationes. Second Edition. 6 vols. Scriptorum Classicorum Bibliotheca Oxoniensis. Oxford: Clarendon, 1905–1918

CLARYSSE, WILLY. "Bilingual Papyrological Archives." Pages 47–72 in The Multilingual Experience in Egypt, from the Ptolemies to the Abbasids. Edited by A. Papaconstantinou. Farnham: Ashgate, 2010

CLASSEN, CARL JOACHIM. Recht–Rhetorik–Politik. Untersuchungen zu Ciceros rhetorischer Strategie. Darmstadt: Wissenschaftliche Buchgesellschaft, 1985

CLEMENS, DAVID M. Sources for Ugaritic Ritual and Sacrifice. Alter Orient und Altes Testament 284/1. Münster: Ugarit-Verlag, 2001

CLEMENTZ, HEINRICH. Des Flavius Josephus Jüdische Altertümer. Orig. 1899–1923. Repr. Wiesbaden: Fourier, 1994

–. Flavius Josephus, Geschichte des jüdischen Krieges. Orig. 1900. Repr. Wiesbaden: Fourier, 1984

CLERMONT-GANNEAU, CHARLES. Discovery of a Tablet from Herod's Temple. PEFQS 3 (1871): 132–33.

–. Une stèle due temple de Jérusalem. RAr 23 (1872): 214–234, 290–296

CLINES, DAVID J. A. The Esther Scroll: The Story of the Story. JSOTSup 30. Sheffield: JSOT Press, 1984

COHEN, SHAYE J. D. The Beginnings of Jewishness: Boundaries, Varieties, Uncertainties. Hellenistic Culture and Society 31. Berkeley: University of California Press, 1999

–. Josephus in Galilee and Rome: His Vita and Development as a Historian. Orig. 1979. Repr. Columbia Studies in the Classical Tradition 8. Leiden: Brill, 2002

–. Pagan and Christian Evidence on the Ancient Synagogue [1987]. Pages 244–65 in The Significance of Yavneh and Other Essays in Jewish Hellenism. TSAJ 136. Tübingen: Mohr Siebeck, 2010

COHN, LEOPOLD, ISAAK HEINEMANN, MAXIMILIAN ADLER, and WILLY THEILER. Philo von Alexandrien. Die Werke in deutscher Übersetzung. 7 vols. Berlin: De Gruyter, 1962–1964

COHN, LEOPOLD, PAUL WENDLAND, and SIEGFRIED REITER. Philonis Alexandrini opera quae supersunt. Editio Maior. 7 vols. Orig. 1896–1930. Repr. Berlin: De Gruyter, 1962

COLES, REVEL A. Reports of Proceedings in Papyri. Papyrologica Bruxellensia 4. Bruxelles: Fondation égyptologique Reine Élisabeth, 1966

COLLINS, ADELA YARBRO. The Charge of Blasphemy in Mark 14:6 [2004]. Pages 149–70 in The Trial and Death of Jesus: Essays on the Passion Narrative in Mark. Edited by G. Van Oyen and T. Shepherd. CBET 45. Leuven: Peters, 2006

COLLINS, JOHN J. The Date and Provenance of the Testament of Moses. Pages 15–32 in Studies on the Testament of Moses. Edited by G. W. E. Nickelsburg. SBLSBS 4. Cambridge: Society of Biblical Literature, 1973

COLLINS, MARILYN F. The Hidden Vessels in Samaritan Tradition. JSJ 3 (1972): 97–116

COLSON, FRANCIS H., GEORGE H. WHITAKER, and RALPH MARCUS. Philo. Works. Greek Text and English Translation. LCL. London: Heinemann, 1929–1962

CONRAD, JOACHIM. נכה. TDOT 9 (1998): 415–423

COOK, JOHN GRANGER. Crucifixion and Burial. NTS 57 (2011): 193–213

–. Crucifixion as Spectacle in Roman Campania. NovT 54 (2012): 68–100

–. Crucifixion I. Greco-Roman Antiquity. EBR 5 (2012): 1085–1086

–. Crucifixion in the Ancient Mediterranean World. Bibleinterp.com. June 2014. Accessed October 12, 2014. http://www.bibleinterp.com/PDFs/CrucifixionAncientMed.pdf
–. Crucifixion in the Mediterranean World. WUNT 327. Tübingen: Mohr Siebeck, 2014 [abbr. Crucifixion]
–. Envisioning Crucifixion: Light from Several Inscriptions and the Palatine Graffito. NovT 50 (2008): 262–285
–. John 19:17 and the Man on the *Patibulum* in the Arieti Tomb. Early Christianity 4 (2013): 427–453
–. Review of Crucifixion in Antiquity, by Gunnar Samuelsson. RBL (2014). http://www.book reviews.org/pdf/9718_10735.pdf
–. Roman Attitudes Toward the Christians: From Claudius to Hadrian. WUNT 261. Tübingen: Mohr Siebeck, 2010
–. Roman Crucifixions: From the Second Punic War to Constantine. ZNW 104 (2013): 1–32
COTTON, HANNAH M. The Impact of the Roman Army in the Province of Judaea/Syria Palaestina. Pages 393–408 in The Impact of the Roman Army (200 BC–AD 476): Economic, Social, Political, Religious and Cultural Aspects. Edited by L. de Bois and E. Lo Cascio. Impact of Empire 6. Leiden/Boston: Brill, 2007
–. Some Aspects of the Roman Administration of Judaea/Syria–Palaestina. Pages 75–91 in Lokale Autonomie und römische Ordnungsmacht in den kaiserzeitlichen Provinzen vom 1. bis 3. Jahrhundert. Edited by W. Eck and E. Müller-Luckner. Schriften des Historischen Kollegs 42. München: Oldenbourg, 1999
COTTON, HANNAH M., and WERNER ECK. Roman Officials in Judea and Arabia and Civil Jurisdiction. Pages 23–44 in Law in the Documents of the Judaean Desert. Edited by R. Katzoff and D. Schaps. JSJSup 96. Leiden/Boston: Brill, 2005
COTTON, HANNAH M., LEAH DI SEGNI, WERNER ECK, BENJAMIN ISAAC, ALLA KUSHNIR-STEIN, HAGGAI MISGAV, JONATHAN PRICE, ISRAEL ROLL, and ADA YARDENI, eds. Corpus Inscriptionum Iudaeae / Palestinae. Vols. I–II. Berlin: De Gruyter, 2010–2012
COUSIN, JEAN. Cicéron. Discours. Tome XV: Pour Caelius, Sur les provinces consulaires, Pour Balbus. Collection des universités de France 166. Paris: Belles Lettres, 1962
COWLEY, ARTHUR E. Aramaic Papyri of the Fifth Century B.C. Oxford: Clarendon1923. Repr. Osnabrück: Zeller, 1967
CRANFIELD, C. E. B. The Gospel according to Saint Mark. Cambridge Greek Testament Commentary. Cambridge: Cambridge University Press, 1963
CRAWFORD, MICHAEL H., ed. Roman Statutes. 2 vols. Bulletin of the Institute of Classical Studies Supplement 64. London: Institute of Classical Studies, University of London, 1996
CRAWLEY, RICHARD. Thucydides. The Peloponnesian War. New ed. Edited by W. Robert Connor. London: Dent, 1993
DĄBROWA, EDWARD. The Governors of Roman Syria from Augustus to Septimius Severus. Antiquitas Reihe 1, Abhandlungen zur alten Geschichte 45. Bonn: Habelt, 1998
DALMAN, GUSTAV H. Aramäisch–Neuhebräisches Handwörterbuch zu Targum, Talmud und Midrasch. Orig. 1938. Repr. Hildesheim: Olms, 1967
DANBY, HERBERT. The Bearing of the Rabbinical Criminal Code on the Jewish Trial Narratives in the Gospels [1920]. Pages 51–76 in The Historical Jesus: Critical Concepts in Religious Studies. Edited by C. A. Evans. London: Routledge, 2004
–. The Mishnah. Translated from the Hebrew with Introduction and Brief Explanatory Notes. Oxford: University Press, 1933
DAVID, JEAN-MICHEL. Du *comitium* à la roche Tarpéienne. Sur certains rituels d'exécution capitale sous la République, les règnes d'Auguste et de Tibère. Pages 131–176 in Du châtiment dans la cité: Supplices corporels et peine de mort dans le monde antique. Table ronde organisée par l'École française de Rome avec le concours du Centre national de la recherche scientifique (Rome 9.–11. novembre 1982). Edited by Y. Thomas. Collection de l'École française de Rome 79. Rome / Paris: École française de Rome / Boccard, 1984

DAVIES, WILLIAM D. / DALE C. ALLISON. *The Gospel According to Saint Matthew*. ICC. Edinburgh: T & T Clark, 1988–1997

DAY, JOHN. Molech: A God of Human Sacrifice in the Old Testament. Cambridge: Cambridge University Press, 1989

DAY, LINDA. Three Faces of a Queen: Characterization in the Books of Esther. JSOTSup 186. Sheffield: Sheffield Academic Press, 1995

DE LA VILLE DE MIRMONT, HENRI. Cicéron. Discours. Tome II: Pour M. Tullius, Discours contre Q. Caecilius, dit 'la divination', Première action contre C. Verrès, Seconde action contre C. Verrès. Livre premier, La préture urbaine. Collection des universités de France. Paris: Belles Lettres, 1922

DECKER, WOLFGANG. Pythia. BNP 12 (2008): 291–94

DEGRASSI, ATTILIO. Sull'iscrizione di Ponzio Pilato. Pages 59–65 in Rendiconti dell'Accademia Nazionale dei Lincei Ser. 8, Classe di Scienze morali, storiche ee filologiche 19. Rome: Accademia dei Lincei, 1964

DEISSMANN, ADOLF. Licht vom Osten. Das Neue Testament und die neuentdeckten Texte der hellenistisch-römischen Welt. 4., völlig neu bearbeitete Auflage. Tübingen: Mohr Siebeck, 1923

DELARUE, CHARLES. Origenis opera omnia. 4 vols. Paris: Vincent, 1733–1759

DELITZSCH, FRANZ. A New Commentary on Genesis. Translated by Sophia Taylor. 2 vols. Edinburgh: T.& T. Clark, 1888–1889

DELZ, JOSEPH, ed. Sili Italici Punica. Stuttgart: Teubner, 1987

DEMANDT, ALEXANDER. 'Hände in Unschuld'. Pontius Pilatus in der Geschichte. Köln: Böhlau, 1999

DERENBOURG, JOSEPH. Essai sur l'histoire et la géographie de la Palestine. Paris: Imprimerie impériale, 1867

DEXINGER, FERDINAND. Josephus Ant 18, 85–87 und der samaritanische Taheb. Pages 49–60 in Proceeding of the First International Congress of the Société d'Études Samaritaines. Edited by A. Tal and M. Florentin. Tel Aviv: Chaim Rosenberg School for Jewish Studies, University of Tel Aviv, 1991

DI STEFANO MANZELLA, IVAN. Pontius Pilatus nell'iscrizione di Cesarea di Palestina. Pages 209–215 in Le iscrizioni dei cristiani in Vaticano. Materiali e contributi scientifici per una mostra epigrafica. Inscriptiones Sanctae Sedis 2. Città del Vaticano Roma: Monumenti, Musei e gallerie pontificie Distribuzione esclusiva, Edizioni Quasar, 1997

DÍEZ MACHO, ALEJANDO. Neophyti 1: Targum Palestinense MS de la Biblioteca Vaticana. 5 vols. Madrid: Consejo Superior de Investigaciones Científicas, 1968–1979

–. Neophyti I. Targum Palestinense MS de la Biblioteca Vaticana. 6 vols. Textos y Estudios Cardinal Cisneros 7–11.20. Madrid / Barcelona: Consejo Superior de Investigaciones Cientificas, 1968–1979

DÍEZ MACHO, ALEJANDO, LUIS DÍEZ MERINO, EMILIANO MARTÍNEZ BOROBIO, and TERESA MARTÍNEZ SÁIZ. Biblia Polyglotta Matritensia IV: Targum Palestinense in Pentateuchum. 5 vols. Madrid: Consejo Superior de Investigaciones Científicas, 1977–1988

DÍEZ MERINO, LUIS. La crocifissione nella letteratura ebrea antica (Periodo intertestamentale). Pages 1:61–68 in La Sapienza Della Croce Oggi, Atti del Congresso internazionale Roma, 13–18 ottobre 1975. La Sapienza Della Croce Nella Rivelazione e Nell'Ecumenismo. Turin: Leumann, 1976

–. La crucifixión en la antigua literatura judía (Periodo intertestamental). EstEcl 51 (1976): 5–27

–. El suplicio de la cruz en la literatura Judia intertestamental. LASBF 26 (1976): 31–120

DIGGLE, JAMES. Euripidis fabulae. 3 vols. Scriptorum classicorum bibliotheca Oxoniensis. Oxford: Clarendon, 1981–1994

DIGNAS, BEATE. Economy of the Sacred in Hellenistic and Roman Asia Minor. Oxford Classical Monographs. Oxford New York: Oxford University Press, 2002

DILLMANN, AUGUST. Genesis: Critically and Exegetically Expounded. Translated by Wm. B. Stevenson. 2 vols. Edinburgh: T.& T. Clark, 1897

DINGEL, JOACHIM. Seneca [2] L. Annaeus S. DNP 13 (2008): 271–278

DINKLER, ERICH. Kreuzzeichen und Kreuz – Tau, Chi und Stauros. JAC 5 (1962): 26–54.

–. Zur Geschichte des Kreuzsymbols. ZTK 48 (1951): 148–72.

DOBSCHÜTZ, ERNST VON. Jews and Anti-Semites in Ancient Alexandria. AJT 8 (1904): 728–755

DODDS, ERIC R. Plato. Gorgias. A Revised Text with Introduction and Commentary. Oxford: Clarendon, 1959

DOERR, FRIEDRICH. Der Prozeß Jesu in rechtsgeschichtlicher Beleuchtung. Ein Beitrag zur Kenntnis des jüdisch-römischen Provinzialstrafrechts. Orig. 1908. Repr. Berlin: Kohlhammer, 1920

DOGNIEZ, GILLES, and MARGUERITE HARL. La Bible d'Alexandrie. Vol. 5: Le Deutéronome. Traduction du texte grec de la Septante, introduction et notes. Paris: Cerf, 1992

DOREY, THOMAS ALAN. Titi Livi Ab urbe condita libri XXI–XXII. Bibliotheca Scriptorum Graecorum et Romanorum Teubneriana. Stuttgart: Teubner, 1971

DORNSEIFF, FRANZ. Zum Testimonium Flavium. ZNW 46 (1955): 245–250

DOSSIN, GEORGES, ed. Archives royales de Mari. Vol. 13, Textes divers. Paris: Geuthner, 1964

DOUDNA, GREGORY L. 4Q Pesher Nahum: A Critical Edition. JSPSup 35. London: Sheffield Academic Press, 2001

DOWLING, MELISSA BARDEN. Clemency and Cruelty in the Roman World. Ann Arbor, MI: University of Michigan Press, 2006

DOYLE, A. D. Pilate's Career and the Date of the Crucifixion. JTS 42 (1941): 190–193

DRIVER, GODFREY. R. Review of Ancient Israel's Criminal Law: A New Approach to the Decalogue, by Anthony Phillips. JTS 23 (1972): 160–164

DRIVER, GODFREY R., and JOHN C. MILES. The Assyrian Laws. Ancient Codes and Laws of the Near East. Oxford: Clarendon Press, 1935

DRIVER, GODFREY R., and JOHN C. MILES. The Babylonian Laws. 2 vols. Ancient Codes and Laws of the Near East. Oxford: Clarendon, 1952–1955

DUBOULOZ, JULIEN, and SYLVIE PITTIA, eds. La Sicilie de Cicéron. Lectures des Verrines. Presses universitaires de Franche-Comté: Besançon, 2007

DUFF, JAMES D. Silius Italicus. Punica. 2 vols. LCL. Cambridge: Harvard University Press, 1927–1934

DUNN, JAMES D. G. Beginning from Jerusalem. Christianity in the Making II. Grand Rapids: Eerdmans, 2009

–. Jesus Remembered. Christianity in the Making I. Grand Rapids: Eerdmans, 2003

EBELING, HANS JÜRGEN. Zur Frage nach der Kompetenz des Synhedrion. ZNW 35 (1936): 290–295

ECK, WERNER. Administrative Dokumente: Publikation und Mittel der Selbstdarstellung [1998]. Pages 3–24 in Judäa – Syria Palästina. Die Auseinandersetzung einer Provinz mit römischer Politik und Kultur. TSAJ 157. Tübingen: Mohr Siebeck, 2014

–. Aelius [II 16] Ae. Lamia, L. BNP 1 (2002): 205

–. Appuleia. BNP 1 (2002): 903

–. Apronius [II 1] L. BNP 1 (2002): 911

–. Beförderungskriterien innerhalb der senatorischen Laufbahn, dargestellt an der Zeit von 69 bis 138 n. Chr. ANRW II.1 (1974): 158–228

–. Die Benennung von römischen Amtsträgern und politisch-militärisch-administrativen Funktionen bei Flavius Iosephus: Probleme der korrekten Identifizierung. ZPE 166 (2008): 218–226

–. Caecina [II 8] C. Severus, A. BNP 2 (2003): 888–889

–. Caligula. BNP 2 (2003): 955–957

–. Domitianus. BNP 4 (2004): 635–639

–. Fannius [II 1] F. Caepio. BNP 5 (2004): 351

–. Kaiserliches Handeln in italienischen Städten. Pages 329–51 in L'Italie d'Auguste à Dioclétien. Actes du colloque international organisé par l'École française de Rome (25–28 Mars 1992). Rome: École Française de Rome, 1994

–. The Language of Power: Latin in the Inscriptions of Iudaea / Syria Palaestina. Pages 123–144 in Semitic Papyrology in Context: A Climate of Creativity. Edited by L. A. Schiffman. Culture and History of the Ancient Near East 14. Brill: Leiden, 2003

–. Latein als Sprache politischer Kommunikation in den Städten der östlichen Provinzen. Chiron 30 (2000): 641–60

–. Die Leitung und Verwaltung einer prokuratorischen Provinz [1988]. Pages 327–40 in Die Verwaltung des römischen Reiches in der Hohen Kaiserzeit. Ausgewählte und erweiterte Beiträge. Band 1. Arbeiten zur römischen Epigraphik und Altertumskunde 1. Basel / Berlin: Reinhardt, 1995

–. Lucceius [II 1] L. Albinus. BNP 7 (2005): 835

–. Marcellus [II 2] M. BNP 8 (2006): 299

–. Pomponius [II 10] L. P. Flaccus. BNP 11 (2007): 579–580

–. Pontius [II 4] M. P. Laelianus Larcius Sabinus. BNP 11 (2007): 597

–. Pontius [II 6] C. P. Paelignus. BNP 11 (2007): 597

–. Pontius [II 7] P. Pilatus. BNP 11 (2007): 597–598

–. Pontuis [II 3] M. P. Laelianus. BNP 11 (2007): 597

–. Porcius [II 2] P. Festus. BNP 11 (2007): 636

–. Praefectus. BNP 11 (2007): 751–756

–. Presence, Role, and Significance of Latin in the Epigraphy and Culture of the Roman Near East. Pages 15–42 in From Hellenism to Islam: Cultural and Linguistic Change in the Roman Near East. Edited by H. M. Cotton, R. G. Hoyland, J. J. Price, and D. J. Wasserstein. Cambridge: Cambridge University Press, 2009

–. Procurator. BNP 11 (2007): 928–930

–. Ein Prokuratorenpaar von Syria Palaestina in P. Berol. 21652 [1998]. Pages 266–274 in Judäa – Syria Palästina. Die Auseinandersetzung einer Provinz mit römischer Politik und Kultur. TSAJ 157. Tübingen: Mohr Siebeck, 2014

–. Prosopographica II. 1. Zur Laufbahn des C. Pontius Paelignus. 2. Lucilius Capito oder Cn. Vergilius Capito auf Cos? ZPE 106 (1995): 249–254

–. Die religiösen und kultischen Aufgaben der römischen Statthalter in der Hohen Kaiserzeit [1992]. Pages 203–217 in Die Verwaltung des römischen Reiches in der Hohen Kaiserzeit. Ausgewählte und erweiterte Beiträge. Band 2. Arbeiten zur römischen Epigraphik und Altertumskunde 3. Basel / Berlin: Reinhardt, 1997

–. Rom und Judaea. Fünf Vorträge zur römischen Herrschaft in Palaestina. Tübingen: Mohr Siebeck, 2007

–. Die römischen Repräsentanten in Judaea: Provokateure oder Vertreter der römischen Macht? [2011], in Pages 166–185 in Judäa – Syria Palästina. Die Auseinandersetzung einer Provinz mit römischer Politik und Kultur. TSAJ 157. Tübingen: Mohr Siebeck, 2014

–. Silius [II 3] C., S. A. Caecina Largus. BNP 13 (2013): 459–460

–. Ein Spiegel der Macht: Lateinische Inschriften römischer Zeit in Iudaea/Syria Palaestina. ZDPV 117 (2000): 47–63

–. Sulpicius [II 13] P. S. Quirinius. BNP 13 (2008): 939–940

–. Vitellius [II 3] L. V. BNP 15 (2010): 476–477

ECKSTEIN, ARTHUR M. Senate and General: Individual Decision-Making and Roman Foreign Relations 264–194 B.C. Berkeley: University of California Press, 1987

EDEN, PETER T. Seneca. Apocolocyntosis. Orig. 1984. Repr. Cambridge Greek and Latin Classics. Cambridge: Cambridge University Press, 2002

EDER, WALTER, and JOHANNES RENGER. Chronologies of the Ancient World: Names, Dates and Dynasties. Brill's New Pauly Supplements. Brill: Leiden, 2007

EDWARDS, CATHERINE. Suetonius. Lives of the Caesars. A New Translation. Orig. 2000. Repr. Oxford World's Classics. Oxford: Oxford University Press, 2008

EDWARDS, WILLIAM D., FLOYD E. HOSMER, and WESLEY J. GABEL. On the Physical Death of Jesus Christ. Journal of the American Medical Association 255 (1986): 1455–1463

EFRON, JOSHUA. Studies on the Hasmonean Period. SJLA 39. Leiden: Brill, 1987

EGGER, PETER. "Crucifixus sub Pontio Pilato". Das "crimen" Jesu von Nazareth im Spannungsfeld römischer und jüdischer Verwaltungs- und Rechtsstrukturen. NTA 32. Münster: Aschendorff, 1997

EGGER, RITA. Josephus Flavius und die Samaritaner: Eine terminologische Untersuchung zur Identitätsklärung der Samaritaner. NTOA 4. Fribourg / Göttingen: Editions Universitaires / Vandenhoeck & Ruprecht, 1986

EHLING, KAY. Zu Th. Mommsens Auswertung der Münzzeugnisse im Judäa-Kapitel des 5. Bandes seiner Römischen Geschiche. Jahrbuch für Numismatik und Geldgeschichte 53–54 (2003–2004): 1–14

EHRENBERG, VICTOR, and ARNOLD H. M. JONES. Documents Illustrating the Reigns of Augustus and Tiberius. Second Edition. Orig. 1955. Repr. Oxford: Clarendon, 1976

EICH, ARMIN, ed. Die Verwaltung der kaiserzeitlichen römischen Armee. FS Hartmut Wolff. Historia. Einzelschriften 211. Stuttgart: Steiner, 2010

EISLER, ROBERT. Ἰησοῦς βασιλεύς οὐ βασιλεύσας. Die messianische Unabhängigkeitsbewegung vom Auftreten Johannes des Täufers bis zum Untergang Jakobs des Gerechten. Nach der neuerschlossenen Eroberung von Jerusalem des Flavius Josephus und den christlichen Quellen. 2 vols. Religionswissenschaftliche Bibliothek 9. Heidelberg: Winter, 1929–1930

ELLIOTT, JAMES K. The Apocryphal New Testament. A Collection of Apocryphal Christian Literature in an English Translation based on M. R. James. Oxford: Oxford University Press, 1993

ELON, MENACHEM. Jewish Law: History, Sources, Principles. 4 vols. Philadelphia: Jewish Publication Society, 1994

ELVERS, KARL-LUDWIG. Cluentius [2] C. Habitus, A. BNP 3 (2003): 483

–. Cornelius [I 6] C. Balbus, L. BNP 3 (2003): 809

–. Cosconius [I 1] C., C. BNP 3 (2003): 859

–. Fabius [I 28] F. Maximus Rullianus, Q. BNP 5 (2004): 293

–. Pontius [I 4] P.Telesinus. BNP 11 (2007): 597

–. Pontius. BNP 11 (2007): 596

EPSTEIN, ISIDORE, ed. Hebrew-English Edition of the Babylonian Talmud. New Edition in 30 vols. London: Soncino, 1967–1989

ESHEL, HANAN. 477. 4QRebukes Reported by the Overseer (Pl. XXXII). Pages 474–85 in Qumran Cave 4.XXVI: Cryptic Texts and Miscellanea, Part 1. Edited by S. Pfann. DJD 36. Oxford: Clarendon, 2000

EVANS, CRAIG A. Excavating Caiaphas, Pilate, and Simon of Cyrene: Assessing the Literary and Archaeological Evidence. Pages 323–40 in Jesus and Archaeology. Edited by J.H. Charlesworth. Grand Rapids: Eerdmans, 2006

–. Jesus and His Contemporaries: Comparative Studies. AGAJU 25. Leiden: Brill, 1995

–. Jesus and the Ossuaries. Waco: Baylor University Press, 2003

–. Jesus in Non-Christian Sources. Pages 443–78 in Studying the Historical Jesus: Evaluations of the State of Current Research. Edited by B. Chilton and C. A. Evans. NTTS 19. Leiden: Brill, 1994

–. Mark 8:27–16:20. WBC 34B. Nashville: Nelson, 2001

EVANS, CRAIG A., and DONALD A. HAGNER, eds. Anti-Semitism and Early Christianity: Issues of Polemic and Faith. Minneapolis: Fortress, 1993

FAIN, GORDON L. Ancient Greek Epigrams: Major Poets in Verse Translation. Berkeley: University of California Press, 2010

FARMER, WILLIAM R. Maccabees, Zealots, and Josephus: An Inquiry into Jewish Nationalism in the Greco-Roman Period. New York: Columbia University Press, 1956

FELDMAN, LOUIS H. Jew and Gentile in the Ancient World: Attitudes and Interactions from Alexander to Justinian. Princeton: Princeton University Press, 1993

–. Judean Antiquities 1–4. Translation and Commentary. Flavius Josephus: Translation and Commentary 3. Leiden: Brill, 2000

–. On the Authenticity of the *Testimonium Flavianum* Attributed to Josephus. Pages 13–30 in New Perspectives on Jewish-Christian Relations. Edited by E. Carlebach and J. J. Schacter. Leiden: Brill, 2012

–. Philo's Portrayal of Moses in the Context of Ancient Judaism. Notre Dame: University of Notre Dame Press, 2007

–. The *Testimonium Flavium*: The State of the Question. Pages 288–293 in Christological Perspectives. FS H. K. McArthur. Edited by R. F. Berkey and S. A. Edwards. New York: Pilgrim, 1982

FENSHAM, F. CHARLES. The Books of Ezra and Nehemiah. NICOT. Grand Rapids: Eerdmans, 1982

FERRARY, JEAN-LOUIS. The Powers of Augustus. Pages 90–136 in Augustus. Edited by J. Edmondson. Edinburgh: Edinburgh University Press, 2009

FESTUGIÈRE, ANDRÉ JEAN. Artemidore. La clef des songes: Onirocriticon. Collection Bibliothèque des textes philosophiques. Paris: Librairie Philosophique J. Vrin, 1975

FIELD, FRIDERICUS. Origenis Hexaplorum quae supersunt. 2 vols. Oxford: Clarendon, 1875

FINEGAN, JACK. The Archeology of the New Testament: The Life of Jesus and the Beginning of the Early Church. Rev. ed. Princeton: Princeton University Press, 1992

FINKELSTEIN, LOUIS. Sifre ad Deuteronomium. H. S. Horovitzii schedis usus cum variis lectionibus et adnotationibus. Editio nova. Orig. 1939. Repr. Corpus Tannaiticum III/3. New York: Jewish Theological Seminary of America, 1969

–. Hashpaʿat Bêt Shammai al Sifrê Debarim. Pages 415–426 in Sefer Assaf. FS Simcha Assaf. Edited by M. D. Cassuto, J. Klausner, and J. Guttmann. Jerusalem: Mossad Harav Kook, 1953

–. The Pharisaic Leadership after the Great Synagogue (170 B.C.E.–135 C.E.). Pages 229–244 in The Cambridge History of Judaism. Vol. 2: The Hellenistic Age. Edited by W. D. Davies and L. Finkelstein. Cambridge: Cambridge University Press, 1989

FISCHER, CURTIUS THEODOR, and FRIEDRICH VOGEL. Diodori bibliotheca historica. 6 vols. Bibliothea Scriptorum Graecorum et Romanorum Teubneriana. Leipzig: Teubner, 1888–1906

FISHER, CHARLES D. Cornelii Taciti Annalium ab excessu divi Augusti libri. Scriptorum classicorum bibliotheca Oxoniensis. Oxford: Clarendon, 1911 [1906]

FISHWICK, DUNCAN. The Talpioth Ossuaries Again. NTS 10 (1963): 49–61

FITZMYER, JOSEPH A. Crucifixion in Ancient Palestine, Qumran Literature, and the New Testament. CBQ 40 (1978): 493–513

FLAIG, EGON. Tacitus [1] (P.?) Cornelius T. BNP 14 (2009): 105–111

FLUSSER, DAVID. Caiaphas in the New Testament. ʾAtiqot 21 (1992): 63–71

–. Jesus in Selbstzeugnissen und Bilddokumenten. Hamburg: Rowohlt, 1968

–. Jesus. Jerusalem: Magnes, 1997

–. The Sage from Galilee: Rediscovering Jesus' Genius. Grand Rapids: Eerdmans, 2007

FONTANILLE, JEAN-PHILIPPE, and SHELDON LEE GOSLINE. The Coins of Pontius Pilate. Warren Center, Pa.: Shangri-La Publications, 2001

FORD, J. MASSYNGBERDE. 'Crucify him, Crucify him' and the Temple Scroll. ExpTim 87 (1975–1976): 275–278

FORNARO, SOTERA. Dionysius [18] D. of Halicarnassus. BNP 4 (2004): 480–484

FORSTER, EDWARD SEYMOUR. Lucius Annaeus Florus. Epitome of Roman History. Orig. 1929. Repr. LCL. Cambridge: Harvard University Press, 1984

FOSTER, BENJAMIN O. Livy. Ab urbe condita. Books VIII–X. LCL. Cambridge: Harvard University Press, 1926

FOSTER, BENJAMIN O., FRANK GARDNER MOORE, EVAN TAYLOR SAGE, ALFRED C. SCHLESINGER, and RUSSEL M. GEER. Livy. 14 vols. LCL. Cambridge: Harvard University Press, 1919–1957

FOSTER, HERBERT B., and EARNEST CARY. Dio's Roman History. 9 vols. LCL. Cambridge: Harvard University Press, 1914–1927

FOSTER, PAUL. Do we know how Jesus died? ExpT 123 (2011): 122–124

FRANCE, R. T. The Gospel of Matthew. NICNT. Grand Rapids: Eerdmans, 2007

FRANKE, PETER ROBERT. Dolmetschen in hellenistischer Zeit. Pages 85–96 in Zum Umgang mit Fremdsprachlichkeit in der griechisch-römischen Antike. Edited by Carl Werner Müller, Kurt Sier, and Jürgen Werner. Palingenesia 36. Stuttgart: Steiner, 1992

FRAZEL, THOMAS D. The Rhetoric of Cicero's "In Verrem". Hypomnemata 179. Göttingen: Vandenhoeck & Ruprecht, 2009

FREEDMAN, HARRY, Midrash Rabbah: Genesis. 2 vols. London: Soncino, 1939

FRESE, BENEDICT. Aus dem gräko-ägyptischen Rechtsleben. Halle: Niemeyer, 1909

FRIEDMANN, MEIR. Sifrè debè Rab, der älteste halachische und hagadische Midrasch zu Numeri und Deuteronomium. Wien: Selbstverlag, 1864

FROMENTIN, VALÉRIE, and JACQUES-HUBERT SAUTEL. Denys d' Halicarnasse. Antiquités Romaines. Collection Budé. Paris: Les Belles Lettres, 1998

FRÖSÉN, JAAKKO, ed. Papyri Helsingienses I. Ptolemäische Urkunden (P. Hels. I). Commentationes humanarum litterarum 80. Helsinki: Societas Scientiarum Fennica, 1986

FROVA, ANTONIO. L'iscrizione di Pontio Pilato a Cesarea. Pages 419–434 in Rendiconti dell' Istituto Lombardo, Accademia di Scienze e Lettere. Classe di Lettere e Scienze Morali e Storoiche 95. Milan: Istituto Lombardo, 1961

FUHRMANN, MANFRED. Marcus Tullius Cicero. Die Prozeßreden. Lateinisch-deutsch. 2 vols. Sammlung Tusculum. Zürich / Düsseldorf: Artemis & Winkler, 1997

–. Marcus Tullius Cicero. Die Reden gegen Verres. In C. Verrem. Lateinisch – deutsch. 2 vols. Sammlung Tusculum. Zürich: Artemis & Winkler, 1995

–. Marcus·Tullius Cicero. Sämtliche Reden. 7 vols. Bibliothek der Alten Welt. Römische Reihe. Zürich / Stuttgart 1970–1982

FUHS, HANS F. שאל. TDOT 14 (2004): 249–264

FUKS, GIDEON. Again on the Episode of the Gilded Roman Shields at Jerusalem. HTR 75 (1982): 503–507

FULDA, HERMANN. Das Kreuz und die Kreuzigung. Eine antiquarische Untersuchung nebst Nachweis der vielen seit Lipsius verbreiteten Irrthümer: zugleich vier Excurse über verwandte Gegenstände. Breslau: Koebner, 1878

FÜNDLING, JÖRG. Pontius [I 3] P. Aquila. BNP 11 (2007): 596–597

FURNEAUX, HENRY. Tacitus, Cornelius. Annalium ab excessu divi Augusti libri. The Annals of Tacitus. Second Edition Revised by H. F. Pelham and C. D. Fisher. 2 vols. Orig. 1896. Repr. Oxford: Clarendon, 1907

GAINES, ROBERT N. Roman Rhetorical Handbooks. Pages 163–181 in A Companion to Roman Rhetoric. Edited by W. Dominik and J. Hall. Orig. 2007. Repr. Chicester: Wiley-Blackwell, 2010

GALSTERER, HARTMUT. The Administration of Justice. Pages 397–413 in Cambridge Ancient History. Volume X: The Augustan Empire, 43 B.C.–A.D. 69, Second ed. Edited by A. K. Bowman, E. Champlin, and A. Lintott. Orig. 1996. Repr. Cambridge: Cambridge University Press, 2006

GAMBETTI, SANDRA. The Alexandrian Riots of 38 C.E. and the Persecution of the Jews: A Historical Reconstruction. JSJSup 135. Leiden: Brill, 2009

GARCÍA MARTÍNEZ, FLORENTINO. 4QpNah y la Crucifixión: Nueva hipótesis de reconstrucción de 4Q 169 3–4 i, 4–8. EstBib 38 (1979–80): 221–235

GARCÍA MARTÍNEZ, FLORENTINO, EIBERT J. C. TIGCHELAAR, and ADAM S. VAN DER WOUDE. Qumran Cave 11.II (11Q2–18, 11Q20–30). DJD 23. Oxford: Clarendon, 1998

GARCÍA MARTÍNEZ, FLORENTINO, and EIBERT J. C. TIGCHELAAR. The Dead Sea Scrolls Study Edition. 2 vols. Leiden: Brill, 1997–1998

GARDNER, ROBERT. Cicero. Pro Caelio. De provinciis consularibus. Pro Balbo. Orig. 1958. Repr. LCL. Cambridge: Harvard University Press, 2005

GARLAND, ROBERT. The Greek Way of Death. Ithaca: Cornell University Press, 1985

GARNSEY, PETER. Social Status and Legal Privilege in the Roman Empire. Oxford: Clarendon, 1970

GEIGER, JOSEPH. Titulus crucis. Scripta Classica Israelica 15 (1996): 202–207

GERTZ, MARTIN C. L. Annaei Senecae Libri De beneficiis et De clementia. Ad Codicem Nazarianum. Berlin: Weidmann, 1876

GEVA, HILLEL. Jerusalem: The Second Temple Period. Water Supply. NEAEHL 2 (1993): 746–747

–. Jerusalem: The Temple Mount and its Environs. NEAEHL 2 (1993): 736–744

GHIRETTI, MAURIZIO. Lo 'status' della Guidea dall' età Augustea all' età Claudia. Latomus 44 (1985): 751–766

GIBSON, JEFFREY B. The Function of the Charge of Blasphemy in Mark 14:64. Pages 171–187 in The Trial and Death of Jesus: Essays on the Passion Narrative in Mark. Edited by G. Van Oyen and T. Shepherd. Leuven: Peeters, 2006

GIBSON, SHIMON. The Final Days of Jesus: The Archaeological Evidence. New York: HarperOne, 2009

GINSBURGER, MOSES. Pseudo-Jonathan (Thargum Jonathan ben Usiel zum Pentateuch). Nach der Londoner Handschrift (Brit. Mus. add. 27031). Orig. 1903. New York: Hildesheim, 1966

GINZBERG, LOUIS. Some Observations on the Attitude of the Synagogue Towards the Apocalyptic-Eschatological Writings. JBL 41 (1922): 115–36

GIZEWSKI, CHRISTIAN G. Coercitio. BNP 3 (2003): 508–509

–. Ambitus. BNP 1 (2002): 568–569

–. Maiestas. BNP 8 (2006): 185–187

GLARE, P. G. W. Oxford Latin Dictionary. Oxford: Oxford University Press, 1982

GNILKA, JOACHIM. Das Evangelium nach Markus. EKK II/1–2. Zürich / Neukirchen-Vluyn: Benziger / Neukirchener, 1978–79

–. Jesus von Nazareth. Botschaft und Geschichte. HThK Sup 3. Freiburg: Herder, 1990

GODLEY, ALRED D. Herodotus. 4 vols. Orig. 1920–1925. Repr. LCL. Cambridge: Harvard University Press, 1963

GOLDBERG, ABRAHAM. Commentary to the Mishna Shabbat: Critically Edited and Provided with Introduction, Commentary and Notes. Jerusalem, 1976

GOLDENBERG, DAVID M. The Halakhah in Josephus and in Tannaitic Literature: A Comparative Study. Ph.D. Dissertation. Philadelphia: Dropsie University, 1978

GOLDIN, HYMAN E. Hebrew Criminal Law and Procedure: Mishnah: Sanhedrin–Makkot. New York: Twayne, 1952

GOLDSTEIN, JONATHAN A. I Maccabees. AB 41. Garden City: Doubleday, 1976

–. The Testament of Moses: Its Content, Its Origin, and Its Attestation in Josephus. Pages 44–52 in Studies on the Testament of Moses. Edited by G. W. E. Nickelsburg. SBLSBS 4. Cambridge: Society of Biblical Literature, 1973

GOLDSTEIN, MORRIS. Jesus in the Jewish Tradition. New York: Macmillan, 1950

GOODENOUGH, ERWIN R. Jewish Symbols in the Greco-Roman Period. 13 vols. Bollingen Series 47. New York: Pantheon, 1953–68.

GOODMAN, MARTIN. Judaea. Pages 737–81 in Cambridge Ancient History. Volume X: The Augustan Empire, 43 B.C.–A.D. 69, Second ed. Edited by A. K. Bowman, E. Champlin, and A. Lintott. Orig. 1996. Repr. Cambridge: Cambridge University Press, 2006

–. The Ruling Class of Judaea: The Origins of the Jewish Revolt Against Rome A.D. 66–70. Cambridge: Cambridge University Press, 1987

GOODSPEED, EDGAR J. Dialogus com Tryphone. Pages 90–265 in Die ältesten Apologeten. Texte mir kurzen Einleitungen. Orig. 1914. Repr. Göttingen: Vandenhoeck & Ruprecht, 1984

–. Die ältesten Apologeten. Texte mir kurzen Einleitungen. Göttingen: Vandenhoeck & Ruprecht, 1984 (1914)

GOODYEAR, FRANCIS R. D. The Annals of Tacitus. 2 vols. Cambridge Classical Texts and Commentaries. Cambridge: Cambridge University Press, 1972

GOOLD, GEORGE P. Chariton. Callirhoe. LCL. Cambridge: Harvard University Press, 1995

GÖRGEMANNS, HERWIG. Plutarch. Drei religionsphilosophische Schriften. Über den Aberglauben. Über die späte Strafe der Gottheit. Über Isis und Osiris. Griechisch-deutsch. Sammlung Tusculum. Düsseldorf /Zürich, 2003

GRAETZ, HEINRICH. Geschichte der Juden von den ältesten Zeiten bis auf die Gegenwart. 11 vols. Leipzig: Leiner, 1853–76

GRAMAGLIA, PIER ANGELO. Il Testimonium Flavianum: Analisi linguistica. Henoch 20 (1998): 153–177

GRANT, MICHAEL. The Annals of Imperial Rome. Sixth Revised Edition. Orig. 1956. Repr. Penguin Classics. Harmondsworth: Penguin, 1989

–. Tacitus: The Annals of Imperial Rome. London: Penguin, 1996

GRAVES, ROBERT. Gaius Suetonius Tranquillus. The Twelve Caesars. Revised by Michael Grant. London / New York: Penguin, 1989

GRAY, REBECCA. Prophetic Figures in Late Second Temple Jewish Palestine: The Evidence from Josephus. New York: Oxford University Press, 1993

GRAYSON, ALBERT KIRK. Assyrian Royal Inscriptions. 2 vols. Records of the Ancient Near East. Wiesbaden: Harrassowitz, 1972

–. Assyrian Rulers of the Early First Millennium BC I (1114–859 BC). The Royal Inscriptions of Mesopotamia 2. Toronto: University of Toronto Press, 1991

GREEN, JOEL B. The Death of Jesus: Tradition and Interpretation in the Passion Narrative. WUNT 2.33. Tübingen: Mohr Siebeck, 1988

GREENE, WILLIAM CASWELL. Scholia Platonica. Philological Monographs 8. Haverford: American Philological Association, 1938

GREENHUT, ZVI. The Caiaphas Tomb in North Talpiot, Jerusalem. Pages 219–222 in Ancient Jerusalem Revealed, Reprinted and Expanded Edition. Edited by H. Geva. Jerusalem: Israel Exploration Society, 2000

–. Discovery of the Caiaphas Family Tomb. Jerusalem Perspectives 4 (1991): 6–11

GREENOUGH, JAMES B., G. L. KITTREDGE, A. A. HOWARD, and B. L. D'OOGE, eds. Allen and Greenough's New Latin Grammar for Schools and Colleges, Founded on Comparative Grammar. College Classical Series. New Rochelle: Caratzas, 1983

GREENWOOD, LEONARD H. G. Marcus Tullius Cicero. The Verrine Orations. LCL. 2 vols. Orig. 1928. Repr. London: Heinemann, 1988

GRENFELL, BERNARD P., ARTHUR S. HUNT, ET AL., eds. The Oxyrhynchus Papyri. London: Egypt Exploration Fund, 1898

GRESSMANN, HUGO. Altorientalische Bilder zum Alten Testament. Zweite, völlig neugestaltete und stark vermehrte Auflage. Berlin/Leipzig: De Gruyter, 1927

GRIFFIN, MIRIAM T. Nero: The End of a Dynasty. Orig. 1984. Repr. New York: Routledge, 2000

GRIFFITH, FRANCIS L. The Abydos Decree of Seti I at Nauri. Journal of Egyptian Archaeology 13 (1927): 193–208

GRIMAL, PIERRE. Cicéron. Discours. Tome XVI: Contre L. Pison, Pour Cn. Plancius, Pour M. Aemilius Scaurus. Collection des universités de France 16. Paris: Belles Lettres, 1966

GRUBE, GEORGE M. A. Plato's Republic. Indianapolis: Hackett, 1974

GRUEN, ERICH S. Heritage and Hellenism: The Reinvention of Jewish Tradition. HCS 30. Berkeley: University of California Press, 1998

GRÜLL, TIBOR. Pilate's 'Tiberiueum': A New Approach. Acta antiqua Academiae Scientiarum Hungaricae 41 (2001): 267–278

GUGGENHEIMER, HEINRICH W. The Jerusalem Talmud. Fourth Order: Neziqin. Tractates Sanhedrin, Makkot, and Horaiot. Edition, Translation, and Commentary. Studia Judaica: Forschungen zur Wissenschaft des Judentums 51. Berlin/New York: De Gruyter, 2010

GUILLET, P.-E. Les 800 'Crucifiés' d'Alexandre Jannée. Cahiers du Cercle Ernest Renan 25 (1977): 11–16

GUMMERE, RICHARD M. Seneca. Ad Lucilium epistulae morales. 3 vols. LCL. London: Heineman, 1917–1925

GUNDRY, ROBERT H. Mark: A Commentary on His Apology for the Cross. Grand Rapids: Eerdmans, 1993

–. The Old is Better: New Testament Essays in Support of Traditional Interpretations. WUNT 178. Tübingen: Mohr Siebeck, 2005

GÜNTHER, LINDA-MARIE. Theodotos [5]. BNP 14 (2009): 478

GUSSMANN, OLIVER. Das Priesterverständnis des Flavius Josephus. TSAJ 124. Tübingen: Mohr Siebeck, 2008

HAAG, HERBERT. חָמָס. TDOT 4 (1980): 476–487

HAAS, NICO. Anthropological Observations on the Skeletal Remains from Giv'at ha-Mivtar. IEJ 20 (1970): 38–59

HACHLILI, RACHEL. Jewish Funerary Customs, Practices and Rites in the Second Temple Period. JSJSup 94. Leiden: Brill, 2005

HAENEL, GUSTAV. Lex Romana Visigothorum. Leipzig: Teubner, 1849

HAGNER, DONALD A. Matthew. WBC 33. Dallas: Word, 1993–1995

HALL, ROBERT G. Epispasm and the Dating of Ancient Jewish Writings. JSP 2 (1988): 71–86

HALLOTE, RACHEL S. Death, Burial, and Afterlife in the Biblical World: How the Israelites and Their Neighbors Treated the Dead. Chicago: Dee, 2001

HALM, KARL. C. Cornelii Taciti libri qui supersunt. Tomus prior qui libros ab excessu divi Augusti continet. Editionem quintam curavit Georgius Andresen. Orig. 1855. Repr. Bibliotheca Scriptorum Graecorum et Romanorum Teubneriana. Leipzig: Teubner, 1913

–. Valeri Maximi Factorum et dictorum memorabilium libri novem. Leipzig: Teubner, 1865

HALPERIN, DAVID J. Crucifixion, the Nahum Pesher, and the Rabbinic Penalty of Strangulation. JJS 32 (1981): 32–46

HAMILTON, EDITH, and HUNTINGTON CAIRNS. The Collected Dialogues of Plato. Princeton: Princeton University Press, 1961

HAMILTON, VICTOR P. The Book of Genesis. 2 volsl; NICOT. Grand Rapids: Eerdmans, 1990–1995

HAMMER, REUVEN. Sifre: A Tannaitic Commentary on the Book of Deuteronomy. Yale Judaica 24. New Haven / London: Yale University Press, 1986

HAMMOND, MASON, ARTHUR M. MACK, and WALTER MOSKALEW. T. Macci Plauti Miles Gloriosus. Edited with an Introduction and Notes. Orig. 1963. Repr. Cambridge: Harvard University Press, 1997

HANHART, ROBERT. Esther. 2. Auflage. Septuaginta VIII.3. Göttingen: Vandenhoeck & Ruprecht, 2008

HARMON, AUSTIN M. Lucian. 8 vols. LCL. Cambridge: Harvard University Press, 1913–1967

HARNACK, ADOLF. Geschichte der altchristlichen Literatur bis Eusebius. Vier Bände, 2. erweiterte Auflage. Orig. 1893–1904. Repr. Leipzig: Hinrichs, 1958

HARRIS-MCCOY, DANIEL E. Artemidorus' Oneirocritica: Text, Translation, and Commentary. Oxford: Oxford University Press, 2012

HÄRTEL, GOTTFRIED. Aus den Digesten. In Römisches Recht in einem Band. Edited by L. Huchthausen. Orig. 1975. Repr. Berlin: Aufbau, 1989

HASE, CHARLES BENOÎT. Valerius Maximus De dictis factisque memorabilibus et Jul. Obsequens de prodigiis cum supplementis Conradi Lycosthenis. 2 vols. Bibliotheca classica latina. Paris: Lemaire, 1822–1823

HAUKEN, TOR. Petition and Response: An Epigraphic Study of the Petitions to Roman Emperors, 181–249. Monographs from the Norwegian Institute at Athens 2. Bergen: Norwegian Institute at Athens, 1998

HAVERKAMP, SIWART. Flavii Josephi quae reperiri potuerunt, opera omnia graece et latine cum notis et nova versione Joannis Hudsoni. 2 vols. Amsterdam: Wetstenios, 1726

HEINEMANN, JOSEPH. Early Halakhah in the Palestinian Targumim. JJS 25 (1974): 114–122

–. The Targum of Ex. XXII,4 and the Ancient Halakha [Hebrew]. Tarbis 38 (1969): 294–296

HELLER, ERICH. Tacitus. Annalen. Lateinisch und deutsch. Orig. 1992. Repr. Sammlung Tusculum. München / Zürich: Artemis & Winkler, 1997

HENDIN, DAVID. Guide to Biblical Coins. Fifth ed. New York: Amphora, 2010

HENGEL, MARTIN. The Cross of the Son of God. London: SCM, 1976

–. Crucifixion in the Ancient World and the Folly of the Message of the Cross. Translated by John Bowden. Philadelphia: Fortress, 1978

–. E. P. Sanders' 'Common Judaism', Jesus, and the Pharisees [1995]. Pages 392–479 in Judaica et Hellenistica. Kleine Schriften I. WUNT 90. Tübingen: Mohr Siebeck, 1996

–. Gewalt und Gewaltlosigkeit. Zur 'politischen Theologie' in neutestamentlicher Zeit [1971]. Pages 245–288 in Jesus und die Evangelien: Kleine Schriften V. Edited by C.-J. Thornton. Tübingen: Mohr Siebeck, 2007

–. Das Johannesevangelium als Quelle des antiken Judentums." Pages 293–334 in Judaica, Hellenistica et Christiana. Kleine Schriften II. WUNT 109. Tübingen: Mohr Siebeck, 1999

–. La crucifixion dans l'antiquité et la folie du message de la croix. Translated by A. Chazelle. LD 105. Paris: Cerf, 1981

–. Messianische Hoffnung und politischer 'Radikalismus' in der 'jüdischen-hellenistischen Diaspora'. Zur Frage der Voraussetzungen des jüdischen Aufstandes unter Trajan 115–117 n.Chr. [1983]. Pages 314–343 in Judaica et Hellenistica. Kleine Schriften I. WUNT 90. Tübingen: Mohr Siebeck, 1996

–. Mors Turpissima Crucis. Die Kreuzigung in der antiken Welt und die 'Torheit' des 'Wortes vom Kreuz' [1976]. Pages 594–652 in Studien zum Urchristentum. Kleine Schriften VI. Edited by C.-J. Thornton. Tübingen: Mohr Siebeck, 2008

–. Rabbinische Legende und frühpharisäische Geschichte: Schimeon b. Schetach und die achtzig Hexen von Askalon. Abhandlungen der Heidelberger Akademie der Wissenschaften. Philosophisch-historische Klasse 1984,2. Heidelberg: Winter, 1984

–. The Zealots: Investigations into the Jewish Freedom Movement in the Period from Herod I until 70 A.D. Edinburgh: T & T Clark, 1989

–. Die Zeloten. Untersuchungen zur jüdischen Freiheitsbewegung in der Zeit von Herodes I. bis 70 n. Chr. 3., durchgesehene und ergänzte Auflage. Edited by R. Deines and C. J. Thornton. WUNT 283. Tübingen: Mohr Siebeck, 2011

HENGEL, MARTIN, and ANNA MARIA SCHWEMER. Jesus und das Judentum. Geschichte des frühen Christentums Band I. Tübingen: Mohr Siebeck, 2007

HENNIG, DIETER. L. Aelius Seianus. Untersuchungen zur Regierung des Tiberius. Vestigia 21. München: Beck, 1975

HENSE, OTTO. L. Annaei Senecae ad Lucilium epistularum moralium quae supersunt. L. Annaei Senecae opera quae supersunt 3. Leipzig: Teubner, 1898

HENTEN, JAN W. VAN, and FRIEDRICH AVEMARIE. Martyrdom and Noble Death: Selected Texts from Graeco-Roman, Jewish, and Christian Antiquity. Context of Early Christianity.

London: Routledge, 2002

HERFORD, R. TRAVERS. Christianity in Talmud and Midrash. 1903. Repr. Jersey City, NJ: Ktav, 2006

HERRMANN, PETER. Hilferufe aus römischen Provinzen. Ein Aspekt der Krise des römischen Reiches im 3. Jhdt. n. Chr. Berichte aus den Sitzungen der Joachim-Jungius-Gesellschaft der Wissenschaften 8/4. Hamburg / Göttingen: Vandenhoeck & Ruprecht, 1990

HERZER, JENS. Zwischen Loyalität und Machtstreben: sozialgeschichtliche Aspekte des Pilatusbildes bei Josephus und im Neuen Testament. Pages 429–449 in Josephus und das Neue Testament. Wechselseitige Wahrnehmungen. Edited by C. Böttrich and J. Herzer. WUNT 209. Tübingen: Mohr Siebeck, 2007

HESELTINE, MICHAEL, and WILLIAM H. D. ROUSE. Petronius; Seneca: Apocolocyntosis. Orig. 1930. Repr. LCL. Cambridge: Harvard University Press, 1987

HEUBNER, HEINZ. P. Cornelii Taciti Libri qui supersunt. Tom. I. Ab excessu divi Augusti. Zweite Auflage. Orig. 1983. Repr. Bibliotheca Scriptorum Graecorum et Romanorum. Stuttgart / Leipzig: Teubner, 1994

HEUSLER, ERIKA. Kapitalprozesse im lukanischen Doppelwerk. Die Verfahren gegen Jesus und Paulus in exegetischer und rechtshistorischer Analyse. NTA 38. Münster: Aschendorff, 2000

HEWITT, JOSEPH W. The Use of Nails in the Crucifixion. HTR 25 (1932): 29–45.

HILLEN, HANS JÜRGEN. T. Livius, Römische Geschichte. Buch VII–X. Fragmente der zweiten Dekade. Sammlung Tusculum. Zürich: Artemis & Winkler, 1994

HINARD, FRANÇOIS, and JEAN-CHRISTIAN DUMONT. Libitina: Pompes funèbres et supplices en Campanie à l'époque d'Auguste. Édition, traduction et commentaire de la Lex Libitinae Puteolana. Paris: Boccard, 2003

HIRSCH, EMIL G. Crucifixion. Pages 4:373–374 in The Jewish Encyclopedia. New York: Funk and Wagnalls, 1903

HIRSCHFELD, OTTO. Die kaiserlichen Verwaltungsbeamten bis auf Diokletian. 2. Auflage. Orig. 1878. Repr. Berlin: Weidmann, 1905

HÖCKER, CHRISTOPH. Rostrum. BNP 12 (2008): 741–742

HODGE, HUMFREY G. Cicero. Pro lege Manilia. Pro Caecina. Pro Cluentio. LCL. Cambridge: Harvard University Press, 1927

–. Cicero. The Speeches. LCL. Cambridge: Harvard University Press, 1927

HOFFMANN, CHARLOTTE. An Introduction to Bilingualism. Longman Linguistics Library. London: Longman, 1991

HOFFMANN, DAVID. Midrasch Tannaïm zum Deuteronomium. 2 vols. Berlin: Poppelauer, 1908–1909

HOFTIJZER, JACOB, and KAREL JONGELING. Dictionary of the North-West Semitic Inscriptions. Boston: Brill, 2003

HOLUM, KENNETH G., AVNER RABAN, and JOSEPH PATRICH, eds. Caesarea Papers 2: Herod's Temple, the Provincial Governor's Praetorium and Granaries, the Later Harbor, a Gold Coin Hoard, and Other Studies. JRASup 35. Portsmouth, R.I.: Journal of Roman Archaeology, 1999

HOLZMEISTER, URBANUS. Zur Frage der Blutgerichtsbarkeit des Synedriums. Bib 19 (1938): 43–59, 151–174

HÖNLE, AUGUSTA. Munus, Munera. BNP 9 (2006): 301–312

HONORÉ, TONY. Justinian's Digest: Character and Compilation. Oxford: Oxford University Press, 2010

–. Ulpian. Oxford: Clarendon, 1982

HOOKER, MORNA D. The Son of Man in Mark: A Study of the Background of the Term "Son of Man" and Its Use in St. Mark's Gospel. London: SPCK, 1967

HOPE, VALERIE M. Death in Ancient Rome: A Source Book. Routledge Sourcebooks for the Ancient World. London/New York: Routledge, 2007

HOPE, VALERIE M. Roman Death: Dying and the Dead in Ancient Rome. London/New York: Continuum, 2009

HORBURY, WILLIAM. The 'Caiaphas' Ossuaries and Joseph Caiaphas. PEQ 126 (1994): 32–48

HORGAN, MAURYA P. Nahum Pesher (4Q169 = 4QpNah). Pages 144–155 in Pesharim, Other Commentaries, and Related Documents. Edited by J. H. Charlesworth. The Dead Sea Scrolls 6B. Tübingen: Mohr Siebeck, 2002

–. Pesharim: Qumran Interpretations of Biblical Books. CBQMS 8. Washington: Catholic Biblical Association, 1979

HORN, FRIEDRICH-WILHELM. Das Testimonium Flavianum aus neutestamentlicher Perspektive. Pages 117–136 in Josephus und das Neue Testament. Wechselseitige Wahrnehmungen. Edited by C. Böttrich and J. Herzer. WUNT 209. Tübingen: Mohr Siebeck, 2007

HORNUNG, ERIK. History of Ancient Egypt. Translated by David Lorton. Ithaca: Cornell University Press, 1999

HOROVITZ, HAIM SAUL, ed. Siphre ad Numeros adjecto Siphre zutta. Cum variis lectionibus et adnotationibus. Orig. 1917. Repr. Corpus Tannaiticum III/3: Siphre d'be Rab 1. Jerusalem: Wahrmann, 1966

HOROVITZ, HAIM SAUL, and ISRAEL ABRAHAM RABIN. Mechilta d'Rabbi Ismael. Orig. 1931. Repr. Corpus Tannaiticum 3.1(3). Jerusalem: Bamberger & Wahrmann, 1960

HORSLEY, GREG H. R., and STEPHEN R. LLEWELYN, eds. New Documents Illustrating Early Christianity. Macquarie University: North Ryde, New South Wales, Australia, 1981–2012

HORSLEY, RICHARD A. High Priests and the Politics of Roman Palestine: A Contextual Analysis of the Evidence in Josephus. JSJ 17 (1986): 23–55

HORSLEY, RICHARD A., and JOHN S. HANSON. Bandits, Prophets, and Messiahs: Popular Movements in the Time of Jesus. Orig. 1985. Repr. Harrisburg: Trinity Press International, 1999

HORST, PIETER W. VAN DER. Philo's Flaccus: The First Pogrom. Introduction, Translation, and Commentary. Philo of Alexandria Commentary 2. Leiden: Brill, 2003

HOSIUS, CARL. Geschichte der römischen Literatur. Erster Teil: Die römische Literatur in der Zeit der Republik. HdA VIII.1. München: Beck, 1927

–. Annaei Senecae Opera quae supersunt. I/2: De beneficiis libri VII. De clementia libri II. Bibliotheca Scriptorum Graecorum et Romanorum Teubneriana. Leipzig: Teubner, 1914

HOWARD, DAVID M. Joshua. NAC 5. Nashville: Broadman & Holman, 1998

HUBBELL, HARRY M. Cicero. De inventione. De optimo genere oratorum. Topica. LCL. London: Heinemann, 1949

HUDE, CARL. Herodoti Historiae. Editio tertia. 2 vols. Scriptorum classicorum bibliotheca Oxoniensis. Oxford: Clarendon, 1927

–. Xenophontis Expeditio Cyri: Anabasis. Editionem correctiorem curavit J. Peters. Bibliotheca scriptorum Graecorum et Romanorum Teubneriana. Leipzig: Teubner, 1972

–. Thucydidis Historiae. Editio Minor. Leipzig: Teubner, 1903

HUNTER, RICHARD. History and Historicity in the Romance of Chariton [1994]. Pages 737–774 in On Coming After: Studies in Post-Classical Greek Literature and Its Reception. Part 2: Comedy and Performance, Greek Poetry of the Roman Empire, the Ancient Novel. Trends in Classics Sup 3/2. Berlin: De Gruyter, 2008

HURLEY, DONNA W. Suetonius. The Caesars. Translated, with Introductions and Notes. Indianapolis: Hackett, 2011

HURTADO, LARRY W. The Earliest Christian Artifacts: Manuscripts and Christian Origins. Grand Rapids: Eerdmans, 2006

–. The Staurogram in Early Christian Manuscripts: The Earliest Visual Reference to the Crucified Jesus?. Pages 207–226 in New Testament Manuscripts: Their Texts and Their World. Edited by T. J. Kraus and T. Nicklas. Texts and Editions for New Testament Study 2. Leiden: Brill, 2006

HUSS, WERNER. Geschichte der Karthager. HdA III.8. München: Beck, 1985

HYAMSON, MOSES. Mosaicarum et romanarum legum collatio. With Introduction, Facsimile and Transcription of the Berlin Codex, Translation, Notes and Appendices. London: Oxford University Press, 1913

IHM, MAXIMILIAN. C. Suetonius Tranquillus Opera. De vita Caesarum Libri III. Orig. 1907. Repr. Bibliotheca Scriptorum Graecorum et Romanorum Teubneriana. Stuttgart / Leipzig: Teubner, 2003

ILAN, TAL. Lexicon of Jewish Names in Late Antiquity. TSAJ 91.126.141.148. Tübingen: Mohr Siebeck 2002–2012

ILLIFFE, JOHN H. The ΘΑΝΑΤΟΣ Inscription from Herod's Temple: The Fragment of a Second Copy. QDAP 6 (1938): 1–3

ILLMAN, KARL-JOHAN. שָׁלַם. TDOT 15:97–105

ILLMAN, KARL-JOHAN, HELMER RINGGREN, and HEINZ-JOSEF FABRY. מוּת. TDOT 8 (1997): 185–209

INNES, ALEXANDER T. The Trial of Jesus Christ: A Legal Monograph. Edinburgh: Clark, 1899

INSTONE-BREWER, DAVID. Jesus of Nazareth's Trial in the Uncensored Talmud. TynBul 62 (2011): 269–94

–. Traditions of the Rabbis from the Era of the New Testament. Vol. 2A: Feasts and Sabbaths: Passover and Atonement. Grand Rapids: Eerdmans, 2011

İŞKAN-IŞIK, HAVVA, WERNER ECK, and HELMUT ENGELMANN. Der Leuchtturm von Patara und Sex. Marcius Priscus als Statthalter der Provinz Lycia von Nero bis Vespasian. ZPE 164 (2008): 91–121

JACOBITZ, KARL. Luciani Samosatensis opera. 3 vols. Orig. 1903–1905. Repr. Bibliotheca scriptorum Graecorum et Romanorum Teubneriana. Leipzig: Teubner, 1913–1921

–. Dionysius Halicarnaseus. Antiquitates Romanae. 4 vols. Orig. 1888–1905. Repr. Bibliotheca Scriptorum Graecorum et Romanorum Teubneriana. Stuttgart / Leipzig: Teubner, 1997

JASNOW, RICHARD. Egypt: New Kingdom. Pages I, 289–356 in A History of Ancient Near Eastern Law. Edited by R. Westbrook. Handbook of Oriental Studies: The Near and Middle East 72. Leiden: Brill, 2003

JASTROW, MARCUS. A Dictionary of the Targumim, the Talmud Babli, and Yerushalmi, and the Midrashic Literature. Orig. 1903. Repr. Peabody: Hendrickson, 2005

JEEP, JUSTUS W. L. Iustinus. Trogi Pompei Historiarum Philippicarum epitoma. Bibliotheca scriptorum Graecorum et Romanorum Teubneriana. Leipzig: Teubner, 1859

JENSEN, MORTEN HØRNING. Herod Antipas in Galilee: The Literary and Archaeological Sources on the Reign of Herod Antipas and its Socio-Economic Impact on Galilee. WUNT 2/215. Tübingen: Mohr Siebeck, 2010 [2006]

JEREMIAS, JOACHIM. Die Abendmahlsworte Jesu. 4. Auflage. Göttingen: Vandenhoeck & Ruprecht, 1967 [1935]

–. The Eucharistic Words of Jesus. Orig. 1966. Repr. London: SCM, 1976

–. Neutestamentliche Theologie. Erster Teil: Die Verkündigung Jesu. 4. Auflage. Orig. 1971. Repr. Gütersloh: Mohn, 1988

–. Zur Geschichtlichkeit des Verhörs Jesu vor dem Hohen Rat. ZNW 43 (1950–51): 145–150

JOBES, KAREN H. Esther. NIVAC. Grand Rapids: Zondervan, 1999

JOBES, KAREN H., and MOISÉS SILVA. Invitation to the Septuagint. Grand Rapids: Baker, 2000

JONES, BRIAN W. The Emperor Domitian. London: Routledge, 1992

–. Suetonius. Domitian. Edited with Introduction, Commentary and Bibliography. Bristol: Bristol Classical Press, 1996

JONES, HENRY STUART, and JOHN ENOCH POWELL. Thucydidis Historiae. 2 vols. Scriptorum classicorum bibliotheca Oxoniensis. Oxford: Clarendon, 1942

JONES, HORACE LEONARD. The Geography of Strabo. 8 vols. LCL. London/Cambridge: Heinemann/Harvard University Press, 1917–1932

JÖRDEN, ANDREa. Eine kaiserliche Konstitution zu den Rechtsprechungskompetenzen der Statthalter. Chiron 41 (2011): 327–356

JOSSA, GIORGIO. Jews or Christians? The Followers of Jesus in Search of their Own Identity. WUNT 202. Tübingen: Mohr Siebeck, 2006

–. Jews, Romans, and Christians: From the Bellum Judaicum to the Antiquitates. Pages 331–342 in Josephus and Jewish History in Flavian Rome and Beyond. Edited by J. Sievers and G. Lembi. Supplements to the Journal for the study of Judaism 104. Leiden / Boston: Brill, 2005

JOSUA, MARIA, and FRIEDMANN EISSLER. Das arabische Kindheitsevangelium. Pages 963–982 in Antike christliche Apokryphen in deutscher Übersetzung. I. Band: Evangelien und Verwandtes. Edited by C. Markschies and J. Schröter. Tübingen: Mohr Siebeck, 2012

JUDGE, EDWIN A. The First Christians in the Roman World: Augustan and New Testament Essays. Edited by J. R. Harrison. WUNT 229. Tübingen: Mohr Siebeck, 2008

–. The Regional *kanōn* for Requisitioned Transport [1981]. Pages 348–359 in The First Christians in the Roman World: Augustan and New Testament Essays. Edited by J. R. Harrison. WUNT 229. Tübingen: Mohr Siebeck, 2008

–. What Kind of Ruler Did the Greeks Think Augustus Was? [1992]. Pages 385–394 in The First Christians in the Roman World: Augustan and New Testament Essays. Edited by J. R. Harrison. WUNT 229. Tübingen: Mohr Siebeck, 2010

JUEL, DONALD. Messiah and Temple: The Trial of Jesus in the Gospel of Mark. SBLDS 31. Missoula: Scholars Press, 1977

JUNK, TIM. Python I. BNP 12 (2008): 12:298

JUSTER, JEAN. Les Juifs dans l'empire romain. Leur condition juridique, économique et sociale. 2 vols. Paris: Geuthner, 1914

KAJANTO, IIRO. The Latin Cognomina. Orig. 1965. Repr. Commentationes humanarum litterarum 2. Rome: Bretschneider, 1982

KALTSAS, DEMOKRITOS. Ein Streit zwischen Epergoi in P. Hels 1. ZPE 142 (2003): 214–220

KASER, MAX. Das römische Zivilprozeßrecht. Zweite Auflage, neu bearbeitet von K. Hackl. Orig. 1966. Repr. HdA X/3,4. München: Beck, 1996

KASTEN, HELMUT. Gaius Plinius Caecilius Secundus. Briefe: Epistularum libri decem. Lateinisch und deutsch. 7. Auflage. Sammlung Tusculum. München / Zürich: Artemis & Winkler, 1995

–. M. Tulli Ciceronis epistularum ad familiares Libri XVI / Marcus Tullius Cicero an seine Freunde. Lateinisch / Deutsch. Orig. 1964. Repr. München: Heimeran, 1989

KATZOFF, RANON GEDALIA. Law as *Katholikos*. Pages 119–126 in Studies in Roman Law in Memory of A. Arthur Schiller. Edited by R. S. Bagnall and W. V. Harris. Columbia Studies in the Classical Tradition 13. Leiden: Brill, 1986

–. Sources of Law in Roman Egypt: The Role of the Prefect. ANRW II.13 (1980): 807–844

KEENER, CRAIG S. A Commentary on the Gospel of Matthew. Grand Rapids: Eerdmans, 1999

–. The Historical Jesus of the Gospels. Grand Rapids: Eerdmans, 2009

KEHNE, PETER. Legatus. BNP 7 (2005): 354–355

KELLY, BENJAMIN. Petitions, Litigation, and Social Control in Roman Egypt. Oxford: Oxford University Press, 2011

KEMPF, KARL F. B. Valeri Maximi Factorum et dictorum memorabilivm libri novem. Cum incerti auctoris fragmento De praenominibus. Berlin: Reimer, 1854

KENNEDY, DAVID, ed. The Roman Army in the East. JRASup 18. Ann Arbor: Journal of Roman Archaeology, 1996

KENNEDY, GEORGE A. A New History of Classical Rhetoric. Princeton: Princeton University Press, 1994

KENNETH, WELLESLEY. Cornelii Taciti Libri qui supersunt. Tomus I pars secunda: Ab excessu divi Augusti Libri XI–XVI. Stuttgart / Leipzig: Teubner, 1986

KENYON, FREDERIC G., and H. IDRIS BELL. Greek Papyri in the British Museum: Catalogue Vol. III. London: Frowde, 1907

KER, WALTER C. A. Martial. Epigrams. 2 vols. LCL. London: Heinemann, 1919

KERKESLAGER, ALLEN. Maintaining Jewish Identity in the Greek Gymnasium: A 'Jewish Load' in CPJ 3.519 (= P. Schub. 37 = P. Berol. 13406. JSJ 28 (2011): 12–33

KIENAST, DIETMAR. Augustus. Prinzeps und Monarch. 4. Auflage. Orig. 1982. Repr. Darmstadt: Wissenschaftliche Buchgesellschaft, 2009

KING, LEONARD WILLIAM, and REGINALD CAMPBELL THOMPSON. The Sculptures and Inscription of Darius the Great, on the Rock of Behistûn in Persia. A new collation of the Persian, Susian, and Babylonian Texts, with English Translations. London: Harrison, 1907

KINZIG, WOLFRAM. Justin Martyr. RPP 7 (2010): 127–128

KIPPENBERG, HANS GERHARD. Garizim und Synagoge. Traditionsgeschichtiche Untersuchungen zur samaritanischen Religion der aramäischen Periode. RVV 30. Berlin: De Gruyter, 1971

KIRBY, JOHN. The Rhetoric of Cicero's Pro Cluentio. Amsterdam: Gieben, 1990

KIRNER, GUIDO O. Strafgewalt und Provinzialherrschaft. Eine Untersuchung zur Strafgewaltspraxis der römischen Statthalter in Judäa (6–66 n.Chr.). Schriften zur Rechtsgeschichte 109. Berlin: Duncker & Humblot, 2004

KITCHEN, KENNETH A. Ramesside Inscriptions Translated and Annotated. Series A: Translations. 8 vols. Oxford: Blackwell, 2000–2014

KLAERR, ROBERT, and YVONNE VERNIÈRE. Plutarque: Œuvres morales. Vol. II/2Paris: Les Belles Lettres, 1974

KLAUSNER, JOSEPH. Jesus of Nazareth: His Life, Times, and Teaching. London: Allen & Unwin, 1925

–. Jesus von Nazareth. Seine Zeit, sein Leben und seine Lehre. 3., erweiterte Auflage. Orig. 1907, 1922. Repr. Jerusalem: Jewish Publishing House, 1952

KLEIN, MICHAEL L. The Fragment-Targums of the Pentateuch According to their Extant Sources. 2 vols. AnBib 76. Rom: Biblical Institute Press, 1980

KOCH, KLAUS. כּוּן. TDOT 7:89–101

KOESTERMANN, ERICH. Cornelius Tacitus. Annalen. Erläutert und mit einer Einleitung versehen. 4 vols. Wissenschaftliche Kommentare zu griechischen und lateinischen Schriftstellern. Heidelberg: Winter, 1963–1968

–. Ein folgenschwerer Irrtum des Tacitus (Ann. 15,44, 2ff)? Historia 16 (1967): 456–469

–. Die Majestätsprozesse unter Tiberius. Historia 4 (1955): 72–106

KOESTERMANN, ERICH, STEPHANUS BORZSÁK, and KENNETH WELLESLEY. P. Cornelii Taciti libri qui supersunt. 2 vols. Bibliotheca Scriptorum Graecorum et Romanorum Teubneriana. Leipzig: Teubner, 1965–1962

KOETSCHAU, PAUL. Contra Celsum. Die griechischen christlichen Schriftsteller der ersten drei Jahrhunderte. Origenes Werke I–II. Leipzig: Hinrichs, 1899

KOKKINOS, NIKOS. The Herodian Dynasty: Origins, Role in Society and Eclipse. JSPSup 26. Sheffield: Sheffield Academic Press, 1997

KOLB, ANNE. Angaria. BNP 1 (2002): 693

–. Transport und Nachrichtentransfer im Römischen Reich. Klio Beihefte NF 2. Berlin: Akademie Verlag, 2000

KÖNIGSBERGER, B. Miscellen aus der juedischen Alterthumskunde. Das Juedische Literaturblatt 20 (1891): 40

KOOIJ, ARIE VAN DER. Isaiah in the Septuagint. Pages 513–529 in Writing and Reading the Scroll of Isaiah: Studies of an Interpretive Tradition. 2 vols. VTSup 70. Leiden: Brill, 1997

KÖSTENBERGER, ANDREAS. John. BECNT. Grand Rapids: Baker, 2004

KRAELING, CARL HERMANN. The Episode of the Roman Shields at Jerusalem. HTR 35 (1942): 263–289

KRAUS, WOLFGANG, and MARTIN KARRER, eds. Septuaginta Deutsch. Das griechische Alte Testament in deutscher Übersetzung. Stuttgart: Deutsche Bibelgesellschaft, 2009

KRAUSS, FRIEDRICH S. Artemidor von Daldis. Traumbuch. Bearbeitet und ergänzt von Martin Kaiser. Basel / Stuttgart: Schwabe, 1965

KRAUSS, SAMUEL. Griechische und lateinische Lehnwörter im Talmud, Midrasch und Targum. Berlin: Calvary, 1898–1899

—. The Jewish-Christian Controvery from the Earliest Times to 1789. Volume I: History. Edited by W. Horbury. TSAJ 56. Tübingen: Mohr Siebeck, 1996

—. The Mishnah Treatise Sanhedrin. Edited with an Introduction, Notes and Glossary. Semitic Study Series 11. Leiden: Brill, 1909

—. Sanhedrin/Makkot. Die Mischna IV/4–5. Gießen: Töpelmann, 1933

KRAUTER, STEFAN. Bürgerrecht und Kultteilnahme. Politische und kultische Rechte und Pflichten in griechischen Poleis, Rom und antikem Judentum. BZNW 127. Berlin: De Gruyter, 2004

KREINECKER, CHRISTINA M. How Power and Province Communicate: Some Remarks on the Language of the (Non-)Conversation between Pilate and Jesus. Pages 169–185 in Light from the East: Papyrologische Kommentare zum Neuen Testament. Edited by P. Arzt-Grabner and C. M. Kreinecker. Philippika 39. Wiesbaden: Harrassowitz, 2010

—. 2. Thessaloniker. Papyrologische Kommentare zum Neuen Testament 3. Göttingen: Vandenhoeck & Ruprecht, 2010

KRIEGER, KLAUS-STEFAN. Geschichtsschreibung als Apologetik bei Flavius Josephus. TANZ 9. Tübingen/Basel: Francke, 1994

—. Pontius Pilatus - ein Judenfeind? Zur Problematik einer Pilatusbiographie. BNot 78 (1995): 63–83

—. A Synoptic Approach to B 2:117–283 and A 18–20. Pages 90–100 in Internationales Josephus-Kolloquium Paris 2001: Studies on the Antiquities of Josephus. Institutum Judaicum Delizschianum. Edited by J. Kalms and F. Siegert. Münsteraner Judaistische Studien 12. Münster: Lit, 2002

KRIMPHOVE, DIETER. "Wir haben ein Gesetz ...!" Rechtliche Anmerkungen zum Strafverfahren gegen Jesus. 2. völlig bearbeitete Auflage. Orig. 1997. Repr. Ius Vivens B: Rechtsgeschichtliche Abhandlungen 5. Münster / Berlin: LIT, 2006

KROLL, WILHELM, and FRANZ SKUTSCH. Iulii Firmici Materni Matheseos libri VIII. 2 vols. Bibliotheca Scriptorum Graecorum et Romanorum Teubneriana. Leipzig: Teubner, 1897–1913

KRÜGER, PAUL, and THEODOR MOMMSEN. Corpus iuris civilis. Editio stereotypa quinta. 3 vols. Berlin: Weidmann, 1889

—. Digesta Iustiniani Augusti. 2 vols. Berlin: Weidmann, 1870

KÜBLER, BERNHARD. Maiestas. RE XIV/1 (1928): 542–559

KUHN, HEINZ-WOLFGANG. Die Bedeutung der Qumrantexte für das Verständnis des Galaterbriefes aus dem Münchener Projekt: Qumran und das Neue Testament. Pages 169–221 in New Qumran Texts and Studies. Proceedings of the First Meeting of the International Organization for Qumran Studies, Paris 1992. Edited by G. J. Brooke, F. García Martínez. STDJ 15. Leiden: Brill, 1994

—. Der Gekreuzigte von Giv'at ha-Mivtar: Bilanz einer Entdeckung, in: Theologia Crucis – Signum Crucis. FS E. Dinkler. Edited by C. Andresen and G. Klein. Tübingen: Mohr Siebeck, 1979, 303–334

—. Die Kreuzesstrafe während der frühen Kaiserzeit. Ihre Wirklichkeit und Wertung in der Umwelt des Urchristentums. ANRW II/25.1 (1982): 648–793

—. σταυρός, σταυρόω. EDNT 3 (1993): 267–272

KUHN, KARL GEORG. Sifre zu Numeri. Rabbinische Texte II/3. Stuttgart: Kohlhammer, 1959

KÜMMEL, WERNER GEORG. Verheißung und Erfüllung. Untersuchungen zur eschatologischen Verkündigung Jesu. 2., völlig neu bearbeitete Auflage. AThANT 6. Zürich: Zwingli, 1953

KUNKEL, WOLFGANG. Prinzipien des römischen Strafverfahrens [1968]. Pages 11–31 in Kleine Schriften zum römischen Strafverfahren und zur römischen Verfassungsgeschichte. Weimar: Hermann Böhlaus Nachfolger, 1974

–. Quaestio [1963]. Pages 33–110 in Kleine Schriften zum römischen Strafverfahren und zur römischen Verfassungsgeschichte. Weimar: Hermann Böhlaus Nachfolger, 1974

KUNKEL, WOLFGANG, and ROLAND WITTMANN. Staatsordnung und Staatspraxis der römischen Republik. Zweiter Abschnitt: Die Magistratur. HdA X/3.2.2. München: Beck, 1995

KURTZ, DONNA C., and JOHN BOARDMAN. Greek Burial Customs. Ithaca: Cornell University Press, 1971

KYLE, DONALD G. Spectacles of Death in Ancient Rome. London/New York: Routledge, 1998

LABBÉ, GILBERT. Ponce Pilate et la munificence de Tibère: l'inscription de Césarée. REA 93 (1991): 277–297

LACY, PHILLIP H. DE, and BENEDICT EINARSON. Plutarch. Moralia VII. LCL. Cambridge: Harvard University Press, 1959

LAMBERS-PETRY, DORIS. How to Become a Christian Martyr: Reflections on the Death of James as Described by Josephus and in Early Christian Literature. Pages 101–24 in Internationales Josephus-Kolloquium Paris 2001: Studies on the Antiquities of Josephus. Edited by F. Siegert, J. U. Kalm. Münsteraner Judaistische Studien 12. Münster: Lit, 2002

LAMBERT, ANDRÉ. Sueton: Caesarenleben. 7. Auflage im Rahmenteil bearbeitet von R. Häußler. Orig. 1955. Repr. Stuttgart: Kröner, 1986

LAMPE, GEOFFREY W. H. A Patristic Greek Lexicon. Oxford: Clarendon, 1961–1968

LAMPE, PETER. From Paul to Valentinus: Christians at Rome in the First Two Centuries. Minneapolis: Fortress, 2003

LATTE, KURT. Römische Religionsgeschichte. Orig. 1967. Repr. HdA V.4. München: Beck, 1992

LAUTERBACH, JACOB Z. Jesus in the Talmud. Pages 473–570 in Rabbinic Essays. New York: Ktav, 1973

–. Mekilta de-Rabbi Ishmael: A Critical Edition on the Basis of Manuscripts and Early Editions with an English Translation, Introduction and Notes. 3 vols. Library of Jewish Classics. Philadelphia: Jewish Publication Society, 1933–1935

LEBEC, A. Physiological Study of the Passion of Our Lord Jesus Christ. Catholic Medical Guardian 3 (1925): 126–132

LEE, BERNON P. Leviticus 24:15b–16: A Crux Revisited. BBR 16 (2006): 345–49

LEFÈVRE, ECKHARD. Plautus. BNP 11 (2007): 361–366

LÉGASSE, SIMON. Le Procès de Jésus. I L'histoire. II La passion dans les quatre évangiles. LD 156. Paris: Cerf, 1994/1995

LEGRAND, PHILIPPE-ERNEST. Hérodote: Histoires. 11 vols. Collection des universités de France. Paris: Belles Lettres, 1932–1954

LEHMANN, CLAYTON M., and KENNETH G. HOLUM. The Greek and Latin Inscriptions of Casearea Maritima. Joint Expedition to Caesarea Maritima: Excavation Reports 5. Boston: American Schools of Oriental Research, 2000

LEHNARDT, ANDREAS. Ta'aniyot. Fasten. Übersetzung des Talmud Yerushalmi II/9. Tübingen: Mohr Siebeck, 2008

LEICHTY, ERLE, ed. The Royal Inscriptions of Esarhaddon, King of Assyria (680–669 BC). The Royal Inscriptions of the Neo-Assyrian Period 4. Winona Lake, Ind.: Eisenbrauns, 2011

LÉMONON, JEAN-PIERRE. Pilate et le gouvernement de la Judée. Textes et monuments. EBib. Paris: Gabalda, 1981

–. Ponce Pilate: documents profanes, Nouveau Testament et traditions ecclésiales. ANRW II.26/1 (1992): 741–778

–. Ponce Pilate. Ivry-sur-Seine: Atelier, 2007

LENFANT, DOMINIQUE. Ctésias de Cnide. La Perse, l'Inde, autres fragments. Collection des universités de France 435. Paris: Belles lettres, 2004

LENGER, MARIE-THÉRÈSE. Corpus des Ordonnances des Ptolémées. Second Edition. Orig. 1964. Repr. Mémoires 64.2. Bruxelles: Palais des Académies, 1980

LENGLE, JOSEF. Zum Prozess Jesu. Hermes 790 (1935): 312–321

LENTZ, AUGUST. Herodian De Prosodia Catholica. Grammatici Graeci III.1. Leipzig: Teubner, 1867

–. Herodian Περὶ Κλίσεως Ὀνομάτων. Grammatici Graeci III.2. Leipzig: Teubner, 1870

LEO, FRIEDRICH. T. Macci Plauti Comoediae. 2 vols. Orig. 1895–1896. Repr. Berlin: Weidmann, 1958

LEONHARDT, JÜRGEN. Cicero II. Cicero as Orator and Writer. BNP 3 (2003): 321–327

LEVEAU, PHILIPPE. Aqueduct Building: Financing and Costs. Pages 85–101 in Frontinus' Legacy: Essays on Frontinus' De Aquis Urbis Romae. Edited by D. R. Blackman and A. T. Hodge. Ann Arabor: University of Michigan Press, 2001

LEVICK, BARBARA. Claudius. New Haven: Yale University Press, 1990

–. Tiberius the Politician. Second Edition. Orig. 1976. Repr. New York: Routledge, 1999

LEVINE, ÉTAN. The Aramaic Version of Ruth. AnBib 58. Rome: Biblical Institute Press, 1973

LEVINE, LEE I. Jerusalem: Portrait of the City in the Second Temple Period (538 B.C.E. – 70 C.E.). Philadelphia: The Jewish Publication Society, 2002

LEVY, ERNST. Pauli Sententiae: A Palingenesia of the Opening Titles as a Specimen of Research in West Roman Vulgar Law. Ithaca: Cornell University Press, 1945; repr. New York: Kelley, 1969

LEWIS, C. T., and C. SHORT. A Latin Dictionary. Oxford, 1955

LEWIS, NAPHTALI. The Compulsory Public Services of Roman Egypt. Orig. 1982. Repr. Papyrologica Florentina 28. Florence: Gonnelli, 1997

–. Emperor or Prefect? Pages 760–65 in Le monde grec. Pensée littérature histoire documents, vol. Brussels. FS C. Préaux. Edited by J. Bingen, G. Cambier, G. Nachtergael. Travaux de la Faculté de Philosophie et Lettres de l' Université Libre de Bruxelles 62. Éditions de l'Université de Bruxelles, 1975

–. Un nouveau texte sur la juridiction du préfet d'Égypte (P. Yale inv. 1606 = SB XII 10929). RHDFE 50 (1972): 5–12

–. On Government and Law in Roman Egypt: Collected Papers. ASP 33. Atlanta: Scholars Press, 1995

–. The Process of Promulgation in Rome's Eastern Provinces. Pages 127–139 in Studies in Roman Law in Memory of A. Arthur Schiller. Edited by R. S. Bagnall and W. V. Harris. Columbia Studies in the Classical Tradition 13. Leiden: Brill, 1986

LEWIS, NAPHTALI, and MEYER REINHOLD, eds. Roman Civilization. Selected Readings. 2 vols. Third ed. New York: Columbia University Press, 1990

LICHTENSTEIN, HANS. Die Fastenrolle. Eine Untersuchung zur jüdisch-hellenistischen Geschichte. HUCA 8–9 (1931–32): 257–351

LIETZMANN, HANS. Der Prozess Jesu. Pages 313–322 in Sitzungsberichte der preussischen Akademie der Wissenschaften Nr. XIV. Berlin: Verlag der Akademie der Wissenschaften in Kommission bei Walter de Gruyter, 1931

–. Der Prozess Jesu. Pages 251–263 in Kleine Schriften II. Texte und Untersuchungen 68. Berlin: Akademie-Verlag, 1958

LIGHTFOOT, ROBERT H. History and Interpretation in the Gospels. The Bampton Lectures. London: Hodder & Stoughton, 1935

LINDSAY, WALLACE M. T. Macci Plauti Comoediae. 2 vols. Orig. 1903. Repr. Oxford Classical Texts. Oxford: Clarendon, 1910

LINDSAY, WILLIAM M. Nonius Marcellus. De Conpendiosa Doctrina. 3 vols. Orig. 1903. Repr. Bibliotheca Teubneriana. München / Leipzig: Saur, 2003

LINDSKOG, CLAES, and KONRAT ZIEGLER. Plutarchi Vitae parallelae. 4 vols. Bibliotheca Scriptorum Graecorum et Romanorum Teubneriana. Leipzig: Teubner, 1957–1980

LINTOTT, ANDREW W. Equites Romani. BNP 5 (2004): 1–4

LIPIŃSKI, EDOUARD. רָכִיל. TDOT 13:498–99

LIPOSVKY, JAMES. A Historiographical Study of Livy Books VI–X. Monographs in Classical Studies. Salem: Ayer, 1984

LIPSIUS, JUSTUS. De cruce libri tres ad sacram profanamque historiam utiles. Editio ultima. Orig. 1594. Repr. Paris: Beys, 1598

LLEWELLYN-JONES, LLOYD, and JAMES ROBSON. Ctesias' History of Persia: Tales of the Orient. Routledge Classical Translations. London / New York: Routledge, 2010

LLEWELYN, STEPHEN R., and DIONYSIA VAN BEEK. Reading the Temple Warning as a Greek Visitor. *JSJ* 42 (2011) 1–22

LOEWY, J. Die drei Jacobus. Das Juedische Literaturblatt 7/4 (1878): 15

LOHFINK, NORBERT. חרם. TDOT 5 (1986):180–199

LOHSE, EDUARD. Märtyrer und Gottesknecht. Untersuchungen zur urchristlichen Verkündigung vom Sühntod Jesu Christi. 2.durchgesehene und erweiterte Auflage. Orig. 1955. Repr. FRLANT 64. Göttingen: Vandenhoeck & Ruprecht, 1963

–. Der Prozeß Jesu Christi [1961]. Pages 88–103 in Die Einheit des Neuen Testaments. Exegetische Studien zur Theologie des Neuen Testaments. Göttingen: Vandenhoeck & Ruprecht, 1973

LÖNNQVIST, KENNETH A. Pontius Pilate – Aqueduct Builder? Recent Findings and New Suggestions. Klio 82 (2000): 459–475

LORTON, DAVID. The Treatment of Criminals in Ancient Egypt: Through the New Kingdom. Journal of the Economic and Social History of the Orient 20 (1977): 2–64

LÖWE, GUSTAV, GEORG GÖTZ, and FRIEDRICH SCHÖLL. T. Macci Plauti Comoediae. Recensuit, Instrumento Critico et Prolegomenis. Tom. IV. Casina, Miles gloriosus, Persa, Mostellaria, Cistellaria, Fragmenta. Bibliotheca Scriptorum Graecorum et Romanorum Teubneriana. Leipzig: Teubner, 1890

LUCKENBILL, DANIEL DAVID. Ancient Records of Assyria and Babylonia. 2 vols. Chicago: University of Chicago Press, 1926–1927

–. The Annals of Sennacherib. Oriental Institute Publications 2. Chicago: University of Chicago Press, 1924

LUNDBOM, JACK R. Deuteronomy: A Commentary. Grand Rapids: Eerdmans, 2013

LUZ, ULRICH. Das Evangelium nach Matthäus. EKK I/1–4. Zürich / Neukirchen-Vluyn: Benziger / Neukirchener, 1985–2001

MACH, MICHAEL. Demons. EDSS (2000), 199–192

MACLEOD, MATTHEW D. Luciani Opera. 4 vols. Scriptorum classicorum bibliotheca Oxoniensis. Oxford: Clarendon, 1972–1987

MAGDELAIN, ANDRÉ. Paricidas. Pages 549–571 in Du châtiment dans la cité. Supplices corporels et peine de mort dans le monde antique. Table ronde organisée par l'École française de Rome avec le concours du Centre national de la recherche scientifique (Rome 9.–11. novembre 1982). Collection de l'École Française de Rome 79. Rome: École française de Rome, 1984

MAGIE, DAVID. The Scriptores Historiae Augustae. 3 vols. LCL. Cambridge: Harvard University Press, 1922–1932

MAGNESS, JODI. Stone and Dung, Oil and Spit: Jewish Daily Life in the Time of Jesus. Grand Rapids: Eerdmans, 2011

MAHIEU, BIEKE. Between Rome and Jerusalem: Herod the Great and His Sons in Their Struggle for Recognition. A Chronological Investigation of the Period 40 BC–39 AD with a Time Setting of New Testament Events. Orientalia Lovaniensia Analecta 208. Leuven: Peeters, 2012

MAIER, JOHANN. Jesus von Nazareth in der talmudischen Überlieferung. EdF 82. Darmstadt: Wissenschaftliche Buchgesellschaft, 1978

–. Die Qumran-Essener: Die Texte vom Toten Meer. 3 vols. UTB. Reinhardt: München/Basel, 1995–1996

–. Die Tempelrolle vom Toten Meer und das "Neue Jerusalem". 3., völlig neu bearbeitete und erweiterte Auflage. UTB 829. München: Reinhardt, 1997

MAIER, PAUL L. The Episode of the Golden Shields at Jerusalem. HTR 27 (1969): 109–121

–. The Inscription on the Cross of Jesus of Nazareth. Hermes 124 (1996): 58–75

–. Pontius Pilate: A Novel. Grand Rapids: Kregel, 1968

MANDELBAUM, BERNARD. Pesikta de Rav Kahana: According to an Oxford Manuscript with Variants from all Known Manuscripts and Genizoth Fragments and Parallel Passages with Commentary and Introduction. Second Edition. 2 vols. New York: Jewish Theological Seminary of America, 1987

MANNING, JOSEPH G. The Last Pharaohs: Egypt Under the Ptolemies, 305–30 BC. Princeton: Princeton University Press, 2010

MANTEL, HUGO D. Fastenrolle. TRE 11 (1983): 59–61

MARCHANT, EDGAR C. Xenophontis Opera omnia. 5 vols. Scriptorum classicorum bibliotheca Oxoniensis. Oxford: Clarendon, 1900–1920

MARCOVICH, MIROSLAV. Iustini Martyris Dialogus cum Tryphone. Patristische Texte und Studien 47. Berlin: De Gruyter, 1997

–. Origenes. Contra Celsum libri VIII. VCSup 54. Leiden: Brill, 2001

MARCUS, DAVID. 'Lifting up the Head': On the Trail of a Word Play in Genesis 40. Prooftexts 10 (1990): 17–27

MARCUS, JOEL. Mark. AYB 27. New York: Doubleday / Yale University Press, 2000–2009

MARK, GÜNTER. Jesus 'Was Close to the Authorities': The Historical Background of a Talmudic Pericope. JTS 60 (2009): 437–466

MARTIN, RONALD H. Structure and Interprtation in the 'Annals' of Tacitus. ANRW II.33.2 (1990): 1550–1581

MASLEN, MATTHEW W., and PIERS D. MITCHELL. Medical Theories on the Cause of Death in Crucifixion. Journal of the Royal Society of Medicine 99 (2006): 185–188

MASLOWSI, TADEUSZ. M. Tullius Cicero Scripta quae manserunt omnia. Fasc. 24: Oratio de provinciis consularibus. Oratio pro L. Cornelio Balbo. Bibliotheca Scriptorum Graecorum et Romanorum Teubneriana. Berlin: De Gruyter, 2007

MASON, STEVE. Contradiction or Counterpoint? Josephus and Historical Method [2003]. Pages 103–137 in Josephus, Judea, and Christian Origins: Methods and Categories. Peabody: Hendrickson, 2009

–. Contradiction or Counterpoint? Josephus and Historical Method. RRJ 6 (2003): 145–188

–. Flavius Josephus on the Pharisees: A Composition-Critical Study. SPB 39. Leiden: Brill, 1991

–. Josephus and the New Testament, the New Testament and Josephus: An Overview. Pages 15–48 in Josephus und das Neue Testament. Wechselseitige Wahrnehmungen. Edited by C. Böttrich and J. Herzer. WUNT 209. Tübingen: Mohr Siebeck, 2007

–. Josephus and the New Testament. Second ed. Peabody: Hendrickson, 2003

–. Josephus as Authority for First-Century Judea. Pages 7–43 in Josephus, Judea, and Christian Origins: Methods and Categories. Peabody: Hendrickson, 2009

–. Judean War 2. Flavius Josephus: Translation and Commentary 1B. Leiden: Brill, 2008

MAURENBRECHER, BERTOLD. C. Sallusti Crispi Historiarum reliquiae. 2 vols. Leipzig: Teubner, 1891–1893

MAYR, ROBERT VON. Der Prozeß Jesu. Archiv für Kriminal-Anthropologie und Kriminalistik 20 (1905): 269–305

MAZAR, AMIHAI. A Survey of the Aqueducts to Jerusalem. Pages 211–244 in The Aqueducts of Israel. Edited by D. Amit, J. Patrich, and Y. Hirschfeld. JRASup 46. Portsmouth, RI:

Journal of Roman Archaeology, 2002

–. Die Untersuchungen über die Wasserleitungen nach Jerusalem. Pages 165–194 in Wasser im Heiligen Land. Biblische Zeugnisse und archäologische Forschungen. Edited by W. Dierx and G. Garbrecht. Mainz: Zabern, 2001

MCGING, BRIAN C. Pontius Pilate and the Sources. CBQ 53 (1991): 416–438

MCLAREN, JAMES S. Power and Politics in Palestine: The Jews and the Governing of their Land, 100 BC – AD 70. JSNTSup 63. Sheffield: JSOT Press, 1991

MEEK, THEOPHILE J. The Code of Hammurabi. Pages 163–180 in Ancient Near Eastern Texts Relating to the Old Testament, Second ed. Edited by J. B. Pritchard. Princeton: Princeton University Press, 1969

–. The Middle Assyrian Laws. Pages 180–188 in Ancient Near Eastern Texts Relating to the Old Testament, Second Edition. Edited by J. B. Pritchard. Princeton: Princeton University Press, 1969

MEIER, JOHN P. Jesus in Josephus: A Modest Proposal. CBQ 52 (1990): 76–103

–. A Marginal Jew: Rethinking the Historical Jesus. New York: Doubleday, 1991–2009

MEIER, MISCHA. Petronius [7] M. P. Mamertinus. BNP 10 (2007): 880

MEISTER, KLAUS. Adranodorus. BNP 1 (2002): 153

–. Hieronymus [3] H. of Syracus. BNP 6 (2005): 315

MELO, WOLFGANG DE. Plautus. The Merchant. The Braggart Soldier. The Ghost. The Persian. LCL. Cambridge: Harvard University Press, 2011

MENDELSON, ALAN. Philo's Jewish Identity. BJS 161. Atlanta: Scholars Press, 1988

MENDELSSOHN, LUDWIG. Appiani Historia Romana. Editio altera correctior. Leipzig: Teubner, 1905

MERKEL, JOHANNES. Die Begnadigung am Passahfeste. ZNW 6 (1905): 293–316

MERRILL, ELMER T. C. Plini Caecili Secundi Epistularum Libri Decem. Leipzig: Teubner, 1922

MERRITT, ROBERT L. Jesus Barabbas and the Paschal Pardon. JBL 104 (1985): 57–68

MESHORER, YA'AKOV. A Treasury of Jewish Coins: From the Persian Period to Bar Kokhba. Jerusalem/Nyack: Yad ben-Zvi Press/Amphora, 2001

–. Ancient Jewish Coinage. 2 vols. New York: Amphora, 1982

METZNER, RAINER. Kaiphas: der Hohepriester jenes Jahres: Geschichte und Deutung. Ancient Judaism and Early Christianity 75. Leiden: Brill, 2010

–. Die Prominenten im Neuen Testament. Ein prosopographischer Kommentar. NTOA 66. Göttingen: Vandenhoeck & Ruprecht, 2008

MEYER, EDUARD. Ursprung und Anfänge des Christentums. 3 vols. Orig. 1921–1923. Repr. Darmstadt: Wissenschaftliche Buchgesellschaft, 1962

MEYERS, ERIC M., and MARK A. CHANCEY. Alexander to Constantine: Archaeology of the Land of the Bible. Anchor Bible Reference Library. New Haven: Yale University Press, 2014

MEYER-ZWIFFELHOFFER, ECKHARD. Πολιτικῶς ἄρχειν. Zum Regierungsstil der senatori-schen Statthalter in den kaiserzeitlichen griechischen Provinzen. Historia Einzelschriften 165. Stuttgart: Steiner, 2002

MICHEL, OTTO, and OTTO BAUERNFEIND. Flavius Josephus, De Bello Judaico. Der jüdische Krieg. Griechisch und Deutsch. 3 vols. Darmstadt: Wissenschaftliche Buchgesellschaft, 1959–1969

MIGNE, JACQUES-PAUL. Patrologia Graeca. 161 vols. Paris: Imprimerie Catholique, 1857–1866

MILLAR, FERGUS. The Background of the Maccabean Revolution: Reflections on Martin Hengel's Judaism and Hellenism. JJS 29 (1978): 1–21

–. The Roman Near East, 31 BC – AD 337. Cambridge: Harvard University Press, 1993

–. State and Subject: The Impact of Monarch [1984]. Pages 292–313 in Rome, the Greek World, and the East. Vol. 1: The Roman Republic and the Augustan Revolution. Edited by

G. M. Rogers H. M. Cotton. Chapel Hill: University of North Carolina Press, 2002

MILLARD, ALAN R. Latin in First-Century Palestine. Pages 451–58 in Solving Riddles and Untying Knots: Biblical, Epigraphic and Semitic Studies. FS J. C. Greenfield. Edited by Z. Zevit, S. Gitin, and M. Sokoloff. Winona Lake: Eisenbrauns, 1995

MILLER, JOHN B. F. Convinced that God had Called Us: Dreams, Visions, and the Perception of God's Will in Luke-Acts. Biblical Interpretation 85. Leiden/Boston: Brill, 2007

MILLER, NORMA P. Tacitus. Annals Book 1. Methuen's Classical Texts. London: Methuen, 1959

MILNE, HERBERT J. M. Greek Shorthand Manuals: Syllabary and Commentary. Egypt Exploration Society. Graeco-Roman Memoirs 24. London: Egypt Exploration Society, 1934

MITCHELL, STEPHEN. Requisitioned Transport in the Roman Empire: A New Inscription from Pisidia. JRS 66 (1976): 106–131

–. The Requisitioning Edict of Sex. Sotidius Strabo Libuscidianus. ZPE 45 (1982): 99–100

MITCHELL, STEPHEN, DAVID FRENCH, and JEAN GREENHAIGH. Regional Epigraphic Catalogues of Asia Minor II: The Ankara District. The Inscriptions of North Galatia. British Archaeological Reports International Series 135. Oxford: British Institute of Archaeology, 1982

MITTEIS, LUDWIG. Ägyptischer Schuldprozeß v. J. 84/86 p. Chr. Zeitschrift der Savigny-Stiftung für Rechtsgeschichte. Romanistische Abteilung 27 (1906): 220–227

–. Miszellen: Neue Urkunden I. Zeitschrift der Savigny-Stiftung für Rechtsgeschichte. Romanistische Abteilung 26 (1905): 484–87

–. Reichsrecht und Volksrecht in den östlichen Provinzen des Römischen Kaiserreichs. Orig. 1891. Repr. Leipzig: Teubner, 1935

MITTEIS, LUDWIG, ULRICH WILCKEN. Grundzüge und Chrestomathie der Papyruskunde. Berlin: Teubner, 1912

MODRZEJEWSKI, JOSEPH. Droit impérial et traditions locales dans l'Égypte romaine. Aldershot: Brookfield, 1990

MOEHRING, HORST R. Novelistic Elements in the Writings of Flavius Josephus. Chicago: University of Chicago, 1957

MOLINIÉ, GEORGES. Chariton. Le romain de Chairéas et Callirhoé. Orig. 1979. Repr. Collection Budé. Paris: Les Belles Lettres, 1989

MØLLER-CHRISTENSEN, VILHELM. Skeletal Remains from Giv'at ha-Mivtar. IEJ 26 (1976): 35–38

MOMMSEN, THEODOR. Gesammelte Schriften. 8 vols. Berlin: Weidmann, 1905–1913

–. Iustiniani Digesta. Corpus Iuris Civilis. Editio stereotypa quinta. Volumen Primum: Institutiones, Recognovit P. Krueger. Digesta, Recognovit T. Mommsen. Berlin: Weidmann, 1889

–. Römisches Staatsrecht. 3 vols. Dritte Auflage. Orig. 1871–1888. Repr. HdA III.1. Leipzig: Hirzel, 1887–1888

–. Römisches Strafrecht. Orig. 1899. Repr. Darmstadt: Wissenschaftliche Buchgesellschaft, 1961

MONTEVECCHI, ORSOLINA, and MARIADELE MANCA MASCIADRI. Corpus Papyrorum Graecarum I: I Contratti di baliatico. Milan: Tibiletti, 1984

MOORE, CLIFFORD H., and JOHN JACKSON. Tacitus. The Histories. The Annals. 4 vols. LCL. Cambridge: Harvard University Press, 1931–1937

MØRKHOLM, OTTO. Antiochus IV of Syria. Classica et mediaevalia – Dissertationes 8. Copenhagen: Gyldendalske, 1966

MOSSHAMMER, ALDEN A. Georgii Syncelli Ecloga chronographica. Bibliotheca Scriptorum Graecorum et Romanorum Teubneriana. Leipzig: Teubner, 1984

MÜLLER, CARL F. W. M. Tullii Ciceronis scripta quae manserunt omnia. 10 vols. Bibliotheca Scriptorum Graecorum et Romanorum Teubneriana. Leipzig: Teubner, 1885–1891

MÜLLER, CHRISTIAN. Larcius [I 2] L. (Flavius?), Sp. BNP 7 (2005): 245

–. Papirius [I 15] P. Cursor, L. BNP 10 (2007): 487–488
–. Pontius [I 1] Pontius, Gavius. BNP 11 (2007): 596
MÜLLER, GUSTAV ADOLF. Pontius Pilatus, der fünfte Prokurator von Judäa und Richter Jesu von Nazareth. Stuttgart: Metzler, 1888
MÜLLER, KARLHEINZ. Möglichkeit und Vollzug jüdischer Kapitalgerichtsbarkeit im Prozeß gegen Jesus von Nazareth. Pages 41–83 in Der Prozeß gegen Jesus. Historische Rückfrage und theologische Deutung. Edited by K. Kertelge. Quaestiones Disputatae 112. Freiburg: Herder, 1988
MÜLLER, KARL, ed. Oratores Attici: Fragmenta Oratorum Atticorum. Paris: Didot, 1888
MUSURILLO, HERBERT, The Acts of the Christian Martyrs. Oxford: Clarendon, 1972
–. The Acts of the Pagan Martyrs I: Acta Alexandrinorum. Orig. 1954. Repr. Oxford: Clarendon, 2000
MYERS, JACOB M. Ezra, Nehemiah. AB 14. New York: Doubleday, 1965
MYNORS, ROGER A. B. C. Plinius Caecilius Secundus: Epistularum libri decem. Scriptorum Classicorum Bibliotheca Oxoniensis. Oxford: Oxford University Press, 1963
NABER, SAMUEL ADRIANUS. Flavii Iosephi Opera Omnia. 6 vols. Bibliotheca Scriptorum Graecorum et Romanorum Teubneriana. Leipzig: Teubner, 1888–1896
NAVEH, JOSEPH. The Ossuary Inscriptions from Giv'at ha-Mivtar. IEJ 20 (1970): 33–37
NAVEH, JOSEPH, and SHAUL SHAKED. Magic Spells and Formulae: Aramaic Incantations of Late Antiquity. Jerusalem: Magnes, 1993
NEALE, DAVID A. Was Jesus a *Mesith*? Public Response to Jesus and his Ministry. TynBul 44 (1993): 89–101
NELSON, W. DAVID. Mekhilta de-Rabbi Shimon bar Yohai. Philadelphia: Jewish Publication Society, 2006
NETZER, EHUD. The Architecture of Herod, the Great Builder. Grand Rapids: Baker, 2008
–. The Architecture of Herod, the Great Builder. Grand Rapids: Baker, 2008
NEUSNER, JACOB. Eliezer ben Hyrcanus: The Traditions and the Man. 2 vols. Leiden: Brill, 1973
–. A History of the Jews in Babylonia. 5 vols. SPB. Leiden: Brill, 1965–1970
–. A History of the Mishnaic Law of Damages. 5 vols. SJLA 35. Leiden: Brill, 1982–1985
–. The Rabbinic Traditions about the Pharisees before 70. 3 vols. Leiden: Brill, 1971
–. Sifre to Deuteronomy: An Analytical Translation. 2 vols. BJS 98.101. Atlanta: Scholars Press, 1987
–. Sifré to Numbers: An American Translation and Expansion. 2 vols. BJS 118/119. Atlanta: Scholars Press, 1986
–. The Talmud of the Land of Israel. 35 vols. Chicago: University of Chicago Press, 1982–1994
–. The Talmud of the Land of Israel. Volume 18: Besah and Taanit. Chicago: University of Chicago Press, 1987
–. The Tosefta. Translated from the Hebrew, with a New Introduction. Orig. 1977–1986. Repr. Peabody: Hendrickson, 2002
NEWMAN, HILLEL. The Death of Jesus in the *Toledot Yeshu* Literature. JTS 50 (1999): 59–79
NICKELSBURG, GEORGE W. E. An Antiochan Date for the Testament of Moses. Pages 33–37 in Studies on the Testament of Moses. Edited by G. W. E. Nickelsburg. SBLSBS 4. Cambridge: Society of Biblical Literature, 1973
NICKLAS, TOBIAS. Die 'Fratze' des Feindes: Zur Zeichnung des 'Nikanor' in 2 Makk 14–15. SJOT 17 (2003): 141–155
NICOLET, CLAUDE, ed. La mémoire perdue. A la recherche des archives oubliées, publiques et privées, de la Rome antique. Série histoire ancienn e et médiévale 30. Paris: Sorbonne, 1994
–. The World of the Citizen in Republican Rome. Berkeley / Los Angeles: University of California Press, 1988

NIEMAND, CHRISTOF. Jesus und sein Weg zum Kreuz. Ein historisch-rekonstruktives und theologisches Modellbild. Stuttgart: Kohlhammer, 2007

NIESE, BENEDIKT. Flavii Josephi Opera. 7 vols. Berlin: Weidmann, 1885–1895

NISBET, ROBERT G. M. M. Tullii Ciceronis in L. Calpurnium Pisonem Oratio. With Text, Introduction, and Commentary. Oxford: Clarendon, 1961

NITZAN, BILHAH. The Laws of Reproof in 4QBerakhot (4Q286–290) in Light of their Parallels in the Damascus Document and Other Texts from Qumran. Pages 149–165 in Legal Texts and Legal Issues. Proceedings of the Second Meeting of the International Organization for Qumran Studies, Cambridge, 1995. FS Joseph M. Baumgarten. Edited by M. J. Bernstein, F. García Martínez, and J. Kampen. STDJ 23. Leiden: Brill, 1997

NIXON, PAUL. Plautus. 5 vols. LCL. Cambridge: Harvard University Press, 1916–1938

NOACK, BENT. Jesus Ananiassøn og Jesus fra Nasaret. En drøftelse af Josefus, Bellum Judaicum VI,5,3. Tekst og Tolkning 6. Copenhagen: Gyldendal, 1975

NODET, ÉTIENNE. Flavius Josèphe. Les Antiquités juives. 4 vols. Paris: Cerf, 1990–2005

–. Jésus et Jean-Baptiste selon Josèphe. RB 92 (1985): 321–348, 497–524

–. Josephus and Discrepant Sources. Pages 259–277 in Flavius Josephus: Interpretation and history. Edited by J. Pastor, P. Stern, and M. Mor. JSJSup 146. Leiden: Brill, 2011

–. Pharisees, Sadducees Essenes, Herodians. Pages 1495–1543 in Handbook for the Study of the Historical Jesus. Vol. 2: The Study of Jesus. Edited by T. Holmén and S. E. Porter. Leiden: Brill, 2011

NOORT, ED. Child Sacrifice in Ancient Israel: The Status Quaestionis. Pages 103–125 in The Strange World of Human Sacrifice 1. Edited by J. N. Bremmer. Studies in the History and Anthropology of Religion. Leuven: Peeters, 2006

NOWACK, WILHELM. Schabbat (Sabbat). Die Mischna II/1. Gießen: Töpelmann, 1924

NÜSSLEIN, THEODOR. M. Tullius Cicero. De inventione. Über die Auffindung des Stoffes. De optimo genere oratorum. Über die beste Gattung von Rednern. Lateinisch und deutsch. Sammlung Tusculum. Düsseldorf / Zürich: Artemis & Winkler, 1998

O'COLLINS, GERALD G. Crucifixion. ABD 1 (1992): 1207–1210

OAKLEY, STEPHEN P. A Commentary on Livy, Books VI–X. 3 vols. Oxford: Clarendon, 1997–2005

OEHLER, FRANZ. Qu. Septimii Florentis Tertulliani Apologeticum et Ad nationes libri duo, ex fide optimorum codicum manuscriptorum aut primum aut denuo collatorum cum adnotatione perpetua et indicibus. Halle: Anton, 1849

OGILVIE, ROBERT M. A Commentary on Livy. Books 1–5. Oxford: Clarendon, 1965

OLDFATHER, CHARLES HENRY, CHARLES L. SHERMAN, RUSSEL M. GEER, and FRANCIS R. WALTON. Diodorus of Sicily. 12 vols. LCL. Cambridge: Harvard University Press, 1933–1967

OLDFATHER, WILLIAM ABBOTT. Epictetus: The Discourses as Reported by Arrian, the Manual, and Fragments. 2 vols. LCL. Cambridge: Harvard University Press, 1928

OLIVER, JAMES H. Greek Applications for Roman Trials. AJP 100 (1979): 543–558

OLIVERIO, GASPARE. La stele di Augusto rinvenuta nell Agorà di Cirene. Notiziario Archeologico del Ministero delle Colonie 4 (1927): 15–67

OLSON, KEN A. Eusebius and the Testimonium Flavianum. CBQ 61 (1999): 305–322

OMERZU, HEIKE. Der Prozeß des Paulus. Eine exegetische und rechtshistorische Untersuchung der Apostelgeschichte. BZNW 115. Berlin: De Gruyter, 2002

ORIGENES. Commentarii in epistulam ad Romanos/Römerbriefkommentar. Lateinisch-Deutsch. 5 vols. Edited by Theresia Heither. Fontes Christianae 2/1–6. Freiburg: Herder, 1990–1999

–. Commentary on the Epistle to the Romans. Edited by Thomas P. Scheck. The Fathers of the Church 103–104. Washington, DC: Catholic University of America Press, 2001–2002

OTTO, CARL EDUARD, BRUNO SCHILLING, CARL FRIEDRICH FERDINAND SINTENIS. Das Corpus juris civilis in's Deutsche übersetzt von einem Vereine Rechtsgelehrter. 7 vols. Leipzig: Focke, 1830–1833

OTZEN, BENEDIKT. בְּלִיַּעַל. TDOT 2 (1975): 131–136

PACK, ROGER A. Artemidori Daldiani Onirocriticon Libri V. Bibliotheca Scriptorum Graecorum et Romanorum Teubneriana. Leipzig: Teubner, 1963

PAESLER, KURT. Das Tempelwort Jesu. Die Tradition von Tempelzerstörung und Tempelerneuerung im Neuen Testament. FRLANT 184. Göttingen: Vandenhoeck & Ruprecht, 1999

PAGET, J. CARLETON. Messianism and Resistance amongst Jews and Christians in Egypt [2007]. Pages 103–122 in Jews, Christians and Jewish Christians in Antiquity. WUNT 251. Tübingen: Mohr Siebeck, 2010

–. Some Observations on Josephus and Christianity [2001]. Pages 185–265 in Jews, Christians and Jewish Christians in Antiquity. WUNT 251. Tübingen: Mohr Siebeck, 2010

PALUMBO, ARTHUR E. A New Interpretation of the Nahum Commentary. FO 29 (1992–93): 153–162

PARKIN, TIM G., and ARTHUR J. POMEROY, eds. Roman Social History: A Sourcebook. Routledge Sourcebooks for the Ancient World. London: Routledge, 2007

PARKINSON, RICHARD. The Rosetta Stone. London: British Museum Press, 2005

PARRY, DONALD W. Notes on Divine Name Avoidance in Scriptural Units of the Legal Texts of Qumran. Pages 437–449 in Legal Texts and Legal Issues. Proceedings of the Second Meeting of the International Organization for Qumran Studies, Cambridge, 1995. FS Joseph M. Baumgarten. Edited by M. J. Bernstein, F. García Martínez, and J. Kampen. STDJ 23. Leiden: Brill, 1997

PARVIS, SARA, and PAUL FOSTER, eds. Justin Martyr and His Worlds. Minneapolis: Fortress, 2007

PASTOR, JACK, PNINA STERN, and MENAHEM MOR, eds. Flavius Josephus: Interpretation and History. JSJSup 146. Leiden: Brill, 2011

PATON, WILLIAM R. The Greek Anthology. 5 vols. LCL. Cambridge: Harvard University Press, 1918–1927

–. Polybius: Histories. 6 vols. LCL. London: Heinemann, 1922–1927

PATON, WILLIAM R., MAX POHLENZ, and WILLIAM SIEVEKING. Plutarchus Moralia III. Orig. 1929. Repr. Bibliotheca Teubneriana. München / Leipzig: Saur, 2001

PATRICH, JOSEPH. The *Carceres* of the Herodian Hippodrome/Stadium at Caesarea Maritima and Connections with the Circus Maximus. JRA 14 (2001): 269–283

PATRICH, JOSEPH, and DAVID AMIT. The Aqueducts of Israel: An Introduction. Pages 9–20 in The Aqueducts of Israel. Edited by D. Amit, J. Patrich, and Y. Hirschfeld. JRASup 46. Portsmouth, RI: Journal of Roman Archaeology, 2002

PEET, THOMAS ERIC. The Great Tomb-Robberies of the Twentieth Egyptian Dynasty. Orig. 1930. Repr. Hildesheim: Olms, 1977

PERRIN, BERNADOTTE. Plutarch's Lives. 11 vols. LCL. Cambridge: Harvard University Press, 1914–1926

PESCH, RUDOLF. Das Markusevangelium. 2 vols. Orig. 1976–1977. Repr. HThK 2. Freiburg: Herder, 1980

PETERSON, WILLIAM. M. Tulli Ciceronis Orationes III. Divinatio in Q. Caecilium. In Verrem. Editio altera recognita et emendata. Orig. 1917. Repr. Oxford Classical Texts. Oxford: Oxford University Press, 1993

PETERSON, WILLIAM, and MAURICE HUTTON. Cornelius Tacitus. Dialogus; Agricola; Germania. LCL. Cambridge: Harvard University Press, 1914

PFANN, STEPHEN. The Essene Yearly Renewal Ceremony and the Baptism of Repentance. Pages 337–52 in The Provo International Conference on the Dead Sea Scrolls. Technological Innovations, New Texts, and Reformulated Issues. Edited by D. W. Parry and E. Ulrich. STDJ 30. Leiden: Brill, 1999

PHILLIPS, ANTHONY. Ancient Israel's Criminal Law: A New Approach to the Decalogue. Oxford: Blackwell, 1970

PHILLIPS, EDWARD J. Roman Politics during the Second Samnite War. Athenaeum 50 (1972): 337–356

PIEPKORN, ARTHUR CARL. Historical Prism Inscriptions of Ashurbanipal. Vol. 1: Editions E, $B_{1-5}$, D and K. Assyriological Studies 5. Chicago: University of Chicago Press, 1933

PIETERSMA, ALBERT, and BENJAMIN G. WRIGHT, eds. A New English Translation of the Septuagint and the Other Greek Translations Traditionally Included unter that Title. Oxford: Oxford University Press, 2007

PINES, SHLOMO. An Arabic Version of the Testimonium Flavanium and its Implications. Jerusalem: The Israel Academy of Sciences and Humanities, 1971

PLAULT, MICHEL. Affaire Jésus. Rapports de Ponce Pilate, préfet de Judée, à la Chancellerie romaine. Paris: Calmann-Lévy, 1965

PLEPELITS, KARL. Chariton von Aphrodisias: Kallirhoe. Eingeleitet, übersetzt und erläutert. Bibliothek der griechischen Literatur 6. Stuttgart: Hiersemann, 1976

PONTET, RENATUS DU. C. Iuli Caesaris commentariorum. 2 vols. Scriptorum classicorum bibliotheca Oxoniensis. Oxford: Clarendon, 1900

PORATH, YOSEF. Herod's 'Amphitheater' at Caesarea: A Multipurpose Entertainment Building. Pages 15–27 in The Roman and Byzantine Near East: Some Recent Archaeological Research. JRASup 14. Ann Arbor, MI: Journal of Roman Archaeology, 1995

PORTEN, BEZALEL, and ADA YARDENI. Textbook of Aramaic Documents from Ancient Egypt. 4 vols. Winona Lake, Ind.: Eisenbrauns, 1986–1993

POUNDS, BRIAN. Review of Crucifixion in Antiquity, by Gunnar Samuelsson. JSNT 33 (2011): 398–405

PRÉCHAC, FRANÇOIS. Sénèque. De la clémence. Orig. 1921. Repr. Budé. Paris: Belles Lettres, 2005

–. Sénèque: Des bienfaits. De Beneficiis. 2 vols. Orig. 1926–1927. Repr. Budé. Paris: Belles Lettres, 1972

PREMERSTEIN, ANTON VON. Alexandrinische und jüdische Gesandte vor Kaiser Hadrian. Hermes 57 (1922): 266–316

PRICE, JONATHAN J. Jerusalem Under Siege. The Collapse of the Jewish State 66–70 C.E. BSJS 3. Leiden: Brill, 1992

PRIEST, JOHN. Testament of Moses (First Century A.D.): A New Translation and Introduction. Pages 919–934 in The Old Testament Pseudepigrapha I. Edited by J. H. Charlesworth. Garden City/London: Doubleday/Darton, Longman & Todd, 1983–1985

PUCCI BEN ZEEV, MIRIAM. Jewish Rights in the Roman World: The Greek and Roman Documents Quoted by Josephus Flavius. TSAJ 74. Tübingen: Mohr Siebeck, 1998

PUECH, ÉMILE. A-t-on redécouvert le tombeau du grand-prêtre Caïphe? Le Monde de la Bible 80 (1993): 42–47

–. Die Kreuzigung und die altjüdische Tradition. Welt und Umwelt der Bibel 9 (1998): 73–75

–. Qumrân Grotte 4.XVIII: Textes hébreux (4Q521–4Q528, 4Q576–4Q579). DJD 25. Oxford: Clarendon, 1998

PUMMER, REINHARDT. The Mosaic Tabernacle as the Only Legitimate Sanctuary: The Biblical Tabernacle in Samaritanism. Pages 125–150 in The Temple of Jerusalem: From Moses to the Messiah. FS L. H. Feldman. Edited by S. Fine. Leiden: Brill, 2011

–. The Samaritans in Flavius Josephus. TSAJ 129. Tübingen: Mohr Siebeck, 2009

PURSER, LOUS C. Cicero. Epistulae ad familiares. Orig. 1901. Repr. Oxford Classical Texts. Oxford: Oxford University Press, 1952

QIMRON, ELISHA. The Dead Sea Scrolls: The Hebrew Writings. 3 vols. Jerusalem: Yad Ben-Zvi, 2010

QIMRON, ELISHA. The Temple Scroll: A Critical Edition with Extensive Reconstructions. Judean Desert Studies. Beer Scheva/Jerusalem: Ben-Gurion University of the Negev Press / Israel Exploration Society, 1996

RABBINOWITZ, J. Ebel Rabbathi Named Masseketh Semahoth: Tractate on Mourning. Pages 325–400 in The Minor Tractates of the Talmud: Massekthoth Ketannoth, 2 vols. Second Edition. Edited by Abraham Cohen. Orig. 1965. Repr.. London: Soncino, 1971

RABIN, CHAIM. Alexander Jannaeus and the Pharisees. JJS 7 (1956): 3–11

RACKHAM, HARRIS. Cicero. De finibus bonorum et malorum. LCL. Cambridge: Harvard University Press, 1931 [1923]

RAD, GERHARD VON. Das erste Buch Mose: Genesis. Zehnte Auflage. Alte Testament Deutsch 2/4. Göttingen: Vandenhoeck & Ruprecht, 1976

RADERMACHER, LUDWIG. Fünf Erlässe des Augustus aus der Cyrenaica. Anzeiger der Wiener Akademie der Wissenschaften (Phil.-Hist. Klasse) 10 (1928): 69–82

RADICE, BETTY. Pliny the Younger: Letters and Panegyricus of Pliny. 2 vols. LCL. Cambridge: Harvard University Press, 1969

RAHMANI, LEVI Y. A Catalogue of Jewish Ossuaries in the Collections of the State of Israel. Jerusalem: The Israel Antiquities Authority, The Israel Academy of Sciences and Humanities, 1994

RAJAK, TESSA. Josephus: The Historian and His Society. Philadelphia: Fortress, 1983

RAMSAY, GEORGE GILBERT. Juvenal and Persius. LCL. Cambridge: Harvard University Press, 1918

RAU, PETER. T. Maccius Plautus. Miles gloriosus. Der glorreiche Hauptmann. Lateinisch / Deutsch. Stuttgart: Reclam, 1984

RAWLINSON, GEORGE. Herodotus: The Histories. Edited by Hugh Bowden. London: Everyman, 1992

RAWLINSON, HENRY C. The Cuneiform Inscriptions of Western Asia. 5 vols., 1861–1884

REA, JOHN R. The Oxyrhynchus Papyri. Volume LI. Graeco-Roman Memoirs No. 71. London: Egypt Exploration Society, 1985

–. Two Legates and a Procurator of Syria Palaestina. ZPE 26 (1977): 217–22

REARDON, BRYAN P. Chariton Aphrodisiensis. De Callirhoe narrationes amatoriae. Bibliotheca Scriptorum Graecorum et Romanorum Teubneriana. München / Leipzig: Saur, 2004

REARDON, BRYAN P. Chariton: Chaereas and Callirhoe. Pages 17–124 in Collected Ancient Greek Novels. Orig. 1989. Repr. Berkeley: University of California Press, 2008

REICH, RONNY. Ossuary Inscriptions from the 'Caiaphas' Tomb. ʾAtiqot 21 (1992): 72–77

–. Ossuary Inscriptions of the Caiaphas Family from Jerusalem. Pages 223–225 in Ancient Jerusalem Revealed, Reprinted and Expanded Edition. Edited by H. Geva. Jerusalem: Israel Exploration Society, 2000

REINBOLD, WOLFGANG. Der älteste Bericht über den Tod Jesu. Literarische Analyse und historische Kritik der Passionsdarstellungen der Evangelien. BZNW 69. Berlin: De Gruyter, 1994

REINHARTZ, ADELE. Caiaphas the High Priest. Studies on Personalities of the New Testament; Minneapolis: Fortress, 2013 [2011]

REYNOLDS, LEIGHTON DURHAM. L. Annaei Senecae Ad Lucilium epistulae morales. 2 vols. Scriptorum classicorum bibliotheca Oxoniensis. Oxford: Clarendon, 1977 [1965]

RICCOBONO, SALVATOR, et al. Fontes iuris romani antejustiniani in usum scholarum. 3 vols. 1940–1943. Repr. Florence: Barbera, 1968–1969

RICHARDS, E. RANDOLPH. The Secretary in the Letters of Paul. WUNT 2/42. Tübingen: Mohr Siebeck 1991

RICHARDSON, M. E. J. Hammurabi's Laws: Text, Translation and Glossary. Sheffield: Sheffield Academic Press, 2000

RICHARDSON, PETER. Herod: King of the Jews and Friend of the Romans. Orig. 1996. Repr. Fortress: Minneapolis, 1999

RIEDO-EMMENEGGER, CHRISTOPH. Prophetisch-messianische Provokateure der Pax Romana. Jesus von Nazaret und andere Störenfriede im Konflikt mit dem Römischen Reich. NTOA 56. Fribourg / Göttingen: Academic Press / Vandenhoeck & Ruprecht, 2005

RIESSLER, PAUL. Die Fastenrolle. Pages 346–347 in Altjüdisches Schrifttum außerhalb der Bibel. Orig. 1928. Repr. Heidelberg: Kerle, 1982

RIGATO, MARIA-LUISA. Il Titolo della Croce di Gesù. Confronto tra i Vangeli e la Tavoletta-reliquia della Basilica Eleniana a Roma. Second ed. Tesi gregoriana. Serie teologia 100. Rome: Gregorian University Press, 2005

RIGATO, MARIA-LUISA. I.N.R.I. Il titolo della Croce. Biblica. Bologna: Edizioni Dehoniane Bologna, 2010

RILEY, HENRY THOMAS. The Comedies of Plautus: Literally Translated into English Prose, with Notes. 2 vols. London: Bell, 1882

RIST, JOSEF. Gratus [2] Valerius G. BNP 5 (2004): 996

RITMEYER, LEEN, and KATHLEEN RITMEYER. Akeldama: Potter's Field or High Priest's Tomb. BAR 20 (1994): 22–35,76–78

RIVKIN, ELLIS. What Crucified Jesus? Nashville: Nelson, 1984

ROBERT, JEANNE, and LOUIS ROBERT. Fouilles d' Amyzon en Carie. Tome 1, Exploration, histoire, monnaies et inscriptions. Paris: Boccard, 1983

ROBINSON, OLIVIA F. Criminal Trials. Pages 229–242 in A Companion to Justinian's Institutes. Edited by E. Metzger. Ithaca: Cornell University Press, 1998

ROBSON, E. ILIFF. Arrian. 2 vols. Cambridge: Harvard University Press, 1929–1933

ROCHETTE, BRUNO. Le latin dans le monde grec. Recherches sur la diffusion de la langue et des lettres latines dans les provinces hellenophones de l'Empire romain. Collection Latomus 233. Bruxelles: Latomus, 1997

–. Traducteurs et traductions dans l'Egypte greco-romaine. Chronique d'Égypte 69 (1994): 313–22

ROKEAH, DAVID. Ben Stara is Ben Pantera – Toward the Clarification of a Philological-Historical Problem. Tarbiz 39 (1970): 9–18.

ROLFE, JOHN C. Quintus Curtius. 2 vols. LCL. Cambridge: Harvard University Press, 1946

–. Sallust. LCL. Cambridge: Harvard University Press/, 1931

–. Suetonius. Lives of the Caesars. Orig. 1913–1914. Repr. LCL. Cambridge: Harvard University Press, 1998

ROOS, ANTOON G., and GERHARD WIRTH. Flavii Arriani quae exstant omnia. 2 vols. Orig. 1967–1968. Repr. Bibliotheca Scriptorum Graecorum et Romanorum Teubneriana. Leipzig: Teubner, 1907–1928

ROSÉN, HAIIM B. Herodoti historiae. 2 vols. Bibliotheca Scriptorum Graecorum et Romanorum Teubneriana. Leipzig: Teubner, 1987–1989

ROSENBACH, MANFRED. L. Annaeus Seneca. Philosophische Schriften. Lateinisch und deutsch. 5 vols. Darmstadt: Wissenschaftliche Buchgesellschaft, 2011 [1969–1984, 1999]

ROSENBLATT, SAMUEL. The Crucifixion of Jesus from the Standpoint of Pharisaic Law. JBL 75 (1956): 315–321

ROSS, WILLIAM DAVID. Aristotelis politica. Oxford: Clarendon, 1957

ROSTOWZEW, MICHAEL. Angariae. Klio 6 (1906): 249–258

ROTH, MARTHA T. Gender and Law: A Case Study from Ancient Mesopotamia. Pages 173–184 in Gender and Law in the Hebrew Bible and the Ancient Near East. Edited by V. H. Matthews, B. M. Levinson, and T. Frymer-Kensky. JSOTSup 262. Sheffield: Sheffield Academic Press, 1998

–. Law Collections from Mesopotamia and Asia Minor. Second ed. SBL Writings from the Ancient World 6. Altanta: Scholars Press, 1997

–. The Laws of Hammurabi (2.131). Pages 335–353 in The Context of Scripture. Vol. 2: Monumental Inscriptions from the Biblical World. Edited by W. W. Hallo and K. L. Younger. Leiden: Brill, 2003

–. The Middle Assyrian Laws (2.132) (Tablet A). Pages 353–360 in The Context of Scripture. Vol. 2: Monumental Inscriptions from the Biblical World. Edited by W. W. Hallo and K. L. Younger. Leiden: Brill, 2003

ROWLANDSON, JANE, ed. Women and Society in Greek and Roman Egypt: A Sourcebook. Cambridge: Cambridge University Press, 1998

ROWLEY, HAROLD H. 4QpNahum and the Teacher of Righteousness. JBL 75 (1956): 188–193

ROYSE, JAMES R. The Spurious Texts of Philo of Alexandria. A Study of Textual Transmission and Corruption with Indexes to the Major Collections to Greek Fragments. ALGH 22. Leiden: Brill, 1991

RUIZ MONTERO, CONSUELO. Chariton von Aphrodisias: Ein Überblick. ANRW II.34.2 (1994): 1006–1054

RUNIA, DAVID T. Philo's *De aeternitate mundi*: The Problem of its Interpretation. VC 35 (1981): 105–151

SABATIER, PIERRE. Bibliorum Sacrorum Latinae versiones antiquae. 3 vols. Rheims: Florentain, 1743–1749

SACCO, Giulia. Il graffito blasfemo del Paedagogium nella Domus Augustana del Palatino. Pages 192–194 in Le iscrizioni dei cristiani in Vaticano. Materiali e contributi scientifici per una mostra epigrafica. Edited by I. Di Stefano Manzella. Inscriptiones Sanctae Sedis 2; Città del Vaticano Roma: Monumenti, Musei e gallerie pontificie Distribuzione esclusiva, Edizioni Quasar.

SALLMANN, KLAUS. Die Literatur des Umbruchs. Von der römischen zur christlichen Literatur, 117 bis 284 n. Chr. HdA VIII.4. München: Beck, 1997

–. Suetonius [2] S. Tranquillus C. BNP 13 (2008): 918–922

SALOMONSEN, BØRGE. Einige kritische Bemerkungen zu Stauffers Darstellung der spätjüdischen Ketzergesetzgebung. ST 18 (1964): 91–118

–. Die Tosefta. Seder IV: Nezikin, 3: Sanhedrin–Makkot. Übersetzt und erklärt. Rabbinische Texte. Erste Reihe: Die Tosefta. Stuttgart: Kohlhammer, 1976

SALVESEN, ALISON. Symmachus in the Pentateuch. JSS Monograph 15. Manchester: University of Manchester, 1991

SAMUELSSON, GUNNAR. Crucifixion in Antiquity: An Inquiry into the Background and Significance of the New Testament Terminology of Crucifixion. Second Revised ed. WUNT 2/310. Tübingen: Mohr Siebeck, 2013

–. Crucifixion in Antiquity: An Inquiry into the Background of the New Testament Terminology of Crucifixion. Skrifter utgivna av institutionen för litteratur, idéhistoria och religion, Göteborgs universitet. Göteborg: University of Gothenburg, 2010

SANDARS, THOMAS COLLETT. The Institutes of Justinian, with English Introduction, Translation, and Notes. Eighth Edition, Revised and Corrected. London / New York: Longmans, Green, 1888

SANDERS, E. P. The Historical Figure of Jesus. London: Penguin, 1993

SARGEAUNT, JOHN. Terence. 2 vols. LCL. Cambridge: Harvard University Press, 1912

SARNA, NAHUM M. Genesis. JPS Torah Commentary. Philadelphia: Jewish Publication Society, 1989

SARTRE, MAURICE. L'orient romain. Provinces et sociétés provinciales en Méditerranée orientale d'Auguste aux Sévères (31 avant J.-C – 235 après J.-C.). L'Univers historique. Paris: Seuil, 1991

SASSON, JACK M. Treatment of Criminals at Mari. Journal of the Economic and Social History of the Orient 20 (1977): 90–113

SATTLER, PETER. Augustus und der Senat: Untersuchungen zur römischen Innenpolitik zwischen 30 und 17 v. Christus. Göttingen: Vandenhoeck & Ruprecht, 1960

SCHAAF, LOTHAR. Der Miles Gloriosus des Plautus und sein griechisches Original. Ein Beitrag zur Kontaminationsfrage. München: Fink, 1977

SCHACHTER, JACOB, and AARON M. FREEDMAN. Sanhedrin. Hebrew-English Edition of the Babylonian Talmud. New ed. Edited by I. Epstein. London: Soncino, 1969

SCHÄFER, PETER. Jesus im Talmud. 2., durchgesehene Auflage. Orig. 2007. Repr. Tübingen: Mohr Siebeck, 2010

–. Jesus in the Talmud. Princeton: Princeton University Press, 2007

SCHÄFER, PETER, and HANS-JÜRGEN BECKER. Synopse zum Talmud Yerushalmi. Tübingen: Mohr Siebeck, 1991

SCHANZ, MARTIN, and CARL HOSIUS. Geschichte der römischen Literatur. Zweiter Teil: Die römische Literatur in der Zeit der Monarchie bis auf Hadrian. Unveränderter Nachdruck der 4., neu bearbeiteten Auflage von Carl Hosius. Orig. 1935. Repr. HdA VIII.2. München: Beck, 1980

SCHARBERT, JOSEPH. זוד ,זִיד. TDOT 4 (1980): 46–51

SCHÄRTLI, MONIKA. Das Nikodemusevangelium, die Pilatusakten und die 'Höllenfahrt Christi'. Pages 231–261 in Antike christliche Apokryphen in deutscher Übersetzung. I. Band: Evangelien und Verwandtes. Edited by C. Markschies and J. Schröter. Tübingen: Mohr Siebeck, 2012

–. Die sonstige Pilatusliteratur. Pages 262–279 in Antike christliche Apokryphen in deutscher Übersetzung. I. Band: Evangelien und Verwandtes. Edited by C. Markschies and J. Schröter. Tübingen: Mohr Siebeck, 2012

SCHEIL, JEAN-VINCENT. La stèle de la chaussée royale du Roi Sennachérib. Revue d'Assyriologie 40 (1914): 188–192

SCHENKL, HENRICUS. Epicteti Dissertationes ab Arriano digestae. Bibliotheca Scriptorum Graecorum et Romanorum Teubneriana. Leipzig: Teubner, 1916

SCHIEMANN, GOTTFRIED. Accusatio. BNP 1 (2002): 65

–. Crimen. BNP 3 (2003): 940–942

–. Damnatio in crucem. BNP 4 (2004): 59

–. Death Penalty. BNP 4 (2004): 136–137

–. Delatio nominis. BNP 4 (2004): 199

–. Lex, leges. BNP 7 (2005): 460–66

–. Peregrinus. BNP 10 (2007): 750–751

SCHIFFMAN, LAWRENCE H. The Courtyards of the House of the Lord: Studies on the Temple Scroll. Edited by F. García Martínez. STDJ 75. Leiden: Brill, 2008

–. The Deuteronomic Paraphrase of the *Temple Scroll* [1992]. Pages 443–469 in The Courtyards of the House of the Lord: Studies on the Temple Scroll. Edited by F. García Martínez. STDJ 75. Leiden: Brill, 2008

–. Laws concerning Idolatry in the *Temple Scroll* [1994]. Pages 471–486 in The Courtyards of the House of the Lord: Studies on the Temple Scroll. Edited by F. García Martínez. STDJ 75. Leiden: Brill, 2008

–. Pharisees and Sadducees in *Pesher Nahum*. Pages 272–290 in Minḥah le-Naḥum. Biblical and Other Studies. FS Nahum M. Sarna. Edited by M. Brettler and M. Fishbane. JSOTSup 154. Sheffield: JSOT Press, 1993

–. The Prohibition of Judicial Corruption in the Dead Sea Scrolls, Philo, Josephus, and Talmudic Law [1998]. Pages 189–212 in The Courtyards of the House of the Lord: Studies on the Temple Scroll. Edited by F. García Martínez. STDJ 75. Leiden: Brill, 2008

–. Qumran and Jerusalem: Studies in the Dead Sea Scrolls and the History of Judaism. Studies in the Dead Sea Scrolls and Related Literature. Grand Rapids: Eerdmans, 2010

–. The Relationship of the *Zadokite Fragments* to the *Temple Scroll* [2000]. Pages 149–62 in The Courtyards of the House of the Lord: Studies on the Temple Scroll. Edited by F. García Martínez. STDJ 75. Leiden: Brill, 2008

–. Reproof as a Requisite for Punishment in the Law of the Dead Sea Scrolls. Pages 59–74 in Jewish Law Association Studies II. The Jerusalem Conference Volume. Edited by B. S. Jackson. Atlanta: Scholars Press, 1986

–. Sectarian Law in the Dead Sea Scrolls: Courts, Testimony and Penal Code. BJS 33. Chico: Scholars Press, 1983

–. The Zadokite Fragments and the Temple Scroll. Pages 133–45 in The Damascus Document: A Centennial of Discovery. Edited by J. M. Baumgarten, E. G. Chazon, and A.

Pinnick. STDJ 34. Leiden: Brill, 2002

SCHIFFMAN, LAWRENCE H., ANDREW D. GROSS, and MICHAEL C. RAND. Composite Text of the Temple Scroll. Pages 266–405 in Temple Scroll and Related Documents. Edited by J. H. Charlesworth. The Dead Sea Scrolls 7. Tübingen: Mohr Siebeck, 2011

SCHIFFMAN, LAWRENCE H., ANDREW D. GROSS, and MICHAEL C. RAND. Temple Scroll Defining Edition 11Q19 (11QTempleᵃ): Hebrew Text. Pages 1–173 in Temple Scroll, and Related Documents. Edited by J. H. Charlesworth. The Dead Sea Scrolls 7. Tübingen: Mohr Siebeck, 2011

SCHILLER, A. ARTHUR. Legal Commentary. Pages 35–101 in Apokrimata: Decisions of Septimius Severus on Legal Matters. New York: Columbia University Press, 1954

SCHIMANOWSKI, GOTTFRIED. Juden und Nichtjuden in Alexandrien: Koexistenz und Konflikte bis zum Pogrom unter Trajan (117 n. Chr.). Berlin: Lit, 2006

SCHNABEL, ECKHARD J. Sanhedrin. NIDB 5 (2009): 102–106

SCHNEIDER, GERHARD. Das Verfahren gegen Jesus in der Sicht des dritten Evangeliums (Lk 22,54 – 23,25). Redaktionskritik und historische Rückfrage. Pages 111–130 in Der Prozeß gegen Jesus. Historische Rückfrage und theologische Deutung. Edited by K. Kertelge. QD 112. Freiburg: Herder, 1988

SCHNEIDER, JOHANNES. σταυρός, σταυρόω, ἀνασταυρόω. TDNT 7 (1971): 572–584

SCHOEPS, HANS-JOACHIM. Simon Magus in der Haggada? HUCA 2 (1948): 257–74

SCHONFIELD, HUGH J. The Passover Plot: New Light on the History of Jesus. New York: Random, 1965

SCHÖTTGEN, CHRISTIAN. Horae Hebraicae et Talmudicae in universum Novum Testamentum. 2 vols. Dresden / Leipzig: Hekel, 1733–1942

SCHUBERT, PAUL. Vivre en Égypte gréco-romaine. Une sélection de papyrus. Chant du monde. Vevey: Aire, 2000

SCHULZ, RAIMUND. Herrschaft und Regierung. Roms Regiment in den Provinzen in der Zeit der Republik. Paderborn: Schöningh, 1997

SCHUOL, MONIKA. Augustus und die Juden. Rechtsstellung und Interessenpolitik der kleinasiatischen Diaspora. Studien zur alten Geschichte 6. Frankfurt: Antike, 2007

SCHÜRER, EMIL. Geschichte des jüdischen Volkes im Zeitalter Christi. 3 vols. 4. Auflage. Leipzig: Hinrichs, 1901–1911

–. The History of the Jewish People in the Age of Christ (175 B.C. – A.D. 135). Revised by G. Vermes, F. Millar, M. Black, and M. Goodman. Edinburgh: T & T Clark, 1973–1987

SCHUSTER, MAURIZ / RUDOLPH HANSLIK. C. Plini Caecili Secundi Epistularum libri novem, Epistularum ad Traianum liber, Panegyricus. 3. Auflage. Orig. 1958. Repr. Bibliotheca Scriptorum Graecorum et Romanorum Teubneriana. Stuttgart / Leipzig: Teubner, 1992x

SCHWARTZ, DANIEL R. Agrippa I: The Last King of Judaea. TSAJ 23. Tübingen: Mohr Siebeck, 1990

–. Composition and Sources in *Antiquities* 18: The Case of Pontius Pilate. Pages 125–146 in Making History: Josephus and Historical Method. Edited by Z. Rodgers. JSJSup 110. Leiden: Brill, 2007

–. The Contemners of Judges and Men' (11Q Temple 64:12) [1982–1983]. Pages 81–88 in Studies in the Jewish Background of Christianity. WUNT 60. Tübingen: Mohr Siebeck, 1992

–. Josephus and Philo on Pontius Pilate. Pages 3:26–45 in The Jerusalem Cathedra: Studies in the History, Archaeology, Geography and Ethnography of the Land of Israel. Edited by L. I. Levine. Jerusalem: Yad Izhak Ben-Zvi Institute, 1983

–. Josephus on Albinus: The Eve of Catastrophe in Changing Retrospect. Pages 291–309 in The Jewish Revolt Against Rome: Interdisciplinary Perspectives. Edited by M. Popović. JSJSup 154. Leiden: Brill, 2011

–. Pontius Pilate's Appointment to Office and the Chronology of Josephus' *Antiquities*, Books 18–20 [1982/1983]. Pages 182–201 in Studies in the Jewish Background of Christianity. WUNT 60. Tübingen: Mohr Siebeck, 1992

–. Pontius Pilate's Suspension from Office: Chronology and Sources [1981/1982]. Pages 202–217 in Studies in the Jewish Background of Christianity. WUNT 60. Tübingen: Mohr Siebeck, 1990

–. Pontius Pilate. ABD 5 (1992): 395–401

–. Reading the First Century: On Reading Josephus and Studying Jewish History of the First Century. WUNT 300. Tübingen: Mohr Siebeck, 2013

SCHWARTZ, JACQUES. Traductions en Égypte gréco-romaine. Pages 379–86 in Mélanges Pierre Lévêque. Vol. 2, Anthropologie et Société. Edited by M. M. Mactoux and E. Geny. Annales littéraires de l'Université de Besançon 82. Paris: Belles lettres, 1989

SCHWARTZ, JOSHUA J. Peter and Ben Stada in Lydda. Pages 391–414 in The Book of Acts in its Palestinian Setting. Edited by R. Bauckham. The Book of Acts in Its First-Century Setting, Volume 4. Exeter: Paternoster, 1995

SCHWEMER, ANNA MARIA. Die Passion des Messias nach Markus und der Vorwurf des Antijudaismus. Pages 133–63 in Der messianische Anspruch Jesu und die Anfänge der Christologie. M. Hengel and A. M. Schwemer. WUNT 138. Tübingen: Mohr Siebeck, 2001

SCHWENDNER, GREGG W. Literary and Non-literary Papyri from the University of Michigan Collection. Ph.D. Dissertation. University of Michigan, 1988

SCHWIER, HELMUT. Tempel und Tempelzerstörung. Untersuchungen zu den theologischen und ideologischen Faktoren im ersten jüdisch-römischen Krieg (66–74 n.Chr.). NTOA 11. Fribourg / Göttingen: Universitätsverlag / Vandenhoeck & Ruprecht, 1989

SCOTT, SAMUEL P. The Civil Law, including the Twelve Tables, the Institutes of Gaius, the Rules of Ulpian, the Opinions of Paulus, the Enactments of Justinian, and the Constitutions of Leo. Translated from the original Latin, edited, and compared with all accessible systems of jurisprudence ancient and modern. 17 vols. Cincinnati: Central Trust Company, 1932

SCOTT-KILVERT, IAN. Cassius Dio. The Roman History: The Reign of Augustus. Penguin Classics. London: Penguin, 1989

SEAGER, ROBIN. *Maiestas* in the Late Republic: Some Observations. Pages 143–153 in Critical Studies in Ancient Law, Comparative Law and Legal History. FS A. Watson. Edited by J. W. Cairns and O. F. Robinson. Oxford / Portland: Hart, 2001

SEELIGMANN, ISAC LEO. Zur Terminologie für das Gerichtsverfahren im Wortschatz des biblischen Hebräisch. Pages 251–278 in Hebräische Wortforschung. FS W. Baumgartner. VTSup 16. Leiden: Brill, 1967

SEEVERS, BOYD. Warfare in the Old Testament: The Organization, Weapons, and Tactics of Ancient Near Eastern Armies. Grand Rapids: Kregel, 2013

SEGAL, ALAN F. Two Powers in Heaven: Early Rabbinic Reports about Christianity and Gnosticism. SJLA 25. Leiden: Brill, 1977

SEGAL, ERICH. The Braggart Soldier *(Miles Gloriosus)*. Pages 65–179 in Plautus. The Comedies. Volume I. Edited by David R. Slavitt and P. Bovie. Complete Roman Drama in Translation. Baltimore: Johns Hopkins University Press, 1995

–. Roman Laughter: The Comedy of Plautus. Second Edition. Orig. 1968. Repr. Oxford: Oxford University Press, 1987

SEGAL, PERETZ. The Penalty of the Warning Inscription from the Temple of Jerusalem. IEJ 39 (1989): 79–84

SEIDL, ERWIN. Eine neue kaiserliche Konstitution über die Apellation. SDHI 38 (1972): 319–320

–. Rechtsgeschichte Ägyptens als römischer Provinz: Die Behauptung des ägyptischen Rechts neben dem römischen. Sankt Augustin: Richarz, 1973

SELAND, TORREY. Establishment Violence in Philo and Luke: A Study of Non-Conformity to the Torah and Jewish Vigilante Reactions. Biblical Interpretation 15. Leiden: Brill, 1995

SÉLINCOURT, AUBREY DE. Livy. The War with Hannibal. Books XXI–XXX of The History of Rome From its Foundation. Penguin Classics. London/New York: Penguin Books, 1965

SHACKLETON BAILEY, DAVID R. Cicero. Epistulae ad Familiares. 2 vols. Orig. 1977. Repr. Cambridge Classical Texts and Commentaries 16. Cambridge: Cambridge University Press, 2004

–. M. Tulli Cicero. Epistulae ad familiares libri I–XVI. Bibliotheca Scriptorum Graecorum et Romanorum Teubneriana. Stuttgart: Teubner, 1988

–. Valerius Maximus. Memorable Doings and Sayings. 2 vols. LCL. Cambridge: Harvard University Press, 2000

SHEMESH, AHARON. Scriptural Interpretations in the Damascus Document and their Parallels in Rabbinic Midrash. Pages 161–75 in The Damascus Document: A Centennial of Discovery. Edited by J. M. Baumgarten, E. G. Chazon, and A. Pinnick. STDJ 34. Leiden: Brill, 2002

SHERK, ROBERT K., ed. The Roman Empire: Augustus to Hadrian. Translated Documents of Greece and Rome 6. Cambridge: Cambridge University Press, 1988

–. Roman Documents from the Greek East: Senatus Consulta and Epistulae to the Age of Augustus. Baltimore: Johns Hopkins University Press, 1969

–. Rome and the Greek East to the Death of Augustus. Translated Documents of Greece and Rome 4. Cambridge: Cambridge University Press, 1984

SHERWIN-WHITE, ADRIAN NICOLAS. The Letters of Pliny: A Historical and Social Commentary. Orig. 1966. Repr. Oxford: Clarendon, 1985

–. The Roman Citizenship. Second ed. Oxford: Clarendon, 1973

SHOREY, PAUL. Plato. The Republic. 2 vols. Orig. 1930. Repr. LCL. Cambridge: Harvard University Press, 1969

SIEBERT, ANNE VIOLA. Piaculum. BNP 11 (2007): 227–229

–. Lituus. BNP 7 (2005): 737

SIEVERS, JOSEPH. The Hasmoneans and Their Supporters: From Mattathias to the Death of John Hyrcanus I. SFSHJ 6. Atlanta: Scholars Press, 1990

SIEVERS, JOSEPH, and GAIA LEMBI, eds. Josephus and Jewish History in Flavian Rome and Beyond. Supplements to the Journal for the study of Judaism 104. Leiden ; Boston: Brill, 2005

SIMPSON, ROBERT S. Demotic Grammar in the Ptolemaic Sacerdotal Decrees. Oxford: Griffith Institute, Ashmolean Museum, 1996

SMALLWOOD, E. MARY. The Jews under Roman Rule: From Pompey to Diocletian. A Study in Political Relations. Orig. 1976. Repr. SJLA 20. Leiden: Brill, 2001

–. Philonis Alexandrini Legatio ad Gaium. With an Introduction, Translation, and Commentary. Second ed. Leiden: Brill, 1970

SMITH, CHARLES FOSTER. Thucydides. 4 vols. LCL. Cambridge: Harvard University Press, 1919–1930

SMITH, GEORGE. History of Assurbanipal, Translated from the Cuneiform Inscriptions. London: Williams and Norgate, 1871

SMITH, HARRY S. Fortress of Buhen: The Inscriptions. London: Egypt Exploration Society, 1976

SMITH, MORTON. Jesus the Magician. San Francisco: Harper & Row, 1978

SMITH, PATRICIA, LAWRENCE E. STAGER, JOSEPH A. GREENE, and GAL AVISHAI. Age Estimations Attest to Infant Sacrifice at the Carthage Tophet. Antiquity 87.338 (2013): 1191–1199

SMITH, PETER L. Plautus. Three Comedies: Miles Gloriosus, Pseudolus, Rudens. Translated and with an Introduction. Ithaca: Cornell University Press, 1991

SONTHEIMER, WALTHER. Tacitus. Annalen. Stuttgart: Reclam, 1964–1967

SPEISER, EPHRAIM A. Genesis. AB 1. Garden City, NY: Doubleday, 1964

SPERBER, ALEXANDER, The Bible in Aramaic Based on Old Manuscripts and Printed Texts. 4 vols. 1959–1973. Repr. Leiden: Brill, 1992

SPIEGELBERG, WILHELM. Der demotische Text der Priesterdekrete von Kanopus und Memphis (Rosettana) mit den hieroglyphischen und griechischen Fassungen und deutscher Übersetzung nebst demotischem Glossar. Heidelberg: Winters Universitätsbuchhandlung, 1922

SPRUIT, JOP, ROBERT FEENSTRA, KAREL BONGENAAR, JEROEN CHORUS, and LUUK DE LIGT. Corpus Iuris Civilis. Tekst en vertaling. 12 vols. Amsterdam: Royal Dutch Academy of Sciences / Amsterdam University Press, 1993–2011

STANTON, GRAHAM N. Jesus of Nazareth: A Magician and a False Prophet Who Deceived God's People? Pages 164–180 in Jesus of Nazareth: Lord and Christ. FS I. H. Marshall. Edited by J. B. Green and M. Turner. Grand Rapids/Carlisle: Eerdmans/Paternoster, 1994

STAUFFER, ETHELBERT. Christ and the Caesars: Historical Sketches. London: SCM, 1955

–. Christus und die Cäsaren. Historische Skizzen. Orig.1948. Repr. Hamburg: Wittig, 1966

–. Jerusalem und Rom im Zeitalter Jesu Christi. Dalp Taschenbücher 331. Bern: Francke, 1957

–. Jesus and His Story. London: SCM Press, 1960

–. Jesus: Gestalt und Geschichte. Dalp-Taschenbücher 332. Bern/München: Francke, 1957

–. Neue Wege der Jesusforschung. Wissenschaftliche Zeitschrift der Martin-Luther-Universität Halle-Wittenberg 7/2 (1958): 451–476

STECK, ULRIKE. Der Zeugenbeweis in den Gerichtsreden Ciceros. EHS 2/4839. Frankfurt: Lang, 2009

STEMBERGER, GÜNTHER. Die Umformung des palästinischen Judentums nach 70 – der Aufstieg der Rabbinen. Pages 172–86 in Judaica Minora II. TSAJ 138. Tübingen: Mohr Siebeck, 2010

STERN, MENAHEM. The Province of Judea. Pages 308–376 in The Jewish People in the First Century. Historical Geography, Political History, Social, Cultural and Religious Life and Institutions. Edited by S. Safrai and M. Stern. CRINT I. Assen: Van Gorcum, 1974

STERN, SACHA. Jewish Identity in Early Rabbinic Writings. AGAJU 23. Leiden: Brill, 1994

STEUDEL, ANNETTE. Die Texte aus Qumran II. Hebräisch/Aramäisch und Deutsch. Mit masoretischer Punktation, Übersetzung, Einführung und Anmerkungen. Darmstadt: Wissenschaftliche Buchgesellschaft, 2001

STOLL, OLIVER. Der Adler im 'Käfig'. Zu einer Aquilifer-Grabstele aus Apamea in Syrien [1991]. Pages 13–46 in Römisches Heer und Gesellschaft. Gesammelte Beiträge 1991–1999. Mavors Roman Army Researches 13. Stuttgart: Steiner, 2001

STRACK, HERMANN L. Der Babylonische Talmud nach der einzigen vollständigen Handschrift München Codex Hebraicus 95, mittelst Facsimile-Lichtdruck vervielfältigt. 2 vols. Leiden: Sijthoff, 1912

–. Pesaḥim. Der Mišnatraktat Passafest. Mit Berücksichtigung des Neuen Testaments und der jetzigen Passafeier der Juden. Nach Handschriften und alten Drucken herausgegeben, übersetzt und erläutert. Schriften des Institutum Judaicum in Berlin 40. Leipzig: Hinrichs, 1911

STRACK, HERMANN L., and PAUL BILLERBECK. Kommentar zum Neuen Testament aus Talmud und Midrasch. 6 vols. München: Beck, 1986

STRACK, HERMANN L., and GÜNTHER STEMBERGER. Einleitung in Talmud und Midrasch. 7., völlig neu bearbeitete Auflage. München: Beck, 1982

STRACK, HERMANN L., GÜNTER STEMBERGER, and MARKUS BOCKMUEHL. Introduction to the Talmud and Midrash. Second ed. Minneapolis: Fortress, 1996

STRASSLER, ROBERT B. ed. The Landmark Herodotus: The Histories. Translated by Andrea L. Purvis. New York: Pantheon, 2007

STRASSLER, ROBERT B. ed. The Landmark Thucydides: A Comprehensive Guide to the Peloponnesian War. Translated by Richard Crawley. New York: Free Press, 1996

A CompHerodotus: The Histories. Translated by Andrea L. Purvis. New York: Pantheon, 2007

STRECK, MAXIMILIAN. Assurbanipal und die letzten assyrischen Könige bis zum Untergange Niniveh's. 3 vols. Vorderasiatische Bibliothek 7. Leipzig: Hinrichs, 1916

STRELAN, RICHARD E. Strange Acts: Studies in the Cultural World of the Acts of the Apostles. BZNW 126. Berlin: De Gruyter, 2004

STROBEL, AUGUST. Die Stunde der Wahrheit. Untersuchungen zum Strafverfahren gegen Jesus. WUNT 21. Tübingen: Mohr Siebeck, 1980

STRÖBEL, EDUARD. M. Tulli Ciceronis scripta, quae manserunt omnia. Fasc. 2: Rhetorici libri duo, qui vocantur De inventione. Orig. 1915. Repr. Bibliotheca Scriptorum Graecorum et Romanorum Teubneriana. Stuttgart / Leipzig: Teubner, 1965

STRONK, JAN P. Ctesias's Persian History. Vol. 1: Introduction, Text, Translation. Reihe Geschichte 2. Düsseldorf: Wellem, 2010

STROTHMANN, MERET. Augustus – Vater der res publica. Zur Funktion der drei Begriffe restitutio – saeculum – pater patriae im augusteischen Principat. Stuttgart: Steiner, 2000

STROUX, JOHANNES, and LEOPOLD WENGER. Die Augustus-Inschrift auf dem Marktplatz von Kyrene. Abhandlungen der Bayrischen Akademie der Wissenschaften, Philosophisch-philologische und historische Klasse 34.2. München: Verlag der Bayerischen Akademie der Wissenschaften, 1928

STRUGNELL, JOHN. Notes en marge du volume V des 'Discoveries in the Judaean Desert of Jordan'. RdQ 7 (1970): 163–276

STUHLMACHER, PETER. Biblische Theologie des Neuen Testaments. Band 1: Grundlegung. Von Jesus zu Paulus. 3., neubearbeitete und ergänzte Auflage. Göttingen: Vandenhoeck & Ruprecht, 2005

SUERBAUM, WERNER. Die archaische Literatur von den Anfängen bis Sullas Tod. Die vorliterarische Periode und die Zeit von 240 bis 78 v. Chr. HdA VIII.1. München: Beck, 2002

SWAIN, SIMON. Bilingualism in Cicero? The Evidence of Code-Switching. Pages 128–167 in Bilingualism in Ancient Society: Language Contact and the Written Text. Edited by J. N. Adams, M. Janse, and S. Swain. Oxford: Oxford University Press, 2002

SYME, RONALD. The Augustan Aristocracy. Orig. 1986. Repr. Oxford: Clarendon, 1989

–. Tacitus. 2 vols. Oxford: Clarendon, 1958

Syrie, mémoire et civilisation. Paris: Institut du monde arabe: Flammarion, 1993

TADMOR, HAYIM. The Inscriptions of Tiglath-pileser III, King of Assyria: Critical Edition, with Introductions, Translations, and Commentary. Jerusalem: Israel Academy of Sciences and Humanities, 1994

TADMOR, HAYIM, and SHIGEO YAMADA. The Royal Inscriptions of Tiglath-pileser III (744–727 BC) and Shalmaneser V (726–722 BC), Kings of Assyria. The Royal Inscriptions of the Neo-Assyrian Period 1. Winona Lake, Ind.: Eisenbrauns, 2011

TANTLEVSKIJ, IGOR R. The Reflection of the Political Situation in Judaea in 88 B.C.E. in the Qumran Commentary on Nahum (4QpNah, Columns 1–4). St. Petersburg Journal of Oriental Studies 6 (1994): 221–231

TAUBENSCHLAG, RAPHAEL. The Law of Greco-Roman Egypt in the Light of the Papyri 332 B.C. – 640 A.D. Second Edition, Revised and Enlarged. Ristampa Anastatica. Orig. 1955, 1944. Repr. Milan: Cisalpino Goliardica, 1972

TAYLOR, JOAN E. Pontius Pilate and the Imperial Cult ult in Roman Judaea. NTS 52 (2006): 555–582

TAYLOR, JUSTIN. The Role of Rhetorical Elaboration in the Formation of Mark's Passion Narrative (Mark 14:43–16:8): An Enquiry. Pages 11–26 in Greco-Roman Culture and the New Testament. Studies Commemorating the Centennial of the Pontifical Biblical Institute. Edited by D. E. Aune and F. E. Brenk. NovTSup 143. Leiden: Brill, 2012

–. The Roman Empire in the Acts of the Apostles. ANRW II.26.3 (1996): 2436–2500

TCHERIKOVER, VICTOR A., and ALEXANDER FUKS, eds. Corpus Papyrorum Judaicarum. 3 vols. Cambridge: Harvard University Press, 1957–1964

THACKERAY, H. ST. JOHN. Josephus, the Man and the Historian. Orig. 1929. Repr. New York: Ktav, 1967

THACKERAY, H. ST. JOHN, RALPH MARCUS, and LOUIS H. FELDMAN. Josephus. 10 vols. LCL. Cambridge: Harvard University Press, 1926–1965

THEISSEN, GERD, and ANNETTE MERZ. The Historical Jesus: A Comprehensive Guide. London/Minneapolis: SCM/Fortress, 1998

–. Der historische Jesus. Ein Lehrbuch. Göttingen: Vandenhoeck & Ruprecht, 1996

TIGAY, JEFFREY H. Deuteronomy. Philadelphia: Jewish Publication Society, 1996

TISCHENDORF, CONSTANTIN VON. Evangelia apocrypha. Orig. 1852, 1876. Repr. Hildesheim: Olms, 1987

TOMEI, MARIA ANTONIETTA. Museo Palatino, English Edition. Rome: Electra, 1997

TORALLAS TOVAR, SOFÍA. Linguistic Identity in Graeco-Roman Egypt. Pages 17–43 in The Multilingual Experience in Egypt, from the Ptolemies to the Abbasids. Edited by A. Papaconstantinou. Farnham: Ashgate, 2010

TOV, EMANUEL. The Dead Sea Scrolls Electronic Library. Rev. ed. Leiden: Brill, 2006

TOYNBEE, JOCELYN M. C. Death and Burial in the Roman World. Aspects of Greek and Roman life. London: Thames & Hudson, 1971

TRAPP, MICHAEL. Artemidorus [6] of Daldis. BNP 2 (2003): 60–61

TROMP, JOHANNES. The Assumption of Moses. A Critical Edition with Commentary. SVTP 10. Leiden: Brill, 1993

TRZASKOMA, STEPHEN M. Two Novels from Ancient Greece: *Callirho*e and *An Ephesian Story*. Translated, with Introduction and Notes. Indianapolis: Hackett, 2010

TSEVAT, MATITYAHU. חקר. TDOT 5:148–150

TZAFERIS, VASSILIOS. Jewish Tombs at and near Giv'at ha-Mivtar, Jerusalem. IEJ 20 (1970): 18–32

USSISHKIN, DAVID. The Conquest of Lachish by Sennacherib. Publications of the Institute of Archaeology 6. Tel Aviv: Tel Aviv University, Institute of Archaeology, 1982

VAN VOORST, ROBERT E. Jesus Tradition in Classical and Jewish Writings. Pages 2149–2180 in Handbook for the Study of the Historical Jesus. Vol. 3: The Historical Jesus. Edited by T. Holmén and S. E. Porter. Leiden: Brill, 2011

VANDERKAM, JAMES C. From Joshua to Caiaphas: High Priests After the Exile. Minneapolis: Fortress, 2004

VARNER, WILLIAM. Ancient Jewish-Christian Dialogues. Athanasius and Zacchaeus, Simon and Theophilus, Timothy and Aquila: Introductions, Texts, and Translations. Studies in the Bible and Early Christianity 58. Lewiston, N.Y.: Mellen, 2004

VAUX, ROLAND DE. Ancient Israel: Its Life and Institutions. Translated by John McHugh. 2nd ed. London: Darton, Longman & Todd, 1961

VEH, OTTO. Cassius Dio. Römische Geschichte. 5 vols. 2., überarbeitete Auflage. Orig. 1985–1987. Repr. Bibliothek der Alten Welt. Berlin: Akademie Verlag, 2012

VERMES, GEZA. The Complete Dead Sea Scrolls in English. Fiftieth Anniversary ed. London: New York: Penguin, 2011

–. The Jesus Notice of Josephus Re-Examined. JJS 38 (1987): 1–10

VERNUS, PASCAL. Affairs and Scandals in Ancient Egypt. Translated by D. Lorton. Ithaca, N.Y.: Cornell University Press, 2003

VERSTEEG, RUSS. Early Mesopotamian Law. Durham, N.C.: Carolina Academic Press, 2000

VICENT CERNUDA, ANTONIO. La Conversión de Caifás y el Hallazgo de sus Huesos. Estudios Bíblicos 54 (1996) 35–78

–. Jesús perseguido a muerte. Estudios exegéticos sobre las personas y los hechos. Monografías 82. Madrid: Fundación Universitaria Española, 2002

–. Jésus ante Anás. Pages 53-71 in Cum vobis et pro vobis. FS M.R. Cabanellas. Edited by R. Arnau-García and R. Ortuño Soriano. Valentina 27. Valencia: Facultad de Teologia San Vicente Ferrer, 1991

VICTOR, ULRICH. Das Testimonium Flavianum. Ein authentischer Text des Josephus. NovT 52 (2012): 72–82

VIEL, HANS-DIETER, ed. The Complete Code of Hammurabi. 2 vols. München: LINCOM Europa, 2005

VIERECK, PAUL, ANTOON GERARD ROOS, and EMILIO GABBA. Appiani Historia romana. Editio stereotypa correctior. Addenda et corrigenda adiecit E. Gabba. 2 vols. Bibliotheca Scriptorum Graecorum et Romanorum Teubneriana. Leipzig, 1939–1962

VINCE, JAMES H. Demosthenes. 7 vols. LCL. Cambridge: Harvard University Press, 1926–1949

VINE, WILLIAM E. An Expository Dictionary of New Testament Words with their Precise Meanings for English Readers. 4 vols. London: Oliphants, 1939

VISSCHER, FERNAND DE. Les édits d'Auguste découverts à Cyrène. Recueil de Travaux d'Histoire et de Philologie III.1. Louvain / Paris: Bibliothèque de l'Université / Les Belles Lettres, 1940

VITELLI, GIROLAMO. Papiri Greco-Egizii. Volume Primo (No. 1–105). Papiri Fiorentini: Documenti pubblici e privati dell'età romana e bizantina. Supplementi filologico-storici ai Monumenti antichi. Pubblicati per cura della Reale Accademia dei Lincei. Milan: Hoepli, 1906

VITELLI, GIROLAMO, MEDEA NORSA, and VITTORIO BARTOLETTI, eds. Papiri greci e latini. Società Italiana per la ricerca dei Papiri greci e latini in Egitto. 15 vols. Florence: Ariani, 1912–2008

VOGEL, MANUEL. Herodes: König der Juden, Freund der Römer. Leipzig: Evangelische Verlagsanstalt, 2002

VOIGTLANDER, ELIZABETH N. The Bisitun Inscription of Darius the Great: Babylonian Version. Corpus Inscriptionum Iranicarum II.1. London: Lund Humphries, 1978

VOISIN, JEAN-LOUIS. Les Romains, chasseurs de têtes. Pages 241–292 in Du châtiment dans la cité. Supplices corporels et peine de mort dans le monde antique, Table ronde organisée par l'École française de Rome avec le concours du Centre national de la recherche scientifique (Rome 9.–11. novembre 1982). Collection de l'École Française de Rome 79. Rome: École française de Rome, 1984

VOSS, WULF ECKART. Digesta. BNP 4 (2004): 407–410

WACHOLDER, BEN ZION. The New Damascus Document. The Midrash on the Eschatological Torah: Reconstruction, Translation, and Commentary. STDJ 56. Leiden: Brill, 2004

WAGNER, SIEGFRIED."דרשׁ. TDOT 3 (1978): 293–307

WALDE, CHRISTINA. Rutilus [II 4] M. R. Lupus. BNP 12 (2009): 797

WALDSTEIN, WOLFGANG. Untersuchungen zum römischen Begnadigungsrecht. Abolitio–Indulgentia–Venia. Commentationes Aenipontanae 18. Innsbruck: Universitätsverlag Wagner, 1964

WALKER, HENRY JOHN. Valerius Maximus. Memorable Deeds and Sayings: One Thousand Tales from Ancient Rome. Indianapolis: Hackett, 2004

WALLACE, SHERMAN L. Taxation in Egypt from Augustus to Diocletian. Orig. 1938. Repr. Princeton: Princeton University Press, 1969

WALSH, PATRICK G. Titi Livi Ab Urbe Condita Libri XXVIII–XXX. Bibliotheca Scriptorum Graecorum et Romanorum Teubneriana. Stuttgart: Teubner, 1986

WALTERS, CHARLES F., and ROBERT S. CONWAY. Titi Livi Ab urbe condita. Tomus II. Libri VI–X. Orig. 1919. Repr. Scriptorum Classicorum Bibliotheca Oxoniensis. Oxford: Clarendon, 1961

WALTKE, BRUCE K., and CATHI J. FREDRICKS. Genesis: A Commentary. Grand Rapids: Zondervan, 2001

WALTON, JOHN H., ed. Zondervan Illustrated Bible Backgrounds Commentary. 5 vols. Grand Rapids: Zondervan, 2009

WALTON, JOHN H., and VICTOR H. MATTHEWS. The IVP Bible Background Commentary: Genesis–Deuteronomy. Downers Grove: InterVarsity Press, 1997

WANDREY, IRINA. Gessius Florus. BNP 5 (2004): 826–827

WANKERL, VERONIKA. Appello ad principem. Urteilsstil und Urteilstechnik in kaiserlichen Berufungsentscheidungen (Augustus bis Caracalla). Münchener Beiträge zur Papyrusforschung und antiken Rechtsgeschichte 101. München: Beck, 2009

WARDLE, DAVID. Suetonius' Life of Caligula. A Commentary. Collection Latomus 225. Bruxelles: Latomus / Revue d'études latines, 1994

WATSON, ALAN, ed. The Digest of Justinian: Revised English Language Edition. 4 vols. Orig. 1985. Repr. Philadelphia: University of Pennsylvania Press, 1998

–. The Digest of Justinian. Latin Text Edited by Theodor Mommsen, With the Aid of Paul Krueger. English Translation edited by Alan Watson. Philadelphia: University of Pennsylvania Press, 1985

WATT, WILLLIAM S. M. Tulli Ciceronis Epistulae. Tomus I: Epistulae ad familiares. Oxford Classical Texts. Oxford: Oxford University Press, 1982

WATTS, NEVILLE H. Cicero. Pro Milone. In Pisonem. Pro Scauro. Pro Fonteio. Pro Rabirio Postumo. Pro Marcello. Pro Ligario. Pro rege Deiotaro. Orig. 1931. Repr. LCL. Cambridge: Harvard University Press, 1953

WAY, A. G. Caesar. Alexandrian War. African War. Spanish War. LCL. Cambridge: Harvard University Press, 1955

WAZANA, NILI. 'For an Impaled Body is a Curse of God' (Deut 21:23): Impaled Bodies in Biblical Law and Conquest Narratives. Pages 69–98 in Law and Narrative in the Bible and in Neighbouring Ancient Cultures. Edited by K. P. Adam, F. Avemarie, and N. Wazana. Forschungen zum Alten Testament 2/54. Tübingen: Mohr Siebeck, 2012

WEBB, ROBERT L. The Roman Examination and Crucifixion of Jesus. Pages 669–773 in Key Events in the Life of the Historical Jesus: A Collaborative Exploration of Context and Coherence. Edited by D. L. Bock and R. L. Webb. WUNT 247. Tübingen: Mohr Siebeck, 2009

WEBER, WILHELM. Eine Gerichtsverhandlung vor Kaiser Traian. Hermes 50 (1915): 47–92

WEBSTER, GRAHAM. The Roman Imperial Army of the First and Second Centuries A.D. Totowa, N.J.: Barnes, 1985

WEISSENBORN, WILHELM. Titi Livi Ab urbe condita libri. Editio altera quam curavit Moritz Müller. Bibliotheca Scriptorum Graecorum et Romanorum Teubneriana. Leipzig: Teubner, 1887

WELCH, JOHN W. Miracles, Maleficium, and Maiestas in the Trial of Jesus. Pages 349–383 in Jesus and Archaeology. Edited by J. H. Charlesworth. Grand Rapids: Eerdmans, 2006

WERNER, ROBERT. Der Beginn der römischen Republik. Historisch-chronologische Untersuchungen über die Anfangszeit der libera res publica. München: Oldenbourg, 1963

WERRETT, IAN C. Ritual Purity and the Dead Sea Scrolls. STDJ 72. Leiden: Brill, 2007

WESTERMANN, CLAUS. Genesis: A Commentary. Translated by John J. Scullion. 3 vols. Minneapolis: Augsburg, 1984–1986

WEVERS, JOHN W. Deuteronomium. 2. Auflage. Septuaginta III.2. Göttingen: Vandenhoeck & Ruprecht, 2006

–. Leviticus. Septuaginta II.2. Göttingen: Vandenhoeck & Ruprecht, 1986

WEWERS, GERD A. Sanhedrin. Gerichtshof. Übersetzung des Talmud Yerushalmi IV/4. Tübingen: Mohr Siebeck, 1981

WHEALEY, ALICE. Josephus, Eusebius of Caesarea, and the Testimonium Flavianum. Pages 73–116 in Josephus und das Neue Testament. Wechselseitige Wahrnehmungen. Edited by C. Böttrich and J. Herzer. WUNT 209. Tübingen: Mohr Siebeck, 2007

–. Josephus on Jesus: The Testimonium Flavianum Controversy from Late Antiquity to Modern Times. Studies in Biblical Literature 36. New York: Lang, 2003

WHISTON, WILLIAM. The Works of Flavius Josephus. Complete and Unabridged. Updated Edition. Orig. 1737. Repr. Peabody: Hendrickson, 1987

WHITE, HORACE. Appian's Roman History. 4 vols. LCL. Cambridge: Harvard University Press, 1912–1913

WHITE, JAMES. The Orations of Marcus Tullius Cicero against Caius Cornelius Verres, Translated from the Original. London: Cadell, 1787

WHITE, ROBERT J. Artemidorus. Oneirocritica. The Interpretation of Dreams. Translation and Commentary. Second Edition, Revised and enlarged. Orig. 1975. Repr. Torrance, Calif.: Original Books, 1990

WIEACKER, FRANZ. Römische Rechtsgeschichte. Zweiter Abschnitt: Die Jurisprudenz vom frühen Prinzipat bis zum Ausgang der Antike im weströmischen Reich und die oströmische Rechtswissenschaft bis zur justinianischen Gesetzgebung. Ein Fragment. Edited by J. G. Wolff. HdA X/3.2. München: Beck, 2006

WIEDEMANN, THOMAS E. J. Emperors and Gladiators. Orig. 1992. Repr. London: Routledge, 1995

WIEDER, NAPHTALI. Notes on the New Documents from the Fourth Cave of Qumran. JJS 7 (1956): 71–76

–. Rejoinder. JJS 8 (1957): 119–121

WILCKEN, ULRICH. Ein Aktenstück zum jüdischen Kriege Trajans. Hermes 27 (1892): 464–480

–. Zu den Florentiner und den Leipziger Papyri. Archiv für Papyrusforschung 4 (1907): 423–486

–. Zum alexandrinischen Antisemitismus. Pages 781–839 in Abhandlungen der königlich-sächsischen Gesellschaft der Wissenschaften, Band 27/23. Leipzig: Teubner, 1909

WILCKEN, ULRICH, and LUDWIG MITTEIS, eds. Griechische Urkunden der Papyrussammlung zu Leipzig. Erster Band. Archiv für Papyrusforschung und verwandte Gebiete 10. Leipzig: Teubner, 1906

WILCKENS, ULRICH. Das Evangelium nach Johannes. NTD 4. Göttingen: Vandenhoeck & Ruprecht, 1998

WILKER, JULIA. Für Rom und Jerusalem. Die herodianische Dynastie im 1. Jahrhundert n. Chr. Studien zur alten Geschichte 5. Frankfurt: Verlag Antike, 2007

WILL, WOLFGANG. Claudius [I 24] C. Pulcher, Ap. BNP 3 (2003): 394–395

WILLIAMS, GLYNN W. Cicero. Letters to his Friends. Epistulae ad familiares. 3 vols. Cambridge: Harvard University Press, 1927–1929

WILLIAMSON, HUGH G. M. Ezra, Nehemiah. WBC 16. Dallas: Word, 1985

WINCKLER, HUGO. Die Gesetze Hammurabis in Umschrift und Übersetzung. Leipzig: Hinrichs, 1904

WINTER, JAKOB, and AUGUST WÜNSCHE. Mechiltha. Ein tannaitischer Midrasch zu Exodus. Orig. 1909. Repr. Hildesheim: Olms, 1990

WINTER, PAUL. On the Trial of Jesus. Second Edition. Edited by T. A. Burkill and G. Vermes. Orig. 1961. Repr. Studia Judaica 1. Berlin: De Gruyter, 1974

WISE, MICHAEL O. A Critical Study of the Temple Scroll from Qumran Cave 11. SAOC 49. Chicago: Oriental Institute of the University of Chicago, 1990

WOLFF, HANS JULIUS. Das Justizwesen der Ptolemäer. Zweite, durchgesehene Auflage. Orig. 1962. Repr. Münchener Beiträge der Papyrusforschung und antiken Rechtsgeschichte 44. München: Beck, 1970

–. Plurality of Laws in Ptolemaic Egypt. Revue internationale des Droits de L'antiquité 3 (1960): 191–223

–. Das Recht der griechischen Papyri Ägyptens in der Zeit der Ptolemäer und des Prinzipats. Band 1: Bedingungen und Triebkräfte der Rechtsentwicklung. HdA X/5.1. München: Beck, 2002

WOLTER, MICHAEL. Das Lukasevangelium. HNT 5. Tübingen: Mohr Siebeck, 2008

WOODMAN, ANTHONY JOHN. Tacitus: The Annals. Indianapolis: Hackett, 2006

WRIGHT, N. T. Jesus and the Victory of God. Christian Origins and the Question of God Vol. 2. Minneapolis: Fortress, 1996

WROE, ANN. Pontius Pilate: The Biography of an Invented Man. Orig. 1999. Repr. New York: Random / Modern Library, 2001

YADIN, YIGAEL. Epigraphy and Crucifixion. IEJ 23 (1973): 18–22

–. Pesher Nahum (4QpNahum) Reconsidered. IEJ 21 (1971): 1–12

–. The Temple Scroll. 3 vols. with Supplementary Plates. Jerusalem: Israel Exploration Society, 1977–1983

YARDLEY, JOHN C. Justin. Epitome of the Philippic History of Pompeius Trogus. American Philological Association Classical Resources 3. Atlanta: Scholars Press, 1994

–. Tacitus. The Annals: The Reigns of Tiberius, Claudius, and Nero. With Introduction and Notes by A. A. Barrett. Oxford World's Classics. Oxford: Oxford University Press, 2008

YIFTACH-FIRANKO, URI. Law in Greco-Roman Egypt: Hellenization, Fusion, Romanization. Pages 541–560 in The Oxford Handbook of Papyrology. Edited by R. S. Bagnall. Oxford: Oxford University Press, 2009

YONGE, CHARLES DUKE. The Orations of Marcus Tullius Cicero, literally translated. London: Bell, 1903

YOUNGER, K. LAWSON. Ancient Conquest Accounts: A Study in Ancient Near Eastern and Biblical History Writing. JSOTSup 98. Sheffield: JSOT Press, 1990

ZANGENBERG, JÜRGEN. ΣΑΜΑΡΕΙΑ. Antike Quellen zur Geschichte und Kultur der Samaritaner in deutscher Übersetzung. TANZ 15. Tübingen/Basel: Francke, 1994

ZEITLIN, SOLOMON. The Christ Passage in Josephus. JQR 18 (1927–28): 231–255

–. The Crucifixion of Jesus Re-examined. JQR 31 (1941): 327–369

–. The Dead Sea Scrolls: A Travesty of Scholarship. JQR 47 (1956–57): 1–36

–. Josephus on Jesus. Philadelphia: Dropsie College, 1931

–. Megillat Taanit as a Source for Jewish Chronology and History in the Hellenistic and Roman Periods. Philadelphia: Dropsie College for Hebrew and Cognate Learning, 1922

–. The Phrase יתלה אנשים חיים. JJS 8 (1957): 117–118

–. Who Crucified Jesus? Orig. 1942. Repr. New York: Harper, 1947

ZIAS, JOSEPH. Human Skeletal Remains from the 'Caiaphas' Tomb. ʾAtiqot 21 (1992): 78–80

ZIAS, JOE, and JAMES H. CHARLESWORTH. Crucifixion: Archaeology, Jesus, and the Dead Sea Scrolls. Pages 273–289 in Jesus and the Dead Sea Scrolls. Edited by J. H. Charlesworth. Orig. 1992. Repr. New York: Doubleday, 1995

ZIAS, JOSEPH, and ELIEZER SEKELES. The Crucified Man from Givʿat ha-Mivtar: A Reappraisal. IEJ 35 (1985): 22–27, plates 5–7

ZIEGLER, JOSEPH, and OLIVIER MUNNICH. Susanna, Daniel, Bel et Draco. Zweite Auflage. Septuaginta XVI.2. Göttingen: Vandenhoeck & Ruprecht, 1999

ZIEGLER, KONRAT. Plutarchi vitae parallelae III/1. Zweite Auflage. Bibliotheca Scriptorum Graecorum et Romanorum Teubneriana. Leipzig: Teubner, 1971

ZLOTNICK, DOV. The Tractate "Mourning" (Regulations Relating to Death, Burial, and Mourning). Translated from the Hebrew, with Introduction and Notes. Yale Judaica 17. New Haven: Yale University Press, 1966

ZUCKERMANDEL, MOSES SAMUEL, ed. Tosephta. Based on the Erfurt and Vienna Codices with Parallels and Variants. With Supplement by Saul Lieberman. New Edition with Additional Notes and Corrections. Jerusalem: Wahrmann, 1970

ZUGIBE, FREDERICK T. The Crucifixion of Jesus: A Forensic Inquiry. New York: Evans, 2005
–. Two Questions About Crucifixion. Does the Victim Die of Asphyxiation? Would Nails in the Hand Hold the Weight of the Body? BRev 5 (1989): 34–43

# Ancient Sources

The page numbers in *italics* indicate numbered items in which the text is treated

## I. Old Testament

## II. New Testament

# III. Ancient Near Eastern Texts

Babylonia

Code of Hammurabi

# IV. Second Temple Jewish Literature, Qumran, Josephus

# V. Rabbinic Literature, Midrashim, Targumim

# VI. Greek and Roman Authors

| | |
|---|---|
| 69–71 | *567–568*, 577, 613, 715, 729, 738 |
| 69 | 564 |
| 348–361 | *563–565*, 567, 672, 675, 676, 713, 729 |
| 359–360 | 729, 743 |
| 677 | 745 |
| 741–744 | *568*, 673 |
| 742–743 | 568, 673 |
| 743–744 | 729 |
| 745 | *568* |
| 849–851 | *729* |
| 852 | 729 |
| 1065 | 569 |
| 1067 | 569 |
| 1128–1134 | *569*, 713 |
| 1070 | 569 |
| 1114 | 569 |
| 1128–1134 | 673 |
| 1133 | 729 |
| 1167 | 569 |
| 1172 | 567 |
| 1174 | 569 |

*Persa*

| | |
|---|---|
| 37 | 732 |
| 127–165 | 731 |
| 289 | 730 |
| 292–295 | *730* |
| 349–354 | *730–731* |
| 352 | 572, 575 |
| 405–426 | 732 |
| 437 | 732 |
| 506–507 | 730 |
| 507 | 730 |
| 685–686 | 732 |
| 794–798 | *731–732* |
| 794–795 | 733 |
| 809–818 | 733 |
| 814 | 733 |
| 815 | 317, 566 |
| 853–857 | 613, *732–733* |
| 854–855 | 567, 721 |
| 855 | 733 |

*Poenulus*

| | |
|---|---|
| 191 | 734 |
| 264–270 | 734 |
| 264 | 734 |
| 271–273 | *733–723* |

| | |
|---|---|
| 339–340 | 734 |
| 343–347 | *734–735* |
| 449–466 | 738 |
| 491–497 | *735* |
| 504 | 736 |
| 510–512 | *736* |
| 519–520 | 736 |
| 520 | 736 |
| 536–537 | 736 |
| 746 | 737 |
| 748 | 738 |
| 779–795 | *736–738* |
| 784 | 567 |
| 789 | 567, 738 |
| 794–795 | 738 |
| 795 | 566 |
| 796–800 | *738–739* |
| 799 | 567, 738738 |
| 816 | 739 |
| 1036–1309 | *739–740* |
| 1341–1343 | 741 |
| 1351–1354 | 741 |
| 1401 | 741 |
| 1407 | 741 |

*Pseudolus*

| | |
|---|---|
| 170–229 | 742 |
| 193 | 567 |
| 196–201 | 741 |
| 265–269 | 741 |
| 326–335 | *740–741* |
| 331 | 741 |
| 360 | 567 |
| 790ff | 742 |
| 808–809 | 742 |
| 829–830 | *741–742* |
| 836–847 | *741–742* |
| 839 | 742 |
| 846 | 742 |
| 1179–1183 | *743–744* |
| 1294–1295 | *744* |

*Rudens*

| | |
|---|---|
| 174–180 | *744–745* |
| 516–518 | *745–746* |
| 518 | 572, 575, 746 |
| 938–1126 | 747 |
| 996 | 567 |
| 1065–1072 | *746–747* |
| 1131–1147 | 747 |
| 1160–1162 | *747–748* |

# VII. Inscriptions and Papyri

# VIII. Early Christian Literature

# Modern Authors

# Subjects